Dear Patty,
To my darling valentine.
All my love,
Maw
February 14, 1978

REFLECTIONS WITHOUT MIRRORS

An Autobiography of the Mind

By Louis Nizer

THE IMPLOSION CONSPIRACY

THE JURY RETURNS

AN ANALYSIS AND COMMENTARY ON THE OFFICIAL WARREN
COMMISSION REPORT

MY LIFE IN COURT

WHAT TO DO WITH GERMANY

THINKING ON YOUR FEET

BETWEEN YOU AND ME

NEW COURTS OF INDUSTRY

Louis Nizer

REFLECTIONS
WITHOUT
MIRRORS

An Autobiography of the Mind

DOUBLEDAY & COMPANY, INC.
Garden City, New York 1978

Grateful acknowledgment is made for use of the following: material adapted and abridged, with permission of Farrar, Straus & Giroux, Inc., from *This Timeless Moment: A Personal View of Aldous Huxley*, by Laura Archera Huxley. Copyright © 1968 by Laura Archera Huxley.

Material written by Edward Balmer, Igor Cassini, and Jacqueline Susann, all used by permission.

ISBN: 0-385-12670-0
Library of Congress Catalog Card Number 77-79559

CONTENTS

Dedicated
to
The Dedicated
to Law
and Justice

REFLECTIONS
WITHOUT
MIRRORS

An Autobiography of the Mind

BEGINNINGS

There are few men important enough to recount their lives. Almost everyone, however, has some experience worth telling. If an autobiography of such selected experiences could be written, there would be profit, learning, and excitement for all of us. Is this not the secret of the novelist? By a combination of events from his own life and those of others, he constructs a single story. His observation enables him to write an imaginative autobiography, enriched by the texture of many lives. The historian and philosopher employ the same device; without simulating the origin of time and persons.

I have shunned writing an autobiography, considering such an enterprise an arrogant exaggeration of ego. But I have toyed with the idea of a selective series of incidents and my thoughts about them, which might contribute something to an understanding of man and his times. Indeed, in *My Life in Court* and *The Jury Returns*, I wrote such a selective autobiography of a few of my experiences as a trial lawyer. But no man's horizon is limited by his profession. A full and turbulent life, and this I have led, sweeps one into the presence of great men and women, famous men and women who are not great, and sometimes great events. Coincidence is more fascinating than planning, because its consequences are beyond expectation. I shall recite some of these in the following pages. But I do not justify this book by such unique accidents. Experiences which may appear mundane become significant and universal if a sharp eye and a memory-filled pen can re-create them; especially if they are interpreted by reflection, the gift of time. These abound.

So I shall eschew the usual trappings of autobiography. The fact that I was born in London on February 6, 1902, is of no importance, even to me; but the fact that I have a vivid recollection of Whitechapel Road, on which my mother carried me when I was one year old, is of some interest because it deals with the mystery of the mind and its computer recordings. Since I emigrated to the United States at the age of three, my parents used to ascribe my recollection to descriptions I may have overheard in later years from them. But when I filled in detail, which even they did not recall, and which was confirmed by their friends, such as that of a pub at the end of the walled street, at which a bobby in a chin-strapped high cup hat would regularly have his ale, or the horse detached from his wagon which was fed outside the market nearby, they were less skeptical though still confused about the indelible imprints which the mind can make before even a semblance of maturity has begun.

Similarly, my description of what I wore when I arrived with my mother at Ellis Island, the entrance funnel to the United States, was so accurate that only a daguerreotype, taken of us in London on departure and later found, demonstrated that I was not inventing. Invention, it would have seemed, considering that I had on a blue velvet Lord Fauntleroy suit, across the front of which ran a pink brocade cord ended by a whistle, high button shoes needing only two buttons for my size, and all topped by a Napoleonic hat, with a huge pompon on the front. The only accouterment in the photograph which I did not recall must have been a photographer's prop, a tennis racket, which lent the final incongruity to the whole attire. Yet, my mother was certain that the enigmatic smile and knowing eyes which peered from the photograph indicated that I was amused by the outfit and was already demonstrating the trait of being above such nonsense.

But when the blond curls which hung underneath my emperor's hat ultimately had to be cut off at the ripe age of six, my alleged insouciance abandoned me. I joined my parents in tears, though I grew to hate those curls, for they were framed under glass and hung over the living-room door for years and years. (What makes hair so hard to grow and so indestructible when severed?)

These early recollections indicate that every scene and word is recorded (perhaps programmed is the word) in brain cells to be released when we know how to do so. But how? For we use only 10 or 15 per cent of our capacity (whatever it be, as determined by the genes and chromosomes at birth). If we could more effectively explore our inner selves, perhaps we might improve human nature so that we could cope with our scientific achievements. Then we would not be in the desperate plight of creating forces so great that they ought to belong only to God, and putting them in the hands of man, still bedeviled by his own inadequacies.

The miracle of brain storage has been demonstrated by hypnotism. When it emerged from the entertainment world into the medical, we learned that men under hypnosis could repeat the foreign language which, at the age of five or six, they had learned from their nurses, even though when out of hypnosis they could not recognize a single word. When one also considers the physical feats of which the body is capable under hypnosis, such as holding up heavy weights with extended arms, controlling pulse, withstanding pain, stiffening the spine so that the body can be supported by head on one chair and heels on another while carrying a man's weight on the stomach, and much more, it becomes evident that we have not begun to exploit our potentials either of mind or body.

I learned this lesson in a peculiar way when I was about thirteen years old. My father owned a cleaning and dyeing store on Sumner Avenue in Brooklyn, New York. For some reason I do not yet understand, it was called the California Cleaning and Dyeing Establishment. Perhaps it was an augury of my later designation as counsel to the Motion Picture Association of America, Inc. which made Hollywood a laboring vineyard.

My father had emigrated a year ahead of us from London to the United States and quickly saved enough to send for my mother and me, greeting us in a bowler hat, which sailed off his head as we flew into his arms to be smothered with kisses, tears, then laughter and more kisses. He had also saved enough money to buy a steam pressing machine. He worked eighteen to twenty hours a day, and during holiday rushes, all twenty-four hours at the machine, disappearing every few seconds in a cloud of steam as the foot lever closed the jaws of the contraption and made a huge pants sandwich. He seemed proud of the steam explosions, and the hisses which announced them because they represented not only progress over the old-fashioned hand iron, but also his progress in being able to afford it. I vowed then, although I considered it a child's fantasy, that I would free him from his slavery. Before he was fifty years old, I was able to fulfill this dream. At my insistence, he retired. Thereafter he tried to use up his enormous energy in household chores, trimming lawns, stripping fruit trees, and shopping. I was never sure his "freedom" wasn't a burden to him.

But back to my early lesson about the body's untapped skills. We lived in one room behind the California Cleaning and Dyeing Establishment. Later we prospered enough to lease a few rooms above, and ultimately to buy the building, although heavy mortgages made ownership a verbal concept. To meet the added burden of the mortgages, my mother and I worked nights at home for a nearby manufacturer, scalloping the edges of laces with small scissors. We grew so adept at maneuvering the curves that reams of laces flowed from our hands and piled high on the floor. Since we were paid a few cents for a specified number of yards, speed was of the essence, and we sang songs of quick tempo to stimulate the rhythm of our flashing blades.

Behind the room in the rear was a yard. How can I call it that? It was paradise. To me it was a park. We planted flowers there. A tree on the property beyond spread its burdened branches across the fence, and we were grateful for the intrusion.

So after school, I retreated to this paradise, playing with my dog Nellie and enjoying reveries in this wild outdoor, fifty yards in length and twenty-five yards in width.

I took to bouncing a ball off a side wall. Probably this training later made possible my being on the handball team at Columbia College. One day a slat of wood broke in a wooden door of that wall. It left a small lateral opening, barely big enough to have a ball go through. To amuse myself, I invented the game of hitting the ball into that slot. At first, it took forty or more bounces before I could score. With practice, this came down to thirty, and then twenty. Finally, I could hit the ball through that slot every second shot, and frequently would score in one shot. When I invited my friends to play, they were astonished by the proficiency which endless practice had produced. There is no limit to what the human body can achieve in dexterity and accuracy. Sharpshooters, who hit bull's-eyes looking into a mirror and aiming over their shoulders, acrobats who leap and tumble in incredible fashion, balancers who spin plates from sticks resting on their chins, soccer players, basketball stars, pitchers and fielders, football runners who dodge and twist while changing speeds, and, of course, golfers, who allow for wind and terrain and club a ball to within a few feet of the hole, two hundred yards away, all attest to the artistry of the muscle.

Many years later, when I represented Robert Young, the railroad magnate, he invited me to play golf at Greenbrier Country Club, a resort in West Virginia owned by the Alleghany Railroad Company. Sam Snead was the golf professional there and we played a foursome. I oohed and aahed as he shot a 68 (he replied, "But can I write a brief?"). When we finished, it was pretty dark, and Young followed the happy tradition of inviting us to the "19th hole"—the bar. Snead excused himself. He headed for the practice tee to hit his 5 iron because it was "not crisp enough." The stories are legion of Ben Hogan practicing six and eight hours a day, until he could place a caddy at an instructed distance for each club, and hit directly to him.

Aside from the body's untapped capacity, I learned a far more critical lesson on the streets of our tough neighborhood. It was to remain with me for life. It dominated my legal work. Curiously, it was learned in a fistfight.

The Williamsburg gang was headed by a brutal kid only fifteen years old, called Leo. He had climbed to the top because of his prowess as a fighter. He was short, but had the torso of a man at least a foot taller. His muscles bulged out of the short-sleeved shirt he always wore, undoubtedly to exhibit them and add to the terror of his hoarse voice. His crew haircut, a novelty then, a flattened nose, and a slit where his lips should have been made him look like a powerful gnome. He later turned to professional fighting.

He was not content with his domination. A cruel streak in him required that he beat up one of his adherents whenever there was the slightest sign of disobedience. Sometimes when obeisance afforded no opportunity to vent his rage and skill, he would provoke or invent a grievance and then punish the imagined offender. To widen his domain, he took to bullying every child in the neighborhood, forcing him to join his gang, and always attending to the initiation personally by exhibiting his punching prowess. Parents complained. Police pulled in Leo once or twice. But revenge was meted out to those who had complained. Ultimately, the neighborhood was cowed by this one bully. What a microcosm this was of the future Hitlers, Mussolinis, and Stalins, although we did not realize it then.

Like others, I wanted nothing to do with Leo or his gang. I kept out of their way. I sought no heroic confrontation. I was afraid of them.

But my turn came. Leo waited for me one day, as I went on a mission to the grocery store. He blocked my path, and demanded that I report to his gang that evening in front of the pool parlor. I told him I could not come. Immediately, a group of his "soldiers" formed a circle around me. Leo was so eager to administer a beating he did not wait for my possible change of mind. He leaped into action with his fists. Within seconds, a gash over my eye sent hot streaks of pain through my body. Then my lips were split and felt a foot wide. A pleasant warm feeling on my face and neck turned to horror when I saw the blood. I was repeatedly knocked down but got up again and again to be rewarded for my audacity by being pelted with blinding blows. Leo's grunts as he belabored me added terror to the attack, like the karate fighter, who utters piercing screams to stun his enemy for a fraction of a second, thereby delaying the defensive move. I felt weak. A blow in the stomach folded me in half and a blow on the top of the head felt as if I had been hit with a hammer. There were hissing noises in my throbbing head, which made the onlookers' wild yells sound distant. Although I was semiconscious and staggering, the outrage of it all released an uncontrollable flood of anger. It was an anesthetic which made me impervious to pain. I charged him furiously. If nothing else, my blood smeared over him and gave the illusion of a contest. My right eye was completely closed, but I kept coming at him the more I was pummeled.

He grew tired punching me. His grunts were no longer auditory attacks but signs of exhaustion—as I continued to rise after each knockdown. Occasionally, I reached him with wild flailing fists. Since I would not stay down, Leo decided to take further measures. He reached into his pocket for brass knuckles. I seized his wrist, twisted it, and as they fell to the ground, I kicked them away. In so doing, I staggered and fell. He came forward and kicked me, but nothing hurt anymore. I got up again and as I weaved toward him in slow motion, I looked into his eyes. They were different! Instead of the squint of joy at the punishment he was handing out, they registered fear. It was as clear even to my one usable eye as if a film had obliterated the satisfaction of cruelty and written doubt on them. The bully, true to his character, began to cringe and for the first time backed away.

I have read that the most vicious animal will not attack man unless he shows fright. A steady look will keep even a lion at a distance. In the case of animals, they probably smell fear. I saw it. The effect was the same, however. It released a new charge of adrenalin. My hands, which had been so heavy that I could not lift them, suddenly became light. My dragging feet took on speed. I clenched my teeth behind the puffed lips and redoubled my effort. The fear in his eyes grew. I rushed him again and I could almost see his disintegration. Panic was written all over him. Within seconds, although really not hurt, he fell from a blow which ineptitude made a shove. He remained on his knees shaking his head helplessly. He was unbloody but bowed. Even through the thumping noises in my head, I realized that silence had descended on the scene. We all remained frozen in our postures, like a motion picture which has turned into a still. After minutes, only Leo moved, looking up as if expecting pity for his plight.

The gang around him, which must have had mixed feelings of satisfaction as well as astonishment, lifted him and restrained him, as he wished, while he pretended he wanted to continue.

I had to be carried home. One of my ribs was broken. There was a huge gash on my scalp which required stitches. The scar remains to this day. I was in bed for a week, attended by a doctor. My parents were furious at me. Love can create anger as well as sweetness. My father threatened to administer a thorough thrashing if I ever got into a street brawl again. They saw no humor in my comment that if I did the thrashing would be administered in advance.

The police hauled Leo in again. But his real punishment was the abdication of his Fuehrer's role. A junta of three ambitious toughs took over. Leo disappeared from the neighborhood. Many years later, I read that he had been convicted of murder and died in the electric chair at Sing Sing.

But I had learned the lesson—he who will not be beaten can't be beaten. Sheer *will* can triumph over great odds. In later years, I saw my contest with Leo on television dozens of times. The contestants were different but the story was the same. In those days, Friday night was fight night on television. It is a cruel sport that should be barred, but I must admit its fascination, a token of the belligerence, if not cruelty, in each of us. Time and again, some inferior fighter would receive a trouncing but would refuse to surrender. My father and I always rooted for him, calling his opponent Leo. Indeed, few fighters are ever knocked unconscious for the count of ten. It is their determination which gives out and paralyzes them with fear. Then they are really helpless, like the hypochondriac who really suffers from his imaginary disease. Of the dozens of ring contests I have seen on television, I think of only two fighters who were actually knocked senseless, Ingemar Johannson by Floyd Patterson and Rocky Graziano by Tony Zale.

A determined will can hold off even death. The stories are not apocryphal of men doomed to die in hours, who lived for several weeks until they could complete some task or duty they had set for themselves. Conversely, those with a good chance to survive, but who give up the fight, die quickly. There can be a will to die as well as to live.

During a matrimonial contest between Marquesa de Portago and her husband, I attempted an amicable resolution and arranged to see the Marquis. He was about twenty-five years old, and as dashing as his reputation foretold. He had a Spanish nobleman's brooding, dark face with a long nose, high forehead, an aggressive mane of black hair. His eyes were deep and shone brilliantly and his flashing white smile gave an appearance of gaiety to an otherwise somber and diffident appearance. The over-all impression was that of vitality. He was proficient in all sports, but was particularly eager to win the top prize in auto racing. No one could have given a better impression of the will to live and live fully.

But when I discussed financial terms, he startled me with an unexpected answer. "As you know, I am entering another race in Mantua, Italy. You may not have to worry about these things." His casual, unheroic manner removed the melodramatic implication of his statement. The next week, we read that the Marquis de Portago had been killed on the last lap of the Mille Miglia race. I believe he had willed to die.

My father had a surfeit of determination—we called him obstinate—and he had successfully weathered surgery at the age of seventy-four. But he was tormented by continuous tests which were not only painful but frightening. One Saturday night, during my visit at the hospital, I watched a procedure which couldn't have been calculated to be more alarming. A huge needle, looking like a thin dagger, was plunged into his chest to draw some marrow or fluid from his breastbone. I barely suppressed a scream as the dagger went in. I saw my father's eyes open wide with horror as if he were being stabbed to death. The doctors made light of it. It hadn't even required an anesthetic. They later declared the test negative. Oh, these tests! Is there not some better evaluation of whether the anguish exceeds the necessity? Or must every book procedure be applied to make sure like a new toy that must be used. When our pallor had subsided, I did everything to cheer him up. Then I left saying, "See you tomorrow, Pa." Instead of the smile and happy wave of the hand, which usually greeted these words, he merely shrugged his shoulders in an unaccustomed gesture of "What's the use of all this torture?" Fright was still frozen in his eyes. That night unaccountably (?) he died.

Long before the emergence of psychology as an independent science, philosophers recognized the peculiar power of the "will to live." Nietzsche wrote, "He who has a *why* to live for, can bear with almost any *how*."

Just as some species will persevere to produce young and then die, there are people who wish to complete tasks for posterity and expire when they have fulfilled their mission. Goethe believed in this theory. He also exemplified it. He began to write Faust when he was in his twenties. He finished it when he was eighty-two years old, and died the next year before it was published. It can also happen at an early age. Mozart and Raphael, being prodigies, achieved their mission early and each died at thirty-five.

It may be significant that prisoners in camp who expected that advancing Allied armies would free them by Christmas, 1945, died in greater numbers than previously when their deliverance did not eventuate.

On the other hand Winston Churchill observed the phenomenon of survival when London was blitzed:

I feared that the long nights for millions in the crowded street, shelters . . . would produce epidemics of influenza, diphtheria . . . and what not. The fact remains that during this rough winter the health of the Londoners was actually above the average. Moreover, the power of enduring suffering in the ordinary people of every country, when their spirit is roused, seems to have no bound.

Dr. Arnold Hutschnecher presented the extreme thesis that "We die only when we are ready to die. If we truly wish to live . . . then no matter how sick we may be, no matter how close to death, we do not die."

History presents no more vivid illustration of "finis" when the task is ended than the death of Thomas Jefferson and John Adams on July 4, 1826, the fiftieth anniversary of the Declaration of Independence. Or was it a coincidence?

Court trials, being contests, depend upon will, courage, or determination—call it what you wish, even though they are battles of the mind, rather than brawn. In every trial in which I have ever participated, there is a revelation which destroys the topography of the original plan. Despite the most thorough preinvestigation, some unknown document or unexpected witness shows up. I do not recall a single trial, among the hundreds I have been in, where this does not happen. After all, it is not so surprising. Complicated court battles involve periods of time from two to twenty years, thousands of documents, and thousands more of conversations. The lawyer is like an archaeologist who must exhume the past. But what archaeologist can ever be certain that his diggings have uncovered *everything* in the locale of a great find?

So, as I tell my assistants, they may be sure that sooner or later, no matter how smoothly things are going, "we are going to be hit over the head." I feel this warning may insulate them against the inevitable shock, so that they will not facially register their distress in the presence of the jury. For jurors may be more affected by the impact upon counsel than by the damaging evidence.

In every trial there is a moment, sometimes many, when sheer will must see us through. Often it turns out to be a psychological rather than a factual crisis, because every new development leads us by the very rule of probability to further facts which may reconcile it with the original plan. It is unlikely that a long train of events which we know about would have taken place if there was a preceding contradiction. Usually, what has happened is that a missing segment in the mosaic has turned up, and because the segment is not complete, it appears to be inconsistent with the rest of the structure. It becomes our duty to uncover the rest of the missing data so that the mosaic may be complete, and present a fuller picture of the truth as originally conceived.

Absent the determination to see it through, the unanticipated revelations can be fatal. There is a rush to surrender, usually in the form of settlement—that graceful disguise of defeat. I have seen many sacrificial settlements made because resistance and persistence had been unnecessarily undermined. So the rule should be, "In smooth sailing keep a careful watch of the horizon; in a gale keep a careful watch of your own head."

It is not only in trials, but in the more peaceful pursuits of commerce, that the same quality of never giving up pays off the largest dividends. Time and again an acquisition of a company or a merger arrangement is stymied by antitrust laws, SEC regulations, unyielding union contracts, required approval of two thirds of the stockholders, prohibitive financing demands, accounting restrictions, or, worst of all, the choice of predominant management among executives each of whom considers his business a child he has reared through infant's diseases to virile manhood, not to be lost by adoption by a stranger.

Time and again, one reads that such transactions have fallen through, although the insuperable obstacles are seldom listed. The formal announcement is as uninforming as the customary statement of voluntary resignation of a government official, together with profound regrets and compliments from the President, who has fired him.

But it is rare that the obstacle to the deal cannot be overcome by resourcefulness and will. The latter is always more important. Not to brook defeat is more than half the battle.

When Thomas Edison was searching for a filament that would not burn out in the electric bulb, he attempted by empirical means to test various metals and other substances seriatim. After ninety-odd experiments had failed, his discouraged assistants regretted that they had not learned anything after weeks of sweaty work. "Wrong," was Edison's undaunted answer. "We now know ninety-four substances that won't work."

His will ultimately lit the world.

IT DOES NO GOOD FOR SHEEP TO PASS RESOLUTIONS IN FAVOR OF VEGETARIANISM WHEN THE WOLVES THINK OTHERWISE

There was another lesson to be derived from my combat with Leo. I was a pacifist at heart. What good did it do me?

When I read of the peace marches, and the noble sentiments expressed by the speakers, who chant "Let's make love—not war," I reflect on the futility of unilateral peace drives. As long as there are Leos in the world, whether individuals in the neighborhood, or nations preying on their neighbors, is there any alternative to defensive violence? Only man's emergence from the animal's lust to kill the weaker of the species can free us from the horror of killing the attacker in order to survive. That emergence may be hastened artificially at least so far as nations are concerned by restraints imposed through international force. I refer to a revised United Nations charter which will substitute pre-emptive collective force for *post hoc* resistance.

The foremost advocate of pacificism in the Western world was Bertrand Russell. He advocated surrender to brute force rather than waging war even in defense: "It is better to be Red than dead." But when Hitler ravaged Europe and appeared on the verge of worldwide conquest, Russell thought World War II to resist was justified. Then what happens to his principle of pacifism? If war becomes justified, depending on subjective judgment of the pacifist, then aren't most wars justifiable according to the differing evaluations of their moral objectives? Or may only Russell and his disciples decide for us which wars are indefensible?

If we contract the lens, the issue of violence becomes more clearly focused. Hundreds of times each day, decent citizens are mugged and robbed on the streets or in their homes. No longer does the marauder wait for the protection of darkness or the isolated path. He operates in

sunlight and in the most traveled areas. His brutality is indescribable.
Old men and women are stomped to death. Others are stabbed dozens
of times in frenzied attacks. It is surmised that dope addiction is responsible for such sadistic outbursts. However, in many instances, when
the attacker is apprehended, the explanation is not so simple. Men can
be incredibly cruel while in full possession of their faculties. They are
driven by devils, which cannot be identified by the name of poverty, environment, or lust for excitement.

Well, shall we of the community be pacifists? Shall we surrender to
nihilists because we are above their tactics? Must we not resist even if to
do so means more violence and bloodshed? Even Woodrow Wilson,
who was elected on his pacifist pledge to keep us out of war, ultimately
found that one cannot always be "too proud to fight." The moral imperative which motivates the pacifist may operate in reverse.

I have proposed a "Good Samaritan Law," which would make it a
criminal as well as a civil offense not to come to the aid of one in distress. If a child was drowning in a lake, and a good swimmer walked by
without helping him or throwing him an available life preserver; or if a
child was playing on railroad tracks and someone saw a train approaching but didn't warn him; or if a worker was backing into the jaws of a
dangerous machine and was not warned by a fellow worker who saw the
impending tragedy; or if the captain of a ship failed to give aid to a
man adrift in a small boat; should not such passivity be deemed a
crime?

Van Heflin, the great actor, was walking in Central Park on a bright
Sunday afternoon, when he was blocked and surrounded by a group of
hoodlums. Dozens of people saw his predicament but did not protest or
intervene. Having once served in the Navy, Van Heflin knew a few
tricks of defense. He kicked one assailant in a vulnerable spot, and got
away. No one near him had even cried out for help.

In the well-known Catherine Genovese case thirty-eight persons
heard the cries of this twenty-eight-year-old girl when she was knifed to
death, but they did not even call for help. In another case an eighteen-
year-old secretary was stripped, raped, and beaten in broad daylight in
the Bronx. Forty witnesses watched silently and did not even telephone
for the police.

Who can approve such pacifism? We have no right to require mar-
tyrdom. An unarmed citizen has no duty to attack a criminal who
brandishes a gun or knife. Reasonable standards must apply.

This proposition is not entirely novel. In 1945 France amended its
penal code to provide that anyone who was able to prevent bodily
harm, without risk to himself, and failed to do so was punishable by

three years imprisonment or a fine of twelve to five hundred thousand francs, or both.

If we adopted the crime of violating the dictates of humanity, yes the crime of passivity, we might ultimately apply it to the international scene.

Voltaire expressed the principle eloquently: "We must not be guilty of the good things we did not do."

A GOOD TEACHER'S INFLUENCE AFFECTS
ETERNITY

Of all the teachers before whom I sat, two left indelible impressions upon me. While all others have disappeared from memory (I hope their teachings haven't), these two are as clear in my mind as if I had spent a lifetime with them, although I took only one course of several months with each fifty-nine and forty-seven years ago.

Undoubtedly, this is due to the impact an unusual personality makes on an impressionable mind. It has nothing to do with teaching as such. Others whose names I cannot remember taught more effectively. Still others like Professor John Dewey, Professor John Erskine, Professor Thomas Gifford, Dean Harlan F. Stone of Columbia University were world-famed authorities. But they never made their subjects exciting stimuli which inflamed the mind and produced a quenchless curiosity.

I remember Mr. Bishop (the first name *does* escape me), who taught geometry and trigonometry at Boys High in Brooklyn, New York. He was about forty-five years old, and bore no mark of distinction in his thin face. He was sallow, with deep, heavily lidded eyes, a short, roundish nose, and a slightly jutting chin. His voice was unresonant and inclined to fade off in a whisper. It had a matter-of-fact quality perfectly suited to the uncompromising logic of mathematics, as if, of course, the result was Q.E.D.—*quod erat demonstrandum.*

All of this should have made him the most forgettable character I ever knew. But no. When he taught, the unimpassioned lucidity of demonstrations created sheer beauty in the triangles and logarithms. He was continuously voted the most popular teacher in the school. Perhaps kindness had something to do with it. A pupil who failed to understand was led tactfully onto the right path, as if it was the most natural thing to have missed originally, and how bright he was to arrive at the corrected conclusion.

The writer who later influenced me most was Emerson. His elegance

and grace of diction added verve and beauty to his thought. As Judge
Benjamin Cardozo once observed, style cannot be separated from substance. An argument well phrased is more persuasive than the same argument prosaically phrased. Substance can titillate the mind, while
style thrills it.

I refer back to Emerson, because Bishop had the same quality in
explaining figures which Emerson had in explaining thoughts. We felt
a fire built under us by this quiet man's expositions. We could not be
certain how the fire was lit. Was it skill with which the problem was
dissected so that the solution seemed to burst upon us with the excitement of a mystery unraveled? Was it the purity of mathematical logic,
the beauty of which caressed the mind? Was it Bishop's own dedication and concentration which set higher ideals for us than his instructions? Or was it that supreme gift of all great teachers, a fatherly concern for their pupils which accompanies the joy of teaching? Whatever
the mystery of personality, there was no doubt about Bishop's achievements. At reunions for a half century—only one teacher was remembered affectionately. It was he.

The second teacher who left his mark on a whole generation of students, including myself, was Professor Thaddeus C. Terry, who taught
"Contracts" at Columbia University Law School.

Curiously enough in almost all physical respects and personality, he
was the opposite of Bishop. He was about sixty-five years old. He had a
clubfoot, and his limping and later use of a cane had developed powerful shoulders, which malformed him, since they jutted out horizontally.
His face was so ugly that there was almost beauty in its rugged asym-
metry. He was in the penultimate stage of complete baldness, only a
few strands holding out. The heavy flesh over his eyes made them look
slanted. His nose could not make up its mind whether to be hooked or
flattened, so it was both, and looked no better from wearing an
unrimmed pince-nez with a black ribbon which shivered down to his
vest. Each of these features, which could have aspired for predominance, was put into shadow by his mouth. It was a thick-lipped wide
permanent scowl and the red glistening inner skin, which showed when
he talked, completed the ferocious face. As one would expect, no sweet
voice could emanate from that face. A deep baritone sound came forth,
and its resonance was constantly squeezed by sarcasm. Such sarcasm.
He was a master at it. When he called out your name, it sounded as if
you were an illegitimate child who had adopted a false name to disguise
the bastardy.

Instead of Bishop's kindliness, there was unremitting cruelty. He humiliated. He taunted. He ridiculed—but how he taught! How he made
you understand the majesty of the law and its philosophical striving for

justice. In his hands, the law was "a sorcerer's wand which created a new world of equity."

He used the Socratic technique, asking questions, never giving answers. You had to find your own way, but he deliberately led you into byways so that you would learn your own way back and really understand the terrain. No matter which way you answered, a barrage of questions threw doubt on your conclusion. Sometimes you were compelled to change your mind. Then the questions pushed you back to your original conclusion. At the end, you knew that the law was not a precise science, but a process of reasoning in which diverse answers might all be right depending on the perspective and social objectives which subjectively provided the greatest moral satisfaction.

So he would begin with the most elementary lesson in contract.

"Mr. Nizer, what is a contract?"

"It is a meeting of the minds, sir."

"Is a meeting of the minds enough?"

"I don't understand, sir."

"If you and I agree who should be President, is there a contract?"

"No, sir. There must be an offer by one party which for a consideration is accepted by the other."

"Does the contract come into existence the moment when the minds meet?"

"Yes, sir."

"Oh, it does, does it?" The snarl that accompanied this question was like the sudden appearance of dark clouds preceding a storm.

I was silent.

"Suppose A offers to sell his car for $3,000 and sends his offer in writing to B, who is in another city. Suppose that B writes his acceptance and puts it in the mail. Is that a contract?"

"Yes, sir."

"Why?"

"Because their minds have met on the deal."

"Even despite the fact that A has not yet received B's letter of acceptance?"

Hesitantly, "Yes, sir."

"Suppose that A has changed his mind and sent B a telegram withdrawing his offer and the telegram is received by B before his letter of acceptance reaches A? Is there a contract?"

"Yes, sir. Their minds had met when B mailed his acceptance."

Angrily, "Their minds had met on *what?*"

"On the offer made by A."

"How could the offer be accepted which has been withdrawn by telegram? What was there to accept?"

"But B had already mailed his acceptance," I reply with a little acerbity.

"Doesn't the meeting of the minds require communication of acceptance? How can the minds meet if A doesn't know that B had agreed?"

"I suppose that's right, sir."

"Has not the offerer the right to withdraw his offer before the contract has been consummated?"

"Yes, sir."

"Then doesn't it follow that A's offer having been withdrawn by telegram, there was nothing to accept, and that B's intention to accept was ineffectual?"

"I can see that, sir."

"So you would change your previous answer, Mr. Nizer?" The name was pronounced so as to be synonymous with dunce.

"I believe I would. Yes, sir."

"And you would now say the opposite of what you previously said, namely that there was no contract under the circumstances?"

"Yes, sir," spoken with the resignation of one who permits his shoulders to be pinned to the mat.

Professor Terry stared at me for a long time. Then he called on another student.

"Mr. Thomas, do you agree with Mr. Nizer's last answer?"

"Yes, Professor Terry."

"Why?" The challenge was flung at him as if nothing had happened in the past several minutes.

"For the reason you gave, sir."

"I gave no reason. I asked questions. Stand on your feet! I have asked you why?"

"Well, the offer being withdrawn by telegram there was nothing to accept."

"But hadn't B already accepted when he wrote that he did?"

"But his writing had not been received by A."

"Why is that necessary?"

"Well, until received, there was no meeting of the minds."

"Where do you get that idea from? If I hold out a proposal to you and you agree, even without mailing such agreement to me, haven't our minds met at the instant you accepted?"

"Sir, I might agree one moment and then change my mind the next."

"In the hypothetical case I gave, B's acceptance was not a mere mental concept. He wrote it out and placed it in a mailbox, beyond his power to control. Would that make a difference?"

"Yes, sir, perhaps it would."

"Perhaps? It would, wouldn't it?" The booming voice sounded like an explosion of a cannon shot, reverberating around the room.

The mental and physical assault was intimidating.

"Yes, sir, it would."

"Furthermore, if each party must learn that the other has agreed, wouldn't A's receipt of B's acceptance have to be communicated to B? And then would A have to learn that B got it? Wouldn't it be an end-

less chain which would prevent a contract from ever being consummated?"

"Yes, sir," almost inaudibly.

"So you would say that the withdrawal of the offer was too late, because the minds had already met as evidenced by the overt act of
mailing the acceptance, is that right?"

"Yes, sir."

"And you would go back to Mr. Nizer's original answer, which he
changed after questioning?"

"Yes, sir. I would."

A long stare. "Mr. McGraw, who do you agree with—Mr. Nizer's
final answer or Mr. Thomas' *final* answer?"

The word "final" put the spotlight back on Thomas and me, just
when we were recovering in the darkness of inattention.

"I think there is a contract when B mails his letter of acceptance.
Nothing thereafter can change that fact."

McGraw's jaw jutted out. His voice was angry as if in anticipation of
the harassment he was about to endure. Having seen the fate of his
predecessors, he was determined to take a position and stick to it. If he
had to go down, he was going to do so with flags flying, not in a surrendering whimper. We could sense the impending battle.

"Nothing can change that?" asked Professor Terry, his voice slow and
ominously sweet. He smiled at McGraw for what seemed hours. We
could see McGraw quiver, as Terry finally turned angry and the red glistened from his inner lower lip.

"Suppose two minutes after B has mailed his letter of acceptance, he
calls up A and says, 'I've decided not to buy your car. By the way, I
mailed a letter of acceptance to you a short while ago—just ignore it
when you get it.' Is there still a contract?"

McGraw was defiant and definite.

"Yes, sir. When B mailed his acceptance, A's offer ripened into a
contract. The fact that B called later can't change that."

Professor Terry's face lit up, announcing to one and all that the trap
had been sprung.

"Suppose then that A, having received the telephone call from B,
sells his car to C—Can B sue A for breach of contract?"

"Well—"

"Well—what?"

"I don't think he can. After all, he told A he was not buying. So A
had a right to sell to someone else."

"But if the offer had 'ripened into a contract'—nice phrase Mr.
McGraw [the compliment could not assuage the distress on the recipient's face]—then no call thereafter could wipe it out—wouldn't you
agree?"

"No."

"Didn't you say a few moments ago that when a contract comes into being nothing can change that?"

"Yes, sir."

"Well, if nothing can change it, isn't B entitled to sue A for having breached his contract by selling the car to someone else?"

"I suppose so."

Terry turned away in disgust.

"Mr. Harrison, do you agree with that?"

It didn't matter which position Mr. Harrison took. He was run down just as mercilessly. And this was only the first and most elementary lesson. What fireworks awaited us, as the really involved problems of contract law were explored.

It eventuated that all our answers were right. Some states follow one rule, and some the other. What would be held to be a contract in Massachusetts would not be in New York. That was why one of the courses still to be taken was called "Conflict of Laws." Which of the conflicting rules applied under varying circumstances? For example, does the rule of the forum where the case is tried prevail, or the rule where the contract was consummated? So, even in the very first session, we learned that the law was not an exact science. It was a philosophical pursuit of moral precepts, and the logic used in the quest was not irrefutable. We were to become sculptors molding the law to desirable ends, and we would thus be engaged in an art not a science.

Entering Professor Terry's classroom was an adventure, and a frightening one. We studied with particular care the cases he had assigned the previous day. Yet we knew that if called upon we would be stripped mentally and compelled to stand nude and foolish in the presence of witnesses. We dared not laugh at our neighbor's discomfort because we knew our turns would come, and the exposure would be as inexorably embarrassing.

Despite our fear (which we did not experience in any other course), we were thrilled by the intellectual exercises Terry put us through. If we had more such teachers, students wouldn't want to turn to pot and LSD for excitement. We literally trembled as we entered his class. And later, for hours, we would talk among ourselves about the brilliance of the technique which made us turn somersaults, as if we were animals being put through our paces by the trainer. Only then could we afford to laugh at ourselves.

Strangely enough, Professor Terry's uncompromising pressure, which often seemed tinged with viciousness, did not make us bitter toward him. A deep affection set in for the man. We understood that he was dedicated to us; that he was determined to equip us for our profession, not by drumming some rules of law into our heads (for anyone can go to the library and find them), but by developing our reasoning powers, so that we would rule the law and not the law rule us; so that we could become interpreters of the law, not its reciters; so that we would be historians of the law who would divine its future; in short, so that we could achieve the highest standard of the profession to be wise enough to be *advisers*.

Professor Terry encouraged discussion with him after the lecture, as if he recognized that a runner who had run a hard race could not stop suddenly, but must taper off. So we crowded around him continuing the discussion. Then for the first time, we knew he was our friend, and that the punishment he had meted out was for our own good. And when in the course of that more informal exchange at the podium he put his hand on our shoulders, we felt as if we had been knighted. Finally, he would limp off while we stood around in small groups too stimulated to leave.

Professor Terry became a legend at Columbia Law School. Thousands of students who passed through his classroom over the years remembered him above all other teachers. But our class was privileged to participate in a special event, which revealed a dimension no others had seen.

He announced his retirement. Dean Harlan F. Stone and the faculty decided to give him a farewell at which an oil painting of him would be hung in the library. Terry asked that the students be invited. We crowded into the library eagerly, but had no inkling that what would happen would be so startling that it would become the most moving experience of our young lives. But, then, that was Professor Terry.

Seated on a raised tier, with the professors, was a lady all in brown. Even her lace collar was dark brown. A beautiful young girl is an accident of nature, but a beautiful old woman is a work of art. She was a work of art and inexpressibly beautiful. Her perfectly proportioned features were enhanced by gentle curving white hair which added aristocracy rather than age to her face. Her neck was long, and she held her head regally high, but without a trace of hauteur. She sat motionless and attentive, a faint smile on her lips, which did not fully disguise her emotions. We wondered who she was. All eyes were upon her until the ceremonies and speeches drew attention away. When they were concluded, with grace and not a little solemn dignity, Professor Terry rose to speak.

He stood motionless for a long time. We observed that his face was different than we had ever seen it before. It had lost its severity. It was flushed and looked pink and kind. The mouth was not a snarl. One could actually see his lips as if they had finally triumphed over the scowl which had suppressed them. He took off his ribboned glasses, which we knew he needed, and placed them slowly in his vest pocket, as if he wanted to remove anything which would interfere with direct eye-to-eye communication. His voice, too, was different. It was soft without a trace of belligerence or sarcasm.

After expressing gratitude for the painting "which would keep memories fresh of the torture I have imposed," he explained that he loved the law, and he had the feeling that every student who had committed himself to the greatest of all professions was his son. He could best express his love to his many sons by training them for excellence. The law deals with every facet of human experience, and cannot brook mediocrity. There is enough of that wherever one turns. One who aspires to be a lawyer must recognize his obligation to become a social philosopher, a leader of thought, a cultured and cultivated man worthy of his profession. For he becomes a minister of justice—justice, "the bread for which the nation hungers." Therefore, out of *love*, he had been remorseless in his training. The mind can only grow if it is challenged, if it must exert itself. Then, in self-defense, it calls upon the reserves of imagination and resourcefulness. These were the reasons he used the Socratic method, always asking, never answering. The student must find his own way as he will have to do in the outside world. That was why he was abrasive. The world outside would be more abrasive. He could not afford to be tolerant with anything but the best that was in us. His great satisfaction in life was to see his students later become brilliant lawyers, judges, and public servants, giving leadership to a society which sorely needed it. He continued in this vein, an unaffected outpouring of idealism. He put into words the high purpose which had motivated most of us to enter the law, but which we never mentioned because it would be striking a posture of nobility, and, therefore, suspect, like the soldier who spoke of his exploits in battle. So he continued, for the first time in declarative sentences instead of questions to fill our minds with inspiration. Our hearts were next.

He expressed his gratitude to the dean and the professors who had been his "intellectual colleagues and personal friend all in one." He said good-bye to the law school, speaking of it not as a building of red bricks, marble, and rooms, filled with student chairs which had one swollen arm to make place for notebooks, but as a huge person throbbing with exertion, and sharing emotions with him over the decades. In my dimmed eyes, there was a picture of tiers of bookshelves drooping in sorrow, the walls waving good-bye to him, and the oil paintings in the alcoves turning their heads toward their new neighbor to greet him for posterity.

Then the unexpected happened. He took one of his long pauses, which had been so meaningful in the classroom, like an exclamation point of silence. He turned toward the beautiful woman in brown:

"I have been expressing my gratitude to you, my students, my colleagues, and my school. But it is all only a very tiny portion of the gratitude which fills my heart. I cannot bid you all good-by and leave unsaid that which is the most important thing in my life."

He took a deep breath and continued, his voice hoarse with emotion.

"At the age of twenty, I met the most beautiful girl I had ever seen, or seen since. Looking at her, no one could be certain whether her charm, warmth and brightness of mind and spirit made her beauty unique, or whether her breathtaking beauty deprived us of the appreciation of her other qualities.

"I was stunned and in love with her immediately. I am sure every other young man who saw her felt the same way. But I considered her unattainable for one such as me. Nature had not endowed me with any of the graces of appearance."

He looked down at his foot and continued.

"I dared not even contemplate the audacity to befriend her, and certainly not to confide my feelings to her. Most impossible of all was to dream of her reciprocal love. I was happy just to think of her, and this gratification I indulged in day and night.

"But she ordered events so as to bring us together. She overcame the inarticulateness which my awe and worship of her created. With delicacy and sensitivity, she told me that she knew how I felt about her, and that she had to tell me, she was more in love with me than I could possibly be with her. I have been blinded by ecstasy ever since.

"Through the years which followed, we have reared a family in supreme happiness. She has dedicated her life and her love to me without reservation or pause even for the vicissitudes of life. I have functioned in the aura of her love. Teaching, writing and practicing law at times, have been temporary absences made bearable only because I knew I was returning to her. Every thinking moment has had the silent musical accompaniment of her presence."

His voice grew hoarser as he struggled to eliminate the quiver which was entering it.

"So, although it is farthest from my nature to discuss the most private of all emotions in public, I cannot in this leavetaking do other than tell you that I owe all my happiness to her, that she has—"

He turned his head toward her and his eyes completed the sentence, as if words could not possibly convey the depth of his feeling.

Tears were running down her cheeks, but she did not move. Her eyes were clear despite the streams and she looked steadily at him. Their gazes met and locked in long silence. Then without another word, he sat down.

No one applauded. We just sat there. After a few moments, everyone got up slowly and left.

The phenomenon of attractive women falling in love with unattractive or older men is not as mysterious as it seems. The answer is power; not because of power itself but because of the energy and brilliance required to achieve it. Energy is all attractive. It connotes sexual power, protective power, and security. I have sought common characteristics among people of great accomplishment. There is only one common denominator—energy. Whether it be the business tycoon, the great painter, or dramatist, the performer, the professional man, the political leader, they are as different in personality as infinite variations of color and form in nature's creations—except one. They are alike in their boundless energy.

I recall seeing Pablo Picasso, his friends, and wife, young enough to be his granddaughter, in Juan les Pins. He was close to eighty years of age, tiny and bald. But his round black eyes blazed, and impishly he led the others in singing songs, among them, surprisingly, *Hatikvah*, Israel's anthem. Even if one did not know who he was, he would have been impressed by the sheer energy which spurted from him.

So the question "What does she see in him?" may be answered by "Perhaps nothing, but she feels much in him." Some cynical people rush to the conclusion that such women are calculating, rather than in love. Undoubtedly, there are such. But more often there is real love, engendered by a captivating power. For many women, despite their declarations of independence, want to be dominated, and only the powerful man, not the handsome man, or the noble one, or the considerate one, can gratify this secret and sometimes unconscious yearning. Sometimes the power involved is an evil one. Nevertheless, fine women have been unable to resist it and have devoted themselves to criminals. Great wealth also gives power, but if it has not been earned, but merely inherited, the qualities which accompany the acquisition are lacking, the power is not real, and the disillusionment is as cold as the metal.

All this may explain many divorces which to the outside eye are perplexing because the fine and handsome husband is dropped for one not nearly as attractive. I shall not supply the names of many public figures who have been involved in such mysterious "changes for the worse."

So, Professor Terry, despite his razor-sharp mind, had missed the real point of his wife's love. It was no miracle, as he considered it to be. He need not have been self-deprecating, despite his ugly countenance and clubfoot. She had been overwhelmed early by the power which he exuded and which made him the most unforgettable teacher and man to almost two generations of students.

Professor Terry's farewell outpouring was as beautiful as it must have been embarrassing to him and to her. I can well understand that she chose not to reply or was unable to do so. But I imagine that if she had she would have added still another dimension to his joy, for she could have told him that it was she who was fortunate to have him confer his deep love and passionate nature upon her; that she had made no conscious choice for which her judgment and discretion should be honored with gratitude; that she could do no other than love him, for he had captured and captivated her—and it was she who was grateful.

Maybe, if she had so spoken, the circle of revelation would have been completed, and we could have emerged from our stunned condition to cheer them both.

The journey from sentiment to science is sometimes short. The inspirational stimulus in education is more valuable to building character than acquiring knowledge.

As for learning—the science of absorption—we are as backward as the Neanderthal man's rock is to a hydrogen bomb. The vista before us is so immense that even though we have learned that science has erased the word "impossible" from the dictionary, what will soon be here would be deemed an insane fantasy.

The impending miracle began with the epoch-making discovery of the cryptic DNA code, which explained the building blocks of life itself. This new science of molecular biology has now taken us to the brink of molecular neurology, the innermost secrets of the brain rather than the body generally.

Were it not for the credibility of renowned scientists like Dr. Francis O. Schmitt of M.I.T., Dr. Holger Hyden of the University of Göteborg in Sweden, Dr. James V. McConnell of the University of Michigan, Dr. Allan L. Jacobson, and Dr. David Krech of the University of California, Dr. Georges Ungar of the Baylor University College of Medicine, Dr. William L. Byrne of Duke University, Dr. David Samuel of

Israel's Weizmann Institute, Dr. D. Ewen Cameron of the Veterans Administration Hospital in Albany, New York, Dr. Alexandre Monnier and Dr. Paul Laget, researchers in France, and a brilliant synthesis of their achievements by David M. Rorvick, what is now projected as a new method of acquiring knowledge would be incredulous to the most hardened science-fiction writer.

It appears that man's brain has a capacity for storing knowledge exceeding several million miles of magnetic tape of a computer. The brain accumulates a million billion bits of information in a lifetime. How? The molecule responsible for storing memory is nucleic acid, called RNA.

Can this stored memory be transferred? Little worms known as planarians were taught by electric shock to avoid certain parts of their training mazes. Later, they were chopped up and fed to untrained planarians. These unschooled cannibals were able to learn the maze, avoiding "forbidden" turns in far fewer trials than other planarians. They had eaten their education!

The next experiment was with rats and hamsters. They were taught certain skills. Then they were killed. RNA was extracted from their brains and injected into untrained rats and hamsters. They acquired the same skills with extraordinary speed. For example, Swiss mice were taught to ignore loud noices which would normally make them cringe in fear. Protein-like molecules from their brains were injected into unconditioned mice, who thereupon became completely unmindful of noise.

Cautious experiments have now begun with man. First, there was the effort to strengthen or restore memory. RNA was extracted from yeast and administered to patients who, due to age, suffered from extreme forgetfulness. There was marked improvement, although it did not last when the treatment ceased. Since then, magnesium pemoline, a chemical designated as Cylert, has been very efficient as a "memory pill." It works by stimulating a brain enzyme which is vital in the manufacture of RNA. Patients who could not remember how to turn on their television sets or how to tie their shoes were able again to play bridge after taking Cylert.

All this presages the transfer of accumulated knowledge directly into the brain by injecting specific RNA memories into the bloodstream. This could be done by using benign viruses, which are nothing more than protein-coated RNA, and which would easily "infect" the brain. Given time, synthetic RNA is virtually a certainty, thus facilitating the development of transferring memories.

Since memories are the receptacle of knowledge, we can foresee learning French, algebra, organic chemistry, music, law, and athletic know-how by taking a pill, or an injection no more painful than a polio vaccination. Indeed, the development of genetic engineering may make it possible to be born with a college education, fulfilling J. B. S. Haldane's prediction that someday our children will come into the world "speaking perfect English."

The minds of great savants can be made imperishable and immortal. To cornea, kidney, and heart "banks," we may add molecular memory libraries. They would consist of synthetic copies of brain molecular RNA extracted from leading men of arts and sciences. The originals would be preserved in vaults. A scholar who wished to benefit from the genius of a predecessor could go to a library for an appropriate pill or injection. This possibility would also overcome the fear that because the most ignorant people breed freely, we are doomed by the survival of the least fit.

The transfer of memory even crosses the line of different species. This is due to the fact that DNA is common to all life on earth. So rats were able to acquire new skills from the RNA of hamsters and vice versa.

If the species barrier can be overcome, then man may be able to acquire the memory and knowledge of a leopard or dolphin. As David M. Rorvick says, such experience would surpass the most profound hallucinogenic "trip." When one speaks of "acid" in the future, he may be referring to nucleic acid.

The science of "grafting" memory onto the brain also makes possible its erasure. The RNA factor can be reduced by an antibiotic called puromycin, which halts the synthesis of protein molecules. Experiments have been conducted with goldfish who were trained to ring bells in order to obtain their food. When puromycin was injected into their brains, they completely forgot this intensively conditioned skill.

If more refined drugs could be developed to selectively blot out crippling memories, what a boon this would be to neurotics and psychotics. Thus, the pattern of chemical cure for mental disease is revealed again.

So there lies before us, and not too far away, the possibility of a new and instant education of man. For centuries, we have been told that only education will lift us out of animalism to humanism. Civilization was the slow process of learning to be kind—but oh how slow. Pedagogic sciences crept along with imperceptible gains. We had to learn to substitute patience for frustration, and hope for failure. Now, suddenly, we face what was once thought to be the millennium, man's emergence from the wilderness of ignorance.

Most significant is the fact that this scientific achievement is different from all previous ones in that it has a built-in *moral* factor.

In the last fifty years science has made more "progress" than in the one million years of man's supposed existence on earth. Indeed, if we made a list of all the great scientists who have ever lived, 90 per cent would be alive today! That is how acceleratingly dominant science has become in this half century.

Yet has man's nature improved similarly? Of course not. We need only look at the prevalence of wars during the very period of scientific accomplishment. Fifty-five million people were killed in World War II. Professor Friedrich Foerster once observed that German virtues—industriousness, obedience, efficiency—were all put in the service of the devil. Similarly, modern science has been put in the service of the devil. We are constantly improving the techniques of slaughter, so that even hydrogen bombs seem obsolescent for most effective killing. Gases, bacteria, laser rays, neutrons, and a concoction of electronically controlled multiple-delivery systems which can attack any point of the earth's surface, from the sky or from the depths of the sea, threaten the annihilation of two hundred million people in a half hour, and perhaps man's extinction in one great suicidal holocaust.

This gap between science and humanism is the greatest dilemma and challenge to mankind. How can we improve man's inner nature so that he will provide moral direction to the forces now available to him? How can we reverse the trend in which the more powerful the vehicle, the more insane the driver? Until now science equipped us, but did not guide us. Science illuminated our path to the farthest star, but left our hearts in darkness.

Even when science was beneficent, prolonging life by eliminating disease, providing food by eliminating pests, creating the highest standard of living if not yet *for* living, increasing the American national product in one year to a trillion dollars—even then we now find resulting heavy entries on the other side of the ledger sheet. For just as Einstein discovered that there was one unifying equation which explained magnetism, electricity, time, and space, I suspect that there is one central explanation for what appears to be disconnected and variegated crises of our century, such as population explosion, race antipathy, pollution, poverty pockets, and war. The central link is that amazing technology descended on man before he was ready to absorb it.

Smokestacks were once the proud symbol of a burgeoning city. Now we suddenly realize that they destroy oxygenization. Jet planes, buses, and automobiles were the wonderful shrinkers of time and space. Now our admiration turns to disgust as we watch the trail of poison they dump into our air.

Large cities were the triumph over the loneliness and hardship of farm life. Now the very crowding of masses of people in close proximity creates nervous tensions greatly responsible for the fact that one out of every ten Americans occupies a bed in a mental hospital at some time in his life. (Experiments with animals have demonstrated that those living in a large cage remain normal, while those living under the same conditions but in confined quarters become neurotic, violent and attack each other. Perhaps restricted space alone is one of our somewhat hidden problems, and yet in many places in the world we are facing geometric increases of population.) The hustle and bustle of city life was once deemed a necessary stimulation, now we discover that boundless and continuous noise alone can disrupt our nervous systems. Even though we marveled at the Concorde, which has made the previous jet planes look slow, we worried about our ears. We forbade it to land in New York City, thus provoking an international crisis and court review. The extension of life's span was medicine's proudest boast. Now we find our mental institutions, our hospitals for the incurable, our welfare and medical rolls jammed, while we struggle with the population explosion.

Even when we attain the objective of technology—leisure—it presents a new problem. For what will non-Renaissance men and women, who have no cultural and versatile interests, do with time on their hands? The treasure of leisure turns into corroding boredom, and some psychiatrists predict we may ultimately start wars for excitement. Already we see the lure of violent movements, permissive and distorted sex, and drugs. The pace and tensions of a speeded-up technologically improved world have made millions of men and women escapists. In the United States, we consume annually $320,000,000 worth of tranquilizers, $280,000,000 of sleeping pills, 350 million gallons of hard liquor, and a billion dollars of drugs. In New York City there are 200,000 drug addicts. The need to escape from life has even infected children, who still in their teens turn to LSD and heroin, dying by the dozen before they have even become mature enough to savor the beauty of life. Machines have made it unnecessary to use the body fully. There is an alarming state of unfitness even among our young, as we discover when they are examined for army or other service.

We were proud of our technological genius in agriculture, which gave us abundance of all good things and enough to feed a large part of the world. Now we find that DDT and other sprays which have killed "harmful" foliage and pests have fouled our streams, killed our fish, eroded our soil, and even put poisons into the delicious technologically produced fruits and meats we eat. New words become universal. Ten years ago, it was gerontology. Now it is ecology. We have a new concern, but the source of all is the same, a burgeoning technology before man was conditioned to accept and absorb it.

Just as we were despairing that every new scientific achievement moved us farther away from man's control of his own belligerency, envy, and greed; just as scientists, recognizing the nihilism of their own inventiveness, were beginning to boycott their own creation, along come scientific achievements, hypnotic induction, subliminal learning, and neurological biology with none of the defects of the past to offer possible solution for its own evil.

In a sense it was inevitable. The gap between science and humanism had to be filled by science itself. Instead of drawing away in an increasingly uneven race, science had to teach humanism how to keep pace. Frankenstein, because of his power, must tell his master how to bring him down to size.

Man only uses 10 to 15 per cent of his capacity. If by new scientific techniques we can teach him to utilize more of his untapped capacity, and even utilize the capacity of others, what a new world awaits us.

THERE IS NOTHING IN THE WORLD SO MUCH LIKE PRAYER AS MUSIC

Back to my childhood and an essential phase of any education—music.

I was the fortunate inheritor of a great Jewish tradition in music. Most Jewish children learn the violin or piano. I can only speculate whether such concentration among a relatively few explains why so many of the great concert pianists and violinists are Jews.

My parents were too poor to provide such training for me, but not too poor to sing. The voice is an instrument which need not be paid for in installments, and it is mobile. I cannot remember talking to my father in my early years, but I clearly remember singing with him from infancy on. It was a customary means of communication, and since song frees the spirit, it was a dialogue of beauty and joy.

Memories are like paintings and each one of us has his own gallery. One such indelible scene is the Seder on Passover night. My father is dressed in a white robe and high satin skullcap worn by cantors. A sofa laden with white pillows has replaced his chair, so that he may recline in kingly fashion as the Haggada requires. The table is filled with gleaming dishes and wine-filled glasses which shine like huge rubies. The matzohs are covered by a gold brocaded satin cloth. The lit candles, over which my mother has waved her hands in prayer, flicker back and forth as the rush of song bends them. My father holds a silver chalice and sings the *Kiddush* so exuberantly that the wine flows over his hand and upon the spotless white tablecloth. With his other hand, he leads all others to sing "amen" at appropriate places.

There is magic and joyousness in the air. The room is transposed into a golden palace. The ceremonies require the youngest to ask the four questions, *koshis,* which are preceded by the introductory question, "Why is this night different from all other nights?" "Why on all other nights do we eat matzoh and bread, but tonight we eat only matzoh?" "Why on all other nights do we eat other vegetables but tonight we eat bitter herbs?" "Why on all other nights do we simply eat food but to-night we dip it into bitters and salt water?" "Why on all other nights do we eat either sitting upright or in a reclining position, but tonight we eat only in a reclining position?" I ask these questions in Hebrew in appropriate intonation. Then I translate into English for the assembled guests (for it is a tradition to invite even some strangers to the feast—to symbolize that all men are brothers).

The answer to the questions is read from the Haggada, the bible of the occasion. It is a historical recital of the bondage of the Jews under Egypt and the miraculous achievement of their freedom, and re-establishment of their country.

During the reading the symbols of the events are partaken by the guests. My father hands out pieces of matzohs, which he has dipped in *harosess* (apples chopped with nuts and soaked in wine) to denote the sweetness of life; matzohs with sharp horseradish to denote the bitterness of life; and lamb to denote sacrifice.

The children are fascinated by the ritual. When the text describes the ten plagues which God visited on Pharaoh and those who killed each firstborn son of the Jews, we spill a bit of wine from the cup ten times.

At one point a child is directed to open the door so that "Alya Hanuva," God's invisible visitor to every Seder, may enter and sip the wine. A special glass for him stands in the center of the table, and the children's eyes open wide as they "see" the wine in the "becher" go lower. I remember this when many years later I am in Italy and am pushed by thousands of devout peasants who have trudged many miles to the Cathedral of Naples on St. Gennaro Day. There, in a semidark corner behind an iron gate, stands a statue of St. Gennaro and the cup in his hand fills with Christ's blood on this holiday. We peer through the gate, to pierce the darkness, and in the fierce heat created by the throng, we see moisture on the outside of the cup and a glistening within. Women faint. Men try to fall on their knees and pray, but cannot because they are wedged in by others who cry out hysterically. Yes, not only is seeing believing. Believing is seeing—something I remember when I cross-examine witnesses.

The Haggada is divided into two "acts." The intermission is dinner.

First, my mother brings a pitcher of water and a large bowl. All in turn pour water over their hands and recite a prayer of cleanliness. Then follow the *gefilte* fish, chicken, and *tsimmes* (cooked carrots and prunes).

There is one unique Passover dish served on no other occasion. It is soup, consisting of salty cold water. Into it a whole hard-boiled egg is placed after peeling the shell at the table. It is sliced in the "soup," no mean feat as it slips around. Small pieces of matzoh are crushed and sprinkled into the water, like croutons, to give it body. The taste is deliciously exotic. Gourmets vow that it is better than the finest hot soups and superior to cold soups like gazpacho or vichyssoise.

Invariably someone asks why in the world we don't make this dish during the year. Always the answer is that "it only tastes good on Seder night." Either superstition or forgetfulness has prevented us from ever testing this explanation. I don't know of a single instance where it has been tried on more prosaic nights. Before I am through I intend to engage in an extreme act of daring by ordering a plate of cold water, salting it, and cutting a hard-boiled egg into it. If it tastes as bad as it sounds, I won't scoff at Passover superstitions anymore.

After dinner a prayer is read silently in thanksgiving for the bounties of life. Then follow the Haggada songs. They can be disposed of quickly or made into a lengthy "concert" by skipping no verses and teaching the assembly by sheer repetition to become a choir and give orchestrated effect to the rhythms. Of course, my father followed the path of most persistence. We caught the spirit and sang until two or three in the morning. The children enjoyed not only the escape from customary bedtime, but the harmonies which they learned to create. The elders simply had a rip-roaring singing time, for here was their initiation into jazz, rock, and soul singing, long before these words were known.

The melodies for *"Adir Hu," "Ekhod Mi Yode-ah," "L'Kho-af-L'Kho," "Khad Gadyo,"* and others are centuries old. Yet they contain rhythms and tempos more modern than anything sung by the Beatles or pop groups, including skipped beats and inventive varying pace. It is not surprising that Irving Berlin made his breakthrough in "Alexander's Ragtime Band," or that Al Jolson, the son of a cantor, produced the rhythm within a rhythm in "Mammy," or that there are so many Jewish composers of popular music, from George Gershwin to Burt Bacharach. They came by it through long inheritance. Examine Gershwin's "Get Happy" and you will find a well-known chassidic melody and rhythm. Phil Baker adopted an identifying melody for his television program which my father used to sing Friday nights before *Kiddush.* "The Anniversary Song" is a melody sung by Jews in Poland a century ago. This is not to decry the originality of modern composers. Their inventions stem from a memory stimulated by their talents. But the genre is as traceable as a Chinese song is distinct from Western music.

My father was not content with his own gusto. He beat a spoon against any glass object near him, creating beats in different pitches. Sweating and joyous in conducting, he drove everyone to participate, his hands waving toward those whose voices were timid, until they rose with him in swelling sound. When the sopranos had the upper hand, he provided the bass accompaniment, sometimes with humorous gestures. When the harmony was lacking, he turned tenor, or even soprano. And when the notes were false, he held his ears in pain, while the children burst into laughter. My mother sang too, she wouldn't dare not to, but her eyes roamed around the room observing the scene knowingly and happily.

The Haggada service always concluded with the singing of "My Country 'Tis of Thee" or "The Star-Spangled Banner." The contrast between the ancient religious ritual with its Hebraic rhythms and the American anthem was sharp and telling. We were transported from history and imagery to the reality of today. But there was one constant, the emotion of gratitude for freedom.

My father sang this paean of dedication to the United States with eyes closed and deep feeling in his by then hoarse voice. Those who immigrated here have by their choice evidenced an appreciation for our country which those born here may lack because they take its opportunities for granted. This was certainly true of my parents. My father worked sixteen hours a day for a pittance in London and seldom saw me awake as an infant. The contrast with life in this country caused his gratitude to overflow. He was unreservedly patriotic. I recall him posting a huge American flag in front of our summer home in Bethlehem, New Hampshire, every day. Even after his doctors cautioned him against exertion, he insisted on climbing a ladder at sundown to remove the flag and fold it tenderly for the next morning's display. When he died, we found in his will the most unusual provision I have ever seen. No one who had been a communist could be buried in our family mausoleum.

My musical education was not entirely homegrown. It stemmed from a great religious tradition. Synagogue music is as distinct and developed an art as that of opera or ballet.

The rabbi was vested with the formal conduct of the services and delivered the sermon. But the cantor was the musical exponent of the prayers. He was chosen because of his great voice as well as his interpretive skill. Like opera stars, cantors came from all parts of the world. The eastern part of Europe produced many of the famous ones. As their fame spread, they were invited to the leading synagogues in Kiev, Warsaw, London, and ultimately the United States.

Here they were eagerly awaited by the cognoscenti. So Cantor Sirota, he of the golden Caruso voice, Cantor Kwartin, whose pure tones shattered chandelier globes, Cantor Reutman, famed for the sweetness of his lyrical tenor, Cantor Koussevitsky, and others were invited to occupy the singing pulpits of leading synagogues in the United States.

Some of the American cantors like Richard Tucker and Jan Peerce became Metropolitan Opera stars. Others trained in Jewish musical lore, like Robert Merrill, also joined the Metropolitan. However, despite their careers, Rosh Hashanah and Yom Kippur services were performed by Richard Tucker, Jan Peerce, "Leibele" Waldman, and other concert or opera singers who returned to their earlier profession on the holy days.

The most famous cantor to arrive on our shores was Josef ("Yosele") Rosenblatt. He had scored triumphs throughout Europe. His arrival in the United States was awaited in Jewish circles with the same breathless anticipation as balletomanes welcome a Pavlova, Fonteyn, Nureyev, or Baryshnikov, or opera buffs greet a Chaliapin or a Sutherland.

Like all supreme artists his performance exceeded the exaggerated claims made for him. He was immediately signed by RCA Victor Records to record his religious renditions, and his platters broke sales records all over the world. In a sense he was a freak, but what a magnificent freak. He had three voices, a most beautiful hearty and distinctive tenor voice of clarity and power. Also, he could sing in the baritone range, and his tones were just as pure as they were deep, even descending to a basso range. But most astonishing of all, he could transfer to a falsetto soprano of incredible beauty.

Enrico Caruso used to play and replay one of Cantor Rosenblatt's records because he was fascinated by the sheer virtuosity of what seemed to be an impossible vocal feat. Rosenblatt recorded a prayer in which he performed a vocal exercise beginning with a low baritone note and rolling in coloratura style up the scale, until he reached the tenor range, which he passed into without the slightest break, continuing to ascend until he shifted into the soprano range, where he engaged in trills which would have made Tetrazzini, Galli-Curci, or the modern Beverly Sills proud; then without a pause or taking a breath, he descended through the tenor and baritone ranges, concluding with a vibrant basso tone of profound purity.

I heard about all this when I was a child because I sang in a choir and the sensational stories of Cantor Rosenblatt's brilliance were bruited about in all Jewish circles, as indeed they were recognized by lovers of music everywhere.

An essential part of the cantor tradition was the development of great choirs. The directors of these choirs also became well known, and their names were featured with those of the cantors. Their art was as distinctive as that of a motion picture director in his medium. Often they were composers of devotional music. Two of them, Joseph Rumshinsky and Abraham Ellstein, later became leading musical comedy composers of the Jewish theater. They produced the shows which starred Molly

Picon and Ludwig Satz, and many of their songs, like *"Bei Mir Bist du Schoen,"* have since acquired English lyrics and become popular American standards.

Usually the "basement" auditorium of the synagogue was filled with worshipers, who had to be content with the performance of a gifted *gabbay* or a rabbi who could intone the prayers without vocal virtuosity. To reduce the unpleasantness of the monetary distinctions which entitled some to enjoy the great cantor and choir, while others had to express their religious devotion in more prosaic style, the rabbi would repeat his sermon to the congregation "below." At least the mental stimulation was equalized.

Great cantors, like stars in other fields, were highly paid. So were choir directors. On high holy days, those synagogues which featured a famous cantor and a choir under a well-known director assessed members for the privilege of maintaining their regular pews for what was not merely a service but a unique religious concert. For others tickets were at a premium. A private police guard was usually placed at the entrance to control the crowd, which was motivated by musical appreciation rather than by religious devotion.

Jews had a sense of humor about all this. A favorite joke was about the man who sought admission without a ticket because he "must talk to his brother, for only a minute." The guard finally yielded but warned him, "Don't let me catch you praying."

The money problem in religious activity was solved in ingenious ways. It was the practice at an intermission in the formal service to read portions of the Torah. Members of the synagogue and visitors were called to the pulpit and were honored by reciting a brief passage from the holy scroll. After the reading, they could donate money to the synagogue, the rabbi, the cantor, and others. Eighteen dollars was a favorite contribution because the Hebrew word for eighteen is *chay* which also means life. Thus charity and long life were linked—a happy symbol. Since it was forbidden to write or to handle money on the Sabbath, gifts were recorded by using prepared cards for various denominations or by other devices. So a pragmatic approach was found for financial support of religious institutions, even though a collection box could not be passed around to parishioners.

Choir directors had to find fine voices to achieve effective musical ensembles. So tenors and baritones who aspired to be cantors or concert or opera performers first rendered their services in leading choirs. Children with beautiful alto and soprano voices were in particular demand. If they were vocally gifted, they were trained by the choir director and his assistants in private and group sessions. They were taught to read music, to place their voices correctly, which meant to produce tones not merely from an open throat, but in such a way as to create the resonances from the cavities in the head and chest, to understand the nuances of rhythm, and to express feeling.

A few were gifted enough in voice and talent to become soloists. The cantorial art permitted alto and soprano solos to contrast with the cantor's broad tenor and the symphonic arrangements of the choir.

I qualified as an alto soloist and received my training under Cantor Isaac Kaminsky, who occupied a post in a leading synagogue in Brooklyn, New York.

Cantor Kaminsky was a distinguished composer of devotional music. His choir and cantor compositions were sung all over the world. Since he was more talented as a musician than as a singer, he trained and led his own choir.

So I went to a special kind of musical school and was taught by a master. I learned to read notes. I learned the variations of harmonies and, above all, the importance of rhythms, which Kaminsky broke, changed, and restored with such skill that the listener thought his own pulse was adjusting to the momentum of each change.

During services, I watched Cantor Kaminsky closely. With limited vocal equipment, he created a thunderous voice. This he achieved by singing softly, and then approaching the climactic note with gradual increase of volume until the listeners' anticipation supplied the effect when the final note was taken.

Later, I stood in the balcony at the Metropolitan Opera House and heard Enrico Caruso use the same technique to give an enlarged effect even to his naturally powerful voice. Listen to his record of the fisherman's song *"Sur le mer"* for a perfect illustration of this technique. The drawn-out, ever-increasing, but slow approach to the high note lifts you out of your seat and you are actually relieved that the destination has been reached.

Also, I observed Kaminsky's knowledge of the physical aspects of producing sound. By twisting his mouth and forcing the voice to reverberate against the roof of his mouth, he created resonances which were deceiving in their volume.

The by-products of any education are sometimes as important as the formal training itself. That is the principle of gestalt philosophy—the total exceeds the sum of its parts. This is particularly true in music. A symphony conducted by Toscanini is not merely the sounds which emanate from the individual instruments. A by-product of my studies was a realization of the entirety of a composition. I was taught the alto part and it sounded unmelodious and strange. Later, when I heard the prime melody to which my contribution was addressed, I perceived the beauty of the continuously varying harmonies, sometimes due to the even more grotesque basso thumping or the baritone's single note holding through a series of variations.

After a while, I could detect the whole composition merely by studying the alto section. My ear and imagination supplied multiple constructions. I became bold enough to suggest some of these to Kaminsky. Even when he didn't adopt them, he was struck enough by my attentiveness and understanding to call me affectionately, "my little artist." He composed special duets for us, one of which was so entrancing and modern in conception that I hope to reproduce it in his name, if I ever fulfill an ambition to write the lyrics and music of a musical comedy.

I am grateful to Kaminsky, not only because he opened a new horizon of the joys of music for me, but because his training has been greatly responsible for such forensic skill as I have. For speaking is also a form of music. About this—more later.

The schism between Orthodox and Reform Judaism is typical of the differences in other churches. The Orthodox synagogue permits voices but no instrumental music. However, in Reform temples, organ music may be played. In Orthodox synagogues, men must keep their heads covered with hats or *yarmulkahs* but not in Reform temples. Women may not sit with men in truly Orthodox synagogues. Their distracting influence is avoided by seating them in the balcony or in a separate section in the rear.

The psychological aspect of somber dress being a sexual reminder is interesting in our current drive toward nudity. The designer Coco Chanel was not being prim when she turned to basic black. Women covered to the neck in satin and black lace can be more enticing than in the most revealing minis. So when women dress decorously for religious functions, whether to have an audience with the Pope or to attend church or synagogue, they draw special attention to their charms. The practice in the East of women covering even their faces with veils adds mystery to sexual curiosity. Perhaps it is the posture of innocence which is exciting. What is more intriguing than a gold cross or other religious symbol resting in the shadow of a low-cut gown?

So the Orthodox practice with respect to women in the synagogue is only one of many with which the Reform Jewish temple disagrees. In most religions, the divisions and sects multiply, each being certain that its form of worship is more consonant with God's will.

For example, on Chanukah, a gay holiday observance, even Orthodox Jews permit instrumental music. So Cantor Kaminsky, his choir, and a full orchestra, which he had rehearsed for weeks, gave a three-evening concert. By this time, I was featured as a soloist in the announcements.

The "dirigeant" of Cantor Rosenblatt's choir had heard of my performances and sent for me. I was auditioned by him and the great cantor himself. With Cantor Kaminsky's blessing, since he was proud of his handiwork and did not wish to stand in my way, I was engaged for the high holidays to sing in Cantor Rosenblatt's choir.

So I met Cantor Rosenblatt, a legend in his day, and more, I was trained to sing several duets with him, as well as solos on my own.

The cantor was a short man, about five feet five inches in height. He was also surprisingly slight, without the broad chest which is the chamber for most great singers. That is why women opera stars who slim down to meet theatrical standards suffer in voice production. Vocal chords cannot stand diets, no matter how good they are for health and the rest of the body. One can tell on the telephone by the hollow voice that the person on the other end has lost much weight.

Cantor Rosenblatt was respected for his religiosity as well as for his voice. He followed the true Orthodox practice of not shaving. So his ascetic beautiful features were almost completely hidden by a black beard which left only his blazing black eyes and a small portion of his pink cheeks visible. When he sang, he was immovable. Only his mouth formed a circle as if suddenly an opening was discovered in his hirsuteness. And from that dark opening, miraculous sounds poured out. Only when he engaged in his soprano coloratura did he close his eyes as if to add prayer to the angelic effect of his incredibly pure trills.

Then after a suitable pause, he opened his eyes and concluded with a most lionesque tenor high C.

It is the tradition of a synagogue service, as in all churches, to have the audience repeat in unison the prayer uttered from the pulpit. But when Cantor Rosenblatt had concluded one of his renditions, one heard not the responding chorus of the worshipers but a widespread gasp, then a chuckle of wonder, and finally, as if collecting themselves, a disorganized reading. Often his prayers were so moving that one heard sobs in the audience.

Yet he was a naïve and simple man. I was amused when we were in the dressing room, where the cantor's and choir's robes were put on, and he asked me for a cherry drop from my five-cent box. This was how he treated that precious voice. Later when he sang, I saw the red dye from the cheap candy on his tongue.

The Metropolitan Opera House tried on numerous occasions to engage him, but he would not shave his beard or agree to sing on Saturdays, and no amount of persuasion or money could induce him to do so.

Instead, he gave himself freely to charities of all kinds. He sang for the Police Benevolent Association, and they rewarded him with an engraved police whistle. This was the pride of his life. He showed it to all who would listen, and blew it frequently. His manager, who took care of his frequent recording sessions to meet an insatiable and growing demand, was beside himself, bemoaning the fact that any organization could save itself $10,000 by giving him a token toy instead.

His naïveté ultimately ruined him. He was induced to go into a large Jewish publishing venture. He lost his enormous earnings, and in addition was obligated on notes totaling almost a million dollars. He would not think of bankruptcy. He decided to accept a vaudeville and concert tour, where he could retain his beard and not sing on the Sabbath, to earn the money to pay his creditors in full. Also he performed marriage ceremonies, and although the fee was $2,500, he was besieged with such engagements. Many a bride and groom mistook the crowd which filled the synagogue or ballroom, and overflowed into the street, as a tribute to them.

The strain of his concert tour not only affected his voice but drained him of his energy. I went to hear him at the Academy of Music, in Brooklyn. The huge auditorium was filled to capacity. Since his audiences were non-Jewish in large part, his program was arranged accordingly. First, he sang Jewish lieder, such as the moving description of a rabbi teaching the Hebrew alphabet to his pupils:

> *Afn pripetshik brent a fa-ye-rl*
> *Un in shtub iz heys*
> *Un der Rebbe lernt kleyne kinderlekh*
> *Dem Alef Bes.*

> *Zogt zhe kinderlikh gedenkt zhe ta-ye-re*
> *Vos ir lernt do*
> *Zogt zhe nokh a mol un ta-ke nokh a mol*
> *Kometz—alef—"O"!*

> *Az ir vet, kinderlekh, elter veren*
> *Vet ir aleyn farshteyn,*
> *Vif'l in di oysyes lig'n trern*
> *Un vif'l geveyn*

> In the fireplace a fire burns
> And the room is hot,
> And the Rebbe is teaching
> Small dear children the Alef Bes [Hebrew alphabet].
> [Refrain]
> Say now children, remember dear ones
> What you are learning here.
> Say now and repeat again
> The vowel *Kometz* together with
> The letter *Alef* is pronounced "O"!

When, dear children, you become older
You will understand on your own
How many tears lie in these letters
And how much weeping.

Then he sang a song for the Irish in the audience. His accent destroyed the lyrics of "Mother Machree."

"I luv the dear sil-vaire dat
shines in her hair."

But his voice overcame all. The audience cheered in never-ending ovations for the lonely little black-bearded figure with skullcap on his head, who stood next to a piano on a huge stage, too dignified to bow. He walked off awkwardly, and when he was dragged back on the stage by his manager, he shuddered at the screams which his appearance evoked. Unsmiling, he stood for a minute and sauntered off again.

He learned to sing encores, which he gave freely not only because of his generosity but because it was the best escape from the embarrassment of applause. (In synagogues, it was forbidden to applaud, and the repressed feeling was expressed in head wagging, tears, and murmurs of appreciation and wonderment, which, when multiplied, I learned to recognize as a special form of applause.)

After he had paid his indebtedness, rescuing his honor with his throat, Rosenblatt went to Israel to replenish his spirit—or perhaps he went there to die. For sudden death came to him in the Holy Land at the age of fifty-two.

Fortunately his recordings, reorchestrated like Caruso's, to give them the utmost background fidelity, are available, so that his unique talents survive. Thanks to the accidental discovery by Edison when a dust-encrusted point scratched one of his turntables covered with wax, death no longer stills the voice.

Cantor Kaminsky also came to a sudden and tragic end. When he had retired on meager means to Florida, he came to New York to visit his friends and two of his alumni. I was one. General David Sarnoff, who had preceded me in his choir, was the other. The General loved to talk Yiddish, and Kaminsky's visits afforded an excellent opportunity. The cantor was also an amusing companion, being an excellent storyteller. His timing and long pauses, derived from his musical talent, were expressive enough to cause gales of laughter, before the punch line produced a second explosion of merriment.

By this time the cantor's blond Vandyke beard and mustache had turned grayish. His fine features prospered with age—except his eyes.

He had trouble with his eye ducts, and I was never sure when his characteristic blotting of his eyes with a large white handkerchief was to wipe away tears or was an emotionless gesture.

One day, he stepped off a curb in Miami Beach and was instantly killed by a speeding car. Little notice was taken of his passing, but Sarnoff and I grieved for our teacher.

Most talents develop with age, but a child's voice is the victim of its own growth. The last time I sang in public was at my high school graduation exercises.

I doubled in brass. I was to deliver an address and later sing John McCormack's famous ballad "I Hear You Calling Me."

My voice was changing. I had no trouble with the lower register, although it had acquired unaccustomed heavy shading, but when I reached the high notes, which once flowed so easily, my vocal chords, growing thick, resisted. I was almost in panic, but strained and got by, though not without a telltale crack in what was to be the glissando finish.

Vocal experts told me to be as silent as possible for a year, so that a mature singing voice could develop. One cannot predict for a caterpillar what its coloring will be when it turns into a butterfly. The voice is just as mysterious. One doesn't know whether the change in structure will produce a tenor or baritone, or what distinctive colorations the new voice will have; indeed, whether any singing voice will develop at all. So the voice doctor, like other doctors, depends on nature to supply the answer. He counseled the avoidance of strain so as not to interfere with the process.

I had entered Columbia College and had ambitions to be an athlete. Since I was very small, I qualified to be coxswain on the crew. Weight was a handicap and I fanatically trained by running from the campus to Grant's Tomb and back several times a day until I got down to a hundred pounds. I made the crew.

Running in freezing winter, and then practicing in the shell on the Hudson River, screaming counts to the crew through a megaphone were exactly what the voice coach had not ordered. Nor did the periodic dunkings of the coxswain in the ice-cold Hudson or Harlem River, a tradition after crew races, help the changing voice. But such are the values of youth. I would have sacrificed much more than my voice to make the crew.

While I lost whatever singing voice I was destined to have, the law of compensation—or is it of averages?—rewarded me with a satisfactory speaking voice. I feel fortunate, for what is more disconcerting than a scratchy, cracking, or high-pitched, nonresonant voice?

A whole army of motion picture stars discovered this tragedy when sound came to motion pictures. Almost all of them disappeared overnight. The impression of heroic men and alluring heroines disappeared the instant they spoke. Their voices registered weakness, and their diction betrayed their breeding. It was ludicrous to have the virile hero talk up in a squeaking voice. Just as suddenly actors who had fine speaking voices, like Conrad Nagel, became stars.

Nature has played tricks in real life, too. The redoubtable Jack Dempsey shocked you the first time you heard his high-pitched voice. Political figures, too, depend largely on their vocal chords. Thomas Dewey and President Nixon were fine baritone singers, and always spoke as if they were producing recitative in an opera. Roosevelt had a bell-like voice which was distinctive and beautiful. Who besides Coolidge, with his nasal twang, and Truman ever achieved high public office without an appealing voice?

So despite my foolishness in college, I did not lose the voice instrument so necessary for my life's work.

While I regret not having learned the piano or some other musical instrument, a skill which would not have been lost at puberty, my musical training has afforded me an enjoyable avocation.

For years while traveling on vacation, I would compose songs about the places I visited. Several of these, "Hawaii" and "Jamaica," were published and my wife and I had the pleasure of dancing to them when they became popular on the islands. Some of my songs, under a fictitious name, were bought by Paramount Pictures for one of its pictures, and by a television producer for his series.

Since then I have composed songs for each of our grandchildren. These were published, and RCA made a record of them under the title "Songs for You." It was interesting to watch a child listening to a song bearing his or her name. The universal reaction was one of embarrassment, shyness, and pleasure. Perhaps this was the evolution of the ego drive—shame at being so self-centered, but lured by the pleasure of adulation.

So I am a member of ASCAP, The American Society of Composers and Publishers, and the small checks I receive periodically for my compositions seem very large and gratifying. Doesn't every comedian want to play Hamlet, or is it too conceited to say, and vice versa?

Fates decreed that I should be trial counsel for the motion picture companies to defend them in an antitrust suit brought by seventy-one composers on behalf of their class for 300 million dollars in damages. Neither our opponents nor I considered my standing as a composer serious enough to constitute a conflict of interest. It was an insult I gladly bore, rather than be disqualified.

HE TOOK SUCCESS LIKE A GENTLEMAN AND DEFEAT LIKE A MAN

Two mayors have become famous national personalities. Municipal government being closest to the people but also to the local political boss, it has demonstrated the best and worst in democracy. The electorate has swung from one extreme to another in the same city. Can anyone imagine a greater contrast in appearance, personality, and devotion to duty than James J. Walker and Fiorello H. LaGuardia? Each represented the true mood of the city at a particular time. But conditions changed. That is why Walker could easily defeat LaGuardia the first time he was challenged by him, and then lose decisively to him in his second attempt, though the issues were the same. Since I had the opportunity to observe both from an intimate vantage point, and become an adviser to one of them, it is worth describing and evaluating two unique political characters on the American scene.

If an artist with great insight had to personify New York City during the gay twenties, he would have drawn Jimmy Walker. He was never a mayor. That was only his title. He was Mr. New York, jaunty, fun-loving, and not bothering too much about standards or morals while entertaining himself and the populace. He loved. He drank. He spoke wittily. He flaunted his sybaritic nature at the expense of dreary municipal caretaking. He took care of his friends, and we shall see that they didn't reciprocate. He was loyal to the worthy and unworthy alike.

He was emaciated as well as dissipated-looking, and he made a virtue of both. Being frail and narrow, he specialized in carefully tailored suits which hugged his waist and made his shriveled frame look dapper— that was the word applied to him. He wore his fedora hat with brim turned down rakishly on one side. He skillfully made his contrived appearance look like devil-may-care casualness. As if to make up for his sunken chest, his dark blue or black shiny satin ties, thinly knotted, curved out at least three inches before tucking into his pearl gray vest.

Obviously, he was the bane or envy of well-built men, whose bulging muscles prevented stylish fits, while his clothes clung to his skeleton frame, as if they were "poured on." All this was made consistent by his face. It was puckish. He had a thin nose which tipped upward roguishly at the very end. His black hair was flattened down in shiny precision and contrasted with his eyes, which were light or dark blue depending on the colors of his suit and tie. They really twinkled. Indeed, he laughed with them, while his lips would purse in comical appreciation. His most robust feature was his voice—low-pitched, distinctive in its half-hoarse, half-resonant quality, with variety of shadings, used as skillfully as an organist plays his keys to surprise and please the ear. Just as effective as his voice were his silences. When making a speech, he would not hesitate to pause for twenty or thirty seconds before the conclusion of a sentence, shaking his head slowly up and down, challenging the audience's anticipation of the jest or point he was about to make. Audiences would respond to his long silence with laughter and applause. He would finally utter the conclusion, in which event there was a renewed burst of appreciation; or not end the sentence at all shrugging as if to say, "Need I say more?" Then he would nod his head in *his* appreciation of the audience. This brought forth another sally from those who now felt they were participating in the speech. He made every speech a two-way affair. It was unique milking of an audience.

Of course, it could only be carried off by one who had supreme self-confidence. A long silence usually breaks concentration and the listeners' attention wanders off. Only masters can make silence a continuation of thought processes. Like telegraphic communication, dashes as well as dots fill out the message. It is all called timing, but very few can practice the art. The only actor I ever saw who dared to be silent for long stretches and not lose his audience was George M. Cohan. He applied the same technique on the stage that Walker did on the dais. I recall his performance in Eugene O'Neill's *Ah, Wilderness!* There was a scene in which the father explained the facts of life to his son. When the son asked a question, Cohan did not follow the author and reply. He inserted his lengthy silence, looked quietly at the boy for what appeared on the stage to be hours, while occasionally nodding his head as if weighing the question, and gazing again intently into the child's eyes. The audience was forced to appreciate his embarrassment and imagine the impending reply. The audience became the author. There was laughter and suspense. His reply was matched against the audience's anticipation and set off heightened reactions as the guessing game was played out. It became dialogue not only between the characters on the stage, but between them and the audience.

Most performers feel that they must be doing or saying something to hold attention. They act as if a pause represented forgetfulness. Comedians, particularly, practice a frenetic delivery to keep momentum going. But silence properly used is part of momentum, because it provides contrast and opportunity for appreciation. Comedian Jack Benny claimed that the most sustained laugh he ever received, in his many sketches depicting himself as a miser, was when a stickup man confronted him with "Your money or your life"—and there was an endless radio silence, while the laughter mounted at the mental struggle he was going through in making his decision.

Walker was cut out to be an actor, not a statesman. His talents ran to writing songs and exuding charm. Unfortunately, he had studied law, the most arduous and exacting profession, and totally unsuited to his aversion to drudgery. His disposition was to savor the final achievement if the effort necessary to attain it could be evaded. Someone should have told him that this is about as possible as winning the Nobel Prize for Literature without writing a word. Shrewd Tammany leaders decided to exploit his personality politically. He became a senator in the New York State legislature. His nimbleness of mind enabled him to read only the title of a proposed bill and make a creditable speech for or against it as party dictates required. He did not hesitate to be cryptic. Once, in opposing a censorship bill, his oration consisted of thirteen words: "I have never heard of a girl who was ruined by a book."

He had the gift of pleading guilty in such a way that the sins of all were epitomized by him, thus evoking sympathy for the many, not merely himself. Once, when he was Mayor, and his escapades with Betty Compton were reaching scandalous proportions (his limousine bearing the No. 1 license plate was continuously parked overnight in front of her apartment, an available target for newspaper photographers of which he never deprived them), Cardinal Hayes summoned him and appealed to him as a Catholic heading the greatest city in the world to be more upright in setting an example for others. He replied, "Your Excellency, there are dozens of confessional booths in St. Patrick's Cathedral. They can't all be for me."

When critics attacked his neglect of city business, he replied, "I don't understand this. You can see lights burning in my office hours after I leave."

He understood that he was violating political psychology, but he was delighted because he could get away with it. He said, "My wisecracks rose many times to plague me, but I couldn't help laughing, even though I well knew that the public does not trust a banker who is gay, a clergyman who smiles, or a politician who forgets to frown at the news camera."

He made a virtue of what others would have hidden. "I've read not more than fifteen books from cover to cover. What little I know, I have learned by ear!"

Al Smith once said to Walker, his protégé, "Why can't you be like Jim Foley? His light is burning late and he studies. While you . . ."

"I'm lit up, too, Al, at that hour."

But he was the perfect mayor in extending the city's hospitality to the world's celebrities whose greatest reward was a ticker tape parade down Broadway. So Lindbergh and channel swimmer Gertrude Ederle, General Foch and Babe Ruth, Queen Marie and Bill Tilden, President Coolidge and Red Grange, King Leopold and Jack Dempsey, and dozens of others in the limelight received their ultimate glow when he bestowed his luminous presence and felicitous praise and wit upon them on City Hall steps, while newsreel cameras recorded and spread the event to the far corners of the world. Wherever people saw his slim figure overshadowing the celebrities he honored, they recognized the sophisticated good will of New York City. He was the symbol par excellence of a teeming cosmopolitan center, prosperous and joyous.

It seemed in those worriless days that the city belonged to the world and that its main function was to be a port of celebration for those who had achieved fame, even of a transitory nature.

Some countries exist on tourism. New York City, under Walker, was the forerunner of the United Nations, apparently with no more difficult task than to honor headliners. This function was so important that there was an official greeter, Grover Whalen, aristocratically mustached and carnation buttonholed, who added the Old World touch before presenting the guest to Jimmy, the king of the New World. Walker's greetings became a feature of newsreels shown around the world. To Guglielmo Marconi he said, "It is gratifying that you did not send a wireless but came in person. Here we do not know much about transmission but we have fine receptions." And when he was invited for reciprocal visits abroad, which he eagerly accepted with the comment that "A Mayor is not fully performing his duty until he leaves town," he charmed everyone there too. He was shown on a newsreel talking to a woman in Paris who asked him whether he spoke French. "Fluently, madam," he replied, "but the ignorance of these natives is deplorable. They can't understand a word I say."

Of course, no ballroom dinner was complete unless adorned by Mayor Walker. Here his official status and special gifts melted perfectly. He attended all the important ones. Sometimes this meant seven nights a week and two or three a night, not to speak of cocktail parties. If only he had been as conscientious about his other duties.

The reason for the plethora of testimonial dinners was the discovery that the easiest way to raise funds for any cause was to select a guest of

honor who could command a large attendance at twenty-five, fifty, or a
hundred dollars a ticket. This resulted in some peculiar guests of honor.
The head of a buying concern for department stores, like John Block of
Kirby, Block & Company was a surefire bet to sell a thousand tickets.
He was the most frequently honored guest in New York. Fortunately,
he was a fine man, who understood that he was lending himself to charity, and his only difficulty was changing his acceptance speech to express differently his awareness that he was merely the bait to bring in
the fish. Often a good cause would be enhanced by $100,000 or more
derived from these functions.

However, there were many occasions when distinguished men in science, literature, art, and government, some from abroad, were honored.
Curiously, the attendance was in inverse proportion to the importance
of the man. When the grand ballroom of the Waldorf was not filled, a
fact disguised by leaving a large dance floor space in the center (as if
discriminating guests needed more *lebensraum* than the hoi polloi
when they danced), one knew that the attendance was voluntary to
honor the guest, and not just to raise money. To correct the imbalance
of attendance, the price of a ticket was modest, just to cover the cost of
the occasion.

Since charitable causes abound, and New York City attracts the great,
there was not and is not an evening when the ballrooms of the large hotels are not being used by Heart, Cancer, Cerebral Palsy, Psychiatry,
Catholic Charities, Federation of Jewish Philanthropies, Protestant Big
Brothers, Greek Relief, Old Age Homes, and dozens of other charity organizations.

Irrespective of the cause or personality involved, it became the custom for entertainers, officeholders, important business executives like
Bernard Gimbel, sport figures, and writers to bestow their presence on
these occasions. The gregariousness of men and women of accomplishment is not of the ordinary kind. Except for a few so introspective
that they cannot bear exposure, they enjoy being introduced from the
dais, hearing the gasp of recognition, and the following salute of applause to express appreciation. It is the only direct confirmation that
someone out there likes them.

So there were large daises to seat the attending celebrities and sometimes two tiers of them. What better symbol of brotherhood is there
than a city composed of more Italians than in Venice or Genoa, more
Jews than in Jerusalem or Tel Aviv, more Irish than in Dublin, more
Germans than in Bonn, and huge black, Puerto Rican, and other ethnic
groups living side by side. Until recent outbursts, huge metropolitan
centers like New York were a living example of a world community living in peace and mutual respect. The multiple daises at these dinners

were microscopic reflections of this reality, and of something else. Democracy and tolerance applied to achievement, as well as race, religion, or color. Of course, all were not to be evaluated equally, but the prizefight champion Jack Dempsey sat next to author John Gunther, the Metropolitan Opera star Martinelli chatted with the chief executive of the J. C. Penney Company, James Farley, once a political manager for Roosevelt and later a Coca-Cola executive, conversed with Dr. Schick, whose findings eliminated the scourge of diphtheria. Judges of the highest courts sat next to nationally famous pop singers. Governors, senators, members of the Cabinet rubbed shoulders with concert violinists or pianists. The dais was a melting pot of talents as well as races. Propinquity can create warmth as well as distrust.

Jimmy Walker often acted as toastmaster, or if Harry Hershfield, George Jessel, Eddie Cantor, Milton Berle, or later Bob Hope or other stars presided, he would be a speaker. In order to give the entertainers fuller scope, and add a more "dignified" touch to the proceedings, nonentertainers with some felicitous gifts were invited to be toastmasters. Authors like Fannie Hurst and Quentin Reynolds, judges like Ferdinand Pecora, laywers like myself served this function.

Over the years, I introduced Walker and he me at these dinners dozens of times, interchanging our roles as toastmaster and speaker. Since honesty is the best policy in speaking as well as in conduct, I never alluded to him as a great or even competent public official. He did not mind. Few would have believed me if I had claimed he was. On the other hand, exchanging witticisms with him, for he never failed to reply effectively, pleased him and titillated the audience. And one could go as far as one wished in praising his charm and warm qualities, symbolic of the good heart of New York, without straying one iota from the truth. He was less discriminating when the time for reply came. For he indulged in lavish introductions of me (usually involving the name of Judge Benjamin Cardozo, probably because he knew I hero-worshiped him and despite the fact that coupling Cardozo's name with those of men far more worthy than me was still preposterously inappropriate).

There are a few traditional annual dinners which bring out the foremost citizens in the land, including the President of the United States—for example, the Al Smith dinner. One such occasion, requiring a triple dais, was the annual McCosker-Hershfield dinner for a cardiac home in their name. The cause was good but hardly pre-eminent. However, Alfred McCosker, who was the president of a radio network, was a most popular and charitable man, and Harry Hershfield lived up to his unique billing, "He walks with the highest and is loved by the humblest." Except for a dinner greeting a Churchill or De Gaulle, no function regularly attracted more "celebrities" from every walk of life than this one. The attendance overflowed each year, filling the Waldorf-Astoria's tiers of boxes and flowing into the corridors. People reserved tickets months in advance. The foremost entertainers and artists from the concert and operatic stages came forth to volunteer their services, and many were resentful because they were not invited.

The perennial trio at this function for twenty years were Jimmy Walker, Bishop Fulton Sheen (then Monsignor) and myself as toastmaster. Sheen and Walker contrasted and complemented each other in an extraordinary way. Walker, with his ubiquitous wit, graciousness, and charm, and Sheen with his hypnotic eloquence. He fulfilled the classic definition of an orator—the flashing eye and philosopher's brow. He could emotionalize the simplest aphorism and move the audience to tears (for example, his description of a muddy pool on a dirty street; but God shines the sun on it, purifies it, and lifts a single drop triumphantly out of the stagnant pool to His heart).

But there was a day of reckoning—literally. Moneys were missing. While the Mayor was fulfilling his social duties brilliantly, greedy contractors, bus operators, and others serving a teeming city were gaining control of the captainless ship of state. And they did not steer it in the direction of the public's interest. Scandals spewed from many city departments. Now Walker's amber-lit romantic goings-on suddenly had ominous green lights cast upon them. There were recitals of Betty's expensive jewelry and contrasting reference to the Mayor's salary. Rumors spread that there was a bagman with more than a million dollars held for Walker in a sort of dis-trust fund.

An investigation was ordered by Governor Franklin D. Roosevelt, and Judge Samuel Seabury, formerly of the highest court in the state, acted as counsel, really prosecutor, before a State Legislative Committee headed by Samuel H. Hofstadter (who later became a judge in the State Supreme Court and upon his retirement after thirty years of scholarly service joined my law firm).

If a dramatist reveling in contrast had invented two contestants, he could not have excelled the diversity between Judge Seabury and Jimmy Walker. The judge was stocky, heavy, white-haired, and white-faced from study, dressed in the most conservative old-fashioned clothes, dignified to the point of stiffness, aristocratic in bearing, humorless, courteous even when irate, severe even when friendly, impeccable in speech, but neurotically paying a price for his rectitude by a most annoying automatic clearing of his throat between words, as if his larynx stuttered.

Of course, as we have seen, Walker's trimness, dark Irish countenance, advance-style clothes, wit, easy bearing, and felicity made a per-

fect foil. When they confronted each other on the stand, Walker
evaded, parried with humor, respectfully mocked the Judge, and
squirted charm all over the hearing room. But Seabury had documents
in his hand; bills for jewelry and expensive gifts, contracts granting
franchises to friends, some of whom were not distinguished for honorable conduct, millions of dollars of deals approved by the Mayor about
which he had no knowledge, and so on, like dripping water which
seemed to make a louder and more unbearable noise by sheer repetition.

"There are three things a man must do alone," Walker said, "Be
born, die, and testify."

The contest was uneven even though Seabury never raised his voice
and Walker was brilliantly flamboyant. But as Walker himself once
said, "If you must fight, never choose the quietest person in the saloon
—the little fellow sitting in a corner minding his own business. The
chances are he is the ex-welterweight champion of the world."

Governor Franklin D. Roosevelt was not unmindful of the co-junc-
ture of official duty and political opportunism. Rumors from authentic
sources indicated that he would remove the Mayor from his post.
Walker resigned. Worse still—since Seabury's relentlessness might have
resulted in criminal action, Walker exiled himself by leaving for London with Betty Compton, his last gesture of defiance, loyalty, and love.

Ironically, the Democratic convention for the selection of a nominee
to succeed Walker was taking place. Powerful political leaders pleaded
with Walker to head home at once, saying that he could be nominated
and elected. Like Mayor Curley of Boston, he probably could. But
Jimmy did not wish vindication. He was pleased to be rid of responsibilities, which constricted his life, interfered with his pleasures, unless
the public was ready to enjoy them vicariously. Reformers had made
this impossible. The price of the spotlight he loved had become too
high because it followed him even when he sought the darkness of privacy.

Much later, I was taking an annual European trip with my friend
Jack Alicoate, the publisher of a motion picture trade magazine called
Film Daily, and we decided to visit Walker, who was living in Dorking,
a suburb of London. We were astonished to find him, Betty, and her
mother in a typical country squire's home, with thatched roof, rose garden, hedges, and gravel road leading to the fenced-in grounds. Walker
was wearing an English tweed jacket with leather elbow patches (I
have never understood this style. Do English gentlemen lean more on
their elbows than others—doing what, playing chess, drinking, or thinking?). Jimmy was delighted to see us. His exile must have been particularly painful because of the contrast between his former turbulent life

and the quiet countryside. Our presence made the memories of New York more real. He grasped my hands with fervor. For a moment, I thought I saw his eyes glisten with a tear. But instantly, they changed into that familiar laughing twinkle, while his face remained solemn, and he advised us that soon the vicar was to arrive and we would all have tea and crumpets. Jimmy Walker, the vicar, and tea and crumpets! He enjoyed our chuckles. Later, the vicar did come, and Walker acted the part of a well-bred English gentleman as if he were to the manor born. And he did so delightfully, without making fun even subtly, but causing everyone to fall into the gentle mood of religious good will and warmth.

Alicoate and I urged him to come back to New York. He asked me in mock melodramatic voice whether the coast was clear. But he meant it. Friends had told him that he better let more time intervene, or he might face trouble (the euphemism for criminal indictment). He confided in me that he was broke and that he lived on the beneficence of Betty's mother, whose house it was. I believed him. I did not think he was merely refuting the stories of the million-dollar bag money he was supposed to have accumulated.

Later in October 1935, he did come back to New York. He was hailed affectionately by almost everyone. There was no talk of any retribution. Once more, he became the darling of the dais. He did not need the title of Mayor to give him status on the public platform.

He talked to me about earning a livelihood. It was obvious that the stories of his secret booty were a myth. He did not have a cent. He had done favors for friends, acquaintances, and strangers, but not for personal aggrandizement. They had profited. He and the city had lost. The city owed him no gratitude, and those who did had no interest in him at all.

He was a lawyer. Emissaries came to suggest that he be taken into my law office and that almost any salary would do. But he had never practiced law and the slurs on his name further disqualified him in a profession requiring supreme character as well as competence to match it. Charm never hurt a lawyer, but where it is the chief reliance, he better look for other weapons. Surely, it would have been more appropriate for Walker to be engaged in some corporate good will mission where his popularity could overbalance his shortcomings. But no such proposal came from any of the myriad of "friends" whom he had freely served at so high a cost to himself.

I wanted to be of help. There was the possibility of his obtaining a post as impartial arbitrator in the garment industry to determine disputes between employers and the union. I sent word to President Franklin D. Roosevelt of Walker's plight and the possible solution. He appealed to the president of the International Ladies' Garment Workers' Union, David Dubinsky, who complied with the request. Walker had a job at a salary of $25,000 a year.

It was Walker's idea that Roosevelt, of all people, would help him. Why? Because he had never criticized or attacked Roosevelt for his hostile conduct toward him. Indeed, he had spoken favorably about Roosevelt when he ran for President and thereafter. All this was due to Walker's philosophy, which he once expressed to me in this way. "The worst thing a politican can do is get acid in his blood. When he developes a hate for his enemies, it will ultimately destroy him, not them. One can never tell in diplomacy, politics, or for that matter other relationships, when yesterday's enemy must become tomorrow's ally.

"Look at Al Smith," he continued, "he got sore at Roosevelt, whom he considered his protégé, for not consulting him when he reached the top. He got acid in his blood. It made him come out for Landon when he ran against Roosevelt. He didn't hurt Roosevelt. He destroyed himself. Al never had any influence after that, and he died a bitter man.

"I never bore a grudge against Roosevelt despite what he did to me. After all, what else could he do under the circumstances? Ruin his career by standing up for me? Roosevelt's friends have told me how he appreciates my attitude and is sorry that things worked out as they did —and that he is very fond of me."

I never forgot his "acid in the blood" philosophy and I have seen its truth demonstrated time and again; John Lewis, the powerful labor leader, condemned his benefactor, Roosevelt, and lost his unique hold on the labor movement; or farther back, Teddy Roosevelt was so galled by his protégé President Taft that he formed the Bull Moose Party and ran on a third ticket, thereby preventing Taft's re-election and squeezing in Woodrow Wilson as President. But also thereby ending his own career. Taft wasn't destroyed. He went on to be Chief Justice of the Supreme Court of the United States.

In less portentous situations, the same principle holds true. Wives or husbands who get "acid in their blood" in divorce preceedings pay a price in ulceration and nervous exhaustion. The tragedy of a broken marriage is thus elongated, so that later their visits with their children at graduation, marriage, and the event of grandchildren become hateful confrontations, the only amelioration of which is avoidance. Without "acid in the blood," time heals the wound, and pleasant memories of early love make it possible to share the joy of its consequences.

I have urged husbands to make property settlements on their wives in settlement of the matrimonial controversy even where courts have no power to do so, because, aside from tax and other advantages, such a gesture of affording security to the wife pours balm upon exacerbated feelings and prevents the acidulous grudge. If a doctor or psychiatrist could measure the injury to health from a protracted contest which is filled with frustration and hatred against the money differences which separate the disputants, he would find that the cost in health (and ultimately the doctor's bill) often outweighs the money over which the quarrel persists. Indeed, there is such a medical condition as a litigation neurosis, which manifests itself in all sorts of nervous disorders or other malfunctioning, and disappears the moment the litigation is ended. I once tried a case for a woman whose hand was convulsed into a "clutching hand" by an injury. Foremost specialists for both sides examined her and pronounced her condition permanent. They agreed it was not a form of hysteria. Nevertheless, the moment the suit was settled, her tendons relaxed and her hand opened up. She and her doctors were as surprised as we were. Mysterious forces which had responded to her deep anxiety about the outcome of the suit had similarly unlocked her hand when she derived inner peace from the end of the litigation. We suspect the result would have been as Lourdes-like even if she had lost the suit but knew it was over.

In other types of litigation, the same phenomenon can be observed. After a controversy has been decided, the contestants prosper physically. They sleep better, eat better, and recapture their perspective and balance.

Time and again, women who refuse to give their husbands a divorce, which would only free him to marry the proverbial blonde, have insisted that they are not condemning themselves to permanent spinsterhood. "You may be sure," they say, "that as soon as I meet someone I can fall in love with, I'll grant the divorce and reconstruct my life." But curiously, they rarely fall in love, while psychologically they consider themselves bound to their straying husbands. However, when they yield to advice not to have "acid in their blood" against their husbands, but think of themselves and end a meaningless marriage, they frequently marry shortly thereafter. In the same mysterious way, their emotions which have clutched tight open up, when the anxiety and frustration of a legal holding operation is ended.

One day, I invited Walker and Betty Compton to my home. On announcing to my wife, Mildred, at the last moment, as was my inconsiderate custom, whom we would have for guests that evening, she expressed her dissatisfaction, although, unlike the Russians, she never exercised a veto. It wasn't the belated notification which bothered her. Long experience had inured her to this injustice and the maids were always ready with extra plates and would have been stunned by reasonable notice. No, it was that Mildred didn't care for the Mayor. She had never been impressed with celebrities as such and she said some plain words about his frailties as a public official.

It was an interesting test of Walker's prowess with people. Within five minutes after he arrived, not only Mildred, but Alberta and Nora, the cook and maid, the doorman, the elevator man were completely charmed by him. Here he was no platform personality.

His affectations which were so effective had become second nature to him, and therefore appeared to be natural. Thus, he salvaged their charm and yet eliminated the irritation of their artificiality. He could posture and be sincere, all at the same time. He was chummy with the help without the slightest condescension, and he was respectful to his equals or superiors without pretended servility. And when, as the evening warmed up, he sat down at the piano, and played and sang his own well-known composition, "Will You Love Me in December as You Did in May," everyone melted.

Throughout all this Betty sat silently, like a beautiful poster of a composite show-girl beauty, unemotional and uninvolved almost to the point of aloofness. She did not, like other women, fawn over Walker, or reflect the glow he gave out. Her manner was almost a challenge to him, unintended, I am sure, that he better do something more if he wanted her adulation. Some men are intrigued by such resistance. Bobo Rockefeller, in the marital strife with her husband, revealed that when she first met him, he asked her, a coal miner's daughter, for a date, she refused. Aside from her beauty, which had won a prize, and her other qualities, it was the beginning of his pursuit.

Jimmy's dissipation in his early years invaded the later period of his good habits. He gave up drinking because of his ulcers. "Just when a man can afford a steak, his doctors put him on a milk diet," he said. Arthritis plagued him. His frail body became even more boyishly thin, but his posture and hesitant walk gave away his age.

He took sun lamp treatments every day to hide his sallowness. When I saw his ruddy face and commented on how well he looked, he replied, "I am like an old house that is painted on the outside, but the plumbing is no good."

I introduced him at the last public dinner he ever addressed. It was a function to aid a charitable cause, and the guest of honor was Ben Sherman, of the A.B.C. Company, which owned the candy machines installed in theaters and elsewhere. So, still responding to the loyalty one owed to a friend, the first commandment in Walker's decalogue, he got out of a sickbed against doctor's orders, to confer his unique luminosity on the occasion. He had been told, and rightly enough, that his presence would "make the dinner."

The poor man was in pain, which at times doubled him up. The audience appreciated his being there. They sensed the sacrifice he had made. When he was introduced, he received a standing ovation that seemed endless. Perhaps they intuitively realized that it was the last time he would hear applause. Men and women cheered and some cried as they did so.

He was tremendously moved, but in characteristic fashion, he hid his embarrassment with wit. When the pandemonium, which had several lives, rising to a new crescendo each time it seemed to have subsided, finally yielded to his finger-to-the-lips gesture for silence, he began for the tenth time, "Ladies and gentlemen." There was a hush. There he stood bent over from arthritis, but his head jaunty and his eyes looking sideways mischievously. It was signal enough, like a comedian's funny hat, that he was not going to respond emotionally. But what he said surprised everyone:

"You will forgive me for being bent over this way. [long pause] After all, why should I at this late stage of my life start going straight!"

The explosion of merriment turned into another ovation, to assure him that they believed in him and loved him.

A few weeks later he was dead.

ONE WHO BRAGS THAT HE IS A SELF-MADE MAN RELIEVES GOD OF AN AWFUL RESPONSIBILITY

The pendulum swings. The Mayor who succeeded Walker was Fiorello H. LaGuardia.* Democracy is not a perfect system, but it is a self-correcting one. It is the forerunner of the computer which miraculously detects that one of its parts is not functioning, announces the fact, and sometimes corrects the defect. Where the pendulum is fixed, as in a dictatorship, there can be no swing to reform, only to force and revolution.

How could the people have reversed themselves more completely than in choosing LaGuardia? In every way, he was the antithesis of his predecessor.

He was chubby, tending toward the roly-poly type. He was so small that Napoleon could have seen the top of his head. Like other ungainly men (Heywood Broun and Thomas Wolfe, for example), he made a fetish of being careless about his clothes, which were baggy and ill-fitting.

He had a thin, shrill voice, which reached shriek proportions when he was excited, and that was almost always. His chunky head squatted necklessly on his shoulders. He was swarthy, and his eyes blazed with blackness. Instead of poise, he had fury.

His most outstanding characteristic was the way he spoke. His mouth would open wide and one could see his tongue forming the words. The impression was that his mouth was filled with tongue. It gave him an unusual accent. It was not Italian. It could not be identified, except that it was LaGuardian or tonguish. There is a psychological reason for speech mannerisms. Usually, as in his case, it is to hide an accent. Boris Morros, the Russian composer of "The Wooden Soldiers," who later

* The unfulfilled term left by Walker was filled in by Joseph McKee and John O'Brien.

became head of the music department of Paramount Pictures, tried to disguise his accent by whispering. Only when he spoke so softly that he became inaudible did he succeed. The tongue has more muscles than any other part of the body, but early training is not easy to overcome. Some speak dialect with an accent. The French and English are proud of their accents and make a special effort to preserve them. If the word charm is ever applied to Italian and Jewish accents, perhaps they too will struggle not to eliminate them.

LaGuardia's squeezed high pitch and labored pronunciation made him instantly identifiable. He recognized early the power of radio and whenever he appeared there could be no doubt who was uttering the words.

He had come up the hard way, courageous flier in World War I, interpreter at Ellis Island, and Republican congressman in a Democratic district. His restlessness spilled over party lines. He had frequently changed political parties, at one time running as a Socialist. Appropriately enough, he wound up combining all on a fusion ticket.

Having no funds and no political support from the leaders who detested him, because he railed against them, he practiced all the arts of showmanship to attract attention. Although he had enormous ability and a piercing intellectual mind, he was not above demagoguery. He believed in F.D.R.'s political primer, "First, you must get elected. Then you can carry out your idealistic program. A candidate who sticks to his principles even though they defeat him at the polls has betrayed his own mission and his opportunity to serve the people." Political death, like other death, is permanent silence. What good is it to the community to be defeated if you have something good to give it? When Roosevelt was accused of having clay feet, he chuckled. It was not an insult. He deliberately maneuvered politically to be in power.

LaGuardia once said to me during a hot campaign, "Louis, if they try demagoguery, I'll out-demagogue all of them." He could, too.

As a congressman opposing the Volstead Act, he stood on the steps of the Capitol eating grapes, and announced that they would ferment and produce alcohol in his stomach, and he defied the law enforcers to prevent the process. The newsreels (the forerunner of television news) asked him to repeat the performance. So did the newspaper photographers. He ate bunches of grapes for all of them.

On another occasion, he conceived a way to dramatize the high cost of living. He brought a chunk of raw steak into Congress, slapped it on his desk, and announced the price. Again, he drew national attention.

He ran for Congress against a Jewish opponent in a predominantly Jewish neighborhood. As the last week of the desperate campaign arrived, a mysterious handbill appeared, charging that LaGuardia was anti-Semitic. His answer was characteristically unique. He hired a hall and challenged his opponent to appear for a debate. There was only one condition. Both must talk Yiddish. His Jewish adversary couldn't, and failed to show up. LaGuardia, gifted in five languages (and drawing on his Ellis Island experience), addressed his audience in Yiddish and won the election.

It was the era of stunts. The law produced its own practitioner. William Fallon, the criminal lawyer, defended a husband accused of poisoning his wife. A vial of poison in his valise, identical to the poison in her body, was the prosecution's prize exhibit. In summation, Fallon, timing his conclusion to precede the lunch recess, charged that the vial did not contain poison at all, and that the prosecutor had engaged in an outrageous hoax. To prove his point, he picked up the exhibit, which experts had testified was deadly, withdrew the cork, and slowly swallowed its contents, while everyone looked on in horror. He sat down smiling. The Judge was barely able to rap his gavel for recess. Fallon walked out into a nearby empty courtroom where doctors were waiting to pump his stomach, which had been readied previously with special oils for the poisonous invasion. The jury acquitted Fallon's client.

Of course, public relations representatives considered stunts especially suited to their talents. Harry Reichenbach was the acknowledged master in this field. His thick gray hair and hard-lined face gave him a magician's looks, but did not reveal his pixie imagination. Some of his ingenious schemes became legendary guides for his profession. But when reaction set in against his unscrupulous devices, and laws were passed making their repetition a crime, his career ended and with it the stunt era.

One of Reichenbach's exploits was to publicize a visiting Hindu princess by leaving her clothes on the edge of a lake and announcing her disappearance. The authorities dragged the lake for the body. The public followed the tragedy of the missing princess in daily newspaper stories until she suddenly turned up well and hearty, explaining lamely that she had gone for a swim and had returned in a robe leaving her old clothes behind. An ordinance was enacted making it a crime to cause the city huge search expenses through deceptive publicity schemes.

Reichenbach similarly obtained free front page notice for a circus which was coming into town, by ordering two hundred pounds of raw meat to be sent to a suite in a leading hotel, registered in the name of T. R. Zann. When the manager investigated, he discovered that a lion had been smuggled into the hotel in a huge trunk. Of course, dispossess proceedings were instituted but not without the piquancy of the story drawing laughter and reams of newspaper space for Reichenbach's client.

Twice I had to tangle with him legally, once, when he was employed to publicize a motion picture called *The Great Gabbo*, a ventriloquist theme, with Erich von Stroheim. He conceived the idea of a huge sign at Forty-fifth and Broadway, on which scantily clad girls would cling to the iron bars and wave their legs in Roxyette fashion at the gaping crowds below. The live sign stopped traffic at Times Square. The city declared it a nuisance and ordered it to be abandoned. I advised compliance. Reichenbach was in a fury. He insisted that I bring an injunction proceeding against the municipal authorities. "Of course, you will lose," he comforted me, "but we'll get the darnedest front page story you ever saw, and everyone will be talking about *The Great Gabbo*. I told him that the law directs the publicity department and not vice versa, and warned the president of the company, Harry Thomas, that Reichenbach might lead him to jail as well as to higher receipts.

On another occasion, Reichenbach was miffed at William Fox, the motion picture tycoon for not rewarding him adequately for his services. He decided to demonstrate his powers in reverse. He spread the rumor that a new Fox theater was built on sand, and might collapse if too many patrons attended. If a plague had been announced in the environs, the theater could not have been more shunned. I forced Reichenbach to retract the falsehood, and with the aid of Building Department announcements restored attendance. But Reichenbach amused his friends by estimating the cost Fox had incurred, which exceeded the amount in dispute between them many times over.

Perhaps the most original stunt Reichenbach ever pulled resulted from sheer pride in his resourcefulness. He made a bet with an incredulous friend that he could elevate any ordinary girl to a $2,000-a-week booking at the Palace Theater in New York City, the very summit of vaudeville achievement and the dream of every vaudeville entertainer who ever set foot on a stage. To win the bet, he employed accomplices. He had the famous Dolly Sisters drive through the Garment District on the Lower East Side of New York. While halted in a narrow slum street by a flat tire, they heard a nightingale voice floating from a window of a factory. It was of such extraordinary beauty that even the annoyance of the car's breakdown could not deter them from climbing the rickety wooden stairs of a decrepit building to find that the incredible tones were emanating from a dark young girl twisting cloth in all directions under, appropriately enough, a Singer sewing machine. They hurried the bewildered genius into their Rolls-Royce, and ensconced her in a magnificent suite at the Pierre Hotel, where, as fate would have it, the story broke in the next day's newspapers. The background material was not very backward. Co-workers asserted that they had been lulled into heavenly trances by the girl's tones. Never in musical history had such a natural talent been hidden from the world for so long. The question was whether the Metropolitan Opera House could capture this phenomenal voice whose pristine beauty ought not be despoiled by formal training.

The publicity was nationwide. Reichenbach's agents saw to it that the Palace Theater would have the first opportunity to let the public hear the miracle of the golden throat. Of course, tryout was out of the question. Would anyone insult Tetrazzini or Caruso by suggesting an audition before a vaudeville house booker? She was engaged at several thousand dollars a week for an extended engagement. If one had judged by the thousands who stormed the box office at the first performance, she still would be singing there. But the sewing girl reaped as Reichenbach had sown, and she was pulled off the bill the second day. All but Reichenbach, who collected his bet, were indignant, although on reflection a few were amused by his ingenuity and their own gullibility.

Reichenbach's devilish talents played a part in Jimmy Walker's successful first campaign against LaGuardia. During most of the contest, Walker never mentioned his opponent's name. This is an ancient tactic followed by candidates who are decisively favored to win. Why publicize their opponent? It is always the underdog who demands face-to-face debate. Television has put more pressure on reluctant debaters. Programmers find confrontation between opponents exciting and, therefore, offer free time. In view of the effectiveness and high cost of political advertising on this medium, rejection of such offers gives strong hint of fear to face an opponent. And, of course, the adversary exploits this inference and makes the matter a political issue in itself. So it was that after the Nixon-Kennedy debates, which were generally credited with Kennedy's narrow victory, Nixon refused to debate Hubert Humphrey, and the latter charged his opponent with violation of the democratic principle of open discussion of the issues.

However, LaGuardia's taunts and sarcastic effectiveness got under Walker's skin. He told his advisers he was going to take on LaGuardia and give him what he deserved. All the political pros warned him against it. "He hasn't reached the public, but he seems to have reached you," they said. "Just ignore him. He hasn't got a chance."

Walker would not listen. It was not merely his honesty and ability that were being impugned. He might have stood for that. He was being pilloried with wisecracks. That was his game. He would fix the little so-and-so.

Unable to restrain him, Harry Reichenbach, Jimmy's public relations adviser, made a deal with him. "If you must reply, will you let me guide you how?" Walker was relieved to be unleashed, and consented.

"When you have finished your speech on schools tonight, as usual without mentioning his name, announce that you have a question to ask Fiorello H. LaGuardia, 'Why did he leave Bridgeport in 1915?'"

WALKER: "What have you got on him? Why did he leave Bridgeport?"

REICHENBACH: "Nothing. Just do as I tell you."

Walker did. Reporters excitedly rushed to LaGuardia. At last the Mayor had acknowledged his existence. Now the campaign would come to life. LaGuardia contemptuously swept the question aside. "I don't remember ever being in Bridgeport. What has this got to do with the issues? The Mayor better address himself to the terrible conditions in the city. That's what the people are troubled by."

The next night Walker, prompted by his gray-haired Iago, had the following peroration to his speech.

"Yesterday, I asked Mr. LaGuardia a simple question. 'Why did he leave Bridgeport in 1915?' His answer was he didn't remember ever being there. Now my opponent has demonstrated a remarkable memory for all sort of fact and statistics about the city's affairs. But on the subject of my question, he doesn't remember. I think we are deserving of more forthrightness from a reform candidate. I repeat my question: 'Why did Fiorello H. LaGuardia leave Bridgeport in 1915?'"

Now LaGuardia's voice was two octaves higher. He bounced as he screamed that the Mayor was trying to engage in red herring tactics instead of discussing the terrible conditions in the city. "This is all nonsense. I had no reason to leave Bridgeport or any other city. If Jimmy Walker knows any let him state it, instead of engaging in dishonest insinuations. I'll match my record of honesty with him or any other Tammany politician. This is no game. Let's talk sense. Let's discuss the issues. I challenge him to a face-to-face debate."

WALKER: "At first, he didn't remember being in Bridgeport. Now he admits he was there but doesn't remember any reason for leaving. I think it is time Fiorello H. LaGuardia came clean with the people of this great city. No more evasions, Mr. LaGuardia. I still have had no answer to my question, 'Why did you leave Bridgeport in 1915?'"

So it continued. LaGuardia was driven to distraction, the people were amused, Reichenbach laughed, and Walker was elected.

When LaGuardia ran for mayor again on a fusion ticket, he asked me and four others to act as his kitchen cabinet. I agreed. His headquarters were in the Paramount Building, where I had my law office. He would dash into my office unannounced and unmindful of other activities, and throw himself on a couch, bouncing once or twice, thus con-

tradicting his claimed exhaustion (I never saw him tired or subdued).
Then he would talk out loud about the next speech he had to make or
the proper tactic to use in meeting the usual hourly crises of a political
campaign.

What I suggested had to be interlaced with his continuing diatribe
in which he rejected, modified, or accepted the proffered idea, as if he
were just talking out loud to himself all the time. He was either too
proud to accept advice, or it was part of his volatility to absorb outside
voices into his thinking process without the usual station stops to listen
and acknowledge that a dialogue was taking place.

He won the election. I had arranged for him to appear first at The
Motion Picture Club, since our Entertainment Division for LaGuardia
had rendered yeoman service for him. We went to the Bond Building,
where the club was situated. It was a very cold night. All but the new
Mayor wore winter coats. He traveled in his suit. It was not bravado. His
wife, Marie, confided in me that he had no coat. A few of us chipped in
and the next day she presented him with an overcoat. It was a symbol
of his penniless condition. That was the way he left the office. He was
fanatically scrupulous about money. There could be no Seabury investigation of *his* regime.

There was such a crush at The Motion Picture Club that he disappeared in the crowd and had to be rescued by two burly police captains
who had already been assigned to him. But his dramatic ingenuity made
him one of the most visible public officials this country ever had.

He brought to his mayoral task a feverish dedication to city business.
Aside from being a good administrator and delegating duties to others,
he strove to be a one-man army. He was everywhere. When fire engines sirened their way down the streets, he was speeding after them in
the fire chief's car, making a clanging racket greater than theirs. Newsreels delighted in shots of him, in a black raincoat, water from the
hoses pouring down on him, while he peered up from under a fire hat
many sizes too large for his head.

If a murder occurred, there he was with the inspector of police, giving directions.

Suddenly, he would appear at eight-thirty in the morning in one of
the magistrates' courts, and, finding no judge there at the opening hour,
he would exercise his right as Mayor to sit as magistrate, dispose of
cases in his unique way, threatening "a tinhorn gambler," bawling out
"a punk," appealing to an alcoholic and sending him to a rehabilitation
center while inviting the wife and children to come to see him at City
Hall. Finally, when the magistrate arrived a half hour late and found to
his surprise that court was functioning, LaGuardia would publicly ad-

monish him that he owed a full day's work for the city's pay, and if the unfortunates and the police could be there on time, so could he.

No department was safe from such flying visits. He set a personal example of conscientious service, stimulating, driving, threatening, imploring, and generally raising hell, because the people were entitled to be served. The city was too large for such physical personal direction, but he stormed to his task as if by his own energy he would do the job tens of thousands were assigned to do. He was King Canute standing at the foot of the ocean sweeping back the waves of inefficiency and neglect, and by sheer dint of a furious broom keeping a little of the water from flowing too high on the sand.

But he also understood the importance of obtaining the foremost experts to man the departments. He scorned selections from political ranks, and often went out of the city to bring in a competent executive.

It was interesting to watch him lure a specialist into city service at reduced salary. Suddenly, his imperious manner was gone. Butter would melt in his mouth. He flattered. He cajoled. He subtly held forth promise of national recognition—and perhaps a cabinet post. He appealed to the ideals of the reluctant expert. Didn't he want to demonstrate his theories in real life rather than in a classroom or in a book and do something for the suffering people? If he came from another city, didn't he want to apply his unique talents in the biggest arena of all? He suggested that the acceptance would be heralded across the nation as a breakthrough in city management, and precipitously called in his secretaries to have the newsreels and newspapers alerted for a special announcement. He told the now wavering executive that he would be his personal confidant, and at the center of a great new experiment in civic reform. He offered cigars (for a new baby was coming into the administration); he brought in coffee and personally poured it like a solicitous hostess and inquired how much cream and how many lumps; he had a city car (of whose use he was most sparing) to be at the beck and call of the soon-to-be Commissioner. He was jovial, earnest, respectful, and even sycophantic (the most difficult of all roles for him) until he got his man. I doubt that any woman could have resisted such consummate wooing.

In this way, he induced Professor Russell Forbes, who taught at New York University, and had written a book on municipal purchasing, to become the head of the City Purchasing Department, and he imported Health Commissioner John L. Rice, Correction Commissioner A. M. McCormick, as well as Park Commissioner Robert Moses, the most redoubtable builder of them all. Had the law, which forbids raiding of corporate executives, been applicable to him, he could have been subject to wholesale suits.

But when the conquest had been achieved and the stunned victim had been personally ushered out with an intimate shoulder hug, he astonished those present by a lightning reversal. His easy, gracious tempo of but a moment before became a bouncing fury of action, as if a picture in slow motion had been turned into high speed. His dulcet ingratiating tones disappeared, and one heard the shriek of a football coach on the sidelines commanding his players to perform beyond their capacity. He was rude to any show of slowness or incompetence, and he didn't give a damn about hurt feelings. I heard him humiliate a high police official, who had brought him a sandwich to gobble, because the dressing was wrong and he did not even know how to fulfill such a simple order correctly.

Yes, his personal force and leadership verged on the dictator complex. Mussolini had once been a Socialist and reformer, but found his boundless energy too strong for subservience to democratic processes. Lenin, Castro, and other revolutionaries also had programs to free the people from oppression, and wound up enslaving them so that they would not resist the good medicine *they* prescribed. The path of idealistic movements often continues right on to a police state, without a detour.

Perhaps I do him an injustice, for it is only a psychological reading, but, given other circumstances, I can imagine LaGuardia, honest and devoted to high ideals, believing that he could do better if unrestrained by a system of checks and balances. He had the impatience of a strong leader.

This is a constantly recurring phenomenon. The weak executive lives under the shadow of the legislative and judicial branches. The strong executive chafes at the restraints and delays they impose. The people are protected in both instances by checks and balances. Democracy rejects the notion of the elite, not because it may not produce brilliant results, but because there is no assurance of its constancy or that with all good intention it won't abuse its power. We prefer less spectacular achievement with the guarantee that the people will determine their own fate. Still our constitutional structure permits the Chief Executive to be strong. Indeed, there are very few leaders in the world who have the powers of our President. But power tends to be absolute and this we never permit.

I am partly led to the surmise of LaGuardia's propensity for personalized government by an incident which ought not to be taken literally because he was not above playing games to achieve results. He didn't float balloons. He pushed them up like kites, and he knew that kites rise only against the wind.

"The March of Time" was a popular motion picture documentary which treated with personalities and issues very much like the special documentary on television does today. It chose LaGuardia for one of its subjects. It was a compilation of newsreel shots of his varied roles, combined with personal interviews with him and others about him.

It showed the full dimension of the man. It jumped from the comic and colorful to his genius for serious administration. There he was, the midget fireman, or cutting Tammany leaders to shreds with his sharp tongue (fully visible as always), the futile replies of the politicos (if they were dignified, they lacked manliness in the face of his tirade; if they were angry, their bad English betrayed them and caused laughter); and then scenes of him closeted for a full week with sheafs of documents higher than he was, working on the city budget, his sleeves rolled up, his shirt collar open and dirty, and his hair disheveled (he dramatized the event as a personal ordeal), looking up sleepily and telling the interviewer, that he was determined to take the fat out of each department, to relieve a long suffering public. Then he was shown addressing a large group of the nation's accountants at the Bar Association Building in New York, and without a note reeling off dozens of figures of the city's budget, funding, interest, bond, and other complex financial plans, with such profound grasp of their complexity that the conservative audience of professional men stood and cheered the tour de force they had just witnessed. All in all, the film was a fascinating document. It was booked into the Radio City Music Hall.

The only trouble was that election time was approaching. Tammany Hall, which was supporting William O'Dwyer, was horrified by this special pleading for the opposition. It felt that the reel was a campaign document and that it was unfair to project it at that time. "Show it after election," they urged, "but not now, or else equalize the situation by showing a Democratic document we'll supply." Great pressure was put on the Music Hall to discontinue the showing of the film. At the end of the week, and before the feature picture had completed its run, the "March of Time" reel was taken off the program.

The next day, I got one of the panic calls from LaGuardia. They were never less than extremely urgent. The fact that he wanted to discuss something immediately elevated it to an emergency.

When I arrived at City Hall, he did not greet me. His first words were, "Louis, who is Leo Spitz?" I was taken back at the inquiry. "Why, he is president of R.K.O. Pictures," I replied, searching his face for the significance of the question.

"He is a gangster!" he yelled. "He is a Chicago gangster!"

"Oh, come now, Fiorello, Spitz is no gangster. He is a distinguished Chicago lawyer, who became president of the R.K.O. motion picture company. I know him well. He is a fine man. What is this all about?"

"He is a member of a Chicago gang. He is a mobster!" His fist banged so heavily on the desk everything on it bounced. Then he leaned over as if he was going to let me in on an important confidence.

"R.K.O is distributing 'The March of Time' subject about me. The crooks in this city have gotten the Music Hall to take it off the screen. The gangs know how to go about these things. They got to their Chicago bums and Spitz pulled the picture. Now, I tell you what I want you to do. You go to Leo Spitz and tell him they have thirty-eight R.K.O. theaters in this city. They are full of violations, fire violations, building violations, sanitation violations. They are rat traps. Tomorrow morning, the inspectors of these departments are going to serve notice of violations on every single one of them. I am going to close them up! Now you tell Leo Spitz that he better retain you to keep those theaters open, and that he authorize the putting back of the 'March of Time' into the Music Hall. And what's more, I want that 'March of Time' to play in the R.K.O. circuit and all the other circuits in this city!"

He paused breathlessly. I leaned back and smiled. "I am not going to threaten Spitz with violations of his theaters. Of course, I am not going to ask him to retain me. Furthermore, Fiorello, if I said I was going to do all these things and started out of this room, you would stop me. You know better. You're just sore and you are letting off steam. I will find out the facts. I'll get them from Spitz himself."

I went to see Spitz and in a friendly way inquired about the matter. He confided in me that Tammany Hall was so aggrieved at the partisan stunt, as they called it, that they threatened through various building and other departments they still controlled to take it out on R.K.O.'s theaters by filing wholesale violations. I did not dare tell him where I had heard of this idea before. A compromise was ultimately effected whereby those theaters which were friendly to LaGuardia would play the reel if they wished to do so, and those which didn't could abstain.

LaGuardia's skill in dramatizing events knew no bounds. He was as resourceful in publicizing himself and his program as he was devoted to making the city the finest in the country. When there was a delivery strike of newspapers he decided that the children would miss the Sunday comics and he would read them to the tots (and, as if he didn't know, to their parents) over the radio. The resulting newsreel shot of this effort became a classic and was shown throughout the country. It depicted him in a white shirt, horn-rimmed eyeglasses perched on the tip of his nose, describing the panels of the cartoons and reading the balloons with such intensity that even the elders were frightened by the goings on. When the picture had the words "crash!," "bang!," LaGuardia shrieked these words hysterically while his open hand smashed the table, knocking over the microphone and causing more "crashes" and "bangs" than the cartoonist had planned. When the villainous animal approached the young boy stealthily, LaGuardia hunched over, almost shrinking to cartoon size, and in breathless hushes frightened the hell out of the kids as no professional actor could have done.

Suddenly, when his pantomime and portrayal of a hundred moods had ended, he straightened up, took off his glasses, and, looking emotionally into the camera, sermonized in as measured and low a tone as he could muster, "And what does all this prove, my dear children? It proves that those who do wrong are punished and end up unhappy, but that if you live an honest and good life, you will be rewarded." He had turned a cartoon entertainment into a Sunday school lecture. He was John Barrymore, the Big Bad Wolf, and Billy Sunday all rolled into one.

On another occasion, he was faced with a serious crisis. The Nazis had booked Madison Square Garden for a rally. They had applied, as was necessary, for a license from the city to hold the meeting. When word got out of the impending fifth-column gathering, a storm of protest broke over the city. The general hatred and contempt for the Nazis was heightened by the presence of so many Jews and Catholics, who were their special victims. The rally was a provocative challenge to the sensibilities of almost all the people. Yet, a great division of opinion existed as to whether the meeting should be barred. Foremost liberals and anti-Nazi leaders asserted that in a democracy the gathering, no matter how despised, should be permitted.

LaGuardia called me. This time his urgency was real. I skipped lunch and rushed down.

"What do you think," he asked, "should I refuse the license?"

"Yes," I replied.

Before I could say another word, he rose from his desk in a fury, pranced up and down the room in a hopping movement and screamed, "How can you, a liberal, say such a thing? Suppose the next week the Republicans or Socialists want to hold a meeting, can the Democrats stop them? Must I refuse a license to the Catholics because the Protestants don't like their meeting?" It reminded me of the Goldwynism "For your information, I will ask you a question."

I let him expend himself for a while and when the purple receded from his cheeks, I interrupted, "Did you call me down to abuse me or ask my opinion? If you will be good enough to listen, I will tell you my reasons."

He looked at me disdainfully and sat down.

"You have two reasons to reject the license. The first is clear and simple. The second is a philosophical reason which you probably won't accept and I won't blame you. It is strictly a minority view."

"Go ahead, what are they?" he said with a gesture, as if he were granting me permission to speak when I deserved to be dismissed.

"The first reason is that a Nazi meeting in the heart of New York is likely to stir a riot and bloodshed. It presents a clear danger of a nuisance. There are many legal decisions which give a city the right to prevent a provocative act which is likely to cause disorder. No clearer case than a paramilitary meeting of Nazis, in the midst of a populace that is feverishly opposed to them, can be given to bring the preventive riot rule into effect."

I took advantage of his reflective silence and continued.

"The second reason is that we liberals have misconstrued the liberal credo. Voltair's 'I disapprove of what you say, but I will defend to the death your right to say it' is sound but can't be universally applied. It has misled us at times into martyrizing the finest among us. That precept is true for all those with whom we disagree, but who would give us the same right to be heard, if they were in power. But when the Communist and Nazi program, which you can buy for ten cents, asserts that if they ever win, they will kill or imprison all 'counterrevolutionaries,' their phrase for minority dissidents, then the battle is uneven. Ultimately, we must die. For we may win a thousand times and protect their right to oppose us. But if we lose once, they will destroy us.

"Look at Germany. The liberal democratic government threw police cordons around Hitler's gatherings to protect his right to rant. When he won, he killed them all.

"Every philosophy must have the seed of survival in it. If it leads to its own destruction, then it doesn't deserve to survive."

"What happens to the Bill of Rights?" he said quietly.

"I contend that legally the right to assemble has one inherent exception. It is not granted to those who themselves proclaim that they won't grant you the right to assemble."

"And you would say the same for the right of free speech?" He didn't look up.

"Yes," I said. "The right of free speech is guaranteed to anyone, no matter how detestable his views, unless he tells you himself that if he ever succeeds in being in power, he will deny it to you. There are recognized exceptions to the right of free speech too, you know. You can't yell fire in a theater, or run a sound truck in the middle of the night, or libel someone. I know you won't agree with this," I hastened to add. "It is a radical departure from the traditional view, but I have thought this through. More accurately, Fiorello, I have felt it through. Whenever my mind tells me what I must do but my heart aches, I re-examine the proposition. There must be something wrong with it. I would be mortified to have to insist that the Nazi Bund, which has been conducting military drills in our suburbs for months, should be permitted to meet at Madison Square Garden and spew their evil in our midst. I don't think democratic principle requires it. And even if I am a minority of one on this among liberals, that is my opinion. However, you don't have to struggle with so contentious a proposition. You can refuse the license on the first ground. You ought to do so."

For the last few minutes of my "speech," he seemed inattentive and lost in reverie. As if he had concluded his own thinking process simultaneously with my conclusion, he said, "No, I am not going to do that. I have another idea."

Knowing his propensity for startling dramatics, I expected a surprise. But I never anticipated one so unique that it would appear on the front pages of newspapers all over the world.

LaGuardia called in the Commissioner of Police and asked how many Jewish police officers and patrolmen there were on the force. Since the Jewish members of the police force have a social benevolent society called The Shomrim (Watchmen), it was not difficult to provide the answer. There were hundreds, including inspectors and captains. A huge number of police would be necessary outside and inside Madison Square Garden. LaGuardia granted the license, but ordered that only Jewish officers and patrolmen should guard and protect the Nazi meeting!

So it came about that protest marchers all over the city were kept in order by Jewish police. Mobs outside the Garden were fenced off by Jewish police. And dozens of Jewish police stood stiffly on guard inside the huge arena, in the midst of Nazi uniformed troops marching to the platform, while the "Horst Wessel Song" blared hoarsely from loudspeakers. (Why is it that Nazi speeches or songs always had an eerie animalistic hoarse sound?) Swastika flags draped the boxes and hung under searchlights from the rafters, and speakers, interrupted by "Heil Hitlers" and thousands of stiff arms pointing upward, like flesh bayonets, harangued the audience with adulation for "The Fuehrer," which would have been too lavish for God himself.

LaGuardia's solution for the dilemma did not meet the principle involved head-on. But his ingenuity turned indignation into ridicule. It broke the tension. People laughed at the Nazis, and the photographs of Nazis protected by Jewish police appeared in hundreds of newspapers all over the world. They caused mirth or consternation depending on the reader's point of view.

LaGuardia's method of controlling crime was similarly inventive. He knew that the police knew who the leading criminals in the city were. They could not be jailed because it was difficult to prove their criminality "beyond a reasonable doubt." He decided that the best he could do was contain them. So he ordered the police to bring them to City Hall in small groups. Sullen chieftains of crime were brought before him. They summoned their attorneys and were ready to assert their constitutional rights not to speak. Also, they were confident nothing could be "pinned on them."

To their surprise, he told them just that. He had no proof against them. He was not going to ask them to say anything. But he had something to tell them.

"I know you bums and tinhorns are the heads of criminal gangs. As long as you stay below Fourteenth Street, we will not do anything to you, until we can prove what lice you are. But if a single one of you, or your lousy gang steps foot across Fourteenth Street, we're going to pull you in as vagrants. We'll keep you in jail until you can prove how you earn money to drive Cadillacs, have swell homes, molls, and the rest. Now, I've warned you! Stay behind your line. We'll get you anyhow. But if you show your face uptown, in the jug you go, immediately. Now get out of here!"

In this way, he kept the major criminals out of the business and lucrative districts of the city. A gang leader didn't even dare to go to the theater in Times Square. The police knew who they were and they were quarantined.

Similarly, he did not attempt to eliminate prostitution establishments. He regarded them as an inevitable evil, but he confined their number and territory. However, no ladies of the evening marched the streets. Unlike most reformers, he recognized the limitation of the cleansing process. He allowed for the impossibility of perfection and tried to protect the public in a realistic and reasonable way.

This rule of pragmatic compromise did not apply, however, to city employees. He pounced upon any policeman who took graft from prostitution or gambling houses or any building inspector who overlooked a violation.

He understood the temptation to which low-earning city employees were subjected. He didn't depend on moral lectures alone. He continuously shuffled the police force to prevent improper alliances which were made more likely by propinquity. He could not eliminate graft, but he reduced it to the lowest ebb in municipal history. The cynical doctrine that one must accept petty dishonesty in a bureaucracy was rejected by him with such vehemence that hands outstretched for a take, for the first time, trembled.

He developed a resourceful policy for dealing with the race problem in Harlem. While on the one hand he strove mightily to obtain funds from Washington and Albany to build new housing, give relief funds, and eliminate the squalor, starvation, boredom, and humiliation which existed there, this was a long-range program. On the other hand, he devised techniques to control crime and riots which were the immediate consequences of the festering conditions. He went to Harlem and formed co-operation committees of black ministers, writers, businessmen, athletes, stars, and other influential citizens. If anyone whose voice might count resisted, he would be subjected to the LaGuardia tear in the eye—bent knee—wringing-hand treatment, and he didn't have a chance. After all, it was true that the chief victims of disorder were black citizens and businesses. Aside from its preventive function when trouble started, LaGuardia and his squad of black leaders, using bullhorns, would drive through the streets appealing for order and directing the people to go to their homes. He augmented this strategy with the use of black police almost exclusively in black neighborhoods, and, in addition, gave strict orders to use weapons sparingly, if at all. It was the first experiment in compassion before arrest rather than in punishment. Because of extremists in later years, the fruits of this leniency have not been good, but in his day, it was a successful maneuver to keep the kettle from boiling over.

Whatever his views about approximating justice rather than insisting on its absoluteness, he was uncompromising in his personal standards.

He carried his crusade of honesty to extreme lengths. No matter how just the request or recommendation, if it was made by a friend, he rejected it. Only a stranger or enemy received consideration. When I was asked to submit the name of some very worthy candidate with a fine record, for a judgeship, I would refuse, saying that my recommendation would be fatal. I wonder if the sponsors believed my explanation or thought it was an evasion. Dr. Stephen S. Wise, the noted rabbi, and president of the American Jewish Congress, who was an ardent supporter of LaGuardia, as were Dr. John Haynes Holmes and other clergymen interested in a clean city administration, once said to me, "I don't know what's the matter with Fiorello. He will consider recommendations from anyone but those who worked with him and have his interest at heart. He is losing out on some fine people."

I suppose he feared that if anything went wrong he would be charged with yielding to influence. He had denounced political bosses so long, because they exacted tribute for their support, that he would not risk being accused of paying off even to his dearest friend.

Once he appointed a magistrate on the recommendation of strangers. The new judge turned out not only to be incompetent but to have once made a speech expressing his respect for Nazis! Hostile newspaper reporters descended on LaGuardia en masse. They felt they had him. He was not going to squirm out of this one. Why hadn't he investigated the appointee's background more carefully? Who had recommended him? Once more, they underestimated his ingenuity and genius for public relations. He triumphed by uttering only nine words. Before they could begin their assault, he said, "Gentlemen, when I make a mistake, it's a beaut!"

This explanation became famous. Again he had turned indignation to laughter. He had ridiculed himself, and the people joyously accepted the admission of vulnerability from one who had striven so fanatically for high standards.

Just as he personalized his own shortcomings, so he personalized his enemies. When he attacked corporations in his weekly broadcasts, he addressed them as if they were individuals. "Look here, Mr. Western Union," or "Let me tell you something, Mr. Con Edison." He needed personal confrontation to be effective, not the vagueness of corporate enterprise.

I wondered whether he ever slept. He had an eighteen- to twenty-hour schedule, and his pace increased as if to banish tiredness by acceleration. Though his day often started at five or six in the morning (he could be seen inspecting garbage-collection procedures before the sun rose), he also spoke at most of the formal dinners in the evening. Unlike Walker, his day did not start at night.

He was extraordinarily facile at these functions. He had had no time to prepare. When I was on the dais, he would sit down next to me and say, "What are we selling tonight, Louis?" I would brief him in verbal shorthand:

"They are building a new wing at the Bronx Home for the Aged.

"They need two million dollars.

"The guest of honor is Max Schneider, president of the bank— You know him.

"In New York State there are now 1,200,000 people over the age of sixty-five. Most will reach eighty-five.

"There are no facilities for them. The city can't do it alone.

"This home is unique. It has apartments, not cells.

"There are paintings and pianos in some of them. There are no inmates. They can come and go as they wish.

"But there is a communal dining room for those who want it.

"There is a medical and dental department. Gerontology and geriatrics will be two of the most important words in the next generation." I defined both.

"In the new home to be built, old people will be able to *live* out their lives, not *die* out their lives."

"What is that last phrase?" he asked, for he was continuously being interrupted by greeters. I repeated it.

Then, when he arose to speak, usually early, so that he could appear at another function, he would deliver a twenty-minute address, skillfully blending the information he had soaked up into an emotional appeal. The audience must have thought he had prepared himself assiduously for the event. This "instant speech skill," combining a smattering of information with boiler-plate paragraphs previously used dozens of times, often is acquired by public officials and candidates. When listening to television interviews, one can sense that the "personality" interviewed has struggled through a few improvised sentences and reached the secure plateau of excerpts from his previous addresses, citing statistics and ringing conclusions. Sometimes the preprepared data is dragged in although not pertinent to the question. But LaGuardia was extremely felicitous and sufficiently original and inventive to make his speech completely applicable to the event.

I learned from him how to deal with men and women who stream toward the dais to shake hands and speak with the celebrity of the occasion. Invariably, the visitor holds out his hand and says, "I bet you don't remember me?"

"Yes, I do. Glad to see you."

"What's my name?"

"Well, I don't remember it right now, but I do recall you."

"Where did we meet last? Can you remember that?"

This cross-examination continues, while the celebrity loses ground, being trapped by his own kindliness. I have seen Presidents, Governors, Nobel Prize Winners, and dozens of other dais sitters unable to escape this ordeal. I used to think political figures played this losing game because they did not wish to antagonize a constituent or potential voter. But no, famous men in other walks of life are similarly cowed by dais visitors. I suppose the flattery of being approached prohibits a rebuke. So out of goodness of heart they evade, fumble, and pretend, while the person holding their hand in a secure grip remorselessly pursues his inquisition.

LaGuardia was the only one who knew how to deal with this kind of dais pest. To the ubiquitous question "I bet you don't remember me" he replied quickly, "No, I don't. What's your name?"

Taken back by the counterattack, the visitor would give his name and make one more try. "Do you remember where we met?"

"No, I don't. You know how many people a mayor sees. Glad to see you." He would turn to his neighbor and continue his conversation, thus dismissing the visitor, who would linger bewildered for a moment and then leave. It worked like a charm. I wondered why none of us had thought of so simple a device, or, more accurately, why we hadn't had the courage to use it.

LaGuardia was too impatient to have a five-year plan for the city. He had a daily plan and it extended to land and air. He built the first great municipal incinerators (not knowing then that they would be large contributors to the pollution problem and might have to be shut down). He brought in engineers to take advantage of the Catskill Mountain ranges, so that New York City would have the purest and best-tasting water in the country. He contracted for new kinds of mechanized garbage-collecting trucks, which required almost no lifting of cans, and thereby reduced hernias and the city's sick and hospital expense for sanitation workers. He ordered a new kind of snow-removal equipment, firefighting apparatus, and established new police car and communication systems. He believed in mechanization, provided those in charge never became calloused to duty because their labors had been reduced. In his eyes, leisure was just another opportunity to work. He resented those who when they got a job stopped looking for work.

One had to see him testing a new piece of equipment to determine whether it met specifications. He was like a woman in a market who knows quality: touching, smelling, squeezing, examining on all sides. He would work the new machine himself, over and over again. The contractor who had been forced by LaGuardia to outbid his competitors, until his profit margin was tissue paper thin, was nevertheless held to the highest standards. If the equipment was not perfect, LaGuardia would cajole the manufacturer into another effort, and Lord help him if he resisted. He was subjected to a public blast that lifted him into the next county.

He resorted to one of his stunts to improve airplane service. One day he flew from Washington to New York. The plane, according to schedule, arrived at the Newark Airport in New Jersey. LaGuardia refused to get out.

"My ticket says 'Washington to New York' and I want to be taken to New York."

Airline executives pleaded with him to evacuate the plane. He settled back tighter into his seat, closed the safety belt, and ordered, "Take me to New York. That's what your contract says." They did not dare evict him forcibly, especially since by this time photographers were swarming over the plane recording a traveler's sentimental plea to be taken home. He won his point. The plane, with one passenger, arrived at Mitchell Field in New York, and the first citizen of the city stepped out. The event was not unrecorded.

Appropriately enough, the air terminal he later built was named after him. It is a fitting memorial. When one sees the planes roaring in and out of LaGuardia, one is reminded of the restlessness and power which drove him frantically in all directions to achieve a better city.

The mayoralty of New York is generally conceded to be the second most difficult executive post in the United States. Like the presidency, it challenges one human being's capacity to survey, reflect, and decide hundreds of complicated problems in varied fields, any one of which would warrant years of concentrated study. Any decision at all is only possible by dependence on others, who, in turn, delegate to still others. The dilution is dangerous. Final resolutions may be based on the opinion of those far down the line, whose names and competence are not even known at the top. Little wonder, then, that any analyst can demonstrate contradictions, inconsistencies, and duplications among the various departments of government.

We are turning to miraculous computers to reduce the scope of this problem. Time saved in fact analysis, and even recommendations based on hard statistics, are invaluable. Even though experience is thus mechanically supplied, the input and output are still subject to judgment factors—another name for wisdom. As the government enlarges its activities to care for the individual citizen, yes, as it becomes paternalistic, reorganization of our government structure becomes essential. Even our constitutional demarcations, so brilliant and simple for the needs of that day, need overhauling. Some, like Professor Rex Tugwell, have suggested a new Constitution, preserving its imperishable spirit and freedoms, but restructuring the three departments of government to deal with new functions. For example, he proposes that a President and four vice-presidents be elected for a nine-year term and that various streamlined departments report to different vice-presidents. He also proposes that one house of the legislature be appointive and serve for life. Amendments to the Constitution would be facilitated. It is not necessary to evaluate the soundness of these and other proposals. It is significant that the Constitution, resulting from a long series of compromises among the quarreling delegates of that day, is not so holy a writ that it doesn't permit revision to meet exigencies never contemplated by those who drew it. As a statement of general principle, it turned out to be an inspired document (although it didn't forbid slavery). But our phenomenal growth required resort to regulatory agencies, economic control through antitrust, SEC, labor, and a host of other laws, and the curtailment of states' rights in favor of central power, all of which were as unforeseen as our nuclear or space sciences or our involvement as a superpower in international affairs. The Supreme Court established supremacy over the legislative branch, and is interpreting the constitutionality of enactments not defined or remotely envisioned by the generalities of the Constitution. Certainly, it was not anticipated that the President would be required to carry the weight of international and domestic anxieties which today challenge the strength and wisdom of mortal man.

LaGuardia was the last executive who strove by sheer superhuman energy to participate in every function of the city. His irascibility and temper were not due to exhaustion, but rather to his fierce determination that everyone measure up to the highest standard. He was a fanatic for good government. Of course, such torrential effort on so many fronts made him appear impetuous and so quick of judgment that his box score of errors and unjust statements was high, and some of them were "beauts," but, when compared to his accomplishments, his average ranked among the highest for a public official in several generations.

At one time there was much speculation that he would be a vice-presidential candidate. This was quite possible. President Roosevelt was a great admirer of LaGuardia and met with him frequently. Roosevelt suffered in the presence of boring people even though he used their competence. He was refreshed by exciting personalities, and where, as in LaGuardia, ebullience was combined with great talent, Roosevelt was fascinated. Probably he also appreciated LaGuardia's dramatizing ability (opponents would call it demagoguery) especially when it was employed not to deceive but to achieve. Roosevelt, generally, was attracted to intellectual mavericks, like Harold Ickes. LaGuardia's political genealogy was the same. But geographic considerations (Roosevelt and LaGuardia both were from New York) as well as other political factors (after all, LaGuardia wasn't even a Democrat) deprived the speculation of fulfillment.

A favorite fantasy bruited about in Hollywood was that when Cecil B. De Mille, the motion picture producer and director, died, he went to heaven (if that is where movie moguls go). He immediately organized a large corporation to entertain the angels. He ran into only one problem, and that was when he proposed that God be first vice-president.

LaGuardia, whose credentials for admission were excellent, would have reorganized the various departments, and might have encountered the same problem, but we can be sure that under his aegis, things up there would be like heaven.

When one contemplates the two most famous mayors in New York history, the intriguing idea presents itself: isn't it too bad that the city didn't use the unique talents of both; Fiorella LaGuardia as the chief executive, and Jimmy Walker the social mayor? It would have been a gay time in the old town tonight, and an efficient one, too, every day and night.

WHAT WE ARE IS GOD'S GIFT TO US. WHAT WE BECOME IS OUR RECIPROCAL GIFT TO GOD

Interviewers who have made a close study of public curiosity and cater to it have a series of ubiquitous questions. For performers: "What was the most interesting role you ever played?" "What attracts you most in the opposite sex?"

There is a similar catalogue of questions for lawyers: "What is the most exciting case you ever tried?" (I dodge this with "the next one"); "What was the most humorous incident you ever experienced in a courtroom?" In this list of questions, presumed to hold attention at least until the answer is given, is one that deals with "firsts." "What was the first case you ever tried?" is a prototype. Ordinarily, the truth would be, "I don't even remember," or "Really, it was of no significance." What else would one expect from a neophyte?

It so happens, however, that my first case was unique and with unusual consequences. To understand the reason for its being at all, one must understand how a lawyer enters into his profession. Without this background, the painting in the foreground loses meaning.

There are two general branches of law, substantive and adjective. The first deals with the philosophy and principles of law. The second with procedure. For example, adjective law is concerned with which courts have jurisdiction over certain disputes, the form of a complaint or answer, what motions can be made to elucidate the pleadings, within what period of time certain legal steps must be taken, and the like. Since each state has different procedures, set forth in Civil Practice Acts, the bar examination, which each graduating lawyer must take to obtain a license to practice law in the state, concentrates heavily on adjective law of that state.

On the other hand, leading law universities place almost all their emphasis on substantive law. While a course in procedural law is given, it is general and illustrative, because the students come from many states, and one cannot concentrate on any particular state. Furthermore, it is prosaic, technical knowledge, not worth pedagogic emphasis. So, adjective law is left for special bar examination courses outside of the college, given by specialists for the state where the student will seek his license. He pays for this course (and it is a lucrative field for teachers who know how to give a cram course in two weeks. Judge Harold Medina, when he was a teacher at Columbia University, gave such a private course).

So, it comes about that students of the best law universities are least trained for the bar examination of their state, and must seek help in adjective or procedural law before subjecting themselves to the test. When the bar examinations were divided into substantive and adjective parts, many passed the substantive law test with flying colors, but failed the adjective law section and consequently had to take that phase of the examination over again the next year. Chief Justice Charles Evans Hughes flunked his bar examination (of course on adjective law only) three times. Other famous lawyers and judges stumbled once or twice. These historic debacles have been a comfort to thousands of students who fail to pass their bar examinations. Indeed, they get to believe it is an omen for their future eminence, because they are following very large footsteps. The mind is capable of all sorts of ego-salvaging operations.

It is true, of course, that no great lawyer ever achieved high standing by proficiency in procedural law. The great law colleges properly stress the substantive law. However, there are smaller law schools which are local and chiefly attract students who intend to practice locally. These give extensive courses in the adjective law of that state. Their graduating students do not require a special preparatory course for bar examinations. They have had it in their regular studies. So, it eventuates that graduates from the smaller law schools have higher bar examination success than those from leading universities.

Bar examinations are unimaginable ordeals. Students have prepared themselves for seven years of college and law school training, met the severest tests of excellence and have finally graduated with honors. Then their right to enter the profession depends on one lengthy bar examination divided into substantive and adjective law questions.

Having sharpened their reasoning powers, rather than their memory or accumulative skills, they are at a great disadvantage in facing a test in which knowledge of rules of law is a requisite. So they must refresh, review, recapture, and recall years of learning in a few weeks in order to be prepared for a few questions which may be scattered over wide domains of law. I took Professor Harold Medina's cram course.

Preparation must exceed necessity. So it is later in the practice of the

law. I have studied and absorbed for weeks the testimony printed in the
record of a trial, because on the argument of the appeal one of the
judges may ask a question, the answer to which lies buried in some
remote part of the record. Uusually these extensive preparatory efforts
are wasted. The judges either sit in silence or their questions are
addressed to the mainstream of the argument. But, occasionally, the
court inquires whether there was any proof on some offbeat matters.
Counsel can, of course, reply that he does not recall whether such testimony appears in the lengthy record, and not lose any ground thereby.
But if, by heart, he can refer instantly to the page on which the subject
was treated, the favorable impact upon the court exceeds the
significance of the answer itself. Counsel's mastery of the record instills
confidence in the rest of his argument. At such a moment, all the tedious hours of "unnecessary" preparation are fully rewarded. The lawyer
tries to hide his exhilaration, as if the feat he had just performed was
nothing at all, but he can see the glint in the eyes of the most stony-
faced judge, reflecting acknowledgment of the virtuosity he has just
witnessed.

There is no greater anxiety than that which the aspiring and perspir-
ing candidate experiences while awaiting the results of the bar examination. It is almost as if after careful hoarding of his resources for a decade, he put all his money on one throw of the dice. Yet, when the bar
examination is passed, and several years of practice follow, the ordeal
completely disappears from memory. It is an early lesson that anxiety
makes mountains out of molehills and perspective makes molehills out
of mountains. The crisis of the moment most often is an insignificant
incident when viewed through the glasses of intervening time. Of
course, it is not always so, but experience proves this to be true in such
a large number of cases, that it is wise to anticipate that possibility, and
not permit immediacy to act as an artificial enlarging glass.

Harry Hershfield used to tell the story of the coal miner who slaved
twenty years in the dark, cold, and wet underground, and saved up
$5,000 by frugal living. Then he goes to Las Vegas for a celebration,
puts the entire sum on one number, loses, and sighs, "Well, easy come,
easy go."

After the bar examination has been passed, and the character committee has found no flaw, the great moment arrives for the swearing in
before the Appellate Division. As I stood there on the threshold of a
new world I had dreamed of entering all my life, there stirred within
me such deep emotions that I could not hear either the encouragement
or admonition which came from the bench. Once, I dared turn my
head and saw my parents crying unashamedly. It had been a long struggle for them, and all the waiting had suddenly come to one moment of

happy climax. And, of course, profound joy is giddy enough to lose its way and indiscriminately trigger tears as well as laughter.

My wandering thoughts were brought to a halt by awareness that the candidates had all raised their hands. I raised mine and repeated the oath being administered, with all the fervor in my being. Then we were given our certificates. In one magic second, we had become lawyers, although we did not realize then how frail the parchment in our hands was in the steel and iron combat we were about to engage. I have not failed to make this point when I address incoming lawyers before they are sworn in.

The courage essential for future engagements was necessary at the beginning simply to overcome the disappointments which beset a beginner. We could not even get jobs. Despite qualifications which were not unimpressive, there seemed to be no opportunity open anywhere. I searched the law journals for positions, put my own ads there, applied to the placement bureau of the law school, and had friends arrange interviews at law firms. But this was 1925, and there were few openings. Many turned away in disgust from the profession, and entered business or other fields.

I was sorely tempted myself by a business offer. During summer, I had done odd jobs, like working for the Intertype Corporation, which manufactured Linotype machines. The job was thrilling because the office was at Court Street in Brooklyn, two blocks from the Supreme Court Building. So I would skip or curtail lunch hour and gravitate to the Court House, where I peered through the oval-glassed green leather doors into the wondrous land within. Someday, I was determined, I would be inside that arena.

Another summer job was for the Carbona Company, which manufactured a cleaning fluid. It was simply a chemical called carbon tetrachloride, and an excellent cleaner. All the owners did was bottle it and give it the trade name Carbona. I was given a small salary and a commission on sales. I talked my heart out to managers of chain stores, and did fairly well. One day, I discovered by accident that Carbona cleaned typewriters. Since it evaporated quickly, the impressions left by the carbons on the platen could be removed and the typewriter used immediately thereafter. I opened up a new and successful market for Carbona. I then dared to approach steamship companies to buy large quantities for cleaning pistons and other equipment. The small bottles of Carbona customarily made were too expensive for this purpose. The new sales field and need for a wholesale cheaper-priced gallon container brought me to the attention of the president of the Carbona Company, Mr. Weintraub. It turned out that he had a son who, as sons so often do, disliked the business, and thus shattered his father's dream of ultimately turning over his company to him. Instead, Mr. Weintraub must have found my enthusiasm and dedication the very qualities he had hoped his son would have. It may have been this transference, or a guess by the old gentleman, that an investment in me might not be a bad gamble.

So he called me into his office, before my last term in law school, and offered me a contract for five years to begin at a salary of $100 a week and going upwards so that by the time I was out of law school I would be earning $200 a week. Two hundred dollars a week! This was more than brilliant young lawyers earned after five years or more. In addition, I would ascend through various titles to the presidency. My legal training would be helpful, but the Carbona Company didn't need a counsel. I was being offered a business career.

Although I knew what my decision must be, I, of course, discussed this proposal with my parents. My heart was heavy. Might they see in this a desirable career and advise me to enter it? Of course, I should not have underestimated them. There was not a moment of hesitation. My father commanded (I could have hugged him for his anger, and I did), "You finish law school. You are going to be a lawyer. What kind of nonsense is this? If Mr. Weintraub offered you a thousand dollars a week, would you quit school and give up the profession you were cut out to follow since you were born?"

He was getting so angry my mother soothed him, "Zindel-leben [our dear son] isn't going to take it. He just wants us to agree. Of course we do. Money isn't everything." As an afterthought, "And besides, who says you can't earn more if you become a great lawyer?"

So I declined the offer, and was told to return at any time that I had a change of mind, if not of heart.

However, when I could not obtain employment as a law clerk, I began to notice Carbona signs and billboards, to which I had never paid attention before. Finally, one day I answered an advertisement for a law clerk and was hired. It was the office of a woman lawyer, a rarity in those days. Her name was Miss Emily Janoer. She had an office on Fourteenth Street, in Manhattan, which I thought was a strange location, until I found out that her chief occupation was real estate, and that my main function was to serve dispossess summonses on defaulting tenants in buildings she owned. My salary was seven dollars a week. The only indication that I was in a law office were a few lawbooks and the daily *New York Law Journal*. These comforted me, but the $200 a week offered by Carbona was like the beautiful nude temptress which lay herself before St. Anthony to distract him from his duty and holy mission.

My parents were bewildered but not disheartened by the early tough going. "Water always finds its own level," my father said. He didn't finish the thought, as if it was preposterous not to realize that that level would be extremely high. "Just stick to it. Everybody will realize your ability someday." My mother just smiled her assenting opinion.

THE PUSHCART CASE

It is against this background that my first case came to me. One evening (yes, it was night, for I had no office or even a shingle), my mother announced in a voice registering excitement and perplexity that several men were at the door asking to see Counselor Nizer. Could they be clients!

They were ushered into our dining room, but not before the green oilcloth cover on the table was hastily replaced with our finest white tablecloth with the fringes and tassels hanging on the sides. My mother immediately busied herself brewing tea, which, according to her London training, was served not only in the afternoon, but as a pacifier for any crisis, small or large.

Although my heart was pounding, I greeted the visiting dignitaries casually as if this were just another conference in a busy day. The spokesman, Mr. Jacob Bassuck (how could I ever forget his name?), told me that he and the three gentlemen with him were property owners on Ellery Street, in Brooklyn, which was part of a public market area. Pushcarts with all sorts of produce and products were lined up on one side of these blocks. They were not permitted to be stationed on the west side of the street. Consequently, shoppers abounded on the pushcart-lined sidewalks. Stores on that side prospered. Property was valuable.

But my visitors owned buildings on the opposite side. There was little traffic. The stores did little business. Many were vacant. Property values were down in sharp contrast to the buildings facing them across the street. Could anything be done legally to see that pushcarts would be permitted on their side of the street?

I had always thought of discrimination in terms of people. It had never occurred to me that the injustice of discrimination could attach to something as inanimate and prosaic as a pushcart.

"Who forbids the stationing of pushcarts on your side of the street?" I asked.

"The city," replied one of the men. "The Commissioner of Market," added another, narrowing the target.

"Does he give any reason?"

"Sure, lots of them. He says Public School 24 is only a few blocks away and there must be clear sidewalks for children going to school. There is also a firehouse nearby and the street must not be closed in on both sides by pushcarts, or they couldn't run through easily."

"Have you asked him to alternate pushcart placements, one week on your side and the next on their side?"

"Look, we've asked him everything. He won't listen. Go fight City Hall!"

The other members of the committee looked askance at the speaker's tactlessness. Was this the way to encourage the young lawyer to try his hand at an impossible case?

"Certainly, you can fight City Hall," I replied, calling on my vast fund of political inexperience and naïveté. "There is a proceeding called mandamus. It is the remedy used to compel a public official to do his duty properly. We could apply to the State Supreme Court for an order directing the city official not to discriminate against you."

My assertiveness must have stirred the conscience of Mr. Bassuck. "I must tell you," he said haltingly, "that we have been to other lawyers, and they all said nothing could be done." Continuing his confession, he mentioned their names, all well known and able, including Emanuel Celler, who was congressman from that district and who later served for half a century in the House, rising to Chairman of the Judiciary Committee.

It was quite obvious that I was not only not a second, but a last choice. (Like the political leader who told the applicant, "You are my second choice." "Who is your first?" "Anybody.") Apparently, some members of the committee had heard me speak, and on such slight evidence had urged a final try. What did they have to lose?

I was not embarrassed by the revelation that, unlike Abou Ben Adhem, I did not head the list. Instead I was stirred by the challenge. Fools step in where fools have stepped before, but I had not stepped anywhere yet. I was unafraid.

"I think you have a meritorious case," I said. "If you want me to undertake it, I would like to spend a few days investigating the facts thoroughly, with your help, and then we can proceed."

They agreed to pay disbursements and, if I remember, five hundred dollars for my representation.

A lawyer who only knows his own side of the case knows little about it. He must anticipate the defense and be prepared to demolish it. What would the city argue if I attacked? The doctrine of discretion. There is a rule of law that where a public official performs a duty which involves his discretion, the courts will not challenge it, even if they disagree with him, unless—unless there is a clear abuse of discretion. So, for example, a judge who decides a case and specifies that it is not purely a legal matter, but that it involves discretion, is virtually immune on appeal. The burden on the appellant is overwhelming. He must demonstrate either that the matter was one of absolute right and did not involve the exercise of contrary discretion, or that the discretion was so bizarre as to fall within the rule of abuse of discretion. The same, of course, applied to the Market Commissioner. We could be sure that the word "discretion" would permeate the defense, to create an impenetrable shield. The Corporation Counsel of the City might, for purposes of persuasion, even strike a generous pose that he, himself, or the court might have acted differently, but that didn't matter. The Market Commissioner had exercised his discretion, based on many surrounding circumstances, and no court should, under well-established law, substitute its discretion for his. The cases supporting this proposition were legion. Undoubtedly, this was the reason that other lawyers had refused to take the case. Perhaps some of them had another reason more visceral than scholarly—they just didn't think there was a future in suing the City of New York.

I prepared myself by preparing the city's argument. With all the force which I could summon, I constructed the corporation counsel's argument; school access, fire engine lanes, consumer advantage, traffic considerations, and all the rest. Then with these contentions ringing in my ears, I set out on foot to visit other city markets, examining the surrounding territory, wresting a fact here and there. I drove my clients (what a wonderful word when used for the first time) to help me investigate the facts. My objective was definite and limited. It consisted of one word—inconsistency. To me this was equivalent to abuse of discretion. If the Market Commissioner had acted differently under similar circumstances, he could not argue that he had exercised his discretion honestly. Mistaken or not, he could only hold his feet if he had acted the same way in the exercise of his discretion. But if he had not, the suspicion arose that there were other factors which accounted for his conduct, and this negated reasonable exercise of discretion. It spelled out "abuse of discretion."

The task was further complicated by the fact that varying circumstances in each market area might justify varying decisions. This would contradict the charge of inconsistency, and restore his claim that he had exercised his discretion honestly, whether wise or not.

So I not only had to find inconsistent conduct, but eliminate factual distinctions by demonstrating that they were too thin to overcome the accusation of abuse of discretion.

This was my first enlistment and for life in the army of "thorough preparation." The demands of such service (should I say servitude?) are enormous. They had driven me to perilous rooftops to peer down a shaft in which an elevator fell; to a barge cutting through icy water to watch divers looking for a metal box in a murder case; to laboratories making atomic tests of paper to determine its origin; to French archives searching for reports in a plagiarism suit; to a secret attic equipped with electronic devices and hundreds of recordings; to a search of an abandoned villa where a missing diary was found behind a bookcase which the wife had thought was thoroughly emptied; to many countries to persuade a knowledgeable witness that it was his duty to give his testimony in a deposition which would be taken in the local embassy; to a hazardous walk on an elevated railroad to find the hole from which a bolt had plummeted onto a man's skull; to a university's records to find a psychological test taken by a student (killed in a railway accident) to establish damages based on his potential earnings; to chemical tests of textiles in breach of warranty cases; to poring over hundreds of Arabic translations in an oil case, or thousands of clippings from a German newspaper to demonstrate Nazi affiliation; to tedious examination of corporate minute books, or accountant statements in SEC cases; to countless interviews with doctors, psychiatrists, surgeons, economists, geologists, public officials, workers, janitors, teachers, executives and all manner of people, young and old, who the fates had decreed should have been present at certain events or heard some words which needed to be reconstructed so that truth, so easily faded by time, could be salvaged from oblivion.

I have adverted to the slavery of preparation, but oh, its rewards! They exceed the windfall from the largest lottery. Many millions of dollars, and more precious rights than can be measured by money, result from a fact or two unearthed by dedicated research. Not least is the exhilaration from triumph over knave or dupe, and the reassurance that justice is attainable in this imperfect world.

If I needed encouragement for the precept that preparation equates with proficiency, my first case provided it. Treading through the sometimes nonaromatic lanes of the city's markets, I discovered practices totally inconsistent with those in my clients' area. Official duty which compelled discretionary manipulation of pushcarts in our market was not applied with similar fervor in others. Some of them also had nearby schools, and firehouses. Of course they would. These existed in all neighborhoods. Yet pushcarts were permitted on both sides of the street. There was enough lane left for vehicles in streets which measured the same or even narrower than ours. Children coursed over the sidewalks on their way to school, without being impeded by the purchasers at the curb. Why only in our market need there be precautions taken for a one-sided use?

My suspicions turned me to an investigation in the County Clerk's records of the owners of the favored real estate. Yes, among them were the names of some who were influential in Tammany circles. One was a political small-wig in the party. This could not be used in the litigation. It was too remote by properly protective legal standards for an accusation against a public official. But it didn't diminish my clients' skepticism about the city's declarations that only considerations of public welfare lay behind the regulations.

When I had prepared the affidavits and exhibits (which included photographs to give visual support to the discrimination), we sued City Hall. Mayor John F. Hylan, Market Commissioner O'Malley, and the Board of Estimate were all joined as defendants in a mandamus proceeding. It was strange that this form of action, so unique and rarely encountered, and which we learned in law school as a sort of esoteric illustration of the law's comprehensiveness, should be the first vehicle for my ride to court.

Justice James C. Cropsey was sitting in the State Supreme Court, Kings County, where the argument would take place.

God takes care of the innocent. He was a Republican. I would not have thought that the rules of law would be applied differently because of the Judge's political adherence before he was elected. How can there be a Democratic or Republican rule of law? That was and is as unthinkable to me as if the Ten Commandments were tampered with. But my clients were not so trusting. They breathed with relief when they heard that a Tammany judge would not preside.

Judge Cropsey had a reputation for fanatical rectitude. He was the severest judge on the bench. A witness who was an obvious perjurer would be melted in his seat by the verbal lava which the Judge poured over him. Any lawyer who overstepped his bounds was subjected to a scathing denunciation.

The bar feared and admired him at one and the same time. His righteous indignation was a purifying factor in a calloused world. But his temper made him impetuous, and it could be triggered too easily. There was little compassion in the man. He seemed always poised to strike. That is why no judicial system is perfect. It reflects the frailties of those who administer it, and which judicial robes can neither hide nor eliminate.

Lawyers are often good psychologists. Hard experience trains them to be. It becomes well known that in arguing before a judge like Cropsey, it was extremely important to have the opportunity of speaking first. Once he caught fire, it was almost impossible for the defendant to quench the flames of his conviction.

I had all these advantages; a judge who would be outraged by official misconduct; and the right to open the argument because we were the plaintiffs.

Knowing that Judge Cropsey was a legal scholar, I planned to catch his fancy by a daring maneuver. I announced early in the argument that the city would rely on the rule of discretion, and I conceded that no matter how right we were on the merits, it would not avail us if we could not demonstrate a clear abuse of discretion; that this was a heavy burden I had to meet; that I accepted it and would address my entire argument to demonstrating that never in the history of the city had there been such a clear case of executive favoritism; that every excuse offered by the Commissioner of Markets for his discriminatory conduct was hypocritical, and so proven by his own inconsistent conduct. I continued in this vein in the very introduction to indicate at the earliest moment who was on the side of the angels.

I could see the gorge rise in Judge Cropsey as I proceeded. His smooth, angular face became more florid as the heated words reached him. When he looked at the black and white photographs attached to the papers, they seemed to cast a red light on his features. Suddenly, he could contain himself no longer. He interrupted me in the middle of a sentence and announced in a tone reserved for sentence of death, "I'll hear the other side." This was accompanied by slamming the sheaf of affidavits on his desk, with a gesture of anger and disgust.

The poor City Counsel. He knew very well that "I'll hear the other side" was a challenge, not an invitation, and meant he would be given little opportunity to speak, and that it was he who would be listening to a tirade. So it was. He was not aided by his lack of resourcefulness. The situation called for an improvised beginning which might delay the imminent explosion from the bench; some soothing words and promise of a developing argument which would encourage patient withholding of judgment. But he had no such flexibility. He had carefully prepared an address based on an exposition of the rule of discretion, and an analysis of the cases which defined "abuse of discretion." That was his speech. His notes were before him. He stuck to the text as if nothing had happened to make such an approach hollow.

"I know the law," screamed the Judge. "Mr. Neezer [the mispronunciation was innocent] has conceded it. Stop wasting time. What have you to say to the demonstration that the city has applied a standard here not used in any other market?"

When the city's lawyer sought to make distinctions, the Judge furiously rejected them as pretense. It was the first time I was to enjoy the experience of the Judge acting as advocate for our position. It is a comforting feeling. There is no one there to overrule him.

The decision was foreshadowed. The Judge wrote a blistering opinion in a style which Judge Cardozo once described in his book *Law and Literature*, as pronouncement from on high. No careful balancing of conflicting claims, no dissecting of the logic to demonstrate a crack here or there in its façade—just stentorian tones of an inviolate judgment—as if it was being read from engraved tablets handed down from the Mount of Justice. He issued a mandamus order directing the Commissioner of Markets to permit pushcarts to be placed on both sides of the street, or, if he wished, he could alternate them for equal periods and without any discrimination of days or hours from one side to the other. All city officials, including the Mayor, were enjoined from interfering in any way with this direction, and the order explicitly applied to any subsequent Commissioner of Markets. In other words, though the order was personal, it was made to attach to the office, like a covenant running with the land in real estate.

My clients read the newspapers with special pride. They had brought about a miracle. City Hall had crumpled. A lowly pushcart had brought it down. They preened themselves on having picked a lawyer who, because he knew little, had entered into awesome battle unafraid. They considered the victory a greater testimonial to their shrewdness than to my skill. When they came to celebrate and congratulate me and my parents, I acted calmly, like a battle-scarred veteran, and warned them that appeals lay ahead. The city would not take such a defeat docilely. There was the Appellate Division, composed of five judges, and the final Court of Appeals in Albany, composed of seven. The gamut had to be run. We passed the Appellate Division and then on to Albany.

Only few cases reach the Court of Appeals. Many lawyers practice a lifetime without an occasion to appear there. Yet, here I was in my very first case standing before the court of last resort in the State of New York.

What made the occasion paralyzing was that the Chief Judge, Benjamin N. Cardozo, presided. There he was in the flesh.

To understand the impact, one must imagine a musician who has worshiped Beethoven's genius and studied his works all his life. Then, he must appear to perform before a group of masters, and by some miracle, there sits Ludwig van Beethoven also, peering down at him. The analogy is not too fanciful. Some men have such immense reputations that we consider them historic figures. We, therefore, associate them with other geniuses who are dead. One forgets that although by reputation they are already in the pantheon, they are still alive.

Cardozo, like Einstein, Picasso, Edison, and Freud, belonged to this group of assured immortality in their fields. In law school, we had read his precedent-making opinions with awe reserved for Coke and Blackstone; except that their styles were flat compared to his. He was a master of prose, a great writer. One has only to read *The Nature of the Judicial Process* to be fascinated by the grace of diction, the symmetry of structure, the musical acceleration of pace, the flowering of emotion out of fact, the humor used to invade a resistant mind, all adorning profound thought and incredible learning. He was the supreme legal philosopher, and since the law encompasses all social sciences, his philosophy extended to domains as broad as life itself.

It seems unfair to engage in such lavish evaluation without supporting illustration. One has only to turn to any page of his writings for it. I select a few passages from an abundance of riches, choosing these particular ones only because they deal with less involved professional problems.

In *The Growth of the Law* he writes:

Judges march at times to pitiless conclusions under the prod of a remorseless logic which is supposed to leave them no alternative. They deplore the sacrificial rite. They perform it, none the less, with averted gaze, convinced as they plunge the knife that they obey the bidding of their office.

We should know . . . that magic words and incantations are as fatal to our science as they are to any other . . .

Here is his comment on the enormous number of precedents which now confront the lawyer and the judge:

The fecundity of our case law would make Malthus stand aghast. Adherence to precedent was once a steadying force, the guaranty, as it seemed, of stability and certainty. We would not sacrifice any of the brood, and now the spawning progeny, forgetful of our mercy, are rending those who spared them.

He discusses the compartmentalizing of the law with this observation.

One line is run here; another there. We have a filigree of threads and cross-threads . . . We shall be caught in the tentacles of the web, unless some superintending mind imparts the secret of the structure . . . The perplexity of the judge becomes the scholar's opportunity.

His reputation was international. Legal scholars everywhere recognized his eminence. When other courts, whether the Supreme Court of the United States or courts in foreign countries, cited cases he had decided, they made a special point to mention that he was the author of the opinion. That gave it unique authority. He was quoted by courts, law journals, and legal writers more than any other judge in history, and invariably his words cast a light on the text, and gave velocity to its thought.

How had his genius developed? There might have been a psychiatric impulse. His father was a judge in the State Supreme Court and became involved in a scandal of dishonesty. Young Cardozo must have determined to make amends, and restore the honor of his name. This might explain his fanatical dedication and even his distorted ascetic life, but not his brilliance, fecund mind, and felicitous pen.

Judged by other mortals, he lived at least two lives in one lifetime. He concentrated on law to the exclusion of all else. He never married. He lived with his sister all his life. He never went to the theater, to a concert, or even to a social event unless it was a legal occasion. Since he required little sleep, he read and studied law eighteen to twenty hours a day. He was familiar with legal periodicals written in French, Italian, German, and Spanish. Since law is all-encompassing, and he never compartmentalized it, he also studied philosophical and sociological works of foremost authorities, and mastered economic theories, scientific developments, and political tracts. His cultural curiosity embraced the widest domain.

More remarkable than all this was that his mind never became stuffed with the enormous intake. He synthesized, eliminated, and sorted everything in orderly fashion. His learning complemented a liberal mind and a perspective of infinite horizon. Stimuli from hundreds of sources were refined by him and then poured out into his opinions. Little wonder they had breadth and scope, which gave them the stamp of authentic wisdom.

In discussing the philosophy which molds the law, he once wrote:

We do not need to spend pages in an attempted demonstration that Gesetz (law) is not coterminous with Recht (right), that la loi is narrower than le droit, that the law is something more than statute. We are saved from all this because in action every day about us is the process by which forms of conduct are stamped in the judicial mint as law, and thereafter circulate freely as part of the coinage of the realm.

Here is a remarkable observation, confession, and objective squeezed into two sentences:

The inscrutable force of professional opinion presses upon us like the atmosphere, though we are heedless of its weight. How shall we make the most of it in service to mankind?

Cardozo's manner was benign. He was a kind man. Civilization being the slow process of learning to be kind, he was on that and other grounds perhaps the most civilized man of our era.

It is the man who gives distinction to the title, and not the title to the man. When Judge Cardozo presided over the Court of Appeals in New York, it was the most honored court in the land. Ultimately, his distinction caused a clamor for his appointment to the Supreme Court in Washington. Although he was ineligible by geographic and religious standards (two of the judges on the court were from New York and one Jew was already on the bench), his reputation transcended such considerations and he was appointed by President Herbert Hoover to acclaim from judicial authorities and intellectuals all over the world.

He was reluctant to take the post. He was ensconced in Albany in his ascetic way of life, and moving to Washington tore up roots of habit and subjected him to a new environment with accompanying demands to be resisted all over again. But he yielded, and for a long time was unhappy on the highest court. He was even subjected to anti-Semitic crudeness by Associate Justice James McReynolds, who ostentatiously read and rattled a newspaper when Judge Cardozo discussed a case in conference. But he wrote a brilliant chapter in the all too short time of six years he served before his death in 1938 at the age of sixty-seven.

Paintings and statues of him abound. One portrait hangs on the ornately carved light wood wall of the Court of Appeals in Albany, parallel with the lectern where counsel speak, as if he were looking gently at them, as he once did from the high-backed center chair. Another hangs in the study next to the Supreme Court chamber. But no painting can capture the ivory-white pallor of his skin and its translucent quality. He had a shock of white hair which by contrast gave his face faint color. His lower lip protruded ever so slightly and formed a graceful curve with upward indentations at the ends affecting a gentleness which looked like a smile. His chin was large and determined. Some accident or arthritic condition had shrunk his neck, so that his shoulders were high. To diminish the distortion he wore high collars.

The over-all effect of his face was one of complete repose. He seemed spiritually above the din of contentiousness. His voice was soft and nonresonant, almost like a whisper without sibilance. No man I have ever met, whether pope, priest, chief rabbi, or guru, seemed more saintly than he.

Considering my belief in a full and vibrant life, there is no man I would less emulate than him, and no man whose mind I have admired more.

There is an anecdote about a young lawyer appearing before the Court of Appeals and expounding a simple legal proposition at length. Judge Cardozo apologized for interrupting him and in a characteristically noncritical manner said, "May I suggest that you need not use up your limited time on that point. I hope you will give this court credit for being familiar with as elementary a rule as that."

"Oh no," replied counsel, "that's the mistake I made in the lower court."

My dilemma was similar. What could I possibly present that was not known to Judge Cardozo and the six other judges on that bench? The answer was—the facts. An answer which applies to most appeals. Counsel usually bear down on the legal authorities and the distinctions among differing cases. But these are often known to appellate judges, or can best be read in the briefs. A mere indication of the legal umbrella under which the client seeks shelter is sufficient. Quotations at length from prior decisions are boring and rarely productive.

The realm about which the judges know nothing—and are not sensitive to the assumption that they are ignorant—is the facts.

The art of advocacy is to demonstrate that the facts warrant the application of a particular rule of law. The adversary often concedes the legal proposition, but argues that it does not apply to the facts in the instant case, because they are different from those in the case from which the rule stems.

In short, it is the factual terrain on which the battle is customarily fought, and it is here that the lawyer should concentrate his fire. He wastes his ammunition by shooting in other directions.

So I cast my argument before Judge Cardozo and the other judges in terms of a recital of the facts, so interwoven that they exuded the city's unwarranted partisanship, favoritism, and discrimination in favor of one set of property owners, and to the injury of another group of citizens deserving of equal treatment. Here and there the facts bounced off the rule of abuse of discretion, making their own dissonant clangor.

A few months later, Judge Cardozo addressed the Bar Association of the City of New York. As always, when he appeared, the huge amphitheater was fully seated long before the lecture. His talks were literary gems, destined for publication. The script was before him and he read it. Of course, as I have indicated previously, this was bound to make a weak presentation. However, we knew that when we would read his talk someday we would appreciate it fully. Then we could pause over its passages, and savor them to derive fullest pleasure. Some sections would need concentrated attention and absorption. They had passed by teasingly when he pronounced them in even gait and went blithely on. But the audience composed of judges and lawyers was thrilled by being in his presence and watching him closely as he delivered the paper.

His talk was followed by a reception. Although the decision in my case had already come down, I approached him hesitantly. I hoped he would remember me. To my surprise, he took my hand warmly and said, "I would like to see you." I did not know whether this was an invitation to visit him in chambers or to wait. I stood aside.

After a while he approached me. He complimented me on the argument before the court, referring in light detail to its persuasive formulation. He asked me how long I had been practicing, and in view of my choked condition, it was fortunate that the answer was necessarily curt. Then he put his hand on my arm in a half gesture of intimacy, and gave me encouragement for what he hoped would be a distinguished career. He concluded with a deliberate air of casualness to suggest that I should feel free to visit him in his New York City or Albany chambers. He must have seen how moved I was by what to me was the conferring of the Nobel Prize of friendship, even though the only words I could summon were, "Thank you, sir."

Through the years, I did visit him and developed a warm acquaintance. I cannot say friendship, for I doubt that with the exception of perhaps one or two, his immersion in thought and work permitted such a relationship. However, I achieved enough rapport to indulge in a privilege which only close friends can enjoy, to be silent together.

So in my very first case I had sued City Hall and met the legendary Cardozo. What a leap from Emily Janoer on Fourteenth Street to Chief Judge Cardozo in Albany.

My father became a philosopher. "Lawyers in fancy neighborhoods don't get pushcart cases," he said.

Every success breeds an opportunity for another. Clients began to appear with regularity.

I received an invitation to join Louis Phillips' law firm. By one of these strange coincidences, he had known my parents in London, and he was prone to tell everyone in later years that he had once held me on his knee when I was an infant. This gave some the false impression that we were relatives.

Phillips was attorney and executive secretary of the New York Film Board of Trade, which represented the leading motion picture companies. He had the privilege of practicing private law. So the handsome quarters of the trade association and his law office were combined in an impressive suite at 1520 Broadway on Times Square.

I had thought of asking him for an association when I graduated, but this would have been imposing on his acquaintance. I was determined to make my own way. Phillips, on the other hand, had needed a clerk, but he guessed correctly that I might want to be independent and avoid favors. However, word of my progress encouraged him to invite me, for now an offer of a job was recognition of my worth, not friendly condescension.

I came to see him, walked over the plush carpets of his office and into the hushed library with its huge oval table covered with stacks of lawbooks. This was a real law office. I was fascinated by the surroundings. I like Phillips' enthusiasm for law, which I was to learn for the next quarter of a century was his predominating trait. He was happy only when he could talk law. All else in life was interstitial.

So I eagerly accepted the job. But by this time, I had a practice, and it was agreed that in addition to my salary of twenty dollars a week, I would receive 50 per cent of fees derived from my own clients.

Within two years, my fees grew large enough for him to offer me an equal partnership. More important, we realized in each other spiritual brothers-in-law. So the law firm of Phillips and Nizer was founded in 1928, and has grown ever since.

Louis Phillips had a love affair with the law. He was so dedicated to his work that it consumed his every thought, his every minute, whether in the office or out of it. When he visited me for a social evening, he would beg off from the other guests for ten minutes to discuss a legal problem with me. It was not urgent, but his mind was filled with it and there was joy in legal exchange.

His professional excellence was given nobility because it was rooted in integrity. That is such an abused word. It is not likely to convey its ripe meaning as it should when applied to him. He was reared in the orthodox Jewish tradition of right and justice. It was the core of his deep religious feeling. True religion is the life we lead, not the creed we profess. I have never known anyone whose life was guided by purer concepts of honesty, decency, and justice. These were not to him esoteric concepts to be uttered in a house of worship, or paid obeisance in conversation. They were his daily applied standards of conduct, and he never, never deviated from them no matter what the exigency. He would not accept the permissible exceptions established by precedent. On this subject he was quietly fanatical. He would brook no compromise. But there was no holy self-consciousness about this. On the contrary, he would hide his embarrassment about his extreme standards with a jest or the Jewish expression *"Es past nisht"*—"It just wouldn't be nice."

What a wonderful canon of ethics *"Es past nisht"* makes. What a guiding rule for a fine life it constitutes. Particularly for one of his tender sensitivity, it was a severe standard. If anything made him feel uneasy or just slightly embarrassed, or gave his delicately attuned conscience the slightest twinge, why, that was enough. So he would not take a case against someone whom he knew and liked even though he had never been his attorney and was not ethically barred from the retainer. He often pleaded with me to reduce fees to clients. He turned down lucrative retainers because the client or his cause did not fully appeal to him.

His exquisite sense of right and wrong motorized his legal conduct. "Where is there any book of law so dear to each man as that written in his heart?" asked Tolstoy. As general counsel of Paramount Pictures Corporation, he was subjected to an annual checkup by the company's physician, Dr. Leon Warshaw. The doctor was alarmed. All signs indicated extreme agitation and nervousness.

"What is the matter, Mr. Phillips? Is anything troubling you particularly?"

"Not really, but I have been somewhat upset by a company problem. I must admit I haven't slept recently."

"What is it?" asked the doctor, scanning the abnormal blood pressure, pulse, and other readings.

"Oh, I have asked for increases for the lawyers of my staff and due to an economy drive, they have been refused."

"Is that all?" asked the doctor. "And you are so upset?"

"Of course, do you realize what these lawyers have to face in increased living costs for their families? And they have worked so devotedly for the company. I will give them increases from my salary, but that won't be enough."

When Dr. Warshaw got to the checkup of the president of the company, Barney Balaban, he said, "If you don't want Louis Phillips to die of a heart attack, better approve his request for increases."

They were granted.

Laughter came easily to him. He had an eager gaiety of childlike exuberance. But tears also came readily, as he was swept by emotion. Anyone's misfortune, no matter how removed from him, would send him into hushed depression. I learned to control my alarm when he telephoned and spoke in almost inaudible sadness, for it often turned out to be nothing more than that some virtual stranger had suffered a broken leg, or that a preliminary motion had been lost in a North Dakota Federal court. There was no terminus to his great capacity for feeling, and he felt so deeply that one could not distinguish the sad from the truly tragic. To see his face lit up dazzlingly with happy excitement, or to see its funereal caste and hear his shaken voice, was to experience only partly the range of his pure emotionalism.

The only sadness he ever caused anyone was when he died.

I enjoyed the practice of law more when we were a small firm with one clerk. Each client received personal attention at all times. There were no departments to which he was sent for specialized advice to be ushered back to the senior for final decision. But the complexity of society has revolutionized law offices, just as it has the medical profession and business.

Today there is barely a legal service that may not be affected by tax consequences. So there is a tax department—lawyers who have made a life study of the tax laws and their kaleidoscopic changes from year to year.

Modern business is not content with internal growth. Acquisitions and mergers are resorted to for accelerated advancement. So there is an acquisitions department—manned by lawyers who understand the applicable regulations and procedures of the Securities and Exchange Commission.

On the other hand, growth can run afoul of the antitrust laws. So there is a department knowledgeable in the law of monopoly.

The public is now the largest of all corporate investors. So stockholder minority suits and proxy battles for control abound. There is a department trained to defend or conduct such contests.

So it is with wills and trusts, copyrights, divorce, real estate, libel, international law, and myriad other problems a law firm must solve to give a client a full rounded professional service. That is why, unfortunately, the individual practitioner or small law firm is at a great disadvantage. That is why law firms today are composed of fifty, a hundred, and even several hundred lawyers under one firm name and under one roof.

The process is not dissimilar to that which has occurred in business, where the small enterpreneur is at an ever-increasing disadvantage against the chain or huge competitor.

Even in medicine scientific advances make medical complexes with available laboratory services, and specialists in various branches, superior to the individual practitioner. How is one doctor to keep abreast of all the progress daily recorded?

Sometimes people introduce themselves and tell me they are clients of my office. I am always humiliated by such an incident, because I consider the role of adviser and counsel uniquely personal. But a complex society separates us from intimacy. There was a time when if your neighbor was ill, you would bring him soup, a hot-water bottle, and your personal solicitude. Today we live in huge cement cubicles and we do not even know who our neighbor is, though he may reside a few feet away.

I cherish the anecdote of the family doctor in a little town who has delivered children, treated them during infancy and maturity, and brought their children into the world. He has taken care of all ills from surgery to mental disease, and his intimate knowledge of the patient and his forebears have given him insights which no contemporary analyses alone could provide. Having grown old and tired from caring for an ever-increasing flock, he heartily welcomes a new graduate who has come into town to practice medicine. He hopes the young doctor, superbly trained, will relieve him ultimately of his responsibilities, but he soon learns that the newcomer does not intend to be a general practitioner. He will be a specialist. "Of the stomach?" the old doctor asks. "Oh no, that is too large a field for one man to master."

"Of the ears, nose, and throat?"

Of course not, there has been such an accumulation of knowledge in these areas that he cannot hope to absorb it all.

The old practitioner can contain himself no longer.

"What nostril do you intend to specialize in?" he asks.

Despite the growth of legal domains, I have striven with might and main to keep direct contact with each client. For I firmly believe that the psychological comfort which a client derives from his lawyer or doctor is of immense importance. A man or woman in trouble needs more than advice or even ultimate relief. There is the intervening period of deep anxiety which must be bridged. It is unnecessary torment, because it contributes nothing to solution, and enervates the victim, whose cooperation is necessary. I consider it the lawyer's duty to address himself to this problem as much as to the pure legal problem presented.

The client, like a patient, who is in trouble is highly sensitive to the demeanor of his adviser: a smile and confident manner are great therapy. A furrowed brow or pursed lips strike terror in the heart of the troubled. The attorney or doctor may only be gesturing unconsciously about a minor aspect of the difficulty, but to the overwrought, disaster is being registered. Scowls should be reserved exclusively for the adversary. Whether the condition is physical or mental, the body does wonders to ease the suffering, if given a chance.

Of course, the truth cannot be tampered with even to assuage suffering. But what is the truth and how is it to be presented? I tell the client that the problem is serious, and that I do not take a Pollyanaish view of it, but I am confident that it can be solved, that far worse has been overcome, and that he may be sure all our energy and resourcefulness will be applied to correct the situation. This is combined with a direct appeal to leave his worries on our doorstep. If he will realize that the ogres he dreams about are exaggerated shadows cast by him standing in his own light, he will understand that they are not real. Some peace of mind then becomes possible.

There is also the matter of "client relationship." Often lawyers are too busy and harassed taking care of the client's battles to worry about informing him or her of developments. What is more cruel than such suspension? Even adverse news is preferable to the imagined disasters conjured up by silence. Frequently there is no news, nothing but delay, but this is no excuse for not reporting—not if the attorney is sensitive to the client's fears. A telephone call or personal report of developments, even if they are thin or nonexistent, is tonic for the client's nervous system.

In short the lawyer or doctor who ignores the psychological areas of his professional duty is as unfaithful to it as if he were guilty of malpractice. Indeed it is humanistic malpractice to be unaware of the client's or patient's suffering when it is possible to alleviate it.

To overcome the impersonal aspect of a large law office, and mindful of the importance of knowing the client profoundly, I adopt what may be considered an inefficient procedure of inviting the most junior associate who may assist in a case to sit in at the very first conference with the client. The young lawyer is not assigned to a cubbyhole to prepare pleadings or bills of particular, or to research in the library, on the basis of an abstract presentation of the problem. He is introduced to the human side of the law, literally and in person. He hears the original, perhaps disjointed, and self-conscious description by the client, with all its telltale emphasis, evasions, or irrelevant excursions. He observes the client's candor, sometimes significantly burned at both ends. If he is perceptive, avenues for further factual research may open up, and may lead to resourceful legal ideas.

Also, empathy for the client is likely to be created (if it is distasteful, he should be taken off the case quickly), and this stimulates the effort, just as hostility dampens it.

I recall a matrimony case in which my associate dedicated himself at all hours on behalf of our client. However, when we discussed developments privately, he laughingly doubted her protestations of virtue.

The client repeatedly pleaded with me to have a junior, who was assisting in the case, assigned to her. She paid tribute to the talents and devotion of the associate, but she was enamored with the talents of the junior, not half as able.

The associate was flabbergasted by her ingratitude. I suggested that his private opinion of her had come through to her. He remonstrated that this could not be, he was fond of her and had never indicated his skepticism. It was difficult for him to realize that there are emanations which cannot be disguised.

My association with Louis Phillips opened up a door to the motion picture industry. I sat in at meetings of the New York Film Board of Trade. In those days there was a compulsory arbitration system whereby disputes between theater owners and motion picture producers and distributors were arbitrated before boards consisting of exhibitors and distributors evenly divided. I was entrusted to try these cases for the producers. They presented complicated industrial problems of clearance (the number of days of exclusive showing of a picture before the second and subsequent run theaters could show it), and copyright infringements (the showing of a picture in a theater for which it had not been licensed). This was called bicycling because that is how the motion picture print was transported to the theaters in the chain which did not pay for it. It was said that in the early days, a Charlie Chaplin print would not be returned for months. It rode the bicycles. Later the techniques became more sophisticated. Motorboats, and even planes, were used to rush the prints to unlicensed theaters.

To stop this practice, I urged that the damages be not merely the license fee which should have been paid, but damages under the Copyright Act, which were a minimum of $250 and a maximum of $5,000 a showing. Arbitration boards handed down awards of thousands of dollars for the illegitimate exhibition of a newsreel which could have been licensed for $2.50. In one case in Boston, the board awarded $26,000 damages for a film whose license fees ran only in the hundreds of dollars.

There were many other industrial disputes, such as conflicts of booking and deceptive advertising. I tried these cases throughout the country. Later the Government challenged the right of motion picture producers to own theater chains. This was claimed to be a vertical monopoly garnished by conspiratorial division of theater territories, scratching each other's backs in supplying films to each other's theaters, and other practices which were charged to be abuse of power. It was a lethal blow aimed at the motion picture structure. I was too young to be chosen for the defense of this action. Giants of the legal profession were retained—John W. Davis (who had been a Democratic candidate for the presidency), former appellate judge Joseph H. Proskauer, and Fred Wood, a lawyer's lawyer. But they lost.

The Supreme Court directed the motion picture companies to divest themselves of their theater chains or of their producing activities. They could not engage in both. This was called divorcement—a quaint domestic reference to corporations, who were compelled to live apart not because they quarreled but because they did not.

The aftermath was worse than the defeat itself. Dozens of theater owners brought antitrust suits against the motion picture companies, relying on the finding in the Government suit that the producers had violated the antitrust laws. I defended the companies in many of these involved litigations in the federal courts of many states. The risk and responsibility were great. The antitrust laws provide for treble damages. Many millions of dollars were at stake in each contest.

Although each plaintiff had the advantage of the finding of monopoly in the Government suit, he could recover damages only if he could demonstrate that he was injured in his theater operation. He could not throw the cloak of the Attorney General around his shoulders to claim damages he had not suffered. That was a Government privilege, but in a private suit, the plaintiff had to demonstrate that he had been victimized and how badly.

I lived for months in Chicago, Philadelphia, and other cities where these protracted cases had to be tried. We were rewarded for our exhaustive efforts and fared extremely well.

When Louis Phillips was offered a counsel post by Paramount Pictures Corporation, I suggested that despite the tempting offer, he should refuse it, unless he was granted permission to continue the private practice of law. He would agree to give his personal time exclusively to Paramount, but he could remain a partner in our law firm. This was an unprecedented request and it resulted in an unprecedented consent. The battle for independence had been won.

I have never veered from this principle. Later, when my law partners, Robert S. Benjamin and Arthur Krim, took the chairmanship of the board and the presidency of United Artists Corporation, the same reservation was made. They remained partners in our law firm. Their salaries were deemed fees earned for our firm—but not their equities. These were just as deliberately reserved for them, and excluded from our firm.

I never owned a single share of stock in United Artists or in any other motion picture company, directly or indirectly. My personal principle has been that an attorney should have no investment which may cut across his complete objectivity in representing clients—particularly where they are competitors in the same industry. He is necessarily entrusted with confidential information of the highest order and like Caesar's wife he must not only be pure, but avoid any act which may give even a suspicion to the contrary.

Of course, a reputation for absolute integrity is the final assurance to a client. I was retained at different times to represent Metro-Goldwyn-Mayer, Twentieth Century-Fox, and Columbia Pictures in proxy contests for control. These retainers and the struggles which ensued involved intricate maneuvers and confidences. But the clients knew that they were inviolate from disclosure even to my own partners at United Artists. So it was with all other types of litigations in which competitive data came to my attention, when I represented motion picture companies in other suits. This is the norm in our profession. The sanctity of confidence is as honored as that of the confessional booth or the doctor's office.

I shall not detail here any of the cases which I fought—whether they involved the lives and fortunes of corporations or individuals. I have depicted a small number of them in *My Life in Court* and *The Jury Returns*.

This being a more personally focused chronicle, I go back to my point about independence. I believe that any lawyer who casts his lot with one client, usually as corporation counsel, makes a serious error. He may rise as he often does to an executive post, even the vice-presidency or presidency, but his tenure is subject to the uncertainties of corporate control. Time and again, I have seen counsel for large companies displaced not because of any deficiency of their own, but because new interests took over and brought in their own lawyers.

The tragedy is that such counsel have become experts in the specialized field of the corporate enterprise, and, when let out, find very few, if any, similar posts available, where their expertise could be applied. Also, though very competent, they have been away from the general practice of the law so long that they are worse off than a beginner, because their distinction and high earnings are handicaps to new training. "A used key is always bright."

I, therefore, advise young lawyers to join law firms, not corporation staffs, so that when they have earned partnership, they are in professional business for themselves.

On several occasions, partners in my own firm were lured by attractive offers made by companies I represent. In each instance, the earnings were much higher, and the proffered title flattering. I would not stand in their way. Indeed, I had introduced them to the client and developed the relationship. But I advised against acceptance, because the shelter of a law firm is secure, while that of a corporation is subject to all the vicissitudes of changing business climate, absorption by acquisition, growth by merger and new faces at the top, and, of course, proxy battles which, when successful, result in new management and the unceremonious ousting of the old. I have been involved in these battles of corporate democracy and seen the defeated regimes lose power just like defeated officeholders when they lose an election.

I have myself been the recipient of proposals to abandon the general practice of law, in favor of exclusive corporate service. I recite one such offer because it was so unusual. An executive of a large company urged me to quit my law office and become his counsel and personal adviser. He made an offer which he thought I couldn't refuse. He would put two million dollars in a trust for me and pay an annual salary in any amount my conscience would permit me to suggest.

I did not give this an instant thought. My rejection was all the more difficult because he and his wife are charming companions. But my principle held fast. I am willing to be enslaved by each case, but do not wish to be a prince in one man's domain.

CURIOSITY AND ABSORPTION

In my junior year in college, I qualified to teach English to foreigners in night school. It was another way to eke out some money for my own education. But I enjoyed it so I should have paid for the privilege. In the first place, the class consisted of mature people, some of them graduates from the gymnasiums of Europe (what a curious transposition of meaning the word gymnasium involves—exercise in thought, not physical exercise). One or two of my students had doctoral degrees. Furthermore, they were eager to learn.

However, they all had one severe handicap—tiredness. They worked during the day and were exhausted at night. Not all had the energy which I had inherited from a long line of ancestors. I was brimful of enthusiasm for the task. The common experience in night school was that attendance dwindled. Students flocked to the opening sessions. A class consisted of forty to fifty. Within weeks there were only twenty or thirty. Toward the end of the term some classes had only five or six attendees. There were even instances where the course had to be terminated because nobody showed up.

Good resolutions rarely have long lives. There is a large drop-out among those who sign up for exercise courses, diet regimes, nonsmoking cruises, correspondence courses, encyclopedia purchases, and the like. The night students had a better excuse for quitting than others, because some could barely keep their eyes open, and without great concentration it was difficult to learn a new language.

The Board of Education trained its teachers in certain techniques. These were set forth in guidebooks. I disagreed completely with them, so I ignored them and followed my own ideas. They worked. Attendance not only remained steady throughout the term, but actually increased, as other classes declined. Furthermore, I arranged a final debate which demonstrated a mastery of English by students who could barely utter a phrase when they entered the course.

The authorities at the Board of Education used attendance figures as an index to effectiveness, as well they might. They were startled to find one class which had a drop-in instead of a drop-out record. What was going on there?

One day an assistant superintendent and two other dignitaries of the Board of Higher Education paid me a surprise visit. They introduced themselves and said they would like to sit in during the lesson. All seats were taken; indeed one or two were doubled up. The principal brought chairs which were placed in the aisles.

What they saw first was that the two large blackboards were filled with material which I had written and printed a half hour before class was to begin.

The contents were startling. Acting on the principle that memory depends on concentration, and that concentration results from aroused interest, the material on the blackboards had nothing to do with the customary techniques of learning a language. There were no lists of nouns, verbs, or adjectives. There was not a word about grammar, parsing, tense, vowels or consonants. I considered these as dull as the Official Instruction Guides which prescribed them.

Instead the first item was headed Health Hint. Each night a useful suggestion was set forth, so presented that it contained words and usage built on the progression of past lessons.

Then followed in succession an interesting history item, a statement by one of the world's great philosophers, a joke, a science curiosity, an unusual biographical fact about a famous composer, or painter, or writer.

For a full half hour, I read slowly from the boards, explaining, repeating, and restating everything in simple form. I did all the talking. I did not call on a student.

This also violated the guidebook. Its theory was that the student should be compelled to speak as much as possible. This seemed to me to be psychologically unwise. A student called upon to express himself when he is not ready to do so is embarrassed before his audience. Every mispronunciation or wrong word causes a gale of laughter. He feels he is being ridiculed. He dreads the ordeal of being exposed.

In my class he knew he was safe. Only when he volunteered would he have to perform.

I believed in teaching through the ear. Over and over again I repeated a question and answered it. I jested. I walked among the students making comments which became familiar to them by sheer varied repetition. I never used a foreign language to explain. But I permitted them to help out each other with translation. Their curiosity stimulated them. Those who understood the joke on the blackboard laughed, and those who didn't would lean over to a friend to get a definition of a word. One could hear the delayed giggles as comprehension reached some students in installments. This reminded me of a story about Adlai Stevenson when he watched a comedian who performed in Hebrew in an Israeli night club. Stevenson joined the others in hearty laughter. Someone asked him whether he understood Hebrew. "No, but I trust these people," he replied.

As the different items were read from the board, curiosity and excitement spread among the students. Once a brilliant student who had studied astronomy in Berlin challenged my astronomy fact on the board. His expertise compelled him to express himself. I helped him with his English whenever he lapsed into German, so that he could complete his argument. Then I asked him whether he would mind repeating his contention solely in English, because I was proud of his effort, and stood corrected on astronomy.

As the informal atmosphere developed, students began to talk to me and, at times, excitedly to their neighbors. "In English," I always reminded them. With a little help, they would utter whole sentences and laugh at the way their compulsion to express themselves had made English words tumble out of their mouths—usually words which had been absorbed from my constant talking to them.

There were times when the subject matter caused disagreement among the students. They forgot that they were in a class and debated with each other. I never interrupted them, except with the stricture "In English—please—only in English," and when their eyes turned pleadingly to fill in a vacuum in their vocabulary, I supplied it, repeated the sentence with it, expressed the thought still another way—and then turned them loose again.

The students were having such a good time (isn't that the best way to learn?) that I could not help showing off and asking whether they would like to stay longer. They voted for another half hour. The dignitaries from the Board of Higher Education had to stay after school.

After the session I met with the visitors in the office of the principal. He reminded me that I had ignored all the rules, but his superiors were far more friendly. They commented that while my individualistic style might work for me, they doubted that it could be applied generally. I thought it could. I quoted Robert Hutchins: "The purpose of education is to inflame the mind." The corollary was even more important: intense interest was essential to learning. A dull lesson could not penetrate a tired mind. These students were grownups. They were intelligent and mature. They would come alert and concentrate if the content was stimulating. Also, language was similar to music. It literally had a tune. One could learn it better by listening. Of course the ultimate goal was to have the student speak. But premature insistence on his practicing out loud was self-defeating. Self-consciousness wiped out his sparse vocabulary. Why not try a new approach?

They asked whether I would volunteer to help write a new guide-book. I did, but it was compromised down the road by conventional technicians. Still it was an improvement.

I cherished the friendships which developed with some of the students, and which lasted for many years. To this day I receive an occasional letter which begins, "Perhaps you remember me. I was a pupil in your class in night school." The gold pen and pencil presented to me by my last class out of their meager earnings was the most touching gift I ever received.

Next to law and medicine, I would have preferred teaching as a profession.

I have continued to teach sporadically. I give law lectures annually on "The Art of a Jury Trial" or some other subject at Columbia, Yale, Harvard, and other universities. I also have presided at moot court trials at various law schools. On each occasion I meet with the students in private seminars after the talks and engage in a dialogue, which is, I hope, as useful to them as it is to me.

Some years ago, I thought I would share my love for law with teaching. I accepted an invitation to give a law course at Yale Law School to be given only on Fridays. I thought this was manageable. But before it could begin, I was retained to try an antitrust case in the Midwest. I was away for months. The law is truly a jealous mistress. I have only succeeded in stealing a day here and there from her, to address students across the land.

Great developments in pedagogic science have not dented the simple principle that stimulation of the mind increases its receptivity and retention.

THE COSMIC SHELL GAME

For some strange reason, trivial incidents, which ought to pass by in a flash, impress themselves on the mind permanently. Something about them digs so deeply into our consciousness that they survive as pressing and sometimes oppressive memories for the rest of our lives.

For example, I recall a minor incident, when boarding a bus. I was late and eager not to miss it. I rushed up the steps, heedlessly pushing an old man aside, unintentionally, I am sure. He remonstrated loudly at my rudeness, and gave me a deserved dressing down in front of the crowd of passengers. I apologized, but to no avail. He condemned me as one of the younger generation, who had no manners or respect for anyone. I finally thought he was overdoing it, but not the audience he was addressing. Some of them mumbled their disapproval out loud too. It was a fleeting instance, but the man's face and his castigation remain indelibly in my mind. Why this psychic scar, when so many worse transgressions have been obliterated by time?

I am sure everyone has experienced a brush with death or injury. I have had a number of such traumas—a plane whose motor has fallen off, a near-drowning incident in a lake, and other perils. But one minor escapade is vividly haunting to this day. I was walking across Times Square in New York City on my way to lunch at the Algonquin Hotel, where I would "preside" over the Round Table.

My mind was still trailing behind on a legal problem I had wrestled with in my office. Absentmindedly, I stepped off the curb. A huge truck, traveling at irresistible speed, passed by me so closely that it ripped a button off my overcoat and smashed it to bits. I was startled, of course, and blew a sigh of fright, but continued to lunch. There I sat as usual with the writer Konrad Bercovici, publishers Martin Quigley and Jack Alicoate, humorist Harry Hershfield, columnist Dr. Frank Kingdon, owner of the hotel Ben Bodne, and one or two visiting celebrities. The table talk was witty, stimulating, and warm. It did not even occur to me to mention the incident. Hadn't we all gone through the same near accidents many times? But the thought that a few inches forward and my life would have been snuffed out never left me. It is as if my subconscious had registered the imminence of death from which soporific nature protects us otherwise.

Well, two incidents of completely different character left the same deeply etched impression on me forever. They also gave me a better insight to other people's sensitivities, and in that sense have been instructive as well as painful.

The first occurred in 1928. In the New York Film Board of Trade there was an executive who took care of the trade association functions. His name was John Cronin. He was about sixty-five years old, having "retired" to this job after being Mayor of Peekskill, New York. He was a very devout Catholic, with impressive bearing, being tall, gray and not convex in the middle. His slightly bulbous, veined nose (not due to drinking) did not detract from his dignity.

Cronin must have been starved for decent conversation. With my advent in the office, he found the opportunity for discourse. I liked him and was stimulated by his knowledge and his fine mind. So whenever the opportunity presented itself, he would wander into my office, inquire whether I was too busy, and sit down to chat, no matter what the answer was.

I found lunch hour most easily sacrificed. So we got into the habit of ordering a bite at my desk and talking about "life" and all its vagaries.

Of course, we reached religion. He entered into this discussion with zest. He did not fear any inroads of logic, because he had faith, which is the ubiquitous bulwark against the finite powers of the mind.

So in the same innocent and friendly spirit in which I had assailed some of his economic or political views, I challenged what I described as the "superstitions" which abound in all religions. These made for lively if inconclusive discussions. He seemed to cherish and enjoy them and indeed invited their continuation.

One day, he brought up the tenets of his religion. Not without sensitivity, I went at some of them, exploiting what I thought was the intellectual atmosphere which pervaded our discussions. I was sure he knew of my respect for his religion, as he had for mine. I merely took an agnostic view about some of the "miracles" which pervade religious lore, whether it be the splitting of the Red Sea or the Immaculate Conception. I recall the playful manner of some of our exchanges, such as my reference to the quotation "I am an atheist, thank God." However, his face became flushed during our argument, and since he had high blood pressure, I changed the subject. He would not detour. He remained chained in thought to the "cross-examination" to which I had subjected

him. My words now passed him by. Suddenly, he interrupted. His face
was contorted as if he was suffering physical pain, and in a low voice he
said slowly, "Please, don't do this to me."

These words and the incident to which they are attached are engraved permanently in my mind. Cronin was a sophisticated man who
had undoubtedly been through many discussions about Catholic
dogma. He was very able and could give better than he received in any
debate. He also had a sense of humor which gave him imperturbability.
His profound religious convictions were therefore impregnable, I would
have thought. Yet something had happened which threatened to
breach his faith. It was a sin to do this. I never felt more guilty in my
life.

Nor could I ever forget his abandonment of the verbal contest to
plead for mercy. It was so uncharacteristic of him, and revealed the
depth of his anguish.

My apologies exceeded my embarrassment, but every disclaimer of intent to offend his sensibilities only emphasized the injury, since it had
been inflicted despite good will. Like a rent garment, the more one
fusses with it, the worse the tear becomes.

Every person builds shells around himself to protect the inner core.
In Cronin's case it was a shell which protected him from the extinction
of death and assured him everlasting life.

Others surround themselves with an idealistic shell. They would
sacrifice everything for a better world. I can think of nothing more
tragic, for example, than one who sincerely believes in the Soviet Union
as the perfect society, and gladly makes all sacrifices for his belief, only
to discover its corruption and Mafia-like leadership, as evidenced again
right from the bear's mouth—Khrushchev's book.

It is only when one cannot build a shell because he hates himself
that he is really sick. Hating others may be detestable and foolish because every minute of hate is sixty seconds of possible happiness lost.
But hating oneself is permanent unhappiness. The inner core cannot be
protected.

There are certain areas where change of mind is not disruptive. Indeed, it is part of enlightenment to explore one's beliefs. Ideas transplanted in other minds grow better. A mind stretched by a new idea
never returns to its original size. But one must recognize the difference
between opinions which can be shaped or discarded and those protective shells which are vital to survival.

I thought I had learned my lesson. I used to have delightful talks
with Martin Quigley, a lay leader in the Catholic Church. He was a
Jesuit scholar and it was unnecessary to spare his feelings, because his
keen mind could thrust as well as parry. His best weapon was an

enigmatic smile as if to say, "It is too bad you don't understand, but after all, how can a finite mind comprehend the infinite?" Nevertheless, we jousted on politics (he thought Roosevelt's financial profligacy would bring about a Fascist state), the arts (he was the founder of the original motion picture code, and considered the mild permissiveness of those days the beginning of the ruin of the industry), on civil rights (we agreed on its universal application), and on religion (he recognized my own religious feelings and used them to combat my own questions). Though he didn't need solicitude, I treated him tenderly, after the Cronin episode.

But many years later, I repeated my error. I was off guard, because the subject was in a different direction. It involved my sister-in-law Cora.

She and her husband were students and followers of the esoteric philosophers Gurdjieff and Ouspensky.

Through their precepts they sought higher consciousness. Cora, who was goodness itself, nevertheless struggled all her life to improve her soul, to prepare herself for the endlessness of all forces. It is always so. The pure seek purification; the clean bathe most frequently.

Cora also believed in reincarnation. As a result of her intensive studies, she became not only an exemplar but a teacher. She and her husband traveled to many countries, where groups of followers practiced these philosophies. Part of the ritual involved intricate dances and exercises, like those of Indian dervishes, to achieve higher concentration and free the mind for nobler spheres.

On one occasion she sought to enlist me and my wife, Mildred, in "the movement." This was, of course, intended as a compliment, for only those who were capable of banishing negative thoughts could aspire to these teachings. Out of curiosity, I attended a meeting at which Gurdjieff presided.

He was a fat, totally bald Russian, with a flowing white handlebar mustache and an unbelievably insulting manner toward his own followers. I was aghast at the supine subservience of his students. I witnessed a microcosm of a tyrannical domain and was revolted by it, even though I am ready to accede the brilliance of his writings and, particularly, those of Ouspensky, who wrote the highly regarded mathematical work *Tertium Organum*. I expressed some of my resentment with a lowly pun. While lecturing and cursing, Gurdjieff had eaten the head of a sheep, tearing it apart with bare hands. I referred to his huge belly as Sheepshead bay.

Years went by. Cora took the place of esteemed leaders in "the movement" who had passed on. Unlike some of them, she was a model human being, kind, sensitive, and striving ever to be more worthy.

A part of her duties was to give talks. She feared them, and sought my help. This, and her general interest in my activities and opinions, led to friendly discussions. I expressed my skepticism about much of her philosophy. Of course, there was some truth in the precepts she held. There is in every "movement." Christian Scientists, Religious Scientists, Quakers, Mormons, Seventh-Day Adventists, Jehovah's Witnesses, Chasidim, Yogis, all preach some psychological truths. It is presumptuous to concede the same for the dozens of religions and sects. The area of doubt begins when these limited truths are extended into full-blown credos, every tenet of which is required to be accepted.

In any event, I argued out my rejection of some of her theses, from reincarnation, with its familiar argument that child geniuses, like Mozart, can only be explained thereby, to higher consciousness in preparation for soul-like existence.

At one point, she paused and looked at me a long time. I thought she was thinking through a reply. Instead, she said in a voice whose change of octave and vibrancy connoted deep emotion, "Lou, live and let live."

It was an echo of Cronin's plea. She had devoted her life looking for its higher meaning. Like hundreds of philosophers who had preceded her, she could not accept the brief cycle of life and death as a fleeting moment to no purpose. So she searched. And she thought she had found. Now all her dedication at great sacrifice to mundane joys of the unthinking was being challenged. Words were reaching her which threw some doubt on the certainty which sustained her. If the shell of spiritual preparation would be loosened—if the great truth might be an illusion after all, of what avail the years spent in study, teaching, and believing? "Live and *let live*" was a literal cry.

I had assaulted a precious shell. I vowed never to do so again.

I can only hope that her untimely death several years later has solved the great mystery for her, and that she now hovers over this page smiling at my foolish skepticism.

IF A SPEAKER DOESN'T STRIKE OIL IN
FIFTEEN MINUTES, HE SHOULD STOP BORING

I have made thousands of speeches and never used a script or a note. This does not mean that I improvise or am not thoroughly prepared. On the contrary, the preparation is intense. I would no more address an audience without exhaustive preparation than I would try a case without advance mastery of the facts. The "secret" of public speaking, like that of successful trial work, is preparation. In lectures to law schools, I have attempted to impress this on memory by creating a "scientific" equation: I.Q. (Intelligence Quotient)$+$W.Q.^{2} (Work Quotient squared)$=$S. (Success).

I would rather try a case against the most famous lawyer, who by virtue of age and success depends on his assistants for preparation, than against a neophyte, who has slaved to learn every factual and legal facet of his case. As Benjamin Franklin put it, "Never was one glorious without first being laborious."

Unfortunately, the opportunity to triumph over the brilliant but unprepared veteran rarely occurs. For he, too, knows the secret of his success, and he is not likely to abandon it. Sir William Osler once stated this principle felicitiously:

There is an old folk lore legend that there is some mystic word which will open barred gates. There is, in fact, such a mystic word. It is the open sesame of every portal. The great equalizer in the world, the true philosopher's stone, which transmutes all the baser metal of humanity into gold. The stupid man it will make bright, the bright brilliant and the brilliant steady. With the mystic word all things are possible. And the mystic word is "work".

Yes, the trial lawyer has many opportunities to improvise, to triumph because of a sudden inspiration, to balance like a gyroscope in a storm

—but all of these are subordinate planets. The sun around which they orbit is thorough preparation.

The same is true in making a good speech. It is arrogant for anyone to take the time of an audience with unthoughtful improvisation. The least one owes to any occasion is thorough preparation so that some ideas may be projected which will be stimulating to the audience.

So much has been written about public speaking. I have contributed a book myself—called *Thinking on Your Feet*. What is generally overlooked is that the overwhelming requirement for a speech is profound thought. Communication has come to mean the process of transfer, instead of the thought which is transferred. Ideas transplanted in another mind seem to grow better. But original thinking is the rarest to come by—and no amount of forensic skill can substitute for it. Technique is an adornment of substance. It is never a substitute for it.

That is why people groan when the program announces a long list of speakers. We have learned from experience that there is not a thought in a carload, and we do not wish to suffer through bromidic exhortations.

However, if the speaker is thoughtful enough to have an original idea and has made a special effort to develop it, the evening can be exhilarating and informative. But where are they?

Dozens of times I have sat on committees to select speakers. The occasions were important enough to warrant acceptance by the most famous men and women in the nation, not excluding the President of the United States. Yet we have struggled to find a suitable speaker. We usually turned to celebrities instead of thinkers, to pique our curiosity rather than to stretch our minds.

This probably explains a unique American phenomenon which assumes that achievement in one field qualifies a man to be an expert in others. The industrialist makes speeches on international affairs; the nuclear scientist on mores; the novelist on the state of the economy, and the motion picture star on politics. Brilliance in one field is rarely across-the-board versatility, and we traverse arid areas with an impostor.

Henry Ford once sued the Chicago *Tribune* for libel, claiming one million dollars damages. The cross-examiner, aware that Ford was brilliant to the point of genius in his field, sought to bring him down from his pedestal by changing the subject.

"Who was Benedict Arnold?" he suddenly asked.

"He was a writer, I think," replied Ford, thus setting off a laugh which reverberated around the nation for many years. It is doubtful that his error was due to confusion with Matthew Arnold. Even that name was probably beyond his ken. More likely he was thinking of Horace L. Arnold, who had written a shop manual for Ford workers.

Charles Lindbergh similarly revealed that his unique competence as a flier could not be transferred to the political and military arenas. He announced his belief that the Nazis would triumph. He headed an isolationist movement. He had earned the world's adulation for his historic flight, but would many want to shower ticker tape upon him for his other views?

We have become cynical about all this. The public takes it for granted that elected officials do not write their own pronouncements. Experts prepare speeches for them, and even the President can claim no more than that he exercises editorial judgment in adopting one view given to him rather than another.

There is not even an effort to disguise this sorry fact. Official announcements are made that two economic advisers are preparing a policy paper which the President will deliver to the nation in a few weeks.

Granted that the complexity of government requires research and advice of experts, but this does not mean abdication to the opinions of unknown men who never submitted themselves to the electorate.

One had only to learn how Churchill, Roosevelt, and Stevenson made every speech their own, irrespective of what material was prepared for them, to understand the difference between an independent intellect digesting research and a weak executive adopting another's thoughts, and sometimes faltering over the delivery of them.

Having stressed substance as the irreducible requirement for any speech, I turn to the art of delivery. Cardozo once pointed out that form is not a protuberance on substance; it is part of substance itself. An argument or speech well made is not the same as the identical argument or speech poorly made.

Perfectionism requires that no speech be read, and that no notes be used. Why? Because the rhythm necessary to absorption of the spoken word is completely different from that of the written word.

All one has to do to verify this is to use one's ear attentively. Listen to any conversation. It is slow, halting for a thought, full of pauses, and then a sudden torrent of words as the idea develops. Often anticipation by the listener makes it unnecessary to finish the sentence. The parsing is faulty. Speech, which is the conveyor belt on which the thoughts are carried, is slow or fast depending on its comprehensibility. Often a word, clause, or sentence is repeated as the speaker senses that the pace is too fast for the complexity of the thought. In short, the delivery is irregular, adjusting to the absorptive capacity of the audience. The listener cannot do what he does with a passage in a book which confounds him—read it over again or put it down for another occasion. If he cannot follow the speaker *instantly*, he deserts him. That is one of the reasons audiences are lost when speeches are read from a script.

There is the jest, all too true, of the speaker who began, "My duty is to speak, and yours to listen. But if you quit before I do, please let me know."

On the other hand, that which is intended to be read rather than heard should never be dictated to a stenographer or on a machine. It should be written or typed, because the rhythm for the words which are read is different from the rhythm when words are heard. The construction can be more involved and more polished. The style more graceful. Short sentences can be balanced against longer ones; declarative ones against questions. Interest can be created through contrast and coloring of diction. The grammar and rhetoric should be impeccable, and enjoyment can be derived by the reader from the beauty of construction as well as thought. There is almost a mathematical construction, like in music, which, although unnoticeable, creates a rhythm which affects the emotions.

So the firm rule is: a speech should be delivered without a single note, the speaker looking his audience in the eye and timing his delivery to match its immediate comprehension.

A book or document intended to be read should never be dictated orally, but written or typed personally by the author. I have followed these precepts. All my platform speeches have no written crutches lying on the podium. All my writings, as this very page, are written out longhand by pen or pencil.

The only exception I make is to have a quotation or statistical data before me when I use them in a speech. These too are in my mind and I do not need the notes, but I deliberately resort to them to assure the hearers of authenticity. Audiences are so skeptical about memory that they may distrust the accuracy of a long quotation. So I make a special point to read them—putting on my glasses, to be sure this part of the delivery is distinguished from the rest.

Is this the rule for all who make public speeches? Of course not. A busy executive called upon to address a group of his pretended peers may not have time or inclination to reach for perfection. He may not even aspire to be a public speaker. He is content to share his expertise from a written script. But let him not pride himself on an art which he does not practice. And when he is complimented by a request that his talk ought to be printed because it was so good, he might suspect that the audience couldn't follow it orally.

Professor John Dewey drew large classes at Columbia College because of his eminence, but he suffered the highest absences. He was as dull orally as he was profound in his writings. Professor Albert Einstein did not need the aid of his accent to be incomprehensible. His eyes were buried in a script. His words in monotone emerged haltingly from behind his mustache, losing volume as they were sifted through hair. Audiences rushed to see and hear him, and after they had satisfied their eyes, they closed their ears. Ultimately, they turned to small talk among themselves while the great man droned on. His best oration was at a commencement exercise where he was one of the speakers. He arose and said, "I do not have any particular thoughts to express today, so I wish you all success in your future years." Then he sat down. If only others who had nothing to say would follow his example.

The speaker must see his audience, look into their eyes, observe their facial expressions, and communicate directly to them as participants.

Even a stripper, like Gypsy Rose Lee, knew that it was eye-to-eye contact that was important to hold attention. In one of the Follies, she was gowned in Ziegfeld's abundant silks and satins, with a flowing train, and a hat as tall and as shimmering as a fountain. As she made her way down the bejeweled circular stairs, she learned that she had to keep her eyes on the audience to hold their attention. The scene was not for stripping, but the risk was tripping. She dared not look down to ensure a safe journey because it would break eye contact.

This principle is responsible for the wise practice at public dinners to put the most brilliant lights on the banquet room when the speaking program begins. That is why the art of public speaking requires experience before an audience. The more frequently the speaker appears, the more at ease he will be. A speaker's nervousness or distress is the most communicable disease in the world. An audience is immediately infected and suffers with him.

One who has not addressed an audience from a platform, dais, or stage cannot possibly imagine the shock from the unexpected surroundings. There is a sea of faces. The eye can only take in a few at a time. They are moving, talking to one another, or looking up challengingly (it might even appear mockingly). A spotlight on the speaker blinds him and the audience becomes blurred. There are all sorts of noises emanating from the front. Applause or laughter does not sound like individual expression, but like a cumulated roar from some huge beast. If the speaker is inexperienced, and becomes overwhelmed by the terrifying surroundings, there is quickly added to his discomfort a competitive conversational buzz throughout the room which signals him that he is being ignored. If he attempts to shout over it, the noise accelerates just enough to make him unheard. He is like a greyhound chasing a rabbit and he cannot win the race for attention. Only his own poise and "presence" could have compelled attention in the first place. This can come only with practice—not in the home, but before an audience.

It is the old vicious cycle when one seeks experience. He is disqualified because he has none. And he can't acquire it until he has some.

Like the inexperienced applicant for a job who demanded a larger salary than his experienced competitors, because "it is much harder work when you have no experience," the aspiring speaker must pass through a much tougher ordeal than the experienced one.

There is a compensating principle. Each appearance before an audience reduces the fear. It is not a gradual descension from panic to self-control, but a progressive one. Ultimately, the speaker learns not to play the game of obliterating the audience's presence in his mind in order to achieve inner peace. Ultimately, he reaches the sophisticated level; when he can look at their faces and observe their reactions to him without being distracted; when awareness of the audience's presence is a stimulation to him; when he is master of his audience; when the "beast" in front knows the assurance and strength of its rider, and is not tempted by his very panic to challenge him. Only then has he become a public speaker.

Even then appearance in front of an audience must be frequent. A long lapse will cause self-assurance to atrophy. Like exercises for the muscles, there is no lasting benefit without slavish repetition. Know-how in some activities is never lost—driving a car, riding a bicycle, or swimming. But in others, like golf, one begins all over again, after a lapse. The greater the psychological demand upon performance, the less self-replenishing it is. So, the more often—the better.

I was fortunate, therefore, to gain speaking experience at a very early age and to accelerate my appearances over a lifetime. In elementary school, I was selected to recite the Pledge of Allegiance at each morning's assembly gathering (a procedure now challenged in our highest courts on the ground that compulsory patriotism is a violation of individual rights. I have always thought that, irrespective of the legalism, this was a rather humorless approach. Children reciting in unison enjoy their self-expression like their elders enjoy a communal sing-in, and entirely apart from the lyrics. But, unfortunately, good causes often ride on a solemn horse. Is that not why people yearning for a light mood sometimes vote sinners into public office?).

At the age of ten, I had become a soapbox orator. In the Brooklyn district where I lived, the Socialists were making their first advances from proclaimers of a better world to election in the State Assembly. There, they learned that their blueprints, as beautiful as bluebirds, were not easily transferable into reality. The defects in dreams are never visible to the dreamer, only to the interpreter. "Where is the money coming from?" was a question that resisters asked, and while there were many answers, the reformers had thought least about such things and were the least competent to pragmatize their visions.

Still, how could one's heart not beat faster as sincere radicals railed against the evils in our society, and called for a better world.

The leader of the local Socialist party was Morris Hillquit, a mustached intellectual whose calm demeanor and uncharacteristic soft tone made him palatable to the average voter. Only when one saw the fierce light in his eyes was it evident that the revolutionary fire within him was disciplined, not dampened. He ran for Mayor of New York City on a Socialist ticket against a Democrat, John F. Hylan, and polled extraordinarily well. His successful campaign pulled in for the first time several Socialist assemblymen.

Morris Hillquit and Eugene Debs became the heroes of the Socialist movement, and their followers predicted the ultimate triumph of the Socialists in American political life. Fate decreed that they should be virtually eliminated from the political scene. But they did not fail entirely. They were to be the catalysts for recognition by Government of direct, not vicarious and remote, responsibility for the welfare of the people. Except for their extreme notion of Government ownership, their program was not rejected. It was adopted by their opponents. Al Smith, a Tammany-dyed Democrat, built a brilliant career from the sidewalks of New York to the State mansion in Albany and to the threshold of the White House, by putting into law most of their demands. When Smith proposed a Child Labor Law, he was denounced as an IWW (International Workers of the World, scornfully translated as I Won't Work), a more deadly appellation than "Communist" in Senator Joseph McCarthy's day. Later, President Franklin D. Roosevelt's New Deal was, in large part, the old deal of the Socialists, a fact which his bitter opponents did not hesitate to hurl at him. Yet, Republican and Democratic conventions in later years both accepted in their official platforms the whole catalogue of "radical" proposals, such as the National Labor Relations Act (the bill of rights for the "working class"), Government insurance of bank deposits, minimum hourly wage, child labor laws, Social Security, Medicare, Tennessee Valley Authority (Government ownership of utilities), civil rights laws, income tax ("confiscatory" taxes on high income), and more and more. Every new effort was denounced, like its predecessor, as the last blow which would destroy capitalism. Yet books appear regularly in which noted economists demonstrate that Roosevelt saved capitalism, because he lifted the people out of despair caused by the great depression and proved that freedom and welfare could be wed without destroying the sacramental authority of democracy. Yes, the Socialists were like spiders which impregnate and die in the process.

Well, my reputation as a boy orator spread. I rejected the suggestion of the powerful Republican leader John Crews to devote my energies to his club, situated enticingly on Sumner Avenue, opposite my home, and accepted the call of none less than Hillquit's emissary to speak on street corners for the Socialists. I always drew a crowd. Few had political interest. They were mainly neighbors who were intrigued to hear Joe Nizer's son hold forth. They reported back to my mother, who beamed because I had made "a good speech," even if it had been on the subject of cruelty to horses (which if too old or sick were shot on the street by a policeman. Those were the days when horses, not cars, were towed away. That is where the old joke stems from about the policeman who could not spell Koscuisko Street, and therefore reported a dead horse on Bushwick Avenue).

My harangues about poverty and an unjust society were not drawn from personal experience. True, my parents were very poor, but the terrible thing was we were happy. I would wake up in the morning in a cold flat, where the defective window permitted the snow to drift in and form icicles on the inside. I shuddered to get out of the bed, and drew the puffed-up huge feather *perineh* closer around me until I disappeared in its billows. My mother encouraged a courageous venture into the cold world by warming my socks on the stove and handing them to me under the quilt, and throwing a warm sweater, as well as her arms, around me as I emerged. (It does not take a skilled analyst to understand why even in my warm penthouse apartment today, my electric blanket is turned on nearer to high than low.)

True, food was not plentiful. My mother tried to hide the fact that the egg which could be spared was given to me. I knew despite her protest that it was not her lack of appetite which caused her to put up her nose at dairy products while urging me to eat because it was good for a growing child.

True, my mother and I worked evenings scalloping laces, but I could hardly inveigh against child labor, because we sang and joked, to the accompaniment of the scissor blades, and often I felt as if I was playing with a toy.

True, I ran errands for the local Regal Shoe Store in the heat of summer to earn a few dollars, but the romance of a job at that early age was as fascinating as my walking across the Brooklyn Bridge to save a nickel, or eating only rice pudding because it cost only a nickel.

True, my clothes were limited to one outfit, as if it were a uniform which discipline decreed must not be changed. But when, as a birthday gift, I received a shiny black leather raincoat and attached hood, like that worn by heroes in motion picture storms at sea, I got up at dawn each day to scan the skies in the hope of a downpour which would justify such stifling garb against the fierce elements. Finally, the dastardly good weather exhausted my patience, and on a slightly cloudy day, I ventured forth in my new regalia, buttoned up to choking. I chose to regard the stares of passers-by as admiration rather than wonder at my anticipation of a second Noah's flood. But I was happy.

"A happy home," says the Bible, "is an early heaven." Try as I might, I could not build my speech upon my own suffering. So I soaked up the Socialist literature of the working class's grievances throughout the world. From the oppression in Siberia to the "exploitation of the masses" in remote regions of the world. I soon learned that mass statistics and generalizations were not the road to persuasion. They were devoid of emotion. Audiences were held by the novelty of a youngster in knickerbockers holding forth from a short triangular stepladder which provided a precarious platform. Later, as the crowds increased, I was provided the back of an open truck, and still later "stardom" brought me the luxury of an open Ford.

There were no microphones, and outdoor speaking was a challenge to the voice because there were no confining walls to bounce the sounds back. So I had invaluable training in the production of sound which could reach a large audience (they grew to hundreds) in all sorts of weather, including winds and rain.

But an attentive audience did not mean a persuaded audience. Huge crowds stormed to hear the great orator Williams Jennings Bryan, but they voted for his opponent. He ran three times for President because his party could not believe that his popularity as a speaker could not be translated into votes.

Persuasion, I learned in those early days, was a two-layered structure —a solid foundation of fact topped by an emotional appeal. Curiously, fact or emotion alone had the same defect—it was interesting but not moving. But the two combined turned their inactive ingredients into explosive persuasion. "When Brutus speaks, everyone says 'what an extraordinary oration!' When Caesar speaks everyone follows him."

But in that early practice, I also observed that there were gradations of emotional appeal. Fist-waving exhortation, so customary to political harangue, had least impact. There were some orators who literally tore their shirt collars open, screamed until their voices cracked in breathlessness, while their eyes almost popped out of their head. Their delivery was bathed in sweat—while the audience remained quite dry and more fascinated than stirred. There is an epigram which reads "when you're in the right you can afford to keep your temper and when you're in the wrong you can't afford to lose it."

On the other hand, if the emotion flowed from an inner well and shone with sincerity, it could set the audience to weeping and it even helped if the delivery was restrained. Apparently, conviction was achieved in inverse ratio to the frenzy of the speaker, because sincerity was blurred and distorted by hysteria. If a speaker cannot control himself, he has little chance of controlling his audience.

The surest way to an effective peroration was to test oneself. Was I moved? Was I so stirred with emotion that my own difficulty in controlling articulation deepened the sincerity of the statement? I decided early that until this test was met, the task of moving an audience was insuperable. That is why I never resort to the most frequent of all elocutional flourishes, a poem. It is too calculated, too esoteric, too contrived.

So I went to the library and searched for vignettes, aphorisms, epigrams, or historical analogies which made a deep impact on me. Later, I created them myself.

For example, to conclude a speech on a high religious note, I depicted a library late at night when the master had retired to sleep. The books begin quarreling among themselves as to which is the lord of the library. The dictionary proclaims that it is because without it, there would be no words or library at all. The book of science angrily retorts that it is the king of the library because without it there would be no printing press or techniques of publishing. The aristocratic gold-embossed novel insists that it depicts life and gives insights necessary to man's progress. The book of philosophy asserts loudly that it is the lord of the library because it has given meaning to man's existence and purpose. The book of poetry argues that it gives surcease to the master when he is troubled. So the noise mounts as the angry contestants insist upon their pre-eminence.

When the din and contentiousness are at their peak, a small voice is heard. It comes from a frayed, brown-covered book lying on a table near the master's armchair. It is heard to say slowly and in a low, vibrant tone, "The Lord is my shepherd. I shall not want . . ."

All the noise in the library ceases. There is a hush. For all the books know who the true lord of the library is.

By the time I was fifteen I had transferred my speaking appeals to charitable rather than Socialist causes. The United States had entered World War I. There were Liberty Loan drives, and the Government enlisted speakers to make appeals for the sale of these bonds. I was chosen to use my skills in this patriotic endeavor. I was eager to shift my speech from the bonds of slavery to the bonds of freedom.

I was assigned to large motion picture theaters like the Brooklyn Fox at Myrtle Avenue and Keith's Bushwick. The flood of pledges following my appeals impressed somebody up there, and I was told that my next talks would be at the New York legitimate theaters on Broadway.

I had never stepped foot on Broadway, so it was bizarre that my introduction to it should be in front of the footlights on the theater row. I stumbled over the paraphernalia, cables, and ropes backstage to the repeated warnings of stars, or curious chorus girls, to be careful. Then, as if I had emerged from a thicket to a beautiful clearing—there was the stage set, incongruously neat, orderly, and beautiful. However, the curtain was down, for these appeals were made at the end of the intermission. The lights dimmed as if the next act was to begin, but instead of the curtain rising, I stepped in front of it.

I had honed my appeal to present the most interesting facts about our war efforts (how did I know they were interesting? Because they interested me. Everything else I eliminated). The speech accelerated to the sacrifices of our soldiers, their needs and our obligation to make moneys available to meet those needs. "I would not demean you by telling you that in buying a Liberty Bond, you are making a good investment at good interest. You must respond for a higher reason. We are all depressed by the brutality and sacrifice around us, and here is an opportunity to lift your arms as if they were wings and do something to ennoble your spirits!"

I had also learned that the mind's lens could not take in too large a scene and maintain definition. Talking of thousands of soldiers dying or being wounded would make an audience shake its head or cluck its tongues in horror, but they really didn't feel it. But if one soldier could be descriptively isolated and made identifiable as an individual, so that in a few brief strokes the audience got to "see" and like him, and then they were told that this boy's legs were cut off by a shrapnel burst, the emotional impact was heightened by identification with the victim.

The patriotic and humanistic peroration reached a climax. Audiences often stood and cheered. I stopped them and pleaded that the only applause which meant anything was at the end of their fountain pens as they filled out the pledges to buy bonds. The usherettes were showered with pledges—and their baskets overflowed. It became the practice of artists backstage to come out on the stage and announce their pledges, which they gave to me. Being naturally emotional as their professions required, some stood on the stage, tears streaming down their cheeks. Some hugged me, much to my embarrassment. The emotion communicated itself to the audience, and a new wave of pledges ensued, some shouting that they were doubling or tripling their purchases. Some pledges were thrown from the boxes onto the stage and floated like heavy confetti into the pit. The musicians in the orchestra handed up their pledges. Excitement reigned. Government assistants made quick calculations and announced approximate totals. They reached hundred of thousands of dollars, and precipitated new enthusiasm.

There was a story of a midnight Liberty Bond rally at Times Square in New York. A record was established. However, they included five-hundred-million and billion-dollar pledges. Hopheads, alcoholics, and derelicts who had gathered had responded with uninhibited patriotic fervor. If they were going to aid their country, they decided to do so in grand style.

While there was always a percentage of defaults, especially where the pledger had overstepped himself when carried away, the audiences at the legitimate theaters were responsible and we had no fear that the unprecedented pledges would turn out not to be genuine.

The Government awarded me a certificate of merit in acknowledgment of my services. My father, whose intense patriotism I have already alluded to, was prouder of this award then any other honor or even honorary degree I ever received thereafter. He had it framed in finest silver and it hung in the most conspicuous place in our home, a token of his vicarious contribution to his country.

My development as a speaker continued through high school and college. At Columbia, I entered the competition for the Curtis Oratorical Award. This required the contestant to write an original composition and deliver it. Wisely, both the content and the style of declamation were evaluated as a whole. During the year, eliminations were held, judged by a group of professors. Four finalists were selected. The finals were held in the evening at Earl Hall, in the presence of faculty, students, and visitors. It was a formal occasion. The judges were distinguished citizens.

I made the finals and this created a sartorial crisis. White tie and tails were required. My father would not hear of renting the outfit, even though the occasion for ever wearing them again seemed remote. A fine tailor, judged more carefully by my parents than I was to be in the contest, prepared the "costume." My parents thought they must be equal to the occasion too, but practicability, which did not apply to me, took over. My father rented a tuxedo, and my mother bought a blue lace gown.

Among them in the audience sat the judges, Governor Al Smith, Charles Evans Hughes, and Nicholas Murray Butler, president of Columbia University.

I was already a veteran at facing audiences, but the splendor of the event and its significance made me nervous. The sharp edge of the wing collar cutting into my neck and the tails flapping behind didn't help.

I delivered an address on disarmament (forty years later, nations are still negotiating on the subject while the armaments have grown infinitely more potent and the will to curb them more feeble). It would be unfortunate for this chronicle if I had not won, and indeed I did. The

Curtis Oratorical Medal was presented to me. It was a huge oval medallion (later inscribed with my name) in an eight-inch leather box so constructed as to please my parents because it could become a stand for display. The program, which described the medallion, stated that it contained one hundred dollars worth of silver. Although its real worth to my father was incalculable, he surprised me with his greeting. He kissed me but said, "The fellow who spoke last was better than you were." My mother waved him aside with a condemnatory "Oh, Joe!" which expressed shock at such an outrageous judgment, and hastened to assure me that everybody in the hall thought I was best. As they walked away to wait for the congratulatory line to end, I overheard him protest that he wanted me to do still better because he knew I could, and that she would spoil me by her adulation.

Later, when he laughed about his unsuccessful effort to prevent me "from getting a swellhead," he referred to my mother's assurance, based on her neighbor's expressions, and told the joke of the concert pianist who was approached by a member of the audience, with no such benign purpose as those who preceded him had. He told the pianist that he had given a terrible performance, weak in interpretation and faulty in execution. The artist's manager, standing nearby, was horrified by the insult. Quite flustered, he comforted the pianist. "Pay no attention to him. He doesn't know what he is talking about. He just repeats what he hears around him!" My mother's eyes twinkled, but she pretended to be serious. "You can be sure I repeated what everybody was saying about Louis."

The next year, the Curtis Oratorical Contest came around again. Professor Brander Mathews, who taught public speaking (and who had given me an unprecedented A+ at the end of the semester, announcing that he doubted such a mark had ever before been given a student at Columbia), urged me to enter again. I thought it might be unseemly, but he insisted that the rules did not forbid it, and even though I would be handicapped as a prior winner, I ought to try. I did. Again, I made the finals.

The white tie and tails outfit became useful again. This was typical of my father's unreasonable stubbornness. Time and again, he turned out to be right after all, but it never discouraged us from making a new but hopeless stand, as when he bought the property on which our store was situated though he had no funds and undertook to pay an oppressive mortgage by working still harder, as if that was possible; or when later he bought our home in Bethlehem, though hotels abounded for our summer vacations at modest rates; or still later when he built an $18,000 marble mausoleum with the name NIZER inscribed on its

Grecian façade, probably to perpetuate our name in some way, since I was the only child and had no children of my own.

This time I put wax on the wing collar to dull its cutting edge, and I wore the tails as if every week was Curtis Oratorical time.

I chose for my oration the subject of capital punishment. Even then it was a classic debating subject. Yet it remained current until the United States Supreme Court, fifty years later, decided the struggle between humanism and severe punishment in a crime-ridden society. I was to encounter the problem in my professional work (I have described one such struggle in detail in the Crump chapter of *The Jury Returns*).

I presented my original composition, constructed on the two layers of fact and emotion. I won again, and presented the first medallion with a mate.

This time my father left his prophylactic skepticism at home. He embraced me unreservedly though not as profusely as my mother.

From that day on, he was uninhibited in his praise and I found this far more difficult to bear than his critical approach. But my mother reveled in his conversion.

How does one go about memorizing a half-hour speech? The memorization is not of words, but of sequences, with felicitious phrasing or climactic sentences as landmarks in the journey.

If a speech doesn't memorize easily, it is because the structure is wrong. If the logical development of sequence is correct, each suggests the next with no effort. When I review a speech in my mind and find my memory fails me at some particular point, I know that the fault is not my memory, but the defect in the correct chain of ideas. Speech memorization is not, as the memory experts tell us, based on association of ideas. For if the association is out of kilter with logic, memory lapses. It is logical sequence which controls memory.

One can check a speech like one can check the addition of figures. If logical sequence inevitably leads to easy memorization, then the structure is sound. The audience will find it easy to follow, because its anticipation will be gratified.

The techniques of memorization may differ with each individual. Like writing practices, they depend on each writer's personal idiosyncrasies. Joseph Conrad wrote in a bath. Perhaps the thick cigar smoke and water made him feel he was viewing the Indian Ocean. Dostoyevsky wrote his psychological studies in the midst of night. Beethoven soaked his hands in ice water before composing. Balzac and Leibnitz prompted the muse by consuming great quantities of coffee, while many, including Shakespeare and Edgar Allan Poe, preferred goblets of wine. Mark Twain wrote best when reclining in bed, which I find the most sensible because I practice it myself. Some write best in the morning. Others through the night. Some concentrate best with music in the background. Others must have silence. Some like beautiful surroundings, others a blank wall. The variations are infinite and sometimes bizarre, like Schiller's insisting on the smell of rotten apples.

I recall selecting Sun Valley for a writing vacation, because there was a balcony outside the room overlooking an idyllic pastureland with a cool shaded lake in the center. I set myself comfortably in this soothing atmosphere with pencil sharpener handy for frequent use. Then I found myself gazing at the sleek, bronze-skinned horses, their necks stretched twice their size toward the grass, while geese skimmed effortlessly on the lake, giving no hint of the furious paddling beneath. When I looked up at the sky there were faded apple green colors melting into blazing orange and red patches, contrasting with fuchsia and violet streamers running in and out of pink-white clouds. I turned my chair around and spent the rest of my writing endeavors looking at the imitation log cabin wall one foot in front of me.

Some speakers prepare by writing out their talks, because the visual and mechanical process in so doing engraves the words on their minds. I disapprove because the writing procedure, even if only as a preliminary to memorization, distorts the proper rhythm. However, each to his own. Therefore, I do not prescribe my own method as the one suitable to others, but I set it forth. I memorize by walking.

Having gathered my research material and thought through my general thesis, I put on comfortable slippers, and begin walking up and down an isolated room, talking the speech out loud.

As I hear it, I reject, add, and develop, but all with an "eye" to my ear. Does it sound clear? Is it easily comprehensible? I become the audience, reacting to my own words. This sentence is only mildly interesting, even though the thought is acceptable. It must be phrased so as to excite attention. Perhaps an epigram or colorful phrase will give it the necessary emotive power. That sentence is too involved and therefore dull. It must be shortened and simplified. These sentences are clear and interesting, but their rhythm is too even and therefore sleep-inducing (the ear, as well as the eye, is the entrance channel for a hypnotic spell). The tempo must be changed, sometimes only by vocal emphasis.

So the process continues, as if I were an editor blue-penciling my own oral script. Each time I begin over again, like a conductor tapping for order, making a suggestion, lifting his baton to say, "Now, from the beginning." The repetitions cause memorization even though I do not strive for it. It is best to be "loose," phrasing the thought differently when the mood dictates. In this way a lapse will not cause a collapse. A word-for-word memorization is dangerous because it enslaves the speaker. If he forgets a sentence, or even a word, the whole sequence disappears and he is left gaping. He must be master of the content and substance, improvising until he reaches the next logical passage in the chain of thoughts.

A speaker who has memorized his speech word for word has a crowd of critics in front of him. They will notice his mechanical reproduction, his distress when a word fails him, and silence suddenly substitutes for the easy flow. The embarrassment is painful to audience and speaker alike, because the singsong cadence of a memorized delivery is revealed in all its artificiality as a pose without inner feeling or thought. Children rushing through a memorized poem, and suddenly gaping at their parents, whose proud smiles turn to shamed prompting, are the familiar prototype of memorization risks.

However, since speech rhythm, like music, requires ascendancy and contrasting climaxes, there should be an emphatic conclusion of every major point. This should be memorized. Here, the speaker may indulge in the luxury of emotional statement. Such statement must be striking and moving—a sort of summation exclamation point. For example, if the point is that violence cannot correct the evil of prejudice—"Civil wrongs can't make civil rights"; or if the thought is that democracy is based on a scientific principle too little observed—"As you multiply judgments, you reduce the incident of error. Two heads are better than one; a thousand better than a hundred; and on a question of right or wrong (not science or mathematics, in which event I would rely on a scientist or mathematician), I would rather trust two hundred million Americans than the ten most brilliant professors in the world!"

These memorized passages are like landmarks in the topography of the speech. They cue in the speaker to the next sequence. So I find that interstitial memorization of specific sentences, combined with a general mastery of the subject matter, provides the best of all worlds for the speaker. He is thinking on his feet, communicating with his audience as he looks into their faces, and improvises the language of his well-prepared argument. At the same time, he reaches memorized plateaus which give epigrammatic, aphoristic, allegoric, or other felicitous emotional appeal to his words. Even if he is occasionally awkward when he is improvising the phrasing, it matters not. Thereafter, the impact of the memorized sentences will be all the greater, because they will be cloaked with the inherited mantle of spontaneity.

I have seen gifted speakers bring a previous unruly audience to rapt attention within a minute. Even those who have lingered too long and eagerly at the preceding cocktail bar will grow silent if the speaker has "presence," another word for self-assurance and direct contact with the audience. No test is too severe. I recall addressing a gathering in Yuma,

Arizona, immediately after the air conditioning broke down in the banquet room and 120-degree heat took possession of the crowded room. Though I felt the trickles and then streams of perspiration flow down my body, even the waving of menus as improvised fans ultimately yielded to attentiveness. Let no one who aspires to be a speaker ever blame an audience for not being in the mood to listen. It is always the "orator's" fault if he cannot gain silence.

I would not belabor this subject if it were not for my conviction that how a person speaks privately or in public provides the quickest and surest insight to his intelligence and personality. Thought, diction, and the skill of expression are X-rays of intelligence, knowledge, and wisdom. How else is a civilized man to be judged? There are a few exceptions—as there always are: the profound thinker who cannot articulate well. But usually muddled expression reveals a confused mind. One has only to watch the dozens of television talk shows, in which the speakers fumble and mumble "you know's" as a stalling device several times in each sentence. It used to be "you know what I mean," a ludicrous question interspersed between words, since what preceded it could have been understood by a cretin, like "I walked into the room, you know what I mean?" or "So I looked at him, you know what I mean?" The modern contraction "you know" is just as vapid, and because of its brevity permits more frequent use, so that every sentence is filled with stuttering irrelevancy. Those who aspire to be leaders reveal their capacity or lack of it on the public platform.

A partial answer to Jimmy Carter's miraculous ascendancy to the presidency is his excellent selection of words, best demonstrated in press conferences during the give-and-take after the prepared text. His syntax is correct, unlike that of President Eisenhower, who mangled it. His sentences are not only properly completed but lucid. He has none of the artificial mannerisms of Nixon, who covered his uncertainty about his next thought by assurance that it was "perfectly clear," and whose sonorous, dignified delivery contrasted terribly with his talk on the tapes.

Although President Carter tries to give the impression of an ordinary, a very ordinary, citizen (he even signs his letters "Jimmy"), his diction reveals an orderly and cultivated mind. Combined with a simple and low-key delivery, there is an impression of sincerity and ability. The resulting confidence in him may well be the answer to the riddle of how an unknown figure triumphed over his famous political adversaries. Such is the power of speech.

I recall a New York State Democratic dinner at the Waldorf-Astoria preceding the 1952 presidential election. All the aspiring candidates were invited to speak. It was as if they were on display for evaluation not only by several thousand sophisticated faithful, but by the nation's political leaders, who controlled the vital delegations. It was in a sense a preview of the convention struggle. Conscious of the importance of the event, each candidate had prepared his best.

Senator Robert Kerr made a brilliant political address, whipping the audience into frenzied applause by his epigrammatic denunciation of the opposition, his partisan sallies capped by clever phrasing and slogans. His clear, ringing baritone voice rang out in eloquent cadences. But even while one applauded and laughed, there was no great admiration for the man himself. It was a fine performance, but not a profound statement. It was appreciated as political attack geared to a partisan rally, but left everyone in the dark as to the leadership qualities of a man who might be President.

Senator Estes Kefauver spoke. His thin, tall presence and matter-of-fact drawl, deliberately employed to make a virtue of a nonoratorical approach, were more impressive even though less applause-provoking than Kerr's delivery. There were no eloquent flourishes. One felt dedication to good causes, but awareness of the resistance in his home territory of Tennessee, requiring him to surround his convictions with a layer of ambiguity. The raccoon hat which he had selected to hover over his head as an invisible symbol announced during every word he uttered, "Remember, I come from a region which won't accept some of my beliefs, and please allow for my difficulties as you evaluate my statements." Poor man. Like other Southern statesmen, he was imprisoned by prejudices, slowly being eradicated, but which were still strong enough to make him politically dead if he were honestly read.

Senator Lyndon Johnson spoke. His Texan height and congressional record were equally impressive. He spoke in deliberate formal tones, as if to negate the informal explosiveness which one easily sensed beneath the surface. He seemed to be engaging in an exercise of self-discipline, to create the impression of solid judgment, although the passion he suppressed would have revealed the man to much better advantage.

Senator Hubert Humphrey spoke. How unfortunate that his sincerity and mental equipment were beclouded by volubility. Like the great director who destroys his achievement because he is in the forefront of the magic he weaves, Humphrey detracted from his excellent statement of ideals by unwittingly featuring his own fluency and felicity.

Senator John F. Kennedy was introduced. His record in the Senate was undistinguished and afforded no stimulus for any special burst of applause. But no one could fail to admire his handsome presence. His youthful appearance was not an asset in the eyes of the politicos who sought presidential stature. Perhaps—perhaps, the murmur went—he might be a vice-presidential candidate, never more. Another evidence that experts are experts only as long as we assume their superiority and make their predictions come true.

Others spoke. Franklin D. Roosevelt, Jr., presided. Unlike Jimmy Roosevelt, he did not have his father's voice, but he did offer visual reminders of that elegant head, with the discolored skin beneath the eyes revealing the torment of muscleless legs, while every tantivy movement of his head conveyed the gallantry and bouyance of his spirit. He introduced the Governor of Illinois.

Few in that room had ever seen or heard Adlai Stevenson. He arose to a smattering of applause. He was terribly short, bald, and unimpressive in face or voice. Within literally three minutes, the audience was spellbound. Magic had suddenly spread across the room. He began with some witty comments about the rumors that he and Mrs. Roosevelt (who sat next to him) were romantically joined. He treated this sensitive subject so farcically and with such becoming self-deprecation and adulation of Mrs. Roosevelt that the charm and humor made the women's eyes moist, and the men's hearts warm. After some original spontaneous reactions to the speeches which had preceded him, inoffensively poking fun at the political necessities of the occasion, he got down to his message. He spoke of the new challenge to our generation, of the destiny of our country, of the sacrifices and new horizons of thought which would be necessary to meet a social revolution spreading across the world; of the pressures on the prosperous, whether individuals or nations, to correct the injustice of inequality, economic as well as social—I refer the reader to his published addresses in *Call to Greatness*—of which this was one.

As he spoke, he grew in size, as if a giant bestrode the podium. The audience was entranced. In less than twenty minutes, the great qualities of the man filled the air. He was no longer short. He was no longer bald —it was a noble shining head we saw. His voice was no longer squeezed and thin. It had a philosopher's cadence. When he finished, the audience stood to a man, woman, and child and cheered and clapped in an unending ovation. Everyone knew that if the hour called for a leader, he had appeared. All this in a few moments. Yes, speech is an X-ray of a man.

I was just as moved. Little did I know then that I would have the privilege at his invitation to work intimately with him in losing elections and winning causes. As for that—later.

THREE GUNS

When I first began tangling with powerful adversaries, my mother tried to persuade me not to take such "hard cases." Although she pretended that she was worried about my exertions, she revealed her true concern by asking, "Isn't it dangerous to fight such terrible people?" I assured her that no one would dare harm an opposing lawyer, and gently chided her for believing motion picture melodramas in which the villainous gang wreaks vengeance on the district attorney. But, children, Mother was right. On three occasions my life was threatened.

The first was when I represented a group of retail butchers who refused to pay tribute to a gang operating a racket under the guise of a union. I sued the outfit, among whom were a number of notorious gangsters with criminal records. I sought an injunction which would strip them of their bogus union and prohibit the compulsory exaction of "dues." The complaint was a weighty document supported by dozens of affidavits by the victims. The answer was weighty too. It was supported by a bomb thrown into the establishment of one of my clients (Ben Danziger was his name), which destroyed his business and almost his life.

The day arrived to argue the application for a temporary injunction. I had no assistants in those days, but as I ascended the steps of the Supreme Court, I suddenly discovered that I had two companions, one on each side. They fell into step with me, looking straight ahead, in correct Warner Bros. style, and one of them said, "If you argue this case, you won't come out alive." They disappeared as I reached the entrance, sending me on my way, as they must have believed, to request an adjournment, if laryngitis would permit me to speak at all.

I cannot analyze my emotions at this late date. It may have been a swimming head, or more likely a conviction that I hold to this day, that those who openly make threats do not execute them. (The dangerous attack comes from those who do not forewarn.) In any event, I proceeded to make a lengthy, impassioned argument. The court may not have known the true reason for my tremulous voice. But my exit was devoid of bravado. I waited for groups to come out of the courthouse, and slunk into the center, like the halfback who runs behind a phalanx of blockers. Then I dashed down the steps of the nearby subway, and I am sure that if there were such an Olympic event, my time would still stand as a record.

The injunction was granted. Deputy Attorney General William Donovan indicted the entire group of sixty-odd defendants. It resulted in the largest mass criminal trial ever held in this Federal district. They were convicted.

Since no ghost-writer is involved in the present telling, it is obvious that the true author came to no harm.

The second instance was mercifully briefer. A chain of theaters owned by one of the major motion picture companies had a labor dispute with the projectionists. Although I was counsel for the New York Film Board of Trade, this matter did not come under my jurisdiction. Nevertheless, a nonrepresentative of Local 306 did not appreciate such niceties. He decided to visit me.

My practice has always been to keep an open door. I resent secretaries putting those who seek an appointment through a drill to determine whether they may enter the holy sanctum. It reflects badly on the king within. It is at best impolite and at worst arrogant and conceited. Even the telephone test which some executives require their secretaries to make: "May I ask what is the nature of the matter you are calling about?" is irritating. When I am so grilled, my equanimity is most disturbed and I regret not replying, "It is none of your business."

Of course, a policy of easy access results occasionally in my being subjected to kooks and salesmen. It is also a time waster, which I am sure the manual of executive efficiency decries. But it pleases me to amend the declaration that all men are created equal with the corollary that they should have equal access. There are 25 million stars in our galaxy and many galaxies. That should give each executive a better sense of his own great unimportance. Besides, one learns even from meeting the strangest characters, and the day is more interesting if also more aggravating.

So, it was that without any ceremony or advance notice a name was ushered in. He was short, swarthy with sleepy lidded eyes, but despite a studied casualness, he was intense. He approached my desk with quick steps. Then he reached into his breast pocket as if he was about to take out his eyeglasses. Instead he pulled out a snub-nosed black revolver, which he handled familiarly, placed it in front of him on my desk, sat down, and said, "I came to talk to you about my men in the booths."

I had never before had such a calling card. My reflex reaction was to deal with this situation as if he had insulted me by boorish conduct. I buzzed for my secretary, Miss Cunningham. She was a slight blond girl. Obviously her entrance was neither protection nor a threat. Psychologically, however, her frailty was just right. A burly male secretary might have caused the visitor to reach for the little cannon he had added to my desk equipment. Instead, he sat impassively for a moment.

Calling on my need to improvise the proper script for such a ridiculous melodrama, I said, "I don't talk to people who threaten. I want you to leave at once. Miss Cunningham, show the gentleman out and take that damn thing off my desk."

Like all who must retreat, he salvaged his pride by assuring me that I wasn't going to get away with this. *I* wasn't going to get away with what? Under other circumstances, we might have laughed at this prize non sequitur. But his statement was akin to that of the lawyer who after a defeat announces boldly that he will appeal, or, during a trial when the judge rules against him, proclaims angrily, "Exception!" even though it is no longer necessary to use this magic word to preserve one's right on appeal. Why deny the defeated the balm that comes from defiance?

So, the gentleman with the gun left quietly, escorted by a shaking little figure who needed the day off after her unaccustomed service. I never heard from him again.

The third incident was the most dangerous. On behalf of Paramount Pictures, Warner Bros., and Metro-Goldwyn-Mayer, I had obtained a judgment of $27,500 against Nat Steinberg, the owner of the Grand Theatre in New York City, New Dyckman Theatre in the Bronx, the Liljay Theatre, and the Palchester Theatre in Parkchester. The charge was that he had violated the contracts with these companies by playing their motion pictures on more days than licensed for. Motion pictures are copyrighted property and, as I have indicated, the companies were therefore entitled not merely to a proportionate added license fee, but to statutory damages ranging from $250 to $5,000 for each violation. Congress has enacted these heavy damages to protect writers and other artists from having their property stolen by unauthorized showing.

So it was that in the case of Steinberg's theaters, the court had awarded copyright damages which were far larger than what the owner would have had to pay had he contracted for the pictures honestly.

The theory of the copyright law is that merely to recover what the contract fee would have been would not stop the practice of stealing the author's works. It would simply be returning the stolen property.

(There is the story of the jury which found a defendant not guilty of having stolen a mule, but directed him to return it. The Judge rejected the verdict and insisted on a proper one. They returned, "We find the defendant not guilty and he may keep the mule.")

Damages which are not realistic are considered penalties, and in civil actions are illegal. They can only be imposed in criminal proceedings. To get around this the copyright law provides that its high scale of damages "shall not be deemed a penalty."

Nat Steinberg did not appreciate all this. Simplistically, he reasoned that had he bought the right for extra showing in the first place, he could have done so for a few hundred dollars. Now, he had lost his case and there was a judgment of ten times that amount. He didn't understand why his dishonesty (even if he thought of it as such) should be so disproportionately assessed. Unlike most clients who blame their own lawyers when they lose, he turned his venom toward me. He had heard my impassioned plea in court justifying the copyright law, and its wisdom in recognizing that tens of thousands of dollars of stolen time go undetected. The proven infringements are only the tip of the iceberg, and even statutory damages probably constitute a small portion of the unjust enrichment. How else but by severe damages in the case proven at great expense would the practice be stopped which deprived authors, sculptors, painters of the just rewards for the creations of their minds?

Steinberg blamed me for his disaster. So, one day he visited me. He had been a professional wrestler. His muscles pushed his suit away from his body, making him look more ungainly than he was. His sallow cheeks fell in toward his mouth, as if his face had to pay the price for his body development. He was totally bald (perhaps he had completed the process by shaving the surviving fringe). Athletes either wear long hair, the sign of virility, or affect bald domes, which, combined with general muscularity, give the impression of a missile to be launched. Steinberg's neck was a trunk, undoubtedly developed by bridging during his wrestling matches. He was past his prime, if he ever had one. His eyes were small and squinting and his voice hoarse. He got down to business quickly.

"Mr. Nizer, you have this judgment against me. I came to tell you that if you try to collect it, I'm going to kill you."

He spoke in a matter-of-fact manner as if he was discussing the date of payment.

I treated the matter lightly, assuming that he was exaggerating, and explained that he had had a fair trial, that I had done my duty as a lawyer, and that if he needed time to pay the judgment, I would attempt to arrange it.

"You don't understand. You think I'm kidding. I'm not. I am telling you straight and I mean it. If you try to collect this money, I am going to kill you. I have a gun [he tapped his pocket] and I'm going to kill you. So forget the judgment."

I warned him that he could be arrested for his threats, and that my duty as a lawyer would not be abandoned by such outrageous tactics.

"I am telling you it will cost you your life," he said, as he arose to leave. "Think it over."

An hour later, I received a call from Earl Sweigert, branch manager of Paramount Pictures. Steinberg had just visited him and pronounced the same sentence of death on him if Paramount collected one cent of its judgment.

"He told me he would shoot you too," Sweigert said. "This is a crazy man, Lou. Don't take him lightly. I was told that he beat a neighbor to a pulp over some dispute. The poor fellow had to be taken to the hospital, but he has been afraid to make charges against Steinberg because he might be killed if he did. I know he has a revolver. He really might kill both of us. I think we ought to take this up with the company."

I had no intention of yielding either to threat or entreaty. I have the habit of enlarging incidents into international analogy and getting more incensed because of the principle involved. Do we surrender to the Hitlers of the world to save our skins? Experience has taught us that such roads to safety are strewn with more skulls than result from resistance.

I arranged another meeting with Steinberg, but seated at my desk were Inspector Goldman and a captain from the New York City Police Department. When he arrived, I asked him to sit down, and introduced him to the police officials, advising him who they were.

"Mr. Steinberg, when you were here previously, you told me that if I attempted to collect a judgment which several motion picture companies have obtained against you, that you had a gun and that you would kill me. Is it true that you made that threat against me?"

"I did. Do you want me to repeat it? I will. Take it down, go ahead." Then, looking squarely into the faces of the police officers, he said, "I'm telling you again. I'm going to kill Mr. Nizer if he tries to collect a penny of that judgment. What are you going to do about it? Arrest me? Go ahead. I'll tell it to the Judge. Do you want it in writing? I'll write it out. What can you do to me? Put me in jail? For how long? Ten days, thirty days? When I come out I'm going to kill him!"

The police officials were so flustered by this daring assault that they lost their composure and acted as embarrassed and stuttering as one would have expected Steinberg to be.

"Don't do anything foolish," the Inspector said foolishly. "We're

going to watch you"—another opening of which Steinberg took immediate advantage.

"Go ahead and watch. You can't watch me every minute of my life.
You know that's illegal! No matter what you do I'll kill him!"

He pointed to me with his eyes. His quiet demeanor gave credence to
his threat.

"Do you want to arrest me, or can I leave?"

They told him that he could go, and sent continued warnings after
him which seemed to bounce off his back as he walked out slowly without another word.

The inspector turned to me. "Mr. Nizer, this is a dangerous man. I
have dealt with many cranks who threaten but are harmless. This man
is no fake. I think he is crazy enough to do what he says."

"We can provide a twenty-four hour watch for you, but for how
long? I must be honest with you. I don't think we can protect you if
this man is determined to get you. I would advise you to do something
which would relieve this crazy man's mind."

The Captain spoke up. "Inspector, we ought to look up his record.
What happened today is enough to revoke his license for a revolver, if
he has one."

"Absolutely," said the Inspector, his emphasis indicating that he had
had this in mind all the time. "But that is no protection either. You
know how easy it is for anyone to get a gun."

They were chagrined at their helplessness and I comforted them out
of the office, telling them that I did not intend to yield, but I would
think of something and let them know.

"Please, don't take any chances" were their parting words, a sentiment which Steinberg would have heartily approved.

At the next meeting of the New York Film Board of Trade, the
agenda included an item entitled "Steinberg," although for Sweigert
and myself, it could better have been described as "To Be or Not to
Be."

Sweigert reported that his company, Paramount Pictures, had authorized him to compromise or abandon the claim entirely in his discretion.
It did not consider it his duty to risk his life. Warner Bros. and Metro-
Goldwyn-Mayer, which had part of the judgment, joined in this consent. One of the branch managers who had been a college wrestler said
it would be worth surrendering the money if he could just give Steinberg a headlock and squeeze the craziness out of him, to which another
replied, "How do you think he got that way in the first place?" But
behind the banter was solicitude for Sweigert and me.

I protested strongly, giving all the arguments why it would be coward-
ice to surrender to a hoodlum.

"Suppose you had lost the case, Lou. We would be in the same position," argued one of them. "That would be worse for Lou than if he got shot," suggested another of my friends.

When all views had been expressed, I said, "Of course, you as clients have the right to forgive any judgment. You make contract adjustments every day for business reasons. And, I am bound by your decision. But this is action taken out of fear. True, it is fear for me and Earl Sweigert, and I appreciate your concern for us. In a way, you are paying ransom for our safety.

"It just goes against my grain for you to surrender to a blackmailer, who holds our lives as hostage. So, for the present, I do not accept your instruction. Let me think of some other way. I'll report back to you."

I invited Steinberg again to my office. He came. "No cops today?" he said as he sat down.

"No, just you and me. I have a proposition to make to you. Before I do, let me explain something. Neither the film companies nor I as a lawyer can simply forget about the money you owe. You should understand that. Suppose the people who owed you money told you not to ask for it or they'd kill you. What would you think?"

He stirred angrily, as if he was not going to listen to another rejection of his ultimatum. I held up my hand. "Just be patient, I am not finished. I told you I have a proposition. Hear me out."

He settled back sullenly.

"I understand that you consider this different because the judgment is many times greater than you would have had to pay for the contract rights."

I explained why the copyright law exacts such larger sums, and rhetorically asked him whether he hadn't gotten away with many other copyright infringements, which had put thousands of dollars in his pocket. So the judgment against him wasn't as exaggerated as he thought. It was just delayed justice. Then, I suddenly shifted to a question which was so irrelevant that it startled him.

"Do you ever give charity?"

He looked at me a long time as if to make sure he had heard me right. I repeated the question.

"Sure I do," he said.

"Well, that's my proposition. You do not pay one cent to Paramount, Warner's, or M-G-M. But you give the $27,500 in three equal parts to Jewish, Protestant, and Catholic charities."

When his silence ultimately turned to questions, I knew the shooting was over, so to speak.

How long would he have to make the contribution? Would his license for a revolver be reinstated? (He explained that he needed a gun when he took his receipts to the bank, and, I thought, also when he canceled his debts.) Would the gifts be solely in his name? (The film companies must not get any credit.) When he reached the point of arguing that a larger proportion should go to one charity rather than another (he lost that one, too), I knew this strange negotiation was going to be successful. It was.

Within eighteen months, the Federation of Jewish Philanthropies, Young Men's Christian Association, and Catholic Charities each received beneficences from one Nat Steinberg. They never knew the evil origin of the good deed.

It is said that when God examines you he does not look for medals. He looks for scars suffered in doing good deeds. I doubt that Steinberg will ever get credit for this particular charity.

This was the paradoxical solution. The film companies did not collect the judgments, but Steinberg paid them.

HE WHO STEALS MY NAME

It wasn't until the seventeenth century that the law recognized that you could assault a person with a weapon called words. Until then only physical blows entitled the victim to a remedy. Concepts of honor and reputation were cherished long before, but they were supposed to be vindicated by violence. Duels on the field of honor, not courts, were the forum for satisfaction.

Of all the remedies the law has fashioned to redress grievances, the libel law ranks among the noblest. It provides a judicial means to salvage a person's dignity; to recapture the esteem in which he has been held by the community; to restore the victim to his profession and business, and to his family and friends. In addition the libel law provides for a triple-tiered damage structure; actual money loss suffered from loss of job or business or professional activity; recompense for pain, suffering, and humiliation; and if the libel was motivated by malice, punitive damages to teach the perpetrator a lesson and discourage others from similar misdeeds. Indeed libel can also be a crime. The effect of inflammatory words can be so severe that it causes riots. Interestingly enough —under the common law and still in many states—even truthful words can constitute a crime if they are maliciously designed to arouse passions which cause violence. Why not? Much less, like loud music all night, or sound tracks blaring at unearthly hours, has been held to constitute criminal nuisance. Despite the philosophers, truth doesn't justify everything. It, too, must accommodate itself to the peace and safety of the community. Here we begin to see the impending clash between the libel laws and free speech, which I shall discuss later.

Although libel laws do not distinguish between a minor hurt and a serious one, I have always felt that it was good discretion not to launch a suit for every lie uttered. The highest estate which a lawyer can reach is not to be a brilliant technician but to be a wise adviser. Not every grievance should result in a lawsuit. In a crowded competitive world, people will step on each other's toes literally and figuratively. But we ought not to rush into court every time we have been jostled or an angry cussword has been spoken. Legal warfare is expensive and harrowing. It should be resorted to only when there is real damage, not merely high sensitivity to a slur.

The exception, of course, is when an important principle is involved. Then the damage is subtle. It may not injure the individual, but he becomes the vehicle through which the rights of many may be asserted. Sometimes the reputation of the person maligned is so firm that it is impervious to libel. Nevertheless, the target, though unscathed, may recover punitive damages.

Most often, however, the grievance is narrow. It affects one individual and no one else. The air is filled with vituperative gossip. Columnists are more short of material than that devouring monster, television. So in desperation for items, columnists pick up rumors, hearsay, and even invented "information" cloaked in anonymity—"What famous Hollywood star has left his home and board because of a redheaded starlet who has a minor part in his new picture?" I discovered on one occasion that the author of the titillating item had no more idea of the answer than the reader. This procedure is encouraged because reporters consider their source sacrosanct. Unless there is a state statute which gives the same immunity to a reporter as to a doctor, priest, or lawyer, such privilege does not exist. There is much to be said for the protection of newspapermen by means of such laws because the serious reporter might not be able to obtain information if, later, he could be forced to reveal his source. However the unwritten law of silence, which has caused reporters to martyr themselves and go to jail rather than speak, also shields the irresponsible gossipmonger.

Is it not always thus? Every law is like a disc—recorded on two sides. The virtuous purpose is stated on one side, but if we examine the platter on the other side dissonances appear. The libel disc has two sides too. One, the idealistic judicial tool to avenge injury to reputation by civilized means, the other the use of such tool to attack for every petty, inconsequential slight.

As a lawyer I have been engaged in lengthy court battles of the first genre, but on the other hand I have probably discouraged and prevented more libel suits than most lawyers.

Let me give several illustrations. Truman Capote, he of the talented pen and gossipy tongue, made disparaging remarks about the writing ability of Jacqueline Susann, the author of *Valley of the Dolls*, *Once Is Not Enough*, *The Love Machine*, and *Dolores*. (Capote insists that all artistic writing is gossip, citing *War and Peace* and Dostoyevsky. This is a shaky thesis which depends on a contrived definition of history as accumulated gossip.) Capote's comments about Susann were made on Johnny Carson's "Tonight Show," thus assuring an audience of millions for his contemptuous views. Opinions are not generally subject to libel. They may be wrong, but not untruthful. They express the critic's frame of mind accurately, and the reader knows that he is receiving an evaluation, not a statement of fact. If, however, a critic writes that an actor's performance was defective because he was drunk, and he was not, that would be libelous; indeed, as the law says, libelous per se because the libel demeans one in his professional capacity. There is the anecdote of Heywood Broun's review of a play in which he stated that the star gave the worst performance ever seen in a theater. He was sued for libel. A year later, while the suit was pending, the same actor appeared in another play. Broun was cautioned by his lawyers not to write anything which would aggravate the situation. He reconciled his critical integrity with his lawyers' admonition by writing about the star whom he had previously impaled that "his performance was not up to his usual standard."

Although Capote's less than enthusiastic view about Susann's artistry was not libelous, the battle of words was on. Carson, like any interviewer, was not averse to controversy and he invited Susann on his program. She was ready. When asked whether she had heard Capote's comment, she surprised everyone by doing a remarkable takeoff of him. Whatever one might think of her writing, there was no doubt she was a great mimic. Capote lends himself to that art. He is very short, pudgy, puffy, baldly blond and talks in a high-pitched, nasal, slow Southern drawl which outrageously exaggerates his homosexuality. He is like a cartoon of himself. It is only respect for his fine writing talents which prevents audiences from laughing at him. Nevertheless his rolling eyes, giggles, squeaky voice, pursed lips, and feminine gestures provoke stifled laughter even from those most attentive to his views.

Susann captured all this prefectly. Despite her large size and dark visage, she shrank to his gnome-like size, and her whining cadences, interrupted by stretched out "w-e-l-l-s," sent the audience into paroxysms of laughter. It is easy for an imitator to gain recognition of a subject who has one outstanding characteristic. Cartoonists know this well; De Gaulle's long nose, Roosevelt's onesided smile, Churchill's bulldog nose, Nixon's jowels, Carter's teeth (called chiclets by one comedian). But for live imitators, the voice and the musical scale it travels are the trademarks of individuality. They are considered as distinctive as a fingerprint. A gifted mimic can achieve his effect by talking from a dark room. But his virtuosity on the stage includes posture, subtle gestures, and idiosyncratic mannerisms. Susann mastered her subject to the finest detail.

Now it was Capote's turn. He was invited to occupy the same chair from which she had performed and give his rebuttal. His was not the skill of imitation. He was an originator, and he must have given much thought to finding just the right descriptive phrase which would ridicule her and create as much laughter as she had subjected him to. When Carson asked him what he thought of Susann's views, he raised his voice to its shrillest pitch and declared that he paid no attention to her. "A-n-y way, she looks like a truck driver in drag!"

Words are like chemicals. Some combinations fizzle. Others explode. The laughter which burst across the nation drove her and Irving Mansfield, her husband and gifted partner in the dissemination of her works, right into my office. They insisted on an immediate suit. I advised them that in my opinion a slander had been committed. Aside from the falsity of the literal description, the innuendo expressed the animus of the words. What is an innuendo? It is the law's device to spell out the intended vicious meaning of what might otherwise appear to be innocent. So, for example, if one writes, sarcastically, "Oh, sure, he is an honest man," one can sue for slander if spoken, or libel if written, and plead the innuendo that such words meant that he was dishonest. So, the innuendos to be ascribed to "A-n-y way, she looks like a truck driver in drag" were many. One was that she was a lesbian of masculine inclinations, or that she was so unfeminine that she was more like a man who, because of perversity, dressed up as a woman, or that she was as ugly as an uncouth truck driver who aberrationally disguised himself in woman's clothes—all clearly slanderous.

I recognized the anguish the words had caused her, her husband, and many friends. She had been ridiculed. She had been made a laughing-stock particularly in those quarters where envy is the by-product of success. We are hero-worshipers but paradoxically we like to see the mighty fall. It levels us, creating the illusion that we have risen somewhat, rather than those we looked up to have descended. That is why we cheer the champion and yet thrill at his defeat.

So, although Capote's comment was in my opinion libelous (television broadcasts have been held equivalent to written publications and therefore libel rather than slander), and although I was not unaware of the hurt and humiliation they had suffered, I advised against suit. It seemed to me that what was involved was an unfortunate exchange not worthy of the fees, exhaustion of time in extended pretrial depositions, ultimate lengthy trial, and probable appeals. Furthermore, there would be no actual damage. Wasn't she still on the best-seller list? Did she really believe Capote's snide comment would affect her popularity as an author? I saw no principle involved. Also, there had been some provocation, which in law is deemed to ameliorate damages.

All this fell on unsympathetic ears. We are blind to what we do not want to see and deaf to what we do not like to hear. They were determined to attack. Fees were of no consequence. She was fabulously successful. She wished revenge. She wanted to see the day when "the little worm would squirm under cross-examination."

I was losing the battle of persuasion rapidly. In the course of the friendly argument, I learned that they were leaving for Germany to attend a book fair, in which her book was featured. I seized the opportunity to gain time.

"You are leaving in a few days. A complaint cannot be prepared in such a short period. Why don't you wait until you return? We'll confer again. Perhaps you will view this differently by then."

They were well aware of the ruse. For the first time, their tense demeanor changed and they smiled.

"You are not going to talk us out of this," Susann said. "We'll be back," she announced with MacArthur determination. "We expect you to prepare papers. Please, please, we want you to sue the nasty little ——." She used a heavenly phrase not intended to be angelic.

Their visit to the bookfair in Frankfurt was a triumph. Her books were featured. She was honored. International recognition is particularly gratifying to an author. It gives the impression of historic appreciation.

When she and her husband sat again in my office, she was glowing with pride, and he reflected hers as well as his own. Her description of her trip set a different stage for the discussion. There was no longer single-minded insistence prompted by desperation.

I redoubled my effort to have her drop the matter. By this time, recollection of the ridicule to which she had been subjected was less painful. I reviewed her acceptance by the public at large, her increasing invitations to appear on forums and television interviews, her husband's prideful citation of the phenomenal sale of her books, the inescapable jealousy such success produces, including possibly Capote's (this pleased her most), the protective callus an author must develop against the inevitable blows from critics, an experience not unknown to her (unanimous praise is almost impossible), and therefore she ought to rise above the taunt in a television exchange. I felt it was my duty to protect her against an improvident litigation, but if she disagreed, I knew there were many able lawyers who would undertake the matter. They insisted that they would only proceed with me, and resignedly, though good-naturedly, the matter was closed.

So we thought. But we counted without Capote's penchant for gossip and pursuit.

A short time later, the following appeared in a publication called *After Dark*:

"It was Capote who took advantage of television exposure to get in an effective gut-stab at another highly vulnerable 'writer,' Jacqueline Susann. On the 'Tonight Show,' he told the world that she looked 'like a truck driver in drag.'

"It didn't take long for Miss Susann, who isn't exactly a novice at verbal self-defense, to announce she was suing Capote for a million dollars.

" 'Had to drop the whole suit,' Capote says, chuckling with victorious pride. Had to! She and her lawyer, the famous Louis Nizer, went to NBC to watch a replay of the program which they watched and watched, and finally, Louis Nizer turned and said, 'Jackie, forget it. You don't have a case.' She went into a rage and screamed, 'A case? Whaddya mean? It's right there in living color. Libel if there ever was libel!' 'And then Nizer told her that all my attorney would have to do was to get a dozen truck drivers and put them in drag and have them parade into court and that would be all. So, no million-dollar suit from Miss Jacqueline Susann.'"

Immediately thereafter, and as surely as inventive venom begets retaliation, I received a brief note from Susann.

Dear Louis—
Now the little 'capon' has put words in your mouth—it's really wild? What do you think?

Best
Jackie

The restrained tone of this note was undoubtedly due to her belief that she now had an ally. She knew that Capote, by repeating and enlarging the libel, and fictitiously drawing me into the suit to confirm him, had made it difficult for me any longer to plead with her to be forgiving.

Her previous gesture of forbearance had resulted in a gloating repetition of the attack on her. I would have to act. She was right. I sent the following letter to Capote.

My dear Truman Capote:
In the May issue of After Dark you are quoted as describing my rejection of Jacqueline Susann's request that I represent her in a libel suit against you because there was an invulnerable defense; our viewing the broadcast at NBC, etc.

Every statement attributed to you is incorrect. I did not advise her and her husband that she had no cause of action against you. On the contrary, I thought you had libelled her. I did not view the broadcast. It was not necessary.

The reason I persuaded her not to sue was that it is my policy to discourage libel suits unless there is very serious injury to the plaintiff and his or her career, or an important principle is involved (as in the Faulk or Reynolds-Pegler cases). There is always hurt to sensibility, but not every injury, at least in my judgment, warrants a legal war.

I had hoped that my judgment in dissuading a suit would be justified by lettting the matter die with only the sacrifice of hurt feelings. However, you have chosen to revive the matter, claiming to know of the confidential conference between myself and my client, presenting completely false reason for your not being sued, and one which incomprehensibly has me confirming your libelous statement. Thus you involve me too. In addition you give further evidence of malice towards Jacqueline Susann.

I may have to reconsider my decision to discourage litigation even though there was a cause of action. My decision may well depend on your reply. In all fairness I would expect and appreciate a prompt correction of the matter.

Sincerely yours,
Louis Nizer

Truman Capote answered with characteristic verve and wit. He flattered me by saying that he found it impossible not to answer a charming letter from a lawyer even though the burden of the communication was to sue him.

But the point of the letter, all said in good humor, was that he did not see how he might have libeled Miss Jacqueline Susann. He remarked that in the give and take of interview language he had commented, off the cuff, that she bore a striking resemblance in some of her publicity photographs to a truck driver. This he felt was "bitchy, yes; malicious, no." He was of the attitude of one professional to another with admiration for what she did in her field of literary endeavor although he reserved judgment on the virtue of the field itself.

The matter of whether or not I was with her at the screening of a Carson TV show, he covered with clever grace full of artful guile. Maybe it was someone else from my office; maybe the meeting was all fantasy . . .

He then turned his attention to the fact that Miss Susann had made some remarks about him in West Coast interviews that might be reviewed. She had repeatedly referred to him as a homosexual which accusation he turned off with the comment, "Big news." He felt that she had also accused him of sloth and that she suggested that he was green with envy of her energy. This accusation seemed to bother him not at all. That he was unhappy about the quantity of her output compared to his he found totally without merit; as far as he was concerned she could win the world's major literary prize and it would not disturb him.

He was gracious in acknowledging the fact that I had told him about one or two magazine and newspaper interviews of whose existence he was not aware. He did tell me about a specific interview and where it ran.

Once again he thanked me for such a delightful scolding letter and pointed out that correspondence was something he indulged in so rarely that he suggested that I keep his letter for my heirs to sell at some far later date at a literary auction.

It was the kind of letter that brightens one's day and suddenly, by his magical writing ability and disarming candor, he had removed the heat from the whole situation.

Susann was completely appeased by this disarming letter. She had received an apology, been told that he respected her "as a very professional person," had conceded that his comment about her was "bitchy" and confirmed her charge that he was homosexual, by chiding her that she had hardly made a new discovery. She laughed about the whole thing and might even have been charmed by his wit.

But the real reason known to few, that she now saw the matter in better perspective, was that she had been advised that she had cancer and had only one year to live. If we could sense the imminence of death one year or twenty, would not most quarrels subside?

Celebrities are of course the special victims of libels. Also they are more sensitive because thousands and sometimes millions of readers consider them vicarious friends, and wag their heads about some revelation to which they wouldn't give heed if it were about a private person they really knew.

So it comes about that most entreaties for suit come from famous people in one field or another. They are written about most often and their skins are the thinnest.

Two illustrations: Cary Grant was distressed because a magazine quoted him as saying he had never loved anyone. It was a garbled version of an interview in which he commented that he had never "left" anyone. His constancy had been turned into emotional sterility. It would be merely a funny transference of meanings (like the nervous editor who featured the homecoming of a "bottle scarred veteran," and hastened to correct the error by changing the type to battle scared veteran) if it were not so humiliating.

The false item was piquant and therefore carried by U.P.I. and reprinted in many newspapers. Grant was furious. He had been sought out by every motion picture "love goddess" to play the lover's role. His handsome face, charm, and acting skills would have been enough. But there was an added dimension which made him the most famous star in Hollywood. It was his sincerity, an abused word—applied even to inanimate objects, but essential in lovers' roles. It could not be completely simulated. Fine actresses rarely shed glycerine tears. They feel the emotion they are projecting and really cry. Powerful love scenes are made possible by real passions. In acting, the less counterfeit, the better the result, another way of saying that the great actor acts least.

All one had to do was watch one of Cary Grant's love scenes on the screen to realize that in real life, too, he loved. Close-ups, catching every shortened breath, hoarsened voice, trembling lips, and above all the glistening eye (not always the lighting man's trick of having the pupil reflect a shimmering beam) lent unmistakable sincerity to the scene.

Furthermore, he had virtually abdicated from his screen kingdom to devote himself to his nine-year-old daughter. She, too, would read of the false accusation.

Still, I told him it was a misprint of a word, worthy of correction but not a suit.

On another occasion, I instituted a libel suit despite my original advice to abstain. The issue was too close to deny the client. A motion picture magazine of no particular standing had featured Elizabeth Taylor on the cover. This was a usual circulation gambit. Her beauty, dazzling in its even simplicity, and her adventuresome life guaranteed a minimum sale, even if there was nothing else inside. The cover test preceded the polls as a measuring yardstick. For years after President Franklin D. Roosevelt died, his picture, or Mrs. Roosevelt's, on a magazine cover boosted its circulation throughout the world. Elizabeth was accustomed to being featured and exploited. She knew it was the reward and sometimes the penalty for being the face which launched a thousand stories each week. Why then her unmollifiable anger on this occasion? What had turned her violet eyes dark with rage?

It was the appearance of her two children alongside her and a teaser headline which read, "Elizabeth Will Lose Her Children." When one turned to the designated page for the story, there was an ill-written "Psychological" analysis of how children of famous parents break away from home when they grow up, to live their own lives. It was an obvious fraud. Those who bought the magazine because of the promise of sensational revelation would have had the right under consumer laws to demand their money back. But who bothers to do so? And the magazine cared not a whit about alienating the reader, since it was a fly-by-night corporate venture which might be destined for a few issues at best, to resume under another name.

I explained all this to Elizabeth and tried to discourage her from incurring the expense and harassment of a suit against an irresponsible publication of no account.

But she was adamant, and I had to respect her logic. "I don't care what they say about me, true or false. You know I have been silent despite many printed lies. But I will not stand for having my children pictured and exploited. The whole thing is a fake. I don't care what it costs, and I understand that I will never collect a cent. But I want to put them out of business, and I want the world to know that they must leave my children alone."

Her statement of principle overcame the pragmatic considerations. There must be a limit to sensationalism and the line is best drawn at the children. So we sued, won, and the magazine was shut down, never to appear again. Elizabeth was content, even though, as anticipated, there was no one from whom to collect.

Even when the libel is serious enough to warrant suit, there are other reasons not to do so. There is wisdom in the old saw "I take it from whence it comes." The source of the article may be so disreputable and limited in circulation, and the prominence of the victim so great, that a suit would only provide wide dissemination of the lie. Also, it would confer the fame of the plaintiff on an otherwise unknown sheet. There are many such instances. I cite only one.

Dorothy Thompson was the most famous woman political writer of her day. Her column appeared in the New York *Herald Tribune* opposite Walter Lippmann's, whose influence she also shared. She was frequently listed among the most important women in the world. Her columns against Nazism were fiery polemics which won a worldwide attention.

Nature, too, had not disappointed her. She looked the part. Even though she wore the weight of fifty-odd years, as well as some extra poundage, she was beautiful as well as distinguished, from her blue eyes and florid cheeks to her crown of gray hair, which tossed with vehemence when she held forth.

She used to attend private gatherings in my home on election night to celebrate the assured triumphs of Franklin Roosevelt, "again and again." It was interesting to see the inevitable grouping around her. Men and women literally sat in a circle at her feet, while she, in a lounge chair, with a martini in her hand, fascinated them with incessant brilliant talk. To hold a conversation, you must let go once in a while. She rarely did. She lectured and we learned and enjoyed it.

Dorothy was also an activist. When the Bund held a Nazi meeting in Madison Square Garden, which was desecrated with swastikas for the occasion, she appeared in person as a reporter. Fritz Kuhn, Hitler's American leader, recognized her. There was an enemy in their midst.

He ordered her ejected. She refused to leave, announcing that she was there to describe the whole obscene conclave for her newspaper. It took an army of shock troops to carry her out physically. The incident was pictured and reported on the front pages of the world's press. It was ludicrous to see storm troopers, puffing from lack of condition, their gritting faces registering supreme effort, as they heaved the rolling woman inch by inch out of the building. Czechoslovakia was easier to conquer.

Dorothy had been married to Nobel Prize winner Sinclair Lewis. Many years later, a murder mystery played by Elmer Rice called *Cue for Passion* appeared on Broadway. To add spice to the plot, two leading characters were a Nobel Prize author married to a famous columnist. It was as difficult to guess their identity as to answer the quiz "What countries were involved in the Spanish-American War?" Since there was no rhyme or reason for their inclusion in the play; they might just as well have been any suburban couple caught in a murder mystery. Dorothy insisted on an immediate injunction.

Otto Preminger was the director. The play was in rehearsal, about to open in a few days. I prepared the affidavits and proposed order to enjoin the play from opening. But my heart went out to the author, director, and cast. There were enough natural hurdles for a play opening on Broadway to surmount without visiting an injunction disaster upon it at the last moment. I explained to the panicky company that my client's objective was not to destroy the play, but merely to remove the identification of herself and her former husband from participation in a murder mystery plot. Why not rewrite the scenes involving them so as to make them as fictitious as the rest of the play and thus save the production? I offered to withhold the injunction application, and even help in the last minute rewriting. This proposal was accepted, but the required changes were not simple. The author had played with the relationship of the famous couple, deriving humor from their rivalry and self-centered dispositions.

I devoted myself to the needed surgery which would remove Dorothy Thompson and Sinclair Lewis from the scenes while preserving whatever virtues the play had.

A bizarre scene followed. The author, Preminger, and I sat up through the night rewriting the play, while the actors, who always grumble when revisions necessitate new memorization, had a special reason to do so. Sleeplessness was not conducive to a keen mind. The play opened on time.

It would be nice to report that not only was the client's mission fulfilled, but that the play enjoyed a long run. Alas, it was not so. While I cannot, therefore, preen myself on having made meager contributions which catapulted the work to success, I am certain that if the main characters had been disguised as a President in a wheelchair because of polio, and his wife as a peripatetic traveler with an ascending high-pitched voice who wrote a column called "My Day," the run of the play would not have been any longer.

Dorothy Thompson, unfortunately, was also an activist in her personal life. She fell in love with an able Czechoslovakian painter, Maxim Kopf. He was married. His wife refused to give him a divorce. Dorothy resented this. She wrote a letter in longhand to Mrs. Kopf upbraiding her for holding on to a loveless relationship. She denounced her attitude as immoral. She advised her that Max and she were in love and that a thousand Mrs. Kopfs could not stand in the way of their happiness. It was indecent of Mrs. Kopf to interfere. She lectured her as she was accustomed to doing with awed admirers.

But Mrs. Kopf was not an admirer. She suddenly had in her hands not only written proof of her husband's infidelity, but a document which might destroy his mistress. For this was in the 1940s, when the bonds of matrimony had not yet become so loose that they slipped off readily. Also sexual freedom was still called licentiousness. Public figures particularly bore the burden of "setting good examples for the young." It was part of the price of fame, that the peccadilloes overlooked in private life would not be tolerated for them. How could we be sure that Mrs. Kopf, embittered by her husband's desertion, and burning for revenge against the woman who had destroyed her marriage and life, might not use Dorothy's letter as a retaliatory weapon? We might call it blackmail, but a scorned wife would consider it nonpoetic justice.

Dorothy was a controversial figure at best. Now her enemies would be joined by moralists, and even those who might not disapprove would be disgusted with her cruelty. I could see her ousted from her column and stunned by public denunciation, the possibilities of which she seemed totally unaware.

I arranged a meeting with Mrs. Kopf and her attorney. Despite Dorothy's insistence, I forbade her to be present. Brilliant woman though she was, she hadn't any understanding of the human problem. She wanted to confront Mrs. Kopf, with Max at her side, and convince her that her dog-in-the-manger attitude would be of no avail. She was going to shame her into granting a divorce, as if a woman's pride and lost love could be stormed by force.

Instead I adopted a sympathetic attitude toward her, one which I sincerely felt. Only one thing could be more painful to a woman than to lose a husband she loved, and that was to be rejected in favor of another identified woman. To assuage her anguish, the abandoned wife often convinced herself that her husband still loved her but that he was "sick." She expects the illness to be brief and then "he will come to his senses again." This rationalizes her refusal to free him. She will wait until he recovers from his insane infatuation.

That is why it is well nigh impossible to obtain consent for divorce from such a wife. Her obstinacy is strengthened by conscious and unconscious motivations. On the one hand she hopes to outwait his fever until normalcy returns him lovingly and apologetically to her side. On the other hand she is determined not to free him so that he can marry "that whore"—isn't she always that to a betrayed wife?

Still there are countermoves of persuasion. They are effective because they are true. The most important is that the husband has other alternatives to obtain a divorce. If he establishes a genuine residence in another state and sues for divorce there, the wife is in a terrible dilemma. If she appears in the action to defend herself, she confers jurisdiction on the "foreign" state, and she is bound by the decree. If she refuses to appear in the action on the ground that it is brought out of the jurisdiction in which they have lived most of their lives, her husband may obtain a divorce by default. If his residence in the foreign state is held to be genuine, the divorce is effective. Particularly people of means have little difficulty in establishing other residences. For example, Winthrop Rockefeller, in his contest with Bobo Rockefeller, actually built a large home in Arkansas, voted there, joined a local club, obtained local driving and hunting licenses—all to establish a genuine residence. The graft of residence took root so well that he became a leading citizen of the community, entered politics, and was elected Governor. Indeed, he had real residence. It was at the Governor's mansion.

The combination of Kopf and Thompson could well achieve a residence in Vermont, where they lived, and he could bring a divorce suit there. Then Mrs. Kopf would have to take the risk of going to a foreign state to defend, or default. Neither was an enviable choice. Even if she won, there might be small alimony because Kopf was not a large earner.

On the other hand if she yielded to her husband's request for a divorce on legal grounds in the state in which they lived, she would receive appropriate alimony and even a lump sum settlement, not obtainable in most states.

The law could not restore her husband's love, but the least he could do was to provide her with reasonable financial security. This he would do if she consented to a divorce.

These were the hard dollar facts. But there was something more important. She ought to stop thinking about him and Dorothy. There were understandable hate feelings. But they would injure her, not them. She ought to consider her own welfare first and foremost. Holding on legally to a fleeing husband was self-defeating. It bound her but

not her husband and Dorothy. The sooner she freed herself emotionally, the sooner she would rebuild an independent life. To lose a
man she loved was a tragedy. But vindictiveness was not the remedy.
For her own sake she ought to look at her terrible loss in true perspective. It was not the worst evil that had ever befallen a human being.
People are resilient. They survive the death of their dearest, and their
own crippling diseases. She ought to build a new life. At the moment
she could not conceive of a happy existence without him, but it would
happen.

I asked her to confer with her lawyer privately, and determine
whether this wasn't the best course for her.

After a number of sessions, she agreed. Satisfactory financial terms
were worked out. Then came the most difficult task. I wanted
Dorothy's handwritten letter returned to me, and a written agreement
that no copies had been made or issued, and that nothing would be
said about it, at least until after Dorothy's death. Violation would bring
about financial sanctions under the divorce decree.

Having been persuaded that venomous pursuit of either Max or
Dorothy was stultifying, she made this final gesture.

So the Kopfs were quietly divorced. Dorothy and Max married and
lived happily in Vermont.

I won custody of the letter.

Against this background of Dorothy Thompson's assertive personality, I turn to a libel suit she insisted I bring, and which in her interest
I refused to do. An inconsequential half-newspaper, half-scandal sheet,
attacked her. It is always possible to find an ugly photograph of a
much-publicized person. One can often tell a newspaper's view of a candidate by the kind of photograph it selects for the news story. From
thousands of snapshots one can always select a handsome exhibit or a
repulsive one. The malicious intention toward Dorothy could easily be
discerned by the picture accompanying the article. It caught her mouth
wide open, eyes distended, hair standing straight up as if lifted by electric shock, copious breasts without a waistline so that they became part
of a protruding stomach, and a clenched fist on top of a trunk-like arm
to add an extra touch of belligerence to the pose. Beautiful Dorothy
looked like an ogre. She could have tried out for the freak fat lady in a
circus.

As if this wasn't enough, the article, as puerile in expression as it
was venomous, had a phrase about her which even Capote would have
been proud to have coined. It said she was "having her menopause in
public."

"Isn't this libelous?" she raged. Of course it was. I could have filled
five pages of a complaint with innuendos. But was it wise for her to sue

and cause a feature story in hundreds of newspapers which would repeat the ugly phrase? The offending publication was too unknown to be quoted. As it turned out the devilish description had motive power of its own and was circulated widely, but surely it was not advisable to give it the propulsion of an announced litigation by the famous Dorothy Thompson. She insisted. I resisted. It was a curious battle of wills, because our common objective was to protect her. She was fair enough later to appreciate my defiance. I was not the kind of lawyer who asked the client what advice he wanted and then gave it to him.

This is an illustration of why, before a libel suit is launched, the relative positions of the involved parties should be evaluated. An unknown publication with limited circulation can do little damage to a prominent individual. But if the victim loses perspective because of hurt feelings and strikes back, the ugly story is given wide currency and the injury is enlarged in the very course of seeking a remedy.

What better example of this principle can there be than the despicable item some time ago in an Italian magazine that the Pope was a homosexual. Let alone, only a relative handful of people would have read the item, and most of them would disregard it in view of its irresponsible source. But the Vatican chose to issue an official denial. It was published throughout the world. The respectable press had no reason to resist a statement by the Vatican. I read it in the New York *Times*. Millions, perhaps tens of millions of people, were thus made aware of the charge. The Pope needs a good lawyer.

And so did President Lyndon Johnson. His sensitivity to press criticism was a weakness which even his tumultuous years in political life could not eradicate. If an editorial in a remote and small newspaper attacked him, as he felt, unfairly, he would telephone the publisher or editor, or communicate with someone close to them to protest. On one occasion when Mildred and I were at the White House, I heard him chide Senator Magnuson for not replying to an unwarranted criticism of him during a Senate debate. "Why don't you fellows get up and defend the President?" He sounded like a football coach rallying his players to greater effort.

In view of the controversies which swirl around the presidency, I am not surprised that he had a heart condition. Although he was a courageous man who I am sure would risk his life for his country, he could not face criticism. This vulnerability makes understandable why the gale of Vietnam opposition blew him out of office. His was not an Achilles' heel, it was tenderized skin.

For the most part, the American people have chosen complex and neurotic men to be their presidents. Occasionally simple men like Calvin Coolidge or Gerald Ford, who didn't grow, or Harry Truman, who did, come to power; but in each instance through accidental ascendency from the vice-presidency. Our deliberate choices, while varied, have one common denominator—involved personalities. Witness Lincoln, Hoover, Wilson, the Roosevelts, Kennedy, Johnson, and Nixon.

To see Johnson sitting in an armchair in the West Hall next to a cabinet with mysterious equipment which enabled him by stretching his arm to communicate with the leaders of the world, or press buttons which might start air and sea armadas moving thousands of miles away, or, heaven forbid, release the power to powderize the planet, was to get a glimpse of the joy of power.

He made no secret of it. His face aglow with satisfaction, he called attention to the circular cabinet and then reveled in a description of the first use of the Hot Line from Kosygin to him during the six-day Arab-Israeli war. He led to the climax like a good storyteller. The war had broken out. Russia was threatening to intervene on the side of the Arabs. Naturally her objective was to control the Middle East.

The President inquired how far the Seventh Fleet was from the battle shore. It was steaming in the opposite direction, but could be there in two days.

"How long will it take Russian submarines to report that the ships have turned around and are headed toward the war zone?" the President asked.

"About two hours," the high command informed him.

"Order the Seventh Fleet to head back full steam!"

Several hours later the Hot Line telephone rang. The President beamed. The script was going according to plan. Kosygin offered to stay out of the conflict if Johnson did too. (I noticed that the conversation was personalized. It was not Russia and the United States. It was two Herculean individuals pitted against each other.)

The President turned from the recital, as if he had put his hand over the phone and was commenting on his reasoning before he replied.

"I was willing to bet on my horse and let him bet on his."

Then back to the phone, "All right, Mr. Premier, in the interest of containing the conflict, I am willing that we both stay out. That's a deal. You have my word."

His enactment was so real I could see him hang up the receiver and chuckle at the outcome.

The penalty for love of such power is that a day comes when it no longer exists. The loss is excruciating. Singers who entrance audiences and then lose their voices to age; athletes who thrill millions with their prowess and suddenly (to them) find that their bodies do not respond; actors and actresses who captivate millions with their beauty and talent, and who have to retire to character parts or else completely retire; and political leaders whose every word and action affect the course of events and then are relegated to private citizenry, all suffer deeply from the removal of the spotlight. They cannot bear the darkness of anonymity into which they are pitched.

Little wonder that rulers struggle to maintain power, even if they must turn dictatorial and kill to do so. And similarly, little wonder that artists, athletes, and politicians almost never gracefully quit the scene of the triumphs they can no longer repeat. Power is an addictive drug. That is one reason why it corrupts. That is why politicians are forever running. They cannot stand the withdrawal pains.

When Jack Valenti became president, and I counsel, of the Motion Picture Association of America, we took our first trip through Europe to visit the heads of nations. (Motion pictures are our country's foremost good-will ambassadors as well as export. Every foreign government is interested in the cultural economic aspect of the American movie.)

In France we visited André Malraux, Minister of Culture under De Gaulle. I had looked forward eagerly to meeting this great writer and activist. We had to wait. He was ill, and wouldn't be in his office for another week. We returned. There he was in the ornate office Napoleon had occupied, with gold-edged carved wood, chandeliers which glistened without light, hand-pressed glass windows, and all the other trappings of authority and power. One could read Napoleon's ambition by looking at this room. It was that of an emperor, not a general. One could read Malraux too.

He was still ill. He had become an opium addict during the Chinese Revolution, in which he fought. When he overdosed, he was away for weeks. There he sat, pale, dark eyes staring, and his clenched fist tight under his chin to keep his head from shaking. While we conversed, many questions passed through my mind. They involved the mystery of power. The radical who had volunteered to fight in foreign wars had become an ardent supporter of De Gaulle, the supreme nationalist. Undoubtedly he rationalized his role as one who would restore art to its high French estate. Even his execution of an edict that important buildings be steam-cleaned was a symbolic gesture of patriotic purity. But he clung to his title of Minister of Culture even though he had earned more important recognition internationally as a writer.

I had an opportunity to observe this clutching to power close up with Lyndon Johnson. After I addressed the University of Texas, Mildred and I were invited to spend a day with the ex-President and Lady Bird at their nearby ranch on the Pedernales River.

During the entire morning Johnson was straining to get out and tour the ranch. At last lunch was over, and we proceeded to a large jeep. Because of his heart condition, the President had been forbidden by his doctors to drive. Mrs. Johnson, with great tact, took the wheel, chatting away to relieve the President of the embarrassment of his incapacity. For him not to be in the driver's seat was about as acceptable as if someone had suggested while he was in office that the Vice-President preside over a cabinet meeting while he sat by.

He made up for it by being a front seat driver. In sharp commands he told Lady Bird where to go and where to stop. She didn't mind. It was his way of defeating the doctors.

Also he had a shortwave radio speaker system, and he barked out his orders to the superintendents and workers in the field. (He was communicating with faraway lands.)

"Jim, why are there no deer out there? I wanted Louis and Mildred to see some. The fence must be broken and they have gone through. Get to it. Find the hole and fix it!" (Turn the Seventh Fleet back!)

"Yes, sir, right away," came a voice from an invisible spot. (The Hot Line telephone was working.)

"Harry, the brush fire is smoldering. It will spoil the patch. Clean it up!"

"It is out, Mr. President. It's only the smoke you see."

"Well, snuff it out!" (We don't want alibis from our commanders. We want results.)

In his mind, Johnson had never ceased being President. He had simply transferred his authority to the vast acres of his ranch (it wouldn't have surprised me if a map showed them to be the shape of the United States).

He, too, had had a dream. It was to achieve a better life for the people. "The Great Society" was not a platform on which to ride into office, but one to stand on while in office. He aspired to be the greatest benefactor of the people who had ever resided in the White House. His sincerity could not be questioned. He strove to lift the underprivileged whether black, yellow, or white, to improve their health, and see that their pursuit of happiness would not be too long a chase.

The Vietnam involvement, which others began and he sought to bull through by half measures (a contradiction in terms which assured defeat) cast a pall of smoke over his achievements. But history may "snuff out" the smoke sufficiently to appraise him justly.

Truman, too, had suffered megaton criticism for use of a new weapon which we now regard fearfully only as a symbol of terror. History is a selective eraser, rubbing out faults, and thereby emphasizing the virtues of its subjects. Otherwise, Washington, Jefferson, and Lincoln would not have fared as well as they justly do.

Johnson was too impatient for long-range appraisal. He smarted at criticism, no matter how minor or unimportant the source.

One Saturday night, while Johnson was President, Eddie Weisl, a distinguished lawyer, Mildred, and I were at a formal dinner for a charitable cause in the Grand Ball Room of the Waldorf-Astoria in New York. A Waldorf official approached Weisl and myself breathlessly. "The White House is calling Mr. Nizer. The President would also like to speak to Mr. Weisl." This is one of the miracles of White House telephone efficiency. Anyone can be traced anywhere.

We were led to a special telephone. The President was too angry to engage in any introductory formalities. "Louis, I want you to start a suit Monday morning against *The Saturday Evening Post!* An article written by a damned liar quotes me as saying, 'If these niggers want it, I'll give it to them!'

"Now you know I have done more for civil rights than all other presidents combined. I want to teach these lying sons-of-a-bitches a lesson they'll never forget. Sue them for everything they've got. Let's put them out of business."

I made the mistake of starting my cooling down campaign too soon. I should have known that he was too furious to listen to reason in a hasty telephone conversation.

"But Mr. President you can't sue—"

"Why not? It's false. Isn't that a libel?"

"Of course it is, but if you, the President of the United States bring a private suit, it would be a front-page story all over the world. You'll spread the lie and its filthy connotation. On the other hand—"

I was interrupted sharply. "Put Eddie on the phone!"

Weisl, who was a close friend of the President, didn't have a chance even to say, "Hello." He listened to a lengthy tirade, and then said, "I'll tell him."

He hung up and said, "He insists that you start a libel suit immediately."

"But it is not wise to do so," I remonstrated. "Even though *The Saturday Evening Post* is a reputable magazine, how many people do you think will read this article, notice the quoted phrase, or most important, believe it? Everyone knows Johnson's record on civil rights. The article is an obvious lie. But can you imagine the front-page stories, followed by editorials, and special features which a libel suit by the President will provoke? The author of the article, rejoicing in the opportunity to joust with the President, may claim he can substantiate his story. Political enemies will quickly point to lies they claimed the President told Congress about Vietnam. 'How do we know this denial now isn't a lie?' So it will go, about a phrase which won't see the light of day if the President ignores it.

"Furthermore, there will be many who will acknowledge that the article is false, but will attack the President on the grounds of free speech. They will condemn him for trying to muzzle the press. They will insist that it is better for the President to suffer criticism, even false criticism, than use his power to make publications shy of writing about him."

Weisl interrupted with a gesture which indicated he didn't need to be convinced. He had his eye on the complex personality of the President.

"You must wait until he calms down. Come to Washington Monday and we'll talk to him."

"Do you think by then he will be ready to say, 'Come let's sit down and reason together?'" I said, referring to his favorite quotation.

The aftermath was that the President needed little persuasion to drop the matter. The enormous burdens of office, and perhaps a host of other items, distracted him. So far as we could learn, no one paid attention to the quotation which had so riled him.

The irony of it was that without our push, *The Saturday Evening Post* went out of business. I do not consider this a coincidence. I have observed that magazines which are in financial trouble attempt to hype their circulation by sensational stories. When a flood of libel claims suddenly appear against a particular publication, I sense a desperate effort by the editors to salvage their failing enterprise by sensationalism.

All these illustrations of abnegation do not mean that there are not times when libel suits must be brought, when they are the most appropriate and noble means to right a terrible wrong. They cannot only provide justice. More than almost any other legal remedy, they can actually save lives.

During the McCarthy era, artists such as Mady Christians, Philip Loeb, and a number of political figures committed suicide because their reputations and means of livelihood had been destroyed. We shall never know the full cost.

That wonderful woman and gifted artist, Margaret Webster, had been designated the American representative of an International Meeting of the Theater in London. The State Department refused her a visa because she had come under the poisonous cloud of McCarthyism. She was so depressed that she wrote me a lengthy letter in which she at one point said she was contemplating suicide. I was frantic with the responsibility of speedy persuasion. Fortunately her threat might have been the expression of her disgust with the stupidity of the world rather than a resolve to flee it.

She survived, and went on to brilliant achievements in presenting Shakespeare throughout the nation. She was chiefly responsible for making the Bard one to be enjoyed by the populace rather than merely revered by name. She also directed Metropolitan operas, removing the stiffness from the joints of traditional posturing. But how near she and many others came to destruction because "He who filches my good name makes me poor indeed."

So I use the libel sword wherever it is necessary. I shall advert here to two illustrations: one of a private citizen, and one of a public official.

Alfred Strelsin was a successful businessman known only to a small circle of friends and acquaintances. He had never sought nor attained any public notice.

In three minutes one night, his name came to the attention of millions of people. It was not fame which was bestowed upon him by the miracle of television. It was contempt. He was cast in the role of a despicable person. The suddenness and unexpected nature of his debacle made it even more devastating.

It came from a news broadcast on a national Metromedia network. Interspersed with the news was a gossip commentary by Rona Barrett. Its relationship to news was similar to the relationship between a gossip column and the editorial page in a newspaper. Its purpose was to relieve the strain of thinking by tickling the mind. Rona Barrett specialized in stories about Hollywood stars, congressmen who sinned at government expense, and those who used their own money, couples who were heading for "splitsville" and those for "church bells" (with batting averages, her second, his third), and since there are more divorces than ever before, there was no lack of fill-in material. What was needed was sensationalism.

The style was breezy. Posing in a three-quarter profile and adopting a saucy manner, she brought the most unimportant, but titillating, items of the day to the attention of her listeners. Any scandal was precious. Rona Barrett had heard something about Strelsin, or so she claimed. She spurted it out on the network as follows:

First Party givers were those fabulous trillionaires [to Rona Barrett millionaire was not impressive enough], Dorothy Strelsin, singer extraordinaire [etc.] and husband, Al Strelsin who once admitted to friends that he sold guns to Hitler during World War II."

The daring nature of such an accusation gave it verisimilitude. Would anyone risk saying such a thing if she wasn't sure? Everyone knows that network lawyers check the broadcasts to prevent libel suits.

The fact that this statement was passed by counsel indicated that some proof of its accuracy had to exist.

Even Strelsin's friends must have experienced some doubts. Was this a skeleton in his closet no one had known before. Was this how he had amassed his wealth?

Strelsin was Jewish. His brother had died fighting for Israel. He had been active in Jewish as well as other causes. This made the perfidy of his accused conduct even greater.

As a friend of Donald Nelson, the head of the War Production Board under Roosevelt, during World War II, I knew that Strelsin had been designated by him to serve in the economic division of the Board, to prevent strategic materials from reaching Hitler. The destination of such items was scrutinized and traced so that indirect deliveries by other countries would not be made. Also vital goods produced by foreign countries were bought up by the United States, so that they would not fall into Hitler's hands. I have reason to believe that this economic warfare did not stop at peaceful means. Any investigation, which I do not suggest, of our activities in blocking strategic materials from reaching Hitler might provide a saga of unsuspected violence.

So to say of Strelsin that he shipped guns to Hitler was also to charge him with being a traitor to the United States. For his mission was to prevent guns or even cotton or food from arriving in Germany. Also the moral dereliction of aiding the Haman and Hun of the twentieth century to slay his kinfolk was so vile as to make Strelsin an inhuman beast.

When Strelsin came to see me, he had aged perceptibly. He literally trembled as he described the blow which had just befallen him. His sleeplessness and torment made him look ill.

I advised immediate suit. "We'll examine Rona Barrett before trial under oath. We'll find out who in the network had approved the script and on what basis. We'll demonstrate the falsity and recklessness of the inflammatory broadcast."

This was not the kind of libel to ignore in the hope that like a wave it would dissipate itself and roll in harmlessly. His reputation had been destroyed, his health undermined. His business might well suffer the same fate. He had no choice but to fight back, hard and immediately.

We served a complaint on Rona Barrett and the network. It was insured against such claims and experienced counsel appeared. They challenged New York jurisdiction over Rona Barrett, who resided in California. We attached her funds in New York to obtain jurisdiction in rem (of her property if not her person). Then we moved to examine Rona Barrett before trial and under oath.

In a libel suit, the phrase "the moment of truth" is not a mere idiom.

It is the literal point of time when the defendant must demonstrate that he is not a liar.

At that moment, the defendants sought settlement.

We wrote a hard ticket. The money request was substantial but not prohibitive. The defendants would have to pay Strelsin's counsel fees, allowing a punitive sum to Strelsin for satisfaction purposes. But more important, we demanded that Rona Barrett read on her regular broadcast a retraction and apology which I would compose. I made it clear in advance that it would confess gross and inexcusable error and contrition and be as strong as my mastery of language would permit. Not a word was to be changed. Also she was to make a tape of it, so that we could listen to it in advance to be certain that her delivery of it would be as sincere and emphatic as the words required, and that no facial expressions or slurring of words would detract from its effectiveness. Finally, we were to have the right to publish her retraction in any newspaper we chose, or mail it to stockholders of Strelsin's companies or to others, with an accompanying statement of the suit, the surrender and the admission of falsity.

Churchill's precept "In victory—magnanimity" appeals to me, and I derived no joy from insisting on such humiliating demands. Indeed, I thought they would not be accepted; that the defendants would rather subject themselves to a trial and damages, seeking to ameliorate the amount by admitting error, but denying malice.

However, the defendants felt denuded of any defense. The accusation was completely baseless. Rona Barrett claimed that she had heard it at a cocktail party from some unidentified source. Even a drunken man could hardly have had the inventive wit to make up such a whopper. Those who were supposed to check such broadcasts must have had hangovers themselves and been too bleary-eyed to read. Otherwise how could such a story have passed them by?

The defendants had the usual Hobson's choice. Either they accepted "unacceptable" settlement terms, or they risked a disaster at trial. They chose the former.

I wrote the statement to be made by Rona Barrett. No script writer ever had a similar task, to write that which would make the star most uncomfortable. We tested the tape. To her credit, she delivered the lines with sincerity and due emphasis. It was not easy for her. Crow tastes more bitter to columnists than to others. Making a mistake is understandable for businessmen and politicians. But pundits, whose stock in trade is purveying inside news, can lose their influence and jobs, if they are exposed as panderers of fiction.

Strelsin notified as many people as possible to listen to her broadcast at the appointed time. They and millions of others saw Rona Barrett, still in three-quarter profile (but now it looked as if she was turned aside partly in embarrassment) say:

"Some time ago, I broadcast over this station a serious charge against Mr. Alfred Strelsin, one of America's leading industrialists, attacking his patriotism. Unfortunately, I found out too late that the charge was totally unfounded. Tonight Metromedia and I want to set the record straight.

"I have found that Mr. Strelsin's record of distinguished service to our government is unquestionable, including top-level government assignments during World War II. He is a dedicated philanthropist with a record of honor and distinction. There was not and is not the slightest basis for the charge I broadcast against him. I retract it fully and offer my and Metromedia's sincerest apologies to a distinguished American, Alfred Strelsin."

In addition she wrote him a lengthy letter dictated by me, saying that she recognized "the severe anguish and distress my erroneous broadcast has caused you . . . I offer my sincere apology for the injury caused by this unfounded broadcast. I authorize you to make such use of this letter in the future as you may find necessary." Metromedia Inc., whose president, John W. Kluge, had demonstrated his integrity in support of correction, also wrote that "the charge was totally unfounded. We regret that our staff failed to detect and delete this false statement from the Barrett broadcast before it was made."

Another illustration of a libel suit which had to be brought involved a public official. It will introduce a subject which has troubled the Supreme Court more than almost any other conflict between constitutional rights.

Governor James A. Rhodes of Ohio was one of those rare men in public life who appealed to the people so strongly that he rose politically with rocket-like vertical propulsion. He had been Mayor of Columbus four times, and then was selected in 1962 to run against the popular Democratic Governor Mike DiSalle. Ordinarily this would be an invitation to disaster. But Rhodes won by the largest majority ever in an Ohio election. The fact that he was a Republican who had swept a Democratic state brought him to the attention of the nation. He was reelected for another four-year term, and as it was ending, there were plans to run him for the United States Senate, and then for national office. Already he was prominently mentioned for the vice-presidency and even the presidency.

At this moment of increasing momentum for a brilliant career, his future was cut off as if by a single sharp knife stroke. *Life* magazine announced on its front cover a feature story, entitled "Scandal Overtakes the Governor of Ohio." Inside, a two-page spread had the caption "The Governor and the Mobster." Photographs have innuendos too, particularly their placement. One was of Governor Rhodes opening the baseball season in Cincinnati. "He has been mentioned as the next Baseball Commissioner." Immediately alongside were two "mug shots of Thomas (Yonnie) Licavoli, taken in 1934," side and front view, to make sure that their dishonorable origin was clear. On the opposite page was a dramatic photograph of Licavoli taken thirty-five years later, in a stretcher, being wheeled out of Riverside Hospital to return to prison, after he "had reportedly suffered a massive heart attack." On the next page were photographs of four gangsters.

The chief accusation was that Governor Rhodes had commuted Licavoli's life sentence for murder in the first degree to second degree. This turned out to be on the unanimous recommendation of the Parole Board, whose decision the Governor accepted. This made Licavoli eligible to apply for parole. But the article did not reveal this. A subheading in the article gave the flavor of the charge. "Plenty of Money Floating Around to Set Yonnie Free." The innuendo was unmistakable. There were references to $250,000 being available to free Licavoli and that in the past there had been overtures to previous officials to free Licavoli. They had rejected the proposed bribes, although there was a vacuum in the article as to why they had not reported the matter to the criminal authorities. The clear implication was that Rhodes had yielded to temptation.

Life magazine was so proud of itself that it took full page advertisements in various newspapers announcing its scoop. One such advertisement appeared in the New York *Times*. Nine tenths of the page was a huge photograph of Governor Rhodes. Underneath was a large head line: "Ohio's Governor and the Mob." I noticed immediately the subtle change from singular to plural. The *Life* article referred to Mobster. The *Times* advertisement to Mob. The accusation, like amoebas, had multiplied itself in the course of transition. "To top it off," said the rest of the ad, "*Life* presents evidence showing that, while in public office, Governor Rhodes 'has engaged in high handed manipulation of political funds.'"

Governor Rhodes and his executive assistant came to see me at once. He was calm on the surface, although I was sure he was seething with anger. It was quickly evident why he was a popular and effective official. He was sincere, gracious, and charming but very firm. It was quite a combination. My partners, Judge Hofstadter, Vincent Broderick, and Paul Martinson, who sat in at the conferences, had the same high impression of him. At the end of one session, Judge Hofstadter commented, "If he survives this, he can go on to be a presidential figure."

As in every matter, we examined the evidence with deliberate skepticism. Indeed, we cross-examined him and his executive assistant as thoroughly as our opponent would ultimately do. No questions were barred. All were answered frankly and satisfactorily. Whenever we requested supporting data, it was sent immediately. We were convinced that the accusations in the article were completely false.

Licavoli had been convicted of conspiracy to kill two people. Since he was not charged with the actual shooting, the jury recommended mercy. He was sentenced to life imprisonment. His confederates were sentenced to be electrocuted.

The mercy recommendation entitled Licavoli, after he had served twenty years, to apply to the Parole Board for commutation to second-degree murder. If the Board did so recommend, the Governor could commute. The Parole Board then for the first time had the power to hold a hearing and grant or refuse parole. On one occasion the Parole Board recommended commutation, but Governor Rhodes rejected it.

Later, after Licavoli's thirty-fifth year of confinement, and serious illness which was certified by doctors, the Parole Board repeated its recommendation to the Governor for commutation. This time he gave it more consideration. Licavoli had written a personal plea to the Governor in which he said:

"I have a daughter who was born three months before I came to prison. Now she is married, with two lovely girls and a little boy of her own, and none of them have ever seen me except behind bars. My first-born daughter was killed, along with my father, while they were on their way to visit me one day."

For four years Licavoli had been under the psychiatric care of Dr. Anderson. During this period he received commendation from Warden Henderson for initiative and action beyond the normal call of duty on three separate occasions:

(1) When I climbed the outside of "C" cellhouse wall, 80 feet above the ground, and saved a man attempting to commit suicide;

(2) When I entered the cell of a demented inmate who had set his mattress on fire—at this time I had to fight the inmate and ended up losing 90 per cent of the sight of my right eye from an acid burn as a result;

(3) When I overpowered another homicidal inmate who was attempting to kill a guard (Mr. Helles) and was struck with an iron bar by the psychopath, 12 stitches being required to close the wound.

Looking back I realize that it was during this period that my rehabilitation began. I began to think about other people more than myself and my own troubles.

Warden Alvis entrusted him thereafter with narcotics of all kinds which were used on the psychiatric ranges. The trust was never violated.

One of Licavoli's confederates, sentenced to death, had had his sentence commuted and was paroled by a former governor without any fanfare.

Governor Rhodes had attempted generally to apply new humanitarian principles in dealing with the penology. He had ordered a list to be prepared of all prisoners who had served lengthy terms and were over sixty-five years old, that he might give special attention to parole applications. He had reduced the number of inmates in one prison by 50 per cent, saving the state money, but, more important, rewarding those who had undergone rehabilitation. He employed at the Governor's mansion trustees, some of them sentenced to life.

In Licavoli's case, he also received a plea from Chaplain Theodore Gratjohn:

Tom Licavoli is assigned to work as a nurse in our Tuberculosis Ward and has done a commendable job in performing his duties . . .

I am certain that he is neither the type man, nor individual that many would like to picture. Instead I knew him as a truly repentant soul, who is deserving of another chance before his fellowman.

Rhodes, aware of the previous rumors about attempted bribes to spring Licavoli, took the precaution of having a careful check made by his executive assistant, John M. McElroy. He requested and received a letter from Mrs. Licavoli which stated that neither she nor any other person to her knowledge "had paid or promised anything of value to anybody," to assist in obtaining a commutation. Inquiry was also directed to the prosecutor's office which had convicted Licavoli. The Attorney General of the state, Paul A. Brown, in commenting on the commutation wrote that "Governor Rhodes has acted justly and with high moral courage in an area always fraught with the risk of misunderstanding."

The basic fact was that the Governor had not pardoned Licavoli. He had merely accepted the seven-man Parole Board's unanimous report to commute his sentence to life imprisonment for second-degree murder. Thereafter a parole application was made and in view of the press furor it was denied. Licavoli remained in jail. He was one of the victims of the false rumors.

What is the purpose of imprisonment, revenge or rehabilitation? We must make up our minds. All would agree that society's objective is to protect itself from repetition of crime and deter others. So unless the prisoner is truly rehabilitated and becomes safe to society, his sentence should run its course. But in the rare instances in which real rehabilitation has occurred, the prisoner is no longer the same man who was sentenced. We ought not keep him in jail indefinitely if he is no longer a threat to society. It would be as wrong to do so as to keep an insane man confined after he has recovered sanity.

Such a policy would not open the door wide for incorrigibles to be let loose. Genuine transformation of a personality is somewhat of a miracle, and does not occur often. I have had occasion to write about one such extraordinary case, that of Paul Crump. He was a vicious, illiterate killer, who like the beautiful flower which grows in the mud of India, became a literate good man while in jail. He proved it by his deeds. So did Licavoli. Wasn't such a man, who paid his debt for thirty-five years and was old and sick entitled to a few years with his family? Why the outcry? There was not one scintilla of proof that money or influence played any part in the unanimous recommendation of the Parole Board or the Governor's acceptance of it. Indeed, even though the Governor's commutation made it possible for the Parole Board to act, it did not do so. Licavoli remained in jail.

If revenge is the purpose of penology, then let us kill convicted murderers, rapists, and kidnapers and perhaps any repeater of a violent crime. Why not also punish lesser offenders, by cutting off arms, legs, blinding some and cutting out the tongues of others? This is still done in some Arab countries. We could all become Nazis in spirit and revel in torture. We shy away from going all the way, because a civilized society must act decently even when attacked and injured. Otherwise there would be no Manual of War. Prisoners would be shot, women raped, and the enemy's cities plundered.

Life's article piled a few additional charges on the wild claim of mob association. These involved improper use of political slush funds, and income tax involvement, accusations which had been raised and found baseless in the 1962 campaign, when the voters rejected them and lifted Rhodes into office with a massive heave of votes.

The multiplication of falsehoods created a picture of a vile, unscrupulous hypocrite. Our indignation rose at the outrageous attacks. Who could be safe, if such tactics succeeded? But once again we asked the Governor to satisfy us, as counsel, by documentary proof. His accountants forwarded a cent-by-cent analysis refuting every accusation. We advised Governor Rhodes to issue a public statement, setting forth the assets of his wife and family. He did so in detail.* After more than twenty years of public service, he had wound up virtually impoverished. His reward had been the honor of high office and the regard of the people for him. Now even these were taken away.

Rhodes was at the time involved in a primary contest for the Senate with the redoubtable Robert A. Taft, Jr. We could not bring him relief in time to overcome the accusations of corruption and Mafia association which *Life*'s article announced. He nevertheless asked that he be permitted to announce a libel suit immediately.

"Governor," I said "I would like to ask you a blunt question. Is it your main purpose to institute suit in the hope of salvaging the primary campaign, or, even if you lose the primary do you intend to pursue the suit to vindicate your honor?"

"Mr. Nizer," he replied, "I want to nail their lies, which will probably defeat me in the primary. But that is a small part of it. I have a wife, children and a host of friends, in my state and throughout the country. I do not want to go to my grave with a cloud of dishonor over my head. I must clear my name for their sake, even if I never hold a public office again in my life."

I was moved by his statement. Who wouldn't be? Factually, there would be no problem. The article was an atrocious lie. We would prove it. But there were unique legal obstructions. I knew he understood them because before he consulted me, he had issued a public statement in which, after denying every accusation with emphasis which only innocence and sincerity could command, he said, "Whether I intend to sue for libel, I have not decided. Under United States Supreme Court decisions, it is almost impossible for a public official to win a libel suit. These decisions make it plain that it is all right for a publication to lie about a public official so long as there is no malice. I will not sue just for political purposes." I explained that we would endeavor to prove malice, by equating recklessness with malice. This was a difficult undertaking, and the Supreme Court had not yet given even this thin cloak of protection to a public official. Why? First Amendment. The need to protect the press from harassment even when it is mistaken.

The risk of obtaining relief was therefore great. But we believed that the Governor was supported by moral considerations of impelling na-

---

* "I own no corporate stock.
I own one $1,000 bond.
I own no mutual funds.
I own no real estate—not even a home.
I am not the beneficiary of any trust or foundation.
Over the years, I paid into the Public Employee Retirement System $24,867.83. All other assets, including those of my wife, myself and my youngest daughter, come to approximately $40,000. I want to make it emphatically clear that I have paid all my taxes."

ture. We were willing to try. We instituted suit. The complaint set forth the evil innuendos to be drawn from the *Life* article: that Rhodes "had acted in collusion with Licavoli and the Mafia"; that he had been bribed "by Licavoli or the Mafia"; that as Governor "he had finally been exposed in a scandal involving flagrant corruption on his part."

It then asserted that *Life* had made these false statements "with reckless disregard of whether they were true or false," and had done so "maliciously." The defense stressed the special immunity given to the press, in the absence of malice, and asserted that *Life* had no malice toward Governor Rhodes.

In the meantime the Governor lost the senatorial primary to Robert Taft, who then lost the election. Ohio turned Democratic.

The legal struggle continued. Supreme Court rulings worsened our position. New decisions put heavy emphasis on the freedom of the press, even where what it published about a public official was untrue. Only malice could sustain a suit.

The legal war heated up. We moved to examine the writers and editor of *Life* magazine to demonstrate the recklessness with which the false accusations had been made. The defendants sought to examine the Governor, and advised Federal Judge Harold R. Tyler that they might consider moving for summary judgment.

As counsel met to arrange the legal duels on the field of honor, the possibility of ending the lawsuit arose. Would *Life* in writing remove the taint on Governor Rhodes's integrity? We stated that, aside from the legal problems, damages were not our goal. The restoration of Governor Rhodes's reputation was. If this could be achieved we would forgo our determination to take the matter, if necessary, to the highest court, to review the restrictive rule which made public officials open targets for published lies.

The editors were decent men and may have regretted the excesses of the publication. An arrangement was concluded. It protected *Life* against the humiliation of open confession of misdeed, and protected Governor Rhodes by withdrawing the charge or innuendo that he had any association with "the mob" or had been bribed or influenced improperly in his conduct.

By agreement Governor Rhodes issued a press release which stated:

"Life magazine has now acknowledged that it did not state or intend to state that I had acted illegally or dishonorably in commuting Licavoli's sentence. Its attorney has written my attorney, Louis Nizer, that 'you are correct that Life did not state in its article that Governor Rhodes commuted the sentence because of any illegal involvement.' Thus Life has withdrawn the charge which motivated my bringing the lawsuit.

"Under the circumstances, my honor has been vindicated and the cloud over my children and family has been removed."

The litigation was withdrawn without prejudice to Governor Rhodes.

Later, the real verdict was given by the citizens of Ohio. They elected Rhodes to be Governor again.

Life magazine suspended weekly publication soon after. Had the magazine been in trouble and reached out for circulation and the stimulation of advertising? We find a clue in the very full page advertisements headed "Ohio's Governor and the Mob." Underneath the largest photograph of a face I have ever seen in a newspaper (it now seemed to bear a triumphant look) appeared the following copy:

"All this week, advertisers, large and small, share the tension and excitement.

"Again, the vitality of the magazine rubs off on the advertising. The things we put on our pages help sell the things *you* put on our pages."

This unabashed linking of the Rhodes exposé with advertising supported the Nizer rule that there is an equation between daring sensationalism in a publication and its imminent expiration.

In any event Governor Rhodes is politically alive and flourishing. *Life*, the weekly magazine, is dead.

I am appalled by the renewed popularity of capital punishment, and the Supreme Court's decision that, if consistently applied, capital punishment is not a violation of the Eighth Amendment of the Constitution, which forbids "cruel and unusual punishment." Could anyone who actually witnessed an execution of a human being, whether by noose, which breaks the neck, by gas, which asphyxiates, or by electricity, which breaks the lenses of the eyes and cooks the body until the skull emits smoke, say it is not a cruel and inhuman act? "In every one of us," wrote Arthur Koestler, "there lurks a little furry animal who cries out for blood." But we do not want him to make the laws of the land. Understandably, we hear him when we are horrified by an outrageous crime, whether by the Manson killers or the assassination of the Kennedys. There is no doubt that each one of us, if he could have reached Hitler, or the murderer of someone dear to us, would want to destroy him with our bare hands. But this is just the time to resist the little furry killer within us. It is the test of emergence from animalism to a more civilized state. Those who believe in the punishment of death cite the Bible, "An eye for an eye and a tooth for a tooth." I believe a fair interpretation of this phrase is that the punishment should fit the crime, not the literal interpretation that we should poke out a criminal's eye. The Bible in many passages expresses its indictment of the taking of life under any circumstance. The civilized and Christian philosophy is best expressed by St. Augustine, who, when the heretics murdered the Christians, said, "We do not wish to have the sufferings of the servants of God avenged by the infliction of precisely similar injuries in the way of retaliation. Not, of course, that we object to the removal from these wicked men of the liberty to perpetrate further crimes, but our desire is rather that justice be satisfied without the taking of their lives or the maiming of their bodies . . ."

If we do not recognize the possibility of rehabilitation in an individual, what hope is there for all mankind, which also must be rehabilitated or we will continue to murder millions in war?

I detest capital punishment not because of sympathy for the killer, but because it degrades and demeans us. The usual arguments, pro and con, rage around the question of deterrence and the possibility of irrevocable error. These are not the crux of the matter. Our self-respect is. However, I don't believe executions deter. If we really thought they did we would hold our executions in broad daylight in the public square and invite children. They are chiefly the ones to be deterred. But we don't do that. We subconsciously are ashamed of the act and sneak away at midnight in a closed room to commit the deed.

Our uncertainty as to whether we wish revenge or rehabilitation results in self-defeating practices which have made our prison system as obsolete as ancient dungeons. For example, we do not permit conjugal rights, as many other countries do. Men and women deprived of their sexual satisfaction are virtually driven into homosexuality and lesbianism.

Since many serve limited terms, they are freed to join their families, having first been emotionally crippled by their prison experience.

Since I believe in the good sense of mass opinion, how do I reconcile my view with the growing popular approval of capital punishment? Many states are passing enactments to authorize the supreme penalty, particularly if a public official, policeman, or prison guard is killed. I believe the reason for this wave in favor of extreme penalty is due to the public's outrage with crime in the streets which seeps into our homes as well. We dare not walk at night on thoroughfares even in "good" neighborhoods. Muggings occur in broad daylight. Our homes are invaded. Store windows require iron sheaths. Purses are torn from women's arms. Our parks are no longer havens for relaxation. For a few dollars men are killed in the streets. During the 1977 blackout of New York City, the darkest traits of man emerged with looting and burning. I believe that our disgust with this lawlessness has evoked the "kill them" reaction.

However, this criminal plague is not of the usual variety. It is drug addiction crime. When addicts are arrested, many of them inform the authorities that they must mug and steal seven or eight times a day to accumulate one hundred dollars needed for the drug shot. That explains the nature of the petty crimes; a television set carried out of a home and sold in desperate haste for ten or fifteen dollars; a typewriter taken out of an office and sacrificed at one tenth its worth; a purse snatched or a man mugged to obtain a few dollars, and if he has no money, perhaps killed in the frustration of the nerve-screechy addict who is minutes away from unbearable craving.

There are reputed to be two hundred thousand addicts in New York. If only one half of these engage in multiple crimes to pay for the day's drug need, it accounts for a minimum of half a million crimes each day. The problem is proportionately the same in other cities throughout the land. This is the explanation for the new kind of crime wave which has terrorized the population.

The antidote is not stiffer penalties. A drug addict driven by inner devils would kill his own mother at the moment of extremis. He would not be deterred by the threat of capital punishment or even by a guaranteed burning in purgatory.

The solution for this unique problem is to provide free heroin and other addictive drugs under governmental and psychiatric auspices. Heroin, for which the addict must pay one hundred dollars a dose, costs the government only two cents. The by-product of such a free drug program would be to drive the drug racketeers out of business. Its chief virtue would be to reduce if not almost eliminate the chief cause of terror in our society.

Unlike other programs to reduce crime, there would be no interminable delay in obtaining relief. Education, improved social conditions, welfare, and unemployment funds are admirable but long-range programs. We are not resigned to suffering in the meantime. Impatience increases our sense of hopelessness and contributes to wild swinging at the enemy.

If the addict did not have to turn criminal to relieve this uncontrollable urge, we might well have instant peace in our streets, homes, and parks. This would not eliminate the usual type of crime, which has a history as old as mankind and unfortunately a future too. But the special scourge of drug addiction crime would be reduced very substantially overnight.

We might profit from England's experiment of supplying free drugs to addicts. The program suffered because it was under private doctors' supervision, and therefore more subject to the canny ingenuity of addicts in obtaining double dosage and other violations. When the program was put under direct governmental control, it worked.

The resistance to this idea comes chiefly from those who argue that it would make "permanent addicts" and even induce others to try drugs. I do not see much correction of addiction under present conditions, or even the reduction of the disease. If anything, such a program would discourage pushers, who would have to compete against a free product. This ought to reduce the number of new addicts. Finally, even if government and psychiatric supervision did not cure a single addict, our choice must be made between these poor incurable devils and the safety of citizens on the streets. It is not a hard choice, and it ought to be enthusiastically supported by the "severe" advocates, whose concern rightly is the protection of the innocent.

In short, capital punishment is the wrong solution for the problem. Entirely apart from the moral aspects, a policy of hatred would make it impossible to run our prisons, unless we had an armed guard for every prisoner. Caged men, deprived of sex, embittered by crowded conditions (which experiments with animals have shown create hostile neurotic tendencies), fed unpalatable or boring food in mess surroundings, and harboring grievances against society on the theory that "it prepares the crime—we only commit it," are difficult enough to control. Riots, burnings, maiming and killing of guards are frequent occurrences. It is the lure of reward for good behavior which makes discipline possible.

The need for freedom is not a mere political slogan. It is a rule of nature. The mockingbird, learning that its young has been captured and put in a cage, will bring poisoned berries to it to end a life of wingless agony.

THE UNBALANCED SPHERES

Being happily married to lovely and loving Mildred for almost forty years might disqualify me as an authority on why the marriage institution is dissolving before our very eyes. But considerable experience in dozens of matrimonial contests, and observations and analysis (the experience of the mind) encourage me to offer an explanation.

The stark statistics are that in one hundred years between 1860 and 1960, the divorce rate in the United States increased eighteen times.* In the 1970s there were 437 divorces for every 1,000 marriages over a twenty-five-year period. This rate, close to 50 per cent divorce of all marriages, must be enlarged to include broken marriages without divorce; husbands who just leave their wives, or vice versa, and even those who continue to live under the same roof in what sociologists have termed "empty shell families." It is significant that divorces occur in the early years of the marriage. Thirty per cent occur in less than four years; 40 per cent in less than five years, and 66 per cent in less than ten years.† At the same time there were fewer marriages in 1975 than in the preceding six years.

When as ancient an institution as marriage fares so badly in the modern world, there must be many reasons, but also a basic cause. I believe there is, and that it is identifiable.

The poetic vow which binds two people is translated in law as a marriage contract. But it is not an ordinary private contract. It is a contract involving public interest to build and preserve the family. Each party to the arrangement has a function to perform. Traditionally, the husband's function was to be the provider and the protector. The wife's function was to rear children and take care of the home. As long as

* Adams, Bert, ed., *The Family: A Sociological Interpretation*, Rand McNally, 1975, pp. 452–53.
† Professor, Judith T. Younger, "Love Is Not Enough," in *The New Republic*, June 19, 1976.

these two spheres of action were accepted, there was marital balance. It was subject to the various infirmities of marriage, the irritations of illness, unemployment, sexual maladjustment, personality clashes, and the daily conflicts of proximity. So there were always divorces despite the joys and warmth of love and growth. But basically there was a balance of spheres, which gave over-all permanence to the marriage institution.

Then came great changes. They were chiefly on the wife's side. The husband still remained the provider if not the protector. But women sought to change their "subordinate" role. Those who could afford it thought that cooks, maids, and nurses could well substitute for their traditional services, and many who couldn't sought jobs so that they could. This was the first liberation movement, although it occurred without books or fanfare. Millions of women, freed from "menial" tasks, sought to realize their potentials out of the home. They entered the business, professional, artistic, and even sports worlds.

The figures show the extent of this migration. In thirty-three years between 1940 and 1973, 50 per cent of married women who had no children under six years of age got jobs even though their husbands worked.* Many who did not take paying jobs gave vent to their restlessness by engaging in philanthropic, social, and, ultimately, political activity. But the home was no longer the exclusive center of interest.

This emancipation from home work was ideologically, as well as economically, motivated. Ibsen foretold it in *A Doll's House*. When Nora was warned by her husband that "before all else, you are a wife and a mother," she replied, "That I no longer believe. I believe before all else I am a human being as much as you are—or at least that I should try to become one."

The notion that self-fulfillment was primary and the shaping of a family secondary has blossomed into a full-fledged movement. Its banners announced that marriage must not inhibit the woman's role as a member of society. Some denounce marriage itself, charging that it "causes premature deaths of mind and soul through sexual rot and plays for power."†

The movement away from marriage gained momentum from the success which women achieved in their new occupations. Instead of being "protected" by their husbands, they became competitors, often outdistancing them in achievement and earnings. The ugly word "emasculation" came into prominence. The transition was too sudden to permit suitable adjustment. It was inevitable that a political women's libera-

* *Statistical Abtract of the United States,* U. S. Government Printing Office, Washington, D.C., pp. 336–41.
† *Marriage Is Hell,* Kathrin Perutz. William Morrow & Company, 1972.

tion movement would follow. It would demand freedoms already partly won, and equality, where women's superiority had often been established.

Like all revolutions, it was not gentle. Man became a "chauvinist pig," the oppressor, from whom long-denied rights were to be wrested.

The issue is not women's rights to equality. That is about as debatable as whether they should be veiled again and walk seven feet behind their husbands. But the progressive achievement of these rights has disrupted the respective functions in the marriage and thrown them out of balance. It is another instance in which an inevitable revolutionary reform has had unexpected consequences. Marriages are crumbling faster than ever before.

The process was hastened by foreseeable corollaries. If many men for centuries practiced a double sexual standard, then why should not women too? Curiously the drive was not always for monogamy, but for equal freedom from it. Technological advances played a part. The pill had wiped out one of man's "self-justifications" for a double standard. Add a dash of philosophy about the freedom to enjoy, and the marital arrangement of sexual loyalty received another serious blow.

More than this, sexual freedom actually acquired some respectability, thus eliminating the hope of religionists that we were dealing only with a fad. Children in high school, and, of course, in college, entered into relationships with no intention of "death do us part" permanence. Sometimes they did ripen into marriages. The pressure of parents and community was still a factor. But with increasing frequency, there was no shame in convenient temporary alliances. The New York City Department of Health has issued instructions to all secondary schools on what to do if a pregnant student went into labor or gave birth in school. The Department notes that in 1969 there were 2,487 unmarried pregnancies among seventh to twelfth graders. There has been a steady increase since then.

Even more startling was the readiness generally to bear children out of wedlock. Celebrities, who used to set the fashion for dress, set them for immorality. That last bulwark of the marital institution, "You want to have a child, don't you?" yielded to a flood of illegitimacies.

Nationally, more than one in twelve children born in 1967 were illegitimate. In four years between 1964 and 1967, 1,187,400 illegitimate children were born in the United States. The number so born in a ten-year period from 1961 through 1970 was sufficient to populate a city as large as Los Angeles, and, in the five years preceding 1971, to populate a city as large as Detroit.*

* Harry D. Krause, *Illegitimacy Law and Social Policy*, Bobbs-Merrill Company, 1971.

So we are witnessing not only the corrosion of marriage by ever-increasing divorces, but the defiance of the rules of legitimacy which provided a foundation for the marital institution. The increasing number of illegitimacies is tending to make us a nation of bastards.

Unable to change these developments, we have resorted to new laws which eliminate the stigma of illegitimacy. Many states, like New York, prohibit birth certificates from revealing that the birth was out of wedlock. The theory is that it is the parents who are illegitimate, not the child. Even inheritance laws have been tailored to wipe out the distinction between legitimate and illegitimate children. The Supreme Court of the United States ruled that "illegitimate children are not 'nonpersons' . . . but 'persons' within the meaning of the Equal Protection Clause of the Fourteenth Amendment. . . . Why should the illegitimate child be denied rights merely because of his birth out of wedlock? He certainly is subject to all of the responsibilities of a citizen, including the payment of taxes and conscription under the selective Service Act."†

This is society's way of conceding its inability to maintain the historic structures of marriage and legitimacy. By eliminating the disgrace and financial consequence of out-of-wedlock births, we record our helplessness to prevent the crumbling of the marital institution.

The impact of all this on our social structure has yet to be realized. It portends a greater change than political or economic upheavals. It challenges the precepts of all religions.

The disintegration of the marriage institution may contribute to another phenomenon, the extraordinary increase of suicides, particularly of children. The shattering of family unity has added to the psychic pressure of a frenetic age. "When I'm alone, I stop believing I exist." This appears to be a rule of nature. Experiments among rhesus monkeys indicate that if one is separated from the family for only a few weeks, despondency sets in. Biologists call partiality to relatives in the animal world "kin selection." When ants are accidentally isolated from the group, they circle in a suicide mill until they march themselves to death.

Human suicide is the fourth largest killer among those between the ages of fifteen and forty-four, reports the World Health Organization. Suicide is the second leading cause of death among adolescents (accident is first). The increase is extraordinary—more than 200 per cent in recent years.

These figures are deceiving. Actually the percentages are much higher. Many suicides are not recorded. Deaths caused by firearms, drownings, and poisons leave doubt as to whether they were accidental

† *Levy v. Louisiana*, 391 U.S. 68.

or intentional. Children's suicides are often deliberately disguised by
those who fear they may be blamed. Also self-destruction by slow, deliberate methods, like drugs, is not deemed suicide, although Karl Men-
ninger calls it "chronic suicide." In Great Britain, France, Germany,
and Japan there has been an enormous increase in deaths from drugs.
The suicidal intention is indicated by the proportionate decrease in the
previous suicide methods of hanging, drowning, jumping off heights,
and violent self-destruction.

Experts estimate that the reported suicide rate is understated and
should be substantially increased to reflect the true rate. Many sociologists attribute the dramatic rise of suicides among the young to the
breakdown of the home and church. That the religious "hold" on a
child may be an important factor is indicated by the fact that more
Protestant youths commit suicide, fewer Jews, and fewest Catholics.

Of those who attempted suicide unsuccessfully, almost 90 per cent
felt that their families did not understand them. Doesn't divorce, which
is the suicide of a marriage, often begin with a similar charge by one of
the parties against the other? Both involve alienation.

A recent study showed that 71 per cent of young suicides came from
broken homes. Some felt "responsible" for their parents' divorce. A
much larger number came from "disturbed" homes, in which families
quarreled, had severe financial problems, where one parent was absent,
alcoholic, or institutionalized, or where conflict arose with a step-
parent.

All this would indicate that the breakdown of the marital institution
may have unexpectedly caused an epidemic of suicides. Is it only a coincidence that in foreign countries there is a relationship between the
rate of divorce and the rate of suicide, particularly among the young? In
Europe, the countries with the lowest divorce rates, Italy and Greece,
also have the lowest suicide rates. Sweden, which has ten times as many
divorces as Italy or Greece, has five times the suicides of those countries. Denmark's high divorce rate corresponds with its suicide rate.
Norway, which has the lowest divorce rate among Scandinavian countries, also has the lowest suicide rate.*

It is impossible to accommodate ourselves to suicide, as we do to illegitimacy. There, we can by law forbid the recording of the illegitimacy
and preserve inheritance rights. We have tried to deal with suicide legally, by making its attempt a crime. But this is inherently silly. We
threaten an unsuccessful suicide with a jail term when he is eager to
inflict capital punishment upon himself.

To fully grasp the enormity of the suicide phenomenon, one must
remember that it runs counter to the most basic principle of self-preser-

* *United Nations Statistical Yearbook,* 1975.

vation. A psychiatrist in the Nazi camps reported only four suicide attempts of a group of three thousand persons living under terrifying circumstances. Generally the suicide rate in concentration camps was extraordinarily low, despite the indescribable tortures to which the inmates were subjected. It is not external misery which provokes the death wish, but rather inner psychological collapse. Living things struggle to the last gasp (a doubtful description for a microbe) to avoid final oblivion. The occasional exceptions of lemmings drowning themselves in mass suicide, or insects and fish, like the salmon, expiring after their mission of propagation has been fulfilled, are part of nature's mysterious scheme, probably to avoid overpopulation. But a human being's yearning for life is so intense that many attempt by their last testaments to stretch out their hands even after death to direct their property among the living. We have had to prevent this by laws which limit the validity of such directions in wills, to two lives in being plus twenty-one years. If old people use such artifices to give them longer "life," what shall we say of children, bursting with energy, and propelled by nature's forces to growth and fulfillment, who nevertheless want to die before they have even tasted life?

Another consequence of the family unit's destruction is juvenile delinquency. If children grow up "without strong personal attachments, without a consistent structure of discipline, the result is likely to be an inner emptiness for them and increasing violence for society."* This is tragically borne out by figures as cruel as their deeds. Between 1960 and 1974, the number of arrests of juveniles increased astronomically for every type of offense. The percentage of increase during a fifteen-year period by offenders under eighteen years of age was:†

Murder	224 per cent
Rape	147 per cent
Robbery	307 per cent
Assault	221 per cent
Prostitution	372 per cent
Drug offenses	3,777 per cent

So we have surveyed the wreckage from the disintegration of the marriage institution. It is as if a train engine collided with new mores and the cars behind it were derailed, causing painful injuries of illegitimacy, juvenile delinquency, drug abuse, and suicide.

Of course, my theory of "unbalanced spheres" can at best be a partial

* *The Fractured Family*, Leontine Young, McGraw-Hill, 1974, New York.
† *FBI Uniform Crime Reports*, 1974, U. S. Government Printing Office, Washington, D.C.

explanation of divorce. No social revolution ever lends itself to simplistic analysis. For a long time I believed that sexual incompatibility, which does not mean only physical incapacity, but, in most cases, declining sexual interest, was the chief cause of marital disharmony. Where the sexual quotient in the marriage remained high, all other grievances seemed to be overcome. No matter how many reasons were offered by husband or wife for their difficulties, ultimately a frank answer to a sensitive question revealed that sex had failed to rear its beautiful head. But if one pursued the matter further and asked what caused the passions which united the couple to dissipate, the "unbalanced spheres" theory threw a meaningful light on the subject. It encompassed many social phenomena. These ranged from the disruption of the couple's traditional roles to a new consciousness of freedom of action for all human beings.

Women had more ground to make up and were therefore more impatient and aggressive. The impact on the sexual relationship was profound in many ways: a new kind of jealousy, centering on achievement rather than sex; women's realization of equality or superiority in various activities, which sometimes diminished their respect for their husbands, even to the point of contempt; and an evil circle of retaliation by one or the other until sexual feeling was dulled.

Also, men and women in their new quest for independence mistakenly rejected mutuality of feeling as if it were the enemy of their freedom. Love of self cannot really be achieved without dependence on another's love. There is an "inborn Thou," wrote Martin Buber. "The single, solitary being is meaningless." When emancipated men and women considered pleasureful isolation essential to their credo, they further upset the marital arrangement. For that matter, they entered a road of emotional nihilism which depressed them, no matter what their status.

This provides another insight to the suicidal trend, and also why it is not mainly the poverty-stricken, the very ill, or the failing students who are the victims. On the contrary, the statistics show that the well-to-do, the healthy, and the high-grade students supply the highest number of casualties. It is not a paradox that the most intelligent often destroy themselves. To cite only a few of the artists who have killed themselves: John Berryman, Anne Sexton, Hart Crane, Virginia Woolf, Sylvia Plath, Ernest Hemingway, Marilyn Monroe, Vincent Van Gogh, Mark Rothko.

In many instances, those who had won the battle for independence, which they equated with antipersonal dependence, found that the victory had left them with empty lives. They then turned their hatred against an "unjust world" inwards toward themselves. Alienation had become disorientation.

I shall illustrate with a case history. Of course it is atypical. Case histories always are. They are the individualistic combination of facts, moods, and neuroses as different as most fingerprints are from each other. But the roots of atypical cases are typical.

This was a marriage broken by the wife's discovery of her rights and the husband's bewilderment at a new relationship. Her background conditioned her for the ultimate assertiveness. She was a brilliant student and earned her Ph.D., but in the course of her studies, several teachers "made a pass at her," and she felt victimized. Her experiences later made her cry out to her husband, "Because I have a vagina, it doesn't mean you have a right to enslave me." The endearing words of love were replaced by the now banal epithet that he was "a male chauvinist pig."

She joined women's groups in England, where they lived for a while, and then in the United States when they returned. Theoretical conflicts gave way to real life ones when a child was born. She insisted on equal turns in the care of their son and in household chores. "I diapered him this morning. You must this afternoon. I shopped yesterday. It is your turn today." "I washed the dishes last evening . . ." I could only wonder what the demands for equality were in the marital bed.

The strain became so great that the husband, in a fit of frustration, smashed a plate over his own head. Thereupon she claimed she feared that his violence might be outward the next time and insisted that he visit a psychiatrist. She had been a patient of one for a long time. The psychiatrist set forth his principle that a divorce was better than strife and its effect on their child. So they came to see me.

As always, the first effort was for reconciliation. They were two fine people of good breeding and character. The little son was a delight to both of them. I talked to each separately. I told her that the women's liberation movement, to which she was fanatically dedicated, was just in principle, in civic and economic rights, and in equal opportunity in all directions. But how could one derive happiness from a life lived with an abacus, counting each service and deed in a love relationship?

"You say you love your husband. Then it would be no sacrifice, when he is sound asleep and tired, for you to care for your son when he cries at night, even if it is his turn. Similarly would you consider it a lack of affection, if you have a headache, but he insists it's your turn to wash the dishes!"

What I thought was a simple statement of accommodation in a love relationship infuriated her. She didn't vocally assign me to the pig family, but she said I was partisan and lacked understanding. She dashed to her psychiatrist, and when he agreed with me she quit him too.

I do not believe that her fanaticism tells the whole story. He was not blameless. Was there ever a marital dispute in which the cause and effect were not uncertain? The lines for responsibility in a marital breakdown always run in circles. The initiation and the reaction vary according to the perspective of the litigant.

The significance of the case history is only that whatever provoked the wife's "liberation philosophy," the marital spheres were disrupted. They were divorced.

Only one inconsistent note arose in the financial settlement. The wife, or perhaps it was her lawyer doing his proper duty, insisted on alimony and child support in accordance with traditional law, protecting women. She did not protest this relief on the ground that it violated her principles.

The centrifugal force of whirling divorces has cast off family unity. I have recorded some of the observable consequences, but no one can foresee the ultimate events. Will men and women be happier without the classic bonds which have existed for many centuries? This depends upon the value judgment of the word "happiness." Women will derive "happiness" from achievements in fields previously pre-empted by men. Self-fulfillment in other ways, including sexual freedom, may also give them "happiness." But these are in a sense negative factors. They result from contrast with old conventional standards, the satisfaction of fighting for and winning their rights, more than from the glow of the rights themselves.

Will men be happier in the new estate than when they were the binding force in the family unit? My conclusion is the same. They will not be. They will not have to be as surreptitious about their polygamous tendencies, but they will be deprived of the satisfaction of presiding over a growing family, nature's intimate demonstration of the maturing life process until death.

The impermanence of a flitting life is its own defeat. Even the sorrow and disappointments which often beset the family unit are part of the living process. Marriage is not merely a man- (or now, man- and woman-) made convention, but a response to nature's cosmic scheme of herding its inhabitants in units for physical warmth and psychic security. "The true morality is remembering and making visible the tradition that gives you form," wrote André Malraux.

We cannot go back to the old balanced spheres.

The change which has occurred is irreversible. Women's involvement in activities which were previous male monopolies was inevitable. It resulted in part from universal education. Did anyone expect that we would send our daughters to college, broaden their horizons of life, stimulate their cultural ambitions, and then have them follow the confined paths of their grandmothers? Entirely apart from economic motivation, women felt suffocated by the roles assigned to them in marriage.

So a new balance of spheres will have to be accepted by partners in marriage, if the institution is to survive. Men will have to recognize and enjoy the new role of women in society, without considering it an abandonment of their duty to home and children. Women will have to recognize that their independence is not inconsistent with their dependence on the strength of their husbands, and that their "rights" may well be voluntarily sacrificed in sufficient measure to devote themselves personally to their children, for their psychological health, as well as that of the marriage. It has even been suggested that the Government should aid by giving tax benefits and child care allowances to working mothers, to encourage direct parental guidance. Other adjustments will be found, just as we must find them in a new technological era which has severed old customs and traditions in many other fields.

My guess is that the new moral structure will lose the glamour of its sophisticated order, and that we will somehow find our way back to the family unit tradition. The glories and beauty of its commitment cannot be found in any other way. "Repetition is the only form of permanence that nature can provide," wrote Émile Zola.

Even the old horrors were less than those which accompanied the escape from confinement.

AND A CHILD SHALL DESTROY THEM

This is the story of a man who was convicted of sexually abusing a child.

Although I have been involved in all manner of litigations, this case created more emotional impact than almost any other I can recall. It also presents the old question, what is justice? Do we take the hard road of protecting the accused by insisting on his innocence unless overwhelming evidence is presented, or the sympathetic road of protecting the accuser even though his testimony is uncorroborated? How does the law deal with a child who accuses? What is justice in such a case? Does the jury system go wrong at times? If so, how can it be corrected? Do those who cannot afford outstanding counsel and appeals have a remedy? These and other vital questions in the judicial system were all raised in the melodrama which follows.

John Bateman (I shall call him) and his wife and three young sons lived in their own comfortable house in a suburban area. They were a model family, a unit of what economists and orators proclaim "the great middle class, the backbone of the nation." Bateman was employed by a large corporation situated in the city, and one could tell the precise time of the day by the train he caught every morning, after his car had been parked at the station. Consistent with this American apple pie picture of life was his hobby. He loved baseball. There was devotion to the home teams which exceeded that of their owners and players. He knew batting averages better than they knew attendance figures and receipts. This and a sense of service to the community led him to be active in Little League baseball.

He became president of it, an honor his neighbors conferred upon him because of his dedication to the venture and his fatherly supervision of the kids.

One day, a bomb destroyed his house. It was not a dynamite bomb, but the effect was even more devastating. It was the appearance of two policemen who arrested him on the felony charge of having sexually abused a young boy.

What is more sensational than an accusation of sexual perversion? It has all the ingredients of a Jekyll-Hyde story—the normal-looking man, but inside him lurks an evil creature. It is the oldest mystery and the oldest plot. Appearances are not what they seem to be. Since all of us have suppressed yearnings, we are ready to believe the worst in people.

Perhaps they are enacting what some of us have only thought. That is why rape stories seem more believable to men than they should be, and why the victim is looked upon with skepticism by women, when the rapist says he was enticed. While this is not as true of sexual abuse of a homosexual nature, except to the relatively small minority of men with homosexual leanings, the general inclination to believe in animalistic tendencies, under the civilized veneer, creates a prejudice in all sex cases.

The charge against Bateman jumped from the police blotter to the front pages of the local newspapers, and from there to the large circulation city press. The story received lurid touches as if a monster had been discovered in the midst of a normal community.

The Bateman house, which previously was unidentifiable in a uniform row, suddenly stood out alone in the spotlight of publicity. The glare enveloped Constance Bateman and her three children. It had the numbing effect of a shock ray. It dulled them to pain for a while. Then continuous tears washed away the narcotic impact and they were immersed in shame and humiliation. Constance struggled to prevent a nervous collapse. The terrible revelation was the topic of conversation in every home and store, and was carried in sonorous or hushed tones by radio and television announcers. To the Batemans, every head on the street became a wagging head; every gesture, a pointing finger. It was a relief not to sleep because nightmares of jail cells, ruin, and death were thus avoided.

A local attorney was retained. He assured the Batemans that the prosecutor's case was flimsy. Without any preparation in depth, he answered ready for trial.

The prosecutor requested that all witnesses be excluded from the courtroom. This was granted. The theory is that witnesses should not be able to accommodate their own testimony to what they have heard from others. In criminal cases particularly, this precaution is taken.

The prosecutor called the accusing child, Walter, to the stand. He was ten years old, blond, handsome, and well spoken—a very appealing witness. Despite his youth, he was sworn in, because he understood the meaning of an oath. Then under guidance of the prosecutor he told his story.

He had gone to watch his father umpire a championship game between Little League clubs. After the game, he made arrangements with
Bateman's son to come to the Bateman home and stay overnight. This
was a customary practice in the community. Children slept over in the
homes of their friends.

Walter's father drove him to the Bateman home about seven-thirty
in the evening. Mrs. Bateman called his mother to be sure she approved
of Walter's night out. She did. Walter was invited to have dinner with
the family, but he had already eaten. So, he watched television, and
then played Ping-Pong and ran a train set with the Bateman boys.

The time came to go to sleep. He and one of the Bateman boys
shared the same room in separate beds. Before putting the crucial question to the young witness, the prosecutor asked him if he could identify
the defendant in the courtroom. The boy pointed unerringly to Bateman. It was the smallest but most damaging finger among the many
which actually or in his imagination Bateman had faced. Then came
the question:

Q: Now, tell us what you recall about what happened after you
went to bed?

A: Well, we went to bed and I was just dozing off. Mr. Bateman
came in the room and he came over to my bed and he pulled down
the covers and pulled down my pajama bottoms and touched my bottom.

Q: What do you mean by your bottom?

A: My backside.

Q: Please continue.

A: Then he kept touching my forehead like this.

Q: For how long?

A: I don't know—seemed like a pretty long time.

Q: Had he said anything to you or did you say anything to him at
this point?

A: No.

Q: What happened then?

A: He pulled my pajama bottoms partially up and kept the covers
down and went out of the room.

Q: What happened then?

A: He came back in the room.

Q: What happened then?

A: He came in the room, did the same thing. This time, touched
my penis.

Q: What did he do with his hand?

A: Just rubbed it.

Q: For how long?

A: I don't know. Seemed kind of shorter than the first time.

Q: What happened then?

A: He touched my forehead again. He kept touching it, touching my penis. Then he left the room.

He came back a third time but left without coming near him. In the meantime, the Bateman boy was sleeping peacefully in the other bed.

In the morning, Walter ate breakfast with the Bateman boy and was driven home by Bateman.

Q: Did you say anything to Bateman when he asked you how you slept?

A: I said fine.

That was it. The prosecutor called no other witnesses.

The defense called Mrs. Bateman to the stand. Warnings by her own attorney to keep her voice up indicated the nervousness verging on terror that gripped the poor woman who had to defend her husband, her three children, her home, and their future.

She and her husband had "tucked the children in" and together gone to their bedroom for the night. She had shut the door and locked it.

Q: Mrs. Bateman, was there some particular reason why you locked the door?

A: Yes.

Q: What is the reason, Mrs. Bateman?

A: We purchased a king-size bed that was delivered that morning, a gigantic bed and we had discussed all day the fact that as soon as the kids went to bed, the first thing we wanted to do was to go to bed.

Q: Now, Mrs. Bateman, did your husband leave the room?

A: No, he did not leave the room.

The new bed continued to play a part in the story. The next morning, Bateman, his boys, and Walter rode to the local dump to drop off the old mattress and spring. Walter drove back to the Bateman home, and played with the children. There was no accusation or protest made by him for what he later claimed was an unwarranted "touching." Bateman drove him home.

Q: Mrs. Bateman, have Walter's parents called you at any time after this occasion?

A: No.

Then the defendant himself faced the jury. He gave his age, thirty-five, the ages of his three children: ten and a half, nine, and six and a half. Even during these preliminaries he was trembling. "Keep your voice up," he was told. Later, "You have a tendency to drop your voice and the jurors will not hear you." He and his wife tucked in the children, kissed them, said good night, and went to their own room. "I believe I even remember telling Walter the bathroom is down the hall if you have to use it."

Q: Did you go down and pull down the covers and pull down his pajamas?

A: No sir. I did not.

Q: Did you touch his buttocks and his penis?

A: No sir. I did not.

Q: Mr. Bateman, did you leave your bedroom after you went into it that evening?

A: No sir.

Q: Did you have—did you do anything that particular night, Mr. Bateman?

A: Yes, we had intercourse.

So, the new bed, waiting to be tested, played its role for the defense. Natural passions kept the defendant in his room. It made it even more unlikely that Bateman would go wandering downstairs for new sensations.

Bateman's testimony about Walter's behavior when he rode him home the following morning was so inconsistent with the accusation that someone had to be inventing a fanciful tale. He testified that Walter said, "Thanks a lot, Mr. Bateman, I had a great time."

The prosecutor sought to extract a conversation which Bateman had with one Armstrong, to whom he was supposed to have said that Walter did not hate him, thus implying forgiveness or consent. They fenced a long time about this supposed conversation, and then:

Q: Are you able to quote Armstrong precisely? What did he say about this matter?

A: I am able to quote him precisely.

Q: Quote him.

A: He said this whole thing is a "Crock of s—t."

It was on this inelegant note that the testimony ended.

After summations and the Judge's charge, the jury retired to deliberate. An hour and fifteen minutes later, it returned.

THE COURT: Mr. Foreman, would you please announce your verdict?

FOREMAN: We find the defendant guilty.

Later, after a probation report, Bateman appeared for sentence. He said to the court, "I absolutely never touched that child or any child in my entire life."

Because of his previous impeccable record, he was sentenced to "probation for one year, on condition that he undergo psychiatric evaluation and treatment as deemed necessary."

There are cases in which the degree of sentence doesn't matter. Condemnation as a child abuser deepened the tragedy. In a sense it was a life sentence. It would have been easier to wash away bloodstains than the stigma of a jury verdict. Unless he and his family fled the community to seek anonymity in some distant place, how could they ever escape the shame with which they had been branded? The compulsory psychiatric treatment only confirmed his perversity. If he complied and took treatment, he would be confessing his illness.

The Batemans were as desperate as they were numb.

It was at this point that the president of the company for which Bateman worked appealed to me to look into the matter. The fact that his employer for ten years had faith in him, and made an emotional appeal to save him and his family, impressed me.

So it was that Bateman and his wife sat in front of my desk. Their faces were drained and drawn. Their eyes half closed from swelling. Their voices quivered and broke so that they couldn't talk. It was a heartbreaking scene of noncommunication. I asked for the stenographic minutes of the trial, which request gave them hope. After ministering to them with assurance that no problem was hopeless and that they must not permit the enlarged shadows of their own fears to undermine their ability to resist, I asked them to return after we had studied the record.

When we reviewed the trial in cold type, we discovered a number of startling things. For the first time, we understood what had gone wrong.

It began with the selection of the jury, a process called the voir dire. The prosecutor's examination of would-be jurors took sixty-five pages of the record. The defendant's counsel did not ask a single question. He left this critical phase of the proceeding entirely in the unfriendly hands of the District Attorney.

So, it came about that a jury was selected which was predisposed to convict Bateman. The technique used by the prosecutor was to challenge any juror if he indicated that he would examine a child's testimony with care. This, as we shall see, is the law.

Nevertheless, the prosecutor excused seven out of fourteen jurors who as a matter of common sense expressed such caution. One juror said "it would be truthfully hard" to convict anyone beyond a reasonable doubt solely upon the testimony of a child. She was out. Even though another conceded that he would convict if he "firmly believed" the boy, the "firmly" was too much risk for the prosecutor. He excused him. To make matters worse, these jurors were excused "for cause." There was no just cause, such as admitted prejudice, acquaintance with the parties or lawyers, or refusal to follow the law as directed by the Judge. The prosecutor could only have exercised a "peremptory challenge" against such a juror—namely without cause but for psychological reasons. Peremptory challenges are limited to three—sometimes as high as four or five. Challenges for cause are unlimited. In this case the prosecutor exercised an excessive number of peremptory challenges by falsely designating them "for cause," all without an objection by defense counsel. The enormity of this process was capped by the following question put to the jurors by the prosecutor:

"Do I have your assurance that if you find there is a failing of proof or the defense does not meet the law, that you will find Mr. Bateman guilty? Do you all understand that?"

Still no objection by the defense to this garbled and inaccurate statement.

What a jury. It was about as impartial as the juror who was asked whether he believed in capital punishment. "Generally no," he replied, "but in this case, yes."

The selection of jurors should be as much a "contest" between the lawyers as the testimony of a witness. Prejudices are thus detected and eliminated, not perfectly, but substantially. But for one side to default in the choosing of a jury is to distort the process as much as if one side defaulted on all testimony offered by the other. It is even worse, because the jurors are the judges of the facts. Bateman was doomed before the trial began.

To add oversight to neglect, the defense did not call a single character witness. In view of the fact that Walter, ten years old, was the only witness for the prosecutor, and his credibility was thus pitted against that of Mr. and Mrs. Bateman, what could be more helpful than to have leading members of the community speak highly of the Batemans' probity?

The issue was simply who was to be believed? This is the classic reason why, in criminal cases, character witnesses are permitted. The philosophy is that the reputation for truthfulness, which the accused has earned during his life, is a proper weight in the scales of justice. Since the defendant must be proven guilty beyond a reasonable doubt, character testimony may just tip the scale in his favor.

The other approach to the battle of credibility is to attack the accusing witness's reputation for veracity. Nothing was done about this, either. So the defendant did not utilize his weapons in the duel of truthfulness. He neither buttressed his own story nor attempted to undermine the accuser's. The irony of it all was that there was brilliant opportunity for both.

When we announced that we would undertake the appeal, we sought to tap the community's support. The very process of approach and open inquiry cleansed the atmosphere. No accused person should slink away. I advised him to conduct himself as he always had; go to business, to the theater, and keep social engagements. Even if one is innocent, this is hard to do. The sensitive have shame. They believe that appearing in public is brazen and calloused. Nevertheless they must overcome their hermit-ism. Human beings, like other animals, smell fear, and conclude guilt therefrom. The public responds to those who are not crushed by adversity. It is difficult to instruct a client how to look when he emerges after a not-guilty plea. Should he be jaunty? Then he is not sensitive to his plight. Should he look solemn? Then he may register the pressure of guilt. Should he just smile, indicating confidence? This is usually best, but it depends on the person who must carry off the mood so as to be natural.

The Batemans' sensitivity caused their friends to avoid them. Probably it was out of a desire not to force themselves upon them in their hour of distress. What looked like walking on the other side of the street when they saw him turned out to be an effort to avoid the embarrassment of confrontation. It is an open question whether expressions of sympathy do not deepen the wound. Cripples resent being given special privileges. It makes them conscious of their infirmities. What is more humiliating to a proud man than to be told how sorry everyone is for his plight? So when Bateman and my law partner William Reilly frontally approached Bateman's neighbors and asked them whether they would submit affidavits giving their opinions of him, they responded eagerly. The expressed relief that they could assist him because to a man, woman, and child they did not believe a word of Walter's accusation. We gathered in sixty-five pages of affidavits by twenty-six leading citizens of the community. Their laudatory statements about Bateman's integrity and honesty of word contained such words as "impeccable," "top-drawer," "outstanding," "spotless," "excellent," "100 per cent," "superb," "very good," "of the highest." Some who knew him well praised him as a good father and family man. Ten persons stated that despite the conviction they had no hesitancy in permitting their children to stay overnight in the Bateman home. What better vote of confidence could be given than that?

Immediately after Bateman was indicted, he resigned as president of the Little League. The directors hesitated to accept his resignation, but were pushed hard by interviewers who provocatively wanted to know how a man accused of molesting children could hold such a post. The directors evaded the challenge by giving assurance that they would "do the right thing." However, deriving courage from the community's favorable response, the directors rode the momentum to the following resolution by a vote of twenty-two to three:

We firmly believe in John Bateman's innocence and feel we are compelled by our consciences to support him and retain him as our president.

We consider that a conviction based on the uncorroborated testimony of a ten-year old is insufficient ground for Mr. Bateman's removal. We believe John Bateman will be vindicated, completely and irrevocably.

It is difficult enough to restrain the "mob spirit" of condemnation after an indictment, but to receive such an accolade after conviction was a unique tribute to Bateman. What character witnesses could have been paraded at his trial!

This acceptance of Bateman's credibility was automatically a rejection of his young accuser's story. There must have been reason for this, too. We turned our search in the other direction. What was Walter's history? Interviews with the neighborhood's children and parents resulted in affidavits that he was considered by many of the youngsters to be "weird," "strange," a "kook," "a bully," "liar," "cheater," "troublemaker," and "flaky." He was known to be extremely hot-tempered. Some parents would not allow their children to play with him.

On one occasion, "Walter put a rope around the neck of a boy in front of him in the classroom and pulled it with both hands, resulting in a visible mark on his neck. The teacher sent the injured child to see the school nurse."

So this was the angelic child whom the jury believed!

Even a jury prejudiced in his favor might have thought twice had these facts been developed on cross-examination and by affirmative testimony. Without the ugly colors filled in, the youngster appeared lily white.

Not all clues are physical. Great detectives achieve their triumphs from psychological insights. But the law does not recognize inferences drawn from speculation. It insists on hard facts. Our investigation turned up an incident, which though remote and irrelevant in a legal sense, revealed Walter's possible motive for telling an elaborate lie.

Several weeks before he slept over at the Bateman home, a child had been molested in a nearby supermarket. The attack caused a sensation in the community. The molester had escaped, but his victim, to those who knew who he was, became the center of sympathetic attention. He was a schoolmate of Walter's. Is it possible that this planted a seed in

Walter's mind that he could become "prominent" if he made a similar claim?

After the complaint was filed against Bateman, the police called him to a "lineup" for possible identification as the molester in the supermarket. He was completely cleared by witnesses, but he suffered the ignominy of the suspicion that he was a repeat offender on the loose.

When our investigations were completed, we faced the question of how to use them. If what we discovered was new evidence, a motion could be made to open the case. But it was not.

To qualify as new evidence, it must not have been previously available. If a reasonable effort would have discovered it before trial, then its use was forbidden to obtain a new trial.

Typical illustrations of new evidence are the discovery of a witness whom no one had heard of, but who turns up with vital knowledge after the trial; or a document found in a vault, which no one knew anything about, but which comes to light after the trial.

In the Bateman case, there was no doubt that diligent effort could have resulted in obtaining for use at the trial the testimony we elicited after the verdict. Therefore, what we had was informative and provocative but it was not new evidence in the legal sense. The neighbors were known. Their children were known. No one had sought them out. The new affidavits could not be used.

This is not technical folderol, as some laymen might suspect. Unless such a rule existed, it would pay to withhold important evidence in every case. If one won on the limited evidence presented, well and good. If not, there would be a second trial, and perhaps a third and fourth, by trotting out evidence not previously offered, and calling it new evidence. To prevent two or more bites at every trial cherry, the test is "Wasn't this evidence reasonably available to you originally? If you were too confident or too careless to prepare more thoroughly, that is not the court's fault. There must be an end somewhere to a litigation. As it is, the judicial process is extended enough."

But justice finds wondrous ways its miracles to perform. We had a plan to overcome the obstacle. It consisted of three steps.

First, the record of the appeal had to be enlarged to include the affidavits. Otherwise they could not even be mentioned. Appeals are limited to the original testimony. Counsel cannot go "outside the record." He cannot present evidence which was not ruled upon by the original trial judge. If the testimony was not in the record and subject to cross-examination, it is out. The reason is similar to that for newly discovered evidence. Why struggle to present a full case in the lower court if you can augment it on appeal? Also the trial judge's rulings on dismissal, based on the testimony at the trial, could not properly be reviewed on appeal if one could add new testimony at the appellate level which the lower court did not have before it. So, to assure ourselves of having the trial record properly broadened for appeal, we made a motion for a new trial based on our affidavits. When this motion was denied, we appealed *both* from the original jury verdict and the motion denying a new trial. The record was thus enlarged so that the affidavits were in the printed record.

Second, we argued on appeal that even if the affidavits did not qualify as new evidence, they ought to be considered because there was an exception to the new evidence rule. It was this: if trial counsel's carelessness or ineptitude was of such magnitude that a great injustice may have occurred, the courts would disregard the customary rule. We told the appellate court, "We are loath to criticize trial counsel's inadequate representation of his client," but the issue was justice, and in this case an accumulation of errors had resulted in an injustice. There must be a remedy. It existed in the exception we cited. The affidavits should be considered and evaluated.

The third step in our plan was to contend that the guilty verdict must be reversed as a matter of law and irrespective of the facts.

This led us to a discussion of the law. What should the rule be concerning sex offenders of children? Should any person be convicted of a morals charge on the uncorroborated testimony of an infant? The answer is, no. Some corroboration, some substantiation, in addition to the infant's word, must be presented.

Otherwise, none of us would be safe from the imaginative and sometimes malicious irresponsibility of infants who are generally disposed to inventive lies. Child psychologists consider fantasizing, stimulated by budding sexual urges, quite normal. Walter might have had an erotic dream and ascribed "the rubbing" to Bateman. Or he may have masturbated after Bateman tucked him in and associated him with the act.

No man or woman who permitted a child to sleep over would be safe from a child's uncorroborated story of immoral tampering. The law considered the risk too great. So the highest appellate court in New York had held that "no conviction for impairing the morals of a child may validly rest on the uncorroborated testimony of the child victim" (*People* v. *Porcaro*).

We must remember that we are not dealing with an ordinary claim, but with a criminal charge which, because it involves sexual abuse of a child, is particularly inflammatory and evokes feelings of horror. The degradation of the accused is so great that it may well destroy him and his family. Any criminal accusation must be proved beyond a reasonable doubt. How can the unsupported word of an infant satisfy such a standard?

We cited cases in which the evidence was more substantial than that against Bateman, but which the courts held did not meet the test of "proof more than usually clear and convincing." So, for example, in one case (Churgen), the court commented that the ten-year-old female complainant "told a logical, sensible story, and told it well. She was not contradicted the least bit on cross-examination. Except for the age of the child, I seldom have seen a better witness." But there was no corroboration. The conviction was reversed.

Children can be persuasive liars. Their innocence and open-eyed guilelessness can be misleading. Their imagination becomes reality to them and constitutes truth. Their story is therefore less vulnerable to contradiction than the conscious lie of a mature person. Also, a child's malice can be more virulent than a mature person's because it is not inhibited by the tolerance of experience. One court expressed it this way: "There have been countless instances in which children have been known to invent morals charges against individuals who have never been near them." In another case (*People* v. *Oyola*) the court wrote: "It is time that the courts awakened to the sinister possibilities of injustice that lurk in believing an infant witness without careful psychiatric scrutiny."

A leading textbook on evidence (Professor John Henry Wigmore) comments: "The most dangerous witness in prosecutions for morality offenses are the youthful ones (often mere children) in whom the sex-instinct holds the foremost place in their thoughts and feelings. It is just such witnesses that often throw suspicion recklessly on the most worthy persons."

Judge Stanley Fuld, a former prosecutor under Tom Dewey, commented on this quotation, "Anyone who has had experience in prosecuting this type of case can document this observation with graphic illustrations."

The enlarged evidence demonstrated that Walter might well be a "disturbed" young boy. Wasn't the conviction of Bateman solely on this infant's testimony a perversion of justice?

The appellate court unanimously held that it was. It not only reversed the verdict of guilty, but dismissed the complaint in its entirety as unworthy of a new trial.

The District Attorney's office announced that it would not appeal. It even made some amends for its prior pursuit of an unworthy cause by consenting to eliminate the record from the files, so that there would not remain a trace of the disgrace.

I once had a client who became rich by taking waste sludge remaining after oil was refined, and, instead of dumping it in the marshes, mixed it with oils and used it for paving roads, making boards and other products. The residue turned out to be almost as valuable as the original product.

I think of certain trials that way. There were frustrating residues from the Bateman case, but with thought they have instructive value. A number of questions raised about the judicial system are exemplified by that case. Can a good case be lost by a bad lawyer or a bad case won by a good lawyer? Unfortunately the answer is "yes." If a trial was God-ordained and controlled (as the priests thought who determined guilt or innocence by putting the accused's arm in boiling water, and after incantation seeing whether there was a burn), then human intervention by the lawyer would not affect the result. Justice could be self-executing. The truth would prevail. It would not be subject to the vagaries of diligent preparation, and the myriad insights and skills of the art of persuasion. But since our judicial system, like any other enterprise, is administered by men and women, whatever robes they wear, it is subject to the frailties which beset all human activity.

Consider the jury. It is a magnificent device to determine the facts. Its common sense is as good a guide as we have ever found. But its decision can only be sound if the critical evidence is presented on both sides. If one litigant or the other fails in his duty to put vital evidence before the jury, its decision will be a distortion of the truth. The verdict may be a correct reading of the scales, and yet be unjust because many weights were missing.

The Bateman case is a good illustration. The jury was subjected to limited stimuli. Its decision might have been right, based on what it heard. But how much it had not heard! Also, we have seen how in the selection of the jury the defendant's counsel sat back in silence while the very balance of the scale was being tested.

Since the jury is the microcosm of democracy, the lesson learned here can be magnified to throw some light on the national scene. The voting public is a jury. If the crucial facts are put before it, its decision is as reliable as any which can be attained by any other method. But if because of illiteracy, or demagogic exploitation of literacy, or imbalanced presentations, the public-jury has inadequate or mangled information, its verdict can be correctly erroneous; correct on the facts known to it, and incorrect on the total picture. Fortunately this is as infrequent in elections as it is in jury trials.

This view of democracy also indicates why it cannot prosper in soil unprepared for it. It is a sensitive mechanism requiring sophisticated preconditions. It cannot be imposed on emerging countries which haven't a minimum base of education and experience in self-government. Tried too soon, it can result in pillage and rape.

Can we eliminate the defect of partial presentation either in the court or in the political arena? Never. We can only minimize it and thus achieve an approximation of justice. We must have tolerance for that amount of failure which is unavoidable in the human condition. While at the same time we can fulfill our idealistic yearnings by closing the gap between "the impossible" and "the attainable."

Although democracy is far from perfect, it has functioned brilliantly. Witness the two centuries of our country. Despite the nation's infant and mature diseases, scandals from Grant to Harding to Nixon, and enormous growth with its attendant complexities, we have preserved our liberties while becoming the most prosperous and powerful country in history.

Similarly, with all of its faults, our judicial system is still as good, if not better, than any other in the world.

We can attain the most civilized view of any issue by confessing the defects of what we praise, and praising the virtues without resigned satisfaction.

Striving for improvement is gratifying even if unsuccessful. That is why those who sacrifice for a cause are almost never defeated. The effort makes them feel noble and becomes an end in itself. This explains why we will never lack idealists. They are involved in a guaranteed enterprise.

In this spirit let us acknowledge and resolve:

Perfect justice—impossible. Approximate justice—acceptable. Efforts to make justice more perfect—always.

FRIENDLY INEFFICIENCY

There is understandable disdain for people who visit a remote country, like China or Russia, for a few weeks, and return experts. But this does not mean that their observations are valueless. I liken such a trip to a photograph sent by wireless from overseas. It is composed of hundreds of dots of dark and light shades which form a face. If the picture is enlarged sufficiently, one can actually see the dots, in their meaningful formations.

In 1971, as counsel for the Motion Picture Association of America, Inc., I accompanied a committee of stars and executives to a film festival in Moscow. For so many years, I had read about and discussed Russia, "the riddle wrapped in a mystery inside an enigma." Now I was there. Surely the vastness of the land and profusion of hard and soft curtains behind the Iron Curtain made impossible any profound conclusions. But each moment my eye detected a dot. Ultimately there were many dots. They formed an image, even if vague because not complete. I record these dots through these words.

Upon our arrival in Moscow, we, like so many other visitors, were immediately impressed with what would stamp every moment of our stay in Russia—its inefficiency. Although there were interpreters, the porters were endlessly confused about our bags. It took many hours to move out of the airport. We were confronted with similar delays in registering at the hotel, getting into the room, or doing anything else. Some friends who had arrived earlier gave us the password: "Be patient and smile." It was not too difficult to practice this advice, because the colossal waste of time and confusion were not due to hostility or laziness. It was pure, sweating, friendly inefficiency.

In the prime old Moscow hotel, the Moskva, the room was dingy with a bare wooden cupboard of a closet and beds that looked like wooden cots. One wouldn't mind their hardness (there was only some kind of an imitation of a mattress), but who wanted to sleep on a *curved* hard board? The quilt was enclosed in a white sheet with an oval cutout which permitted the color underneath to make a design. This was apparently deemed to be fetching, because in the brand new Rossiya Hotel, the same hard beds and cutout quilts were used. Perhaps it was not a matter of style but of necessity. But even in the Rossiya, the new carpets in the hallways looked like billows. They didn't know how to lay carpets. Someday when there have been some accidents, they will probably import an expert.

The Moskva favored hanging electric bulbs rather than chandeliers, but it had a prize in the "bedroom-parlor"—a television set. Its screen was eight inches and its wooden box was exactly like the oldest Amos and Andy model of a radio when it first appeared in the United States. Sound sometimes mysteriously came out of the set even when it was turned off. This heightened the uneasiness of the bugging in each room, about which we had been fully warned. That rooms are bugged was no illusion. I had the occasion to speak to several Russian artists and newspapermen. They pointed to the ceiling and motioned silence, then took me to the street. The cumulative, depressing effect of this, upon one accustomed to privacy in his home, must be experienced to be fully realized. And this was the new, liberalized Russia.

The bathroom had a huge tub, but we had been advised to bring our own stopper. For some reason, they didn't supply them. But there were two large rough brushes for shoes. This might be a holdover from the days of muddy streets and caked boots. The soap, a luxury not supposed to be there, was a one-inch square which looked like red wax and was unusable. The plumbing worked infrequently, but made up for its delinquency by tremendous noise.

The hotels had no central switchboard. Each room had its own telephone and separate number. Unless one had everybody's individual room number, it was impossible to connect. Whether all this was due again to inefficiency or for reasons of security was hard to figure out. But it may help to know that upon leaving your room, you had to leave your key with a woman at a desk which guarded the entrance to each floor. Thus, your absence from your room was at all times known. When you returned, the woman could not understand the number of the key which you requested. But here was the first sign of business ingenuity. She had a list with numbers on it, and you pointed to the number of your room. This was one of the shortest operations in my stay in Russia.

The telephone was generally a nightmare. This was not so merely for foreigners. Our embassy officials who talked the native language motioned with resigned exasperation, subdued by long experience, when they hung up again and again because the busy signal a second ago was

followed by no answer, and then busy again. It could take fifteen minutes to a half hour to make an ordinary telephone call.

On entering the country, one had to declare all currency and jewelry,
and account therefore meticulously when leaving. One bought coupons
which were used as currency to pay for meals. The result was another
maddening delay while the waiter computed the bill and translated the
price into coupons. Frequently, he brought an abacus to the table to
help him make the addition. It did no good to offer an extra coupon or
two, to avoid the delay. Earnestly, he figured away, while sweat broke
out on his brow, and good-naturedly he told you he must finish. So
every lunch or dinner was delayed an extra half hour or more to go
through the mathematical gyrations.

The menu, in all but a few special restaurants, was the same: caviar
or sturgeon, borsch, hot or cold, fish or chicken, black bread, fruit com-
pote served in a glass, ice cream, and tea or turkish coffee. The food was
edible but not good, and one soon learned that the best thing to order
was an omelet. Even the caviar and vodka were not of the best, because
the prime quality was shipped out as an invaluable export. The ice
cream was exceptionally good and this brought about the question,
why? In the 1930s when Anastas Mikoyan visited the United States, he
tasted ice cream for the first time. He became a devotee of it and ate
pints at a time. He arranged for an expert to come to Russia, build a
plant, and provide the formulas. So, the ice cream in Moscow was better than in London, Paris, or Copenhagen. It was universally popular.
Stands on the streets sold ice cream to the multitudes, who walked
along sucking their cones.

I wandered out at night and within a few blocks came across Red
Square in front of the Kremlin. Whether it was the hugeness of the
cobblestone square which was so impressive or the recognition of the familiar site which newsreels had depicted year after year, filled with endless arrays of marching soldiers, ponderous tanks, and missile carriers, I
could not be certain. My imagination filled the empty platform above
Lenin's tomb with figures of the past, Malenkov, Timoshenko, Beria,
Malinovsky, Mikoyan, Stalin, Khrushchev, and others whose ill-cut suits
were topped with fedora hats, which looked too large contrasted with
the military splendor below. To the right of the tomb were white rows
of low horizontal benches, not wide enough to sit on. They acted as
markers for prominent standees.

The square and streets were deserted, except for a bundle of people
who had gathered in front of Lenin's tomb. I soon learned the reason.
It was almost midnight, and a ceremony was about to take place in
which two guards, facing each other stiffly at the entrance, were to be
replaced. Suddenly, I heard tromp, tromp, tromp. Three Russian sol-

diers, two in front, one behind, were approaching from the tower, about a hundred yards to the left. To my surprise, they were doing a perfect Nazi goose step. Their legs shot out in a straight line as if they had no knees, and came down with tremendous force on the echoing stone. They carried guns with gleaming bayonets in their left hands, while their right hands swung in an automatic semicircle across their stomachs and back again. When they had made a left angle turn and marched to the tomb's entrance, one soldier stood tight against the door. At that precise moment, the clock on the tower struck twelve. The two guards were replaced and the three goose-stepped back, hammering their heels into the stone so that the clanging noise again echoed through the square. The two new guards had become part of the immobile stone façade. On another day, when I visited the tomb, I noticed that an overseer wiped the sweat off the nose and forehead of one of the guards, who could not move, nor even blink an eye.

Why the Russians should adopt the Nazi goose step, which evoked the memory of 22 million of their people killed by Hitler, or why they should engage in a royal ceremonial for the father of the proletariat regime, which made the changing of the guard in London an informal affair, were among the enigmas which abounded in this land.

The knot of people who had watched the ceremony untied and disappeared. But my attention was attracted to a woman dressed in white party clothes, with a bouquet in her hands, exchanging shrill words with a Russian policeman. He had fined her for some transgression and she was protesting. Her two friends, dressed like her, and with bouquets in their hands too, were trying to mollify her, but she would have none of it. Another policeman appeared. She was put in their car and driven off. Before we had completed the circle of the square, the car was back. A large black police wagon had arrived. She was now thoroughly subdued, as she was transferred into it, and her two friends were taken along for good measure. I wondered what would happen to them.

The courts in Russia were presided over by a judge and two laymen who flanked him. However, if the charge was of a political character, the judge sat alone. He was then acknowledgedly not objective. He became the arm of the government and was virtually the prosecutor.

Still I was heartened by the woman's audacity. In Stalin's day, could such an incident have occurred? Even this little zephyr of protest pointed to the relaxation of the former absolute tyranny.

At the end of Red Square was St. Basil's Cathedral. It was built by one of the czars to commemorate the victory over the Tartars when they were driven out of the land. The war consisted of nine battles, and so there are nine chapels in the church. It is the outside of the structure which is fantastic. It consists of turnip-shaped towers, one above and beside the other in haphazard architectural imagery. Each turret is striped with curved gold and green lines, in barbershop design. The top of the Byzantine array is a dome covered with gold which shines blindingly in the sun. At night it is favored by dozens of spotlights which light the square. The effect is as if Disney had built a fairy church for one of his cartoons. It is garishly beautiful. The Russians use their night lighting effectively. The huge red star over the highest tower in the Kremlin against the blue-black sky and St. Basil's sparkling turrets create a magical scene of colored moonlight on the empty square.

The next day I visited Lenin's tomb. It was vacation time and a million Russians come to Moscow each day. The chief attraction was to see Lenin in the flesh. To understand the impact of this event, imagine that we had been able to preserve the body of Washington or Lincoln, and you could see them as they were on the day they died. Even this fails to convey the emotion which gripped the visitors. For Lenin was more than the father of the revolution and of the state. In a country where "religion is the opiate of the people," he had taken on the role of a god. To many Russians, looking at Lenin was almost as profound an experience as if a Christian could see the face of Christ.

The single line of viewers was like a rope which snaked its way through many bustling city blocks and finally reached Red Square. Tourists, accompanied by an official guide, were cut into this line at the outer end of the square. It was then only a half-hour wait as the rope slowly moved into the tomb.

Originally, the tomb was constructed of wood. Later it was replaced by a dark red marble structure built in severe, modernistic simplicity, in contrast to the curving colored spires of St. Basil.

Finally, I was inside the semidark building. A hushed silence enveloped me, except for the noise of shuffling feet, as I descended several small flights of steps. The day was hot, but the temperature dropped precipitously as I approached the crypt itself and it was quite cold. As I followed the barely discernible figures in front, I suddenly saw suspended above us in mid-air (the dark marble on which it rested could not yet be seen), the glass-enclosed body of Lenin, brilliantly lit by spotlights within. The stairs led up to the level of the body, across a short platform and down a flight toward the exit. This afforded a view of Lenin from all sides. Dimly I now discerned at the bottom of the pit on both sides four soldiers guarding the glass coffin.

Lenin lay in formal dark clothes, his head on a red pillow. His pate and face were a healthy pink and white color. So were his hands, the only other flesh visible. They lay on his thighs, the fingers of his left hand straight and those of his right curved under in graceful pose. His beard was neatly trimmed. He was expressionless and the glowing flesh belied the inertness of death. Even allowing for the cosmetic skills of an embalmer, it was a miracle of preservation. It aroused skepticism. Why had no other important person been immunized from decay? Why haven't wealthy Russians used the technique to achieve one of man's fondest dreams—permanence of body? Or was the Lenin we saw a wax statue, while underneath lay his decayed remains? Why was the tomb kept noticeably at cool temperature? Perhaps some enterprising writer will pierce the mystery of this preservation of the flesh.

When I emerged, I was in an area between the tomb and the high brick Kremlin wall, which once protected the czars who lived within. It was a graveyard. Buried in this place of honor were great generals, and former officials of the revolutionary regimes. At the head of each grave was a marble column topped by the sculptured head of the deceased. Stalin's grave was at the end of this line, but significantly, his was the only grave without a column or sculptured likeness. Only a bronze plaque revealed his name.

Immediately after his death, he had been placed alongside of Lenin inside the tomb. Soon, however, disenchantment became vocal, when Khrushchev denounced him as a ruthless murderer and madman. Stalin was then ousted from the tomb and buried unceremoniously in the rear. At that he was fortunate. The Russian practice of erasing their fallen heroes from their history books and effecting their nonexistence might still befall Stalin. Obliterating their former leaders is the highest form of ignominy. Stalin's photograph had hung in every office and home. Millions of Stalin banners had fluttered throughout the land. Thousands of statues and busts of him had decorated the squares. One recalled the jest of Stalin's offer of a prize for the best memorial to Pushkin. The winner designed a huge figure of Stalin reading a book by Pushkin.

Upon ascendancy to power, the technique used to be the issuance of banners of Lenin and, in profile alongside him, Stalin. When the royal succession had been sufficiently impressed upon the public, a new banner was issued, Stalin in front and next to him Lenin. Then the final banner—just Stalin. Thereafter, cities, streets, plazas, buildings, parks, rivers, mountains, ships, planes, books—all named after Stalin. Yet now it would be difficult to find a trace of all these. Huge statues of Stalin on foot, on horse, reading proclamations, protecting Moscow with a sword—all have melted into the night and disappeared. On millions of walls discolored squares appear where once his photograph hung. A thirty-year regime has vanished as if it were all a mirage. Probably, future generations will read his name only in foreign books not in

Russia. Mussolini and Hitler went through similar obliteration of their cults heralded by them to be thousand-year empires.

In the Kremlin wall itself, small holes had been cut to contain urns with ashes of other prominent officials who were identified by a covering square bronze plaque. The newest of these was Vladimir Komarov, the astronaut who perished when his capsule's parachute lines became snarled and he crashed.

A tour of Moscow revealed how drab most of the city was. The landscape in the suburbs was scrawny. With the exception of several new housing developments, the buildings were unkempt and candidates for slum status. One soon noticed iron scaffolding of box design around various structures. At first the impression was of a repair operation, but their number (it looked like about 10 per cent of all buildings) elicited an inquiry. One then learned from circumspect sources that, due to defective construction, many buildings constructed in the last ten years crumbled and leaned toward collapse. The scaffolding was a permanent crutch. It was another illustration of Russian inefficiency.

The monotony of the Moscow tour was broken by two sites. The guide registered excitement as she approached them. The first was a huge swimming pool. It was the largest in the world and accommodated thousands. It was shaped like a half grapefruit with quadrants separating one section from another. In the central circle was a high diving board. Each quadrant had its own. On the outer circular edge were roped-off shallow sections. The triangular distance toward the center was also roped. The people paid a small price to enter, and the water was heated in the winter so that even when there was snow on the ground, thousands swam in the pool.

On the road to this circular compartmentalized artificial lake, the guide pointed to hospitals on both sides. One wondered whimsically whether there was a connection between the outdoor winter pool and the hospitals. The Russian people received free hospitalization and medical treatment, in contrast to the punishing costs in hospitals in the United States. In Russia only medicines which were bought outside of the hospital had to be paid for by the individual.

The other attraction of the Moscow tour was the university. It was a large pink brick complex of buildings. We assumed its educational excellence and were impressed by it, but the guide characteristically stressed its size: "If a student went into a different classroom each day, it would take him ten years to get out," she told us triumphantly. Would we think of describing Columbia University or Rockefeller Center this way?

The striving for size was the revelation of the government's struggle to give the impression of a mighty power. Was it motivated by an inner realization of inadequacy? Was it intended to hide the slow progress of a defective inflexible system which could not even solve its agricultural problem in a vast fertile land?

Size. The Russians were completing the largest hotel in all Europe. It would have 3,100 rooms. It was conceded that there was no need for so huge a structure and that economically it was bound to be a disaster. But it was a government project. The public had no right to a reckoning; and the pride in the "largest" was rich reward for a national inferiority complex.

Size. The subway in Moscow had the largest up and down escalators in the world. It took at least three minutes to ascend or descend one at high speed. The guide visibly thrilled as he escorted us on them and observed that we craned our necks to see the bottom or the top, which were so far away as to be out of sight.

Size. Even Russian humor, as Freud would have been quick to point out, stressed the unconscious desire for bigness. The chief comedy routine in the Russian circus was a machine which enlarged anything put into it. One comedian demonstrated it to another by dropping a small comb into a slot. Immediately the other pulled a three-foot comb out of the other end of the machine. Then a small bread roll was placed in it. Out came a four-foot loaf of bread. The astonished comedian had an idea. He ran offstage and to the delight of the audience returned with a small bottle of vodka. The end product was so huge it could not be taken out of the machine. They lifted the entire mechanism to reveal an eight-foot-high bottle of vodka.

What is the explanation for the paradox of colossal inefficiency and a low standard of living side by side with the hydrogen bomb, huge missiles, the largest tank, the most powerful sputnik, the largest jet plane, etc.? The answer is that when the government concentrated all its resources on a particular project, sparing neither expense nor manpower, it could achieve an outstanding prototype. But this did not signal natural growth. There was seldom mass production or simultaneous progress in many directions. If the government could abandon its military concentration, it might solve the fertilizer, tractor, and scientific agricultural problem. Also, size was raw power. Today miniaturization is the key to scientific achievement. The Russians, who were far ahead in space when shooting heavy loads into orbit was the chief requirement, have now dropped out of sight in the "race," because sophisticated complex scientific systems, requiring technological production of the highest order, are the requirement for planetary travel. This they have not got. Indeed, despite the discount which one must give to Egyptian alibis for their humiliating defeat by the Israelis in the 1973 war, one begins to wonder whether there might not be some truth to their claim

that the "advanced" Russian military equipment shot shells in parab-
olas instead of toward the enemy.

The Russians are pragmatists. Those in power are not likely to
deceive themselves. Perhaps this accounts for Russia's withdrawal
whenever frontally confronted. What greater loss of face in full international view could any nation have suffered than when President Kennedy directed their ships on the high seas to be searched for missiles
and sent back, and their missiles in Cuba moved out? They complied.
In the June 1967 Middle-East crisis, when there was danger of a direct
clash with the United States because of Russia's age-old ambition to
control the gateway to three continents, it was Kosygin who used the
Hot Line to the White House for the first time, and assured President
Johnson he would not intervene directly in the conflict.

To what extent do the controlled news media condition the Russian
people against the West? Does impartial news enter the country and
filter through to the masses? Even with full investigative powers, it
would be difficult to reach a definitive answer. But a number of experiences may be significant.

A short while before our trip, Svetlana, Stalin's daughter, had de-
fected to the United States. Then she had enlarged the gesture of flight
by writing a book exposing the tyranny from which she had fled. The
Russian Government took the position that the Svetlana defection and
book were a plot by the United States to spoil Russia's Fiftieth anniversary celebration of the revolution. Russian diplomats made overtures to
our Ambassador Llewellyn Thompson to postpone the publication of
Svetlana's book at least until the jubilee year was over. Although
Thompson, who was highly respected by the Russians and spoke their
language fluently, had assured them that in our country the Government has no power to instruct a publisher what to publish or when,
they remained unconvinced and bitter. The official line was that
Svetlana was crazy and irresponsible. Kosygin, in his interview following
the Glassboro Conference with President Johnson, revealed only two
moments of exploding impatience. One involved a question of anti-
Semitism, and the other Svetlana, whom he deemed to be emotionally
sick. This position seemed to be swallowed without any reflective chewing by every Russian to whom I talked. One well-educated man contemptuously rejected my assertation that the United States Government had no jurisdiction over such a matter. "What would the
publishing company do if it received an order from the President?" he
asked. "It would go to court and have the order annulled," I replied.
"You sue the government?" he exclaimed. "I and others have done it
many times, and won," I replied. If I had been Lenin, he would not
have believed me. He threw up his hands in a gesture of "What's the

use of continuing this discussion when you are spouting ridiculous propaganda and I am talking facts?"

Our guide, an intelligent college student, similarly asserted that Svetlana was mentally sick. When I told him that I had seen and heard her on television and that she was composed and charming, he replied, "Yes, but right after that broadcast, she had to be taken to a hospital." Astonished, I asked, "Where did you get that notion? She was never put in a hospital." "Oh, please!" he said, with an air of great tolerance for my attempt to deceive him.

A Russian newspaperman of great experience, and not without some empathy for the United States, talked earnestly about Vietnam. When I told him that our President had offered to stop the bombing if the Vietcong would come to a discussion table, he demurred, "Then why hasn't he ever said so?" I told him that the President, Vice-President Humphrey, Dean Rusk, and others had on many occasions proclaimed and embraced unconditional talks as a way of ending the conflict; that once the President had unilaterally stopped the bombing for thirty-seven days without a whisper of reciprocation by the Vietcong. His skepticism (to put it mildly) yielded slightly when I offered to mail to him newspaper reports of these events from several countries. He asked particularly for the New York *Times.*

Knowledgeable Americans and others who spend much time in Russia were unanimous in asserting that Voice of America broadcasts were listened to by millions. This was the real penetration of the fog curtain which hides the truth from the people. Those who discovered the factual integrity of these broadcasts, perhaps because they recited adverse news to American interests as well, accepted it and compared it with the monotone of villainy which emanated from Russian radios. Taxis were constantly spouting controlled news. Even if one didn't know the language, he was struck with the continuous use of "Amerikanski." It was obvious that this dinning of hatred of the West into the head behind the wheel, and millions of other Russian heads, could not be easily overcome. Finally, the broadcast turned to music. Ironically it was American jazz and, just coming into vogue, rock and roll. Occasionally, there was a Russian folk song like "*Shatzy,*" which was far more beautiful to my ears.

The artistic level was high in all the arts. We had become familiar with the superb verve and freshness of the Moiseyev Dancing Ensemble, and the classical perfection of the Bolshoi Ballet. When they performed in the United States they were hailed by American audiences as incomparable. Time and again they received ovations. The performers, in a reciprocal gesture of warmth, applauded the audience from the stage. The artistic bridge of comradeship had been significant in several ways. When these troupes of young men and women returned to Russia, did they not recognize the official line of unrelieved anti-Westernism as propaganda and a distortion of the truth? Cultural exchange was not only a proper expression of the internationalism of art, but a leveler on both sides of the boundary walls of prejudice and falsity which poison the people's good will. It was significant that the United States cherished these exchanges. The Russians called them off arbitrarily whenever they wished to heat up the atmosphere of national hatred. So, during the Middle East crises, several tours of the ballet were canceled by Russia.

The Russian circus was a stupendous show. Here tradition played a great part. The Russians had for generations been great tumblers and horsemen. Their feats continued to be incredible. They leaped on and off horses which were circling at top speed. They climbed under the horses' bellies and up on the other side. They held onto the horses' tails and dragged in the sawdust, finally maneuvering under and through the horses' hooves. They did not pretend that these were achievements under the revolutionary regime. They dressed as czarist Cossacks, and waved gleaming sabers, displaying the skills of cavalry fighters in days of old.

The trained bear was another extraordinary tradition. In a comedy act, he rode in an auto, which continuously exploded and poured out frightening smoke. The bear was unperturbed, as he fixed a tire, telephoned for help, and performed with full understanding of the fun involved.

Russian acrobats and tumblers began where most others left off. Triple somersaults, side cartwheels of such speed that the performer became blurred, and man-constructed mountains were performed with such ease that they almost lost their theatrical effect.

Poetry and other forms of writing were flourishing in Russia. The advance was in direct proportion to the defiant declaration of independence by the artist. Many go to jail for their audacity (how many dozens would be incarcerated for life in the United States if lèse majesté of President Johnson had been a crime?), but occasionally there was enough protest internationally to release a victim from torture.

The control of the artistic field fell under the heading of political control. Thus, when the 1967 Moscow Film Festival was planned, all nations were invited to participate. Whether tourism or a policy of lifting the curtain a few inches was the motivation, it became advisable to accept on pain of injuring the sensitivity of Russian leaders. It apparently didn't occur to them that prior restraints might have affected the sensitivity of others.

The State Department officially encouraged the American motion picture industry to send as impressive a delegation as possible. It agreed to do so. But shortly thereafter the Middle East crisis erupted. Suddenly the United States was denounced with more than customary vehemence as a vicious imperialistic mad dog. The tap which trickled friendship had been turned the other way and a torrent of abuse gushed forth. There was consternation in the American delegation. Should we call off our visit and thus turn the good-will mission into one of reciprocal contempt? Some artists and executives found it impossible to attend and withdrew. Nevertheless, it was decided to go through with the venture lest we broaden the breach. The secure must cater to the insecure. There were anticipatory tremors. Would the head of the delegation, Jack Valenti, be marked for humiliation because of his prior association with President Johnson?

The trip came off well. On arrival, the head of the Russian film industry, a government official, was at the airport with Ambassador Thompson to greet us. Flowers were presented to the ladies. At the conclusion of the Festival, Sandy Dennis was awarded a prize as the best actress, and Paul Scofield an award as best actor for his role in *A Man for All Seasons*.

However, there were also petty meannesses. The American entry, *Up the Down Staircase*, which was scheduled to be shown in an evening, was suddenly reduced to an afternoon exhibit. The picture starred Sandy Dennis as a teacher in a problem school in New York. She presided over a class which included neurotic juvenile delinquents, one of whom threatened her with a knife and another with rape. The real assault was on her idealism. At one point she gave up the struggle to be a teacher, because she didn't wish to cope with the special problems of a rebellious group. She wanted to teach in a normal school or not at all. Finally she triumphed over the morbid and criminal environment and decided to stay.

There could be no doubt that the school and students were atypical. This was the whole point of the picture. Yet *Tass*, the Russian newspaper, reported "American authorities stated that this was a typical American school." To add ingenuity to mendacity, the next sentence stated that Stanley Kramer (who because of *Judgment at Nuremberg* and other pictures, was popular in Russia), had said that " 'Up the Down Staircase' is an honest and true work." Of course, he hadn't subscribed to the first sentence that "it represents a typical American school." Thus, by skillful juxtaposition, he became authority for the original misrepresentation.

At the same time, the Russians at the last moment barred the showing of another American entry, *The Young Americans*. It was a wholesome, gay depiction of America's youth. Ambassador Thompson tried diplomatically to overcome this slur by showing the picture in his embassy home and even inviting Russians to see it.

After each country's exhibit, a party was tendered at which other delegations were invited.

The American dinner and dance took place in the ballroom of the new Russian hotel. The occasion was formal. Robert Mulligan, the director, Tad Mosel, the scriptwriter, Sandy Dennis, the star of the American picture, Jennifer Jones, Sandra Dee, Dmitri Tiomkin, the composer, Stanley Kramer, Anatole Litvak, Abby Mann, George Stevens, Jr., King Vidor, and foreign managers of leading American motion picture companies were present. Ambassador Thompson and his wife attended. So did V. Baskakov, the head of the Russian motion picture industry, who was given a seat of honor.

At an appropriate moment, Jack Valenti, head of the American delegation, made a graceful and eloquent toast to the Russian people. He expressed the genuine good will which motivated the journey. To our surprise, Baskakov did not make a reciprocal toast. Even a cautious word in the most general terms from him would have reduced the strain. His silence was like a roar of unfriendliness. An American producer, who knew Russia and its language well, decided to speak to Baskakov. I watched as he led him into lifting a glass of vodka with him and nudged Valenti into clicking glasses. But it was all silent. Indeed a Russian photographer standing ready for any occasion was about to snap a picture of the incident, but Baskakov called him off with a negative wave of the head.

We were subjected to other picayune discourtesies. There were insufficient tickets for the American delegation to attend the showing of the American entry. Finally this mysterious bureaucratic annoyance was overcome.

The French delegation, in co-operation with the Russians, also snubbed us. De Gaulle, having found another opportunity to berate the United States, had joined the Russian camp in the Middle East crisis. Suddenly he, who supported Israel against their surrounding enemies when they were screaming threats of destruction, now declared that the United States was belligerent. This catapulted him into a position of being an ally of Russia in her drive to control the Middle East. His own countrymen, including some in his cabinet, protested his view. All this made France the darling of the Russian Government at the festival. The ill-will toward the United States, which permeated the Russian-French partnership, spilled over onto our delegation. We were the only nation not invited to the French celebration after the showing of its picture.

It was customary for American motion picture representatives to meet with producers, writers, and directors of every country they visited. This furthered the international aspect of motion pictures and our desire to achieve excellence in the art irrespective of nationality. So our delegation sought a meeting with Russian artists. We were refused. Probably when we were originally invited to the festival, such meetings had been part of the program. But there was on each Russian invitation an unwritten postscript, "Subject to change without notice, in the event political expediency so requires."

However, one day unexpectedly, a handwritten note was slipped under my door inviting me "as a writer" to attend a meeting of Russian motion picture writers and directors. I accepted eagerly. English, Mexican, Peruvian, and other artists attended. A picture of Lenin was the only decoration in the room of the writers' union building. The meeting was in the morning, but there were the usual caviar and vodka, which respected no hour. The chief discussion turned to the respective rights of the author and director to credits announced on the film. Writers claimed that the director's billing was overweening and excluded proper credit for the author. This controversy had been raging in Hollywood too. In the course of the discussion, the freedom of a writer to express himself without directors' or governmental interference was bespoken. The Russians listened attentively and obviously sympathetically to my exposition on American freedom of expression. The discussion thereafter was like a fresh ocean breeze which wafted away stifling air. The union of Russian writers (not limited to the screen) had been in a tumultuous quarrel. Novelist Aleksandr Solzhenitsyn and poet Andrei Voznesensky had openly defied and condemned the union for censorship. The poet had recently jumped on the stage of Moscow's Taganka Theater where *Antiworlds* was being performed for the two hundredth time, and despite official disapproval yelled "How shamefully we hold our tongues, I'm ashamed of things I've written myself." Russians were discovering that a little freedom could be a dangerous thing. Once loosed it could gather unstoppable momentum from long-suppressed yearning.

Russians have preserved their lavish past with great relish. The czars' palaces were exhibited to the public, which filed through the incredibly ornate, bejeweled rooms in wonder and pride. Then they trudged through the gardens stretched out for acres toward the lake, which provided the air conditioning of that era. Fountains were everywhere giving frenzied motion to the surrounding flower beds. In some castles there were collections of paintings which outglittered the columns of malachite, onyx, quartz, and lapis lazuli. The Pushkin Museum in Moscow and the famous Hermitage in Leningrad contained rooms which were filled with Rembrandts, Goyas, Rubens, Van Goghs, Cézannes, Matisses, and Renoirs, and in sculpture, Michaelangelos, Da Vincis, and Maillols. In terms of modern values, the greatest growth stock in the world was the art treasures in these museums.

Yet the Russians sometimes built modern structures which clashed with the symmetry of their architectural past. The most glaring example was the 6,000-seat modern theater with a huge stage where the Politburo met on official occasions, and which was used for the motion picture exhibits of the festival. This building was situated inside the Kremlin wall and contrasted incongruously with the czaristic palace and structures which surrounded it. We wondered why it was not built immediately outside of the wall.

There were three million Jews in Russia, and for years efforts to permit their emigration had been thwarted. Disconcerting reports of their persecution under Stalin had been published. Jewish newspapers were forbidden. Synagogues had been closed (as were many churches). During Passover, matzohs could not be imported. Yet the official line was that there was no governmental anti-Semitism, and that the anti-religious policy was universal rather than specific. So, now that tourism had been encouraged, it was natural that visitors should visit the only Catholic church in Moscow, or the famous large synagogue in Moscow. A group of us did so. In the synagogue we spoke to Rabbi Levine in his study.

We asked him how conditions were, not realizing until we signed the visitors' book at the end of our interview that he had been visited by similar groups many times each week, and had been asked the same questions.

He was a patriarchal figure, with brightly penetrating dark eyes which belied the equanimity of his manner and the peaceful gray of his long beard. He delivered a long paean of praise for the Russian Government. "Everything is fine here. No one interferes with us. Those who work, earn a good living. Of course, none of us are rich but we are well taken care of. The government provides free medical service and treatment for all the people. We are repairing our synagogue, as you can see, and making it more beautiful. There are many scholars here who spend their day and night studying and discussing the Talmud . . ."

We interrupted to ask whether Jews could leave the country if they wished. "Of course," he assured us. "Those who want to leave can do so. Indeed, even after Russia broke off diplomatic relations with Israel, hundreds of Jews were still permitted to go to Israel."

We were becoming more skeptical every moment. Perhaps he was talking for the record. Was his room bugged too? When we pressed him on the government's attitude toward religion, he replied, "The powers that be are generally against religion. That means all religions, not just the Jewish religion. Therefore the youth is largely lost to us. It is the middle-aged and the older generation that attend. But on Saturdays, our synagogue is filled and on the holy holidays, the streets outside are filled with Jews who wish to worship."

We called his attention to an incident in the small synagogue on the ground floor, which was used for study and early morning prayer. Two old scholars were seated there as we entered. We had asked them how they were faring. Both had made a forbidding gesture that it was not wise for them to speak. The rabbi seemed alarmed. He disposed of this with a vehement statement: "I am telling you how it is. If you wish to interpret some old Jews' gesture, you may do so. I am telling you the facts."

A few moments later in answer to another prodding question, he exclaimed, "All that we want is peace. Peace in Vietnam. Peace in Nigeria. Peace in Israel. Peace in the Arab world. Peace in all the world."

Peace in Nigeria! By this time, some of us were convinced that the fine man was making his statements for the bugging equipment and simply to protect his flock. We could not be sure, but we believed that we had been dim-witted in pressing the poor man. Recent reports from Russia, which had broadened its attacks on Israel to include Zionism generally, with implications of the revival of the colossal lies about international Jewish plots, and even horrendous analogies of Hitlerism and Judaism, pointed to the dangers affecting the Jewish population in Russia.

The United States followed a policy of patience with Russia. For example, its embassy was housed on the top floor of a ramshackle building, with an old-fashioned elevator which held only two or three passengers and was self-operated. The quarters were inadequate in size and appointments, and contrasted with our beautiful embassy buildings in Mexico, England, France, Italy, and other nations less important in the political strata. Furthermore, the Russians permitted only a limited number of attachés and assistants. The wives and children of the embassy personnel therefore filled in as secretaries and associates to take care of the enormous responsibilities of such a leading outpost. The private home of the Ambassador however, was magnificent. Averell Harriman once bought this palace from a wealthy Russian businessman and presented it to our government as a residence for its ambassador.

One of the most poignant consequences of Russian rejection affected a choral group from Amherst College. Under the leadership of its dean, it was making a tour of Europe, and had been invited to perform in Moscow and Leningrad. However the Middle East crisis had put frost on

American ventures, and their performances in Russia were canceled and forbidden. This fine group of students, typically American in their friendliness, zest, and good humor, found itself barred after a long trip. It performed in the International House for other foreigners, but Russians stayed away. What a waste and souring of good will?

We departed from Russia by plane from Leningrad to Helsinki. The Amherst choral group was on our plane. So were other foreigners who had visited Russia. As the plane roared out of the airport and away from Russia, the passengers spontaneously and without any prearrangement, sang *The Star-Spangled Banner*. I had never heard it sung with such quiet fervor. Thereafter all the passengers from many visiting countries cheered and applauded, expressing openly the relief of leaving the stifled air of an oppressed country and winging toward freedom. It was no ordinary patriotic gesture. One felt in that unique moment the true meaning of liberty and how essential it was to the very essence of man's existence.

When we had been taken through the customs procedure at Helsinki, we waited for baggage clearance. There was a door leading to a sunlit terrace where taxis were stationed. I asked the Finnish guard whether I could step out. I shall never forget his reply. With a smile he said, "Of course, you are in Finland now," and held the door open.

HOW TO TELL A LIAR

Can a lawyer tell whether a witness is lying? Very often yes. He does so by a variety of means, from advance preparation, which enables him to compare the witness's story with contradictory documentation, to psychological insights.

It is the latter which are most intriguing and which I shall discuss. We all use techniques to judge credibility, even though we may not be conscious of doing so. For example, if you are at a dinner party you may tell your spouse on the way home that you wouldn't trust the man who sat next to you farther than you could throw a piano. How did you come to that conclusion? If we had a tape recording of your conversation with him that evening, it probably would be quite innocuous and would not explain your impression. But you didn't like the way he looked at others while he was talking to you, or his affected flirtation with the woman next to him, or his raucous laughter at what wasn't so funny, or his pretense of knowledge which he didn't have; or his voice, eyes, mannerisms, all spelling out lack of sincerity. On the other hand you might form a very favorable opinion of him—again evaluating everything from his clothes to his speech and his persuasive sincerity. The point is that we gauge credibility not merely by what we hear but what we see while we hear it. That is what a jury does when it *observes* a witness intently. That is why there is a rule that an appellate court will not reverse a jury on a question of *fact*, only on law. The appellate judges have only the printed record of the testimony. They have not *seen* the witnesses as the jurors have. They therefore uphold the juror's determination of credibility, even if they disagree with it.

The jurors too apply psychological tests to determine a witness's honesty, whether they know it or not.

Trial lawyers, because of practice in the arena of contest, often develop special antennae to pick up signals from the witness, which reveal that he is not telling the truth.

Let me illustrate some that I have observed.

1. If a witness puts his hand in front of his mouth before he answers, it might mean "I wish I didn't have to say what I am about to say." Of course it might be an innocent gesture. So I go to another subject and return to the same point. If the hand covers the mouth again, I will cross-examine deeply on the subject, assuming that there is vulnerability even though I don't yet know what it is.

On a number of occasions, this "hunch" proved very rewarding. I recall one such witness, later asking me how I knew the secret dug out of him. Like Cavour, who learned how to deceive diplomats by telling them the truth, which they didn't believe, I told him that he had tipped me off himself. I am sure he rejected this explanation and must have though that I had a phenomenal investigator.

2. Nervous gestures such as scissoring the legs or shifting in the seat whenever a particular subject matter is raised is another distress signal sent out by the witness.

3. The eyes. Poets say they reflect the soul. Perhaps so, but they also reflect fear and confusion. The voice may be steady. The manner confident. But that look in the eyes! Like an animal which senses danger. A combination of an emphatic assertion while the eyes reveal doubt is particularly significant.

4. Undue emphasis. Emotions of course affect the voice, but its tremulousness is not very significant. Anyone sitting in a witness chair facing an audience with a black-robed judge on one side, and twelve jurors watching every flicker of his eyes on the other, will be nervous. But it is a *general* nervousness. It is not related to any particular question. However, when a witness who has testified in a certain vocal range suddenly increases his decibels belligerently for no accountable reason, it is a signal. The question must have touched a nerve and caused a vocal explosion.

5. Instant amnesia. Often a witness who has been answering difficult questions with facility will suddenly stop, look up at the ceiling as if beseeching help from the almighty, then, getting no relief there, shift his gaze to his lawyer, as the second-best bet, and finally in a half stammer say, "I d-don't remember." Particularly when the question appears harmless, the cross-examiner is alerted. Is the sudden loss of memory a revelation of Freud's thesis that one never forgets? He is merely unable to reveal an unpleasant fact.

6. Quarrelsomeness. A witness who protests that he is being harassed or tricked by the cross-examiner reveals his sensitivity to the questions rather than the unfairness of the questioner. Under our system of law, improper questions are ruled out by the judge. If the question is allowed but the witness claims he is being persecuted, he is pitting his

own uninformed view of the law against the court's. Why is he indulging in such an unequal contest, unless he fears to answer the questions?

If a lawyer is earning his bread by the sweat of his browbeating, his adversary, not the witness, should protest. Any unfair tactic provides its own punishment, because the judge and jury will resent it. But the witness's role is to inform, not to control the questioning.

7. Negative pregnants. This is the legal phrase for a denial which appears to be complete but is really partial. For example, to the question, "Didn't you try hard to block the deal?" he answers, "No, I did not." Upon further inquiry, he claims his answer meant he didn't "try hard" to block the deal. He just tried to block it. His answer was negative but pregnant with admission.

Whenever a witness engages in such a ruse, the lawyer's antennae pick up a signal not only of slyness, but of an attempt to evade, which may apply to other answers as well.

8. Candor. A mistake by a witness is readily forgiven by a jury if he is frank to admit it. Memory about dates and details of events years old can be faulty. It is when the witness pretends that he didn't testify as he did, or that he didn't mean what he said, or that he is misinterpreted, that his dishonesty is revealed. Curiously, such feigning does the witness more harm than the frank admission that he was mistaken.

A witness who has erred and is caught will, if he is not honest, invent escape hatches. Such improvisation is almost always fatal. He merely creates more opportunities to demonstrate that he is lying. The witness who can under stress invent an excuse which will be foolproof is rare. As he is forced to retreat from his newly dug trench, again and again, his credibility is completely destroyed.

9. Sincerity. There is an imponderable over-all test of a witness's honesty. Does he look and sound truthful? It is a kind of summation of all the emanations which make him believable. It is his face, voice, directness, and above all his sincerity. That is why credibility has no relationship to education or culture. An illiterate cleaning woman may be impressively honest. A refined executive may appear shifty. Character is a letter of credit written on the face.

10. More useful than any of the other tests for detecting a liar is the rule of probability. If the testimony given by the witness does not accord with common experience, it must be false. Unless the witness is unstable, in which event the bizarre becomes normal, it is extremely unlikely that he will behave in a manner which violates usual standards. This rule is universal. In our daily contacts we apply this test unwittingly. We believe what seems reasonable and disbelieve the "tall story." Why is it "tall"? Because we wouldn't have acted that way under similar circumstances. The rule of probability is also used by the

jurors, though they may not know it. Faced with directly opposite testimony, they accept one version rather than another because it complies more closely with their idea of what would be normal behavior under the circumstances.

It is my favorite litmus test in the courtroom. If testimony violates the rule of probability, I will not let up on cross-examination in an effort to expose the witness.

The rule of probability works its miracles in wondrous ways. Recently the Government brought a suit against wholesale tour operators for violating the regulations which forbid low air fares to charter groups unless their members belonged to a genuine club or organization for at least six months. A Government investigator testified that he had bought a low-priced ticket even though he was not a member of a charter group and had not presented any of the required proof. In defending the case, I was struck by the responsibility of the executives. I was convinced they had given proper instructions to their sales clerks not to sell cut-rate tickets to those who were not members of a qualified group. Yet an experienced salesgirl had broken the rule. The explanation that she had just been careless violated the rule of probability. I pursued the matter and discovered that she had taken a weekend trip immediately after the ticket was sold.

When the Government investigator took the stand to testify to the violation, I drew the following out of him on cross-examination.

Q. You told her you were a schoolteacher?

A. Yes, sir.

Q. Of course that wasn't true, was it?

A. No, sir, it was not.

Q. And you told her you were single, didn't you?

A. Yes, sir.

Q. Now, what relevance did it have that you were single when you talked to her?

A. None whatsoever.

Each admission made it more difficult to resist the next. Momentum prevents a sudden stop of revelation.

Q. You told her you liked her?

A. No, sir, I didn't—excuse me, I did. I did tell her she was a very nice individual.

Q. Did you tell her that you would like to go on the trip and you could spend some time with her in Las Vegas?

A. I said that could—could happen, yes, sir.

Q. What did you tell her about being with her in Las Vegas, if anything.

A. I said perhaps we could get together in Las Vegas.

Q. Perhaps?

A. Yes, sir.

By this time it was too late to retreat. He tried to do so, but found it too embarrassing. The ultimate admission finally tumbled out of him.

Q. So you knew that she was arranging for the flight the two of you would be together on?

A. Yes, sir.

Q. Did you ask her to make an exception to the six-month rule? Did you talk to her about the two of you being together in Las Vegas?

A. Yes, sir, I did.

Not much more was necessary to explain why the pretty salesgirl had violated the CAB rules when she sold a ticket to the handsome young Government agent. It came out that they met at the plane and boarded together.

Q. Were you very attentive to her?

A. Yes, sir, I was.

Q. It was very clear to you that she was attracted to you?

A. Yes, sir.

Occasionally in an effort to protect himself he would announce that he had done it all to perform his duty in uncovering an illegal sale of a ticket. This left him even more vulnerable.

Q. When you told her you were single, did you think that was part of your duty for the CAB?

A. No, sir.

Finally she discovered who he really was. It was the oldest of all plots but it had happened. She thought he was in love, or at least liked her, but he was merely a deceiver gathering evidence for the Government.

Q. Did she tell you that it might cost her her job because she had done that for you, because she liked you and she thought you and she were going to have a good time in Las Vegas together?

A. She may have said that.

Q. Did she tell you she liked you?

A. At some point during the trip there I think she did.

Q. And did she tell you that she had sold you the ticket improperly because she liked you and she felt that you liked her. Did she reprimand you for having deceived her?

A. Something like that, yes, sir.

How could the company which employed her be held responsible for the illegal ticket sale when it was the unauthorized act of a salesgirl who had a rendezvous on her mind, not the company's rules? The Judge and the courtroom were astonished to find that in a prosaic CAB case sex, and not avarice, was the villain. The rule of probability had led directly to evidence of entrapment.

In another case, Roy Fruehauf, president of Fruehauf Trailers, was indicted in 1959 for giving $200,000 to teamster president Dave Beck. Even though the money was a loan, it was a clear violation of the statute. I undertook the defense when it was demonstrated to me that the Fruehauf company had obtained no preference from the union in wages, hours, or in any other manner. Also, Fruehauf was no intimate of Dave Beck. Then why had Fruehauf, quite aware of the law, risked his reputation and liberty by making the loan? The rule of probability told me that something vital was missing.

It turned out that many years before, when a proxy fight was launched against the Fruehauf company to take away Fruehauf's control of the company, he had turned to the Teamsters Union for a large loan to buy in his own stock and stave off the assault. The teamsters had millions of dollars for investment and loans at appropriate interest. The loan was formally made and approved by the union's committee and its counsel. Fruehauf had later repaid it in full with interest.

Years later, Dave Beck was in financial trouble in his personal real estate investments. He turned to Fruehauf to make him a loan. Fruehauf felt that he would be an ingrate if he didn't reciprocate in Beck's hour of distress. The $200,000 he lent was also repaid, although part of the interest was still due.

The legal problem was that the prior transaction might afford a moral explanation but was no legal excuse. The statute forbade gifts or loans to union executives—period. It was, as we lawyers say, draconian. Therefore, the early history would not even be admissible. Fortunately, the Government prosecuter was quite willing to admit this evidence, because he felt that it established a chain of financial transactions which were unholy. The jury acquitted Fruehauf.

Even though the case went to the Supreme Court of the United States before Fruehauf could enjoy his freedom, it was the rule of probability which led us to an otherwise invisible defense.

In another case a gifted top executive was accused of neglecting his office for days at a time. He was a dedicated man, and responsible in every way. Yet there were these occasional absences. His explanation, supported by his family, that he suffered occasional illness did not satisfy the rule of probability. He seemed healthy. There were no doctors' certificates. Persistence revealed that he had a drinking problem. Then the improbable had become probable.

What is referred to as woman's intuition is often nothing but the rule of probability. A wife of a philandering husband will sense a change of relationship which the most cogent explanations cannot overcome. The rule of probability nags at her and finally reveals the naked truth.

Science has attempted to provide lie-detector and chemical tests to expose a liar. Unfortunately, they have not been proved to be reliable. We still depend on the psychological insights of the questioner to reveal the truth.

Cross-examination is still the best scalpel to excise the truth from the brain.

A-OK

In 1966, astronaut Alan Shepard asked me to be the attorney for the astronauts in their personal affairs. There were fifty-two astronauts at the time. (The number grew to seventy-three.) Shepard was their spokesman and he had obtained their authority and that of NASA (National Aeronautics and Space Administration) to approach me, but he had two preliminary questions. What fees would be entailed, and would I come to meet the astronauts and NASA executives in Houston, Texas, for mutual approval of the representation?

I told him that out of regard for the astronauts' heroic service to our country, I would be pleased to represent them without fee, and that I, too, would wish to meet with them and NASA's executives to learn in greater detail the nature of the representation, and the Government's attitude.

So it was arranged. On October 3, 1966, I flew to Houston and had lunch with a large number of spacemen. I addressed them, and then spent hours in private conversation with the most remarkable group of "clients" I had ever encountered.

Thereafter, I was taken by Alan Shepard and Virgil Grissom to the offices of Dr. Robert Gilruth, director of the Manned Spacecraft Center, and Dr. George Low, then the deputy director, for further discussion. They were, of course, concerned with the well-being as well as the welfare of their charges, who were training for feats previously envisioned only in fiction and were now to be attempted with the world in attendance.

I saw the need to assure Dr. Gilruth and Dr. Low that, whatever issues arose, it was necessary to accommodate the astronauts' wishes to the approval of NASA. This was the astronauts' duty in any event.

The astronauts approved my becoming counsel, and NASA did too, and made a public announcement of my designation.

So began a rewarding relationship. It was exciting to know the men who in the millions of years of earth's existence would be the first to attempt to free themselves from nature's forces which bound us to our globe and fly in illimitable space to other planets.

Columbus is held in awe because he dared sail on water into the unknown, where he might fall off the flat earth. Lindbergh is heroized because he dared to do in the air what ships had done countless times on water—reach Europe three thousand miles away. What awaited astronauts who undertook to be blasted off the face of the earth with sufficient force to break the gravitational chains and fly out a quarter of a million miles into the nothingness of space, with sufficient technical skill to find and land softly on another planet?

Innumerable obstacles presented themselves and increased anxiety about an "impossible" task. In a weightless condition, how would the blood circulate without the benefit of gravitational pull? How would the organs of the body function? Would the astronauts perish from unknown physical causes? Would meteorites or radiation or other mysterious forces in outer space crush the capsule, or disorient its equipment or the minds of its inhabitants? Could man, in defiance of nature's plan which separates billions of stars, succeed in invading the privacy of the celestial scheme? Even if the astronauts were not killed by the initial explosion underneath their seats, having a thrust of seven and a half million pounds, and even if by the miracle of miniaturized technology and magnified courage and skill, they landed on another planet, would the lifesaving apparatus which was to replicate the earth's conditions be able to sustain them? And how would they come back? If they did, would they be able to overcome the "bends" of another environment? What visible or invisible injury of deformity would they suffer from having forced themselves in and out of an environment not intended for man?

NASA and the astronauts reduced the overwhelming risks by fanatical preparation.

It began with the most stringent physical and psychological tests which could be devised. Every astronaut had to be less than forty years of age (later thirty-five years), less than five feet eleven inches tall, have a bachelor's degree or equivalent in engineering, and in the early program had to be a qualified jet pilot with at least fifteen hundred hours of flying time.

Then he was subjected to an unprecedented five-day physical examination conducted by the Air Force School of Aerospace Medicine at Brooks Air Force Base in Texas. Astronaut Michael Collins described the process with verve:

Inconvenience is piled on top of indignity, as you are poked, prodded, pummeled and pierced. No orifice is inviolate, no privacy is respected.

Cold water was poured into one of his ears causing his eyeballs to gy-
rate wildly as conflicting messages were relayed to his brain from one
warm and one cold semicircular canal.

Your fanny is violated by the "steel eel", a painful and undignified
process by which one foot of lower bowel can be examined for cancer or
other disease processes. Your eyes and ears are tested with an unbelievable attention to detail, by some of the foremost specialists in the
world.

After blood tests requiring repeated bloodletting (which would have
satisfied an eighteenth-century physician), electrocardiac sensors which
left no privacy for the slightest tick of the heart, and inspections of
every joint, muscle, and organ of the body, the five-day ordeal ended,
only to usher in the psychiatric tests. The endless search for "normalcy"
by abnormal probing caused Collins to turn on his inquisitors. At least
he demonstrated his sense of humor, itself a test of balance.

Then the shrinks take over where their more stable compatriots leave
off. Thrust and parry. What are inkblots supposed to be anyway? Is one
crotch in ten pictures too many? How can I describe the blank, pure
white piece of paper? I said it was nineteen polar bears fornicating in a
snowbank, and the interviewer's face tightened in obvious displeasure
over my lack of reverence for his precious cards.

Michael Collins, Carrying the Fire

The simple external tests of a well-adjusted man were not ignored.
Was he married? Did he have children? Was he a good family man?
Was he religious? Had he functioned well previously? If we were going
to send visitors out into the universe, they were to be as perfect as man
could be, physically and psychologically.

Their preparation therefore included postgraduate courses never conceived of before.

On one occasion, when I visited Houston, several astronauts took me
on a tour. It began prosaically with a visit to classrooms where astronauts sat at desks, while a professor of astronomy sought to make them
familiar with heavens in which they might soon be wandering. Other
classrooms hummed with the intricacies of engineering, geology, orbital
mechanics, rocket propulsion, meteorology, physics of the upper atmosphere, guidance and navigation, digital computer systems, satellite orbits and trajectories, medicine and aerodynamics.

There were unique subjects never before studied by man. The astronauts had to understand each part of the equipment whose development over the years cost twenty-four billion dollars. They had to learn

the ingenious technical means of correcting a defect, and the backup of backups for instruments which might fail when subjected to unanticipated stress.

Panel boards, looking like demonstration models for voting machines, but of course infinitely more complicated, were practiced on, to answer questions which assumed a stream of disasters.

From this college of esoteric aeronautics, I was taken by astronauts Ed White and Virgil Grissom to another building and into a simulator. This was an exact duplicate of the capsule which would fly the Apollo missions. It was on crossrails, so that the rolling motions in all directions could be reproduced. There were three narrow cots for the astronauts. How could they rest on such small beds? I asked, regretting my naïveté before the words were out of my mouth. Of course, they do not lie on beds in outer space. They virtually float over them, and the feeling is euphoric. Indeed, sleeping bags were devised in which their arms were taped down so they wouldn't rise and perhaps be injured. Since there is no up, down, or sides in a weightless environment, one can sleep while attached vertically to a wall, like a suit hung up, or even "upside down" on the ceiling.

In the training capsule, the upper left quadrant opened and the trainee saw the heavens, stars, or planets in precisely the way he would see them from his window in actual flight. A motion picture technique was used to create this outer world. One of the inventions in Hollywood which revolutionized the industry was a screen on which any locale in the world could be shown, full of movement, but integrated with the actors in front of it. By this simple device, actors could be seen walking, or driving in any foreign city, without transporting them. Astronomers and astronauts who had previously invaded the vacuum outside the earth had made it possible to produce motion pictures which enabled the astronauts to experience outer space while in the simulator.

But more was required of him. As I sat in the capsule, various indicators of the panel were deliberately knocked out. The astronaut had to restore them. Then, when this was made impossible for him, he had to "fly by the sky," navigating correctly not only through his knowledge of the stars, but by sunrays called airglow. This is the ionosphere. Of course, the moon and earth provide landmarks. All this while the capsule was deliberately pronated, so that it was flying sideways or even upside down.

Still, this was only a fraction of the drills which astronauts made for months on end. They spent from twelve to fourteen hours a day in the simulators.

A single illustration of the intricacies to be mastered is that the zone of atmosphere re-entry is only forty miles thick, and hitting such a target from 230 miles is, to use Collins' phrase, like "trying to split a human hair with a razor blade thrown from a distance of twenty feet."

Each flight afforded invaluable information for the next, thus narrowing the risk of unknown factors. Who can forget the Apollo 8 flight (Borman, Lovell, and Anders), a 147-hour trip with ten lunar orbits and a Christmas reading of the Bible seventy miles from the moon, "In the beginning God created the heaven and the earth. . . ."?

I know that in law, preparation is more important that inspiration. This was the rule for each astronaut. He was subjected to torturous procedures so that he would be ready for the most gruesome eventuality. To simulate takeoff and re-entry, he was whirled in a centrifuge until he weighed eight times his normal weight, and yet was required to speak into a microphone. During launching, the strain on all body organs compressed his lungs and pushed him toward unconsciousness. By experience he learned that he could overcome these effects and function. He was required to throw balls into a basket while sitting in a speedily revolving room to prove that he was not disoriented.

An astronaut who weighed 160 pounds on earth would only weigh ten pounds on the moon. He therefore had to be taught how to maneuver by training in the near weightless world of water at the naval scuba diving school.

Noise was another hazard. The Saturn V booster created 175 decibels, enough not only to destroy the inner ear, but cause convulsions and even death. So each astronaut was helmeted and bombarded by giant microphones to determine how much noise he could bear and still function efficiently.

The cruelest of all tests was devised to train the astronaut how to gain control of the capsule if it began to tumble in space. He was spun thirty revolutions a minute in three directions at once; head over heels, roundabout, and sideways. This stirred his innards and unhinged his body's balance. His eyeballs fluttered, but he had to train himself to pull and tilt his stick until three needles met at zero, thus stopping the wild descent.

One of the original astronauts with outstanding credentials even in that august group was Donald (Deke) Slayton. When first examined, his heart had functioned perfectly. However, after a centrifuge run, preceded the night before by an innocent beer, he registered fibrillations. He was bumped from the Mercury flight. He stayed in the program and because of his special competence became director of Flight Crew Operations. He was treated by Dr. Paul Dudley White, and by Dr. "Chuck" Berry, the space physician. During the time he was grounded, he repeatedly tried to persuade us not to include him in the distribution of money derived from publication of the flight stories, but neither the astronauts nor I would hear of it. Thirteen years later, in 1975, all doubts about his "heart murmur" were eliminated and he was permitted to fly in the Apollo which rendezvoused with the Russian spacecraft Soyuz.

Another example of overcoming a physical handicap was Alan Shepard. He had pioneered manned space for the United States in a suborbital flight. He had thus become the most famous of the original seven and perhaps of the program. But he developed Ménière's syndrome, which, due to elevated fluid pressure in the ear canal, affects balance and hearing. He was grounded. His leadership was recognized by designating him chief of the Astronaut Office.

Shepard hoped the infirmity would disappear, but after five years of frustration he submitted himself to surgery. A tube was implanted from the ear canal to the spinal column. The pressure was relieved and he was declared fit. He captained Apollo 14, which achieved the third successful landing on the moon.

Spacecraft might be defective too. Even the remote contingency that a crippled capsule might land in wild terrain rather than in the sea was not overlooked. Astronauts were taken to a jungle in Panama and taught how to survive. Indians taught them how to capture an iguana and broil it on a skewer to make it edible. The hazards of king-sized biting ants were explained and the astronauts learned to make a meal of coconut milk and iguana chunks wrapped in a leaf "cone." They had a plastic bag device which used the sun's energy to evaporate sea water, condensing pure drinking water from it. Unplanned incidents filled out the curriculum. While receiving intructions in an improvised classroom in the jungle a huge boa constrictor suddenly appeared. It was merely a pet of the instructor, but the astronauts could not discern its amiable intentions as it curled toward them.

The training of the astronauts did not begin when they were selected from hundreds of applicants. Just as our education begins with our parents, so the astronauts' skills began with their previous occupations.

The first seven astronauts were all test pilots for the Navy, Air Force, or Marine Corps (Lieutenant Commanders Alan B. Shepard, Jr., and Walter M. Schirra, Jr., Captains Virgil L. Grissom, L. Gordon Cooper, Jr., and Donald K. Slayton; Colonel John Glenn, Jr., and Lieutenant M. Scott Carpenter).

Actually, being a test pilot was more hazardous than being an astronaut, except for the terror of the unknown. The astronaut's duty was to take no intentional chance. "Abort the trip rather than risk your life" was the instruction. There were redundant safety systems.

In contrast, a test pilot had to take risks intentionally. His job was to bring the airplane to its ultimate theoretical capacity of speed, altitude, and strength of materials. He would try to put stress on the vehicle to find out whether its wings would break or its controls snap. He was ready to parachute if necessary, but there was no assurance he could. It took a daredevil to be a test pilot. Although he flew in the earth's atmosphere, he challenged the fates. The astronauts sought to avoid them.

Yet, despite guidance by control centers and sophisticated equipment, a test pilot, when he became an astronaut, had to steel himself to overcome fear, a fear which could not be identified, because no one knew what there was to fear. So, the most intrepid test pilots registered a sudden rise in heartbeat immediately before launch, as high as double the normal rate.

Eight astronauts died. Ironically, not a single one in flight.

Four astronauts died when their T-38 jet planes crashed, one in a collision with a snow goose. Another died in an automobile accident. I once suggested a slogan for an airplane company. "Of course, air travel isn't safe. You must get to the airport in an automobile."

On January 27, 1967, three astronauts were burned to death in an Apollo spacecraft atop a Saturn 1-B rocket. It was a practice session. The cause appeared to be a spark from an exposed wire, which set off a deadly conflagration in the pure oxygen atmosphere. The victims were Edward White, the first American to have stepped out in space in a previous Gemini flight. The second fatality was Virgil Grissom, who had been on Mercury and Gemini 3 flights. The third was Roger Chaffee, who had not yet flown on a mission.

The nation was shocked by these three deaths, particularly because it had become familiar with the men. Their agonizing cries for rescue as the flames exploded around them gave poignancy to their death.

The astronauts knew that they were brushing death when they left the earth to venture forth into the heavens, but to die in a stationary capsule on earth deprived them of their heroism and daring.

I had gotten to know these men and their families personally and my grief was deep.

The public was not fully aware of the hazards overcome, only that they had been. The circulation of blood in zero gravity might have been a fatal handicap. At first the heart pumped at the same pace as it did on earth. The astronauts' heads felt "full" as if they were hanging upside down in normal atmosphere. Had this condition continued, it might have become impossible for the men to function, and no trip could have been completed. Fortunately, after a few hours of weightlessness the heart "learned" that it was doing more than necessary and adjusted its pumping rate to the new environment.

However, the body's wisdom worked in reverse, too. It did not need as much blood in weightless condition and it manufactured less. The astronauts returned to earth with insufficient quantity. A simple procedure contributed to the solution—drinking more water. Astronaut Lovell recalled how strange it was that among the sophisticated technical instructions from control center was the cry, "Drink some water."

Similarly, their bodies, sensing that there was less need for the bones to be strong in outer space, reduced their calcium. Exercise was the solution, but how in the constricted space of the capsule? Isometric exercises were devised, and later, when Skylab was built, there was enough cubic footage to accommodate a stationary bicycle-type apparatus. The astronauts returned with less affected bone structure and marrow.

To the surprise of everyone, including the brilliant staff of doctors, swallowing, digestion, and defecation were not problems. Urine was expelled and feces were sealed in sanitary bags to be returned to earth.

What did cause annoyance was unexpected. Eye tears would not flow out because of lack of gravity. Being acidic, the retained fluid caused irritation and more need for drainage. There was nothing to do but remove the tears mechanically by blinking hard and rubbing the eyes.

The unexpected could also be as humorous as frightening. On one occasion, Pete Conrad pulled down the shades of Skylab so that he could go to sleep. Later Pete awoke and saw a green-eyed monster moving in the cabin. He pushed up the shades and saw his watch with a luminous dial floating in space.

The astronauts were troubled by contract problems. In 1959 a contract had been made by the original seven astronauts with *Life* magazine, giving it exclusive rights to the astronauts' personal stories under their by-lines. This involved not only their own experiences but also those of their wives and children. Obviously, the strain on their families was a moving story in itself. They watched their husbands and fathers shot into the unknown, perhaps never to be seen again. This agreement expired in 1962, and was replaced in 1963 with contracts with *Life* and Field Enterprises, Inc., under which *Life* agreed to pay $200,000 a year and Field an additional $320,000 a year to the astronauts.

In addition, *Life* and Field agreed to insure each astronaut for $100,000 a year during the four-year term of the contract.

Misgivings about these arrangements had been expressed in many quarters. President Kennedy, Vice-President Johnson, and a number of senators had been confronted with the ethical problem of the astronauts "exploiting" their military duties for private gains. NASA was deeply involved and sensitive.

The question of renewal in 1963 was not merely a legal but a moral one. The issue had been raised with fervor by those who sincerely believed that their objections were righteous. Did the astronauts have a right to sell their experiences for publication? The scales which measure ethical values do not tip readily one way or the other in all situations. In view of our concern that standards of conduct of officials and private citizens should not be demeaned, it is appropriate to analyze the astronaut issue.

Against the sale were two major arguments:

1. The Government financed the space program, and the story was its property, not subject to private sale.
2. The buyer of the story was put in a privileged position not available to the press generally.

For the sale, there were five arguments:

1. Precedent had established the right of public figures through books and otherwise to exploit their memoirs for private gains.

Eisenhower, Truman, General Bradley, Kissinger, and Churchill and numerous others had done so. Why discriminate against the astronauts?
2. The stories also featured the wives and children of the astronauts. Their reactions were not public property.
3. The astronauts held full press conferences upon their return. The public had immediate access to the men.
4. The astronauts received merely military pay or its equivalent and were grossly underpaid for their special qualifications. Technicians working on boosters at Cape Kennedy received higher salaries. Furthermore, as international celebrities, they had special expenses. An astronaut and his wife told me that they had to outfit the family because President Kennedy had invited them to the White House and they could not afford to do so. Other expenses mounted because they were in the public eye.
5. Finally, their risks were so great that they were uninsurable. Ought we to deprive their families of a little security?

Originally, President Kennedy opposed the astronauts' contracts. However, a presentation to Vice-President Johnson, made him an advocate of private income for the astronauts and their families. When Kennedy learned of the special expenses incurred by the men the nation called upon to be ambassadors of heroism to the world, and who restored the United States to its pre-eminent position of resourcefulness, he shifted his position, particularly when NASA and the astronauts gave continued assurance that there would be debriefing on television for the first full information to the public.

In the meantime, the astronauts voted to divide all income in equal shares. This meant that the newest tyro, who might never fly but who was admitted into the group, received the same as the famous few who had made several flights and landed on the moon. Also the widows of the men who had perished were equal participants. Even when the three men who stunned the world by reaching and cavorting on a satellite wrote a book, *First on the Moon*, the royalties were shared equally by all astronauts.

In 1967 *Life* magazine renewed its contract, but Field Enterprises decided not to renew. The reason that Field dropped out was that it had paid $1 million while the Gemini program, which was to provide readership interest, was delayed. Also, prior to the moon flights, public excitement about "the greatest story in history" was below expectation. This was a mystery to all media. The answer might be the simple psychological fact that perfection diminished suspense and therefore interest. Recently I attended a performance of a Chinese acrobatic troupe which had been hailed for its incredible feats. The performers lived up to their notices with ridiculous ease. The audience applauded politely. Then during the building of a human mountainous structure, one on top of the other, a girl slipped and fell. She was unhurt. They tried again and succeeded. The applause and cheers rocked the theater and were so sustained that the next stunt had to be delayed. Acrobats have discovered this phenomenon and deliberately miss. When they finally "triumph," the audience responds vigorously. That was the trouble, from a public relations viewpoint, with the accomplishments in space. Everything (with one exception) was A-OK, and while we shook our heads in wonder at the pinpointed completion of the space journeys, the excitement was diminished by their very perfection. I could observe this in my own office. When Neil Armstrong visited me, there was a stir among the personnel to see the first man on the moon, but hardly as much excitement as when athletes like Julius Erving, Muhammad Ali, Joe Namath, or motion pictures stars appeared.

The astronauts were simply too successful and they, the public, and we rejoice that they had been.

One would think that men bound together by unique qualifications might have other common characteristics. Not so. The astronauts' personalities varied sharply. Neil Armstrong is taciturn and withdrawn. One of his comrades said that "when Neil says 'good morning' that's a big conversation." He was besieged with dozens of offers which would commercialize his fame, but he chose to be a professor of aerospace engineering at the University of Cincinnati. His home does not display any award or memento of his historic trip.

Charles "Pete" Conrad, the third man to walk on the moon, is at the opposite end of the personality scale. He is full of fun, and as colorful as he is competent. Frank Borman is aggressive and a quick-witted decision maker. Jim Lovell is open, warm, and friendly. "Buzz" Aldrin, the second man to step on the moon, is serious and reflective. So the astronauts are individualistic and as varied a group of men as one can assemble. They shared a common devotion to the space program and old-fashioned values of duty, country, service, and courage, and they were not embarrassed about it.

Tom Stafford, chief of the Astronaut Office, wanted to express his appreciation for the services we rendered to the astronauts. He surprised me by suggesting that if I provided him with a very tiny *mezuzah* it would be taken on the Apollo 13 trip to the moon and presented to me. He was referring to a miniature scroll of scripture which is enclosed in metal, and which many Jews attach to the outer frame of the door of their homes as a religious symbol. Those who are very devout touch the mezuzah with their fingers and bring them to their lips before crossing the threshold. Stafford mispronounced mezuzah, giving it an unrecognizable Oklahoma twang, and it took me some time to know what he was referring to. Even though I would have been gratified no matter what the object was, I was moved by his desire to make it a Jewish religious symbol. I obtained a mezuzah and gave it to him, but when he learned that it had an inner scroll which was inflammable, he suggested, as a substitute, a small metal Star of David. Once more he sought to please me by choosing a religious symbol. I found a tiny star and gave it to him.

On April 11, 1970, Lovell, as commander, Jack Swigert, and Fred Haise took off to the moon on Apollo 13. When they were hundreds of thousands of miles away from earth, an explosion ripped the command module. The mission was aborted, but could the astronauts be brought back in their crippled vehicle? Tens of millions of people watched breathlessly as control center, calling upon the daring, skill, and cool-headedness of the crew, sought to save them from death in a permanent orbit, the first burial in space.

They returned safely. Superstitious commentators referred to "13" as the omen of bad luck, while I chose to consider the tiny metal Star of David the lucky charm responsible for their miraculous return. Lovell sent it to me with a letter which prosaically authenticated that it had been "on board the Odyssey-Aquarius spacecraft during the space flight of Apollo 13 from April 11 to April 17, 1970." Like most heroes, the astronauts were tight-lipped about their exploits.

The qualities and qualifications of the astronauts have not been overlooked. William Anders became Ambassador to Norway; Frank Borman, president of Eastern Airlines; Michael Collins, director of the National Air and Space Museum of the Smithsonian Institution; Charles "Pete" Conrad, vice-president of McDonnell-Douglas Corporation; Donn Eisele, was Peace Corps director in Thailand; John Glenn, United States senator from Ohio; James Irwin, director of High Flight, an evangelical religious organization which he founded; Edgar Mitchell, a student of parapsychology; Harrison Schmitt, United States senator from New Mexico; Thomas Stafford, major general and commanding officer of Edwards Air Force Base; John Swigert, executive director of the Committee on Science and Technology, U. S. House of Representatives; and Alfred Worden, writer of several books of poetry and books for children.

Others will fare as well. They are unique men, but the impression which the public may have had of them as perfectly adjusted supermen is not true. In their midst have been divorces, a nervous breakdown courageously described about himself by Buzz Aldrin, involvement in esoteric studies such as ESP and Eastern religions. They were trained to be as perfect as physical specimens could be, but the frailties of human nature cannot be eliminated by any programs thus far devised.

The greatest resistance to the space program has resulted not from the failure to achieve, but from the question, "Why do we divert so much money, talent, and energy to outer space, when they are so sorely needed on earth?" "Are we guilty of a misdirection?" These are fair questions.

NASA and the proponents for the space program admit that it is a long-term investment, not to be judged by immediate direct benefit to the man in the street. Basic knowledge often results in incalculable gains which were not anticipated. Roentgen was not searching for a diagnostic means when he discovered the X-ray. He was engaged in abstract testing of the effects of electricity passing through rarefied gases.

When the British scientist Michael Faraday was asked what good was one of his discoveries, he replied, "What good is an infant?"

The cost of the space program does not diminish in any significant way the resources for social programs. It cost three billion dollars a year, which is approximately one per cent of the national budget to alleviate poverty, improve health, control pollution, and eliminate hunger.

During the decade which fulfilled President Kennedy's prediction that the United States would place a man on the moon, the program cost $24 billion. During the same period Americans spent four times that much on liquor, more than twice as much on cigarettes, and still more on pari-mutuel betting. Furthermore, the sums spent on the space program were fed back into American industry.

Also with progress, the proportionate cost of the space program is declining. When the first payload in space, Explorer I, was launched in 1956, it cost a half million dollars per pound. Less than ten years later, when Apollo 7 was launched, the cost was only five hundred dollars a pound. With reusable space shuttles by the 1980s the cost will be reduced to fifty dollars a pound.

Where can all this lead us to? Perhaps the greatest boon to mankind. We can get a glimpse of the possibilities by examining past experience. In 1903 the first theoretical study of rocket-powered spaceships was published by Constantine Tsiolkovsky. In that year also, the Wright brothers achieved the first flight in a power-driven aircraft. Would anyone then have thought that only sixty-six years later man would step on the moon?

Only forty years after Lindbergh's flight, twenty thousand people fly across the Atlantic Ocean every day. So his flight in a single-engine plane was not just a stunt of no practical use.

However, we need not wait for unknown future applications of basic knowledge to justify the space program. Its enormous immediate benefits have not been sufficiently appreciated.

Meteorological satellites have expanded our surveys from 20 per cent of the earth to 100 per cent and made weather forecasting more of a science than an art. In one instance, in 1969, they reported Hurricane Camille, the most intense storm to hit North America, and by giving early warning saved fifty thousand lives by evacuation.

Two butterfly-shaped spacecraft called Landsats circle the globe six hundred miles out in space. They detect new oil and mineral deposits and, even more important, hidden sources of fresh water. They can locate schools of fish, and can report pollution and even the source of it.

It is estimated that satellite information of forest fires, crop infestations, and droughts can save more than $5 billion for the United States and as much as $15 billion for the entire world.

Communications satellites made it possible for five hundred million people to see the first moon landing in 1969.

Satellite telephone calls (10 million in one year) have also reduced prices, almost one half from New York to London.

As an educational device the satellites will contribute much to change the world for better. They can beam lessons, as in India, to five thousand remote villages. They are virtually the only means to combat illiteracy in certain areas.

Satellites will, in the not too distant future, make possible audio-visual communications between any two persons anywhere on earth; the availability any place of any volume in any library; or the ability to have the finest doctors or other experts instantly available throughout the world.

How can one evaluate the lives which may be saved by military reconnaissance satellites which are so powerful that they reveal the number on an automobile license plate?

Scientists are studying how to gather solar energy in outer space and beam it to earth by microwave. This is now feasible because we could send up solar energy power stations. There would be no interruptions because of night or inclement weather. Abundant "free" energy would thus be available, and whether it would take thirty years to develop this technique or a shorter time depends on our resolve.

Those who insist that the space program is too far out (symbolically as well as literally) to do any good on earth overlook the industries which space technology has already spawned. The United States has a natural monopoly of every major computer system. This is the result of NASA's stringent requirements and developments.

To cite only two other spin-offs, there is the integrated circuit industry which has created billions of dollars of income, and the structural analysis computer program, which designs trains, bridges, and buildings at a cost saving of hundreds of millions of dollars.

In medicine, the outgrowth of miniaturized solid state circuitry developed for spacecraft has made possible the cardiac pacemaker. Thirty thousand of these lifesaving instruments are implanted each year in the United States and a similar number in the rest of the world. Also NASA's miniaturization requirements have made possible the development of blood-pressure and heart-monitoring systems, which can be inserted by hypodermic needle rather than surgery; remote monitoring systems which enable a nurse to keep continual check on dozens of patients; electrocardiograms by radio or telephone, and the storage of white blood cells and bone marrow needed in treatment of leukemia.

In industry, the space program has given us fire-resistant paints, stronger plastics, heated piping (which we can use to transport oil from Alaska's oil field), super glues, and much, much more.

Theoretical science researchers are rarely aware of their progeny, although later they can trace their origins back to their begetters. Most often they have passed away not knowing that their creations have grown from abstraction to practical everyday miracles.

Even if the space program had not already shown its usefulness in varied ways, we should be confident that the vast new area of knowledge it opens to us will reward mankind in spectacular ways not dreamed of today. It has always been so, when the border of ignorance has been pushed back, and it will be so again.

SICKNESS COMES ON HORSEBACK AND LEAVES ON FOOT

The closest I have ever come to death was in 1947 at the hands of a doctor—and it was a dentist, too.

It began insignificantly enough. A tooth had lost its nerve and died. It could be saved with root canal work. In all fairness, I was warned that the particular molar involved did not lend itself to root canal procedure and there was a risk of infection. But the thought of losing a tooth was in a small way as horrifying as losing a limb. Vanity, not judgment, spurred me to salvage.

The dentist began the drilling operation. In a microscopic way it was similar to the rigs which drill for oil, ever deeper and deeper. Despite all aseptic precautions, it happened. An abscess developed. Concerned, the dentist suggested that I consult a foremost dental surgeon, who taught at one of the universities. He looked his part—white-haired, gray-faced, and with a taut though confident body and manner. He wore gold-rimmed glasses (which didn't matter because special telescopic lenses fitted over them to give him 100-100 vision). An attached blinding light beamed from his forehead as if it was a cyclops' eye.

He was so besieged by dentists who needed his reputation and skill that I had to visit him in the circular amphitheater where he taught. There were no students present, but I imagined the stands were filled with cheering crowds. To get at the abscess, he had to cut underneath the lower jaw, leaving me with a scar for life, not of honor in combat, but a reminder of my indiscretion. He scraped and scraped. Thoroughness in surgery sometimes means doing more than is necessary. Although I was anesthetized, I felt the knife, if not the pain it caused. That was to come later. It was an eerie feeling, like dreams in which one suffers falls or other catastrophes without being hurt, but experiences fear.

Finally it was over. Immense wads of packing filled my jaw. I was directed to stay overnight in the surgeon's private hospital. He would see me in his office forty-eight hours later to remove the packing, and dress the wound.

That night I became acquainted with an old, senile nurse. The poor woman was still dedicated to her task, but she was addled. She wore her nurse's crown backwards. This should have warned me of what was to come. In the middle of the night, she woke me from a daze and somberly announced that she was going to sponge me down. She did this backwards, too. First she dried me with towels, from jaw to foot. Then she sponged me, and when I was thoroughly wet, she left.

I rang the bell. Other nurses came. They knew of their comrade's hard-arteried brain. One of them set up a watch for her, rather than for me. It was a good precaution. The old lady, her spic-and-span nurse's hat, not only backwards but askew, as if she were drunk, returned with a needle, to give me an injection probably ordered for another patient. She was intercepted and led out.

The worst was still to come. I reported to the surgeon, my mouth still agape with cotton. He set me in his unusual chair, which made the electric chair look like a simple contraption. It had arms which collapsed, pedals which rose, a profusion of lamps on extension arms which moved in many directions, water receptacles with fountains which added gurgling noises to the patient's own, and a huge X-ray box which swung overhead and could have crushed the patient, if its supporting arm had slipped from its hinge. Fortunately I do not suffer from claustrophobia. I merely worried that the surgeon would be so hemmed in that he couldn't reach me.

He began to remove the gauze, yard by yard. He looked like a magician pulling hundreds of silk handkerchiefs from an impossibly small container. Suddenly, I felt a rush of warmth fill my mouth. It trickled out of my lips. It was red. The surgeon was shocked. He acted quickly and efficiently to pack the gauze back into the cavity. His nurse hastily supplied a large wad of cotton and helped him press it down hard over the wound. This was no match for the blood which now came in uncontrollable spurts. It washed away the obstruction, like a torrent of water breaking through a dike. It rushed down my throat. Instruments to suck it up were placed in my already crowded mouth and made gasping noises as they attempted to keep pace with the flood. Now towels were shoved into my mouth and pressed down on the gushes. To no avail. They came out soaked.

What had happened was that the surgeon had accidentally cut the carotid artery and when the packing was removed my life's blood began to pour out. In simple words, he had cut my throat.

My mouth was wide open and my head rigid, but my eyes observed the surgeon. As the towels got redder, his face grew paler. I could see that he was panic-striken. He screamed at his nurse to get more cotton. Then after a 180-degree turn, as if he didn't know in what direction to take off, he ordered the nurse to call an ambulance. "No," he countermanded, "that will take too long. Hail a taxi. Hurry."

By this time the alarm had spread. Attendants appeared from all sides. Hasty orders were given to reserve an operating room at Mount Sinai Hospital for immediate surgery. Dr. John Garlock, a foremost surgeon, was called to perform an emergency ligation (tying) of the artery.

A taxi arrived. The chauffeur was unlucky. His car was destined to be a bloody mess. The surgeon and his nurse took me into the cab. The nurse had taken along a handful of towels. They quickly gave out.

I could read in their faces the fear that I might die from the bloodletting before a transfusion and ligation could be performed.

Although I was sick from involuntarily swallowing blood, I decided to do something about the crisis. What? I had to banish the hysteria which surrounded me. Excitement would only make my heart beat faster and accelerate the spurts of blood. I made a conscious effort to be very, very calm. My training as a trial lawyer, who must remain serene in the midst of storms, came to my aid. I deliberately breathed softly (a strange picture came to my mind of Houdini surviving burial by taking shallow breaths). I closed my eyes, and became immobile. I wouldn't even raise my hand to hold a towel. I relaxed every muscle in my body until I was limp. Whether it was an illusion or not, I felt that I had actually slowed my pulse, and that the blood was not gushing with previous fury.

At the emergency entrance of the hospital, a stretcher was ready. A surgeon hovered over me nervously, as I was taken to the operating room. Mildred and my parents had been summoned. Their shocked faces and tears when they saw my ghoulish wide-open mouth packed red challenged my effort to avoid emotional strain. My blood was typed. Nurses were rushing in and out of the surgery room. Doctors with masks were arriving hastily, heightening the impression that I was experiencing a bad dream.

Then Dr. John Garlock arrived. If he was concerned, he hid it like a good psychologist. I was grateful. He smiled, and in a casual tone, as if there was no emergency (I remembered the lecture of a professor to his students, "If a severed artery is not sutured in two minutes, the patient will die. You can do it in two minutes, if you don't hurry!"), he said:

"Louis, I see that they have fixed you up good. Don't worry, I'll take care of it. You'll be all right."

Moving as little as possible, I motioned for a pad and pencil, indicating that I wanted to write something.

He handed me his doctor's notebook and a pencil. I wrote:

I am not alarmed. I feel that the bleeding is slowing down. I really think it will coagulate. Please don't operate. Give me another 15 minutes. It may not be necessary.

His face looked severe as he read the note. Then the vertical lines in his cheeks gave way to a grin, and finally a full smile.

"Anyone who can write a note like this at this time—I'll take a chance on."

He left for a few minutes, to talk with the anesthetist, nurses, and assistants. He had ordered a delay of the surgery, to the dismay of the dental surgeon, who had become so jittery that I wanted to write another note suggesting that he be given a sedative.

Dr. Garlock called for a chair and sat down slowly. I felt he was in tune with my pace. Then he casually held my hand, testing the pulse without looking at a watch. I renewed my concentration on slowing the blood flow. There was no doubt that each heartbeat was no longer accompanied by a gush into the mouth. Dr. Garlock did not want to disturb me even to determine whether time was a healer or a fatal loss. But one could see that the flood had slowed to a trickle. I did not have to write another note. My eyes did the pleading. He gave me another extension, for which I was more grateful than any I had ever received in court.

The bleeding stopped. I was placed in a bed so gently that the pillow hardly dented. Intravenous relief was given. That night, I did not move an inch no matter how uncomfortable it was to lie in one position. We do not realize it, but each of us exercises a good deal during a night's sleep. Our muscles need renewed circulation which can only be obtained by turning and twisting. A good night's rest does not mean what it literally says. It really means some healthy tossing about. So my determination not to move subjected me to a special kind of pain, like that which comes from being forbidden to scratch an itching skin.

Came the day when the packing would again be removed. Would there be another disaster? This time, Dr. Garlock, surrounded by the dental surgeon and nurses, performed the task. His long, stubby fingers, famous for their strength and sensitive dexterity, were applied to the mundane task, usually done perfunctorily by a nurse. He gently, inch by inch, removed the packing. If there was the slightest resistance, he sensed it, stopped, and with faintest movements freed the gauze before proceeding. As the doctors and nurses peered over his shoulder, I had the image of detonating squads during the war removing a pin from a bomb with breath-holding caution. Only this time it was not their lives which were at stake. It was mine.

At last the task was done. There was no mishap. The very blood with which we had struggled became its own healer and sealed the artery. From then on it was nature's process, not knives and sutures, which completed the cure. Of course there was much discomfort, but fortunately it cannot be re-experienced by recollection. Joys can be. Pain can't.

The cure was not perfect. For about six months I suffered from trismus, a partial locking of the jaw. I nevertheless continued to try cases and make speeches. I had to fall back on my singing days, and by forming circles with my lips, I was able to project my voice even though I could only open my jaws two inches. I missed only one early engagement, an introduction of President Truman at a public function at the Waldorf-Astoria in New York. I would have had to talk through clenched teeth, and I didn't want him to think I was a Republican.

The greatest healer I have ever met was a naturopath. His name was Sholem Baranoff. It was by coincidence that I got to know him, but his influence on me, like that of all great teachers, was profound and lasting. To a considerable extent I have followed his precepts for good health, and as much as possible avoided medicines and particularly surgery. I have never taken a headache pill and only on a few rare occasions, in all my life, an aspirin or its equivalent. I shun drugstore drugs like a plague.

My acquaintance with Baranoff started about forty years ago. Mildred and I had returned from a trip abroad which included Israel. There was a white miracle in that land of miracles. It had snowed in Jerusalem. The unseasonable weather caught us with our resistance down. We returned debilitated from our arduous travels and encountered the penetrating freezing cold of a New York winter. We decided to go south. Florida was a natural choice, but Miami and its environs represented the hectic life of its self advertised playground. Was there anything on the west coast of Florida? Yes, Safety Harbor Spa. Every word of the title appealed to me. We tried it.

It was what I had dreamed of, quietly beautiful and isolated. Its feature was a former state building where spring waters of three kinds were bottled. As the state literature did not hesitate to inform, these springs had been discovered by Ponce de León, and might be the fabled fountain of youth. This impressive building had been bought and transformed into a private dining room, the nucleus of the spa. In the center of the room was still a well, from which waters could be tapped. In each room were three large bottles of differently numbered waters, whose taste, after a while, was sufficient identification.

We checked into a simple room, which had none of the grandeur of the state building. Within a few moments, the telephone rang. "Dr. Baranoff would like to see you."

"Who is he?" I asked.

"He is the owner, and you must be examined, so that he can prescribe the food you are to have, and what spa treatments are permissible."

It was the rule. We could not waive it. Reluctantly, we went downstairs and met Baranoff for the first time. The immediate impression was of a slight, thin man with a shock of hair as white as his smock, contrasting with black eyebrows and dark, penetrating eyes. His head was wide on top because his snowy long hair floated sideways but tapered to a triangle despite a strong chin. We couldn't tell his age. Judged by his vitality, he was about fifty, but his drawn, lined face might make him seventy. His kindness and sincere interest in us quickly overcame our resistance.

After a few preliminaries, and before the usual procedure of blood pressure, listing of former illnesses and the like, he carefully wrote down what our eating habits were. He reached for the smallest detail. It was an emphasis, I learned later from his lectures, which was the key to his diagnosis of all ills.

"Your food is the chemistry you give to the body. You are what you eat. But each person is different. Orange juice is excellent Vitamin C for some, but harmful to others. When we discover the needs of your body, we are on the road to good health."

This was not so startling in 1951, but in the early 1900s, when Baranoff first wrote his theories, it was. His other theories, which I shall describe, aroused the scorn of the medical authorities, but he was to live to see many of them accepted by foremost doctors.

After a little while, he ushered me into an adjoining room, where there was a cubicle, to undress. Then he put me on a table and began to press different parts of my body with steel-strong fingers, here gently, there severely. The first words out of his mouth were, "Your thyroid glands are not functioning right."

Doctors had told me after several checkups that my metabolism was low. His accuracy on mere touch surprised me. My lawyer's skepticism came to the fore.

"What makes you say that?" I said casually.

"You winced when I touched you here," he replied, applying a heavier finger which made me jump. "There is a lack of circulation, or you wouldn't feel it any more than when I touch you here."

"Well, I must admit Doctor, you are right. That's the only thing the doctors found that was wrong."

"So, what have they done for you—given you thyroid pills?"

"Yes."

"Of course. And what will that do? They'll just weaken your heart." Angrily, "Throw them away. Has anyone asked why a person as healthy as you are shouldn't be producing sufficient thyroid extract?" Without waiting for an answer, he turned warm and friendly and spoke in a conspiratorial tone.

"I'll tell you what we'll do. I'll give you a simple exercise for your neck which will correct the defect, but only on one condition." He paused. "If you promise to do it every day without fail. O.K.?" He held out his hand to seal the bargain. We shook hands on it. He then illustrated certain exercises which were designed to bring blood to the neck and particularly to the thyroid gland. In my later annual checkups, there has never been a finding of low metabolism.

I was intrigued by his psychological approach, exacting a promise in the interest of the patient. The concern for my well being was an act of friendship which elicited confidence.

"I will write out a diet for you." Studying the notes he had taken of what I like to eat, he prepared a card, which was an instruction not only for the kitchen but for the waitress. His wife, Lisa, was the chief cook. She had to know you, too. Her inquiries were not the mere formal ones, but the gathering of findings, which in consultation with her husband would result in adjustments on the card. Every person at the table was served a different meal, suited to the idiosyncratic needs of his body. We couldn't deviate. The waitress, trained to be polite but firm, would not honor our requests.

This caused some grumbling, but as most victims found themselves feeling and looking better, they yielded to the discipline, while poking fun at it. I induced my father and mother to visit there for a vacation. For many years he had tried to lose some thirty pounds and had been unable to do so. Being a man of will, he tried all sorts of methods. He would fast Wednesdays, but then he caught up with his hunger the rest of the week.

Under Baranoff's regime, he lost weight, but he amused everyone around him by ridiculing the diet. He would look at the plate before him, nine tenths of which was shining porcelain, and announce, "I usually leave more than this," or "No wonder they make money here. There is no expense spared for food." Nevertheless he and my mother were captivated by Baranoff. There was a common old-country tie among them. Baranoff would gather a few aficionados of Sholem Aleichem, or Peretz, or Bialik and in an improvised entertainment he would read some of their writings in English or sometimes in the original Yiddish. All this intimacy was before Safety Harbor Spa became a roaring success, with million-dollar buildings, modern spa equipment from steam to sauna, and from pools to plush paraphernalia.

Occasionally, guests would arrive who knew nothing of Baranoff's dictatorial dedication to their health. We would hear some commotion in the dining room, because they had demanded bread, and the waitress had told them it was against the rules. The Friday night, at his weekly lecture, Baranoff dropped his benign attitude, and pointedly addressed the rebellious guests.

"This spa has certain theories about good health. I have spent a lifetime developing them. Those who come here and want to learn to be healthier live up to these principles. Those who do not believe in them have no right to interfere with the others. They have a perfect right to live and eat as they choose. There are many fine hotels nearby. They are welcome to leave. If they didn't know about our rules, and came here by mistake, we will make no charge for the day they have been here, and we wish them luck and good health."

Each of his lectures dealt with a different part of the body—heart, liver, pancreas, the mind, and why they failed us. The stress always was on prevention, not cure. Underlying all his theories was a simple leitmotif. Proper food intake, which "keeps the blood thin" and therefore circulating freely, and proper daily exercise of a certain kind, which brings the good blood to the vital organs, were the key to health. "A clear flowing stream will wash away impurities. They will never be noticed. But a stagnant pool will sooner or later be filled with rot."

A half century after he first argued this oversimplistic rule, he had the satisfaction of reading to his audience the conclusion of the famous Dr. Paul Dudley White after a lifetime of study and experience, that healthy eating habits and exercise were the best preventives of heart disease and for that matter of other afflictions.

Baranoff was opposed to all diets. He insisted that one must learn to eat properly. Then there would be no need to cut down intake, be tempted back again to excess, and go through the sacrifice again of severe discipline. He saw no need to be deprived at all. Healthy foods were more delicious than unhealthy ones. He had his own way of persuasion.

"When you were a child, and you wanted to paste a picture into a book, what did you use for glue? Flour and water—right? Well, that is what bread is made of—especially after modern processors remove the only nutritious thing in it, the brown wheat. That's the paste that cakes are made of, and they add all sorts of goo on top of it. They are filled with white sugar from which has been removed the only valuable nutrient to make it white, and a chemical added to make it shine."

After a number of such descriptions one was inclined to look at bread or cake as pretty revolting objects. Then he described a beautiful pear, a rose-tinted peach, a ripe purple plum, grapes filled with sunshine, dates and figs bursting with sweetness, toasted almonds and other variety flavored nuts, before he ennobled the taste of a tomato, artichoke, asparagus, squash, and other exotic-tasting vegetables. Finally he turned to the protein family, in which richly flavored broiled pompano, or juice-covered lean meat crowned the meal and delighted the stomach. One had to hear the saliva flowing dulcet tones in which these descriptions were given to understand why listeners developed a love affair with foods they couldn't stomach before.

"Now, when instead you eat highly peppered and salted pastrami and corned beef, inside two thick pieces of bread, and then some ice cream with whipped cream or chocolate cake, what happens to all the paste which you pushed into your stomach? Your digestive process cannot get rid of all of it. Ordinarily a mound of paste would form which could obstruct your bowels and perhaps kill you. But nature protects you. To prevent this from happening, it passes it into the bloodstream, which then spreads it thin along the arteries to which it adheres. For a long time, you don't notice it. But with the years, the coated arteries get narrower and narrower. Your blood supply to the heart and other organs diminishes. They become undernourished and weak, and victims of all sorts of diseases. The doctors fill you with medicines. But the underlying cause not only continues, it gets worse, because of your suicidal eating habits. Then one day, the blood can't get through the artery at all. You get a heart attack and die. The doctors call it an occlusion. Your friends say, 'He was such a strong, healthy person, and suddenly he dropped dead.'

"Suddenly? It took years of stupid eating to bring it about. You were killing yourself surely but gradually. Your body is the greatest doctor you will ever know. Why do you abuse it? Why don't you give it a chance to keep you healthy."

He interrupted with an epigram, "Nature cures and the doctor sends you the bill."

His nontechnical and, I am sure, at times, nonmedical analysis aroused resistance and sometimes abuse from doctors. I recall my partner, Walter Beck, who knew much about medicine (and had tried malpractice cases), reacting to one of Baranoff's lectures. Baranoff had resorted to his homey analogies, which lent themselves to ridicule from sophisticated, medically trained men.

"Your arteries are like the plumbing in your house. Fatty deposits are like rust that close the openings and make the water come slowly, then in drips and then not at all."

Beck laughed at the plumbing analogy. It demonstrated Baranoff's lack of medical knowledge, which had been such a boon to better health. Our longevity span is constantly increasing, he pointed out.

Several years later, CBS network announced a special program revealing the first motion picture X-ray technique. It enabled the viewer to see blood actually flowing through an artery. It looked like a river running through a ravine. A number of famous doctors and scientists were commenting on the improved opportunity to make observations. The same artery was photographed at different intervals, many months apart. One could see a little hill form inside the artery which obstructed the natural speed of the blood. A later X-ray motion picture showed the hill, considerably enlarged, and the adjoining tissue much thicker. A still later picture clearly showed a narrowing of the artery which impeded the flow. The accompanying lecture by the professor explained that it was cholesterol or other fatty substances which were responsible for the closing of the artery, so that in the last demonstration the blood was desperately trying to get through a pinhole in the clogged artery.

Then the lecturer, apparently as a concession to the assumed low intelligence of the mass television audience, decided to simplify the matter for easy comprehension.

"You see," he said, "the arteries are exactly like the plumbing in your house. When rust gathers on them they grow smaller, and one day we have to clean them out or replace them. Well, it is not as easy to remove the fatty deposits which coat the artery, though we have tried, and of course it is even more difficult to replace them. So the lesson is, ladies and gentlemen, avoid food with saturated oil. Stay away from breads, sweet desserts, chocolates and fats."

Baranoff had his own ideas about what he called compatible eating, more accurately, compatible foods. He contended that there were two kinds of digestive systems. Tigers and lions could digest only meat, not grass or carbohydrates. On the other hand cows could only digest grass, not meat. Man was one of those animals who could digest both. However, the digestive juices required for meats were different from those for carbohydrates. Our bodies produced pepsin and hydrochloric acid to break down meat. But to digest bread, spaghetti, or other carbohydrates other juices were required, such as saliva and pancreatic juice. It was incompatible to mix the two. So, if one ate bread with steak, he was eating incompatibly, because the digestive juices necessary for meat were useless to digest bread, and vice versa. Hydrochloric acid needed to

break up meat molecules was unnecessary and inimical to carbohydrates. They clashed. This was the cause, he argued, of heartburn, gas,
and indigestion. He therefore counseled that it was all right to eat a
protein meal or a sensible carbohydrate meal of spaghetti or potato,
vegetables, whole-wheat bread, and even ice cream or fruit, but not
with bacon, steak, or other proteins. These were incompatible.

"A piece of bread begins to be digested in the mouth. Saliva is essential. It should therefore be fully chewed before swallowing. But a piece
of meat, which doesn't need saliva, could be swallowed without injuring the digestive process. Use one or the other of your digestive
systems. Don't mix them."

Baranoff did not claim to be the originator of the compatible eating
theory. It came from the old Hays diet. I was never convinced of its
soundness. Many authorities insist that our bodies adjust to far greater
"clashes" of intake. It had one virtue, however. It reduced the quantity
of food we ate. If one eliminated bread or a potato from his meat meal,
it might or might not avoid digestive incompatibility, but it surely reduced the calorie consumption. This in itself was desirable. On this
point he was adamant and I don't believe contradictable. He insisted
that our bodies needed much less food than any of us thought, and that
by constantly overstuffing ourselves, we compelled the body needlessly
to struggle with burning up the food to turn it into glucose. This was a
waste of our energy. It was counterproductive to "thin blood" and good
health.

"When you sit down to dinner in a restaurant with your friends,
what do you do? You have a cocktail. You are hungry. So while chatting and waiting for the menu, you eat a roll, maybe two, with plenty
of butter on it. You do not realize it, but you have already eaten a full
meal and not a very wise one, either. You ought to get up and go home.
Then the waiter arrives, and you begin all over again. If you put a duplicate of everything you ate thereafter into a pail and under the table,
you would be ashamed to carry it out of the place."

Another basic, perhaps oversimplistic theory of his was that in essence there was only one disease, toxicity.

"We have many names for diseases. Wherever there is a weakness in
the body, the poisons of toxicity cause trouble. If the frailty is in the
shoulder, we call it arthritis; in the blood supply to the heart, we call it
heart disease; in the lung, pneumonia; in the eyes, cataracts, but the
cause is all the same. If the blood is pure from right eating and you circulate it properly with exercise, none of these conditions will occur."

His lectures were never just strictures for health and longevity. They
were accompanied by stirring assertions of the joys of living, of being of
happy disposition, of love and generosity. He caused laughter, by mim-

icking the sour face of someone suffering from dyspepsia; his nastiness
to his wife and children, his crotchety walk, and his general misery.
Then he enacted a healthy man. His eyes glistened like those of a
young lover. He pranced about nimbly, and held out his arms as if he
would embrace the world. "Which one do you think will succeed in his
business? Which one will be popular? Which one will make everybody
around him happy? Which one will love and be loved?"

I noticed that he eschewed references to the word spiritual. It was
too ephemeral. His convictions were based on physical perfection. He
pored over anatomy books day and night, comparing their learning with
his own tactile observations. He strove for the impossible. One had to
experience his "treatment" on a table. It was chiropractic or osteopathic. It was uniquely Baranoff. His fingers touched, probed, and
explored endlessly. They were as sensitive as the heralded sandpapered
fingers of a safecracker. Patients dubbed them X-ray fingers. When he
thought he discovered a knotted muscle, or a slight swelling, or a lack
of elasticity, his whole body stiffened, like a hunter who senses his prey.
He soon knew. When he touched more deeply there was pain: the
body underneath him coiled and reacted. Then he would massage the
area, ignoring the agonized outcries of the patient. He became remorseless. He would press still harder. It was his only streak of cruelty.
His dedication to the patient's health overcame his sympathy for the
writhing body. Time and again he would return to the same spot.
Each time the pain was less.

"You see, I have forced circulation there and it is bringing you relief."

Sometimes after such a treatment the patient would go to his room
and fall soundly asleep for an hour or two. I had this experience a number of times. Could it be not only that the muscle or tendon had been
relieved, but that the nerves involved in the area also responded?
Baranoff thought so. He claimed that there were "plexuses," or nerve
centers, which fed various organs. If one of these was constricted, he
knew that the organ dependent on it, whether kidney or liver, bladder
or prostate, could not be functioning right. This was his method of detecting that a vital organ in the body was not functioning as it should.
The patient almost jumped off the table with pain when he dug ino a
plexus which was related to the defective organ.

Although Baranoff may not have known it, this theory had ancient
origins. In effect it was related to acupuncture, but without "insulting"
the body with piercing needles. I have heard of it since as "zone therapy," pressing certain nerve ends, particularly in the toes, which indicate by pain that the organs of the body "fed" by them (echoes of
Baranoff's nonscientific explanations) are not functioning properly. A

touch of a specific area of a toe, "connected with the ear," will not hurt one who has no hearing problem. However, another person, troubled with slight deafness in his left ear, will register intense pain from the same touch. To this extent, credence in zone therapy is heightened. Is it possible that we will develop techniques for bringing nerve energy supply to our organs, as we bring blood supply to our muscles to improve them?

I do not know whether the plexus response explained Baranoff's deduction or whether his general highly developed "instincts" about the body informed him. I am sure that he was sincere, and my skepticism was reduced by some extraordinary cures I witnessed with my own eyes. I shall cite only a few, although there were others.

A woman arrived who was so crippled that despite the sympathy she aroused, there was grumbling by a number of guests that they had come for a vacation and not to a sanitorium. She was bent over so low that she used two small canes to prevent her from toppling over. She was apparently a woman of means and had had treatment by foremost doctors and neurologists at leading clinics. They could not straighten her up. It was a gruesome sight to see her practically on all fours like an animal. She had been recommended to Baranoff. Several days later, she walked into the dining room, straight up. At first no one was sure it was she. Then when a murmur went through the room that indeed it was, everyone stood. Cheers broke out. Women cried. Some yelled it was a miracle. It was a hysterical scene. Baranoff had to quiet the audience and address them. He severely chided them for nonsensical talk about miracles. There were none. The human body is a remarkable machine, and when it breaks down, a good mechanic, that's all he was, can sometimes find the defect and straighten it out. "It only proves that despite the fact that we abuse our bodies, it is never too late to make them function right."

Another case was that of a car dealer who had become well known through radio advertising as "The Smiling Irishman." He was Jewish, but I suppose it wouldn't have sounded as well had he called himself "The Smiling Jew" or "The Smiling Italian." Perhaps the compliment to the Irish persuaded them to overlook the deception. He had such a severe heart condition that he had to retire from his business. He was not even permitted to drive a car. Baranoff insisted that he had no heart condition at all. His heart was quite strong. It was a circulation problem. There wasn't enough blood flowing to it. He put the man on a "cleansing" diet, taught him mild exercises, and spent hours kneading him with those X-ray fingers of his. The man recovered. He drove his car again, and went back to his business.

Baranoff had his failures, too, and it was my own senior law partner,

Louis Phillips, who was the victim of one of them. Louis had a family history of heart disease. The inexorable code written in his genes and chromosomes did not except him from his fate. Five years before he died, from hardening of the arteries around his heart, Baranoff detected the condition. He did not want to alarm Phillips, but he told me, "Your partner has a very serious condition. The muscles near his heart are so rigid they feel like stone."

He attempted to dig deeply into them to soften them with blood supply. His powerful fingers cracked one of Phillips' ribs. Understandably, Louis would have nothing more to do with Baranoff. "Let him illustrate how strong he is on somebody else's ribs," he said. But he was tolerant enough to permit his wife, Helen, to go to Safety Harbor, which she continued to do long after Louis died.

Another illustration involved Wilbur Wood, the sports editor of the now defunct New York *World Telegram*. He had a severe case of diabetes and administered his own insulin injection daily. Baranoff disagreed with the medical theory that once the pancreas stops functioning it cannot be revived. He believed that sometimes it can be induced to produce its vital extract. By careful exercises, deep finger therapy, and a special diet in which onions were heavily favored, he stimulated the pancreas, constantly reducing the insulin intake. Finally he told Wood he could give up the needle. Wood was scared. Baranoff invited him to be tested daily in a nearby hospital. The miracle had happened. When Wood returned, his doctors couldn't believe what had happened. They considered it one of those rare remissions which occur even in cancer. I saw the letter one of them wrote to Baranoff, expressing his delight and surprise and asking for information of the treatment.

Baranoff rejected uniformity in exercise as he did in food. Every individual was just that to him, an individual, not a type. He improvised exercises for each person to correct some particular defect. One could see him experiment until he found the movement which would affect the part of the body he "was after."

"Let's see, hold this leg down and move your right leg out to the side." His fingers tested the result. He was unsatisfied. He tried again and again, until he literally felt that the exercise was reaching the desired result. I was round-shouldered. This he explained was due to a "sway" in the spine. He struck a harmless blow with the side of his hand, like a karate chop into the lower spine.

"There's no use working on the shoulders. They are the result of this down here. Now we can straighten that curve a little. Let me show you how."

He made me get off the table. He bounced on, got on his knees, dug his head inward, and then pushed his hands forward as far as they could reach. He asked me to put my hand on his lower back. I felt the convex curve rise and get flatter. He assured me that even at my age the spine could be straightened, provided I did this exercise at least five minutes a day.

"The body is good to you. It never gives up. It's you who give up."

When he lectured on Friday nights, his enthusiasm broke through all formalities. He stressed mobility.

"If you're forty and you walk like this, you're an old man." He imitated a slouching shuffle, which looked very much like the gait of some of the young men in the audience who laughed embarrassedly.

"But if you walk like this when you are ninety, you are a young man."

This was true of arms as well as legs. He said not one of a hundred persons could lift his arms straight up, alongside and touching his ears. He demonstrated. Suddenly, he took off his tweed jacket, opened his tie, and lay flat on the floor, illustrating knee movements to the chest. "This," he would say from a prone position, "is wonderful for your liver." He held up a fist and closed the fingers tight. "That's the effect of bending your knees tight to your stomach. It squeezes the liver. You ought to do this every morning without fail."

He disapproved of typical American exercises, which developed the biceps and other muscles, not needed for the sedentary life we led. In this respect he was in harmony with yoga theories that exercises should be mild and directed toward stimulating blood flow to vital organs. For example, he advised just simple stretching in the morning and several times a day as most beneficial. "Watch a cat or dog after it has slept. It stretches . . ." He pushed out his hands as if they were paws, threw back his head, and registered relief. Then he lay down and stretched his legs as if they were the hind legs of an animal. "This brings the blood to all parts of the body. It is wonderful." He looked so happy we imagined he had grown healthier in our presence.

When he prescribed numerous exercises which I should do every morning, I would laughingly comment that I would never get to the office. He saw no humor in this. With utmost earnestness, he said, "Have you an appointment diary in your office?"

"Of course."

"Well, write in every morning from nine to ten the name of your most important client. It is you."

After his lectures he would invite questions. There was no lack of skeptics in the audience. "Don't you believe in any medicines? Hasn't medical science eliminated many diseases?"

"Of course, I believe in medicines, chiefly those that nature provides.

They are in every food. The water, after parsley is boiled, is a diuretic. Grape juice is nourishing for the nerves. Grapefruit cleanses the blood. Onions stimulate the pancreas and produce nature's insulin. The trouble with synthetic medicine is that you don't know its complete effect on the body. Medicines are necessary when you are sick. But why should you be? Man's natural state is to be in good health. Live right and you won't need doctors' medicines. They will be in your food."

The year after penicillin was discovered, Baranoff included it as a topic in his talk.

"It will save many lives, so it is a blessing. People torn apart in an automobile accident will survive because of it. Mastoid operations may become unnecessary.

"But, I warn you, ladies and gentlemen, it will also kill hundreds of people. Already hospitals report many deaths of people allergic to it.

"Every time a new drug or pill is discovered, we are in danger that later, it will be learned that it caused cancer, or blindness, or lord knows what. No drug is intelligent enough to attack only the virus that we don't like. Before we sing Halleluja about a patient cured by penicillin, we ought to examine the lacy tissue of his kidney and see what happened to it.

"Please, please, don't ask your doctor or permit him to give you penicillin unless there is no alternative to save your life. There almost always is. The oldest remedy is still good. Sweat out the disease. Fever is nature's way of burning up the germ. Don't kill the fever with aspirins. It is a warning signal, and you don't cure the disease by silencing the alarm bell. Medicines often sweep the disease under the rug. That is why colds reappear again and again, during the winter. You have deceived yourself by thinking you have got rid of it.

"If you must take penicillin, be sure to drink a lot of orange juice with it."

Some of his warnings about food provoked challenging questions.

"Why do you condemn eggs and milk? The whole world knows that eggs are a healthy food. If you believe in nature, how about the fact that babies are nourished by milk at their mothers' breasts?"

Almost half a century earlier, Baranoff had written severe criticism of eggs. He did not know the word "cholesterol," but his study of the content of food and, above all, his knowledge of the human body learned by touch, combined with detailed information about the food intake of each patient, made him suspicious of certain foods. Eggs were one of them. He was not a laboratory scientist. His was an empirical approach. He experimented and observed until he reached a conclusion. He applied the Thomas Edison method to health research, using trial and error. Today, the great laboratories have confirmed the high cholesterol content of eggs, seafood, butter, liver, and meats and other foods with saturated fats. So very respectable medical authorities now agree with Baranoff that eggs should be eaten sparingly.

He was opposed to shellfish, chiefly because they were scavengers. He pointed out that scaled fish ate plankton, and not the filth at the bottom of polluted waters. He warned that scavengers would sooner or later infect us. Much later hepatitis, unfortunately, became a well-known word.

As for Baranoff's opinion about milk: "It is too concentrated a food for a mature person. It has a high calcium content. This is necessary for growing children, whose bones are growing. In an older person, it is not needed, and nature deposits the excess calcium near joints. Then you have arthritis.

"Also, notice that while we swallow a glass of milk like water, a child doesn't drink milk. It chews it. It knows instinctively that it is a very concentrated food, not to be gulped down.

"Besides, once we take the child away from the breast, we cut down the concentration in milk. We devise formulas. That is really a way of diluting the milk."

At one time he had been impelled by devotion to principle as well as to purity of food to be a vegetarian. But, as always, he bowed to nature, the final arbiter. Man belongs to that species of animals whose digestive tracts prospered on meat, even raw meat (witness steak tartare). Also, meat has the highest concentration of protein of any food. So be it, then.

There was no liquor bar at Safety Harbor. There were grapefruit bars. At four o'clock, one opened around the pool. Others were strategically placed inside. You also had a choice of apple or grape juice, depending on the instruction on your card. Dull? Surprisingly not. The cold, juicy half grapefrut with a little honey on it hit the spot after a day outdoors and a receptively empty stomach. Still, there was a thrill in sneaking directly across the street where there was a bar, whose owner understood temptation and the excitement of violating rules. He was the kind of man who would build an oasis in the desert. Guests of the spa ran into each other there, and the sinners laughingly exchanged recriminations.

Actually, Baranoff was not opposed to alcohol. He considered it a natural food and a healthy stimulant, preferring scotch to Bourbon because the former tended to dilate the arteries, while the latter to constrict them. When, after several weeks of discipline, we bade farewell to return to New York, he would share a scotch or, preferably, a little brandy with us. "I am opposed to the cocktail hour, not the cocktail," he would say. "It comes at the worst time. Liquor stimulates the appetite, and we do not need such artificial stimulation before sitting down to eat. We eat too much anyhow."

The only time a question embarrassed him was when he was asked about smoking. He said it was a terrible habit. What could be worse than substituting smoke for clean air in the lungs? Smoking had increased lung cancer enormously. It injured the eyes. It caused bronchial conditions and sometimes fatal emphysema.

Then why was he embarrassed? Because he smoked. He explained that once this awful habit had been acquired, it might take more toll of the nervous system to quit than to cut down. He therefore had reduced his smoking to a few cigarettes a day. He sought to mollify his confession with a little philosophy: "Nothing done in moderation can be very harmful."

In a negative way, he had provided another lesson. That a man of his adamant convictions buttressed by an iron will should not be able to give up the filthy weed only demonstrated what a powerful addiction smoking was. True, he had a habit of sixty, perhaps seventy years to overcome. I could tell he came from Russia by the way he held his cigarette between the middle two fingers, so that when he put it between his lips the rest of the hand covered his lower face. I am sure that he also bit a piece of sugar before sipping his glass of russet-colored tea. Age, and I suspect illness, finally freed him from his only inconsistency. In later years, he has not smoked at all.

He was such a blind lover of nature that even when it contradicted him he yielded. After all the interdictory lectures, he would nevertheless say:

"Your body is your best instructor. If you feel a terrible urge to have chocolate, eat some. It means that you need sugar badly. Or if you are dying for pickled herring, have it. Your body may need salt and vinegar. Ordinarily highly seasoned food eats at the lining of your stomach and helps to bring on an ulcer. But occasionally, it will not hurt you. Moderation in everything is your best protection."

I liked this deviation from fanaticism, even if it had not been justified as another rule of nature, because I distrust any theory, whether in religion, politics, economics, or health which holds itself out as a perfect solution. There are no panaceas even in heaven, or why would we need guardian angels?

Baranoff scorned psychiatry. If I have not already subjected him to discredit as a "kook" because of his theories, this should alienate another large segment of the population. He did not believe that the mind was any less physical than the heart or liver. If it did not function well, there was a physical cause. He would have rejected the couplet:

What is mind
No Matter
What is Matter
Never mind.

If the brain was not functioning normally, it might be due to defective blood supply, inherited weakness of a lobe, physical abnormality in some part of the body which deprived the brain of nerve or blood supply, "a twisted nerve" (again Baranoff's atrocious similes), but he would not accept what to him was a mystical theory that the mind was spiritual and not to be classified in the same way as any physical organ of the body. In response to the flood of criticisms which this evoked from his listeners, he held his ground tenaciously.

"True, shocking news of a sudden death may affect the mind. There is no physical blow, you say, but there is. For example, it will affect the solar plexus, a group of nerves, here near the stomach. That is why such news can cause diarrhea. A shock to the nervous system is the same as a physical blow, and may therefore affect the brain. Often it will shut off blood supply. That is why a person faints when he hears terrible news. Phobias have similar physical causes. The chemistry of the body can be affected, causing disease, or even insanity. But," his voice turned to sarcastic ridicule, "it has nothing to do with tracing how your mother treated you when you were five years old."

He once made a daring experiment in a lunatic asylum, and got into trouble for his pains. He had persuaded the head of such an institution that he could improve the conditions of many inmates, and perhaps cure some of them, by applying simple health measures. Since no surgery or medicines were involved, the open-minded "warden" permitted him to try. Baranoff studied the eating habits of the inmates. What was outstanding was the number of pills of all kinds which they took each day. Most of them were sedatives to calm the unruly population, and really for the benefit of the keepers rather than the residents. Others were laxatives to overcome the sedatives, and there were many others of varying colors and purposes. The inmates were pimply. Their rashes and skin revealed the "poisoning" to which they were subjected.

Baranoff ordered that all these medicines be stopped. Simultaneously he installed high colonics to cleanse them. Then he prescribed food designed to remove toxicity—grapefruit, grape juice, apples, celery, etc.— but with as much individual adjustment as was possible under the circumstances. The result was remarkable. So much so that the state authorities discovered the unauthorized interference by one not even a M.D. but only a "naturopath." The rules had been violated. The head of the institution was reprimanded. Baranoff, after a hearing, was lucky to escape the cancellation of his license. I do not know whether any attention was given to the demonstration, but I suspect not.

Over the years, our friendship grew. A group of doctors, impressed by the results he was getting in healing, and with the possibilities of growth and profits, bought into Safety Harbor Spa. Baranoff neither needed nor wanted much money. His real mission and satisfaction in life were to preach and practice his theories and teach people how to be healthy. He was induced to make the deal not because it gave him and his family financial security, but because he saw the possibility of enlarging his influence in a greater institution.

As in all things in life, there was bad with the good. Magnificent modern buldings were constructed over the years. New spa equipment was installed, featuring an indoor hot jet pool, whirlpool baths, solariums, massage areas in the sun and indoors, jet showers, and all the rest now copied by many spas which have sprouted all over the country.

One was no longer examined by Baranoff alone. He sent you for the customary medical checkup to one of two resident physicians. Lisa was no longer the cook, presiding lovingly over each preparation. She retired. There was a staff which had to be more impersonal with the increase of guests.

Baranoff could only give his special treatments to a relatively few of the new flood of guests. He worked as hard as he could, never rushing, however. But how could he keep up with the growing clientele? Some came who did not even know of him, except for his Friday night lectures. Many skipped them in favor of motion pictures and prize entertainments offered in other rooms. I could see Baranoff growing unhappier with success and prosperity. He was of course making much more money, but this meant nothing to him. Indeed, he was offered far more attractive contracts by other spas which were being built throughout the country, and this despite his age.

What was his age? No one knew. He always taught that there was no reason why people couldn't live to the biblical one hundred and twenty years "at least." Some thought he was approaching that himself. I recall once sitting in a steam room, chatting with a friend of Baranoff's in tones made hollow and echo-like by the visible heat. He knew him from the old country, Russia. He computed his age by disaster landmarks: a collapsed bridge, a fire which destroyed the vegetable shed, an overflowed river which swept away a child on its bank, and other unhappy events which fixed the dates in memory. By such a circuitous route, he was certain Baranoff was at least eighty years old. That was more than twenty years ago, and Baranoff is still tossing bodies around on his table.

Baranoff's relationship with the doctor-owners sometimes created conflicts. There was such a thing as incompatible association as well as incompatible eating.

One Christmas holiday, the professional managers, not imbued with his theories, arranged a children's outdoor party. Frankfurters and Coca-Cola were served. When Baranoff heard of this, he dashed to the scene and condemned the desecration of his temple with the same passion with which Moses had castigated the revelers around the golden calf. The blow was deeper than his new associates could understand. He had dedicated his life to an ideal, and now the children who should be educated early were being led along the same old path which made Americans physically unfit despite the highest standard of living. His fury astonished the staff. They could not quite understand why a frankfurter and a Coca-Cola should cause such turmoil. They did not understand that he felt his life's work being destroyed before his very eyes and in his own home. Nevertheless, they were moved by the purity of his convictions. When the hall where lectures were given to listeners who sat on hard folding chairs was replaced in 1964 by a modern, one-thousand-cushioned-seat theater, rivaling the finest Broadway structure, with a curtained stage, blazing with lights as varied as the moods he depicted in his lectures, the owners voted that it be called "The Baranoff Theater" and arranged a dedication ceremony.

There are men, like Baranoff, known only to limited thousands whom he taught and touched healingly over a long span, but not known to the multitudes. It is one of the misfortunes of a troubled world that "Full many a flower is born to blush unseen."

Many worthy men make their impact in limited circles, while generals, athletes, and politicians, who ought to be proud to stand in their shadows, achieve worldwide fame. The world's spotlight is not very discriminating. Its beam follows the television wave and thus lights on the sensational, the titillating, and the morbid more often than on the scholarly and profound.

The auditorium reflected two groups. Those who knew, and those who ought to have known. Gathered were many of Baranoff's patients who owed either their health or even their lives to him. They had come from all sections of the country. Also, there were his friends in the community, headed by the city leaders of Safety Harbor, Clearwater, Tampa, and other environs, who had recognized him as a good man, dedicated to all worthy causes. Religious leaders of all denominations had come to honor him as a Jew who actually lived up to the Judeo-Christian ethic.

There were also present "new guests" who knew little about him and who were impelled chiefly by curiosity. In the front row on the side sat Baranoff, an effulgent vision, as if a white cloud had settled on his head while his piercing eyes, shaded by black eyebrows, glowed mostly. Next to him sat Lisa, much younger in years, emotionally moved and struggling to maintain her usual smile, nature's permanent make-up for beauty.

I arose to introduce him. I thought it best to describe his life by describing his theories of nature's preventive medicine. After all, the two were the same. His teaching and his life were one. He had only an osteopathic diploma. He had been ridiculed as a freak because of his food and exercise preachment.

However, the scientific mind, like a parachute, functions only when it is open. There were great physicians who overcame their prejudices inculcated by the aristocracy of formal learning, and supported Baranoff. Dr. John W. Knowles, president of the Rockefeller Foundation, had recently said that gluttony was the cause of most of our ills. We spend billions on "after-the-fact medicine" instead of avoiding disease. Last year, the country's health bill rose by more than $14 billion to $118 billion, but less than 3 per cent went toward the prevention of disease. The next major advance in the health of the American people, he said, "can only come from self-imposed changes in the way individuals live." Spoken like a Baranoff, but fifty years later.

So, at last his life had come to fruition. He was recognized in scientific circles and honored for his achievements.

He rose to an ovation, and ascended the stage. He kissed me ostentatiously on both cheeks. He stood still as the applause, like a stormy sea, rose again, each time a previous wave flattened out. He took advantage of the time to try and compose himself. He could not stop the tears, and there was no use pretending they were not there. The spotlights revealed their glistening paths down his cheeks. He wiped them away with a handkerchief, blew his nose, and finally he was permitted to speak.

In a few moments, his quavering voice strenghtened. He was on his subject. I doubt that the audience listened very attentively to what he was saying. Rather, they were intrigued by his vitality and intensity. He forgot the nature of the occasion. He was not conscious any more of the honor being paid him. There was a large audience out there. The opportunity must not be lost. If only he could put each one of them on a table and make them healthier. He pleaded with them to develop new habits which would make them more useful to themselves and to their families. His concern for their welfare was so deep and sincere that everyone in the room felt enveloped by his love. He forgot all about the new theater and its new name. He never mentioned them.

It was the most gloriously inappropriate "acceptance" speech I ever heard.

One day I received confirmation of the theory of self-restraint in eating habits from an unexpected source. It was from Salvador Dali, the great painter. It is sometimes thought that artists, being under great strain, seek release in dissipation. Not so. There are exceptions, but most creative people know that good health is essential to their achievements and go to great lengths to be fit. I would have thought that Dali, noted for his designed "eccentricity," would be an exception, but I learned otherwise.

We were having lunch in my office to discuss a lawsuit in which he was unjustly involved. He was being sued for his failure to deliver paintings to be drawn on the backs of tarot cards used for fortunetelling. He arrived in a purple-satin-lined Russian sable cape. He wore a lavender shirt with a mustard yellow tie, demonstrating that there was no such thing as a wrong color combination. Even during lunch he would not put aside his silver-nobbed cane. His famous mustache, waxed upwards in bicycle handlebar manner to two sharp points which almost pierced his nostrils, gave no hint of his conservative views on health.

He would not touch the rolls and butter before him. He wanted only a simple salad and fruit. He would not even drink coffee. I thought it would be appropriate to serve fine Spanish wine to complement the lunch. He refused it.

"Don't you drink any liquor?"

He held out his hand, pulselessly steady, his forefingers and thumb clutching an imaginary paint brush. He peered steadily with shining eyes into the distance to symbolize the imaginative visions which had stirred the artistic world.

He continued, dropping articles and prepositions as if they were extra luggage. "There are two kinds people, romantics and realists. Romantic thinks if he takes alcohol, pills, marijuana he find artificial heaven. No find. Realist knows here is heaven." For the first time he dropped his tremorless hand and pointed the imaginary paint brush to the earth. "No interfere clear mind and imagination."

When we concluded our conference, I offered to have my car take him to his hotel. Again he refused, adding that he would walk, walk, walk because it was a necessary exercise for him. He held up his cane, not, as I suspected, a symbol of support, but of protection.

During our discussion I had, as is my habit, drawn his head on a napkin. He noticed it and approved. That was kind enough, but he made a Dali gesture. "I sign generously," he said.

I did not know what that meant but I was pleased to hand him the napkin. He drew a long vertical line with a little knob. It was his cane, but it also was the stem of the letter "D." Then in large script which covered three quarters of the napkin, he wrote the rest of his name. The drawing appropriately shrank in size by comparison.

There could be no more incongruous figures than Baranoff and Dali, but I realized by the very contrast how remarkably their creative theories coincided.

LOOKING INTO THE FUTURE

As a lawyer I have trained myself to anticipate the future developments in every case, even appeals which may take place years after the trial. The habit of looking ahead sometimes enables me to present evidence which at first blush might appear irrelevant but which, in the light of later analysis, may protect the original verdict.

Carrying forward this habit, I have thought about the future of mankind in the next seventy-five years.

It is difficult to peer into the future. H. G. Wells in 1901 wrote that an airplane would never be invented but if it were, it could never be a practical conveyance. Two years later the flyer took to the air at Kitty Hawk.

When Fulton's steamboat stood poised on the Hudson River to make its first demonstration, the cynics stood on the bank of the river and said steam could never move a heavy object. When the stack began to breathe heavily with smoke, and the ship began to glide, imperceptibly at first, and then slowly down the river, the same cynic, his jaw agape, yelled, "They'll never be able to stop it!"

So I know that it is hazardous to predict the future, but I also know that in man's battle against reality, imagination is his greatest weapon. And I also know that never in my lifetime have we lived in a time when our doubts were greater than our problems.

Therefore, I hope that by looking into the future we can lift our spirits and regain our confidence. I will therefore engage in an imaginary exercise. Assume that it is the year 2053 and that we are looking back seventy-five years to the year 1978.

In the year 2053 there are no electric lights or chandeliers in our buildings. They are lit by phosphorescent, luminescent walls.

People do not wear suits or dresses. They are draped in comfortable materials which have the property of either warming or cooling them as they wish. No overgarments are needed. Furthermore, these soft, beautiful clothes are disposable, being made of a synthetic paper material.

The tables at which we eat and the chairs on which we sit are at least a half foot higher, because the average height of men and women is seven feet.

One quarter of the people are over the age of 110, since the longevity average has reached 150, and scientists tell us that in another 25 years it will be 160.

Since we have also developed supersleep, one hour will suffice. So we are conscious and active twenty-three hours a day, thus adding to our span of life.

We wear rings which contain microscopic transistors enabling us to telephone from our hands.

We can determine in advance the sex of children. Because of larger brain development, it has become necessary to resort to Caesarean births.

Around our waist we wear a laser-beam fob which enables the brain, the greatest computer of all, to send brain wave messages for short distances.

We travel in invisible capsules with radar equipment to prevent collision, which fly us to our homes, where the walls part to admit us into the landing room. It is next to a huge circular room, the walls of which, at your choice, are filled with knowledge from a central bank of information, with news and with entertainment sent by satellite.

Weather conditions and temperature are determined by our government, based upon farm and environmental considerations. In some areas we travel north for the warm weather.

There is no race problem, not only because we have overcome the stupidity of prejudice, but because scientists have learned how to change the pigmentation of our skin so that people can be any color they choose to be. The predominant choice is not white or black but rather a suntanned kind of light brown.

We have virtually free energy. We now know the secret of fusion as previously we knew fission, so that we duplicate the process of the sun.

We talk of second and third generation artificial organs and limbs as once we talked of second generation computers.

Our food supply is abundant due to the extraction and creation of protein and other essential vitamins from the air, sea, and laboratory, as well as from the earth.

On our wrists are discs which send a record of our bodily functions twenty-four hours a day to a central medical computer. Every morning we read on the white circular wall a report of any deficiency and the precise remedy.

We do not begin functions by singing *The Star-Spangled Banner*, because the United States has become one of 153 states of a World Federation in which the votes of each state are based upon four factors:
size, population, productivity, and educational and cultural standards.
The nation-states vie with each other to improve their voting power by
improving their ethical, cultural, and productivity standards rather than
their armaments. We sing the world anthem entitled *A United World
Among the Planets*. Next to the flag of the United States stands the
flag of the World Federation, which depicts the globe on which all
boundary lines are deliberately eliminated. It is surrounded by 153 stars
against a blue background.

Does all this seem incredible? Well, make this simple test. Suppose
that in 1903 someone predicted that in the next seventy-five years the
following would happen:

That antibiotics would be discovered which would eliminate diseases
which had plagued mankind for centuries:

that this nation and the rest of the world would be laced with pave-
ments so that horseless carriages by the millions would drive upon them
with no visible means of propulsion;

that huge birds would be built on which hundreds of people would
perch, and though they weighed thousands of tons, these mechanical
birds would lift into the air and fly across mountains and rivers and
even across oceans;

that electronic waves, which circle the globe seven times in one second, would be harnessed so that they would go through brick, glass,
steel, iron, and millions of human bodies without injuring them, and
come out in a little box so that words spoken thousands of miles away
could be heard distinctly;

that human beings would be able to see tens of thousands of miles by
simply looking into the same box;

that even after a person died, his voice could still be heard by having
a needle scratch a piece of wax;

that a surgeon would cut the heart out of a man without killing him,
and then sew in another man's heart to preserve his life;

that an infinitely small particle of matter could be broken in two and
would release as much power as thousands of tons of dynamite, and
that this discovery would be used to destroy two whole cities and one
hundred thousand people in a few seconds;

that three men would be placed in a cabinet which would be shot
from the face of the globe, and while traveling at fifty thousand miles
an hour toward a planet, one of them would step out of the cabinet
and walk in space, and that we would sit in our homes and watch these
men cavort on the moon.

And a hundred other miracles. Would all of this have seemed more credible than what I have depicted for the next seventy-five years? And yet, those wild predictions have become commonplace in our lives. So take heart. We will not be the pallbearers of the past. We will create a new glorious future.

There is only one respect in which we will not have achieved our goal in the year 2053. That is the substantial improvement of human nature. Darwin wrote that there are tame animals and wild animals, and that man is a wild animal, and it will take five million years of evolution to tame him. We will cut down this prediction by millions of years.

Indeed, we will by the year 2053 have made considerable progress in this direction. There will be an educational revolution, for we will have learned to infuse knowledge into the brain by electronic stimulation. Thus, we will learn instantly. Universities will be discarded as slow mechanisms. They will be used only for discussion and cultural development.

Also, biological engineering of the human personality will be greatly developed by 2053. The secret of matter and life having been wrested from nature, there will be all sorts of programs to change the genes and chromosomes in the hope of improving the human being. There will be sperm banks as well as brain banks, but who shall determine what the standards of improvement shall be?

This will be the great problem of the next century. For we have learned that while science can equip us, it cannot guide us. Science can illuminate our path to the farthest stars and leave our hearts in darkness.

We will have explored the outer planets of space and built colonies on some of them. We will have traveled to the bottom of the oceans in nuclear craft and excavated untold treasures. But we will not yet have succeeded in exploring the inner continents of man himself.

We will have to, in the words of Pindar, the Greek poet, "exhaust the limits of the possible." And everything is possible.

CONSTITUTIONAL CONFLICTS

In sports, it is only close contests which arouse excitement. Clear superiority breeds disinterest. That is why there was the cry about the original Philadelphia Athletics and later the Yankee baseball dynasties, as well as the Green Bay Packers football dynasty. "Break them up." Monopoly of power in sport is more objectionable than in business. Paradoxically, teams which are too successful sometimes attract small audiences.

If this rule was universal, we would be hanging on the rafters over the contest between constitutional amendments. I hope to convey the excitement which not only grips the scholar, but would envelop every citizen if he understood the neck and neck race among the various constitutional rights which compete with each other.

The First Amendment guarantees free speech. The Sixth Amendment guarantees a fair jury trial. The two conflict. May the press reveal in advance of a trial that the defendant has confessed? Suppose that the confession was obtained by duress and is not later admitted in evidence. How can the jury trial be fair where the jurors have been drenched with the prejudicial press report of confession, which should never have been brought to their attention? Or suppose that the press, exercising freedom of speech, reveals that a man about to be tried had a previous conviction.

Under our law, this would not have been admissible at the trial, because it does not prove that he is guilty of the present charge. For all we know, he may have been arrested because of his prior history, rather than because of evidence supporting the charge for which he is being tried. It is only if the defendant takes the stand in his own defense that he can be confronted with a prior conviction (not indictment) and only for its effect on his credibility, not as proof of guilt.

But if the press publishes his prior conviction, then the jury is advised of an irrelevant fact, which prejudices it, even though the defendant does not take the stand.

The same close contest exists between the First Amendment, guaranteeing free speech, and the Fourth Amendment, which guarantees against illegal search and seizure, and the Fifth Amendment, which protects against self-incrimination. There is a similar conflict between the First Amendment and the right of privacy. Every individual has the right "to be let alone." Is this precious right invaded when the press publishes his history even though he is not involved in any current news?

The most vivid illustration of conflict is that between the right of free speech and the right of an individual not to be injured by lies.

Which right shall be given predominance in each of these conflicts? Neither. They are both precious. There must be an accommodation between these conflicting rights. The courts have struggled to find the proper line to be drawn. In its search for a balanced rule, the Supreme Court has veered one way and then another over the years. The issue is still in flux. Choose which side you will cheer for as I trace the close and fierce contest which is being waged between the free press and the individual's right not to be slandered.

For 188 years, from 1776 to 1964, if the press printed a falsehood about an individual, he could sue, and if the press couldn't prove truth, it was liable. This seemed right enough. A citizen could be destroyed by a vicious accusation. He could suffer the loss of his job. His family could be reduced to starvation. His wife and children shamed. The perpetrator of the wrong ought to pay damages, in the same way as if he had crippled the man by negligently running over him with an auto.

But in 1964, the law was changed. It came about because of a hard case, which legal philosophers say often makes bad law. This means that in order to give relief because of special circumstances, we adopt a rule of law which does mischief when applied generally. Such special circumstances occurred in the famous case of the *New York Times Company* v. *Sullivan*. There, a commissioner in charge of the Police Department of Montgomery, Alabama, won a half-million-dollar verdict against the New York *Times* for merely publishing an advertisement part of which was false. There was no actual damage. The award was for punitive damages. The advertisement, in the name of the "Committee to defend Martin Luther King and the struggle for Freedom in the South," was signed by sixty-four persons, many of whom were well known in public affairs. Three were black clergymen, who were made co-defendants with the *Times*. The Commissioner who obtained the judgment was not even mentioned in the advertisement, but he claimed that the references to the action of the police against protesting students of Alabama State College reflected on him. Even the errors in the advertisement were not gross. For example Dr. King had not been arrested seven times, as the ad said, but only three. The cost of the advertisement was $4800. The *Times* had accepted it at the request of A. Philip Randolph, a responsible chairman of the Committee.

It can readily be seen why this was a hard judgment to uphold. It cried for relief. In this way there was fashioned the doctrine that unless there was malice, a public official could be criticized even falsely, and he would have no remedy.

The public interest, it was argued, required that the press publish without fear of retaliation. The word "press" includes books, television, radio, or any other means of expression. A rationale was given for this departure from the previous rule that the press, like any other individual or corporation operating for profit, was liable if it lied. It was that a public official sought the limelight. He was involved in public issues. He exposed himself to the acclaim of the citizenry, and thus waived the ordinary standards of privacy. His was a public trust, and was subject to scrutiny and criticism not applicable to private citizens. Also he had a better opportunity to have his reply published than a private citizen. Unless the press could be uninhibited in attacking a public official, it could not serve its highest purpose. "Let there be news. Let there be the right to publish without fear." These were biblical type pronouncements for the holy mission of the fourth estate.

This reasoning spilled over into the area of public figures who were not public officials. So the exception was widened and the press received even greater immunity. This came about in two cases decided by the Supreme Court. The first, in 1967, involved college football. An article in *The Saturday Evening Post* charged that Wallace Butts, a well-known football coach and athletic director of the University of Georgia, had fixed a game against his own team by giving to Alabama's coach "Bear" Bryant, "all of the significant secrets Georgia's football team possessed." The article heralded the exposé with these words: "Not since the Chicago White Sox threw the 1919 World Series has there been a sports story as shocking as this one." The rivalry between Georgia and Alabama had the intensity which only pride of students and alumni can generate. Championships sometimes hung in the balance. Adherents of each took loss with despair more fitting for the death of dear ones, and victory with elation which verged on hysteria. In such an atmosphere, one can imagine the scandal created by the story.

What was the authority for such a damning accusation (aside from our old friend, sensationalism to increase circulation and obtain a reprieve from the magazine's death)? It was based on an electronic mishap. An Atlanta insurance salesman, George Burnett, claimed that by error he was cut into a telephone conversation between Butts and Bryant and that "Butts outlined Georgia's offensive plays . . . and told . . . how Georgia planned to defend. . . . Butts mentioned both players and plays by name."

Burnett claimed he made notes, and gave specific examples of the divulged secrets.

The article added the necessary dramatics to what turned out to be a false story. It discussed the Georgia players' reactions to "the frightful beating" they suffered, "like those rats in a maze."

Experts compared Burnett's notes with the films of the game, and his claims were severely contradicted. Also the players' remarks had been misrepresented. Furthermore Burnett had been placed on probation in connection with bad-check charges, and *The Saturday Evening Post* knew this, but trusted his affidavit without independent investigation.

The defense of truth was rejected by the jury, which awarded $60,000 in general damages, and $3,000,000 in punitive damages. This award was cut to $460,000. The Supreme Court held that Butts was a public figure, rather than a public official, and that it would apply the same rule to both. Malice had to be proven. But it found that malice had been demonstrated because the publisher had "vented his spleen." Therefore it upheld the Butts verdict. It said that "the basic theory of libel has not changed, and words defamatory of another are still placed 'in the same class with the use of explosives or the keeping of dangerous animals.' "

Naturally, one could find contradictions in this analysis. The judges of the Supreme Court upheld the Butts decision but differed among themselves as to the right reason for doing so. Seven out of nine agreed that a public figure was entitled to the same protection as a public official, but they split as to whether the test of malice had been met.

The second case involved General Edwin A. Walker, who, in 1967, sued the Associated Press because in describing the riot which occurred when a black man, James Meredith, attempted to enter the University of Mississippi under a court order, it charged Walker with leading the violent crowd. At the time Walker was a private citizen, although he had been in charge of Federal troops, years earlier during a school segregation confrontation in Little Rock, Arkansas. He denied the story. He claimed that he had actually counseled restraint and peaceful protest. The reporter who gave the dispatch was on the scene. He had a good record for responsibility. The situation required an immediate report. There was no evidence of improper preparation or of personal prejudice.

The jury rendered a verdict of $500,000 compensatory damages, and $300,000 punitive danages. The trial court set aside the punitive award because there was no evidence of malice, but permitted the half-million-dollar verdict to stand. The Supreme Court, however, held that General Walker was a public figure and, like a public official, could not recover even if he was lied about, unless there was malice. There being none, the verdict was set aside, and he received nothing.

The logic for bunching public figures with public officials, to protect the press, seemed impeccable on the surface. Public figures, like public officials, have access to the press. They can defend themselves better than private citizens. So, theoretically, can public figures.

The trouble was definition. There is no doubt about identifying a public official. But what criterion is there to decide who is a public figure? How much fame must attach to him? How wide must the public be, local, state, national? The courts soon found themselves in a maze of conflicting decisions on this point.

Nevertheless, an attempt was made to increase the press's immunity even farther. In a suit brought by one Rosenbloom, in 1971, against Metromedia, Inc., the defendant argued that because Rosenbloom had involved himself in a public *issue*, he could not win a libel suit unless he would prove that the false statement was made with malice. The court extended the immunity it had conferred on the press, when sued by a public official, or public figure, to include one who had discussed a matter of public interest.

Let me take a compass reading of where we are at this point. We start with the inviolable proposition of the precious nature of free speech. It is the bulwark of democracy. It is not necessary to ring the bells on this proposition and relate how many have died for this right. (Thomas Huxley's "It is better for a man to go wrong in freedom than to go right in chains"; Thomas Mann's "Speech is civilization itself"; and of course Thomas Paine's "Give me liberty or give me death"). It is as superfluous to augment the point as to defend motherhood. The real question is how to accommodate this right with other constitutional provisions which are just as precious. Edmund Burke said that the foundation of government is compromise. Where shall we draw the line between competing rights?

The philosophical support for favoring the press is powerful, but not conclusive. If public officials can be libeled with impunity, unless they can prove the lie was born of malice, will not our political and judicial ranks be deprived of many outstanding men?

Distinguished citizens usually earn much more than they can in public service. Most men are willing to make financial sacrifices in return for the honor of leadership and the satisfaction of public service. But if instead of honor, they must look forward to the indignities of "dirty politics" and slander, the price is too high.

I cite a personal experience. Although I had been involved in politics "at the top," writing speeches for Presidents and others, I had sought to maintain my independence by practicing law. Judicial and political posts had been suggested if not offered (the technique is to obtain consent in advance). I refused. It was not modesty, but the love of practicing law which guided me. One accustomed to contest in the arena of justice would find umpiring it a tame affair. The judge cannot experience triumph or defeat. He can only impose it. True, he has the exhilaration of scholarship and writing, but these are not denied to the lawyer. Indeed without them he can neither be a successful office lawyer nor an advocate.

George Medalie, a leading trial lawyer of his day, was appointed by Governor Thomas E. Dewey to the Court of Appeals, the highest court of the State of New York. I met him after he had served a year.

"George, how do you like your new duties?"

"I am not sure," he replied. "The trouble is I don't know which side I'm on."

I did not care to don robes which would make it necessary for me to decide to which side my neutrality would yield. Also, the sedate life of a judge did not suit my temperament.

My resolve weakened one day, while I was on vacation in Colorado Springs. President Truman wanted to appoint me to the Federal bench. I received a series of telephone calls from emissaries conveying the honor. With expressions of appreciation, I declined. It was not difficult to do so. But the calls continued. My senior law partner, Louis Phillips, tempted me with the news that he had checked with the Bar Association, and I would be entitled to income from the law firm for at least two years in matters I had handled. This would reduce my financial sacrifice. I told him it was not money at all that governed my declination. When I set forth my real reasons, he countered that I ought to try the judicial post. "If you don't like it after a year or two, you can resign and return to private practice."

Next, my friend, Austin Keough, the general counsel of Paramount Pictures, Inc., telephoned to urge my acceptance. "The chances are you will not remain a district judge. If you are a distinguished judge, you may rise to the Court of Appeals, and perhaps even to the Supreme Court." I laughed. Knowing that Keough was a devout Catholic, I asked him whether he would have entered the priesthood if his father had held forth the possibility of his becoming Pope. I promised to think it over and reply the next day.

Mildred, who always thought I worked too hard, urged my acceptance on the mistaken notion that judgeships are sinecures. How little the public understands that conscientious judges work evenings and weekends studying voluminous briefs and trying desperately to stay afloat on the ever-increasing flood of litigations which inundate them.

Then a coincidence made up my mind. Judge Charles C. Lockwood of the State Supreme Court was also vacationing in Colorado Springs. He was in the dining room having dinner, when he heard me paged to the telephone a half-dozen times within the hour.

"What is the matter, Louis, anything wrong?"

I told him of the judicial offer and my negative view, although I was beginning to have doubts. He asked me to sit down with him. Then he proceeded in the most earnest terms to set forth the reasons why I should accept. He knew, he said, that I could make contributions to the judiciary which it needed, and which would give me greater satisfaction than repeating my endeavors as a trial lawyer. No matter how much one rejects flattery, some of it by osmosis induced by vanity seeps through and becomes conviction. When one has a good opinion of himself, resisting compliments is a losing struggle.

Everyone in the profession had great respect for Judge Lockwood, not merely as an able judge and good man, but because he had the parent of all gifts—sound judgment. I thanked him for his opinion of me and decided to accept the judgeship.

I returned to New York, and with a heavy heart proceeded to end my activities in the office. FBI reports, checking Federal appointments had been concluded. I was informed that the two senators of the state who had to approve and recommend the appointment were in line.

Then I was advised that as a final step I must visit Ed Flynn, the Democratic leader.

"Why?" I asked with naïveté that was more befitting a novice.

"You must have the approval of the Democratic leader, to get the appointment," I was told.

"I have nothing against Flynn. I don't know him. I have been induced to take this judgeship, because it offered a new opportunity for service in a field in which I have some expertise. But if I now have to cater to a political chief to pass muster, I'm not going to do it."

My sponsoring friends were exasperated with my eccentric behavior.

"For God's sake, Louis, no one is asking you to cater to anybody. It takes one visit. It is political protocol. He knows of you. We're sure he will be delighted to meet and approve you."

"I don't want his approval. I don't recognize the distinction between a Democratic and Republican judge, any more than between a Democratic doctor and Republican doctor, or for that matter a Democratic street cleaner and a Republican one. If I must go through the political routine to be a judge, I'd rather not be."

That was the end of my judicial career.

Men of standing invited to run for office must take into account the vicious attacks made on public officials. The honor of these posts, whether executive, legislative, or judicial, is drained by the debased standards of reckless and crude criticism which now pervades the political scene. The Watergate revelations of dirty tactics were more publicized, but were only the continuation of such practices for many years before Nixon.

Senator Joseph McCarthy's successful demagogy had led to two United States Senate subcommittees looking into the problem of campaign excesses. Senator Guy Gillette's committee recommended the adoption of a Code of Fair Campaign Practices promoted by a nonprofit private organization, to be called the Fair Campaign Practices Committee. Candidates for major offices would be asked to sign a pledge "to conduct my campaign in the best American tradition."

The Code condemned "the use of personal villification, character defamation, whispering campaign libel, slander or scurrilous attacks on any candidate on his personal or family life."

It also condemned "creating doubts, without justification" concerning an opponent's "loyalty and patriotism" or "any appeal to prejudice based on race, creed or national origin." Finally, it denounced any unethical practice "which tends to corrupt our American system of free elections."

Every President of the United States has lent his name as honorary chairman of the Committee. I was pleased to serve on it. It is one of the least publicized but most valuable organizations in our democracy. It is as important to prevent the pollution of our political streams as of our natural ones.

Since 1956 this committee has processed hundreds of complaints. It gathered the facts from both sides and publicized them. Some cases were sent to the American Arbitration Association for impartial finding by qualified arbitrators. It is significant that "dirty campaign tricks" have been about evenly divided between the two major parties. In the 1966 campaign, thirty-six complaints were filed by Republicans against Democrats, and twenty-nine by Democrats against Republicans. The total complaints for three elections of 1966, 1968, and 1970 were ninety-six by Republicans and eighty-nine by Democrats. The Republicans won 59 per cent of their complaints, the Democrats 43 per cent. So iniquity, like nobility, is not the monopoly of either of the major parties.

Robert Kennedy involved me in a controversy of unfair campaigning in the New York senatorial contest between himself and Senator Kenneth Keating. It arose from three campaign speeches which Kennedy made in Syracuse, New York, on October 20, 1964. Among other things he charged that Keating had failed to support the Nuclear Test Ban Treaty, which "Averell Harriman, Hubert Humphrey, and Adlai Stevenson labored to make a reality." Keating had voted for the treaty. He therefore filed a complaint with the Fair Campaign Practices Committee, and did not hesitate to publicize that he had done so. The Committee advised Kennedy of the complaint. Keating used a press release that the Committee "was angered and shocked" by Kennedy's distortion. Kennedy's defense was that he was guilty of nothing more than an ambiguity, because although Keating finally voted for the treaty, it was true "that when President Kennedy was fighting for it, Keating never once rose to speak in its favor before the United States Senate." The trouble with this defense was that in one of his speeches, Kennedy had also charged that "Keating ridiculed the Treaty and did not speak out for it until after passage was assured." Keating denied ever ridiculing the treaty.

Kennedy saw my name on the Committee stationery, and called me. He was terribly agitated. He feared that a public exposé of his error and condemnation by a responsible committee might cost him the election. Having been counsel to the McClellan Committee, he knew the impact of a charge which could be misunderstood as deliberate foul tactics.

When people are in trouble, fear, like a hyperactive thyroid, makes the problem grow. Kennedy sounded panicky.

"This kind of thing can cost me my career," he said. "Louis, please take care of this, will you? It was an innocent mistake. Do you think I ought to call Cardinal Cushing?" (who was also a member of the Committee).

I advised against it. It seemed to me that he felt he was in extremis and wanted to appeal to God for succor, but that he would turn to the Cardinal for more immediate results. It was the wrong approach. I presented his explanation to the Committee. It was a candid admission of his overstatement in the midst of a campaign.

The Committee regretted the publication of its letter of complaint to Kennedy before all facts had been gathered, thus enabling Keating to exploit it as if it were a finding. This pleased the Kennedy forces, while the Keating adherents objected that the matter was not properly resolved.

If a mistake is looked upon as a teacher rather than a progenitor for alibis, it can be valuable. The Committee reviewed its faulty procedures and tightened them, so that its very inquiry could not be exploited by either party to the dispute. In the meantime, however, two members of the Committee, Ralph McGill and Cardinal Cushing, had resigned.

Gratified by his extrication, Kennedy asked my judgment about another problem which he was facing. He had been challenged by Keating to a television debate on a Columbia Broadcasting channel. His brother's experience against Nixon had taught the lesson that the underdog had everything to gain and little to lose in such a confrontation.

Bobby was a clear favorite. Why should he confer his fame as a Kennedy and former Attorney General on the relatively unknown Senator Keating? Going by the rules, his committee had decided to reject the invitation.

Keating took advantage of the situation. He announced that he was going through with the debate just the same. An empty chair would represent his absent opponent. He would accuse the spotlight, which substituted for Kennedy in the chair, with lack of courage to meet him on the issues even though Keating was paying for the program. He would point to the chair and quote some of Kennedy's speeches, and reply to them. In effect he was going to make a campaign speech, dramatized by his opponent's "flight."

I had a different view of proper tactics. Kennedy was impressed by it and invited me to his home, where the Committee heads were gathered, to repeat it. There was Stephen Smith, his brother-in-law; Alex Rose, the leader of the Liberal Party; democratic chieftains, speech writers, and workers. They were milling about in every direction amidst a babble of noise punctuated by a distinct word or phrase which rose above the din thereby adding to the incoherence of the scene. It was not a smoke-filled room but it gave me the same feeling of wonder how anything could be decided sensibly in such a confusing atmosphere. Bobby asked me to state my views. I did. I urged that he should appear on the program and smilingly fill the empty chair. It would give a touch of grace and courage to the event, and upset Keating's prepared speech based on the formula of Kennedy's fear to face him. As to the debate, Kennedy had discussed the issues in dozens of appearances. He could hold his own easily against the ponderous Keating. Why not act boldly?

"But it is too late," came the warning from all sides. "The debate begins in an hour and a half. It's down at the CBS studio."

"All the better," I replied. "We'll show up at the last minute. It will take Keating by surprise."

Bobby's long-toothed smile indicated his approval. All agreed, though not with uniform enthusiasm. Kennedy rushed into the bathroom to shave. He asked that I sit with him there for last-minute preparation. He stripped to his shorts, revealing a very hairy chest, applied lather quickly, and despite the grimaces of shaving, which distorted his words, prepared for the encounter as if he were a witness about to take the stand. And I as a lawyer, accustomed to my soft high leather chair, sat on the hard cover of the toilet bowl, an inappropriate throne for the discussion of principles.

The news media had been advised that Kennedy was coming to the CBS station. Television and news cameramen appeared immediately and escorted our small party to the studio. There a large crowd had gathered. Kennedy was cheered and he waved happily, all recorded for the nightly news. He was already ahead. But surprising developments were to come.

Inside the building, we announced that Kennedy was ready to debate and wanted to be taken to the Keating studio. There was little time, and the executives in charge of the event were taken aback by the change of schedule. There were hasty telephone calls back and forth. At last we were invited to the floor where the studio was. Behind the closed studio door, Keating was already seated opposite the empty chair. Word was sent to his assistants inside, that Kennedy was ready and wished to enter. Distressful voices were heard. Then came the answer.

"It is only five minutes to broadcast time. Mr. Keating will not permit a last second change of heart. Mr. Kennedy will not be admitted."

Kennedy needed no prompting. He exploited the situation with professional skill. With television and flashlights pouring on him outside the locked door, he said, "I demand to be admitted. Mr. Keating challenged me to a debate. I am ready. I am eager to discuss the issues with him. It takes only a second to open the door, and another second for me to occupy that chair. There is plenty of time. If Mr. Keating refuses, who is running away? The people will consider his talk to the empty chair a fraudulent act. With one hand he shuts me out, with the other he gestures I did not show up."

From one of his astute assistants came a loud cry. "Bobby, we have reserved fifteen minutes in another studio for reply. Let's pick it up and tell the people how you were locked out!"

"Let's do it," said the triumphant candidate, waving his hand with disgust at the closed door. Turning to the press:

"Gentlemen, you see that Keating doesn't want to debate me." He knocked at the door for the last time. "I ask again for admittance."

"There you are, it is not a silent chair, but a silent Keating we have inside."

We headed for another CBS studio to hear Keating and then reply. Kennedy asked me to appear on the program with him. I agreed. We were hastily "made up," a technique which always makes me feel like a fop, but is justified by the television personnel on the ground that if you don't, the contrast with those who do is horrendous. ("You don't want to look worse than you are?" I was once comforted by a make-up man who needed a Dale Carnegie course.)

We heard enough of the Keating broadcast to improvise a reply. Kennedy and I decided quickly who would answer a particular argument. He took the issues of the campaign, I the personal references to Kennedy. We wrote out hastily Kennedy's opening, which was a vivid recital of how Keating had locked him out of the studio to which he had been challenged to debate. He told how the press had witnessed his demands for entry, and Keating's pretense that it was too late to live up to the original plan. He characterized Keating's broadcast in which he addressed an empty chair as a shabby trick unworthy of a senatorial contest. He was dry but effective. The camera must have caught his eyes, which turned steel gray with anger.

Keating's main thrust had been that Bobby was cashing in on his brother's reputation. I addressed myself to this. I used a technique known in law as "confession and avoidance." What is wrong with emulating a father or brother who had achieved world recognition for his great qualities? Is filial devotion and the continuation of a great family tradition an argument against electing Robert Kennedy? Then I proceeded to recite and analyze the official positions Bobby had held with distinction, his achievements as counsel to congressional committees, as Attorney General, and particularly his wise advice to his brother during the Cuban crisis. The fact that the President leaned on him during those crucial hours indicated that he recognized in Bobby those qualities which the nation needed. Thus I was able to say things for and about him which would have come with ill grace from his lips. Then I passed the baton to him and he expressed movingly his hopes for the people of the state which he wished to represent.

When we emerged, Ethel Kennedy was there to kiss him and thank me. The campaign squad acted as if a triumph had been achieved, and the cameras continued to roll as he pushed his way through a cheering mob, his slight body disappearing at times among the burly bodyguards and then suddenly emerging as if he had come to the surface after a deep dive.

Much later when Bobby was assassinated while trying to pass through a similar wall of adulating flesh, I thought of the scene at CBS. Why must our public men risk their lives in crowds which may include a mad fanatic bent on notoriety through murder?

Despite the salutary restraints which the Fair Campaign Practices Committee, the press, and the public impose on candidates, their eagerness to win drives many to abominable practices. As election day grows nearer, the fever chart shows a sharp incline of reckless and desperate statements. Moreover, the loser's hope for a better day prompts continuing attacks on the victor. A partisan press and disgruntled opponents join the chorus of criticism which often crosses the boundary of decency. The refusal of many outstanding men to enter the political arena as candidates may well be due to their resentment of the abuse which they consider inevitable, and for which there is no remedy. Should there not be? The libel laws had been the traditional tool therefor. Its edge has been dulled. Was it in the public interest to keep it so?

We are all committed to the First Amendment and free speech, but the press, like other valuable institutions, is capable of perpetrating abuse and injustice.

The framers of the Constitution recognized that none of our institutions is so sacred or safe, not the Presidency, not the Congress, and not the judiciary, that absolute power may safely be reposed in any of them. Fear of absolutism dictated the very system of constitutional checks and balances, which is the most important safeguard of all our fundamental freedoms. Should not the press be subject to the check provided by the libel laws?

Thomas Jefferson thought so. He saw clearly the dangers of journalistic abuse. I quote him:

It is a melancholy truth, that a suppression of the press could not more completely deprive the nation of its benefits than is done by its abandoned prostitution to falsehood.

Jefferson believed in absolute press freedom on matters of opinion (the "public judgment will correct false reasonings and opinions"), but he deplored false factual reporting as "demoralizing licentiousness," an abuse of freedom of the press.

Jefferson believed that curbing of the press to prevent lies was so important that he spoke about it in his second inaugural address. After referring to the "wholesome" remedies against defamation he said a citizen "renders a service to the public morals and public tranquillity in reforming these abuses by the salutory coercion of the law"—in other words by suing for libel. This, coming from the foremost champion of freedom of the press, was not a retreat, but a declaration of a balance between the press and the individual's rights.

Benjamin Franklin agreed. With characteristic felicity he wrote:

If by the liberty of the press were understood merely the liberty of discussing the propriety of public measures and political opinions, let us have as much of it as you please; but if it means the liberty of affronting, calumniating, and defaming one another, I, for my part, own myself willing to part with my share of it . . . and shall cheerfully consent to exchange my liberty of abusing others for the privilege of not being abused myself.

No talk here of the need to prove malice in order to recover for a lie. Unless truth could be proved, the press was to be held liable. Much later the Supreme Court echoed this view when Justice Potter Stewart wrote that "the reputation of a man or woman rises to constitutional dimensions."

We have understandably ennobled the press's service and the priorities it requires for its guardianship of officialdom and its service to the public interest. For example, we will under no circumstances permit an injunction to prevent a newspaper, book, or telecast from publishing a story. Such advance "shutting of the mouth" is abhorrent to free speech. When it is published, and it is actionable, suit can be brought. Otherwise we anticipate a violation, and this may well be a means to cut off permissible opinion or factual criticism. The rule against "prior restraint," as it is called, is firm and should remain so.

On the other hand, how much protection should the press enjoy after it publishes? If we were dealing only with the majority of great journals, we might consider diminishing the individual's rights in their favor, on the theory that such sacrifice would rarely be needed. But there are yellow newspapers, "sensational" journals, pornographic magazines, scandal columns, trade publications which engage in blackmail ("unless you place ads with us, we'll expose you"), and all sorts of vicious sheets to which printing presses are hospitable. They abound in lies which often are motivated not by malice, but by greed. The editors and writers may know little about the victim and care less about him, but they repeat irresponsible gossip published by a similar reckless source, embroider it with invention, and exploit it for "a buck." Malice in the legal sense may really not exist. Avarice does. This brings about a situation in which the very false accusations which ought to be most subject to remedy are the most immune.

"Muckraking," like "ambition," is one of those words in the English language which can connote good or evil, depending on its usage. Usually we shade our meanings with two words. Persistent-good; obstinate-bad. Generous-good; spendthrift-bad. Self-respect-good; vain-bad. Prudent-good; stingy-bad. Confident-good; conceited-bad. Insight-good; self-centered-bad.

Ordinarily we would consider raking up mud about people a pretty unsavory undertaking. But when the digging exposes facts which, in the public interest, should never have been buried, muckraking becomes a virtue. Then we cherish the glitter, after the caked mud has been removed, and we honor the muckraker.

The trend to teams (in surgery, economics, and politics) has spread to muckraking. It was such a team that was responsible for the "Governor and the Mob" story.

The Supreme Court has taken note of the "muckraking" technique, and decided that it indicated malice under certain circumstances. In the Butts case, the court said:

The Saturday Evening Post was anxious to change its image by instituting a policy of "sophisticated muckraking," and the pressure to produced a successful exposé might have induced a stretching of standards. In short, the evidence is ample to support a finding of highly unreasonable conduct constituting an extreme departure from the standards of investigation and reporting ordinarily adhered to by responsible publishers.

Chief Justice Warren spelled it out more bluntly:

. . . an editorial decision was made "to change the image" of the Saturday Evening Post with the hope that circulation and advertising revenues would thereby be increased. The starting point for this change of image was an announcement that the magazine would embark upon a program of "sophisticated muckraking" designed to "provoke people, make them mad" . . .
Freedom of the press under the First Amendment does not include absolute license to destroy lives or careers.

President Johnson must have relished this slap at the same magazine which made him so "mad." Governor Rhodes must have been interested in the reference to "muckraking," because *Life*, in his case, had ascribed its story to a newly formed "muckraking team."

And I, noting that the Supreme Court said the motive for the libel was "advertising revenues," and observing also that both magazines expired, consider this a confirmation of the Nizer theory of relativity.

As the law stands at the present writing, one could say of the President or the Chief Justice that he is a cocaine user, or has been improperly influenced in his official duty. Even though the accusation was totally false, if the President or Chief Justice sued, a defense could successfully be interposed that the plaintiff, being a public official, could not recover unless he could demonstrate that the charge was made with malice. The defendant would insist there was no malice. Witness the fact that he voted for the President, or previously wrote an article praising the Chief Justice. He merely relied in good faith on a muckraking investigator. The President or Chief Justice could not even obtain a favorable verdict of six cents, thus vindicating his honor. The suit would be dismissed.

This is how far the pendulum has swung in favor of the press and against a public official or public figure. But, I believe the pendulum's arc is at its zenith. Already it is beginning to swing back in favor of the individual's rights. First it reversed its position that a private person involved in a public issue was to be treated like a public official or public figure. In other words, that he too, if lied about, had no remedy unless he could prove malice. At last, the ever-increasing immunity for the press came to a halt. It even moved back somewhat.

The Supreme Court weakened its public figure ruling by redefining what a public figure was. It laid down a narrower test, so that even many prominent persons could not be qualified as public figures.

It did so in a case in Chicago, in 1974, where a policeman named Nuccio shot and killed a boy. He was convicted of murder in the second degree. The family brought a civil suit for damages against Nuccio. It was represented by a well-known lawyer, Elmer Gertz.

The John Birch Society attacked Gertz, in its monthly magazine, as a "Leninist" and a "Communist-fronter" who was in a conspiracy to discredit local law enforcement agencies. He sued the publisher Robert Welch for libel.

The charges were untrue. But was "malice" required before Gertz could recover? If he was a public figure, yes. If not, the jury verdict of $50,000 could stand, even though there was no proof of malice.

The Supreme Court began its opinion with a frank admission:

This Court has struggled for nearly a decade to define the proper accommodation between the law of defamation and the freedoms of speech and press protected by the First Amendment. With this decision we return to that effort.

The effort resulted in whittling away the immunity to the press which had gradually been broadened. The court held that Gertz was not a public figure. Even though he had written three books; had appeared "very frequently" on radio and television programs, had served on various city commissions, and had represented Jack Ruby, who had killed Oswald, the assassin of President Kennedy, he did not come within the court's new definition of what a public figure is:

Although Gertz was well known in some circles, he had achieved no general fame or notoriety in the community. None of the prospective jurors called at the trial had ever heard of Gertz prior to this litigation.

We would not lightly assume that a citizen's participation in community and professional affairs rendered him a public figure for all purposes. Absent clear evidence of general fame or notoriety in the community and pervasive involvement in the affairs of society, an individual should not be deemed a public personality for all aspects of life.

In a recent divorce case, in 1976, the Supreme Court set a still higher standard for declaring a person a public figure. It involved Russell Firestone, the scion of the famous tire company family. He was sued by his wife, Mary Alice Firestone, for separate maintenance in a Florida court. He fought back with a counterclaim which charged her with cruelty and adultery. She denied the charges. There was a lengthy trial, in which venom flowed freely. The court granted him a divorce and engaged in vivid descriptions which such cases sometimes stimulate:

According to certain testimony in behalf of the husband, extramarital escapades of the wife were bizarre and of an amatory nature which would have made Dr. Freud's hair curl. Other testimony in the wife's behalf would indicate that the husband was guilty of bounding from one bedpartner to another with the erotic zest of a satyr. The court is inclined to discount much of this testimony as unreliable.

So the Judge indicated that both parties had exaggerated. He did not find either party guilty of adultery. Nevertheless he concluded that "neither party is domesticated," which was sufficient reason to grant the divorce. "The equities," said the Judge, "were with the husband." He granted the divorce, ordered the husband to pay the wife $3,000 a month alimony.

Time magazine mistook the decision. It reported that Firestone, "heir to the tire fortune," was granted a divorce because his wife was guilty "of extreme cruelty and adultery," and that the "testimony of extramarital adventures on both sides, said the Judge, was enough 'to make Dr. Freud's hair curl.'"

Time was so certain that it had correctly reported the decision that it refused to issue a retraction. Mrs. Firestone then sued *Time* for libel. A jury awarded her $100,000 damages. The highest court of Florida affirmed the judgment.

Obviously it would be difficult to prove that *Time* was motivated by malice. Therefore, if Mrs. Firestone was a public figure, and had to prove malice, she had failed and the verdict would be set aside.

The Supreme Court reviewed the case and held that she was not a public figure. True, she was prominent in the affairs of society, but only Palm Beach society. She had not thrust herself to the forefront of any particular public controversy in order to influence its resolution. True, she was involved in a sensational trial which was characterized by the Florida Supreme Court as "a cause célèbre," but controversies interesting to the public are not necessarily public controversies. Even the holding of several press conferences in the course of the sensational trial did not make either party a public figure. The doctrine would not be extended to such a situation.

So the pendulum has been swinging back toward the individual's rights. In the center of the arc is an uncontested proposition. Ideas are always protected. There is no such thing as a false idea which is not protected by the First Amendment. No matter how pernicious the opinion, we depend on competing ideas to correct it.

Immediately adjacent to this calibration is "fact." Here we are still in the process of finding a proper equilibrium with the First Amendment.

Charles Rembar, a leading fighter for freedom of the press, said in a Bar Association forum in which I recently participated:

We are pushing the First Amendment too far. My credentials are that I happened to try some cases in which the law was profoundly changed in the direction of more freedom of expression. People who have been principally engaged in furthering the scope of the First Amendment . . . are getting a little sanctimonious . . . We have to watch out that we are not the Anthony Comstock and John Summers just on the other side.

We talk of the sovereignty of nations and states, but who talks of the sovereignty of man, for whom all laws are created? Libel is the legal shield of his reputation, the remedy for the invasion of his sovereignty.

The dignity and worth of the individual is at stake, and they deserve the foremost consideration in a civilized society.

The difficulty with the philosophical discussions concerning freedom of speech is that, like all esoteric evaluations, they are bloodless. To understand the issue, one must climb down from the Olympian heights of generalization, and meet a victim of a vicious lie, face to face; see in his bloodshot eyes, his tossing sleepless nights; meet his trembling wife empty of tears, and his children, sullen with sudden maturity, ashamed to go to school; know that friends were calling to give him comfort and thereby emphasizing the injury; know that others were shunning him, and that his employers were discussing how to fire him without giving the real reason—in short, to see him and his distraught family as the world around him collapses.

He comes to his lawyer and explains that he is fighting for his very life. He wants justice. Under the present state of the law, the lawyer must say to him, "I'm sorry. Because of the freedom of the press, you have no real remedy. You are a public official (or public figure) and you would have to prove malice, or your case will be dismissed."

"Even though they lied?" he asks.

"Yes, even if they can't prove truth. The Supreme Court has given the press immunity."

"Press," he says bitterly. "This was an article in a filthy pornographic magazine. But it has a larger circulation than the New York *Times*, the Washington *Post*, and *Time* magazine put together. Yet you tell me that although my family and I are ruined, we have no remedy?"

I hope to contribute something to see that he does.

THE SPARROW THAT TURNED OUT TO BE AN EAGLE

I first met Harry Truman when he was a senator from Missouri. That he would become President of the United States seemed too remote to contemplate. That I would be present at the White House and witness one of his historic decisions was even less imaginable. But it all happened.

The way for a senator to attract a national spotlight was to be chairman of an important investigating committee. Like Hugo Black and Estes Kefauver before him, and John McClellan and Sam Ervin after him, Truman overcame public inattentiveness to the processes of legislation by chairing an investigating committee. It sought to expose improprieties in war contracts.

The role of an active prosecutor-detective was sure melodrama. Phillips H. Lord discovered the device in his television program "Mr. District Attorney." This was no mere desk-sitting official, assigning footwork to others. He was a crusader, going forth with gun and enlarging glass to track down the villains. The program ran five years. I became aware of its potent formula when I defended it against a claim of plagiarism by a writer who claimed he had originated the idea. Ideas are not copyrightable. Only the execution of them, the language and the incidents which covered the idea's bone structure, was protected and could not be copied. "Mr. District Attorney" spawned many surefire television programs, and whether by coincidence or precept, there were many House and Senate investigating committee prototypes. The best of them were actually carried on television and out-Nielsened the fictional ones.

This is a curious phenomenon, because Senate committee hearings are solely for the purpose of formulating legislation. This would appear to be a dry search for the need of a "new or better law." But it was soon learned that sensational revelations might be hidden under the dust-covered stastical data.

Famous scenes abounded. In a Senate committee hearing John Pierpont Morgan and other millionaires testified that they did not have to pay one cent income tax, and to top it off, a midget placed himself on Morgan's lap while he was in a witness chair. The resulting photograph of the somber financial giant who didn't pay taxes, and the grinning midget who did, must still be the most piquant lesson in civics.

The gangster Frank Costello objected, on grounds of right of privacy, to television cameras and lights blinding him as he testified, so they narrowed the focus to his squirming hands. Thereby they made Hollywood directors envious of a most dramatic effect.

Witnesses, yelling the Bill of Rights over the hoots and applause, defied Senator Joseph McCarthy, who cited them and had them thrown out by guards.

As a senator, Truman had worked his way up on the investigating committee ladder from small bit parts, to feature roles and finally to stardom. He was chairman of a subcommittee which wrote the Civil Aeronautics Act of 1937. Then he became vice-chairman of a subcommittee of the Senate Commerce Committee which proposed the Transportation Act of 1940. So far there was no "sex appeal" in his efforts. But when he headed a special committee investigating the National Defense Program, which was called the Truman Committee, the revelations dealt with nothing less than the safety of every citizen.

It was January 1941. The United States was putting its industry to war. Ships, tanks, and planes began to roll off production lines as if we were mass producing glasses or coat hangers. Technology was demonstrating its prolific nature with a literal bang. But the Nazis had prepared their war machine for many years. We had been jolted into a sudden drive.

Truman warned that the defense effort would fail unless thousands of small manufacturers were utilized. He charged favoritism and inordinate profits in granting contracts to large companies. His committee, originally budgeted for only fifteen thousand dollars, was credited with saving the nation fifteen billion dollars by preventing waste and unnecessary expenditures. More important, by harnessing the incredible resources of our producers, small and large, and our technology, often inspirited by individual entrepreneurs, the flood of armaments swept over the Nazis like a tidal wave.

So Truman emerged from the somewhat obscure mass of senators to become, if not a household word, at least a newspaper and radio word. His qualities of simplicity, forthrightness, and no-nonsense personality were attractive. He was the little man fighting huge, unscrupulous forces who were cheating the American people in making war equipment. He represented plain honesty, and undemagogic patriotism as he exposed the miscreants. There was a new shining hero, not on a white horse, but appropriately walking fast in that chesty, straight-backed gait, as he gave interviews. He was the forerunner of the austerity school in politics whose graduates later included Governor Jerry Brown and President Jimmy Carter.

It was through a book that I first came in contact with him. The war was coming to an end. Although the night sky in Europe was still filled with lightning flashes from artillery, and although tanks, like huge ungainly bugs, were still lumbering over fallen trees, and planes could still be imagined in front of long white vapor trails, we all knew that we had reached the epilogue. I had made an intense study in anticipation of the question which would soon confront us, and entitled my book with that question, *What to Do with Germany*.

The publisher sent advance copies to those whose opinions would be meaningful. Truman was one. He responded with extremely enthusiastic praise which he authorized to be used as a blurb on the jacket. Still, the publisher, while displaying it proudly there, placed it underneath those of Walter Winchell, Clifton Fadiman, and Rex Stout, although ahead of Somerset Maugham, Louis Bromfield, and Maurice Maeterlinck. Such were the ratings in those days. But Truman's status was soon to change.

Roosevelt had to choose a running mate. Jimmy Byrnes aspired to be Vice-President and thought he was the President's choice. He asked Truman to nominate him. Truman agreed and came to the Chicago convention with a prepared speech. But Roosevelt exercised the President's prerogative to change his mind. Byrnes had been born a Catholic but had converted to Protestantism. This might create a problem. Roosevelt pronounced his verdict: "It's Truman!" It was tantamount to election. He ascended to the vice-presidency. The fact that he was only the proverbial heartbeat away from the Presidency made him a popular invitee at public functions. His was the eminence of possibility. It was then that I met him in person. I introduced him at several dinners. He responded with references to my book, and revealed that President Roosevelt had sent copies to Prime Minister Churchill and the British cabinet.

He invited me to visit him in Washington. He was burdenless, and chatted easily. With self-conscious contradiction he showed me his desk diary to emphasize his busy day.

Then that heartbeat away became a reality. Suddenly (suddenly? We had refused to recognize the slowly approaching death on Roosevelt's drawn and quivering face and the hollowness in his voice as if it came from a subdued echo chamber), the plain man from Missouri was the President of the United States. There is no greater contrast than the emergence from the darkness of the powerless vice-presidency to the blazing prominence of the most important political office in the world.

It took a long while for the people of the world to get used to the contrast between Roosevelt's patrician head, bell-like voice ringing in metronomic cadences, and Truman's average, undistinguished features, his nasal tones, as if in the last stages of a cold, his chopping hand gesture for emphasis, and his plainness, which he showed off because he excelled in it. "Indeed, the eagles," Churchill and Roosevelt, were gone, and "the sparrows," Attlee and Truman, had taken their place. Or so it appeared at the time.

Sudden acquisition of power can paralyze a man with fright, or stimulate him with confidence. No one can know a man's psyche to predict what his reaction will be. Like the mysterious action of a new ingredient on a chemical compound, it can reduce or activate it. Truman actually grew cocky, when faced with immense responsibility. It may have been due to his knowledge of history, which he did not flaunt, because it might give him an intellectual appearance. He felt more comfortable being known for "common sense" than for learning. Nevertheless, from his immense reading, he realized that great leaders in history followed their instincts, acted firmly, and were not torn apart by indecision and worry. He once expressed this to me, offhandedly, shunning profound psychological exposition. He defined it as a combination of judgment and courage. But how does one acquire them and how often are they confused with recklessness?

The President agreed to make an address at the University of California, where he would receive an honorary degree. He chose to speak on the dangers of Communism and asked me to prepare a draft for his talk. I did so, phrasing his own view, which I admired, that we would not interfere with any nation which chose a totalitarian government for itself. It was only the insistence of fanatics, whether on the right or left, that they must subdue their neighbors in order to bestow upon them the blessings of their totalitarian notions, which we would resist. It was the difference between a benign tumor, which was relatively harmless, and a cancerous, metastasizing one, which invaded the other organs of the body.

Looking back now more than thirty years to Truman's words gives one the eerie feeling not only that history repeats itself, but at times that it is a mere extension of the past. He said:

No action by the United States has revealed more clearly our sincere desire for peace than our proposal in the United Nations for the international control of atomic energy. In a step without precedent, we have voluntarily offered to share with others the secrets of atomic power. We ask only for conditions that will guarantee its use for the benefit of humanity and not for the destruction of humanity.

The speech was dotted with epigrammatic passages. Addressing Russia, he said:

No nation has the right to exact a price for good behavior . . . . it is possible for different economic systems to live side by side in peace; provided one of these systems is not determined to destroy the other by force.

Truman's earnestness and sincerity were his own brand of nonoratorical eloquence.

The only expansion we are interested in is the expansion of human freedom and the wider enjoyment of the good things of the earth in all countries.
The only prize we covet is the respect and good will of our fellow members of the family of nations.

His address was well received. The New York *Times* reported, "The speech was easily the most important of the more than forty talks the Chief Excutive has delivered so far on this wide-ranging topic."

On another occasion, I was invited through his special counsel, Clark Clifford, to submit a draft for a new address. I went to Washington for this purpose only. It was Friday, May 14, 1948. I did not know that the day would have historic significance. After I was briefed on the subject matter, I thought I would informally greet the President, if he was not occupied at the moment. I was ushered in. The President was in a tense mood. He had known for some time that on that very day Israel would declare its statehood. He had been under enormous pressure for months by conflicting forces concerning the creation of a Jewish state. On one side were England, the Arabs and their oil, even then a crucial factor, the State Department particularly the Middle East desk, which accepted the Arab view. As Truman later wrote in his memoirs:

Like most of the British diplomats, some of our diplomats also thought that the Arabs, on account of their numbers and because of the fact that they controlled such immense oil resources, should be appeased. I

am sorry to say that there were some among them who were also inclined to be anti-semitic. (p. 164)

On the other side were a great majority of senators, representatives,
and Jewish leaders who bombarded him with pleas to assist in bringing
the Balfour Declaration for a Jewish state to culmination. As far back
as 1937, Winston Churchill had said to the House of Commons:

It is a delusion to suppose that the Balfour Declaration was a mere act
of crusading enthusiasm or quixotic philanthropy. It was a measure
taken . . . in dire need of the war with the object of promoting the
general victory of the allies, for which we expected and received valuable and important assistance.

Still, when faced in 1948 with Arab threats to attack if a Jewish state
was formed, the Balfour Declaration, which had been described as "humanitarian," of "tactical political advantage," and "long range strategic
interests," and therefore "an irresistible combination to any imaginative
Anglo-Saxon Statesman," ceased to be attractive to Britain, which
could not keep order in Palestine with ninety thousand troops.

Truman similarly experienced the conflict between an ideal and the
realities which loomed like obstructive mountains to its effectuation. As
senator, he had no difficulty with the concept of a Jewish state. ". . .
when the time comes," he said, "I am willing to help make the fight for
a Jewish homeland in Palestine." Prophetically the time came, and he,
as President, more than any person in the world, was in a position to
make that dream of Herzl come true. But the Middle Eastern region
had become a political hot spot of intrigue, boiling in oil. Truman expressed his exasperation:

I surely wish God Almighty would give the Children of Israel an Isaiah,
the Christians a St. Paul, and the Sons of Ishmael a peep at the Golden
Rule.

He had vigorously favored the admission to Palestine of one hundred
thousand Jewish escapees from the Nazi terror. With unbelievable
callousness, England and other countries were rejecting boats filled
mostly with women and children, who, through the heroism of the underground, had escaped the Nazi extermination program. The defective
immigrant status of the passengers was such an immoral legalism, in
the light of the burning ovens which awaited them, that it should have
yielded to the ordinary dictates of humanity. Instead, with few exceptions, there was unwitting but real co-operation with the Nazi hunters.

Truman was indignant. In 1945 he so wrote Clement Attlee, Britain's Prime Minister. Truman's grandparents had been displaced persons, uprooted during the Civil War, who had fled to Missouri. He had been moved and fascinated by their reminiscences, of the misery of dislocation. The impression on his child's mind added poignancy to his compassion for the Jews' plight.

When Ibn Saud protested Truman's sponsoring the immigration of a hundred thousand Jewish refugees into Palestine, he received a blunt rebuke. Truman expressed the hope that countries outside Europe, including the United States, would admit the survivors of Nazi persecution. "The United States," he wrote, "which contributed its blood and resources to the winning of the war, could not divest itself of a certain responsibility . . . for the fate of people liberated at that time."

There was no equivocation. That was not the Truman way. He continued, ". . . a national home for Jewish people should be established in Palestine."

What a contrast with President Roosevelt's communications with Ibn Saud. They were so ambiguous that all conflicting parties drew encouragement from them and later denounced them, or vice versa. First, it was reported by Colonel William Eddy, United States Minister to Saudi Arabia, that Roosevelt had given a pledge to Ibn Saud that he would not support any move to hand Palestine over to the Jews. Later Roosevelt confided to James Byrnes that when he mentioned Palestine to Ibn Saud, "That was the end of the pleasant conversation." Congress was assured that American policy for the establishment of a Jewish homeland remained firm.

Nevertheless Roosevelt wrote to Ibn Saud that "no decision will be taken with respect to the basic situation . . . without full consultation with both Arabs and Jews." Thus the Arabs were given a veto. This was the difference between Roosevelt's diplomatic ingenuity, which operated in circled lines, and Truman's straight point-to-point candor.

Although Truman favored Jewish statehood, he became involved in a conflict with his own State Department and with his most trusted and revered adviser, General George Marshall.

Both the Democratic and Republican parties had planks in their platforms supporting the creation of a Jewish state. Congress was overwhelmingly pledged to it.

On July 2, 1945, a petition signed by fifty-four senators and two hundred fifty-one members of the House of Representatives urged his support of the United Nations resolution for partition, a plan which created two independent states in Palestine, one Jewish and the other Arab. But the "striped pants boys" of the State Department, as Truman called them, would not have it.

The conflicting pressures became so painful that Truman resolved to see no one, outside the Government, on this subject. He would make up his own mind, eschewing political and emotional considerations. It so happened that Dr. Chaim Weizmann had come from Palestine to visit Truman. He was the scientist who had increased the effectiveness of explosives to make them more devastating than ever before. This aided the Allies to win World War I, as much later, Professor Einstein's formula led to the creation of the atom bomb, which Truman used to end World War II.

Weizmann had obtained the Balfour Declaration, the charter which was England's promise to support a homeland for the Jews. He was destined to be the George Washington of Israel, its first President. When I later visited him in the President's office in Rehovat, near the great scientific institute named after him, his bearded head, ineffable charm, and humor ("We are becoming a real nation. We haven't any horses yet, but we already have horsethieves.") gave me the impression that Disraeli must have been like him.

Truman stuck by his instruction to his staff, that he would see no one on the subject of Palestine, not even Weizmann, whom he admired. Eddie Jacobson, Truman's former partner in a haberdashery store and friend for thirty years, came to plead for Weizmann's reception. Truman, who had great affection for Jacobson, nevertheless warned him not to talk about Palestine. Jacobson was desperate. He was not a Zionist, and he had never met Weizmann, but he felt it was important for Truman to be informed in a matter which involved the remnants of his destroyed people.

He avoided Truman's injunction by a ruse. He launched on a discussion of Truman's hero-worship of Andrew Jackson; how he remembered him reading about Jackson whenever there was time in the store, and how he had later put Jackson's statue in front of the Kansas City Courthouse. Then he made his point. Weizmann had been Jacobson's hero all his life just as Jackson had been Truman's. Now, Weizmann, although old and sick, had come thousands of miles to talk to the President. How could he refuse to see him? There were tears on Jacobson's cheeks.

Truman thought a while. Then he said, "I'll see him, you bald son of a bitch." To prevent a new flood of visitors, Weizmann was ushered in through the East Gate, without public or press announcement.

Truman saw the creation of a Jewish democratic state in the Middle East, not merely as a moral debt to six million slaughtered Jews, but as an essential part of American counteraction to Communistic designs on the Middle East and its oil. By 1947, Communists dominated Poland, Latvia, Lithuania, Estonia, Rumania, Czechoslovakia, Yugoslavia, and

Bulgaria. Britain had announced that she was ending her economic and military aid to Greece and Turkey. The President announced the Truman Doctrine and, shortly thereafter, the Marshall Plan to prevent further Communist penetration of Europe. The Middle East and its precious oil had likewise to be immunized from Communist take-over, not only to protect Europe, but because it was in itself the gateway to three continents and was coveted by the Soviets.

In this large strategy, a democratic, modern state with outstanding capabilities, in the midst of feudal Arab regions, which were susceptible to Soviet blandishments, was a great gain, if not indeed a necessity. On the other hand, if it resulted in war, the desired stability would be endangered. It was these considerations of Kennanism and Marshallism which concerned Truman, not, as the critics of the day charged, domestic considerations of the coming election.

So he had overruled the State Department and directed that the United States vigorously support the creation of a Jewish state. Even then, through a strange misunderstanding, Warren Austin, our ambassador to the United Nations, made a contrary public statement. In protest, Mrs. Eleanor Roosevelt resigned as a member of the American delegation to the United Nations. Truman refused to accept her resignation. He was furious with the State Department. He had been made out to be a liar to those he had talked to on the subject. The impression in the United Nations and in the capitals of the world was that the United States was confused, vacillating, and incapable of taking a firm position in a situation fraught with danger.

Curiously, the Soviet Union, through its chief delegate to the United Nations, Andrei Gromyko, denounced Warren Austin's "treachery," and urged the creation of a Jewish state. Anything to oust England from Palestine. That was why Russia had previously sent military equipment to the Haganah, Israel's army, aiding it in capturing Haifa on April 24, 1948. It was not until years later that it served Russia's purpose to become Israel's chief antagonist. This is another illustration of the Soviet Union's inconsistent tactics to achieve a consistent objective.

Truman's difficulty with the State Department merely repeated the experience of other Presidents. The State Department considered itself the repository of historical institutional policies. Presidents came and went. It "taught" the President what should be done, and if he was not assertive enough, it contrived to bypass his contrary views by subtle involved instructions to our far-flung embassies. Roosevelt had coped with this problem by organizing his own little State Department at the White House. Nixon and Ford were to use Dr. Henry Kissinger for the same purpose, much to the distress of the Secretary of State, William Rogers, until Kissinger absorbed the office. Truman struggled to establish the authority of the presidency over the entrenched power of the "striped pants boys" as he continued to call them contemptuously. He finally established his dominance in the Israeli issue.

Despite the formidable opposition of George Marshall, who later relented, James Forrestal, Admiral Leahy, Edward Stettinius, Loy Henderson, and others, Truman, with the advice of his special counsel Clark Clifford, who dared to challenge the impressive opposition, gave full support to the Partition Plan in the United Nations. On November 29, 1947, by a necessary two-thirds vote of thirty-three to ten, with ten abstentions, the General Assembly passed the resolution which gave international sanction of the United Nations to the creation of a Jewish state.

On May 14, 1948, the Union Jack was hauled down from the Government House in Jerusalem and the British mandate came to an end. The English commander, General Cunningham, withdrew his troops to the mournful music of Scottish bagpipers. The Jews decided not to lose a moment in declaring their independence as a state. Egypt and other Arab states had threatened repeatedly that such an act would bring immediate attack. This did not deter them. Fearing an Arab air raid which might snuff out the infant state before it was born, the founders arranged a meeting with great secrecy at which the momentous announcement would be made to the world. The site was designated to be the Tel Aviv Museum and was revealed only one hour before assembling. Soldiers with Sten guns guarded every approach to the building. There, under a picture of Theodor Herzl, the Austrian Jew who fifty years earlier had founded the Zionist movement, Ben-Gurion banged his gavel with the same power with which he had split the rocks on the desert and declared, "We hereby proclaim the establishment of the Jewish State in Palestine, to be called Israel." Then in a frieze tableau, as if staged for reproduction for centuries to come, they stood to the strains of *Hatikva*, the national anthem.

Word of the new state fled on radio wings to every man, woman, and child in the land, setting off hysterical jubilation. The screams of elation were suddenly suppressed. It was Friday evening. The Sabbath had begun and would last until sundown the next day. It was a time for prayer, not for shouting and dancing. So with superhuman restraint, they disciplined their fervor and turned it into reverent silence and prayer.

But the next day, as soon as the sun dipped into the Mediterranean, Hassidic joy burst forth with violent abandon. Men hugged each other, kissed women, whoever they were, formed circles and danced the hora. Individualists ran into the circles with waving arms and high-prancing feet to add to the frenzy. Young boys and girls, many of them in the

army, marched in file in and around the swirling masses, singing patriotic songs. Old religious Jews sang their odes to God to express the holy
joyousness of Hassidic belief. Their vigorous whirling dervish spins
defied their age, and their long satin caftans flew high in the opposite
direction of their feet as if they were wind-borne. Flags and flaming
buntings appeared everywhere waving the revelers on, and in cafes and
homes toasts rang out. At times the fury was stemmed momentarily by
tones of the *Hatikva*. But its patriotic solemnity could not long quench
the wild joy of the populace.

The name Israel had been chosen because of the legend in Genesis
(32:24), according to which the Patriarch Jacob and an angel engaged
in an all-night wrestling match. Jacob triumphed and extracted from
the helpless angel the mysterious blessing, "Thy name shall be called
no more Jacob, but Israel; for thou hast striven with God and with men
and hast prevailed."

The emotions of the historic birth, which was a reincarnation of a
nation two thousand years old, were understandably overwhelming. For
centuries, one of the prayers in every Jewish service throughout the
world was for the re-establishment of the Temple and a Jewish state.
"If I forget you, O Jerusalem, let my right hand wither. Let my tongue
cleave to the roof of my mouth." At last a nation had risen from ashes
laden with sacrificial bones. The prayer had come true. To Jews it was
the fulfillment of God's grant, set forth in the Book of Genesis.

On that day a covenant was made with Abraham that said to your children I shall give this land from the River known as the River of Egypt
until the great river Euphrates. (15:18) And I shall give this land to
your children after you; the land of sojourning; the entire land of
Canaan as eternal inheritance. (17:8)

The land authorized by the United Nations was only a sliver of the
Bible's promise, but it fulfilled a biblical promise of the creation of a
state.

The prosaic political task of choosing a form of government and
filling its contours with men and women was still to take place.
Truman had received notification on the letterhead of "The Jewish
Agency for Palestine" (the nation did not yet have its own stationery)
that "The State of Israel had been proclaimed as an independent
republic . . . and that a provisional government has been charged to assume the rights and duties of government."

It advised him that "The Act of Independence will become effective
at one minute after six o'clock on the evening of 14 May 1948, Washington time."

It expressed "The hope that your government will recognize and will welcome Israel into the community of nations."

The letter was signed by Eliahu Epstein, "Agent Provisional Government of Israel."

Truman had several alternatives. He could withhold recognition entirely. He could grant *de facto* recognition to the Provisional Government. He could wait for the finalization of the Government apparatus and grant full *de jure* recognition. Or he could, in anticipation of the formal completion of the Government, grant immediate *de jure* recognition even though there was only an interim "provisional government."

Truman leaned to recognition. But to blunt the opposition in the State Department and the possible criticism that he was acting hastily, he was inclined to await the formal election of an Israeli parliament (the Knesset) and the election of a President. Then he would grant *de jure* recognition. This would give him time, because, as he knew, it would take many months to achieve such a status. Actually, it took six months. Not until January 25, 1949, was a duly constituted Israeli Government completed.

It was about five o'clock, Washington time, Friday, May 14, 1948. In about an hour the Provisional Government of Israel would be announced in Tel Aviv.

It was in this atmosphere that I found myself at the President's desk in the oval office. Clark Clifford had been urging the President to grant full recognition to Israel immediately. He thought this might deter the Arabs from executing their threats to attack the new state. Moreover, this would fulfill the American promise, continuously expressed in the platforms of both the Republican and Democratic parties, supporting the creation of a Jewish state. Truman had given his word. That was enough.

Truman rose agitatedly from his desk and walked to a globe of the world which Roosevelt had kept in the office. He twirled it and indicated the refueling ports and bases for our Navy, and said that Admiral Leahy had warned him that antagonizing the Arabs might deprive us of essential support points and distant oil depots for our ships.

I commented that even if this was so, would it not be advantageous to American security to have a democratic bastion of loyalty in the Middle East with its own shoreline, to offset feudal Arab rulers who were notoriously undependable. Communist expansion in the area would also be discouraged by an Israel which could not be turned into a Soviet satellite.

Truman returned to his desk and gestured with his thumb toward the State Department Building, saying that Secretary of State George Marshall and the rest were firmly opposed to recognition. He would take care of that but he was inclined to wait until Israel was a formally constituted government entitled to *de jure* recognition.

Clifford had urged him to act immediately, pointing out that there was a strong likelihood that the Soviet Union would recognize Israel during the weekend, and thus be the first nation to do so. He was right in his warning. The Soviet Union and Poland recognized Israel the very next day.

Truman spoke reflectively, like a man who was appealing to himself rather than to his hearers. He expressed his profound biblical conviction that Israel's emergence was the fulfillment of a prophecy. I commented that he was in a unique position to make that prophecy come true, and that history would remember him for the historic act he could now perform, perhaps more than for any other thing he would do in his life. He was deeply moved. He authorized Clifford to draft a recognition *de facto*.

Clifford, who during White House meetings that week with George Marshall, Robert Lovett, and State Department officials had stood up to the opponents of recognition and relieved the President of replying to their intemperate statements, had met with Bob Lovett for lunch the day before. Lovett had had a change of heart, and in anticipation of the catapulting events, he and Clifford had drafted a formal recognition statement. Clifford was ready. Eleven minutes after Israel's declaration of independence, the following statement was released by the White House:

May 14, 1948

STATEMENT BY THE PRESIDENT

This government has been informed that a Jewish state has been proclaimed in Palestine, and recognition has been requested by the provisional government thereof.

The United States recognizes the provisional government as the de facto authorized of the new State of Israel.

Although a copy of this announcement was sent to the Secretary of State, none of the United States delegates to the United Nations knew anything of the decision in advance. There were consternation and surprise in the diplomatic fraternity. Many were dumfounded, since they were still engaged, as they believed with United States support, in a debate for trusteeship, the opposite of the creation of a Jewish state. Some thought the report was a joke. Dr. Philip C. Jessup, of the

United States delegation, checked the report and assured the delegates it was true.

The Washington *Post* commented that:

Diplomats were shocked because the United States flipflopped from a policy of confusion and indecision on Palestine to a positive act taken in unprecedented haste.

There was precedent for Truman's action. The United States had granted full *de jure* recognition to the Soviet Union in 1917, even though it was only a provisional government. It had recognized *de jure* the provisional government of Poland after World War II. So that Truman's granting only *de facto* recognition to Israel was unusually cautious. The United States was the only country in the United Nations, except South Africa, which did not grant *de jure* recognition to the Provisional Government of Israel. It finally did so in January 1949, when Israel completed its constitutional procedures with presidential and parliamentary elections.

However, Truman's instant recognition of Israel after its birth, even though *de facto*, was deemed by the Israelis a glorious and unforgettable chapter in their two thousand years of struggle.

It did not deter Egypt and four other Arab states from carrying out threats to invade Israel. The nation had been born in agony and would have to survive infancy against overwhelming numbers of antagonists. The people were calm and inured to strife. An anecdote illustrates this. One evening, a fierce storm broke. Jagged daggers of lightning seemed to pierce the clouds to release torrents, accompanied by tremendous peals of thunder. The next morning, a mother asked her five-year-old son whether he had been frightened during the night. "No," he replied, "I thought it was guns."

Within hours after the pronouncement of the state, Egyptian bombers struck a bus station in Tel Aviv killing forty men and women. The blood which flowed from them was to spread through the small nation.

On Friday nights, it had become a happy custom for Mildred and me to visit the well-known couturier Maurice Rentner, his wife, family, and other guests for dinner. It was a quasi-religious occasion, with candles on the table and a traditional feast. But it was very quasi. After dinner, the candles and dishes were cleared away, leaving only fresh pineapple and plates of candies for the gin players who took over. I was due there as usual that Friday evening.

When I left the White House, I stopped to telephone Mildred at the Rentners' in New York, to tell her that I would be late for dinner. More important, I was bursting with the news that Israel had just been recognized by the United States. The Rentner guests included outstanding executives of department stores and other enterprises. They were quite knowledgeable and apparently as incredulous about the story as our own delegates at the United Nations. They turned on the radio and television sets, and by the time I arrived, the news had flashed across the wires. Yes, a radio wave goes around the world seven times in one second, and the whole world knew that a new state had been born, and that it, the youngest democracy, had been recognized by the oldest modern democracy.

I delayed the dinner further to call my father and mother. They were in their summer home in Bethlehem, New Hampshire. They had just returned from the synagogue situated down the slope on Strawberry Hill. Sensitively my father caught the excitement in my voice and was alarmed by it. "Is anything the matter?" "No," I replied, "it is wonderful news." I gave it to him. "Bella!" he cried out. "Come here, listen to what Zindel-leben has to tell us." She listened and all she could say in a choked voice was "God bless you." I learned later that they had alerted the rabbi and many of their friends who gathered in our home. My father led the singing and schnapps flowed freely. The celebration in Tel Aviv had an echo in a town in New Hampshire appropriately called Bethlehem.

It must have had similar echoes in gatherings throughout the world, many of them among non-Jews, for a biblical prophecy had that day come true.

Truman was a student of the Bible. He had read the St. James Version twice while he was a young man. He had evidenced a special interest in history of the Middle East and had spoken movingly about it on many occasions.

A year after the recognition of Israel and after it had repulsed the invaders, the patriarchal white-bearded Chief Rabbi Herzog of Israel visited Truman. He had previously been the Chief Rabbi of Ireland and spoke with a thick Irish brogue. He expressed the sentiment I had offered to the President on the fateful recognition day. But he did it with mystical eloquence. He said to the President:

"God put you in your mother's womb so that you could be the instrument to bring about the rebirth of Israel after two thousand years."

THERE ARE MANY ECHOES BUT FEW VOICES

It has been my good fortune to be engaged in politics at the top. During the first Eisenhower-Stevenson campaign in 1952, I was invited to introduce the Governor at a number of meetings. I did not resort to the usual political hyperboles. Instead I analyzed the needs of the hour and the qualities of the candidate, as if destiny had offered up the man to suit the occasion. Each introduction carried this theme farther, making a series of political expositions whose connections were not evident to separate audiences but did not escape Stevenson's perception. He told me that they virtually outlined a campaign theme, and invited me to elaborate on them and submit them to him.

Of course, he eliminated the references to himself, although candidates usually unashamedly speak of their own capacities and accomplishments in the most laudatory terms. Somehow the theory has developed that a candidate who is modest about himself forfeits the electorate's support, because then he has no business aspiring to powerful office.

Even John Kennedy, whose grace and taste were impeccable, deemed it politically wise to retort to President Truman's comment that he was too young and inexperienced to seek the presidency, by proclaiming that he was fully qualified and ready to assume the highest office. I was surprised not only by the unabashed declaration of his own ability, but the asperity with which it was announced. He commented sarcastically that apparently no one was qualified for the office unless he obtained the approval of Truman.

But Stevenson could never engage in a gauche gesture irrespective of political dictates. He continued to be self-deprecating and there was more sincerity than humor in his attitude. This did not mean that he held himself in light esteem—certainly not when compared to the rivals on the scene. Rather it evidenced his recognition of the enormity of the problems our generation faced and the inadequacy of any man to cope brilliantly with all of them. His modesty was the expression of a fact of life, not lack of confidence to do as well or better than any other man. But could the people sense those distinctions?

The same problem was presented by his thoughtfulness. He knew that only a demagogue could be sure about solutions for century-old problems made more complicated by rising nationalisms and the developments of science. So he weighed both sides. He pondered. He admitted his doubts. He wanted more information and the opportunity to reflect. This was nothing but an intelligent approach. It didn't mean paralysis of thought or inability to make up his mind. Indeed, he was firm as a rock when he had reached a decision. Who could have been more direct and aggressive than he was with the Russian representative at the United Nations when he demanded that he say "Yes" or "No" whether Russia had placed missiles in Cuba. When the representative paused to gather his thoughts for an evasive answer, Stevenson pushed him with "Don't think—just answer, did you or didn't you?"—and "I am ready to wait for your answer until Hell freezes over!" Did this come from a vacillating man who could not make up his mind?

Yet during the campaign, and until this day, one hears that Stevenson had a Hamlet defect, forever asking "To be or not to be" and never coming to a conclusion. Men who reach decisions carefully and after searching their souls are more resolute than impetuous executives who give the appearance of strength but veer readily under pressure. Woodrow Wilson is another example of a "slow to conclude, but hard to dislodge" (I almost wrote dis-Lodge) type of personality.

I am convinced that Stevenson would have been a strong and decisive President.

Most public men have two personalities, or at least shadings which are different in their public and private appearances. President Johnson, for example, immediately became a different man when he appeared on television. It was as if he put on a cloak of deliberateness and dignity, and temper and passion were washed out of the picture. Unconsciously, he revealed his notion of his ideal by using over and over again the quotation from Isaiah, "Come, let us reason together." In action, he was the opposite. For a good cause he would twist arms mercilessly. Pressure, not reason, was his technique when he was leader of the Senate.

Hubert Humphrey once told me the amusing story of his experience when he first entered the Senate. Senator Johnson called him to a caucus meeting to line up the votes for a bill. Humphrey indignantly announced that he had been elected senator by the people of Minnesota, and would exercise an independent judgment on every piece of legislation. He was not going to be instructed what to do, even by the President himself, let alone the leader of the Senate.

"Of course, of course, Senator," said Johnson. "I merely thought it was a good bill and you would want to be told about it."

Later, there was an opportunity for a junior senator to be appointed to one of the Senate committees. Humphrey was passed over.

On another occasion, he was summoned to a caucus meeting. Again he declared that only his conscience would guide him. "I might vote for the bill when I study it, but I don't want to be pushed," he declared. Again the leader understood, but when a post office had to be built in Minneapolis, the project was held up.

So it went. Finally Humphrey said he realized that he had voted for every piece of legislation proposed by the caucus. The next time he was summoned, he laughingly announced "I am with you, Senator." A great friendship began which ultimately made him Vice-President but cost him the presidency.

On another occasion President Johnson described to a group of visitors, who met in the Cabinet Room, how he wanted the president of one of America's great corporations to serve on a committee with a labor leader and a public representative to control inflation. The executive replied that he would have to consult with his board of directors, and called later to decline. The President gathered some facts and called the executive again. "I hope you will reconsider," he said, and reeled off the precise amounts of payments made to his company under government contracts in the past several years, and the current applications pending.

"Would you believe it," the President smiled mischievously, "this awakened his duty to render some public service, and he accepted the assignment without even going back to his directors."

"Come let us reason together"—indeed? One certainly can't be angry at such use of presidential power for the public weal, but unlike Truman, who bragged of such tactics, Johnson's public demeanor negated his true and often better personality. So did Eisenhower's. But Stevenson's charm, warmth, humor, reflectiveness, and felicity were precisely the same whether on the platform or at the dinner table. He laughed readily. He was flattering, and sincerely so, to others when his generous spirit caused him to believe they deserved it.

Above all he had a large perspective. Some call it a historical sense. To hear him discuss any subject was to be lifted immediately above shallow consideration and see the problem in full dimension. Thus his deliberation for a solution began where others had ended, since they had not even perceived the depth of the difficulty.

Another extraordinary quality was that he would not compromise with himself. "To thy own self be true," was a natural and unshakable principle by which he lived. Despite frenzied pleas by his political advisers, he would not cater to voters by ambiguous statements or subservience to the wishes of a particular group. It was in Madison Square Garden, at an American Legion convention, that he delivered a talk on true patriotism. Those who read his speech in advance had a fit. They feared he would be hooted out of the hall. They knew he wouldn't cater to any jingoistic spirit and cause the rafters to ring with a Fourth-of-July oration. But why couldn't he save this speech for the Civil Liberties Union or the Americans for Democratic Action? Why risk offending an audience which represented a huge following, when it was so easy to sing the glories of America and its flag and bring the house down?

Stevenson would not budge. It took courage to deliver that speech because he might have been hissed off the platform, and the campaign would be lost before it began. He said:

"Consider the groups who seek to indentify their special interests with the general welfare. I find it sobering to think that their pressure may one day be focused on me. I have resisted them before and I hope the Almighty will give me the strength to do so again and again. And I should tell you, my fellow Legionnaires, as I would tell all other organized groups that I intend to resist pressures from veterans also."

He told me that he was not being defiant. He believed in the American Legion. He believed in their constituency. They were the American people, conservatives and liberals. There was no reason to trim his sails.

He was right. The audience recognized his greatness, and even those who disagreed with some of his pronouncements stood and cheered. It was an ovation and gave impetus to the campaign instead of destroying it.

So it went. It was to labor that he talked on the excesses which disserved their best interests. It was to businessmen that he talked of responsibility to the public and the shortsightedness of a greedy policy in a modern world. It was to the South that he talked of the brotherhood of man which could not be abnegated by color, and to the North, that hypocrisy in civil rights was a sin against the Constitution as well as against blacks.

He talked where it did some good for the nation's welfare, not for himself as a vote getter.

Compare Eisenhower's posing for a picture with Senator Joseph McCarthy, whom he detested. When the senator took advantage of the opportunity by putting his arm around the General's shoulder and hugging him like a buddy, Eisenhower nearly spit. He warned his clever political strategists that if McCarthy ever did that again, he would punch him in the nose. But even his unfailing good instincts had yielded to political expediency. He was like the lawyer who found out what advice his client wanted and then gave it to him. It was impossible to conceive of Stevenson in this light. He abhorred political pap. It offended not only his cultured appreciation of our language, but his integrity. "A politician," he jested, "is a man who approaches every question with an open mouth." He insisted on "talking sense to the people." He respected them too much to treat them like fools or infants. In this sense there was no self-sacrifice in his "highfalutin" campaign. The people would understand. They deserved nothing less than the best. That is why he would polish every word of his speeches to its highest gloss, while his assistants were driven to distraction, waiting for the script to be put through the vast communication process.

Four sentences in his acceptance speech at the convention revealed the exquisite qualities of his mind and his deep feeling. "The potential of the presidency for good or evil now and in the years of our lives smothers exultation and converts vanity to prayer. I have asked the merciful Father to let this cup pass from me. But from such dread responsibility one does not shrink in fear, in self-interest, or in false humility. So, 'if this cup may not pass away from me, except I drink it, Thy will be done.'"

He was doing more than running for President. He was lifting the national spirit, appealing to the ideals which he knew were responsible for American's greatness, setting before the people moral standards toward which they could repair from all directions, thus enhancing their unity without obliterating their differences. He aroused their conscience. To be complacent in the face of injustice was to be guilty of indecent composure. Had he been President, he would have utilized the moral power of that office to better effect than any other Chief Executive with the exception only of Lincoln.

The fact that he lost did not disprove his faith in the democratic process. He himself recognized the wisdom of the people in choosing Eisenhower. In intimate discussion, he expressed the rationale for his own defeat. The great problem facing the nation was Russia, and the selection of the victorious general in history's greatest conflict provided an invaluable power symbol which would command Russia's respect and caution. Eisenhower had used his authority to create good will. He was a friend of Marshal Zhukov and other Russian military figures. He was better known than Stalin to the peoples behind the Iron Curtain.

In contrast, Stevenson was an unknown figure internationally, and indeed hardly known to the American people. The Russians might be tempted to test him, as later they did Kennedy—a probe which brought us nearer a holocaust than we have ever been before or since. So the people, in electing Eisenhower, were buying insurance. The premium was reasonable. He had a kind heart and an ingratiating smile. He had demonstrated his diplomatic skill. He was not a martial figure like Mac-Arthur, who was admired as a general, but would have been unthinkable as a President. Indeed, Eisenhower's later valedictory warning against the military establishment corroborated Stevenson's analysis of him as devoid of military impetuosity or arrogance.

Thus, Stevenson rose above his own defeat to understand and justify the wisdom of the people.

Why then did he run a second time against Eisenhower? I participated in that decision, though I was a minority of one. Stevenson invited me to attend a meeting in his law office in Chicago in 1956. Present were his most intimate advisers and friends—among them Colonel Jacob Arvey, his law partners William M. Blair, Jr., and Newton Minow.

Arvey was recognized as the man who had brought Stevenson into the political arena. He was properly honored for his acuity and high-mindedness in attracting such a star into a firmament which usually shone with lesser lights. He, too, however, suffered from the unorthodoxy of his candidate. He told, with a mixture of exasperation and pride, how Stevenson turned down a large contribution from a union when he was running for Governor of Illinois. Every cent was precious, but when the visiting committee requested a promise that, if elected, he would appoint their candidate for Water Commissioner, he respectfully dismissed them.

"Mr. Stevenson, here is his record. He is the best qualified man for the post. Look into it."

"I will," he said, "and perhaps I will appoint him, if I am lucky enough to be elected. But I will make no advance promises."

They withheld their contribution. "He is one of those impracticable idealists," they told Arvey. "He will never be elected dog catcher."

But he was elected Governor. Later, he did appoint the union's choice because he was the best man on the merits.

On the other hand, his principles compelled him to support a member of his administration even though there were rumors of a scandal about him. An opposition newspaper threatened to expose him, unless Stevenson dismissed him. The evidence was circumstantial and did not convince the Governor of guilt. "If I had to appoint him today, I would not do so. There are those about whom there are no suspicions. But I will not dismiss him, and thereby brand him for life."

The headline broke. Stevenson would not budge. Nothing was ever proved, and the accused served well and honorably the rest of the term.

Since then he had become a national figure. It took the exposure of a presidential campaign to lift him to recognition.

I recall the shrewd words of the motion picture pioneer Adolph Zukor, whose hundred-year celebration I attended. Carried away by Stevenson's campaign, I predicted that he could win over Eisenhower. "Never," said Zukor. "You have the best actor but he is unknown. He is running against a star, a Clark Gable. Wait until you see the box office returns!"

But now as a new election approached, Stevenson was no longer an unknown actor. If he wished the Democratic nomination again, there was no doubt he could have it. The question was, should he accept?

Those around the table agreed on two propositions. First that the Governor should run. He was the strongest candidate the Democrats had. If he withdrew, the party would never forgive him. He would be dead politically. If he ran and lost, he would still have to be reckoned with in the future. The most politically knowledgeable men there pronounced this proposition with a certainty that one would ascribe to a logarithmic axiom. When my turn came, I demurred. It was evident that President Eisenhower was a more formidable opponent than he was the last time. Economic conditions favored him. The foreign scene was reasonably quiescent. His much-discussed fatherly image had matured into a more lovable grandfather image. Why court defeat a second time? If the Governor sat this one out, he would be a powerful, perhaps inevitable choice to run four years later, when Eisenhower would not be his opponent. The chances are that after eight years of Republican rule, a Democrat would win, and Stevenson would be an overwhelming choice, over any other Republican than Eisenhower.

As for the political shibboleth that a candidate owed his party the duty to lead it even if in defeat, I confessed my amateur standing in such a matter, but I could not understand why it would serve the party or the Governor to destroy its foremost personality by another defeat when he might well be salvaged for victory in the next campaign.

Everyone turned to Stevenson. He said he had given the matter long and earnest thought. He described his distaste for campaigning. It was an ordeal he would wish to avoid if he possibly could. Even the presidency was not worth it to him. It put a premium on stamina rather than thought. The hoopla, the posturing, the handshaking, the ubiquitous need to beg for support, the humiliating fund-raising functions, the pull and tug to be everywhere and cater to every influential politician—all violated his sense of propriety. Nevertheless, he felt he had to accept the nomination if it were tendered to him.

The reason was somewhat different from that urged upon him. He recognized Eisenhower's increased popularity. He foresaw the great possibility of defeat. If he refused to run, it would appear that he was running away from the battle. He could not act in this cowardly way. He would lead the party as ably as he could if it wished him to do so.

I could not agree with his conclusion. It seemed to me to be based upon a concept of chivalry rather than upon higher and more realistic considerations. But the political experts and the idealist agreed. Such a parallelism was impressive. I kept my peace.

The discussions then turned to the kind of campaign Stevenson should wage if, as seemed a foregone conclusion, he was nominated. Once more, I found myself in a minority of one.

Everyone urged with varying degrees of tact that the Governor should change his campaign style. In effect, they were saying that he talked "over the heads of the people," that he must stop appealing solely to intellectuals; that instead of a few carefully prepared addresses, he ought to make ten to twenty short talks a day to small groups at whistle stops, at shopping centers, and to any whirlpool gathering which a candidate attracts; that he was a warm human being and he ought to communicate this quality by mixing with people, shaking hands, making small talk and seeking out the leaders of the local community. Less humor wouldn't hurt either. Levity and statesmanship don't go together, according to public relations experts.

Of course, there would be the opportunity for important pronouncements on television and at great rallies, but even here, he ought not to write speeches for enshrinement in political literature. He ought to talk to the people in their terms.

It was evident that these were not improvised suggestions. They seemed to be carefully worked out plans for a "down to earth" campaign which would reach the masses, and which would give him a chance to win.

I expressed my dissent, but far more vigorously this time. Often a man's strength is also his weakness. Stevenson's intellectual, idealistic, and felicitous appeal made him a unique figure on the political scene. True, it was not the customary mass appeal. That may have been its weakness. But he had polled more than twenty-seven million votes against a national hero and the most popular candidate of the century. So there must have been considerable comprehension of his stature even if not always of his words. Also his personality had evoked an enthusiastic following rarely seen in political annals. The people loved Ike, but those who admired Stevenson were fanatical about him. Such dedication and loyalty ought not to be sacrificed, which it would be if the gold of idealism turned to the dross of political stratagem.

History has proved that "intellectual candidates" can win and "people's candidates" can lose. But one cannot be transposed into another. The people called Roosevelt, "Teddy"; Smith, "Al"; Truman, "Harry"; Eisenhower, "Ike," but no one called Wilson, "Woody"; Hoover, "Herbie"; or Hughes, "Charlie." Indeed, Stevenson had not done too badly by this test of public identification. They had cheered "Adlai," even though no one would scream at him, "Give 'em hell!" as they affectionately did at Truman.

Furthermore, even if the "humanizing" tactic were wise, it could not be carried off. We had already heard how distasteful the knockabout bruises of campaigning were to him. If he quickened the pace and ran an even more frenzied schedule, without the opportunity for rest and thought, he would become dull, and his infectious zest for a debate of the issues would be drowned in the trivia of public relations gimmicks.

I concluded by turning to Stevenson and saying, "Governor, if you start kissing babies, you'll be embarrassed and so will the babies. It just isn't your style."

He threw back his head, a little like Roosevelt, and laughed heartily. There was no decision on this point. It was considered premature. The matter had been aired. That was sufficient for the time being.

When he was nominated, he gave no hint in his magnificent acceptance address that he was acting out of loyalty to the party. On the contrary, in a typically gallant and witty passage, he said that last time he had been reluctant to accept the nomination conferred upon him, but "this time you may have noticed, the honor was not entirely unsolicited by me."

Weeks later the nation was shocked by the announcement that President Eisenhower had suffered a heart attack. He had been rushed to Bethesda Hospital. The world's attention was focused on the daily bulletins which were issued from his bedside. Affection and alarm were the prevailing mood. Vice-President Nixon was filling the vacuum of the presidency, while announcing that the President was still at the helm and being consulted on anything of major importance.

Whatever the medical outcome, it seemed certain that the President could not run again. The ordeal of a campaign and the burdens of the Presidency were taxing enough for a well man. How could one stricken do justice to the office, and how could he expect the people to take the risk? How could an enfeebled President be trusted to react in a crisis?

Such are the uncertainties of life in general and political life in particular. Like a tropical storm which comes with such suddenness that the sun is still shining as the black clouds drench the land, the Republican Party was inundated by despair at the very moment when the shining countenance of its invulnerable son was at its brightest. There was no other candidate who could beat Stevenson. In one tragic instant, he appeared certain to be the next President of the United States.

"My God, my God," I kept saying to myself. "Suppose he had been talked out of accepting the nomination." I was never so grateful for having lost an argument.

However, Eisenhower's recovery was more startling than his illness. And his courage in staying in the race exceeded both. So desperate was his party to retain him as its candidate, and so confident of his hold on the people, that he even announced the restricted schedule of his activities in the future. With admirable candor he was telling the nation that, if elected, he would be a part-time President.

Here was a new clear-cut issue. Could the nation afford to take the risk of a sick President and perhaps worse? Stevenson decided as a matter of principle that he would not even discuss the subject. He admired Eisenhower as a man, and he would not indulge in morbid speculation about his short life expectancy, or his possible incapacity. He conducted the campaign as if the shadows over the President's health were nonexistent. As always, his punctilious instincts were right. But he abandoned them on the closing night of the campaign. I shall come to this.

It was clear then, and even more so in retrospect, that Stevenson's second campaign was far less effective than the first. He resolved the strategy dispute in his office by adopting both views. He would stick to the high road. Nothing could perusade him to abandon that. His speeches were still sculptured elegance. He still sought perfection as he made last-second changes in the television studio, while his assistants clamored for a finished version. He still put his personal stamp on every paragraph, no matter what the staff handed him.

At his request, I prepared a talk on the Middle East. It was an analysis of Russia's penetration into an area which Napoleon once said was the key to world domination. Despite his feverish schedule, he had somehow found the time to rewrite and improve on my best effort.

So he had rejected the plea to talk down to the people. He would not compromise with excellence whether it be thought or diction. Yet in an effort to make a more pervasive campaign, he had also accepted the advice to appear more often, make improvised, short speeches, which could be repeated ad nauseam to small groups, shake hands, and generally be more a man of and with the people than above them. He had weighted the alternative of limiting his campaign in the main to television, even though that meant relatively few appearances. He asked me whether stumping in person had not been made obsolete by technology. I told him that experience in motion pictures proved the opposite. The more a star's image appeared on the screen, the more eager audiences were to see him in person.

I believe it is a false political concept of democracy that its leader must be reduced to the common denominator (if not the lowest common denominator) in order to be accepted by the people. They look for humaneness in their representative. In this sense he must be one of them. It is a wise insistence because without it he can govern but not lead. But the American people aspire to high estate in whatever occupation they are in, and are flattered that from their midst can arise an exceptional man. They admire and honor men of achievement in art, science, music, business, and sports. They are natural hero-worshipers. They certainly expect their President to be a uniquely gifted man, whom the world can admire and respect. Mediocrity in the White House reflects adversely on the American people and they are chagrined by it.

So it is an error, when one has as sensitive and brilliant a man as Stevenson, to gripe about his articulateness, and worry that he is not performing the rituals to make him a regular guy. I have commented on the lawyer who seeks favor with his client by matching cussword for cussword with him. He may have the illusion that he is effecting a closer tie, but I believe the client would prefer to look up to his lawyer as a cultured man. So, too, the electorate and their leaders.

Nevertheless, Stevenson drove himself in all sorts of nonsensical gyrations to do his duty as an energetic candidate. He mixed with the people, but I saw him wince every time someone slapped him on the back to demonstrate approval or familiarity, neither of which he needed. His schedule was so frenetic that he had no time to think—and this was as necessary to him as breathing. He was pummeled, shoved, lifted, and cranked, until his arm ached from being squeezed, his feet from standing, and his voice from shouting above the din which surrounded him. He made so many appearances in such rapid succession that he did not know whether he was arriving, leaving, or had been there. Cars sped him to unscheduled destinations, because some committee had requested his appearance, and the local managers thought they could squeeze it in.

Some public officials are refreshed by crowds. Truman, Kennedy, and, especially, Johnson reveled in crowd commotion and excitement. Johnson's secretary would come home and collapse from the strain of watching him go through a tumultuous day. But the President was stimulated and stayed up talking or dancing late into the night.

Others, like Stevenson, are dulled by noise. Every conversation used up part of his attentive capacity. It eroded his energy. He related to people. He could not go through the motions without expending himself. Unlike the judge who said he could look a lawyer in the eye for a full hour and not hear a word he said, Stevenson never mastered that art.

The result was that he became numb. Numb with tiredness, with boredom, and with an election process which seemed to him to have been corrupted into a circus. The inner spark of the man, which lit every word with feeling, burned low. He was like an actor who recites his lines from memory but without emotion, and therefore cannot create any in the audience.

I introduced Stevenson to several audiences toward the end of the campaign. One was a huge rally of women. When he arose to speak, they screamed their adulation for Adlai for, at least, five minutes. I thought this might arouse him from what almost appeared to be torpor as he was crushed by the guests on his arrival. Even the police could not extricate him from the pawing men and women who sought his hand, slapped him on the shoulder, sometimes by error a little too high, and yelled their support close into his ears. I thought he looked dazed, having just come from several other such affectionate, crushing exhibitions.

So I tried to shield him for a few minutes while the traditional chicken and cold peas were placed before him on the dais. But it was impossible. A crowd gathered and almost pushed the table over upon him. Each one told him of his or her work in the campaign, or asked for his autograph, or made a twenty-second critical analysis of one of his speeches.

There was only one moment of comic relief. A lady, who perhaps had attended the preceding cocktail hour a little too early, said, "Adlai, I'd put my slippers under your bed any time." He looked startled for a second, then laughed heartily and said, "You might want to use them sooner than you think." When she was led away, the line behind her continued with more dignified and more boring approaches. Some pleaded for autographs for their children and insisted on dictating what he should write on them. He pretended not to hear, or perhaps he really didn't. Certainly the crowd didn't hear or obey when the chairman announced that no more autographs would be given.

Stevenson didn't eat. He couldn't. And so the ovation which greeted his introduction was only more noise to burden his spirit.

He spoke like an automaton. His opening jests, which usually sent a receptive audience into spasms of glee, got only a titter. Nothing is funny when the speaker is uncomfortable and the words fall tired from his lips. His serious comments were memorized recitals without inner feeling. When he finished, he received respectful applause, which was like a dim echo of the ovation which had greeted him.

A few officials approached me and asked what was the matter with

Stevenson. I explained that he was simply exhausted. One of them advised that he go to bed for two days, so that he could wind up the campaign with spirit. I passed on this recommendation, but the howl of protests from those loyal workers who had arranged "wonderful schedules" for him every hour of the day and night almost blew me out of the room.

Perhaps it was his tiredness which put him in a noncombatant mood one night. "The trouble with this campaign, Louis, is that there is nothing we can tell the people about Eisenhower which they don't know. And they're still for him."

How true this was. Even before his illness, every one knew that Eisenhower was not doing his homework. Time and again this would be revealed at his press conferences. A question would be put about a matter which had been on the front pages for days. Despite last-minute preparatory cramming, he would look blank and then begin by saying that he was not aware of the incidents involved in the question. Before he could go farther, a friendly correspondent would tip him off that the fact had been officially reported. Eisenhower, always honest, would then state that unfortunately he was not familiar with it and would reserve judgment until he had looked into the matter.

If delegation of authority is the sign of a good executive, he was the greatest executive the White House ever had. Dulles made and executed foreign policy. So it went with all other departments.

When he did take the helm, his customary good judgment would often yield to impetuosity which only his illness could explain. Heart conditions often trigger bursts of temper. I recall that Federal Judge Archie O. Dawson, who had been a mild and kind man all his life, suddenly developed a fearful temper after he had "recovered" from a heart attack. The outburst was over in a flash. Without warning his fist and voice would explode without any apparent provocation. Then he was contrite and sometimes offered an apology. I cite this illustration because I think it explains Eisenhower's noted temper tantrums. Of course, they affected policy.

In a quick move in July 1958 Eisenhower sent marines to faraway Lebanon to counter a threatened take-over of the government. Fortunately, we didn't get mired in a long struggle, but it is an interesting commentary on Republican criticism of Democratic involvement in Vietnam without congressional approval.

Also, Eisenhower's reputed rude instruction to Prime Minister Eden to "get the hell out of Suez" was uncharacteristic of his proven psychological skills in dealing with disparate forces.

Now, after a serious heart seizure, it was even more evident that he would spare himself. Even if he were not an invalid, he would give only part time to the presidency. Yet, the magnificent symbol of power and goodness remained, and the people accepted it despite all handicaps.

At the very end of the campaign, extraordinary news came to Democratic headquarters about Eisenhower's health. The source was absolutely reliable. I do not identify it because it resulted from a professional leak which might involve the doctor in an ethical violation. A man of Eisenhower's age who had suffered a by-pass ileitis surgery had only a few years of life expectancy. If on top of that one added the specific kind of coronary he had since sustained, the life expectancy shrank alarmingly. The precise figures were given. It meant that, according to the most authentic medical opinion and longevity tables, Eisenhower could not finish his term in office if he were re-elected.

This information was forwarded to Stevenson. The question was whether his sensitive silence ought to yield to the national interest. It was no longer a matter of Eisenhower's illness in general terms. Now there was scientific evidence which made the previous fears a high probability, if not indeed an inevitability. Was it fair to the people not to know that they were electing Nixon and not Eisenhower for a part of his term? The President could not be faulted for keeping this information from the public. Obviously he could not be informed of the fatal news. But why had those high in the party councils, who must have known the facts, permitted him to run? Was it now the duty of the "loyal opposition" to speak the truth in a matter of such importance? Stevenson struggled with the issue. It was more bizarre than the hackneyed plots of duty versus love, or honor versus loyalty. It presented a novel question of the public's right to know versus heartless revelation about the President's heart.

If his exposure of the facts might not also benefit his campaign, the decision would have been easier. What caused him anguish was that he would be accused of exploiting the issue for political gain. This was the very reason he had previously refused to mention the subject. But now the medical portent was so ominous that he felt as a citizen, as well as a candidate, it was his duty to warn the people of the tragic facts. He could have dodged the dilemma by having someone else break the story. But he would not play games. The responsibility was his. Having decided to accept it, he would speak of it himself at the only opportunity he still had—on his election eve telecast.

So in that broadcast he said: "And, distasteful as this is, I must say bluntly that every piece of scientific evidence we have, every lesson of history and experience indicates that a Republican victory tomorrow would mean that Richard Nixon would probably be President of this country within the next four years." It was too little, too late, and too vague. Executed in such a halfhearted manner, it lacked persuasion and seemed to be nothing more than a political ploy, and a dirty one at that. If the revelation had to be made, it required scientific verification, and a decent opportunity for reply. Then, the motivation for so daring a statement might have become clear. But too much delicacy and restraint in such a matter were self-defeating. Better not to have touched it at all. Problems are like illnesses. The worse they are, the bolder the solution must be. One cannot be delicate with a cancer. Extensive and dangerous surgery must be used. Poultices, or just a little cutting to be considerate of the patient, won't do.

Another factor which militated against the strategy was the timing. Unfortunately, the news had come to Democratic headquarters at the last minute. This may not have been accidental. Troubled consciences may have been responsible for the "leak," and they must have been subjected to the same struggle in which Stevenson became engaged. Imminence of disaster puts an end to indecision. So no time was left. But it has always been considered unfair to make a serious charge on the eve of election, when the opponent cannot reply. Stevenson could not have afforded less opportunity for rebuttal than to say what he did at eleven o'clock at night preceding the next morning's voting.

This was not by design. Such sharp tactics were not in him. But he should have considered the appearances. The surrounding circumstances were incriminating. For months he had not referred once to the health issue. Now, at the very last instant, he abandoned his principles and indulged in morbid predictions of his opponent's life-span. If he considered it his duty to give warning, why didn't he do so earlier? The answer, which could have been given, was not supplied. If he knew how serious the matter was, how could delicacy have prevented him from speaking out a long time ago? Again, the ready answer was not given.

It may well be that Stevenson's exhaustion contributed to the error of making the attack, and the greater error of making it in an inadequate and half-baked way.

He would have suffered a bad defeat anyhow, but many experts believe, and I agree, that this incident cost him millions of votes. It appeared to be a revelation that the idealism and high spirit of the first campaign, which made it a glorious enterprise, irrespective of the outcome, was tarnished in the second campaign by political expedients.

The irony of it all is that the scientific data, which had come from the most reliable sources, was completely wrong. Eisenhower not only lived out his term but survived to put his golf instruction on the White House lawn to full test in the Palm Springs sun and elsewhere, as he so richly deserved.

In 1968, twelve years after the dire prediction, a new series of heart attacks struck him. He lapsed into coma. The medical reports indicated that the end was near. Obituaries lay on editors' desks ready for instant use. Headlines reported "Ike sinking." Again the doctors were wrong. He pulled out several times in what were described as "miraculous recoveries." He sat up, received visitors, and left the hospital.

Finally he succumbed. He had been first in war, first in popularity, and perhaps first in the hearts of his countrymen, but far from first among the Presidents of the United States.

The final irony was that Stevenson, who was only fifty-six years old at the time of the second campaign, and in good health, fell dead while walking on a London street. He, who had warned against Eisenhower's fate, died four years before Eisenhower.

This is the trouble with mortality tables and averages. They never apply to the individual case. If they did, they would not be averages. Family counselors succeed in healing broken marriages in less than 5 per cent of the cases, but for the lucky couple in that statistic, there is a 100 per cent result. The local philosopher who was asked what the death rate was in his town, and replied one to a person, was not so foolish. Particularly unreliable are statistics about span of life when applied to a single individual. There are mysterious life forces in each of us which defy prediction, at least by the scientific evaluations available today. Inheritance factors, which are unmeasurable, seem to play an important, perhaps decisive role. We do not yet know what they are. Nor do we know to what extent dissipation or health habits reduce or enhance our inherited treasure.

We are all concerned with longevity, but insurance companies have business reasons to learn as much as possible about it. Theirs is a "life and death" business need to know the answer. Their profits or losses depend on accurate guessing. In the past, medical examinations were the guiding test. How did the heart, kidney, liver function?

But more and more, we have learned to rely on the "life force." It is the mysterious "x" factor in the equation. Many decrepit people live long. Many healthy ones suddenly die. The vitality to overcome disease and malfunctioning organs of the body is the apparent answer. But how to measure it?

One way has been found. It is an inherited factor—a strain such as we seek in horses or cattle. Therefore the ages of one's parents, averaged out, are a significant factor. The statistics bear out the correlation. It has been suggested that if we knew the longevity of our grandparents and parents and divided by six, we would come closer to one's own span of life than medical reports could provide. Even the theory that in the past people succumbed to diseases which are now extinct and therefore not a fair test is offset by the fact that a strong life force overcame those scourges even before antibiotics were discovered. Similarly, even in the case of death by accident, it can be argued that in many cases a vital life force would have overcome broken bones and infections.

Many years ago, my French law partner, Pierre Gide, recommended to me a doctor who claimed that he could measure one's "life force" by a simple sputum test which he had devised. It registered one to ten, somewhat like a litmus test, by color. If you registered five you were average and reasonably safe for a long life. If you were seven or over, you could smoke, dissipate, be obese—nothing would mow you down. It reminded me of the comedian Ed Wynn, who claimed his uncle was so strong that they had to beat his liver with a club for hours after he died to put an end to him.

The doctor also contended that if the sputum test registered one to three, it was certain that the person had a fatal disease, like cancer, even if it had not yet appeared, and would die within a few years. I tried to introduce him to medical authorities who would permit him to test patients in hospitals, as he claimed he had done in France, but he was rejected as a quack and went the Laetrile way. I never heard of him again. Will his name someday be resurrected, like Semmelweis?

Medical books record unexplainable remissions of fatal diseases like cancer and leukemia. On the other hand, strong and healthy individuals have broken under the slightest strain when there was no prior history of weakness.

So Eisenhower's survival and Stevenson's collapse proved only one thing about medical prediction—that it is unpredictable.

The same might be said for most political predictions. It turned out that Stevenson's second defeat did not destroy his opportunity to run again, as I had thought it would. Of course he was not the irresistible choice he would have been had he sat out the second Eisenhower election. More important, he would have been ready and eager to carry the banner in 1960. As it was, he announced firmly that he would not be a candidate a third time and that opportunity ought to be given to others.

This decision was a composite of sincere principle and the horror he had of another maddening campaign effort. But when it seemed that the prize, and this time it was a prize, would fall to a young senator with no distinguished record, and the burden of cracking prejudice against a Catholic, many leaders of the party turned to Stevenson. He had earned a real chance at the presidency. Who couldn't beat Nixon?

Mrs. Roosevelt spearheaded the effort to get Stevenson to change his mind. We all helped. She emerged from a personal conference with him to announce that he would accept the nomination if it were tendered. There was an explosion of elation among the delegates and the people.

Apparently her anxiety to obtain his consent had misled her into interpreting his gratitude for acquiescence. There was an embarrassing contradiction by Stevenson. She had misunderstood him.

The crowds in front of and in the convention hall were ready to stampede the convention for Stevenson. They were confused by the Stevenson-Roosevelt exchange. Many were in tears. But they continued to scream and hope for Stevenson's acceptance. There is little doubt that, despite the excellent groundwork of the Kennedy forces, had Stevenson said "Yes" he would have been lifted on a wave of wild acclaim to the nomination.

When he entered the convention hall, the greatest and only real unorganized ovation greeted him. The rank and file of the party, including many delegates pledged to others were pleading with him to run again. But he stood firm. Kennedy was nominated—and even he, not yet recognized for the great qualities he later exhibited, and with handicaps which no other candidate was burdened with—beat Nixon. There can be little doubt that had Stevenson, like Williams Jennings Bryan, chosen to run a third time, he would have been nominated and elected President by a far greater margin than Kennedy.

Would he have lived out his term or would he have fallen as he did, but in the White House? Who can tell? He had been disappointed in not being designated Secretary of State. He had served his President and country well at the United Nations, but not without misgivings and embarrassment because he was not the recipient of confidences which later grieved him.

He might have lived had he been President. Even more poignant is the virtual certainty that John F. Kennedy would be alive today if Stevenson had not withdrawn. So, fate is a grimaced visage. Both men might have lived had they been defeated in their purpose. Both died when they succeeded.

In political life, pygmies abound—giants are rare. This is not surprising. When the people rule themselves, their representatives reflect them in all their grandeur and ignorance. We abhor an exclusive elite class, but we welcome the elite when they rise from the people. Stevenson came from a distinguished background. His grandfather was Vice-President under Cleveland. Whatever the derivatives of his qualities, they were unique and brilliant. Due to his sensitivity, he may never have emerged on the political scene. A career as professor, or scholarly international lawyer, or writer might have been more natural. He was not built for the turmoil and aggressive scheming of political warfare. He did aspire to serve in the diplomatic arm of the Government. But a turn of fate catapulted him into public office, and then his outstanding gifts came to the nation's attention.

Such men are rare. They are particularly rare in politics. What a pity that they appear so infrequently, and when they do, they do not attain the presidency. We seek men of vision, and when we find them we call them visionaries. Such men would be the answer to the restless quest of all of us, even though the youth movement claims it as its own, for nobler ideals in government, for higher standards of ethics. For greater intellect in creating new means to meet novel problems, and for the purity of purpose and prose to lead the nation to more worthy goals.

The nation should be grateful to Stevenson. He was a breath of fresh air in a morally polluted atmosphere. His qualities shone so brightly that his opponents had to attack his virtues as weaknesses in a tough world. We must learn before it is too late that the idealists are the real pragmatists. Every castle on earth was once a castle in the air. Men like Stevenson can achieve the nation's highest aspirations, and give such moral and spiritual leadership that the "establishment" would be an honored word.

IMPEACHMENT OR CENSURE?

"Mr. Chief Justice and Senators, I rise as counsel to speak for the President. More importantly I rise to defend the Presidency, and the Constitution.

"I shall not ask you to acquit the President. Too much evidence has been presented to you of unworthy conduct to do that. But I do ask that you not remove him from office, and that censure is the appropriate penalty. He has appeared before you in defense of himself. He was contrite. His explanations were not evasions but the candid statement of such ameliorating circumstances as exist. You may be sure there will be no repetition of the conduct which brought about these charges.

"Removal from office is the extreme remedy. It is capital punishment. Not every offense requires the maximum sentence. A resolution of reprimand for certain conduct is humiliating enough. It would fulfill the moral imperative. At the same time, it is consistent with constitutional restraints which I shall analyze.

"Before I do so I hope you will not consider me presumptuous if I call attention to your special role. In view of the fact that this is the first impeachment trial of a President in more than a century, and only the second in our history, there is little experience to guide us.

"The House of Representatives is the only body, under Article I, Section 2, of the Constitution, which has the power to issue an impeachment. It has done so. That impeachment was equivalent to an indictment in a criminal case. A trial was required. The Senate has been designated by the Constitution to try the case. So you are not sitting merely as senators. You have been transformed into a court, and you have taken a special oath as jurors, if you will, in addition to your original oath as senators. That oath is significant. You are to 'do impartial justice according to the Constitution and laws.'

"During this trial, the Vice-President is not presiding as he ordinarily would. The Constitution designated the Chief Justice of the Supreme Court to sit in his place. Here again, your powers are unique. In a criminal trial, the judge's rulings would be binding on you, subject only to appeal to a higher court. But in an impeachment trial, you can by a majority vote overrule the Chief Justice.

"Also, the ordinary rules of evidence do not apply. Even hearsay may be admitted, to be sifted by you for the inherent weakness in such evidence, or accepted by you.

"Most importantly, your decision cannot be judicially reviewed by the Supreme Court. You are the court of last resort. Some scholars differ on this, particularly if the proceeding had not accorded with the directions of the Constitution. As defense counsel I ought not forgo the possibility of an appeal, but as I have said, I am defending the presidency and the Constitution, not merely the President, and I consider the present proceeding punctiliously correct. I can therefore see no right of judicial review.

"This view is supported by tracing the origin of the impeachment clause in the Constitution. The first draft of the Constitution, in 1787, provided that an impeachment trial should be by the Supreme Court. This was changed to substitute the Senate as the trial forum. One of the reasons must have been that the President on trial may have appointed some of the justices. Also, the Supreme Court might have to review a criminal conviction if the President were tried after he was removed from office. The history of the impeachment clause therefore indicates that you are the final arbiters. There is also a common sense reason for this conclusion. If the Senate removed a President from office, and the Supreme Court reinstated him, the confusion during the interim period when no one would be sure who the Commander-in-Chief was, and later the doubtful authority of a restored President, might be fatal to the nation's security. Therefore, you have the responsibility of an irrevocable decision.

"Finally, your role as jurors is unique. Ordinarily, a juror is disqualified if he knows the defendant. Most of you know the President personally. Most of you, like myself, belong to the opposite political party and are therefore opposed to many of his programs. Some of you, like myself, have even spoken and written critically, if not indeed bitterly, about him. A few of you have even expressed in advance your opinion about the issues in this trial. Yet you are not disqualified. You sit as his judges.

"Thus, there is placed upon you an extraordinary responsibility. You have many things to remember. Remember that you are the final court. If you err, there is no appeal to correct your decision. Remember that you must overcome your political partisanship, your possible personal animosity, and that you are sitting as judges of the facts and law, although by usual standards you would be disqualified to do so. You must shed preconceived notions, your bias, the passions of the day, and in the words of your solemn oath, 'do impartial justice according to the Constitution and laws.'

"You must be inspired by the ideals of our Constitution to rise above any prejudice. You must vindicate that Constitution which expected you to act in such a crisis as only men of the highest character could. There is a special call for your conscience to guide you; you are truly acting for the ages and, as you judge, so shall you be judged.

"To put it simply, I plead with you, in the name of our noble Constitution, to keep your minds open. Yes, to keep your hearts open, to what I shall say.

"How shall we decide when a President has so violated his duty that no other remedy but removal from office is necessitated? Under what circumstances may a lesser punishment be given?

"I believe that the test for removal is that the President's continuance in office will imperil the nation. Anything less than that may permit either acquitting him or censuring him. That is in your discretion. But if he is not an immediate danger to the nation's security, you cannot overrule the will of more than two hundred million Americans who elected him. Your disapproval cannot encompass his removal.

"Let me support this conclusion. First we look at the impeachment clause in the Constitution. It gives three grounds for impeaching a President: 'Treason, Bribery and Other High Crimes and Misdemeanors.' The last phrase is vague and requires interpretation. If a President is guilty of maladministration is he impeachable? We can find the answer to this question in the debate on the impeachment clause in 1787. Originally the committee recommended that the only grounds should be 'Treason and Bribery.' It even rejected 'corruption' as a ground for impeachment. Then the following debate took place:

Col. Mason: 'Why is the provision restrained to treason and bribery only?'

He moved to add the term 'maladministration.' James Madison objected. 'So vague a term,' he said, 'will be equivalent to a tenure during the pleasure of the Senate.' Colonel Mason then withdrew the word 'maladministration' and substituted the phrase from English law, 'High Crimes and Misdemeanors.'

"There you have it. Our founding fathers rejected the firing of a President by the Senate even if he had committed sins of maladministration or even corruption. They feared the possibility of the Senate saying what Congressman Gerald Ford later said concerning a proposed impeachment of Supreme Court Justice William Douglas, that 'impeachable offenses are what the House and Senate jointly consider them to be.' They didn't want this body to have the arbitrary power to create its own definition of impeachment. They specified treason and bribery, most horrendous crimes, to be serious enough to throw a President out of office. By adding, 'and *other* high crimes and misdemeanors,' they surely were referring to equally shocking acts. 'Misdemeanor,' in this context, has been held to mean 'felony.'

"The law has rules to construe language. These rules of construction are based on common sense. One such rule is that when specific words are followed by general words, the general words take on the same shades of meaning as the words which they followed. The Latin scholars among you will recognize this rule by its name '*eusdem generis*,' meaning 'of the same kind.' Thus the general words 'high crimes and misdemeanors' related to the preceding specific words, 'Treason and Bribery.' In short, 'high crimes and misdemeanors' meant crimes generally as serious as treason or bribery. So we begin with the proposition that the Constitution lists only the most serious charges as grounds for impeachment.

"Must these charges be crimes, or can lesser misconduct be sufficient for impeachment? No less an authority than Blackstone said that only a crime could justify impeachment. He wrote that an impeachment 'is a prosecution of the already known and established law.' This view was expounded by President Andrew Johnson's attorney, who argued, at the impeachment trial in 1868, that 'no impeachment will lie except for a true crime.'

"I do not agree. I believe you have wider latitude. There may be misconduct which imperils the nation, even though it is not a violation of any law. I stress again that the test is whether the nation is imperiled, not whether there is any common law or statutory dereliction.

"So, for example, if a President announced that he would veto all legislation because of his contempt for Congress; or if he closed all foreign embassies and refused to communicate with nations because he regarded them as selfish or treacherous; or if he became a psychotic, or an alcoholic, and no one knew what military directions he might give; he would not be committing a crime under the criminal code, but he certainly ought to be impeached.

"If impeachment could result only if the President committed a crime, then the Constitutional protections for a criminal trial would have to be observed. A jury trial would be necessary. None exists here. Unanimous agreement would be required among the jury or there could be no conviction. This does not apply here. A two-thirds vote of this body is sufficient for conviction. There would be the right of appeal. There is none here.

"The proper interpretation of your powers is more important for the welfare of our nation than the defense of any particular President. Your authority is larger than narrow constructionists contend. In justice to this President, he is aware of my position and supports my contention for the broad concept, although it puts him in greater jeopardy.

"Does this mean that no matter what crime a President committed, even murder, that his only punishment would be removal from office? No. When he was no longer President, he could be indicted and tried in the regular way in a criminal court. Then he would be accorded all the protections of due process. But in an impeachment trial there is no due process in the traditional sense. He cannot even be sentenced. He can only be removed from office. It is a political process. As Mr. Justice Story of the United States Supreme Court wrote, 'an impeachment is purely of a political nature. It is not so much designed to punish an offender as to secure the state against gross official crimes. It touches neither his person nor his property, but simply divests him of his political capacity.'

"Indeed, if impeachment could only be based on the commission of a crime, then a later criminal trial would be barred, because it would constitute 'double jeopardy.'

"So, I concede, gentlemen of the Senate, that you have the power to remove the President, even if his conduct did not constitute a crime. You could do so if his deeds or lack of action were so serious and dangerous that the nation was in jeopardy from his continuing in authority even another day or week.

"As you will see from this test, the opposite is also true. Just as a crime is not necessary to impeach, so not every crime requires impeachment and removal. For example, adultery is a crime. There are current revelations that several of our most revered Presidents committed this crime repeatedly. Had they been charged while they were in office, would anyone think they should be impeached and removed?

"Suppose a President obstructed justice by deliberately concealing the fact that one of his aides had a supply of marijuana, should be thrown out of office?

"Suppose that the President treated valuable gifts given by other governments as his own or his wife's, should he be removed because the crime of thievery was charged?

"As we go up the scale of crimes, the answers become more difficult. But the test isn't. It remains the same. Does the President's continuance in office imperil the nation? If it doesn't, then he may not be ousted even though he may fall in our regard, fail in his ambition for high historical appraisal, be shunted aside for re-election, or, if he is not eligible for a new term, prejudice his party's continuance in power. The public may eagerly await the coming election to 'throw the rascals out,' but the Constitution does not permit the Congress to usurp that privilege of rejection. It resides in the ballot box. Otherwise there might be horrendous proceedings against almost every President elected.

"You might have had President Franklin D. Roosevelt sitting here in a wheel chair, with ten pounds of steel around his legs, facing the charge that he violated our country's declared neutrality by selling weapons to the Allies and that his Lend-Lease deal, giving England fifty destroyers, was a tricky evasion of the Neutrality Act passed by this Congress. You would hear arguments that such abuse of power risked catapulting the United States into a world war. True, he would have contended that his acts were morally necessary to preserve England from being overrun by the Hun. Such a defense is not entirely dissimilar from President Nixon's claim that the bombing of Cambodia was essential to save the lives of American soldiers placed there by other Presidents. Incidentally, in judging this charge, remember that after you found out on March 27, 1973, about the bombing of Cambodia you waited until August 15 of that year before acting to end it. To what extent was your delay acquiescence, or at least uncertainty?

"Remember also that during the entire Vietnam War, Congress had the power to cut off funds for its continuance, and that you did not do so. I am not arguing the merits of the President's or your actions. After all, three previous Presidents and Congresses were involved in initiating and prosecuting the growing Vietnam War. I merely point out that he who points a finger at someone else has three fingers pointed at himself, and that your judgment must be tempered by your own uncertainty as these events were unraveling.

"You might also have had sitting before you President John F. Kennedy, charged with an invasion of the Bay of Pigs, secretly planned and executed without approval of Congress, which is the only body authorized to declare war. There might have been added the charge that the gross incompetence and failure of the undertaking caused great injury to our nation's standing in the world. And you might have had to pass on a count charging the electronic surveillance of Dr. Martin Luther King authorized by Attorney General Kennedy.

"If brazen lying by a President warranted removal, you might have had sitting before you a grinless President Dwight D. Eisenhower, charged with public denial that a U-2 spy plane had flown over Russia, while unknown to him, the Russians had already captured that plane and its pilot, Gary Powers, and could reveal to the world the plane's extraordinary spy equipment.

"If a claim of personal aggrandizement were enough to bring on an impeachment proceeding, the list of tractors, bulls, and other valuable articles listed by Drew Pearson, an 'investigative columnist,' as having been presented to President Eisenhower for his farm in Gettysburg, would have required him to suffer the anguish of an impeachment trial, although he was universally known to be a man of the highest integrity. Errors of judgment are to be distinguished from venality. If "cover-up" were a fatal charge then we would have been deprived of the lifelong services of a great Supreme Court justice, Hugo Black. During confirmation proceedings, he and his supporters remained silent about the charge that he had joined the Ku Klux Klan. It was deemed unproved and he was confirmed. A month later, an enterprising reporter of the Pittsburgh *Post-Gazette* exposed the evidence that Black had attended a secret Birmingham Klorero. Justice Black then went on the air and said, "I did join the Klan. I later resigned. I have never rejoined." Had President Nixon acted similarly, would he have had to resign?

"I could continue these analogies, but a few will suffice to make my point that we do not expect perfection from our chief executives any more than we do from our executive chiefs in business. To put it another way, we may hope for the best, but not every disappointment permits the punishment of removal from office. Ladies and gentlemen of the Senate, there is no Federal law, such as a few states have, which upon a sufficient number of petitioners requires a special election to recall the elected officer in the midst of his term.

"My plea that removal of the President from office is not the appropriate penalty in this proceeding is supported not only by a study of our Constitution, but by the profound philosophy of our form of government. Let me analyze the governmental design of the Presidency.

"Democratic government has many forms. Generally there are two plans to determine the tenure of the chief executive. The first is the parliamentary system. The second is the definite term approach.

"In the parliamentary system, the premier, as he is usually called, has no specific term. He holds his office only as long as the elected parliament chooses that he should. If it votes 'no confidence,' he must submit himself to a new election. Notice, please, that so must the parliament. It has not the privilege of putting him out and remaining in office itself. The entire government falls. The people are invited to elect new representatives and through them a new leader. England, France, Israel, and many other countries have chosen this form of democracy.

"The second democratic system is the election of the President for a fixed term. Congress cannot by a 'lack of confidence' vote to shorten his term. Even when Congress and the President are at odds, and he vetoes its bills, it can overrule him only by a two-thirds vote, but it has no power to interfere with his office, let alone end his term.

"Similarly, Congress has a definite term. It, too, cannot be 'dissolved.' It cannot under any circumstances be made to stand election before its prescribed term has ended.

"Which is the better system? Each has its advantages and defects. The parliamentary form is sensitive to the public's changes of heart. Under it President Nixon would probably have 'fallen' a long time ago, as have prime ministers in Europe. Then the Vice-President and congressmen and senators would also have to face election.

"The greatest defect of the parliamentary system is that in a turbulent world, the moods of the populace change frequently. This may result in a series of governments within a short period. At one time France had six within two and one half years. It is difficult for foreign governments to deal with a head of government who by ordinary majority may be ousted the next month. How can domestic or foreign policies be adopted in such an atmosphere of uncertainty?

"It has been argued that immediate response to the public's will does not allow the maturing of public opinion. This principle of avoiding precipitous action which one may regret has been applied in other areas. For example, many states have passed laws which do not permit the institution of a divorce suit until the husband or wife has filed notice of intention to sue, and a number of months intervene to permit a cooling-off period. In political life, too, there is precipitous public reaction which may change. Compulsory patience may prove that an unpopular President was right all along.

"You recall that when President Harry S Truman fired General Douglas MacArthur, the public condemnation was so intense that a poll showed the President to be at the lowest ebb in modern times (23 per cent) lower than the present incumbent, despite the tirade of criticism and abuse aimed at him for at least a year.

"Incidentally, there were cries to impeach President Truman at that time. Yet recently, a group of historians ranked Truman the ninth greatest President in our history, and in listing his virtues made special mention of his courage in dismissing the nation's revered military hero, in defiance of public adulation for him. So much for the volatility of public reaction. Perhaps immediate response to public clamor is one of the defects of the parliamentary system. Virtue and fault often interchange position.

"Our founders, having surrendered the advantage of continuous citizen control in favor of stability, imposed upon us the strengths and weaknesses of a fixed term. As a people, we are aware that when we elect a President, we are taking him for better or for worse for four long years. We know that only in the most extraordinary circumstances can we even try to dislodge him.

"We also know that in the coming years of his administration unanticipated problems will arise, concerning which he will have no mandate from us. There can be no advance guidance for the unforeseeable. Therefore in choosing a President, we vote more for his character and judgment than for his position on issues. Indeed, we have learned that Presidents, once elected, have often reversed themselves on issues they had announced as unshakable. This has not been due to treachery or even light-mindedness, but to changing circumstances, or caution which the power to act instills in the theoretician without responsibility, or perhaps access to better advisers, or even a larger perspective of the whole, from the height of the presidency.

"Many Presidents have abandoned the platform on which they rode into office, from Wilson, whose emphatic promise was to keep us out of war, to the President who sits before you, who reversed himself on wage and price controls, détente with Russia, approaches to China, a balanced budget, and more. Flexibility and a ventilated mind may be better than consistency. Certainly we are forewarned by experience that we must depend much more on the kind of man we elect than on the kind of speeches or promises he makes.

"All this has made us searchingly cautious in our choice of a President. The men who aspire to our highest office have faced scrutiny for decades. They have been senators, governors, and in public service all their lives. They have made hundreds of speeches on radio and television, written articles and books, and been dissected by opposition critics. Finally, to achieve the nomination of their party, they have had to trudge across our immense country, submitting themselves in the most intimate way to the view and touch of millions of citizens. It is a test of ruggedness as well as intellect and personality.

"Then, those rare few who achieve the nomination begin a grueling campaign of more than three months, in which they talk to more people in one night than all the religious, political, and military leaders in nineteen centuries reached in a lifetime. Through enlarged visualization which penetrates their skin, every flicker of the eyelid, every involuntary muscle movement of the face, every hoarsening inflection or hesitancy of the voice, we learn about them as if a thousand psychiatrists had given us the benefit of their scientific insights.

"Why do I recite all this, which you know so well? Because our democracy, more than any other, gives us an opportunity to judge the character of the man we elect. The doctrine of *'caveat emptor,'* 'buyer beware,' applies to people as well as to things.

"Therefore, having had the opportunity for evaluation of our chief executive to a greater extent than is afforded by any other government, we must take responsibility for our choice and abide by it for the fixed term, even if we have regrets. I suggest that there is an equation between knowledgeable selection and the right of rejection. The larger the former, the smaller the latter.

"This principle applies with double, nay, triple force to the incumbent President. Not only was he a congressman, a senator, sitting among you, but for eight years he presided over this body as Vice-President. In that capacity he traveled to many countries, thus giving the people further insight into his capacity and character. Yes, and they also were made aware of defects, recounted with paradoxical gleeful anger by political opponents. He was pilloried with rhymed meanness as 'tricky Dick,' and ridiculed as an untrustworthy secondhand car salesman, just as Thomas Dewey was reduced to a pygmy comical role of a bridegroom on a wedding cake. Such is the vituperation our public figures must endure, I suppose on the theory that in a land of free speech, humiliation begets humility, and lightning is the proper precaution against those who think their heads are in heaven.

"The people weighed it all, and he, a Republican, was elected President after eight years of Democratic rule. He was chosen in a three-way race by a minority vote, and even then by a margin so thin it was almost invisible. So he had to prove himself all over again to the American people, at that time deeply divided by its most unpopular war.

"Then, after four years of laser-lighted examination of his every mood and movement, of every word and worth of his pronouncements, of leadership which expanded from national parameters to the free world and even made deep inroads into vast areas previously deemed too hostile or enigmatic for democratic approach, he received the most phenomenal endorsement of a public figure in American history. He won forty-nine of the fifty states. He received five hundred twenty-one electoral votes, almost twice the number required for election. His popular vote total of more than forty-seven million gave him a plurality of eighteen million. From a minority vote in his previous election, he won by a 60 per cent plurality. This was more than a landslide. It was an avalanche. And the roar of approval of the American people must still echo in this chamber today.

"The impeachment process has been heralded as democracy's safeguard, but it must not become the nullifier of the will of the people, the source and strength of democracy itself.

"Frankly, the presidency is not the only branch of our government which is in low estate. Polls indicate that Congress itself is held in less regard than even the beleaguered President. Under these circumstances we must take mutual measures to lift the ethical standards of all representatives, whether they wear legislative or presidential robes. This is not the first administration in which shoddy practices have occurred. Self-criticism leads to necessary reform. It heals, no matter how severe the wrench from accustomed practice. On the other hand, punitive attacks only widen the breach and may give the false impression that democracy itself has failed. At one point during these developments, bumper stickers appeared, reading 'Don't re-elect anybody,' a disturbing jest. We can overcome such cynicism by raising the moral standards of all branches of government. At the same time, we must respect the will of the electorate, even if it errs, unless, in the words of minority counsel Albert Jenner of the Watergate Committee, 'the conduct of the President is so grave that it amounts to a subversion of government.'

"Consider the consequences throughout the world of the removal of the President. American leadership requires stability abroad as well as at home. The world would be shocked by the disgrace and disappearance of the President in the midst of vital treaty negotiations.

"Foreigners are more resigned than we are to human frailty among their leaders. If the President were censured, but maintained in office, other nations would respect our sensitive standards, but not feel that they had been left adrift. If we throw him out, the consequences abroad cannot be foreseen. It might even trigger aggressive action in some part of the world by adversary nations who have in the past seized any moment of weakness to act boldly and swiftly to fill a power vacuum. Can we afford the risk of such a disaster, perhaps even a third world war, when the remedy of censure would leave at the helm a strong President, respected and feared abroad? Continuity has its own momentum. I sit wise to assert our concern with domestic chicanery in such a way that we tempt, almost invite, hostile nations to miscalculate our Constitutional strengths and overestimate our confusion? The remedy of reprimand is safer and better.

"It may be in your minds that censure, too, may so injure presidential prestige that he will be unable to conduct foreign affairs. This might argue for acquittal, particularly since acquittal does not mean approval. It merely means that the charges have not been proven. But as I have said, too much has been demonstrated to claim that the misconduct does not rise to a level requiring condemnation. The question is what form it shall take.

"As to the fear that this President will no longer be able to conduct foreign affairs, the evidence to the contrary should comfort you. Even while the Watergate scandal was our daily headline to be swallowed with our morning coffee; even when the scandal stole the front pages of the press abroad, the President's travels were greeted in foreign lands with unprecedented curb-cheering people. It may well be that this was

326 *Reflections Without Mirrors*

due in large measure to the world's regard for the office more than for its occupant. This, too, is encouraging. It is another illustration of the advantage of a fixed term. Due to the power and stability of his office, the President's influence can survive even crisis. Indeed, the President has derived so much strength from his trips abroad that his opponents fear he may continue long journeys to overcome the ordeal at home.

"Has he been so distracted by his troubles that he cannot attend to the inundating duties of his office? If so, that might imperil the nation. But the record is to the contrary. While the Watergate revelations were beginning to blaze, the Vietnam War was being wound down and tens of thousands of soldiers brought home; the great wall in China was being scaled, the Iron Curtain in Russia partly lifted, the Middle East hostile forces parted, and the Cyprus melee subdued; the President's declaration that our country would avoid direct military involvement in remote corners of the globe evoked praise from the House and from this body.

"The domestic scene was filled with recommendations of bills, imposition of wage and price controls, the devaluation of the dollar, a new trade policy which imposed a 10 per cent surcharge on most imports, addresses to the nation, and appointments of administrators of new programs, all of which appealed sufficiently to the electorate to evoke a cascade of favorable votes. Whether one approves or disapproves of the administration's policies, it has not been slothful or moribund.

"If you examine the sequelae of removal, it is more likely that the ousting of the President may imperil the nation, than that his retention after reprimand will.

"There is another guideline to determine when an extraordinary remedy, like impeachment, should or should not be applied. For example, an injunction, which is the use of the chancellor's equitable sword, will not be issued unless two tests are met. First, the proof must be overwhelming and beyond ordinary standards. Second, it must be demonstrated that the wrongs are continuing. If there is no real danger of repetition, then lesser remedies may lie, but not an injunction.

"Let us apply these two criteria to an impeachment. I have said that the rules of a criminal trial need not be followed. Therefore it is not necessary to prove the President's guilt beyond a reasonable doubt. But neither should the standard be that of an ordinary civil trial, that a preponderance of evidence is sufficient. We are engaged in a unique procedure of momentous consequences, and the proof required for removing a President should be unusually persuasive, even if not beyond a reasonable doubt. Otherwise public divisiveness would flourish. The awesome power to cancel the deliberate choice of the people must be supported by the strongest kind of proof. This is particularly true where it is charged that the impeachment decision in the House of Representatives was made by a group dominated by the President's political and philosophical enemies. It was just such an accusation which undermined public confidence in the impeachment of President Andrew Johnson. The main charge, that he had removed Secretary of War Edwin M. Stanton without senatorial consent, and Johnson's escape from conviction by only one vote short of the two-thirds majority required were further warning that the passions of the opposition party are not to be trusted, and that public approval must be courted by fair procedure. I would say that unimpeachable evidence is essential to impeachment. Otherwise, the highest court of all, the people, may not accept the verdict.

"Assume that you have winnowed the various charges to eliminate those which are not established by overwhelming evidence, and assume further, as I do, that some remain; is the second test met? Is there a danger of continuing violations? Surely not.

"When a man has achieved the highest and most powerful political office in the world, his ambition turns to historical appraisal. That is why recent Presidents have made plans to construct libraries of their works. So the President would wish to live down his censure, to demonstrate his integrity; to prove that the achievements of his administration will outweigh its desultory aspects; to salvage the President's name and reputation for the history books.

"Far from taking a desperate risk of 'more of the same,' we would be assured that the chastisement of censure would stimulate the President to live up to the highest precepts of his office for the remainder of his term.

"I come now to the most painful aspect of my appeal. Punishment is not and should not be equal for all. This is a common error I hear all about me. If it were so, we would not have probation departments which investigate every facet of a man's life and background, to report to the sentencing judge. If it were so, judges would not have to weigh facts extraneous to the crime itself, to determine whether the punishment should be lenient or severe. If it were so, there would be no wide discretion vested in the judge to impose either a suspended sentence or fine or a long prison sentence for the same crime. We punish the man, not the crime. Men who commit wrongs are as different from one another as nature intended good men to be, too. We must therefore consider the condition of each to make the punishment fit not only the crime but the man who committed it.

"One of the facts which you should weigh, as every judge does, is the suffering which the defendant has already endured.

"I don't think any of us are in a position to evaluate the anguish the

President has suffered. We can only use our imagination, and it too must fail in this instance. Why? Because there is only one person in a world of hundreds of millions of human beings who can be President. He stands alone at the apex of the international complex of nations. We can only truly feel and understand that which touches our experience. And none of you, even though you hold exalted positions yourselves, can grasp the unique feelings of a man who knows in every waking second of his existence as President that he wields unprecedented power, is held in awe by people all over the world, and is destined for history. It is a glory and a responsibility which challenges the sense of reality of the most balanced man. Intimate friends address him as Mr. President. Kings and ministers seek his nod. Trumpets blare and guns salute when he appears abroad. Every word he utters is sent across the world. No matter how prosaic his movement or deed, it is recorded for millions to read. He sleeps in Lincoln's bed. He is surrounded by mementos of George Washington, Thomas Jefferson, and every historic name since then. He is seen and heard by tens of millions of people in the remotest regions of the world, and when electronics are not available, the printing press features his utterances as well as his features in newspapers and magazines wherever they are printed. Even all this is only a glimpse of the Olympian heights on which he resides.

"So when such a man faces disgrace, the hurt is magnified to the same degree that his pre-eminence separates him from other citizens. This is true in lower echelons as well. The more distinguished the defendant, the more painful his fall. But when the man who stands before the bar is the President of the United States, the indignity is almost unbearable—unbearable for our country and unbearable for him.

"The President has suffered the torment of turning his mind backward to make a different choice. It is a painful reliving of events because the outcome cannot be changed by reverie. Such dreams become nightmares of futility. 'If only I had to do it over again' is a self-inflicted penalty, there being no second chance.

"The suffering of the President cannot be alleviated by his intimates. The reflected agony of friends is as difficult to bear as the gloating of enemies. Added to his own burden of guilt is the pain he has caused to those loyal to him. One can see on the President's face this magnification of sorrow.

"And as for his family, I would like to think their grief is private, and not the proper subject for this matter of state. But I cannot. We do not elect the President's wife, but she has been weighed in the public judgment of his choice during her campaign travels. She must be equal to the title of First Lady we confer on her and the ceremonial duties she performs. So her suffering is not irrelevant in considering what she and the President have endured. He must also bear the tears of his lovely Julie. I need not tell you who, by proximity, see the pain etched on their faces and its transference to him.

"The people understand all this. I have heard over and over again that it is a wonder the President can stand this pressure; that it would kill an ordinary man. When Napoleon was defeated, disgraced and exiled, he told an aide that he would 'kill himself.' The aide replied, 'No, Your Majesty could not do that. A gambler kills himself. A king faces adversity.' The President has lived up to the greatness of his office by facing adversity. He knew that an advance estimate of the votes to be cast against him in this chamber would reach the two-third minimum required to remove him from office. But he has come here to express apology and face humiliation bravely. He has been able to do this because he believed that you were open-minded; that some of you would yield to the moral imperatives of the democratic process which elected him; that you would hesitate to destroy the principle of stability which has protected us at home and abroad; that you would weigh his candor and his contrition; that you would not forget his past deeds when you consider his failings; that you would be comforted by the assurance that being recondite there would be no repetition of misconduct; that therefore the nation would not be imperiled by his continuance in office; and most important of all that there is an alternative to removal, namely, reprimand, or censure, and that this would best serve the Constitutional structure.

"If you censure but maintain the President in office, he will never again wield the power he once exercised. Oh, his Constitutional powers will be the same, but that power, which derives from the full trust and affection of the people, will be withheld until he proves himself again worthy of it. Such loss of power is in itself an unendurable death. Francis Bacon wrote, 'Who can see worse days than he yet living, doth follow at the funeral of his own reputation.'

"That march of penance will continue. Its pain is ineradicable. Indeed, it is the true measure of his penalty and you need not fear that a lesser punishment than removal from the Oval Office, will be inadequate.

"The very fact that merciful consideration is extended by you, the members of the opposition party, will attest to its nonpolitical nature. It will soothe the feelings of millions of Americans who, although not condoning his wrongs, would resent the extreme penalty of divestiture of office. It would be healing in a moment when our country desperately needs it. It would provide continuity of authority, in a strife-ridden world, in which the symbol of America's power and influence resides uniquely in the President. It would at the same time be a declaration of high principle, and a warning to this and future Presidents that the President is no king, and that the law is the true majesty.

"I beseech you to abstain from removal or acquittal, and as to those charges which you feel were proven by overwhelming evidence, that you express your condemnation in the form of censure.

"In that way, you will have fulfilled your special oath. You will have served our country best."

Of course, such a summation was never made by any counsel. It was not necessary. Nixon resigned. As he later put it, "I impeached myself."

Whenever public officials quit under fire, they attempt to turn their surrender into noble sacrifice. They declare that they want to spare the public the ordeal of a disrupting contest. Actually, Nixon resigned because the most careful tabulation of votes, after an incessant drive for support, convinced him that he would lose the impeachment trial. Had he had the courage to face his accusers, without dissembling, he might have won them over to a lesser penalty and salvaged his presidency.

I have illustrated in an imaginary exercise this Constitutional and persuasive possibility. But the preconditions for such an appeal required his appearance and testimony with uninhibited forthrightness. It would also require his consent that his counsel should not spare him. His wrongdoing could not be denied, although, of course, it could be stated without unnecessary animus. When a tree is down everyone runs with his hatchet. His counsel had to wield a merciful one. But the catharsis had to be complete. No acquittal could or should have been sought.

If Nixon could have brought himself to such a posture, he would not have been in this dilemma in the first place. So perhaps even strong legal guidance in the right direction would have been of no avail.

This appears to be the fact, because there was a subsequent test. Tempted by money, he emerged from seclusion to explain himself on television in a David Frost interview. I saw three Nixons in that one broadcast. The first continued to evade, quibble about the true meaning of words, claim that the quotations from the tapes were taken out of context, assert his "understanding" of his enemies' motives in a self-pitying way, and suggest conspiracies against him, by "an impeachment lobby," a media "fifth column" and the "peccadilloes" of the CIA—while at the same time disavowing his belief in the conspiracy theory and otherwise disporting himself in the manner which had set the desultory tone of the White House conversations.

Also, he continued to add to the truth, thus really subtracting from it. He added his motives to the facts, thereby subtracting from their true nature, for he failed to distinguish between motive and intent. One may have the motive of a Robin Hood but his intention to rob makes his act a crime nevertheless. Particularly offensive was his attempted justification of his instructions to his assistants, to be sure to utilize the "I don't remember" evasion. He claimed that every defense lawyer instructs his witness not to volunteer if he is not sure. Indeed! The difference between restraining a voluble witness who spouts irrelevancies of which he has no knowledge, and an instruction not to reveal what one knows, is so basic that only moral astigmatism could confuse the two.

The second Nixon who emerged from the broadcast was the one who engaged in what is known in law as confession and avoidance. Under great stress, he conceded that he had lied, "let my country down," "let my friends down," and had "screwed up" the mess (he could not get away from the inelegant language which had flooded the tapes). Yet, having confessed, he sought to avoid the consequences. He insisted that he had not committed a crime or an impeachable offense.

Nevertheless, this second Nixon moved us to compassion. His face quivering with suppressed tears, which his eyes betrayed, one felt the anguish which racked him. The prosecutor of Warren Hastings, who was impeached in Parliament in 1787, expressed the feelings which, nearly two centuries later, many Americans experienced: "To see that man, that small portion of human clay, that poor feeble machine of earth, enclosed now in that little space, brought to that Bar—and to reflect on his late power! . . . What a change! How he must feel it!" Sympathy went not so much to the man as to the tragedy of the great fall.

The third Nixon was one who gave us psychiatric insights to himself. The most revealing was his statement that he had "brought himself down." He said that he had given his enemies a sword and they stuck it into him "and twisted it with relish." Here was the picture of a vicious assailant. Who was he? His next sentence identified him. "I would have done the same in their place." So he really plunged the sword into himself "and turned it with relish," a remarkable revelation of suicidal intent. The continued taping even while the scandal was mounting and the preservation of the tapes were also illustrations of a subconscious desire to be caught and destroyed.

The nation was fortunate not to have suffered worse from the transference of presidential power to a Vice-President who had replaced Spiro Agnew, a felon, and who had therefore himself not been elected to office. The vacuum of authority and a dismayed citizenry might well have invited adventurers abroad, or disorganization at home.

The greatest accolade to democracy is the peaceful transition of power. It is due to centuries of education and a new tradition of graceful acceptance by the defeated. That is why sudden installation of democracy in territory unprepared for it causes a reversion to bullets and conspiratorial coups.

The Nixon resignation tested our constitutional tradition most severely. We had to accept a transition in bitter atmosphere, and where legitimacy was strained. We succeeded. Fortunately, the risk was not enlarged by hostile opportunism abroad. In retrospect, it was fortunate that Nixon had not challenged the extreme remedy of ouster. As it turned out, we were saved the ordeal of a trial, while escaping the dangers to which the abrogation of a fixed presidential term might have subjected us. From a viewpoint of precedent, the result is not cheering. Is there the danger that a partisan legislature may someday seize upon the misdeeds of a President, even if they do not clearly come within the ambit of the general proscription of the Constitution, to force him to resign, rather than face ouster?

The rarity of such a situation, even when Presidents have acted beyond their traditional authority, should limit our fears. Ultimately, it is the common sense of the people which is the true motive power. Consent by the governed also applies to procedures like impeachment, in which they are not directly involved. The genius of democracy is that the people's representatives hear the thunder of election day long before it approaches.

The imaginary defense summary, which I have presented, might really have taken place. Only an accident of time prevented it. Unexpectedly, I became involved in the critical developments.

After the House voted impeachment, I thought that there would be an extensive period of preparation and a trial before the Senate. I had not anticipated Nixon's resignation, especially because he declared over and over again that he would fight to the last. Perhaps I should have learned from Vice-President Spiro Agnew's similar assurances, before he resigned, that the emphasis on resistance to the very death was a ploy to discourage the pursuer and encourage the pursued.

In any event, anticipating a Senate trial, I was troubled and intrigued by the constitutional questions presented in such a proceeding. Having been invited by the *Reader's Digest* to write an article of my choosing, I wrote one entitled, "Impeachment or Censure?" Then I decided it would be more appropriate for the New York *Times Magazine* and might thereafter be reprinted in the *Digest*.

On August 6, 1973, I was on the phone with a Washington client concerning a legal matter. He could not keep his mind on the subject. He was a friend of Julie Eisenhower, and he described her distress, because her father had decided to resign. An announcement was soon to be made on television. He asked my opinion about the clash of views between the President and his advisers as to whether he should stand trial or quit.

"In my opinion," I said, "if he went to trial, and the right argument was made, he might not be removed from office."

The voice at the other end became urgent. "Why?" he asked.

I explained, with appropriate telephone brevity, my theory that the test of removal was nothing less than imperilment of the nation, and that Nixon's wrongs might warrant censure or reprimand and not ousting from office.

"Can you dictate this immediately?" he asked.

"I have already written it as an article."

He pleaded with me to deliver a copy at once to the White House. He would call Julie and arrange for its immediate transfer to the President. "Perhaps it is not too late," he said. To save minutes, my article was Telecopied for immediate delivery to the White House by special messenger. It arrived there shortly before four in the afternoon.

The scene at the White House was chaotic. The die had been cast. Nixon's television announcement of his resignation had been scheduled. Everyone was emotionally drained by the preceding indecision, and numb from the decision itself. In tears and shock, the family and staff were busy packing for the first nonpresidential journey to San Clemente. An article on constitutional alternatives was hardly suitable reading matter in the midst of such a mournful crisis.

At first, I was advised that General Al Haig had shown the article to the President, who had commented, "Why didn't this come two weeks ago?" Later, I was informed that in the stress of events, the article had not been read by Nixon until much later in San Clemente.

In law, we use the phrase "Time is of the essence." It is a peculiar phrase, because time is always precious and the most unrecoverable asset in life. But the legal phrase has a special connotation. Even delay of hours may be fatal. It is possible that, had my article been mentioned earlier to my Washington friend, it would have been received at the White House in time to be evaluated. Then my imaginary summation plea to the Senate might have been made by some attorney. Perhaps history would have been changed.

ILLUSORY SYLLOGISMS

"I know you don't believe in ESP or parapsychic phenomena," said one of my law partners, "but how are you going to explain this?" "This" was almost impossible to explain as a coincidence. The facts come best from a skeptic like me.

One day a lady in distress called from Monte Carlo. Her immensely wealthy husband was acting strangely. He was apparently trying to get rid of her. She was terrified. Could I send someone to meet with her surreptitiously at an appointed place to guide her? My law partner Gerald Meyer, gifted in foreign languages and laws, took off to Monte Carlo on this mission of matrimonial mercy. Later he was joined by my partner Julia Perles. They returned with a bagful of legal problems. The most important was jurisdiction. In what country would her rights to share his wealth (a matter of intense personal concern, euphemistically called community property) be best protected? Where should her suit be brought?

As befits the very rich, they had residences in many lands. Why experience the inconvenience of foreign travel when you can arrange to be at home everywhere? So, they had mansions in Switzerland, England, France, United States, Monte Carlo, and, in addition to some others, South Africa, where they had been married.

The legal research therefore required knowledge of the matrimonial law of South Africa, and if that law was favorable, what other countries would apply the law of the country of marriage, rather than their own? How to find out the matrimonial law of South Africa? To communicate with a law firm there was hazardous to the secrecy required. The husband was so influential that important law firms might well have represented him in his multifarious enterprises (unlike some women, she didn't pronounce it nefarious enterprises). There would be a conflict of interest. They would disqualify themselves, but somehow the husband might learn that his wife was not a complacent sufferer, ready to surrender. So we had to find the law ourselves.

We reasoned that there must be a legal textbook on South African matrimonial law. We were determined to find it, if there was one. Search soon revealed that there was. Its author was Professor H. R. Hahlo. The title was literally precise, *Husband and Wife*. But neither the law libraries of the leading bar associations, the university law libraries, nor the comprehensive public libraries possessed this esoteric book. We called our Washington office and stressed the importance of obtaining Professor Hahlo's work. Researchers who had previously found the thinnest and smallest needle in the largest haystack scoured all possible sources, from the Library of Congress and Copyright Office, to the law libraries of the many law firms in Washington. All to no avail. Calls to lawyer-friends in California and other states ended the same way: "Never heard of it." We began to suspect that Professor Hahlo's publisher had only printed a few copies and confined them to the country of their special interest.

On Thursday, June 17, 1976, the client was to call us for advice at 4 P.M. On an untraceable private phone in Monte Carlo. We would have to confess that we were not ready to guide her.

At 2 P.M. my secretary put upon my desk a huge book (it had 674 pages) with old-fashioned heavy leather black-brown mottled covers. "What is that?" I asked.

"It just arrived without a letter."

I rose from my desk to look at the almost invisible title. It was *Husband and Wife*, by Professor H. R. Hahlo!

On the left inside cover was scribbled a flowery compliment signed "C. K. Friedlander."

We didn't know who the inscriber was or how he came to send this rare book so that it would arrive at the critical hour. The mystery would have remained forever unsolved were it not for a search of a file marked "miscellaneous correspondence" which revealed a letter from C. K. Friedlander, dated April 21, 1976. On the letterhead of the law firm of C. K. Friedlander, Kleinman and Shandling situated in Cape Town, South Africa, he wrote that he had just read my book *My Life in Court* (thirteen years after it was published), and hastened to express his compliments. (That is one of the satisfactions of authorship. The work is never stale to one who reads it for the first time. Books enable us to reach across centuries and touch the reader intimately. Perhaps the arts receive our special homage because they provide this unique possibility of immortality.)

I answered the letter with formal expression of appreciation for his graciousness. (When it is a friend who sends such a note, I can indulge in a light-mannered reply of complimenting him for being a discriminating reader.)

Generally there are two classes of correspondence each day; the worrisome, which requires thought and treatment, and the pleasant, which induces rereading and filing. So this letter was filed.

It was almost a month after that verbal bouquet was filed that the lady in Monte Carlo found herself distraught, and we in equally desperate need for Professor Hahlo's book. Friedlander could not, therefore, have known all this, and certainly could not have known that we had only two hours before the client would seek the answer locked in that book.

We devoured the pertinent contents of the huge book which had just arrived. It described the Dutch-Roman law, a source as remote as the book itself. We were ready with a stream of advice to the lady in distress when she called.

I wonder if she, like me, doesn't believe in telepathy or other mysterious forces of communication?

A similar eye-opening coincidence occurred in the very preparation of this book. Because of its autobiographical nature, Ken McCormick, Doubleday's senior editor, suggested that childhood photographs might be appropriate. Theoretically, as a man gets older he acquires the face he deserves. What was his face before it was molded by his conduct? Also, early photographs of my parents might be instructive. Aside from the quaint outfits they wore in London in 1900, their physiognomies might reveal unseen genetic clues. I had seen a few such memorabilia in the past, but where was one to find them now? My parents were long dead. If there ever were photographs sixty or seventy years old, they had been washed away by the currents of time.

Only Ripley's title *Believe It or Not* is suitable for what follows. Within a week after Hahlo's book on South African law materialized on my desk, a grayish-blue suitcase appeared in my office. Upon opening it, I would have been less surprised to find a treasure of ancient jewels and gold than to see what the contents were: photographs of myself from infancy to adulthood, photographs of my parents, some taken in London, still clear in their somewhat faded sepia color. Where had they been? How had they suddenly shown up?

Like great magic tricks which have simple explanations, mysteries often have obvious solutions. My parents' summer home in Bethlehem, New Hampshire, had a brick path entrance, difficult to traverse because the chrysanthemum bushes on both sides jutted toward each other affectionately, and an orchard of apple and pear trees. Most important for this recital, the house had what is a rarity these days, an attic. My parents had gradually discarded old possessions, but somehow several barrels of things, too sentimental to leave behind, found their way to the attic.

I recall, on one occasion, Mildred and me climbing to the attic on a shaky wooden ladder to explore the unknown region. There, beside albums of old phonograph records, Mildred found in one barrel London dishes ringed with raised gold, issued for the coronation of Edward VII, teacups with a mustache protector (so that a gentleman could drink his tea without wetting his adorned lip), a brass vessel with accompanying brass pestle which druggists used to mash pills, and sundry other items which justify the existence of the word "miscellany." Mildred selected a few to be saved from the strewn confusion, and with care we lowered them in a sling. Some are in our home today.

My parents were astonished at our interest in these items, even after I told them of a sign in an antique shop which read, "If you think this stuff is junk, come in and price it."

This reminds me of a semantic problem which caused Mildred much hurt. The Yiddish word for delicious is antique (with a broad "a"). Used about a person, the idiom is "She is an antique"—a doll. Bragging about her one day, my father resorted to this Yiddish expression. Mildred overheard it. It took a long time to convince her that my explanation wasn't an artful lawyer's device to extricate my father from an insulting reference; although all she had to do was look in the mirror to know that what she heard was not what she thought it meant. "*Interpretare est prodere*"—to translate is to betray.

Our groping in the attic revealed no photographs. When my parents died, I presented the property to the community. Various couples lived there in the next two decades. The present occupants are a Mr. and Mrs. Bressman. A short while ago the admission committee of our law firm had selected a number of young graduates, among them one David Bressman, the son of the Bethlehem occupants. I knew nothing of this relationship or even who the occupants of our former home were. But the Bressmans, aware of the link, and having come across photographs, a tennis trophy I had won in 1933, and other personal items, felt that their son ought to deliver them to his senior. So it was that a suitcase suddenly showed up in my office out of nowhere. I shudder to think that the reader might otherwise have been deprived of the visual nostalgia which surrounds this book.

Another incident hovering between coincidence and mystery occurred on my birthday. It is possible now to trace the disparate facts which converged to create the result.

Scene 1: In Woodstock, New York, a man by the name of Ed Balmer was in the business of building swimming pools. One day when he was preparing a hole for an installation, he accidentally dug up an electrical feed line. He had to repair it at considerable expense. He decided to eliminate such risks in the future by inquiring about devices which could detect metal underground. The most efficient metal detector was produced by the Garrett Company in Texas. He not only bought one but became a dealer for the product. Whenever a new model came out which detected metal at a lower depth, he would test it at Woodstock Recreation Field.

This was a site which the troops of the Revolutionary War used for drilling. Later traveling circuses and carnivals camped there.

It became a favorite place for men in the area to go "treasure hunting" with metal detectors. Balmer had found a silversmith hammer, an old hand-forged stirrup, and an aluminum medallion with a portrait of Lincoln on one side and a motto, "Death to the Traitors," on the other.

Three years ago, his metal detector discovered a fourteen-carat gold charm four inches underground. Imprinted on it was the calendar month of February. The date of the sixth had been drilled through and a tiny amethyst, the stone of Aquarius, shone where the number had been.

Scene 2: A young lady, by the name of Monelle Richmond, became a secretary of one of my associates in our law office in March 1976. Her mother had been an astrologer for twenty-five years and Monelle was therefore interested in horoscopes. Because she worked in our office and had read my books, she wanted someday to prepare a horoscope about my future. She learned that I had been born on February 6, and entered that date on her Rolodex for future use.

Scene 3: Monelle Richmond and her mother had lived in Woodstock for many years. They knew Balmer. Recently he asked Monelle when she was born. She told him February 11. He told her about the February 6 date on the charm. The next day when she returned to New York, as she described it:

"Something snapped in my mind. I looked on my Rolodex, and sure enough! I told him when I next saw him that it was your birthday."

Scene 4: Since February 6 fell on a Sunday, my law partners decided to tender me a birthday luncheon two days in advance on February 4. At twelve-twenty, just as I was leaving for the party at the Park Lane Hotel, a letter arrived from Balmer. It read:

Dear Mr. Nizer,
    An unexpected birthday present is always fun, particularly from somebody you never laid eyes on.

He explained the link with Miss Richmond, whom I had also never met, and concluded:

I am old enough to remember that bastard McCarthy and your part in his comeuppance, which is most of the reason you are getting this. Enjoy a very happy birthday with my best wishes!

Enclosed was the beautiful gold calendar charm.

Scene 5: I took it to the luncheon, where I was presented with a Steuben glass decanter with an eagle cover, and more glittering speeches with sentimental covers. After I explained that I had felt uneasy about the event, but enjoyed its warmth so much that I would appreciate semiannual repetitions; and after I commented that my dislike for birthday parties was not because I minded others knowing about my age, but that I did not want to learn about it myself; preferring to cling to my illusion that I was only thirty-five years old, and after telling my family of thirty-eight partners-in-law that growing old is a bad habit which I was too busy to cultivate, I told about the remarkable incident of the unexpected gift from a stranger.

It gave a surprise note of mystery to a warm event.

Even those who believe in mental telepathy may balk at the notion that the dead can communicate with the living. I don't believe in either, yet Aldous Huxley involved me in a message he sent after his death to his widow.

Huxley, brilliant author and extraordinary man, was fascinated with the extensions of consciousness. He experimented with hypnotism (called mental passes) and later with mescaline and LSD. Shortly before he died, he said, "It is a little embarrassing that after forty-five years of research and study, the best advice I can give to people is to be a little kinder to each other."

But that was for the living. Huxley's sense of the cosmos convinced him of a continued consciousness after death. He sought to bridge the gap by psychedelic (a word he used first) experiments which he described in *The Doors of Perception*; by visionary experience, meditation, and deep hypnosis about which he wrote in *Heaven and Hell* and finally synthesized in *The Island*.

His wife, Laura, an author in her own right, has written a remarkable book about him called *This Timeless Moment: A Personal View of Aldous Huxley*. It is a tender, sensitive description of that handsome, gifted man. It has many photographs of him revealing the penetrating eyes, the deep-nostriled nose, and high brow with distinguished gray curved hairline, the small hollow in the cheeks like masculine dimples, and the full lips—all of which constituted a combination of superior intelligence and sensuality. The photographs featured his hands, which were as artistic as his face. Indeed, there was one photograph of only his right hand, with its long slender fingers, above which he had written

"Aldous." It may have been a symbol of his reaching out to the here-after.

Huxley had long preparation for his death. He was afflicted with cancer of the tongue, and after he declined surgery, which would have made him speechless, he recovered. But then his glands developed a new cancer, and for months he knew he was dying.

Although the knowledge of the ultimate end is always with us, its imminence often sets off the terror of dying. Huxley's search for greater consciousness in life led him to the mysteries of survival after death. His poetic sense of purposefulness provided a rationale for each individual's permanence, in spirit if not in flesh. In a letter to his doctor he wrote: "The emphasis, in the last rites, has to be on the present and post-human future, which one must assume—and I think with justification—to be a reality."

A medium, aware of these convictions, advised his wife that "Aldous says that you are going to receive . . . *classical evidence of survival* of the personalty and consciousness—not something that can be explained by telepathy or other theories."

Since Laura Huxley had no predilection toward spiritualism or messages from disembodied spirits, how had the "classical evidence of survival" been given to her?

A young man she identified as K.M.R., who was doing research in parapsychological aspects, had sought her out for a television interview in her home. He discussed mediumship, ESP, and reincarnation. He explained that he was a medium and headed a foundation in Seattle for parapsychological research. Then he offered a reading. She declined in a kindly way, suggesting that she would take "a rain check" until he returned from Europe, where he was headed for more television interviews. But this was not the last of it, as is often the case and intended to be, from vague postponed appointments. He returned. He had obtained a television interview with Bertrand Russell, then ninety-four years old. Russell was a dear friend of Huxley, and the fact that he spared his flagging energies for K.M.R. impressed Laura.

Once more he offered her a private reading. She declined, but when he suggested a group reading for the five guests who had come to dinner, she accepted, probably because it would be an entertaining oddity. The guests were skeptical but curious, and agreed.

He gave each of them a card on which was printed "Direct your billet to loved ones . . . write full names; place questions in center, sign your full name at bottom. Thank you." These cards were placed in sealed envelopes, and given to him unopened. He was thoroughly blindfolded. Then he went into a trance for an hour and a half.

He reported personal messages from disembodied spirits to each of the questioners. They were not merely astonished. They were over-whelmed. The words conveyed intimate information which could not have been known to the medium. For example, Laura asked about an old friend. The medium's face registered suffering and he said that the man had been brutally murdered. This was the fact. He even men-tioned Ensenada, a place which Laura and the man had visited, and other details she did not recall, but which photographs taken by a friend later confirmed.

Each guest encountered replies of similar startling information. When incredulity is breached by the inexplicable, there is either confu-sion or shock. All guests were in this state. The medium told Laura that Aldous Huxley had been present throughout the session and he reminded her of his offer to give her a private reading.

But first, motion pictures of his interviews abroad were to be shown. While threading the projector, the medium suddenly said, "Please give me a pencil and paper. Aldous is saying I must write this down."

He wrote:

17th page
6th book from left
3rd shelf
    or
6th shelf
3rd book from left
23 line

He told Laura that Aldous wants her "to look up those books."

She and a "witness" proceeded immediately to the library. The first book designated was in Spanish. Page 17, line 23, began as follows (translated into English):

Aldous Huxley does not surprise us in this admirable communica-tion . . .

Laura commented that she was "speechless," especially because she was certain Aldous had never seen this soft-cover book in a cardboard container, sent after Aldous had been unable to attend a conference in Buenos Aires.

She decided to make the "book test" again by counting the shelves from the opposite direction. The book so designated was titled *Proceed-ings of the Two Conferences on Parapsychology and Pharmacology*: Page 17, line 23, read:

Parapyschology is still struggling in the first stage. These phenomena are not generally accepted by science although many workers are firmly convinced of their existence. For this reason the major effort of parapsychological research has been to demonstrate and to prove that they are working with real phenomena.

Once more the quotation was pointedly meaningful. Then Laura writes:

One more book was found that met the requirements of location and page. It was *My Life In Court* by Louis Nizer.

There I described a man six feet five inches tall, which approximated Aldous Huxley's unusual height, and as his wife wrote: "It is as though the intelligence that motivated the two previous events wanted now to give also a physical proof. We were stunned."

The book then concluded with a quotation from Huxley's grandfather that one must "sit down before fact like a little child, and be prepared to give up every preconceived notion . . ."

What shall we make of all this? As a nonbeliever, I nevertheless accept Laura Huxley's assurance that she made "an objective report without opinions or emotions—only facts." This is the classic approach to credibility of the incredible. Not only those engaged in search for truth as she was, but fiction writers use the device of having a character in the book express his disbelief more emphatically than would the most skeptical reader. Later the impossible occurs and breaks down the character's resistance and therefore, the author hopes, the reader's as well.

One thing caught my eye, when I read the instruction on the medium's printed card, "place questions in center." It recalled an experience I had with an entertainer called the "X-Ray Mind." He astonished audiences by reading their minds.

One day he came to see me professionally. Of course, his very presence in my office was disproof of his mental powers. Why would one with his professed gifts need advice? I did not consider my jaundiced view of his telepathic readings to be pertinent, and treated him like any mortal whose brain did not simulate the Roentgen ray.

Somehow his pride was hurt. He needed awe as well as advice. So he opened the subject:

"Have you seen me perform?" he asked.

"Yes." My tone denied him the admiration he sought.

"You don't believe in mental telepathy, do you?"

I did not flinch from the question, put as if it were an accusation. I confessed I did not.

"Well, suppose I give you a reading right here."

I had other things to do, but how could I dodge the challenge and convict myself of closed-mindedness. I agreed.

It was early afternoon. My room was lit bright by copious windows. He continued to make the test severe. "I'll do it right at your desk. I'll use any piece of paper you give me, so you won't think I have something prepared."

There was a small yellow pad on my desk, a printed form to be filled in with data. I tore off a sheet, turned it on its blank side, and handed it to him. He drew a circle in the center and said:

"I'll leave the room until you call me. Write any question you wish in the circle. Fold the paper four times, so no one will know what you have written."

I did, and buzzed my secretary to send him in. He took an ashtray on my desk and put it in front of him. Then he lit a match and held out his hand for the tightly folded sheet. I gave it to him and he set it afire. He watched the smoke intently as it curved upward, while the black ashes fell into the ashtray.

Then he proceeded to answer the question I had put on the folded sheet. There was no doubt that he knew what the question was, although his answer could not be checked at that time.

He gazed at me triumphantly, awaiting my surrender. I told him I was impressed, but I still believed it was a trick, conceding mystification but not the phenomenon of a penetrating X-ray mind. I would give it thought and try to learn how it was done.

He left with a shrug, which meant that obstinacy can make an intelligent man a fool.

Having amateurishly practiced the art of magic, which, despite my lack of dexterity, amused children, I knew that the right way to solve the puzzle, if it could be solved, was to trace back in detail everything that had happened. My mind lit on the circle he drew on the piece of paper and his instruction to write my question within it. Was it possible to burn the folded paper and leave the center palmed in the hand for a quick glance? Indeed it was. I did it myself. A magician told me that there was a shorter cut to the trick. Any skillful magician could palm the entire folded paper and substitute a similar one without detection. The burning of the fake paper would prevent checking its authenticity. I believe the former method was used. That is why the instruction was not simply to write a question, but to do so within a predrawn circle.

The medium's card likewise instructed "place questions in center." But that is as far as I could get in deduction because Laura Huxley told us that she put each card in an opaque envelope, and that the blindfolded medium held the closed envelope in his hand while the disembodied spirits spoke the answers through him. The incident is too remote for further investigation, but the question arises, why in such supernatural goings-on was it necessary to write out a question? Why couldn't the incarnate spirit indulge in the elementary power of reading the questioner's mind? One would think that a mind which could pierce an envelope, and isolate a spirit among billions of dead to reply, would also divine the question without mundane script.

What force is it that draws an intelligent mind to a preposterous belief such as spiritualism? It is the force of logic! Yes, logic so brilliantly deceptive and enticing that its logic is not detected. I call it the illusory syllogism.

It is a series of reasoned steps which seem irresistibly right and which lead to an inevitable conclusion. But it is an illusion. If you spot the error, the syllogism collapses.

Laura Huxley, her bright and talented mind notwithstanding, unwittingly gives us a good illustration. How does she induce the reader to believe in her husband's message from beyond?

The first step in the syllogism is her comment:

A medium is similar to a telephone, he is a channel of communication between different states of consciousness—possibly the living and the dead.

This is a modest statement. It merely states a possibility—fair enough.

The second step is to cite an illustration of disbelief in some other phenomenon which was overcome by miraculous facts: She writes:

If a few telephones had suddenly appeared in the Middle Ages, people would have considered them the work of the devil—and their users burned at the stake. What? Speak to someone in Florence when you are in Sienna? . . . no one can speak *that* loud—it is *impossible!*

Having shown that people who disbelieved were terribly wrong, the syllogism proceeds to analogize the telephone with spiritualism:

What? To be able to communicate between this, our universe, and the invisible universe of the dead—we are not sure it even exists! Exceedingly suspect!

By this time, the logic is pressing hard, the reader is beginning to feel almost ashamed of his skepticism. The next step in the syllogism is to pry the mind open a little more; to weaken resistance to a belief which earlier seemed preposterous. This is done by exploiting a current example, an event which almost everybody considered implausible even to contemplate, and yet happened in front of our eyes:

Suppose we had not been informed, through press, radio and television, of the preparation of the last eight years for trips in outer space; suppose we had not seen on the TV screen the launching of space vehicles. How would we react to a man who showed us a blurry photograph of sands and pebbles and announced, *'This is the moon'*? It is easy to predict. We would call him a charlatan or a madman. Now, secure in our knowledge, we all agree that the famous blurry photograph is indeed the moon!

So, we have reached our destination. Discarnate entities may well exist and they speak to us through a medium who is nothing but a telephone communicating the message. If you doubt this, you are guilty of the same error which caused people to reject as a charlatan's claim every great invention before it became a reality. You belong to the embarrassed multitudes who were willing "to bet their heads" that man would never step on the moon. Your mind is closed to the miracles all around you. You are a reactionary, devoid of imagination and prejudiced against cosmic possibilities. You reject the mysterious although life is filled with mystery, being unveiled to us day by day. Etc., etc.

Yet, all this is based on an illusory syllogism. The fundamental gap is that before one can talk of disembodied spirits communicating messages to us through an anointed medium, there must be some evidence that living animals not only survive after death but have all the communicating and other attributes of life except physical embodiment. To merely assume such a conclusion by an analogy with physical phenomena which previously astounded the skeptic is an unwarranted leap. It begs the question. It assumes that the miracle of splitting the atom or computerizing a trip to the moon automatically makes reasonable a belief in discarnate bodies yearning to speak to us. It is an illusory syllogism because it equates the fact that some things did eventuate which we once thought were impossible, with the conclusion that we should believe anything at all. It is an illusory syllogism because it assumes that because we were in error before, we must surrender all judgment and accept everything or we may err again.

The illusory syllogism isn't confined to spiritualism, reincarnation, and such. It has misled us in law, medicine, politics, indeed in any area where reasoning fashions our beliefs.

An illustration of the illusory syllogism in politics is the betrayal of Czechoslovakia. Hitler's voracity would permit nothing but the annexation of the neighboring state. England and France, unprepared to resist and desperate for time and peace, went to Munich and sacrificed

Czechoslovakia to save themselves. Munich became a symbol of the villainy of appeasement. Clearly, this was ignoble, if not indeed treacherous. So, we heard on all sides condemnation of them. "They are no better than Hitler." "They are just as amoral."

The syllogism was false. What was overlooked was the distinction between the aggressor and the amoral conduct of those who should have aided the victim. The murderer who invades a home and threatens to kill is not to be equated in venality with the policeman who is too cowardly to interfere.

The illusory syllogism is active in the arts. Isn't present tolerance of mediocrity and even fakery partly the result of its application? Why do we accept a blue line across a white canvas as a possible masterpiece? Why do we hesitate to condemn it as a hoax? Because prior new directions in painting were ridiculed and later were recognized as the work of genius. Listen, for example, to a respected critic writing about the Impressionists in 1876:

An exhibition has just been opened at Durand-Ruel which allegedly contains paintings. I enter and my horrified eyes behold something terrible. Five or six lunatics, among them a woman, have joined together and exhibited their works. I have seen people rock with laughter in front of these pictures, but my heart bled when I saw them. These would-be artists call themselves revolutionaries, "Impressionists." They take a piece of canvas, colour and brush, daub a few patches of colour on them at random, and sign the whole thing with their name. It is a delusion of the same kind as if the inmates of Bedlam picked up stones from the wayside and imagined they had found diamonds.

Far more savage criticism was written about these Fauvists, whose works now are hailed as unique and beautiful revelations of nature (and, incidentally, turning the critic's sarcastic comment about inmates of Bedlam picking up stones and imagining they were diamonds into a tribute to their imagination). Nevertheless, does it follow that, because many were once artistically blind, we must now see virtue in trash, as if *we* were blind? Only the illusory syllogism pushes us to an abandonment of discretion. Out of fear that we may reveal our ignorance, we see gold raiment where there is only nudity.

The same is true in music. We refrain from holding our ears, and instead listen reflectively to cacophonies of weird dissonant noises (sometimes made by scratching a tin washboard) because we dare not pit our judgment against historical precedent which exposed the most vociferous critics as stupid.

None of the geniuses escaped abuse. Had it come from minor critics it might not have mattered. But they were seared and humiliated by the foremost musical critics of the day. To read these attacks is to appreciate the vitriolic virtuosity of the critics, if not their judgment. Friederich Dionys Weber, the respected musical theorist, considered Beethoven's ninth symphony "pure nonsense." Another famous critic wrote that Wagner's *Tannhäuser* overture was "only a commonplace display of noise and extravagance." Lohengrin was denounced as "a frosty, sense-and-soul-congealing tone-whining." *Meistersinger's* overture was an "ugly rioting of dissonances" whose effect was "caterwauling." *Parsifal* reminded one eminent critic of "piano-tuning with impediments," and another of "The howls of a dog undergoing vivisection."

The famous critic Eduard Hanslick was more comprehensive: he lumped Beethoven, Wagner, and Mozart together and shot them down with one bullet: "There has been nothing of any interest since the classicists."

Of course Stravinsky was an even more inviting target. Appropriately enough his music was compared to the paintings of the Fauvists and called "The music of the Fauve." This was not intended as a complimentary allusion. His works were condemned for their savagery and brutality. The critics' anger spread to the people. At the premiere performance of *The Rite of Spring*, at the Théâtre des Champs-Élysées in Paris, on May 29, 1913, an enraged audience rose in mass, hooting and stamping their feet. Blows were exchanged. One woman spat in the face of a demonstrator. The music was drowned out by noises more dissonant than that which came from the stage.*

So it is understandable that some current critics, knowledgeably indoctrinated by the past, may be slow on the trigger. Who knows, they think, but what grates on their eardrums and offends their minds may soon be recognized as brilliant representation of the discordant times in which we live? Furthermore, it is chic to be avant-garde, to hear into the future, even if one cannot see into it. The result is caution, a lack of confidence to state their true feelings, and sometimes even a struggle to find talent in the very revolutionary formlessness of a creator without the power to create. That is why it is always possible to find somewhere a kind word for rubbish.

The illusory syllogism takes many forms. Here it is expressed in the syllogism that great artists break through traditional barriers; that we are repelled by the unfamiliar; that everything new meets resistance until we educate ourselves to appreciate it; and therefore that we must not scoff at the aberrational or even at emptiness. It is new and when we accustom ourselves to it, perhaps we will learn that it is an ad-

* David Ewen, *The World of Twentieth Century Music*, Prentice-Hall, N.J., 1968. P. 789.

vance in art. Therefore we abandon our discriminating judgment. Don't reject. Don't denounce. Accept with tolerance the possibility that what you believe is trash may turn out to be gold.

As between the risk that posterity will prove us fools and the risk of surrendering our judgments, I prefer the former.

So in matters of the occult—no equivocation. I don't believe in extra-sensory perception, astrology, reincarnation or spiritualism.

If I am wrong, the first words uttered by a medium some future day, when he summons my voice from beyond, will be "I apologize."

LAUGHING AT OURSELVES

A human being is distinguished from all other animals by his capacity to laugh. By this standard, Harry Hershfield was one of the great human beings of our time.

Most comedians have musical identifications, like "Thanks for the Memory" or "Everybody Loves Somebody." Harry's was prose: "He walks with the mighty but has never lost the common touch." Five Presidents of the United States called him their friend. Kings and statesmen, from Winston Churchill and Charles De Gaulle down, paid him tribute. The foremost scientists, writers, and painters honored him. But it was the people who took him to their hearts.

This is a great American tradition, to choose a humorist by popular choice and make him the folk hero of his generation. His duty? To tell us the truth about the mighty and ourselves without offending us. To cleanse the democratic process by making us laugh at ourselves. Hershfield belonged to this long line of aristocracy in our democracy; Mark Twain, Josh Billings, George Ade, Robert Benchley, and Will Rogers.

I had good opportunity to observe his hold on the people. We often ate together at the Algonquin Round Table. Ate is a bad description— we choked and gasped for breath from laughter between bites. On one occasion he had just arrived from Washington, where he had been a guest of President Nixon. He exhibited White House cuff links which had been presented to him. "Mr. President," he had said, "the country doesn't need cuff links. It needs shirts!"

Even his food order sent the waiter into spasms. "Let me have something that will give me heartburn now, not two in the morning."

After lunch, he would walk me back to the office. When we passed the Lambs Club, we would encounter prominent stars, all of whom, men and women, embraced him with enthusiasm out of all proportion to the need for professional recognition. As we continued, the street cleaner raised his brush in salute. The shoeshine boy lit up with a smile brighter than his shine. And sometimes, when we passed the alleyway of the Belasco Theater, a drunken derelict would open his swollen eyes and greet him, "Hello, Harry." I got to imagine that the policeman's horse neighed his greeting too. Harry belonged to all, because he made us all happier.

There are people who carry germs and infect others with disease. Harry was a carrier who infected people with good will. If you were morose or moody, you had to be wary of him. If you carried your business burdens on your shoulders, you had to shun him. You didn't have a chance, if you met him. For whether he was telling a story to one or to 25,000 at Madison Square Garden, his enthusiasm, gaiety, and boyishness infected you. You lost your sad face. You walked away with a stronger back, if not a lighter burden.

You could observe this phenomenon at any of the thousands of banquets at which he presided. A distinguished foreign dignitary, public official, or artist would approach him ponderously. Within a moment, Harry would be telling him a story. You would see a smile and then the explosion—the diaphragm moving violently up and down. The visitor had been infected with good humor. Now he had become a carrier himself. When he returned to his seat, he repeated the story to his neighbors. Thereafter, Harry acted as toastmaster, and the laugh germ spread to the whole audience. For more than seventy years, he spread such epidemics throughout the nation.

In 1955, Mayor Robert Wagner designated Harry officially as "Mr. New York." At a brilliant dinner in the Grand Ball Room of the Waldorf, overflowing to the highest tier, Times Square was designated "Hershfield Square."

Even in appearance Harry represented the conglomerate qualities of the city. He had Irish gray hair, Scandinavian blue eyes, Greek pallor, French vivacity, Italian love of music, Jamaican gaiety, and he was thoroughly, wonderfully Jewish. New York is a huge melting pot and Harry seemed to be standing over it with an enormous stirring spoon pouring humor into it to prevent it from boiling over.

Freud commented on what he called "the peculiarly liberating and elevating effect" of humor. Harry didn't tell jokes because of social consciousness. He simply enjoyed making people laugh. He breathed laughter, as ordinary mortals breathed air.

Harry was born in Cedar Rapids, Iowa, in 1885, two weeks after his parents arrived from Odessa, Russia. His parents were gifted. His father, Michael, was a musician and linguist and head of a "gymnasium" in Russia. His mother, Alta, came from a family of musicians and physicians. Harry was one of thirteen children. He had aspired to become a doctor, but he quit high school because the study of drawing was irresistible. (One of his later lines was "Educated he is, but smart he isn't.") It was his brother Alex who became a distinguished physician in Chicago.

At the Frank Holme School of Illustration, Harry's classmates were the cartoonists, H. T. Webster, Will B. Johnston, and LeRoy Baldridge.

He obtained a job on the Chicago *Daily News* as an illustrator, but was suspended when he retouched a photograph of the Leaning Tower of Pisa to straighten it up.

Harry became not only a repository of stories but a creator of humor. One could tell by his bemused look that a "new" joke someone eagerly told him was one he had invented and used in a Kabibble cartoon a half century earlier.

Unlike most raconteurs, he carefully measured the possible hurt of a story, and his kindliness prevailed over laughter. So he would check with his friends Cardinal Spellman and Bishop Sheen before making a talk at a Communion breakfast. (Is it all right to say that you make holy water by boiling the hell out of it, or that the donkey carrying Mary stumbled and Joseph cried out, "Jesus Christ, he almost fell" and Mary said, "You know, that's a better name than Irving.")

He took more liberty with Jewish groups, as if to cure their hypersensitivity:

"A child brought home a poor report card. Facing the tirade of his parents, he explained, 'The teacher is anti-Semitic. She picks on me.'

"The next morning the irate mother visited the teacher and upbraided her for bigotry. 'It isn't true. Your boy just doesn't know his lessons. Let me prove it to you. Sammy, how much is 10 and 10?'

" 'There she goes, Ma, picking on me again!' "

And so by the thousands, stories poured from him. He was an inexhaustible geyser of humor. For years he demonstrated his prowess on radio and television programs called "Can You Top This?" If anyone doubted the authenticity of his instant recall, all one had to do was be in his presence and witness the spontaneous flood of stories from his computerized brain.

He was an etymologist of jokes and his books on humor developed the theory that basically there were only six stories. He would illustrate professorially. A Mussolini story (a pollster reported to him that 99 per cent of the people were for him, "but I must say I constantly ran into the other 1 per cent") could be used for Stalin, Hitler, or any other dictator. He could illustrate ten offshoots of a basic war story ("Don't be scared. Every bullet has a name on it. If your name is not on, then you're safe." Frightened soldier, "I'm worried about the bullet which has on it 'To whom it may concern,'").

He was a humorist, not a comedian.

The common denominator of virtually all his stories was their meaningfulness. They pointed up the foibles, weaknesses, or surprise ingenuity of the underdog. The point may have been washed away with the first burst of laughter, but then reflection, like the tide, brought it back and we enjoyed the intellectual aftertaste.

Harry had no compulsion to be "on" all the time. He would listen respectfully to serious discussions. He would sit back reflectively, his lips pursed as if he were savoring good wine. It was interesting to watch him as others tried to tell him a "new" joke. Inevitably he knew it, but not once did he embarrass the teller by stopping him. He would listen appreciatively, and comment, "Isn't that wonderful." His tolerance was like that of a lover of opera who can enjoy the same music over and over again. When he was challenged to admit that he had known the story all the time, he would reply, "But I like the way you told it."

His generosity was unlimited. He practiced the greatest exercise of all —to bend down and help someone up. He was the softest touch wherever he was. Although it was his profession to make appearances and entertain either as toastmaster or speaker, he made hundreds of talks without compensation, either because a friend (and who wasn't his friend?) asked him, or because the function was charitable.

He was the quickest draw in the land, in picking up a check at the dinner table. If it weren't for the rule of the Algonquin Round Table that all guests signed their own checks, he would have paid everyone's bill every day.

As a toastmaster, he was overgenerous in introducing others, but his exaggeration was forgiven because it stemmed from his goodness. But when he was introduced, he turned compliments aside jestingly. "I am not as good as you have been told, but I am not as bad as you out there are thinking."

He never told a joke which had daggers in it. He never told an off-color joke in public.

He could be given to pixieish mischievousness, but, as always, it was harmless. Once he presided at a public dinner at which Congressman Sol Bloom was a speaker. The politician glowed in the aura of his appointment by Roosevelt as the head of the George Washington centennial celebration. This made him more verbose than usual. After forty-five minutes, the audience was getting exceedingly restless—a step preceding their abandonment of the speaker to converse among themselves. Harry put a note before Bloom, "Time." Bloom ignored it.

Fifteen minutes later, another note, "Time." Bloom continued with what Harry used to describe as his eighth "In conclusion."

Finally, Harry scribbled another note. Bloom read it, and sat down instantly, hardly finishing his sentence.

We on the dais had watched this. The audience had long before retired. (Harry used to tell of the speaker who looked at his watch, and someone in the audience yelled, "There's a calendar behind you!")

"What did you write on that last note?"

"I just wrote 'Your fly is open!' "

He had been attracted to the theater and tried his hand at it. In 1912 he appeared at Hammerstein's Victoria Theater with Eddie Cantor and Lila Lee. His column "Broadway Unlimited" earned him one of the first appearances in talking pictures, with President Coolidge and Adolph Zukor, in 1926.

He also appeared on the first television program, sent to Times Square from Jersey City, which starred George Jessel and Sid Grauman. At one time he was a theater reviewer on a radio program called "One Man's Opinion."

Nevertheless, the artifices of performing were inimical to his sincerity and simplicity.

Therefore, he did not practice the art of embellishing a story with dialect, elaborate descriptive language, or Thespian skills. To him, the joke "is the thing." He did not wish to dazzle. It was the story which was front stage. The spotlight must be on it. I sometimes thought he practiced economy in the telling, so as to have more time for more stories. Only once did I hear him "stoop" to performing. It was the story of the Jew on line with hundreds milling about the United States Bank, which had closed during the 1929 crash. He was screaming imprecations at the officers of the bank. Harry imitated his hysterics, "Even hanging was too good for such villains!"

A passer-by asked him how much money he had in the bank.

"None—if I had had any money in there, would I be taking it so lightly?"

He appreciated art. He was a collector and his home and office were filled with fine paintings and sculpture. He was also a collector of memorabilia. I drew dozens of drawings of him on napkins and he saved them all. Once, not realizing his collecting mania, I drew his head on a tablecloth. He insisted on cutting it out and offered payment to the owner.

Although his humor directed him to cartoons (the famous Abe Kabibble, Desperate Desmond, Homeless Hector, and According to Hoyle), he was a good draftsman and could have had an art career. At one time for three years he was a scenario writer for Warner Brothers and, later, editor of animated cartoons for M-G-M. However, to be in Hollywood was like being banished from New York, the great banquets and the teeming excitement which were essential environment to his well being. His constitution could not stand the sun. He needed Broadway electric lights.

He was the author of a serious novel about New York. On the flyleaf, he wrote "Where everyone mutinies and no one deserts."

In his early days he was a sports writer and artist of sports events for the San Francisco *Chronicle*. Among the hundreds of photographs which crowded each other off the walls, onto the tables and floor of his home and office, were poses with every champion boxer of the last sixty years, his slight figure throwing a punch upwards, while his opponent feigned distress. But also there were dozens of photographs picturing his dais companions, the foremost public officials of this country and abroad.

He had unusual eating habits. He could not touch butter or any dairy product. His translucent pale skin revealed his sensitive organism. Captains and waiters in all the grand ballrooms knew of this eccentricity. As the food was paraded to the tables in military file, one waiter would head for the dais with a special Hershfield plate. It was a perquisite of his fame and popularity. For he had entertained them, too, dozens of times and they loved him.

As he neared his ninetieth birthday, he changed in only one respect. He became good-naturedly philosophical. "I have lived and experienced everything. Now I enjoy everything more because I understand better." His phenomenal good nature prevailed over his age and he really believed it was the best period of his life.

He had practiced joyful serenity all his life. He, like everyone else, had suffered tragedy. But he was dauntless. In 1917 he had married Jane Isdell, a beautiful actress whom he met in Chicago, where she was appearing in *The Girl Question*. But she became mentally ill, suffering from all sorts of phobias. He loved and cared for her for a half century, until she died. Few ever saw her. He always appeared alone. No one would have suspected his private anguish.

Even his own illness could not dampen his bubbling spirit and gaiety.

His heart failed and he was desperately ill. No visitors were permitted. But he persuaded the nurse to permit him to take my telephone call.

"Hello, Harry. I'm delighted I can visit you on the phone."

"Oh, Lou, I am so glad, so glad to hear your voice."

"How are you feeling?"

"Lou, I'm too weak to collapse."

He joined me in laughter but his was weak.

"Harry, you're incorrigible. I understand they're going to give you a heart pacer. That should make you feel better."

"Yes, I'll try it for ten years. If it doesn't work I'll throw it out."

"I can hear the nurse telling you to hang up. I'll talk to you again soon. Feel well."

"Don't worry. In a few weeks I'll be back to abnormal!"

Two days later, December 15, 1974, he was dead.

Few people can go through life without making an enemy. The process of achievement is abrasive. To excel is to rise above others reaching for the same pinnacle. We are reared in the tradition of competition—in business, arts, and sports. We try to assuage the loser by honoring "good sportsmanship"—which usually means, to lose gracefully. But the psyche does not yield to slogans.

We envy the victor and often hate him. And it is easy to find or imagine a grievance to justify the violation of the loser's ethic.

Harry was unique not only because of his talents as raconteur, columnist, and artist, but because of his personality.

He combined sophistication, guilelessness, and goodness. He was truly loved and thus he lived a fulfilled life.

Measured by customary standards of greatness, he was not a great man. But he was the foremost philanthropist of our day because philanthropy does not mean giving money. The word is derived from *philo* (love) and *anthropos* (man); to love man.

When one evaluates the joy he brought to millions, the realization grows that this warmhearted man came closer to the mysterious purpose of life than most of us.

PORNOGRAPHY—OBSCENITY

Is pornography or obscenity a crime? It is under certain circumstances, but the Supreme Court of the United States has admitted that it is "an intractable problem." Several dissenting judges have criticized the Court for being "mixed" in definitions of obscenity. Justice Jackson sarcastically referred to his own tribunal as the "High Court of Obscenity," which reviews erotic and scatological material. Other judges have expressed concern that any obscenity conviction violates the First Amendment guarantee of free speech. Yet, the Supreme Court has upheld criminal statutes which make obscenity a crime punishable by jail.

However, the road to this conclusion has had so many detours that one traveling it didn't know whether he was coming or going. The definition of obscenity has been changed time and again. On some occasions a majority of the Court could not be found to reach a decision, there being so many splintered views.

Justice Harlan in the Dallas "censorship" case, which I argued, wrote of "a variety of views among members of the court unmatched in any other course of constitutional adjudication."

The Court has held that free speech requires "breathing room" and any limitation upon it must be made with "sensitive tools." How sensitive? And what is obscenity?

The word derives from the Latin *obscaenus*, meaning filth. My Webster's dictionary defines it as "disgusting to the senses, grossly repugnant to the generally accepted notions of what is appropriate."

Pornography derives from the Greek *porné*, harlot, and *graphos*, writing. Literally it means a description of prostitution, of lewdness, a portrayal of erotic behavior designed to cause sexual excitement.

These are dictionary definitions, but they do not determine the legal test of when the state will consider them criminal.

The reason that this subject so intrigues the public is not only because, like all subjects of sex, it arouses interest, but for more profound reasons. It poses questions of our values, moral, ethical, and philosophical. Is there a point at which permissiveness endangers the structure of civilized society? We are warned that the decline of empires is preceded and accompanied by general licentiousness, and that this is no coincidence. On the other hand, we are also warned that free expression is democracy's strength and ensures the possibility of change while preserving fundamental values. Is there a line which can be drawn between these two precepts without sacrifice of either?

I have argued a number of motion picture pornography cases in the Supreme Court, and have engaged in "debate" with the judges, who initiate and encourage it, in preference to be passive listeners of a prepared speech by counsel. I have participated to some extent in the evolution of the prevailing rule and deign to enter and explore this mined territory.

I begin the journey with a decision in 1957 (Roth case) that obscenity was not protected by the First Amendment. How did the Court justify this apparent encroachment on freedom of expression? Simply by saying that obscenity didn't qualify as the kind of expression worthy of constitutional protection. It didn't rise to the level of ideas, good or bad, which would be shielded by the guarantee of free speech. It was just garbage. This still left the need for a definition. When would the words or scene be deemed obscene? The answer was when the dominant theme appealed to prurient interest (aroused sexual feelings), which an average person, according to community standards existing at the time, would find patently offensive.

Little wonder that these generalities did not put the matter to rest. The Court proceeded to search for a more precise definition. Nine years later in 1966, the Court fashioned one in the famous case of *John Cleland's Memoirs of a Woman of Pleasure* v. *Massachusetts*. Material would be considered obscene if it contained three elements:

One, the dominant theme as a whole appealed to prurient interest in sex.

Two, it was patently offensive because it violated contemporary community standards.

Three, it was utterly without redeeming social value.

The word "utterly" in the third test left a loophole so large that even complete nudity, sexual intercourse, and oral sex could be depicted and still not be condemned as obscene. The reason was that in books or motion pictures where all this was vividly depicted, there were other scenes which were not "utterly without redeeming social value." Resourceful producers had no difficulty beginning a picture with the heroine fully dressed, interviewing men and women in various strata of life about socialism, marriage, children, and politics, and then being frustrated by their opinions, while the viewers were bored by them, proceeding with her lover to the bedroom where her resourcefulness could be better illustrated. The first breakthrough picture which used this device was *I Am Curious Yellow*. In 1968 the Federal Court of Appeals, by a two-to-one vote, held that it was not obscene; that it came under the protective arm of that phrase, "not utterly without redeeming social value."

The Court expressed its discomfort at its own decision, saying: "There are scenes of oral-genital activity . . . The film is presented with greater explicitness than has been seen in any other film produced for general viewing." But the Court said that it was bound by the definition in the *Memoirs* case.

Judge Friendly agreed, although he argued with himself in the course of writing his opinion, as brilliant judges often do, by commenting "A truly pornographic film would not be rescinded by inclusion of a few verses from the psalms." But he too found some redeeming social value in the girl's search for her identity. Both judges warned, however, that if the producer's promise that children would not be permitted to see the picture was broken, or that if the advertising stressed the sexual aspect of the picture, they would be subject to criminal action such as sent the publisher Ralph Ginzburg to jail, because he had "pandered" his wares by offensive advertising and thus refuted his alleged serious purpose. Judge Friendly concluded by saying, "With these reservations and with no little distaste, I concur in the reversal." Chief Judge Lumbard wrote an indignant dissent: "The participants indulge in acts of fellatio and cunnilingus. Needless to say these acts bear no conceivable relevance to any social value, except that of box-office appeal."

A Danish sex film virtually mocked the "redeeming social value" test by claiming that it consisted of an appeal from the screen by one of the characters to the audience, to sign a petition which would be supplied in the lobby, protesting against the prudery which put any limit on sex depiction. This was, to say the least, an imaginative device of an inverted automatic compliance with the test. If the same resourcefulness had been applied to the sex scenes, the picture would have been a greater success.

The "utterly without redeeming social value" requirement pleased the advocators of absolute First Amendment rights much more than those who sought to curb pornography, because it was almost impossible to convict under it. In a way there was satisfaction for both sides. The law condemned obscenity. On the other hand, the definition of obscenity permitted very wide latitude. An uneasy truce descended on the battleground. As permissiveness gained during the lull, a cry went up again for restraint.

President Johnson appointed a commission which after lengthy study rendered its report. It found that "society's attempts to legislate for adults in the area of obscenity have not been successful" and that "exposure to explicit sexual material" does not cause criminal behavior among youths or adults insofar as evidence can demonstrate.

By the time this "Report of the Commission on Obscenity and Pornography" was filed, President Nixon was in the White House. He denounced it because he claimed it overstressed freedom of expression instead of recommending restraint. In doing so, he was reflecting public indignation. Of course his strictures on moral rectitude could hardly have come from a less appropriate source:

I have evaluated that report and categorically reject its morally bankrupt conclusions and major recommendations. So long as I am in the White House, there will be no relaxation of the national effort to control and eliminate smut from our national life . . .

If an attitude of permissiveness were to be adopted regarding pornography, this would increase the threat to our social order as well as to our moral principles . . .

American morality is not to be trifled with . . . I totally reject its report.

However, it was not a report or Nixon's views which would control. It was the Supreme Court's search for a definition of obscenity which would be sound enough to obtain concurrence of a majority of the Court. The opportunity arose when a man called Marvin Miller was convicted by a jury of distributing obscene material in California. The case went to the Supreme Court in 1973 and became so famous that it is referred to merely as *Miller*, an intimacy reserved only for landmark cases.

What had Miller done? He had conducted a mass mailing campaign to advertise the sale of four books entitled, *Intercourse, Man-Woman, Sex Orgies Illustrated,* and *An Illustrated History of Pornography*, as well as a film entitled *Marital Intercourse*. The brochures consisted chiefly of pictures and drawings explicitly depicting men and women in groups of two or more, engaging in a variety of sexual activities, with genitals often prominently displayed. A recipient of the brochures and his mother complained to the police. Indictment and conviction followed.

When the case came to the Supreme Court, it said that it had re-examined its earlier decisions. It repeated that obscene material was not protected by the First Amendment, and was a crime. However, it carefully set forth a new definition of pornography or obscenity, which it said would protect the public against smut and nevertheless comply with free speech requirements. The break with the previous rule was complete. Chief Justice Burger, who wrote the majority opinion, conceded that there wasn't a single judge who still supported the *Memoirs* test. Even Justice Brennan, who had written that decision, abandoned it.

The new test substituted for the famous "utterly without redeeming social value" the following: to be obscene a work, taken as a whole, must lack serious literary, artistic, political, or scientific value. If it had any one of these values, it could not be obscene irrespective of what else it portrayed. The serious quality, like an antitoxin, made it immune from attack.

Even if a work failed to have any of these qualities, it could be obscene only if two other conditions existed:

One, would an average person, applying contemporary standards, find that it appealed to prurient interest; and second, did the work depict in a patently offensive way sexual conduct specifically defined in the state statute?

The Court for the first time defined what would be considered "patently offensive":

(a) Descriptions of ultimate sexual acts, normal or perverted, actual or simulated.
(b) Descriptions of masturbation, excretory functions, and lewd exhibition of the genitals.

The decision attempted to still the concern of extreme free speech advocates:

No one will be subject to prosecution for the sale or exposure of obscene materials, unless these materials depict or describe patently offensive "hard core" sexual conduct . . . Today for the first time . . . a majority of this Court has agreed on concrete guidelines to isolate "hard core" pornography from expression protected by the First Amendment.

The villain had been identified. It was "hard-core pronography." It was sheer (to avoid the unfortunate word "pure") smut. Everything else would be exempted from punishment, either because it had literary, artistic, political, or scientific value, or because it was not patently offensive.

Chief Justice Burger anticipated the attacks which would be made on this formulation. He argued that just because no one could define regulated material with "god-like precision" didn't mean that the states or

Congress should not be able to strike at "hard-core" pornography. His opinion did not spare the dissenting members of the Court.

I have always thought that it was unfortunate when, during oral argument, judges of the Court argued with each other. Sometimes they attacked their "brothers" on the bench, by addressing the hapless lawyer, who then received a reply from the "brother," the lawyer becoming an unwilling conduit. The attorney dared not agree with either judge, but had to exhibit the kind of tact which an English solicitor once demonstrated when he said to the Court, "Last month your honors decided a case for the plaintiff, and this week you decided an identical case for the defendant; and may I say, your honors, in both instances, most admirably."

Ordinarily differing opinions would evidence vigorous intellectual discussion. But the Supreme Court has deservedly been held in greater awe than some of our Presidents. Unlike the White House, the Court is visited by people from every part of the nation who observe how it functions during argument. They may not understand the quarreling among the judges. It strips the Court of the aura of infallibility, a psychological, if not realistic, expectation. Clash of views, sometimes angry ones, should be reserved for the conference room. Indeed great Chief Justices have striven to achieve unanimous decisions because dissents weaken the persuasive effect of the majority. For example, the ruling against President Nixon on the production of tapes derived special force from the absence of any dissent.

The obscenity debate, however, was so volatile that the opinions themselves in *Miller* reflected the contentiousness and fiery disagreements which pervaded the conference room. By reading them one could almost hear the bitter exchanges behind the closed door. The Chief Justice took on Justices Brennan and Douglas directly. Mentioning them by name, he wrote:

The dissenting justices sound the alarm of repression. But, in our view to equate the free and robust exchange of ideas and political debate, with commercial exploitation of obscene material, demeans the grand conception of the First Amendment and its high purposes in the historic struggle for freedom . . . Civilized people do not allow unregulated access to heroin because it is a derivative of medicinal morphine.

Justice Douglas, as eloquent as he was extreme in advocating free speech, dissented:

There are no constitutional guidelines for deciding what is and what is not "obscene" . . . What shocks me may be sustenance to my neighbor. What causes one person to boil up in rage over one pamphlet or movie may reflect only his neurosis, not shared by others . . .

The First Amendment was not fashioned as a vehicle for dispensing tranquilizers to the people.

The four dissenting Justices saw "dark days" for America if obscenity was made an exception to the rule that free speech was absolute. They predicted that zealots would raid libraries to remove offensive works, and that motion pictures, which were not hard-core pornography, would nevertheless be attacked.

Soon we would see. It did not take long. Within eight days after the *Miller* decision, the District Attorney of Albany County acted against *Last Tango in Paris*, starring Marlon Brando and Maria Schneider, and directed by Bernardo Bertolucci. This motion picture had been playing for almost two months in the Towne Theater in Albany. It was rated "X" by the Motion Picture Producers Association. The rating code, and how it came about, I shall discuss later. Suffice it to say that the "X" rating merely meant that children would not be admitted. It was no evaluation of the quality of the picture. Indeed, three "X"-rated pictures, *Midnight Cowboy*, *The Damned*, and *Clockwork Orange* had won Academy Award nominations.

The reason that children were barred from *Tango* was that it had scenes of nudity, sexual intercourse, and sodomy.

Curiously enough, most of the coupling was done while fully dressed. This was to emphasize the sudden impulse devoid of personal relationship. Its dehumanizing aspect was accented by the "butter" sodomy scene. It was only later when the man's feelings turned to love that he derived real gratification.

Clearly, the picture had a genuine story in which the sexual scenes advanced the plot rather than dwarfed it. The film took two hours to show, of which time eight minutes were devoted to sex scenes. True, the test is not merely time. A hard-core pornographic motion picture may have the same proportion of actual sex scenes, but they are the dominant characteristic of the film. The rest is flimsy excuse for its real purpose. In *Tango* the reverse was true. Sex was incidental to the story. The film was a study of a man whose wife had committed suicide after betraying him, and who at the age of forty-five found himself tormented and embittered. He met a girl accidentally in an empty apartment which both were trying to rent. Almost without communication, and while fully dressed, they indulged in intercourse while standing up. The erotic relationship continued on his insistence that they should not know anything about each other, not even their names. The impersonal, animalistic nature of their sex relationship "leaves no room for lying, deceit or treachery," but it turned out to be unsatisfactory. What began as a quest for the assertion of male mastery moved on to love. She wanted to be free of him and when he pursued her she killed him. As one literary expert testified, if the film was considered in its entirety, the plot was the coat. The sexual scenes were the buttons. Clearly the film had serious literary value.

The *Christian Century* described it as "a parable of man seeking release from inner anguish through sexual catharsis and finding that love, not sex, is the answer." When *Tango* was shown at the New York Film Festival at Lincoln Center, New York, Pauline Kael, the film critic of the *New Yorker*, equated its impact on cinema with the effect of Igor Stravinsky's *Rite of Spring* upon modern music.

The critic of the New York *Times*, Vincent Canby, called it a "beautiful, courageous, foolishly romantic and reckless film . . ."

Judith Crist, the distinguished critic, wrote that "Tango is not about sex . . . it is about the things man lives by."

Lavish praise came from all sections of the country. As if anticipating the impending struggle, Max Lerner, teacher and author, wrote: "No one will dare to ban 'Last Tango' and get away with it. The critical audience won't let them, and that is what counts."

But, critical audiences don't fight legal battles.

The prosecutor, believing that *Miller* gave him an opportunity to strike at the hard-core pictures in the Albany area, and confusing *Tango* with *Deep Throat* and its lurid progeny, because they all had an "X" designation, summoned theater owners to his office. He gave them a summary of *Miller* to read and announced that all "X" films would be submitted to the grand jury for possible prosecution.

So there it was. The District Attorney went fishing for pornography and *Tango* was caught in the net.

The exhibitor who was playing *Tango* was told that if he ceased playing the picture, the subpoena would be withdrawn. He "pulled" the picture immediately even though under his contract with United Artists it had many weeks to run. The result was that all other bookings of *Tango* were jeopardized. Why should a theater owner risk criminal involvement? There has never been an abundance of martyrs (even though it has been said that martyrs should not be pitied because they liked their job). The expense of a legal test would be severe. The case might have to be taken to the Supreme Court. There were many other pictures available. This was a perfect example of the "chilling effect" so often bespoken by those who argue that encroachment on free expression frightens off others from expressing themselves.

United Artists, however, decided to test the issue. As its counsel, I rushed to Albany to argue before a three-judge panel which we had demanded, because of the constitutional question involved. After some skirmishing, *Tango* triumphed and continued its unmolested career.

In reflective terms, the dissenters in *Miller* could point to *Tango* to support their prophecy that repressive efforts would follow that decision. The majority could reply that that effort had failed, and that the beneficent effect of curbing hard-core pornography must not be sacrificed because of misguided application of the law. In a sense, it was a standoff. Soon, however, there was a more severe test which would come before the Supreme Court in 1974. Then it could look at its handiwork empirically. How did the clashing theories really work out in the field?

The motion picture involved was *Carnal Knowledge*. It boasted the combined talents of some of America's leading contemporary artists. It was directed by Mike Nichols; written by Jules Feiffer; acted by Jack Nicholson, Candice Bergen, and Ann-Margaret, who won an Academy Award nomination for her performance in this very picture; and produced by Joseph E. Levine. Even the cost of the picture, $9 million, distinguished it from the $25,000 to $100,000 budgets of most of the skinflicks.

Carnal Knowledge had played to seventeen and a half million people in some five thousand theaters, including cities in Georgia, enjoying popular and discriminating acceptance.

However, during an engagement in a theater in Albany, Georgia, the local sheriff seized the film. The manager, Billy Jenkins, was arrested on the charge of "public indecency." The case was tried by a jury. No doubt it was shocked. Words not generally bandied by men except in the proverbial smoking car (I wonder what has happened to this release of profanity now that people fly) emanated from the screen to the mixed audiences sitting in the dark theater. There was a youthful petting scene in which he pleaded to touch her breast and then guided her hand to himself. There were obvious scenes of intercourse, and a final scene in which the impotent "hero" engaged in a fantasy with a woman so that she could talk him into turgidity.

The jury, ignoring all the rest of the film, found Jenkins guilty. He was sentenced to one year's probation and fined seven hundred fifty dollars.

This decision caused little stir because it was the finding of a local jury, which probably would be corrected. Jenkins' lawyers took an appeal to the Supreme Court of Georgia. When that court upheld the conviction by a vote of four to three, an alarm arose throughout the creative world. If a theater manager could be criminally convicted for showing *Carnal Knowledge*, how could anyone dare to produce anything but "kiddy" pictures? Who knew but that some other local jury might find a passionate kiss or a deep-shadowed cleavage a crime? One of the judges of the United States Supreme Court had said "that distributing books should not be a hazardous occupation." The same applied to motion pictures. But now it clearly was.

Also private interest had been placed in jeopardy. What would happen to future bookings of *Carnal Knowledge?* Would other theaters risk exhibiting it in the face of the warning by the highest court of one of our states that it was criminal to do so? Was this multimillion dollar project to be mummified as a historic example of the fate of unconventional artistic effort?

The clashing opinions of the majority and minority of the Georgia Supreme Court were like jagged lightning flashes preceding the thunder in the world of creative artists.

The majority of four judges rested on the foundation laid down by the United States Supreme Court that "obscenity is not within the area of constitutionally protected speech or press." It pointed out that the Georgia legislature had enacted a statute which adopted the *Memoirs* test of "utterly without redeeming social value." The *Miller* case had come down since then and actually provided a more restrictive test. But *Miller* had also held that a jury "can consider State or local community standards 'in lieu of national standards.' " The jury therefore had the right to evaluate the local standard according to which the picture was obscene.

The majority wrote in stentorian tones reserved for conclusions from on high:

We hold the evidence in this record amply supports the verdict of guilty by the showing of the film "Carnal Knowledge" in violation of the definition of distributing obscene material under our Georgia statutes.

The decision added moral justification for the jury's verdict. The showing of an obscene picture, it said, "involved the welfare of the public at large since it is contrary to the standards of decency and propriety of the community as a whole."

It referred to the "legitimate interest" of the state to regulate commerce in obscene material. In this way, "states' rights" and "public welfare," like pepper and salt, were added to the brew.

The minority opinion was legalistically phrased, but Judge William Gunter could not disguise either his emotions or acerbity. *Carnal Knowledge* had been shown to all seven judges of the court. Four thought it was "obscene, pornographic material, unprotected by the First Amendment." Three thought it was not obscene and therefore constitutionally protected as free expression. He then quoted Chief Justice Burger's retort to the minority of his own court:

The dissenting Justices sound the alarm of repression . . . Their doleful anticipations assume that Courts cannot distinguish commerce in ideas, protected by the First Amendment, from commercial exploitation of obscene material.

Could they? Judge Gunter didn't think so:

My experience with this case teaches me that the "alarm of repression" was validly sounded.

To think that judges could distinguish ideas from commercial exploitation of obscenity was, he said:

a too optimistic assumption. The Jenkins case is the proof of the pudding: material is pornographic and unprotectected in the subjective mind and senses of one judge; and the same material has serious literary or artistic value in the subjective mind and senses of another judge.

He referred to an old saw which mocked the Supreme Court. That court's decision is not final because its members are infallible. It is infallible because it is final. For good measure, he sounded a louder alarm of repression than even Justices Douglas and Brennan:

"If the motion picture 'Carnal Knowledge' is not entitled to judicial protection under the First Amendment's umbrella, then future productions in this art form utilizing a sexual theme are destined to be obscenely soaked in the pornographic storm."

The alarm was heard. Authors, book, magazines and newspaper publishers, motion picture producers, directors, actors, theater owners, television companies, unions in the art industry, libraries and others expressed their determination to join in the battle to reverse the Jenkins conviction.

I was requested by the Motion Picture Association of America Inc. to represent Billy Jenkins. With his consent and that of his lawyers, I undertook to appeal and argue the case in the Supreme Court of the United States.

But first, that court's permission to appeal had to be obtained. It had refused to do so in some twenty obscenity cases, sending them back to the state courts to comply with the new standards of the recently decided *Miller* case. The Jenkins case had also preceded *Miller*, but we nevertheless filed a petition (*certiorari*, it is called) requesting the Supreme Court to hear our appeal. This was opposed by the State of Georgia.

The Supreme Court announced that our petition was granted. We were delighted to have passed the first hurdle. *Carnal Knowledge* would be the first case argued and reviewed by the Supreme Court since its *Miller* decision.

Intense preparation and brief writing began. Dozens of obscenity cases were dissected to derive every nuance. Articles on the confused law of pornography which had appeared in the law reviews of leading universities were analyzed for their errors as well as insights. Hundreds of pages of preparatory legal data were reviewed. Our briefs went through the critical process of more than a dozen lawyers, and their suggestions were weighed for acceptance or rejection.

Although only Tony H. Hight, counsel for the District Attorneys Association of Georgia, would argue for the State of Georgia, and I for Billy Jenkins, many briefs were filed by organizations not parties to the controversy but having a large stake in the outcome. These are called *amicus curiae* briefs, submitted "as friends of the court." It is a quaint phrase because one must obtain permission from the Court to be its "friends." The reality is that amicus curiae briefs are intended to aid one of the litigants. In this case, the Court granted petitions to listen to its "friends" on both sides. So briefs were filled by the Authors League of America, Inc.; the Directors Guild of America, Inc.; the National Association of Theater Owners; the American Publishers, Inc.; Magazine Publishers Association, Inc.; American Booksellers' Association, Inc.; the National Association of College Stores, Inc. All these supported Jenkins' position.

The State of Georgia was supported by only one friend-of-the-court brief, filed by Charles H. Keating, Jr. founder of Citizens for Decency Through Law. The plethora of briefs indicated to the Court the enormous concern in many quarters about the case.

Each of these briefs, as well as our own, had a different color for identification. They were like warning flags. The shades of opinions in them were as different as the covers.

One of my tasks was to cajole excellent counsel for these organizations to be consistent with our strategy in the case. Otherwise, as has not been unknown, your ally may do you more injury than your opponent. For example, the brilliant dissenters in the Georgia Supreme Court had lined up with the dissenters in *Miller*. They sounded an alarm of repression. They contended that the *Miller* majority was wrong. We welcomed the dissent of Judge Gunter in favor of Billy Jenkins, but should we too attack Chief Justice Burger and the majority which voted with him?

I thought this was wrong strategy. On principle as well as persuasive wisdom, we ought to agree with *Miller* that hard-core pornography should be ruled out. Our position ought to be that *Carnal Knowledge* was not hard core, and that the majority of that court ought to give emphatic warning that the true meaning of its decision could not be debased. Such a trumpet call denouncing those who stretched and distorted the *Miller* decision would dissuade district attorneys from instituting futile prosecutions. *Miller* needed a follow-up, not a chastisement. Such an approach would not antagonize the majority, and might even win over some judges on the minority side.

Also this would be consistent with the position of the leading motion picture producers, none of whom made or approved hard-core films.

Some of our *amicus curiae* friends were purists. They wished to see *Miller* destroyed. They wanted to point up its failure in the Jenkins case and to predict the inevitability of other repressions.

It took as much energy to unify our comrades as to prepare our own briefs. A lawyer, particulary when he deals with eminent co-counsel, whose talents and achievements warrant strong egos, must be a consummate diplomat.

What else must he be? He must be an archaeologist who exhumes evidence; a psychologist who strengthens his client and weakens his enemy; a paragon of patience to withstand the unreasonableness of troubled clients; a man of endurance to withstand the strain of the most arduous profession; an optimist in the darkest hours and a pessimist in the brightest, so that momentum doesn't slacken; a historian of the law so that he can better predict its future; an idealist in the service of justice and a practical man who may forgo litigation in his client's interest; a precisionist who must draft documents which defy ambiguity; a negotiator who makes deals not breaks them; an administrator who can recommend corporate efficiency and achieve it in his own office; a pleader whose eloquence is harnessed by sincerity; a scholar who is not confused by his learning; a lover of the law so that sacrifice for it becomes a selfish act; a visionary who uses legal tools to sculpt a better society; and a realist who knows that it is impossible to attain any of these except to a small degree but who never stops trying.

Well, many of these attributes were needed the night before the argument in the Supreme Court. Gathered in the huge living room of a suite in the Hay Adams Hotel in Washington were more than twenty lawyers and some executives to help prepare the argument for the morrow. I sat behind a desk with briefs and pads to make final notes, while around me swirled a brilliant coterie of experts unhesitant about their suggestions. Present were Jack Valenti, the president of the Motion Picture Association of America, Inc., who appeared before congressional committees frequently, to argue as well as to observe, and who sat with lawyers continually in the problems that beset his worldwide industry; who traveled in all directions of the compass whether to the Shah of Iran, the Soviet Union, South America, to the heads of state in Europe, with sufficient peripatetic zeal to qualify him to be Secretary of State; Sidney Schreiber, general attorney of the Association, who was a storehouse of motion picture law and lore; James Bouras on his staff; my law partners Gerald Phillips and Gerald Meyer, who had worked on the brief with me; Tench Coxe, Atlanta counsel and his associate, attorneys who had submitted *amicus curiae* briefs, and other executives and wives who wanted to share what might be a historic moment, and who looked to me like people who were not content to see the meal offered up but wanted to watch the chef as he prepared it.

To be helpful, everyone anticipated questions which the Court might put to me, so that we could review the proper answers and cite the appropriate authorities. Naturally, there were differences of opinion concerning the right reply, sometimes very vehement ones. I drank it all in, making up my own mind in silence. The exercise was useful because it paraded every conceivable attack which the judges, differing among themselves, might launch, but one could not decide what tack the answer should take by argument with a committee. That would be more wearing on my throat and energy than was advisable. As the clock hands stiffened at midnight, the group thinned out. Finally at about 2 A.M. only a few stalwarts were left. I packed my voluminous notes, knowing that if they had not been stored in my mind, they would be useless in the give and take of oral argument, and we retired.

The next morning, I had breakfast in bed, as always while reading a newspaper. This was not an ice-in-veins demonstration. I simply function better if I awake without shock of an alarm bell, and slowly recapture consciousness. Even if I have been up through the night working on a case, I eat breakfast leisurely, and deliberately read the morning news in the same way as when there is no anxious court engagement. It is a discipline helpful to me because it eases tension. Just as there is an erosion limit to listening, so there is an erosion limit to strain. The longer it is delayed, the more effective one is. When contrasted with the sleepless witness or his nerve-racked counsel, the advantage is enlarged.

This, of course, is not an equation applicable to judges, for they "don't know what side they are on," and their tension is of a different character. It is one of concern about true performance of duty. I recall a judge of the highest court of a state consulting me about his unbearable headaches. He felt it was due to his misgivings about decisions he had rendered. Doubt tormented him day and night.

"I have watched you in court, Lou; and observed your equanimity. How do you do it? Is it a born trait, or can you learn it? If I don't, I may have to resign from the bench. I simply can't stand it any more."

I told him that it was not an inherited characteristic at all. It was the result of persuading oneself (call it self-hypnosis if you wish) of the stupidity of a worrisome disposition.

Self-control comes from perspective. It can be trained like a muscle. It banishes fear and induces calm. Freud discovered that learning why we are neurotic is itself a catharsis which eliminates the neurosis. Similarly, learning that we exaggerate our fears eliminates them. I advised the learned Judge to render judgment on himself; to recognize that he was inducing migraine headaches by overblown fears about his decisions; that he was enervating his function as a judge, which required a steady, confident mind, by torturing himself into inefficiency, ill health, and resignation.

"You don't need advice from the outside," I said. "You are intelligent enough to give yourself a lecture and wise enough to accept it."

I do not know whether our talk was responsible or his headaches ran their course and stopped (doctors always claim credit for cures of coincidence, so why shouldn't lawyers?), but he became well and continued to serve on the bench with great distinction.

In this spirit of self-induced calm, I arrived in the Supreme Court. A lengthy line of visitors from many areas of the nation were waiting for admission to the two hundred seats. It would have been wise if the architects of the fairly recent courthouse had provided thrice that number. Like airports which become obsolete before they are finished, we underestimate people's interest in their government, particularly the Supreme Court. Many were turned away in disappointment.

Counsel who are scheduled to argue are led by attendants to front row desks on which are pads and inkwells with feather quill pens. This reminded me of the Congressional Room preserved in Philadelphia where the Constitution was enacted, and where stood similar desks and inkwells with quill pens. There is also on each desk a card indicating by squares the names of the judges as counsel faces the bench. This is about as necessary as the identification letter Lindbergh presented when he landed at Orly in Paris. More useful is an instruction of how to address the Court: "Mr. Chief Justice, may it please the Court." The Chief Justice acknowledges this greeting by nodding and greeting counsel by name. It is the first time the lawyer is sure that he is not speaking to the photograph in his office.

There is also instruction about the light signals on the podium, white to indicate that only three or five minutes are left in accordance with advance request to the Clerk, and the red light, which requires immediate completion of the sentence and withdrawal. Counsel is admonished not to inquire of the Court how much time is still available. Furthermore, time used to answer questions by the Court is not deductible. It is part of the argument and not deemed by the judges an intrusion of counsel, as he may feel. However, if the Chief Justice feels that the lively questioning by the justices may have been too pervasive, he will volunteer to counsel that a few more minutes are granted him. This is a matter of mercy on the part of the Chief Justice, although many a lawyer would be better off without his beneficence.

There was a low-keyed buzz in the room, which disappeared into frozen silence when a gavel descended loudly three times. There followed the deep somber voice of the clerk, "The justices of the Court."

The burgundy-red plush curtain behind the bench quivered and one by one the nine judges emerged to stand in front of their seats, the most recent appointees at the end, and the others according to their seniority on the bench nearer to center on both sides of the Chief Justice. The effect was not dissimilar to that which occurred when the lace curtains on the balcony window in Castel Gandolfo fluttered and the Pope in white satin splendor stepped forward.

The Clerk, his voice now stronger and tinged with emotion, announced, "Oyez! Oyez! Oyez! All persons having business before the honorable, the Supreme Court of the United States, are admonished to draw near and give their attention, for the Court is now sitting. God save the United States and this honorable court." This ceremonial opening did not help to release the voice of counsel, already locked in his throat.

Our case was called. I stepped up to the podium, which was equipped with a microphone and light gadgets. In the preliminary description of the case, I stressed that children under the age of eighteen had not been admitted to see *Carnal Knowledge,* and also that there was no "obstrusive exhibition to unwilling persons." This was to eliminate other problems which bedeviled consideration of pornography and to which I shall address myself later. I quickly isolated the issue and put it in the simplest form.

The *Miller* decision had expressed sensitive regard for First Amendment rights by clearly announcing that "hard-core pornography—*and only hard-core pornography*—may be suppressed." Would this Court now permit its decision "to be stretched and grievously misinterpreted so as to strike down a work of serious literary and artistic achievement, such as *Carnal Knowledge?*"

I attempted with economy of words to describe the apprehension which had swept through all the creative elements of our nation "from producers who fear to risk production; to theater owners who fear to exhibit on pain of criminal involvement; to book publishers who fear to print beyond the safe norm; to authors who fear to be innovative; and most important of all, the public which may be deprived of access to athletic diversity which flourishes best when the artist is not reined in and must conform to the lowest common denominator of safe presentation."

I spoke not only of *Carnal Knowledge* but of the visible and subtle encroachment—chiefly self-censorship—induced by uncertainty.

So very early in the argument our position was not critical of *Miller* or of the majority which had passed it, but rather a condemnation of the Georgia decision, which would have "a chilling, indeed a freezing effect on the First Amendment right of expression, unless the Supreme Court vigorously renounced that holding. I asked the Court to repeat and emphasize that hard-core pornography was "the sole exception to the protective shield of the First Amendment."

The motion picture print of *Carnal Knowledge* had been deposited with the Clerk and the Court would later view it—all but Justice Douglas, who believed that the Constitution protected even hard-core pornography from molestation and therefore saw no purpose in viewing the picture. But for the rest of the justices it was nevertheless necessary to summarize the film, so as to give meaning to my statement that "it is unthinkable that this picture should be confused with hard core pornography."

I gave a frank word picture of its contents.

"The film depicts the lives of two college students over a span of thirty years. They grow older, but they don't grow up. They are preoccupied with sex, but the picture isn't. It does not bombard the senses with erotica driving all other ideas out of the mind (which is characteristic of hard core pornography).

"The picture deals with the human predicament resulting from the enthronement of impersonal detachment, the inability to love, and the sequellae of cruelty and psychic illness.

"It is an artistic treatment of a problem which has beset this decade and has evoked many social and philosophical studies. It has been the subject of plays from Strindberg to Tennessee Williams."

I followed this thumbnail sketch with thumbnail quotations from the reviews. The New York *Times* called it "profound"; the *Saturday Review*, "mature," the Atlanta *Journal*, "One of the best films in a long time," and the Catholic *Film Newsletter*, despite some reservations, "a perceptive and brilliant put-down of a certain style." The many critics throughout the nation who shared these views couldn't all have been fantasizing.

I believe that every argument should be punctuated with a telling sentence which by its forcefulness becomes an exclamation point. Having concluded that the dominant effect of the film was of a sincere and earnest effort to create a literary and artistic work, the exclamation point was:

"To confuse this picture with pornographic imbecility is cultural illiteracy!"

I was going along swimmingly. The Court was attentively silent. Then it came. The Chief Justice unerringly put his finger on the most vulnerable spot in our armour.

Chief Justice Burger: "Mr. Nizer, we are dealing here with a jury's finding of obscenity. Hasn't it been recognized that the jury represents the conscience of the community? If so, do we not have to accept its judgment rather than impose our own?"

Mr. Nizer: "Mr. Chief Justice, I fervently believe in the jury system. I think jurors have seven senses, not five—they add horse and common. But there is a distinction between ordinary facts and what this Court has called constitutional facts.

"Here we are dealing with First Amendment rights which involve constitutional facts and this Court has stated that in such a case, the Supreme Court will reserve to itself independent review . . . If a jury decided that Michelangelo's statue of "David" would be obscene unless a fig leaf was used, this Court would be heard from.

"In short, your Honor, in the ordinary commercial world, we give special weight to the common sense of the jurors, but when we are dealing with the precious rights of the First Amendment and a constitutional question is involved, this Court should not hesitate to express its paternal care of the constitution which is exclusively vested in it."

I turned to another error in the Georgia decision. It assumed that just as one tests offensiveness by community standards, one can test literary value the same way. Here again was our friend, the "illusory syllogism." I argued that this wasn't so. Even if a majority of people in a community thought otherwise, Chaucer, Boccaccio, Rabelais, and Fielding still had literary value. The test was quality, not popularity. Then the exclamation point sentence:

"A literary work survives even the illiteracy of its reader."

Carnal Knowledge had literary value and therefore had the impregnable shelter of the First Amendment. Even if it hadn't, it did not meet the two other tests of pornography; its appeal was not to prurient interest, nor was it patently offensive. It was not designed to exploit sex for its own sake. The camera was almost always on the faces of the characters, not below. The camera angles were deliberately discreet, picturing the least, not the most, and avoiding explicitness. Sex was treated as a sometimes baffling and exasperating part of life, but without lewdness or lasciviousness.

MR. JUSTICE WHITE: "Mr. Nizer, assume that a work is pornographic, do you see any other inquiry that we are required to make under the Miller decision?

MR. NIZER: "If a work has literary, artistic, scientific or political value, it cannot be obscene no matter what else is in it. The Constitution protects it even if it offends the public, because the right of free expression is not limited to those who approve.

"Therefore, I would put it this way: that the inquiry ends when it is found that the work has literary or artistic value. It must enjoy the protection of the First Amendment.

"If the work has no literary or artistic value, then it still may not be obscene unless it has explicit sexual scenes which are patently offensive and appeal to prurient interest. So, in such a situation where there is no literary value, the inquiry doesn't end. We must still examine the other two tests which may make it obscene."

Soon, the argument lost its unilateral character, and became a question-and-answer period, if not indeed a debate. The transformation was caused by a geographical consideration. How large must the community be whose standard governs? Was it local, statewide, national?

Miller had rejected the national test because "our nation is simply too big and too diverse" to permit a standard for all fifty states in a single formulation. It accepted the state as an appropriate unit for determining the community standard. Even then, it held it would not be error if a local standard was applied.

Motion picture producers and book publishers were alarmed by this. They had to make a product for national distribution. How could they risk running the gamut of local prejudice? They couldn't make different versions to meet the views of various sections of the country. During the preceding evening's preparation, this question caused the longest and loudest differences. Some thought I should boldly argue for a national standard. Others replied heatedly that in view of the express language in *Miller* rejecting it, "You will have your head torn off if you try that." Others urged that I should attempt to sway the Court to rule out "local standards" and plump for a state standard. Still others contended that I should leave it alone. "It's too hot a potato." I resolved not to ask affirmatively for a national standard, but, if the opportunity arose, to test the waters. But no one had foreseen how the argument would develop.

When the argument reached this sensitive area, I attacked the "local standard" test of the Georgia decision. Did "local" mean county, city, or neighborhood? It was a void test because it was constitutionally vague.

Furthermore, there were 78,200 separate political subdivisions in the fifty states. There were almost 15,000 theaters and many more bookstores which were situated in areas which overlapped. There would be a crazy quilt of conflicting standards if the local standard was applied. This would put an intolerable burden on the dissemination of communication. It was not feasible to prepare different versions of books and films for different parts of each of the states.

This loosed a barrage from the Court.

MR. JUSTICE REHNQUIST: "Wouldn't you have the same problem if we decided that the state, not the local community, should be the geographic unit to determine community standard?"

MR. NIZER: "No, your Honor. There would be a decided difference in degree and that is very important in this matter because we are not dealing with absolutes. We must apply a rule of reason. A State is a natural sovereignty with well-recognized boundary lines. The confusion which would result from barring overlapping local areas would be avoided to a very large extent if the State were the required area."

MR. JUSTICE MARSHALL: "Would you have the rule of one state determine the rights of another State?"

MR. NIZER: "No, your Honor. I am talking about state statutes and each state would determine the community standards of the entire State in deciding what is patently offensive.

"Where there is a State statute isn't it more reasonable to insist upon a State standard, thus also avoiding the constitutional burdens of continuous query to this Court whether the varying fragmented hodgepodge of local areas constitutes a constitutionally viable standard?"

MR. JUSTICE STEWART: "Mr. Nizer, if we adopted a state standard and this Court upheld a decision by a state court holding the picture obscene, wouldn't the theaters in other states be just as much inhibited from playing the picture as you say they would be within the state if we upheld an obscenity decision of a local community?"

MR. NIZER: "Psychologically, the States are sufficiently jealous of their own sovereignty not to be overly impressed with a standard set by another state. But if the highest court in a state upholds a conviction in one of its localities, it is unlikely that other localities in the same state will test their own standards. They are more likely to consider the announcement of their highest court conclusive upon them.

"There are illustrations of this, your Honor. When "I Am Curious Yellow" was decided to be obscene in Maryland, other states nevertheless played the picture and many upheld it.

"We are dealing with imprecise factors, but the rule of reason would indicate greater safety for First Amendment rights if state standards are adopted."

MR. JUSTICE REHNQUIST: "But legally it would be no inhibition either upon the local community or on another state to make their own test, would there?"

MR. NIZER: "No, your Honor, that is why I used the word 'psychologically.' This Court said in the Freedman case that it is very easy for an exhibitor not to play a picture. The fact that the situation is imponderable does not give comfort to this Court, which is concerned with the free access to commerce and thought."

MR. JUSTICE STEWART: "Mr. Nizer, you recognize however, don't you, that it is more difficult for a jury to determine a community's standards for a State than it is for its own locality."

MR. NIZER: Mr. Justice Stewart, we leave to juries more difficult tasks than this every day in the courts. In a certain sense, the struggle of the jury to discover the State community standard causes it to avoid too narrow a view."

I felt that these questions by the justices had opened the door to a try for a national standard. Since it was supposd to be a forbidden subject, I trod softly. But despite the warnings the night before, an advocate must feel his way in the maze of argument. So continuing my answer to Mr. Justice Stewart, I said:

"Indeed, the question may arise why not a national standard? Your Honors have held that a national standard is inappropriate because our country is too big and diverse for such a standard. If this court would entertain any reconsideration of that holding, I would respectfully suggest three reflections:

1. There is a technological equalizer which reduces the national diversity. Television, the same columnists in different newspapers, national magazines like 'Time' and 'Newsweek', the ease of travel, have made for homogeneity.

2. Such diversity as survives is not much different from that which exists within a State.

3. And most important, the larger the circumference of geographical parameters, the less likely an infringement of First Amendment rights.

"After all, we are dealing with a national constitution, and national standards accepted in Federal Obscenity Statutes such as Customs, Interstate Transportation, Mailing, Broadcasting ought with the same ease be applied here."

There was no vocal reaction from the Court. My "head was not torn off" because I had dared to request a reconsideration in favor of national standard. However, silence was not agreement, as we shall see.

Then in two brief sentences, I sought to gain the next best result:

"Coming back to the need for at least a State standard, as against a local standard, I would point out that a Balkanized application of the Constitution would make impossible a uniform standard of criminal justice."

The white warning light flashed.

"Time no longer supports me and I must lean on our brief for due process deprivations which abound in this case.

"We request this Court to make doubly clear that only hard core pornography may be suppressed and that such works as "Carnal Knowledge" were not intended to be caught in the net of obscenity."

An angry red light told me I had one sentence left before retiring:

"Only thus can we preserve the Constitutional rights of free commerce in ideas; the right to communicate them and the right to receive them."

I sat down, removing my papers and water alongside the podium to make room for my adversary's equipment.

Mr. Hight, who argued for the State of Georgia, had the advantage or disadvantage, depending on the angle of prejudiced sight, of the Court's comments on the chief point he was about to argue. That was, that a jury had heard, and in this case seen, the evidence, and decided the case. That decision involved a fact. Was *Carnal Knowledge* obscene? No appellate court should interfere with factual findings of a jury. It would only review errors of law. He insisted that the jury's decision, upheld by the highest court of his state, was final. It should not be tampered with.

The Chief Justice had anticipated this contention by a question to me, perhaps only to explore this vital issue. Echoing still was the answer that constitutional considerations raise certain facts to a constitutional level which *would* be reviewed. As in flashbacks in motion pictures, I hoped the words would come back, that if a jury found that Michelangelo's statue of David was obscene because it lacked a fig leaf, the Supreme Court would not be precluded from reviewing such a decision. Professor Alexander Bickel of Yale University had once written that if a jury found the calf of a woman's leg obscene, the Supreme Court "would be heard from."

Mr. Hight also contended that the question of obscenity was not before the Court, because it had not been properly raised in the lower court. One of the judges disposed of this with asperity:

"Counsel, I see on one page of your brief the word obscenity five times."

Finally the impartial red light signaled him too that his argument time, if not his argument, had expired.

The next case was called. Clerks appeared behind the judges carrying new sets of briefs, and removing our multicolored ones on which some judges had written their notes. Hopeful counsel stepped up as we hurriedly gathered our papers and tiptoed out.

In an alcove outside the building were television cameras and Fred Graham of CBS. I declined to be interviewed. When a matter is pending before the Court, I do not consider it fair for either or both counsel to condition the public to his view. Only if the rule is violated by opposing counsel is it permissible to reply, in order not to be at a disadvantage. Also, outside I met Billy Jenkins for the first time. This also was strange. Usually counsel "lives" with his client for weeks, and sometimes months, in a legal struggle. Here the issue was abstract. Jenkins had become a mere symbol of a constitutional battle.

Two and a half months later, the Supreme Court's decision came down. It unanimously reversed the conviction and held that *Carnal Knowledge* was not obscene. The reasons for the reversal, however, still differed.

Justice Douglas reversed because he refused to recognize any limitation of free speech, including hard-core pornography.

Justice Brennan reversed because he agreed with Justice Douglas except that he would recognize the right of the Supreme Court to interfere where children were involved, or where "unconsenting adults" were subjected to "obtrusive exposure." Otherwise he rejected the doctrine of "Constitutional fact," which required the Court to review, case by case, every obscenity decision. He argued that this placed an undue "institutional stress upon the judiciary." Two other justices agreed with this view. They were Mr. Justice Stewart and Mr. Justice Marshall.

Five justices, Chief Justice Burger, White, Blackman, Powell and

Rehnquist reversed because they upheld *Miller,* and found *Carnal Knowledge* not obscene.

Mr. Justice Rehnquist wrote the opinion. He quoted the *Saturday Review*'s description of the picture, which he considered accurate:

Nicholson has been running through an average of a dozen women a year but has never managed to meet the right one, the one with the full bosom, the good legs, the properly rounded bottom.

This was hardly comstockian language. It reminded me of Federal Judge John Munro Woolsey's description of the Betty Boop doll which we claimed had been infringed. "She has the most self confident little breasts," he wrote. It must not be assumed, as some fighters for free speech do, that judges are old fogies, or, as in the case of Mr. Justice Rehnquist, young fogies.

In denying patent offensiveness, he pointed out that although there were "ultimate sexual acts" in the picture, the camera did not focus on the bodies of the actors at such times. "There is no exhibition whatever of the actors' genitals, lewd or otherwise. There are occasional scenes of nudity, but nudity alone is not enough to make material legally obscene under the *Miller* standards."

Writing for the majority of five, Mr. Justice Rehnquist rejected the argument that the jury verdict was not subject to review because it dealt with a question of fact which was final. There was no hedging. Juries have not "unbridled discretion" where First Amendment rights are involved. The Court embraced tightly the doctrine of "Constitutional facts," which require "the appellate courts to conduct an independent review." The Court substituted another illustration for my Michelangelo statue argument. It would not "uphold an obscenity conviction based upon a defendant's depiction of a woman with a bare midriff."

As to the "community standard," the Court said the jury had the right to consider the national, or state, or even local area. No geographic area had to be specified. The trial court had the right simply to instruct the jury to apply "community standards" without more. If a state legislature, as in *Miller,* prescribed a state standard, that was permissible.

Although at first blush this might appear indecisive, or an evasion of the national vs. state or local test, it actually gave the creative world much comfort. It really meant that, irrespective of what geographic standard was used, a finding of obscenity would be reviewed by the Supreme Court. It would not be deemed beyond its protective arm, even though it involved a fact decided by a jury. First Amendment rights had to be guarded. They were too precious to be precluded by a jury verdict.

The Court's over-all conclusion was sounded in resonant terms:

We hold that the film "Carnal Knowledge" could not, as a matter of constitutional law, be found to depict sexual conduct in a patently offensive way, and it is therefore not outside the protection of the First Amendment . . ."

It repeated the *Miller* admonition that "no one will be subject to prosecution . . . unless the materials . . . describe patently offensive hard core sexual conduct . . .

"We reverse the judgment of the Supreme Court of Georgia."

Before considering the effect of this discussion on the general problem of pornography which persists, I turn to a unique development in which the cultural industries sought to deal with permissiveness outside of the courts.

The motion picture industry was the first to do so. When Jack Valenti was installed as president, and I as general counsel of the Motion Picture Association of America, Inc., we encountered the changing tides of public tolerance. Gone was the Hays Code, which limited the number of seconds a kiss could be shown on the screen, the strict limitations of cleavage exhibition, the prohibition of words such as "virgin," which caused a denial of a Code license for the picture *The Moon Is Blue* and United Artist's withdrawal from the Association the insistence that all villains be punished, abolishing thereby the antihero.

Permissiveness was on the march. Yet as I look back, hardly the first tentative step had been taken. The first picture which confronted the new president was *Who's Afraid of Virginia Woolf?*, starring Elizabeth Taylor and Richard Burton. The dialogue was unprecedented. "Screw you," "frigging," "son-of-a bitch," "goddamn," and "hump the hostess," a game bitterly announced by the betrayed husband, assaulted our ears from a screen which had never before yielded to such verbal realism. Valenti and I were shocked. Would there not be a public revolt against excessiveness in motion pictures, particularly in the Bible Belt and Midwest.

Our reaction was not personal sensitivity. Valenti had been on Capitol Hill, where swearing was a grand tradition coming from Benjamin Franklin and the other founding fathers, and carried on by no less than Abraham Lincoln, Andrew Jackson, and our later Presidents. Legislators were not to be outdone by their historic ancestors.

As for myself, how could an active lawyer escape the bruises of foul language on all sides?

Our concern was censorship. To anyone dedicated to free speech, that word is anathema. It was one thing to have the courts deal with offensive material. There would be a trial, judicial review, and appeals. That was due process. But to have a private censorship board cut into the flesh of a book or picture was an atrocity.

So we concluded that self-restraint by our own companies was necessary; or censorship boards, goaded by religious organizations, would multiply like viruses in a conducive environment. Valenti felt that unless he asserted his captaincy at once, the ship would zigzag uncontrollably into rocky waters. At this time there was no rating system. A seal was issued by the MPAA or refused. If a picture was not granted a seal, many theaters might not wish to book it for fear of offending their patrons.

Warner Brothers was the producer of the film *Who's Afraid of Virginia Woolf?*, Jack Warner was a personal client. I would appeal to him in the larger interest of the industry's defense against censorship, to make some cuts. The picture would still remain powerful. The furious, drunken, hate-love quarrels between husband and wife would still be there. Warner, who disguised his large vision and pioneering achievements behind a clownish exterior, was not too difficult to convince. However, he felt that he could not undermine his general sales manager, Ben Kalmenson, and that we ought to have his consent too. When we met with him, he told us in choice four-letter words, which were part of his vocabulary even in friendly discussion, what we could do with ourselves. He was adamant. He raised technical problems of recalling all the prints out in the field, the alignment of the music track with the dialogue, all of which was not only costly but would delay bookings contracted for and submit his company to hundreds of suits. All this was punctuated with expletives which made us grateful for the few in the picture. Suppose Kalmenson had written the entire script? Indeed, judging by the dialogue in pictures released years later, maybe he was the disguised author of all of them. Valenti stood his ground. Warners agreed to delete "screw you" and "frigging" but not the other objectionable words pleading that it was impossible to reshoot the picture with fitting music track, contract violations, and all the rest. A seal was refused.

The procedures permitted an appeal. The Appellate Board was composed of producers, independent producers who were not members of the Association, and theater owners, who would have to take the brunt of criminal proccedings and were, therefore, highly sensitive. When they viewed the picture, they thought it was an artistic work of the highest order. It was based on a play by Edward Albee which had won the New York Drama Critics Award and played throughout the country. Warner offered to insert a clause in its contracts with theater owners prohibiting children under eighteen from attending.

The Appellate Board granted a seal on the express condition that this was not to be a general precedent which would apply to "a film of lesser quality . . . This exemption does not mean that the floodgates are open for language or other material. Indeed, exemption means precisely the opposite. We desire to allow excellence to be displayed and we insist that films, under whatever guise, which go beyond rational measures of community standards will *not* bear a seal of approval."

The picture played throughout the country and was an enormous success. No lightning flashed from distant territories to strike dead those responsible for the desecration of the screen. But the intended limitation could not be isolated. Other works had artistic merit too, and now they were condimented with audacious dialogue. The threshold of permissibility was lowered, or should I say raised to public acceptance. Perhaps the "floodgates" were not opened, but the trickle breached the dam, letting through an ever-broadening stream until it reached torrent proportions in which restraints on language were swept away.

This was not impeded by Supreme Court rulings, which gave special protection to use of words no matter how much they violated previous norms of public expression.

For example, in one case a writer with the implausible name of Kois wrote a "Sex Poem" giving a detailed account of his experience and sensations during intercourse. It was completely uninhibited, including vulgarisms which expressed passion's candor. His style was as affected as its content. The writing ran in vertical columns, like Chinese script, one word under the other, often repeated three or four times to simulate the rhythm of thrusting.

In 1971, he was indicted and convicted under a Wisconsin statute which forbade dissemination of "lewd, obscene or indecent written matter." He was sentenced to one year in jail and one thousand dollars fine. The highest court of Wisconsin upheld the conviction.

The Supreme Court of the United States reversed. It acknowledged that the poem was "an undisguisedly frank, play-by-play account of the author's recollection of sexual intercourse. But sex and obscenity are not synonymous." The Court thought that the poem had "some of the earmarks of an attempt at serious art" even though "the author's reach exceeded his grasp."

Still publishers and authors feared criminal prosecution under the various state statutes. They did not look forward to legal struggles which would require the Supreme Court to free them from jail.

When John O'Hara submitted his script of *A Rage to Live* to his publisher, Random House, in 1948 they were advised by their counsel that the bedroom description of the wedding night would subject the publisher and O'Hara to possible criminal charges under the New York statute. They cited cases. O'Hara was asked to eliminate some of the vivid detail. He refused. In desperation, Bennett Cerf, the president of Random House, turned to me. He thought that, as O'Hara's attorney, I might overcome his artist's principled stubbornness. After all, he urged, O'Hara didn't want to go to jail.

O'Hara sent me a mound of his typewritten yellow sheets of *A Rage to Live*. The wedding night was described in lyrical, erotic terms, which, like his other descriptions, whether of the silverware on the table, the furniture in the room, or the clothes of the characters, omitted not a single detail. This was one of his gifts. He saw and noted everything, so that trivia fitted into a mosaic which ultimately gave the reader a sense of presence and the very feel of the atmosphere. In the same way, the bed scene was so realistic that the reader almost felt every touch, heard every sigh and cry, and experienced the waves of passionate love that came from the pages. O'Hara was persuaded to eliminate some phrases, on the ground that his original script was selective too. He had not included everything that took place. Therefore, the issue was not really an artist's integrity, but rather the degree of selectivity. Perhaps a little more shading might enhance the effect and still satisfy the frightened publisher. As one can still see by reading the slightly cut published version, the intended impact remained. Actually, O'Hara, by economy of words, achieved the emotional effect which Ernest Hemingway (his greatest hero, whom he compared with Shakespeare) did in *The Sun Also Rises*: when the heroine says she must leave her lover for another man, he protests. She says:

"Do you still love me, Jake?"

"Yes," he said.

"Because I'm a goner," she said, "I'm mad about the Romero boy. I'm in love with him, I think."

"Don't do it."

"I can't stop things. Feel that?" Her hand was trembling. "I'm like that all through."

Still, in later years, before O'Hara had to give up drinking, when we sat at the bar of Dune Deck, near his Quogue home, we would laugh at the recollection of the furor about the bed scene in *A Rage to Live*, in view of what the current books contained.

Despite the liberal view of the courts toward "offensive" language, motion pictures were mass enertainment, and there were sufficient thousands, perhaps millions, who vocally resented it. The larger the audience, the greater the risk that it will encompass unsophisticates and prudes. Organizations of all kinds, often headed by church and social workers, put pressures on legislatures. Censorship boards grew by leaps and bounds. The board of one city or state would demand certain cuts, another would approve the same scenes but demand other cuts. The inconsistency and confusion of censorship standards wreaked havoc on the industry, not to speak of the expense of submitting films to each board, with all the attendant horrors of delay and bureaucratic application of imprecise moral standards.

The motion picture industry had, together with other art industries, fought censorship for many years. The new standard of permissiveness made this effort a losing one. At times we succeeded. In the United States Supreme Court I argued against the Dallas ordinance which was held to be too vague and therefore unconstitutional. We were sweeping back the ocean of oppressiveness with a broom. However, during the argument of this case, there was the usual exchange with the judges. One of them remarked that if the motion picture industry could protect children, the Court might have less difficulty in upholding works of daring content. This theory of a separate standard for children had been suggested by the Court in other cases. It was called the doctrine of variable obscenity.

Valenti decided to act upon it. He invited all elements of the industry to co-operate in setting up a rating board. No motion picture would be barred from being shown, no matter what its contents were. But a label would be put upon it, so that the public would know what to expect. The label was in the form of initials. "G" meant suitable for all. "GP" suitable but parental guidance suggested. "R" meant restricted, children under seventeen would not be admitted unless accompanied by adults. "X" meant that children would not be admitted under any circumstances. An enormous educational program was projected so that the public would understand the symbols. Theater owners volunteered to display these symbols at their box offices, and bar children when the symbols required.

Was this censorship? Of course not. Government-imposed restrictions of what we may see or hear is censorship. Self-imposed restraint in the interest of protecting children and guiding adults is not. If I am told I may not view a picture or read a book, I am censored. If I decide I would rather not see such a picture or read such a book, that is my privilege, not to be condemned. The rating code merely applied the old doctrine of *caveat emptor*, buyer beware, to motion pictures. It was a label on the bottle, "not suitable for children," or for adults who had prudish inclinations, but the bottle was not barred.

Nor was the rating an evaluation of quality. That was solely for the audience and critics to determine. The rating system was voluntary. A producer who chose not to submit his picture for rating did not have to do so. True, he might then encounter resistance from some theaters which desired to advise their patrons what an impartial rating board had considered was the nature of the picture. Walter Reade, Jr., a distributor of films and a chain theater-owner, did not believe in the rating system and ignored it. He remained a member in good standing in the theater association and his own pictures and others were exhibited. If there was any protest, it had to come from his patrons, who were deprived of information they might have thought helpful for their choice.

The public appreciated the classifications, which the rating system provided. Furthermore, the effectiveness of the rating system as an antidote to censorship can be judged by the fact that since 1968 not one of the many proposed censorship statutes passed any state legislature. Nor have the bills for classification (mimicking the industry's rating system) passed in any state except Rhode Island; and that has never been implemented.

We knew that sooner or later the legality of the Rating Code would be tested. There are always those who believe that no limitation of any kind of free expression, even to "protect" children, should be countenanced. They are purists and undoubtedly believe in their hearts that any compromise, no matter how modest or reasonable, destroys principle. It is to my mind another example of the "illusory syllogism"; free speech is good, therefore any exception, no matter how mild and morally pragmatic, violates it and must be fought. It does not matter that the shielding of children by voluntary action helped also to defeat censorship, the real enemy of free speech.

Soon the test came. It was made by the motion picture producer of Henry Miller's *Tropic of Cancer*. The book had been considered by many a classic and variously by the courts, when it sought entry into the United States. One court described it as "a kind of grotesque, unorthodox art form," and another, "a filthy, cynical, disgusting narrative of sordid amours." Now it had been brought to the screen.

Paramount Pictures had contracted to distribute it. When it was submitted to the Rating Code administration, it was designated "X." There was no doubt in Paramount's judgment or those of theater owners that children under sixteen ought not to be admitted to see the film. The language was Milleresque, that is to say, completely uninhibited. Nudity and fornication gave visual support to the words and vice versa. Scatology abounded, from vermin to turds. It was an adult picture if ever there was one. This did not mean that it was hard-core pornography. It was a serious description of Henry Miller's early days in

Paris, when he starved for food and sex, and gratified the latter more than the former. While Miller's experiences crackled in words, the visualization of them had a double impact. Some were harmlessly ingenuous. For example, behind the titles, one saw a beautiful fountain. As the camera focused to detail, the fountain turned out to be a bidet.

In 1970 the producing corporation sued Paramount and the Motion Picture Association of America, Inc., for having designated the picture "X," claiming that the Rating Code was an illegal group boycott and that the producers and exhibitors who participated in it were guilty of violating the antitrust laws. Treble damages were demanded. An injunction was sought in a Federal court. The battle to legitimize the Rating Code had begun.

I took the testimony under oath of the able producer and director of the film, Joseph Strick. In order to demonstrate the extremity of his position, I developed that he had objected to deletions which Paramount had made in the advertising trailers shown in theaters. In one scene, the character was about to make love to the girl depicted with nude breasts. Paramount deleted her comment, "Did I tell you I have the clap?" Similarly, he objected to the deletion from the trailer of "fuck you" and "hard-on." In another scene Miller was shown teaching a class of young children and he said, referring to a whale, "This noble beast has a penis two feet long." Paramount's deletion of this line was strenuously protested.

What made the producer's insistence in these matters bizarre was that some of these phrases were not in Miller's book. "They were dialogued in," the witness explained.

So, for example, Miller in the book had a "reverie" about animals, but the scene was transposed in the picture to a schoolroom and made the subject of an illustrated lecture.

I asked, "In the Henry Miller book, that reference to the whale and his prodigious qualification are a general reverie, but in your picture you inserted that line when he was talking to the children in the classroom, right?"

ANSWER: "I would say the young adults."
QUESTION: "Some look 10 and 12?"
ANSWER: "I would say 12 to 14."

. . .

QUESTION: "In other words, you felt that since Miller made a general comment, not even in Miller's Milleresque terms of four-letter words, but referring to the fact that when he taught children he didn't bar any subject . . . that you would use the dramatic license to fill in at that point something that he had mentioned in reverie about a huge penis of an animal and have him tell that to the children, that is what it amounts to, in a transposition?"

ANSWER: "In effect, yes."

. . .

QUESTION: ". . . it is a scene which by transposition is different from what Miller wrote about that particular whale?"

ANSWER: "That's correct, sir."

QUESTION: "And you do recognize that if I transposed words from one scene to another, I can change the content of the subject matter very easily, this is commonly done, isn't it?

ANSWER: "That is quite so, sir."

QUESTION: "And who was it that made the decision to transpose the reverie statement about the whale into the classroom, you?"

ANSWER: "Yes, sir."

The theory that the rating system was an illegal restraint of trade was false for two reasons: First, there was no restraint. No picture was barred. It was merely labeled. Second, not all restraints of trade are illegal. Only unreasonable ones are. Every contract restrains trade. It automatically limits the contracting parties' dealings with others. But that is not unreasonable. Also, there are beneficent combinations to hold fire drills, contribute to charity, or protect children from adult entertainment. These are not unreasonable restraints of trade, and therefore legal.

When the injunction application was argued before the Federal court, I pointed out that this principle had been upheld when Howard Hughes tested the right of the Motion Picture Association of America, Inc., to refuse a seal to his picture. The court upheld the right of the Association to maintain such a system in the public interest. It was a reasonable restraint of trade. This, of course, was more true of the rating system which did not bar pictures no matter what their content. Judge Morris Lasker candidly wrote that the objective of the rating system was to make possible the exhibition "of films dealing frankly with sexual matters, and at the same time wishing to avoid what they felt might constitute an onslaught of legislative censorship."

The Court denied a temporary injunction, adding for good measure that the plaintiff had not demonstrated a probability of success. The Judge also commented that the television networks' refusal to book the picture was due to its contents, not its rating. The rest of the opinion was so devastating that the suit was dropped "with prejudice," meaning it could not be reinstituted. The Rating Code had been legitimized and has been in effect every since.

So, the struggle for artistic freedom has fared well, even though it has suffered setbacks. Persistence and ingenuity have overcome the efforts of well-intentioned protectors of morals who would delimit expression because it was offensive to some. The same vigilance necessary to protect political liberty must also be exercised to protect artistic liberty. But this does not mean that the line between excessive (some won't recognize this word at all) permissiveness and freedom of expression has been accepted generally.

It is argued that morals can't be legislated. But we do. Adultery becomes a test for the dissolution of marriage. So does homosexuality or lesbianism. Even the refusal to bear children is a ground for annulment under certain circumstances. Also, we forbid exposure of genitals, fornication in public, or intercourse with animals. Indeed, moral considerations are the basis of all laws, from Sunday closings to child welfare. The real question is what quality of life and what kind of a society we prefer. Absolute freedom of expression was supposed to enhance social and intellectual progress. I fervently believed this. But now we find that it protects pornography, which blights entire neighborhoods, fills them with massage parlors, "adult" bookstores, "adult" movies, prostitutes, pimps, live sex acts, drug addicts, narcotic pushers, simulated homosexual rape, co-ed wrestlers engaging in sodomy, lewd magazines, all of which attracts mob control of a foul billion-dollar industry.

Even the contention that those who disapprove need not participate is no longer valid. The blazing neon signs, the advertisements, the handbills handed out on corners, the pervasive invasion of large areas such as famous theater or fine restaurant districts where audiences still wish to visit, make it impossible to escape the obscene pollution. The Supreme Court's denunciation of the intrusion of pornographic material on unconsenting families applies equally to the intrusion of physical presence in public streets of the pornographic plague. This is no isolated evil. From Times Square, New York, to the Barbary Coast in San Francisco, and almost every city, large and small in between, the infestation of smut has driven out decent enterprises, despoiled living conditions, increased crime, corrupted the law-enforcing authorities, and achieved an antisocial result. Where are we heading? If someone was willing to commit suicide on a stage, or if consenting adults agreed to fight to the death, should society be indifferent to the brutalizing entertainment? We forbid cockfighting and bearbaiting not only because of cruelty to animals, but because it debases us.

Must we, in the name of an abstract principle, close our eyes to the ugly view, and our noses to the stench? Or shall we, by modest interpretation, which declares that hard-core pornography is not protected by the First Amendment, or by zoning which isolates the evil to limited territory, sweep back the filth which inundates us?

I have observed previously that when logic leads me to a conclusion which offends my sense of rightness, I am alerted to re-examine the intellectual process for some unobserved flaw; to search for the illusory syllogism. The pornography question is such an instance. Intellectually, it is difficult to resist the contention that free expression must not be compromised, no matter what the consequence. Someday it can be argued that what we thought was offensive may turn out to be acceptable and even desirable. "One man's vulgarity is another man's lyric." Perhaps, it is contended, it will be proven that pornography provides a healthy sexual outlet and properly breaks down sexual taboos. Nevertheless, the reality is that today the injury to our society and the moral order which is essential to it (or else crime and anarchy will take over) justifies the Supreme Court's exclusion of hard-core pornography from constitutional protection. It is a reasonable limitation in the interest of a healthier social structure.

I believe that such a limitation will not affect the very broad area of free expression, sexual or otherwise. A work which has any literary, artistic, or scientific value will enter the "market place" of ideas, no matter what else it contains. By localizing our blows to hard-core pornography, we not only limit its antisocial impact, we protect freedom of speech generally from indiscriminate attacks. This is the real danger. Provocation begets countermeasures, which unintentionally injure liberty itself.

FOREIGN AGENT

A criminal case involved me with President Kennedy and Attorney General Robert Kennedy. It gave me insight to their characters and personalities from a rare vantage point. One of the fascinations of law is that almost every case radiates beyond its natural boundaries in the most unexpected ways. Such was the situation in the indictment of Igor Cassini, for failure to register as a foreign agent.

Cassini was a columnist for Hearst newspapers under the name of Cholly Knickerbocker. It was a newsy gossip column, with an unlimited range of social events, unsocial marriages, data of who was dating whom (expecting the reader to supply the appropriate inference) and who was just expecting (where no inference was necessary), inside revelations, called news if it was national, and intrigue if it was international, exploits of the jet set, a phrase Cholly had coined to denote speedy living, although bore set might have been more accurate, and much more, which Cholly would call "gutsy." The large circulation, which the column enjoyed, transformed its popularity into commercial value. But even though Cassini had a public relations firm called Martial and Company, there was no correlation between the names in the column and the clients of Martial. Ethical conduct has its rewards. When a crisis arose, I was able to demonstrate that fact to Bill Hearst, and maintain Cassini's position in the newspaper during the proceedings.

Igor, who was called Ghighi, was married to Charlene, the daughter of a prominent social family, the Wrightsmans. Joseph Kennedy and his clan (a favorite column description) were next estate neighbors of the Wrightsmans, and visited each other. John F. Kennedy had once dated the beautiful Charlene.

Joe Kennedy had been fond of Igor Cassini and his talented brother Oleg, and had become their adviser and intimate friend. Later, Oleg became the clothes designer for Jacqueline Kennedy when she became the first lady of the land.

Allen Dulles was the Wrightsmans' lawyer, and when Kennedy became President, he was made head of the CIA. The President, Igor Cassini, and Allen Dulles played golf at Palm Beach. One of Igor's friends was Porfirio Rubirosa, who had become an aid of Generalissimo Rafael Trujillo, the dictator of the Dominican Republic, and married his daughter. He had been ambassador from the Dominican Republic to Cuba, Belgium and held other important posts for that island. His diplomatic career was not so exacting that it prevented him from achieving a reputation as the leading playboy in the world.

One day, Igor recalled, Rubirosa confided in him that there was danger of a coup against Trujillo, and the seizure of the island by troops supported by the Communists. According to him, another Cuba was in the offing. The Cassini family, which had to flee Russia when the Communists took over, continued to be implacable enemies of its tyranny. They apparently had a sharpened sense of foreboding. Igor had denounced Castro as a Communist, before he was recognized as such by many who were taken in by his sweet, democratic intentions when he spoke in the United States. So when Igor was alerted by as close a source as Rubirosa that the Dominican Republic might turn Communist, he reported this to his friend Joseph Kennedy.

The White House took due note. It designated Robert Murphy, former ambassador and Under Secretary of State for Political Affairs under Eisenhower, to visit Trujillo, the dictator of that island, secretly and find out whether he would install certain democratic reforms, so that the United States might improve its relations with him. The implication was that if he would voluntarily curb his powers by permitting a free press and elections, President Kennedy could throw a protective arm around him. Was it not better for Trujillo to be an eagle with clipped wings rather than a dead bird?

The designation of Murphy for this task was natural and admirable. He was then an executive of Corning Glass, but he had once performed a heroic military mission which would not have been expected from a man in striped pants. During World War II, he had been landed in dark of night by submarine off the Normandy coast to meet the French underground chiefs in a deserted old house in preparation for the invasion. The Nazis had become suspicious, and sent a few soldiers to investigate the candlelit house on the shore. Murphy and the French leaders hid in a cellar, while the French family held off the investigators. Below they stood ready to shoot it out if the Nazis decided to make a search. Yes, movie scenarios are not always fiction.

Joseph Kennedy advised Igor Cassini that, in view of his close friendship with Rubirosa, the President wanted him to accompany Murphy. So it came about that a society columnist was designated on a confidential, international mission.

Murphy and Igor urged upon the dictator the admission of foreign correspondents and their right to file uncensored reports, as a beginning to his new role of elder statesman. They reported to President Kennedy that Trujillo was giving some thought to the matter of democratic reform since it would not affect the enormous wealth he had improperly accumulated. However, less than three months later, in May 1961, Trujillo was ambushed on a visit to his mother. He was assassinated by General Juan Tomás Díaz and his troops.

Two years before this, in 1959, Trujillo, probably on the recommendation of Rubirosa, had offered Igor's company, Martial and Company, a contract to render public relations services in the United States for the Dominican Republic. Igor was about to accept, but when, as always, he consulted Joseph Kennedy, he was advised to reject the offer. The reason was that Martial and Company represented a number of South American countries, and they might resent such a liaison. Igor had more to lose than gain by representing a country hostile to his other clients. He refused.

He so advised his attorney, Paul Englander. Their relationship was unique. Englander not only represented Igor and Oleg legally, he was their sponsor and intimate friend. He had their power of attorney to pay their bills, even household expenses. He was a wealthy man and lent them moneys. He was over seventy years of age and treated the Cassinis as if they were his sons. The relationship was one of complete trust. It was Englander who had suggested to Igor that he open a public relations company.

It was, therefore, natural for Igor to suggest that, rather than have another public relations firm inherit the $160,000 Dominican account, why didn't Englander take it? He did, organizing a corporation called Inter-American Company, hired several South American specialists, and registered the company and his manager as foreign agents.

Englander offered Igor a finder's fee, but he refused it. Englander had been his benefactor too long to modify a long overdue gesture of appreciation. However, Trujillo would not accept an unknown agency and Igor had to recommend Englander's new company to the dictator. In order to persuade him, Igor assured him on a letterhead of Martial and Company that the service would be excellent. He did not anticipate that a copy of his letter of recommendation would later be used by the FBI and prosecutor to claim that it was really Cassini's company which was the principal, and Englander's company was merely a blind. If Igor was the real owner, then it had been his duty to register Martial and himself as foreign agents. Since he did not do so, it was claimed he had violated the statute. The innocent color of events glows guiltily when subjected to a dark light from future developments.

To make things worse, after Trujillo had met the fate of tyrants, and democratic reforms were in the offing, Igor anticipated recognition of the new regime by the United States. This would enable him to accept a contract from the new government without conflict of interest with his other South American clients. So he arranged a contract with the new regime in the name of Englander's company to await the happy event. Then he would take over. Again he didn't register.

In 1962, Senator Fulbright's committee, incensed by "the sugar lobby," began an investigation of foreign agents and their reported payments to American officials. The matter had no relationship to the Cassini situation, but Martial and Company and Inter-American Company came under inquiry. Newspapermen saw an opportunity for an exposé. Bobby Kennedy, as Attorney General, was given data which seemed to implicate Cassini at least on the technical charge of not registering. Bobby was driven not only by duty, but by fear that if he did not act, it might appear that because of the Cassinis' friendship with the President and the Kennedy family, he was being treated favorably.

Joe Kennedy learned that Igor was under investigation. He called him to ask whether he had received money from the Dominican Republic while he was on the diplomatic mission with Murphy. Igor assured him that he had not received a cent.

Now Bobby was convinced Igor was lying, because he had evidence of moneys passing from Englander to Igor. These were part of the general loans from Englander to Igor which were repaid, but without explanation they seemed incriminating.

Bobby dispatched an army of FBI agents who swooped down on every employee of Inter-American and Martial, their bank accounts, and even Oleg's bank accounts, much to his embarrassment.

Word spread that the charges would soon be submitted to a grand jury, and Igor would be indicted. Failure to register as a foreign agent was a felony punishable by a long jail sentence.

Igor retained me to defend him. While my staff was digging into the facts and law, the grand jury indicted him on four counts. The press reported "the item" in sensational style, often featuring an old smiling photograph of Igor, as if he took the matter lightly. Actually he was distressed to the point of panic. He knew that the struggle would be destructive even if he won. He immediately offered his resignation from the Cholly Knickerbocker column to Dick Berlin, the head of the Hearst organization. William Randolph Hearst, Jr., who was married to Igor's second wife, "Bootsie," and Berlin refused to accept it. However, it was just a matter of time. He was suspended until he could be cleared.

His clients in the Martial Company began to melt away. How could a public relations company be effective in exploiting its good will and influence when it was under a cloud of a criminal charge itself?

The condition at home reflected the disaster. Charlene, too frail under any circumstances to withstand pressures, was particularly vulnerable at the time. She had sustained a fracture of her leg in a skiing incident. Before it healed, she fell and suffered a concussion. Her mother had died within twenty-four hours after an inconsequential quarrel with her. Her ski instructor and friend had committed suicide. She was taking psychiatric treatments.

Suddenly there was added to this pyramid of misfortune Igor's "disgrace," the cutting off of his earnings, her father's request that she and Igor not visit him when the Kennedys might drop in, and, worst of all, their son, Alexander, coming home from school in tears because children taunted him about his father.

I suggested that I talk to Charlene. Perhaps it would give her confidence and strength. I have found this a useful and often necessary legal "therapy" for a man who is in deep trouble. The suffering of his loved ones add to his distress and thereby increase their concern. A circle of anguish is set up, growing constantly as it feeds on mutual reactions. So I have frequently invited the wives and children of a client to visit me, and I spend hours analyzing the case fairly, and reducing their fears to proper perspective, and, whenever I can, expressing confidence in the outcome. It is especially interesting to observe the reaction of children, some of them in their teens, asking pertinent questions and registering relief because of better understanding. The circle of suffering is then reversed. Hope and an occasional smile light up the intense faces. One realizes then that it is the impact of the tragedy which must be overcome as much as the tragedy itself.

I arranged a dinner meeting at the Forum of the Twelve Caesars Restaurant for Charlene, Igor, Mildred, and myself. I did my utmost to assure Charlene that Igor would be completely vindicated. I should have been successful because I was absolutely certain of this, based upon the research we had by then completed. I shall describe the reasons below. But I watched Charlene's placidity (not to be confused with serenity), and I knew that while she smiled and was charming, nothing was reaching her. Her malaise was deep and rooted, and although her love for Igor made the instant crisis unbearable, its removal would not leave her in peace.

Later, Igor sent me a copy of Charlene's handwritten letter to the President. She apparently had decided to solve Igor's problem by direct action rather than through legal channels. She began the letter, "Dear Mr. President," but before she was through, she was calling him "Jack."

March 31, 1963

Dear Mr. President,

I have hesitated writing you before, but now I feel I must appeal to you. I don't know if you fully realize what have been the repercussions of Ghighi's indictment. Brushing aside the personal embarrassment it has caused our family—it has completely ruined us financially. Ghighi has not only lost his job at the newspaper, but his public relations company has completely disintegrated. And this just at a moment when there are staggering lawyers bills to meet. My father hasn't made a gesture to help us, and if it were not for Oli who lent money, Ghighi couldn't even have afforded a lawyer for his defense.

I tell you this simply because this alone should satisfy Bobby, who seems to be hell-bent in punishing Ghighi. I cannot tell you how surprised and shocked I have been by Bobby's harsh and punitive attitude. We always considered ourselves good friends of the Kennedys, and Ghighi still cannot understand why the son of a man whom he considered one of his closest friends for 17 years, and who so often advised him in all matters, should now be determined to bringing him down to total ruin.

I realize, of course, that Bobby as Attorney General has duties to perform that take precedence over his loyalty to friends. But my husband is not an arch-criminal, and whatever mistakes he may have made they don't warrant the kind of investigation he has been subjected to—with dozens of F.B.I. men scurrying around and harassing all his employees and friends for weeks, and all sorts of people, some who hardly knew Ghighi were called before the Grand Jury—the leaks to magazines and newspapers that have but already totally destroyed him, and finally the staggering preparations being made for the trial by the Justice Department. Frankly, I don't think the Justice Department could have acted with more vigor if the entire Communist Party had been involved!

It has come back to us directly that Bobby has stated that Ghighi and his co-defendant Paul Englander, are going to get the "full treatment", and that the Government is out for a win and that special counsel will be hired by the Government to prosecute this case. You would think that Ghighi was another Hoffa, or that he had conspired for the overthrowing of the United States Government. The reason for this massive retaliation, we have heard again and again from Bobby's friends is Ghighi lied to Bobby and, therefore, he should be punished.

Ghighi had no chance to lie to Bobby because he never talked to him. What happened is that one day Oli came back from Washington and told him to send a memorandum of his Dominican activities to Bobby.

In this memo, Ghighi explained his relationship to Englander and explained about the 1959–1960 contract that he had helped Englander secure. He omitted saying anything about the 1961 contract because that was well known to your father—in fact your father advised Ghighi and complimented him for the great assistance he had given Bob Murphy during that entire period—and Ghighi naturally believed that this was well known to you and Bobby. Besides, Ghighi was still under the impression that Bobby wanted to help him, and he didn't realize that this document was going to be turned over to a Grand Jury and used against him!

I have been told that you believe that Ghighi was offered a chance to come forth and tell his story but he refused. That is not so. Ghighi was told he could go before a Grand Jury, that had been convened expressly to indict him, and his lawyers did not permit him to do so, although he himself was most anxious to tell the whole truth.

I am not trying to say that Ghighi did not make some foolish mistakes. Evidently he did, otherwise he wouldn't be in the trouble he's in now. Certainly he surrounded himself with people who later betrayed him in order to cover their own guilt. And the Government gave these people immunity in order to indict Ghighi.

But no matter how you look at it, Ghighi's mistakes do not warrant such punitive measures. He has registered for other Governments, and if Dean Acheson can be an agent for Communist Poland, and Franklin D. Roosevelt, Jr. could be an agent for Trujillo, Ghighi would have done so had he been so told or advised. Instead he was made to understand it was not necessary. That is the crime he's accused of.

If you think it is advisable, I will be glad to go and speak to the Attorney General and appeal to him directly, for evidently he had taken this as a personal matter. I know it is up to the Government to take either a harsh or lenient attitude. Therefore, it's entirely up to the discretion of you and Bobby to what extent you want to go against Ghighi.

I hope, Jack, that you will not resent my writing you this letter. We've been friends for so many years, and in this terrible moment in which our family needs help, I appeal to you.

Sincerely,
Charlene

The President was moved by this letter. I received word that he wanted to see me. He was warm and gracious.

He quickly told me that, of course, he would not interfere with the Attorney General's duty to enforce the law. But that formal statement having been made, he showed his deep feeling for the Cassinis' plight. He wanted to know what my view was of the case. As briefly as possible, I told him that Igor and his company had previously registered when they represented Brazil and Italy. There was, therefore, no reason why he would not register again, had he undertaken the representation of the Dominican Republic. Due to a conflict of interest, he did not accept the Dominican offer, and had turned it over to Englander and his company, Inter-American, which had registered.

I knew Robert Murphy, and had recently talked to him, and he would assure the President that Igor had been helpful and loyal in his mission. Allen Dulles would do so too. It was a matter of discretion whether Bobby should have sought indictment in such a technical matter. No prosecutor can act on all the violations brought to his office. He must choose those cases for prosecution which will best serve the public interest. I could not understand why there had been such concentration on a matter of such little consequence and, in my opinion, which could not be won by the Government.

"You don't think the Government has a good case?" he asked.

"No, Mr. President, there isn't a jury in the world which will convict under these circumstances, with Murphy, Dulles, Rubirosa, and others testifying for Ghighi. However, in the meantime, Charlene and Ghighi have already been punished as if a serious crime was involved."

He suggested that I should see the Attorney General and have a talk with him. I, of course, agreed to do so.

I had a psychological block about John F. Kennedy. I never really believed he was President. I thought of him as a young, handsome Hollywood star who was playing the role, like Jimmy Stewart being a senator in his early pictures. This impression continued as I saw him behind Franklin D. Roosevelt's and Dwight Eisenhower's desk in the White House. His blue eyes, abundant hair giving off red tints from the bright light, his large white smile which searchlighted his face long before Jimmy Carter tried it, and his surprising height and slimness when he arose, all added to my illusion that he was too young and handsome to be President.

But his Lincolnesque compassion during our talk brought me back to the reality of his position. In the midst of all the problems which fill the President's office, it was obvious that he was suffering for Charlene and Igor and was trying to correct an overzealous attack upon them.

The very next day, I received a call from the office of the Attorney General to come to see him. An immediate appointment was arranged.

The physical layout of that office is more impressive than even the President's. Whoever originally constructed it wanted to express the majesty of the law more earnestly than those who built the Supreme Court building. A large anteroom leads into an office so enormous that couches and stuffed chairs galore abound to avoid the embarrassment of size. The architects must have envisioned that no one less than basketball center size would ever hold the post.

So when one entered and found the small figure of Robert Kennedy almost blocked out of view by the high desk except for the feet perched on it, coatless, sleeves rolled above his elbows, tie hanging inches below an opened collar, and an unruly lock of hair over his forehead, the incongruity of the office and the occupant was plain. President Carter was not the first to install informality in Washington.

He greeted me as a friend without reservation. He was interrupted during our talk by a telephone call. "Check whether they'll have lights on tonight," he said. Then, "Louis, do you want to go ice skating with us tonight?" I declined with thanks, curbing my impulse to make a smart comment about skating on thin ice.

When we turned in earnest to the case, his demeanor changed to sheer ugliness. He cussed and denounced Igor and I had to retort sharply that the facts did not warrant his anger. The most charitable view I could take of his personal venom was that he resented the Kennedys being drawn into the matter. He must have known that his father was responsible in the first instance for Igor's designation to the diplomatic mission. Also, the President must have told him how concerned he was about Charlene if not Igor. On the other hand, a Senate investigation and newspaper stories compelled him to act. At one point, he expressed his frustration when he yelled, "Do you think I like this? Do you think the President should be bothered with this? It's a pain in the ass!"

He was getting angrier by the minute. I thought I read his fears, and assured him with utmost sincerity that I would try the case on the merits. No extraneous references to the family friendship would be mentioned. He could hardly hide a look of relief on his face.

In the less bitter atmosphere, I struck hard with the most persuasive argument which can be made to any prosecutor. "You can't win this case," I said, and developed some of the reasons. There were two objectives in the Registration Act: one to ensnare spies or informers for hostile governments; the other to register any representative for friendly governments. The statute should never have confused the two. It ought to be redrawn. In Igor's case, we were dealing with a technical requirement of an innocent service. Almost every large law firm in Washington was registered as a "foreign agent." Igor had done so when he sought publicity for other governments. At worst, his failure to do so for the Dominican Republic was an innocent oversight, even if the Government was right that he should have registered. I told him why, in our opinion, he was not obliged to register at all. After reviewing the law, I said:

I have not come here with hat in hand asking for a favor. I am here because the President asked me to see you. If you feel you cannot drop this matter, very well, we'll try it.

As the discussion continued, I could not help but remind him that the Government had lost an infinitely stronger case against Roy Fruehauf of the Fruehauf Trailer Company, who gave a huge loan to Dave Beck of the Teamsters Union. But because Fruehauf's moral position was sound, he not having received a single benefit in his labor contract, the jury acquitted him. That decision had come down only a short time before, and I knew Bobby's deep disappointment. I reminded him that I had to try that case under the handicap of having Dave Beck, the predecessor of Jimmy Hoffa, brought into the courtroom daily from prison, where he was serving a sentence for another crime. How in the world could the Government prosecutor expect to prove Igor guilty beyond a reasonable doubt on the hocus-pocus technicality with which he was being charged?

Bobby would not yield. He had to do his duty. Igor was not worth consideration. He had lied to him. He would think about it, which meant to me that he would report to the President, but I sensed it would be a negative recommendation.

The contrast between the two brothers was startling. Jack had responded with heart. Bobby with bile. Both were honorable, but feelings are part of honor. Even a judge who does not leaven his interpretation of the law with considerations of human frailties becomes an automaton. Heartlessness is not an essential ingredient of judicial or executive objectivity. A great official or judge must first be a noble man, and there can be no nobility without compassion.

The great crisis was still to come.

I had urged Igor to continue his social activities as if nothing had happened. Psychologically, the withdrawal of a man under charges calls attention to his plight and gives the impression that he is immobilized because he is weighted with guilt. So Igor put on a smiling face and continued the rounds and parties, which were part of his professional life. Charlene, however, was not strong enough to engage in charades. I observed this the evening we met for dinner. She smiled, but her eyes remained sad.

On April 8, 1963, the Cassinis were to attend a birthday party. Charlene begged off, as she had on other occasions, but insisted that Igor should go. She had a better excuse than usual. It was Academy Award night on television. She and their fourteen-year-old daughter, Marina, preferred to have the Hollywood party visit them in their bedroom than venture out. Igor yielded. Later he telephoned just to be sure everything was all right.

After Marina's nurse had retired, Charlene sent Marina to the drugstore to fill a prescription. The nurse had been under instructions not to do so, but the child obeyed. When she returned with the bottle,

Charlene went into the bathroom. After a long while, she emerged and lay back again in bed. Her gasps alerted the child. She could not waken her mother, and called the doctor in alarm. He summoned an ambulance and dashed to the house, arriving almost simultaneously with Igor's return. An empty bottle which had contained thirty sleeping pills left no mystery as to the cause of her unconsciousness.

Through the night the customary emergency treatments were applied, and she responded well to them. In the morning, the doctors who were reporting the gradual progress to Igor appeared again. It was a final report. Her heart had given out. Charlene was dead.

If only we could have as true a perspective of human struggle as death imposes on us. How puny and unnecessary the strife over a technical registration seemed when beautiful Charlene, thirty-eight years old, did away with herself.

The shock reached into the White House. I received another call to visit the Attorney General. But now I was to receive another kind of shock.

After my first meeting with Bobby, I had reported to Igor on my private telephone. I had explained the President's sympathetic reaction and Bobby's stubbornness. He exploded. Between stuttering expletives, he threatened to tear the robe of respectability from Bobby, and proceeded to give me a bill of particulars. I interrupted him. I knew that his outburst was to relieve the pressure within him, like the primal scream healers advise. It was not a serious program of retaliation. Nevertheless, I told him firmly that his idea was unthinkable, and that if he really meant it, he would have to get another lawyer. "We will win this case on the merits," I assured him, and added that I understood his resentment. He quieted down and we discussed the hiring of accountants to analyze Englander's accounts with him and Oleg and other preparations for the trial.

When I visited Bobby after Charlene's suicide, I had expected that tragedy to be the opening fulcrum for our discussion. I was, therefore, taken back when instead he launched a bitter attack on Igor.

"Now you have found out," he said, "that your client is a blackmailer at heart." He combined this condemnation with praise for my rectitude in curbing him. It was clear that my telephone talk with Igor had been tapped. I was stunned by this violation of law by the Attorney General in the course of trying to prove a violation by Igor. I grew more sullen when his reference to Charlene was merely another jumping-off place for his berating Igor. I had to curb my impulse to tell him just what I thought of his tactics and venom. But always in such moments, the lawyer's thoughts must be of his client. I would injure Igor if I "broke" with Bobby. A lawyer can afford to be emotional on behalf of his client, but not to his injury.

Also, the President was behind these appointments. I could not expect him to continue his benign influence if I defied his brother. So I suffered in silence. He must have observed my mood, because he changed his tone abruptly. He suggested that he would set up an appointment for me with Assistant Attorney General Nicholas Katzenbach, to determine whether the case could be resolved without trial.

Katzenbach was summoned. Bobby said, "See if you can get together with Nizer and straighten out the Cassini matter." I arranged to meet with Katzenbach and Kevin T. Maroney, the Government attorney in charge of the case, at Katzenbach's home. I had permission to bring my Washington law partner, Lawrence Lesser, with me. We met at eight-thirty in his living room in front of an active fireplace and talked until midnight.

Katzenbach's and Maroney's integrity and fairness warranted letting down my guard. I virtually tried the case before them, revealing factual and legal points which ordinarily a defense advocate would not present to a prosecutor.

There is a saying in law that one should go "for the jugular." This ugly phrase, suitable for military warfare, is an unhappy allusion in law, where the objective is justice, not death to the enemy. Nevertheless, the principle is sound that if an argument which is the basis of other contentions can be destroyed, the whole case collapses.

I began with such a legal argument. The Government assumed that it was Igor's duty to register. I surprised its counsel by arguing that under the statute Igor was exempted from registering. Why? Because the statute said that it was not necessary to do so if the foreign country is deemed by the President "vital to the defense of the United States." I contended that the Dominican Republic met this test. In 1936, the Buenos Aires conferences had established the principle of hemispheric solidarity. In 1940, the Act of Habana provided that an aggression against one American state should be considered an aggression against all.

When the bombardment of Pearl Harbor catapulted the United States into World War II, the Dominican Republic, faithful to its commitment, declared war on the Axis powers, and became an ally of the United States.

Furthermore, whether the President "deems" a country vital to our defense may be determined by whether he enters into defense treaties with it. My research showed that on January 1, 1962, there existed 139 bilateral and multilateral treaties between the United States and the Dominican Republic. They covered such defense matters as atomic energy, the Atlantic Charter, GATT (General Agreement on Tariff and Trade), the Organization of American States, and one actually called "Defense."

I pointed out to Katzenbach, and he agreed, that it was not a violation to represent a foreign country. The only wrong was not to register. But the Dominican Republic was one of the exceptions which did not require registration. I predicted that the indictment would be dismissed.

Sometimes the legal escape route is like a thin string which is too feeble to hold a man, but if it is attached to a thicker and thicker cord, ultimately a defendant can climb out of his dilemma on a sturdy rope.

There was a continuation of the logical cord which lent strength to the argument. Suppose it was contended that the Dominican Republic, being a dictatorship and for other reasons, was not a country vital to our defense, despite its proximity and strategic position. Who would decide whether it was or not? The statute made the test subjective. It was what the President, and only the President, thought that counted. The language is, "If the President deems the defense of the foreign country vital to the defense of the United States . . ."

How could a citizen find out whether the President "deems" it so or not? There was no declaration to which anyone could point. The President's intention did not appear in the Federal Register, where sometimes similar matters are recorded. A citizen would, therefore, not be sure whether he had to register or not. He would have to guess. Such vagueness in a statute made it unconstitutional. Katzenbach and Maroney were familiar with Supreme Court decisions which had so decided.

Under our law, no person may be put to the risk of interpreting an ambiguous statute and find himself guilty of a crime if he guessed wrong. That would be entrapment. Criminal laws must be clear and precise so that an ordinary citizen would know what he may or may not do. If they are vague they are held to be unconstitutional. So, for example, a statute which forbade the carrying of a three-inch knife was held not to apply to a three-inch razor. If the legislature intended to include razors, it should have said so. A citizen should not have to guess or interpret on pain of committing a criminal act. Similarly, a statute against pornographic "writings" was held not to include a private pornographic letter. An indictment against the letter writer was dismissed. True, a letter is a "writing," but if the legislature intended to bar private communications, it could have said so explicitly. We do not slap people into jail if the prohibited conduct is not clearly expressed.

How was Igor to know whether the President "deems" ("Notice the present tense," I said) the Dominican Republic vital to our defense? If he guessed it was, he did not have to register. The statute was too vague to be the basis of a criminal charge.

I cited Italy as an illustration. In 1942, it was an ally of Hitler and at war with us. In 1944, Italy made peace with the United States and became our ally. Surely a President would "deem" Italy differently in those years. Suppose, as has been feared, Italy became a Communist country. Again, the President would "deem" it differently in making this test. The need for current reappraisal made the statute even vaguer. One could not guide himself by the past attitude of the President, even if it had been recorded, for example, in the Congressional Record, which it was not.

Katzenbach suggested that Cassini should have resolved the doubt by registering. But the law placed no such burden on the citizen. The Government would have to prove "beyond a reasonable doubt" that he had violated the law, not that he could have avoided the problem by doing what he was not obliged to do.

At one point, Maroney asked whether I had copies of all the letters Igor had sent. The inference was that there was an incriminating one, and I suggested that in the spirit of mutual revelation, he show it to me, rather than hoard it for a day which might never come. He looked at Katzenbach, whose impassivity was consent and pulled out a huge folder. He turned to a letter dated April 27, 1961, signed by Igor and addressed to "His Excellency and the Dominican Republic," in which he urged the acceptance of Englander's Inter-American Company for public relations services. Maroney stressed the word "we" in the letter to indicate that Cassini was really the principal and, therefore, evidence that the moneys derived from the contract were coming to him and his Martial Corporation.

It was easy to demolish this contention. The accountants' records which I submitted to him showed that Cassini did not receive one cent from the Dominican Republic account directly or through his company. He had even refused a finder's fee from Englander.

True, there were checks from Englander's special account to both Igor and Oleg, but these followed the same pattern which had existed from 1947, fourteen years before the Dominican contract. Igor and Oleg had given all earnings to Englander, who invested for them. He sent them checks for their needs. When they were short of funds, Englander lent them moneys, and repaid himself when there was a surplus. It was an unusual lifetime, paternal relationship. However, the checks from Englander to Igor and Oleg had no relationship to the Dominican matter. The amounts were the same as previously and their innocent purpose had been identified by an accountant's study. Katzenbach freely admitted that this showing was impressive and might well undermine the Government's theory.

Besides, I asked him not to forget that the issue was not whether Igor received moneys from the Dominican contract, but whether he had a duty to register. The legal point, that he did not have to do so, superseded any factual argument. The Government might seek to color its claim at the trial with irrelevant money considerations. "If color was going to be the order of the day," I said, "let us not overlook Igor's two battle stars, for his services in the war and his and Oleg's impeccable record."

After midnight we left. Katzenbach and Maroney were to report to the Attorney General and we would hear.

It was too late to return to New York. I stopped at the Mayfair overnight and called Igor to report the developments. Before meeting with Katzenbach, I had told Igor at dinner that his phone had previously been tapped, and cautioned him to keep his feelings to himself lest what he said in anger might again be misunderstood. So after my midnight report, he remained eloquently silent.

Having thus tried the case before a jury composed of prosecutors didn't mean that we could sit back and await their verdict. There was a real jury verdict still to be won. We continued our preparation for trial.

Although Trujillo had disappeared in a flash of bullets, there was one knowledgeable link to him still available to us. It was Porfirio Rubirosa, his former son-in-law and for thirty years an ambassador for the Dominican Republic. I wanted vital testimony from him. He was a friend of Igor, but would he come forth in his hour of need? Rubirosa was a traveler and not easy to track down, but we found him, of all places, at Frank Sinatra's home in Palm Springs, California.

I called Sinatra, who had retained me several times to protect his ex-wife, and others—typical of his expansive friendship. He was pleased to invite me for the weekend, but cautioned me to bring my golf clothes. His home was on the fairway, in this case, a sign of new preoccupation, like the tennis or golf novice who is outfitted with the finest equipment. Naturally, specially crafted clubs and a "limousine" golf cart would not be enough for Sinatra learning the game. A home on the course was indicated.

Rubirosa was heavily built but trim. He was a two-goal polo player and moved with ease and grace. The sun had emphasized his swarthiness and given it a glow. He exuded vitality. A quick snack ushered the three of us right onto the golf course. The legal work could wait. Rubirosa, poor man, thought he could transfer his athletic skill to golf. If he could hit a speeding ball with a mallet while riding full speed on a pony, plunging against other ponies, how ridiculously easy it would be to strike a stationary ball from a standing position, while no one harassed him. He couldn't believe it when he failed to make contact at all, swinging right over the mocking ball (Sam Goldwyn used to explain that his home course was two inches higher than the one he was playing on). Soon he was jumping up and down and screaming in exasperation. It was quite a picture of the glamorous playboy, former husband of Danielle Darrieux, Doris Duke, and Barbara Hutton, squealing and carrying on like a petulant child.

When the nine holes with the two great lovers were finished (something I thought would never happen, what with balls finding their way into forests and lakes and everywhere else than on the green), we proceeded to the magnificent nineteenth hole, which Sinatra called home. Finally, we got down to the purpose of my visit.

Rubirosa's recollection of events was a complete refutation of the Government's case. I wrote out his statement and he signed it unhesitatingly. After explaining that he had made many visits to the United States over a period of ten years and would have knowledge of any arrangements or contracts between the Dominican Republic and any public relations firm or individual through the period of 1959 to 1961, he asserted:

To my knowledge, neither Messrs. Igor Cassini nor Martial Corporation, directly or indirectly represented the Dominican Republic in the United States or elsewhere. I can also state that to my knowledge neither Igor Cassini nor Martial Corporation directly or indirectly received any money or other compensation from the Dominican Republic for any representation or for any other service whatsoever.

It was part of Rubirosa's duties to be familiar with efforts to improve the image of his country in the United States. He was, therefore, able to say:

I know that Igor Cassini recommended Mr. Englander's firm, Inter-American, as the representative for the Dominican Republic; that a contract was made between the Dominican Republic and Mr. Englander's firm for one year; and that later when Cassini recommended a renewal of this contract, such renewal was not made.

His final paragraph would have served as an excellent summation to a jury:

I can sum it all up this way: that to my knowledge, Mr. Igor Cassini and his company (Martial) never represented the Dominican Republic in the United States, or performed services for the Dominican Republic, or received any compensation from the Dominican Republic.

How could the prosecutor overcome such testimony from the only other party to the claimed contract with Igor? Also, Rubirosa was well and favorably known to Bobby and the President. He and his wife, the beautiful French actress Odile Rodin, had been guests at the White House on more than one occasion. His diplomatic standing qualified him, and his playboy reputation apparently didn't disqualify him. Who knows, perhaps it made him more attractive and adventurous to the Kennedys.

To think how star crossed they all were, the President and Bobby assassinated, and Rubirosa killed in a car crash shortly thereafter.

When I reviewed our preparation, I knew that our confidence in winning was justified both on the facts and the law. More important, I believed the prosecutor knew it too. The problem was how he could retreat. If he dismissed the indictment, would it not appear that Igor's and Oleg's friendship with Joe Kennedy, the President, Jackie, and Bobby was responsible? In politics and law, appearance can be as deadly as reality. I knew we were all trapped by the very friendship which should have assisted us. We would have to go through with a trial.

I was wrong. The President, Bobby, and Katzenbach came up with an idea. The prosecutor would drop three counts of the indictment and press only one, the technical charge of failing to register. Igor would plead *nolo contendere*, which meant that he would stand mute. He would not plead guilty or not guilty; he would simply remain silent. He would not contest the charge. The prosecutor would not request a jail sentence. Under such circumstances, the chances for a mere fine were overwhelming. That is how the whole matter would be resolved.

It was now up to us to decide whether to accept this offer and change the "not guilty" plea to *nolo contendere*. It was an agonizing decision. Igor, Oleg, and we as counsel weighed the advantages and disadvantages of the plan. The most serious negative aspect was that *nolo contendere* was equivalent in law to a plea of guilty insofar as the Judge's power to sentence was concerned. I did not want to alarm Igor, but I had in mind a case in the Midwest in which the president of a corporation pleaded guilty to a criminal charge of violating the antitrust law. He did so on the express promise of the prosecutor that no prison sentence would be imposed and that the prosecutor would recommend only a fine to the Judge. The prosecutor lived up to his promise, but the Judge disagreed, and sentenced the defendant to five years in jail. The defendant fell dead at the counsel table.

I had related this lurid story to Bobby, but was assured that such rejection by the Judge was extraordinary and would not reoccur, especially on the limited charge which would be asserted in our case. More important, the President felt the same way.

Another objection to *nolo contendere* was that it deprived Igor of full vindication. True, it was less offensive than a plea of "guilty," although even if the plan required such a plea, it would be worthy of consideration.

There were a number of arguments in favor of accepting the plea of *nolo contendere*. Such a plea, when accepted by the prosecutor, was, as Attorney General Herbert Brownell once said, "an admission by the Government that it has only a technical case at most and that the whole proceeding was just a fiasco."

Also by withdrawing the three more serious counts in the indictment, the Government eliminated the risk, no matter how infinitesimal, of a maximum penalty of twenty years in jail. Newspapers always liked to give importance to a story by asserting the top figure of incarceration if found guilty. They would be deprived of an impressive number.

The acceptance of a *nolo contendere* plea would avoid a long and costly trial, and above all emotional exhaustion. One who has not experienced the tension of facing a trial, or been sufficiently involved with the participants, either as counsel or family, cannot feel the nerve-tearing strain involved. The witness knows he will be questioned endlessly by friend and foe. Can he hope to be letter perfect in his recollections? Will he with one slip of the tongue destroy the case on which so much depends?

Having dealt with actors, I am aware of their desperate fear of blotting out on their memorized lines. Even those who can hold an audience enthralled with confident declaimer become nervous wrecks if asked to speak impromptu at a luncheon. Think then of the witness who cannot seek the shelter of well-memorized fiction but must hold his own against a cunning cross-examiner hurling questions at him in rapid succession to disorganize his defenses. The risk of making a fool of himself in the presence of an audience is as frightening as losing the case itself. Even the lowliest of us doesn't want to be marked stupid. Notice how often the ignorant protest, "Do you think I'm an idiot?" Fortunately they are spared a frank answer.

Since a confused answer may send a defendant in a criminal case to jail, his fear grows, further disorganizing his thought processes, and increasing the percentage of error which he is struggling to reduce. Thus is set up a circle of confidence erosion. The more one considers the hazards, the more they are likely to occur.

Being aware of this, I do everything possible to overcome the distress which I know is building in the witness. First there is thorough, thorough preparation. Every letter, every document, every date, every conversation and act is patiently reviewed, over and over again, until the witness has relived the past so often that it has become the present. Then I drill him in cross-examination. After he has withstood the bolts from my merciless questioning, he feels more competent to deal with the attack of an opposing lawyer, which often turns out milder than what he has experienced with me. This mental device is not dissimilar to the physical one of swinging a heavy club, so that a normal one will feel light. Finally, I assure him that even if he slips, it will not be fatal. There is redirect examination, which can rehabilitate him.

Nevertheless, despite all this, I know that as the day of battle approaches, he sleeps fitfully, eats mechanically, and worries continually. Yet he must be driven to approach witnesses, so that through personal contact their reluctance will be overcome, and to review developments into the early hours of the morning. The trouble with the formula for success is that it is the same as for a nervous breakdown.

All this was present in Igor's case, and, added to it, the sentence, inflicted in advance, of his suspended job, his upended public relations firm, and his never-ended tragedy at home. The temptation of relieving him of the ordeal of trial was therefore great, especially because the plea was comparatively innocuous. I had to tell him that the chances of a dismissal of the charge, without his even taking the stand, were good. But in view of the virtual certainty that only a fine would be imposed (which would be much less than the cost of a trial) and that there was no moral turpitude involved in the reduced charge, I would not oppose his wish to accept a *nolo contendere* plea. He registered relief.

I can only guess that Bobby Kennedy received this decision with relief, too. He was under pressure from the President and probably from his father (who by that time had suffered a stroke), to dispose of the matter mercifully, and without too much fanfare. After all, despite my determination to try the case strictly on the merits, one could not prevent the newspapers from drawing the Kennedys into it. They knew that the President had designated Igor for the diplomatic mission to the Dominican Republic. They also knew of the intertwining relationships of the Cassinis, the Wrightsmans, and the Kennedys. The suicide of Charlene would not go unnoticed. Rubirosa, a true original, always made good copy. The case was bound to create a field day in the press. From a legal viewpoint, Katzenbach's report must have dimmed Bobby's enthusiasm for a successful prosecution.

Under the new plan, the indictment would not be dropped entirely, and thus the prosecutor would be "vindicated." Yet for all practical purposes, Igor would be let off. Also, the President's heartfelt impulse to do something, no longer for Charlene but in her memory, would be achieved.

The details were worked out. On October 8, 1963, Igor appeared before Chief Judge Matthew F. McGuire in the Federal District Court in Washington, D.C. He pleaded *nolo contendere* to the single charge. The prosecutor approved the special plea and the Judge accepted it. Sentence was scheduled for January 10, 1964, three months later, to allow the Probation Department to prepare a presentence report, and also to skip the intervening holiday season.

We used the time effectively, meeting with the probation investigators to submit the facts of Igor's impressive background. A probation official's duty is to be nosy. He learned that Igor had been born thirty-nine years before in Sebastopol, Russia; that he was a member of the Russian Orthodox Church; that after fleeing Russia he had attended the University of Florence, in Florence, Italy, for three years, and had thereafter attended law school at the University of Perugia in Perugia, Italy, for another three years; that he had served as sergeant in the United States Army in the Battle of the Rhine and Nuremberg, and had received the European Theater Medal with two campaign stars; that he had three marriages and other scars such as from an appendectomy; that he held newspaper posts on the *Times-Herald* in Washington, D.C., and on the *Journal-American* for eighteen years; that he was proficient in golf, tennis, and skiing, and on endlessly.

We obtained letters of commendation for Igor from people whose opinions would carry special weight. Allen W. Dulles was so eager to be of assistance that he overcame his reticence as a former director of Central Intelligence to write that he was "quite prepared to talk to the probation officer" and he confirmed Robert Murphy's views about Igor's service during their visit to Trujillo. Murphy had written an uninhibited letter of praise for Igor. Other telling letters were submitted by Richard Berlin, president of Hearst Corporation; J. Kingsburg Smith, publisher of the New York *Journal-American*; Franklin D. Roosevelt, Jr., Under Secretary of Commerce; Robert Lehman, investment banker; Earl E. T. Smith, former Ambassador to Cuba; Ray Stark, motion picture producer; Vincent Garibaldi, president of Fiat Corporation; Father George Grabbe, priest of the Russian Orthodox Church; Liz Smith, columnist; Clyde Newhouse, art dealer, and many others.

"Too bad," I teased, "that we can't submit letters from Joe Kennedy, the President, and Jackie."

A presentence report is addressed to the wide discretion which a sentencing judge must exercise in the degree of punishment. One who has committed a crime, no matter how serious, is entitled to the consideration of the ameliorating circumstances of his life. If it is his first "fall from grace," he should be treated more mercifully than if he is a recidivist. Also, his previous good works and normal, crimeless life are a consideration in judging the public's safety if he is returned earlier to society. The presentence report strikes a balance of good and evil, not unlike the compassionate balance which religion teaches will be struck in the hereafter in determining how much angel and devil was in each of us.

Came the day. Igor stood before Chief Judge McGuire. The Court invited me to address it on the subject of sentence. It was an opportunity to reduce the charge to the technical triviality which was involved. Contrasted with the minor aspect of the accusation was the major punishment already suffered by the defendant; the loss of his wife, his profession, his business. I believe the Judge, too, felt the enormity of the disproportional grief already imposed on Igor. He imposed a fine of $10,000 and a six-month probation period.

Igor walked out free. His ordeal had ended. But Charlene could not be restored to life, nor even could his column nor his public relations firm.

Igor has since written an autobiography entitled *I'd Do It All Over Again*. I could suggest a slight amendment or two which would interrupt the inexorable repetition of his life, and save him from unnecessary anguish. Couldn't we all stand such an amendment?

Every case is unique. Like human beings, there are no replicas. This one unexpectedly buffeted me from the President to his brother, the Attorney General. It preceded Kissinger's shuttle diplomacy to create a new genre, "shuttle advocacy."

TYCOONS

The business tycoon is a growing American phenomenon. He has replaced the Alexanders and Napoleons to conquer new worlds—industrial worlds. Governments have set up defenses against him—to no avail. Theodore Roosevelt began the major assault against "the malefactors of great wealth." Antitrust laws were enacted. Political platforms uniformly promised to curb business "predators." Franklin Roosevelt created a Maginot Line of legal obstructions from the SEC to the Federal Trade Commission. President Truman seized one of their plants illegally and had its president removed from office. Kennedy became so angry with one of the tycoons who raised steel prices despite White House appeal that he lost his verbal elegance and called him a "son of a bitch."

What do the tycoons desire? Wealth? Not entirely, because after they have amassed uncountable millions they redouble their efforts if that is possible. Power? Not entirely, because after they have built industrial empires, they drive on to create conglomerates, absorbing unrelated industries in their original companies. Ego satisfaction? Not entirely, because many, like the old Rockefeller, Harriman, Carnegie, Gould, Morgan, and Howard Hughes, are shy men avoiding publicity and genuinely seeking anonymity.

Yet, it is all of these in some way or other, but with no terminal point. The game never ends. The struggle persists, lending credence to the theory that the strife and excitement in the course of achieving are the goal itself.

What makes all this more curious is the sacrifice gladly made for an objective so ephemeral that it is difficult to define.

Every tycoon, without exception, gives complete dedication to his task. There are not enough hours in the waking day, so sleeplessness is gladly endured. The luxury rewards of money and power are either eschewed entirely or are not enjoyed. They are workoholics, accepting slavery willingly. They surrender more than their freedom. They give up their health, suffering ulceration, heart disease, and mental breakdown, but they will not stop. They cannot stop. They are builders who cannot put down the hammer. I knew one such man who in his spare time, as if there were any, literally built houses on his estate. Without cease, he built a "doll's house," as he called it, for his wife; one for himself; a large one where both could live; a playhouse for the children; a bowling alley for the grownups; a boathouse on the lake; dressing rooms at the pool; a game room; and on and on. His estate later became a resort, it never having been a home.

Arde Bulova did the same in his Connecticut estate. After he had built guesthouses and a four-hole golf course, he constructed a large adjoining open-aired dining platform. He wanted the outdoor pool to be covered by a huge Plexiglas dome for use in winter. But the dome had to be on rails, so that it could be moved over the dining area. However, in cold weather, the steam heat would cloud the Plexiglas, cutting off the view outside. So he created air currents which kept the glass clear and permitted us to see the trees shadowed white with snow, while we swam and enjoyed the orchid plants on the inside.

I have noticed that some of these driven men lose their restlessness and high-tensioned tantivy when they are on water. The transformation is extraordinary. Put some tycoons on a boat and they calm down as if sedatives had been administered. Perhaps it is the feeling, as the boat takes off, that the world has moved away from the stationary object on which they sit, leaving them isolated in outer space. There is nothing but lonely water—nothing to conquer. The horizon is empty. The challenge has disappeared and a new perspective has taken its place.

Tycoons have been changed by social evolution. Once they were ruthless in their climb. "The public be damned" was their motto. I recall representing Robert Young, the railroad magnate, who gathered in department stores and motion picture companies. I was to make a plea to a congressional committee for tax relief so that roadbeds could be rebuilt and the American railroads freed from palsy type rides accompanied by deafening staccato noises as the cars jumped over the gaping cracks in the rails. I suggested a memorandum which would emphasize public convenience. "Say it, if you want to," he said, "but actually I don't give a damn about that. We are interested in a decent return on our investment and we are entitled to it, just as much as a public utility is." This was in the 1950s. It was an echo from the early tycoons who were not abashed by the adjective "ruthless."

Those who sought to conquer a rugged continent had to be as roughhewn as the "enemy" they were determined to subdue. They had a worthy adversary. Nature fought back. Railroads built around the curves of mountains were attacked by rock slides. Forests cut down to create passageways summoned up nature's fecundity and overran the cleared area. Rainstorms washed away embankments and swelled streams which hurled themselves against the dams and broke them. Mines resisted being disemboweled, caving in on their invaders and crushing them.

But the tycoons won the desperate battle. Only personal tragedy could daunt them. They were human after all. Young's severity accompanied his quiet frenzy. But he softened in the presence of his beautiful wife and daughter.

His daughter went up in a private plane with her fiancé and both were killed in a crash. Young seemed to take even that blow stoically. But a year later, he blew his brains out with a gun. Financiers sought an explanation in possible hidden reverses of his financial empire. There were none. He died extremely wealthy, but impoverished by deprivation of the joy of conquest.

Tycoons had to be brilliant, as well as determined, to earn the title. This brings me to the social evolution I mentioned. New generations set new standards. A business could not succeed unless the good will of the public was earned.

Telephone companies sponsored concerts and operas on television even though their excellence kept people away from telephones. Oil companies spent millions to tell the people how they spend billions to find oil and provide cheaper power. Huge corporations sponsored television specials on public issues, often warming the hearts of their liberal antagonists with civil rights contents. (In 1975, Xerox produced a two-hour television special of the John Henry Faulk trial, which eliminated blacklisting. In support of this drama it published one million educational booklets for schoolchildren. It was presented on CBS network, which had been involved originally in the blacklist.) Manufacturing companies advised the public of their concerns about pollution and their huge expenditures to protect the environment.

Symphonies, ballets, modern dance teams, instrumental soloists, like Heifetz, Menuhin, and Horowitz, singers like Beverly Sills and Robert Merrill, all were brought before huge TV audiences by commercial enterprises which sought nothing more than recognition for their public spiritedness. Why don't stockholders who sue management at the drop of a financial statement attack the enormous expenditures for such projects which often do not even describe their product, let alone extol it? Because the good will of the public is money in the bank. It is a real asset created by the awareness of the buying public of new values. From "the public be damned" we have come to "the public is our first concern."

This evolutionary process is startlingly illustrated in the labor field. Tycoons used to consider unions illegal, radical intrusions upon their sacred property rights. They felt fully justified in organizing counterforces to quell the workers' insurrections. As public reaction to strikebreaker goons and scabs mounted, sales were affected. The evolutionary process of making the tycoon conscious of customer good will accelerated.

Today, almost every large corporation installs a vice-president in charge of labor relations. He often comes from union ranks, understands the workers' psychology and needs, and negotiates contracts with union leaders on a sophisticated brotherly basis.

Not only that, but it is deemed advantageous to employers to install pension plans, health programs, escalated vacation periods, bonuses, stock acquisition plans, coffee breaks in leisure rooms, lecture and promotion programs, severance pay, etc. The good will of the worker is sought as eagerly as that of the customer, because often the two are the same.

But although evolution changed attitudes, it didn't change human nature. The arrogance which accompanied employers' power was just as evident when employees became dominant. Exceptions of course abounded in both. In the so-called "needle industry," unions made loans to employers so that they could survive and give employment. Unions accumulated hundreds of millions and even billions of trust funds. They retained economists to make financial studies and guide them just as employers did. They lobbied in Washington just as traditionally employers had always done. There was no greater virtue, efficiency, or farsightedness in one group than in the other. Even the selfish manipulations of corporate management which the Securities and Exchange Commission was created to curb, found its counterpart in corrupt practices of union leaders.

The fact that neither honor nor evil is a monopoly of any class is the idealist's tragedy. He needs a clearly defined enemy to overcome; some thing and some one to sacrifice for; the satisfaction of destroying oppressive forces. But when what he lances against is found also in his own midst; when, as he triumphs, he absorbs the enemy and his iniquity, he is frustrated and confused.

Resignation is not the answer. A tolerant understanding of man's imperfections is. Then one can be a reformer and not an absolutist. Then one can try to better the world and not become a fanatic. Then one can fall short of the goal and not be disillusioned.

We might learn from scientists who, despite the miracles of technology, allow tolerance for all instruments. If we similarly allowed tolerance for human frailty, we would not suffer disappointment so often. We would be less neurotic and wiser.

I have represented and studied businessmen of all types. The most remarkable businessman I have ever met is Dr. Armand Hammer.

His life touches so many distant shores of excitement, involving legendary personalities and events, that a mere mention of them defies credibility. Born poor on the East Side of New York, he became a millionaire while attending Columbia (by acquiring a bankrupt pharmaceutical company and guiding it to success in spare evening hours). He gave up a possible musical career as a concert pianist to become a doctor (he was designated "the most promising" in his graduating class).

While he was in medical school an incident occurred which could have changed the course of his life. It involved obstetrics. Seniors were required to put their studies and observations to actual test by delivering several babies. They were moved into the New York Nursery and Child's Hospital for Women, near the medical school. There they could treat women as outpatients during pregnancy and ultimately deliver their babies.

One midnight, a nurse woke him and gave him a card which directed him to a woman in labor at Sixtieth Street and Tenth Avenue. He took his bag of instruments and rushed for his first delivery. Climbing several flights of the tenement located in the poor Italian neighborhood, he was ushered to the bed by a distraught husband. Although his instruction card recited a normal pregnancy, the woman was screaming from pain.

Hammer put on his gown and rubber gloves and after extensive examination discovered that he was confronted by an unusual condition, a breech delivery. The child was upside down. The feet would emerge first instead of the head.

There had been a lecture on breech deliveries, but his preoccupation with his pharmaceutical enterprise had caused him to miss it. However, he had had the foresight to pack a textbook, Cragin's *Obstetrics*, with his instruments. He rushed into the bathroom with the book, indexed it to the section on breech deliveries, and saw the illustration of the technique. He also learned that when the labor progressed to the point of expulsion, that unless the head, the largest part of the body, could be released immediately, the infant would be strangled.

He dashed back to the woman and found that meconium (feces) was being released. This meant that he only had minutes to save the child and perhaps the mother. Following Cragin's instructions, he inserted the index and middle fingers of his right hand into the womb and into the child's mouth. With this grip, he rotated and slid the head gently in one direction and then the other until he swiveled it out of the womb. He cut the umbilical cord, washed the protective coating from its body, slapped it, and heard the most pleasant noise of his twenty-two years on earth. As he placed the child next to the exhausted mother, the father and neighbors who had gathered burst into song and dance. A great breakfast was prepared, but incongruously, wine, not coffee, was served. His ears ringing with praise, Hammer left and returned to the hospital. It was four in the morning. He arose hours later to attend Professor Loeb's class in pharmacology.

Word had spread that Hammer had successfully made a breech delivery. He was congratulated by the students. They called him "Professor" and good-naturedly teased him about doing things "ass backwards."

While in the classroom a message arrived that the dean, Dr. Samuel Lambert, wanted Armand Hammer to come to his office. When Hammer arrived, he found many members of the faculty seated alongside the dean. He was about to put on his modest manner—"Really, I don't deserve all this"—when he was startled by Dr. Lambert's announcement: "Mr. Hammer, you have been summoned here to answer why you should not be expelled." "Expelled?" The thud from the sudden descent stunned him. He sat speechless.

"You risked the lives of a child and its mother in a dangerous situation. You should have called for a staff doctor or a member of the faculty. How dared you undertake a breech delivery without any experience."

The injustice of it all shocked him into articulateness.

"The diagnosis and treatment card given to me gave no indication that this was not a normal pregnancy."

Dr. Lambert waved this excuse aside irately.

"But when you discovered it was a breech you should have called for help at once."

"There was no telephone. Besides, I realized that there was no time. The child would have strangled before anyone could arrive."

"You could have found out much sooner that this was a breech case. Then you would have had time to call for an experienced obstetrician."

"Dr. Lambert, this woman was treated by your staff here for months." He took a long look at the judges sitting before him.

"If they couldn't discover that the baby was in an abnormal position during this long period, how do you expect a novice like me to do so on a moment's notice?"

He had achieved a logic breech. It was the dean and his staff who were on the defensive. They dismissed the charge and sent him back to his studies.

What they did not know was that they had almost cost the college millions of dollars. How could they know? It was a half century later, in 1977, that Dr. Hammer arranged with my partner Arthur Krim (who in addition to being a special adviser to Presidents had by then become chairman of the Board of Trustees of Columbia University) to give a $5 million gift to Columbia Medical School.

At the age of twenty-three, Dr. Hammer decided to visit Russia, which was famine-ridden and in need of medical services. The pragmatic aspects of this startling decision were that he could do his internship on a large scale, and try to collect moneys due him for pharmaceutical sales. He brought with him a $100,000 World War I surplus field hospital stocked with medicines and instruments, and also a $15,000 ambulance. The daring of such a trek to the hostile Bolshevik country which was still in the agony of a revolution can only be compared to that of pioneers who headed west into Indian territory. He encountered mass starvation (one Russian was chopping wood for his own coffin in anticipation of his death). Hammer broke through the European economic blockade, and imported a million bushels of wheat in a barter deal. The feat came to the attention of Lenin, who invited the young American doctor to see him.

Thus began a friendship as warm as it was bizarre between the five-foot-three, bald, brown-eyed founder of the new Russian state and an American capitalist. Lenin talked English fluently. Incredibly his affinity with Hammer was in the economic realm. Lenin picked up a scientific American magazine and urged that American technology and know-how were what Russia needed. He saw no reason why the two countries couldn't do business together. He appointed a committee for concessions and gave Hammer the first concession of asbestos. Later Lenin wanted to confer on his friend another concession. Hammer surprised him by requesting the pencil concession, because "I know you will want to wipe out illiteracy, and everybody will need pencils." Lenin was warmed by the gesture. In the papers left after his death, he wrote about Hammer fourteen times.

Hammer persuaded Henry Ford, as bitter an enemy of Bolshevism as could be found on the globe, to sell tractors to Russia. Hammer then became the agent for thirty-seven other companies which sought entry into the virgin market, including U. S. Rubber, Allis-Chalmers, Ingersoll-Rand, Underwood (typewriters), and Parker Pen. Later Ford actually built a plant in Russia which turned out 100,000 cars a year.

When the first Ford tractors arrived, Hammer climbed on one of them and led the parade into Novorossisk. The people mistook them for tanks and the Communist guard was called out. When it was explained that these were friendly machines which would make possible more food, cheers and tears replaced their fears.

In 1922, Lenin suffered a severe stroke. His right side was paralyzed: Lenin doggedly conquered his aphasia and learned to speak again. His right hand was dead. He learned to write with his left. But two years later he died.

Hammer also met Leon Trotsky, but found him cold and unlike Lenin. Due to the killing of twenty members of the Moscow Communist Committee, by a bomb thrown through a window, Trotsky's windows were covered with steel netting. He sat in a darkened room, with only an electric light over his head. He conversed with Hammer in German. He, too, following Lenin's lead, wanted to interest American capital, contending that investments there were safer because the revolution had already taken place, whereas it was yet to come to the United States. It was one of those inverted arguments like the cynical jest that it is better to re-elect a corrupt politician because he has already taken his graft.

What came through Hammer's experience, supported in part by Lenin's writings, was that had he lived longer, he might have set Russia on a path of amity with the Western world, deriving economic strength from capitalism, to buttress his impoverished people. Perhaps he would have been content with that achievement, without exporting Communistic revolution by force of arms and infiltration. There might have been true détente. Who knows, revolutionaries are fanatics and unpredictable.

After the Stalin freeze, Russian leaders, Khrushchev, Kosygin, and Brezhnev, all greeted Hammer eagerly and dealt with him. The fact that he was a friend of Lenin was a unique passport which pierced all reserve and suspicion of a noted capitalist. Brezhnev announced on an NBC documentary, while standing next to his friend, "Armand Hammer has expended considerable effort. I help him, he helps me. It is mutual. We do not discuss secrets—just business." That business involved a $20 billion deal in which superphosphoric acid would be shipped to Russia in return for ammonia, urea, and potash. Also, natural gas was to be shipped from Siberia enough to heat two million American homes for thirty years, while a hundred-million-dollar trade center with offices for American firms would be erected in Moscow.

The hope was that trade coexistence might lead to military and political coexistence.

What a triumph that would be for capitalism. The Communist prophecy of the collapse of capitalism would be defeated by Russia's need to utilize the efficient productivity of the system it hated. On the other hand, Communist states could point to the triumph of socialist policies adopted by capitalistic countries which paternalistically cared for the masses. One is reminded of President Franklin Roosevelt's observation that Russia was moving toward capitalism and the United States toward socialism, and the two would meet midway.

One of the chief architects of the former has been Armand Hammer, who, due to his friendship with the George Washington of the Russian state, now deemed god-like by its mystically inclined people, has bridged the commercial chasm.

A man's life is colored by the dye of his imagination. Hammer's ventures in other directions were no less challenging than his "Russian connection." Roosevelt's secretary, General "Pa" Watson, once told the President that he ought to use Hammer because "The man is just plain lucky." This was a superstitious imprimatur, which might be more flattering than the prosaic explanation of imagination harnessed by hard work. Roosevelt assigned Hammer to Harry Hopkins, with whom he developed the fifty-destroyer lend-lease for Great Britain in return for some bases. This broke the U-boat stranglehold, and might well have saved the Allies.

Hammer's "luck" included staying out of the stock market in 1929, turning a rotting Maine potato surplus into alcohol, and later selling out his liquor business to Schenley for six and half million dollars cash, discovering phosphate in northern Florida, where none had been found before, combining it with sulphur, by buying the Jefferson Lake Sulphur Company in Texas to create a leading fertilizer company, accidentally becoming interested in breeding bulls, which resulted in his acquisition for $100,000 of the world's prize black Angus bull, Prince Eric (whose picture is next to Lenin's autographed photograph on Hammer's shelf and whose one thousand calves in three years, by means of artificial insemination, resulted in $2 million profit); and buying the Mutual Broadcasting System, signing Walter Winchell and Kate Smith and selling it one year later for $1,300,000 profit.

"The most versatile tycoon of the century," as Hammer has been called, demonstrated his imaginative flair, in the most dangerous of all enterprises—oil. He had retired at the age of fifty-eight, to devote his time to his art gallery and the gathering of masterpieces for gifts to museums, $25-million bequest to the Los Angeles County Museum and drawings to the National Gallery in Washington, D.C.

A tax accountant suggested oil investment because the inevitable dry holes would provide tax relief (one of the curious consequences of a high tax bracket). So he bought into a defunct little company called Occidental Petroleum Corporation, worth $34,000, with three employees, and built it into the twentieth largest corporation in the United States, with thirty-five thousand employees, three hundred thousand stockholders, six billion dollars annual revenues, and an after-tax profit of several hundred million dollars.

What kind of alchemist is this who turns everything he touches into gold? Like all tycoons he is tirelessly dedicated to his venture, whatever it be. Like all achievers he spouts energy in greater bursts than his oil gushers. There are other attributes and the usual faults.

His nervous system is protected by mental shock absorbers which enable him to be serene in the midst of turmoil. He can talk in sequence to ministers, kings, and business royalty in distant countries at hours normal there and appropriate for sleep here, read reports, write shorthand notes, all without nervous strain. He increases his capacity by avoiding tension. But how eliminate stress when so much is at stake? One way is to take a ten- or fifteen-minute nap in the midst of work, I learned the signal. When during a hectic conference, he asked for a private room to telephone, he would be given an office with a couch. In a few seconds he was sound asleep. He would return shortly, refreshed, and eager for the fray with less rested adversaries.

Reflective calm is another antidote to the wear and tear of activity. Those upon whom others lean for decision must not waver. Confidence in their wisdom brings out the best in them, and gives impetus to execution, which often makes a questionable instruction come out right. Hammer, like all tycoons, has this quality of decisiveness.

His personal habits are sound. Every morning, there is the one-half-hour naked swim in his indoor pool followed by five hundred stomach contractions, rubdown, and cold shower. Then to bed for breakfast. He eats moderately and drinks less. But when travels abroad require feasts, he returns to a strict diet regimen, until the bulges disappear.

However, concentration, like that of most tycoons, is directed with laser beam narrowness to the particular venture he is guiding. He will listen and even participate in general discussion but his heart isn't in it and his eye is dull. It is only politeness which prevents him from revealing his boredom. But mention his enterprises and animation sweeps across his face and body. This one-trackedness can freeze a man but in his case it is relieved by a readiness to laugh and a capacity to enjoy.

He has had three wives. The first was Baroness Olga Vadina Von Root, a blue-eyed beautiful daughter of a Czarist general whom he met in Moscow. She was a concert singer. She bore him a son. The marriage was stormy and unsuccessful. A second marriage, to a beautiful society girl with a weakness for drink, also failed, but his third, to Frances Tolman, has been one of rare complementary affinity. They share common interests in finance, art, and joy of achievement. She gladly suffers the 300,000 miles of travel a year to all corners of the earth, to be near him, and he feels at home whenever she is beside him.

Hammer's serious demeanor, made somewhat forbidding by the knowledge of his accomplishments, changes to charm when he is on a persuasive tear. He is irresistibly insistent. He could have been a fine advocate. I know. I have been the target of some of his pleas.

Once Mildred and I were on vacation in Monte Carlo. Hammer called. His soothing solicitous voice warned me that an unusual request was coming. There was an important case scheduled for trial in Midland, Texas. He set forth the complicated facts pithily to demonstrate how just Occidental's cause was. He wanted me to try the case.

"When?" I asked.

"Tuesday."

"Today is Friday. That is impossible. I never try a case without thorough preparation. You have prominent Texas counsel. Why not proceed with them?"

"They'll collaborate. This is a case you must try. Please, Lou, do this for me."

"Can you adjourn it?"

"No, and besides it is important to us not to delay it."

So the conversation continued. When I pleaded that I could not even get a reservation on a plane on such short notice, the reply was that he would send his plane. The result: I flew to Midland, studied the files for forty-eight hours without sleep, and tried the case. Lest this be deemed a demonstration of low resistance by me, I can report that I have seen tough executives lured to hazardous posts abroad; others cajoled into deals they had forsworn, by the persistence, charm, and pleas to which they were subjected from the same source.

On the other hand, if he feels he has been wronged, he is no respecter of powerful forces arrayed against him. He is unabashedly litigious. He has started suits against the mighty and earned their enmity. He has dared as an "independent" to challenge the giants, and it has taken a long while for some of them to accept him as a fellow giant, or at least an independent not to be tampered with. In the meantime, we had fought successfully various legal battles, one of five years' duration against Armour & Company over a patent infringement involving superphosphoric acid, another against Standard Oil Company of Indiana, which had attempted a take-over of Occidental, one against Tenneco, and a number of others.

In the course of Occidental's growth, Hammer has left strewn behind him many adversaries. They have not hesitated to injure him public relations-wise whenever they could. He is vulnerable because he has President Johnson's sensitivity to criticism. So he fights back with threats of libel suits and corrective letters to the publications.

In view of his optimism and enthusiasm, his anticipatory claims, while sincerely made, are not always realized.

There is no reluctance in many quarters to pounce upon "his exaggeration" and try to discredit him. Ultimately, in almost every instance, he has exceeded his promise, but his "enemies" have no desire to be patient. So it came about that probably the most gifted businessman of our time, who has earned unprecedented accolades, has also been subjected to embarrassing skepticism. There is only one way to avoid criticism: to say nothing, do nothing, and be nothing. Anyone who violates all three cannot escape the lash.

I have referred to the tycoons' gratification from battle, as much as from victory. Hammer qualifies. Like Al Smith, who was known as the happy warrior, Hammer has the joy of combat. He and only one other person, in all my experience, are eager to testify. I have seen men who risk their lives readily but quail at taking the stand to face cross-examination. It takes a special kind of courage akin to super-self-confidence salted and peppered with an arrogance and conceit to face a trained cross-examiner. The lawyer's scalpel which cuts into the mind is painful enough, but to have the surgery performed in the presence of a judge, jury, audience, and worst of all a gloating adversary is purgatory to most people. Yet Hammer looks forward to taking the stand. As in his business deals, he prepares thoroughly. Hours mean nothing. I have been called "slave driver" by many clients (the first to so dub me was Harold Lloyd), but Hammer doesn't understand why we quit at three in the morning. He studies every fact, every date, and the principles of law involved. Then in a quiet way, hiding his exultation, he corrects the examiner on some misstatement, parries every point, frequently referring to a document by memory, which proves him right and embarrasses the less prepared attacker. He comes close to being the perfect witness; politely devastating and disarmingly persuasive. And he enjoys every minute of it, particularly the postverdict reminiscences of the verbal thrusts which felled the enemy.

Being intrepid himself, he despises lawyers who are nay sayers because they see the dangers and wish to avoid the risks. Lincoln used to bemoan the timidity of his generals, until he found Grant, whiskey and all. Eisenhower and Bradley appreciated the daring Patton, neuroses and all. There is a time to settle and a time to fight, and sound judgment in making the choice is an invaluable attribute of an adviser. But Hammer has a nose for sniffing out advice motivated by fear and supported by a catalogue of possible disasters, to which every important controversy lends itself. He would endorse the great Elihu Root's statement that the function of a lawyer is not to tell you that it can't be done, but how you can do it legally. In short he glories in resourcefulness as much as in the goal it achieves.

When principle is involved, he rejects compromise. No matter how prudent it might be to make a settlement which would be "a premium on an insurance policy against an enormous risk," he insists on a verdict to vindicate his position. It does not matter how great the gamble. I shall cite one example which engaged us in an eight-year litigation. At stake was a quarter interest in Occidental's great oil strike in Libya. The damages sought against Occidental were "in excess of a hundred million dollars" and an accounting which might well increase the claim to a quarter of a billion dollars. A defeat would be a crippling blow to Occidental.

Yet Hammer, feeling that Occidental's honor had been impugned, because he was charged with welshing on a written contract, refused to settle. As his trial counsel, I agreed, although the responsibility of advising and supporting his stubbornness was a burden which kept me sleepless beyond preparation necessity. The litigation war was fought before fourteen Federal judges and took us to Italy, Switzerland, England, Germany, and Belgium.

The author of the *Arabian Nights* could not have provided a more engrossing scenario. We were engaged in a fascinating struggle, filled with mystery, intrigue, forged documents, and miracles, such as the discovery of an ocean of water beneath the Libyan desert. Naturally, then, Hammer enjoyed the drama while hiding his anxiety, while I, as lawyer, shared the anxiety without appreciating the drama.

It all began in 1964 when the highly regarded Allen brothers (Charles and Herbert), heads of one of the foremost investment companies, advised Hammer that a friend of theirs, Ferdinand Galic, could be very helpful in obtaining oil concessions which were about to be granted in Libya. Galic said that he was a friend of General de Rovin, who was represented to be in the good graces of the Libyan Government. A meeting was arranged in London. A draft of an agreement between Hammer and the Allens was drawn, granting them a 25 per cent interest in any concession which "Galic turned up." Costs and profits were to be shared in the same proportion.

The Allens did not wish to subject themselves to costs which might run to millions of dollars and wind up with a dry hole. So after consultation with their lawyers, they inserted, in ink, after the word "costs," "to be mutually agreed upon."

In returning the letter for Hammer's signature, Allen referred to this insertion as a "major change," as indeed it was. It was known that two American oil companies each had expended $50 million exploring previous concessions in Libya without getting a single barrel of oil. A French company had a similar experience to the extent of $25 million. The Allens knew, as they later acknowledged in cross-examination "that hundreds of millions could be sunk into the ground in a vain search for oil." As prudent businessmen, they wanted to have a veto on how much risk they would take. The condition they inserted gave them this protection.

Hammer accepted the condition which permitted the Allens to be let out if they so chose. He signed. With uncanny instinct he took the burden for Occidental alone of millions of dollars for seismograph and other expenses, and later enormous drilling costs, without assurance that there would be a barrel of oil.

Then came the first melodramatic incident. It was discovered the General de Rovin was an impostor. He was no general. He was a notorious crook with a long criminal record. Galic, too, had no real standing in Libya. Besides, it was learned that the concessions were not to be granted by negotiation. They were to be awarded on sealed competitive bids, so that influential negotiations were not necessary.

Hammer decided to get rid of the disreputable promoters who had been foisted on him. He terminated their representation. Since Galic would therefore no longer be in the picture, he could not "turn up" any concessions and the letter agreement with the Allens also fell. Hammer so wrote them. They never protested this cancellation in writing. Not until eighteen months later, when one of the greatest oil gushers in the region's history flooded the sands, and floated Occidental's stock upwards, did they decide that they were 25 per cent partners, although they had not put up a cent of risk capital.

In the meantime, how had Occidental obtained two choice concessions, which many of the one hundred twenty sealed bids sought? Imagination and resourcefulness carried the day. Libya requested that bidders offer not only money, but other considerations called "preferences."

Occidental submitted unique preferences in the form of sheepskin diplomas rolled and bound with silk ribbons of red, green, and black, the national colors of Libya.

The wrapping caused the Libyan minister who opened the sealed bids in public to comment that he hoped the inner contents were as interesting. They were. The suggestions were so intriguing that he asked Occidental's representative, Richard H. Vaughan, to explain them out loud.

Occidental offered to earmark 5 per cent of its net operating profits derived from oil exploitation in Libya for the agricultural development of Kufra, which was King Idris' birthplace and where his father was entombed. (The King has not yet been overthrown by Qadaffi.) Later the King, in appreciation of the redemption of Kufra, offered to change its name to "Hammer," but with self-abnegation suitable to the occasion, Hammer declared this would be "too much of an honor" and suggested that the newly discovered oil site be called Idris Field. The King, not wanting to hurt Hammer's feelings by rejecting his suggestion, overcame modesty and consented.

Also, Occidental offered to build an ammonia plant in Libya to manufacture fertilizer. This structure would cost $30 million and would be spent even if oil was not discovered in the concession area. In addition, Occidental offered to use its Oxytrol process for the transportation of vegetables and produce over long distances without spoilage. Finally, it offered to use modern technology to search for water in the desert.

The total offer was so appealing in its mixture of economic advantage, national pride, and general welfare that one of the competitors was heard to remark, "Why didn't we think of something like that?"

All councils of the King and finally the King himself approved the grant of two highly promising concessions to Occidental.

After $5 million of drilling there was only a dry, a very dry hole. Then, near the very sight where Mobil had previously abandoned hope, a rare, geological phenomenon occurred. A reef was punctured. It contained so much encapsulated oil that it would flow almost indefinitely without the use of pumps. A single well produced 72,000 barrels of the finest quality of low-sulphur oil a day. Hammer immediately ordered a crash $150 million pipeline, one hundred and thirty miles long, capable of transporting a million barrels of oil a day.

When the first oil reached the sea, Occidental arranged a celebration attended by eight hundred Cabinet ministers, robed local chieftains, diplomats, a United States senator, and many others. The King presided proudly in a specially built air-conditioned building in the desert. Flowers flown from abroad decorated the entire region. Food was imported. The party cost $1 million.

Occidental stock took wings and soared to one hundred dollars a share. After splitting amoeba-like three for one, the stock still climbed to fifty-five dollars a share in 1968. Those who believed in Hammer's luck, from servants to friends, became millionaires.

The Allens could not resist the temptation to lay claim to some of this wealth. They had been there at the conception, even though Occidental had made an earlier application for Libyan oil concessions. They brought suit in the Federal Court in New York.

Still Occidental's position appeared invulnerable to attack. The Allens had avoided the risk of investment. They had not protested Occidental's cancellation notice until a year and a half later when the Libyan sands were drenched black with oil. The cancellation was not frivolous. Notorious crooks had been interposed as agents and Hammer had the right to get rid of them.

All looked well for a victorious defense. But was there ever a suit in which a surprise witness or document didn't suddenly appear to upset all calculations?

The Allens produced such a document. It detonated in our midst and almost drove us to surrender. Then we recovered our stance and fought on more determinedly than ever.

What was it? Nothing less than a letter from the Minister of Petroleum Affairs of Libya, Fuad Kabazi, on the official stationery of the Libyan Government, addressed to Ferdinand Galic and indicating their intimate relationship and Kabazi's reliance on the Allens' financial ability. He advised Galic that Occidental would receive two concessions. The letter could not have served the Allens better if it had been prepared by them to create a perfect claim against Occidental. That was the trouble with it. It was too pat.

When we had recovered our breath, we launched a counterattack to demonstrate what we suspected, that Kabazi, who no longer was a minister, had backdated his letter to aid Galic and the Allens in winning their suit and probably share in the result.

The Allens' counsel sought to take Kabazi's testimony in advance of trial. The court designated London as the site of the deposition. We welcomed a chance to get at him. We might as well know whether we could survive his damaging testimony.

The examination took place in the American Embassy building so that the American Consul could swear in the witness and preside, if necessary, over formal matters, acting as an extension of the United States courts.

Kabazi was a handsome, academically bearded man, with eyes which could have qualified him as a hypnotist. He prided himself on being a poet, which he announced frequently to offset his difficulties with the commercial issues. He had not the slightest idea of Anglo-Saxon judicial procedure. He did not understand the function of cross-examination and considered my questions an insult to his integrity. He had previously been interviewed by the Allens' lawyers, in a friendly manner. He kept chiding me for not being as courteous, by which he meant believing, as "the other lawyers."

Cross-examination is often effective when its purpose is not discernible, and the witness readily steps into traps. Only later does he discover his predicament. So, for example, Kabazi testified that he was in Tripoli when he typed the letter. It seemed to be an innocuous statement. He was sure of it. In much later testimony, unaware of any contradiction, he testified that he had attended Council meetings in Beida (seven hundred miles from Tripoli) on dates which included the very day of the letter's date.

Similarly, he said that he had always communicated with Galic in

Italian, addressing him "Dear Ferdo," and received replies in French. English was never used. He overlooked the fact that the questioned letter, was in English, and addressed Galic, "Dear Sir.—"

He conceded that neither Galic's name nor the Allens' was mentioned in Occidental's application, and that the attached letter of the Chase Manhattan Bank in support of financing was satisfactory, and yet his letter claimed he was relying on Allens' financial standing. The internal contradictions in the letter escaped him. There was a more subtle contradiction. His testimony was in broken English, the kind one speaks when he must mentally translate Italian, in which he thinks, into a language and grammar of which he is unsure. But the letter, which he claimed he personally typed, was in perfect English.

When the cross-examination became really cross, and I confronted him with a section of the Libyan criminal law which would send him to jail for six months, for leaking the grant of concessions in advance, as he had done in his letter, he rose in mighty indignation at the insult to his honor, and stormed out of the room.

I moved to strike his entire testimony, if the witness did not return to complete his examination in accordance with the Court order. This caused the Allens' lawyers to join with the American Consul in pleading with Kabazi to continue. He finally returned, sulking in his chair as if it were a tent. He continued to make speeches about his being an artist and resenting the insinuations against his honor. But as admissions were wrung from him (such as that he could not have voted as he claimed for Occidental concessions in the Council meeting because he only had a vote if there was a tie and there was none), his protestations of a poet's honor began to sound more and more hollow.

We were moving closer to our conviction that Kabazi had dated back a letter bearing the imprimatur of Ministry of Petroleum Affairs to make it appear that Galic's friendship with him was responsible for the award of concessions to Occidental. In short it was a forgery. It was neatly constructed to prove that Galic, through his influence, had "turned up" the concessions.

Like the conceited counterfeiter who was finally caught because he put his own face on the twenty-dollar bill, Kabazi had left the stamp of his perfidy on every word of his testimony. He claimed that he typed the letter on his portable Olivetti typewriter. Where was the typewriter? He fumbled around, resentful of the probing questions, and finally said he had given it as a gift to a friend in Rome, whose name he could not remember. Did he think we would stop there? We retained an expert, Ordway Hilton, who provided objective evidence that the type on the letter was not that of an Olivetti. Even plaintiffs' experts, including one brought in from Scotland, conceded this fact. So both sides condemned Kabazi as a liar on this point.

Kabazi claimed that he had made a copy of his letter and filed it in the Ministry of Petroleum Affairs. We obtained an authenticated statement from the ministry that no such copy was found in its files.

Furthermore, we challenged his statement that he had made a carbon copy at all. It was necessary to submit the original letter to experts for microscopic and ultraviolet-ray tests to determine whether any traces of carbon could be detected in the indentations caused by the keys striking the paper. The plaintiffs' attorneys refused to surrender the letter to us for such purpose, claiming we might mutilate an important exhibit. We battled before three judges before we could wrench the letter from the plaintiffs' hands.

A court-appointed expert, J. Howard Haring, reported that no carbon copy had ever been made. The plaintiffs brought an expert from Texas to give another view.

Thus the legal contest raged to overcome the surprise Kabazi document presented by the Allens. But the shock of newly discovered documents was not ended. This time it was Occidental which provided the surprise.

A rumor had reached us that "General de Rovin" and Galic had split. The thieves had fallen out. Galic, we learned, had obtained a 10 per cent interest in any judgment which the Allens would recover in the suit. De Rovin apparently felt he was entitled to part of the loot. This was denied to him and the betrayer felt betrayed. I asked my partner Neil Pollio to visit de Rovin in Italy to find out whether his bitterness could be turned to our advantage.

De Rovin was so eager to do Galic in that he delivered to us his personal file of correspondence with him. When we read its contents, we could not believe our eyes. There, set forth in Galic's own handwriting, was a detailed description of the fraudulent arrangement to make it appear that Galic had "turned up" the concessions through his association with Kabazi, and thus give substance to the Allens' suit. I do not believe the Allens were participants in this scheme. They had blind faith in their personal friend Galic, and he deceived them too, in order that they would win and he and Kabazi could share in the bonanza of tens of millions of dollars.

Trial lawyers dream of a future invention which would enable them to lift out of the airwaves words spoken years before, a sort of automatic recording, so that truth could be accurately reconstructed. That wish was fulfilled in this instance by words inscribed by Galic himself.

Armed with Galic's letters, we laid a deep trap for him. I examined him for days, as if I did not have his writings, which were hidden, like explosives, under the table. He felt free to paint a fictitious picture of his intimacy with Kabazi and the way he was responsible for everything good which had happened to Occidental. I actually encouraged him to do so, each question being phrased closer and closer to the contradictions in his own handwriting, which I had memorized.

Then when the examination seemed to have been exhausted, and opposing counsel asked whether we would be through in an hour or so, I began all over again. But this time, after quoting his previous days' answers (from stenographic minutes delivered overnight), I confronted him with his letters to de Rovin. They were in French and each had an English translation, which he conceded was accurate. His own words gave the lie to almost every answer he had made. Instead of "palship" with Kabazi while he was minister, he wrote to de Rovin that he had tried to arrange a meeting with Kabazi twice but that he would not see him.

Instead of learning in advance from Kabazi that Occidental's concessions would be awarded Occidental, he confessed knowing nothing and suggesting that perhaps someone else might find out for him.

At one point, he wrote ruefully, "I wanted to be the first to announce to Dr. Hammer but I see he is informed before everybody. I do not know from where . . . He is always in advance of anybody."

In another letter he said he had learned that "Kabazi did nothing at all" to obtain the concessions.

The most embarrassing of all was Galic's letter to de Rovin, revealing the Allens' predicament. Galic wrote:

I relied on your [de Rovin's] statement that the concessions could be obtained by negotiation and then it was by tough bidding. This is what Mr. Allen reproached me yesterday. You could have avoided that. That will be the weak point in my lawsuit.

As he was confronted with these devastating letters, Galic's face seemed to turn the colors of the Libyan flag. Then in order to salvage his prior testimony, he condemned his own letters as lies, "all lies." After a while, he got tired of calling himself a liar, and shifted to "baloney." He stuttered and fumed as his words struck him.

More revealing than Galic's disintegration was his lawyer's conduct. He put a wood pencil in his mouth, and as the letters unfolded, he actually chewed the pencil in half.

Federal Judge Edward Weinfeld, who is recognized throughout the nation as a scholar, concluded in his forty-seven-page opinion that Galic's testimony "is belied by his own statements in letters and cablegrams sent to de Rovin. Caught in a web of falsehood by this cor-

respondence, Galic sought to extricate himself by testifying that he lied
to de Rovin to mislead him and keep him out of the deal. But there is
more than this perfidious conduct which mars his testimony. His glib
and facile explanations of falsehoods and contradictions are implausible. A careful word-by-word reading of the record compels the conclusion that Galic's testimony is utterly lacking in credibility."

Kabazi, who was also impaled by Galic's lies, fared no better in the
court's opinion. The Judge found his testimony replete "with inherent
contradictions and implausibilities." Much worse, the court condemned
the Kabazi letter as "deliberately contrived and written some time after
the awards were announced, predated, and sent to Galic in an effort to
aid Galic in a contemplated lawsuit against Occidental."

The cross-examination of both Allens consumed a large part of the
three-week trial. They suffered not only from the Galic-Kabazi debacle,
but from their own inconsistent conduct.

When Occidental floated a $61 million debenture issue, its friends,
the Allens, were one of the underwriters. As such, Allen & Company,
Inc., had to sign a statement to reveal whether it had any financial
interest in Occidental. Had they believed that they had a 25 per cent
interest in Occidental's Libyan concessions, they would have so stated.
But they answered that they had no "material relationship" with
Occidental. This, we argued, demonstrated that they had accepted
Hammer's cancellation letter, and did not consider themselves partners.
Also, in reports filed with the SEC the Allens did not list any assets or
contingent liabilities involving Libyan concessions.

So it always is. The truth is a thicket for prevaricators. Past conduct
of no special significance becomes an accusing finger of inconsistency.
The court rejected the Allens' testimony.

The court also found that "The proof is overwhelming that by their
acts and conduct they acquiesced in and consented to the termination
of the claimed agreement with Occidental," and further that Occidental
had the right to cancel the agreement.

As in every case there was an equitable principle at the core. Can one
lie in wait to see how a risky enterprise turns out and then announce
that he was a partner all the time? The courts have dealt with many
such cases, particularly in mining, where millions may be lost or won.
One judge expressed this age-old principle in colloquial terms: "Heads I
win and tails you lose, cannot, I fancy, be the basis of an equity." Judge
Weinfeld put it another way: The Allens "sought the best of two
worlds. If oil was struck they could claim a 25% profit in the joint venture; if it turned out to be a dry hole, it could disavow liability for 25%
of the loss, pointing to Occidental's termination letter. The Allens cannot have it both ways."

There was an appeal and the Court of Appeals, composed of three judges, unanimously affirmed the judgment.

Above all, from Hammer's viewpoint, he had taken an enormous risk involving approximately a quarter of a billion dollars, in order to be vindicated. He was.

So the drama ended. Occidental struck a great oil gusher. Libya received something more precious than oil income. Occidental had taken a drilling rig and crews five hundred miles across the burning desert, and 250 feet below the surface found an underground ocean of beautiful clear spring water larger than the flow of the Nile for two hundred years. Hammer immediately ordered miles of aluminum irrigation pipes, sprinklers, and chemical fertilizers. Occidental planted alfalfa and it grew as if planted in rich soil. The desert bloomed.

So did Occidental's wealth, which Hammer utilized to buy Island Creek Coal Company, the third largest in the United States, for a mere $150 million. It had annual sales of almost that much, with reserves of over three and half billion tons of coal. Its profit in 1976 alone was approximately $100 million.

After other triumphs and acquisitions like the Jefferson Lake Sulphur Company, Hammer's star had risen so that he was as honored as he was feared as a business adversary.

He lavished his attention and money on public interest and artistic endeavors. He made a $5 million grant to the Salk Institute for Biological Studies to seek a solution for cancer, as immunization had solved polio.

He has not lacked recognition. President Truman appointed him to the Citizens' Food Committee, President Eisenhower to the Council for the Study of Peace in the World, and President Kennedy to the Eleanor Roosevelt Memorial Foundation. Rulers of many nations have welcomed and decorated him.

At this point of his life, nearing the age of seventy-eight, he was struck with disaster. A criminal charge was made against him by Watergate Special Counsel. He faced the possibility of losing command of the company he had built, and the high regard of distinguished friends all over the world. Much worse, he faced the possibility of spending his final years in jail.

His vaunted fighting spirit was undiminished. He felt he was innocent and insisted upon a trial so that he would not end a creative life in disgrace. But the strain of this totally unexpected threat was too much for his heart. He collapsed, and was put in a hospital. His very life was imperiled.

What was the charge which had caused such havoc? Hammer, who had made beneficences in the tens of millions, was accused in a matter involving $54,000. The charge grew out of a contribution to the Nixon campaign. It was a purely technical claim. Campaign gifts after April 7, 1972, could not be anonymous. Hammer was accused of making such a gift without revealing his name. He claimed he had made it before April, and, therefore, did not have to announce his name. There was no moral turpitude involved. Were it not for the Watergate aspect, I doubt that any prosecutor would have given the matter much attention. But Watergate prosecution was the great news of every day. Any prominent name added to the sensationalism which justly filled the Washington air, and floated speedily throughout the nation.

Like most tragedies, the beginning was uneventful. One of Occidental's vice-presidents was Tim Babcock, Governor of Montana from 1962 to 1968, a leading Republican figure, well known to President Nixon.

When Nixon's second campaign got under way, an intense drive for funds was conducted as if a desperate election struggle, rather than a sweep, was impending. Maurice Stans was the generalissimo of the insistent sell. Executives were called in and were virtually told, rather than asked, what their financial duty was to re-elect "a great President." Babcock was assigned by Stans to hit Hammer. An appointment was arranged in Washington. Hammer had reported his Russian deals to Nixon. He had resolved to make a $50,000 contribution from his personal funds. Stans thought $250,000 was more appropriate for one of his standing. Hammer didn't appreciate the compliment. Under pressure, he agreed to increase his contribution to $100,000. He paid $50,000 immediately to Babcock, on March 31, and promised to pay the balance when he arrived in Los Angeles a few days later.

It had been widely announced in the press that, due to a new statute, Section 440, any campaign contribution *after* April 7 would have to bear the donor's name. Hammer knew this. He wished his substantial contribution to Nixon to be anonymous because he himself was a Democrat.

The opposite number to Babcock in his company was Marvin Watson, former Postmaster General in Johnson's cabinet. Hammer had contributed more to Nixon than he had anticipated and did not want the Democrats to seek similar largesse. He, like many executives who contribute to both political parties, preferred no publicity about his dual gifts. In general, I have found that many important entrepreneurs avoid publicity like a plague. It is not their modesty but their instinct for self-preservation which motivates them. They fear provoking tax authorities, kidnapers, charity seekers, and jealous competitors. Anonymity achieves the same protective coloration that animals use to avoid predators.

So Hammer hied himself to his vault in Los Angeles on April 3, as the record there shows, to obtain the balance of the payment and deliver it to Babcock before April 7.

However, Babcock later contradicted Hammer. He insisted that he had received the balance of the contribution after April 7. At first, he thought it was July and later August or September. If so, it would be claimed that Hammer had violated Section 440 by not revealing his name as donor. If Hammer's recollection was right there was no violation. He had the right to give his contribution without a name.

But it wasn't as simple as that. Whenever it was that Babcock received the money, he did not pay it over immediately, as he should have, to the Republican Campaign Committee. He only turned over the first $46,000. The rest of the $100,000 he paid in three installments over a period of many months, the last so late that the election was over.

Investigation later revealed that Babcock had suffered severe losses in his business enterprises in Montana. He was sorely pressed for money. Could it be that he had utilized Hammer's money to satisfy creditors, instead of turning it over immediately to the Campaign Committee?

Babcock had a different explanation. He said he was delayed because he was seeking friends who would give their names to the contributions. He would pretend that he had loaned them money to make the contributions. Then, when he feared that the FBI would inquire where he had obtained the money to lend to his friends, he arranged through an associate in Occidental to obtain a fictitious loan for which he gave a note. Hammer claimed that he knew nothing of this silly charade, but now the original charge had grown to include the deadly word "cover-up."

To conform to the new statute, questionnaires were sent by the Senate Select Committee to investigate Presidential Campaign Practices, called the Ervin Committee, to donors to state the amount of their campaign contributions. Hammer had previously received a letter from Stans's office advising that he had made a $46,000 contribution. That is how he learned that Babcock had not delivered the additional $54,000 he had given him. So he answered the questionnaire by adopting the figure supplied by him by the Committee, namely $46,000.

Had he answered $100,000, would it have been correct, when only $46,000 was registered as his contribution? At worst, this was an ambiguous matter. Yet, the prosecutor added the charge that Hammer had lied to the Senate committee, violating Section 1001 of the Criminal Code. A minor matter involving a date had grown, like Topsy, into a series of felony accusations, made more ominous by the inflamed Watergate atmosphere.

The central issue still was whether Hammer had delivered the

$54,000 before or after April 7. I thought of a lie detector test. Like many courts which will not admit it in evidence, I had doubts about its infallibility. But the psychological significance of a willingness or fear to take the test was real. Would Babcock take it?

I called Hammer long distance and asked him whether he would submit himself to such a test. He almost flew across the wires in his eagerness to consent. There was no doubt that he sincerely believed that he had complied with the law. Why should he not have? Certainly, he was not lacking the money to make the contribution. He knew it had to be made before April 7 if it was to be anonymous. What reason did he have to delay and involve himself in a criminal charge?

We retained Scientific Lie Detection, Inc., an outstanding company whose president, Richard O. Arthur, had headed the polygraph examiners of New York State, taught 1,800 polygraphists, and coauthored a leading book, *Lie Detection and Criminal Interrogation.* He had a reputation for integrity and objectivity.

Hammer answered questions while the levers recorded his pulse variations. As Mr. Arthur reported, "In order to verify the consistency of the polygraph reactions, Dr. Hammer was requested to return the following day for additional tests. This was agreeable to Dr. Hammer."

The written report gave the following conclusions:

On April 3, 1972, did you give Tim Babcock that $54,000?
ANSWER: Yes.
By April 7, 1972, had you then already actually given Tim Babcock that $104,000?
ANSWER: Yes.
On September 6, 1972, did you give Tim Babcock $54,000?
ANSWER: No.
On both examinations there were definite indications of truthfulness when Dr. Hammer answered the same pertinent test questions.

During one of our conferences with the special prosecutor, I gave this report to him and offered to have him select any polygraphist of his own to repeat the test, and to invite Babcock to do so. We heard nothing more from him on this subject.

While searching his mind for proof that he had delivered the money before April 7, Hammer recalled a visit to the White House several months after that date, on July 20, 1972. He had just returned from Russia with his first trade agreement and was invited by Nixon to report on the event. At the end of the conference, as he was leaving, Hammer said, "Mr. President, I am glad to tell you that I am a member of the $100,000 club."

Now that it was learned that everything was taped, could not his comment be proved? Would this not indicate that he had already delivered the $100,000? If, as the prosecutor charged, and Babcock claimed, he completed the contribution months later, in September, it was unlikely that he would have made the comment, which could be so easily checked, to the President.

We asked the prosecutor to review the tape to confirm the incident. He did, and Hammer was borne out by it. But, whatever impact it made was not revealed to us any more than that of the polygraph test.

On the contrary, the prosecutor was preparing to present the matter to a grand jury. Then if indictments were handed down, the story would break for the first time in the press. Hammer wanted to volunteer to appear before a grand jury and tell his story. He was convinced that he could persuade the jury that he was telling the truth and that it would not indict him. It was our painful duty to forbid him to do so. Why? Because experience had shown that when a prosecutor wants an indictment, a grand jury will almost always hand one down. If the target of the indictment testifies, and others like Babcock in this case, contradict him, the prosecutor can add a perjury charge to the original accusation. And he often does. For example Maurice Stans and John Mitchell offered to appear and testify before a grand jury. They were then indicted for perjury. The trial took place in New York and they were acquitted by a jury, but they had to defend themselves on a felony charge of perjury, which their voluntary appearance before a grand jury made possible. (The defects in the grand jury system are another example of how a noble procedure may become ignoble in practice. The grand jury was created to avoid the tyranny of a king, but over the centuries it has become tainted by another kind of tyranny, the power of overambitious prosecutors. In too many instances, the grand jury becomes a rubber stamp for a prosecutor who sheds his obligatory neutrality and seeks indictment.)

Hammer did not yield readily to our precautionary advice. His self-confidence was buttressed by his certainty that he was innocent. He distinguished other cases from his own. He had not used one cent of corporate money in making his contribution. He had used his personal funds only. This was in accordance with his general principle of personally absorbing most corporate expenses when he traveled. He felt that a grand jury would not submit him to a criminal charge in so technical a matter, but this was one time our insistence overcame his.

In the meantime, Babcock had sought mercy from the prosecutor by pointing a finger at Hammer. He entered into a plea bargain which involved him only in a misdemeanor charge. He was advised by his counsel that his punishment would be limited to a fine. This appeared sound enough, especially since the prosecutor agreed to make no contrary recommendation. But when Babcock appeared before Federal Judge George L. Hart, Jr., in Washington, everyone was stunned when the court sentenced him to four months in jail. The Judge held forth as follows:

"Mr. Babcock, in your case, you were not some untutored underling who had to dance to the tune of the boss. You are independently wealthy, you were decorated for bravery at Remagen Bridgehead, you could have told Hammer that you had no intention of assisting him in breaking the law, and been impervious to any penalty of any sort that would have meant anything."

Thus Hammer, who had not yet been charged with anything, had not appeared in any court, or had an opportunity to defend himself, was condemned by the court!

The press and media prominently carried the story. Often it was Hammer's picture, not Babcock's, which accompanied it.

It was an unbelievable and unjust blow. Almost everything about the pronouncement was incorrect. Babcock was not "independently wealthy." He was in a severe financial bind. He had solicited $5,000 from Hammer for senatorial campaigns. Four thousand dollars of this sum was deposited in his own corporate account in the Commerce Bank in Helena, Montana, as was verified by the prosecutor. As Hammer later wrote to the probation officer, "The fact is, I was the victim, not principal."

Now we had to overcome another burden. Would not the jail sentence to Babcock put a psychological burden on any court to do likewise? Only an acquittal could avoid the danger. It made a trial inevitable. I was convinced that he would be acquitted, even by a Washington jury understandably drenched with deep feelings about any Watergate charge. (This was before Edward Bennett Williams demonstrated this possibility when he represented Governor Connally.)

Hammer was ready for the fray. But his heart wasn't. We were advised by two eminent cardiologists who had to be called in that he could not stand the strain of a criminal trial. We were forced to reveal our dilemma to the prosecutor, requesting that he designate his own cardiologist to verify the finding. He selected Dr. Meyer Texon, who in two reports confirmed the medical condition of Dr. Hammer.

Babcock appealed his prison sentence. He appeared to have a cogent argument that a misdemeanor precluded anything but a fine, and that the prosecutor had so understood the consequence of his plea. Suddenly Hammer found himself rooting for a victory for Babcock, who had been hoisted on his own sword, the point of which, however, was also thrust into Hammer.

We faced a new dilemma. Our client insisted that he was innocent and yet he could not stand trial. The doctors forbade it. We were not going to risk his life, although he was recklessly willing to do so. What was the solution for such an impasse?

The law, in its wisdom, provided one. It is called "The Alford Plea." It permitted a defendant to assert that he was innocent, but that he was willing to plead guilty in order to avoid the ordeal, expense, and uncertain outcome of a trial. It was the perfect instrument to extricate us from our predicament. But it required the agreement of the prosecutor, and then the approval of the court. The prosecutor would not accept such a conditioned plea. We were left with one alternative, to negotiate a plea of guilty for the smallest offense possible. It would have to be a misdemeanor. Under no circumstances would Hammer consent to a felony plea. If it came to that, we might have to yield to Hammer's insistence for vindication by trial, even if we had to bring him into court on a stretcher. But it was not yet necessary to face this agonizing decision. We were just perplexed about how a technical dispute about a date had cancerously enlarged itself into a life and death struggle.

After long negotiations with the special prosecutor, a plea bargain was struck, whereby Hammer would plead guilty to three misdemeanors involving the campaign contribution by him of $54,000 without revealing that he was the donor. He also had to accept a prejudicial, historical recital of the surrounding events, even though it was stated they were not relevant to the charges to which he pleaded.

There would be no grand jury hearing; no indictment. It would all be processed by the filing of a mere information, suitable to the minor nature of the charge. Furthermore, as some protection against any punishment, except a fine, the prosecutor agreed not to ask for a jail sentence and to recommend to the court that it "should take into consideration as a relevant factor in imposing sentence" the medical opinions concerning Hammer's ill health.

With heavy heart, physically and psychologically, Hammer agreed to this agreement. It was not easy for us, as counsel, to recommend it. In preparation for a trial, before the deterioration of Hammer's health, I had written more than twenty briefs demonstrating that even as pure legal matter there were no violations. For example, even assuming a lie in the questionnaire sent to the Ervin Committee, it was not a criminal violation under Section 1001. Not every misstatement is a crime, or a large part of the population would be in jail. The test is one of perjury, the strict standards of which could not be diluted. So Judge Gerhard

Gesell, in Washington, later ruled in another case involving a lie to an FBI agent.

Similarly, even the giving of a campaign contribution anonymously after April 7, was not a crime, because a fictitious name did not accompany the gift. It was later supplied by Babcock's friends. I demonstrated in a brief that the gift and false name must be simultaneous, or there was no violation. I found authority for this argument in a case where an elected senator who had not yet been sworn in was charged with bribery. His conviction under the public official section was reversed. He had not yet become a senator, and his subsequent swearing in could not be referred back to constitute a crime. The prosecutor could not "retroject." We had the same defense under the doctrine of "retrojection."

These and other arguments might be deemed by a layman technical defenses, but could there be anything more technical than the charge; before April 7—valid, after April 7—a crime? In dealing with men's liberties, the burden of proving the specific accusation "beyond a reasonable doubt" lies heavy on the prosecutor. Also, he had to rely on Babcock as his chief witness, and he knew that we would welcome a test of credibility between him and Hammer.

Our client had carefully read my briefs. He was persuaded that we even had a chance for a directed verdict in his favor at the end of the Government's case. Then it would not be necessary for him to testify at all.

However, health considerations prevailed over everything else. The mere pendency of the proceeding was a pressure on Hammer's nervous system which communicated itself to an arrhythmic heart. We persuaded Hammer to take the misdemeanor plea.

So Hammer appeared before Chief Judge William B. Jones in the Federal Court in Washington to plead guilty. The court, in accordance with required procedure, questioned him closely to be certain that he knew the possible consequences of his plea. He wanted Hammer to understand that the court could sentence him to jail, even though only a misdemeanor was involved. Hammer protested that he had been advised by counsel that the only punishment was a fine. The judge insisted that although he was not saying that he would impose a jail sentence, he had the power to do so. Hammer grew more edgy. The court recognized his dilemma and suggested a recess for a half hour so that he could consult with his counsel in a private conference room.

The scene that followed was chaotic. The majority of counsel agreed with Hammer that he should plead not guilty and stand trial. The minority vociferously opposed. Washington counsel Edward Bennett Williams interpreted the letter agreement with the prosecutor as to require a plea of guilty without reservation and threatened to withdraw from the case (later he did). The argument grew so strident that a court attendant bade us to lower our voices, because they could be heard in the adjoining courtroom.

When I looked at Hammer, pale-faced and shaken by divided counsel and knowing the doctors' forebodings, I shifted my position. I advised that the plea of guilty be taken. I felt that nothing was more important than to accelerate the end of the proceeding. It was desirable to have a vindicated client but only if he was alive. Hammer announced that he would follow my advice. He returned to the courtroom and answered every question docilely. The court then accepted the plea, and adjourned for another date so that he would receive the probation officer's report before imposing sentence.

At last we thought we were nearing the end of the struggle. Little did we know that it had just begun. Extraordinary intervening events made everything that preceded a mere interlude.

Hammer was interviewed by the probation officer, James Walker, in Los Angeles. He was invited to open his heart and his mind and set forth fully all the circumstances surrounding the events which led to the misdemeanor plea. This and any other statements about his background, age, health, achievements, and the opinions by others about his character were solicited, so that Judge Jones would have before him a full history upon which to exercise his discretion in meting out punishment.

Probation reports are based on the theory that not all the same crimes should be punished equally. It is a common misconception that they should. The law punishes the individual, not the crime. One who has lived an exemplary life and has strayed under unusual circumstances should not be punished equally with one who has previously been an enemy of society and who has no redeeming record to warrant mercy.

Thus invited, Hammer wrote a letter which was virtually a stream of consciousness.

Did my intention to make the payment before April 7 become confused with the actual deed? In the hectic life I lead, with problems of global scope often engaging me day and night, this matter could conceivably have been overlooked although I had it checked off in my mind as done. I know that such memory quirks can occur—for example have we not all had the experience of being sure of having sent a letter, when it turns out that the intention to dictate it was never executed?

In view of his illness he was willing to resolve all doubts in favor of the prosecutor and plead guilty

Judge Jones was angered by this letter. He did not consider it "the outpouring of the heart of a very troubled man," but rather a protestation of innocence inconsistent with the plea of guilty. He directed Hammer to appear under oath and reaffirm the answers he gave when the plea was taken.

Hammer's condition had grown worse, and a trip from Los Angeles to Washington was not advisable, but we imposed on Dr. H. J. C. Swan, past president of the American College of Cardiology, and professor of cardiology at U.C.L.A., to come with him. The doctor, having no authority to practice in Washington, took the precaution of retaining a heart specialist in the capital to attend, in the event that some incident occurred, in the courtroom. Also Arthur Groman, Hammer's able California counsel, who had participated from the start and knew his condition best from daily observation, and conferences with the physicians, flew in to present the medical evidence to the Judge.

Dr. Hammer volunteered to take the stand under oath to confirm his plea. The court refused to hear him. The court also refused to permit Dr. Swan to testify, "The continued strain could easily produce . . . a catastrophic illness in Dr. Hammer." The physician designated by the Government had agreed.

The court ruled that "I am unable to find a factual basis for the plea of guilty." Even though neither the prosecutor nor defense counsel sought to change the plea, the court on its own motion (*sua sponte*) vacated the guilty plea, entered a "not guilty" plea for Hammer, and set the case down for trial.

Thus forced to a decision which, except for Hammer's health, we would have welcomed, we sought the doctors' views about the risk. The prosecutor ended our indecision. He announced that, the plea bargain having been set aside, he was convening a grand jury and would indict Hammer on two felonies to be added to the misdemeanors which had been set down for trial. This was too much.

We immediately applied for a stay which would enjoin the prosecutor from indicting Hammer. We appealed from Judge Jones's decision and requested that the plea bargain be reinstated. The prosecutor moved to dismiss our appeal and argued that a stay could not be granted which would enjoin a law enforcement agency from pursuing a criminal prosecution.

The Court of Appeals, composed of three judges, granted a stay until argument could be heard. We faced a new crisis. At the argument the judges indicated their perplexity as to why Judge Jones had been so offended by the letter to the probation official. It was obviously intended, like so much other material, to aid the court in deciding the degree of punishment. I offered to withdraw the letter. The judges directed that the plea be reinstated, thus forbidding the prosecutor from seeking felony indictments. I was asked how soon Hammer could appear before Judge Jones to complete the procedure. I commented how eager we were, for reasons of his health, to expedite the matter. I would try to have him appear within three days. So it was ordered.

I telephoned the good news to Hammer, who was elated with the reversal. We were confident Judge Jones would recognize the conclusive findings of five leading heart specialists, including the Government's, which ruled out any jail sentence particularly for a misdemeanor.

This time we were sure we were nearing the end. What else could happen? The worst of all. Judge Jones issued an order transferring the case to another judge. He designated Judge Hart, who had previously condemned Hammer when he sentenced Babcock to jail! It appeared that we had not been cast from the proverbial frying pan into the fire, but directly into jail.

A lawyer cannot afford to surrender to either physical or emotional exhaustion. Hammer had heart disease, but we could not be disheartened. Our adrenalin was flowing freely. We had learned of Judge Jones's order at 4:00 P.M. I asked the staff of my Washington office to stay through the night. We dictated a motion to disqualify Judge Hart from sitting in the case, and supported it with affidavits and briefs recounting the tormented history of the case. We asked in the alternative to transfer the proceedings to California.

At 6:00 A.M., the voluminous papers were typed and bound. Two attorneys were assigned to wait at the prosecutor's office to serve them at 8:30 A.M., and then to file them in the courthouse immediately thereafter. If Judge Hart refused to disqualify himself (recuse himself, is the legal phrase), we had also begun preparation for an appeal.

An hour later, when Judge Hart ascended the bench, I was ready for argument, any dishevelment of appearance offset, I hoped, by the stimulation derived from the effort.

"May I say at the outset—and with great sincerity, and not as lip service, that it is a great honor to appear before Your Honor, and I am grieved that my application must be made to recuse, but a lawyer's duty to his client often requires very embarrassing tasks."

THE COURT: "Well, don't be embarrassed. Just give me your point of view."

MR. NIZER: "Very well, I will, sir."

I quoted his previous condemnation of Hammer.

Then I read from the statute that a judge should recuse himself when "his impartiality might reasonably be questioned." I emphasized that it was not partiality which was the test but the appearance of partiality which had to be avoided.

"How can the defendant feel when the Judge before whom he comes has already condemned him with respect to matters which our affidavit now shows were incorrect?"

The Judge assured me that he had no personal knowledge of the disputed facts:

THE COURT: "Counsel, what you are arguing is something that, in the event that the plea was accepted, and he comes up for sentence, you could argue in connection with the sentence but it has nothing to do with this matter so far as I can see."

I urged again that:

"in the interests of this court and generally, that there be no punishmen of Dr. Hammer, at your hands, in the light of your prior condemnation of him."

Furthermore, I contended that if Judge Jones wanted to transfer the case, the rules required that the new judge be selected at random from a revolving wheel. It had been improperly assigned directly to him.

Despite the sensitivity of my requests, the argument had proceeded with admirable professional objectivity. Judge Hart was known for his fairness and he accepted my contentions with tolerance. But suddenly I realized that he was riled, not by my challenge of him, but what he understood was my challenge of Judge Jones:

THE COURT: "Mr. Nizer, this is a fifteen Judge Court. Normally, whenever a defendant asks me to disqualify myself I am inclined to do it, but let me ask you a question: Did you or did you not ask the United States Court of Appeals to remove Judge Jones from this case?"

I explained that Judge Robb in the Court of Appeals had commented that apparently Judge Jones had felt imposed upon by Hammer's letter, which he thought repudiated his plea. I replied that "we had the greatest regard and respect for Chief Judge Jones" but that if he felt imposed upon by the defendant, the court might consider sending the case back to another judge, as was the practice, for example, in the Second Court of Appeals, so that a judge who was reversed might not harbor resentment. The issue was the same—the avoidance of the appearance of partiality. So I concluded my answer to Judge Hart, saying that I had not volunteered my request about Judge Jones, but responded to a statement that he might feel resentment. "To that extent I made the application."

Judge Hart was not appeased.

"I certainly have no desire to have this case; I would be very happy to get rid of it, but I have a duty to take it.

"I have a duty to see that judge-shopping is not permitted, and I will therefore not disqualify myself in the case."

MR. NIZER: "I assure your Honor with the greatest earnestness that we are not judge-shopping.

"On the contrary, we think that inadvertently the assignment of this case, not in the regular manner by random choice was much closer to the selection of a Judge than anything we wished to do, and we would respectfully submit that we wish any Judge who was impartial and might not give the appearance, no matter what the fact is, of partiality to sit in a matter of this kind.

"So I respectfully except to your Honor's ruling."

This exchange was an example of confrontation, which sometimes occurs between counsel and the court, in which daggers fly, disguised though they be in courteous sheaths.

The bitter exchange having ended, Judge Hart immediately addressed himself dispassionately to the medical problem, with equal concern for Hammer's health and the prosecution's rights. This, despite my provocative statement (necessary to protect our client) that I would proceed, "but we do not thereby wish in any way to acquiesce in Your Honor's sitting in the matter ultimately."

The Judge's duty also had to be performed without rancor.

THE COURT: "Well, you have your remedy there, if you wish to pursue it."

An appeal to a higher court was in the air again. But in the meantime we were invited by the court to discuss Hammer's physical condition and our motion to transfer the case to California.

Groman, who had again flown in with the latest sad tidings, submitted an affidavit of Dr. Rexford Kennamer, who for seventeen years had been Hammer's personal physician. He described an attack his patient suffered at ten in the evening, two days previously, which required him to be brought to the Los Angeles Hospital. His condition was diagnosed as preinfarction angina, congestive heart failure, and disturbance of his cardiac rhythm. The affidavits of three other pre-eminent cardiologists and one selected by the prosecutor attested to the seriousness of Hammer's condition.

The prosecutor suggested that the Judge appoint an independent physician to examine Hammer and report. I said that "we would welcome that."

Judge Hart announced that he had selected four "outstanding" cardiologists, and he would designate any two that the prosecutor and I agreed upon. It was time for a grand gesture;

"We will consent to any doctor that the prosecutor selects—do that blindly—he doesn't have to consult me because I know what the tragic facts are."

The heated session came to an end on a hopeful note.

MR. NIZER: "Perhaps Your Honor might still consider in the light of the health situation, the advisability of transferring the matter to California."

THE COURT: "That could be. It would depend on the physical situation, I guess."

The prosecutor selected from the Judge's list Dr. George A. Kelser, Jr., director of cardiology of the George Washington University Medical Center, and Dr. Ross D. Fletcher, chief of cardiology of the Veterans Administration Hospital in Washington, D.C. They flew to California, submitted Hammer to the most rigorous examinations and tests, and filed a seventeen-page report.

Judge Hart set another hearing. He bade us present the medical evidence. I put his appointed physicians on the stand. Their findings confirmed in every detail those made by five other outstanding cardiologists including one previously designated by the prosecutor. Hammer was "threatened with acute myocardial infarction due to coronary artery atherosclerotic disease." Surgery might be necessary.

The very pending of the proceeding "contributed significantly to a life-endangering situation." The unanimous conclusion was that:

The nature of his disease is such that he will need to remain close to his physicians for an indefinite period of time. If feasible, consideration should be given to possible arrangement of transfer of the court appearance to Los Angeles when the acute phase of his illness has abated.

The prosecutor accepted the doctors' report. Judge Hart was fully convinced by the independent judgment of his own designated physicians, as well as those of the pre-eminent cardiologists who had treated Hammer.

The Judge issued an order transferring the case to the Federal Court in Los Angeles County, and indicated his solicitude for Hammer's survival, by directing that his order be expedited "forthwith" so that the proceeding there could be hastened, thus relieving Hammer as soon as possible of the anxiety which worsened his condition.

The motion to disqualify the Judge became obsolete.

In Los Angeles, the turn of the court wheel designated Judge Lydick. He was a severe disciplinarian, insisting on precise conformity with the rules. He refused to accelerate the proceeding by holding court in Dr.

Hammer's hospital room, as some judges had, in their discretion, done in other cases. There was fretting delay. Finally Dr. Hammer was taken to the courtroom, wired invisibly with telemetered electrocardiographic equipment, so that he could be monitored secretly in an adjoining room.

The court not only had before it the voluminous medical reports forwarded by Judge Hart, but questioned Dr. Swan under oath. He accepted Hammer's plea.

Then he weighed the appropriate sentence. He considered the probation report, and the more than one hundred letters which had been sent to Judge Jones recommending the greatest consideration for Dr. Hammer. These letters came from men in the highest stations in all walks of life, from clergymen like James Francis Cardinal McIntyre, Rabbi Edgar Magnin, and Norman Vincent Peale (who called him "one of the most creatively inspirational persons I have ever met"), to public officials like Secretary of the Treasury William E. Simon (who wrote that "Hammer is a man of the highest character and integrity who would not consciously or knowingly violate our laws"), six United States senators, presidents and deans of universities, ambassadors, Federal judges and two former presidents of the American Bar Association, publisher Arthur Ochs Sulzberger of the New York *Times*, public figures like Lady Bird Johnson, Henry Ford II, Lowell Thomas, and Bob Hope, business executives, and many, many others.

The outpouring of high regard and good will for Hammer offset the anguish of the occasion to some extent. It was a gratifying by-product of a criminal charge. How else could a man solicit such letters? Like flattering obituaries of ourselves, we would like to read them, but are pleased to forego the pleasure.

The Judge fined Hammer $3,000, and provided for one year probation. Hammer was free.

Then occurred the most startling of all developments. Within weeks, Hammer was dismissed from the hospital forty pounds lighter from his regimen there. He began his exercises to tone his muscles (a musical reference as if the body would sing). Sing it did.

He took vigorous charge of his business duties. He began to fly across the globe, although he diminished the risks by an oxygen tank and a resuscitating machine in his private plane, the three pilots trained in its use, catnaps on a comfortable bed, and for a while a doctor alongside him. Even the visual change was remarkable. He looked ever younger, as if his age retreated with the lost hours of his far-flying travels. He resumed his around-the-clock schedule.

Lest this be confused with mere nervous energy, the medical reports confirmed what the doctors considered an impossible recovery. They were astounded. Understandably, laymen and readers of his continued exploits became skeptical of the prior prognoses, particularly in the midst of a criminal proceeding.

Due to several experiences I had witnessed of litigation neurosis caused by stress, I was not as mystified. I had seen a young woman with a clutching hand (called syndactilism), diagnosed as permanent by opposing insurance company doctors, open her hand a week after a verdict. I had seen men and women in matrimonial and other disputes, seriously ill from bleeding ulcers, high blood pressure, diabetes, paralysis, and even dangerous tumors, recover when their problems were solved. We simply have not sufficiently evaluated the effects of "stress"; the cruelties it can inflict and the miracles resulting from its banishment.

The Thirteenth Report, No. 275, of the World Health Organization asserts that 70 per cent of all patients currently being treated by doctors are suffering from conditions which have their origins in stress (*Stress Disease*, by Peter Blythe).

Dr. Hans Selye, in his book *The Stress of Life*, has traced many diseases directly to stress, particularly cardiovascular disease. Predisposition to a disease increased the vulnerability to stress. This factor existed in Hammer's family history. His father and one brother had died of heart attacks, and his younger brother had suffered a stroke and had undergone carotid endarterectomy. We do suffer the ills of our fathers.

Also, studies have revealed that in evaluating the intensity of over forty types of "life-stress" events, the fear of a jail term ranked first, death in the immediate family second, and divorce third. So the "miracle" of Hammer's recovery was not as mysterious as it seemed, in the light of science's discovery of litigation stress.

But the "miracle" of his "luck" in developing new enterprises remained. After his heart and honor were rehabilitated, he devoted himself largely to solving the energy crisis, not through conventional oil drilling and coal, but by means of a new technology.

Nature has endowed the United States with more oil than exists in the entire Middle East. It is located in the Rocky Mountains. In three states, Colorado, Utah, and Wyoming, there exist one trillion, eight hundred billion barrels of oil, two and a half times the entire oil reserve of the world, and sufficient to supply the needs of the United States for one hundred forty years at its 1973 rate of consumption.

Why had this "black gold" not been tapped? Because the oil is encased in shale rock and the former method of extracting it was uneconomic. The technique was to dig into the mountain, excavate tons of shale, reduce it to rubble, heat it to release the oil, and then cool it with water. This was known as aboveground shale oil mining. It was not only prohibitively expensive but left surface shale debris, offensive to any ecologist. To produce fifty thousand barrels of oil a day by the aboveground method would require moving twenty-five million tons of shale rock a year to a plant for refining. Thereafter, the spent shale rock would have to be transported to a dump. Veritable mountains would have to be moved.

Some years ago, Hammer became interested in a new technology to extract shale oil. The mining took place inside the mountain. It was called in situ (in place) mining. The process was to dig a chamber, called a retort, and fragment the shale by use of explosives. Then the shale rubble was lit with a gas flame so that the heat separated the oil from the shale, which then flowed to the bottom of the chamber. From where it was pumped to the surface and sent to a refinery. This method cut the cost in half and made it competitive with imported oil. It avoided the ecological effect of shale mounds left on the surface, and it did not require the large use of water.

Hammer acquired the technique for Occidental, obtained nine patents on the process, and has spent approximately fifty million dollars to develop it. Three agencies of the Government have passed on the new development. The Department of Interior, the Federal Energy Administration, and the Energy Research and Development Administration have reported that "Occidental Petroleum has developed the modified in situ process that offers economic and environmental advantages over conventional processing techniques."

With characteristic flair, Hammer offered this technology to the United States Government for defense purposes at no cost. He offered to license private firms at a reasonable fee, namely 3 per cent of the selling price of the oil. He also suggested a national plan like GOPO (Government Owned Private Operated), which President Roosevelt developed to meet the rubber crisis during World War II.

There are other potential sources of energy. After all, it was American ingenuity which turned the barren sands of Arabia into a rich oil reserve. We may learn to send solar energy by laser beams from outer space, as one astronaut told me could be done. Energy from the sun captured on the "beads" of windmill-like arms of Skylab provided the power upon which it operated while in earth orbit. In addition to nuclear, coal, wind, and water power, we may even get free and abundant energy from the air itself, or from the sea. A national concentrated effort, similar to the one that produced artificial rubber or the atomic bomb, could tap the vast resources of oil beneath the Rocky Mountains.

In the meantime, a tycoon who had to fight for his freedom may have made possible energy independence for the United States.

MIRROR WITHOUT REFLECTIONS

Many people fear to make their last will and testament. Family and business planning look to future living. Wills look to death. The subconscious evasion of that uncertain certainty is pierced by every word in a will, from the customary provision that funeral expenses shall be paid first, to the painful disposition of assets. The older one is, the greater the reluctance. It appears to be, as a child said of his grandmother reading the Bible, "preparation for the final exam." To rationalize their fears, some people turn to superstition: "It is a bad omen to make a will." Picasso, for example, who died at ninety-one, and therefore must have anticipated the need for a will to dispose of his $750-million fortune, refused to make one. He shrank from the mere mention of death. The same was probably true of Howard Hughes.

In a sense, an autobiography, even a semiautobiography such as *Reflections Without Mirrors,* presents the same problem. The implication is that a final summary of one's life is being written.

Well, I don't feel that way. The gifts of vitality, I have previously bespoken, are overflowing.

There is a custom followed in many religions that upon death mirrors are covered or turned to the wall. Presumably this is to defeat the vanity of those who come to pay condolences.

As I end *Reflections Without Mirrors,* I have no thought of writing "finis." There are many cases I will still try, many landscapes I will paint, music I will write, and more books within me to release before the final day of that mirror without reflections.

INDEX

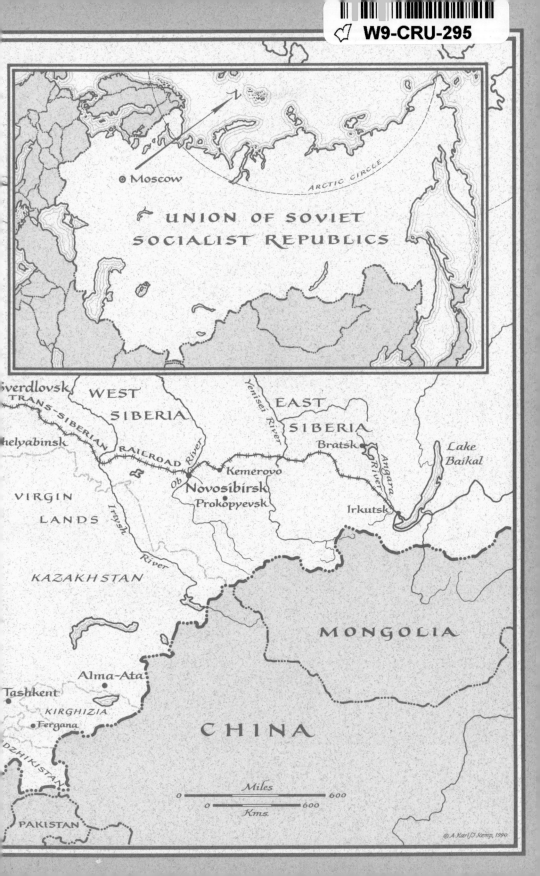

Moscow

UNION OF SOVIET
SOCIALIST REPUBLICS

ARCTIC CIRCLE

Sverdlovsk
TRANS-SIBERIAN
Chelyabinsk

WEST
SIBERIA

Yenisei River

EAST
SIBERIA

Bratsk

Lake
Baikal

RAILROAD

Ob River

Kemerovo

Novosibirsk

Prokopyevsk

Angara River

Irkutsk

VIRGIN
LANDS

Irtysh River

KAZAKHSTAN

MONGOLIA

Alma-Ata

Tashkent

KIRGHIZIA

Fergana

CHINA

TADZHIKISTAN

PAKISTAN

Miles
0   600

0   600
Kms.

© A. Karl / J. Kemp, 1990

THE
NEW
RUSSIANS

THE
NEW
RUSSIANS

HEDRICK SMITH

RANDOM HOUSE
NEW YORK

Grateful acknowledgment is made to the following for permission
to reprint previously published material:
Thurlbeck Productions, Inc.: Seven lines from the song "Revolution" by DDT.
Reprinted by permission of Thurlbeck Productions (DDT).

Library of Congress Cataloging-in-Publication Data

Smith, Hedrick.
    The new Russians.
    Includes index.
    1. Soviet Union—Social life and customs—1970–
2. Soviet Union—Social conditions—1970–
DK276.S527   1990   947.085   90-53127
ISBN 0-394-58190-3

Manufactured in the United States of America

Book design by Jo Anne Metsch

To my children,
Laurie, Jenny, Scott, and Lesley

May you enjoy a lifetime
of genuine peace
and love

ACKNOWLEDGMENTS

Whatever the shortcomings of this book, they would have been much greater without the generous help, advice, and comments of many friends and colleagues.

Five people deserve special acknowledgment. My friend Greg Guroff, a Russian historian with a fund of knowledge and personal acquaintances in Moscow, not only opened the doors of his many friends for me but read the entire manuscript and infused each section with his understanding of Soviet society and Russian history. Bruce Parrott, director of Soviet Studies at the Johns Hopkins School of Advanced International Studies, also read the manuscript, sharing with me his insights and steering me from missteps in the world of Soviet high politics.

Anne Lawrence, my chief researcher and an accomplished student of Soviet society, provided me not only with organized, detailed chronologies of rapidly changing developments in many fields, but also with rich memoranda on many special events, people, and topics—all of which made the swift writing of this book not only easier but possible. Kate Medina, my editor at Random House, mingled her infectious and supportive enthusiasm with wise comments about its architecture and suggestions about making it more alive and accessible for the reader. With history literally in the making, she persuaded an entire publishing house to move with unusual speed so the reporting would be fresh to the reader. My wife, Susan, not only gave me her many acute observations and personal reflections during months of our traveling together, but then sat up into the wee hours many a morning, reading the new pages and offering her suggestions and, best of all, her encouragement.

I am indebted to two institutions: WGBH-TV in Boston, and in particular to Peter McGhee, manager for national productions, for backing my documentary series, *Inside Gorbachev's USSR with Hedrick Smith,* and putting me in the Soviet Union at the most fascinating period of change since the Russian Revolution. The commitment of WGBH made possible much of the reporting in this book; and the support of people at WGBH such as Marcia Storkerson and Paul Taylor made the effort more fruitful and more pleasant.

Each of the four series producers, Martin Smith, Sherry Jones, Marian Marzynski, and David Royle—and especially Martin Smith as executive producer—shared with me their reporting and their ideas; in the collaborative process of fashioning films and working out scripts with them, I honed many of my own concepts. I thank them for their help and tip my hat to them as first-class professionals. I gained much, too, from the knowledge and experience of Louis Menashe, professor of Soviet studies at Brooklyn's Polytechnic Institute, and from the reporting of Natasha Lance, who, with Louis Menashe, served as associate producer.

I am indebted as well to the Foreign Policy Institute of the Johns Hopkins University, to its president, Harold Brown, to executive director Simon Serfaty, and to George Packard, dean of the Johns Hopkins School of Advanced International Studies, for giving me an academic home and a congenial working atmosphere. I benefited particularly from the knowledge of three Johns Hopkins colleagues: Bruce Parrott and Charles Fairbanks, Jr., of the Foreign Policy Institute, and David Calleo, director of European studies, SAIS. Linda Carlson, the reference librarian at SAIS, provided invaluable assistance on innumerable occasions.

Scholars in the field of Soviet studies at other institutions were very generous. Two deserve special note for their highly regarded expertise and generosity: Ed Hewett, a specialist on the Soviet economy at the Brookings Institution, and Paul Goble, a specialist on Soviet nationality issues, formerly with the State Department and now with Radio Free Europe/Radio Liberty.

I am also grateful for the assistance and advice of many other scholars, especially Stephen F. Cohen of Princeton University; Nancy Condee of the University of Pittsburgh; Murray Feshbach of Georgetown University; William Fierman of the University of Tennessee; Ken Gray, U.S. Department of Agriculture; Gregory Grossman, University of California at Berkeley; Nicholas Hayes of Hamline University; Jerry Hough of Duke University; Gail Lapidus of the University of California at Berkeley;

Robert Legvold of Columbia University; Ellen Mickiewicz of Emory University; Vladimir Padunov of Pittsburgh University; Peter Reddaway of George Washington University; Gertrude Schroeder of the University of Virginia; Anatole Shub of the United States Information Agency; Vladimir Treml of Duke University; Don Van Atta of Hamilton College; Josephine Wool of Howard University; and Steve Wegren of Duke University.

In the Soviet Union, three officials were unusually important in helping me gain wide access and in sharing their own life experiences and ideas: Leonid Dobrokhotov and Nikolai Shishlin of the Central Committee staff, and Valentin Lazutkin, deputy chairman of the State Committee for Television and Radio.

I could not have completed this book without the assistance of my research staff: not only Anne Lawrence, but those who worked with her so closely and devoted many long hours to my book—Louise Keefe, Jeffrey Lilley, and Sue Thornton. At the Library of Congress, I owe special thanks to Grant Harris of the European reading room; and at Radio Free Europe/Radio Liberty, to Jane Lester, Julie Moffett, and Brian Reed.

I owe thanks as well to my translators: Aleksei Levin, Julie Moffett, Moira Ratchford, Conrad Turner, Michele Berdy; to Randa Murphy, who transcribed many interviews; to Maryliss Bartlett, my secretary, who did countless chores; and to several interns—Jon Ballis, Paul Poletes, Christine Feig, Anastasia Urtz, Cynthia Kop.

At Random House, I am grateful to Amy Edelman for her painstaking copy editing of my manuscript and for keeping me from many missteps, and to Jon Karp for his shepherding of my work through the byways of Random House, often under considerable pressure but always with good cheer. And finally, my thanks to Julian Bach, my literary agent, who was enthusiastic about my writing about the Russians long ago, and to Ann Rittenberg, his associate, for their strong support.

Sovietologists will contend that this book should not be titled *The New Russians* because it is the Soviet peoples, all nationalities, and not just the ethnic Russians, who are engaged in massive transformation of their country. They will assert that with the Soviet Union now breaking up, readers should not mistakenly identify Russia with the whole Soviet Union.

That is correct, but I believe that Gorbachev, who set free the process of *perestroika,* is very much an ethnic Russian, not only in lineage but also in psychology, and that ultimately, success or failure of the process of reform will be decided by how it is handled by the Russians, who are the dominant people. Other nationalities, for example in the Baltics and in the Caucasus, were much more ready for reform, almost like the East Europeans. It is the Russians who have to remake their society and themselves. I have tried, as well, to make it clear to readers when I am talking specifically about Russians, and when about Soviets in general. And because of my earlier book, *The Russians*, I wanted to make explicit that *The New Russians* was a comparison of the same people and culture over time.

Finally, there are several systems of transliteration for Russian into English. I have adopted the practice of American newspapers, such as *The New York Times*, which generally follow accepted academic rules but make minor adaptations, for example, inserting the *y* before vowels (as in *Y*eltsin or *Y*evgeny) in personal names. My standard has been to make names and terms easier for the general reader.

HEDRICK SMITH
Chevy Chase, Maryland
September 6, 1990

CONTENTS

INTRODUCTION: AFTER THE WALL CAME DOWN

When I left Russia and the Russians in December 1974, after three years as Moscow bureau chief for *The New York Times*, I thought that vast country and its people would never really change. As a people, they were so Russian, so different from people in the West.

Having lived since 1971 under the oppressive orthodoxy of Communist party leader Leonid Brezhnev, and having endured numerous personal scrapes with the chill and arrogance of Soviet officialdom, I had come to see authoritarian rule as something firmly embedded in Russian society and ingrained in the Russian psyche. A solid wall separated the rulers and the ruled. In 1956, Nikita Khrushchev had eased the raw despotism of Stalin, but he had left intact the granite citadel of power that was the self-perpetuating hierarchy of the Communist Party.

Five long centuries of absolutism—from Ivan the Terrible to the Soviet seventies—had left the Russian masses submissive. In their personal lives, I found them ingenious in beating the numbing inefficiency of the state economy. Their black market was so vast that it operated as a countereconomy, even to the extent of producing underground millionaires. But in the sphere of political action, grass-roots initiative was moribund.

In Russian history, tiny shoots of democracy had sprung up briefly from time to time, but none had taken root. Except for a handful of dissidents, most of the intellectuals I encountered in the seventies were politically passive: Fear had taught them to save cynical jokes for private company. Ordinary people might grumble about shortages or injustices, but they never took action. As I was told time and time again, Russians would choose stability over chaos, order over freedom.

The Chinese are known as a nation of traders and businessmen, but I learned firsthand that the Russians had little entrepreneurial know-how. Underground centers of illicit private enterprise were in the non-Russian republics of Georgia, Azerbaijan, and Uzbekistan, or in the more Western-oriented Baltic regions of Latvia or Lithuania. In places like Moscow or Leningrad, Jews or transplanted Georgians or Armenians showed more of a knack for commerce than most Russians did. The vast majority of Soviet people expected the state to take care of them—especially of their economic needs, however poorly—and to tell them what to do. For despite its revolutionary conceits, the Soviet Union was a profoundly conservative society. Most Russians were not driven by Western appetites for the new and trendy; they were held back by the dual weights of inertia and dogma.

I did know some intellectuals who were desperate for a bit of fresh air, some room to breathe, for a modest "thaw" such as the one initiated by Khrushchev in the late 1950s. But it seemed to me that even a modest reform would be long in coming. Like others who had lived among the Russians, sent children to their schools, studied their history and their institutions, come to know their ways and their mentality, I left Russia sixteen years ago thinking that fundamental change was impossible. And I wrote that in my book *The Russians.*

The decline and stagnation that sank into place for the next decade, into the mid-eighties, seemed to confirm this judgment. Soviet politics appeared as frozen as the Siberian tundra.

As it turned out, of course, I was wrong.

Never had I imagined that the Soviet Union would undergo the kind of seismic transformation that became apparent a couple of years after Mikhail Gorbachev came to power in March 1985.

In the name of reforms that would modernize, humanize, and ultimately save Soviet socialism, Gorbachev cracked open the wall between the rulers and the ruled and let loose massive popular discontent; he shook the very foundations of the system that Stalin had imposed from above. He provoked the Soviet people to begin taking their destinies in their own hands. He summoned a democratic spirit that aroused the slumbering giant of Russia and then swept across Eastern Europe, toppling Communist governments like a row of helpless toy soldiers—Poland, Hungary, East Germany, Czechoslovakia, Romania. When these puppet governments looked to the Kremlin for protection, they got none. Gorbachev let the tidal wave roll on, until it swept over the Berlin Wall and carried the Iron Curtain out to sea.

He called this vast undertaking *perestroika*. But like any shrewd political leader who is improvising strategy as he goes along, Gorbachev has kept manipulating the definition of that word to suit his purposes. In his hands, it is a slogan for the general urge for reform, and also a label for whatever measures he chooses to implement. Sometimes, when Gorbachev is on the offensive, his *perestroika* rings with what he loves to call "revolutionary" change; it harbors gossamer promises of democracy, of private enterprise—and it smacks of heresy to the Soviet power establishment. At other times, when Gorbachev is on the defensive, the term has more limited, cautious connotations—of modernization, of readapting Soviet socialism without dismantling the system founded by Lenin. Then, Gorbachev uses the term *perestroika* in ways that include protection of the establishment.

In talking with Gorbachev's colleagues and following his course closely, I have come to see Gorbachev not as a theorist with a pure vision of the future, but as a pragmatist, who pursues what works and is ready to junk what does not. *Perestroika* is a process, not a fixed and finite objective. Literally, it means "reconstruction" or "restructuring." But on a deeper level, it is the Reformation. Think of Gorbachev, then, as a kind of Martin Luther, setting out to cleanse, purify, and renew a corrupt and failing Socialist Church, but instead forever changing its nature and its destiny.

Because, in fact, *perestroika*, in its essence, represents a sweeping and profound change, far more extensive than a specific program of reforms. It is the catalyst for a wholesale societal transformation, analogous to the opening of Japan by Commodore Perry in 1854, or Bismarck's forging of the modern German state in the nineteenth century. It has parallels with Kemal Atatürk's disciplined drive to modernize the remnants of the Ottoman Empire and thrust Turkey into the twentieth century, and with Mahatma Gandhi's sounding the death knell of British colonialism with his nonviolent campaign to free India from Imperial England. These were not passing trends that flashed brightly for a few years and then disappeared. They were major bend points in the path of history. So, too, is Gorbachev's *perestroika*.

Initially, of course, many in the West were skeptical. For several years, people wondered: Was Gorbachev a Communist charlatan, a masterful media politician whose changes were cosmetic, but not cosmic, not real, whose "new thinking" was transitory, not fundamental? At first, both President Reagan and then President Bush were cautious, and careful not to embrace Gorbachev too hastily. But with the stunning collapse of

Communist power in Eastern Europe in the latter half of 1989, it became clear to almost everyone that the long, painful period of the Cold War was ending, and that the world was crossing an important historical divide.

Overnight, it seemed, the world order was transformed and our global agenda reshaped. The old structure based on East-West confrontation became obsolete. German reunification replaced the Cold War as the number one concern of the major powers. Subtly at first, but then very dramatically, the world was shifting from an era in which international affairs were driven by the arms race and the threat of a nuclear apocaplyse, to a new epoch in which the principal driving force of global affairs was economic competition.

In the American psyche, the threat of Soviet nuclear missiles was replaced by anxiety over the economic challenge from Japan and the fear that the United States could not compete well enough in the global marketplace. Gorbachev's *perestroika* did not create these trends, but it accelerated them. It vaulted us all into a new era.

What was so striking about Gorbachev's approach, when I finally had a chance to see it up close, was that he was daring to trust the people; and he was daring to disassemble the pyramid of power in the Soviet Union. His strategy represented a reversal of much of twentieth-century history, for this has been the century of totalitarian governments, epitomized by Adolf Hitler and Joseph Stalin. Dictators, parties, ideological movements, have single-mindedly set about accumulating power, concentrating power—total power—in their own hands. Yet now, near the century's end, both Gorbachev in the Soviet Union and Deng Xiaoping in China have tried to head in the opposite direction. Each has attempted the controlled dispersal of power, but when those attempts got out of control, as they were bound to, Deng pulled back; Gorbachev has kept going.

Once Gorbachev lifted the threat that Soviet tanks would roll out to suppress the democratic spirit in Eastern Europe, the pent-up rage of masses of people who took to the streets shattered dictatorships and converted the Berlin Wall from the world's ugliest barricade into a bandstand for the celebration of freedom.

In a less visible way, Gorbachev is responding to popular pressures at home. The sullen discontent and stubborn lethargy of millions of Soviet workers and a cynical, disenchanted Soviet intelligentsia have forced Gorbachev to embark on reform—to try to energize his people and revitalize his country. At each stage, when he has hesitated, popular pressures have impelled him forward. In his fifth year, for example, he was provoked to do what Khrushchev could not or would not do, and what he himself had hesitated to do—attack the Communist Party's lock on power.

In December 1989, he admonished the dissident physicist Andrei Sakharov for demanding a multiparty system, but within two months, after political uprisings in Lithuania and Azerbaijan that showed the Party's loss of authority, Gorbachev reversed his course. He summoned the Party bosses in early February 1990 and told them that the Party would have to change or it would perish; that it would have to give up its constitutionally guaranteed monopoly on power and prove itself in the competition of a multiparty system. On the eve of that Party session, in the largest spontaneous gathering in Moscow since the Bolshevik Revolution, nearly two hundred thousand people massed outside the Kremlin to demand that the party *apparatchiki* yield to popular will. *Perestroika* had come full circle. Gorbachev was being propelled forward by the very forces he had unleashed.

My personal introduction to this new world, the world of the New Russians, so different from the world I had known in the early 1970s, came at one of the high tides of *perestroika,* in May 1988, when I went to Moscow for President Reagan's summit meeting with Gorbachev.

For Americans, Reagan's venture to the Kremlin was big news. His strolls on Red Square with Gorbachev, his luncheon for Moscow dissidents, his speech to university students, all made great television soap opera: the old Cold Warrior playing in the heart of "the evil empire."

But the Russians I talked with then were blasé about the summit. They saw Reagan's visit as a sideshow; the much more compelling battle was the one within their own country, over internal change. Its outcome that May was most uncertain. The Russians knew that Reagan's coming was important for Soviet-American relations, but it stirred no real excitement. They were glad for his courtesy call, especially after all the harsh things he had said about them, and they were polite to the president for a few days. But they could hardly wait for him to get out of town, so they could get back to their own unfolding political brawl, a struggle over their national destiny.

That 1988 trip to Russia was my first to Moscow in nearly fourteen years, and the ferment and electricity astonished me. It began an adventure of discovery and rediscovery that would take me to the Soviet Union nine times in the next two years, to do the reporting for this book and to film a series of documentary programs for American public television, *Inside Gorbachev's USSR.*

On the way into Moscow from Sheremyetovo Airport that first visit back, I remember looking for immediate evidence of Gorbachev's supposed earthquake, but at first I couldn't see any. Along the main highway I saw the same massive, naked apartment buildings that I had remembered from the seventies, huge, impersonal, thirteen- and twenty-story tenement blocks that looked like a vast construction site, a sprawling, gargantuan Levittown, balconies aflutter with the wash, buildings crying out for paint, for trees, for shrubbery, for any tiny bit of decoration. These behemoths had been designed with one object in mind: to pack in as many people as possible, with little thought for individual convenience, human scale, or diversity. Along Gorky Street in Moscow proper were the same old concrete block constructions of the Khrushchev era, the same impersonal signs that I knew so well: MYASO (meat), APTEKA (drugstore), KHLYEB (bread). I searched in vain for signs of individuality—VANYA'S BAKERY or GORKY STREET GROCERY—something that would convey a new spirit of entrepreneurship; but there was none.

Later, with producer Martin Smith and writer Paul Taylor from WGBH-TV in Boston, I went up to the Old Arbat, a long strolling mall, hunting some more for evidence of material change. But in one state store after another, we found only a paltry selection of staples—potatoes, cabbages, cucumbers, a few carrots, and some sad-looking green oranges; in the meat store, one brand of fatty salami, one brand of fatty bologna, each at over $5 a pound. Otherwise, the meat counter was empty. Chances were that the state-store butchers were sneaking the better cuts of meat under the counter to sell for private profit, and, of course, for very steep prices, peasants were selling meat and produce at the farmers' market. Nevertheless, the food situation in the heart of Moscow looked no better than it had fourteen years earlier.

I was eager to talk with old friends, so I phoned Zinovy Yuryev, a science-fiction writer and for a long time deputy editor of *Krokodil,* the Soviet humor magazine. During the seventies, I had often visited Zinovy and his wife, Yelena Kornyevskaya. Following my old precautions, I did not call Zinovy from my hotel, where the lines might be bugged. Instead, I went to a pay phone on the street. Yelena was away, but Zinovy was eager to meet for dinner. He asked a question that caught me by surprise: "What restaurant shall we choose?"

I had never met with Zinovy and Yelena in public; always we had talked at their apartment, and often, when going there, I had taken precautions: I had used the metro or had driven my car partway there, then had parked some distance from their home and taken a taxi or a metro the rest of the way. In those days we foreign correspondents sometimes saw unmarked cars tailing us; one American reporter found a radio device under his car that sent out a signal, letting the KGB secret police know where his car was at all times. We had assumed such devices were planted somewhere on all our cars, so we did not drive directly to the homes of Soviet friends, unless they had official reasons for meeting us. Zinovy, as a Jew with a high-level press job subject to Communist Party oversight, had had to be careful about private contacts with foreigners.

So his willingness now to meet in a public place signaled a change in the political climate. Moreover, he suggested Kropotkinskaya 36, a new cooperative (privately owned) restaurant. This was a treat for me because I had not yet eaten at a Moscow cooperative, and the service and food turned out to be unusually good, the atmosphere quiet and intimate—unknown in the Moscow of my day—even if the prices rivaled those in Manhattan.

"Two years ago, I would not have been here and seen you in public like this," Zinovy told me after we greeted each other with warm Russian hugs and kisses.

Zinovy is a short, intense man in his early sixties, with thick graying hair and the energy of someone much younger. His English is excellent, his accent sharp and choppy. With me, he has never minced words. He is a satirical writer, ironic and sophisticated in conversation, but never indirect. He speaks in staccato bursts, either with great passion or with acid cynicism—and during the Brezhnev era he found ample cause to be cynical. He believed in nothing, trusted virtually no one, had little good to say about the leadership or the system. But now he was brimming with enthusiasm. He told me that he had left *Krokodil* and was trying his hand at writing movie scenarios as well as books.

"The director of Gorky Studio phones me and says, 'Zinovy, I'd like to see you. Come over,'" Zinovy reported. "To you, it's nothing. But to me it is as if Buddha were calling me—these bureaucrats never call anyone. So I go to see him and he says to me, 'I've looked at your script and it seems to me that it can be a good movie and it will make money.' To you, that's nothing. It's a natural idea. But to me, it's *astonishing* to think that this will be the standard—to make money. These idiots have produced so much rubbish over the years, never worrying a damn about wasting billions of rubles. Now suddenly they want to make money. If they really stick to this, it's a revolution."[1]

But Zinovy had an even more surprising story to tell about the revolution going on in his country. It involved his son Misha.

I remembered Misha as a boy of eleven, with large brown eyes and a mind that matched the intelligence of his parents. So brilliant was he, in fact, that he had later graduated from the Moscow State University biology department at nineteen, headed for a career as a geneticist—until he found himself in serious political trouble.

I knew from my earlier experience that many free-thinking Soviet intellectuals had faced a dilemma in raising their bright adolescent children. They could simply keep silent, hiding their honest beliefs and opinions from their children. This guaranteed that under the political pressures for conformity their children wouldn't be induced to expose the parents as hidden dissenters. This would spare their children from having to grow up living double lives—speaking their minds in the privacy of their families, and toeing the Party line in public. Or they could do what Zinovy did, be honest and open with his two sons, Yura and Misha. He had talked candidly with them and let them dip into his extensive personal library of contraband literature—modern American and British fiction and nonfiction as well as dissident Soviet writers like Solzhenitsyn, Sakharov, and others.

So it was only natural that Misha, working in 1986 as a young biologist in his early twenties, had borrowed his father's copy of Tom Clancy's novel *The Hunt for Red October* and taken it to his office at a prestigious scientific institute. Of course, as the story of a Soviet submarine captain defecting to the West, *Red October* is not a book on which Party watchdogs or security officers looked kindly. Unfortunately for Misha, he lent it to a friend, and either the friend or somebody else reported Misha to the KGB for possessing and disseminating anti-Soviet literature. The incident occurred in Gorbachev's early period, when his emphasis was not so much on reform as on work discipline and the drive against alcoholism and corruption. So the investigation blossomed and eventually led the KGB to Zinovy's private library of forbidden books.

One morning a KGB major and several workmen arrived in a truck to do an *obysk*—a search of Zinovy's apartment. When the KGB do an *obysk*, as Zinovy explained, they do it methodically, top to bottom, meticulously listing all the materials they confiscate for an investigation. This morning, they went through Zinovy's entire collection, not only his books but his Western videotapes and cassettes. They took everything, cataloging every single item, and they expanded their original investigation of Misha to include Zinovy as well.

Investigations such as this one have a way of dragging on, with all the various complications and interrogations. The family used what connections it had with Communist Party higher-ups to get the matter dismissed, but the situation looked grim for both father and son. Although formal charges had not been filed, Misha appeared headed for Siberia, and Zinovy likely to lose his job and perhaps worse.

Then suddenly, on December 17, 1986, Gorbachev called Andrei Sakharov at his enforced exile in the city of Gorky and invited the famous dissident to come back to Moscow and help enlist the intelligentsia for Gorbachev's reforms. That phone call was a dramatic harbinger of cultural liberalization to come, as Zinovy was soon to find out.

Within a few weeks, the KGB investigator in Zinovy's case telephoned Misha and said, "Why don't you write us a letter asking us to drop your case?" Misha, who had steadfastly refused to write or sign any paper for the KGB, balked at first, but eventually Zinovy persuaded him to go ahead and do it.

More weeks went by, and then a phone call came from the KGB telling Zinovy and Misha to be at their apartment on a certain morning. Once again, the KGB major appeared with the workmen in a gray truck—but this time they began to unload Zinovy's books and tapes, and then systematically put them back on the shelves. When they had finished, Zinovy noticed that the KGB had kept two of his videotapes.

"One was *Pretty Baby,* which they considered porno," Zinovy recalled with a chuckle. "Too dangerous, they evidently thought, for an old guy like me. And the other was *Aliens,* which they considered too violent."

All the books were returned, except one. "They said that was a mistake," Zinovy reported, "and they apologized!"

Zinovy sat there shaking his head in wonder and disbelief at this weird new KGB politesse. And at the somersault in his own family's fortunes.

"Imagine it, Rick," he said. "The KGB *apologized* to an ordinary citizen! Now you see why Gorbachev is the first Soviet leader I have believed in."

It seemed a fantastic story, worthy of Zinovy's satirical fiction, but this time it was true. And it conveyed a wider message about the mechanism of state terror and the climate of fear that had ruled Russia for seven decades of Communist power, and for centuries of Russian absolutism before that. For if the KGB were truly to be held in some check, and Gorbachev really to lift the threat of arbitrary arrest for the mere possession of liberal writings, then gradually ordinary people might gain the nerve to speak their minds in public.

On the day that President Reagan arrived for his summit meeting with Gorbachev, my colleagues from WGBH and I decided to try to talk to some ordinary Russians. We went out to the Great Stone Bridge, which crosses the Moscow River on the southern approach to the Kremlin, to mingle with the crowds along Reagan's motorcade route. As executive producer of our documentary series, Marty Smith had a minicamera and wanted to try out some man-in-the-street interviews. I wanted to see whether the Russian people would talk to us openly.

I was recalling my arrival in Moscow in 1971. During my first week, Nikita Khrushchev died an anonymous pensioner, and Western reporters had been tipped off within hours by friends of the Khrushchev family. Nothing appeared in the Soviet press for two days; obviously, Khrushchev's successors could not decide what to say about him, so they did not print even the news that he had died. Of course *The New York Times* had the story, and we wanted to get reactions from ordinary Russians.

So, fresh from Russian-language tutoring, I went to find out firsthand what the people had to say about old Nikita, the bumptious upstart peasant who had dared denounce Stalin, had put missiles into Cuba, and had banged his shoe on his desk at the United Nations.

No one would talk.

People scurried away when I mentioned Khrushchev's name. I managed to lure people into conversation by asking for telephone change, but when they got my drift, they fled with vague mumblings of "I'm not from around here," or "I don't know what you're talking about." Then I tried cornering vegetable vendors at stands in the farmers' market, but they, too, were full of evasions. "Poor old man," said one grandmother. A middle-aged man parried, "Where was he all this time?" But more typical was a ticket seller in a movie house. Eyeing me suspiciously, she demanded, "How do you know he died?" I realized that people were so wary that it was ridiculous to put together a story.

So with that memory still in mind in 1988, I headed out to the Great Stone Bridge, skeptical at our prospects for a genuine give-and-take. I figured the camera would be an extra handicap, more likely to attract police interference than talkative Muscovites.

But my experience from the seventies was a poor guide. As soon as I explained to people on the bridge that we were American public-television reporters here for Reagan's visit and eager to sample public opinion, they wanted to talk. The sight of the camera drew a crowd. Moscow suddenly seemed like New York or Los Angeles.

At first, their comments were safe and obvious, sentiments about wishing Reagan well. People said they were glad he was in Moscow; they hoped his visit would strengthen peace. It was far better, they said, to have our leaders talking than preparing for war. When I edged toward more controversial territory, such as questions about their personal lives, there was a moment's hesitation; then a wiry little man in a straw hat, with the almond-shaped eyes and Oriental face of a Tatar, started delivering a rapid-fire speech from the back of the crowd.

"We ought not to be talking about this—this is not what's number one on our minds," he declared. "What's number one is that our economy is in terrible shape. These people are *Moskvichy,* Muscovites—they're well taken care of compared to the rest of us. I come from near Kazan on the Volga River [six hundred miles east of Moscow], and our situation is a nightmare. We can't find sugar or tea in our shops. Coffee is hard to get. Housing is terrible. . . ."

And he went on. I kept expecting someone to object, or to put a hand in front of Marty's camera. That's what would have happened in the 1970s. Some Soviet patriot or some militia officer would have grabbed this little Tatar by the scruff of the neck, pulled him out of the crowd, and lectured him about washing dirty linen in front of foreigners. But instead, his tirade touched off a kvetching session. Others chimed in with pet peeves—the lack of meat, the shortage of baby clothes. One serious young man began to preach that there was too much materialism, that more people should turn to religion, now that Gorbachev was letting churches reopen. Suddenly, we were in the midst of a mini–Hyde Park. People were pushing and shoving to get to the camera to give America a piece of their minds.

Then a sturdy, middle-aged matron with black hair tied back severely in a bun pushed aggressively through the crowd and demanded to speak. She had the authoritarian aura of a school principal. Her iron back and steely eyes reminded me of a type I had encountered all too often in years gone by: the ideological vigilantes, self-appointed keepers of order. Her advance to the front rank signaled a moment of reckoning. There will be no more self-indulgent whimpering, I thought to myself; this woman will cuff the ears of any who would sully the honor of the motherland.

I was trying to figure out how to finesse her. "I don't think we need this one," I said to Marty Smith. "Let's just take a little bit," he replied; and so I asked her to state her problem, and her script began as I imagined.

All the others had spoken anonymously. But with the abrupt efficiency of a military officer giving name, rank, and serial number, this woman self-confidently reeled off her name, address, and occupation: "Tretyakova, Olga; Stavropol Territory; teacher, retired." For special effect, she emphasized that she came from the home province of Mikhail Sergeyevich, using Gorbachev's first name and patronymic, the normal Russian way. Obviously, not a lady to be trifled with.

Then, with stentorian oratory, she commenced to deliver a pitiful indictment of the Soviet health system. To my astonishment, she was speaking out not to defend the system but to drive a nail into its coffin. "Eleven years ago my only son died in a hospital," she began, "a victim of corruption." She was outraged not only at faulty diagnosis and bad treatment but also at the arrogance of one doctor who had demanded a bribe for treatment that was supposed to be free under Soviet socialism. When she took her case to a public prosecutor, she said, he, too, demanded a hefty bribe, of 1,600 rubles (practically a year's pay for her), and then disappeared with the money.

"Later, he was arrested and convicted," she said, apparently for other crimes. But the doctor, whom she condemned as "a killer in a white coat," was still unpunished because of a "cover-up" in the Stavropol prosecutor's office.

Initially, Olga Tretyakova's riveting story and commanding presence kept the others silent. Then people began to grumble. Several uniformed militia men at the fringe of our group pressed in closer to listen just as Mrs. Tretyakova was emphasizing that this scandal had taken place practically under Gorbachev's nose, in his home province.

"I have written the Communist Party Central Committee," she complained, "but they just pass the buck."

One onlooker cautioned her to be careful or she might get in trouble.

"Let them arrest me!" she blurted out.

I fully expected a militia officer's gray-uniformed arm to reach over the crowd and lead her away, but the police made no move. Eventually, she became frustrated that we, the Americans, would not promise to right the wrong and investigate the doctor; she reluctantly relinquished her hold on the camera and the crowd, and made her way out along the street—still a free woman, for as far as I could see.

In the end, it was we, not the Russians, who ended the dialogue.

For me, the episode was a revelation. In the 1970s, I had heard Russians gripe about terrible living conditions, but they had been wary of expressing individual criticism too freely in front of strangers, especially other Soviets. Indeed, as we strolled away that afternoon, a young blond workman in rumpled clothes tagged along after us. When the militia were out of sight, he approached me with a story of being fired from his job and blacklisted because his bosses condemned his complaints as a political protest. He was having trouble getting work; he wanted us to help him emigrate. His furtive contact was typical of my encounters in the 1970s, a symptom of a system of repression, some of the effects of which obviously still lingered on.

But the openness of the others, their willingness to voice their criticisms in public, on camera, was a striking change. In three and a half years of roaming the country in the 1970s, I had heard many candid and sordid stories from Soviet citizens, but if they had a negative message to deliver, they were usually careful to check that no one was eavesdropping and to protect themselves with anonymity. In a crowd, Big Brother was always assumed to be present. Fear had been palpable.

As we returned to our hotel that afternoon, I had to admit that even if the food selection was still grim and other material conditions had not improved three years after Gorbachev's ascent, people's psychology had changed. I found it remarkable that Russians, who have almost no tradition of tolerance for differing opinion, would let each other speak without shouting each other down, and without some Communist Party busybody stepping in to set the record straight or call a halt. The notion of public dialogue had obviously gained some legitimacy, but what impressed me most of all was that these people had lost much of their old fear. If Gorbachev had done nothing else, he had created a whole new world merely by lifting people's fear.

It is tempting for us in the West, especially Americans, to witness such sea changes in events and in people's psychology and then to interpret them through the prism of our own values, our own political framework. We assume we understand what is really going on inside the Soviet Union; we assume that as soon as Soviet people are given freedom, they will behave as we do. Our framework is capitalism and multiparty democracy; our way of life seems so natural, so right to us, that we take for granted that once dictatorship is removed, Russians will reflect and assert our same values.

When Gorbachev talks about democratization and greater freedoms, we mishear his rhetoric because few of us understand that Russian history has given those words different meanings for him and his people. We expect that people who have been politically inert for decades will immediately know how to operate democratic institutions, how to take charge of their destinies. We imagine that only an entrenched Old Guard is blocking them, that once a few "bad guys" at the top are removed, the world of the average Russian will look like ours. To us, Gorbachev's *perestroika,* or casting off of the old Stalinist dictatorship, makes so much sense that we cannot fathom how deeply embedded is the resistance to change among the vast majority of people, even those dissatisfied with the past.

The swiftness of political change in Eastern Europe only compounds our misperceptions of what is happening inside the Soviet Union. The governments of Poland, East Germany, Czechoslovakia, and Romania fell with such electrifying speed in the fall of 1989 that it fostered the illusion that tyranny can be replaced by democracy overnight. A banner waved aloft by exuberant street crowds in Romania on their most fateful day captured the lightning tempo with which the old world was being turned upside down. It read: POLAND—TEN YEARS. EAST GERMANY—TEN WEEKS. CZECHOSLOVAKIA—TEN DAYS. ROMANIA—?

On our television screens, we see the same massive street marches in Lithuania, Azerbaijan, and in Russian cities that we saw in Prague, Leipzig, and Bucharest, and we are tempted to assume the Soviets will transform their country as swiftly as East Europeans have.

But as the past five years have shown, the Soviet Union, and at its heart, Mother Russia, is different from its neighbors. As a society and a people, Russia is more difficult to change. Even the largest street demonstrations in Moscow have been nowhere near as large or universal as the demonstrating masses in the smaller capitals of Eastern Europe—a sign that Muscovites, indeed most Russians, are not as swept up by the magnetic attraction of a new way of life as are Poles, Germans, or Czechoslovaks.

Eastern Europe faces a torturous process in its move from socialism to capitalism and revival of working democracies, but at least in Eastern Europe there was a relatively recent tradition of democracy, within the memories of people now alive. As World War II began, governments in Eastern Europe included the institutions of democracy. But Russia has been ruled by czars and Communist dictators for five centuries, with only brief interludes of democratic reform.

What is more, the dictatorial brand of Soviet socialism had its roots in Russia. It was not imposed by an alien army, as the Soviet army imposed Communist dictatorships on Eastern Europe. It was fired and hardened in the crucible of war, famine, terror, and hard sacrifice, and it has its committed legions. Moreover, the Russians are a people who historically have needed a belief system, an ideology to live by, whether Communism or Russian Orthodoxy. Many are uneasy with a political system in which the guiding principles of public life are concerned with means, not ends.

When I have described our political ethic to Russians, many of them have said that they felt something was missing; they have been uncomfortable with our notion that while the wider society establishes process—the institutions of government, its legislatures, division of powers, and free press—the individual himself is left to develop philosophy, faith, and the meaning of life. That is not the Russian tradition. Most Russians look to the state and the ruler to provide an ideology and a purpose as well as law and order.

So the collapse of the wall—both the Berlin Wall and the wall in the Soviet Union between the rulers and the ruled—is not the whole story; it is just the beginning. The story now is what happens after the first massive political tremors; what happens after the wall comes down. That is the story which has fascinated me most, the human story, the story of personal transformations: how people cope with reform, some promoting it, others resisting it or mouthing its slogans but secretly sabotaging it, still others floating in uncertainty, voicing hope for change but unwilling to take risks to make it happen.

In pursuit of that story, I have spent nearly nine months in the Soviet Union over the past two years, traveling more than forty thousand miles, visiting twenty-five major cities and nine republics. I have ranged from Siberia to the Baltic republics, from Central Russia to Uzbekistan, from Armenia and Azerbaijan to the Ukraine. I have tried to probe the innards of Gorbachev's U.S.S.R., talking to coal miners, farmers, high school students, listening to city officials and industrial bosses, reformers and hard-liners, questioning taxi drivers and members of the Politburo. My own reactions to what was happening have passed through several stages of deepening awareness. My opinions of Gorbachev have changed several times.

What follows in this book are the stories of what it is like in the Soviet Union today; what it is like for individuals to live through a cultural convulsion, a wholesale change in their society and environment.

There is the story, for example, of a local Communist Party leader who for the first time stands for election in a genuine contest, and loses. There is the story of an industrial manager who is suddenly told, "Run your own business and make a profit"—but first he must struggle to extricate himself from the web of a state-run economy. There is the story of high school teachers who dutifully preached the dogma of the past, but are suddenly told the old textbook is full of lies and that they must invent a new version, using disclosures in the daily newspapers.

I write about students who have heard one orthodoxy from early childhood, taught by both teachers and parents, only to discover that, actually, their teachers believed one thing, their parents another. What is it like for a television producer to be given license by Gorbachev to tackle any topic, but then to discover she is being held back by the taboos of her own superiors? How do older people, who once worshiped Stalin and made sacrifices in his name, react when their idol is discredited—when their own lives are discredited? To whom does a mine worker turn if he shares Gorbachev's infectious dream but sees, after five years, there is still little food on the shelves? Or a farmer who would like to till his own land but cannot be sure that the state will not snatch it back from him if Gorbachev disappears tomorrow?

From afar, there's a tendency to see things in either utopian or apocalyptic terms: success or failure, stability or collapse, dictatorship or chaos, black or white. We don't necessarily see the shades and the fluctuating currents that swirl around ordinary people. The epic story of Russians today has been personalized around Gorbachev: Is he winning or losing? Will he survive or not?

But in truth, the struggle in the Soviet Union, and within individual Soviets, has become far more complex than that; change is operating on so many levels and in so many directions simultaneously. There is no single hero, no single plot line to follow. All too much of the time, our focus has been on Gorbachev and whether he will "make it"; but the most important questions reach beyond Gorbachev personally.

In fact, one of the most important things I hope this book will show is that whether Gorbachev "makes it" or not, the process of change has taken root in the Soviet Union. It may be halting, untidy, embattled, and its course unsteady and sometimes uncertain, but whether or not Gorbachev survives, reform has now acquired a momentum of its own, and it will carry on regardless of his individual fate.

The transformation of a society as large as the Soviet Union, and as enmeshed in the habits and traditions of authoritarian rule, will inevitably take so long to run its course that no single leader can hope to see the process to the end. The old dictatorial order of Soviet Communism has been broken, and the process of forging a new social and political order will be painful, turbulent, and prolonged. The battle will ebb and flow over two or three decades and more, for it is impossible to crack an entrenched dictatorship without peril and bloodshed. Some leaders, frightened by the powerful forces that Gorbachev has unleashed, have already tried to check or reverse the process, and at some point they may succeed for a while; but I believe that others, now maturing and learning the skills of democracy, will emerge to carry reform forward to another stage, further than Gorbachev himself either intended or was capable of realizing.

In time, we may come to see Gorbachev as a transitional figure, who uncorked the process and set the yeast of change to work in the Soviet body politic. In fact, as we shall see, fundamental change had been gestating within Soviet society for years before Gorbachev appeared. He fostered its birth, and now, finally, reform has taken on a life and dynamism of its own.

PART ONE

ROOTS OF REFORM

That fact comes through most clearly in the personal experiences of the people you will meet in this book.

Even from afar, the transformation now under way in the Soviet Union holds a special fascination for all of us, and not only because its success or failure affects our destiny, our survival, even the changing nature of our own society. What is happening there rivets our interest for a deeper reason: It is a modern enactment of one of the archetypal stories of human existence, that of the struggle from darkness to light, from poverty toward prosperity, from dictatorship toward democracy. It represents an affirmation of the relentless human struggle to break free from the bonds of hierarchy and dogma, to strive for a better life, for stronger, richer values. It is an affirmation of the human capacity for change, growth, renewal.

This book is about how that story of change began and what it is like to live through it today. And it is about what this change means for the New Russians, and for the rest of the world, in the 1990s and beyond.

For more than five years, events in the Soviet Union have raced past all of us so rapidly that we have hardly had time to absorb their long-term meaning.

We have noted certain milestones: the first elections offering choice in seventy years; the rise of the independence movements in the Baltic republics; coal miners in Siberia and the southern Ukraine staging the first mass strikes since the time of the Revolution.

We have watched Gorbachev force the Communist Party to renounce its constitutional monopoly on power and gradually shift to a new Soviet parliament and presidency. But what has been less noticeable is that city governments in Moscow, Leningrad, Gorky, and Sverdlovsk have been taken over by reformers, who are now quietly at work building the infrastructure of democracy.

We have followed the incredible political fall and redemption of the populist leader Boris Yeltsin, who defied Gorbachev once and lost his post in the Politburo, defied him a second time and won the leadership of the Russian republic. But we know little about political movements at the grass-roots level, movements that have forced the opening of churches, taken charge of neighborhoods, stopped the construction of half a dozen nuclear reactors since the accident at Chernobyl.

We have seen an inefficient, top-heavy economy convulsed in crisis, ordinary people in despair over chronic shortages and panic-shopping out of fear of higher prices. But it has been harder to catch sight of the new private sector, which now employs five million people, making textiles, developing inventions, building highways.

In short, the headlines of the week have so dominated our attention that it has been hard to fathom and comprehend the fundamental transformations that are taking place throughout Soviet society; to piece together what has really happened and why; to understand what is merely transitory and what trends will begin to define the future.

The purpose of this book is to look beneath the surface of events, to try to see how deep and wide the process of reform runs: how much of it is likely to endure, and who will be the carriers of reform in the future.

The seeds of that future were in fact germinating in the Soviet past, largely unseen. Before we can understand the New Russians and where they are heading, it is necessary to understand the roots of the present reforms, and the forces that have propelled change inexorably forward.

CHAPTER I

THE HIDDEN WELLSPRINGS OF REFORM

"Problems snowballed faster than
they were resolved. On the whole,
society was becoming increasingly
unmanageable. We only thought that
we were in the saddle. . . . The need
for change was brewing."[1]

—Gorbachev, 1987

"*Perestroika* is like a spring
bursting from the rocks in this
mountainside of ours. . . . It comes from
an underground stream flowing somewhere
beneath the surface of the soil."[2]

—Tatyana Zaslavskaya
Sociologist
September 1989

When Gorbachev burst upon the world stage to proclaim a Soviet New
Deal under the trumpet call of *perestroika,* it seemed as if he and his ideas
about reform had emerged from nowhere. But it is now clear that under
what seemed like the dark, still surface of Soviet life in the seventies,
wellsprings of reform were churning, and the vision of dramatic reform
slowly beginning to take shape.

Many Americans were tempted to think that Moscow had been forced into reform by Washington's policies. In this view, Ronald Reagan's toughness toward Brezhnev, Andropov, and Chernenko, the aging Kremlin leaders of the early 1980s, had compelled the Politburo to pick a younger leader, to change the Party line and scrap the Communist system.

But the evidence is overwhelming that Gorbachev's reforms blossomed forth from forces germinating within Russia itself. The impulse for change was homegrown. It took a generation for the forces favoring reform to gather and for a broad base of support to develop. Because of the secretive way in which Soviet society moved in the past, this process was almost entirely hidden from view. And so it took us all very much by surprise.

In fact, by the time Gorbachev became the top man in the Kremlin, reform had hidden constituencies at every level of Soviet society: mine workers and housewives incensed about and weary of chronic consumer shortages and the dismal quality of Soviet goods; farmers and teachers demoralized by rural decay; little people outraged by the arrogant, pervasive, Mafia-like corruption of ministers and high Party officials; others embittered by the rampant black market, and by underground millionaires profiting from the gaping inefficiency of Stalinist economics.

Scientists and engineers were worried about the Soviet Union's industrial stagnation and its growing technological inferiority to the West. Intellectuals and young military veterans were sickened by the futile war in Afghanistan. Army generals, intelligence chiefs, and civilian technocrats were alarmed by the Soviet inability to compete in the world market and by the prospect of becoming a fourth-rate power in the twenty-first century, outstripped not only by the United States, Western Europe, and Japan, but even by China. Cab drivers and poets alike were sick of the blatant hypocrisy of Soviet propaganda. There was a pervasive cynicism about the widening chasm between the pompous pretensions of Brezhnev and the bleak reality of a Russian's everyday life.

Still, these forces were dormant, inchoate, until Gorbachev set them free, galvanized them, and gave them direction and form. They were the tinder, he the match. The kind of astonishing political explosion that took place in the mid-eighties required both ingredients; until the match was struck, that undergrowth of social disenchantment lacked fire and force. But without a vast reserve of incendiary disaffection, the match could have been struck and the flame of reform would have flickered out and died.

Reform of the bold and sweeping nature attempted by Gorbachev was not inevitable; the changes could have been more modest—indeed, Gorbachev himself began modestly. Or reform could have been postponed.

But historically some thrust toward reform was overdue. For within Soviet history, there is an alternating rhythm, a pattern of repression-and-thaw that goes back centuries to the time of the czars, and then up through the Soviet era.

In 1989, a Soviet philosopher told me a bit of folk wisdom. According to an anecdote then making the rounds in Moscow, he said, the Soviet state oscillates between bald leaders and hairy ones—between reformers and conservative tyrants. He ticked off the pairs: Lenin, the bald revolutionary, was followed by Stalin, the tyrant with thick, bristling brush-cut hair and menacing mustache. Nikita Khrushchev, the peasant reformer, who was bald as a potato, gave way to Brezhnev, the conservative, whose bushy eyebrows and headful of hair were parodied by cartoonists in the East and West. Yuri Andropov, a wispy-haired puritan bent on modernism and efficiency, was succeeded by Konstantin Chernenko, a defender of the Old Guard, who even in senility had an abundant head of white hair. So it was only natural that Gorbachev, whose birthmark gleams from a naked pate, should usher in a new era of radical reform. And of course, the philosopher said, smiling, nervous liberals were already beginning to speculate about what hairy hard-liner would succeed Gorbachev.

In Russia, as elsewhere, history moves with a rough Newtonian logic—action and reaction, one generation reacting to the policies and practices of the previous generation. By Gorbachev's takeover in 1985, it had been nearly a quarter of a century since the heyday of the last major reformer, Nikita Khrushchev, who had dethroned Stalin and challenged the Communist Party apparatus. Khrushchev's successors had reacted against him; Brezhnev had largely restored Stalin and enthroned the Party hierarchy.

But now it was time for Khrushchev's political children to come to power and carry on from where he left off.

If America and the West played any role in provoking *perestroika*, it was not through any specific policy of the 1980s, but rather because of our long-term economic success. For contrary to Khrushchev's vain boasting of the early 1960s, the Russians did not "bury" us or even come close to catching up. The capitalist world did not falter and collapse as Marx and Lenin had predicted and scores of Soviet ideologists had dutifully echoed. Just the opposite had occurred. The West had leapfrogged ahead into the Information Age, so that by the early 1980s, the brightest people in the Soviet system could see the telling contrast between Soviet stagnation and Western progress. They could see that the world was passing them by—and that realization forced them to reexamine their own system, to try to find out what had failed and discover ways to shake their nation out of its despotic lethargy.

What has fooled so many Westerners is that this Soviet soul-searching and dissatisfaction had long remained intensely private. Open, incremental evolution—that we understand. Covert, subterranean shifts within the body politic of an authoritarian regime are much harder to detect and comprehend. When grumbling private discontent and dissent become audible, we wonder: Are these just black moods, which a dictator can hold in check? Or do they indicate a gathering storm of irresistible forces? And if so, when, if ever, will it break?

Of course, this is precisely the purpose of censorship—not only to block unwanted views, but to keep people who are unhappy from knowing how many millions of others share their unhappiness; to keep the dormant opposition from awakening to its own developing strength.

THE SAFE HAVENS OF HIDDEN DISSENT

One person who, in the seventies and early eighties, nursed the idea of reform and eventually broke through the veil of secrecy to awaken others to the need for dramatic economic and social change was sociologist Tatyana Zaslavskaya. Her analysis of the ills of Soviet socialism and her ideas for reviving the Soviet economy certainly influenced Gorbachev's thinking. She was among the first people, if not the very first one, actually to use the term *perestroika.*

"Perestroika," Zaslavskaya said years later, "is like a spring bursting from the rocks in this mountainside of ours. It comes shooting out of a specific spot, and you can tell where the water is coming from. It comes from an underground stream flowing somewhere beneath the surface of the soil. Then some kind of opening appears, a chance to burst out into freedom—and then suddenly out of nowhere, a spring emerges and turns into a river."

Zaslavskaya, herself an innovative iconoclast, had been part of that underground stream. She had graduated from the economics faculty at Moscow State University, having first studied physics, and in 1950 she began to do research in Moscow. Then, in 1963, restless and intrigued by the challenge, she had been lured to Akademgorodok, or the Academic City, outside the Siberian industrial center of Novosibirsk. The man who had lured her there was Abel Aganbegyan, just beginning to gain a reputation as a free-thinking economist with maverick ideas about the Soviet system.

The Academic City, a community of twenty-two scientific institutes, had been set up under Khrushchev in 1957. It was peopled largely by younger scholars and discontented free-thinkers prepared to give up the prestige and cultural attractions of Moscow and Leningrad for more opportunity and a bit of freedom, permissible because it was nearly two thousand miles from the Kremlin and because its scientific founder, the physicist Mikhail A. Lavrentyev, had been canny enough to locate it just far enough away from Novosibirsk proper that it did not fall constantly under the prying eyes of regional Party bosses. Akademgorodok was popular with those who had savored Khrushchev's cultural thaw in the 1960s and were gagging under Brezhnev's sterner rule. It had quickly gained a reputation within the Soviet Union as a place with some degree of intellectual freedom, with fairly lively discussion groups, Western rock and jazz, and the Soviet abstract art that its scientists hung in their homes.

But after the Soviet invasion of Czechoslovakia in 1968, the screws were tightened.

I visited Akademgorodok in 1972, and the mood there was no longer as heady as it had been in its early years. For example, Club Integral, a discussion group for university students and junior scholars, had been shut down for something as mild as organizing a concert featuring politically risqué songs by Aleksandr Galich, a playwright recently expelled from the Writers' Union.

Even so, for the Brezhnev years, Academic City was still a relatively safe haven for developing unorthodox ideas. Zaslavskaya, for example, had become a sociologist and was practicing that heretical science without excessive political interference. That was unusual. In most places, Brezhnev's ideologists had banned sociology as a "bourgeois pseudoscience," because its concepts of group interests and conflicts and its empirical methods were a challenge to orthodox ideology and the Party's monopoly on social information. During the Brezhnev crackdown, sociology departments had been shut down at universities in Moscow and Leningrad, and many academic institutes had been purged of sociologists. Yet in distant Siberia, Zaslavskaya had managed to keep on doing her research, but so invisibly that I had not even known then that she existed.

I had gone to Akademgorodok to search out the more independent political climate of Siberia and talk with such intellectuals as the economist Aganbegyan, then head of the Institute of Economics and Industrial Organization, and already known, even then, for having an independent-minded slant on the Soviet economy. Aganbegyan, an Armenian and a great bear of a man, was a maverick, a loyal socialist who nonetheless refused to bend economic facts to fit ideology. He had taught himself statistics and mathematical economics in defiance of Stalinist strictures; Stalin had not wanted people collecting hard economic data that could be used to challenge his claims.

I did not know it then, but years later, traveling with Aganbegyan in America after he had become an adviser to Gorbachev, I learned that he had incurred the wrath of the late Prime Minister Aleksei Kosygin in the early seventies. Aganbegyan had insisted at a private Kremlin conference that Kosygin's halfhearted reforms were failing, and that the country was suffering from hidden inflation, inflation that was disguised by official statistics on the economy. When Kosygin started to dress him down, Aganbegyan had sent cold shock through the room by having the nerve to assert: "Mr. Minister, I want you to take a pencil and paper and write these numbers down. It's my job to get these numbers. If you want to check them and they're wrong, you can fire me." To the astonishment of others, Kosygin had proceeded to take notes; Aganbegyan was not fired, but because of his open impertinence, Kosygin banished the outspoken Armenian from his group of outside consultants.[3]

Aganbegyan's diagnosis back then, refined over the years, was that the Soviet economy was not capable of continuing its rapid postwar growth through the old formula: massive investments and constant expansion of its labor force. Aganbegyan did not back down when Brezhnev or Kosygin blamed economic setbacks on bottlenecks in transportation, bad weather, poor use of new technology, or the ineptitude of individual managers. Long before Gorbachev's emergence, Aganbegyan saw fundamental flaws: straitjacket controls on industrial managers, the rigidity of central planning, low productivity caused by the abysmal morale of workers. In October 1981, for example, Aganbegyan had written in the official trade-union newspaper *Trud* that the main drag on the economy, a major cause of the alarming drop in Soviet economic growth rates, was "people's attitude toward their work." One crucial indicator, he said, was endemic alcoholism, including widespread drinking on the job.

But during my first interview with Aganbegyan back in 1972, he had kept his most heretical thinking to himself, shying away from any spectacular statements. I remember his brown eyes as impassive and wary. At that time, he had been more interesting than ideologues, but still cautious, careful not to go beyond what he had already said in published articles, which contained what I now know was only a fraction of what he really thought and knew. Aganbegyan clearly felt he had troubles enough without sounding off to *The New York Times*. Typical of many Soviet establishment figures in that day, he preferred to work through private channels, occasionally publishing troubling statistics in his institute's magazine, *Eko*.

Aganbegyan was one, almost invisible tip of what was actually an under-surface archipelago of the Soviet scientific and cultural intelligentsia, and his caution had kept me from penetrating the island of free thinking at Akademgorodok. But in Moscow, Leningrad, and elsewhere, I had become acquainted with others in that archipelago: writers, poets, and artists who had let me, like Alice, pass through the looking glass into their own private, underground worlds of discussions, readings, and other little gatherings.

During those years, I had learned that Russia was a split-level society, with an official public facade and another reality in private. I had come to understand that I could not judge someone by what he said in public. It was clear to me that after Stalin's death in 1953, and probably during Stalin's reign as well, the U.S.S.R. was not as monolithic as most people in the West assumed. Even the Communist Party was not as monolithic as I had once thought, though in the seventies it was still pretty opaque. Repression and fear, and the Party's siege mentality, its compulsion for secrecy toward external enemies, papered over the cracks.

In those years only a tiny band of courageous dissidents dared to shatter the pretense of unanimity in public—Andrei Sakharov, Aleksandr Solzhenitsyn, Roy and Zhores Medvedev, Vladimir Bukovsky, a few Ukrainian dissidents, Crimean Tatars, and Lithuanian Catholics. Or Jews such as Volodya Slepak and Aleksandr Lerner, who wanted to emigrate but were refused permission, and became known as *refuzniki*. Their voices were like bolts of lightning crackling against a darkened sky. Yet in a nation then numbering 220 million, these were an infinitesimal sliver of Soviet society.

I had sensed from my travels and contacts that there must be thousands upon thousands of other clandestine objectors, scattered pockets of malcontents who could not unite because they were afraid to expose their views. In the Brezhnev years, these people saved candor for their families and perhaps one or two trusted friends. Ever fearful of informers, they had pulled the curtains, turned on a radio, and locked the doors to bare their hearts. From Moscow to Siberia, from the Baltics to Georgia and Armenia, I had listened to such people share irreverent jokes about Brezhnev's chest full of medals and his slobbering peasant speech, or tell heartrending stories of how Stalin's terror had shattered their families. The most desperate and daring had huddled in small circles like conspirators to read Solzhenitsyn's contraband book about Stalin's camps, *The Gulag Archipelago*, typed secretly and laboriously, page by page, on onionskin paper. Sometimes they would read all night, passing pages from hand to hand, exhilarated and terrified by the risks they were taking.

Of course, many of these invisible dissenters were at the fringe of the system, but I knew from my acquaintances, or theirs, that there was ideological dry rot even in the pillars of the establishment; it affected editors, diplomats, established writers, scientists, actors, the children and grandchildren of the political elite. There were ideological defectors-in-place, who hid their real views and sold their souls to the Communist Party in order to get good jobs and bargain their way for trips to the outside (Western) world as diplomats, trade officials, physicists, economists, regional leaders, university administrators, tour guides, ballerinas, poets, hockey players. Most of these philosophical defectors kept their heads down low, shying away from political activism.

One training ground for reform in the late 1970s was the environmental movement to save Siberia's world-famous Lake Baikal from industrial pollution. This was an issue on which some establishment liberals and conservatives could unite, and it was one that the Communist Party hierarchy, for some reason, did not find threatening—perhaps because the problem was localized and far from Moscow. Then, too, there were occasional daring snippets of poetry or theater, or politically salty songs by such underground balladiers as Vladimir Vysotsky, Aleksandr Galich, or Bulat Okudzhava. But basically, the Soviet intelligentsia had almost no safety valve, and things were at the bursting point when Gorbachev came along.

THE HUMAN FACTOR

By the late 1980s, when I finally met Tatyana Zaslavskaya, she was a tall, distinguished woman in her early sixties. In an odd way, she reminded me of a taller version of Winston Churchill, with white hair and without the jowls. Her large, alert, unblinking eyes gazed out over roundish Churchillian cheeks, and her high forehead and erect posture gave her the air of a British aristocrat. She wore a woman's black-and-white-checked business suit, and she carried a handsome imported briefcase. She was nearly six feet tall in sturdy two-inch heels, vigorous in stride and vigorous in conversation, chortling with a kind of lusty enjoyment at her scrapes with authority.

Zaslavskaya had achieved great distinction in the last few years, becoming one of a handful of women members of the Soviet Academy of Sciences, a consultant to Gorbachev, head of the Soviet Sociological

Association, and director of a center for the study of public opinion. But in the 1970s she had operated in the hidden archipelago, studying why young people left the countryside, why workers were so unmotivated. She was busy developing concepts of economic sociology. During what seemed like a decade of darkness, she was part of the gathering intellectual streams that Gorbachev would eventually tap into for *perestroika*.

Under Brezhnev, Zaslavskaya recalled matter-of-factly, there was harassment. Many intellectuals, she told me, had tasted the relative freedom under Khrushchev. But when Brezhnev clamped down, most adjusted and played along. Others, like herself, had been unwilling to conform. Unable to publish their most cherished work, they labored in private, developing new concepts invisibly, talking only among small groups of trusted colleagues.

"My colleagues at work constantly grappled with the fact that it was impossible to publish the results of their research in an original, unmodified form," she said. "Harsh censorship simply rooted out every stimulating idea. Any phrase that sounded in the least bit unusual would have the censor crossing it out, deleting it. . . . The censorship was quite thorough. But while censorship could, of course, prevent the release of certain materials, it could not prevent ideas from taking shape. And so, ideas continued to develop, and because of this people continued to discuss things among themselves, to get involved in debates, and to type lectures in five copies, to share with each other. The thought process did not stop."[4]

For the group of nearly fifty sociologists who eventually took refuge under Zaslavskaya's umbrella at Akademgorodok, the key was to *unlearn* many of the official teachings—the teachings of a lifetime—and learn anew about Soviet society, sifting fact from fiction. "Ideological propaganda tried to establish certain precepts: that we were building fully developed socialism, that nowhere else did people live better than we did in the Soviet Union, that in the West there existed widespread poverty," she said. "However, we *saw* what real life was like and naturally we drew our own conclusions. Still, it took time for people to free themselves from ideas that had accumulated over the course of many years and decades."

This little group of scholars quietly pursuing their research was hampered by the difficulty of exchanging views with others, of learning from academic work done elsewhere. The Novosibirsk group had heard that there were others doing serious work, the economist Gavril Popov at Moscow State University, Boris Kurashvili of the Institute of State and Law in Moscow, the sociologist Vladimir Yadov in Leningrad. But in the seventies, independent-minded scholars dared not speak out openly at large academic conferences, for instance, because they knew that among the participants were not only intellectual hacks but also informants who would take notes and report to Party watchdogs on anyone who deviated from the Party line.

Nonetheless, by 1981, the Aganbegyan-Zaslavskaya team felt confident enough of their work to launch a broad, interdisciplinary study of the Soviet economy. Over the course of the next two years, Zaslavskaya developed a searing indictment of the centralized Stalinist command system and an argument for major reforms. Her work was more advanced and heretical than what Aganbegyan had done previously, and in early 1983 she circulated a 150-page report to a limited number of like-minded economists, sociologists, and lawyers at ten major institutes in Moscow, Leningrad, Novosibirsk, and elsewhere.

By her account, about 150 scholars, each one hand-picked, came to Akademgorodok in April 1983 for a closed seminar at which Zaslavskaya's report, among others, was debated.

By another account, Zaslavskaya's reform-oriented paper also circulated to specialists in the economic departments of the Communist Party Central Committee, and in Gosplan, the state planning committee.[5]

Her paper, which became known as "The Novosibirsk Report," was leaked to Dusko Doder of *The Washington Post* by an official in Moscow close to the Politburo faction of Konstantin Chernenko, who was then number two in the Party. Doder waited four months before publishing a story about the report, but when his story did appear, high officials in Moscow denied there was any serious talk of reform and launched a KGB investigation to track down the leak.[6]

"There were deep reverberations [to the story] here," Zaslavskaya told me. "The KGB hunted down and confiscated every copy of that report, down to the last one."

"They conducted searches?" I asked.

"Well, not in people's homes, but at the institute," she replied. "They went through everything, because they were short two copies. They never found them. The documents had been published for official use, and each copy was numbered. So two copies were missing, and they found out how they ended up in the West. Many participants in the seminar experienced extremely unpleasant consequences as a result of the report."

When I read Zaslavskaya's report, I was struck by how much of its thinking was later reflected in Gorbachev's general approach. Zaslavskaya diplomatically disavowed any claim that she was an architect of Gorbachev's reforms, but she told me she had good reasons for believing that

Gorbachev and other Politburo leaders had read her paper after the *Washington Post* story appeared.

In her document, Zaslavskaya had depicted the Soviet economy as being at a dead end and headed for even worse disaster. She blamed the iron hand of the rigidly centralized Stalinist system for the economic mess; she asserted that the tinkering and piecemeal reforms of previous Soviet leaders had proven inadequate; and she called for "a serious reorganization of the system of state management of the economy. . . .

"It is impossible to improve the mechanism of economic management, arrived at years ago, by gradually replacing the more outmoded of its elements with more effective ones," she argued. Past reforms had failed, she said, because the system had not undergone what was needed—"a qualitative restructuring"—and her term for this restructuring was *perestroika*.

Although in 1983 Zaslavskaya had stopped short of explicitly advocating market economics, she had damned the Soviet system for its weak market relations and for putting prices on goods that "bear no relation to their social value." She had made no mention of political reforms; hers was an economic paper. But as a sociologist, her central thesis was that the Soviet economy was being crippled by what she called, and what Gorbachev would later emphasize as, the human factor—the laziness, incompetence, and apathy of masses of workers who were alienated from their jobs by a system that offered them no personal stake in or connection with the enterprises where they worked.

Zaslavskaya argued that the old Stalinist method of command might have been successful in the 1930s, with a work force that was obedient, passive, and poorly educated, but it no longer fit Soviet workers in the 1980s, who were more skilled, educated, mobile, and conscious of their interests and rights. It was in society's interest, she asserted, to give workers, and presumably managers too, a "wide margin of freedom of individual behavior" to make them more productive.

Zaslavskaya's report was prophetic in many ways. She warned that sweeping reforms "cannot run their course without conflict"; she predicted with precision that among the powerful forces that would oppose reforms would be central ministries and subagencies "that have grown like mushrooms in recent decades" and whose armies of bureaucrats occupy "numerous 'cosy niches' with ill-defined responsibilities, but thoroughly agreeable salaries." Surprisingly, she said nothing about the likely reaction of the Communist Party apparatus, either in Moscow or around the country. But she did forecast that important support for reform would come from the people, especially from the most qualified, energetic, and active workers and from the managerial staffs of industrial enterprises.[7]

Overall, as she said to me later, her message was that the Soviet economy was in "no small crisis, that it wasn't a matter of sewing arm patches on an old suit in order to extend its wearability. I argued that the suit was no longer usable, and that an entirely new one had to be purchased. But to obtain this new suit you needed a restructuring of ideas, the development of market forces, the economic independence of enterprises."[8] In other words, and in her words, the country needed *perestroika*.

Her message reached a receptive audience, both among intellectuals and on high, and it was to have profound reverberations.

CHAPTER 2
THE BREZHNEV GENERATION: SLIDE INTO CYNICISM

The responses of three Soviet leaders when the "train" of Soviet Communism stalls:

STALIN: Shoot the engineers. Exile the crew. Get someone new.

KHRUSHCHEV: Pardon the crew and put them back to work.

BREZHNEV: Pull down the shades and pretend we're moving.

—Soviet political joke

Gorbachev's reform movement was successful not only because it tapped into important and hidden intellectual wellsprings; it also struck a resonant chord with millions of people in Soviet society. *Perestroika* has been called "a revolution from above," but it is not a cabal mounted by a single leader and a handful of disaffected intellectuals. Such a narrow group could hardly have inspired the wave of popular upheavals that swept across the country in the mid-1980s. For that populist response, Gorbachev's reform needed a mass base.

This mass support had been gathering slowly for two decades, gestating amid the mass discontent and developing with the social changes brought by the process of modernization. Tatyana Zaslavskaya's report was one of several pointing out that a transformation had occurred in Soviet society, providing not only fertile soil for change, but also an army of followers ready to respond when Gorbachev sounded the trumpet call of reform.

For in spite of all of the shortcomings of the Soviet economy and the stagnant inertia of the Brezhnev period, the Soviet Union had changed greatly in the decades since World War II. It was no longer a predominantly peasant society with a primitive work force comprised largely of unskilled manual laborers, and commanded by primitively undereducated political leaders. It had become a predominantly urban society, still dominated by smokestack industry but with a sizable middle class and a growing professional intelligentsia trained at the university level.

And while Soviet political culture was still at a very low level compared with the West, it had undergone a social sea change since the Stalin era. Millions of Soviet citizens were now more receptive to the politics of modernization.

Raw figures reveal an important part of the story. At the end of World War II, only 56.1 million people lived in cities; by 1987, that figure had more than tripled to 180 million. In Khrushchev's time, there were only three cities with a population of more than 1 million; in 1980, there were twenty-three. That massive shift from country to city has slowly worn away the peasant mentality that long characterized the Russian *narod*, or masses. In the early 1970s, this peasant mentality had been a prime source of the political passivity and fatalism of many Russians.

But during my recent travels, one provincial leader after another complained to me that large numbers of young people, especially those with some education and skills, had left dreary villages for big cities in search of better jobs, housing, clothes, stimulation—the latest movies, rock music. Such middle-class urges now made these younger urban transplants dissatisfied with the old, ossified ways of doing things; they were susceptible to the promise of change, impatient and ready to lash back when reforms failed to deliver a better life.

The reemergence of Solidarity, the Polish workers' movement, undoubtedly had an impact both on Soviet intellectuals, inside and outside of the Communist Party, and on the blue-collar proletariat. In her 1983 essay, Zaslavskaya pointed out that in the 1980s, Soviet blue-collar workers were no longer as obedient nor as moved by fear or Communist sloganeering as they had been under Stalin. The Soviet proletariat was now more skilled, more likely to have finished high school, more conscious of its own interests. And, in a distant, muffled echo of Solidarity, it was more assertive.

What is worth noting is that at least in some instances, fear of repres-

sion was not enough to check the economic disillusionment of the working class and their fury at the privileges of the Party and government
elite—their cars and drivers, special stores, country *dachas,* special clinics,
trips abroad. In sum, by the early eighties, even before Gorbachev took
over, Soviet society was no longer as docile as it had been. Not only were
people more open with their wisecracking jokes about Brezhnev and the
regime, but workers as well as intellectuals were getting feedback from
abroad, learning that workers in Eastern Europe were living much better
than they were. That fed Soviet dissatisfaction and led to some acts of
daring unheard-of during my earlier stay in Moscow, though only rarely
did active mass dissatisfaction rumble to the surface.

During my Moscow tour from 1971 to 1974, I had not heard of a single
serious labor strike. Fear had stifled what was in fact desperate economic
discontent. But several years later, even with Brezhnev's repressive apparatus still in place, the situation had changed, inspired in part by Solidarity.
In 1980 and 1981, there were wildcat strikes at auto and tractor plants
in Gorky, Togliatti, Tartu, Cheboksary, and Naberezhnye Chelny; among
coal miners at Vorkuta and Donetsk, where an illegal union was briefly
formed; in industrial plants at Vyborg, Riga, and Krivoi Rog; and at three
different factories around the Ukrainian capital of Kiev. This phenomenon spoke not only of widespread disaffection among blue-collar workers
but also of a new activism, even in the face of possible arrest and punishment. This message cannot have been lost on reform-minded leaders in
the Kremlin.[1]

But the most natural source of support for reform, in the late 1970s and
early 1980s, was the growing, university-educated urban middle class. Fed
up with Party exhortations in the face of obvious stagnation and decline,
this growing stratum was eager for a better life, not only in material terms
but also in terms of greater personal freedom and flexibility, of more
respect and protection for the individual, of more openness and honesty
in Soviet political and cultural life.

For years, Moscow and Leningrad intellectuals have charged the Soviet
leadership with a deliberate decimation of the Russian intelligentsia and
professional classes by cycles of violence, beginning with the Bolshevik
Revolution, continuing through civil war, collectivization, the Stalinist
purges, and on up through World War II. Then the Brezhnev crackdowns
of the 1970s prompted new waves of a cultural diaspora to the West. All
of this took a devastating toll on the most talented portion of the Russian
population. Quite a few of my Russian friends said that it literally "depleted the Russian genetic stock," leaving the Soviet Union genetically
inferior to the West. Even if the notion of genetic inferiority seems

extreme, the national brain drain has been enormous. Some Russian intellectuals have begun to feel that only recently has their stock begun to be replenished.

The increase in the numbers of people getting a higher education is striking, even though the quality of that education is uneven. In 1950, there were 1.2 million university-level students in the Soviet Union; by the mid-1980s, that number had multiplied over four times to 5.4 million students being taught by half a million professors and instructors.

The Soviet Union now has one of the largest bodies of scientific researchers in the world: 1.5 million scientists and engineers doing research work.[2] In the past decade, new fields have gained acceptance—systems analysis, ecology, social psychology, mathematical economics, ethnicity, political science. Even though sociology was long under a cloud, there are now fifteen to twenty thousand sociologists, not only doing research and public-opinion polling, but also employed in factories across the country advising industrial managers on how to cope with their changing work force.[3]

Under Stalin, law had low status. In 1940, Soviet universities produced only fifty-seven hundred economists and lawyers a year. But by 1974 that figure had jumped to seventy thousand a year, enough to produce a million lawyers and economists since the mid-1970s. So much interest has developed in the law that the magazine *Chelovyek i Zakon (Man and Law)* has a monthly circulation of ten million.[4]

Gorbachev himself is part of this burgeoning educated middle class. He is the first university-educated Soviet leader since Lenin, born the son of peasants and, like Lenin, educated in the law. Despite Gorbachev's rural roots and his Party career, the intelligentsia see him as their champion. Some of his concerns—the rule of law, the rights of individuals, freer expression—match the concerns of professionals and the intelligentsia—individual self-expression, personal development, and impatience with the heavy-handed imposition of state morality. This group was a natural constituency for reform aimed at increasing citizen participation and decreasing the role of the state and an entrenched bureaucracy.

In the dynamics of change within the Soviet Union, the most important segment of the intelligentsia is the so-called Khrushchev generation—people who from 1953 to 1964 experienced the excitement of the political and cultural thaw under Nikita Khrushchev.

Some of these people are now in their fifties and early sixties; they were liberated from the heavy pall of Stalinism during their formative university years, and were given hope for greater cultural freedom and personal autonomy. And then they watched in horror as these changes were stolen away from them by the retrogression of the Brezhnev years.

Another stream of reformers are younger, now in their forties; they were schoolchildren under Khrushchev, but nevertheless were caught up in the optimism of that era.

For both groups, hope in the future and faith in Soviet socialism had soared in the years after the first Soviet sputnik in 1957 and of Yuri Gagarin's first manned space flight on April 12, 1961. Despite Khrushchev's bumptious saber-rattling, his shoe-pounding at the United Nations, millions of middle-aged Soviets believed him when he boasted that the Soviet Union would catch up with and then overtake the West, and Gagarin's orbital flight had marked the zenith of that feeling.

"I was in school. All the lessons ended. Even today I can remember that tremendous joy, literally the tears we all had in our eyes—because we were the first, because we were in space," recalled Leonid Dobrokhotov, later one of the most articulate, candid, and thoughtful followers of Gorbachev in the Communist Party Central Committee apparatus.

"We felt our power," he told me. "We felt that there were no limits, that all tasks would be accomplished, and so on. It's no wonder that in 1961 the third program of the Communist Party of the Soviet Union was published. That program stated that we would achieve Communism in twenty years. It was like President Johnson's Great Society program, which many Americans believed in. But here, almost *everyone* believed that in twenty years we would surpass the U.S. in every way—in living standards, in food production, housing, in meeting spiritual needs, in everything.

"We would become Country Number One in the world—and socialism would be utterly victorious. Almost everyone believed that. That was in 1961."[5]

THE POLITICS OF LIES

The heady optimism of this Khrushchev generation set them up for the crushing disillusionment of the long, painful decline under Brezhnev. The Brezhnev period had actually begun in 1964 with a certain optimism—attempts at managerial reform in the economy, slow but steady improvements in the general standard of living; communal apartments were slowly being replaced, and better clothing, washing machines, and refrigerators became available. But in Brezhnev's second decade, economic reform was dead, strangled by the party apparat; cultural controls tightened. In every sphere, reality fell short of people's expectations and public morale took a nosedive. This was true even among the most loyal and optimistic Communists, such as Leonid Dobrokhotov, people who were making their way up the ladder in the Communist Party.

Leonid's terse description of his own disenchantment is etched in my mind, his pale blue eyes locked on mine, his slender arms thrown out wide, his slender pianist's fingers gesticulating. A member of a theatrical family, Leonid is more expressive, and more sensitive to the moods of the intelligentsia, than most Communist Party officials. For many years, his job involved dealing with the Academy of Sciences, which put him in contact with the intellectual and scientific community. His recollections, therefore, reflect a wider perspective, both within the scientific intelligentsia and within a reformist element in the Communist Party apparatus.

I asked how Leonid felt at the end of the 1970s.

"It's the exact opposite of the feelings I described in 1961," he replied. "I wouldn't call it disenchantment with socialism, but it was certainly disenchantment with our country's leadership, and an understanding that the program to build Communism in twenty years was a total fiction. That that program had not been carried out at all, that it *couldn't* be carried out. That everything was very bad in the country. The economy was bad. There was no real provision for the population's needs. There was no democracy. The leadership was corrupt. And finally, there was Afghanistan."

But if segments of the intelligentsia were disillusioned by the early eighties, Leonid said the masses were not quite; they were more skeptical than disillusioned. "People saw that things were bad and that the system didn't work, but why it didn't work was unclear to the overwhelming majority of people. So it's true to say that almost everyone continued to believe in socialism, in the foundation of the system." What they didn't believe in was Brezhnev. "They simply thought that Brezhnev had not justified the hopes pinned on him. And that the people working with Brezhnev were not the right people. So they thought it would be rather easy to replace those people, and leave the mechanism essentially the same. Only an insignificant number of people understood that the system had to be radically changed—that it wasn't a matter of people, but rather of the system. I think that was understood only by a minority, mostly the intelligentsia."[6]

The majority view is in many ways understandable. In his eighteen years of power, Brezhnev had concentrated the country's efforts on a few high-priority areas, and had driven the Soviet Union to accumulate an enormous nuclear arsenal. The Soviet Union had surpassed the United States in such yardsticks of industrial might as steel output and oil production. And the living standards of Soviet people had actually improved during the first dozen years of Brezhnev's rule. However much the West was offended by the invasion of Czechoslovakia in 1968, most Russians were proud that Brezhnev had asserted Soviet power and kept the empire intact.

But sometime in the mid-seventies, the tide began to turn. By the end of the decade, the economy had quite clearly lost momentum. Four bad agricultural harvests, from 1979 through 1982, made food shortages endemic. There was rationing of meat and milk in some regions. Industrial sectors went into decline; labor productivity went flat. The free health-care system, a much-vaunted pride of Soviet socialism, had deteriorated so much that infant mortality rates rose while male life expectancy went down. The statistics were covered up, but people could experience for themselves the horrible inadequacies of the health system: shortages of medicine, unbearably long waits for treatment, serious infections picked up in hospitals, the bribery necessary to secure treatment. The press occasionally reported stories of corruption by middle-level officials. Moscow was full of unseemly rumors that reached into Brezhnev's own family and entourage. Later it turned out that even the army, Party officials, and the KGB, headed by Brezhnev's eventual successor, Yuri Andropov, were embarrassed and angered by the corruption and sloth of the Brezhnev era. The whole country was sliding into cynicism.[7]

"That was an awful time," recalled Roy Medvedev, the dissident Marxist historian who had dared, in the Brezhnev era, to write and publish in the West his devastating book on Stalin, _Let History Judge._ Roy, a Communist idealist whose father had been executed under Stalin and whose twin brother, Zhores, had gone into exile in London, had squirreled himself away in a cubbyhole writing den in his fifth-floor apartment. Basically isolated, he was nevertheless still fed information and documents for his archives by covert Khrushchev-style reformers within government institutes and the Party apparatus. I had known Roy in the early 1970s as one of a handful of outspoken dissidents; he told me how much worse things had gotten after I left.

"People did not believe in anything," Roy recalled. "Brezhnev was so cynical, his whole policies and politics were full of lies. Power was more important to him than ideals. He was a vain, stupid person. When people saw him come on the screen, they just switched off the TV. Not just when he became sick, but before he was sick. So you could say those years were lost for politics. People focused on their personal lives, because culture, politics, and art, especially social sciences, were not developing anymore. Nobody wanted to take part."[8]

The same was true in the economy. Workers, managers, everyone, went through the motions of working in the official economy, but when consumers really wanted something they turned to the black market, which was so massive that it really amounted to a countereconomy. People turned to this for meat, fresh vegetables, toothpaste, caviar, women's boots, baby clothes, rugs, wall lamps, ballet tickets, spare parts to fix the refrigerator or the car, medicine, tutoring for the kids, a decent apartment. Entire underground industries flourished, illegal factories within legal ones, operating with the same workers and the same raw materials, but this time efficiently because for private profit. There were underground millionaires managing wholesale production and marketing enterprises with links all over the country. This is where people's energies were going, where they were applying their ingenuity. Just as in academic life and the world of culture, progress did not stop. People pursued their own ends in private, underground, ignoring or eluding the regime's threats of prosecution. In fact, the practice was so much a part of everyone's daily life that most Russians I knew believed that Brezhnev and his cronies counted on the black market as a safety valve for people's frustrations.

The gap between real life and Communist dogma yawned ever wider. As the problems grew worse, the regime became more boastful. As official propaganda became more pretentious, as Brezhnev held ceremonies to have decorations pinned on his chest, ordinary Russians mocked him. I remember several jokes poking fun at the Brezhnev cult. The first lampooned the nation's immobility under Brezhnev; the second mocked his dim wit.

In the first joke, a train carrying Stalin, Khrushchev, and Brezhnev stalls somewhere in the steppes. People turn to Stalin, as the senior leader, to ask how to get the train moving. Without hesitation, he gives a characteristic command: "Shoot the engineers. Exile the crew. Get someone new." But a short while later, the train stalls again. This time, responsibility falls on Khrushchev, who pardons the crew members exiled by Stalin and puts them back on the job, and the train resumes its journey. Inevitably, it stalls a third time. This time Brezhnev has to deal with the problem. The others turn to him, he thinks a moment, and then orders: "Pull down the shades and pretend we're moving."

In the second anecdote, Brezhnev is congratulating some Soviet cosmonauts after a successful space flight. But conscious that the Americans have landed on the moon and are leading in the space race, he discloses that the Soviet Union intends to leap ahead with a special new mission. The Politburo, he announces, has voted to send out a Soviet cosmonaut team—to the sun!

"But, comrade leader," one cosmonaut protests, "we'll be burned alive."

"Do you think we understand nothing?" Brezhnev replies. "Don't worry. We have planned every detail. We have arranged for you to land at night."

By the early eighties, Brezhnev's senility had become an embarrassment. When I went to Vienna to cover President Carter's summit meeting with Brezhnev in 1979, I remembered the Brezhnev who had visited America six years earlier. He had been vigorous then, cavorting with husky Western movie star Chuck Connors, who had hoisted Brezhnev off the ground in a Russian bear hug. But in Vienna he seemed a walking corpse. He hobbled off the plane from Moscow, his gait unsteady, his face sallow and waxen. Then, when I followed him to a ceremony at a monument honoring the Soviet dead in Austria during World War II, I was even more shocked at his infirmities.

He was supposed to march past a gathering of Soviet officials and embassy families, make a right turn, take half a dozen steps, and then symbolically touch a huge green wreath that had been placed before the monument. I watched him approach, moving mechanically, like a windup doll. His feet shuffled in short little steps from the knees down, arms pinned to his sides, his hands flapping back and forth. His loyal lieutenant Konstantin Chernenko was a step behind, followed by other dignitaries.

Then, as I watched from fifteen feet away, Brezhnev missed the turning point and plowed helplessly into a group of onlookers. There was an audible gasp from the people around me, as Brezhnev was rescued by Chernenko, who pulled him back and manually steered him onto the correct path. The rest of the ceremony went all right, but I was left astonished by Brezhnev's obvious incapacity.

Nevertheless he stayed in office three more years, his geriatric decline a symbol of the general stagnation and drift that was afflicting his country.

THE HALF-LOST GENERATION

Periodically, Brezhnev—and the Kremlin—would lash out, as if to assert the regime's power, to ward off the developing urge for change. But these assertions of power only added to the growing hunger for reform. The

December 1979 invasion of Afghanistan was the most violent of these power moves, and it served to alienate a new generation, the young people of the 1980s.

"It was a shock for us, the Afghanistan invasion, an absolute shock," one of them told me. Sergei Stankevich was in his mid-twenties in 1979, teaching at Moscow Pedagogical Institute. "It was a very bad New Year— the invasion took place on the eve of the New Year. It was a time of mourning for us. In my circle, everyone was ironic about the official rhetoric—that we were 'invited' in by the Afghans. At the same time we were terrified, because we understood that when the war starts outside, the war also starts inside. The war against truth, openness, against liberals. We understood that it meant a long period of tightening the screws. Still, almost nobody had enough courage to protest openly—except Sakharov, of course. We heard about him by foreign radio. At that time, everybody listened to foreign radio. Our reaction was blaming: We blamed the whole system and Brezhnev personally. But blaming in the kitchen, a typical situation for us, kitchen blaming. There was absolute rejection of Brezhnev and all that he was doing."[9]

Stankevich and his friends confined their protests to the kitchen, because they knew that public protests over the Afghan war would result in a trip to Siberia and the end of their careers.

Stankevich had entered the university in 1972, at the dawning of détente between Nixon and Brezhnev. He and his classmates were hoping for a real opening to the world, and not just through government-to-government agreements. They were encouraged by the Helsinki Accords on human rights, signed in 1975. And they were devastated by Brezhnev's subsequent repression of human-rights activists, and by the invasion of Afghanistan.

"Afghanistan was a watershed for our generation," Stankevich told me. "It was the funeral of hope."

Stankevich turned thirty before Gorbachev came to power. He felt cheated out of freedom and out of the new opportunities his generation had expected from détente. He said that he and his friends felt that their lives had been half wasted under Brezhnev and his geriatric successors, Andropov and Chernenko.

"We are the half-lost generation," he said bitterly.

Still, Stankevich and his friends thought the war in Afghanistan might eventually work to their benefit. Remembering that the Crimean War in the 1850s had been the undoing of Czar Nicholas I, and the Russo-Japanese War of 1905 had begun the unraveling for Czar Nicholas II, they saw the Afghan war as a potentially fatal mistake for Brezhnev and company.

"It was a kind of sunset of the regime, because they were involved in such a bad business," Stankevich said. "[We thought,] 'They can never prevail in this war, and it can only aggravate the crisis.' We felt that sometime, sooner or later, radical changes would be inevitable."

"Really?" I asked. "You felt that even before Brezhnev died?"

"Even before Brezhnev died." Stankevich replied. "You know when the government of a regime in crisis goes to war, it's also an attempt to postpone the crash. But in practice it accelerates the crash."

FERMENT WITHIN THE PARTY

And so the intellectuals, in both the middle and younger generations, as well as consumers and workers, were disaffected by economic misery, but they were still politically inert. What about the hidden world of the Communist Party?

Contrary to the Western perception of the Soviet Communist Party as a monolith that operates with Nazi-like discipline, by the late 1970s feelings of grievance, failure, and the need for change had penetrated and fragmented the Party as well. Many Soviets have told me in recent years that the inner life of the Party reflects a range of popular moods. On basic economic issues, the views of rank-and-file Party members are likely to be fairly close to those of the public at large. The prevailing views of people in the Party apparatus are dominated by older, more conservative career-ists, including regional power barons and *apparatchiki* who have a vested interest in the status quo. But throughout the Brezhnev period, and certainly by the end of it, there were already several different tendencies within the Party: Old Guard conservatives like Brezhnev protecting the status quo; neo-Stalinists who wanted a return to a tougher line; Khrush-chevite reformers who wanted Stalin and Stalinism explicitly rejected; a growing stream of newer reformers; and a preponderance of opportunists feathering their own careers by going along with the Brezhnev line.

By 1980, many of the brightest people rising through the Party hierar-chy shared the disenchantment of non-Party intellectuals. Within the Party, morale was sagging and ideological cynicism was on the rise. Many were sickened by official corruption; others were fed up with the two laughable old fools Brezhnev and Chernenko. Although they dared not speak out publicly, they were deeply offended by the fatuous personality cult fostered by Brezhnev, reminiscent of Stalin, and by the false claims of the Brezhnev regime.

"The first three years of Brezhnev's rule had offered some hope," recalled Aleksandr Yakovlev. Now Gorbachev's closest political ally, Yakovlev was a powerful figure even back in the late 1960s, when he was acting chief of the Party's propaganda department. "Brezhnev said the right things; I didn't know he was speaking someone else's words. He seemed open to reforms, to fresh ideas. And then later it all turned out so obscenely. I remember that certain comrades in his entourage began to call me and ask why I wasn't promoting Brezhnev. That astounded me. It was simply impossible for me to do—it was physically unbearable."[10]

Yakovlev's refusal to play along with Brezhnev and his entourage on issues important to Brezhnev and his ideological attack on Russian nationalism, to which Brezhnev was sympathetic, cost Yakovlev his job. He was banished to Canada, as ambassador, in 1972; Gorbachev rescued him in 1983.

Other high-ranking officials, such as Andropov, the KGB boss whose intelligence role required him to study the West as well as manage internal security, and army marshals such as Chief of Staff Nikolai Ogarkov, who saw Western advances in modern technology, knew the U.S.S.R. was slipping badly. Internally, the Communist Party was full of ferment as the 1980s began.

"I can speak only for myself and my comrades, but at that time, we talked only politics," recalled Leonid Dobrokhotov, who at that time was a rising Moscow Party functionary in his mid-to-late thirties. "We argued. Everyone was dissatisfied. Everyone saw that the situation wasn't getting better, it was getting worse. We argued about what to do. The majority of us felt [our national crisis] was due to a lack of discipline, to insufficient demands, insufficient control over how people fulfilled various laws and decisions, because Brezhnev was not capable. His policy was too liberal. So we came to the conclusion that we had to make tougher demands, improve discipline. Of course, this was not truly deep, analytical thinking, and it did not uncover the real reasons for the country's problems. But that's the way the majority thought. Only a few understood that the fault was not the lack of formal discipline; the fault was the system—it didn't work, or it was working worse and worse all the time."[11]

Even very near the top, the spirit of reform was gestating. In Brezhnev's final year, agencies such as Gosplan (the State Planning Committee) and the Committee for Science and Technology set up study groups to look at the option of decentralized economic management. In 1983, Vadim Medvedev, rector of the Academy of Social Sciences, the main domestic think tank of the Communist Party Central Committee, published a book advocating new attempts at economic reform. Medvedev, an economist who would emerge as a member of Gorbachev's Politburo, praised Kosygin's reforms of 1965 but said they did not go far enough. He urged more autonomy for state enterprises, more material incentives for workers, letting consumers have more say in determining output, and introducing "commodity-money" relations (a code term for market economics).[12] His book was not as blunt and radical as Zaslavskaya's "Novosibirsk Report"; it was couched in vaguer, more technical wording. But it pointed in the same direction.

Some experimentation was already under way in Soviet Georgia, under Eduard Shevardnadze, the innovative Georgian Party boss who had been a close political friend of Gorbachev since the two were leaders of Komsomol youth organizations in the late 1950s. In the early 1970s, I had known of Shevardnadze as a Party puritan. He had purged the corrupt Georgian Party apparatus and sent scores of officials and businessmen to jail for illegal economic operations. But by 1979, he was known as a liberal who had set up a public-opinion center under the Georgian Party Central Committee and used public-opinion polls to help monitor the quality of state services and then fired high officials who got bad reports from the public. Later, Shevardnadze allowed experiments in enterprise self-management, in market-oriented pricing, in leasing small businesses to families, and in legalizing industrial black-market industries so as to tap their entrepreneurship.[13] Shevardnadze began by liberalizing controls over the arts, cinema, and the press.

Dobrokhotov, intrigued by an article about Shevardnadze's unorthodox approach, went to Georgia in 1979 for a firsthand look.

"In Georgia, I saw the *perestroika* that is now going on here," Dobrokhotov told me. "So that even during the worst period of stagnation in our country, democratization was going on in Tbilisi, Georgia. They were chasing out bureaucrats. The jails were filled with almost all of the former leaders of the republic—they were jailed for corruption and theft, for deception. There was a battle against bureaucracy. The press was extremely critical of these negative elements. I was inspired, awed by what I saw in Georgia. When I came home, I started to report about this to the leadership; I said that we should do what they were doing in Georgia. But my boss at the time was a rather shrewd leader, as I understand now, and he told me, 'Leonid, under no circumstances should you tell anyone about your impressions.'"[14]

In short, even if Shevardnadze was testing out a mild version of Gorbachev's future policy of *glasnost* in the provinces, it was not smart for a rising Party official like Dobrokhotov to risk his career by going out on a limb with the Brezhnev regime.

But times were changing. By the time Brezhnev died in November 1982 and Yuri Andropov took over, there was substantial sentiment for change within the Party as well as among the people.

Widely regarded as the smartest member of the Politburo, Andropov seemed aware of the country's paralysis and bent on restoring a national sense of purpose. He began like a man in a hurry, intent on breaking the economic logjams and stirring up an apathetic society. He immediately launched a purge of Brezhnevite corruption and a campaign for greater work discipline and more economic efficiency. He injected a sense of momentum. But essentially, his reforms were conservative—tightening rather than loosening control. And in just fifteen months, his rule was cut short by death.

Reformers' hopes were dashed, then, when Politburo conservatives proved powerful enough to impose as the new leader Konstantin Chernenko, Brezhnev's old lieutenant and a doddering apparatchik in his seventies. Chernenko was a throwback, his rule an embarrassment. He revived Brezhnev's personality cult, pomposity, inertia. The old Brezhnev jokes were recycled and applied to Chernenko. Everywhere lay the dead hand of the oppressive bureaucracy grown fat under Brezhnev. People were ashamed of the past, frustrated by the present, fearful for the future.

It was doubly painful for the older people, whose hopes were raised by Khrushchev in the 1950s and then dashed by Brezhnev, only to have that cycle repeated by the quicker up-and-down of Andropov and Chernenko.

By the time Chernenko died in March 1985, the gloom was pervasive, the pressure for reform explosive. Aleksandr Yakovlev, by then an adviser to Gorbachev, described to me the mood of that time:

"I had a sense of foreboding, like before a storm. That there was something brewing in people and there would be a time when they would say, 'That's it. We can't go on living like this. We can't. We need to redo everything.' "[15]

CHAPTER 3

GORBACHEV AND THE KHRUSHCHEV GENERATION

"The main social forces behind *perestroika* are people in that generation. Those are the people that we call the Children of the Twentieth Party Congress—Khrushchev's Congress, where he gave his secret speech denouncing Stalin. These were the people who came out of Khrushchev's thaw, which formed their mentality, and of course, he—Gorbachev—was part of that generation."[1]

—Vladimir Tikhonov
Economist
September 1989

While a political storm had been gathering, it took Gorbachev to unleash its fury. A new kind of Soviet leader was needed to pry the lid off and deal with decades of discontent, to legitimize protest, permit free expression, restrain the KGB and police from scooping up the first new demonstrators and starting to refill Stalin's old gulag. It took a political visionary, one who was both desperate and self-confident, to declare that it was impossible to rescue Soviet socialism and pump life back into its decrepit carcass without also injecting political freedoms and giving people, especially educated people, a voice and a stake in the Soviet system. It took Gorba-

chev, idealistic, bold, and supremely agile, to set the match to the fuse
of political dynamite that had been building up. It took Gorbachev to
proclaim the Grand Reformation of the Soviet system.

But where had this Mikhail Gorbachev come from?

How had such a daring innovator wriggled his way up through a bureaucracy that had put a premium on orthodoxy, had ground individuality
out of its apparatchiks?

Once Gorbachev emerged as the leader, we began to see for ourselves
some of the traits that led to his success: strong beliefs, strict candor about
the failures within the system, intellectual curiosity and openness, an
ebullience, and a penchant for change and experimentation. Gorbachev
became a political trapeze artist who defied the normal laws of gravity.
But how did such a risk taker get himself chosen by his Politburo peers
to preside over a conservative, self-protective power pyramid that had
habitually hidden behind lies, punished political deviation, and routinely
quashed anything that smacked of intellectual independence?

What was the crucible that forged the steel in Gorbachev's character?
Where had his notions of reform come from, and how had he struck such
an exquisite balance between the need to conform and the need to be
open enough to think anew? How had he been cunning enough to preserve a vital core of belief deep inside himself, while showing sufficient
obedience to satisfy his superiors? What intellectual and biographical
origins had shaped his inner mental world?

Many of Gorbachev's most important traits came from his family and
took root in early childhood: his honesty and realism, his outspokenness,
his tolerance for religion, his breathtaking self-assurance, his driving ambition, and most important, his astonishing resilience, his capacity to survive. At the pinnacle of power, Gorbachev stunned Westerners with his
ability to ride over the turbulence of *perestroika,* to buck with confidence
the waves of reaction. He seemed to thrive on crisis, as if crisis were his
natural state.

The truth is that from the day of his birth, Mikhail Sergeyevich Gorbachev was tutored in the arts of biological and political survival in a hostile
world. His life story evokes Abraham Lincoln's odyssey from log cabin to
the White House, except that the death and famine from Stalin's farm
collectivization, which engulfed the early years of Gorbachev's life, was
far more devastating than anything Lincoln experienced growing up.

In 1931, the year Gorbachev was born in the village of Privolnoye,
Stalin's terror and his collectivization reached a climax. Gorbachev's
home was a little hut on a gentle rise in the open prairie, or steppe, of

the Northern Caucasus, now called Stavropol Territory, or Krai. It is a place of broad expanses, like northern Texas, and the independent-minded people whom I met there speak of *prostor,* or space, the same way that Texans limn their romance with wide open spaces. The town's name, Privolnoye, means "free" or "spacious," alluding not only to the broad pastoral landscape stretching off in all directions, but also to a certain free-booter spirit among its people.

The land, lying nearly one thousand miles south of Moscow and stretching north from the Caucasus mountain range, is fertile, framed by the deltas of two great Russian rivers, the Volga and the Don. The soil is a rich ebony; with a kind of peasant reverence, the Russians call it *chernozem,* black earth. The long temperate growing season is a bit dry, but the favorable soil has made this one of the richest grain-producing areas in the entire country.

The people of this southern frontier region have a wilder, freer history than the more settled peasantry of central Russia. When they came to the region around the Don River in the sixteenth and seventeenth centuries, they became known as the Don cossacks, legendary as independent yeoman farmers and fierce horsemen, who settled the wild frontier and, as mercenaries, defended this southern outpost of the Russian Empire against Muslim peoples from the south. The cossacks were not ethnic stock but freedom seekers, runaways, even escaped criminals. A century later came the forebears of Gorbachev, peasants from central Russia and the Ukraine, again people escaping the yoke of serfdom and in search of better land and more freedom. Throughout the nineteenth century, the Northern Caucasus thrived on a tradition of independent homesteading, which was continued even by Lenin, only to be shattered by Stalin's violent collectivization of the land and his bloody repression of the kulaks (so-called wealthy peasants, even though their wealth might have consisted of no more than a home, a few acres, and a couple of cows).

In Privolnoye, the leader of collectivization was Gorbachev's maternal grandfather, Pantelei Yefimovich Gopkolo. By many accounts, he was the pivotal influence on Gorbachev's life. Family friends describe Grandfather Gopkolo as an active, dynamic Ukrainian, gregarious, persuasive, a good public speaker, with a self-confident manner, a masculine stride, and the presence of a natural leader. These qualities plus Grandfather Gopkolo's ability to swing pragmatically with the violent tides of history were an obvious model for Gorbachev.

Born in 1882, Gopkolo had to follow a zigzag course merely to survive to the age of seventy. On a trip to Great Britain in 1984, Gorbachev revealed that even though his grandfather was a Communist, his grandparents hid religious icons in their home behind portraits of Lenin and Stalin. This was hardly a unique experience; it was done in many families. But clearly, their way of secretly protecting something that was vital to them was an object lesson in political behavior that stuck in the mind of the grandson, and served as an example for his own dealings with higher authority.

As a young man, Grandfather Gopkolo had to adapt to the violent crosscurrents that swept through Privolnoye. As he moved into young adulthood, the region was benefiting from czarist land reforms of 1906 that legalized private farming. In the next few years, Russia become the world's number one exporter of grain, enriching the countryside. After the Bolshevik Revolution and during the civil war from 1918 to 1921, Privol-noye was caught in the crossfire between the Red Army and the counter-revolutionary Whites (many of them Don cossacks), who were battling for control of the region. Monuments to the civil-war dead, a few miles from Privolnoye, attest to the heavy toll in lives. When the Reds won, Grandfather Gopkolo cast his lot with the Communists. Lenin's New Economic Policy of the mid-1920s permitted the peasants to continue private farming.

By Gorbachev's later account, his family were not "wealthy" kulaks, but "middle peasants," who made a moderate but decent living. Yet when Stalin commanded collectivization, Grandfather Gopkolo was among the first to step forward.

The village elders told me that the peasantry were persuaded by roving Communist Party workers that collectives would be the most efficient way to work their modest plots of land. Some said that Gopkolo and others willing to form a new collective were offered the incentive of a few Ford and Caterpillar tractors, obtained from America.[2] Undoubtedly, some were also influenced by the ominous warnings dropped by Stalin's agents roaming the area. But according to Grigory Gorlov, a warm and craggy-faced old local Party leader who knew the Gorbachev family well, even before Stalin's campaign began in earnest in 1929, Gopkolo contributed his own land to what was initially a small farm cooperative of about twenty families.[3] As a respected figure in the village, someone to whom people turned for advice, Gopkolo actively went about recruiting others. Eventually, their cooperative became a full-fledged *kolkhoz,* or collective farm, of about three hundred families, with Gopkolo as its chairman.

The process was painful, Gorbachev's uncle Sergei Gopkolo told me. "Collectivization was a very hard time," he said. "Some people did not want to join, especially those who were 'rich.' "[4] What he meant was that many homesteaders, especially the cossacks, had to surrender not only their land, but often horses and other livestock and wagons. In many areas violence was used. But the village elders insisted to me that Gopkolo was a man of moderate temperament, opposed to using force and preferring "the course of persuasion."

If true, then Privolnoye was unusual and extremely fortunate, because the general devastation wrought by Stalin's policies was horrifying. In the Northern Caucasus, people are full of stories about terror against cossacks and peasants. Some Western experts have estimated from Soviet accounts that, during the forced collectivization, as many as six million peasant families disappeared nationwide between 1929 and 1934. The Northern Caucasus, with its cossack traditions of independence, was especially hard hit.[5]

What is more, the land and people were ravaged by what became known as the Great Famine. By the winter of 1932–33, Stavropol Krai had become a famine disaster zone. Conditions were harsher than during the American Great Depression. "The repressions of the 1930s hit the rural areas of the North Caucasus badly," wrote Zhores Medvedev, who grew up not far from Stavropol Territory. "Almost every family lost relatives, friends or neighbors during this period and Privolnoye was no exception."[6]

Each year, Stalin winched up his demands for ever more grain from the countryside, to feed urban factory workers—46 percent of the total harvest in 1930, 63 percent in 1931. Peasants were left without enough food for themselves. To survive, they went on grain strikes, hiding their grain from state procurement agents; yet Stalin tightened the vise of collectivization to capture every kernel. It was a vicious cycle. In Privolnoye, food virtually disappeared in the winter of 1932–33. People now claim that something like one third of the village's six thousand residents perished, some buried crudely in collective graves. A wizened old farm agronomist named Nikolai Lubenko told me, "The raw hunger was terrible."

This was the apocalypse into which Gorbachev was born, on March 2, 1931. His mother worked on Grandfather Gopkolo's *kolkhoz* as the leader of a team that raised vegetables. His father, Sergei Andreyevich, was a combine operator. Eventually he became the head of a tractor brigade of thirty workers at a machine tractor station, a Stalinist innovation that helped monitor all farm production.

On my two visits to Privolnoye with a television crew, I found a village of rough-hewn houses made of brick or wood, lined up on plots fifty feet wide behind weather-beaten wood fences. Only a few of the town's roads are paved. Today, Gorbachev's mother, now in her late seventies, lives on one of the paved roads in a brick house with a special telephone line to maintain contact with her son. The mother's house is under the watchful eye of security men and off limits to foreign visitors, at Gorbachev's personal request.

He has also obviously decreed that the town make no visible cult over its famous son. It is a very ordinary-looking village, in the center of which stands a Soviet "House of Culture." The whole scene looks like a village in Ohio or Wisconsin sixty years ago.

But back when Gorbachev was born, his family lived in a much more primitive, two-room hut made of mud bricks, dung, and straw, about three or four miles from the main village. Grigory Gorlov told me that the Gorbachevs had an outhouse, a small barn, a cow, a few pigs, and chickens and turkeys running around the yard. Next to the house was a grape arbor. Out back was a vegetable garden for growing potatoes, cucumbers, onions, and tomatoes; also there were some fruit trees—apricot, cherry, apple. The kitchen had a stove and table, but no running water. The main room had one big bed and heat, but the room given to young Misha (Gorbachev's Russian nickname) was unheated. It was his alone, until he was seventeen, when his brother, Aleksandr, was born.

The fierce deprivation he witnessed in the countryside left an indelible impression on Gorbachev. Years later, to fellow students at Moscow State University, he exposed the hypocrisy of Stalin's propaganda about the happy life on Soviet collective farms, recalling the forced labor and the meager meals of his own childhood. His family managed to endure the famine years, thanks to their backyard plot and to their favored standing at Grandfather Gopkolo's *kolkhoz*. But that experience hardened young Misha for the future. It taught him the basics of survival, while inculcating in him candor about the infirmities of the system that he had seen firsthand.

THE INSTINCT FOR CENTER STAGE

Misha Gorbachev was far from an average farm boy. His record, in and out of school, was impressive, but nothing that caused people to mark him as a future national leader. "He was not like a special person," his high school history teacher, Antonina Shcherbakova, told me. "He was just a regular guy. He liked games. He liked laughing. He liked soccer. He used to run barefoot in the grass. Even without pants, only in his shorts. He walked to school on foot."[7]

A hometown chum, Aleksandr Yakovenko, a combine operator with a twinkle in his eye who now looks a decade older than Gorbachev, recalled normal boyhood pursuits with Misha—splashing in a great wooden rain barrel, pulling the pigtails of the village girls, playing a Russian game like baseball called *lapta,* sitting on the bench outside his house singing folk songs while Misha played the stringed balalaika. As Yakovenko plucked one of those songs for me, "Bread First of All," tears welled up in his eyes. In those days, Yakovenko said, Misha loved munching on salted watermelon and gulping down cold *kvas,* a Russian peasant brew made by dripping water through burnt toast. Their boyhoods were hard, but not without pleasure, and Misha was known as a cheerful lad.

Still, by the time he finished high school, a discerning eye could pick out characteristics that would distinguish him later—his zeal for learning, his self-righteous contempt for alcohol, his ambition, his ability as a leader and organizer—and his instinct for center stage.

No one who has ever met Gorbachev comes away without mentioning his penetrating eyes. Gorbachev's gaze is commanding—his retinas sometimes a deep brown, sometimes a shining charcoal-black. These magnetic eyes radiate power, intensity, and energy—abnormal energy. I spoke with him briefly during his visit to Washington in December 1987, and I remember that his eyes were like lasers, locking onto mine, never shifting, never blinking. He was looking directly at me, yet through me. Family friends remember that Gorbachev's father had those same eyes, and in fact, that penetrating gaze stares out from beneath Misha's high forehead and over his round, fleshy cheeks in snapshots taken when he was only four years old.

Gorbachev's father, according to accounts given me, was a simple, practical, hardworking man, at home on his tractor in the fields, but rather shy. Like all the others in the family, he had no more than a few grades of education in a local village school. He was well regarded enough to be a trusted member of the Communist Party District Committee, but he intensely disliked making speeches, and would offer to work extra days in the fields if that would excuse him from making an oral report.

Young Misha took after his mother, old Gopkolo's daughter, Mariya Panteleyevna. She was—and is—a strong woman, sturdy, outspoken, self-confident, and self-righteous. People in the village know her as a religious believer who had young Misha baptized and probably inculcated in him tolerance of religion, although she did not make a believer out of him. But she did set a powerful example in speaking out. At district Party meetings, with her husband silently cringing beside her or trying to talk her out of making a fuss, she would rise to her feet and launch into a speech, bombarding her fellow farmers and local officials with questions and criticisms. She spoke at almost every meeting; no one was exempt from her tongue-lashings. Descriptions of her bring to mind the modern Gorbachev.

An aggressive teetotaler, "she would scold drunkards and people who worked badly," recalled Grigory Gorlov, the district Party secretary in those days. "She even argued with the chairman of the *kolkhoz* and the head of the machine tractor station. I recall one session vividly. There was a big fat farmhand named Kabakov, who had gotten drunk and left the barn door open. It was winter, and half of the *kolkhoz*'s flock of poultry perished in the cold. Mariya Panteleyevna demanded: 'Why are all the poultry frozen to death and why didn't *you* freeze? I tell you why. You're not frozen because you were drunk, you were so full of alcohol!' "[8]

Temperance was the rule in the Gorbachev household. On holidays, the men might take one shot glass of vodka or cognac in celebration, no more. It's small wonder that, half a century later, Gorbachev would initiate, as one of his first priorities after taking power in March 1985, an anti-alcohol campaign combined with a drive to improve work discipline.

The hard life on the farm and the onset of World War II forced Misha to become an adult at an early age, gaining maturity and self-confidence. His father was called to the front in 1941; he served as a minelayer, from Smolensk to the end of the war in Prague, and was wounded three times. In 1942, when Nazi forces occupied the region around Privolnoye, Gorbachev, now the man of the house, left school for a year and went to work in the fields with the old folks and the women. He was then only eleven, having just passed the local rite of puberty—jumping off the rickety wooden bridge over the Yegorlyk River into the muddy waters fifteen feet below.

The Nazi occupation, part of Hitler's attempt to cut southern Russia off from the north and capture the important Soviet oil center at Baku on the Caspian Sea, lasted only five months, from August 5, 1942, to January 21, 1943. In Privolnoye, about three hundred Jews who had fled the German occupation of the nearby Ukraine were gathered up and deported by the Germans. Two or three local Jewish families, including a doctor and a teacher, were taken away and shot, according to Grigory Gorlov. But for most Ukrainians and Russians in the village, the German presence was not harsh. The local people were protected by a villager of German stock, whom the Germans used as a middleman; he ordered the Soviet peasants to turn over collective harvests of vegetables, corn, and sunflower seeds, used in making bread.

Grandfather Gopkolo, by then the village headman, tried to rally the peasants to passive resistance against the Germans, urging them to hide grain and refuse to cooperate. But most people thought they had little choice; even grandson Misha had to help supply the Germans. Practically every day, German soldiers would come through the village on motorcycles with sidecars, searching peasant homes, including Gorbachev's, and commandeering food for the troops.

"It was scary," Aleksandr Yakovenko recalled. "They took everything—meat, milk, eggs. Whether the family had kids or no kids, the Germans didn't care. There were two [German] pilots here. Their plane had crashed on our field. And this one pilot lived in our house for a couple of months."[9]

By the time Sergei Gorbachev returned from what Russians call the Great Patriotic War in 1946, his son was fifteen, a self-reliant young achiever who knew how to operate a Soviet S-80 harvester and seemed to thrive on a hard day's work in the fields. During the war years, curly-haired young Misha had grown in other ways. He had followed the course of the war in regional newspapers. Older people, only half-literate, brought Misha the papers so he could read aloud to them. He would figure out the various battles and explain the progress of the war. So Sergei returned to find a young man already developing an acquaintance with the world beyond Privolnoye.

Each summer, all summer long, the two worked together as a team. The father drove a harvester, and the son was assigned the dusty, dry, backbreaking work of pitchforking grain into the path of the combine. Years later, Gorbachev was to comment that "joint work with adults from a young age" had molded his inclination for hard work and taking responsibility.

The high point for the father and son came in 1948. Stalin wanted to recover from the severe drought and postwar hunger in Russia, and that whole summer, Misha and Aleksandr Yakovenko worked like slaves with their fathers, in a four-man harvest brigade. The wheat crop had been damaged by wind and rain. The stalks were bent over.

"We worked twenty to twenty-two hours a day, only stopping when the dew set on the grass," Yakovenko recalled, his face creased and red even today from working the fields. "We had only two hours of break, and then we had to clean the combines. If we slept at all, we'd dig holes in the haystacks and cover ourselves with straw. We didn't even have a place to wash our faces. We didn't have meat, just bread. For soup, we just had millet in water."[10]

The extraordinary effort paid off. The four-man brigade brought in a record yield, five or six times the average, and won national recognition. That fall, when national honors were passed out for outstanding work, both fathers and sons got the prestigious Order of the Red Banner of

Labor award. Normally, this award was given to veteran Party leaders, factory bosses, outstanding "shock workers," as the culmination of a lifetime career. It was unheard-of for a pair of teenage farm boys in Privolnoye to receive it. They were being held up to the nation as models.

They were decorated with medals at an official ceremony in Stavropol, the territorial capital one hundred miles away. Just going to Stavropol was an adventure for the two country boys.

"We didn't have a movie house here in Privolnoye, so we went to the movie in Stavropol just to celebrate," Yakovenko recalled. "Then, at the store, we told people we were going to be decorated and we wanted to have suits. The suits were too big and made of coarse wool, but we were still the best-looking guys in our village." Yakovenko stayed on in Privolnoye but, of course, Gorbachev did not.

If any single person fired Gorbachev's ambition, his drive to rise above the crowd and strike out beyond Privolnoye, even beyond Stavropol, it was Grandfather Gopkolo. Strange, perhaps, for a family in which no one had a formal education beyond fourth grade, but old Gopkolo constantly fueled young Misha's hunger for education. Understanding that for an ordinary peasant boy, education was the only ticket to a new life, he supplied Misha with books such as Pushkin's poetry, and Lermontov's novel *A Hero of Our Time.* He urged the boy to go on to high school when he finished the seven-grade school in Privolnoye.

"His grandfather practically forced him to learn," recalled a girl named Lyubov Grudchenko, the only other student from Privolnoye at that time to make it into the high school at the district town of Krasnogvardeisk, fifteen miles away. "Misha said, 'I don't have shoes.' And his grandfather said, 'Take these,' handing him a pair of boots. And Misha said, 'I don't have anything to wear.' And the grandfather said, 'Take this,' and gave him a shirt."[11]

Every week, spring, fall, winter, and spring, Misha and Lyubov walked to school, four or five hours across the open steppe, stopping halfway at the monument to the civil-war dead for a rest and a talk. During the school week, Gorbachev boarded with relatives or friends and returned to his village home for the weekend.

In school, Misha was always near the head of his class; he was diligent about his homework, a bit of a teacher's pet, a voracious reader who was always going to the dictionary. Even in first grade, he had won the biggest *yolka,* New Year's tree, for being the best student. Like all Soviet school-children in the thirties and forties, he was drenched in propaganda about Stalin, who assumed grandiose titles such as the Benevolent Friend of All Children, the Mountain Eagle, the Leader and Teacher of the Workers of the World, the Greatest Genius of All Times. But Misha's boyhood hero was Lenin. When the high school principal ran an art contest, other youngsters drew portraits of literary figures, but Misha Gorbachev drew Lenin and won first prize. Teachers recall him as a natural mediator, a boy who broke up fights on the playground. Fellow students in primary school remember him as their intermediary with teachers when they had not finished their homework. He would get up and ask questions, stalling off a test on their behalf. Later, after the Nazi occupation, other students resisted learning German, seeing it as the language of the invader, but Misha was curious about the outside world and, after his year off from school, belatedly threw himself into studying German.

His grades were good. His teachers, now white-haired, proudly show off his high school report cards, a string of A's, except for a B in German, when his lost year put him behind. His record won him a silver medal, but not the coveted gold for straight A's, which his wife, Raisa, won at her high school. "He was gifted in history," his teacher Antonina Shcherbakova remembers. "Other students were learning material only from mark to mark, for tomorrow's lesson. He wanted more. He really wanted to understand. He was very curious to learn about life, and he did." Studying history in Soviet schools meant studying the Revolution, reading Marx and Lenin. Gorbachev pored over those texts, and Shcherbakova remembered him being especially taken with Lenin's slogan "One Step Forward, Two Steps Back"—justification for temporary retreat for the sake of the longer-term objective. In short, Gorbachev was absorbing Lenin's political pragmatism. Yet despite his diligence in class, it was not academics that set Misha Gorbachev apart. He was the Big Man on Campus, popular and active in everything—literary club, history club, drama club, political debates, the Komsomol youth organization.

"He was very interested in politics, in international affairs," recalled Mariya Grevtsova, former head of the high school teachers' union. "In those days, we had what we call polboi, political battles. The students divided up into teams to debate political questions. Mikhail Sergeyevich always gave very thorough answers. If some other student did not answer well, he would add something. One of his character traits was showing great respect for other people, older people. If there was some controversy, he did not force people to accept his opinion."[12]

If Gorbachev was a natural polemicist in high school debates, the drama club exposed his instincts for center stage, foreshadowing his future as a media politician. Teachers and fellow students remember his love of acting and how naturally he came to it. With his deep brown eyes, soft full lips, and commanding presence, he was a hit, playing the lead roles in Russian prerevolutionary classics. In a dashing czarist-era uniform with gold epaulets, he played the Grand Prince Arbenin in Lermontov's *Masquerade.* He was the lovelorn Mezgir in Ostrovsky's *Snow Maiden,* Chatsky in Griboyedov's *Woe from Wit.*

"When people watch Misha on television these days, they somehow think he is so natural, so self-confident," Gorbachev's high school sweetheart and fellow actor Yuliya Karagodina told David Remnick of *The Washington Post.* "Well, he was always that way, even forty years ago, when he was a handsome prince, wearing his fake mustache in our drama club. He had a kind of aura around him, the sort of person you just naturally listen to and even follow."[13]

But if the young Gorbachev had charm and charisma, he also had a hard edge. As a disciplinarian, he was a puritan who did not let friendship interfere with duty and the rules. Like his mother chastising errant farm workers, Lyubov Grudchenko told me, Misha would scold other high school students for not finishing their homework. One morning, she said, as leader of the morning calisthenics at school, he upbraided her and another girl for arriving late. "We thought that probably as a friend, he would disregard it," she recalled. "But he noticed it and said, 'Okay, we've done our morning exercises without them. Now let them do the exercises and we'll watch them. That will be a lesson to them. Next time, they'll be on time.' "

"He could be so cool and businesslike sometimes," added Yuliya Karagodina. "Once at a Komsomol meeting, in front of everyone at the local cinema house, he was angry with me for not finishing on time a little newspaper we put out. And despite our friendship, he reprimanded me in front of everyone, saying that I'd failed, that I was late. Then afterward, it was as if nothing had happened. He said, 'Let's go to the movies.' I was at a loss. I couldn't understand why he did what he did, and I said so. He said, 'My dear, one thing has nothing to do with another.' "[14]

Generally, however, he is given credit for having been diplomatic and skillful at handling people. In high school, he became the Soviet equivalent of senior-class president—secretary of the Komsomol, the Communist youth organization. And at nineteen, a very early age, he was chosen a candidate member of the Communist Party. The fact that he applied to join even before graduating from high school was a strong indication of his ambition.

Precisely how Gorbachev landed in the law faculty at Moscow State University is still a riddle. During the Stalin era, law was not a profession held in high esteem for a young achiever such as Gorbachev. Those who knew him well in school said history and international relations were obviously his first loves. "His dream was to be a diplomat," Ivan Manuilov, his high school geography teacher, told my television colleague Louis Menashe. By Manuilov's account, Gorbachev actually entered the faculty for international relations at Moscow State University and studied there for a year, but he had such a rough time, including a spell of severe headaches, that he fell back to the law faculty.[15] No one else with whom I talked confirmed that story. In retrospect, some who had known him speculated that he picked law because his hero Lenin had studied law and it was a good entrée to a political career.

Many years later, Gorbachev admitted that law had not been his first choice, saying that he preferred physics, or even mathematics, history, or literature, but "it was my weakness" to be a generalist and not enough of a specialist.[16] The clear implication was that he was not strong enough in science to be accepted into the physics faculty, and he had to fall back on law, along with a lot of returning Soviet war veterans who were preparing for political careers. As in Europe, Soviet universities are organized by faculties, or departments; competition for entrance is to each department, not to the university as a whole. Law was an easier faculty to enter than international relations, natural sciences, or his best subjects, history and literature. Because the quality of education at a small provincial high school was so modest, getting into Moscow State University—the nation's top university—was a very long shot even for a top rural student like Gorbachev.

Misha was understandably nervous as he headed off on the thirty-six-hour train ride to Moscow for the entrance examinations. According to his uncle Sergei, Grandfather Gopkolo gave the boy a pep talk.

"Don't be nervous," the grandfather coached. "You will pass all the exams. If you don't know something and you stumble, have confidence. Just keep going."

When Gorbachev came home, old man Gopkolo demanded the results: "How did you do?"

"I passed them all, thanks to your coaching," Misha replied.[17]

But the competition was so severe it was not enough merely to pass; Gorbachev was put on a waiting list.

Grandfather Gopkolo, having invested his dreams in his grandson, got impatient. As a veteran farm and Communist Party leader in Privolnoye, he put pressure on the Komsomol organization in Stavropol City to use its influence in Moscow, according to Grigory Gorlov, the old family friend. It was not just a matter of Gopkolo's pulling political strings. The Communist Party then, as now, was on the lookout for outstanding young people from humble beginnings and with the right political credentials.

In the university entrance competition, well-connected children whose parents were big-city officials had a built-in advantage, and quotas of university slots were set aside for proletarian youth. Gorbachev's agricultural medal and his work for the Komsomol, coupled with his academic record, marked him as an excellent candidate for one of these slots. That his parents and grandfather were longtime Party activists helped too.

"Why don't they take our guy?" Gopkolo demanded of the provincial higher-ups. "He was decorated with a silver medal in school and with the Order of the Red Banner of Labor for his farm work. Please take it up with the Central Committee of the Komsomol in Moscow." The top Komsomol youth officials in Stavropol took his advice, Gorlov said. "They called Moscow and the Komsomol in Moscow called the university."[18]

The odds against a farm boy from southern Russia making it into the nation's top university were tougher in 1950 than they would be for an American black from an urban ghetto getting into Harvard University in 1990. Gorbachev's making it not only testified to his personal success as a young man; it also put him into a politically sophisticated world that would reshape his outlook and serve as a springboard for his career.

"TELL ME, WHAT IS BALLET?"

The university years are a formative time in anyone's life, and in Gorbachev's case, that was especially true. For Gorbachev belongs to a special generation in Soviet history, the generation whose university careers roughly spanned the time of Stalin's death in March 1953 and Nikita Khrushchev's denunciation of Stalin, in a secret speech to the Twentieth Communist Party Congress in February 1956. Both events were watershed moments in the life of the nation and especially in the lives of impressionable young adults; they broke the iron grip of Stalinist tyranny and sowed the seeds of reform. They were earthquakes whose tremors are still being felt three decades later.

It is no accident that Gorbachev and other leaders of the *perestroika* reforms now under way come from a generation born between 1925 and 1935; they are people who are now fifty-five to sixty-five years old, not a typical age for reformers. But Khrushchev's secret speech was the seminal political event in their young lives; it jolted them out of their early belief in Stalin and the old dictatorial system, and opened up their minds to experimentation. Khrushchev's rule brought a cultural and political thaw that not only fostered intellectual ferment but also fired hopes for greater cultural freedom, economic flexibility, and social justice. Khrushchev himself was too disorganized, too impulsive, and too much the political loner to fulfill the expectations he raised. His attempts to break up the power of the Party apparatus helped provoke the political coup that ousted him in 1964. Still, the ideals of liberalization and democratization that he had inspired took root, and would resurface long after he was gone.

Those momentous events lay ahead for Misha Gorbachev when he arrived at Moscow State University in September 1950. He was a country hick, with one coarse, gray pin-striped wool suit that he would wear during all five years at the university. He was so tan from working in the fields that other students took him for a non-Russian, perhaps from one of the Caucasian hill tribes. His class was full of veterans returning from the war and gold-medal high school valedictorians. Perhaps hoping to be noticed, Gorbachev, following Soviet custom, wore his medal of the Red Banner of Labor on his suit. Some city sophisticates from Moscow and Leningrad snickered behind his back about his uncultured ways, and he worked terribly hard to catch up with them academically and culturally.

Conditions in Moscow then were primitive. The Soviet capital was still digging itself out of the devastation left by war. At the university, the monthly student stipend of 290 old rubles (29 current rubles, now worth less than $5) was barely enough to buy two meals a day in the student cafeteria, let alone clothes or luxuries. The diet in the canteen was spartan—on good days, dark bread, borscht or cabbage soup, and kasha, a buckwheat gruel, and very occasionally ground beef lost in watery stews. With other students from the provinces, Gorbachev shared a dorm room with no closets at the Stromynkha student hostel, a run-down building that had been a military barracks at the time of Peter the Great.[19]

"We were sixteen students in one room at Stromynkha—sixteen!" recalled Gorbachev's law classmate and roommate Rudolf Kulchanov, now deputy editor of the *Trud* newspaper. "Of course it was impossible to study there, but we had a reading room downstairs. This room was also too small for all of us, so we worked there in two shifts, one studying until nine. Misha was there pretty often until one or two A.M. We were poor, simply poor. At the end of each month we usually didn't even have enough money for dinner. We resorted to black bread and sweet tea, what people usually eat for breakfast. But that was all we got. Some used to get parcels from home. Sometimes I got potatoes. Misha received homemade salami. He used to put it on the mutual table and we all shared."[20]

Stalinism was omnipresent. Portraits of the leader hung in every room; his words were constantly quoted in the press, on the radio, in the lectures. The law faculty, like any other, had required courses on Soviet history and the classics of Marxism-Leninism, which included Stalin's speeches and writings. Typical of the time, one textbook, *A Course on Soviet Criminal Law* by Professors A. A. Piontovsky and V. D. Menshagin, presented the Stalinist show trials of the 1930s as true examples of "socialist legality."

There were a few broader courses in the humanities, taught by professors educated before the Bolshevik Revolution; they opened a window on a wider intellectual world. Several students spoke warmly—and said Gorbachev had also been an admirer—of Professor Stepan Kechekyan, one of the pre-Bolshevik lecturers. Kechekyan taught a two-year course in the history of political ideas (four lecture hours and four hours of tutorials each week). This course exposed the law students to such philosophers as Aristotle, Plato, Aquinas, Machiavelli, Hobbes, Montesquieu, Rousseau, and Hegel, and to concepts of international law from the Code of Hammurabi and Roman law to the American Constitution. Accounts differ on how free the discussion was, but there seems to have been more flexibility on writers before Marx because they were not censored if Marx himself had studied them.

"Speaking of this faculty of the 1950s, I wouldn't say that it gave a lot in terms of the understanding of law and the notion of law," commented Zdenek Mlynar, a classmate of Gorbachev. "Nevertheless, some remnants of the historical or economic approach did exist. They gave us a general picture of the significance of law in the life of civilized society, although at that time, law was totally superseded by politics."[21]

Mlynar, a gray-haired intellectual living in Vienna when I saw him in March 1989, was a particularly thoughtful observer of Gorbachev during their university years. Mlynar, who was Czech, had made it to Moscow as one of a small group of promising young East European Communists. He lived across the hall from Gorbachev. Taking a considerable risk at a time of Stalinist Cold War paranoia about spies and outside influences of any kind, Gorbachev formed a close friendship with Mlynar. They were often in the same classes and small study groups, and they spent hours talking together, comparing experiences. Mlynar, who would eventually become one of the leaders of the Prague Spring of 1968, was struck by Gorbachev's intellectual curiosity and openness.

"He was, of course, a country boy," Mlynar told me that balmy spring afternoon in a park outside Vienna. "What really separated him from the others, I felt, was that he was naturally intelligent, gifted, able to overcome all the limitations and barriers of a peasant boy coming to Moscow for the first time. He possessed a kind of open-mindedness, not merely an adaptability, but an openness.

"I remember, for instance, his asking somebody, 'What's ballet? Tell me, what is it about? Take me with you to see it. I've never seen it in my life.' He was not embarrassed to ask. I think that is characteristic of him until today. He is a person who is never embarrassed if he doesn't know something, but who always wants to know. When he learns something new, it gives him a sort of self-assurance. To some extent he has the mentality of what in English is called a self-made man. That was his mentality."

Other students, such as Nadezhda Mikhailova, who had a crush on Gorbachev at law school and is now a bubbly teacher of law, echo that assessment. They remember Gorbachev as always interested in improving his mind, asking them to take him along to symphony concerts or to art galleries. Soon Raisa Titorenko, who was in the philosophy faculty, had more polished ways, and came from a better social background, would take on the broadening of Misha's cultural horizons. They met at a dance in 1952. Gorbachev had gone along to make fun of a friend, an army veteran named Volodya Lieberman, who had been taking dancing lessons, but saw Raisa and was smitten with her at once. Two years later, they were married, and they celebrated with raucous singing and dancing in Gorbachev's dorm room. For their wedding night, Gorbachev's roommates cleared out, but the next day, everything went back to normal, and the two newlyweds lived separately for several months until they could get a room together in a residential hall for married students.

As time wore on, Gorbachev became known not only as a serious student, a workaholic with a phenomenal memory, but also as a young man of some intellectual independence and candor, who was willing to take risks for his own ideas about honesty and fairness. Fellow students remember his favorite saying, from Hegel, "Truth is always concrete," by which Gorbachev meant that truth had meaning in concrete situations. Many of those who knew him well retell the story of his violent reaction to the glossy Stalinist glorification of life in the countryside, in the movie *Cossacks of the Kuban.* The film showed peasants happily joining collective farms, their dinner tables groaning with plentiful harvests. This hypocritical whitewash of his own childhood experiences infuriated Gorbachev.

"We were big Communists with a capital *C,* but Gorbachev was always a person who saw the truth," Mlynar recalled. "When he saw that movie *Cossacks of the Kuban,* he spoke openly about the discrepancies, about miserable dinner tables rather than the depicted abundance. It was from Gorbachev that I learned that collective farm life didn't look the way it was depicted in movies or in propaganda. The reality was really frightening. People were forced into labor. He definitely didn't make any public statements, but he spoke to his friends pretty openly."

A cautious attitude was understandable; Stalin was still alive, and any deviation from the Stalinist line could be punished by expulsion, Siberian exile, even execution. During their study of the Stalinist purges, Mlynar recalled that Gorbachev pointed out to him privately that Lenin had allowed one foe, the Menshevik leader Julius Martov, to emigrate rather than be executed. The contrast with Stalin was implicit. Even though Gorbachev was speaking privately, Mlynar regarded it as risky, and highly unusual, for Gorbachev to confide such a critical view to a foreigner.

In 1952, his third year in law school, Gorbachev caused a scandal in class. A visiting professor arrived to deliver a special two-hour lecture on Stalin's new tome, *Economic Problems of Socialism in the U.S.S.R.* The students, already exhausted from the normal six hours of lectures, became furious at the visitor's droning on and on, merely reading aloud Stalin's numbing phrases, without comment or discussion. Gorbachev and Volodya Lieberman wrote an anonymous note of protest: "We are university students. We can read the material by ourselves. If you don't have anything to add, please take this into consideration."

The two upstarts, both active in Party and Komsomol work, hoped the visitor would simply stop lecturing, but instead he blew up and declared that the note showed hostility to Marxism-Leninism. The author, he said, was "un-Soviet." Who was it? he demanded.

First Gorbachev rose. Then Lieberman.

"I wrote it," Gorbachev said.

The lecturer stalked out, and within minutes, Gorbachev was summoned to the office of the university provost; Lieberman waited out in the corridor, as members of the Party committee for the university were summoned.

The other students were stunned, and quickly denounced the two renegades for criticizing a teacher.

"It was considered unethical to write such messages," Kulchanov recalled. "[Gorbachev] could easily have kept silent. But he stood up and admitted that he did it. I was scared. Nobody knew what would happen. Dismissal, perhaps."

After a while, Gorbachev emerged from the meeting to say, quite unexpectedly, that the Party committee had heard the students' complaint about the lecturer and had accepted it.

"Everything is all right," he said.

Gorbachev's stature suddenly rose in the eyes of the other students. According to Kulchanov, they were awed by his courage, his independence, and his ability to handle a tough situation, although several took the episode as evidence that his political conformity had limits.

"All of us, his schoolmates, had suddenly discovered that he was a brave guy," Kulchanov said. "We all began to respect him very much."22

Gorbachev's willingness to stick his neck out politically was even more dramatically demonstrated when, in the midst of a fever of Stalinist anti-Semitism, he defended his friend Lieberman, who was a Jew.

It was a dangerous time—February 1953, a month before Stalin's death. The press was full of fabricated accusations that Jewish doctors were plotting to kill Stalin. Arrests were being made, a witch-hunt was beginning, perhaps even a new purge. Party opportunists were speaking out against "the Judases of medicine" and "cosmopolitanism," a euphemism for Jewish influence.

As Lieberman tells the story, he and Gorbachev, as members of the Communist Party (Gorbachev had become a full member in 1952), were at a Party meeting at the university when a Communist named Balasayan suddenly launched a vicious personal attack on Lieberman, the only Jew in the room. Lieberman recalled that Balasayan "suddenly jumped on my neck, mentioning that in spite of my good marks I had lots of foibles, and in particular, I was talking too much." To others, there was no apparent reason for the attack other than the anti-Semitic campaign. Gorbachev broke in, scolded Balasayan, and denounced him as "a spineless animal" for stooping to such opportunism. His words were enough to deter others, and Lieberman was spared further harassment.23 In Lieberman's eyes, Gorbachev's actions were a sign not only of personal loyalty but also of courage and willingness to stand behind the principles of honesty and fair play.

Over time, whether in class or in discussions back at the dorm, Gorbachev became known in his group for his rationality, logic, and skill at establishing group consensus. When arguments in the crowded dorm room became heated, especially when some of the older army veterans would take sharp positions, Gorbachev emerged as a kind of moderator. "He was a good listener," Kulchanov said, "and he tended to find some mutual background in our debates, to touch a mutual base, without giving up his principles. He was always looking for some consensus." In class, Lieberman recalled, "he used to say, 'This issue requires a dialectic approach. That is, first we have to consider one side, and then, on the other hand, we have to consider the opposite side.'"

Gradually, too, Gorbachev became a student leader. Many in his law-school group had their eyes on political careers. "We were all hand-picked cutters, so-called—people with a future," said Mlynar. "He is a man that always possessed an informal authority. You know, when there is a party of five people and he is one of them, everybody tends to listen to him, even though he has no formal position. He is persistent, single-minded, and he knows how to achieve. . . . Sometimes some of our schoolmates used to joke, 'Misha will someday make it big; he'll be at the top,' because they knew that we were all longing for politics. But I couldn't say I ever thought that in Stalin's place, we would get Gorbachev. It didn't seem possible at that time."[24]

There is a considerably less flattering side to Gorbachev's political ambitions and activities at the university—that of an officious disciplinarian, a Stalinist zealot in the university Komsomol organization. As a country boy in the fast world of Moscow, Misha seems to have lain low during his first year, but during his second year, 1951, he set out to become the Komsomol organizer, *komsorg*, for his class. He wanted the job so badly, according to a fellow activist, Fridrikh Neznansky, that he got the incumbent drunk one night and then denounced him the next day at a Komsomol meeting for behavior unworthy of a Communist youth leader.[25] Gorbachev got himself chosen Komsomol organizer for the law faculty as a whole, and served from 1952 to 1954. But in his senior year, the law faculty was merged with the Moscow Law Institute and he lost the top job to the Komsomol leader from the institute, a well-connected Muscovite.

Like Gorbachev's high school friends, some former law classmates recall his hard side, his martinet strictness as a Komsomol apparatchik. One law-faculty graduate outside Gorbachev's personal circle portrayed young Misha as a dogmatic defender of Stalinist orthodoxy who curried favor with Party higher-ups. "He was one of the boys with his colleagues, and he played up incredibly to those in authority," recalled Lev Yudovich, who later emigrated and became a teacher at the U.S. Army Russian Studies Institute in West Germany.[26] Yudovich, who graduated in 1953, two years ahead of Gorbachev, said that during the Stalin years, Gorbachev's ideological zeal was well enough known that Yudovich and his friends tried to steer clear of Gorbachev. Neznansky recalled Gorbachev's strict, formal reprimands for Komsomol members arriving late to meetings. Vivid in his memory was the "steely voice of the Komsomol secretary of the law faculty, Gorbachev, demanding expulsion from the Komsomol for the slightest offenses, from telling political anecdotes to shirking being sent to a *kolkhoz.*"

A dual portrait of Gorbachev seems inevitable, in part because friends saw Misha sympathetically, and he let them in on his doubts, his skepticism, whereas others saw him only from a distance, exercising an official role and toeing the Party line. Beyond that, Gorbachev had by then developed two sides to his character—a personal intellectual openness and an organizational conformity. He had split his life, public and private. Like his peers, including Neznansky and Yudovich, who served as hard-line prosecutors before emigrating to the West many years later, he had learned the need to conform and play by the rules of the Party's political game.

But most fundamentally, like everyone in his generation, he was a believer. He believed in Stalin and Stalinism. It was a religion ingested from birth and indoctrinated daily ever after.

"We were all Stalinists," Mlynar admitted to me, "all convinced of the necessity of the leading role of the Party led by Stalin. Stalin was the leader of the world proletariat."

Since Gorbachev had confided so much to this friend of his youth, I wanted to know: "Did Gorbachev have any doubts about Stalin during Stalin's lifetime?"

"I wouldn't say so," Mlynar replied. "During Stalin's life, we were dedicated Stalinists."

BREAKING FREE FROM STALINISM

That faith in Stalin, so all-enveloping, made the eventual break with Stalinism all the more shattering for true believers. The first blow fell powerfully, on March 5, 1953, with Stalin's death. For the overwhelming majority of Russians, that was a day of emotional trauma. It is hard for Americans, who see Stalin as an evil tyrant, to understand how differently Stalin was seen at that time by his own people.

Stalin's death was personally even more devastating for Russians than the assassination of John F. Kennedy was for many Americans a decade later. To this day, Russians can remember what they were doing when they heard Stalin had died, where they were standing, how they were feeling—as if it were yesterday. For most of them, Stalin was not the paranoid dictator of the purges, but their infallible leader, the Father of their country. Stalin had industrialized the country, had led them to victory in war. Millions had gone into battle shouting, "For the Mother-land, for Stalin!" He was the linchpin of their universe, their compass, their czar, the ruler who held life together and gave it meaning. His death shattered their national self-confidence, leaving them feeling bereaved and abandoned, vulnerable to external enemies, uncertain of a future without him. On the day of his funeral, millions stampeded in the center of Moscow in a frenzy of anxiety and grief.

When Stalin died, Gorbachev and his friends "were all gathered in one room and some of us were crying," recalled Nadezhda Mikhailova. "None of us really knew what to do next. We'd been brainwashed up to the level of idiocy. You have to understand. To us, yesterday's schoolchildren, he meant more than God. And we didn't really know how to survive after his death. So some of us were crying. Misha was silent."

"Yes, Misha remained silent," another classmate, Vladimir Kuzmin, added. "We didn't discuss it but we were thinking what would happen after Stalin's death."

"We were saying that now, after Stalin's death, the opportunists and careerists will take over," said Rudolf Kulchanov. "They will ruin socialism. We will forget our dreams about Communism. And I remember when we all went to see Stalin's body exposed in the Hall of Unions, there were tanks and troop carriers. I don't remember whether Misha managed to go. That was a terrible night. Lots of people died, crushed by the crowd."

"Here in the university, we had a memorial meeting," Mikhailova went on, "and somebody, I don't remember who, said that if all of his blood would be required in exchange for one hour of Stalin's life, he wouldn't think twice and would give all of his blood. And the same for me, you know; I would have given my blood in exchange for one hour of Stalin's life."[27]

Mlynar remembered standing next to Gorbachev at the time of Stalin's funeral. "There were two minutes of silence or something like that—and we thought of Stalin," he recalled. But shortly afterward, "when we discussed Stalin's death, we didn't really know what to do next. It was a real shock. Everything was just a big question mark."

"For Gorbachev too?" I asked.

"Yes, of course," Mlynar replied. "Yes, many people spoke that way. Nobody knew what would happen next, since God had died."[28]

Stalin's death occurred during Gorbachev's third year in the university. Gradually over the next two years, the atmosphere changed.

The charges against the Jewish doctors were found to be fabricated and the doctors released. By that first June, portraits of Lavrenti Beria, Stalin's feared secret-police chief, were taken down from prominent places in Moscow. In a power struggle with Khrushchev and others, Beria had been killed, and the bloody terror he had led exposed in documents circulated to Communist Party members. Privately, people began to suspect Stalin of involvement and to criticize him. Neznansky recalled that Gorbachev, as university Komsomol leader, spoke for the first time of injustices done to "middle peasants"—people who owned and farmed their own land—

during Stalin's brutal collectivization drive in the 1930s, and he even mentioned that one of his relatives had been arrested unjustly.[29]

"I knew that something had happened to his family," Mlynar told me. "But I don't think it happened to his father. Rather, to his grandfather. I didn't know any details. We never discussed family matters. But it was not that unusual for some member of a family to be repressed during the Stalinist purges in the early thirties."[30]

In later years, Gorbachev practically never mentioned that a relative had been repressed under Stalin, but with some bitterness he brought the matter up a few years ago at a small gathering of high Communist Party officials. "There were only about a hundred people present," Nikolai Shishlin, one of Gorbachev's speech writers, told me. "It was after he had become general secretary. When the Stalin period was being discussed, he told us, 'Although I was a child, I remember these times. I remember my *ded*, my grandfather, was arrested and taken away to the camps. And when he returned, he was silent, always sitting and thinking, and very sad.' "[31] According to Shishlin, Gorbachev said his grandfather Andrei Gorbachev had been arrested at the peak of the purges in 1937, when the secret police were headed by Nikolai Yezhov, and had been incredibly lucky to be released eighteen months later. As Shishlin reminded me, Lavrenti Beria had succeeded Yezhov as secret-police chief, had executed Yezhov and his sinister coterie, and then released some of those recently jailed by Yezhov, among them Gorbachev's grandfather.

The details of this incident are puzzling. There was little reason for a peasant to be arrested in 1937; by then, Stalin was going after high officials. By one published account, Gorbachev's paternal grandfather, Andrei Gorbachev, was arrested in 1931 and sentenced to nine years in the camps after an informer in the village of Privolnoye had accused him of hiding forty pounds of grain for his family, evading the Stalinist requisitions of grain. That timing sounds more appropriate for the arrest of a peasant, though the actual charges could easily have been a trumped-up pretext for his arrest.[32] Like Mlynar, Shishlin told me that Gorbachev had never cited the reason for the arrest. "It's impossible to say why. You know, it was Stalin!" Shishlin said emphatically, assuming that was sufficient explanation for any act of repression.

There is little question that the experience left a searing impression on Gorbachev and that he nursed a personal grievance against Stalin's mass repression of the peasantry—and he still does. In a major speech on November 2, 1987, the seventieth anniversary of the Revolution, Gorbachev sharply criticized Stalin's "excesses" against "middle peasants"—

average people, the group from which his own family came. Gorbachev extolled these people—the middle peasantry—who were given land under Lenin, who tilled their own modest plots, and whose lives were improving until Stalin's henchmen victimized many of them during the campaign against the kulaks, or rich peasants. "Gross violations of the principles of collectivization acquired a ubiquitous character," Gorbachev thundered. "The policy of struggle against the kulaks, which was in itself correct, was often interpreted so broadly that it also caught up a significant proportion of middle-level peasants."[33]

In short, Stalin's death allowed the young Gorbachev to draw on his own experience, and edge away from idolatry.

The real jolt to his thinking, however, came three years later, after Khrushchev bluntly denounced Stalin's mass terror at the Twentieth Party Congress on February 20, 1956. Khrushchev focused on Stalin's repression against high Party officials and on crimes that followed the murder of Leningrad Party leader Sergei Kirov in 1934, thereby excluding the crimes of collectivization and earlier political purges. Even so, the effect of his exposé was an enormous shock to the entire country, and especially to Gorbachev's generation.

Gorbachev, who by then had graduated from law school and gone back to his native Stavropol to begin a career in Komsomol and Party work in the provinces, would not have been a delegate to the Congress, but his future friend and Politburo colleague, his alter ego, Aleksandr Yakovlev, also a young Party worker in 1956, was at the Congress as a guest. He described to me the hall's stunned reaction to Khrushchev's speech. Particularly shocking, he said, was that Khrushchev talked not so much about mass terror, but about Stalin's arbitrary violence against the upper echelons of the Communist Party itself.

"There was a deathly silence," Yakovlev told me. "People stopped looking at each other."

Yakovlev was sitting on a couch a few feet from me during our on-camera interview in one of the private upstairs rooms of the Foreign Ministry's press center in Moscow. At first, he leaned back reflectively, talking of his boyhood, his childhood faith in Stalin, then some doubts arising when he was a teenager because of the mistreatment of an honest peasant in his village. Then later, his disapproval of Stalin for punishing returning Soviet prisoners of war. But his mother's admonition was: "Speaking ill of the czar is bad business." Then he recalled the fateful day when Khrushchev exposed Stalin. Leaning toward me to emphasize the details, he said:

"I remember I was sitting in the balcony, and when we went down, I heard just one word uttered by people around me: 'Yes.' Then after a while, 'Yes.' No conversation. People didn't even look at each other. They hung their heads, and left.

"That is, to hear what had happened, and understand, and accept it in full, after what had been! Yesterday like this, and today like this!" Yakovlev gestured first one way with both arms and then far in the other direction, illustrating the old lies about Stalin and the new truth. "It was very hard, especially for those who believed. For young people. And then to destroy it with that information, which would change radically the entire development of the society. It was, of course, very hard for everyone—emotionally very hard. And to make sense of it required much time, much time."

Yakovlev recalled the ideological body blow that he himself had felt. "I had thought of Stalin as a great man, a great intellectual, a profound thinker, and so on—and all that was destroyed. I had received some moral blow. . . . It gradually turned out that [what Khrushchev said] was the way it truly was. And it's right that it was destroyed.

"Gradually," he went on, "those convictions consolidated, the sense that many mistakes had been made. But after the Twentieth Congress, the process was very contradictory. It was like two trains, or two airplanes, or two carts—depending on the speed—traveling next to each other. One went the old way, and the other went in the direction of the maturing of civil consciousness."[34]

Again and again, I have heard Communists of Gorbachev's generation echo these sentiments. Khrushchev's speech was the seminal event in their young lives. Emotionally, it hit them as if they had been struck down by a train, shattering their beliefs to their very foundations, leaving them stunned at first but then, later on, open to new ways of thinking and more flexible than the generation that had preceded them, and even those that followed. So powerful and formative was the impact, on Gorbachev's generation, of Khrushchev's unmasking of Stalin in February 1956 that they became widely known as "the children of the Twentieth Party Congress."

"For those people, the Twentieth Congress was a shock because, you know, Stalin was like God to them," recalled Roy Medvedev, the historian whose disillusionment came earlier, after his father's arrest by Stalin. "It was as if they had lost their religion. You believe in Christ, or in Allah, or in Buddha, and all of a sudden something happens. Your whole life is changed and your beliefs are lost. And you are trying to look for something else to lean upon, some other foundation. So for the whole generation, this Twentieth Congress was such a blow I cannot describe it to you. Such a blow for them when they were very young people, just at the age of twenty to thirty."[35]

As a member of the Communist Party, Gorbachev was in the center of this ideological upheaval. He was summoned to a Party meeting where Khrushchev's speech was read aloud; then he had to take part in many discussions with Party members about Stalin's crimes, his prison gulag, his assault on the very apparatus of the Party itself.

"Gorbachev admired Khrushchev as an unbelievably courageous political leader," recalled Rudolf Kulchanov, who later saw Gorbachev on visits to Stavropol.[36] This was confirmed by Mlynar, who also went to Stavropol to see Gorbachev.

In short, Gorbachev's inner mental world had been reformed too. After the initial shock, he and his generation were caught up in the ferment and excitement of Khrushchev's early years—a time of hope and reform, of political and economic experimentation as well as cultural liberalization, even if far from real democratization. These were trends that not only appealed to some of Gorbachev's own youthful instincts, but also nurtured in him the desire for reform, for the dismantlement of the Stalinist system. These urges were to flower three decades later, with his final ascent to power and the beginnings of *perestroika*.

CHAPTER 4

How Did Gorbachev Make It to the Top?

"It's impossible to imagine
that Gorbachev would emerge at
the top of this system. There are so
many pitfalls he had to avoid, so many
traps he had to pass through,
so many obstacles to foil him.
One single little blemish could
have stopped him. How he made it
is one of those historical mysteries."[1]

—Zinovy Yuryev
Soviet Writer
June 1988

During the early seventies, neither I nor any of the Western specialists I knew spotted Mikhail Gorbachev as a future contender for national leadership.

By 1971, Gorbachev had become a member of the Communist Party Central Committee—one of the regional barons who comprise the backbone of the Party's power across the country. There are about 150 of them, reigning as Moscow's proconsuls over the nation's far-flung political fiefdoms.

But rarely does any individual in this powerful group stand out. While they all have power greater than governors of American states, they lack national visibility—if they are smart. For in traditional Soviet power politics, the route to the top is a quiet game of tough, inside politics, serving the apparat and fashioning alliances; it is more like old-fashioned American machine politics than modern American media politics, with its splashy speeches, telegenic style, and speculation about one's presidential intentions. Soviet politics are more covert, which makes it hard for outsiders to pick out the rising stars inside the system.

As Party boss of Stavropol Krai, Gorbachev was as far from the center of power as an American governor in South Carolina or Maine (those states are roughly the size of Stavropol Krai). But Gorbachev was blessed by fate. If he had come from Murmansk or Vladivostok, far off the beaten political track, he might have gotten lost in the crowd. But his home territory was more happily situated. For Stavropol Krai is not only one of the country's richest agricultural regions, but also contains the favorite health spas and mountain resorts of top national leaders. And so Stavropol's Party leaders have a chance to hobnob with the Politburo elite when they come for rest cures, a favorite vacation pastime of the Soviet elite. Not surprisingly, then, Stavropol, like Ohio, or Texas, or Massachusetts, is a promising springboard to national leadership. And some of Gorbachev's predecessors there had made the leap—no small advantage for a man who aspired to follow them.

In the twenty-three years Gorbachev spent in Stavropol, from his university graduation in 1955 to his selection for the upper reaches of Party power in 1978, he proved an intriguing amalgam—a loyal apparatchik who also nursed the germ of reform, an organization man with a streak of daring. He was both able and nimble. He could be an innovator or wear the veneer of the sycophant. As he climbed the Party ladder, Gorbachev maneuvered successfully through the twisting turns of policy, from the rambunctious reformism of Khrushchev to the gray conformity of Brezhnev and beyond.

People describe him in those years as being both a good political infighter who risked direct confrontations with powerful figures in Moscow and a canny master of the arts of flattery and concealment. He was able to cultivate high-level patrons from different factions. He was too intelligent, honest, and open to be a typical apparatchik of the corrupt Brezhnev era. He grew impatient, even alarmed, at the ineptitude and meddling of Moscow. But he never betrayed the radical urges of a maverick; he didn't upset the applecart.

Gorbachev's career in Stavropol also had a very fast start. He came home from law school and worked only a few months in the state prosecutor's office before shifting to political work in the Komsomol. Within a year, at twenty-six, he was named head of the Komsomol Communist youth organization for Stavropol City (population 123,000). Three years later, he had shot up to Komsomol chief for the entire Stavropol Krai (population 1.9 million). This put him in the inner cabinet of the regional Party boss in the late fifties, when Khrushchev was riding high.

Gorbachev rode the Khrushchev bandwagon, conveying to the young the leader's message of idealism and economic experimentation. Fellow Komsomol workers told me that in those years, Gorbachev promoted Khrushchev's line with a reformer's zeal.[2] As Komsomol chief of the krai, he had the singular honor of serving as one of the five thousand national delegates to the Twenty-second Communist Party Congress in 1961. Khrushchev, still feeling threatened by the Stalinist wing of the Party, played to Gorbachev and his generation as the hope of the future. In a highly symbolic gesture, the delegates—Gorbachev included—joined Khrushchev in a new act of de-Stalinization: They voted to remove Stalin's body from its honored place beside Lenin's in the mausoleum on Red Square.

Like many a rising young politician, Gorbachev found a political patron close to home. He hitched his wagon to the star of the Stavropol regional Party boss, then a veteran of Moscow infighting, Fyodor Kulakov, who would help Gorbachev climb the rungs of power. "He learned his lessons from Kulakov," old family friend Grigory Gorlov told me.[3] Kulakov had his eye on the top. To get there, he was intent on making Stavropol an agricultural showcase. In 1962, when Khrushchev launched a new agricultural experiment, setting up large regional farm units that embraced twenty-five to thirty collective farms, Kulakov persuaded Gorbachev to leave Komsomol work and step up into the Party hierarchy as one of the Party's sixteen new regional farm organizers in Stavropol Krai. From that post, Gorbachev began his climb up the Party's ranks.

And, in other ways, he followed Kulakov's pattern. Kulakov had gone to night school to get an agricultural degree, thereby boosting his career. In 1962, Gorbachev, to whom self-improvement came as second nature, signed up for a night-school degree at the local agricultural institute. Ironically, his wife, Raisa, was one of his instructors.

Raisa had come to Stavropol with her Moscow University degree in philosophy, a good cut above locally trained teachers. She quickly got an appointment at the local institute and plunged into the study of sociology, specializing in rural areas of Stavropol Krai. Eventually, she wrote the Soviet equivalent of a Ph.D. thesis on the problems, attitudes, and conditions of the peasantry—an unusual topic for a scholar in those days. Despite her schoolmarmish manner, her former colleagues respected her academically, and some spoke of her warmly as a person who took an interest in others. When I visited the institute in 1988, they proudly showed me her charts on the methodology of Marxism-Leninism, which were still hanging in her former classroom; her monographs were in the library.[4]

In class, Raisa proved herself Gorbachev's intellectual peer; she gave him no quarter. Grigory Gorlov, who was also in her seminar, recalled her correcting her students, including Gorbachev, if he strayed off the mark in some discussion of philosophy. "That's not correct," she would say. "You should understand it more like this." Gorlov said she was firm, without being a martinet. "She corrected us all in a comradely way," he told me.[5] Other instructors were equally demanding with Gorbachev, even though he was becoming an important local Party boss. Valentina Brelova, a fellow student, said Gorbachev asked for no special treatment, and he got none. She recalled one teacher eyeing him before an examination, and saying half in jest, "Ah, so you're the Party boss. Well, let's see. Let me check your brains."[6] It took him five years to get his degree; he finally received it in 1967.

That same year, the Gorbachevs had a visit from former law-school classmate Zdenek Mlynar, who had risen to become a member of the Czechoslovak Communist Party Politburo in the reformist government of Alexander Dubček. Mlynar flew into Mineralnye Vody, the heart of Stavropol's resort area. Gorbachev, then Party boss of Stavropol City— one notch above the mayor—met him at the airport.

"He had a fedora, you know, like these Soviet apparatchiks," Mlynar recalled, grinning at the thought of a pudgy Gorbachev in the baggy business suit and wide-brimmed hat that was the uniform of Soviet officials in that era. Even though Khrushchev was gone, Gorbachev looked like a mini-Khrushchev.

"The first thing I said to him was, 'Hey, Misha, you've got this fedora already.' And he said, 'Okay, forget it,'" Mlynar recalled. "He hadn't changed a lot.

"After that, we traveled across the steppe, and I enjoyed the landscape. You see, I had a hobby—I used to collect beetles, and I was collecting them during my meeting with him in the steppes. And he was helping me. He could even distinguish some basic species. 'After all,' he said, 'I am a graduate of the agricultural college.'

"We were talking all day long—lots of questions. As for politics, first and foremost, I asked him about Khrushchev's failure. It had been only [three] years since Khrushchev was dismissed. At that time, his opinion was that Brezhnev was just a transitional figure."

Mlynar was keen to get Gorbachev's assessment of Khrushchev because he was looking for reform ideas for Czechoslovakia. By his account, Gorbachev, then thirty-six, praised Khrushchev's anti-Stalin line but was impatient with his zigzagging agricultural policies and his interference in provincial affairs. In the end, Gorbachev had not been unhappy to see Khrushchev ousted. Mlynar told Gorbachev that the Czechs had considered Khrushchev a guarantor of their reform movement, and now, after his removal, they lacked a protector in Moscow. Mlynar complained that the Soviet Embassy in Prague was staffed with "ignoramuses who didn't understand one iota about Czech reality" and he feared they were sending Moscow reports "bad-mouthing our people.

"And Misha laughed and said, 'Okay, there are lots of idiotic bureaucrats. We have to take into consideration the local conditions for each socialist country.'" This remark foreshadowed Gorbachev's subsequent liberalism toward Eastern Europe. But it was heresy at a time when Brezhnev was trying to rein in Prague; within months he would launch an invasion to snuff out the reformist trends in Czechoslovakia.

"Today that sounds like a quotation of some legitimate central newspaper," Mlynar observed. "But at that time, it sounded almost revolutionary."

The two old schoolmates talked on and on into the night, arriving back at the Gorbachev apartment very late and a bit under the influence. Raisa was furious and bawled them out.

As they had talked, Mlynar had been struck by Gorbachev's interest in reform in Czechoslovakia. "Misha mentioned that things were possible in Czechoslovakia, but it would be quite different in the Soviet Union, though the Russians also need some changes," Mlynar recalled. "So I got the impression that not only he but his generation were against the stagnation then. They were looking for something newer. . . . I remember his wife, Raisa, was helping him do sociological research. He told me that she was visiting collective farmers and asking them questions. They were very surprised that anyone was actually asking peasants questions. Even at that time, you see, he was a person who tried to employ new methods."[7]

THE PRAGMATIC INNOVATOR

At that stage, Gorbachev was probably more candid with Mlynar than he was with Soviet colleagues about his reformist inclinations. For he was making his way up the ladder in traditional loyalist fashion; he wasn't making waves. His patron, Kulakov, had helped the plotters who threw

out Khrushchev in 1964, and two years later was rewarded with an important job in Moscow as the Party's national chief for agriculture. From
there, Kulakov could promote Gorbachev's career. Apparently, in 1970 he
helped Gorbachev get Stavropol's top job—Party boss for the whole krai.
This made him more powerful than an American governor—at the young
age of thirty-nine.

During eight years in that job, Gorbachev established himself as a
political leader of unusual integrity, and one with catholic intellectual
tastes. By many accounts, he seems even then to have enjoyed lecturing
journalists on economics or ideology and telling them to make their
articles interesting. He was known for allowing several Russian Orthodox
churches to operate in Stavropol and for mingling with visiting Moscow
writers to discuss the latest books. According to Mikhail Novikov, a
playwright and former theater director, Gorbachev was instrumental in
opening a new cultural center. He and Raisa were regulars at Stavropol's
Lermontov Drama Theater. They were fans of Shakespeare, of such
American plays as Neil Simon's *Barefoot in the Park* and Tennessee
Williams's *A Streetcar Named Desire*, and of the Russian classics that
Gorbachev had played in in his own youth. Once, Novikov recalled, the
company put on a controversial play, *Love, Jazz, and the Devil*, in which
a playwright from the Baltics argued that young people should decide
their own destiny. Some older people were offended and wanted the play
banned. Gorbachev went to see it and was asked what should be done
about it. According to Novikov, his reply was characteristic: "If this
performance evokes arguments and makes people think about the problems of bringing up our children, then it should remain on stage."[8]

Unlike many provincial Party leaders who lived as feudal lords, aloof
from ordinary people and protected by security men, Gorbachev was
known as an approachable, populist-style leader. He enjoyed mixing with
the people. As Party chief, he lived in a handsome old aristocrat's house,
an ample residence down a side street lined with maples and poplars,
about half a mile from his office in a massive Communist Party building.
Valentin Mezin, a linguist, told me that Gorbachev used to jog and do
exercises in the wooded park across the street from his house. He walked
to work every day. He became well known for casual encounters with
people on the street, who would accost him along his route, bringing him
their problems directly rather than battling the bureaucratic apparatus.

"He was very open and free . . . and typical of the people of this
region—he was dynamic and optimistic," Mezin told me as we strolled
along Gorbachev's route. "I personally saw him walking to and from his
office several times—no bodyguards. He was usually carrying his office

folder and wearing a lamb's-wool *shapka* [hat]." Sometimes Gorbachev and Raisa would go shopping in the local department store just up the street from their house.[9]

As Party leader, Gorbachev's first priority was Stavropol's farm crop. Others now remember him for overseeing the installation of a major irrigation system to offset the dry climate, or battling Moscow ministries, convincing them not to impose inflated production quotas but settle for more realistic ones. He experimented with small work brigades and other measures to give farmers and factory workers greater incentives and more autonomy than the rigid Soviet planners usually allowed. Like an American governor, Gorbachev worked hard to diversify his region's economy, pushing Moscow higher-ups to invest in the construction of a huge chemical fertilizer plant and new electronics factories. He took a personal interest in stimulating local development—more along Western lines—of a massive broiler-chicken industry, the Stavropol Broiler Association.[10] Viktor Postnikov, the association's ruddy-faced, white-haired general director, credited Gorbachev with giving him, in the seventies, great autonomy as an industrial manager and then encouraging him to experiment with self-financing and profit-oriented business operations similar to those Gorbachev tried to introduce nationwide a decade later. Over the years Postnikov himself has come to act and talk more like a Western businessman than most Soviet managers.

Gorbachev was not a radical reformer in those years, Postnikov said. Rather, Gorbachev wanted what worked, and when one approach failed to produce results, he tried something new. He was a pragmatic innovator. In the early seventies, Gorbachev had taken trips to Italy, France, and Germany on various Communist Party delegations, once spending several weeks with Raisa motoring around France. That exposure to the West apparently opened him up to new ideas.

But he was also a canny politician, and a strong bureaucratic infighter. "He studied the bureaucracy well," observed Postnikov, with a knowing laugh. "He was always going to Moscow to get something. Often he would take me along. I could see he knew how the various ministers worked."[11]

Gorbachev's most celebrated fight with Moscow, recounted to me by Postnikov and others, came over his proposal that a portion of the territory's farmland should lie fallow every year. This ran counter to the policies of Brezhnev's agricultural advisers in Moscow, and of economic planners, who insisted on farming every acre for maximum output. On their advice, the Politburo had barred fallow lands. But Gorbachev, drawing on the experience of peasants working Stavropol's arid land, warned that constant planting was exhausting the soil. Productivity would rise,

Gorbachev said, if the land were allowed a periodic rest. He took the highly unusual—and risky—tack of appealing personally to Brezhnev, in effect putting his job on the line by openly bucking his Party superiors and the minister of agriculture.

"There was a standoff," Postnikov recalled. "The scientists demanded that we use the land every year; they said we'd have a better harvest. Those opinions were in conflict in the Politburo—two camps, the experts versus Gorbachev. . . . I remember how upset he was. I was in his office and he said, 'I don't know if I'm going to work today, or if I should look for a new job. I don't know if I'm going to be taken out of my job tomorrow for this.' But, fortunately, Brezhnev and his entourage allowed Gorbachev to carry out that experiment, and it has been tried on millions of acres since the seventies, and right now, the harvest has doubled. He started that surge."[12]

But at other times Gorbachev played along with Moscow, especially with Kulakov, and he benefited from his old patron's glory. In 1977, Kulakov decided to test a new method of harvesting winter wheat; he used a traveling armada—five combines, fifteen trucks, repair units, mobile homes, showers, and food services. This was a Soviet-style tactic—throwing big resources at a problem. Tapping his Stavropol connections, Kulakov decided to test the experiment in the Ipatovo District of Stavropol Krai. His approach became known as "the Ipatovsky method."

In July 1977, the method scored a great success—a harvest of two hundred thousand tons was completed in a record nine days. In Moscow, the Central Committee quickly passed a decree declaring that the Ipatovsky method should be copied nationwide. Kulakov was a hero—and so was Gorbachev. *Pravda* ran a front-page interview with Gorbachev, and the following March he was decorated with the Order of the October Revolution. Then, in May 1978, Mikhail Suslov, the Party's ideological chief and number three in the Kremlin hierarchy, came to Stavropol to award the city a special honor, and he spent several days traveling around the region with Gorbachev. There was talk that Kulakov, now sixty, might eventually be in line to replace Brezhnev. Actually, the success of the Ipatovsky method depended on favorable local conditions, and it never worked that well in much of the country. But it was a couple of years before this was apparent.

In July 1978, Kulakov died quite unexpectedly, seemingly in the peak of health. So odd was his death that some suspected suicide or foul play. Gorbachev, as his protégé and friend, flew to Moscow to give a eulogy at Kulakov's funeral, his first nationally televised speech. It was a pedestrian speech; more important was the fact that Kulakov's death left an opening in the Politburo, and in the Party secretariat, for a new agriculture secretary. It was a rare opportunity for someone to make a leap upward.

Gorbachev was a contender for the position, but he was not the most obvious one. Several Politburo members favored Agriculture Minister Valentin Mesyats, with whom Gorbachev had frequently crossed swords in bureaucratic infighting. Others in Brezhnev's circle suggested two Party bosses from southern Russia, Ivan Bondarenko and Sergei Medunov. Gorbachev had an excellent record, especially riding the publicity of the Ipatovo experiment, but his candid, teetotaling style did not fit in with the Brezhnev clique, with its reputation for partying and corruption.

Over the years, however, Gorbachev had carefully cultivated high-level connections. His honesty and intellectual style appealed to the spartan, puritanical, brainier members of the Politburo, such as Suslov, Prime Minister Aleksei Kosygin, and KGB Chief Yuri Andropov. All three of them had been regular visitors to the ornate hilltop sanitariums around Kislovodsk and Pyatigorsk in Stavropol. Suslov, as a former Party chief in Stavropol, took an interest in Gorbachev, especially revived by his visit that May. Andropov had been born and raised in Stavropol and had a *dacha* in Kislovodsk, where he enjoyed the pompous Stalinist architecture of the sanitariums, with their marbled baths and fountains. Kosygin, too, liked to take the Caucasian mountain air, and was so fond of his walks there that years later, one path was named "Kosygin's Walk," in his memory. As far back as 1971, Gorbachev been drawn to Andropov, who, despite his KGB job, was widely regarded as the brightest, most intellectual member of the Politburo. According to Postnikov, the two men often talked when Andropov came to Stavropol; they shared concern about the deteriorating economy and dissatisfactions with the corrupt, inflexible bureaucracy.

Back in May 1978, presumably emboldened by the Ipatovo success, Gorbachev had set out his thinking in a confidential twenty-page memo to Kulakov. With surprising bluntness, Gorbachev complained about the "incredible red tape" of overcentralized control; he said it was choking Soviet agriculture. "It takes the abilities of a gladiator to overcome the bureaucratic barriers standing in the way of resolving the smallest and most obvious questions," he groused.[13]

Typical of farmers and politicians from farm regions anywhere in the world, Gorbachev sounded the litany that farms were caught in a cost-price squeeze: Equipment prices were rising rapidly while the government's procurement prices for produce were fixed. Those prices had to be raised, he said. He also called for big new agro-industrial complexes that would bring the food-processing industry to the farms—an approach that Brezhnev later adopted.

But more intriguing is the fact that in 1978 Gorbachev was proposing reforms in agriculture that were a rough version of steps he would take in 1985–86, in the early phase of *perestroika*. He was applying the lessons of eight years as Stavropol Party boss, and while he paid lip service to the existing system of economic planning in Moscow, he asserted that there were too many output targets and quotas set by the centralized plans. "This discourages an increase in production," he said, "because people naturally spend all their time trying to reduce these excessive targets and shift responsibility." He called for more streamlined planning and decentralized economic management.

"In our opinion, we have to grant enterprises and associations greater independence in settling various questions of production and finance," Gorbachev wrote. "We must develop democratic principles, local initiative, free upper echelons from petty concerns, and maintain . . . flexibility in decision-making."[14]

Perhaps most characteristically, Gorbachev admitted there were many unprofitable farms, and he focused on what later would be called "the human factor" as the major reason for disaster in the farming sector. Presumably drawing on some of Raisa's research on the low morale and poverty of farm workers and the flight of young people from rural areas, Gorbachev asserted that material incentives and living conditions were insufficient to motivate farm workers.

This obviously very self-confident provincial chief told his superiors: "We must guarantee a growth in agricultural production not by administrative methods but rather by . . . a mechanism of material incentives and material-technical supply."[15] His language was stilted and bureaucratic, but his message was clear. If Moscow wanted better results from the farms, farm workers were going to have to be given better housing, better roads, better schools, and some decent health clinics ("material-technical supply") and investment was going to have to be increased to improve rural living standards.

Only Kremlin insiders can know how this memo affected Gorbachev's hopes for the Party's top national job in agriculture—or even whether anyone except Kulakov and his aides read it. Gorbachev's candor would hardly have gone over well with some members of Brezhnev's entourage, especially Agriculture Minister Mesyats, at whom Gorbachev was pointing an accusing finger. But the memo was the kind of constructive criticism that appealed to Andropov, who not only ran Moscow's spy operations and cracked down on dissidents, but also followed the Soviet Union's economy and built dossiers on the corruptive practices of the Brezhnev "mafia."

"Gorbachev talked with Andropov," Postnikov told me one morning as we sat in a park near the Kremlin walls. "And Andropov understood that [Gorbachev's] views were the same as his own. . . . Their views on what the Soviet Union needed were the same —two things: We need the country to be well fed and clothed, and we need defense. That's what Andropov said. Of course, [Gorbachev] was upset and dissatisfied [at the bad economic situation]. I think that was his view then. But he couldn't say publicly what he felt."[16]

Publicly, Gorbachev played along with Brezhnev, obliging him with the kind of flattery that the aging Party leader demanded as a political tithe from underlings all across the country. Brezhnev's later years were especially marked by vanity and fatuous self-glorification, as well as by the hyperbole of Soviet propaganda. Gorbachev bowed to the degrading necessity of delivering false hosannas to *The Little Land,* Brezhnev's ghostwritten war memoirs, which were published in 1978. "In terms of the profundity of its ideological content, the breadth of its generalizations, and the opinions expressed by the author, *The Little Land* has become a major event in public life," Gorbachev told an ideological conference in May, the same month that he wrote his blunt memo on economic mismanagement. "Communists and all the workers of Stavropol express limitless gratitude to Leonid Ilyich Brezhnev for this literary work."[17]

That September, the enfeebled Brezhnev made his way by train around southern Russia, meeting candidates for Kulakov's vacant post. When he arrived at the spas in Stavropol, Andropov was there, with Gorbachev, to endorse his candidacy. Later, back in Moscow, according to Kulakov's widow, the Politburo argued for three days over who would replace Kulakov in the Politburo and the Secretariat. Initially, the majority favored Mesyats, but Andropov pushed Gorbachev and gradually brought the others around.[18]

Years later, visiting Washington, Raisa Gorbacheva saw a picture of Andropov in the home of the late Ambassador Averell Harriman, and she remarked quietly, "Oh, yes, how much we owe him."

And so in November 1978, Gorbachev was summoned to Moscow. At forty-seven, he joined the national leadership as Party secretary for agriculture; two years later he became the youngest member by far of Brezhnev's geriatric Politburo. Gorbachev was an exception to the Brezhnev policy of keeping younger leaders down and replacing dead or retiring leaders with other officials who were just about as old, and this gave him an unusually long period to rise to the very top.

GATHERING A BRAIN TRUST

During the next seven years, Gorbachev developed his ideas for what Foreign Minister Eduard Shevardnadze would call the Soviet "New Deal," a program comparable to Franklin Delano Roosevelt's American model. Sweeping reforms were aimed not at scrapping the existing system, but at saving it. Gorbachev's style of work in these years, his leap over the final hurdles to supreme leadership, offer a rare glimpse into the inside workings of the upper reaches of the Communist Party hierarchy.

In those years, Gorbachev built a network of allies in his own generation of rising Party leaders, and recruited the intellectual brain trust that would help formulate his concepts for *perestroika*. For one of Gorbachev's trademarks throughout his career—and it is striking because it was then unusual for a Communist Party administrator—was his way of reaching out to scholars and academics for new ideas, and his obvious enjoyment of the company of Party intellectuals.

Reminiscent of his grandparents' hiding religious icons on the backs of portraits of Stalin and Lenin, Gorbachev let only a trusted inner circle of advisers and allies in on his thinking. The Moscow intelligentsia heard a few promising things about him, but during his first years in the capital they saw little external evidence that Gorbachev would become an extraordinary leader.

"Under Brezhnev, Gorbachev was a careful man, very careful—because at that time it was dangerous to be open and frank," I was told by Sasha Gelman, a well-known playwright who caught Gorbachev's favor and became a people's deputy during the later period of reform. "He always came to the theater to see the sharpest plays. He comes less now—he has no time. But he was a big fan of the theater. One nice thing about him was that—you know how these big shots come to a performance and say, 'It's good' or 'It's bad,' and everyone takes that as a big signal from on high. Well, the nice thing is Gorbachev would come and then leave without making any comment. That was the right thing to do."[19]

But a handful of Party insiders, those trusted by Gorbachev, quickly got a different picture of him. "When he arrived in Moscow, very soon it was clear that Gorbachev was really a new kind of person with a fresh look, with fresh ideas," recalled Nikolai Shishlin, who became a speech writer for Gorbachev and more recently a Soviet television commentator on world affairs. Shishlin has a deceptively sleepy-eyed, boyish look, but he is extremely bright, long a hidden reformer within the Central Committee apparatus.

"As I remember, our people began to say, 'He's too bold,'" Shishlin said, recalling Gorbachev circa 1980. "He had his own ideas on every problem—especially on agriculture and the economy. It was easy to talk with him because he knew life. He had seen in Stavropol that something was wrong. Everything at that time had to be decided through long discussions with Moscow, with different ministries, and that had bothered him. So he was interested in fresh ideas, in experiments in Hungary, in Bulgaria. He would travel there and bring back ideas. I liked reading notes of his conversations. They were real conversations with concrete ideas."[20]

At home, Gorbachev began to gather Soviet agricultural economists with innovative ideas and get them to formulate new approaches for coping with the nation's farm problems. One of those economists was Vladimir Tikhonov, who had been fighting the Brezhnev bureaucracy, unsuccessfully, for years. His view was that greater efficiency required that the massive state and collective farms be broken down into smaller work teams—"links," he called them—that would share the profit from their harvest, and thus have an incentive to produce more. Gorbachev had experimented with something similar—he called them "contract brigades"—in Stavropol Krai. The idea was that a brigade of workers would sign a contract with a state farm, take a plot of land, and promise to deliver so many tons of grain. If they could cut costs and manpower, or boost their yield per acre, they could increase their earnings, both as a group and individually. The idea was slowly catching on when Gorbachev left Stavropol. To reform-minded experts like Tikhonov, Gorbachev was a breath of fresh air in the Party hierarchy, especially when Gorbachev began seeking Tikhonov's advice in the early 1980s.

"We liked this young secretary of the Central Committee," the craggy-faced Tikhonov told me one morning as he chain-smoked in his book-lined study. "Because when he came here he manifested a clear, lively interest in economics, in social problems, in the development of rural areas and society as a whole. At that time, he rather frequently invited prominent economists home. And we got many instructions—directly from him—to carry out assignments, to study the most urgent, most essential, and most profound problems that the agrarian economy was suffering at the time."[21]

One of half a dozen economists whom Gorbachev assembled in April 1982 to prepare a new farm policy for Brezhnev was Tatyana Zaslavskaya, the sociologist from Novosibirsk, who was even then preparing her explosive report on the collapse of Soviet economic growth and the need for massive reform.[22] For Gorbachev, she became a bridge to Abel Aganbegyan, the maverick chief of the Novosibirsk Institute of Economics. And Zaslavskaya herself quickly became a favorite of Gorbachev because her outspoken ideas matched his private thinking.

How like-minded they were was evident from his behavior at a closed, high-level conference on agriculture in September 1982. The conference was sponsored by the Academy of Sciences and was attended by several Politburo members. In a fifteen-minute report to that session, Zaslavskaya gave a partial preview of the dynamite she was about to explode. Her key point was that Soviet agriculture could not be improved through technology, machinery, fertilizers, or administrative reorganizations, as the Party leadership had long contended. Rather, above all else, it would have to be improved by giving the peasant "an interest in his work . . . and normal living conditions." In short, she said, "everything depends on the people involved"—not on empty Party slogans.

Her analysis was candid and caustic enough that a senior Party official told others she had "overstepped the boundaries" of the permissible. In fact, when the full conference report was later published, her speech was so heavily censored that she found it unrecognizable.

Zaslavskaya's consolation was that the private audience of higher-ups was her primary target. Yet to her great disappointment, Gorbachev was called out of the room while she was speaking. For her, he was the most important person at the conference, and he had missed her report. What she did not know, and only learned later from Yuri Ovchinnikov, vice president of the academy, was that on his return, Gorbachev was given extensive notes on her analysis. "He read them, turned them over and read them a second time, got to the end, and then read them yet a third time," Ovchinnikov told her. "So I congratulate you. Even though he missed your presentation, I saw him read the entire thing three times."[23]

But if Zaslavskaya was frustrated to have missed a face-to-face exchange with Gorbachev on that occasion, Gorbachev's own frustration was even greater when Brezhnev and his Politburo rejected the reform program that Gorbachev had put together with her and the other agricultural economists.

Gorbachev's years as national agriculture secretary were not good ones. The grain harvests of the late 1970s and early 1980s were disastrous. Imports from the United States had been rising until President Carter's grain embargo of 1980. As Gorbachev's private memo indicated, he felt drastic steps were necessary. Brezhnev, who really made agriculture his own personal bailiwick, knew that food shortages were endemic and promised the people dramatic improvements. To great fanfare in May 1982, he announced his ten-year "food program," full of ambitious targets and high-sounding rhetoric.

With his team of agricultural economists, Gorbachev had tried to put together a comprehensive reform package. It promised less central planning, improved living standards for farm workers, plus more autonomy and more financial incentives for local units. In sum, he proposed liberalizing the farm sector. But the plan was shot down in the Politburo. They did not see the same urgency he did.

"He went up against strong opposition from Kosygin," Postnikov told me. "Kosygin had the view that agriculture was like a bottomless barrel: You put in a bunch of money at one end and you get nothing back. Kosygin was an industrialist. Industry was something else: Invest money and you get something back. . . . Gorbachev tried to prove to [Kosygin] that without food for people, you couldn't have anything—not defense, not industry. So he had a run-in with Kosygin and Brezhnev was constantly making peace between them."[24] Still, Brezhnev was no reformer at heart; that spring he was constantly sick, and too tired even to think of reform, let alone fight for it.

Gorbachev was flexible and pragmatic enough to try to get Politburo approval for individual proposals—the development of agro-industrial complexes, more investment in the rural infrastructure, some increases in state subsidies to farms and procurement prices. Some piecemeal measures were accepted. But the Brezhnev plan's targets were wildly unrealistic, and there was almost nothing of Gorbachev's ideas for real reform: no relaxation of centralized planning, no passing of decision-making to lower levels, no independence for individual farms, no real push for small, profit-oriented work brigades. Everything was still to be run top-down from Moscow and locked into the old inefficient superstructure left by Stalin.

Gorbachev gamely bit his tongue, even with his small team of advisers, but they sensed his deep disappointment at the Politburo's rejection. "It seemed to me that when they turned down that whole series of measures in this one very fundamental document, he was very upset," Tikhonov recalled. "In those high levels, leaders train themselves to be very reserved. But we saw his reaction, and we imagined what it was." Gorbachev's behavior betrayed his feelings. Brezhnev unveiled the plan and Gorbachev distanced himself from it. He seemed content not even to deliver a speech at the key Party meeting, although that was expected of him. Afterward, he always referred to it as Brezhnev's program.

"After Brezhnev's speech, no one was satisfied," Zaslavskaya recalled. "It was full of half measures rather than radical policies. But that was no longer Gorbachev's fault."

GROOMING FOR THE TOP

After Brezhnev died in November 1982 and Andropov took over, Gorbachev's star shot into ascendancy and his responsibilities suddenly mushroomed. He was then fifty-one and Andropov, sixty-eight and ill, began grooming him for the top job. Although Andropov also promoted a potential rival to Gorbachev, Leningrad Party boss Grigory Romanov, he made Gorbachev his deputy, gave him the ideological portfolio, expanded his mandate from agriculture to the entire economy, put science and technology under his wing, and had him oversee a purge of the Party apparatus to replace corrupt Brezhnev hacks with younger, more zealous, more honest leaders. Andropov was called a reformer, but his were traditional conservative reforms—demands for discipline and campaigns to fight corruption and inefficiency, to sweep deadwood out of the government, and to institute a crackdown against sloth and drinking among workers. In other words, no reforms of substance. He did not touch, let alone shake, the underlying structures of the Soviet system, as Gorbachev later would.

What served Gorbachev's development especially well was Andropov's decision to charge Gorbachev with developing a program for genuine reform of the management of the economy—a program that Andropov would not live long enough to begin to carry out. But its preparation enabled Gorbachev to surround himself with intellectual advisers and to expand his growing network of reformist allies within the Party hierarchy. Gorbachev's voracious appetite for intellectual input was reminiscent of the zeal for self-education evidenced by Peter the Great, who borrowed heavily from the West and used science to initiate a famous period of reform in czarist Russia.

In the field of economics, Zaslavskaya led Gorbachev to such new advisers as Aganbegyan, Leonid Abalkin, and Oleg Bogomolov, who generated more detailed critiques of the economy and began to discuss reform measures. Gorbachev's new responsibilities in science and technology brought him into contact with Yevgeny Velikhov, a specialist in computers and information technology and a vice president of the Academy of Sciences; and with Roald Sagdeyev, the outspoken, free-thinking head of the nation's space institute. As Sagdeyev said to me, "We scientists were being treated as very important people—and that would have been impossible without Gorbachev's personal interest. We talked to him about Reagan's 'Star Wars.' Our first written assessment was produced in August of 1983. We had a task force of ten or fifteen top people advising him."25

At the Academy of Sciences, a graceful old building constructed under Catherine the Great and still pale yellow, trimmed with white woodwork, Velikhov recalled Gorbachev's fascination with computers when Velikhov first showed him how they worked. "It was on a Saturday, a day off," Velikhov explained. "He was the agriculture secretary. I had called him and told him we were having this meeting that might interest him. He came over and then became very interested in how to promote systems analysis of agriculture. Later, he asked to see many scientists, not only me. He developed very rich relations with everybody. He does not want just a fifteen-minute protocol meeting, as with a lot of Party leaders. Gorbachev wants to understand, to go to the depths. Since that first meeting, I have met with him many times. We have discussed many issues, especially arms control. His grasp, his understanding, has steadily deepened."26

Within the Communist Party itself, Gorbachev developed another circle of advisers. He became a frequent visitor at the Party's Academy of Social Sciences, which was then headed by a political economist, Vadim Medvedev, whom Gorbachev eventually pulled into the Central Committee apparatus, and finally, the Politburo. Valentin Lazutkin, then an academy scholar and now deputy chief of the State Committee for Television and Radio, recalled that Gorbachev enjoyed giving a speech on some broad topic and inviting a sharp exchange with Party intellectuals at the academy. "He came there often in the early 1980s," Lazutkin said, "and seemed to thrive on lively debate of issues with us. He has a high regard for scholars, and a very analytical cast of mind."27

In 1983, Gorbachev traveled to Canada, his first exposure to the West in several years. There, he renewed his friendship with Aleksandr Yakovlev, who would become Gorbachev's alter ego in the Politburo. They had met in 1971, when Yakovlev had been a much more powerful figure than Gorbachev as chief of the propaganda department in the Central Committee. But Yakovlev had gotten in trouble for attacking Russian nationalism in a published article, and Brezhnev banished him to Canada in 1971 as ambassador. A decade in the West had made Yakovlev even more of a free-thinker than he had been in Moscow. When Gorbachev visited, their roles were reversed—this time Gorbachev was the big shot. Yakovlev told me they hit it off extremely well, talking late into the night about their country's problems. Others revealed that Yakovlev, looking over the main speech Gorbachev was going to give in Canada, advised Gorbachev that it would not go over well with a Western audience and wrote a new draft for Gorbachev overnight. Gorbachev liked Yakovlev's version so well, he delivered it and then recruited Yakovlev for his brain trust. He got Yakovlev reassigned as the head of Moscow's prestigious Institute on International Relations and World Economics, and moved him from there into a series of high Party posts.

"In Canada, we talked very, very candidly about everything," Yakovlev told me. When I asked whether Gorbachev was as critical of Brezhnev then as Yakovlev had been, Yakovlev sidestepped a direct answer. "Oh, I don't remember now what specifically he said, but the understanding that society should be changed and built on other principles—that was there."[28]

Gorbachev's visits to Canadian farmers were an eye-opener and added to his conviction that change in the U.S.S.R. was imperative. According to Canadian officials who accompanied him, Gorbachev was impressed by the initiative of the private Canadian farmers. At one stop, he tested one farmer: "Who makes you get up in the morning?" The farmer, non-plussed, said he got going on his own. At home, Gorbachev knew it would take the hounding of state farm supervisors and the threat of disciplinary action to get many farm workers on the job. In another encounter, he asked to see a farm's labor force, expecting the typical Soviet collective, and was taken aback when the farmer replied that he farmed several hundred acres with just his family and a few hired hands. Sharing his secret, the farmer showed Gorbachev his tractors and other modern farm machinery, close to $100,000 worth. "Do they trust you with all this?" Gorbachev asked, assuming that the equipment belonged to some government agency because he could not imagine a single farmer's owning such an expensive array of equipment. By the accounts of Canadian officials, Gorbachev walked away muttering, "We'll never have this for fifty years."

Gorbachev had good reason for more than a passing interest in the Canadian family farm. Back in Stavropol he had tried to stimulate individual initiative through a Soviet variation on family farming. His idea was not outright private ownership of the land, but a step in that direction—and a step away from massive collective farms. In his Stavropol experiments, a parcel of land was assigned to a small work "brigade," under a contract with the collective farm. If their harvest exceeded the contract, the family brigade could pocket the profit. This was known as the "brigade contract" or, when done by families, the "family brigade" system. In 1982, Gorbachev had tried to get this idea adopted as part of Brezhnev's food program, but he had failed. A year later, with Brezhnev out of the way and his patron Andropov in charge, Gorbachev won Politburo approval for it.

With Andropov's blessing, he was moving ahead on other fronts too, forming alliances with newcomers to the national Party leadership who had been promoted by Andropov. One who would become a significant figure in the Gorbachev era was Yegor Ligachev, a successful party boss in the big Siberian centers of Tomsk and Novosibirsk—whose streak of incorruptible puritanism appealed to the strict Andropov. A second was Nikolai Ryzhkov, a successful economic manager who had been chief of Uralmash, the huge heavy machine–building plant in the Ural Mountains city of Sverdlovsk. For Andropov, Ligachev was running the Central Committee's organization department, replacing the old Brezhnev mafia with new faces, while Ryzhkov was becoming the Party's top expert on the economy. Their roles in Andropov's regime foreshadowed the roles they would play in the future in Gorbachev's Politburo: Ligachev became number two to Gorbachev, and the Party watchdog, running the apparatus and serving as its pointman in the Politburo; Ryzhkov, the technocrat, became prime minister, running the economy and policing and protecting the ministries. In the late eighties they were often at odds with Gorbachev, but back in 1983 they were a team of rising reformers, impatient to shake off the corrupt lethargy left by Brezhnev.

Andropov fell so ill within a few months of his rise to the top that he had to abdicate much of his power and make Gorbachev his de facto deputy. As proxy, Gorbachev ran Politburo meetings and the Party Secretariat, relaying Andropov's orders and then reporting back to his chief. Andropov lay bedridden, tied to a kidney dialysis machine, either at his *dacha* in Usovo, west of Moscow, or at the Party elite's well-hidden hospital in the town of Kuntsevo. In addition to the day-to-day running of the country, Andropov assigned Gorbachev the crucial mandate: to begin preparing plans for revamping the system of economic management. Even better than Gorbachev, at first, Andropov understood that the whole economy was in a shambles, and that Russia was falling disastrously behind the West.

In what ultimately became essential preparation for his own future reforms, Gorbachev began to organize task forces. He drew on his widening circle of brain-trusters, in Soviet institutes and think tanks in Moscow, Leningrad, Novosibirsk, and other major cities. Working in tandem with Ryzhkov, he commissioned 110 different policy studies; he sought advisers on overall economic policy, experts in science and technology, computer scientists, agricultural specialists, labor sociologists, educators. Some of the topics covered were the space race, arms control, and foreign policy, but the bulk of them, by Gorbachev's account, were concerned with domestic affairs, especially the economy. Andropov's death in February 1984 did not interrupt that work, which continued until Gorbachev's ascension to power. More than once, Gorbachev has emphasized that the intellectual springboard for reform was prepared several years before he actually launched *perestroika*.

"[T]he appearance of the trends of restructuring," he would later recall, "was preceded by a specific period of analytical studies and moral assessments. All this was being prepared and was coming to a head within the Party, in science and culture, and in broad social circles. It has to be stated directly that a substantial reserve of fresh ideas was developed. We all sensed that it was impossible to live as before."[29]

Except, of course, for the Old Guard, which was powerful enough to impose Konstantin Chernenko, the doddering Brezhnev toady and life-long apparatchik, as Andropov's successor, in February 1984. Chernenko was even more of a geriatric embarrassment than Brezhnev had been. Gorbachev was formally named number two, the stand-in chairman at Politburo meetings and the Party Secretariat when Chernenko was too feeble to attend.

It was Gorbachev who went to London in December 1984, captivating the Britons as the leader of a new generation of Soviets and prompting Prime Minister Margaret Thatcher to gush, "We can work with him." It was Gorbachev that same month, in an astonishing speech to a Soviet ideological conference, who declared the need for openness (*glasnost*), for more self-management in the economy, for the use of such market levers as prices, profits, and credits, to make the system work. And it was Gorbachev who declared war on inertia and on the "moribund conceptions" of Party dogmatists—all reflecting the provocative work of his brain trusts.

It was also Gorbachev whom the outside world took to be the obvious heir apparent when Chernenko died after thirteen feeble months as general secretary. As Gorbachev's ally Aleksandr Yakovlev remarked to me, "It was historically logical" for the Kremlin to pass the torch to a new generation, and to signal the changing of the guard by anointing Gorbachev.

But as the Politburo met through the night of March 10, 1985, Gorbachev's prospects were touch and go. He had exposed his own beliefs more and more, dropping the double life he had carried on within the Party for so many years. Now, on the threshold of power, he faced the final obstacle. He was almost blocked by the aging, conservative Moscow Party leader

Viktor Grishin, whom Chernenko had tried to anoint before his death.

Ligachev, then a strong supporter of Gorbachev, has reported that the Politburo was closely divided on the critical choice, and passed "very anxious hours" that could have come out with very different people on top. I have been told by well-connected Party officials that Gorbachev's circle anticipated the close division as they watched Chernenko sink into a coma in the final days of his life and that Chernenko's vital life-support systems were pulled at a time when three Politburo conservatives were far from Moscow and unable to vote on the new leader. Vladimir Shcherbitsky, the Ukrainian Party leader, was in San Francisco; Vitaly Vorotnikov, future head of the Russian republic, was in Yugoslavia; and Dinmukhammed Kunyayev, the Kazakh Party leader, was in his capital of Alma-Ata, several hours away from Moscow by plane. Whether or not it is true that Chernenko's life support was removed at a politically propitious time, the fact that Shcherbitsky, Kunyayev, and Vorotnikov did not reach Moscow until March 11—after the Politburo had made its selection—unquestionably helped Gorbachev. By virtually all reckonings, at least two of them, if not all three, would have voted against him. Mikhail Shatrov, the playwright, has reported that the eight Politburo members voting that fateful night were evenly split until the deadlock was broken by threats from KGB Chief Viktor Chebrikov to expose corruption in Grishin's family. At the Central Committee meeting held to confirm the Politburo vote, the scales were tipped by former Foreign Minister Andrei Gromyko's stunning endorsement of Gorbachev as a skilled leader of the Politburo, nearly brilliant in foreign policy. Significantly, Gromyko did not review Gorbachev's record in agriculture, which was far from brilliant; in fact, Gorbachev had not been a good economic manager. But Gromyko praised his political finesse and hailed Gorbachev as a tough partisan, despite his nice smile—"a man with iron teeth."[30]

The moment for reform had arrived, and Gorbachev was unusually well prepared—by conviction, life experience, temperament, and the process of high-level analysis he had commissioned. He embarked, as he later said, with the understanding that "cosmetic repairs would not do; a major overhaul was required."[31]

Only the self-assurance that he had developed over a lifetime would have made him bold enough to tackle such a daunting task. If anything, his own success had made him overoptimistic about the chances for reform and overrational about how to go about it. "Gorbachev's main failing," one of his Party aides and admirers conceded to me privately, "is that he's too intellectual, too rational. He does not understand ordinary people well enough—what makes them tick." Gorbachev has, at times, been transparent in his own surprise at the difficulties. Nearly four years after taking power, in the midst of national turmoil, he admitted that "we are *only now* [emphasis added] truly understanding what *perestroika* is . . . the huge scale of the work to come."³²

But if Gorbachev's failing would be political miscalculation and underestimation of the difficulties, his extraordinary talent as a political leader would be his capacity for survival, his ability to ride the tiger, to outflank his opposition, to sidestep catastrophe and improvise new solutions, to cast off policies that did not work and constantly to change the national agenda to make himself once again the vector of history—even if only long enough to keep the process of reform alive and deepen its hold on his society so that, if necessary, it could outlive him.

PART TWO

THE AWAKENING

A central element of Gorbachev's strategy to rebuild and modernize Soviet society was the marshaling of public opinion. For Gorbachev understood, if not initially, then by 1987, that to set in motion his economic and political reforms, he had to arouse his country from silence, to awaken his people and give them voice. Gorbachev could not hope to compete with the world in the twenty-first century—he could not hope to move his nation—without freeing up ideas and information.

For decades, orthodoxy had stifled initiative, had suppressed creativity in politics, the arts, the economy. For reform to flourish, the dead hand of dogma had to be lifted; the stimulus of intellectual ferment had to be fostered. In place of Party slogans, Gorbachev needed fresh thinking; in place of the Party line, a diversity of opinions; instead of a political monolith, pluralism.

Achieving these things required a political high-wire act.

Most Soviet leaders rise to the top on the power base of the Communist Party apparatus, and Gorbachev was no exception. Once he was installed, however, he had to reverse course; as the agent of change, he had to take action against the interests of the Party apparatus. In order to free up the creative energies of his people, he had to break the power monopoly of the very hierarchy that had chosen him.

To do this, he needed to create an army of supporters, to tap into the pent-up frustration of the masses. And so, very deliberately, he revived the people—especially the intelligentsia—from their slumber by liberating the press, television, the world of books and cinema.

CHAPTER 5

"WHAT DO YOU THINK?"

"Russia was deep in sleep and nothing was
happening. Then the people woke up
about two or two and a half years ago [1987]."[1]
—Yuri Levada
Sociologist
March 1990

"Before, I thought our people had
forgotten how to think. But our research
and the elections and campaigns have
shown that it just isn't so. Maybe
after all, we should trust our people more."[2]
—Leonid Sedov
Sociologist
September 1989

Yuri Levada does not look like a bomb thrower. He could be anybody's
friendly Dutch uncle—an ample, amiable man with engaging warmth, an
open manner, and an air of genial self-confidence. Given to wearing
turtleneck sweaters and zippered suede jackets rather than a coat and tie,
he looks like a French film director. In fact, Levada is a sociologist, and
that vocation puts him at the leading edge of Gorbachev's peaceful political revolution. Levada is one of the vital links between the leader and the

masses. His version of bomb throwing, suppressed in the 1970s, is political opinion polling.

His first mass experiment, a full-page questionnaire printed on February 1, 1989, in *Literaturnaya Gazeta (Literary Gazette)*, the weekly of the Soviet Writers' Union, touched off an avalanche of responses, precisely the kind of popular reaction that Gorbachev needed to power his drive for reform. Levada's story, over the past quarter of a century, also illustrates how Soviet society has changed from the enforced orthodoxy of the Brezhnev era to Gorbachev's new openness.

In the late 1960s, Levada had created a stir by becoming the first Soviet scholar to teach sociology at Moscow State University. After Khrushchev's thaw in the early 1960s, sociology was no longer the forbidden territory it once had been, but it was still an academic black sheep; there was no sociology department at any Soviet university. But Levada, a philosopher by training who was always interested in "how people live" (as he put it), was permitted in 1966 to give lectures on sociology in the journalism faculty of the university. And at the Institute for Applied Social Research, he led a seminar in the theory and methods of sociology.

Levada's classes and seminars were immensely popular. Students flocked to him, attracted by his undogmatic thinking and his intellectual daring; he became a mentor to many. Testing the limits of the permissible, Levada had also dared to invite the American sociologist Talcott Parsons to lead some seminars in Moscow in 1967. Levada's own popularity grew to the point where the university published his lectures as a paperback book in 1969. But as the first thousand copies circulated, Levada found himself in trouble with the Party.

After the invasion of Czechoslovakia in August 1968, Brezhnev's line had hardened; the KGB was cracking down on dissidents and the Party was tightening up. Not that Levada was an open dissident like Andrei Sakharov or Aleksandr Solzhenitsyn; his political credentials were impeccable. He was an establishment scholar, a Communist Party member, and the ranking Communist in his institute—the secretary of the institute's Party committee.

Levada's sin was not personal; it was something more menacing—professional free-thinking, and the challenge to Soviet Party dogma inherent in sociology. His book was no flaming tract; it was a basic introduction to sociology, one that today's Soviet students find pretty tame. Yet in the Brezhnev era, another sociologist observed, simply by eschewing dogma, "Levada showed himself underneath as a real enemy of the system."[3]

Years before, Stalin's ideologists had branded sociology a "bourgeois pseudoscience." Their Marxist-Leninist argument was that historical materialism explained all reality and thus sociology was unnecessary. In practice, the danger for Communist ideology was that sociology presumed society was composed of competing interest groups, and the very idea of group antagonisms threatened the Communist Party's precious myth of the classless society living in monolithic harmony.

What is more, empirical sociology as practiced in the West sought data that inevitably challenged the Party's political claims. Indeed, Levada had cited some early, very limited opinion polls conducted by other Soviet sociologists such as Vladimir Shlyapentokh and Vladimir Shutkin, who had found that, contrary to the Party's boasts, few children of workers and peasants made it into decent universities; also that most readers of *Pravda* did not even bother to read its party-line editorials.

At bottom, of course, independent opinion polling posed too much of a threat to Kremlin leaders, who had rarely if ever worried about what the people thought. And after Czechoslovakia's spring of ferment, the Brezhnev leadership was pulling back from the risks of having to deal with public opinion at home.

Levada, whose impish candor rarely deserts him, compounded his problems with the wry comment, "You cannot solve ideological issues with the help of tanks." To the Kremlin, that remark, reprinted in his book, sounded like a slam on Moscow's military suppression of Czechoslovak liberalism. In reprisal, *Pravda* made Levada the first scapegoat of what became a broad purge of Soviet sociology. He was denounced at meetings at the Academy of Social Sciences and the Communist Party Central Committee. In the end, not only Levada but about two hundred other sociologists were fired from various institutes and universities in the early 1970s.[4]

By the time I arrived in Moscow in late 1971, Yuri Levada was something of a mystery man, beyond the reach of Western correspondents. He had become a symbolic target of the ideological hangmen of the Brezhnev era. Communist Party watchdogs had forced him off the faculty of Moscow State University and gotten him expelled from the Institute for Applied Social Research. He had slipped out of view and was lying low at another institute. Politically, he lived in a forbidden zone; and for close to fifteen years, he remained hidden in this way beneath the surface of Russian political and intellectual life.

Now, under Gorbachev, Levada has made a political and professional comeback. He is operating freely, though even now he is not easy to find. I found him, with considerable difficulty, tucked away in an unmarked room on the fourth floor of a third-class hotel, the Central House of Tourists, far from the center of Moscow. It was an unlikely place for an office, but apparently the only thing available with space so short in Moscow.

At sixty, with a white fringe of hair circling his head, Levada radiated vitality. In a system where senior academics are often formal and pretentious, Levada was relaxed and informal. He was born and brought up in the Ukraine, then went to Moscow State University. He comes by an intense interest in politics naturally: Both his parents were journalists and essayists. His mother was Russian, his father, Ukrainian. Of course, he speaks both those languages, but also Polish, French, and accented English. I knew in advance that he was considered a father figure by many young Soviet sociologists; when I met him, I could readily see why he was so popular with younger colleagues.

Six of them were clustered around Levada in what was once a skimpy double room; the Levada team was practicing sociology out of a garret. The place was crammed with old wooden school desks, file folders, piles of questionnaires, wall charts, and stacks of miscellaneous papers. Levada had the corner desk and his own chair; I'm not sure there were enough chairs to go around for all the others. Some of Levada's now middle-aged acolytes sat on their desks while we talked; the smokers spilled ash into cupped hands or onto the floor; someone made tea on a hot plate.

But there were no computers. Things were so tight financially and their operation so new that they had only a few computers, far too few to go around, and those were all three or four miles away, in the basement of an aristocrat's former mansion, which their technical department shared with several other agencies. Someday soon, they said, they hoped the whole operation would have new premises. I first visited them in April 1989, but a year later, their office situation had not improved.

Under the direction and political protection of Tatyana Zaslavskaya, Levada's group was now part of the All-Union Center for the Study of Public Opinion on Social and Economic Issues, with twenty-three suboffices scattered across the country to organize on-the-spot polling. When the center was set up in 1988, "politics" had been deliberately left out of its title and mandate, I was told, because Kremlin hard-liners mistrusted Zaslavskaya's radical tendencies; indeed, they were still making periodic attempts to remove her as the center's director. But, as she proudly told me, she was too well known to be knocked off easily.

THE UNEXPECTED AVALANCHE

Despite the inevitable obstacles, the Levada group exuded an ebullient sense of camaraderie and the enthusiasm of people finally doing what they had been forbidden to do for close to twenty years. Like excited children, they were sitting on the edge of history, watching a great democratic experiment unfold.

As Levada and two of his former students, the black-bearded, analytical Alex Levinson and close-cropped, sandy-haired, pragmatic Lev Gudkov, explained, the center had ignored the formal restrictions and plunged almost immediately into political polling. In the previous two decades, there had been some industrial polls on social and economic issues—jobs, education, problems in the workplace. But Levada's group was no longer content with dabbling. They wanted to get to the gut political questions. So they printed their full-page questionnaire in *Literaturnaya Gazeta* under the headline WHAT DO YOU THINK?

By American standards, the questionnaire was as daunting as a mortgage loan application: thirty-four questions, with many detailed, multiple-choice answers. Most Americans would have balked, refusing to devote more than half an hour to answering such a poll. But the Levada group hoped that by using a newspaper with six million subscribers, they could get enough responses for an adequate national sample. In the West, that would require roughly three thousand respondents.

Levada's team was wholly unprepared for the reaction: They received two hundred thousand responses in all!

When they told me the figure, I simply could not believe it. It was so incredible that we all broke out laughing.

In one stroke, the Soviet Union had gone from one voice to many, from orthodoxy to pluralism. The hold of dogma, long since weakened, had been destroyed.

Levada and his team had never in their wildest dreams imagined that their questionnaire would touch off such a Niagara. It was as if someone had thrown open the floodgates. Before, no one was sure whether there was even a trickle of public opinion to be measured. Now, overnight, a flood.

Levinson led me into the bathroom, where the tub was piled high with nine or ten huge mail sacks. The Levada group had carefully selected three thousand responses to tabulate, but they did not know what to do with the remaining mountains of replies. It was such a precious testament to the country's political awakening that it seemed criminal to throw the letters away. So they kept them, and a year later, when I peeped into the bathroom, those letter sacks were still there.

"Through the decades," Levinson remarked, "people have never been asked *anything*. All of a sudden their opinion is being counted—someone is seeking their answers. They feel this is some sign of trust toward them, a demonstration of their worth."

Gudkov added, "People write us: 'We see your questionnaire as a referendum' and the possibility of a referendum on major topics compels people to answer."

"People are saying things like, 'I have lived for eighty years and no one has ever wondered about my opinion. For the first time in my life I have experienced that moment,' " reported a third member of the group, Aleksandr Golov.[5]

Several times over the past year and a half, I have visited Levada and his group, and each time their wonder over that first poll, and its implications for the new world that Gorbachev is trying to open up, remained undiminished.

STUDYING A SOCIAL REVOLUTION FROM THE INSIDE

"Russia was deep in sleep and nothing was happening," Levada observed. "Then the people woke up about two or two and a half years ago."

As others have, Levada dated the real start of popular involvement in Gorbachev's reforms not from 1985, when Gorbachev first came to power, but 1987, when Gorbachev began to build toward a more open press and democratic reforms.

"It [the *Literaturnaya Gazeta* poll] was a tremendous event for us. For the first time we saw that our people are not only ready to answer a bold question but they actively want to speak out. The main result of *perestroika* is the disappearance of mass fear."

I suggested to Levada that this sudden eruption of public opinion must have seemed miraculous, a great discovery.

"Yes, yes," he said. "For the first time in history, we can study a social revolution from the inside. Because at the time of the American and French and other great revolutions, there were no sociologists out polling. But we . . ." He smiled broadly. "It's *verry* interesting."[6]

Even these maverick liberals were astonished that after decades of silence and repression, so many ordinary people were willing to risk political reprisal to express their views—something inconceivable even two or three years before.

"On the envelopes [mailing back questionnaires], people put their full names and addresses," Alex Levinson said. "And according to existing laws, these people could be brought to trial." What he did not say, but what I well understood, was that during the Brezhnev years, many dissidents had been sent off to Siberia, and in the Stalin years, many intellectuals had perished, for openly stating political opinions about the leadership. The great poet Osip Mandelstam had gone to his death in the mid-1930s for a fourteen-line poem that mocked Stalin's "cockroach whiskers leer" and his sycophantic circle of "fawning half-men for him to play with."[7] To underscore his point, Levinson fished out a letter.

"Here," he said, handing me a letter to inspect. "Someone writes something sharply critical about the Communist Party, about Gorbachev, about politics—and then he signs his full name and address. This could be used as evidence against him. So I think [this shows] the fear of the past has just disappeared. That's why, when our interviewers do their interviews, people speak very openly with them."

If this openness came as a surprise to free-thinking academics, it must have been even more of a shock to Communist Party higher-ups. I asked if Party officials had been interested in their findings, and they all nodded, adding that the poll results had gone to branches of the Central Committee.

"How does the Party apparatus react to all this?" I asked.

"Extremely negatively, of course," Gudkov replied.

The apparatchiks had of course ample cause for concern. The readers of *Literaturnaya Gazeta* were delivering a stinging indictment of the system and of the Party hierarchy. In answer to an open-ended question about the main reasons for the country's "current difficulties," the number one villain mentioned was the Party—government bureaucracy. With a choice of nineteen different reasons, plus a blank space to write in another explanation, responses broke down as follows:

63% cited the dominance of bureaucrats;
60% listed corruption, drunkenness, black-market speculation, and thievery from the state;
56% mentioned the country's technological backwardness;
45% cited a mistaken strategy of national development;
35% pointed to loss of faith in the ideals of socialism;
33% cited the consequences of Stalinism.[8]

What intrigued me especially was that only 1% chose a favorite whipping boy of Communist Party propaganda—the policies of "countries of imperialism"—that is, the West.

Of course, Levada and his group understood that the newspaper's subscribers were overwhelmingly intellectuals and the people who wrote in were self-selected; and so the poll was not entirely representative, no matter how many responses they received. It was not the kind of random or weighted sample that pollsters normally require. Indeed, the training and experience of Soviet sociologists and pollsters is a good deal less sophisticated than that in the West.

In the interests of greater accuracy than is possible in a reader's poll, the Levada group ran a second poll of forty-five hundred people, a sample of the general population that they selected to match the nation's various ages and social, economic, and demographic groups. In seventeen regions across the country, interviewers went door to door. In this poll, the number one villain cited was corruption and drunkenness (57%), closely followed by technical backwardness (42%) and the hated bureaucracy (41%). This more working-class-oriented sample was far less likely than the intellectuals to blame the country's ills on the wrong development strategy and popular loss of faith in the ideals of socialism. But surprisingly, even though there were plenty of workers polled, 28% blamed the nation's economic mess on the laziness or "shirking," as Russians say, of Soviet workers.

At the end of the national poll, I noticed figures about Soviet living standards that were stunning. Two thirds of the people reported that the per-capita income in their families was less than 125 rubles a month—about $200 at the official rate of exchange, but more like $20 on the free market. All but 3% made less than 250 rubles. Even allowing for some exaggeration, these were dismal living standards, and those of a Third World country, not of a superpower.

The two polls also confirmed an important divergence in attitudes between the intelligentsia and the working class. Differences cropped up on many questions, but most significantly on a question that asked people to choose ways to make "decisive changes for the better" in the nation's situation.

The national poll, which the Levada group saw as dominated by working-class opinion, showed little taste for reform. By far the largest number (50%) said the most important step was to restore *tvordy poryadok*— "strict order." In short, their cure for the current crisis was to run the nation like an army, show everybody a tough fist, impose discipline, and head back toward the Stalinist system. In a similar vein, they also wanted an improvement in central planning, rather than abandonment of it. Reforms came far down the list.

The intellectual readers of *Literaturnaya Gazeta* were on a different track. First of all, they said, give peasants the right to own land (66%) and cut army and military expenditures (55%). They also strongly favored breaking up the centralized power structure and giving more autonomy to minority republics and more authority to local governments. One third wanted a cutback in Soviet foreign aid and urged efforts to attract foreign capital investments in the U.S.S.R. In short, they had more appetite for reform than Gorbachev himself.

Rippling through the responses in both polls was what Gudkov called a civic rage over miserable living conditions—bad housing, a bad health system, shortages of all kinds—and a demoralizing sense of futility about the future.

The Levada group had touched the raw anger of the population, suppressed but accumulated over decades. As Levada observed, what the Russians call the *narod*, the masses, had finally awakened—and with a vengeance.

"They began to wake up with something of a hangover, not with a clear head," he explained to me. "The main form of consciousness, from what we can determine, is a wild hostility toward the apparat, which they feel fills its pockets, takes bribes, enjoys privileges. The main enemy is the corruption, the privileges of the apparat bureaucracy."

THE MAFIA

Everywhere I went in the Soviet Union, people simply called it the "mafia," not literally meaning organized crime in the Western sense but having that dark connotation. In Soviet parlance, the mafia is a stratum of society that includes powerful Party and government officials, economic managers, and criminal elements, an amorphous, privileged layer held in popular contempt for its corrupt life-style and evil tentacles that reach into all walks of life. The "mafia" is an epithet constantly on people's lips, but hard to get them to define with any precision; it almost always links political power and illicit economic advantages. When I tossed out names of political leaders who might be possible symbols of the mafia to the public, Levada rejected them all.

In 1990, the Levada group did a special survey to try to induce people to say more about what they meant by the term. "Let them put down anything they want—crime, the Party clique, retail trade," he said. "In general, it's hazy: some unclear powers-that-be. You know how Russians express themselves, as if there were some kind of sorcery, black magic. One third thinks the mafia is the main reason for all evil. This invisible, secret, universal, omnipresent mafia is considered responsible for whatever you please."

In subsequent polls conducted by the Levada group, some of which I witnessed, they found such mistrust among the people toward the bureaucracy and Party leadership that large majorities were demanding direct elections. Initially, Levada's team had been hesitant to ask people about a multiparty system. "It's not really necessary to ask such a question now," Lev Gudkov told me at our first meeting, in April 1989, when the Levada group was still feeling its way.[9] But within a few months, the idea of a multiparty system was no longer taboo. And once a choice was put to them and they had to answer a question asked by a poll taker, people started taking positions and then hungrily reading the results of the polls in which they had participated.

"We present a mirror for society," Gudkov remarked. "We show them what they are. And looking at that mirror, a person thinks about what he sees."

Leonid Sedov, one of Levada's longtime colleagues, who had paid for his own dissenting views in the Brezhnev era with a term of Siberian exile, remarked to me that the results of the new polls had changed his once-skeptical view of the Soviet people, whom he had always regarded as politically inert.

"Before, I had a much worse opinion about my countrymen," he said, stroking his weatherworn face and soft beard.

"I thought our people had forgotten how to think, how to want things, how to organize themselves, how to be active," he admitted a bit tensely, recalling his earlier disenchantment with others less radical than he. "But our research, and the elections and campaigns, have shown that this just isn't so. Maybe, after all, we should trust our people more—which is something that I'm going to do from now on."

What struck Alex Levinson especially forcefully was the synergy between polling and public opinion. The act of polling, he said, prompted people to think about issues they had long left to others; they had to formulate their own attitudes about elections, about relations among nationalities, about national priorities, and then to speak out. In short, polling stimulated what Gorbachev wanted—the formation of public opinion.

"We are needed first of all by the people who don't really know what they think until they find out what everybody else thinks," he observed.

"When someone knows that 'I'm not the only one who thinks this should be done; the whole country thinks that way,' this is extremely important.

"In a way," he concluded, "this [polling and publishing polls] is a quiet revolution."

The revolution, of course, is the emergence of a civil society—the very notion that society at large has legitimate interests and opinions, apart from the Communist Party's or the state's definition of what is good for society. In the nineteenth century, the appearance of this notion among the Russian intelligentsia was crucial for efforts to oppose and reform the czarist state. Granted legitimacy by Gorbachev, this same notion of the public's interests and opinions has reappeared—a foundation stone for a democratic society.

CHAPTER 6

GLASNOST: A MARRIAGE OF POLITICAL CONVENIENCE

"In short, comrades, what we are talking about is a new role for public opinion in the country. And there is no need to fear the novel, unconventional character of some opinions. . . ."[1]
—Gorbachev, June 1988

"*Glasnost* comes from the Russian word *glas,* or voice. So it literally means voiceness, or speaking out."[2]
—Vladimir Pozner
TV Commentator
June 1988

In his assault on the existing Soviet power structure and the stultifying effects of enforced ideological orthodoxy, Gorbachev did something unconventional for a Communist ruler: He reached out to form a political alliance with the intelligentsia.

He was moving beyond his well-developed habit of tapping small academic brain trusts for private advice, to embark on open political warfare. The marriage of political convenience he sought—engaging intellectuals as his main allies against the Party hierarchy—required a much bolder political stroke, and one not without risks, as Gorbachev later discovered.

Intellectuals were natural partisans of reform, far more so than the disgruntled masses. The most progressive of them were well ahead of Gorbachev and his circle in their desire for fundamental changes in the Soviet system. Broadly speaking, the liberal Soviet intelligentsia were united by a common revulsion toward Stalinism and its hallmarks: terror, censorship, the arbitrary *ukaz*—or dictatorship—of the state bureaucracy. More than other segments of Soviet society, they valued individual rights, freedom of expression, the rule of law. And since Khrushchev's demise in 1964, they had been a frustrated, latent political force.

No less a Communist icon than Karl Marx had put his finger on the reason for their disenchantment. "A censored press only serves to demoralize. That greatest of vices, hypocrisy, is inseparable from it," he had written back in 1842. "The government hears only its own voice while all the time deceiving itself, affecting to hear the voice of the people while demanding that they also support the pretense. And on their side, the people either partly succumb to political skepticism or completely turn away from public life and become a crowd of individuals, each living only his own private existence."[3]

Americans have often asked me, "Where were all these Gorbachev liberals before he appeared? Where did they all come from?" The answer is that they were hidden, an army of defectors-in-place. They were smirking at the sallies of poets and playwrights; they were desperately venting their anger to a few trusted friends. In the seventies, I had heard them describe how their fathers were carted away in the night by Stalin's henchmen; I had listened to their disapproval of the invasion of Czechoslovakia, laughed at their brutal lampoons of Brezhnev's slobbering speech. The ideological dry rot, extensive even then, indicated that Soviet society was not the monolith it appeared to be from afar. Among my personal acquaintances in those days, I could count poets, writers, artists, actors, journalists, musicians, scientists, historians, linguists, teachers, and university students. Their disaffection made them a veritable army, awaiting a new political moment, ready to be summoned into battle against the hated apparat.

Vladimir Pozner, the Soviet television commentator, told me a political anecdote that captured this cynicism and frustration. A man goes to a local health clinic and demands to see "the eye-ear doctor." The nurse explains there is no such thing—there is either a doctor who examines your eyes or a doctor who examines your ears and throat, but not one eye-ear doctor. But the patient is insistent. They argue, and finally the nurse says, "Well, there isn't one but if there were one, why would you want to see him?" The man replies, "Because I keep hearing one thing and seeing something very different."

Hypocrisy had bred disillusionment.

Gorbachev had another built-in advantage: The connection in Russia between the world of culture and the world of politics has long been much closer than it is in the United States. Americans generally regard culture as entertainment, a diversion, perhaps even a source of individual development; culture rarely plays a central role in national political life, except perhaps at times of mass protest, such as the Vietnam War. Not so in Russia. Through much of Russian history, culture has been a proxy battleground for politics. Russians have always turned to artists to reveal the truth behind official lies. Poetry and fables have served as Aesopian subterfuges when open political communication was impossible. So important was literature to Czar Nicholas I that he was Pushkin's personal censor; Dostoyevsky was exiled and faced a firing squad before being spared at the last minute by order of the czar. One reason the biting nineteenth-century satires of Nikolai Gogol and Mikhail Saltykov (Shchedrin) have played to enthusiastic modern audiences in Russia is that they mock the same political diktat and pretentious habits of rulers as modern underground balladiers do. Under dictators, life and thought do not cease; art becomes the substitute outlet for politics.

In the Khrushchev thaw of the 1960s, poets such as Andrei Voznesensky, Yevgeny Yevtushenko, and Bella Akhmadulina led the way. A decade later, underground balladiers such as Vladimir Vysotsky, Bulat Ozudzhava, and Aleksandr Galich stirred excitement with their off-color political songs and poetry. But this was esoteric politics, usually played behind closed doors for select audiences, rarely produced on an open stage. It was titillating to the cognoscenti, but it had no wide political impact. In the pre-Gorbachev period, the audience was very limited. The Party held the reins of control so tightly that disaffected Soviet intellectuals lacked any real notion of their strength.

Fear and suspicion kept most people from knowing the true opinions of their neighbors across the hall. Often, in the seventies, I found Russians more willing to talk candidly to me, a foreigner, than to each other, because they knew I would not inform on them to the secret police. My Russian friends taught me never to bring together in private company two Soviets who did not know each other well. In fact, they also taught me not to bring together two who *did know each other*—unless *they* initiated the idea. This was because there were so many informers that they could not afford to trust anyone but blood relatives and a few tested soul mates.

So they had no way of knowing how many millions of other people agreed with them.

In time, I concluded that the most important function of the Soviet press during the 1970s had been to keep these latent dissenters isolated and feeling impotent. Their disillusionment had progressed to the point where most university-educated big-city intellectuals were too cynical to be inspired by the endless outpouring of official ideology in the press, but the suffocating foam of the Party press kept them powerless. They plodded along obediently, out of inertia, fear of economic blacklisting or Siberian exile, and ignorance of their own numbers. The Party line numbed them, choked their voices, denied them the means of communicating with each other and thus of beginning to coalesce as an opposition opinion.

Gorbachev needed ways to activate this inchoate army, to summon the pressure of public opinion to help him break the power of the party apparat. Aleksandr Yakovlev, then the most philosophical and the most radical reformer in the Politburo, encouraged Gorbachev to open up the press and to recruit the intelligentsia as activists for reform.

Glasnost became Gorbachev's strategy for arousing his countrymen to action, but not *glasnost* meaning freedom of speech or freedom of the press, as we know it in the West. Despite Gorbachev's promise in early 1987 of a law guaranteeing the rights of the press, it was more than three years before such a law was passed, on June 12, 1990. It took relentless pressure from liberal reformers in the Supreme Soviet to draft and then push through a progressive piece of legislation lifting censorship and granting the right for individuals to start newspapers—the first law in the nation's history to provide guarantees for journalists. But in a society uneasy with the notion of journalistic freedom and lacking experience in libel law, high officials had trouble giving up the habit of control. Gorbachev himself was not immune. During the 1990 May Day parade, he was angered by catcalls and taunts from marchers; his response was to demand a tough law barring criticism of the Soviet president. Reformers toned it down so that punishment—up to six years in jail—could be imposed only for insulting the Soviet president "in an indecent way." The implication was obscenity, but the wording was so vague that no one could be sure that the new law did not bar political criticism as well.[4]

But even though *glasnost* does not connote the full freedoms that American newspapers and television networks take for granted, it has been a crucial and essential catalyst for Gorbachev's reforms. "*Glasnost* comes from the Russian word *glas,* or voice," to quote Vladimir Pozner. "So it literally means voiceness, or speaking out." And this speaking out, even with its imperfections, has broken down political taboos. It has given legitimacy to pent-up popular grievances, and stimulated that provocatively Western democratic notion called pluralism. It gave all those isolated critics a chance to build political networks. It made possible the watershed election of March 1989, which sent dozens of high regional Party officials into the shock of defeat. Without *glasnost,* the entire range of Gorbachev reforms would not have been possible.

In December 1984, even before he rose to supreme power, Gorbachev had called for *glasnost,* asserting the need for political candor and hinting at his future use of the media as a tool for reform. "Broad, timely, and frank information is testimony to trust in people, respect for their intelligence and feelings, their ability to interpret various events themselves," he told a conference on Communist ideology. "It raises the activeness of the toilers. *Glasnost* in the work of Party and state organs is an effective means of struggling against bureaucratic distortion. . . ."[5] In short, Gorbachev recognized the enormous gap between the dismal realities of Soviet life and the fatuous pretensions of Party propaganda, and recognized that he could not gain credibility until he had closed that gap.

Yet strangely, Gorbachev did not begin as boldly as he had foreshadowed. His reform program has gone through several stages. In the first of these, for most of 1985 and 1986, Gorbachev tried conservative reforms, picking up where his mentor Yuri Andropov had left off. In 1985, he launched a campaign against alcoholism, pushed for work discipline, purged corrupt Brezhnev hacks, and promoted progress in science and technology. In the economy, he began not by dispersing power or breaking up ministries but by creating new superministries and superagencies. In the media and in cultural life, there was a relaxation of controls. He and other political leaders spoke more openly about current problems and past mistakes. But these were very modest beginnings.

On April 26, 1986, a little more than a year after Gorbachev took over, the nuclear accident at Chernobyl showed that when a catastrophe occurred, the reflexive reaction of the Soviet leadership—Gorbachev included—was to hide behind a shroud of secrecy. Even with neighboring countries clamoring for information because of alarming rises in nuclear radiation and satellite photos of the damaged Chernobyl reactor, it was four full days after the reactor explosion before Moscow made a minimal acknowledgment that there had been a nuclear accident. In mid-May, Gorbachev spoke of the dead, but in a defensive, chauvinistic tone, he criticized Western reaction to the incident. It took time for the real story of Chernobyl, and the radiation hazards it released, to dribble out.

Even today, activists and experts in the surrounding areas complain, with good reason, that the Ministry of Health and other government agencies covered up their failures to evacuate people rapidly, and are still sitting on the terrible truth about radiation sickness among tens of thousands of people in the Ukraine and Byelorussia. On October 15, 1989, *Moscow News* ran a major story on the cover-ups at Chernobyl, headlined THE BIG LIE.

If nothing else, the embarrassment of the cover-up helped propel Gorbachev in late 1986 into a full-blown strategy of *glasnost*. In the fall, the Soviet press reported the sinking of a passenger ship on the Black Sea with the loss of some four hundred lives—an unprecedented admission for the Soviet government. In December, Gorbachev dismissed the state overlord of the movie industry, months after an upheaval in the cinematographers' union. Around the time of his October 1986 summit in Iceland with President Reagan, Gorbachev released a dissident poet, Irina Ratushinskaya. There were other partial gestures.

But the real signal of a major change in the works, and of Gorbachev's open political alliance with the intelligentsia against the Party bureaucracy, was his celebrated telephone call on December 16, 1986, to Andrei Sakharov, the dissident Soviet physicist and winner of the Nobel Peace Prize.

Sakharov had been banished to exile and political isolation in the city of Gorky for nearly seven years; KGB agents had grabbed him off a Moscow sidewalk, jammed him into a car, and shipped him out of town without a trial or a hearing. As the most vocal domestic critic of the Brezhnev leadership and, specifically, of Brezhnev's decision to send Soviet troops into Afghanistan, Sakharov was a genuine hero to the Soviet intelligentsia. He was revered as the country's most outspoken exponent of human rights and intellectual freedom. He spoke with such courage and integrity that even as a solitary individual, he was a moral force to be reckoned with.

Gorbachev's decision to lift the ban on Sakharov, his invitation to the physicist "to return to work for the public good" as a willing partner in *perestroika,* was a crucial symbolic gesture. In the West, this move was immediately seen as a sign of Gorbachev's liberalism. But it was more than that. It provided the Soviet leader with a bridge to the liberal, reformist wing of the intelligentsia and signaled a new phase in his move toward democratic reforms. The changes Gorbachev wrought in the political institutions of his country reached a crescendo in 1989 and 1990; but the ground was prepared by Sakharov's release and the acceleration of *glasnost* that took place in the winter of 1986–87.

CHAPTER 7
TROUBADOURS OF TRUTH

FIRST DOG: How are things
different under Gorbachev?

SECOND DOG: Well, the chain is
still too short and the food
dish is still too far away to reach,
but they let you bark as loud
as you want.

—Soviet political anecdote

"It's more exciting right now
to read than to live."[1]
—Tankred Golenpolsky
State Publishing Committee
June 1988

When Gorbachev broke the dam with *glasnost,* he caused a deluge.

Suddenly, criticizing the Soviet past, the Soviet present, even the Soviet leadership, was not only tolerated, it was encouraged—in the press, books, theater, and films, and on television.

The press switched from being Party cheerleader to being Party watchdog. It was like a coiled spring suddenly released.

Especially from 1987 onward, newspapers and magazines blossomed forth with exposés about crime, prostitution, and high-level corruption.

The weekly magazine *Ogonek* ran confessions by former KGB investigators and prison guards. In the Party's theoretical journal, *Kommunist,* a senior KGB official conceded that political abuses of power had been caused in part by excessive secrecy. In mid-1989, the government admitted, after more than thirty years of denial, that the world's worst nuclear accident, an explosion of waste from the production of plutonium, had taken place in 1957 in the remote Ural Mountains, two thousand miles east of Moscow. The main military newspaper, *Krasnaya Zvezda,* revealed that in 1953, the Soviets had tested atomic bombs near some of their own military units, to check the psychological effects on combat troops.

Instead of promulgating false hosannas to Party leaders, television, too, began to carry candid political debates, live man-in-the-street interviews about such topics as housing conditions and whether to continue the military draft; they broadcast films of the Stalin show trials of the 1930s.

A number of movies long blocked by censors were released, among them *Scarecrow,* an allegory about Stalinist-style group persecution of an innocent schoolgirl by her classmates; *Rasputin,* a movie that depicted Czar Nicholas II not as a cardboard villain but as a well-meaning yet emotionally troubled and weak-willed man; *Commissar,* a sympathetic view of Jewish humanism and suffering, bottled up for twenty years; *Confession,* a chronicle of the bleak life of a Soviet drug addict; and *Is It Easy to Be Young?*, a documentary about Baltic youth who go on a rampage and the squalor of their lives.[2]

Books long banned by censors, such as George Orwell's *1984* and Boris Pasternak's *Doctor Zhivago,* started appearing in print.

In 1989, the literary event of the year was the serialization of *The Gulag Archipelago,* Aleksandr Solzhenitsyn's devastating record of prison-camp repression and cruelty, from Lenin and Stalin to Brezhnev. It took Sergei Zalygin, chief editor of the magazine *Novy Mir,* more than a year of relentless pressure to persuade the Politburo that under *glasnost,* the Soviet Union's most famous living author could not be ignored.

As recently as late 1988, Vadim Medvedev, then the Politburo's czar of press and culture, had declared that Solzhenitsyn would not be published. Many ranking Communist Party officials thoroughly detested Solzhenitsyn for his self-righteous defiance of the Kremlin from his exile in Vermont, as well as for his openly anti-Communist, monarchist views.

Of all Solzhenitsyn's works, *Gulag,* which explicitly blamed Lenin for the evil violence of Soviet dictatorship, was the hardest for Party leaders to swallow. In the early 1970s, mere possession of a few typescript pages of the book was enough to risk one's being sent to Siberia. Back in February 1974, Solzhenitsyn had released to me one then-unpublished portion, for an article, and he was arrested the next day and ejected from the country. But in the late 1980s, Solzhenitsyn was insisting that *Gulag* be the first of his banned works to be published in the U.S.S.R. and rebuffing suggestions that his novels *Cancer Ward* or *The First Circle* be published first, to break the ice. The argument raged on for months.

Ultimately, a Party official confirmed, it took Gorbachev's personal intervention for *Novy Mir* to begin publication of *Gulag.* And Party conservatives retaliated by holding up the magazine's paper supply in the spring of 1990, blocking publication of the March, April, and May issues.[3]

Other books hidden away by Soviet authors came off the shelves. In the dark years of heavy censorship, the most liberal novelists had written "for the drawer," as Soviets say, producing books they knew would never see the light of day and stashing them away in desk drawers. *Glasnost* brought them out into the daylight. One of the first was Anatoly Rybakov's novel about life during the Stalinist purges, *Children of the Arbat,* which the author kept in the drawer for twenty years. Even more politically shocking was the scathing portrait of Lenin, the most sacred icon in the Communist pantheon, in Vasily Grossman's *Forever Flowing,* written in 1963. In language previously unthinkable in Soviet literature, Grossman harshly portrayed Lenin's fanatic drive for power, his "intolerance . . . his contempt for freedom, his cruelty toward those who held different opinions and his capacity to wipe off the face of the earth, without trembling, not only fortresses but entire countries, districts and provinces that questioned his orthodox truth."[4] Just printing Grossman's short novel, starting with the November 1989 issue of the magazine *Oktyabr,* nearly cost chief editor Anatoly Anayev his job. Hard-liners went after his scalp, but he survived.

FRONT-LINE DISPATCHES FROM AFGHANISTAN

The liberal faction of the press was using Gorbachev's *glasnost* for an open assault on current policy—specifically, Soviet intervention in the Afghan war.

During a television roundtable in mid-June 1988, Fyodor Burlatsky, a former speech writer for Khrushchev, asserted that the Soviet intervention in Afghanistan had been a mistake. *Izvestia* columnist Aleksandr Bovin added that sending one hundred thousand troops into Afghanistan was typical of the excessive use of force in Soviet foreign policy.

Several months later, the weekly *Ogonek* ran an interview with General Valentin I. Varrenikov, for four years the Soviet commander in Kabul, who disclosed that the Soviet General Staff "did not support the idea of sending our troops into Afghanistan" until it was overruled by the Brezhnev Politburo.

This interview with General Varrenikov was the work of Artyom Borovik, one of the new breed of reporters, a jaunty twenty-eight-year-old who is impatient with the old-style Soviet propaganda-journalism formerly practiced by his father, Genrikh Borovik, and who even chafes at the limits of *glasnost.* In July 1987, Borovik had caused a sensation by filing the first honest, graphic dispatches from the front. He described how the flower of Soviet youth was dying, their boots oozing with blood, their stomachs pierced by bullet holes, their armored vehicles crumpled by land mines. "War tears the halo of secrecy away from death," Borovik wrote in his "Diary of a Reporter."

For the first time, the readers of *Ogonek* could see the war from the inside; they could sit in the foxholes, feel the fear and loneliness of Soviet troops dying far away from home. Borovik wrote about the cold terror of a night ambush, the gunfire, and the darkened sky lit up by tracers. He quoted from the diary of a dead helicopter pilot, who described how his flight suit had smelled for two days of charred flesh, from the corpses of three comrades he had recovered from the burned ruins of their downed helicopter.[5]

To get his unprecedented dispatches past the military censors, Borovik had hooked General Varrenikov himself into helping him.

Borovik told me that when the censors had balked at the pieces he had written, he had phoned the general and said: " 'Listen, I've written a big, big documentary and these guys in censorship won't let it go because they think you guys are, you know, staging a ballet in Afghanistan, raising flowers and nothing else. They don't want to show real life.'

"The general got angry," Borovik recalled, "because guys die there, they're risking their lives, and the press writes ridiculous things. So he helped me. He didn't read the articles. He just phoned them and said, 'Let Borovik publish what he saw, you know, the truth of what he saw.' Probably he wouldn't have made this call if I'd shown him the articles. But this is how I got the visa—we call it a visa—of approval from the military."[6]

Borovik's editor, Vitaly Korotich, told me that the whole project had even higher-level political approval—from Gorbachev himself.

"I have a hot-line phone—Gorbachev gave me this phone." Korotich is a chain-smoker whose flat, pudgy face looks as beaten as a prizefighter's but whose soft brown eyes betray his vulnerability. "I can call anyone on this phone," he bragged. "So I called Akhromeyev, chief of the General

Staff. I told him, 'I want to do a story on our boys in Afghanistan, a real story.' He said, 'Screw you and your journalists. They always want to make a story without taking any risks.' I told him, 'No, I want my boy to be in the front line with your boys.' He said, 'And if he gets killed, they'll all get angry at the army.' But I pushed him, and for the first time Akhromeyev gave me permission to send a reporter to the front. If he did not, he knew I would print that he refused. I understood that I must publish something about the end of this war to prepare the public. You see, it was already understood that the war must be finished."[7]

In short, he explained, Gorbachev, who had publicly lamented that the war in Afghanistan was "a bleeding wound," was using *glasnost* and specifically Korotich to prepare public opinion for the withdrawal of Soviet troops. The stream of articles on Afghanistan, just like articles criticizing Stalin, the Red Terror, and official secrecy, all suited Gorbachev's policy.

This interplay between the press and public opinion was a deliberate part of Gorbachev's new strategy of overturning old institutions as well as old policies. He was manipulating the press just as surely as American presidents do—but in ways that Soviets were unaccustomed to.

This pressure on public opinion continued for several years, turning the troop withdrawal from a political blow to Gorbachev into a public-relations triumph. In May 1988, Tass, the official Soviet news agency, revealed for the first time official Soviet casualty figures in Afghanistan—13,310 killed in action, 35,478 wounded, and 311 missing in action. To see such figures printed in the Soviet press, which in the seventies could not even reveal the number of traffic deaths in Moscow, was almost unbelievable—not only for me, but for Russians as well. Each new press revelation set people abuzz. Back in the seventies, people used to buy official newspapers to use as toilet paper; they were cheap, only three cents apiece. Now people were lining up to read the latest editions, displayed on billboards and walls, because there was so much news.

When I arrived in May 1988, I found it difficult to reach people by phone; friends told me it was because they were all so busy calling each other with the latest disclosures. One acquaintance, Tankred Golenpolsky of the State Publishing Committee, said exuberantly: "It's more exciting right now to read than to live! The oxygen of democracy is intoxicating and contagious."

There was a joke making the rounds those days about the newspaper *Moscow News (Moskovskiye Novosti)*, which had gone from a pap and propaganda sheet for tourists to one of the hottest newspapers of *glasnost*, full of juicy items and hard to find before it sold out. In the anecdote, one Muscovite calls a friend to ask if he has managed to buy the latest issue.

"Yes, I got it," answers the friend, with a certain pride.

"What's in it?" the first man inquires.

The second man pauses, obviously thinking things over, and then replies: "Can't talk about it on the telephone."

Russians love that story because it is so rich with irony about their old fear of saying anything controversial or revealing on the telephone, for fear of listening devices. They were amused that those same old habits lingered on in the new era, even though the press was printing things they had previously not dared to mention on the phone.

The public hunger for news had generated a genuine competition among the press for readers. The hot new liberal publications that were pushing the limits of *glasnost* gained readers, while the circulation of orthodox, Party-line outlets fell. From 1985 to 1989, *Izvestia*'s circulation nearly doubled from 5.7 to 10.1 million, while *Pravda*'s stayed steady at about 9.6 million, and was always slow to sell at newsstands. *Komsomolskaya Pravda*, which went after younger readers with a liberal slant on the news, jumped from 12.8 to 17.5 million; the radical weekly magazine *Ogonek* shot up from 596,000 subscribers to more than 3 million; and the weekly *Argumenty i Fakty* skyrocketed from 1.4 to 20.4 million within four years. At the same time, the army newspaper, *Krasnaya Zvezda (Red Star)* drifted down from 1.6 to 1.4 million. People shunned the propaganda peddlers; they were drawn to real news.[8]

All of this was a remarkable change; fifteen years earlier it had taken a microscopic search to find and decipher nuggets of interest in the Soviet press; *Pravda* and *Izvestia* had left intellectuals numbed with boredom. I was stunned now to read about thousands of people marching in the streets of Tomsk, Omsk, and Irkutsk, defying Party leaders deep in the Soviet heartland, and to see pictures as well. In the seventies, protests never were written about in the Soviet press. Now *Izvestia*, the government paper, was reporting that in Sakhalin, on the Pacific coast, popular protests had become so strong that a regional Party boss had been forced to resign. The news described hundreds of thousands of people demonstrating in the capitals of Armenia and Azerbaijan, where violence had broken out over control of the mountainous region of Nagorno-Karabakh, an Armenian enclave turned over to Azerbaijan by Stalin. Party leaders in both republics had been fired. The Baltic republics were also exploding with unrest—"the singing revolution" in Estonia, the stunning rise of the national front Sajudis in Lithuania.

In Moscow, it was reported that the Supreme Soviet, for seven decades one of the most supine legislative bodies in the world, had taken the unprecedented step of refusing to rubber-stamp a law proposed by the government. A handful of delegates had the temerity to protest that the 90 percent tax rate proposed by ministry bureaucrats for economic cooperatives was strangling the new private sector. The government, evidently surprised by the opposition, backed off and promised to rewrite the law.

Reading *Pravda* one morning at breakfast, I laughed out loud at the impertinence of one letter to the editor. Gorbachev had been lecturing Communist Party officials to stop interfering in the day-to-day operation of the economy and government. Now one reader suggested that Gorbachev (who was not mentioned by name) follow his own advice and that the Politburo, holy of holies, pinnacle of Soviet power, stop poking its nose into other people's business.

More sweeping in its implications was the sudden announcement that all across the country, history examinations for high school seniors were being canceled because the old textbooks were so full of lies about Stalin, Brezhnev, and the Soviet past.

Russians were suddenly catching up with their own history, and learning what we in the West had known for decades. It was a time warp; the papers were bringing out daily disclosures about Stalin's tyranny and the Red Terror, debating how many millions had perished, urging the rehabilitation of Stalin's old rival Nikolai Bukharin, an advocate of a mixed economy.

Television, too, carried scenes never shown before to a mass Soviet audience. The talk of Moscow was a documentary called *Protsess (Trial)* that included segments of Stalin's show trials, depicting the insanity of the Stalinist purges of the 1930s. There on the screen was prosecutor Andrei Vishinsky, looking like a speeded-up Charlie Chaplin figure, sending old Bolsheviks to certain death based on trumped-up charges or on confessions extracted by torture. There, suddenly, mingling with Lenin and the others, were Trotsky and Bukharin, one murdered by Stalin, the other purged, and both nonpersons for sixty years now. The new *glasnost* television had people glued to their sets.

More bombshells exploded in leading literary magazines. A small group of intellectuals were pushing the limits of *glasnost* beyond officially encouraged attacks on Stalin, questioning the very legitimacy of Soviet Communism by tracing the roots of Stalinist tyranny back to Lenin and Marx. In the May 1988 issue of *Novy Mir,* an economic writer named Vasily Selyunin was the first to implicate Lenin for justifying the systematic use of state terror. "First, it was used to suppress opponents of the

Revolution, then it shifted to potential opponents, and finally it became a means of solving purely economic tasks," Selyunin wrote.[9] In a daring bit of ideological heresy, Selyunin suggested that Stalin's despotism was not accidental, but virtually inevitable under the Soviet system. Any system that concentrates all power in a single party and where the state owns all means of production, he argued, has a tendency to produce despots.

This seditious logic was carried another step by Aleksandr Tsipko, a philosopher and former Central Committee staff official, who suggested that Marxist theory was the root cause of Stalinism. "Stalin didn't just create his kingdom and strengthen his own one-man rule," Tsipko wrote in a scholarly journal. "He built socialism in accordance with prescriptive theories." Pointing his finger at Marx, Tsipko asserted, "When cracks appear in the walls of a new building," it is time to reexamine the foundations and the architecture. "We must doubtless begin . . . at the beginning, with the word, the blueprint, with our theoretical principles."[10]

GLASNOST OF THE STREETS

Even on the streets of Moscow, I could feel the ferment of *glasnost.* Pushkin Square, right outside the offices of *Moscow News,* had become the Soviet equivalent of London's Hyde Park. In the 1970s, a handful of dissidents used to gather there on Human Rights Day, December 5, but back then there were usually more foreign correspondents than dissidents—and both groups were outnumbered by plainclothes police agents. A dissident speaker would begin to read a statement, his colleagues would unfurl a banner, and usually before the banner was completely unfolded, KGB agents would have grabbed the demonstrators and hustled them off to jail.

But in 1988, the sidewalks in the square were jammed with people: They were reading the latest editions of *Moscow News,* buying and selling all sorts of unofficial—and previously underground—newspapers. Occasionally, the Old Guard still showed its muscle; the militia would swoop in to make some arrests. But this no longer seemed to intimidate the dissidents, or the crowd of people debating every conceivable issue—from how to fix the economy to the right of minority republics to secede from the Soviet Union.

Elsewhere in the city, the atmosphere on the streets was palpably more relaxed. On the strolling mall of the Old Arbat, crowds flocked around young groups with guitars, singing songs that mocked the political elite, the Afghan war, or the love affair Westerners were having with Gorbachev. "Perestroika, perestroika," sang Nikita Dzhigurda, a husky-throated youth. *"Our new GenSek [Party Leader], powerful or not, goes from one unfinished stroika [construction site] to another. The dumbfounded foreigners are naïve about him, my brothers. The foreign serenaders sing and toast to Russia."*

What struck even deeper resonance was an old favorite, an illicit song from the seventies by the late writer Aleksandr Galich, but always sung clandestinely back then. Now here it was out on the streets, this song about the life of the elite in their luxurious country *dachas* outside Moscow:

> *Grass is green there*
> *And Stalin's eagles*
> *Eat shish kebab and fine chocolates*
> *Behind seven fences.*
> *Bodyguards and informants*
> *Protect them from the people.*
> *They make us watch films*
> *About factories and collective farms*
> *And at night, they watch imported films about whores,*
> *And they like Marilyn Monroe.*

The bitter truth of that song got a laugh—and a grimace—from the crowd.

In the hotels, I found that both foreigners and Soviets had become less suspicious of each other. In the old days, we always assumed that the "key ladies" on each floor of Soviet hotels, who insisted on holding our keys whenever we left our rooms, kept a close eye on us and opened our rooms to allow the KGB to search whenever we were out. On walks, we would look over our shoulders to see if people were following us. At the National Hotel one day, my colleague Louis Menashe was talking with the maid about what differences she noticed now. "Oh, the Americans are much less nervous now," she said. "They are not looking over their shoulders all the time." Nor were the key ladies any longer demanding our keys.

Strolling in the wild, wooded meadows of Izmailovo Park, I noticed other changes. Not long after I had left Moscow at the end of 1974, underground artists had tried to hold an exhibition of forbidden paintings in the park; the KGB had used bulldozers to break it up. Now the park was a giant flea market, its pathways jammed with once-forbidden items—easel after easel of abstract and irreverent paintings, religious icons, old czarist medals and emblems, miniature statues of Christ on the cross, of Gorbachev as the Statue of Liberty. There were political buttons poking fun at the KGB, at Yegor Ligachev—then the Politburo's number two figure—at Raisa Gorbacheva, at Gorbachev's reforms (*Perestroika:* 2 + 2 = 5), playing on an old line of Dostoyevsky's, mocking the dreamy Russian notion that the world is what you want it to be. Favored items, at 25 rubles (officially $42), were rubber masks lampooning the faces of Brezhnev and other former Soviet leaders. Foster Wiley, one of the cameramen for our television series, caught a mask maker peeling off a series of masks—Brezhnev, Khrushchev, and Stalin, each with a punch line mocking Stalin's contempt for the people: BROTHERS AND SISTERS, GO TO HELL!

I found that, as always, Muscovites told wry jokes about their predicament; in fact, their lives had not improved under Gorbachev, even though they now were freer to speak out about it. One old political joke, revived with a new twist, was about a Soviet dog, back from a long trip. The dog asks an older, wiser mutt how life is different under Gorbachev.

"Well," says the old-timer, "the chain is still too short and the food dish is still too far away to reach, but they let you bark as loud as you want."

Even out in the provinces, different regions had their own symbols of *glasnost.* One of my favorites, pointed out to me by Pavel Nikitin, a newspaper correspondent in Yaroslavl, concerned the bells of the ancient city of Rostov, a rich musical chorus that ranged in size from modest to massive and required a team of ringers.

Bells have great symbolic importance in Russian history. As Greg Guroff, a friend and Russian historian, observed, historically bells have been used to summon Russians—to worship in their churches, to gather in town meetings, or to defend their cities against fire, or invaders. The famous Russian émigré writer Aleksandr Herzen named his nineteenth-century democratic newspaper *The Bell.* In the 1930s, Stalin ordered that thousands of churches all over the Soviet Union be closed, and their bells destroyed or their clangers removed. Among those silenced were the famous bells of Rostov.

In silencing those bells, Stalin was metaphorically silencing the people of Russia.

Not until Gorbachev's clarion call of *glasnost* did the bells of Rostov ring out freely once again.

Pavel Nikitin smiled as he remembered the ringing of the bells of Rostov in 1987—for the first time in more than half a century. "That," he told me, "is the sound of *glasnost.*"

THE PIED PIPERS OF THE CINEMA

If the primary vehicle of Gorbachev's drive to awaken his people was the mass media, movies and television were in the forefront.

During Khrushchev's cultural thaw, plays or novels such as Solzhenitsyn's *One Day in the Life of Ivan Denisovich* were the primary signs of new freedom. Young poets, especially Yevtushenko and Voznesensky, were the pied pipers of intellectual excitement, their poetry readings at times bringing out five or ten thousand people, filling soccer stadiums. But in the 1980s, Gorbachev had to reach audiences in the *millions* to create the kind of wide popular upheaval he needed.

Moreover, in terms of the media's power and influence, life inside the Soviet Union was becoming more like the rest of the world. The tube and the screen had the biggest impact; movies could draw audiences of eighty million, national television 150 million. Gorbachev needed to tap into that power.

If there was one movie that changed the climate and the popular political mind, it was *Repentance,* a powerful surrealist allegory of Stalinist terror and the cult of Stalin, produced in Soviet Georgia by Tengiz Abuladze. Its appearance in late 1986 caused a political earthquake. *Repentance* became the cinematic flagship of *glasnost.*

Tens of millions of people flocked to see the film. They broke into applause at the parody dictator who looks fat (Mussolini) and has a brush mustache (Hitler), but is modeled on Stalin and his last secret-police chief, Lavrenti Beria. They wept at the terror. Gorbachev himself, I heard, had cried on seeing the film, perhaps remembering his own grandfather's arrest.

One poignant scene portrayed the pitiful efforts of families hunting for scraps of news about loved ones sent off to Stalin's forced-labor camps. In the movie, a mother and daughter scramble frantically among logs that have floated downriver from the gulag. Prisoners have carved their initials on the logs, and these two women search frantically for some sign that their husband and father is still alive; but they search in vain.

The making of *Repentance* is revealing about Soviet cultural politics at the dawn of the Gorbachev era. The film had been written in the early 1980s, and was produced by 1984—a year *before* Gorbachev came to power. It had the political blessing of Gorbachev's close friend Eduard Shevardnadze, who was Georgia's Communist Party leader until Gorbachev appointed him foreign minister.

Shevardnadze told me that in 1982, while Brezhnev was still alive, Moscow censors had rejected the script as unacceptable for nationwide production and distribution in the Russian language. But Shevardnadze, who read the script himself three times, decided to permit the film to go into production in the Georgian language and for Georgian television—a domain under his control.[11] At least, he indicated, that was the pretext under which the film was permitted. Production took place while Andropov was in power, and things were starting to open up a bit. But by 1984, when production was completed, Andropov had died, and the winds from the Kremlin had turned chillier. As a result, *Repentance* was not released after its completion; in fact, it wasn't until eighteen months after Gorbachev came to power that the movie was finally shown in Georgia, and distributed, with Russian voice-overs, across the nation.

Another body blow to the old taboos was dealt by *Little Vera*, a box-office sensation that included nude scenes and explicit sex. Its twenty-eight-year-old director, Vasily Pichul, has a dark, gypsy-like face and a *dolce vita* air. I thought at first that he seemed like one of the petulant young offspring of the Soviet elite, derisively nicknamed the "golden youth" by others. But it turned out that Pichul was the son of a blue-collar worker from Mariupol, an industrial wasteland far from Moscow and more desolate and depressing than the South Side of Chicago. The real power of *Little Vera*, released in the West after it was seen by more than forty million Soviets, is its candid portrayal of the caldron of frustration and rage among Soviet workers. The father in the movie family is driven to uncontrollable drinking bouts and domestic violence, and the daughter, Little Vera, sleeps around and lives such a morally bankrupt, aimless existence that she winds up taking an overdose of pills.

Pichul's wife, María, whose Spanish ancestors came to Moscow after the Spanish Civil War, wrote the screenplay as a biting indictment of the misery to which the "heroic proletariat" was consigned by the Soviet leadership. When Pichul went home for the premiere, he was expecting a hero's welcome: He had shattered the hypocritical pretenses, promulgated by Soviet propaganda, that Mariupol was a model city; he had presented the unvarnished truth on behalf of the workers in his hometown. But he found instead that his parents and other workers were furious, resentful at what they took to be an exposé of the tawdry emptiness of their lives.

"My parents were insulted!" Pichul told me. "My mother said, 'You have insulted us. You have put our family's whole life up on the screen in front of the whole Soviet Union.' When my parents walked down the street, people pointed at them. One woman pointed at my mother and said, 'Is your family life really such a nightmare? Is your daughter so awful?' My mother couldn't handle it."[12]

I later learned that this reaction was typical of the response that Gorbachev's reforms produced among many people, especially blue-collar workers. In theory, these people were demanding change—they were fed up with the degrading misery of their lives, or they were infuriated with having to work for dictatorial bosses in inefficient factories. But when someone came along and offered them a chance to go out and work on their own, or exposed their misery in order to reform it, they recoiled, denouncing those who spoke the truth. They recoiled from change, preferring the old, familiar hell.

"Of course, this film is *not* about my own family," Pichul said, and it sounded as if he'd repeated this hundreds of times to his relatives and friends. "But I know this life. I am not a stranger from America, or a man from Mars. I have put in this movie what I have seen with my own eyes, and reflected about. Everybody knows this life; they recognize it in my film. Some people just don't like to *see* it up there on the screen. But *Little Vera* is very popular. Millions and millions go to see it. So you see, most people are sick of lies and half-truths."

Little Vera represented an important breakthrough for both artistic freedom and economic reform, and it was powerful because it was so close to real life. For in the unending trench warfare that Gorbachev's policies have triggered between radical advocates of change and Old Guard hardliners, documentaries have generally become more effective weapons than feature films. Once Gorbachev brought the political battle out in the open, fact had more persuasive force than fiction—especially after so many decades of censorship. The mere admission of reality had shock effect; it changed the nature of public dialogue.

In terms of the Afghan war, for example, the most powerful stories, aside from Artyom Borovik's front-line dispatches, were moving documentaries such as *Pain* and *Homecoming*. One portrayed the palpable grief of parents who had lost their sons; the other showed legless and armless veterans being helped off troop transports, and then later living as civilians, enraged by their country's indifference and ingratitude for their sacrifice in a distant and ugly war. The harsh atrocities of the gulag were dramatically brought home by documentaries such as *Greater Light* and *Solovetsky Power*. These films were pieced together from archives and from the bitter remembrances of onetime true believers, still incredulous and pained by having been unjustly jailed and by having seen so many comrades go to their deaths.

Documentaries became powerful weapons, too, in shaping reactions to current events. Reformers used them to expose the repressive instincts of Party hard-liners seeking to stem the tide of change.

When Soviet troops used poison gas and pick shovels to crush a peaceful demonstration in Tbilisi, Georgia, in April 1989, killing at least sixteen people, Georgian filmmakers put together footage of the brutality and made the army's excessive use of force a national cause célèbre. Eldar Shingalaya, head of the Georgian Filmmakers' Union, showed the documentary to Western correspondents and to deputies in the Congress of People's Deputies, creating a political storm and bringing about an investigation.

When Gorbachev sent massive forces to occupy the city of Baku in Azerbaijan in January 1990, killing more than one hundred civilians, the Azerbaijanis made their case against the Kremlin with gruesome films of the fighting and the dead.

In both these cases, films that were at first circulated privately became part of the national political debate. When the national press was giving skimpy or slanted coverage of events in the minority republics and Soviet authorities were denying that they used excessive violence, the films undercut their credibility and exposed the truth.

One filmmaker who has seized on the opening of *glasnost* to produce several politically potent, journalistic-style documentaries is Arkady Ruderman. Before Gorbachev, the richly bearded, forty-two-year-old Byelorussian was a quiet-spoken, laconic, rather conventional director at the Byelorussian studios; he had never attracted attention for political daring, nor was he known as a fighter by nature. But since 1987, Ruderman has come out with three striking films. One, developed from footage and interviews, told the real story of the Soviet invasion of Czechoslovakia, months before the Kremlin was prepared to admit that the incursion had been a brutal suppression of Prague's experiment in democracy. Eventually the official line embraced that view, and the Ruderman film has now played successfully in official Soviet theaters.

But the fate of two other Ruderman films has been more problematic.

One film concerned the violent suppression of a peaceful demonstration in Minsk by hard-line Byelorussian authorities. In October 1988, police were sent out with billy clubs to break up a peaceful rally calling for a memorial to local victims of Stalinist mass killings. At considerable risk, three local cameramen shot pictures, on amateur video cameras, of the police brutality, and Ruderman put their material together, along with sequences of a court battle over charges and countercharges about Stalin's actions and role in history. That documentary was called *Counter-Suit*.

Ruderman's second film, *Theater in the Time of* Glasnost *and* Perestroika, also made the case that neo-Stalinists were still running Byelorussia, describing the repression of the works and life story of the artist Marc Chagall, a native Byelorussian. The film detailed how authorities had blocked an exhibit of Chagall's paintings and fired an editor of the Byelorussian encyclopedia because she approved a favorable article about the painter. According to Ruderman, a top Communist Party official in Minsk claimed that Chagall was part of a "subversive intrigue," and the encyclopedia wound up printing a tendentious attack on Chagall.

I was interested not only by what Ruderman was reporting and his difficulties in trying to get the films shown, but also by what his experience illustrates about the difficulties of carrying out Gorbachev's policies at the local level. I was told in Moscow and Minsk that both films offended Byelorussian authorities, and that they were blocked by censors there. Even under *glasnost*, this was enough to keep the films from being circulated to regular movie houses through the state-run distribution system. But Ruderman got some help from powerful reformists at the national level.

Even in 1988, Byelorussian film studios, obviously under political pressure, had refused to do technical work on Ruderman's films, so he had shifted to a more sympathetic studio in Leningrad; he managed this with the help of a famous, well-established filmmaker, Aleksei Gherman, whose own film of life in Stalinist times, *My Friend, Ivan Lapshin*, was kept under wraps from 1971 to 1987, when it was finally shown. Andrei Smirnov, then leader of the national Cinematographers' Union, told me that he had personally taken Ruderman's film about the Chagall episode and shown it at a Soviet film festival in Sverdlovsk, where it caused a great stir. Smirnov also helped Ruderman enter *Counter-Suit*, the other film, in the 1989 Leningrad film festival, where it won a prize, although it had still not been officially released by the censors.[13]

Ruderman also became his own distributor, like other documentary filmmakers I met around the country. When censors stop them, they become traveling minstrels of the cinema, troubadours of truth going from city to city, republic to republic, with their contraband films hidden in their luggage. They show the films to film clubs, reformist groups, or sympathetic political activists—small but usually enthusiastic and influential audiences. This is done primarily for exposure, not profit. Sherry Jones, one producer of our American documentary series *Inside Gorbachev's USSR*, found Ruderman showing his movie *Counter-Suit* to an unofficial film club in Yaroslavl, a city north of Moscow, and about six hundred miles from Minsk. These people had seen no press coverage of the events Ruderman portrayed, and they were fascinated both by the news of the Byelorussian demonstration and its suppression and by the ways in which Ruderman had managed to gather his material. He described to them how the three cameramen had taken pictures, trying to keep their amateur cameras hidden from the police. He said the boldest of the three had been spotted by the police and arrested—and he had managed to keep his camera operating all the while, so that he filmed his own arrest. The police took away his cassette, but then, inexplicably, gave it back to him without destroying the film.

Ruderman also entertained the film club with a story of how he had outwitted the censors. When he had submitted *Counter-Suit* to the Leningrad film festival, he had left in a segment where the poet Yevgeny Yevtushenko was moving his lips but saying nothing, because the censor, a woman whose face had turned white at Yevtushenko's words, had banned that one piece of script. Instead of removing the picture, Ruderman had just cut out the words. Journalists covering the film festival had asked about the missing words, anticipating some stunning disclosure, but Ruderman told them Yevtushenko was only talking about a famous Russian writer whose name begins with *S*. He knew everyone would immediately realize that he meant Aleksandr Solzhenitsyn. Typical of the confused situation in the Soviet Union today, approval had been given for Solzhenitsyn to be published in Moscow, while censors in Leningrad were still excising the mere mention of his name!

Even stranger was the fact that press coverage of the episode won Ruderman an appointment at the office of *glavlit*, the chief censor of Leningrad, where he could argue for release of his film.

"The head censor turned out to be the most pleasant and well-mannered person," Ruderman told the film club. "He told me that my profession was an absolutely wonderful profession, but these journalists are scoundrels: They care only about hot facts and sensational news; they are always hired to attack the censors!"

Ruderman went on to describe their dialogue:

"He looked at the piece in the script and said, 'I don't see anything special about it.'

"I said, 'I don't see anything special about it either.'

"He said, 'It was a mistake. I'll give an order. Don't worry. Everything will be all right.'

"I said that I would work on the film and that I thought this scene was a bit too long and that I would make it shorter.

"Then he said, 'Yes, I think the film is much too long. Why don't you cut it here, here, and here.' "[14]

The audience roared with laughter, because they could see from the version Ruderman had just shown them that he had not cut it at all—and that Yevtushenko was heard to utter the forbidden name, Solzhenitsyn.

"I think that the Soviet Union is now an interesting place for documentary filmmakers because everything is moving, everything is bubbling," Ruderman remarked later. "People are turned on to politics because they finally realize that politics is not an abstract understanding of something far from their personal lives. All of a sudden we understand that politics is our life, that politics decides how we are going to live."[15]

As Ruderman explained it, *glasnost* had given his documentary filmmaking a new purpose—to present object lessons to people. It was his view that if his film on the 1968 Soviet invasion of Czechoslovakia had appeared in the early 1970s, it might have prevented the Soviet invasion of Afghanistan in 1979. And, had his film on the brutal suppression of the demonstration in Minsk in October 1988 gone on television right away, it might have prevented the bloody events of Tbilisi in April 1989. Ruderman now saw himself not only as a filmmaker but as an active participant in politics—and in the formation of public opinion.

A CLASSROOM IN DEMOCRACY

Gorbachev, of course, was the prime exponent of using the media to give object lessons in the new politics. Among his most sensational object lessons for the Soviet people were the nationally televised sessions of the most remarkable Communist Party meeting in seven decades—the Nineteenth All-Union Conference of the Communist Party of the Soviet Union, a truly open debate about the country's future.

For the first time since the Bolshevik Revolution in 1917, the nation was getting from Gorbachev the chance for mass participation in politics—both in the election of delegates to that conference and in its debates. The conservative Party apparat blocked many reformers from becoming delegates, but enough made it into the conference to cause confrontations entirely new to a public session of the Communist Party.

The conference lasted four solid days and became, for the Soviet people, an astonishing classroom in democracy. Occurring relatively early in Gorbachev's sequence of major political reforms (June 1988), it set the stage for the country's first contested elections in March 1989 and the beginnings of a real parliamentary system in the summer of 1989.

Gorbachev called the conference to win a mandate for political reforms, and he got from it formal backing for a two-term limit for government executives and Communist Party leaders; separation between the work of the Party apparatus and the government; mandatory retirement age of seventy for the Party's Old Guard; elections with multiple candidates.

In the West, a two-term limit for political office-holders might seem natural enough, but it was unprecedented in Russia, where for centuries czars and dictators either died in office or were removed by a coup d'état.

In addition, the concept of multicandidate elections was a crucial breakthrough toward democracy.

But beyond these steps, the major achievement of the conference may have been its impact on the public, thanks to television. People were riveted to their sets, incredulous at what they were seeing. They drank in the spectacle of their leaders' meeting in the open and engaging in fractious debate and disagreement. They had never seen this process in their lifetimes, and that they should do so was central to the entire thrust of what Gorbachev was trying to achieve.

Even before the conference convened, people were consumed with preliminary skirmishes over reform. Gorbachev's proposals were not enough to satisfy popular demands, and the press was bursting with more radical proposals that, under previous Soviet rulers, would have earned their authors a long term in frozen Siberia: abolish the Stalinist system of internal Soviet passports; control the KGB with legislative watchdogs; publish the Communist Party's secret budget; have the prime minister do a regular radio call-in show; eliminate the privileges of the Party elite, the *nomenklatura,* hand-picked, self-appointed, and self-perpetuating inner core of the Party at all levels; allow new political organizations to compete with the Party.

"Last January, I would not have dreamed that this May such things would be happening, that change would be taking place so fast," Genrikh Borovik, a longtime Soviet press commentator, remarked to me.

The conference was full of shockers, a political circus. It was like a massive, freewheeling town meeting, a laboratory for Gorbachev's new politics. Philip Taubman, then *New York Times* Moscow bureau chief, described the atmosphere as a cross between a revivalist gathering, a graduate-school seminar in politics, and a national catharsis.[16] Gorbachev began by admitting that in the first three years of his rule, his reforms had not achieved many tangible results. Then he bluntly told the nation: *"Perestroika* is not manna from heaven. Instead of waiting for it to be brought in from somewhere, it must be brought about by the people—themselves."[17]

The delegates, taking him literally, grabbed the microphone and rewrote the traditional script for Party gatherings. For decades, the hallmark of Communist Party meetings had been harmony; they were famous for their leaden monotony, for droning, turgid speeches filled with sycophantic adulation for the leader and endless paeans to unity. But this time, no sooner had Gorbachev surrendered the lectern than the session turned into a political free-for-all.

With an entire nation watching in awe, Leonid Abalkin, normally a scholarly, mild-mannered academic economist, publicly shattered taboos by having the temerity to criticize Gorbachev for proposing to serve as head of the Communist Party and head of the government simultaneously. He questioned whether democratic reforms could be achieved under a one-party system.

Then Vitaly Korotich, editor of *Ogonek,* announced he had evidence that four conference deputies from Uzbekistan were criminals. Amid conservative catcalls aimed at the media, filmmaker Yuri Bondarev lashed out at the press, especially *Ogonek,* for excessive negativism. Mikhail A. Ulyanov, an actor made famous for playing Lenin, retorted with a demand for increased protection of the press from censorship. Gorbachev, wagging his finger like a schoolmarm, granted the press its freedom, but rasped that freedom required responsibility too.

For a public accustomed to the facade of Party unity, such a political brawl was grand entertainment. There were shockers every day. Vladimir Kabaidze, head of a huge machine-building plant and one of the country's most successful industrial leaders, delivered a blistering speech against government economic ministries, and called for their abolition. "To tell you the truth, we don't need ministries," Kabaidze declared, to the delight of millions of viewers. "We earn our own feed. We earn our own hard currency. What can they give us? Nothing. . . . Let the ministries catch the mice. If they don't, they don't eat. . . . I can't stand this proliferation of paperwork. It's useless to fight the forms; you've got to kill the people who produce them. . . . I'll probably catch hell from them for saying this."[18]

An even more astonishing moment came when Vladimir Melnikov, a regional Party leader from Siberia, stood at the dais, just a few feet away from Soviet President Andrei Gromyko, and called for his ouster as well as those of three other high Party figures—Politburo member Mikhail Solomentsev, *Pravda* editor Viktor Afanasyev, and Georgy Arbatov, director of the Institute of the U.S.A. and Canada. Russians talked about Melnikov's audacity for months afterward.

But the climax came with verbal fireworks between Boris Yeltsin (the radical reformer and former Party boss of Moscow, who had been ousted from the Politburo several months earlier) and his Politburo nemesis Yegor Ligachev (then leader of the conservative faction). They had clashed the previous fall in the secrecy of closed Party sessions at the Kremlin, and rumors had continued to circulate of their rivalry after Yeltsin was fired from the Politburo. Suddenly, their political blood feud exploded on the tube.

On the final morning of the conference, Yeltsin, tall, husky, and silver-haired, strode to the podium to cry out for political rehabilitation. Unrepentant, he renewed his assault on the slow pace of reform, and once again fingered Ligachev, another white-haired veteran, who had begun the Gorbachev era as a reformer but then slid to the right, the chief villain.

In an angry rebuttal, his voice thick with anger, Ligachev savaged Yeltsin. He denounced the fallen leader as "a destructive force," who had implied "that the work of the Party and the people is in vain" and was "playing into the hands of our enemies." Wrapping himself in Party loyalty and solidarity, Ligachev—and eventually the conference delegates—spurned Yeltsin's appeal to have his honor restored by the Party.

The television broadcast of their clash was delayed for six hours, but people all across the country stayed awake into the wee hours to watch it.

As he closed the conference, Gorbachev himself was moved to remark that "nothing of the kind has occurred in this country for nearly six decades." In short, not since Stalin had consolidated his control over the Party in the 1920s had the nation seen such a tumultuous Party gathering. Gorbachev had thrown the door of debate wide open.

The example was there for all to see, and to follow in their own cities and provinces. The image of Yeltsin and Ligachev trading body blows was etched in the Soviet public's mind. Wherever I traveled over the next two years, people had fixed those two figures in their minds as champions of rival forces—Yeltsin the avant-garde, Ligachev the Old Guard. What struck me as especially significant was that Ligachev retained the formal power of a commanding Politburo position, but Yeltsin was the one who had forged a populist bond with the man in the street.

In this era of media politics, the televising of that conference is a classic lesson in the power of television to change the political dynamics of a society and alter the mind-set of a nation. It is a case study in the interaction between the media and public opinion. For that conference not only formed public opinion, it also opened up the country to debate, and ultimately to breaking the power monopoly of the Communist Party, though it would take nearly two more years to achieve that revolutionary step.

CHAPTER 8

STALINISM: THE OPEN WOUND

"I agree with Solzhenitsyn that
without repentance, we cannot change
ourselves or our society. We must
feel responsibility for our history.
Who was it who made Stalin's terror?
It was we—our fathers—and we must
now pay for our fathers. But this is
repulsive to most people. They want to blame
others. They accuse Jews or someone else.
They do not want to accept responsibility."[1]

—Andrei Smirnov
Film Director
March 1990

"At Kuropaty, even the trees cry."[2]

—Nina Soboleva
TV Producer
April 1989

Kuropaty does not look like Auschwitz. At Auschwitz, the ovens remain ugly carcasses, standing as grisly testimony to the Holocaust. But the killing ground at Kuropaty, about five miles northeast of Minsk, capital of the Slavic republic of Byelorussia, is a forest of tall pines sighing peacefully in the wind. It looks deceptively ordinary and tranquil. From the road, on a spring afternoon, it looks like the kind of place where people go picnicking or pause to play with their children or take a nap under the trees, soothed by a woodpecker tapping out his tattoo. A chance visitor might pass by, pine needles gently rustling underfoot, and not understand what happened here.

But go deeper under the trees, and the silence grows eerie; there is a feeling of desolation, of emptiness. Then, as the eye adjusts to the darkness, graves come into view—scar upon scar upon scar, gouged into the earth. These graves are not mounds, but unmarked hollows, as if a giant had clawed out enormous scoops of loam and left the face of the earth scarred by some hideous, deadly pox. These are not normal graves; they are great gaping holes, sagging like hammocks with weatherworn edges. They are huge graves—each one large enough for 50 or 100 or 250 corpses, stacked layer upon layer.

These malevolent hollows stretch in all directions, as far as the eye can see, for half a mile this way and hundreds of yards that way, acre after acre of graves, all hidden from view by the woods.

"Over the course of four and a half years, they shot people here every day. Literally every day. When people were driven to the graves, the pits were already dug. They were very deep—up to ten feet deep—and about ten feet wide by ten feet long, sometimes fifteen feet or even thirty feet long. People were taken out of the trucks. Their hands were untied. NKVD (secret police) officers stood around the pits, revolvers ready so that no one could run away. Pairs were led up to the pits and shot in the back of the head. Usually, people, when they were untied, understood that they had been brought to be killed. They threw themselves on their knees and usually began to ask why they were being killed, what they were guilty of. They appealed to God, prayed, remembered their families."[3]

My guide was Zenon Poznyak, a tall, gaunt Byelorussian archaeologist. His brown eyes blazed, his jaw was set, his voice was brimming with hatred for the killers who decimated his people. In a knee-length smock and a blue beret, Poznyak looked disarmingly like an artist loping across the countryside in search of some quiet spot to set up his easel. But Poznyak is a fighter, one of those dissenters who spring up miraculously under dictatorships: a moralist, daring, uncompromising, and forever challenging the authorities because his independent spirit will not be quelled.

"Around Kuropaty," Poznyak said, "there was a tall wooden fence, over ten feet high, and on top of that fence was barbed wire. Over beyond the fence there were guards and dogs, and the gates were tightly shut. They brought prisoners in the morning and at night, after dinner. So the people in the villages—it's less than a mile to the nearest village—they constantly heard those who were being shot, the screams, the shrieks of the women, men, young people, 'Oh, God, why?' 'We're innocent.' 'Please help us.' Every day for five years people living in the villages heard these shots, heard these screams. In the evening, they would walk outside. It was quiet, and they could hear everything—how the people were being murdered.[4]

"Two hundred people who saw and heard these shootings are alive—more than two hundred. All their accounts are recorded. Several villagers said they counted up to sixteen truckloads a day. The shootings continued over four and a half years, from 1937 to 1941, to the very beginning of the war [in Minsk]—July twenty-third. When the German planes had begun bombing the city, they [Stalin's men] were still shooting people. . . .

"Farmers were annihilated. The intelligentsia were annihilated. People who graduated from the university in Prague or some other place abroad were annihilated. People who had earlier belonged to some party or some movement were annihilated. People who protected Byelorussian culture were annihilated. They annihilated the believers—Russian Orthodox, Catholics. They annihilated priests. They annihilated ordinary people when it was necessary to fulfill their quota. And many people were annihilated simply under this system of secret informers or denunciations. . . .

"Every investigator was given a quota: One or two people per day should be unmasked as 'enemies of the people.' If he did not expose 'enemies,' he himself was killed. . . . And as far as the 'seksot'—the secret informer—was concerned, he would go get paid on the very day that he wrote the denunciation of an 'enemy'—one hundred and fifty rubles in old money. That is, around fifteen rubles today. This was the price of a human life.

"They shot about two hundred fifty thousand people here, a quarter of a million," Poznyak said to me. "People were shot like flies."[5]

Crisscrossing the Soviet Union, I encountered a handful of people like Poznyak, militants whose zeal, even fanaticism, to expose Stalin's terror, has emboldened millions of others. In Byelorussia, Poznyak led a team of archaeologists and a network of activists who were investigating the horrors of Stalinism. They called themselves Martyrologists, *Martyrolog* in Byelorussian. Later, Poznyak was chosen leader of the Byelorussian Popular Front, which was openly challenging the Communist Party hierarchy. By the elections in March 1990, Poznyak had won a sufficient following to be elected to the Byelorussian parliament.

I suspect that Poznyak is a restless soul by nature. Forty-six and unmarried, he has no family except his mother; he has adopted the descendants of Stalin's victims as his family. Some of them almost worship him for what he has dared to expose. He is married to their cause, has made it his personal crusade, and he pursues it with fierce passion and the single-minded commitment of a Jesuit.

I could not help wondering whether Poznyak's vibrant anti-Stalinism sprang from the sufferings of his own family.

"What happened to your family?" I asked him. "Did they perish here?"

"My mother is alive, but my father was killed by the Nazis," Poznyak replied matter-of-factly. Then his face hardened, and he said, "The Bolsheviks killed my father's father. He was the editor of a newspaper, a true intellectual, and they were trying to destroy the intelligentsia. So they shot him."

As a devout Catholic, Poznyak has never forgiven the Bolsheviks either for murdering his grandfather or for their desecration of Christianity, and he took up his grandfather's cause, defending Byelorussia against the alien anti-Christ. In 1962, when he was a college freshman studying acting in the drama faculty of the Byelorussian Central Institute of Art, he was expelled for criticizing Khrushchev. Somehow he wangled his way back into the institute, but in a different faculty, and he was expelled again in a post-Khrushchev purge of liberals. He became an archaeologist as a last resort, and eventually unearthed the terrible evidence of the slaughter at Kuropaty.

Mass murders were conducted not only at Kuropaty, but all over Byelorussia. In April 1989, when we met, Poznyak took me to Kuropaty, but when I returned to Minsk that fall, he told me there were other killing grounds, a ring of eight of them in the countryside surrounding Minsk. Despite dreadful weather, Poznyak, the missionary, led me and our film crew out in the chill rain to all eight gravesites—four in various forests, one in a swamp, one now plowed under a highway cloverleaf, another in a ravine asphalted over for a parking lot, and the last in a popular Minsk park.

With us was Maya Klishtornaya, a soft-spoken architect, whose father, beloved Byelorussian poet Todor Klishtorny, had been arrested during the Stalinist purges and "liquidated," as the Soviets say, at the age of thirty-two. After all these years, she still seemed incredulous at her father's fate.

"He saw everything through rose-colored glasses," Maya recalled. "He was surprised when he was arrested. He could not understand why, and they never told him. . . . He wanted only good things, pure things. That was the Revolution for him. . . . My mother literally ripped out her hair. She had long black hair, in braids. My mother went everywhere, tried to get through, asked questions. But nobody could explain anything to her, except one thing—your husband is an enemy, an enemy. This word didn't fit him, didn't, no way. . . . I was born when my father was already gone. He was in prison."[6]

Maya is a small, gentle, attractive woman gray beyond her years. She never saw her father. With her mother, she spent the first seventeen years of her life in exile in Kazakhstan and Siberia, in concentration camps for relatives of "enemies of the people." She never knew her father's precise fate, but she is convinced that he was shot at Kuropaty. And so now she makes a pilgrimage there every week, often planting red and white roses by the anonymous graves.

As I walked with her through the woods of Kuropaty, I noticed that at one grave someone had put up a crude wooden frame bearing a wreath and a handwritten note, now faded from the rain. It said something Maya herself might have written:

Mother and Father,

I have searched for you since your disappearance in 1937. At last, after 52 years, I have found you.

Galya

Nearby, close to other graves, there were crosses, handmade from small stones laid out on the earth, and farther on, the simple legend REMEMBER FOREVER.

By then we were barely noticing the terrible weather. It seemed fitting that raindrops were falling from the branches of the pines; and I was reminded of something a TV producer in Moscow had said to me: "At Kuropaty, even the trees cry."

After Kuropaty, Poznyak took us to another cemetery, where the graves are marked, some with expensively cut stones. Here, Maya came face-to-face with a truth that millions of other Soviets now confront: The evil that killed their families was not the work of an invader; it was inflicted from within. Some of the people buried in this cemetery took part in the Stalinist murders.

Poznyak showed us one gravestone on which had been etched the almost photographic likeness of a youthful, square-jawed military officer with a crew cut—the stereotypical Soviet hero. This man's widow had recently admitted that in 1937 and 1938 her husband had been an NKVD officer and had participated in the Stalinist killings.

"Imagine this life-style," Poznyak said, drawing on a description he'd heard from another NKVD wife. "This person comes home from work every night, very late. He's tired, very drunk. The wife meets him. She is disgusted, of course. He smells like blood. And how do the kids react to that—'Daddy, how many did you kill today? Seventy or eighty?' It's hellish, surrealism. It's a nightmare that these people have lived in, destroying our society, destroying our people. . . . You know, maybe this person has killed Maya's father."[7]

Maya was in a state of shock, her face revealing unbearable pain. She looked as if she wanted to scream, but she spoke only in a murmur.

"They shouldn't have buried this one so close to the other graves," she said. "They shouldn't put him in a common cemetery."

Others like this man, Poznyak observed, are still alive.

"What do you think should be done with them?" I asked.

"We should investigate and start criminal cases against them," he replied, "and if their guilt is determined, we should judge them. We should start a criminal case and prove their guilt. Otherwise, it will be the same kind of killing all over again."

The threat of this kind of retribution paralyzes Soviet society, and so far those in power will not permit any such investigation to take place.

Poznyak emphasized that most important is the moral judgment of guilt so that historical truth can be established.

By his own reckoning, the Stalinist massacre in Byelorussia—"genocide," he calls it—took 2 million lives. The census counted 12 million Byelorussians in 1920, but only 9.8 million in 1940, before the war, and Poznyak blames Stalin and the Bolsheviks for those who vanished. If death from Stalin's violent collectivization of the farmlands and the famine that ensued is included along with the actual police killings, Poznyak may be right.

"I want to tell you, Hedrick," he said, "that a normal, civilized person cannot comprehend deliberate, cold-blooded, mass extermination of innocent people on a national scale. Stalin, after all, was a criminal. His psychology, his mentality, was criminal. There has never been anything like it."

"Even Hitler?" I asked.

"Even Hitler," he answered. "No comparison. If you compare the victims—fifty million lives in the U.S.S.R. annihilated by Stalin—that's an enormous number. Also, Hitler fought basically with external enemies." The greater horror of Stalin, in Poznyak's view, was that he had devoured his own people.

BITTER TRUTHS, COMFORTABLE LIES

Zenon Poznyak's campaign to dig up the truth about Kuropaty represents much more than a local struggle of Byelorussians to seek justice for the violence perpetrated against them. Poznyak's unearthing of the corpses at Kuropaty is a metaphor for the entire process of *glasnost*—for Gorbachev has been digging up the past and forcing Soviet society to confront the political skeletons in its history.

Sadly, Kuropaty and the ring of killing grounds around Minsk are far from unique. I have been taken to other mass graves, in forests outside of Kiev and Moscow, and there are many more, from Leningrad in the west all the way across Russia and Siberia to the Pacific. These have been unearthed in the past two or three years under the stimulus of Gorbachev's new openness and under his political protection.

Gorbachev understood that before his people could begin to define and build their future, transform the Soviet system, they had to consciously reject the legacy of Stalin, to confront the nature of the society that Stalin had created. Khrushchev had begun the task in 1956 when he dethroned Stalin personally, exposing the raw terror of his reign. But Gorbachev had a larger target: not just Stalin the person, but Stalinism, the entire Stalinist system. He was intent on digging deeper, on uprooting and casting off the Stalinist system by discrediting it morally, especially among generations in their middle and younger years.

Gorbachev and his liberal allies in the leadership, principally Eduard Shevardnadze and Aleksandr Yakovlev, encouraged Poznyak and other political radicals to come forward with the bitter truths that unmasked the long-held lies. This not only provided an outlet for pent-up grievances, but also helped legitimize the break with the Soviet past that Gorbachev needed; putting Stalin's terror and authoritarian rule under fire also served to discredit Stalin's militaristic management of the economy, and his one-man political rule. So the zealous anti-Stalinism of people like Zenon Poznyak served Gorbachev's broader reform movement in several different ways.

Nevertheless, there were formidable obstacles, and perhaps more in Byelorussia than elsewhere. That republic is widely known as a bastion of the hard-line Old Guard, much as Alabama and Mississippi were known as hard-core segregationist states during the American civil rights movement of the 1960s. Like the Ukraine and much of western Russia, Byelorussia was occupied by the German army during World War II, so Soviet authorities in these regions could blame all mass killings and mass grave sites on the Nazis. The Minsk park that Poznyak took us to, for example, has a monument to the victims of Nazi occupation, but Poznyak, and many others, dismiss this as "a mock monument" because by their reckoning German killings were minor compared to the slaughter inflicted by the Soviets themselves. Yet Byelorussian authorities refused to recognize that with a new monument to the innocent victims of Stalinism.

Another obstacle has been fear—a fear so keen that Poznyak himself was intimidated for many years. He confessed to me that he had first learned about Kuropaty about fifteen years ago, from the villagers. But he kept silent until 1988, doing nothing to publicize the horrible secret.

"Why did it take so long to come out?" I asked. "You had the opportunity to open this up."

We were standing only a foot or two apart, and I could see that his breathing was heavy. I sensed his anger and tension over my pressing him on this point. He fixed me with a stare.

"It was impossible to say anything out loud," he said finally. "In order to understand me, you need to live in this society, under Communism. Then you will understand everything. It was an absolutely impossible situation—to know everything but not be able to say anything. You can go mad, but still not say anything. The whole ideology, the whole press, the whole information—it's all in *their* hands. If a person comes out with that type of information, nobody's going to listen to him, or worse yet, they pronounce him crazy, or they take him to prison, or kill him. And they just say that he's stupid, he's crazy, he just made it all up, and that's how evil he is. This is how millions of people were destroyed."[8]

Beyond that, after the war the NKVD, forerunner of today's KGB, tried to cover up their crime—and nearly succeeded. According to what the villagers told Poznyak, NKVD troops came back to Kuropaty, dug up the graves, and carried away tens of thousands of corpses and dumped them somewhere else. That is why the mass graves at Kuropaty all sag like hammocks. Bodies have been removed and there is not enough earth to make the graves level. Eventually, Poznyak was able to confirm the villagers' story through archaeological detective work. The NKVD had done a sloppy job, leaving traces not only of the original crime but of the cover-up as well. Initially, however, the NKVD cover-up foiled Poznyak's efforts.

"We did the excavation, dug to about five feet, and not one bone—empty graves," he told me. "We discovered the corpses only by chance. Some children dug deeper in one pit than we had, to about six or seven feet, and they came upon the corpses. Then everything fell into place. Digging to the lower levels of the graves, we found bones, human skulls shot in the back of the head—every skull in the back of the head."

What apparently happened, he said, was that the original graves had been constructed in layers—first bodies, then a layer of earth and lime, then more bodies and another layer of earth, for several layers. When the NKVD came after the war, they dug down only to the normal depth of a grave, and removed the top layer or two, especially in the center of the graves, thus leaving the lower layers intact. Poznyak's investigations turned up those lower levels, confirming the villagers' stories.

But when Poznyak tried to go public with his findings on Kuropaty, the Byelorussian Communist Party Central Committee forbade all newspapers and magazines from printing his article. Only one Byelorussian magazine, *Literatura i Mastačtva (Literature and Art)*, was brave enough to try. Its editors warned Party officials that if the article was not printed, they would write a collective protest to the Nineteenth Communist Party Conference in Moscow. Even then, only by agreeing to cut about 20 percent of the article were they able to publish "Kuropaty—Road to Death," on June 3, 1988.

Poznyak is convinced the Party bosses relented only because this was the high tide of *glasnost,* during the buildup to the Party conference, and Byelorussian authorities were afraid to be caught too far out of step with Gorbachev's line.

"Our authorities did not know what to expect from the Party conference," he told me. "If they had not been so busy with the conference, they would have crushed this article. If it had been after the conference, they would have crushed it. Timing saved it, and it was a bombshell, because it became clear to people what a genocide had taken place."[9]

The Party leadership tried to discredit Poznyak personally, and to blame the Nazis for the Kuropaty killings. One Party activist claimed that thirty-eight thousand German officers had been shot after the war, so outlandish a story that it had no credibility. A rising public outcry forced the formation of a government commission to study Poznyak's charges. Some of the younger investigators took the charges seriously enough to dig up six graves, with the help of Poznyak's archaeological specialists. The evidence, as Poznyak knew it would be, was devastating.

"We found shells from Soviet revolvers—Nogam brand," Poznyak recalled. "We found bullets, homemade high boots, rubber galoshes from Soviet factories—Red Hero, Red Triangle, truck hubcaps, lights.[10]

"We found a lot of rubber boots—all made in '37, '38. Our population was pretty poor and at least half of them wore rubber rain boots. We found combs, little mugs. Some graves had toothbrushes, glasses, women's hair, remnants of clothes. We found wallets, a little bit of metal money made in the thirties. Then we found leather jackets, neatly folded, and inside them there were women's shoes, slippers, wrapped up. They even found chicken bones. Do you understand what happened? A person took some chicken and didn't have time to eat; he was shot and thrown into the grave, and the chicken bones were left over. When you make this analysis, you realize that these people were very poor, mostly farmers, locals, because all of the articles were local . . . basically people just taken in the middle of the night."[11]

The investigation confirmed the thrust of Poznyak's story, but officials then disputed his figures. He calculated the death toll at 250,000, having measured out that there were 250 corpses in each of the 1,000 graves that he estimated filled the fenced-in area at Kuropaty. The authorities put the figure at 30,000 because only 510 specific graves had been located; moreover, they only counted actual bodies found in the lower layers—excluding the larger numbers that had been removed from above.

To verify the death toll and help people learn the fate of their relatives, Poznyak and his organization Martyrolog demanded that the KGB open its files; the KGB insisted there were no documents because all files had been destroyed in the war. "All lies," Poznyak retorted. "There are people who clearly know that their parents were shot here, and these people applied in 1959 to the Minsk KGB for [political] rehabilitation of their parents. The documents were there, and they received rehabilitation. Aside from that, all documents on the shootings in the 1930s existed in four copies—two for Moscow and two for Byelorussia."

The Minsk press knows less about the details than Poznyak and Martyrolog, and Party leaders refuse to talk about the mass killings. I made repeated efforts to see them, but they completely stonewalled my requests; I did not encounter such total avoidance anywhere else in the Soviet Union.

To Americans, who have known of Stalin's Red Terror for decades, Poznyak's determination to pry out every last historical fact may seem obsessive. But to Soviets, Stalinism is a burning issue today because for the first time in their lives they can finally talk about it. Moreover, in fighting over the past, Poznyak and his allies see themselves as locked in battle with the neo-Stalinists of Byelorussia today.

"Stalinism will be dealt a mortal blow only when all the documents are revealed," Poznyak contended. "What we now relate, based on people's recollections—they can claim it was not so, that it is invented, it is a personal opinion, subjective. Even now, Stalinism still clamors for the right to exist. So one of the most important issues in dispute is whether to publish all documents about the crimes of Stalinism. *They* understand the importance of this. The system itself understands that the publication of these documents, and the unmasking of Stalinism, is the unmasking of that same system now."[12]

STALIN—DEMON OR DEMIGOD?

Half a century after the purges, Stalinism is still an open wound. No other issue cleaves Soviet society quite the same way. It defines the political spectrum. It lies at the heart of the country's struggle to recover its soul—a struggle that reaches deep into the personal lives of almost every adult over forty, testing the beliefs of a lifetime. Gorbachev's new openness may liberate some people, but it points the finger at others. Because tens of millions of people alive today enthusiastically supported or reluctantly collaborated with Stalinism, the painful questions being raised are about *their* responsibility and guilt, *their* pride or shame.

And what makes Stalinism still such a vibrant issue is that its influences continue to permeate Soviet life, shaping and coloring the mentality of most people. I saw this, and heard it, all over the country, from many thoughtful people, including Yuri Solomonov, a senior editor at the weekly newspaper *Sovetskaya Kultura.*

"Why do we have such arguments about Stalinism?" Solomonov echoed my question. "Because all the institutions of our society were created at that time. When we argue about Stalin, it's not just about the past, it's about the present. We have a part of Stalin in all of us. Stalinism is the living past, and the worst poison is here," he said, pointing at his head.[13]

From an eminent and elderly Soviet physicist, Andrei Borovik-Romanov, I heard how it felt to reflect on one's own role in the Stalinist period, after Khrushchev's revelations about Stalin.

"That was for me a very difficult moment," he said. "I felt guilty. All honest people have problems with this guilt. Every citizen is responsible. I knew innocent people were arrested. I knew at the time that my friend"—he paused, but gave no name—"who was arrested, was innocent, that it was a mistake. But you think that the others who were arrested were actually guilty. Most of the people in the thirties were interested in building a new world. What we need now is to formulate new policies. But it is much easier to criticize the past."[14]

People's views of Stalin are a touchstone for their political loyalties and their attitudes toward the Soviet future. For if there are millions like Zenon Poznyak who believe that Stalin was a demon, there still are millions of others who revere him as a demigod.

It was Stalin, they declare, who built the Soviet Union into a superpower. It was Stalin who industrialized a peasant country, took it from wooden plows to atomic weapons, thrust it into the twentieth century, and made the West tremble at the might of Russia. Above all, it was Stalin who won the war, destroyed Hitler, beat the Germans. As they talk of Stalin, his admirers romanticize the exploits of their own youth, when, with Stalin at the helm, they were building a Brave New World. And now, amid the disarray of Gorbachev's *perestroika,* they long nostalgically for the order and discipline imposed by the strong boss in the Kremlin. Those were times, they assert, when factories worked—and so did workers— unlike today!

The battle over Stalin and his legacy rages in virtually every level of society, and between two ideologically opposed camps—from the higher reaches of the Communist Party to factories and neighborhoods. In the Soviet Writers' Union, the neo-Stalinist Right battles the anti-Stalinist Left for control of the union and the editorship of major newspapers. In the streets on March 5, the anniversary of Stalin's death, rival demonstrations of the anti-Stalinist popular movement Memorial and the pro-Stalinist right-wing group Pamyat ("Memory") have ended in shouting matches and fisticuffs.

In the corridors of power, Memorial, which seeks to rehabilitate the victims of Stalinist repression and establish memorials at eight mass graves across the nation, including Kuropaty, has been waging a struggle for more than two years to be legally registered with the government and thereby be allowed an office, a bank account, and normal organizational facilities and rights. But it has been blocked, some of its leaders fear, by Stalin's defenders in the bureaucracy, who want to keep popular anti-Stalinism in check. Memorial's top priority is erecting a monument to Stalin's victims on Red Square; it has raised large funds from private donations to do this. It has even publicly exhibited the scores of designs submitted for the monument, only to have its unregistered bank account frozen by the Ministry of Culture.

Angered by a stream of articles on Stalinist repression, former Stalinist officials have gone to court, their chests lined with medals, to file lawsuits against Stalin's accusers. In September 1988, a retired prosecutor named Ivan Shekhovtsov created a sensation by charging the prominent writer Ales Adamovich with slandering Stalin and his henchmen by calling them "butchers" in a newspaper article. Among other things, Adamovich had accused Stalin of deliberately organizing the famine of 1930–31, in which millions died. Shekhovtsov retorted that this was illegal defamation because Stalin had never been found guilty by a legal tribunal. His case was dismissed, but when Moscow television ran a documentary on the trial, its producer, Nina Soboleva, received seventy-five hundred letters supporting Shekhovtsov.[15]

"It's a battle for power," Alla Nikitina, the editor of a monthly magazine for teenagers, asserted. "There's not just an effort to rehabilitate the victims of Stalin, but there is the battle [of reformers] against the Stalinists of today, the people who still use Stalinist methods. If they did not consider themselves Stalinists, they would not worry about that old society. But these people see a real danger to themselves."[16]

As Poznyak suggested, the most rigid and unyielding neo-Stalinists are people still in power who feel threatened by the drive to expose Stalinism. There are also the true believers, who are still in the grip of dogma, and the superpatriots, who take any criticism as a slur on the nation. There are the zealots of law and order, for whom crime, prostitution, gaudy television, rock music, and the loose ways of modern Soviet youth are evidence of decadent Western influence. The numbers are legion, especially among the older generation, who are defensive about their own lives, both what they did and what they did not do.

"Many people don't want to know the criminal things about Stalin because it means they have fought for a lost cause," observed Genrikh Borovik, a veteran news commentator.[17]

And there are those who simply find it too hard to change and who do not like the confusion of democracy. "Many people like a totalitarian regime," was the comment of Andrei Borovik-Romanov, the physicist. "You don't have to think about anything. You don't have to be responsible for anything. It is like being in the military. It's an easier life."

Soviet opinion polls indicate that Stalin's critics significantly outnumber his defenders. A December 1988 telephone survey done in five major Soviet cities by Moscow's Institute of Sociology found 65 percent had an unfavorable view of Stalin and only 10 percent were willing to state a favorable view. Another 20 percent had mixed feelings about him, or were unsure.[18] However, Vadim Andreyenkov, a sociologist at the institute, suggested that Stalin was probably viewed more favorably nationwide than this poll indicated. The reason, he said, is that this poll and others like it either leave out rural areas or underrepresent the elderly, two groups among whom sociologists have found that political conservativism—and approval of Stalin—runs higher than average.[19]

Stalin's most celebrated grass-roots defender is Nina Andreyeva, for years an ordinary chemistry teacher at the Leningrad Technological Institute, who sent political chills through the ranks of reformers in early 1988 with a bold defense of Stalin and an attack on Gorbachev's *glasnost* policy. Panic rose among anti-Stalinist liberals when Andreyeva's forty-five-hundred-word letter was printed in the newspaper *Sovetskaya Rossiya*, a conservative stronghold, and when it was warmly endorsed by Yegor Ligachev, then number two behind Gorbachev in the Politburo. It is a well-known maneuver in Kremlin infighting to use the views of an ordinary person—a real or fictitious letter-writer to a newspaper—as a proxy to promote the cause of one Politburo faction against another, so for days, many of the most daring liberal editors interpreted the publication of Nina Andreyeva's letter as a signal that a right-wing power play against Gorbachev was under way and that their own days might be numbered.

In her letter-essay, titled "I Cannot Forsake Principles," Andreyeva voiced alarm that her students had been plunged into "ideological confusion" and "nihilist views" by the press and by liberal writers. She chastised these groups for debunking Stalin and "falsifying" Soviet history, contending that Stalinist "repression has become excessively magnified" and that some writers sounded like "the professional anti-Communists in the West, who long ago chose the supposedly democratic slogan of 'anti-Stalinism.'

"Too many things have turned up that I cannot accept, that I cannot agree with—the constant harping on 'terrorism,' 'the people's political servility,' 'our spiritual slavery,' 'the entrenched rule of louts,' " she wrote. "Take the question of the position of J. V. Stalin in our country's history. . . . Industrialization, collectivization, and the cultural revolution, which brought our country into the ranks of the great world powers . . . all these things are being questioned."[20]

While paying obligatory lip service to the existing Party line, Andreyeva took issue with it. She challenged the tendencies of "leftist liberal dilettantish socialist" reformers—Gorbachev seemed implied but was not named—to abandon the "class struggle" against the West and indulge in heretical preaching about the superiority of capitalism over Soviet socialism. In frustration, she declared: "Against proletarian collectivism, the adherents of this trend put up 'the intrinsic worth of the individual'—with modernistic quests in the field of culture, God-seeking tendencies, technocratic idols, the preaching of the 'democratic' charms of present-day capitalism and fawning over its achievements, real and imagined. [They] assert that we have built the wrong kind of socialism. . . ."[21]

KTO KOGO—WHO WINS?

When Nina Andreyeva's bombshell landed in the press, Gorbachev was in Yugoslavia, and his close Politburo ally Aleksandr Yakovlev in Mongolia. Ligachev, the Politburo's leading conservative, who was acting as Gorbachev's temporary replacement, moved into the power vacuum.

On March 14, the day after *Sovetskaya Rossiya* printed the letter, Ligachev summoned leading newspaper editors to a meeting, excluding some important liberals. According to Valentin Chikin, chief editor of *Sovetskaya Rossiya*, Ligachev drew attention to the Andreyeva letter as something to be emulated. By Chikin's account, Ligachev merely said: "Undoubtedly, you did not read *Sovetskaya Rossiya*, but I saw a very interesting article there by Nina Andreyeva." That was enough to start a stampede. Ligachev's move was read by many editors as a dramatic reversal of Gorbachev's line.[22]

Tass, the official news agency, sent regional papers an advisory note, "authorizing"—that is, virtually instructing—them to reprint it; many did so. In closed lectures to Party activists, a common way the Party line is transmitted, speakers began citing the Andreyeva article approvingly. This was also done in military channels.[23]

Within days, there were reports that Ligachev and his staff actually had drafted the Andreyeva letter and planted it. I heard from Yuri Solomonov of *Sovetskaya Kultura* that his paper had received a copy of an original, fifty- to sixty-page version, directly from Nina Andreyeva. The published version, he said, was shorter and better written, showing extensive rewriting.[24] Chikin said his staff had contacted Andreyeva before publishing the letter, and although he tried to minimize their role, two other journalists, one on Chikin's staff, told me the letter had been largely reworked by Chikin's editors, including Vladimir Denisov, who had close links to Ligachev. Denisov had gotten to know Ligachev during four years as a correspondent in the Siberian city of Tomsk, where Ligachev had been the regional Party boss in the early 1980s.

Once Gorbachev and Yakovlev returned to Moscow, it took them several days to react to Ligachev's challenge. They did not immediately issue a high-level repudiation of the Andreyeva letter, despite strong appeals from liberals. For three weeks, the situation dragged on, delay fueling the reformers' sense of danger. Vitaly Korotich, whose magazine had been publishing revelations about Stalinism, told me that he became so worried there would be a conservative crackdown and he would be exiled to Siberia, that he actually made preparations for his own arrest. "We understood that an article like this is a sign to prepare a satchel of clothes for a long trip," he told me months later, with his boyish, crescent-moon grin. "We understood that if we lost our power and lost *perestroika*, it would be a catastrophe, for the government and for us personally."[25]

By the end of March, Politburo member Aleksandr Yakovlev and his staff had created a strong reply to the letter, and word was passed to leading editors that an authoritative Party statement would run in *Pravda* on March 31. But it did not appear that day, or the next, or the next.

Several months later, Roy Medvedev, who as a dissident in the 1970s had written the devastating history of Stalin *Let History Judge*, told me the Politburo had been split on publishing an answer to Andreyeva. Medvedev learned from his high-level Party contacts that Gorbachev had pushed hard, first lobbying Politburo members individually and then summoning the Politburo into session, in the first days of April. His difficulties indicated that there was resistance from Ligachev and others. I was told that Gorbachev broke the deadlock by playing his trump card: He warned the others that he could not continue to lead if they did not back him on this issue, and he stalked out of the Politburo meeting, going off to his *dacha* to await their verdict.[26]

On April 5, with Politburo approval, *Pravda* printed a stinging six-thousand-word rebuttal to Nina Andreyeva and her high-level backers. It denounced her letter as "an ideological platform and manifesto of anti-*perestroika* forces," namely "the conservative resistance to restructuring," which does not accept "the very idea of renewal." It mocked their view of history as "a nostalgia for the past when some people laid down the law and others were supposed to carry out orders without a murmur." It declared that "the guilt of Stalin and his immediate entourage . . . for the mass repressions and lawlessness they committed is enormous and unforgivable." In uncompromising language, it insisted that "those who defend Stalin are thereby advocating the preservation in our life and practice today of the methods he devised for 'resolving' debatable questions . . . but most important, they are defending the right of arbitrary action." It dismissed Andreyeva's letter as the work of a "blind diehard dogmatist" who confuses patriotism with "jingoism." As for the "nihilism" of today's youth, *Pravda* declared, "its roots go back into the past."[27]

This was one of those telltale moments in what Russians call the endless Kremlin struggle of *Kto kogo*, literally "Who is over whom?" Put more simply: "Who wins?" Gorbachev had forced Ligachev to back down.

The crisis was over—but the debate was not. Within ten days, Chikin had reprinted the *Pravda* article, along with his own editorial conceding that running the Andreyeva letter had been a mistake. In Stalinist times, Andreyeva would have vanished in a trice for crossing the Party leader so brashly. But no steps were taken against her, and within a month other letter writers, even those who disagreed with her, were defending her right to be heard under Gorbachev's policy of "socialist pluralism of opinions." A year later, in April 1989, I was told that Chikin was boasting to his hard-line staff at *Sovetskaya Rossiya* that they had brought Nina Andreyeva to five million readers "and the heavens opened up on us. The terrorists [evidently Gorbachev and Yakovlev] bombarded us. But that didn't dampen our spirits."

Far from being chastened by *Pravda*'s verbal caning, Nina Andreyeva became more outspoken. She was a national celebrity by the time I went to see her in September 1989. A hero, a symbol and rallying point for hard-line Stalinist and Russian nationalists, she was now the leader of a mass movement called Edinstvo—"Unity."

I found her and her husband, Vladimir Klushin, in a modest one-room apartment. They were swamped with mail—seven thousand letters, she said. A constant stream of Stalin loyalists made pilgrimages to her home. Only the day before, there had been someone from Tashkent, she said; and now there was an American television crew.

Andreyeva looked less like the nation's most notorious street-corner polemicist than a stocky, chubby-cheeked matron in her fifties. I had seen hundreds of women who resembled her, standing as self-important sentries at the entrances of government buildings, warily checking visitors. More stylish than they, she was decked out in tight-fitting slacks, platform heels, a short, upswept hairdo. She had a small mouth that was given to laughter as well as to smug little grins at the expense of her enemies—and she had them, for, as Moscow Party officials told me, she had been expelled from the Communist Party unit in her institute some years back for writing anonymous denunciations of colleagues and pretending they were written by students. With me, she was full of righteous talk about defending the working class, even though she and Klushin displayed distinctly bourgeois tastes: lacquered cabinets, cut crystal, and ten-year-old Georgian cognac, which they served along with a modest lunch of cold cuts and eggplant pâté.

Their apartment was only a few hundred yards away from the battlefield that marked the deepest penetration of German forces during the nine-hundred-day blockade of Leningrad in World War II. She and Klushin took me through a war memorial and to a nearby park, where he described the fighting and recalled that Russians had gone to their deaths shouting, "For the Motherland! For Stalin!"

Andreyeva had lost her father and brother in the war, but Klushin revealed that his father had been arrested, interrogated at the Lubyanka (the KGB headquarters prison), and sent to the gulag after being pressured into signing a false confession that he was part of a gang plotting against Stalin. Actually, Klushin said, his father was arrested because, as an officer, he had absentmindedly taken some classified data out of a secret room. When I asked Klushin his reaction to the false confession, he evaded my question, saying that, after all, his father had been guilty of something and had himself "felt they were correct to imprison him." But later, in another context, Klushin said his father's investigator had not been honest and he disclosed triumphantly that during the shadowy postwar intrigues of secret-police chief Lavrenti Beria, the investigator and, in fact, "all four who were on my father's case, were shot—deservedly, absolutely deservedly, shot!"[28]

Nonetheless, his father's fate had left Klushin strangely unaffected, his devotion to Stalin undimmed. Now beefy and white-haired, he has pursued a career as an instructor in Marxism-Leninism, one of several hundred thousand ideological instructors nationwide. This group is widely regarded as among the most simple-minded dogmatists in the system. Like an overgrown puppy, he would offer his comments whenever his wife permitted.

Andreyeva, now expert at her own public relations, was on her best behavior for our filming. Her original letter had included some anti-Semitic remarks about Trotsky. In a subsequent interview with David Remnick of *The Washington Post*, she had openly attacked what she regarded as excessive Jewish influence in Soviet life. "Why is the Academy of Sciences, in all its branches, and the prestigious professions and posts in culture, music, law—why are they almost all Jews?" she had complained, though exaggerating the facts. "Look at the essayists and the journalists—Jews mostly?" She had also fumed about the corrupting influence of rock and roll, especially about a male singer named Yuri Shevchuk, who performed with his shirt unbuttoned, his chest and belly button showing, "and down below his male dignity was protruding . . . in front of all those young girls."[29]

With the camera running, she was careful how she put things. But she made it plain that her famous letter had been provoked by a sense that the country was disintegrating. In the months since, with all the strikes, political movements, nationalist demonstrations, and violence, she saw the nation sliding into the abyss of anarchism.

"Now, what's the worst thing?" she demanded rhetorically. "Disorder! Disorder! It's in everything. You've noticed. It's everywhere. And to imagine that a state can exist in conditions of anarchy, that's ridiculous. Even take capitalists—they get profits because everything is well organized. We need to learn labor discipline from capitalism . . . discipline that we unfortunately don't have."

"There wasn't such disorder under Stalin or even under Khrushchev, and to some degree even during Brezhnev's time," Klushin chimed in. "Real disorder has come now. People have become irresponsible."

Both now saw a political division that was sharper and more open than at the time of Andreyeva's original letter. The differences of the spring of 1988 had become "irreconcilable contradictions," which were now being fought out at all levels, top to bottom, Klushin said. "We don't accept the switch to the capitalist economic system," Andreyeva proclaimed. "And no matter what the leaders of *perestroika* do to pull us in that direction, it still won't work. It's bad. Of course, there's only one solution out of this crisis, only one in the interest of the worker, if you examine our society. It is to stop the current ruinous economic reforms. . . . Only one path is acceptable—the path of further socialist development, our development as a socialist power."

Andreyeva dismissed *Pravda*'s reply to her letter as the work of the intelligentsia, whom she derisively termed "the superintendents of *perestroika*." But I pointed out that the letter was in the Party newspaper, written by Politburo member Aleksandr Yakovlev. She waved me off. "It wasn't his style," she sniffed. Her cocky self-assurance indicated she still had powerful support from higher-ups as well as from the masses.

Both she and Klushin repeatedly criticized the press for picking on Stalin. "Such stupid things they publish now," she fumed. She ridiculed articles that said Stalin had "grabbed everything for his own good," saying that one of Stalin's KGB bodyguards had told her that the dictator did not even have shoes for his own funeral. But their pet peeve was the ever-mounting Stalinist death toll cited by their hated rivals.

"Khrushchev spoke of eight hundred thousand—Khrushchev, who directly knew about these issues," Andreyeva insisted to me. "Now in the period of *glasnost* and democracy, these eight hundred seventy-five thousand, it seems, have turned first into ten million, then twenty million, then thirty million. Everyone is trying to shock the listener, the reader, with these wild numbers."

"What about Stalin himself?" I asked. "As Khrushchev, and even Gorbachev said, Stalin gave the orders [for the killings] himself."

"You understand, the thing is there were no such orders," she shot back. "And there couldn't have been because this stupid thing that the press is saying now, that Stalin destroyed his own people, this prejudiced juggling of the facts, it's disinformation which is aimed at our very impressionable man in the street."

She raced on.

"If you say that all those generations that enthusiastically built our society, that they were all slaves, dehumanized, understood nothing, and that task number one is to rid yourself of this slavish part, drop by drop, what does this say? That all our past generations didn't understand what they were doing? It's criminal, just criminal. People lived a hard life. We didn't have a lot of material things, but the society which we created in 1917, it was building itself. It was hard. It was difficult. But with each day, people lived better, no matter what. The quantity of consumer goods increased, prices decreased, the problem of housing was solved, for we built huge amounts in the civilian sector. So to spit on all this, it's immoral."

The press was to blame, she said, for one-sided sensationalism. "*Glasnost* for the sake of *glasnost* isn't worth anything," she asserted. "It's a direction that leads to the collapse of society. If you accept that everyone can, excuse me, blather anything he wants, then we can say that psychiatric hospitals are the clearest example of *glasnost.* That would be utterly absurd."

"Is this the cost of freedom?" I asked.

"No," Klushin shot back. "It's the ugly face of freedom."[30]

TEACHING THE NEXT GENERATION

Some Russians say, "It's easier to live with comfortable lies than face the bitter truth." There are the comfortable lies of Andreyeva, the bitter truths of Poznyak. The choice ultimately lies with the next generation, teenagers now in high school. And what they are taught will be crucial in shaping their outlook ten or twenty years down the road. Then, they will be influencing the Soviet future.

One of Gorbachev's most far-reaching reforms—and one that is the least noticed in the West—is the dramatic change being made in the history that these Soviet high school students are taught. In what struck me as an incredibly daring step, because it was so visible and so sweeping, the government canceled history exams for Soviet high school students in May 1988. As *Izvestia* put it, the current textbook was "full of lies" and students should not be tested on that version of history. The textbook was out of sync with what the press was now writing about Stalinist repressions; there were gaping holes in Soviet history. A new textbook was needed. In the spirit of *glasnost,* Gorbachev's supporters in the Ministry of Education came up with the unusual idea of having rival teams of historians produce competitive versions of a new textbook; they would publish not one version, but two.

"We're talking about reeducating the teachers themselves, as well as the writers and historians." This according to Galina Klokova, a member of one team that is developing a text for high school seniors. She is a historian and former teacher.

"It is extremely difficult for a new approach to make headway, even on a personal level," she said. "The saddest thing of all is that a large portion of the teachers and students don't think for themselves. They have not been taught to analyze or to compare. They just accept. If they get a textbook, *any* textbook, they will teach whatever is in it. Unfortunately, teachers sometimes still try to work the old way, because it is more comfortable."[31]

I found it hard to imagine a Russian better suited to rewriting Soviet history than Mrs. Klokova. Or rather, she would be trying to write it honestly for the first time. For Mrs. Klokova is both a charming, gentle-spoken, white-haired woman of fifty-eight, with ruddy cheeks and a warm smile, and a scholar who combines intellectual rigor with a streak of tolerance and an instinctive feel for democracy, unusual among Russians. So many Soviets have grown accustomed to orthodoxy that they demand the single-textbook solution and get upset when it is not fed to them.

Galina Klokova is not only undogmatic, she is also untroubled by historical uncertainties and ambiguities.

"Dogma distorts history," she said simply. "It is important that history be opened clearly, vividly, to bring people into history. History should help to create a free person."

Her sentiments were echoed in principle by one of her textbook-writing colleagues, Oleg Voloboyev, an intense fifty-year-old who had long been an instructor at a citadel of historical orthodoxy, the Higher Communist Party School. Even so, he was willing to say that the teaching of Soviet history had suffered from excessive "mythologizing" (he meant hyperbole), and from dependence on one history book—the infamous *Short Course,* Stalin's own version of people and events.[32]

The problem was that textbook writing was to be a collective endeavor, and before they could write their textbook, Klokova, Voloboyev, and the rest of their team had to agree on the truth. I quickly discovered, however, that even these two could not see eye to eye on the fundamentals—for example, how many people had died at Stalin's hands.

"What will you tell your students?" I asked. "I've heard nine million, twenty million, forty million."

"I don't think we will ever be able to calculate those figures," answered Voloboyev. "We can only approximate."

Klokova had a far different notion. "Even forty million may be short of the mark," she said, "if you take figures connected with the civil war, the destruction of the countryside in the 1920s, the famine, the poverty. The figure forty million could include deaths from the Great Patriotic War [World War II]."

Voloboyev immediately objected: "You shouldn't lump together the civil-war dead with Stalin's repression. They are totally different things."

They got into a squabble. She held Stalin responsible for the millions who died from the rural famine, the millions of minority people who were forcibly relocated by Stalin, as well as those who were shot at places like Kuropaty or perished in forced-labor camps.

"These are all victims of Stalin's repression," she asserted.

"No, no, no," he interjected.[33]

They disagreed, too, over whether to teach high school students that the Red Terror had started in 1918; that meant not only Stalin, but Lenin, too, was culpable. Klokova believed that was true; Voloboyev adamantly objected.

Their argument was instructive not only because of their clashing views but also in terms of the problem historians have rewriting history. The press was far quicker than the historians in breaking new ground on Soviet history; the professional historians were already in print with books and articles that were now being discredited. They had a vested interest in the old orthodoxy, so they were slower to make amends than publicists or poets. Moreover, textbooks are always subject to political pressure when there is a monopoly customer—the state educational system. Decades of experience had schooled the professional textbook writers in political orthodoxy; the new freedoms were baffling for them.

Yet while the historians argue, teaching goes on, and the teachers who venture into the classroom every day, with history literally changing before their eyes, need immediate help.

For two years now, teachers have been sent periodic history bulletins for their courses through a teachers' magazine put out by the Ministry of Education. These instruct teachers how to deal with what Soviets call "the white spaces" in their history: Stalin's purges, the secret protocols of the 1939 Hitler-Stalin pact, the invasion of Czechoslovakia. Many teachers also clip newspaper and magazine articles to use in class, just to keep pace with what their students are reading or hearing at home. For many old-time teachers, the process of adjustment is painful.

In Yaroslavl, a city of half a million people about two hundred miles north of Moscow, I visited a provincial school that reminded me of the one my children attended in Moscow in the early seventies. Neither the uniforms nor the rules seemed to have changed much in fifteen years. The boys were still wearing navy-blue suits, the girls' uniforms consisting of dark brown sweaters and black skirts that I was told dated back to czarist times.

When I arrived in Yaroslavl, Viktoriya Kulikova, a heavy-set teacher with dyed red hair, was running her class with the order and formality of a German gymnasium. She lectured and the children stood to recite. She told me she felt it important to instill habits of work and discipline. Kulikova has been teaching for thirty years, and has been a member of the Communist Party all her adult life. She was trying to be tolerant of the changes, but they clearly made her uncomfortable.

"Indoctrination in citizenship—that's my most important task," she told me. "Basically that means, despite all our problems, love your motherland and its people, and respect their achievements."[34]

After class, several students, boys and girls of sixteen and seventeen, said that Kulikova's teaching was tame and orthodox compared to the candid, freewheeling discussions in their own homes. Their family talk revolved around revelations in the press and sometimes drew on personal recollections of older people in the community who were victims of Stalinist repression. Though Viktoriya Kulikova knew all this was going on, she was protective of the past. She spoke in terms of the students, but I think she was really speaking about herself.

"The kids suffer," she said. "Of course, I can't speak for all children, but I know in our school the children suffer from such recollections. They suffer because it seems to them that the history of their homeland should be just so, should be beautiful. . . . My position is this: We should show everything about our history, the bad and the good, the very bad and the very good. But nevertheless, we should try to instill in young people an image of something positive. . . . Too much criticism is dangerous. That's my opinion."[35]

At School No. 45 in Moscow, I met an educator with a very different cast of mind. For thirty years, Leonid Milgram has been the principal there. To see the energy of the kids running and talking in the corridors is to sense an unusually democratic school for the Soviet Union, despite the large gold profile head of Lenin with the slogan LENIN EVEN NOW IS MORE ALIVE THAN ALL THE LIVING.

Milgram is in his sixties, balding, potbellied; he looks as casual and approachable as the sleeveless sweaters he wears. Serious math and science students come into his office with schemes for computer hookups with high schools in Los Angeles. Younger children run up to him in the hall to show off their Michael Jackson buttons.

When I asked Milgram how things were going with the new teaching about Stalin and the purges, he admitted great problems. "The old teachers were indoctrinated with one textbook. You know the one," he said. "They can't reorient themselves and they don't want to. They respond well to Nina Andreyeva—to her views. They reflect those views. That's one problem. Others, the younger ones, are so far from that period that they don't know much and they didn't study the new history. They don't know how to study."[36]

Like Kulikova, Milgram is a lifelong Communist. He is still a believer in the socialist ideal of a humane society in which the goal is not profit but people. But he has been sorely disillusioned by how much has gone wrong, and above all, by the tyranny of Stalin. His own father was shot in 1937, at the peak of the purges; Milgram's disillusionment came two decades later.

"I don't trust people who say they always understood what Stalin was," he told me.

"I believed," he said. "I believed. You know, I'm not alone. In the class where I studied, thirteen of us ended up without parents. And still everybody believed. No one took it into his mind to say anything against Stalin. The tragedy is that we blindly believed Stalin, and even more painful was that we kept believing. That's where the tragedy is.

"I can say one thing: I never lied to the kids. Never. On the other hand, I was also mixed up in certain ways. Although I said what I thought, I might not have been correct. But I never intentionally lied. I could say, 'I don't know.' But I could never lie. It seemed to me that one could—and had to—remain a decent man.

"We need *perestroika* because we must create a new person—a person, I would say, with straight shoulders. Here for decades a person was taught to believe that if there's someone giving orders, you should obey them. Russia only touched democracy for several months in 1917, from February to October. Both before that and afterward, our politics always had the style of command. Command was its essence."

Milgram let that sink in, and then went on.

"To deny the beliefs that we grew up with is very difficult," he said. "So now we have to try to democratize society and to raise democrats anew. It's a hard road."[37]

Milgram has a natural talent for getting young people to think for themselves. He had wanted to take a class of his oldest students to Mikhail Shatrov's play *Dictatorship of Conscience*, a searing indictment of the development of the Communist Revolution that puts no less a figure than Lenin on trial. But Milgram could not get tickets, so our film crew videotaped the production and then took the film and a VCR to his class. Milgram used Shatrov's play to provoke thoughtful debate among his seniors. They were not typical—an unusually bright group, mostly from professional families. Nonetheless their reactions gave me an insight into the thinking of Soviet teenagers.

"The fact that Stalin appeared, this kind of tyrant, was it natural or wasn't it?" asked a pretty girl in a purple turtleneck named Marina. "That is, if it weren't Stalin, would it have been someone else? It's a very important question."

"And how do you answer it?" prodded Milgram.

"I don't know," said Marina. "It's a tough one."

A hand went up, and Milgram pointed to Masha, a girl with long blond hair. "It seems to me that Stalin was a product of the system," she suggested. "The system presupposed tyranny at that time."

"Generally, we must not say whether Stalin's coming to power is either natural or unnatural," added Alex, a dark-haired boy in a blue uniform. "When any man concentrates an unlimited amount of power in his hands, when there are no controls on him, he gradually of his own accord turns into a tyrant. Sooner or later, being intoxicated with power and having no controls, this is what happens."

Milgram put in his own word: "Haven't you noticed there's something dramatically opposed to this, which we're going through right now— being intoxicated by freedom?"

"It's not yet clear what that can lead to," young Alex replied. "It's pretty understandable that people like Sakharov and Yeltsin are concerned about what Gorbachev has concentrated in his own hands. He has taken for himself the key powers and in general has concentrated power in his hands."

A curly-haired boy named Boris saw historical parallels. "It seems to me the coming to power of Stalin was completely natural," he said. "The October [1917] Revolution was basically the first revolution in which power passed not to the middle class but to the very lowest class, and the lower class was not ready for this power. And right when people were unprepared for democracy, that's when, according to any law of history, some man of steel must appear to bring order. Right now, we can see approximately the same thing. Now, a kind of freedom has appeared. Most people use this freedom the wrong way. And now, once more we hear voices saying that we need another dictatorship, we need another firm hand."

"Criticism is crucial," Milgram advised. "Without that, without criticism, without external influence on those who are in power, there can be no movement forward. . . . Democratization leads to greater responsibility on the part of each individual. Otherwise, there will be anarchy."

"A dictatorship is in our future," said a dark-haired girl in the back. "Dictatorship is inevitable."

"We are pessimists," Marina, in the turtleneck, commented. "If we believe that everything that awaits us is terrible, if we really believe that, we should either leave this country or go and shoot ourselves. Why go on living if you think like that?"

Andrei, a thoughtful boy with glasses, wanted to go back to Shatrov's play and to history. "At the time when the country was being led by Lenin, was he guilty for all this?" he asked. "If he was guilty, then the whole foundation is destroyed."

"I would like to say that there's a famous saying, 'Create no idols,' " said a girl with a ponytail. "I think the followers of Lenin should have understood not only Lenin, not just believed in him blindly, but also understood his ideas."

Outspoken Boris had a response. "With Lenin's separation of the Church from the State, he removed all thinking people—except those who backed him," he asserted. "In this sense, he was very close to Stalin."

"You're out of bounds here," Milgram interjected, still defensive of Lenin, "because you don't know anything about Lenin, and you're confusing Stalin with Lenin and grouping them together. You should study both Stalin and Lenin."

"About Lenin, we should know more and study more," offered a pig-tailed girl. "Not just about Lenin. We should generally just know more. And if there were mistakes in the past, they should not be repeated today."

"That's what school is for, right?" Milgram said.

Turning to the class as a whole, he went on. "This was a very interesting conversation," he said. "But one thing depresses me a little bit. You have very little optimism. That's tough; that depresses me. You know, my friends, future society depends on your optimism or pessimism. It's very serious.

"You know, there is socialism and there is socialism. What is socialism? From the point of view of an economic system, socialism is a system in which there is no private ownership. From the point of view of everyday socialism in society, in which there is a maximum of democracy and satisfying the demands of people, that kind of socialism is possible. Something else—command socialism—can also be. But we shouldn't allow it.

"The choice depends not on me, because I'm old, but on you," he said. "Therefore, it's very important that you understand everything correctly and look at things correctly. . . ."[38]

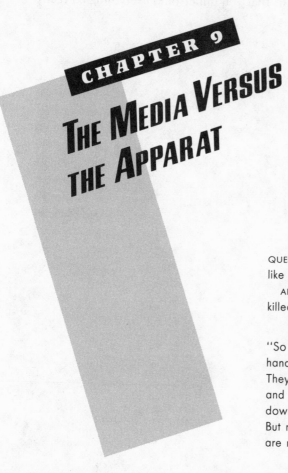

CHAPTER 9

THE MEDIA VERSUS THE APPARAT

QUESTION: Why is a minister like a fly?

ANSWER: Because both can be killed by a newspaper.

—Soviet riddle

"So far, *glasnost* is in the hands of the Party apparatchiks. They set limits for what we can and cannot do. We try to break down the walls they have erected. But no matter what we think, we are not completely free."[1]

—Bella Kurkova
Leningrad TV
September 1989

Bella Kurkova has the feisty, rebellious temper of a Bolshevik—especially when she is fighting Bolsheviks.

Bella is executive editor of *Fifth Wheel (Pyatoye Koleso)*, Leningrad's most daring television program, and when I first saw her in April 1989, she had just announced her candidacy for the Congress of People's Deputies in Moscow.

Having taken on the Leningrad Communist Party apparatus on the tube, she was now taking them on at the ballot box.

She bustled into her office, shaking hands all around, looking less like a radical than like a suburbanite. In her late forties, she has a soft, open face, her bleached blond hair done in a modified bouffant. With traditional Russian femininity, Bella was all dolled up in a pale peach blouse with a huge bow at the throat—yet she radiated the hyperkinetic energy of a short-order cook at lunchtime rush. She was about to have a campaign photograph taken, but even so, she headed for her desk, and without sitting down began to give instructions to assistants, answer the phone—all the while conversing with me and my companions, Martin Smith and Louis Menashe. Primping for the photographer, she motioned him into position with one half-free hand.

I decided to start right in on my questions. "Isn't it a conflict of interest for a journalist to be an elected member of Congress at the same time?" I asked.

"Excuse me . . . the photographer," Bella said, and she posed primly, before turning to my question. "Before, I never would have thought about this—about becoming a candidate. I'm doing it to defend my program and to defend *glasnost* for journalists in general. If everything were going smoothly for *Fifth Wheel,* I would never have gotten into this. But we cannot work normally. And so I have to take the risk."[2]

She was referring to the fact that in the first round of the elections on March 26, 1989, the Communist Party hierarchy in Leningrad had been savaged—and Party apparatchiks were blaming the media, specifically *Fifth Wheel,* for the fact that seven top figures in the provincial and city leadership had been rejected by the voters. "Certain press organs joined with anti-Marxist forces," one speaker complained at a Party meeting. Another accused Leningrad television of "gaining popularity on the cheap by pandering to the narrow-mindedness of the man in the street." He zeroed in on the culprits: "We can point to many shows, including *Fifth Wheel.* There are many instances where they behave in a truly ugly fashion."[3]

The media clearly were functioning at the forefront of political opposition to the Communist Party hierarchy.

No organized political force had yet emerged to galvanize mass support. And so muckrakers in the media, especially those on television who had a mass following, were leading the challenge against the Party apparat. They were exposing official corruption, the privileges of the elite, and the inept mismanagement of the economy, as well as giving vent to public grievances.

Party conservatives were now lashing back, trying to stifle the media. They were demanding that Bella be fired, and *Fifth Wheel* shut down.

To fight back, Bella felt that going to the public as a candidate would be the strongest tactic. According to Soviet law, she was allowed to become a second-round candidate in districts where no one had won the election in the first round. And so she had happily cast herself as a foe of the apparatus, even though she was a Communist Party member and held a *nomenklatura* appointment—meaning that she had been picked for her job by the ideological department of the Leningrad Province Party Committee, the very same officials she was now fighting.

As a print and television journalist, for twenty years Bella had been boiling with indignation at the tactics of her Party overlords. "I want to kick the apparatchiks out of the Communist Party," she declared. "We live for the day when the apparatchiks don't boss us around."[4] Years of chafing at ideological control now mingled with bitterness at the miseries of everyday living and fueled her protest.

"Every day I give thanks to our government for our terrible transportation system," she told me, barely containing her fury. "It takes me an hour to get to work—first on the bus, then on the subway, and finally on the trolley. And I live pretty close to the center of the city. But I have three transfers, so it's a terrible struggle. I never find a seat. But I thank God, because it puts me into a fighting mood. You can't make great art if you are completely satisfied. You only get great art when there's a sense of crisis. We always have that sense of crisis.

"And it's not just a matter of transportation. My pay is great—eight hundred rubles a month[5]—from my salary as chief editor, plus extra fees for my own scripts and appearances. But what can I do with the money? I can't find the books I love. I can't buy good-quality records. I can live without sugar or meat or vegetables, or a car, but I can't live without food for my mind. I love Italian culture and I want to get good books or subscriptions to Italian magazines. I can't do it. It's hard to get good tickets to the theater—I can't simply go to the box office and get them. I'm an executive editor so I have ways of getting tickets, but it's a struggle. If I could go to Italy or Spain or wherever I want, then everything else would be tolerable. Once, for six days, I got to Italy on a delegation from Leningrad. We shot twenty-four hours of videotape in six days. Imagine how intense that was. I saw it as a unique opportunity, so I worked eighteen hours a day. But I can't get out now."[6]

There was an explosive excitement among the team at *Fifth Wheel*. Bursting with ideas, they had the wild enthusiasm of an American university campus in the 1960s. To be with them was like being at Berkeley—a swarm of producers and reporters milling about in their jeans, with the hair of flower children. Rebellion was in the air.

Bella and her crew knew which side they were on: They were the "antis"—the people against the "power structure." Their programs amounted to unabashed advocacy journalism. Long suppressed, they had a sudden sense of power, having just shaken up the Party establishment, yet they also had a sense of vulnerability. Fear of retaliation was palpable; in the darkened hallway of her television studio, Bella told me the Party was after her scalp. "The situation is dangerous," she said.

While that danger was partly romantic, it was also realistic. The new muckrakers of Gorbachev's *perestroika* had known life under a repressive dictatorship. Until the spring of 1988, when *Fifth Wheel* began, they were hidden away in the interstices of safe programs on the Hermitage Museum or czarist palaces, on filming theatrical classics, doing shows for children or a few risqué programs—Western jazz, features for young people. They had fresh memories of hiding in the shadows, recalled one wine-filled Russian evening at the apartment of a producer named Natasha Sereva.

"The most important thing is to get rid of the feeling of fear," said Sasha Krivonos, a rumpled, chain-smoking producer, still infectiously boyish after twenty years in television.

"It's important to heal the soul inside us," he went on. "It's a terrible feeling—this horrible fear which makes you turn back now and then to make sure you are not being followed. No matter how we behave, the feeling of fear is deep in our souls. We are trying to overcome it. We try to argue with our superiors. We tell them, 'We don't give a damn about you. We will air our show.' But we still have this feeling of fear. Each of us has this censor inside, which prevents us from doing many things. We ask ourselves, 'Can we do it or can't we do it? Will it be allowed or not?' "

"Oh, Sasha, speak for yourself—not everybody's afraid," blurted out Tatyana Smorodinskaya, a slender reporter with long thin hair, sharp eyes, and a tense face. "We are absolutely not afraid. We have an opportunity to make basic changes, to try to change the political system and to get new laws."

But what had they all been doing and thinking before Gorbachev came to power?

"No matter how we are suppressed by the ideologists, they haven't yet invented a way to ban thinking," replied the hostess, Sereva, a strong-looking woman with dark hair. "They can't forbid us to think. Even before, it was possible to use one's brains."

"You had to resort to all kinds of tricks," chirped Zoya Belyayeva, an aggressive young reporter. "The more they banned, the more tricks we invented. Remember how, when we gave them our scripts to approve, we would drop phrases they could object to, and then we would use them during the shooting?"

"Do you think that we didn't understand what was going on ten years ago, twenty years ago?" Natasha Sereva asked. "We were no different ten years ago than we are today. We were exactly the same. But we lived, then, in the atmosphere of a concentration camp. We could take a step in this direction, but we could not take a step in that direction. They set limits for us. We *always* wanted to work the way we do today."

"Then, everybody was silent," Sasha Krivonos added. "Now, more things are made public. If they stop it tomorrow, it will be terrible."

"Five years ago, I lost my job," Zoya Belyayeva said.

"Yes," Natasha said, "Zoya lost her job because she did a show about an American musician. I don't remember who—was it Bob Dylan?"

"No—it was B. B. King," Zoya corrected her. "He came to Leningrad."

The reporter Tatyana Smorodinskaya grew philosophical. "It would be difficult for you to understand what it means to be a stranger in your own country," she said. "That's how many of the intelligentsia existed, as 'internal exiles.' "

It was a phrase that I had often heard in the seventies, for intellectuals who had withdrawn from involvement in public life because they rejected the system.

"To tell you the truth," Smorodinskaya added, "the only purpose of our lives then was not to turn into mutants—into deformed people." And she went on to explain how "the system," with its pressures to conform, had divided people into two groups.

In one group there were in every field the "careerists—those who wanted to serve the regime and be rewarded. They gave something, and they got something for themselves—and they were morally destroyed. Those who lived according to this pattern turned into mutants."

Then there was another group. "The people you are talking to here went out of their way not to become mutants. It was hard. You had to keep your behavior under control constantly. You had to maintain a very delicate sense of ethics. A great number of people did not turn into mutants, thank God. But the rest did. It's a terrible drama—a terrible historic drama."

"Now [on TV] we can cover more themes," Natasha Sereva said, "but the symbol of our time is still struggle—struggle, just as before. Freedom is still limited. Our leaders tell us, *This* you can do and *this* you cannot. The general structure hasn't changed. They only expanded the range of subjects and themes we're allowed to cover."

It was a thought that sobered everyone.

Natasha began to talk about Soviet intellectuals who had emigrated to the West during years of repression.

"All of us here could have emigrated to your homeland and lived very well there. We stayed here. We're not fanatics, we're not idiots. We stayed here because we must tell people the truth."

"The flow of truth is powerful," Sasha Krivonos observed, "so powerful that it knocked a lot of people off their feet."7

"A CLASS STRUGGLE AGAINST *GLASNOST*"

Leningrad is a natural battleground for the struggle between the media and the apparat. Its rich cultural tradition and its large intelligentsia have made it a city with pretensions to cultural leadership of the entire nation. The fact that it is now Russia's second city gives it an inferiority complex, and this has spurred its radicals to cause a splash that would outdo Moscow.

Arrayed against those cultural forces and ambitions is a powerful, hidebound Old Guard political leadership, one of the most autocratic in the Soviet system.

So sparks were bound to fly in Leningrad when Gorbachev kindled the ferment of *glasnost.*

The Party kept control of the main newspaper, *Leningradskaya Pravda,* but the film studios and the television station became hotbeds of radicalism.

Fifth Wheel is one of three major television programs that are on the cutting edge of new media freedoms. These programs play to an audience of twenty million people in and around Leningrad, northwest Russia, and the Baltic republics.

The most widely watched program is the nightly *600 Seconds (Shestsot Sekunduv),* a graphic, ten-minute news kaleidoscope, featuring crime, corruption, and sensation. Its anchor, Aleksandr Nevzorov, was once a movie stuntman and singer in a church choir. Now, at thirty-one years old, he is a full-tilt ambulance chaser. He can cover thirteen news bits in ten minutes. His topics range from how rotting meat is ground into sausages at a Leningrad factory, to how radioactivity emanates from old Soviet helicopters in a children's park, to a trip to the morgue to report on the tragic suicide leap of a woman and her two small children. The reporting is aggressive, if skimpy, and the camera work looks like an amateur imitation of *60 Minutes*.

Nevzorov, whose brash disclosures and leather-jacketed cockiness have made him the best-known figure in Leningrad, brags that he once did a piece from a hospital, about a man whose dog bit off his genitals after the man had tried to bugger the dog.[8] People with grievances to air insist that Nevzorov shakes news free and gets action. "He names names," one youthful admirer said. "One line from Nevzorov will kill three apparatchiks."

But critics suggest that he may be the unwitting tool, or secret ally, of hard-liners among the police who want to oppose *perestroika:* His steady drumbeat of bad news feeds popular pessimism.

The second program in the Leningrad TV troika is *Public Opinion (Obshchestvennoye Mneniye),* a three-hour call-in show that combines debates among experts on topical issues, live man-in-the-street interviews, and a running poll of call-ins on the issue of the night. Its anchor is Tamara Maksimova, who comes on like "Miss Gollywood" (the Russians, having no *H* in their alphabet, use *G* instead); she wears almond-shaped dark glasses and thick black leather slacks. Her husband, Vladimir, more modest and self-contained, is the producer. Their show, which went on the air in early 1987, has discussed the death penalty, alcoholism, the economy, the terrible pollution of Leningrad's water system, and *perestroika.*

On one show, Soviets and Yugoslavs debated whether it was better to live in Yugoslavia, where the stores had plenty of goods but inflation was so bad that many people could not afford to shop, or in the Soviet Union, where many people had cash but the stores were so empty there was little worth buying.

In another show, "Blackboard of Democracy," people were invited to write their own political slogans on a huge board in downtown Leningrad. Among those that appeared were: DOWN WITH LIGACHEV; AFGHANISTAN IS OUR SHAME; and GIVE US A MULTIPARTY SYSTEM.

Some Party progressives had backed *Public Opinion* as a way of monitoring the general mood, but they went into shock one night when a listener mockingly asked how there could be *perestroika* if Gorbachev and Politburo colleagues like Yegor Ligachev could not agree on what the word meant. Any mention of breaches at the top was beyond the tolerance of even progressive Party members. Tamara Maksimova saved her career by smothering the question, and the program became a bit more cautious after that.[9]

Fifth Wheel was different from the other two programs in the way it used investigative documentaries to discuss both current issues and Soviet history. First aired in the spring of 1988, it soon built a popular following; its twice-a-week, two-hour shows were penetrating, in-depth reports. The name *Fifth Wheel* symbolized the supposedly superfluous people in Leningrad television who covertly created the first show and then persuaded their bosses to run it.

In one short year, *Fifth Wheel* ran shows on the problems of returning Afghan veterans; the maltreatment of children at an orphanage run by the police; dangers posed by a nuclear-power station near Leningrad; the problems of poor, disabled, and lonely people; the battles of rebel artists; communal tensions in Soviet Georgia; the execution of Czar Nicholas II and his family; recollections of Stalinist purge victims; unprecedented footage on the destruction by Stalin of the famous Church of Christ the Redeemer in Moscow; and Arkady Ruderman's interview with former Czechoslovak leader Alexander Dubček.

In one of *Fifth Wheel*'s most unforgettable scenes, Bella Kurkova and Sasha Krivonos tracked down a former Stalinist executioner, who was living in the cramped poverty of old age. Sasha persuaded him to show, on camera, how he shot people.

"Tell me, Andrei Ivanovich," Sasha coaxed the former gulag guard, "from what distance were people shot?"

The bald old man moved around behind Sasha and raised his arm, not quite straight. He made a gun with his hand and pointed his index finger at the back of Sasha's head.

"Bang in the head," he said, eyes staring wildly. "At approximately this distance."

"At the distance of an outstretched arm?" Sasha asked.

"No," the former executioner replied. "Arm slightly bent. You can't shoot with a straight arm."

Then he described how guards later stripped the corpses of jewelry and gold fillings.

"You'd put some sort of spirit, alcohol, on the gums, and the teeth came out easier," he said.

Later in the program, as the camera panned the smokestack of the crematorium at Moscow's Donskoi Monastery, Bella Kurkova took up the narrative, telling viewers that in the dark of night, "trucks with crates marked MEAT or VEGETABLES or FURNITURE would pull up to the crematorium and dump the bodies in the fire. The place where they finally buried the bones and ashes was paved over a few years ago."[10]

Politically, the most explosive broadcasts were a series of three programs on the privileges of the Leningrad Communist Party elite. The first, focusing on Party leaders' exclusive, well-furbished *dachas* in the wooded areas of Stone Island near Leningrad, was called "Silent Walls," for the seven-foot-high walls and fences built to hide these opulent residences from public view. Some of the estates had separate housing for servants. Zoya Belyayeva, the reporter fired for doing the program on B. B. King, climbed the walls with a cameraman to show the lavish mansions that Party leaders had built for themselves, while nearby, a hospital and a historic home of Pushkin's languished in disrepair, for lack of funds.

Stung by the public outcry, Party leaders lashed back at *Fifth Wheel*. They denounced it in the press, and set up an ideological commission to investigate it. A battle royal was on, the Party trying to silence Bella while she made more accusations, more appeals to the public, on her show; and the public egged her on. The first broadcast in December 1988 was followed by two more, on official graft; each was cut by censors, but they were still powerful. The third one ran on March 17, and nine days later was the fateful election in which seven Party bigwigs lost. In the Soviet system, it takes at least 50 percent of eligible votes to win, so there were lots of runoffs that spring.

Fighting for her life and for the survival of *Fifth Wheel* in the second round of the election, Bella Kurkova became a political candidate and carried the battle directly to Yuri Solovyov, the top Party boss in Leningrad and a junior member of the Politburo in Moscow. During a televised debate, Bella attacked Solovyov, who was not present. "I criticized him severely for interfering in our work," she recalled. "I spoke about the fact that when he takes part in an event in town, we are stripped of all the good equipment—cameras, cutting rooms, everything—because the authorities require other crews to shoot him with three cameras." Bella told me she had seized the candidate debate to criticize Solovyov, even in his absence, because she assumed he would never agree to see her.[11]

In the elections, Bella Kurkova was beaten by an even more outspoken foe of the Party apparat, a criminal prosecutor pursuing official corruption named Nikolai Ivanov.

On May 16, two days after the election, Solovyov sent an official car to bring Bella to Party headquarters; the Party was demanding a written explanation for her criticism of him. She refused to go, advised by Anatoly

Sobchak, a lawyer and people's deputy, that her campaign statements were protected by law. But the heat was on, and the campaign to strangle *Fifth Wheel* resumed. Leningrad Mayor Vladimir Khodyrev, who had lost in the election, declared Bella Kurkova and *Fifth Wheel* his personal enemies.

"Can you imagine—who he is and who I am?" Bella said, sharing her astonishment with me. "*We* are dangerous for *him*? The man who is in charge of TV in the Obkom Province Party Committee told me that in the committee offices they jump every time they hear my name. They are afraid of us! The humor is in the fact that *they* are afraid of *us*."[12]

Despite that fear—or because of it—Bella was told that the provincial Party committee had decided to shut down *Fifth Wheel* and fire her. At a closed Party meeting, she was informed, sixteen of twenty-two speakers had come out against the program; only one defended it. "My colleagues tried to console me but the situation was really serious," she told me later. "I remember May twenty-fourth, twenty-fifth, before the opening of the People's Congress [in Moscow]. It looked like our program could be banned."

She went on: "It's a real class struggle against *glasnost*. The apparatchiks think the press is given too much freedom. They don't want the public to learn about their doings. For seventy years, they have been so used to giving orders which are fulfilled. Now the time has come when their orders are ignored. They can't take it. . . . They fan up hatred toward Jews. To divert people's hatred from the Party bureaucrats, they blame Jews. I'm Russian but I am considered a Jew because I think that all nationalities are equal. I receive letters in which they call me a kike."

During the campaign, Party hard-liners had tried to whip up the anger of workers against the intelligentsia, and specifically the media, as a force for liberalization. Neo-Stalinist conservatives, joined by Russian nationalists from the right-wing Pamyat, meaning "Memory," organized a rally near television headquarters, attacking the most aggressive programs— and *Fifth Wheel* was a prime target. Placards declared: THE KGB AND MINISTRY OF INTERNAL AFFAIRS ARE THE STRONGHOLDS OF DEMOCRACY; DOWN WITH *FIFTH WHEEL*; DOWN WITH THE RUSSOPHOBES FROM *FIFTH WHEEL*.

Fifth Wheel put out the word that it was to be closed down.

The public response was overwhelming. Liberal cultural organizations called a counterrally in support of the program. "Many, many people came to that rally," Bella recalled. "The whole square was filled with people. The apparatchiks saw that we were stronger than they were. And that is why they hate us." Other protest meetings were held at institutions and factories. One huge plant sent a telegram to Party leaders: IF YOU TOUCH *FIFTH WHEEL* AND KURKOVA, WE WILL GO ON STRIKE.

Not only did *Fifth Wheel* escape the guillotine, Bella told me triumphantly, but its bête noire, Leningrad Party boss Yuri Solovyov, was removed by Gorbachev for being so out of step with Gorbachev's own policies and, as the elections had shown, with the public.

"I always said either he would outlast us or we would outlast him," Bella said. "Thank God we're the ones who lasted."

"You're a politician, Bella, not just a journalist," I observed.

"I don't think I'm a politician," she replied. "But today, any honest journalist is a politician. Because if you want to restore justice, if you want the life in your country changed, it's necessary," she answered. "Each of us has only one life. It's necessary not to waste it. A decent journalist cannot avoid hot issues. . . .

"We are rather amateurish politicians at *Fifth Wheel*. We tried to stay away from politics. We didn't think it was our business. Then, after our first show was broadcast, politics burst into the life of every person [involved in the show]. In the last year and a half, politics has become almost everyone's concern in the country. There are no indifferent people left."[13]

THE LIMITS OF *GLASNOST*

If Party hard-liners could not close down *Fifth Wheel*, they tried, covertly, to squeeze the life out of it by working through Bella's bosses and employers, and through the Leningrad branch of the State Committee for Television and Radio. Bella's staff was cut by one third. *Fifth Wheel* was reduced from two shows a week to one. It was denied financing and good equipment.

Censorship was tightened through a system that was multilayered: military censors, literary censors with their lists of taboo names and topics, and most important, political censors from the Party apparat and the television administration. The first two were the official censors; the last group were not officially called censors, but they were in fact the most important and most controlling.

In *Fifth Wheel*'s first eighteen months, Bella told me, about twenty segments of various programs had been banned outright by censors before the Party's outright effort to shut it down. Included among them were one on the mass graves at Minsk, an interview with a people's deputy who quoted private statements by Gorbachev that were at odds with his public positions, and a program about the repression of a Soviet choreographer named Roman Yakobson. Twenty more programs had been heavily censored, including the program about the Leningrad nuclear-power station and those on the privileges of the Party elite. Still other programs had been delayed for weeks and months—especially several that dealt with tensions among Soviet nationalities.

In September 1989, Bella fought for approval of a powerful documentary on the Leningrad boss of the NKVD (Stalin's KGB). The man was named Litvin, and he had allegedly ordered the murders of twenty thousand people in 1937, and then committed suicide just as he himself was about to be killed. According to Bella, the new head of Leningrad television, Viktor Senin, had been blocking this film for a couple of months, presumably on orders from Party headquarters. On the script, he had written, "Specify the actions of Litvin." Bella had hopes of bringing Senin around because he was a former *Pravda* correspondent, and better to deal with than the ideological watchdogs the Party usually put in such posts. She urged me, and our camera crew, to go with her to Senin's office.

It was huge, with a polished table long enough for twenty people. Senin, a trim, well-dressed man in his mid-forties with a self-confident jut to his chin, greeted us at his desk. We had asked to see him at that very hour, but our arrival with Bella caught him by surprise. Still, he was polite and agile. On that day, with our cameras rolling, Senin cast himself in the role of a man caught in the middle, forced to serve as agent of the Party hierarchy above him but sympathetic to the journalists and people below.

It was instantly apparent that he was no longer going to block *Fifth Wheel*'s exposé of the NKVD. Without even sitting down, he signed off on what had been a suspect script. Bella winked at me, pleased that her ploy had worked.

"This is the first time we have covered this theme—a machine of extermination," Senin bragged to me. "You see we are giving an inside story about the KGB."

Eager to reinstate his liberal credentials, Senin reported how he had recently championed a program on the controversial people's deputy Boris Yeltsin, over the objections of Party apparatchiks for whom Yeltsin was a mortal enemy.

"I signed off a week before the show and they were trying to ban it up to the last moment," Senin said. "An official from the provincial Party committee was sitting right here, in my office, right on top of my head, telling me, 'You should not,' and I was telling him we should."

"What kind of *glasnost* is this, if they are sitting on top of your head?" I asked.

"There are people who dream of the time when it will be possible to go back to the old methods," he replied. "But we have a TV audience today that can't be shut down by any bureaucrats. They can fire me, they can kick me out of this chair, but they can't silence the audience."

"Can they fire her?" I asked, gesturing to Bella. We were all three still standing around his large desk.

"Sure they can," Senin said, then reconsidered. "No, it's more difficult to fire her. It's a very popular program. That's why we have meetings . . . to think what can be done to preserve this program."

That was enough to launch Bella into a diatribe—for her, a relatively mild one—against the whole process of censorship.

"Above him, on the staircase of power, there are many steps which interfere with his work," she said. "Here in journalism a bureaucratic machine has been created which doesn't care to make journalism exciting and interesting for readers and listeners."

She thrust the script about the NKVD chief at me, showing how the censors were holding her responsible for every single word.

"Each line of the script is checked and double-checked," she protested. Then, riffling through it page by page, she raced on: "I must sign every page. Here is my signature. Let me show you how many times I signed. Thirty-one times. Thirty-second time here, and thirty-third on the back. What's next? Then the censor at the city literary censorship office will have to sign. There is a chance that he won't sign because the show is about the KGB. He can send me to the censor of the KGB. They also have a censor."

She was describing a system stuck in inertia, which, out of habits bred over decades, squashed independent-minded journalists and ignored Gorbachev's dictates for greater openness. This system had a reflexive instinct for self-preservation, a natural suspicion of anything new. The state monopoly of broadcasting, which Gorbachev had retained, made Senin's office a natural choke point.

"Bella is right when she says we have too many people who are not responsible for anything but who have a right to ban things," Senin said. "That's how they earn their salaries."

"But what's the reason for it?" I asked.

"Well, they have to do *something*," Senin sputtered. "They aren't qualified to do anything else. They have to demonstrate they are working hard, that they are zealous. If they forbid a lot of things, it means they're doing their job. They can show their superiors at the Party committee that they are zealous, because they censor things."

"How many people are there?" I asked. "Ten?"

"Oh no. About a hundred and fifty, and all over the country about eighteen million," Senin replied, using the figure Gorbachev gave for the entire national bureaucratic apparatus. "I am talking about our provincial committee staff. They must be responsible for something. They must pretend they are working. Do you expect them to show up and say, 'Viktor, go ahead, air the show'? They'll die from fear."

"How often do they visit you?" I asked.

"Every day," he said. "Every day."

"But Gorbachev said there should be more openness," I reminded him.

"For whom?"

"For everyone."

"Excuse me." Senin straightened up. "Gorbachev himself is not quite free to do what he wants. He is tied hand and foot. Even *he* cannot control things."[14]

HOW THEY PORTRAY US

The brawl between *Fifth Wheel* and the Leningrad Party apparat illustrates how the media have become both an instrument of change and a prime political battleground. This is true all across the country. The revolution in the Soviet media, their coverage of the West as well as of domestic affairs, has played a vital role in reshaping public attitudes and in driving the political agenda of *perestroika* in ways that Gorbachev did not anticipate.

In the summer of 1988, nationalist movements in the Baltic republics of Lithuania, Estonia, and Latvia were practically born on local television-discussion shows. In Georgia, Armenia, Azerbaijan, and elsewhere, the spark of nationalism was spread by regional television. In mid-1989, striking coal miners in Siberia and the southern Ukraine forced their demands on Gorbachev and Prime Minister Nikolai Ryzhkov through the visibility and political leverage given them by local and national television.

At Kemerovo, in western Siberia, Aleksandr Melnikov, the regional Party boss, complained to me that the media, especially television, were hounding him, publicizing the grievances of workers and criticizing him.[15] A senior television official, Gennady Metyakhin, openly disagreed with the Party leadership over the sources and cures of trouble in the coal mines. They clashed as well over the proper function of state television: As Party boss, Melnikov wanted his regional television to help mobilize factory workers to go out into rural areas and bring in the harvest; Metyakhin refused to be the Party's mouthpiece, asserting that this would merely perpetuate an inefficient farm system, rather than bring a reform of Stalin's collectivized farm system.

"We don't want to help the bureaucracy," he said, "because if the harvest is brought in that way, then once again the Party will claim, 'Thanks to our leadership, the people are well fed and happy.' "[16]

In Yaroslavl, four young journalists told me how Aleksandr Tsvetkov, a gutsy local television reporter, had battled his skittish TV bosses and forced them to let him broadcast a series that exposed a major construction scandal. The mayor was forced to resign and a slew of Party officials were punished.[17]

What is astonishing is that this fresh breeze is blowing through one of the stalest, most centralized monopolies of the Soviet state—Gosteleradio—the State Committee for Television and Radio. Back in the seventies, Soviet national television was leaden and immobile; it was the most politically orthodox of all the media because the Kremlin worried about the impact of any whimper of dissonance on the immense national television audience. On the stage and occasionally in books, little heresies were allowed to slip through. But not on television.

Only two channels broadcast nationwide across the eleven time zones, from Vladivostok on the Pacific to Kaliningrad near Poland: the First Program, for the most important news and cultural events, and the Second Program, for less important shows. Moscow had two other channels, for several hours a day, one for adult education and another for sports. Minority republics and important regional centers like Leningrad or Novosibirsk were allowed for a few hours a week to broadcast local programming, which was usually heavy on folklore and native costumes. In other words, it was a dull wasteland in the early 1970s, so insufferably dull that a Soviet diplomat, back home after a stint in Washington, admitted to me that his eleven-year-old son, having become accustomed to American TV, was bored out of his wits with Soviet programming and had become practically unmanageable.

The Soviet news, carried coast to coast to what was then estimated to be 100 million viewers (it's now 150 million), was literally read to viewers by announcers who were more notable for buttoned-up reliability than for their ease on camera. Flat and formal, the shows were also heavily censored. *Vremya (The Times)*, the one evening news show, which came on at 9 P.M., was long on official Soviet communiqués, gray bureaucrats in wooden ceremonies, Foreign Minister Andrei Gromyko shaking hands with visiting delegations, and foreign footage of violence in America, protest marchers in Germany or Britain, bloodshed in Vietnam. Interspersed were paeans to Soviet economic achievements, statistics, films of

Soviet harvesters in formation as they swept across fields of waving wheat, blast furnaces belching mightily for the Socialist Cause. Children's programs, sports events, and concerts or ballets provided some relief, but even so the camera work was monotonous.

An anecdote mocked these programs: A viewer tuned in to find, on the First Program, Brezhnev delivering a windy speech. He switched to the Second Program: again, Brezhnev droning on. On the Third Program, a uniformed officer pointed a gun at the viewer and ordered: "Comrade, go back to Channel One."

Today, there are startling changes in form, style, and content. While much of the old wooden programming persists, a host of new shows offer live programming, Western-style visuals and graphics, a sprinkling of ads, and some out-and-out entertainment. Rock music and MTV have arrived with a vengeance. Even the morning news is spiced every few minutes with splashy, non-sequitur cutaways to Soviet rock groups or pop singers in spangly costumes and voluptuous poses. In the old days, women on Soviet TV were dowdy or costumed. Now, willowy young women lead aerobics classes or do suggestive dances in skintight leotards, and on news shows, the anchorwomen dress more stylishly. *Vremya* is still pretty tame, but even it has more on-the-spot reporting and a quotient of controversial material. The rest of the TV programming includes topical talk shows, fashion parades, game shows, film clips of Western stars from the Beatles to Bruce Springsteen, and even an occasional beauty contest.

The hard edges of the old Cold War stereotypes have been rounded off. Just as the American media have found plenty that is positive in the Gorbachev-*perestroika* story, the Soviet media no longer portray the West as a hostile armed camp seething with social tensions and anti-Soviet cabals. For one thing, Soviet television has given its viewer direct, uncensored access to Americans, from former Secretary of State George Shultz or Moscow-based American correspondents, to live satellite telecasts of citizen exchanges between cities like Seattle and Leningrad, or arguments between American senators and Soviet legislators.

What is more, the image of America itself is changing, as coverage becomes more balanced and varied. Typical of the new attitude was the public confessional I heard, in Tbilisi in September 1988, from Melor Sturua, a veteran Washington correspondent for *Izvestia*. Sturua acknowledged that his reporting on America had been deliberately negative, meant to reinforce ideological stereotypes. He voiced personal shame and promised to turn over a new leaf. Later, Valentin Lazutkin, deputy chairman and chief of foreign relations for Gosteleradio, wanted to be sure I took notice of the shift from the bad old days.

"Our picture of capitalist countries used to be very negative," he admitted. "We emphasized the poor and the homeless. From our correspondents in America, we used to order stories such as who is sleeping under the Brooklyn Bridge [an actual report in 1985]. We knew, especially those of us who traveled to the West, that this was a one-sided picture. Now we don't order such stories anymore—although like you we assert our right to cover anything and everything. But we try now to give a more balanced and accurate picture of life in the West."[18]

By the late 1980s, the Soviet press had a flow of favorable stories, especially about how well the American economy was working. Soviet television did admiring portraits of the McDonald's fast-food service, the efficiency of construction projects in Seattle, a well-run American family farm in Iowa, and even the way American political conventions operate. In a three-part documentary series on American farming, Soviet viewers got an impressive look at the modern technology used by family farmers, from tractors to computers—not to mention what to Russians would be an incredible network of businesses serving the farmer. In a report on traffic congestion in New York City, Soviet TV also ran flattering shots of the interstate highway system—light-years ahead of the rutted, gutted Soviet roads. Another documentary took a close look at Congress, showing its inner workings, almost textbook-style, for Soviet newcomers to the world of parliamentary politics. Policy differences on issues such as the American invasion of Panama or the war in Nicaragua have been pointed out, but without the vitriol of the coverage during the Cold War. And, wonder of wonders, given the traditional Soviet treatment of sports, Moscow television has run advertisements showing American athletes winning gold medals at the 1988 Olympics.

Ordinary Soviets have an enormous appetite for realistic pictures of the outside world, both out of curiosity and out of a desire for a standard by which to measure their own lives. At a grass-roots level, I have found them to be far more curious about us than we as a nation have been about them, and their greater interest shows up in the media. Academic specialists have found, for example, that Soviet television has given more coverage to foreign news than American networks have.[19] As Sturua and Lazutkin conceded in the past, the coverage has fit the paradigms of Soviet ideology.

With *glasnost,* and especially with the crumbling of Communist regimes in Eastern Europe in the fall of 1989, Soviet viewers got a fresh slant on events abroad. The breaching of the Berlin Wall, for example, was given timely and candid coverage. Sakharov's widow, Yelena Bonner, compared the opening of the Wall to the capture of the Bastille during the French Revolution. "Our TV showed all of this," she said. "We saw the same things you saw—those people on top of the wall."[20] Tass, the official Soviet press agency, was quick to assure Russians that the collapse of the Wall—and the collapse of the old hard-line regime—did not mean any change in the postwar borders, a sensitive issue for Russians. Before long, their focus, like ours, shifted to Bucharest, and the bloody Romanian revolt, the overthrow of Nicolae Ceauşescu, was played out on Soviet television.

It intrigued me that throughout the tumultuous events of 1989 and 1990, Moscow television was more candid about the political upheavals in Eastern Europe than it was about the nationalist tensions within its own borders. The Moscow media, especially television and its flagship, Vremya, have either ignored or given tendentious accounts of the violent suppression of the peaceful demonstrations in Georgia in April 1989, the bloody occupation of Azerbaijan in January 1990, the Lithuanian drive toward secession in the spring of 1990. Despite such omissions, Vremya remains the most-watched program in the nation, helped by its monopoly on the evening news. But cautious coverage of the most ticklish domestic developments has cost it some credibility. To most people, it is no longer the premier pacesetter of Soviet television.

THE FRIDAY-NIGHT RITUAL

The most popular program—the one that epitomizes the new trendiness and daring—is a brassy weekly magazine show that is like a combination of Nightline, 60 Minutes, and MTV. It is called Vzglyad—meaning "Glance" or "View." My pollster friends say that it is at least six or seven times more popular than any other program, especially with the under-thirty-five crowd. For modish young Muscovites, Vzglyad serves up a blend of cool informality, hot rock, and the most modern video gimmickry on Soviet TV. In bastions of conservatism like Minsk, Kiev, or Ivanovo in the Russian heartland, Vzglyad is a shot of adrenaline to advocates of change. Even its detractors have to watch it, to be in on what's new and controversial. Vzglyad never fails to stir reactions—enough to receive fifteen thousand letters a month and to get the national chief of Soviet television fired.

Shock is its trademark. Since it began on October 2, 1987, Vzglyad has broken more taboos and more exclusives than any other show on television. It has interviewed Gorbachev and Nina Andreyeva, presented Western rock stars such as Pink Floyd and Bon Jovi, and examined both the

Soviet and American armies. If *Fifth Wheel* is made up primarily of documentaries, *Vzglyad* consists of sharp talk and fast-paced movie segments. In an hour and a half to two hours, it rarely lingers with one segment for more than six or seven minutes. Watching it on Friday night has become a ritual all across the country. From Moscow to Yaroslavl, Sverdlovsk to Tallinn, I have watched parties and conversations stop dead in their tracks at 10 P.M. Friday, when *Vzglyad* comes on.

The show on the eve of the March 1990 elections was typical of *Vzglyad*'s kaleidoscopic pace. It opened with quick little sound bites of people telling why they believed in the Communist Party or why they were fed up with it. Cut to the Soviet rock group Nautilus Pompilius, singing, *"We're all soldered together, like pieces of a chain."* Then, over shots of Stalin in pompous poses, a historian asserts that Soviet tyranny began not with Stalin but with Lenin. Cut to a report from Bulgaria about moves toward a multiparty system. Switch to a montage on life in the West, from Michael Jackson to Americans hiking in the forests, scenes of pro football, and Carneval in Rio. Cut to a piece on a would-be Soviet Madonna, a singer named Laima Vaikal, with a throaty voice, high cheekbones, liquid hips, and blond Scandinavian beauty. Switch to mothers in Byelorussia sobbing about the radiation sickness their children suffered in the Chernobyl nuclear accident. Cut to a joint interview—rare for Soviet television—with Moscow Communist Party boss Yuri Prokofyev and former gulag dissident Sergei Kovolev. Cut to an economist urging the formation of private banks. Segue to a sequence from an upcoming movie about a lovers' tryst on a train. And finally, a tongue-in-cheek recitation of great moments in Soviet history on March 2: 1930—Stalin proclaiming the success of collectivization; 1931—Gorbachev born; 1957—Khrushchev saying America could never catch up with the Soviets in space.

To Anatoly Lysenko, *Vzglyad*'s producer and a canny old television hand, this program resembles an original idea of his from the 1970s. He had wanted to create a television show that was as candid and unpredictable as kitchen-table conversation. He dubbed it *In Your Kitchen,* which is where Russians had usually let their hair down. But this was the Brezhnev era, and the television watchdogs were not buying experiments. "We didn't find a common language with the leadership of television at that time," is how Lysenko tactfully put it to me. "Without *glasnost,* this show couldn't have happened."[21]

When Lysenko finally got the go-ahead, he roped in three young comers from Moscow radio, Dmitri Zakharov, Sasha Lyubimov, and Vladislav Listyev, live wires, but inexperienced in television. They became instant anchors, with nothing but a few hours of coaching from a circus clown on how to behave in front of the camera. It worked, Lysenko felt, partly because people were stunned to see a live talk show led by anchors slouching in easy chairs and dressed in jeans and windbreakers rather than sitting at desks in coats and ties.

"I don't like the news so much," observed Zakharov, obviously putting down *Vremya*. "They write a script. It's read. And then it's thrown into a wastebasket. That's too close to life itself."

Zakharov, at thirty-one, is the central figure of the three and the most iconoclastic. He is a wiry, slender intellectual, with a lively sense of the absurd, alert brown eyes, an artful way of staying laid back while he draws people out—and then pouncing on them. He stands in a permanent slouch, his silhouette forming a question mark. It should be forming an exclamation point, for he is given to sudden, dartlike pronouncements. Walking to a coatrack one day, he casually remarked to me: "This is a country of fading fascism, like Spain and Portugal were, only it is fading here later than in those other countries." When I asked about Communism, he mockingly shot back, "Oh, Communism and all that? . . . I don't know what socialism is." While others like Bella Kurkova work at exposing Stalin's Red Terror, Zakharov sees the roots of Soviet violence in Lenin. For him, the execution of Czar Nicholas II and his family was unnecessary. "It made all the later killing possible, if not inevitable," he said.[22]

Zakharov, who graduated from the Maurice Thorez Institute of Foreign Languages, is an avid fan of Monty Python and Alec Guinness. He studied hundreds of hours of Western TV footage to develop concepts for *Vzglyad*. But, he advised me, "you must take into account the Russian mentality."

"What do you mean?" I asked.

"This is a country of poor people, with a distorted psychology, who for seventy years have been deceived and pumped full of ideology."

"So what do you do?" I asked.

"You have to explain everything very simply to them—this was this and that was that," he replied. "I want to have a program showing people that the Revolution was not made for them. This is all very painful. When you tell them that they have been deceived, they don't believe you. It turns out many of them prefer to be fooled rather than to know the truth."

In shattering old myths and stereotypes, *Vzglyad* has used hard-hitting reporting on problems that Soviet propaganda used to relegate to the capitalist West—prostitution, police corruption, and drug addiction. When Soviet forces killed nineteen people while suppressing a peaceful demonstration in Tbilisi, Georgia, on April 9, 1989, *Vzglyad* was the first national television program to run film showing the bloodshed and tying it to the army and security forces. The following January, when a violent right-wing group raided a meeting at the Writers' Union in Moscow, shouting anti-Semitic slogans, *Vzglyad* broke the story. Months before the Soviet government was prepared to admit that Stalin's NKVD had slaughtered thousands of Polish army officers at Katyn, in Byelorussia, at the end of the war, *Vzglyad* presented the evidence. Nikolai Travkin, a people's deputy, suggested on *Vzglyad* that Prime Minister Nikolai Ryzh- kov's wife give up the special stores for the Party elite and get a taste of shortages and standing in line with ordinary folks at the regular state stores.

Vzglyad pioneered one arena after another. In 1987 and 1988, it put more Soviet rock on television than any other program, giving mass exposure to Soviet heavy-metal groups such as Akvarium, DDT, and Brigada S. Their stark, sarcastic lyrics often brought delays from the censors. In "Revolution," DDT sings:

> *Two fingers held high—that's victory.*
> *But it's really a poke in the eye . . .*
> *But, Revolution, you've taught us to believe*
> *That good can be perverted.*
> *How many worlds do we burn up in an hour*
> *In the name of your sacred flame? . . .*
> *How many Afghanis does death cost?*[23]

Vzglyad was the first to report on AIDS in the Soviet Union, revealing that there were eighty-one cases of children with the virus in the provin- cial cities of Elista and Volgograd and pointing the finger at hospitals. Yevgeniya Albatso, a reporter for *Moscow News*, declared on *Vzglyad:* "No mother in the Soviet Union today can be guaranteed that her child will not be infected with AIDS. . . . You see our maternity hospitals are simply made for AIDS to spread uncontrollably. There is filth, lack of disposable medical products, one toilet for a postnatal ward of seventy women. Eighty percent of the maternity hospitals in Moscow are infected with staphylococcus. . . . In our country, however blasphemous it may sound, the main source of AIDS infection is health-care organizations and their polyclinics and hospitals."[24]

While Soviet troops were still in Afghanistan, *Vzglyad* ran powerful footage on the carnage. In one sequence, there was an audio track of a Soviet pilot whose helicopter had been hit. It was plunging out of control, and his words, barely intelligible, became panicked and hysterical, rising to a high-pitched squeal. Then, at the final second, the audience heard his last transmission: "Farewell. Farewell." Then a crash, and a lingering silence.[25]

The military has been one of *Vzglyad*'s spiciest targets, in part because the show caters to a young audience, for whom the draft, the Afghan war, and military spending are hot topics. One program featured the novelist Yuri Polyakov, whose book *One Hundred Days Before Mustering Out* described the violent hazing, gang rapes, and psychological browbeating of raw recruits by older soldiers. *Vzglyad*'s exposés of this often interethnic brutality, known as *dedovshchina;* its repeated critiques of the draft; and its pressures for a professional army so nettled Defense Minister Dmitri Yazov that he summoned Zakharov for a sharp dressing-down. Other military officers accused the program of "slandering the army" and fanning hostility toward career officers. *Vzglyad*'s anchors replied that all three had served in the military, and some of their staff had been in Afghanistan. Zakharov told me that he pursued military stories because it had "dawned on me one day in school that these guys could kill us all someday because they have the button, and I thought they should be under control."

But *Vzglyad*'s biggest political bombshell was its broadcast of the blasphemous proposal that the central shrine of Soviet Communism, the Lenin mausoleum, be removed from Red Square and that Lenin be given a normal burial in Leningrad with his wife, Nadezhda Krupskaya. That bolt of political lightning was hurled not by *Vzglyad*'s anchors but by a guest, Mark Zakharov (no relation to Dmitri Zakharov), director of the Leninsky Komsomol Theater. The mausoleum had been not Lenin's idea but Stalin's—he intended to immortalize Lenin and thereby build the cult of the Party and its leader. Mark Zakharov suggested this was immoral and that the mausoleum was tacky. "No matter how much we hate a person, no matter how much we love him," he asserted, "we do not have the right to deprive a person of burial."

That outrageously seditious suggestion touched off an absolute storm at the Communist Party Central Committee meeting on April 25, 1989, just four days after the broadcast. Party leaders were on a rampage against the press and media after the humiliating defeats many of them had suffered in the March 1989 elections, and *Vzglyad* became the lightning rod for their general fury. The chairman of Gosteleradio, a senior Party veteran named Aleksandr Aksenov, joined in the general condemnation, obviously trying to save his own neck. The suggestion to move Lenin was "rude," Aksenov declared, adding that on television, "political mistakes are especially inadmissible."[26]

A few days later, Vadim Medvedev, the Politburo's chief for press and ideology, paid a visit to Gosteleradio for a two-hour session with the major figures at *Vzglyad,* presumably to roll some heads. Dmitri Zakharov, ever the history buff and quick to live by his wits, was well prepared. "We had a discussion about our program and its influence, and [Medvedev] said, 'By the way, about Lenin . . .' " Zakharov recalled with a wry grin. "I had found some documents from Krupskaya which spoke of Lenin's desire for a normal burial and not to have a mausoleum. And Medvedev couldn't really argue with Lenin."

Somehow the ax did not fall on Mark Zakharov either; Gorbachev seemed to be friendly and approving toward him a few days later at a large reception. It was Aksenov, the head of Gosteleradio, who took the fall. Within a month he was fired, the prime casualty of *Vzglyad's* irreverence toward the sacrosanct figure of Lenin.

Nonetheless, as with *Fifth Wheel,* the noose has tightened on *Vzglyad.* As the months wore on, fewer and fewer of its segments went on live and unrehearsed, leaving fewer chances to slip things past the censors. A white phone was put on the anchors' table, amid phones used for viewer call-ins; this was the line by which management told the anchors, while they were on the air, to get off some sensitive theme. Here and there, Gosteleradio bosses have sheared away offensive material. An interview with historian Vyacheslav Kondratev, which was highly critical of Lenin, was trimmed back sharply. An interview with former Czechoslovak leader Alexander Dubček was stalled six months. Zakharov produced a probing film on the execution of Czar Nicholas II and his family, but the new boss of Gosteleradio, Mikhail Nenashev, refused to let it go on the air. When *Vzglyad* got documents showing that Stalin's NKVD had cooperated with Nazi forces invading Poland, helping them to locate military targets with radio signals, it broadcast that revelation on its first transmissions to the Soviet Far East. But the censors banned it from later broadcasts to central Russia, the Ukraine, Byelorussia, and the Baltics, the regions neighboring Poland. On the same show, September 1, 1989, *Vzglyad's* censor barred an impersonation of Gorbachev by the comedian Mikhail Grushevsky.[27]

But the sharpest blow was the seizure of the tape for *Vzglyad's* year-end show for 1989. Scheduled for broadcast on December 29, it was full of New Year's Eve–style black humor. It opened with a serious segment on the life and funeral of Andrei Sakharov, the physicist who had become the moral leader of the democratic opposition and who had died shortly before. Another segment, more offensive to the television hierarchy, was a parody of a *Vremya* broadcast of government ministers seeking a solution to the nation's economic problems. "In it, I had a discussion with a wizard and a prophet about *perestroika* and the fate of the economy,"

Zakharov told me. "As the discussion ended, a huge spider ran across the stage, and I said, 'We can't put our faith in wizards and prophets. We have to believe in the further development of democracy in our country.'"

The final segment was a melancholy allegory about the ultimate fate of *perestroika*, reflecting the pessimism of the Moscow intelligentsia in the winter of 1989–90. It played out the liberals' nightmare ending for the current era of reform. In this scene the three anchors were sitting around a fictional campfire of the future, representing three advocates of more aggressive reform—deputies Boris Yeltsin and Yuri Afanasyev, and Vitaly Korotich, editor of *Ogonek*. They were deep in the woods, wearing the uniforms of gulag prisoners and mulling over the past. "Once upon a time," they said, "there was *perestroika*. But the president was too kind to take steps against the right-wing extremists." With that, a gulag guard with a submachine gun arrived to order them "back to the barracks"—a symbolic slogan for Stalinism.

"A lot of elements in this program bothered the authorities. So they sent a fat old woman to get the cassette," Zakharov told me. "She was trembling. She said, 'I'm very sorry, but I have to take this.' It was astounding to us. That had never happened before. One of us destroyed the master tape, out of fear of more serious actions being taken. They had seized the show tape the day before the program. The next day, they returned it—we don't know why. But by then, we decided that we did not want to air the program. We felt, 'They did this thing. Let them live with the consequences.' So the program didn't run and Nenashev had to give a press conference to explain why. He said the program was bad, dull, poorly put together."[28]

For the bulk of the Party hierarchy *Vzglyad* represents the worst of the Pandora's box that Gorbachev has opened. As they began their reforms, they accepted Gorbachev's logic that modernizing the country meant allowing greater intellectual freedom for scientists, industry, even the arts, and requiring greater honesty about the past. But the ways of democracy have clearly been more provocative and unruly than they anticipated, and they have fought back.

What is more, Gorbachev himself has been quixotic, sometimes urging the press on and other times warning it not to overstep some vague line. In October 1989, for example, Gorbachev went after Vladislav Starkov, chief editor of *Argumenty i Fakty*. He had published a readers' poll about attitudes toward members of the Supreme Soviet that made Gorbachev look bad. At a closed meeting of senior editors, Gorbachev thundered that Starkov's poll was "divisive" and intolerable and Starkov should quit. In the old days, that would have finished Starkov's career. But in the spirit of the new politics, Starkov stood his ground, backed by his staff and a readership of twenty-six million, the highest circulation in the country. It was ironic that Gorbachev had picked on him, because Starkov, while assertive, was not among the most provocative editors. In the end, Gorbachev relented.

Vzglyad's survival, given its more persistently provocative record, is harder to understand without some appreciation for the factional infighting within the upper reaches of the Communist Party. In Leningrad, the Party apparatus is relatively unified and conservative. That deprived Bella Kurkova of high-level patrons for *Fifth Wheel*. In Moscow, there are Party radicals and progressives in high posts as well as hard-liners. Obviously, *Vzglyad* has had its well-placed protectors. I suggested to Zakharov and Lyubimov that *Vzglyad*'s main patron was Aleksandr Yakovlev, Gorbachev's close ally and the guiding spirit behind *glasnost.* They did not want to say. But others connected with the show privately agreed, pointing as well to influential reformers in the Central Committee apparatus a level or two below Yakovlev, officials who might not have liked the jab about reburying Lenin, but were still ready to protect *Vzglyad* so that it could keep stoking the fires of reform. In other words, *Vzglyad* benefited from the splintering of power that Gorbachev set free, but it has suffered from his failure, or unwillingness, to break the grip of the old system.

Vzglyad's mixture of sensational popular success and unending difficulty with the powers-that-be tells a great deal about how far reform in the media has come and how far it still has to go. New freedoms are there for the bold to grasp and fight for, but they are not complete. Nor are they guaranteed. In 1987, as he was gearing up *glasnost,* Gorbachev promised to provide a law guaranteeing the rights of the press and media. But three years later, editors and broadcasters were still waiting for that law. One quite progressive piece of legislation I was shown provided for the end of censorship and took control of the media away from the Communist Party by allowing any group or individual to operate a publication or a television outlet. That bill was drafted by liberal deputies in the Supreme Soviet and approved by the Committee on Glasnost. But months later, the bill was still bottled up by Party bureaucrats who were keeping it from coming to a public vote under the ruse of having it studied by experts. Even without the press law, efforts were under way to establish an independent television network and outlets—another method of assuring greater freedom and less control. But Gosteleradio was fighting tooth and nail to hang on to its monopoly.

Without legal protection and alternatives to state ownership, the media can be neither free nor secure. As Bella Kurkova said to me, "I don't dismiss the idea we may finish in a prison camp," like the three characters in *Vzglyad*'s banned program. But each new truth the public learns is itself an irreversible step, a small but important widening of the borders of the permissible and a shrinking of the forbidden domain controlled by censors. Ultimately, of course, public opinion—what the public demands and expects—has been and will be the greatest protection and guarantee for ground-breaking programs like *Fifth Wheel* and *Vzglyad* and their counterparts in the print media, such as the weeklies *Ogonek* and *Moscow News*.

"What people are finding out today about the past is the first and greatest guarantee that they will not want to return to that past," was how Yegor Yakovlev, chief editor of *Moscow News*, put it. "The thing is we can adopt any law or decree, and easily change it later. The single guarantee is public opinion. Public opinion has found out so much that only a suicidal person could return to the past. And that's the most important thing."[29]

PART THREE

LOOKING FOR PERESTROIKA

*T*he economy was the real reason for Mikhail Gorbachev's rise to power. It will be the ultimate test of his success.

The economy that Gorbachev inherited was in desperate straits: Growth rates were tumbling, consumer shortages were endemic, the farms were not feeding the Soviet people, smokestack industry was old-fashioned, rigid, inefficient. The Information Age was passing the Russians by.

World competition was a goad, and a challenge. Not only Gorbachev, but his scientists, economists, Politburo colleagues, even his generals, understood that, as a superpower, the Soviet Union was slipping because its economy could not keep pace with the world.

Soviet prospects in the twenty-first century were bleak—unless something dramatic was done. In stark language, Gorbachev spelled out the stakes and the nation's mission to his countrymen: "Only an intensive, highly developed economy can safeguard our country's position on the international stage and allow her to enter the new millennium with dignity as a great and flourishing power."[1]

And yet the messianic Gorbachev set off on his bold effort to modernize the Soviet economy and to catch up with the West without a blueprint, without a model, without even an overall economic strategy. On *glasnost*, Gorbachev's strategy was clear; on economics, he improvised, deferring often to Prime Minister Nikolai Ryzhkov. He proceeded by trial and error.

In his first months, Gorbachev sailed under the banner of *uskoreniye*—

acceleration—intending mainly to tap science and technology to lift the Soviet economy out of its morass. To improve performance, he created new bureaucracies, one of them a huge new agency to enforce quality control. To sharpen work discipline, he launched a drive against alcoholism. To energize the government, he fired old Brezhnev hacks and promoted their deputies.

Only belatedly, when *uskoreniye* failed to produce what he wanted, did Gorbachev turn to structural reform, to *perestroika;* only then did he declare that generating new dynamism would require "scope for the initiative and creativity of the masses and for genuine revolutionary transformations."[2]

Even *perestroika,* however, was a vision, not a program with well-thought-out phases. It was a move away from the old, but Gorbachev never clearly defined the new. By declaring it as his goal, he launched his own search for *perestroika.*

That was enough to stir a battle royal within the Soviet system. On the offensive in 1987 and 1988, Gorbachev tackled one sector after another: promulgating new rules and laws; declaring his desire to tame the massive, centralized superstructure that commanded the Soviet economy; promising new freedom to industrial managers, farmers, even private entrepreneurs. But he quickly discovered that economic change is much more of a test than turning loose the press or declaring elections.

At every inch, his economic measures met resistance and opposition— from ministers, bureaucrats, and Party bigwigs (even from Ryzhkov), who saw their power threatened; from ordinary people, skeptical of yet another leader's promises of a better life and wary of the risks of a genuinely free market; from advisers, who warned of a popular backlash, even civil violence, if state prices were raised; from radical reformers, who pushed for bolder, more sweeping changes.

For Gorbachev, the temptation was powerful to try incremental change, to settle for half measures, to compromise. But this, too, had its risks.

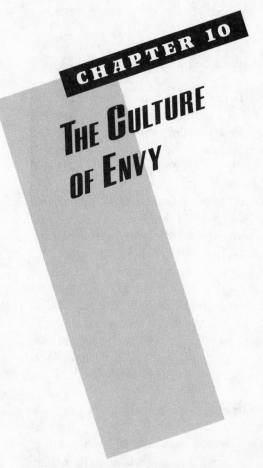

CHAPTER 10

THE CULTURE OF ENVY

PEASANT SAYING: Remember—the tallest blade of grass is the first to be cut down by the scythe.

MORAL: Do not try to stand above the crowd, the collective.

"Perestroika has to happen in the mind. For it to work, people's outlooks have to change."[1]
—Vladimir Pozner
TV Commentator
June 1988

One Saturday evening in the autumn of 1989, when I was working late, alone, in a Moscow office loaned to my film group by an American friend, I heard a knock at the office door. I couldn't imagine who it might be.

It was sometime after ten, and even when I had come in at around six, the building had been so deserted that I could hear my footsteps echoing in the corridor. The *dezhurnaya,* an elderly Russian woman working as the twenty-four-hour watchman, had had to unlock the front door for me. She had emerged from the *dezhurnaya's* room, no bigger than a closet, in which was crammed a cot, a small desk, clothes hooks, a hot plate. Each day, a different *dezhurnaya* was on duty; I'd never seen this woman before.

In Moscow, unexpected knocks at the door can bear ill tidings. I wondered who would be interrupting me at that hour in a locked office in a locked building.

When I opened the door, there stood the *dezhurnaya,* a rather tall woman in her sixties, erect and businesslike. I asked if there was some problem.

"No," she said, "no problem." She paused, then said, "You've been working hard for a long time. You must be hungry. Would you like me to fix you a cup of tea?"

I was startled, not only because she and I were total strangers but also because I have encountered many a *dezhurnaya,* and most have the mentality of a sentry—gruff, suspicious of aliens, protective of turf, and accustomed to reducing human commerce to the inspection of a permit. I mumbled something like: "It's really not necessary. I hadn't realized it had gotten so late. I'll be leaving soon."

She could see my papers spread out, could reckon that I would be there for some time. *"Seichas, prinesu,"* she said—"I'll bring it in a moment."

I was deep into my work again and had almost forgotten her when she returned, not just with a cup of tea but with a whole tray of things, including four small open-faced sandwiches, bologna topped by a slice of cucumber, plus a packet of tasty Polish biscuits. She said in clear but unpracticed English, "I put some strawberry preserves in your tea. We do it that way. Is that right? Is that how you say it, 'strawberry preserves'?"

Understanding that she must have sacrificed part of her own nighttime rations, I thanked her, invited her to sit down, and said her English was quite correct. Not wanting to intrude, she stood by the doorway of our inner office as we talked.

I learned that she was a retired teacher, supplementing her tiny pension. To pass the hours, she was reading *Mezhdunarodnayazhizn (International Life),* a Soviet magazine in which the man whose office I was using, Simon Chilewich, had an article. The magazine also happened to include an excerpt from *The Power Game,* my book on Washington, D.C.

"Oh, I'll look for it," she said. "But I don't even know your name."

When I told her and asked her name, she said, "My name is Anna Ivanovna." Only then did we shake hands, as properly acquainted. In return for her generosity, I gave her a book and some magazines to practice her English, and after that, when I saw her, we would swap stories, comments, little gifts.

That first late-night encounter illustrates an endearing quality of the Russians—their extraordinarily warm hospitality, their love of bestowing gifts on each other and on people whom they choose to befriend, especially foreign visitors. I have often encountered this touching generosity. For example, one night when my wife, Susan, and I were leaving Minsk on a late train for Moscow, two new Soviet acquaintances surprised us by showing up at the station to say good-bye. One, Galina Laskova, arrived with a huge bouquet of flowers for Susan—they must have cost her 10–15 rubles, more than a day's pay. The other, Maya Klishtornaya, presented Susan with a book of Byelorussian recipes, now out of print and a rare treasure, which probably came from her own library.

Flowers are a special hallmark of hospitality in the Soviet Union. Once, a slender, gracious schoolteacher named Nana Batashvili struck up an acquaintance with Susan during a Soviet-American conference in Tbilisi, Georgia, and she subsequently invited us home. She lived in a cramped apartment with six other members of her family—her mother, sister, sister's husband, and their three children. Their furniture was tasteful but limited. The floors were bare. What sticks out in my memory is a shelf stuffed with books. Both teachers, the sisters were surely underpaid. The brother-in-law had been disabled by a heart attack, and disability pensions are below Soviet poverty levels. So their family means were severely limited. Nonetheless, the brother-in-law immediately bought Susan an immense bouquet of roses. The next day, after feasting us on a traditional Georgian meal, Nana pulled two books of illustrated Georgian folk tales from their bookshelf as a gift, and her brother-in-law produced four bottles of Mukuzani, one of Georgia's best red wines. These were gifts the family could ill afford, but when I tried to take no more than one bottle of wine, they sneaked the other bottles into our taxi.

Often, the poorer a person's circumstances, the more generous his or her instincts. One morning, as we entered a government building in Sverdlovsk, about two thousand miles east of Moscow, our talking in English drew the attention of an old woman washing the floors. While the guard checked our credentials, she disappeared, and soon she re-emerged with a container of milk, which she handed Susan. We knew that getting that milk had cost this woman a long wait in line in the early hours of the morning. We tried to deflect her gift, but she insisted. Having spotted us as Americans, she wanted to make this gesture. "Please, take it," she told Susan. "It's fresh. It is very good for you, our milk."

To American travelers who have found Russians on the street to be brusque and impersonal, who have found Soviet officials cold and rigid, and Soviet waiters exasperating in their imperious and surly indifference, this generous side of the Russian character often comes as a surprise. But the Russian character is made up of both coldness and warmth.

Over the years, I have found Russians generally to be a warm and sentimental people, more like the Irish or the Italians than like most Americans. One reason many Russians don't especially like the Baltic peoples—Estonians, Lithuanians, and Latvians—is that they find them too cool and reserved, too self-contained, too Nordic. Russians are more emotional, more likely to strike deep friendships, less superficially gregarious. They make great sacrifices for those within their trusted circle, and they expect real sacrifices in return. Their willingness, indeed their eagerness, to engage at a personal level makes private life in Russia both enormously rich and incredibly entangling. Close emotional bonds are part of Russia's enchantment and also its complexity. It complicates Gorbachev's drive to set up a law-governed state, for example, because people are more readily moved by the partisanship of personal loyalties than by belief in individual rights and a sense of fair play. Within the trusted tribal ring, the bonds are strong, but outside it, the frictions are abrasive and the mistrust corrosive. This often plays havoc with the most obvious steps toward raising the Soviet economy out of its morass.

"THEY PRETEND TO PAY US AND WE PRETEND TO WORK"

While the kindhearted impulses of Russians and most other Soviet nationalities make private life tolerable, there are other less positive and less charitable qualities in the Russian character that tend to make public life intractable and pose formidable obstacles to Gorbachev's drive for reform: their escapism, their impracticality, their lackadaisical attitude toward work, and their vicious envy of people who try to get ahead.

Westerners know, because Gorbachev has made it an issue, that an entrenched bureaucracy of Party and government officials—eighteen million strong, by Gorbachev's count—have been blocking and sabotaging many reforms, clinging to power and privilege. What is far less understood in the West is that the mind-set of ordinary people is an equally forbidding obstacle. My intellectual friends would tell me, "We Russians are long on debating, arguing, philosophizing, or reciting poetry; we are good at feasting, drinking, toasting, and at talking deep into the night; but we have no head for business."

"Russian mentality is not based on common sense. It has nothing to do with common sense," the writer Tatyana Tolstaya told David Royle, one of our producers. "Our thinking is not orderly, logical. We do not have a linear consciousness. . . . In Western culture, European culture maybe, emotions are considered to be on a lower level than reason. But in Russia, no. . . . It is bad to be rational, to be smart, clever, intelligent, and so on. And to be emotional, warm, lovable, maybe spiritual, in the full meaning of that word—that is good."[2]

"It is the Russian soul," the poet Andrei Voznesensky told me one afternoon, as we sat on a park bench talking in a light snowfall. "In Russia, I think we have a love of literature, a so-called spiritual life. We can talk all day and all night long about all kinds of questions, immortal questions. That is the Russian style of thinking.

"I want our economy to be the same as in the West. I want our people to have a good quality of life, a good level, the same as in America, and technology as in Japan and America. But I am afraid to lose this Russian part of our soul, to lose our love of literature and . . . how to put it . . . our impractical character. Maybe too lazy, it is a minus, but it is a plus too."[3]

In this view, which I have heard echoed time and again, Russians are prone to escapism, whether it be the "lazy, dreamy" philosophizing of the intelligentsia, as Tolstaya has put it, or the brutal, destructive, and often self-destructive mass alcoholism of workers and peasants. "We just ruin everything we touch," Tolstaya lamented, contending that Communism had given vent to that destructive streak in the Russian character. Under the hardships of the Soviet era, she said sadly, "people are very cruel with each other, more cruel than I ever encountered anywhere else."

It is only natural, I suppose, for writers and poets to assert the importance of the inner life over pragmatism and creature comforts. As Tolstaya said, it is "better to be poor, unhappy, and suffering" than rich and successful, because such a life is purer. For writers, philosophers, and religious figures, this is true—perhaps.

But among the rank and file, I found that people are fed up with suffering. They are demanding a minimal standard of material well-being. Even among the affluent, such as world-traveled writers Voznesensky and Tolstaya, materialism is thriving. People indulge in reckless bursts of conspicuous consumption, such as blowing a month's salary on a lavish birthday party, living for the moment instead of planning, saving, building for the long term. Soviet people live this way largely because that is just about all the system offers. The shortage of goods is demoralizing; grim prospects for the economy foster hedonism, the search for immediate gratification.

Such escapist habits, however understandable, are powerful handicaps in Gorbachev's drive to energize his people and galvanize them into purposeful initiative.

It is true that over the decades, the Soviet system has turned out regiments of result-oriented engineers, something of a counterpart to Western businessmen. They now fill echelons of the Soviet government and Communist Party, running city councils and Party organizations at all levels. Yet even allowing for this group, Voznesensky and Tolstaya are correct in suggesting that by contrast with people in the West, Russians are not a career-driven people; their primary touchstones are not success, getting ahead, making deals, accumulating material possessions.

In fact, one of the most notable traits in the Soviet Union is the lax national work ethic. Tolstaya's comments about the lazy, dreamy side of the Russian soul made me think of Oblomov, the famous character in the nineteenth-century Russian novel of the same name by Ivan Goncharov. Oblomov is an anti-hero who hates work and is incapable of discipline and effort. It takes him an entire chapter to get out of bed. He is a symbol and paradigm for those Russians who prefer to dream and plan rather than work and take action. Although that literary portrait derives from the slack gentry of a bygone era, even today, a century later, Russians recognize in Oblomov the embodiment of an important facet of their national character.

It is ironic that this should be so, given the extensive Soviet propaganda aimed at inculcating work and discipline as national values. Even so, industriousness, discipline, efficiency do not rank high with most Soviets, whether they be blue-collar workers, peasants, or white-collar bureaucrats.

During my first tour as a correspondent in Moscow, I remember a government economist describing where work stood on the Russian scale of values. "A man can be a good worker, but work is just a *thing*," he told me. "What really matters is his spirit, his relationship to others. If he is too scrupulous, too cold, people will dislike him. We have a word for that, *sukovaly*—dryish—but *sukhoi*—dry—is even worse. And finally *sukhar*, which means dry like a bread crust—no human touch at all—that is the worst."

Such admiration for human warmth is understandable and appealing, but the problem is that Russians tend to slip over the line, turning commendable traits into a justification for avoiding responsibility and initiative, for a slack attitude toward work. If, as psychologists have suggested, America is dominated by workaholic Type-A personalities, the Soviet Union is mired in hard-to-motivate Type B's—no small problem for a leader such as Gorbachev, who is bent on thrusting his people bodily into the twenty-first century.

For decades, the mass output of the Soviet system, especially its concentration on military might and production, masked the inefficiencies of the system. The Stalinist command economy could concentrate enormous national resources on showpiece targets—huge hydroelectric dams spanning great rivers, massive steel plants, machine-tool factories that turned out tanks for the Soviet army in World War II—all built at the cost of enormous sacrifices by the people. During the early Stalinist years, the masses were motivated by the romance of building a New World. Then the war against the Nazi invader summoned Russian workers to a great patriotic effort. Finally, the fear of a demonic dictator drove the people. But once Stalin was gone, and as the postwar years rolled by, the Soviet work force sagged into a now legendary pattern of sloth and shirking.

"Our unemployment is the highest in the world," leading reform economist Pavel Bunich quipped, watching for my astonishment; officially the Soviets admit to less than 1 percent unemployment. "But unfortunately," he quickly added, "all our unemployed get salaries."[4]

FREELOADING SOCIALISM

Stories about the monumental inefficiencies of Soviet workers are legion. In early 1988, I was introduced to Vladimir Kabaidze, long one of the most energetic Soviet industrial managers; at that time he ran a huge plant in Ivanovo, 250 miles northeast of Moscow. A slender, wiry, chain-smoking, canny Georgian, Kabaidze was presented to me by Soviet Party officials as a model Soviet manager, someone able to get much more work out of his people than most supervisors. Given his reputation, I was especially struck by Kabaidze's blunt comments in a speech he made to the Nineteenth Communist Party Conference a few weeks after we met. He spoke about the appalling incompetence of Soviet construction workers and their reckless disregard for deadlines—ironic in a planned economy.

"We think it's normal to take fifteen to twenty years to build a factory," Kabaidze said. "As general director of the Ivanovo–North Korea Machine Building Works [a Soviet/Korean joint venture], I can tell you how they build things in North Korea. The shell is built the same way as ours, and it takes nine months to build a fifty-thousand-square-meter building. Nine months! Our [factory's] project is one of twenty-seven important projects in the country, and it has been under construction for eight years already. I'm afraid they'll still be writing up change-orders when I'm carried out feet first."[5]

The Party delegates broke into laughter, amused that someone of Kabaidze's stature had suffered from the same unbearable delays that they all knew from personal experience, and that he had dared to make fun of them at a nationally televised Party conference.

Economists and political thinkers like Tatyana Zaslavskaya, the sociologist who gained fame from her Novosibirsk report, blame the Stalinist command economy and rigid central control for molding an obedient, passive labor force, a labor force plagued by heavy absenteeism, idleness on the job, poor quality of work, low morale, and serious alcoholism. As Zaslavskaya put it, Stalin's system turned workers into robots. "People were consistently regarded as 'cogs' in the mechanism of the national economy—and they behaved themselves just as obediently (and passively) as machines and materials," she wrote.[6]

"Apathy, indifference, pilfering, and a lack of respect for honest work have become rampant," added the reform economist Nikolai Shmelyov, "as has aggressive envy of those who earn a lot, even if they earn it honestly. There are signs of an almost physical degradation of a considerable part of the population as a result of drunkenness and sloth."[7]

The Kremlin's two would-be modernizers over the past decade, Yuri Andropov and Mikhail Gorbachev, recognized the slack Soviet work ethic as a national Achilles' heel, and they attacked it the moment they took office. Each began his tenure with a loudly trumpeted campaign to tighten work discipline and fight both the indolent torpor of the Soviet working class and its companion disease, mass alcoholism. Andropov, the former KGB chief, closed down liquor stores during working hours and even had his police agents raid the *banyas,* the communal Russian baths, which are notorious hideouts for workers playing hooky. In the *banyas,* people not only bathe, but also drink beer and eat salted fish and play cards or just while away the hours talking. Despite Andropov's attack on such behavior and Gorbachev's even more ambitious battle against vodka drinking, neither one was able to make much of a change in Soviet productivity, primarily because there was no significant change in the attitude of the Soviet proletariat toward their jobs.

Soviet workers themselves have an ironic saying that expresses their open cynicism toward their "social contract" with the so-called workers' state: "They pretend to pay us and we pretend to work."

Cynicism is understandable. The state has conditioned people to perform badly, having given them little incentive to work harder. Soviet workers have faced neither the threat of being fired nor the reward of higher pay for good work. And so they have drifted along—secure, but feeling little or no connection between their performance and their wages. That applies up and down the line throughout the economy, among professionals as well as the proletariat.

Dima Mamedov, one of Moscow television's leading young producers of youth programs, burst out in frustration one night, complaining about his pitiful salary. We were at a private rehearsal of the American rock group Bon Jovi and the Soviet group Gorky Park. Dima was wearing an Italian-made cotton sport jacket, which he said had cost 350 rubles (nearly $600). Either the jacket was a gift from his father, a senior editor on the nightly newscast *Vremya*, or Dima had bought it with extra money made moonlighting for foreign firms. His regular pay from *Good Evening, Moscow*, one of Moscow television's more popular shows, could not support such expensive tastes.

"Even if I don't work hard at it, for my job they pay me one hundred seventy rubles [about $285] a month," he groused. "If the show is no good—boring—they pay me one hundred seventy rubles. If I work hard and kill myself and the show is very popular, they still pay me the same measly one hundred seventy rubles. Does that make sense?"

Lots of Soviet workers make up for such poor pay by stealing from the state. The common saying is, "What belongs to everyone, belongs to no one, so why shouldn't it be mine?" Sometimes, Soviets indulge merely in petty purloining or quick cadging of state equipment where they work.

Late one afternoon at a lumber mill outside Novgorod, a huge industrial truck mounted with a crane came lumbering into the muddy parking area outside the front gate. No one was around. Out of the truck cab spilled a workman, a couple of children, and a mother carrying string bags full of what looked like picnic leftovers. Sure enough, overhearing their talk, we could tell they had filched the lumberyard's crane truck to go off picnicking.

Sometimes, however, the hijacking is on a grander scale. Underground industries have operated on millions of rubles' worth of pirated textile goods, entire warehouses of construction materials and equipment, fresh fruits and vegetables, lockers of meat. So endemic is larceny of state supplies that the Ministry of Internal Affairs has set up a special police force to combat petty pilfering and big-time swindling. Soviets joke openly about fooling the state inspectors.

One of my favorite anecdotes is about a worker who leaves his factory one afternoon with a wheelbarrow covered with a piece of cloth. The guard at the gate lifts the cloth, looks underneath it, and, finding the wheelbarrow empty, waves the worker on. The next day, the worker shows up again with a wheelbarrow covered with a cloth. Again the guard checks. Nothing underneath the cloth, so he lets the worker pass. A third day, it happens again—the wheelbarrow is still empty.

Finally, the guard bursts out, in utter frustration: "Look, comrade, you must be stealing something. What is it?"

"Wheelbarrows," the worker replies.

Another facet of the cynicism about work is the historic collusion of industrial managers and local Party officials to deceive higher-ups about the real levels of output on the farm or in the factory. When Gorbachev came into power, it was clear that practically everyone from the bottom up was cooking the books. In Uzbekistan, for example, investigators found that every year the entire republic had reported to Moscow one million tons of phantom cotton harvest; massive bribery kept officials quiet. Ever since Count Potemkin built fake villages in the eighteenth century to impress the Empress Catherine the Great on her visit to the Crimea, Potemkinizing has become a Russian national pastime. Gogol's famous Inspector General faced the same shenanigans from the locals.

Upon visiting Soviet farms, factories, schools, and institutes, I have often been shown freshly painted buildings, phony statistics, new equipment borrowed for display; I have encountered not typical citizens, but model ones. The modern expression is *pokazukha*—show—that is, putting on a show, a bogus veneer to impress outsiders who are not in the know.

This penchant for falsifying reality can easily be translated into subverting Gorbachev's ambitious reforms. Inevitably, Russians have jokes about how people pretend to reform. In one, a flock of birds is roosting on a tree. Along comes a man with a stick, and he begins banging the branches. The birds all fly off and the man walks away. Back come the birds to their old perches, announcing with satisfaction: "We have 'restructured' ourselves."

In another Soviet anecdote, one man is demonstrating to a second man the meaning of *perestroika*. The man has two pails. One pail is empty and the other is full of potatoes. He pours the potatoes from one pail into the other, very satisfied with what he is doing.

"But nothing has changed," objects the second man.

"Ah, yes," agrees the first, "but think what a noise it creates."

PERESTROIKA IN THE MIND

People are looking for some external transformation to take place, but *perestroika* is first of all internal. *"Perestroika* has to happen in the mind," my friend Vladimir Pozner, the television commentator, remarked to me. "For it to work, people's outlooks have to change, and that happens as society changes. It's a push-pull, gradual process. It cannot be decreed."8

Old habits die hard, even among supposedly reform-minded intellectuals. I recall a visit one Tuesday morning to Vladimir Yadov, director of the Institute of Sociology, reputedly one of the more active academic institutes in Moscow. The place was almost deserted, and as I sat down to talk with Yadov, I commented on the absence of people on a normal workday. Yadov, a sympathetic figure with a craggy, Robert Frost face, is a scholar who, like sociologist Yuri Levada, had nurtured his craft in hiding during the dark years of Brezhnev.

With his wry humor, he said, "This is what my driver calls 'bath day.' " He grinned, assuming I knew that people hid from work in the baths. "No one is around our institute except the director," he went on, pointing to himself, "and a few of my assistants. Everyone else is away. No one is at work. Theoretically, this is library day, when they are all supposed to be at the library." He shrugged, again assuming I understood that this was fiction. "Do you remember what Maksim Gorky told Lenin when Lenin asked Gorky why he did not want to come back from living abroad to work in Russia?" When I shook my head, he went on. "Gorky told Lenin, 'You know, Vladimir Ilyich, at home in Russia they all go around and shake each other's hands and talk all the time and swap anecdotes. No one really works.' Well, that's how it is here on 'bath day.' They all go around and shake each other's hands and swap anecdotes. That's how it is—just what Gorky said."9

Occasionally I ran into middle-aged officials and intellectuals who had begun to think that the Soviets' casual attitude toward work took root during their youth, especially among the educated middle class, which allowed its children to develop an easy dependence on their parents and, later, on the state. In short, they observed, self-reliance comes slowly among the very class of people that in Western societies show the greatest spark of responsibility and initiative. Russians are soft on their children; they spoil them all through childhood, trying to protect them from hardship. They readily make considerable sacrifices for their children's education without demanding that their children earn money; they keep them living at home after the university and often support them financially during those years. This is partly out of necessity: Housing is almost impossible to find, Soviet society provides few part-time jobs, and in a society where there is little to inherit, education is the road to opportunity and therefore an extremely high priority. In short, reality reinforces cultural traits.

The contrast with American young people is so striking that Soviet writers and journalists, reporting on travels across America, have been moved to send home detailed descriptions of the summer jobs taken by American college students. Soviet parents are both horrified and impressed to read about how middle-class American young people take jobs waiting tables, pumping gasoline, baby-sitting, digging ditches, serving fast food. They have told me that they are horrified that well-heeled American parents can be so cold toward their own children as to force them to work to make money. To many Russians, that smacks of exploiting child labor. And they are impressed, I was told, that American teenagers show so much initiative and self-reliance.

Either way, Soviet parents are extremely curious about the American experience. On an all-day car trip through the farming regions of Yaroslavl Province, a senior provincial Party official named Igor Beshev fired questions at me about the jobs my children had taken, the money they had earned, and how I had persuaded them to go out and work.

"I just tell them they have to contribute a part of the cost of their college education," I said.

Beshev approved of their *delavoi*—businesslike—attitude, but he reminded me that Soviet university students got stipends from the state, leaving them with no tuition to pay.

"What about meals, clothing, and other costs?" I asked.

Beshev nodded, but said little, looking uncomfortable. Like many a Russian parent, he seemed to be taken aback at the notion that parents would ask their children to pay for such things.

"Well, our kids earn their own spending money," I said suggestively.

Beshev warmed to that idea. His twenty-year-old son was a university student, but he had never had a job. Like other Soviet young people, he had taken part in various work projects organized by the Komsomol, the youth wing of the Communist Party. Those activities, however, were not a step toward financial self-sufficiency. Beshev was concerned that so far his son had no practical sense of money.

"He's dependent on me," Beshev said. "He never earns any money. Of course, I expect he will have a good career when he finishes university. But I do not think he knows how to take care of himself. And I would like to see him get some preparation now, the way your children have. I'm trying to get him to find some job. But that's a big change, and it's very hard for him, for all of us."[10]

With variations, it was a story I had heard often. Sometimes the young people were eager to find jobs and the older generation was disapproving, saying that children should be cared for and protected.

Of course, total dependence on parents is a prelude to dependence on the state, which the Soviet system encourages. After graduation, univer-

sity students are assigned jobs called *raspradeleniye*—literally, the "distribution"—which they must accept as a way of repaying the state for their
education. Often out of inertia or limited possibilities, they stick with
those assigned jobs for many years, sometimes for the rest of their lives.
They often get housing through their employer, and big factories have
their own health clinics. In the countryside, villages are like old-fashioned
company towns, dominated by the local state or collective farm. The
individual fits into the local hierarchy, which both supports him and
checks his initiative. Dependence is the routine.

Dependence is also nurtured by subsidies for essentials like housing,
food, health care, education. Soviet apartments are spartan and dreary by
Western standards, but they are cheap. The rent for a one-room apartment can be as little as 15 rubles a month, not much more than the cost
of those big bouquets of flowers Susan was given. Even a good-sized
apartment of three rooms may be no more than 25 or 30 rubles a month,
two or three days' pay, a pittance by Western standards. Health care is
poor, but it's free—except for the bribes that people have to pay to get
service. Education, even at the university level, is free. Dietary staples—
bread, milk, potatoes, cheese—are all subsidized. For years, a small but
tasty loaf of Soviet brown bread has cost about 25 kopecks (35 cents). The
state buys potatoes from farmers at 30 kopecks a kilo and sells them to
city dwellers for 20 kopecks a kilo (about 15 cents a pound). The result
is enormous food subsidies, running about 96 billion rubles—about $155
billion—in 1990.[11]

The majority of Soviet workers clamor for greater efficiency, for more
consumer goods, but they react violently to any proposal suggesting that
overall economic improvement means floating prices and an end to state
subsidies on consumer essentials. That is a potent element in the new
politics of public opinion in the Soviet Union. For five years this mass
dependence on subsidized socialism has been a deterrent to Gorbachev's
move toward a free market; and each time he has approached it, he has
backed off or watered down his plans. His caution is in dramatic contrast
to the boldness of the new Polish leaders, who have plunged headlong into
free-market reforms, allowing price inflation.

"The Poles prefer high prices to empty counters," was the response of
Nikolai Petrakov, Gorbachev's personal economic adviser. "In this country, all the opinion polls show quite the opposite. People accept rationing
coupons and standing in line—especially during work time—but not price
increases."[12]

"We all shout in unison—including those who otherwise favor the
market: 'Do not touch prices!' " observed a reform-minded economist,

Otto Latsis. "This is the kind of 'market' we have imagined. Like a rose without thorns. But such a plant does not exist in nature. The market is a rose with thorns. . . . Ours is the only country in the world where there are strong 'anti-market' feelings."

Then he added sarcastically, "Perhaps Albania has them too."[13]

In line with this attitude is a widespread aversion among Soviets to risk taking. As a people, they are economically cautious and conservative. In a society built on job security, the specter of unemployment is terrifying, and Soviet society has little experience and no infrastructure for dealing with it. By government estimates, roughly three million people were thrown out of work by state ministries, agencies, and enterprises from 1985 to 1989, and about fifteen million more jobs will be eliminated by the end of the century.[14] New jobs, of course, are developing in other sectors, including private enterprise hiding behind the euphemistic title of "cooperatives"—that is, group-owned businesses. The more daring workers, especially younger people, are giving this sector a try, but that is still a small minority.

Most Soviet workers are reluctant to make changes. I have been told this countless times, by workers as well as by economic specialists. The vast majority have grown accustomed to leaning on the state. They would rather settle for a meager wage and miserable living standards—and continue to complain about these shortcomings—than quit their jobs and take the chance of shifting to a cooperative with an uncertain future. They would rather pass up higher pay than take the risk of a cooperative's failure, or face the certain knowledge that they will have to work harder. Risk and uncertainty are things most Soviets habitually avoid like the plague.

"The masses expect change to come from the top," my friend Andrei Smirnov, the filmmaker, remarked to me over dinner one night in the Writers' Union dining hall. "They do not understand that real democracy, or real changes in the economy, must come from below. They resist the idea that we must change ourselves."[15]

Dependence on the state and resistance to taking chances reaches far beyond the blue-collar proletariat. It exists at all levels of Soviet society, affecting creative professionals, scholars, and industrial managers as well. Smirnov, head of the Filmmakers' Union for two critical years of adjustment in the late 1980s, described his union as a microcosm of Soviet responses to greater economic freedom.

"Everyone was enthusiastic about overthrowing the old dictatorial system," he told me, "but our directors and producers are fearful of the new system of competition. If we have a choice between the free market and a guaranteed salary, the majority will pick a guaranteed salary. Those who can't compete on the market are unhappy at the prospect of being unemployed. Others who are more talented are unhappy because they think that studio directors will pick friends and favorites to make films, not the qualified people. They want the union to protect them and to go after the studio directors. The really good ones, who can work well in any situation, are unhappy with our poor technology and the bad system of financing in the country."[16]

Rair Simonyan, an adviser to the Council of Ministers and a specialist on industrial management at Moscow's prestigious Institute of International Relations and World Economics, reported similar reactions among industrial managers and even his own efficiency experts.

"Everybody can tell you about the necessity for change, but when it relates to them, it's different," he told me. "As director of the Department of Industrial Economics, I had trouble with my own people. Everybody said we need radical reforms. The first thing I tried to do was to cut our staff—sixty researchers is too many. But people were upset. They told me, 'You can't arrange these jobs purely on the basis of efficiency. You have to balance efficiency and social security. You cannot fire a man in his fifties with no job prospects or a woman with two children. . . . Even our industrial managers, to whom we are trying to give more autonomy from the state to decide their own production—they want the old system of being guaranteed their supplies. Often they will tell us, 'We need one hundred percent state orders, so we will have no problem with material supplies.' "[17]

Leonid Abalkin, deputy premier and Gorbachev's top adviser on economic reform, notes the contradictions even among the advocates of reform at the Supreme Soviet, where new laws and policies are being debated and formulated.

"All the speakers were demanding independence, abolition of the dictate of ministries and departments, reduction of the percentage of state orders," Abalkin said. "I often sat alongside [Prime Minister] Ryzhkov and . . . dozens of deputies would come up to him with written and oral requests to guarantee deliveries, to guarantee material and technological supply, and so on. Although they should have all understood that as soon as you have been victorious in taking from the government [the power to issue] state orders, by which it assembles resources, you no longer have the right to demand supplies from the state."

As Abalkin said, "No one wants to notice the contradictions" between the demand for freedom from state control and the lingering desire to be protected and supplied by the state. They all want to "exert pressure on the government, extort from it supplies, benefits, and resources," he said, "as though the government were the head of a patriarchal commune—a strong, good, and wise father. Just ask and he will make a present to you from his bounty."[18]

Aleksandr Yakovlev, who has a well-deserved reputation as an even more radical proponent of reform than Gorbachev himself, calls this mind-set "freeloading socialism," and cites it as the most debilitating obstacle to Gorbachev's reform program. In Yakovlev's view, this mentality entails not just economic dependence on the state but a broader psychological dependence on state paternalism in general—a mass inertia, unless there are orders from on high.

"Society is accustomed to freeloading, and not only in the material sense," Yakovlev explained to me during a long conversation one afternoon. "A person wants to be sure he'll get paid, even if he doesn't work. But also in politics, he wants to be sure that he'll be given instructions, orders, that people will explain, will show him what to do. In every sphere, this is a society of freeloading—of freeloading socialism.

"If we don't break through that, if a person doesn't accept some inner freedom and initiative and responsibility, if there is no self-governance, in society, in outlying districts, then nothing will happen."

"That means people taking real responsibility themselves," I interjected.

"And people don't feel like taking responsibility," he shot back. " 'Let someone else answer, but not me.' That's also freeloading. And it has eaten into our pores and our life."[19]

THE INDIVIDUAL IS NOTHING

This passive mentality stalls the engine of reform. But this habit of mind, of course, is of the Soviet state's own making. As sociologist Tatyana Zaslavskaya observed, the Stalinist system turned the Soviet worker into a robot. In many ways, the psychic termites of statism have eaten away at the foundations of individual self-esteem and initiative; it is the latter that Gorbachev, Yakovlev, and others now so desperately want to revive. For decades, the all-powerful state has literally dwarfed the individual, and given ordinary people a sense of their own insignificance.

Soviet ideology, of course, exalts the "collective" over the individual. In the 1970s, our *New York Times* Moscow office had two American correspondents and three Soviets. The Russians talked about our office group as the *kollektiv,* as if it had some mystical significance beyond the five individuals involved. One of the high-priest poets of Soviet socialism, Vladimir Mayakovsky, captured the Soviet mind-set when he framed the line *edinitsa nul'*, variously translatable as "the single unit is zero" or "the individual is nothing." In a paean to Lenin, he wrote:

> The Individual: who needs him?
> The voice of one man is weaker than a squeak.
> Who will listen to it? Not even a wife. . . .
> The Party is the all-encompassing hurricane, fused from voices, soft and
>   quiet. . . .
> Misfortune befalls a man when he's alone.
> Grief comes to one man, for one alone is not a warrior.
> Every pair is his master,
> Whether sturdy, or even weak. . . .
> The individual is nonsense,
> The individual is nothing. . . .'[20]

Every time I visited the Soviet Union, I saw this disdain for the individual. It is reflected in the very architecture of Moscow, with acre upon acre of massive, cheerless tenement apartments; twelve-lane boulevards so broad that pedestrians are forced into underpasses; pompous state offices like so many somber banks; and cavernous stores with empty shelves. The Kremlin is mighty too, handsome and historic; it was once a fortress, and the golden domes of its churches lend it beauty and grace. But the rest of the city, especially seven skyscrapers built by Stalin, which look like massive drip castles—the Foreign Ministry, Moscow State University, the Ukraine Hotel, and four others—is simply huge and overwhelming. With a fetish for gigantism, Stalin sought to impress, even intimidate, his people by the sheer magnitude and volume of the awesome structures he had built. Unfortunately, Khrushchev and his successors perpetuated Stalin's tendency toward gigantism in architecture in even more vulgar ways.

"We lost the proper scale in our city," Aleksandr Kuzmin, a Moscow city architect, lamented to me one afternoon as we were looking at models of urban development. "It has lost the feel of a city in many places. It has an inhuman scale."

"All these huge tenement buildings look mass-produced," I observed, and Kuzmin nodded. "And in some places the neighborhoods are so barren, the buildings look as if they had been dropped on the face of the moon."

"You see," Kuzmin said, "Stalin had a plan in 1935. He told the people,

'We are building the world's first Capital of Socialism.' So he destroyed some of the most charming old sections of Moscow and replaced them with these huge new structures. Now we are trying to save the few old areas that remain."

"The individual gets lost in the leader's dreams of glory," I suggested.

"I think it's worse in the new development areas," Kuzmin said, referring to the rows of dreary apartment blocks. "The scale there is especially inhuman. That comes from our desire to get the maximum floor space for the minimum cost. We have this notion of equality of housing, which means we have to build these massive buildings which depress people."[21]

There are other ways the individual gets lost in the Soviet system. Soviet hotels and restaurants are set up to serve groups, not individuals. In Moscow and Leningrad, the better tourist hotels have caught on to the idea of the individual self-serve breakfast, but the Miner Hotel in the coal-mining city of Donetsk in the southern Ukraine is more typical of the country. The majority of foreign visitors there are East German tour groups, Polish schoolchildren, and Bulgarian basketball teams, and the dining room cannot cope with individual tourists for breakfast. One morning, Susan and I appeared and were told by a waitress that there was no breakfast, despite the fact that she was at that very moment setting out breakfast dishes for twenty-five to thirty people. I pointed out the inconsistency to her.

"Oh, but this is for a group," she explained. "Are you a group?"

"Well, we are three Americans," I answered, referring to Susan, Marian Marzynski, and me.

"That's not a group!" she sniffed, turning away.

"But we need breakfast and we are staying in your hotel," I protested. "Where can we get something to eat?"

The waitress shrugged and went back to setting out meals for the group.

Another waitress overheard the end of our conversation and advised us to try a little buffet elsewhere in the hotel. It offered some terrible coffee, tea, cold hot dogs, and cookies. No cereal, eggs, or anything else resembling normal breakfast food. We settled for tea and a very dry cookie, while the group of tourists in the dining room were served pancakes, little *blinis* with cheese, as well as a selection of breads, jams, rolls, and fruit.

The attitude of that first hotel waitress epitomized the attitude of the Soviet state toward customers in general, and the approach of Soviet sales clerks toward shoppers. The Soviet economy is a command economy, not a demand economy. It is run by and for producers, not for customers. Marketing is unheard of. For decades, volume of output has been the yardstick of success; never mind quality or a selection that consumers may want. Tens of millions of tons of potatoes or other vegetables rot in the fields, railroad cars, or warehouses because the Soviet distribution system is abysmally run and central plans and pay bonuses are based on output, not on delivery. Millions of pairs of shoes can be produced, but they sit on shelves unwanted, because the quality is awful or the sizes do not match those of the population. Once again, the state's interest over the individual's.

Even when efforts are made to cater to the individual, the Soviet system is long on form and short on function. For years, Moscow's Sheremyetovo Airport had no pushcarts for luggage inside the customs area. Apparently, Soviet officials were so besieged by complaints that they finally allowed a cooperative firm to bring in luggage carts. But there was a catch. The co-op, being a Soviet firm, was not allowed to accept hard currency as payment, only Soviet rubles. By Soviet law, however, arriving tourists were not allowed either to bring Soviet currency into the country or to exchange money in the customs area. So they had no rubles to pay for the carts. Human ingenuity eventually developed a barter in cigarettes; it took several months before Soviet officials realized the need for a hard-currency cashier to rent the carts.

In another gesture, theoretically designed to spare some tourists from the tedious delays of customs inspections, the Soviets copied other countries by setting up two customs lanes—a red lane for detailed inspections and a green lane for people with no imports to declare. Once again, catch-22. Any foreigners arriving with $50 or more in any foreign currency had to declare it and go through the red lane. So, of course, no one got to use the green lane. It was a nice *pokazukha,* for appearances, but not much use.

Service is not an ingrained notion in the Soviet system. Foreigners quickly discover that many waiters, drivers, and desk clerks working for Intourist hotels are uncaring, petty tyrants. My own encounters with their imperiousness and rigidity would fill a book. Drivers refuse to deviate a couple of blocks from normal routes, even for extra pay, if it is not written on their job tickets. Once, in Baku, I approached a hotel cashier, urgently needing to change a 10-ruble note. "I don't change money," he replied haughtily, motioning me to another, identical cashier's desk three feet away. That cashier was on a long break. I waited for several minutes. The man who had refused to serve me dipped into the cash drawer in front of me to do several transactions. But no appeal from me would get him to change my bill.

Meals often involve a tedious hassle. The pet peeve of Scott Breindel, our sound man, was getting breakfast served in the National Hotel. The dining room had a faded baroque elegance, with a huge wall mirror and gilt molding, but service was nonexistent. After the first round of diners, the tables lay littered with dishes and bread crumbs. Waiters would stand around talking with each other or looking bored, ignoring newcomers at the tables. The menu was fixed, so people were spared the complication of ordering, but it took repeated appeals to break through their indolence and get bread, coffee, one third of a cup of juice (evidently they were saving on juice), and a cold boiled egg.

Dinner at the National Hotel was my Waterloo. Even as a guest in the hotel, it was almost impossible to get a table. Reservations mattered little, except in the hard-currency dining room. One day, when I had invited a Soviet couple to dinner, I took the precaution of ordering a table early in the day. No seats were available in the hard-currency dining room, so I approached the maître d'hôtel in the salon marked for hotel guests and "payment in rubles." But for a table he wanted to blackmail me into paying in dollars or into ordering *zakuski*, Russian hors d'oeuvres, in advance, for 100 rubles. I refused and it took me about ten minutes to get him to quit glaring at me and write down my name. That evening, we were left standing for fifteen or twenty minutes, even though there were free tables in the room. Once seated, we were ignored for another forty-five minutes. When we finally ordered—we chose hot dishes—there was another long wait. Our Soviet guests were mortified by the wretched service, saying that is why they never went out for meals. Finally, in desperation, I demanded, "Bring us anything cold, just bring us something." Out came the *zakuski* for, you guessed it, about 100 rubles. We never got our hot dishes, but we did get ice cream.

Soviet store clerks treat Soviet customers with a similar arrogant indifference. There is simply no culture of service, no tradition of greeting customers by asking, "Can I help you?" or saying, as they depart, "Thank you, come back again." In part, the haughtiness comes from the economics of supply and demand. Chronic shortages make the Soviet Union a seller's market; the buyer is a mere supplicant. The sales clerk is besieged by more customers than she—it always seems to be women in these jobs—can ever hope to satisfy. She feels overwhelmed, harassed, and helpless. Moreover, she is in the driver's seat, empowered by the state and its shortages either to cut down her customers with a crippling *"Nyet*, we don't have any," or to whisper a demand for a fancy under-the-counter bribe for an item in short supply.

There is another reason for the Soviet aversion to service. In the context of socialist equality, one person does not serve another, because that puts the server into a lower social status. It smacks of capitalist exploitation.

Soviet intellectuals are smart enough to realize the hypocrisy of this attitude in a system where state planners grasp all the power of decision-making and relegate the citizenry to economic serfdom. They still relish a joke I heard in the 1970s. One person asks, "What's the difference between communism and capitalism?" The other answers, "Capitalism is the exploitation of man by man, and communism is the reverse."

Humor aside, the haughty disdain of Soviet salespeople for their customers can be exasperating. To me, one of the classic examples is the *pereriv*, or lunch break. In the buffets and cafeterias at Soviet hotels or airports, the staff are fond of taking their break just when most customers want to buy a meal. I cannot begin to count how often that has happened to me. Soviets have simply surrendered to it, and no longer protest. Once, our group had a short layover in Voroshilovgrad during a six-hour trip from Yerevan to Vilnius. We had taken off at 6:00 A.M., been given no food on the plane, and were quite hungry by the time we landed at Voroshilovgrad at 8:30—a normal breakfast time. But the only airport restaurant had a chair in the doorway, blocking the entrance, and a sign announcing CLOSED FOR A BREAK. We had nothing to eat until we landed in Lithuania at noon.

"EQUAL POVERTY FOR ALL"

For the great mass of Soviet people, the years of unrelieved struggle against shortages of goods to meet the most elementary of human needs have bred still other habits and attitudes that go against the grain of reform. Illicit profiteering is as pervasive as crabgrass in a summer lawn; it's an almost universal defense mechanism that has been operating sub rosa for many years. Think of the worker stealing wheelbarrows and multiply him by a million. This pilfering causes many Soviets, even though they regularly benefit from underhanded dealings, to look on anyone who makes a profit as an illicit operator.

Beyond that, the competitive combat that shopping has become has fed a meanspirited streak in the Soviet soul. For if Russians are justly known for their warmth within a trusted circle, and for their hospitality toward guests, they often show an abrasiveness, a churlish spite, toward people outside their circle; the natural breeding ground for this attitude is the floating anger engendered by wretched circumstances. The Russians are long-suffering people who can bear the pain of their misery, so long as they see that others are sharing it. The collective jealousy can be fierce against those who rise above the crowd.

Traveling around the country, I came to see the great mass of Soviets as protagonists in what I call the culture of envy. In this culture, corrosive animosity took root under the czars in the deep-seated collectivism in Russian life and then was cultivated by Leninist ideology. Now it has turned rancid under the misery of everyday living.

On a plane from Sverdlovsk to Moscow, our producer Marian Marzynski struck up a conversation with the young woman next to him, an attractive, jovial person who was full of consumer woes. Her name was Galya Zhirnova, and she was a buyer for the central trade agency of the city of Sverdlovsk; this agency supplied all the state department stores and consumer outlets in her city. Galya was going to a trade fair in Moscow, with a budget of 10 million rubles. She was going to meet with manufacturers to try to contract for shipments of television sets, radios, cameras, records, cassettes, electronic games, sports equipment, and other recreational goods for her city's one and a half million people. The budget did not sound too bad—until I did the arithmetic. It worked out to 7 rubles a head, a little over $10 per person for the entire year 1990. A pitiful amount.

"We have no television sets to sell," she said. "We could sell a railroad car full of TV sets in an hour. Bed linens are impossible to find in our stores. We have people who signed up to buy furniture fifteen years ago and they are still waiting. We could have bought one hundred twenty million rubles of furniture for next year, but they only allotted us twenty million rubles' worth. And we don't have enough storage space for that. So it sits in railroad cars—millions of rubles' worth—because we have no warehouses."[22]

When we landed at Domodyedovo Airport, nearly an hour's drive south of downtown Moscow, the number of taxis was far from adequate. Great droves of people stood in a drizzle waiting for buses. Galya laughed bitterly at the human disarray. "That's Russia," she snorted. "Things don't work. If they worked well, it would be America."

Galya, with her bourgeois tastes, sneered at the poor quality of Soviet products—but she could afford to. Her job put her in an enviable position between suppliers and consumers, an ideal place for skimming off choice items for herself and, if she chose (as any Russian would assume), for a profitable under-the-counter trade. I don't know whether she indulged in graft, but from her conversation, she seemed already to be, at thirty, a canny operator, and her wardrobe hinted at an access to goods far beyond the reach of ordinary Russians. She was wearing a smart black Yugoslav raincoat and a stylish woman's suit. Before we parted, she proudly informed me, "Everything I'm wearing is *importny*—imported."

My driver the next day, Volodya Konoplanikov, commented, "Of course the sales clerks engage in speculation, because there are never enough goods to go around. You go to a sports shop and they have nothing. Then they toss out on the table a hundred pairs of athletic shoes. What's that—nothing! So people speculate. The clerks hold things back. People do business for themselves."

Volodya himself was a repairman at the State Optical Factory, which makes high-quality optical lenses for the Soviet space program. He was moonlighting as a driver on his days off, for extra pay. I was amazed that he had a brand-new Zhiguli, a Soviet variant of the Fiat. He told me that his mother had had to wait nearly twenty years for the car, and only got it through a special allotment to her factory, where she had worked for forty-three years.

Volodya's tone turned to anger. "Everyone knows you can't buy anything," he said. "I want a warmup suit, one of those sports outfits. I can't get one. Really! I should live thirty-five years and still I won't get a warmup suit! People don't want to work—the ruble has lost so much value, there's no point in working. I've put in ten, twelve hours today, for good money, but why should I care? I can't buy anything with my money. Everywhere there are shortages—sugar, soap, tea, shoes. Such a great country, and it's a real problem to buy shoes. Is it really true that with all this space, we cannot grow enough leather for shoes? It is to our shame."

Like many Muscovites, Volodya was working himself up into a virulent sulk, pouring out one old grievance after another. He kept turning around to make sure I got his point—I had to motion to him to keep his eyes on the road!

"You know they turn off the hot-water system in Moscow for two months every summer," he fumed. "What are you going to wash in—cold water? This has been going on for the past twenty-five years, ever since they set up a centralized hot-water system."

Then Volodya turned his venom against the elite, the people on top, or as the Russians call them, the *vertushka*.

"People see how the *vertushka* live—not one *dacha*, but two!" he sputtered. "All kinds of medicines. We can't get such medicines. But *they* get them from you in the West. Why don't they get them for everyone? Why only for the elite? They have much more housing space than ordinary people do. My kitchen is only six feet by six feet. Two people get in there and you can't even turn around. It's like a closet. But *they*—they get three- and four-room apartments with kitchens three times the size of mine. These bureaucrats 'sit' on our backs. They produce nothing. Everywhere there are extra people in those jobs. People get hired because their papa or some political friends protect them. They are incompetent. We have to get rid of them. We have to get rid of those high mucky-muck bureaucrats. And the only way is revolution."[23]

As Volodya built up to his crescendo, my mind flashed to sociologist Yuri Levada, and his description of the popular rage against the "political mafia." This was the rage tapped into by Boris Yeltsin, the renegade Moscow Communist Party boss ousted by Gorbachev and the conservatives in 1987. In the elections of March 1989, the Party apparat had tried to discredit Yeltsin, but Yeltsin, with his brash outspokenness and populist instincts, had gone to rally after rally, savaging the political elite for its privileges. It was a monumentally successful strategy—more than five million Muscovites had voted for him. Yeltsin had provided an outlet for the boiling anger of the masses.

The Soviet ruling class, with their cushy cars, clinics, and country homes, are a natural enough target for the wrath of the little people. But what is ominous for Gorbachev's reforms is that this free-floating anger, the jealousy of the rank and file, often lights on anyone who rises above the crowd—anyone who works harder, gets ahead, and becomes better off, even if his gains are honestly earned. This hostility is a serious danger to the new entrepreneurs whom Gorbachev is trying to nurture. It is a deterrent to even modest initiative among ordinary people in factories or on farms. It freezes the vast majority into the immobility of conforming to the group.

Valentin Bereshkov, a former Soviet diplomat, told me of a farmer he knew in a town outside of Moscow whose horse and few cows were set free and whose barn was set afire by neighboring farm workers who were jealous of his modest prosperity. The Soviet press is full of stories about attacks on privately owned cooperative restaurants and other small service shops, the perpetrators people who resent seeing others do well. In the debates at the Supreme Soviet, the most potent arguments, the ones with the strongest resonance among the general populace, are the passionate accusations that the free market will yield speculators getting rich from profiteering and exploiting the working class.

Such antagonisms, of course, bear witness to the powerful influence of decades of Leninist indoctrination. For great masses of Soviet people, capitalism is still a dirty word, and the fact that someone earns more, gets more, is a violation of the egalitarian ideal of socialism. Tens of millions of Soviets deeply mistrust the market, fearing they will be cheated and outsmarted. They see the profit motive as immoral. After all, Lenin wrote in 1918, "We consider the land to be common property. But if I take a piece . . . for myself, cultivate twice as much grain as I need and sell the excess at a profit . . . am I really behaving like a Communist? No. I am behaving like an exploiter, like a proprietor."[24] That mind-set is strongly entrenched, despite the efforts of Gorbachev and the reformers to uproot it.

But there is more than ideology at work here. There are class and collective instincts, born in the countryside of prerevolutionary Russia, embedded in the peasant psyche, and often carried from the farm to the factory when peasants have migrated to the cities. This hostility toward those who rise above the herd reflects the collective ethic of the *obshchina,* the commune of villagers who in czarist times lived in a small huddle of homes, close by one another, not in single homesteads dotted independently across the open plains. After serfdom was abolished in 1861, the peasantry banded together, working the land together. There is good evidence that the czarist bureaucracy, before the Soviet state, encouraged collective farming because it feared there would be anarchy once the power of the rural lords was suddenly taken away by emancipation.

The peasant commune apportioned to each family strips of land to work, in different fields, some near the village, some off by the forest, distributed so that each family was assigned some good land and some not-so-good land. The *obshchina* decided when they would all plant, when they would all harvest, and often how they would all work the fields. The villagers shared the bad weather. They planted the same crops. They grew accustomed to a common fate. And they reacted warily against anyone who tried to advance beyond his peers. Because the commune members were collectively responsible for paying the "redemption" costs of their emancipation, the elders did not want young people leaving for the cities; they either charged high fees or refused to let them leave the *obshchina.* So the commune imposed a harsh order and maintained a social leveling.[25]

In my travels, villagers have told me more than once: Remember—the tallest blade of grass is the first to be cut down by the scythe. The lesson? Do not try to stand above the crowd, the collective.

Felicity Barringer, a former *New York Times* correspondent in Moscow, put that sentiment into language that drives home the point. At a Soviet-American conference, she made the shrewd observation that "in America, it's a sin to be a loser, but if there's one sin in Soviet society, it's being a winner."[26]

Dmitri Zakharov, the anchor of the Friday-night television show *Vzglyad,* said:

"In the West, if an American sees someone on TV with a shiny new

car, he will think, 'Oh, maybe I can get that someday for myself.' But if
a Russian sees that, he will think, 'This bastard with his car. I would like
to kill him for living better than I do.' When Russians see a cooperative
where people make a lot of money, they ask angrily, 'Why do those people
make so much money?' They do not ask, 'Why does the state pay me so
little?' Instead of making an effort to raise their own incomes, they want
to close down the cooperative."[27]

I heard another slant on that from Anatoly Sobchak, a reformist deputy
in the Supreme Soviet. "Our people cannot endure seeing someone else
earn more than they do," he told me one night in Leningrad, where he
had come for a television interview with *Fifth Wheel.* "Our people want
equal distribution of money, whether that means wealth or poverty. They
are so jealous of other people that they want others to be worse off, if need
be, to keep things equal. We have a story that describes this trait. God
comes to a lucky Russian peasant one day and offers him any wish in the
world. The peasant is excited and starts dreaming his fantasies. 'Just
remember,' God says, 'whatever you choose, I will do twice as much for
your neighbor as I do for you.' The peasant is stumped because he cannot
bear to think of his neighbor being so much better off than he is, no
matter how well off he becomes. Finally, he is struck by an idea and he
tells God, 'Strike out one of my eyes and take out both eyes of my
neighbor.' "

Sobchak paused. I was stunned by the implications of this terrible story,
which I later heard repeated in several variations by others.

"Changing that psychology is the hardest part of our economic reform," Sobchak resumed. "That psychology of intolerance toward others
who make more money, no matter why, no matter whether they work
harder, longer, or better—that psychology is blocking economic reform
on the collective and state farms. Peasants actually smash the machinery
and burn the barns of other peasants who try to work their own land to
make a better living."[28]

Not only that, but—not surprisingly—successful people try to hide
their light under a bushel. Vladimir Pozner put a new twist on something
I had noticed among Russians: the built-in caution of their daily greeting.
"When two Americans meet, they ask each other, 'How are things?' and
they tell each other 'Fine,' " Pozner said. "An American will say 'Fine,'
even if his mother died yesterday. After a while, a Russian will conclude,
'Americans are hypocrites. They have problems. Why don't they admit
it?' By contrast, when two Soviets meet and ask each other how they are,
they will say, 'Normal,' or 'So-so.' Even if things are good—especially if
things are good! You don't want to tempt the devil. You don't want

people to think things are great. Because they might be envious. And if they're envious, there's no telling what they might do."[29]

This impulse for leveling the fate of all, for sharing misfortune and spreading misery rather than letting anyone get ahead, is what radical economic reformer Nikolai Shmelyov has called the syndrome of "equal poverty for all."[30]

"The blind, burning envy of your neighbor's success . . . has become the most powerful brake on the ideas and practice of *perestroika*," Shmelyov asserted in an important analysis of the Soviet economy in the magazine *Novy Mir.* "Until we at least damp down this envy, the success of *perestroika* will always be in jeopardy."[31]

No less a figure than Gorbachev himself has picked up this theme. In April 1990, stumping for a new phase of economic reform, Gorbachev bowed to popular resistance to raising prices on consumer essentials. But simultaneously, he upbraided Soviet workers for lacking "a sense of responsibility" and for resisting wage reforms that would reward good work. Specifically, he warned that the culture of envy would snuff out any spark of initiative and daring and cripple hopes of real economic progress.

"If we do not break out of this foolish system of wage leveling," he declared, "we will ruin everything that's alive in our people. We shall suffocate."[32]

CHAPTER 11

WHY THE RELUCTANT FARMERS?

"As a peasant might say, our
field grew too thick with the weeds
and thistles of bureaucratism,
mismanagement, social apathy, and
irresponsibility. And weeding alone
won't suffice."[1]

—Gorbachev, April 1988

"It's the fifth year of *perestroika,*
and our people should be
confident but they're not. Our people do
not believe in tomorrow. . . . [They have]
never owned the land. . . . They are
afraid of it. It has become alien to them."[2]

—Dmitri Starodubtsev
State Farm Director
September 1989

When I returned to the Soviet Union in 1988, I expected that on the
economy Gorbachev would follow the pattern set by China. As a correspondent, I had visited China when President Reagan went there in 1984,
and that trip gave me not only my first look at that country, but also
firsthand impressions of its daring new economic reforms. That was nearly

a year before Gorbachev took over the Kremlin, and China's resilient, canny, innovative leader, Deng Xiaoping, was already blazing a path away from orthodox Communist economics.

For five years, Deng had been decollectivizing agriculture—dismantling China's infamous peasant communes and turning over land to individual peasant households to farm on their own. After delivering a set quota to local governments, peasants were allowed to sell the rest of their crops for personal profit. To heighten incentive, Deng had raised the prices for farm produce.

A sudden, stunning explosion had taken place in the Chinese countryside. Most of China's roughly three hundred million peasants had seized the opportunity, and generated a great leap ahead in production and living standards. Since 1978, grain output had shot up 33 percent—from 305 million to 407 million metric tons. Overall, the farm sector was rolling along at 7 percent growth a year—certainly enviable in Moscow, and unheard of not only in other Communist countries but almost anywhere in the world. New cottage industries had sprung up all over the countryside—small service shops, little textile mills, and the like—creating an economic boom in rural China: 52.9 percent growth in 1984 alone. Close to seventy million people were now at work in that sector, and the Chinese press carried stories of new millionaire-entrepreneurs in the hinterlands.

Marxism seemed turned on its ideological head.

On a bus trip through the countryside around Shanxi, I had been struck by what seemed like a thriving hive of activity—swarms of Chinese farmers on their bicycles, pushing carts, or on foot, toting produce to market, choking the roadways. Squawking chickens tied by their legs were draped over the handlebars by some cyclists; others had little crates of produce precariously perched on their bikes. The energy and commotion were overwhelming. Those who had studied China or knew it from earlier visits, such as my friend China scholar Doak Barnett, were even more stunned than I by the dynamism of rural China.

"I found the countryside unrecognizable," Doak said. He had returned to China in the late 1980s after an absence of seventeen years. "The physical changes were really impressive. In towns and villages along the Yangtse and Pearl River valleys, there were little shops and township industries. The peasants had all built themselves new houses. Their earnings had doubled and tripled in just a few short years. The whole countryside of east China, and much of west China, too, looked vastly different from what I had seen before."[3]

In Beijing and Shanghai, middle-class urban Chinese—government officials, journalists, and intellectuals—told me how Deng's reforms had changed their everyday lives. Food, of course, was the big change; it was much fresher, more varied, more plentiful. Industrial reform had begun, but essentially Deng was propelling his nation forward with a peaceful revolution in the countryside. At that stage, he had struck together two combustible elements—food and profit—to forge a huge constituency for reform, both among villagers, who were reaping profits, and among the urban middle class, which was enjoying the food.

Four years later, returning to the Soviet Union, I anticipated that Gorbachev would use Deng's example and begin his economic reform by harnessing the energies of tens of millions of farm workers; that he would liberate them from the Procrustean Stalinist regimen of collectivized agriculture. After all, before the Bolshevik Revolution there had been something like seventeen million private farmsteads in Russia; under Lenin's New Economic Policy, the number had risen to twenty-five million. And then Stalin's ax had fallen.[4]

Moreover, Gorbachev had a natural base to build on, smaller in scale than what was going on in China, but a base nonetheless. Back in the 1970s, I had been impressed by the success of farmworkers who cultivated little quarter-acre kitchen gardens and half-acre private plots. The state owned the land, but the *kolkhozniki*—the collective-farm workers—farmed little plots next to their log-cabin homes to feed themselves and make some money by selling their surplus at farmers' markets in the big cities. In the heartland of Russia proper, the *kolkhozniki* raised potatoes, carrots, and cabbages, and tended tiny orchards of apple trees. In the warmer southern climates of Georgia, Azerbaijan, and Uzbekistan, they raised grapes, pears, and citrus fruits. Driving through the Russian countryside, I had often seen several chickens pecking around peasant homes, and here and there a pig; and in Central Asia, goats and sheep.

In a land that falsely trumpeted "the heroic success of socialized agriculture," the government grudgingly let private plots exist, but played down their importance. They were a pragmatic necessity, but an ideological embarrassment. In 1977, Brezhnev increased the legal size of the plots to one acre; typically, local Party bosses kept the actual size much smaller. Nonetheless, by 1985, there were thirty-five million private plots with an average size of half an acre.[5] The private plot was a well-established staple of Soviet agriculture, a throwback, I was told, to the little gardens allowed serfs in czarist times. Farmers' markets functioned everywhere, from Siberia to Moldavia.

The truth was that Brezhnev could not have fed his people unless he allowed in his system this one legal vestige of private enterprise. And the same was true for Gorbachev, of course.

In terms of market value, the private-plot system Gorbachev inherited in 1985 produced 60 percent of the nation's potatoes, 32 percent of other vegetables and meat, 30 percent of the eggs, and 29 percent of the milk.[6] And all this on about 1.6 percent of the Soviet Union's agricultural lands.

Theoretically, that meant that as Gorbachev came into office, private plots were at least twenty-five times as efficient as land farmed collectively.[7] The figures were somewhat misleading because peasants simply stole seed, fertilizer, transport, and other equipment from their state and collective farms, rather than having to buy or rent these items; often, when they could get away with it, they cheated on their collective work time. Even allowing for this mass rip-off of the state, private plots were indisputably the most productive sector of Soviet agriculture.

Many city people, especially the educated middle class, could not live without the farmers' markets. In the 1970s, we had gone to those markets all the time to bargain with fat, nubby-fingered Russian peasant women who offered their dusty carrots and cucumbers beside wiry, swarthy Georgians or Azerbaijanis, who had flown north to Moscow with sweet-smelling suitcases full of ripening grapes or pears and fresh-cut flowers. Prices were steep but it was a relief to find better produce and better cuts of meat, and more of both than were available in the state stores—testimony to the basic marketing ingenuity of cash-crop farmers, with personal profit as an incentive.

By contrast, what Gorbachev inherited on the official side—the collectivized side of Soviet agriculture—was all too palpable, visible in the dismal disintegration of rural life in the core provinces around Moscow, the heartland of central Russia. In the late eighties, it looked much the same as it had in the early seventies. Traveling to such ancient tourist sites as Rostov, Vladimir, Suzdal, and Yaroslavl, I would stop to photograph the colorful carved woodwork of the peasant log cabins, only to be shocked by the primitive living conditions: the absence of indoor plumbing, necessitating freezing trips to the outhouse in the depth of the Russian winter; the peasant women trudging along with two pails of water from the village well hanging from a shoulder yoke; the poor schools; bad health care; empty stores; rutted roads; and the scarred faces of the peasants, as weatherworn as a lighthouse beaten constantly by gale and lightning. This area of Russia is known as the "non–black earth zone," because it lacks the chocolate earth of the more fertile farmlands to the south, such as in Gorbachev's home region of Stavropol. In central Russia, farmers scratch a subsistence from the gritty brown soil. Their life is grimmer than in American Appalachia.

The people of this region looked to Gorbachev for a better life.

During the Brezhnev years, the spirit and vitality had been sucked out of the Russian heartland. There had been the mass exodus of the young, millions of whom—the brighter and more energetic ones—had fled the countryside for the cities. Especially in northern Russia, whole villages had become ghost towns. If a few hardy souls hung on, local authorities eventually came and transferred them to larger towns with tacky dormitories for farm workers. But still the hemorrhaging had continued, a clear sign of the failing agricultural policy. Brezhnev, unlike Deng in China, had never recognized the problem for what it was—the system's failure to motivate its people. The blame was always placed on the weather, the soil, or occasionally backward technology or incompetent local leaders. The system itself was never found to be at fault.

Paradoxically, Brezhnev's sympathies were with the core constituency of the Russian heartland. As a Russian loyalist, he had tried to prop up this huge region with vast infusions of money—for roads, buildings, village administrators, hundreds of thousands of new tractors and combines. He had mounted campaigns, drives, programs, all run from the top down by phalanxes of bureaucrats and Party officials. He had somewhat liberalized the rules for private gardening and the raising of livestock, but lack of grain kept the peasants from developing any decent herds. In the main, Brezhnev's strategy was to throw money at the farm problem, to the exasperation of his prime minister, Aleksei Kosygin, who saw (so Gorbachev's colleagues told me) the farm sector as a rat hole. One Soviet economist reported that the non–black earth heartland received 474,000 new tractors and combines between 1976 and 1980; by 1980, more than two thirds—322,000—were written off as unusable.[8] Kosygin had been right; the funds spent on the farm sector had been sucked up and had disappeared almost without a trace.

By the time Gorbachev took over, the farm sector was a stagnant quagmire, a symbol par excellence of what was wrong with Soviet economic policies. Before the Bolzhevik Revolution, czarist Russia had been an exporter of grain. By the mid-eighties, it was importing from the United States fifty-one million tons of grain annually. As the Chinese grain harvest began to skyrocket upward in the late seventies and early eighties, the Soviet grain harvests were sagging. The most demoralizing failure, however, was not simply the harvest, but the stunning losses in the Soviet storage, transportation, and distribution system. It was so bad that Gorbachev himself estimated that 20–30 percent of the annual harvest never reached consumers; others put the figure at closer to 40 percent.[9] Great volumes of crops were—and are—left in the ground or else rotted in storage or in transit.

What is more, the gross inefficiencies of the farm sector had been perpetuated by government policy. Literally thousands of unprofitable collective and state farms were kept afloat in the Brezhnev era by rising subsidies. Brezhnev had fueled a vicious cycle; the more he propped up failing farms with larger subsidies, the less efficient they became and the more dependent on the state. For example, in 1982, Gorbachev and his colleagues in Moscow had determined that literally half of the fifty thousand state and collective farms in the country were operating at a loss.[10] In 1983, Moscow approved massive new subsidies of 55 billion rubles (about $90 billion) on top of the already inflated state procurement prices—just to keep failing farms from going bankrupt.[11] By the late 1980s, the failing farms were disguised by newer, higher price supports; only two thousand farms were officially listed as unprofitable. But one of Gorbachev's aides, Georgy Shakhnazarov, estimated to me that roughly 40 percent of the nation's farms were actually losing money.[12]

In sum, Gorbachev himself was moved to comment: "As a peasant might say, our field grew too thick with the weeds and thistles of bureaucratism, mismanagement, social apathy, and irresponsibility. And weeding alone won't suffice here."[13]

To me, all these elements—China's new leap forward, the success of Soviet private-plot farmers, and the disaster in the collective farm sector—seemed to give Gorbachev compelling reasons to launch his economic reforms with radical changes on the farm, and specifically to promote private farming.

FIVE "RULES" OF ECONOMIC REFORM

Strangely, that is not what Gorbachev did. For all his liberal, reformist reputation, Gorbachev began his farm reform not at the bottom, with the farmer, as Deng Xiaoping had done, but at the top, with the bureaucracy.

After all those years as Brezhnev's lieutenant for agriculture, Gorbachev took power without any clear-cut economic strategy beyond a drive to accelerate output and demand more discipline. Even as he attacked Brezhnev's old ways, he continued them.

His first big step in farming was to create a superministry—the State Committee for Agroindustry—which swallowed up five other ministries. It was supposed to break bureaucratic deadlocks, but still, this was the tenth—the *tenth*—time the agricultural bureaucracy had been reorganized since World War II. Gorbachev offered one difference from Brezhnev's periodic shakeups: He cut thousands of bureaucratic jobs when he combined the five ministries.

Gorbachev's aim was to integrate farm production and food processing under one umbrella. Back in 1982, he had wanted to create "a unified economic mechanism" for agriculture, but Brezhnev and the Politburo had blocked him.[14] Now, as number one, he could impose his own plan.

The difficulty was that Gorbachev's plan did not address the fundamental problem of motivating farmers at the grass-roots level. It perpetuated the command mentality, and farms continued to get their output plans from the top.

To make matters worse, Gorbachev put in charge an old Stavropol crony, Vyacheslav Murakhovsky, who was stiff, pompous, and not up to the job. In speeches, Gorbachev and Murakhovsky tossed out talk about markets and more flexible wholesale trade, but nothing happened. The Party apparat kept right on giving out detailed orders to farms on sowing and harvesting. Gorbachev's superministry only seemed to deepen the farm mess, not cure it.

For a supposed innovator who advocated decentralization when he was in Stavropol, this was not an impressive beginning. He gambled on administrative readjustments and modifications rather than going for structural reforms.

Irreverent Russian humorists inevitably mocked Gorbachev's bureaucratic white elephant, which was known as Gosagroprom, drawn from its Soviet title, Gosudarstvenni Agropromyishlenni Komitet.

In one joke, a Soviet spy and an American spy get together after retirement for a few drinks. Eventually, Boris, the Soviet, turns to his new American friend and says, "Come on, John, you can tell me now. The CIA caused terrible disasters in our country. You were responsible for Chernobyl, right?"

"No," answers the CIA man modestly, "but we did something much worse. We invented Gosagroprom." Then both men laugh.

The one departure from big collectivized farming that Gorbachev did champion—indeed, which he had pushed as Stavropol leader and as Party secretary for agriculture in Moscow—were "contract brigades." These were small teams who, together, worked a section of land, leased equipment, brought in the harvest, and shared earnings. As Vladimir Tikhonov, a reform economist, told me, Gorbachev "understood very well that these small groups of peasants . . . could give new oxygen to agriculture."[15] This approach had the kernel of reform, but it was applied experimentally and not very widely, it was modest in thrust, and it was easily subverted by Party and agricultural leaders who disliked giving up their control. Most

important, the work team did not get control of a specific section of land
for a period of several years, so the people in it could not begin even to
simulate the pride and profit of private land ownership.

In short, instead of hitting it at the outset, as Deng had done in China,
Gorbachev's program put off real agricultural reform. In early 1988, after
Gorbachev had been in command for three years, industry and the new
privately owned service cooperatives had new laws on the books offering
them autonomy, but there was no new Magna Charta for farmers.

Puzzled by this, I put the question to Abel Aganbegyan, the reform
economist, who had become one of Gorbachev's senior advisers and was
visiting America in 1988; I was writing an article about him and Soviet
economic reform for *The New York Times Magazine*. I asked why Gorbachev's economic reform had not begun with agriculture, and why Moscow
had not copied China's approach.

At first, he tried to put me off with an all-purpose joke: "You know,
everything, every sector in our country, is in crisis, and we have a five-step
strategy for dealing with a crisis. The first thing we do is make the mess
even worse, to intensify the crisis. Second, we look for an outside enemy
to blame. Third, we punish the innocents by firing some bureaucrats.
Fourth, we pass out medals and awards to all of our leaders. And fifth,
we finally recognize the problem."

"Okay," I said, "so it's easy to make fun of Brezhnev and his style of
operating. But this is now the time of Gorbachev and *perestroika;* you are
doing things differently. Why haven't you tried the Chinese approach?"

Then Aganbegyan said, "Chinese farmers are different from Russian
farmers. They have not lived as long under state capitalism and a command economy as our people have. The Chinese still have the habit of
private farming. They are natural traders. So they are suited to private
farming. But our people have lost that habit. They have lived under the
Stalinist system for nearly seven decades and they cannot adapt as quickly
as the Chinese farmers did. It does not make sense for us."[16]

Only a couple of years later, Aganbegyan was singing a different tune,
conceding that it had been a great mistake not to push private farming
at the start of *perestroika.* But his answer to me in 1988 was typical of
what I heard for the next couple of years. And of course, as we will see,
there was some truth in his comment about the attitudes and aptitudes
of Soviet farm workers. But his answer masked the larger, more powerful
reasons for resistance to private farming in the Soviet Union.

First, there is an army of officials and bureaucrats, at least three million
of them, who have a vested interest in the collectivized system. There are
farm chairmen, directors, staffs of technicians, assistants, accountants,

and agronomists, not to mention a parallel structure of Party organizations concerned with agriculture in every province capital, district town, and village.

More than one reformer has accused this powerful pyramid of blocking a shift toward private farming. "Some people who are strong and powerful fear our autonomy, because then we ourselves become strong and powerful within the confines of our economic territory," asserted a reform-minded collective-farm leader. "So who is it? Look and see where the decision adopted at the Party Congress and subsequent Central Committee plenums become bogged down, where they are devalued, and there you will find the answer to that question."[17]

I have met many of these obstructionists, but none who was more personally striking than Valery Romanov, a rugged, good-looking outdoorsman of fifty, who was the agricultural secretary for the important province of Sverdlovsk, in the heart of the Ural Mountains. Poised and self-confident, Romanov was unusual for a Party bureaucrat—when he met me on a Saturday morning in his gleaming, modernistic office, he was dressed in a khaki work shirt and slacks, rather than the normal bureaucrat's gray suit. Romanov had a gruff, masculine charm; clearly he relished the opportunity for verbal jousting with someone he saw as a representative of the capitalist world. His open manner was appealing, but I quickly discovered he was dogmatic when it came to policy.

When the Soviet farm performance had been repeatedly raked over the coals by Gorbachev each year, Romanov admitted to me that he had felt the sting of criticism, which was echoed by the masses. "I take that kind of criticism painfully," he admitted. "I've poured half of my life into agricultural work and when people say that the whole system of agriculture is a mess, of course it's an insult. I don't sleep well at night."[18]

Nonetheless, his own views had not changed. He had no use for market economics. He did not want to shift farmland from state farms to private operators, except for the private plots they already worked. He did not want to raise prices on potatoes or cut subsidies to the farms. He was furious and frustrated that Gorbachev's industrial reforms had taken away from him several thousand workers who, in years past, had helped bring in the fall harvest. The depleted countryside was short of labor.

Under the old system, Romanov had been able to requisition regiments of free labor. As a senior provincial Party leader, he had had the clout to call up local factory managers and give them orders on how many workers to send to the farms for field work during the key harvesting drive in the fall. Now Gorbachev's reforms had deprived Party bosses of that power and lifted that obligation from the factories. Romanov had been left desperately short of manpower, which risked the loss of part of the harvest.

Romanov's solution to the poor productivity of Soviet farms was to import fancy new harvesters and tractors from Holland, and to reimpose the factory corvée labor force for the harvest.

But, I reminded him, there was still the problem of lazy, unproductive workers and inefficient farm management.

"How do you solve that problem?" I asked.

"The old way—with the fist," he asserted, raising a fist in front of my face, an unmistakably neo-Stalinist answer.

Another deterrent to radical change in Soviet agriculture is the brooding fear among the peasants—a fear that the parasitic apparatus of officials and Party workers shrewdly manipulates—that free-market economics will cause thousands of state and collective farms to fail, throwing the mass of peasants into chaos, and leaving them in even worse poverty than they are today.

Yevgeny Sokolov, Byelorussia's top Communist Party leader and a staunch foe of private farming, promoted the stark view in *Izvestia* that: "Breaking up the land into plots is a quick road to nowhere. Not only economically, but also socially. For the peasant himself, it means total slavery!"[19]

The specter of chaos, of being left at the mercy of the unpredictable gyrations of some unknown market, is something that Soviets, especially Russian peasants, desperately fear—and given the violent upheavals of their history, this is understandable. And so, as Aganbegyan implied, they cling to the only structure they know—the state and collective farm system.

LOSING IDEOLOGICAL VIRGINITY

One final source of psychic resistance to farm reform lies in the Leninist stereotypes embedded in the peasant mind—specifically, the stigma attached to the successful peasant farmer as a plush bourgeois, a covert capitalist. Lenin and Stalin created an ideological demon in the countryside: the class of kulaks, about five million individual homesteaders, usually modestly prosperous, hardworking, middle-class farmers, who were forever portrayed in Communist propaganda—often falsely—as rapacious landowners, as opposed to the masses, whose lives revolved around traditional peasant communes.[20]

Lenin, in his militant, postrevolutionary phase, was quick to accentuate class divisions. "The proletariat," he said, "must separate, demarcate the working peasant from the peasant owner, the peasant worker from the peasant huckster, the peasant who labors from the peasant who profiteers. In this demarcation lies the whole essence of socialism."[21]

Having rhetorically sharpened the knives of class warfare, Lenin then issued the call to battle, which was eventually waged by Stalin when he carried out the "liquidation" of the kulak class. Stalin deliberately crushed the private farmers, and in the process he destroyed the most productive elements of the peasantry, with devastating impact on Soviet agriculture for decades to come. He was carrying out Lenin's shrill command: "Kulaks are rabid enemies of the Soviet regime. . . . There can be no doubt at all that [either] the kulaks will cut down an infinite number of workers, or the workers will mercilessly cut down . . . the robbing kulak minority."[22]

Oddly enough, later Lenin had second thoughts; by 1922, he was not only more tolerant toward private farming, but he embraced it as part of his New Economic Policy. Sixty years later, however, his biting attacks on kulaks are more widely remembered. And they are easy for hard-liners to manipulate for their own ends: to ostracize would-be private farmers and intimidate others into keeping their heads down.

A celebrated case, brought to my attention soon after my arrival in Moscow in May 1988, was that of a peasant, or *muzhik,* from Arkhangelsk, a region in the northern tundra that raises only half the meat necessary for its inhabitants. This peasant, an unusually daring small-time farm entrepreneur named Nikolai Sivkov, was lionized in a documentary film called *Arkhangelsky Muzhik* made by Marina Goldovskaya. He was also vilified as a base profiteer by Communist diehards and apparatchiks.

This *muzhik*'s crime, in the eyes of local Party bosses, was that he used initiative and his own cow shed to breed a herd of bulls belonging to the state farm where he worked. He turned a nice profit—not only for himself but for the state farm too. He hacked a grazing area out of the forests and swamps, and gradually he built up a herd of sixty bulls, plus some cows and calves. Economists calculated that, single-handedly, Sivkov accounted for nearly 10 percent of the entire livestock herd of a huge state farm of several hundred people.[23] Thanks in good part to his hard work, his state farm was about the only one in the region that showed a profit.

Sivkov was doing what Gorbachev's program of "contract brigades" envisioned, except that Sivkov was operating alone as what he called a "one-man cooperative." This was not strictly legal, because no one else joined his co-op. But instead of rewarding Sivkov and helping him expand, or holding him up as a model to others, local Party and farm officials, angered by his independent spirit, harassed him and fought him every step of the way.

"For many years, people on the state farm, in the district Party committee, and in regional organs looked at me with suspicion," Sivkov glumly reported. "At first for feeding state-farm bulls in my own cow shed, then for my demands to be given land, and then for my aspiration to set up a cooperative. I heard lots of words—'kulak,' 'money-grubber,' 'capitalist dregs.' . . . I tried to explain that a peasant needs his own arable land, meadows for grazing and hay, his own agricultural machinery, and the unlimited right to buy or sell his output. . . . I failed to convince the [regional Party] secretary; he decided that I'd become a man of property, sort of an owner.

"Since 1982, they have not let me get on my feet," Sivkov complained. "With the greatest difficulty, I managed to get ten calves to fatten. In the district town, they do not want to deal with me. They also turn me down for loans. We are paupers."[24]

In Moscow, I was told that the harassment of Sivkov intensified after the documentary about him ran on nationwide television. Sivkov himself told reporters that local authorities actively intimidated other farmers from joining him in a farm cooperative.

Sivkov sometimes turned the glare of *glasnost* to his advantage. Once, when a French television crew came to film him, he used their presence to press for a loan to build a new house.

"I filled out the form and said quietly: 'Give me eight thousand rubles right away, or else I will tear up the document right in front of the camera,' " he recalled. "I knew that once the French left I would get nothing. The local officials were afraid of an international disgrace, and they gave me the loan. Recently, I filed a petition to lease a tract of woods. They turned me down. Must I wait for the French again?"[25]

The hard-liners showed no sympathy for his appeal. Wherever they detected economic initiative on the farm, they used the conservative wing of the press to attack what they called profiteering. One collective-farm chairman attacked Moscow for backing Sivkov and cried crocodile tears for Sivkov himself, mocking him as an uncouth bumpkin who worked so hard that he didn't "even have leisure time to straighten his hat."[26]

Ultimately, the documentary about Sivkov seemed to cut two ways. Among radical reformers in the big cities, it made him a cause célèbre. But among peasants, his unending problems were an object lesson in the apparat's capacity to victimize peasants who stepped out of line. It was also evidence of the dangers of Gorbachev's timid half measures.

This second message was understood by some of the more radical reformers, among them the sharp, iconoclastic, market-oriented economist Nikolai Shmelyov.

I met Shemlyov at the Institute for the U.S.A. and Canada—a think tank for studying North America—but Shmelyov was not looking overseas; his focus was on the domestic economic mess within Russia. A stocky scholar in his fifties, he spoke with appealing candor and a nasal twang. He was Nikita Khrushchev's son-in-law, which had given him access to high circles early in life and probably reinforced his natural self-confidence. He was an unabashed advocate of family farming. Shortly before our talk, he had laid out his views in a hard-hitting article, a copy of which he gave me.

"Family contracts and leasing [land] may be the only salvation for many farms that have long been 'unworked,' " Shmelyov declared. "How is one to justify the fact that a virtual campaign against personal farming has broken out again in the press? How is one to understand signs that . . . a new pogrom is brewing against personal orchards and hothouse operations, and against breeding personal livestock?

"We must decide finally once and for all what is more important to us: whether to have an abundance of food, or eternally to indulge . . . irresponsible loudmouths and proponents of equality in poverty. We need to call stupidity, incompetence, and active Stalinism by their proper names. We need to do whatever it takes to ensure an ample supply of foodstuffs. . . .

"We need to do these things even if it means losing our ideological virginity. . . ."[27]

GORBACHEV'S TURNAROUND

Late in the game—more than three years after he took power—Gorbachev finally heeded the logic of the reformers and turned his agricultural policy around. Lenin had made "Land to the Peasants" a revolutionary slogan; now, finally, Gorbachev appropriated it as his slogan too.

This move appealed to political progressives, who believed that turning land over to individual farmers was one way to reduce the power of the Party apparatus and bureaucracy, and thereby to promote economic—and hence political—independence among an important segment of the population. Returning "land to the peasants" also appealed to Russian nationalists, mainly conservatives, who saw it as a policy that could revive the dying Russian countryside. And it appealed to reform economists as a way to put food into the shops.

Also, they felt desperate to have Gorbachev's reform program show some tangible results, because the masses were getting restive.

The cornerstone of Gorbachev's new policy, first floated in June 1988, was a proposal to grant fifty-year leases of land to small "lease teams." It was a measure that stopped well short of outright peasant ownership of the land, and short of individual private farming, but it moved significantly in that direction.

Gorbachev's first serious push for long-term leases came at a Communist Party Central Committee meeting in October 1988. After three and a half years of defending the collectivized farm system, Gorbachev seemed finally to agree with such reform economists as Nikolai Shmelyov and Vladimir Tikhonov: The farm sector would never really improve until individual peasants were given strong incentives to produce, over a long period of time, on sections of land they could come to think of as their own.

"Much depends on giving the farmer a greater stake," Gorbachev told the Party conference in June. "Everything depends on how quickly we can interest the people . . . in leasing. We must overcome the estrangement between the farmer and the soil. We must make the farmer sovereign master, protect him against command methods and fundamentally change the conditions of life in the villages."[28]

Under Gorbachev's new proposal, Soviet farmers, like the Chinese under Deng Xiaoping, would get lease contracts on land, be given annual procurement targets, and then be allowed to sell any surpluses above their targets. The "lease team" would run its own business, decide what feed, seed grain, fertilizer, and machinery it needed, and buy or lease it from state and collective farms.

This still-relatively-modest approach was fraught with opportunities for sabotage by bureaucrats; and it met powerful resistance from Party conservatives who saw it as the first step toward dismantling the state- and collective-farm system.

By now, Gorbachev was growing impatient with conservative foot-dragging. There was nothing wrong with making money, he argued, and some incentives were needed to galvanize the peasantry. In the past, Gorbachev said, "the people have been alienated from the soil and the means of production" and turned into mere "wage-earners." To the doubting hard-liners, he declared: "People's desire to take possession of land and facilities, and to set up their own family livestock units, does not contradict socialism, comrades. This kind of owner would be operating on land that is the property of the whole people."[29] Then Gorbachev went on the offensive, denouncing Party and government organizations for resisting reform and "playing a waiting game."

It was typical of the relentless trench warfare that has gone on over the reform program that Gorbachev was unable immediately to carry the day for his new fifty-year-lease proposal, let alone for outright private ownership of the land. His new progressive push landed him in a hot battle with Communist Party dogmatists such as Yegor Ligachev, second-ranking figure in the Party, the conservative champion of collectivized farming and the foe of privately owned property. Gorbachev and Ligachev had begun in 1985 as allies for reform, but as Gorbachev became more progressive, Ligachev grew more outspoken and more resistant, all the while making a pretense of unity with Gorbachev's overall policies. As the March 1989 elections approached—the first Soviet elections in seven decades to offer a choice of candidates—their debate took on the aspect of an American political campaign, charge and countercharge, except that neither side used the other's name.

Barnstorming through the Ukraine in late February, Gorbachev declared: "We have to move on to new forms of life and organization of work. A revolution in our mentality is the most important thing. Vast social energy is needed to overcome the force of inertia and the resistance of the old, to smash braking mechanisms and shift society onto the path of intensive development."[30] Referring to Ligachev's two main areas of responsibility, agriculture and ideology, Gorbachev said that "stereotypes and dogmas" should be put aside. Specifically, he proposed that unproductive farms and other unproductive state-run enterprises should be dissolved in favor of new forms of land leasing and free-market cooperatives.

A few days later, Ligachev voiced his opposition, during a speech to the Party faithful in the Siberian city of Omsk. Ligachev backed leasing and farmers' cooperatives in principle, but not when they threatened the system of state and collective farms, which he insisted be maintained. In what looked like a planted question, Ligachev was asked how he felt about disbanding just the *unprofitable* farms, and he dug in his heels against Gorbachev. "You and I did not establish Soviet power so as to treat people and work collectives so shamelessly," he retorted. "We must find other ways."[31]

During the buildup to an important Central Committee meeting on farm policy in mid-March, Ligachev stepped up his advocacy of the traditional approach, asserting that the Party and government should bolster state and collective farms with large new infusions of money. During a visit to Czechoslovakia, he lavishly praised collective farming in that country and questioned Gorbachev's reform plan. Soviet television showed him walking through shops in Prague with well-stocked shelves and then, as if to offer a lesson for home audiences, Ligachev told the camera: "For all these years there has been no deviation from the Czecho-slovak policy in the agrarian sector."[32] In other words, experience in Prague shows, comrades, that no dramatic changes are needed back in the Soviet Union.

On his side, Gorbachev stepped up the rhetoric. Finally, he said what the experts had been saying all along: that decades of experience showed that massive investments in collective farming had not paid off. "Analysis of history and experience of the past few years offer compelling evidence that if we opt for this as the mainstay of agricultural policy, it will be a serious mistake," Gorbachev declared. What is more, he took note of the conservative tactic of pretending to go along with his reforms while secretly sabotaging them, and he denounced sham lease contracts that assigned land but in practice gave farmers little real freedom—an echo of the nightmare problems of Nikolai Sivkov, the *Arkhangelsky Muzhik.*

At a Party meeting on March 15, Gorbachev called for the dismantling of the huge new superministry he had set up in 1985, and a gradual transition to a new market system that would give farmers "complete freedom" to choose how to market their products. Edging ever closer to outright advocacy of private property, Gorbachev outlined a new principle of "individual ownership" of farmland. In the first major shift in Soviet farm policy since Stalin's collectivization drive in the late 1920s, the Communist Party Central Committee bowed to Gorbachev's pressure and agreed to lifetime leases for farmers, with the right to pass on land to their children. In a burst of optimism, Gorbachev envisioned a gradual transformation of the existing huge state and collective farms into much looser amalgams of smaller independent farm units run by families and small groups of farmers. He argued that this would be a radical turning point, making it possible for the peasant once again to be the master of the land. Anything less, he said, would not work.

Ligachev had the last word. On the issue of long-term leasing, he had been beaten, but at a press conference he emphasized that the collective- and state-farm system remained the keystone of Soviet agriculture and that there should be strict limits on the implementation of Gorbachev's concept of "individual ownership."

In sum, Ligachev, the voice of the Party apparat, asserted: "I want to stress that everything will still be based on the principle of common ownership and common property."[33] His stand left a large question mark over the fate of private farming.

THE HALFWAY HOUSE OF REFORM

A few months after this celebrated clash among the leadership, I went out with my film crew to see how Gorbachev's new policy was faring in the grain-growing regions of the Russian heartland north of Moscow.

In the fall of 1989, a golden Indian-summer sunshine played over the meadows of ripened grain in central Russia, the kind of weather that should bring a bountiful harvest. But Vladimir Dorofeyev, the Communist Party's agricultural chief for Yaroslavl Province, conceded to me that the grain harvest in his domain was "very low" (sixty-five to seventy bushels per acre), barely half of a good Soviet harvest. Dorofeyev told me he was puzzled by the poor showing, but several others, including one state-farm chairman, said much of the grain had been lost in the fields because there were not enough farmhands to harvest it.

On individual farming, Dorofeyev mouthed the new Party line, and even had some astonishing things to say when I tested him by asking his view of the kulaks, so hated by Lenin and Stalin.

"I think they were real good owners of the land," he answered. "The old attitude did a lot of damage. I think that was wrong. Because the people who really farmed the land, who did such a great job on the land, who did it with their own backs, their sweat and blood, so to speak—they were doing a lot, they were dying for that land."[34]

Almost as an afterthought, he confessed under his breath: "I am the grandson of a kulak."

That a Party agriculture secretary would make such a confession was a mark of the changing times; under Brezhnev, this revelation could have cost him his job, and under Stalin, a trip to Siberia.

Dorofeyev gamely tried to walk the new line but inevitably betrayed the attitudes of an apparatchik. Under the new Party policy, he was supposed to promote individual farming, but when I suggested that this would soon eliminate the need for his own job, indeed for any role in agriculture for Party officials, he recoiled.

"The role of the Party is such that the peasant is always under the control of the Party," he said, bristling. "Everything here goes through the Communist Party."

Others in Yaroslavl, a city of half a million about two hundred miles northeast of Moscow, told me the man to see was Dmitri Starodubtsev, director of the nearby Dzerzhinsky State Farm, a man in the Gorbachev mold, one of the new breed of farm managers who was applying progressive methods.

Starodubtsev was a non-Party man, a favorite of the Popular Front reform movement in Yaroslavl, and an outspoken exponent of the new political freedoms. So well known was he as an independent-minded maverick that when he first announced his candidacy for the national parliament in the elections of March 1989, the Communist Party hierarchy in Yaroslavl had tried to torpedo him. Undaunted, Starodubtsev had cast himself as the champion of the little people and had easily beaten a Communist Party regular for a seat in the Congress of People's Deputies. His election had added to his local mystique and prestige.

When I first met Starodubtsev, it was not long after his election, and I quickly understood why he had won. He was a tough little bantamweight, short, strong in the arms, a tireless, kinetic, fifty-five-year-old bachelor with a flair for heroics and a taste for Georgian brandy. For years, he had lived—usually successfully—at the borders of the permissible. He earned an economics degree in night school, served as a jurist in the army, became a farm expert, and then got into trouble, lost his Party membership, and went to jail.

Back in the late seventies, Starodubtsev ran afoul of the system by being too entrepreneurial. The Brezhnev crowd, especially the Party boss where Starodubtsev was working, did not appreciate innovation. He and his two brothers, Vasily and Fyodor, were running a network of collective farms near Tula, south of Moscow; they had their own trading system and set their own prices, different from the fixed state prices. This infuriated the regional Party bosses, especially when Dmitri made deals to obtain farm supplies from outside the region. Dmitri was eventually accused, one of his allies told me, of spending farm funds lavishly to entertain visitors and to help a high Gosplan (state-planning) official repair his country home, in return for a kickback of feed for the cattle on Dmitri's farm. This kind of thing is typical of Soviet mutual back-scratching, and it's notable that it was not for private profit on his part. Starodubtsev insisted the case against him was a frame-up, and he mustered two hundred witnesses in his defense. Nonetheless, he went to jail for two years, from 1980 to 1982, because, he said, the Party bosses wanted him put away—"That's how it was done then." He's still pushing for an official pardon.[35]

After Starodubtsev had returned to normal life and held a couple of regular jobs, the Gorbachev reforms gave him a new chance—he was given control of Dzerzhinsky State Farm. Today, he bounces around his twenty-thousand-acre domain in the Soviet equivalent of a Jeep, barking orders to his office through an old-fashioned walkie-talkie radiophone, inspecting fields of wheat or potatoes, or stopping in to check on some of the farm's two thousand head of cattle. He is equally at home churning on foot through the mud, in his gray fedora hat, coat, and tie, half covered by an open windbreaker.

Starodubtsev is a hard-driving, no-frills, no-nonsense farm manager. Over the past three years, he has begun to turn handsome profits, Soviet-style, at a farm as big as a Texas cattle ranch, a farm that, despite its size, had been stumbling along in the red before he arrived. About six hundred people work on the farm, one of Stalin's creations, which is organized like a factory. The state organizes the farming, the workers punch the clock. Often, entire families are on the payroll. Housing and most of the food are provided.

The workers seem to like Starodubtsev, but they also fear him. He conveys power, and he doesn't mince words. He has won loyalty by being more humane and more concerned with his people's welfare than previous managers have been, building new housing and recreational facilities, offering more pay for good work, and using his political clout to hound local agencies into providing his farm with things it needs. On his farm, the new benefits he has offered have stopped the horrible flight into the cities of the best workers—mechanics, engineers, and other skilled laborers.

By Soviet standards, Starodubtsev runs a good shop. The obstacles for any Soviet farm director are daunting: from terrible roads, inadequate supplies, and shortage of labor to machinery that is antiquated and always breaking down. There are never any spare parts on the market. Many farms have to triple their manpower to compensate; Starodubtsev gets by with doubling it. He has brought in East German tractors and cut back the waste of his potato crop to 10 percent, although his potatoes are still low-grade. He is experimenting with improved strains of cattle and wheat to increase productivity, and he begged us to provide him with a real Idaho potato to upgrade his stock.

For all his drive for modernization, Starodubtsev's state farm is, at best, only a halfway house of reform. Clearly, he has improved efficiency through effective management, but even as a self-proclaimed reformer, he has not yet fulfilled Gorbachev's goal of creating a new body of self-reliant individual farmers. In principle, Starodubtsev supports the idea, but he's also something of a dictator who has difficulty letting real power slip away; he's reluctant to give his farm workers genuine independence.

When I asked Starodubtsev for a progress report on Gorbachev's new approach to individual farming, he said he had put the leasing idea to some of his best workers. He introduced me to the family who had been most successful raising cattle. Lydiya Popova and her teenage son, Sasha, were in the cattle shed that afternoon, feeding 220 head of cattle. Typical of Soviet farm workers, Starodubtsev said, this family had no money to buy cattle, so his idea was to lease livestock to the Popovs, let them fatten up the cattle, turn the cattle back to the state farm at a heavier weight, and make their money from the gain in weight. Or Starodubtsev had milk cows to offer, at about 1,000 rubles ($1,650) a head, and capable of producing 2,000 rubles' worth of milk a year.

"You find me someone to buy a hundred cows and I'll sell," he kidded me.

There was a catch, which Lydiya pointed out.

"I would like to take the cattle, but not the land," she said. "To lease land means I have to work it myself. But if the weather is nasty or something, how will I manage? It's impossible for us to grow enough. We're just three people in our family. What if I do not have enough feed for my cows?"

At the mention of cattle fodder, Starodubtsev was nodding his head.

"We're very short of cattle feed," Lydiya Popova went on. "It's impossible to buy cattle feed."

"Everyone wants to buy grain, but nobody wants to sell it," Starodubtsev agreed. "Everyone in this region grows rye. What they want to buy from us is wheat. We have a problem. We cannot give it to them free. We cannot even sell it to them."

"It's too big a risk for us to take the cattle if we cannot get the feed," Lydiya said.

Clearly, she preferred leaving the risk and the headaches to Starodubtsev, while she continued to draw her 200-ruble-a-month salary from the state farm.

"Too risky even to try?" I asked.

She nodded. "Too risky."[36]

REAL FARMING OR SHARECROPPING?

Starodubtsev had an even better candidate for a leasing deal, Aleksandr Orlov, the head of his twelve-man potato brigade, which worked five hundred acres of land and produced about five thousand tons of potatoes. Orlov had eight children, four of them married and working at the state farm, so he had a strong nucleus for a family farm. He had been farming in this region since 1943, when he was only a teenager. He was so outstanding as a worker that he had been officially designated a Hero of Socialist Labor, a rare distinction for a rank-and-file farm worker, won only by a few hundred farm workers nationwide.

"Orlov—he's a good professional who knows the machinery and how to grow and harvest potatoes," Starodubtsev told me. "I made him an offer: 'Comrade Orlov, lease the land and the machinery. We will give you the seeds and fertilizers. Grow potatoes and sell them to us.' He tells me, 'I'll think about it.'"

I found Orlov in the potato fields, driving a harvest combine. He was a nice-looking man with silver hair, deep-blue eyes, and a strong face, weatherbeaten from long days in the sun. He wore the costume of a field hand—flat visored cap, a faded padded jacket, high rubber boots. As the camera crew and I approached, he climbed off the combine. The September wind whipped around us as we talked among the hardened furrows of earth under a fading sky. It was early evening, and Orlov had been working for close to twelve hours.

"There's great excitement in the Soviet Union, in Moscow, about leasing land to the peasants," I said to him. "What do you say? Are you ready to take the land?"

"No, I'm not ready to take it yet," he replied cautiously. "I don't have a good enough head for it. You have to have a real good head on your shoulders to do that. Of course, it would be nice to be a farmer, to have my own place. I would take good care of everything. I'd get rid of all this stuff—no junk, none of these stones." He kicked his boot at some small rocks.

"I would live here on my own plot of land," he said, chewing over that idea, beginning to relish it. "That would be nice. I would like to buy land, but I don't have enough money. I could make an arrangement with the state somehow, but I'm afraid of it. I'm really afraid."

"Afraid of what?" I asked.

"Well, I'm afraid of . . . everything," he admitted. "I've never seen anyone lease land in my region. I'd like to go someplace and have a look, see how people do it."

"Is it such a huge risk?" I asked.

"Yes, it's a risk," he answered.

"What conditions would you need to make it work?" I asked.

"What conditions?" he echoed. "Conditions that would help me grow more and sell the produce at better prices."[37]

To lease or not to lease was a question for Orlov's entire family. He invited me home to hear their views. He was the patriarch but, at sixty-three, close to retirement. At dinner with Orlov and his wife, Katya, were his two daughters, Natasha and Lida, and their husbands, plus his son, Yuri, a tractor driver, and his wife—all employees of the farm.

"What I don't like," Orlov began, "is that there's no law about leasing yet. It's not written on paper. What if I start farming and then lose the land? . . . We saw on TV and heard on the radio that people leased some land from a collective farm and then the collective farm took it back."

Natasha, his energetic and outspoken older daughter, pointed out the problem of low prices in state stores. "The state people would tell us, 'You must sell your potatoes cheap,' and that won't be profitable to us." she said. "We want our profits."

"But there are great shortages," I pointed out. "Everybody knows you could sell produce that is in short supply."

"Where would I sell it—to the store?" Orlov asked skeptically. "They won't take it. So I'll have to bring everything I produce back home. That's no good. I don't have a warehouse to store it."

Orlov's wife did not want the headache. "I don't want him to work so hard anymore," she said. "In two more years, he goes on retirement. I can't wait until he enjoys himself, sitting on the sofa next to me."

The younger generation were full of practical questions about how they could operate amid a state-run economy, accustomed as they were to orders from above. They all assumed, as did Starodubtsev, that they would have to sell their produce to the state farm.

"Say we decide to grow beets," Natasha suggested. "The state farm may say, 'We don't want you to grow beets. We need potatoes.' But beets are more profitable for us, right? Well, they could say, 'If you don't want to do things our way, okay, we'll just take back the land.' What kind of lease is that?"

I fished for pragmatic motivation: "Wouldn't you like to earn more money so you could, say, buy a car?"

"We have already been on the waiting list for a car for five years," groused Yuri. "My father is not able to buy a car."

"A Hero Worker with no car!" Katya chirped sarcastically.

That phrase echoed around the table; it was obviously a sore point with Orlov's family. Supposedly his distinction as a Hero of Socialist Labor entitled Orlov to some privileges. In practice, however, Orlov had seen none, and that empty promise left his family wary of new promises from the state.

The larger message for Lida was the difficulty of getting farm equipment. "It's impossible to lease a tractor," she said. "When the state farm is short of tractors, they would never lease one to us. So where would we get one?"

As with tractors, so with other machinery, fertilizer, seeds, feed grain.

In an economy of constant shortages, they all took it for granted that the state farm would take care of its own needs first, leaving the family farmer out in the cold. If forced to turn outside their own state farm to try to obtain machinery and supplies, they were even more pessimistic about their chances with the state distribution network. Besides, Orlov pointed out, there was no system of financial credit to help independent farmers buy machinery over time.

Their fundamental worry was that they would wind up too dependent on the state farm and, therefore, not truly the masters of their own land.

"The director would be in the yard every day checking in every pail," said Natasha, "and if you wanted to sell something in the market, on the side, he would never let you. He would be in charge of everything the leasers produce. It wouldn't be like real leasing. It would be like half leasing."

"We have a saying in Russia—'Two bears can't live in one den,'" Orlov concluded. "You can't have two masters for one piece of land. I say, No leasing. Just give it all to us. We'll do everything. We'll farm it. We'll sell it. It's my own property. What I want to do, I do. That would be for real. If I want to grow beets or cabbages, this is my thing. It's just a tiny household but it's mine. I own it."[38]

The next morning I went to see Starodubtsev in his office, to ask why experienced and able farmers like Orlov didn't trust the new Gorbachev plan and didn't trust Starodubtsev himself.

"They don't trust me simply because during so many years of collective agriculture, the peasants have been lied to," he replied candidly. "As a result, they've developed a general mistrust, and they don't trust me because they see me connected to the system of collectivized farming. I'm telling them, 'We'll help you,' and they're afraid. They say, 'Today, Gorbachev is governing the country, and tomorrow he may disappear and there will be another man and a different attitude toward leasing land.' It's the fifth year of *perestroika* and our people should be confident, but they're not. Our people do not believe in tomorrow."

"How about yourself?" I asked. "As someone who was put in jail, do you believe in the system?"

"All my life I believed that there would someday be democracy in our country, democracy based on deeds, not slogans. And that laws would be used not against the people, but for them," Starodubtsev replied. "I believe such times have come. As an elected representative, I will try to fight for laws that promote truth and trust among the people. I believe that in the future we will have laws that will not cheat the peasants or other working people, and gradually people will come to believe in them too."

Starodubtsev's notion was to pit privately run family farms and small-lease cooperatives against the big state-run farms, "and we'll see who is better."

But even in his eyes, the eyes of a proponent of reform, the competition would be stacked in favor of the big farms, with their equipment and other advantages. The new family farmers not only had to overcome the inbred peasant caution against breaking out of the pack and standing out as individuals, but they would have to operate without firm assurances of necessary financing, marketing, and material support.

As for the Orlovs' worries about getting seeds and equipment, or marketing their crops, Starodubtsev said he would help as much as he could, but that as a state-farm director, he was "tied with all kinds of regulations and instructions." He could not, for example, sell the Orlovs tractors and machinery outright. If they turned to the state, he added, they would have to pay very steep prices, twice as much as a state farm pays.

"Your people feel this is all an enormous risk," I observed. "Knowing how the system works, would you be confident?"

"Well, they are afraid of something new and different, because they have grown accustomed to working as employees," Starodubtsev replied. "Now, Orlov works very well and he gets very good pay. Whether the harvest is good or bad, he draws his salary. And he says to me, 'If I lease the land and work hard, and there is no rain, or too much rain, then I lose my harvest, and I go broke.' That's what's worrying him."

Was that the "essence of the problem," I asked, the real reason Gorbachev's leasing plan was not taking hold?

Starodubtsev grew thoughtful.

"You see," he said, "the land was confiscated from the peasants in the thirties, even in the twenties. Sixty years ago. So the new generation never owned the land. They are not used to the land. They are afraid of it. It has become alien to them. The livestock they are willing to take. To breed animals, that's okay. But the land, they're afraid of it. Our people have lost the feeling of being masters of the land."[39]

Starodubtsev's views are shared by many, especially among government officials and leaders of collective and state farms. They put the primary blame for minimal progress in agricultural reform on the farm workers, their mentality and their habits. From what I saw and heard, the farm workers' reluctance is a critical obstacle. As the conversation around the Orlovs' dinner table illustrated, it is very hard to break the habit of dependency.

Even so, in spite of all the problems, some have dared to take the plunge. In Yaroslavl Province, the Ukraine, Siberia, and certainly the Baltic republics, I heard of individual farmers who were working the land on their own or in small cooperatives. Lithuanian and Estonian officials were aggressively trying to return farms to families who had owned the land before the Soviet occupation in 1940 and postwar collectivization. But the Baltics were exceptional in many ways, because individual farming had flourished there so recently and because the new reform governments were not hung up ideologically on keeping land under common state ownership.

Periodically, Gorbachev himself would cite encouraging examples of new farming ventures around the country. In one speech, he pointed with pride to the formation of thirty-three small "primary cooperatives" of three to five people each at the Krutishinsky State Farm not far from the Siberian city of Novosibirsk. Four of these cooperatives were growing grain, four growing feed, six producing milk, a dozen providing services, still others raising fur-bearing animals—all doing things that people on Starodubtsev's farm were not willing to try on their own.[40]

In the Russian heartland, I met some farm workers who had signed "lease contracts" with their parent state farms. The farther north and the more desperate the farming conditions, the more likely local Communist Party leaders were to promote experiments in leasing as a last desperate way of trying to hold younger workers on the land and to keep them from drifting off to the cities.

Yet the more I talked with these "lease teams," the more I came to see them not as the Soviet equivalent of independent homesteaders, but as tenant farmers working at the direction—and at the mercy—of state farms, which were reaping what profit there was. One of the staunchest advocates of private farming in the Communist Party Central Committee called these lease teams "not proprietors in the full sense, but halfway proprietors, or perhaps not even that."[41]

To me, they were simply sharecroppers.

As time wore on, it seemed to me that the fundamental failure was not the mind-set of the farmers but the failure of the reformers, from Starodubtsev up to Gorbachev, to provide attractive and viable conditions for private farming on anything larger than the kitchen-garden scale. The Orlovs had many legitimate worries that the reformers were dismissing all too lightly. Successful farm directors such as Starodubtsev were not eager to encourage real independence for their best farm workers, for fear of undercutting their own success. What is more, Gorbachev's plan failed to make provisions for the equipment, credit, service industry, and marketing support necessary for independent farming, and needed to spur farm workers on to make the leap of faith that Gorbachev proclaimed he wanted.

It puzzled me why Gorbachev and the reformers did not begin simply by increasing the size of the private plots, year by year, and letting the existing network of farmers' markets gradually expand. The main objection was that prices at farmers' markets were so high that few ordinary city dwellers could afford them; they were mainly for foreigners and more affluent Soviets. The ideologues were outraged by what they foresaw as profiteering. Still, gradual expansion of this sector might slowly bring down prices and encourage the development of the service industry that the farmers so badly needed.

The reluctance of the Orlovs was typical. Millions of other farm workers were watching and waiting too. Without greater assurances of support, only a small minority were intrigued by Gorbachev's offer of long-term land leasing. An opinion survey conducted by the government newspaper *Izvestia* in early 1990 found that roughly 40 percent of the rural people polled were willing to "take the land," but closer questioning revealed that only 10–14 percent were actually ready to organize personal farms—and then, *only* if a land law were passed.[42]

Finally, in late February 1990, the Supreme Soviet passed a land law. At Gorbachev's prompting, the new law allowed not merely small cooperative farms but "individual" landholdings—an important addition; it also allowed the right to lease land for life and to pass it on to inheritors.

Significantly, however, the legislation did not permit land to be bought, sold, or owned outright. For despite the urgings of some reformers, the government balked at accepting the concept of private property—an issue on which *Izvestia*'s poll found public opinion almost evenly divided. But it was an issue on which the conservative majority in the Supreme Soviet refused to budge; they gagged at even using the term *private property*.

"We are all children born during a time of meaningless political incantations, of meaningless fetishes, meaningless words, disinformation, and double standards," moaned one disappointed reform economist, Aleksandr Vladislavlev. "When I hear the words 'private property,' I will always be reminded of the helpless expression on the face of [Prime Minister] Nikolai Ivanovich Ryzhkov. He was so shocked by the sound of the words 'private property' being uttered within the walls of the

Supreme Soviet. 'Have you asked the people if they want this?' he asked. What is the point of asking the people when for seventy years the people were told things which had absolutely nothing in common with reality? . . .

"[Public opinion] will have to be remolded. . . . Private property . . . is the only way to achieve the highest work productivity, and this is the task which now faces our society."[43]

This was a minority view at the Supreme Soviet, a view that was rejected. Once again, the spirit of Ligachev and collective property prevailed. Gorbachev himself was either unwilling or not ready to assault the entrenched governmental resistance to genuine private farming, and he settled yet again for a weak compromise.

Over time, this law may persuade some farm workers—the 10 percent found in the *Izvestia* poll who were waiting for legal protection—to take the risk of setting up their own farms. Even 10 percent would mark some progress; but it would leave the vast majority of Soviet farming unchanged. Through the growing season of 1990, the political uncertainties and the resistance of officialdom persisted; so the Gorbachev policy brought no significant change to the face and structure of Soviet agriculture.

Gorbachev's half measures thus fell short of creating the kind of bandwagon surge in enthusiasm, production, and living standards that Deng Xiaoping had produced more than a decade earlier in China.

CHAPTER 12

THE CAPTIVE CAPTAINS OF SOVIET INDUSTRY

"What are we doing, talking about catching up [with the West] when we're two hundred years behind? And we sit and wait, and our bosses sit on their butts, doing nothing."[1]
—Soviet Worker
September 1989

"Extricating our economy from the precrisis state necessitates truly revolutionary transformations."[2]
—Gorbachev, June 1987

"Economic reforms are impossible in Communist systems. What is possible are political reforms that have economic consequences."[3]
—President Tito, Yugoslavia

In March 1988, the government newspaper *Izvestia* reported the startling news that a Soviet enterprise had refused to accept the economic production plan given to it by the State Planning Committee and the Ministry of Heavy Machine–Building in Moscow. That news caught the eye of anyone familiar with the traditional workings of the Soviet economy. Here was a singular act of industrial rebellion: An enterprise out in the provinces was boldly challenging the central hierarchy, daring to threaten the nerve center of the state-run economy.

For six decades, ever since Stalin had imposed the command economy, armies of bureaucrats in Moscow had been drafting annual production plans for every single economic unit in the country: forty-six thousand industrial enterprises, fifty thousand state and collective farms, thirty-two thousand construction associations, plus several hundred thousand other miscellaneous economic units—warehouses, stores, retail outlets, repair shops, distribution centers, and the like.[4]

This herculean undertaking was mounted under the aegis of Gosplan, the State Planning Committee. Throughout the Stalin era, and then under Khrushchev and Brezhnev, the very word *Gosplan* acquired a mystique that conveyed power, authority, gospel. In the eyes of Soviet Marxists, the "Plan" exemplified the scientific, rational organization of the nation's might. It was the formula for achieving maximum growth, for overtaking the capitalist West; it was the unerring mechanism for marshaling the manpower and the resources of a sprawling empire; it was the Utopian device for assuring the coordinated functioning of the world's second-largest economy. The Plan embodied Soviet socialism.

In the highly centralized Stalinist system, the Plan came close to being the fundamental law of the land.

After Stalin initiated the first Five-Year Plans in 1928, each subsequent one became the compass by which the nation was steered, and "fulfilling the Plan" became a national incantation. It was endlessly intoned in speeches, in the press, on television. Back in the 1970s, I was told that it was the whole concept of central planning, epitomized by Stalin's Five-Year Plans, that had multiplied Soviet output manyfold, from 1928 to 1973, had built the backbone of Soviet industry and lifted Russia from backwardness up to superpower status.

The national Plan emanated from the Olympus of Gosplan. It was passed down to various ministries, was expanded and embellished by echelons of ministerial bureaucracies, and then was transmitted to huge industrial conglomerates, or associations. It was then sent further out, to subdivisions or enterprises, and so on down in hierarchical fashion. In short, Gosplan's word was law.

Soviet industrial executives told me that the Plan would arrive at an enterprise in the form of huge books—as large, as thick, and as full of fine print as the Manhattan telephone directory. The Plan spelled out every last detail of what the entire enterprise should produce, and at what cost, made from what materials, for what price, for which customers, on what time schedule, with how many workers, at what wages, and so on. There was both a production plan and a supply plan, one for output, the other for where the enterprise would get its supplies. These fat books, with their sweeping instructions and their picayune detail, were the embodiment of the Stalinist economic system.

Now here, suddenly, was the spectacle of a Soviet enterprise irreverently opposing the system: mailing its set of fat planning books back to Moscow, unopened. As *Izvestia* reported, the Ministry of Heavy Machine–Building saw the episode as "a socially dangerous phenomenon"; they tried to avoid discussing it with reporters, and most desperately tried to get the entire matter hushed up and kept out of the press.

First Deputy Minister R. Arutunyov asked the *Izvestia* reporter directly: "What do we have to do to ensure that your article doesn't appear in print?"

"It was something that had never happened before, and something that it did not seem ever *could* happen," the *Izvestia* reporter commented in his story, with a certain wry amusement at the bold defiance of the enterprise and at the discomfort of the central planners.

"In the view of those we spoke with [at the Ministry], this could plunge not only the industry but the entire economy into chaos. . . . The ministry painted us a downright apocalyptic picture of enterprises refusing en masse to obey orders from Moscow."[5]

This upstart industrial David that was challenging the Gosplan Goliath was no economic pip-squeak. It was Uralmash, one of the mightiest of Soviet industrial giants, a titan of the machine-building industry. What Uralmash was objecting to was one of the basic yardsticks of Soviet central planning, the gross-output target—that is, the total value of production the government was requiring it to turn out in the coming year.

Under Gosplan's supervision, the Ministry of Heavy Machine–Building had assigned Uralmash a 1988 output target of 610 billion rubles, or just a bit more than $1 billion worth of machinery. Uralmash had refused to accept that production target, and it had raised other objections to the ministry's plan. Not only were the overall figures too high, Uralmash argued, but it made no sense to require it to produce items that customers had rejected in the past. Furthermore, Uralmash would not be able to obtain sufficient component parts to produce the items, nor did it have the necessary machinery to do so.

A spokesman for the management and workers of the huge enterprise called the government orders an "unrealistic plan" typical of the old "arbitrary planning" methods of the Brezhnev era, and "at odds" with the new Gorbachev approach. As reported in *Izvestia,* "Uralmash called for realism: Don't succumb to a plan that is obviously impossible."[6] To Uralmash, realism meant cutting its overall output target by about 50 million rubles (about $85 million)—or about two weeks' output for Uralmash. It also proposed various other changes in the ministry's plan.[7]

In years past, enterprise managers had indulged in behind-the-scenes bargaining to try to shave down their output quotas and thus ease their work load. But the kind of open confrontation initiated by Uralmash was economic and political heresy. By going to the press and going public with its complaint, Uralmash was breaking the old rules of the Soviet economic game. Ministry and Gosplan bureaucrats were determined to crush this act of industrial insurrection before the example spread. In fact, seventeen other enterprises tried the same tactic within the ensuing weeks, but they were blocked. Only Uralmash had enough clout to win revision of its plan—and then only after an investigation by a neutral economic commission. What is more, the bureaucrats had their vengeance on other captains of industry: They transferred quotas initially imposed on Uralmash to more obedient enterprises in the automotive industry.

It was a victory—a very rare one; and it happened only because Uralmash shrewdly based its actions on the new bill of rights that Gorbachev and his *perestroika* had promised industrial managers nationwide.

GORBACHEV'S ECONOMIC MANIFESTO

In June 1987, two years after taking over supreme power, Gorbachev issued his major economic manifesto: a stinging indictment of the rigid, Stalinist command economy that he had inherited, and a call for "revolutionary transformations" that would move the Soviet system away from centralized controls and military structure toward freer, more flexible market economics. Gorbachev himself later claimed this was "the most important and radical program for economic reform our country has had since Lenin introduced his New Economic Policy in 1921."[8]

In a speech to the Communist Party Central Committee that rang with talk about efficiency, profit and loss, "real competition," and bankruptcy for losers, Gorbachev raised the banner of "more democracy" in the functioning of the Soviet economy. He offered to industrial enterprises new independence in the form of "economic accountability and self-management." He made it clear that he was bent on shattering the stifling inertia of top-down economics and on unshackling initiative at the enterprise level, and would effect this by curbing the power of the central bureaucracy and guaranteeing greater autonomy and flexibility to industrial managers all across the country. Yet radical as he was, Gorbachev was not ready to abandon centralized economic planning; nor was he ready, by any means, to embrace capitalism.

"We are looking within socialism rather than outside it, for the answers to all the questions that arise," Gorbachev later explained. "We assess our successes and errors alike by socialist standards. Those who hope that we shall move away from the socialist path will be greatly disappointed."[9]

Even so, this new economic program was a major turning point for Gorbachev. He had been pursuing a conservative economic policy, trying to tighten up the old system by firing incompetent people, holdovers from Brezhnev, and by reshuffling ministries, instituting quality controls, fighting alcoholism, and pressing for greater discipline. Under the slogan of *uskoreniye*—acceleration—he had left the old system in place and largely undisturbed. Now he was talking about serious changes in its operation, about breaking the iron grip of the central bureaucracy.

Far more candidly than any previous Soviet leader, Gorbachev used his June speech to lay out the anatomy of the Soviet economic crisis. His critique of existing practices was unusually sharp—focused first of all on the micromanagement of all Soviet industry and agriculture. On previous occasions, Gorbachev had chastised the central ministries for their "petty tutelage" of industry, for "striving to embrace everything down to trifles." Now his rhetorical blows were more sweeping against the pretense of omniscience and omnipotence on the part of central planners. "It is an illusion," he declared, "to think that everything can be foreseen from the center within the framework of such a huge economy as ours."[10] Overall strategy, yes, he said; detailed direction, no.

In language more reminiscent of a Western market analyst than a Communist leader, Gorbachev attacked another sacred cow: the system of fixed prices, set by the central planners for more than two hundred thousand individual commodities, from gargantuan earth movers to tiny nails, a system that he said had produced inflated and wholly artificial notions of profit throughout the Soviet economy.

"Economically unjustified approaches to price formation have led to the emergence and rapid growth of subsidies for the production and sale of a wide variety of products and services," he said. "For many types of output, an unjustifiably high level of profitability has evolved, one that bears no relationship whatsoever to efficiency in production. . . . Those who make products for which prices are unjustifiably low have no incentive to increase their production, and those who obtain surplus profits due to overstated [excessive] prices have no incentive to reduce outlays and increase efficiency. In this situation, normal economic relations are simply impossible."[11]

From there, Gorbachev ticked off a long list of sins of what reformers were now calling the Stalinist "administrative-command system": its encouragement of massive waste, equally massive industrial hoarding, featherbedding, keeping unprofitable enterprises afloat. A few days later, Prime Minister Nikolai Ryzhkov reported that, even allowing for massive subsidies, 13 percent of all Soviet industrial enterprises were operating at a loss, and the government was bailing them out.[12]

Gorbachev's pet peeve, one to which he returned again and again in later speeches, was the mindless "cranking out of large amounts of gross output" to make production figures look good and to fulfill the numerical targets set by Gosplan, regardless of the quality of goods and whether customers really needed or wanted the items. "It is intolerable that enterprises are compelled to produce goods that no one wants just for gross output targets," Gorbachev later declared. Or again: "We don't need tons of oil and cubic meters of natural gas or tons of ore for their own sake. We don't need cubic meters of timber and tons of iron, steel, and so on for their own sake. We need them so that in the end, we have a higher national income, which we could use for improving every walk of life of our society, of our people."[13]

What Gorbachev all but said, and what some radical reform economists wanted him to make explicit, was that the fundamental cause of the nation's economic problems was the entire system of centralized planning to which Gorbachev and the Soviet leadership still clung. Their hang-up was ideological; but more than that, they looked back at what they saw as important gains in decades past from this centralized system. Most of the rest of the Politburo was more cautious than Gorbachev. But he was ambivalent too, even as he launched this ebullient new phase of reform. He wanted something new, but he was not ready to scrap the old.

Gorbachev's generation, for all their disenchantment with Stalin, were now in their late fifties and could remember how this militarized command economy had focused the nation's energies on a few top priorities—arms, space, certain elements of heavy industry—and lifted Soviet Russia from its role as a backward bit player in the game of nations after World War I to a nuclear-armed superpower in the 1980s. In the "Great Patriotic War"—what the West calls World War II—Stalin's economy, run with military urgency, had equipped an army that staved off and then defeated the technologically more sophisticated Germans. After the war, Stalin had set out to surpass the world in steel, oil, machine tools; and the Soviets took great pride when, in terms of raw volume, they had gotten out front in those areas. Centralized planning had worked in a few high-priority areas and in sectors where quantity was a useful yardstick of success, such as in electricity, crude oil, gas, iron ore, tonnage of steel. But unfortunately for Moscow, these were industrial raw materials, not finished products; they were the output of a developing economy, not the sophisticated wares of a modern industrialized nation.

As the years wore on and the running of a modern economy became increasingly complex, the anomalies and drawbacks of the Soviet system became starkly evident. A smokestack economy could not keep up with the Information Age. In 1987, when the United States had 25 million personal computers, the Soviet Union had about 150,000, according to a top Soviet computer expert.[14] The explosion of electronics, not to mention the millions of varieties of modern products, made it ludicrous to think of drafting a single economic master plan and honing it down to the last detail. The planning apparatus had subdivided into many baronies and fiefdoms, often working at cross purposes. Gorbachev himself noted the bottlenecks when one sector, one ministry, intersected with another. Nikolai Federenko, one of Moscow's most respected economists, reckoned only half in jest that even using computers, it would take thirty thousand years to draft a thoroughly calculated, balanced economic plan.

The very notion of producing a single blueprint for a continental-sized national economy was a reflection of the Utopian impracticality of Soviet socialism. As reform economist Nikolai Shmelyov observed, "From the very outset this entire system was marked by economic romanticism, heavily larded with economic incompetence."[15]

Moreover, since "fulfilling the Plan" meant using quantitative yardsticks—not profits—as the measures of economic success, this system often produced ridiculous results. It provided tens of thousands of tractors and harvesters without spare parts; millions of pairs of shoes that were left on the shelves because the sizes did not match up with the population's; television sets that self-destructed, literally blew up. The irrational worship of raw numbers ignored quality and bred inefficiency. For example, construction firms worked to fulfill mandatory quotas that reckoned their volume in terms of their total costs; that gave both labor and management every incentive to jack up wages and costs, rather than try to build things more cheaply. Transportation plans reckoned in ton-kilometers (how many tons of goods were transported over how many kilometers) encouraged both truckers and their customers to ship heavy items over long distances, rather than keep weight down and distances minimal. This "more the merrier" approach tightened national transportation bottlenecks.[16] Health care reckoned in numbers of hospital beds did not work to reduce abnormally high infant mortality or to extend life expectancy of Soviet males, which actually grew shorter during the Brezhnev period.

In industry, the "Plan mentality" discouraged modernization, because interrupting production to install new machinery inevitably meant falling behind prescribed quotas. Inventions and innovations of any kind disrupted the drive toward fulfilling the Plan, so innovation became a nuisance instead of an advance. Another anomaly was that in the Soviet economy, massive waste and enormous shortages existed side by side. For the Plan not only set production quotas but also allocated raw materials and components. Because of perennial shortages, smart industrial managers stocked up on needed parts and components. This led to colossal hoarding, making the shortages still worse, a vicious cycle. Beyond that, it was to everyone's advantage to play the game dishonestly and cover up their real results and activities. Planners won favor with political leaders by setting ambitious economic goals—Nikolai Shmelyov calls them "fantasy plan-targets."[17] And since enterprise managers and their workers were paid bonuses on the basis of fulfilling these targets, they turned to false reporting and outright lying about their actual results. Deception was endemic to the system.

Obviously, one central element of Gorbachev's new economic program was to shock the system into realism through a sharp dose of candor from the top. But in his economic manifesto of June 1987, Gorbachev declared his intentions to make vital changes in four areas: the rights of enterprises, the powers of central agencies, the role of prices, and the development of a wholesale market. The cornerstone of his new policy was the promise of more freedom from bureaucratic control for farms, enterprises, and industrial associations (large Soviet corporate conglomerates).

"The main thing that we should achieve by introducing the new mechanism is to give broad rights to enterprises and to ensure real economic independence for them, on the basis of full economic accountability," Gorbachev declared. "The enterprise itself, proceeding from the real requirements of society, draws up a plan for the production and sale of its output. The plan should not be based on a multitude of detailed plan assignments set in the form of directives by higher-level agencies. . . ."[18]

In order to cut back ministerial interference, Gorbachev said the ministries "must be relieved of their day-to-day management functions" and their staffs cut back. Even though central organs would continue to give "target figures" to enterprises, Gorbachev envisioned that these would be guidelines, not iron laws. These target figures, he said, "should not serve as directives and should not shackle the [enterprise] in drafting its plan but should leave it plenty of room for maneuver in making decisions and choosing partners when signing economic agreements."[19]

In perhaps his most daring declaration, given the universal Soviet dependency on subsidized prices, Gorbachev asserted that price reform was an essential element of the entire process, and he promised early action by 1990, so that a new pricing system would be working by the start of the new Five-Year Plan, for 1991–95.

"A radical reform in the formulation of prices is a very important component of the restructuring of economic management," Gorbachev asserted. In words that would come back to haunt him year after year, he added: "Without this, a complete changeover to the new mechanism is impossible. Prices should play an important incentive role in improving the use of resources, reducing outlays, increasing output quality, accelerating scientific and technical progress, and in rationalizing the entire system of distribution and consumption."[20]

Finally, he advocated moving away from the system of centralized allocation of raw materials and components by the powerful agency known as Gossnab, the State Committee for Material and Technical Supply; and to the establishment of a wholesale market where enterprises could simply buy what they needed from each other. Prime Minister Ryzhkov revealed that as of mid-1987, only 5 percent of industrial supplies were covered by genuine wholesale trade contracts between enterprises; Gorbachev's target was to boost that level sharply, to 60 percent by 1990, and to 100 percent by 1992.[21]

"The quicker we switch to direct ties and wholesale trade, the quicker we will get rid of shortages and of surplus stocks of goods," Gorbachev said enthusiastically. "And this is no armchair talk."[22]

To industrial managers, this was an impressive vision, a far-bolder-sounding mandate than had been attempted in the earlier economic reforms of Nikita Khrushchev in the late 1950s, and of former Prime Minister Aleksei Kosygin in 1965. Gorbachev was telling industrial managers: Be your own bosses, run your own businesses, do your own investments, keep your profits, and make your plants efficient.

There were, nonetheless, some troubling inconsistencies in Gorbachev's outline of the "new mechanism." Central planning would continue, mainly to plot longer-term national economic goals; its targets for various industries would be "nonbinding" guidelines rather than immutable decrees. Ministries could issue "state orders"—goszakazy—for the most essential goods and services. The ministries were to be responsible for ensuring that the nation's needs were met in every sector, and for

checking cost and price inflation among the enterprises under their jurisdiction. Beyond that, the basic priorities and levels of large industrial
investments would still be set in Moscow. Such were the terms that Prime
Minister Ryzhkov, as the principal figure in economic policy-making and
the prime protector of the ministerial bureaucracy, had extracted from
Gorbachev. Ryzhkov had come from Gosplan; he believed the central
machinery of planning was essential to keep the nation's needs and outputs in balance.[23]

Gorbachev himself, moreover, was wary of alarming the blue-collar
proletariat with his ideas of reform. While he drummed on the theme that
Soviet workers had to work and produce more and that managers had to
cut unnecessary staff, he also promised Soviet workers that his new economic mechanism would not cause unemployment. And to prevent catastrophes from befalling firms that operated in the red, the fine print in the
new economic scheme instructed ministries to build up reserve funds to
support these losers—by imposing special levies on profitable enterprises.

In short, Gorbachev's rhetoric was bold and dramatic, but in practice
he was actually straddling: He was embracing two contradictory economic
logics—the logic of market economics and the logic of central planning.
He was endorsing the power of two rival forces—the enterprises and the
ministries.

The real test was how this new scheme would work out in practice. If
there was one place where reform would stand a good chance, I figured
it would be at Uralmash, the upstart giant that had taken Gorbachev at
his word in early 1988—and gotten Gorbachev's minions to back its
challenge to Gosplan.

OPENING A "CLOSED CITY"

Getting to Uralmash was not simple. It is located in Sverdlovsk, the main
city in the Ural Mountains, about two thousand miles east of Moscow on
the western fringe of Siberia. A brawny industrial region, the Urals are
rich in iron, coal, and other minerals, and Sverdlovsk, now a city of 1.6
million people, is a kind of Soviet Pittsburgh. It was also the place where
Bolshevik militants had executed Czar Nicholas II and his family during
the Russian civil war.

For seven decades Sverdlovsk had been a "closed city"—closed, that
is, to foreigners. It is packed with huge defense plants, and it is in a region
of prison gulags, within one hundred miles of the site of the Soviet
Union's—and probably the world's—most disastrous nuclear accident,

which Soviet authorities tried to hush up for three decades. In 1957, the government now admits, an explosion of plutonium waste at a major nuclear-weapons plant, known as Chelyabinsk-40, released massive radiation. From personal contacts and after extensive research, Zhores Medvedev, a Soviet scientist now living in London, disclosed that radiation contaminated hundreds of square miles with strontium 90; hundreds of people were killed, and thousands more hospitalized.[24] For many years, road signs along the 150-mile stretch from Sverdlovsk to the city of Chelyabinsk warned of radioactivity; drivers of state vehicles were instructed to go at top speed and never to leave their vehicles on the highway.

Given Sverdlovsk's "closed" status, people were very surprised to see our film unit when we showed up there.

"Who do you know?" asked Nikolai Antonov, the regional television chief, in some amazement. "Must be someone important."

Antonov told me that only one other American party had ever visited Sverdlovsk: Vice President Richard Nixon, on a swift, three-hour stopover in 1959.

"But Mr. Nixon never spent the night," Antonov said. "You are the first Americans to spend the night here."

Actually, I later found out, some American arms-control inspectors had more recently visited Sverdlovsk to check on a plant that had previously made SS-20 missiles, the ones banned by the Reagan-Gorbachev arms-control agreement of 1987.

Getting permission for us to go to Sverdlovsk had taken six months of my prodding the government and Party Central Committee. In the end, my request had to go up to the office of Prime Minister Nikolai Ryzhkov. He had worked for years at Uralmash, once serving as its general director, and had taken an interest in our going there, thanks to a push from his press aide, Lev Voznesensky, and from Valentin Lazutkin of the State Television Committee.

Once the door opened a crack, it swung open wide. We got VIP treatment. As a closed city, Sverdlovsk lacked one of the standard facilities of most Soviet cities: an official Intourist hotel for foreigners. Our hosts considered the normal Soviet domestic hotels too shabby, so they put us up in the best facility available—the Communist Party hotel. We shared it with Party workers, government officials, and military officers on assignment.

This elite hotel was a handsome, well-built, five-story brick building on a tree-lined side street, with no markings to disclose its function to the unwitting passerby. You had to know in advance what it was and why you were going there. The only clues to its special nature were the black Volgas with gray curtains, a favorite of Soviet bigwigs, that occasionally were parked in the driveway. The rooms were nicely furnished and well maintained, and the service personnel more pleasant than usual; but the sauna did not work, and the food was no better than in our other hotels.

One feature was striking: the phones. They worked flawlessly, better than anywhere else I ever stayed in the Soviet Union. For example, it had taken me days to get a call through to the United States from Tashkent or Kiev; even getting through to Moscow was an ordeal that required several hours. From the Party hotel in Sverdlovsk, we got through with a snap of the fingers, and the line was crystal clear, rather than crippled by static. I attributed the speed of service to the almost military obedience of Sverdlovsk and Moscow operators when a call came from the Party's October Hotel. And I assumed the lines were so clear because they hooked into the military circuits serving Sverdlovsk's defense industry.

Uralmash, literally the Ural Heavy Machine–Building Works, is an industrial showcase, part of what earned Sverdlovsk its special place in the heroic saga of Soviet industrialization.

Uralmash is an industrial giant, literally built from scratch, which went into operation in 1933, a time when throwing up massive plants far from Moscow was a hallmark of Soviet socialism. It became a prime model of the Stalinist command economy: heavy industry built at the expense of ordinary people who were called upon to sacrifice for the might of the state.

In the pantheon of Soviet socialism, agriculture has always been something of a neglected stepchild, but heavy industry, symbolized by enterprises like Uralmash, has been celebrated not only in the ideological cheerleading of the nation's leaders, but quite literally in popular song and legend. Uralmash has its own factory song, and its own two-story museum. In fact, one of the first obligatory stops at Uralmash is the factory museum. Beside models of Uralmash products and displays of "hero workers" in Uralmash history were photos of such Bolshevik leaders as Ordzhonidkize and Sverdlov (for whom the city was named) and large mural-photos of crowds cheering as Uralmash rolled out tanks for the war against the Nazi invaders, and cheering again for victory in the Great Patriotic War.

Today, Uralmash is an industrial behemoth, a kind of Soviet General Motors, with a work force of fifty thousand. It has huge blast furnaces, 180-ton metal presses, blooming mills, rolling mills, slab-casting machines—shop after shop after shop stretching over five square miles on one side of Sverdlovsk. It is not one factory but many; more than one hundred in all, not counting several subsidiary plants at other locations, plus its own state farm. Its internal railroad spurs add up to more than one hundred miles of track. In short, Uralmash epitomizes the Soviet industrial romance with size.

Uralmash also epitomizes the current Soviet economic crisis. It is the embodiment of old-fashioned smokestack industry: an aging plant with antiquated equipment and a style of operation that is way out of date. The brute methods of high Stalinism, which worked in the first years of industrialization and the war, are now too rigid. They have stifled innovation and left the workers unmotivated.

My first strong impression of Uralmash was that the world had passed it by. The whole feel of the place was old: a 1950s factory operating with 1930s equipment. There was astonishingly little activity in some of the shops, which were as cavernous as airport hangars. Others were busy with activity, overhead cranes swinging huge pieces of cast metal into place, massive orange-hot ingots of steel being slammed into shape by metal presses, automated lathes and filers shaving steel parts down to specification. But other shops were as dusty, grimy, and idle as abandoned warehouses, piled high with rusted ingots or iron reinforcing rods bent in so many loops like metal noodles. Here and there, a black-overalled worker manned a blowtorch or a lathe, but others wandered about aimlessly. Smoking on the shop floor was common. Despite the enormous potential for disastrous accidents, safety lanes were rarely marked on the floor. A handful of safety signs reminded workers to wear safety glasses or to ground electrical equipment before using it, but I didn't notice many workers following these rules. It was unusual, too, to see them wearing hard hats, despite all the heavy metal carried overhead by cranes. Even though the plant had obviously been spruced up for our filming, the atmosphere was lax; plant officials who had been abroad knew their whole operation had fallen behind standards even in India, Brazil, or Czechoslovakia, let alone in the West or Japan.

WHERE ARE THE "HERO WORKERS"?

The man with the mandate to bring *perestroika* to Uralmash is Igor Ivanovich Stroganov, a captain of Soviet industry. He was only forty-two when he became general director of the enterprise—comparable to an American CEO—in 1985, the year Gorbachev took power. Just two years later, he had the nerve to face down Gosplan and the Ministry of Heavy Machine–Building.

Stroganov easily fits the image of a Soviet power player. He looks like a tough Irish cop—about five feet eleven and 240 pounds, with a lion-sized head and beefy hands. He speaks with a low, throaty growl and moves with the slow, athletic tread of a weight lifter. His bushy gray curls have been cultivated into a fifties style pompadour.

Despite his overpowering physical presence, I found Stroganov open and gregarious, quick to laugh, unusually willing (for a Soviet manager) to let his subordinates speak, and very friendly toward the United States. At lunch one day, he winced while his chief engineer told stories about drugs and crime in America. Stroganov quickly cut in to mock Russians who believed, as the Soviet press had reported, that there was a murder every fifty seconds in Manhattan. "I was there for two weeks," he said, "and I never saw one."

Like Prime Minister Ryzhkov, Stroganov had started his Uralmash career at the bottom. After army service, he became a welder, went to night school at Sverdlovsk Mining Institute, worked his way up to shift foreman and shop boss, and then, after ideological training, rose to Communist Party secretary at Uralmash, his last post before becoming general director. The Party job is a big one; at places such as Uralmash, the Party secretary hand-picks or has a voice in all high appointments, helps the management run production campaigns, and deals with worker morale. And Uralmash has one of the biggest Party units in Sverdlovsk—eight thousand members.

As boss of Uralmash, Stroganov has one of the largest offices I saw in the Soviet Union, as large as a deputy prime minister's, with a desk the size of a double bed, and a conference table long enough to seat twenty-two aides, whom he assembled for our arrival.

After the preliminaries, it became clear that in applying Gorbachev's economic manifesto, Stroganov had two major problems: people—retaining and motivating his work force; and power—gaining the freedom to pick his own products, set his own prices, choose his own customers.

After my visits to Soviet industry in the seventies, when it was like pulling teeth to get the barest admission of a tiny problem, I was surprised by Stroganov's candor. On the two visits I made to Sverdlovsk—each time for several days—he let me move around the plant with our film crew, to see the operation for ourselves and then ask questions.

Indelibly etched in my memory is a message playfully painted on some iron struts by the workers in Shop No. 15, the metalwork shop. To the customer, they wrote: HAPPY NEW YEAR 1989. These struts had been completed in 1988, in time for the New Year, but here it was July 1989, and they were still there, sitting in the shop. In September, I noticed they were still there. Looking around, I saw great piles of grids, rings, and parts of all kinds, waiting to be shipped.

Perestroika obviously was not working the way it was supposed to. I remembered from the old days that the Soviets divide the month into "decades"—three ten-day work periods. They are nicknamed *spyachka, goryachka,* and *likhoradka,* meaning sleepy time, hot time, and fever, to indicate the pace of work in Soviet factories. The first ten days of the month are pretty slow, the middle of the month things heat up, and the final ten days are a frenzy, as the factory races to complete its production quota, often resorting to "black Saturdays," extra weekend workdays *without* extra pay. The bosses and the Party have to whip the workers into a high tempo. Obviously, Stroganov still had to resort to these old methods, working like a cheerleader to mobilize workers to fulfill quotas. Deliveries were running late. Output was stacking up.

"What's the problem?" I asked Stroganov.

"This is what we call 'unfinished production,'" he said with a snort. "The less time this stuff lies around here and the quicker it is delivered to the customer, the more profit for us."

"How come this happens?" I asked. "What are your main problems?"

He looked at me for a moment, his huge head nodding in acknowledgment of his difficulties.

"We have *billions* of problems," he growled. "First and foremost, shortage of manpower. Look, this is his second shift," he said, gesturing to the shop boss standing nearby. "He now has only enough workers to man forty percent of the available machine tools." To the shop boss, he said, "The third shift has even fewer workers, right?"

"That's right," said the shop boss. "Ten percent of our machinery does not run at full capacity because there are not enough orders from customers. About sixty percent of the machinery cannot be used because there's a shortage of qualified workers. The rest works normally."[25]

In short, Uralmash was bleeding.

As Marian Marzynski, my producer on the economics film, quipped: "The era of the 'Hero Worker' is long gone." The new generation of workers are no longer willing to sacrifice for the state. They want better pay, better housing, better working conditions, and more modern equipment. Dissatisfied, they are looking for greener pastures. According to Georgy Pospelov, a plant sociologist who studies labor relations, Uralmash lost 10 percent of its work force—five thousand people—in a period of eighteen months, a staggering defection.

I ran into many indications that blue-collar morale was poor. In the smelting shop, the workers were threatening a strike for higher pensions and higher pay for night work. There was a brief test of power, then Moscow intervened; the ministry, panicked at the thought of a strike and having granted similar increases at other factories, told Stroganov to agree. But it was his problem to come up with money for the whopping 20 percent and 40 percent differentials, for night pay and other benefits.

Stroganov was trying to apply Gorbachev's reforms by putting each of his large shops on a more independent footing, responsible for its own output, work schedule, pay roster, and costs. As part of this self-management, his economists and supervisors had encouraged workers to organize small production teams and had offered them profit sharing as an incentive to boost production. In a few shops, this approach had begun to work, producing modest increases in output and wages. He had even managed to lease one unprofitable and distant subsidiary to a newly formed industrial cooperative. But in most of his empire, the *perestroika* approach was giving rise to more questions than answers.

"I was told we were getting rid of some bosses here," one dark-haired young metalworker shouted at a management aide. "Shouldn't we get rid of a few apparatchiks up there in Moscow?"

Other workers raised all kinds of dilemmas: What kind of self-management was it when prices were still fixed by the state? Why did the factory still need a central administration if each shop became independent? How could they catch up with the West?

"What are we doing, talking about catching up with them," jeered an older man, "when we're two hundred years behind? And we sit and wait, and our bosses sit on their butts, doing nothing."

The steady departure of dissatisfied workers has become such a serious problem that Uralmash conducts exit interviews with every one of them. The personnel officers who conduct the interviews call themselves "life savers" for Uralmash, because they rescue about one third of those who, as required by Soviet law, file departure notices.

I watched the personnel manager try to keep one young woman by offering her a raise, but after five years at Uralmash she was determined to leave. The manager put her through routine questions about her pay, work, the housing provided by Uralmash, and then came to the jackpot question.

"Have you got a new job yet?" he asked.

"Yes, I go to work for a private cooperative," she replied.

"Private co-op," he repeated distastefully. Then, typical for an official at a state enterprise, he tried to cast aspersions on this new rival economic sector. "Do you think the private cooperative movement will survive?"

Pospelov, the sociologist, objected.

"Wait a minute," he told the personnel manager. "You shouldn't put the question that way."

Then turning to the young woman, Pospelov asked a revealing question: "Are you going to have a very flexible work schedule at the new job, or not very flexible?"

"Well, at that place, it all depends on my productivity," she replied. "The more I do, the more I make."

"So that means it is very flexible," Pospelov said.[26]

Pospelov told me that 12 percent of the departing workers cited low wages as their reason for leaving; 20 percent cited bad working conditions; 40 percent inadequate housing.[27]

In the Soviet system, Uralmash and other big enterprises are expected to provide low-rent housing for their workers—an example of paternalism, Soviet-style. Uralmash was known as "the father of Soviet machine-building," and like a good father, it had financed the construction of an entire region of the city of Sverdlovsk. In recent years, however, the father had not kept pace with demand, and was now being cursed. Stroganov told me that twelve thousand Uralmash workers now lived in substandard housing.

On a Saturday morning, he took us around to see six- and seven-story worker dormitories. Typical of the situation was a family of four living in one room and sharing a bathroom and kitchen with other families. The two children, who were lucky to have a homemade double-decker bed, said it was pretty hard to do homework while their parents were watching television; and the parents never got any privacy. The daytime couch became their bed at night, a situation I saw repeated scores of times.

"How long have you been waiting for a separate apartment?" Stroganov asked the wife.

"Since 1981," she said. Eight years.

"What's your number on the waiting list?"

"Two thousand eight hundred forty-four."

"Well, after three years you'll get a separate apartment," he tried to assure her.

"That's a long time to live in these conditions," she replied.[28]

I could tell Stroganov was embarrassed and disturbed by the housing problem. It gnawed at him, especially since it was a major reason that his work force was draining away. To stem their departure, Stroganov was ready to spend some of his profits to build new housing, schools, and clinics.

But there was a catch. In the Soviet system, money is not enough to build a building. Stroganov did not have his own construction crews; he had to turn to state-owned enterprises, and they were under the thumb of the Sverdlovsk provincial government. So the government controlled all resources for local construction—manpower, equipment, bricks and mortar—and had veto power over every big construction request.

While we were in Stroganov's office, his construction manager delivered the bad news that the regional government had cut two thirds of his $50 million housing proposal.

I could feel Stroganov's frustration. He tried to call his Party connections, to get the decision reversed. The next day was the deadline for final appeals; his best contact was out. Another call; still no luck. Stroganov was chain-smoking, his fingers drumming the table.

"There is no logic to their action," he burst out. "All our problems today are related to the low level of social services for our workers: housing and daily provisions. I can understand the reduction of our industrial construction budget, in the light of recent national decisions. But to deny our request for housing? That makes no sense at all!"[29]

BIG DOESN'T MAKE A PROFIT

The other major problem for Stroganov, and hundreds of industrial managers like him, is how to get control of their own operations so they can turn a profit, modernize their factories, and compete on the world market—Gorbachev's proclaimed goal.

At first glance, Uralmash looks to be in an enviable position. It monopolizes the manufacture of most essential heavy machinery in the Soviet Union: giant mining excavators; deep oil-drilling rigs; turbines for power stations; cranes; struts and spans for bridges; iron wheels for steam engines; ore crushers; huge hydraulic metal presses; and industrial centrifuges—not to mention consumer items such as prefab kitchen cabinets and washing machines. As I wandered through the plant, everything except the consumer items seemed big. The annual volume at Uralmash was big too—over $1 billion.

The problem is that bigness does not equal profit; most of the big items are not making money.

If Stroganov had his way with *perestroika,* he would give up most of the big equipment, change his product mix, and go after the export trade.

He gave me chapter and verse on how the old ways of doing business were hurting Uralmash. Every kitchen-cabinet console, he said, cost him $135 more to produce than he got from the Ministry of Trade, which sold them to consumers through its network of retail outlets. The oil ministry, he said, was buying drilling rigs from Romania for $5 million, but paying Uralmash only 1 million rubles (about $1.6 million) for similar rigs; and it had refused his appeal to raise his price to 2 million rubles ($3.2 million).[30]

The most exasperating, Stroganov said, were the mining excavators. For strip mining, the ministry of coal mining had a passion for a massive mobile excavator with an arm one hundred meters long (just over one hundred yards long) and a scoop with a volume of one hundred cubic meters. The scoop alone was twice as big as a living room. Stroganov told me 250 schoolchildren could fit into it. There was a model of the excavator at the Uralmash museum. The cab was ten stories high; beside it, a human being was dwarfed. Uralmash finished seven of these mechanical dinosaurs each year; it took three years to build just one. And since nobody ever gets rich on the state's fixed prices, Uralmash earned not a single kopeck from their production.

"I won't lie to you—the price only covers our expenses," Stroganov confessed. "We don't make any profit on them."[31]

Stroganov suspected that he might make money if he could market them abroad. Recently, he said, Uralmash had sold a giant excavator to the Kemerovo Coal Combine in western Siberia for 11.5 million rubles (just under $20 million). On a trip to Canada, he had seen a similar one, perhaps a bit more sophisticated, made in America, that had sold for $86 million.

Still, the big ones were an enormous headache. Stroganov wanted to stop making them and, instead, make many more smaller ones (with a five-cubic-meter scoop—the size of a Volkswagen Beetle). Those were popular with foreign customers, in Spain, Austria, and West Germany, as well as in India, Algeria, Iran, and Eastern Europe. For Soviet customers, the fixed price was 190,000 rubles, but abroad they went for no less than 500,000 rubles apiece, according to Stroganov. Uralmash was already exporting sixty a year; he wanted to triple that figure.

"If we could produce another hundred of those smaller excavators and if we could sell them abroad," he said, puffing proudly on a filter tip, "that would be remarkable."

Yet he could not do what he wanted to do; in each case, ministries were blocking him. They said other Soviet industries would collapse without equipment made by Uralmash and unavailable elsewhere.

That was Stroganov's catch-22.

He could not get permission to export oil rigs because the oil ministry said Soviet oil fields would go dry without Uralmash rigs. The ministry would not let him charge more on the domestic market, on the grounds that Soviet prices were set according to technical calculations and could not be increased except for significant modifications.

And then, each ruble had to be justified in excruciating detail. A similar story with the excavators: The coal ministry had him in a bind, insisting on a continuing flow of giant machines, refusing to let him make more small ones for export. Even the Ministry of Trade insisted that Uralmash was obliged to keep making kitchen cabinets, at a loss, because of Gorbachev's drive for more consumer goods.

Where, I wanted to know, were Gorbachev's promises of more autonomy? How could the ministries tie his hands?

First, he explained, Uralmash was a monopoly producer and so it had to accept *goszakazy,* mandatory state orders from the ministries. Each ministry claimed it was following Gorbachev's decree that ministries fill the nation's needs. That was the massive loophole that the bureaucracy won from Gorbachev when he was promising industrial managers their independence.

"So how much do state orders account for?" I asked.

"One hundred percent of our big excavators," grunted Stroganov, "ninety-five percent of our cast-metal products, seventy-eight percent of our rolling equipment, one hundred percent of our consumer goods."[32]

"I thought Gorbachev had promised to cut the Plan," I observed. "Didn't they cut back anywhere?"

"Small excavators," he said. "Only thirty percent state orders."

I searched for a smile, some sign of satisfaction.

"So you can do what you want," I suggested, "produce more small excavators and export them?"

Stroganov shook his head.

Catch-22 again.

To produce what he wanted, Stroganov needed raw materials in great quantities, but only the state could supply them—so he had to produce what the state wanted. Uralmash was caught in the interlocking web of the Soviet economy, still controlled from the top.

The bureaucrats in Moscow were using a gimmick called *limity*—limited or rationed goods allocated by Gossnab, the State Committee for Material and Technical Supply. Under Gorbachev's blueprint, Gossnab was supposed to be fading away by late 1990, but Stroganov said it was as powerful as ever; now, it was even more powerful than Gosplan.

"They gave us freedom, but then through Gossnab they took it away from us," he sighed. "Instead of the Plan, they substitute state orders and state supply. One way or another, they decide ninety-five percent of our output, and we decide only five percent.

"We told them, 'You have to let us sell our production, using direct contracts between us and other companies,' and they told us, 'Yes, you can do it—sometime,' " Stroganov reported. "But at this point they have not permitted us to do that."[33]

The question on my mind, and on Stroganov's mind too, was what had happened to the wholesale market that Gorbachev promised would be working by this time, in late 1989.

"It's very hard for you Americans to understand the specifics of our production," Stroganov explained. "In your country, normal economic relations exist, meaning you have money, the free market exists, you purchase your raw materials, any kind of resources, and you solve any kind of problem. We, on the other hand, in the era of *perestroika,* have to learn from you and introduce this mechanism here. At this point, we don't have the means to develop factories and enterprises. I cannot solve all my problems, because the old mechanism is still in place. I cannot peacefully go and buy the things that I need . . . because, to put it mildly, the open market is very limited."

As Stroganov talked, he became more irked by the trap he was in. He had often clashed with the Moscow hierarchy over these same issues— perhaps one reason, as he later told me, that he had not been given annual pay bonuses above his regular salary of 600 rubles ($1,000) a month. The ministry decided which directors got bonuses.

"I always speak my mind about this situation," he said. "I do not hide my thoughts from anybody."[34]

The next afternoon, I learned of another place where the shoe of central control still pinched, in spite of Gorbachev's promises of autonomy. Stroganov met with some of his economic advisers. Vladislav Grammatin, head of the Uralmash subsidiary for foreign trade, blurted out his frustration at Moscow's stop-and-go policies. Grammatin was responsible for marketing nearly $150 million in exports annually.

"There was the new law saying that we have full independence to do what we want," Grammatin recalled. "They opened the gates wide and we happily entered. And then they slammed the gates shut right in our face. They said, 'Controls and licensing. You have to get a license from the State Committee on Foreign Relations. And they will decide whether each trade is profitable or not.' I said, 'If you trust us to work in this area, trust us all the way. Let them check me once a year and if I break the law, I will answer for that. . . .' But we are not a small firm with a hundred, a hundred and fifty employees. We are not a seedy enterprise, but a serious business with a huge inventory and customers in forty-two countries. Our turnover is so big that we deserve to be trusted and given special worldwide trade permission. At least seventy-five percent of our hard currency from modernization should be left with us."[35]

The point about hard currency was probably the sorest of all. Uralmash was working hard to develop new markets in the West, to earn dollars, yen, and deutsche marks in order to buy state-of-the-art equipment. The issue was more than just buying Western equipment; it was managerial freedom. Uralmash, like many Soviet factories and organizations, had accumulated rubles but it could not spend them on new technology, except by going through the state supply system. Foreign currency gave Uralmash freedom to bypass the clogged state apparatus. But on every foreign deal, Moscow was raking off more than half of Uralmash's hard currency, and then tying strings on the rest.

Stroganov had just lived through a particularly painful example: a promising partnership deal with the Japanese. In 1987, Kobe Steel of Japan had begun discussing a joint venture with Uralmash. The Japanese were prepared to invest $80 million in redesigning and modernizing the main metallurgical shops at Uralmash, with the latest computerized equipment for working cold metal. Uralmash had wanted to modernize that shop in the early 1970s, but the central planners vetoed it. Now, the shops desperately needed updating.

To make the Japanese deal work, Uralmash had to match the Japanese money with a combination of Soviet rubles and hard currency. Stroganov did not have enough hard currency in Uralmash accounts, so he had to ask the Soviet State Bank for a loan. This, in turn, required approval from Gosplan.

Catch-22 again.

The central planners did not want to spend their currency this way, even though Uralmash would have had enough if Moscow had let it keep all of its earnings in the first place. But that was not how Moscow played the game. So Stroganov had to let the Japanese deal slip through his fingers.

The final blow, I found out, was that Moscow's bureaucracy was undercutting Gorbachev's goal of promoting industrial efficiency by draining off most of Uralmash's profits.

According to Stroganov and his top financial deputy, this is how it worked: After all expenses, including the normal ones of Western firms, plus housing construction and reinvestment, Uralmash had a pretax income of $125 million. Its tax bill came to a paltry $13 million. But the bureaucrats had added one more item: *otchisleniye*, literally "the deduction"—a whopping $83 million that Uralmash had to contribute to the state budget and to the Ministry of Heavy Machine–Building. For some reason, no one—neither the bureaucrats nor Stroganov—called this an additional tax, though that's what it amounted to.[36]

What astonished me was that this money was earmarked to help subsidize other industries and companies operating in the red! Not only were the losers being kept afloat, but Uralmash was being punished, rather than rewarded, for its efficiency.

As we stopped by Stroganov's apartment to bid farewell over Russian tea and a thick chocolate cake prepared by his wife, Svetlana, Stroganov tried to put a good face on things.

"I must tell you that lately we have more freedom to decide," he said. "There is some movement forward, so when we start the next Five-Year Plan, we'll discuss all these issues and they will give more independence to the enterprises. But so far, the major issues are decided only through Moscow. Moscow is the master."[37]

It was a gentler echo of his frustration over the restrictions imposed by state orders and state supply.

"This is a very old disease in our country," he said then. "But now we have so much to do, so many problems to solve. So this situation really creates a lot of dissatisfaction."[38]

THE KREMLIN: BEWARE THE SWAMP

After talking with Stroganov and others around the country, I returned to Moscow to talk with top policy-makers, to find out what had gone wrong with Gorbachev's industrial blueprint. The man I saw at the Kremlin was Deputy Prime Minister Leonid Abalkin, chief economic adviser to Gorbachev and Prime Minister Nikolai Ryzhkov. Abalkin is a learned scholar, head of the Institute of Economics, with a reputation in the West as a moderate reformer. A thoughtful, professorial type nearing sixty, Abalkin is cautious in manner, but at times he has been very outspoken, startling Gorbachev. He has had quite a number of fresh ideas, such as paying hard currency to farmers to stimulate Soviet grain production, rather than buying from the West.

Nonetheless, I found him a classic case of the outsider who makes radical pronouncements from the academy, but becomes more moderate once he is invested with responsibility. He was brought into government to inject new thinking and push market-style reforms, but he had to adjust to the inside politics of the Gorbachev leadership, and he seemed to have become a captive of the system; Prime Minister Ryzhkov's resistance to radical measures tempered him more than he was able to spur Ryzhkov.

In addition, like all his economist colleagues, Abalkin has never had the headaches of meeting a payroll, so he is more at home with theory than with practice.

I told Abalkin about the various complaints that I had heard, specifically those from Stroganov, and he retorted quickly that Stroganov was exaggerating his limitations.

"You have to take into consideration the attitude of the Soviet people—we're criticizing everything now," he said. "Nowadays, everybody is complaining they are not in charge. They're saying, 'What can I do? I'm a little man.' "

I offered a specific: "Stroganov at Uralmash says they want to produce for the foreign market and it would be very profitable, but they are not allowed."

"So who would produce for the Russian market then?" Abalkin countered. "Maybe we should make the prices profitable for him, so he would like to deal with our local market."

"If you give him the opportunity to do business, he'll do it," I said. "But if he is not really a free person, he cannot do it."

"Yes, this is really a dead-end situation," Abalkin conceded. "But it cannot all be changed overnight."

He insisted managers had more freedom today than they had a year or two ago: "It's not the government that's tying our hands, it's the shortage of resources. It's deficits of all kinds, including our state budget deficit of one hundred twenty billion rubles."[39]

I was a little surprised at Abalkin's tack. I had met with him in July 1989, about four months earlier, soon after he had come into the government. At that point, he was saying that one major imperative of economic reform was the step-by-step elimination of "production ministries," that is, the very agencies that were tying Stroganov's hands and micromanaging his business.[40] Now Abalkin seemed to be defending the central agencies, or at least defending their current method of operating, which blocked any genuine autonomy for industry.

"What is the major problem?" I persisted.

"The major problem of *perestroika* is that there are some people who want *perestroika,* and there are some people who combat *perestroika,* who want to keep things the old way," Abalkin replied. "And the powers are almost equal. Today, one side is getting the upper hand. Tomorrow, the other side. So we call *perestroika* a revolution. It's a revolutionary fight. It's like the fight of two powers; it's not so simple."

Our discussion got interrupted because Abalkin had to meet with three young economists who were helping him prepare options for a new reform program for Gorbachev and the leadership. The group sat around his huge conference table; Abalkin let me listen in.

"We see very limited time for changes," Grigory Yarlinsky said, breaking the ice. "We should consider the experience of the small socialist countries of Eastern Europe. They've been doing their reforms slowly. In Hungary, it took twenty years, in Yugoslavia thirty years, in Poland ten years. And we see what happened, what mistakes they made. Why should we repeat their history step by step? Look at the Yugoslavs, for instance. They have a new concept. They know what they want to do now. Understanding why the slow pace failed, they have brought to their parliament a new, accelerated concept of reform."[41]

"We really have to organize all the different forms of ownership—state enterprises, cooperatives, individual, and the rest," suggested an Armenian economist, Gennady Melikyan. "We don't want to slip backward."

"It is impossible to provide all economic spheres with the same opportunities at the same time," cautioned Abalkin's aide, Yuri Ivanovich. "But in the area of finance, which is the lifeblood of the entire economy, we need a more radical approach."

They debated markets, freer prices, and measures that would help enterprises like Uralmash and the growing sphere of cooperatives. No one mentioned Sweden, but as they talked that seemed the kind of mixed economy that they wanted to head toward, and Abalkin confirmed later that Sweden was his model.

Urgency was the mood of the younger three. They saw the country in crisis, inflation growing, sharpening people's frustration with consumer shortages, provoking strikes and street demonstrations. One adviser proposed launching a major new reform effort in 1991, but the others, worried about public impatience, pushed Abalkin to act sooner.

"I have just heard your young economists saying that you have to take large steps forward at once," I said to Abalkin as we resumed our interview. "Are you going to do that?"

"Yes, I think we have to go forward rapidly, we have to break the barriers and obstacles that are blocking our way now," he said. "But maybe because I am older than they are, I think that we should make these steps cautiously. When I enter an unknown territory and take my first steps, I must first make one step, feel the solid ground under my foot, and make sure that I am not in the swamp or in the marshes. Only then, after I am sure that I won't slip into the swamp, I'll take my second step. When my foot feels solid again, I'll take my third step."

He was sitting across a table from me. As he spoke, Abalkin did a pantomime—using his hands—of an elephant treading very slowly, very carefully. He advanced one hand, fingers spread, and put it down, palm down, slowly, ponderously, as if the elephant were checking the ground to see if it would bear its weight. Slowly, Abalkin moved up his other hand, again checking the table beneath it carefully, and so on. His slow pantomime, more expressive than his words, was an apt metaphor for the pace of economic *perestroika.*

"We are living now in a highly charged social situation," Abalkin reminded me. "We have no right to make a mistake. Our society won't tolerate a government which makes mistakes."

"Haven't mistakes already been made?" I asked.

"Well, that's why I was transferred from academic life to government—so that there will not be more mistakes," he went on. "You can provoke social unrest and strikes by careless actions. Social disturbances don't come out of a void. They may be the result of ill-conceived decisions."

"But if you walk very slowly, it could also be a mistake," I suggested. "Some people are very dissatisfied with the slow pace of *perestroika.*"

"Everyone wants fast changes now, but you do not promise your people something you cannot do," he countered. "I would say in another year, year and a half, it will improve. But now we have to stop the worsening process. The market is deteriorating. The economy is going downhill. So what we have to do now is slow things down and stop this process."

"What specifically do you want to stop?" I asked.

"Stop the worsening of the economic situation, stop the budget deficit, stop the imbalance in the consumer market," he said. "That's what must be stopped . . . the economic downturn. We cannot let it go the wrong way. We must stop the process of decline."[42]

Abalkin had framed Gorbachev's dilemma.

Here was Gorbachev—roughly five years in office—with the urge to shake up the economic system and free up his most able managers, but the bureaucracy and its protectors in the Politburo, principally Prime Minister Nikolai Ryzhkov, had blocked him. The bold ambitions of the 1987 economic manifesto had been blunted, paralyzed, even sabotaged by the iron resistance of Gossnab, Gosplan, and the ministries, which had no intention of relinquishing power.

As an experienced politician, Gorbachev should have anticipated their resistance: A liberalizing reform, by definition, reduces the power of the bureaucracy and is therefore opposed by the bureaucracy. So Gorbachev had failed to carry through on the single most crucial step for successful economic reform: breaking the power of the bureaucracy by delivering real power to industrial managers such as Igor Stroganov, and by establishing a wholesale market with a system of free industrial prices. Only these conditions would let the better enterprises be rewarded and improve production and quality.

In late 1989, bright young government economists were urging a daring plunge, and even older, wiser heads like Abalkin knew, intellectually, that this course made sense. Within a few weeks of our encounter, Abalkin put before the political leadership a proposal to introduce a market economy—including unregulated prices—by the end of 1991. But arrayed against him was not only the ministerial bureaucracy headed by Ryzhkov, instinctively resistant as a matter of their survival, but also public opinion.

The hopes of Gorbachev's early years had given way to popular disenchantment. Gorbachev had squandered his precious period of initial popularity by settling for conservative economic measures and by failing to carry through on the few progressive measures he had adopted. By the end of 1989, as Abalkin said, the acute economic situation had raised the dangers of a public backlash and popular unrest, should Gorbachev finally get up his nerve to crack state controls and monopolies, and to set markets and prices free, giving Stroganov and his peers the conditions they needed to revitalize their enterprises, and laying the foundations of a new economic system.

Once again, Ryzhkov prevailed in the private Kremlin maneuvering, and on December 13, 1989, he announced an economic program that imposed austerity and centralized control for three more years; a market economy was not to be attempted before 1993.[43]

That, however, did not end the policy fight.

On March 15, 1990, after Gorbachev was elected to the newly established office of the presidency, he promised radical economic reforms. Economists such as Stanislav Shatalin and Nikolai Petrakov, two new advisers to Gorbachev, mounted a campaign to persuade Gorbachev, Ryzhkov, and Gorbachev's new Presidential Council to go for broke, to administer strong medicine: They urged the Kremlin to copy Poland's instant plunge into market economics. In the lingo of the private, high-level Soviet debate, the Polish formula became known as "shock therapy" for the Soviet economy. For weeks, working groups that included sixty economists, lawyers, and government officials debated drafts, options, and proposals in the government *dachas* west of Moscow.[44]

In the end, Gorbachev rejected the most radical proposals, revealing his decision in a series of campaign-style speeches through the Ural Mountains region at the end of April. He told his people that he had rejected "shock therapy" and the radical plans of "impatient" market enthusiasts:

"They want to gamble: 'We must move faster and do everything decisively, opting irrevocably for a market economy. Let everything be thrown open tomorrow. Let market conditions be put in place everywhere. Let's have free enterprise and give the green light to all forms of ownership, private ownership. Let everything be private. Let us sell the land, everything.' I cannot support such ideas, no matter how decisive and revolutionary they might appear. These are irresponsible ideas, irresponsible."[45]

Even so, Gorbachev was brutal in his diagnosis of the economy, in decrying how "the old structures were holding back reforms," and in declaring the need for urgent action: "We cannot wait." At his side, in Sverdlovsk and at Uralmash, was Igor Stroganov, obviously confronting Gorbachev with the same demands for greater economic freedom that I had heard. Gorbachev reported: "The Ural people are all asking for oxygen: 'Give us room to show initiative and enterprise both inside our country and abroad. We are prepared to assume this sort of responsibility.' "[46]

A month later, on May 23, yet another economic program was unveiled by the government; in the hyperole of his initial enthusiasm, Gorbachev called it a historic shift "equal to the October [1917] Revolution."[47]

Indeed, it had a near-revolutionary impact on the people, for what hit them hardest was the announcement that on July 1 the price of bread—stable for three decades—would triple; and come January 1, 1991, there would be 30–130 percent increases in the prices of other food products, clothes, and consumer goods. That news touched off a wave of panic buying and hoarding, which, in the first forty-eight hours, sopped up three fourths of Moscow's food supplies for an entire month. The new Moscow City Council barred sales to anyone from out of town; other regions as far away as Uzbekistan retaliated by imposing similar restrictions on their goods. In Kiev, the Ukrainian prime minister declared his "firm opposition" to the new package. In the Supreme Soviet, dissatisfied reformers clamored for a vote of no-confidence in Prime Minister Ryzhkov, the plan's primary sponsor. Deputy Prime Minister Yuri Maslyukov, a principal architect of the package, said that if it failed, the Ryzhkov cabinet should resign.

Amid the furor, Gorbachev appealed to the public not to "give way to panic," but he distanced himself from the package—leaving Ryzhkov as the scapegoat.

As with previous measures on the economy, this package bore Ryzhkov's fingerprints: He called it a gradual transition to a "regulated market economy," but his emphasis was on the gradualness, and, especially in the early phases, on regulation. He had some progressive-sounding phrases, but for an economy in deep trouble, his pace was a crawl. On prices, Ryzhkov emphasized increases rather than reform. In 1991, for example, his package kept 85 percent of all prices under state control, and left only 15 percent to supply and demand. His plan spoke of converting state enterprises into stock companies, but the shares would initially be held by the government. Only in the mid-1990s, he promised, would there be a major effort to break up administrative controls and to ensure real competition. Overall, Ryzhkov seemed more intent on closing the budget deficit than on reforming the economy.[48]

Not only was the Ryzhkov plan an economic failure, it was a political disaster. In economic terms, it failed to make a genuine shift to a market economy; politically, it caused a massive backlash against Gorbachev from all sides. By beginning with the bombshell of tripled bread prices, Ryzhkov ensured the program would be torn to shreds in the Supreme Soviet, and it was; the deputies flatly rejected the price increases, tinkered with some other elements, and blocked the rest. Gorbachev was finding out what Western politicians have had to contend with: The more democratic he made the Soviet political system, the harder it became to muster a majority for unpopular economic measures.

Gorbachev left Ryzhkov to defend the plan publicly, but even his own advisers admitted later, in somewhat veiled language, that Gorbachev had to shoulder blame because the plan had been so politically inept.[49] Yuri Prokofyev, the Moscow Party chief, was furious because Gorbachev gave him no advance warning to cushion the public shock; he accused Gorbachev and Ryzhkov of arrogantly assuming that people would accept whatever they offered.[50] The problem was that except for the harsh medicine of price increases, it was too timid a program to have been worth risking a public upheaval. Once again, Gorbachev had fallen short. As reform economist and Supreme Soviet deputy Pavel Bunich put it, the Ryzhkov formula offered the worst of all worlds: "shock without therapy."[51]

Gorbachev was thrown back on his heels. Not until the fall of 1990 was he ready to try again on economic reform. This time, he tried teaming up with his old nemesis the resilient Boris Yeltsin. As head of the Russian republic, Yeltsin won Gorbachev's consent for a five-hundred-day transition plan to a market economy, yet again Prime Minister Ryzhkov was resisting, applying the brakes, urging a preliminary six-month stabilization period. But the Soviet people had grown wary of plans and promises. With Moscow suffering bread shortages for the first time under *perestroika*, the people were tired of talk. They were impatient for results.

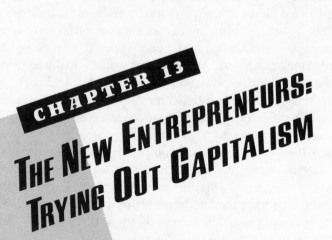

CHAPTER 13
THE NEW ENTREPRENEURS: TRYING OUT CAPITALISM

"A cooperative is private
enterprise in a state economy.
That's like a newspaper in a
prison: It cannot operate freely."[1]
—Oleg Smirnoff
Soviet Businessman
April 1989

"The cooperative creates a
different . . . mentality. . . . Working for a
cooperative makes people independent, free.
. . . [But the] whole system is built
on dependence. . . . That's what the
bureaucrats don't want to see change."[2]
—Gleb Orlikhovsky
Co-op Manager
March 1990

With the heavy-handed state bureaucracy still manacling industrial managers such as Igor Stroganov, Gorbachev tried to inject dynamism into the Soviet economy by inviting a new set of players into the economic game: private entrepreneurs.

Gorbachev was not directly invoking Adam Smith as a guiding spirit for running the Soviet economy, but he was taking the first important step away from state socialism and toward a mixed economy. So that this new element of Soviet economic life did not sound too capitalistic, too heretical to socialist believers, even to Gorbachev himself, the new enterprises were officially designated "cooperatives," a term that maintained the principle of collective property. Some cooperatives actually operated as group-owned businesses in which the workers all shared equally as owners and employees; in others, the cooperative label was merely an ideological veneer to make thinly disguised capitalism—businesses in which private owners hire workers and that run counter to the socialist ethic—seem acceptable.

No other element of Gorbachev's economic *perestroika* has proven so controversial as the cooperatives. Almost as sharply as Stalinism, the new privatized sector of the economy has divided public opinion and kindled passionate disputes. For the cooperative facade neither fooled nor pacified dogmatic Communists.

Spekulatsiya is a catch-all Soviet epithet for virtually any profitable private business, and for three years, the press has been filled with criticism of "profiteering" and "speculation" by cooperatives. Horror stories also abound about mafialike shakedowns and firebombings of cooperative-run restaurants and other establishments of private enterprise. Time and time again, Gorbachev has watched the Supreme Soviet explode into emotional debates over cooperatives. The new entrepreneurs and their defenders accuse the state bureaucracy of trying to strangle infant initiative in its cradle with taxes and harassment; the diehard Communists fling about accusations that Gorbachev has legalized "the plunder of the working class" by infamous capitalists; they demand the excision of this "malignant tumor" from the supposedly healthy body of Soviet socialism.

To one group, the cooperatives are the nation's best hope for economic revival. To the other, cooperatives are a fatal affliction, a mortal threat to their cherished system of command economics and social egalitarianism.

Given all the pain and furor—and the very real obstacles—it is remarkable that in three short years, the cooperative movement has mushroomed so rapidly that Aleksandr Yakovlev, Gorbachev's Politburo ally, has said that the future for the Soviet economy lies in "cooperative socialism."[3]

Gorbachev has not gone that far, but he has thrown his weight strongly behind helping cooperatives develop throughout the economy, even as he has warned against abuses by private operators. In 1986 and 1987, Gorbachev made piecemeal attempts at legalizing limited individual enterprise. Then, evidently not satisfied, in 1988 he moved forcefully to embrace cooperatives as a central element of his economic reforms and as a key to Soviet competition in the world market.[4]

Lashing out at "the scornful attitude" toward cooperatives of some officials, Gorbachev bluntly told one major national gathering: "We need highly efficient and technically well-equipped cooperatives, which are capable of providing commodities and services of the highest quality and of competing with domestic and foreign enterprises."[5]

Under *perestroika*, he said, cooperatives have "a truly golden opportunity to organize their operations." He envisioned that huge collective farms would be broken down into small units, each a cooperative, and that eventually each big farm would become "a cooperative of cooperatives." Technically speaking, the collective farms, or *kolkhozi*, were already cooperatives of farmers who shared property and income and elected their own chairmen, but in fact, practice had rendered this a fiction. The *kolkhozi* actually were run top-down, like factories; the chairmen and officials were selected by the local Communist Party organs, and their workers drew salaries (not profit shares), just like the workers at state farms, or *sovkhozi*. Gorbachev now wanted to inject reality back into this fiction, to make collective farms into genuine cooperatives.

In the consumer sector, Gorbachev was looking to small, flexible, market-oriented cooperatives to fill the gaps in the state economy and to compensate for its lumbering waste and inefficiency. "The potential of cooperatives and the need for them is especially great, not only on collective farms but also on state farms," he said. "And in all spheres—production, technical services, supply, the marketing and processing of products and consumer services."[6] The success of cooperatives, he suggested, would be a boon to local governments, which could collect taxes from co-ops. He subsequently made clear that he felt cooperatives should play an important role in city life too.

In late May 1988, Gorbachev's ideas were embodied in the Law on Cooperatives, the first legal charter for private enterprise in the Soviet Union since the 1920s. It permitted cooperatives to operate in almost all areas of the economy and conspicuously placed no ceiling on the number of members in a cooperative, or on the size of their assets. Both Gorbachev and Prime Minister Ryzhkov suggested that a vigorous, profit-oriented cooperative sector might not only improve the lot of Soviet consumers, but also, through competition, jab some life into the lethargic state sector.

For a conservative Communist country just beginning to edge away from ossified Stalinist command economics, this was a surprisingly liberal law. Cooperatives were legally entitled to set up banks, to sell stocks and bonds, to engage in foreign trade, and to obtain raw materials either from the state supply system—in which case their prices would be set by the state—or through the open market, if they could find one—in which case they could set their own prices.

Before 1988, the Soviet system had modest cooperative housing units and retail outlets, but they were very tightly controlled by state bodies; as commercial operations, they were emasculated. Gorbachev's new law offered cooperatives substantial rights: self-management, self-financing, price setting, the ability simply to go into business when three people agreed to form a co-op. With an eye to past practice of Party and government officials, the law shrewdly instructed local authorities not to interfere with cooperatives, and specifically not to prohibit them. Supposedly registration was unnecessary, although in practice, registering with local authorities became a requirement to get office space, which was controlled by each local government.

And in a remarkable departure from past Soviet practice, the new law gave cooperatives the right of ownership—not of land, but of machinery and equipment used in production.

Other significant changes were the rights given to cooperatives to hire part-time workers on contract, and for co-op members to own different-sized shares in the enterprise, based on their financial investments and on their amount of work.[7]

This was not the first time that Bolshevism had made a virtue out of necessity. As Gorbachev recalled, an early Soviet cooperative movement had helped the nation dig out of the devastation and famine brought on by the civil war in 1918–21; it put people to work, supplied the countryside, provided markets for farmers, and restored financial soundness to an economy racked by war.[8] In this period, Gorbachev recalled, Lenin had equated the growth of cooperatives with the growth of socialism.

In short, for his break with Soviet economic orthodoxy, Gorbachev found precedent and legitimacy in the policies of no less hallowed a figure than Lenin, whose New Economic Policy (NEP), starting in 1921, had leaned heavily on small private enterprise. After a period of nationalization and intense concentration of economic power in the state—known as War Communism—from 1917 to 1921, Lenin reversed direction and established a mixed economy, with small-scale private manufacturing, legalized private trade, and an overwhelmingly private agriculture. By 1923, three fourths of all retail trade was in private hands; the number of private farms rose from seventeen million before the Bolshevik Revolution to twenty-five million in 1927; and there was a handicraft and small-industry sector that employed 2.3 million people.[9] Lenin's example was obviously the model that Gorbachev had in mind.

THE SHADOW ECONOMY

Gorbachev was doing more than borrowing from Lenin; he was bowing to reality. For in a society of chronic and universal shortages, and under a rigid, inefficient state economy, the Soviet people had gone underground to meet their needs. During the Brezhnev period, illegal private trade had grown to enormous proportions; it was no longer merely a black market, but rather a full-fledged shadow economy, and one on which the nation depended. The Russians called it, colloquially, shopping *na levo*, literally "on the left" or "on the side"—under the table. In the early seventies, the physicist Andrei Sakharov estimated that the shadow economy accounted for at least 10 percent of the entire national output. Through the seventies, it kept expanding. An American team, professors Gregory Grossman of the University of California at Berkeley and Vladimir Treml of Duke University, surveyed Soviet émigrés and concluded that as much as 50 percent of the population's personal income in the later part of that decade came from private economic operations outside the state sector.[10]

Soviet estimates, made soon after Gorbachev took over, were almost as stunning and even more detailed. Reform economist Nikolai Shmelyov cited one official estimate that as many as twenty million people provided services through "underground business," mostly moonlighting from their state jobs. Further, that the volume of service business done under the table was 14–16 billion rubles, roughly 30 percent of the state service sector. "In some spheres [previously illegal] private enterprise outdoes the government," Shmelyov wrote. "In 1986, people working *na levo* in repair and construction earned nearly two times more than the state agencies offering those services."[11]

Shmelyov and other Soviet specialists estimated that in major cities, private operators—or *chastniki*—accounted for roughly half of all shoe repairs, nearly half of all apartment repairs, 40 percent of repairs on private automobiles, 40 percent of tailoring, 33 percent of repairs to household appliances.

Private operators also accounted for at least half of all illegal abortions. Shmelyov reported that "every year 4–8 million illegal abortions are performed, for which people pay several hundred million rubles. The entire 'gray market' of medical services is a 2.5–3-billion-ruble business. The black market trades almost 10,000 video titles, while the state market offers fewer than 1,000. Although there are virtually no government construction organizations that make contracts with individuals, 16 to 17 million square meters of private living space (about 15 percent of all the housing built in the country)—private garages, dachas, and other buildings—are built by this sector."[12]

Shmelyov and others sought to draw a distinction between the "gray" and "black" markets—"gray" often meaning the part-time moonlighting of state employees, using state supplies, rather than operations that were wholly illegal, or "black." It was legal but unofficial—"gray"—to buy and sell private cars at fixed state prices; but the real prices were far higher, therefore illegal, and "black."

In the early seventies, construction was a particularly lucrative field for private operators—for floating brigades of construction workers, known as *shabashniki*. As I traveled through Siberia, I was frequently told how local industries and governments were turning to migrant construction teams to complete crash projects. The *shabashniki*, who were in effect little private companies, journeyed from regions where there was excess labor, such as Central Asia or the Caucasus, to labor-short regions such as Siberia. They would sign short-term work contracts with tight deadlines, and their fast, hard work earned them what was colloquially termed "the long ruble"—double or triple the normal pay. By some accounts, as many as three hundred thousand workers were part of this floating construction pool. Their legal status was never quite clear, because they did not belong to official enterprises, yet they were employed openly.[13] Their use inevitably caused friction with regular state construction workers, who resented the fact that the *shabashniki* received higher pay. Early on, the Gorbachev regime tried to limit the *shabashniki* by imposing legal restrictions on them.

Almost every illegal private operation depended on graft and embezzlement from the state, which became such an endemic problem that there was a special branch of the militia to cope with it; in the most serious cases, the death penalty was imposed. In the seventies the press publicized huge operations, such as a ring that had stolen 260,000 rubles' worth of textiles and fabrics in Lithuania; another that had illegally marketed 650,000 rubles' worth of fruit juice in Azerbaijan; a third that had swiped 700,000 rubles' worth of gems from a Moscow diamond-cutting enterprise.[14] However sensationalized, these were not the most sophisticated operations—they were engaged merely in theft and resale.

Far more elaborate were factories-within-factories. One example was textile entrepreneurs who siphoned off raw cotton or wool from state enterprises, and then used these materials to manufacture shirts, dresses, sweaters, sheets, linens. They marketed their goods through illicit retail networks in other parts of the country. In some cases, these enterprises operated right within existing state factories; the same workers and managers worked part of the day legally, part of the day illegally—and they worked slowly for the state and rapidly for themselves.

These operations combined all the ingredients of the shadow economy—from thieving and phony bookkeeping on through manufacturing, sales, and distribution. Occasionally, the Soviet press would expose them—a plant in Bashkiria making plastic goods, tablecloths, women's summer shoes; a gang operating an illegal fur factory in Odessa; whole slews of factories in Soviet Georgia, eventually exposed by Gorbachev's longtime friend, Eduard Shevardnadze, who became the republic's leader after fighting economic crime and political corruption.[15]

I had read about various isolated cases in the seventies, but had not appreciated how extensive were the networks of illegal entrepreneurs until I read *U.S.S.R.: The Corrupt Society,* a book written by Konstantin Simis, a Soviet émigré lawyer who had worked for the Soviet Ministry of Justice and had later become a defense lawyer for some Soviet underground millionaires.

Simis identified Moscow, Leningrad, Riga, Vilnius, Odessa, Tbilisi, Baku, and Tashkent as the centers of illegal private enterprise. In Riga alone, he said, there were seventy to one hundred illegal operations. Nationwide, he estimated there were tens of thousands of modest underground factories, turning out knitwear, shoes, sunglasses, handbags, hosiery, sporting goods, recordings of Western popular music. In virtually every case, he said, they operated with the collusion of local, city, regional, and even national government officials who were on the take, known in Russian as *vzyatka.* His picture of Soviet society, pre-Gorbachev, made Tammany Hall bribery and corruption look small-time.

What upset Simis the most was the interconnection between illegal enterprises and the political apparat of the Communist Party, from the local or district level working up to Politburo members:

> Massive and ubiquitous corruption at the district level of the Party-state apparatus has forged such close ties between it and the criminal world that . . . a system of organized crime has come into existence in the Soviet Union, a system that has permeated the political power centers of the districts as well as the administrative apparat, the legal system, and key economic positions. Although not conceived as such by its creators, this Soviet variety of organized crime naturally is derived from and has become an organic part of the dictatorship of the apparat of the Soviet Union. Organized crime in the Soviet union bears the stamp of the Soviet political system. . . .

The paradox lies in the fact that the underworld is not made up of gangsters, drug peddlers, or white slavers. The criminal world of [the Soviet system] includes store and restaurant managers and directors of state enterprises, institutions, and collective and state farms. They are all members of this ruling monopoly—the Communist Party—and their principal professional activities are absolutely legal and aboveboard. . . . [It is] characteristic of the system that the ruling district elite acts in the name of the Party as racketeers and extortionists of tribute, and that it is the criminal world *per se* who must pay through the nose to the district apparat. Thus it happens that the system of organized regional crime combines with the political regime and the economic system of the country and becomes an inseparable component of them.[16]

Gorbachev, of course, knew all this well enough and had a reputation for honesty and incorruptibility. Several others in the Politburo were also economic puritans, from Yegor Ligachev on the ideological right to Boris Yeltsin on the progressive left and Prime Minister Nikolai Ryzhkov, just right of center. So it was only natural that they combine forces to try to clean up a system riddled with corruption. One strategy was to fire corrupt Brezhnev holdovers and to press ahead with criminal investigations begun in 1983 under Yuri Andropov. Eventually, these exposed massive corruption, most dramatically in Uzbekistan, in a scandal that led to the indictment and conviction of Brezhnev's son-in-law, Yuri Churbanov, for bribes taken when he was first deputy minister of the interior.

Gorbachev had an additional strategy: to tap all this underground business acumen, energy, and entrepreneurship and make it work for *perestroika*. It was with this in mind that he and some of his Politburo colleagues decided to legalize private enterprise in the form of cooperatives. In effect, Gorbachev set out to co-opt the illegal operators, to turn them from law evaders into taxpayers, to reduce demoralizing corruption and bribe taking, and turn its perpetrators into partners in Soviet socialism.

KEEP OUT THE PARTY CELLS

The new strategy worked with surprising speed. Entrepreneurs came out of the woodwork, especially in the Baltic republics, in Soviet Georgia, and in big cities such as Moscow and Leningrad, where illegal enterprises had been concentrated. In late 1987, after only a modest nudge from the Gorbachev regime, there had been 8,000 known cooperatives, with about

88,000 employees; but by the spring of 1989, just eighteen months later, the economist Abel Aganbegyan told me, the number had shot up to 75,000 co-ops with 1.5 million members and employees.[17]

For me, the change from the seventies was stunning.

Now I encountered cooperatives everywhere: a number of new restaurants, with far better food and service than in state restaurants—and some with prices that rivaled those in Manhattan; interpreters and translation services; copying co-ops with Xerox machines; beauty salons and little boutiques; and co-op bathrooms, in railroad stations or on Moscow streets, which charged just 15 kopecks, and which replaced some of the horrendously filthy public lavatories with relatively clean ones.

I met Soviets who were working in co-ops providing a wide variety of services: advertising co-ops beginning to edge into the world of modern marketing; biology co-ops, in which bright young Soviet scientists were inventing and marketing industrial and agricultural chemicals; banking co-ops engaged in financing new business ventures; information co-ops, such as Koop Fakt, engaged in instructing others on how to organize co-ops, or on where to get services from other co-ops; computer co-ops such as Micro-Contour, which was operated by the computer whiz Stefan Pachikov, whose team of twenty-five young computer programmers was developing software for Soviet industrial enterprises. Even striking coal miners whom I met in the Siberian mining town of Prokopyevsk wanted to form a cooperative to take over their mines.

"The driving force for me was to get away from the state system," said Sergei Vladov, a linguist from Kiev who is in his mid-thirties. Sergei, who speaks flawless English, joined five other linguists to form a language co-op that provides translation services and language instruction in Ukrainian, Russian, and several Western languages.

"I taught for the state system for ten years—literature, Russian as a foreign language, and English," he told me. "I did not make a decent salary—I had to supplement it with odd jobs. So when *perestroika* came along, I got together with a few friends and we set up a school to teach foreign languages. At the start, six of us broke away from the state language institute. Then our co-op got popular. Lawyers joined us. Computer experts. In all we have eighty people in six offices, not only in Kiev but in Minsk. Soon we will have branches in Leningrad and in Kishinev [Moldavia].

"For us, this co-op is not just for the money we make," Sergei explained. "It has meant freedom. For the first time, we are managing our own lives. One young woman told me that the first six months in the co-op was the best time of her life. She felt she had grown up, she had a sense of her own individuality. You know, a lot of people get their salary from a regular state job, but they get no sense of individuality from that job. The main group of people who went into co-ops at the start were people who wanted that, people who had done jobs *na levo* under the old system, people who had learned to rely on themselves."[18]

Almost inevitably, the change in economic life-style affects a person's whole life. Sergei told me about a Communist Party member who had been working part-time under contract for the co-op and wanted to work full-time. "We had two Communist Party members in our co-op already and we could not afford to have a third because [of the Party rule that] three Communists means they have to form a cell," he explained. "And we didn't need a Party organization in our co-op. So we told him, 'You can continue to work for us on a contract basis, or, if you want to be full-time, then you have to quit the Party.' The next day, we got a call from him saying, 'I'm on my way to the Raikom, the district Party Committee, to quit the Party.'"

Vladov's cooperative sprang out of nowhere, but many new cooperatives are the unprofitable subsidiaries of major state enterprises that the enterprise managers want to spin off. Ministries will not permit closing down these economic losers, but large factories have learned they can get rid of deadweight divisions by leasing their buildings and equipment to cooperatives. At Uralmash, Igor Stroganov told me that he was preparing to lease the Red Guard Crane Factory, a subsidiary about one hundred miles to the north, to a new cooperative being formed by fifteen of the factory's senior staff who wanted to fire their incompetent manager.

"We think that factory will work better with a new cooperative running it under a leasing arrangement from Uralmash," Stroganov told me. "That factory is working badly. It would simply die without some reorganization."[19]

When I visited the Red Guard Crane Factory, I could see why Stroganov was so willing to unload it. It was a mess. The buildings were old and decaying; mounds of scrap were piled outdoors, rusting in the rain; a new structure begun four years before was still no more than an empty shell of four exterior walls; next to it stood the hull of another shop, badly damaged by fire. Two large metalworking shops were busy, but their equipment was old; by comparison, the main factories at Uralmash looked modern. It took state subsidies to keep this plant operating.

The self-proclaimed spark plug of the new cooperative that was going to run the Red Guard Crane Factory was a toothy, potbellied, tired-looking forty-five-year-old engineer named Stanislav Dailitko. After fifteen years at this factory, Stanislav was now its deputy director, and he had ideas for making it more efficient. First, he planned to fire about 150 of its 870 workers, mainly in the overstaffed administration. When I tried out that idea on the women in the accounting office, they protested that it would be unfair to let older women go after years of loyal service, or to fire young mothers raising children. Like all the workers at the plant, they were people from the local villages, and they saw no other job prospects in the area. Several workmen in the machine shop, who agreed with Stanislav about the need for cuts, were skeptical that he could go through with firings in a such a small community.

Stanislav also imagined that the new cooperative could wriggle free of state orders for 20 percent of its output and instead sell that directly to other Soviet enterprises for a profit. But he acknowledged resistance among the workers to the cooperative idea. "At first, people were very cautious," he said. "But they were partly appeased when they heard that the highest authority would be the general assembly of the cooperative, and that the workers themselves would decide how to divide the profits—how much for reinvestment, how much for pay bonuses, how much for social funds."

How would he get people to work harder?

"We need to change the psychology of people," he said, mouthing the standard patter of *perestroika;* it was hard to tell if he really understood what he was saying. "We have to get people to see that to live better, you've got to work better. I think it will take about two years before we can see clear results."[20]

Neither Stanislav nor his factory inspired great confidence about the future of the Red Guard cooperative. If he did not succeed, it would be a real test of Gorbachev's policy: Would the state or Uralmash keep this loser factory afloat, or would they let the workers go unemployed and force them to find work elsewhere?

"THIS—THIS IS LIFE!"

Aleksandr Smolensky is a type whom many Americans would recognize: a quiet-spoken, fast-moving loan shark with golden hair, a golden mustache, a pocket calculator, leather jacket, and a wry view of the life and times of *perestroika.*

"My pay is twice Gorbachev's—I get twenty-five hundred rubles a month, he gets twelve hundred as a Politburo member, maybe some more as president," Smolensky quipped. His own financial success at the ripe young age of thirty-five amused him, but there were frustrations. "My ruble is not Gorbachev's ruble. I can't buy anything with my rubles. In our country, we have a sea of money, but a famine of goods."21

Still, Sasha Smolensky likes to make money—and fast. He and his cooperative, the Moscow Capital Bank, which only began operating in February 1989, move on a fast financial track. They have no tellers, computers, deposit windows, or cash machines. In fact, their cooperative doesn't look like a bank. The only physical hint that this is a bank is an old green safe stuck in the corner of one of the bare, high-ceilinged offices. Smolensky opened the safe to riffle through a couple of hundred thousand rubles in tightly wrapped packets of ten-ruble notes just to prove to me that they had money there.

I saw other evidence of this. Smolensky made a 1-million-ruble loan in about half an hour, and he charged 130 percent interest. His customers were from the All-Union Council of the Interbranch Association of Industrial Construction. They needed the 1.32 million rubles in a hurry, to finance the purchase of forty fax machines from a Soviet middleman who had imported them somehow from Singapore and was now reselling them at 33,000 rubles apiece ($55,000 at the official rate of exchange). Fax machines are practically unheard of in the Soviet Union; hence the sky-high price. In effect, the price acknowledged an exchange rate of about 60 rubles to the dollar, one hundred times the official rate.

When I asked how the deal to buy and then sell the faxes would work, Igor Karminsky, head of the group, explained: "We buy forty faxes, sell thirty-eight to our member enterprises, and keep two faxes for ourselves."

"So you make big money selling those thirty-eight faxes?" I asked.

"No, not on this deal," he replied. "But we have an urgent need for two faxes. That's what we get out of it." They wanted the two machines, not the money made in selling off the others.

And since they were reselling those thirty-eight faxes immediately, they did not need to borrow the money for long—only for two weeks.

Smolensky said he would charge 5 percent interest and, pulling out his calculator, reckoned that the loan would cost 66,000 rubles; the fine for late payment would be double the interest rate. Since the 5 percent was being charged for only two weeks, I privately calculated that this worked out to 130 percent annual rate of interest.

"That's a lot of interest," I said to Smolensky after his customers had left. "Wouldn't a state bank charge much less? Why didn't they go to the state bank?"

Smolensky allowed a smile to curl his golden mustache. "Because it would take them about six months just to do the paperwork at the state bank, and they needed the money right away or they would lose the deal."

The day before, Aleksandr Friedman, one of Smolensky's deputies, had explained that all their loans were very short-term: six months or nine months at most, preferably less. Quite a few loans are to help new cooperatives get started. "Six months is usually enough," Friedman said. "All cooperatives are based on quick profit. If it takes them five or ten years to be profitable, they'll never make it in our system."[22]

I got a quick lesson in why speed was so important. In the middle of the loan bargaining, Smolensky had gotten a call from Moscow City Hall telling him that his bank was being evicted from its offices—at once. Actually, Moscow Capital Bank had leased its office space from a state enterprise, but Lev Zaikov, then Moscow Party boss, had slammed cooperatives at a Party gathering and, according to Smolensky, Party functionaries were now trying to prove their loyalty by harassing co-ops. Smolensky sought protection from the city council, where he had many contacts because he had worked for years in reconstructing city buildings; in fact, initially he had run a construction co-op for building renovation, but, not finding that profitable enough, had switched to banking. Now he had to drop the loan business for several days to search for new office space and thus avoid being thrown out on the street.

Smolensky took it all in stride. It was a nuisance, but it was par for the course, not an overwhelming catastrophe. The bank had been formed by five cooperatives that had put up about 10 million rubles in capital; it had another 3 million rubles from about fifty large private depositors; and using that as collateral for credit from a state bank, Smolensky said his cooperative could loan up to twelve times its assets. It already had branches operating in distant cities such as Kharkov, Novgorod, Ryazan, Kiev, and Lvov—all cities where Smolensky saw promise for private commerce, and not too much risk of political interference from overzealous Party bosses. He had shied away from the Baltic republics, Georgia, and Armenia, he said, "because one fine day we'll need visas to get to those places." In short, they were expected to secede from the Soviet Union.

Over an expensive lunch of caviar, smoked salmon, and other hard-to-get delicacies, Smolensky told me and my colleagues Marian Marzynski and Natasha Lance of his ambitions. He had recently been approached for two very sizable loans (about 50 million rubles) from some generals at a defense factory that produced equipment for chemical weapons. Now, he said, they wanted to convert to making equipment for environmental protection for both Soviet and foreign markets.[23]

Foreign deals intrigued Smolensky, but he had discovered they involved more obstacles than domestic transactions did. An Austrian firm had signed a contract with the Soviet Ministry of Energy to deliver ten thousand computers for 500 million rubles and deposit the proceeds in Smolensky's bank. "The Austrians have a joint-venture enterprise in Simferopol and they want to set up an ice cream factory and other facilities," Smolensky said. "The whole deal got to the Ministry of Finance and . . ." He rapped the table, meaning it got killed. "They found a 1937 law passed under Stalin that a foreign firm cannot open a bank account in a Soviet bank without the agreement of the Ministry of Finance."

I had trouble understanding why the ministry would object; here the Ministry of Energy was getting badly needed Western computers, and the Austrian firm was willing to take payment in Soviet rubles rather than insisting on hard currency. It looked like a good deal for Moscow. When I saw Deputy Prime Minister Leonid Abalkin, I raised the question, and he agreed that the deal worked to Soviet advantage; he wrote down the details and said he would look into it. As I was leaving his office, Valentin Pavlov, the minister of finance, appeared, so I put the matter to him. With a crew cut and built like a tank, Pavlov was not to be outtalked, even by a deputy premier who was nominally his superior. He asserted that the deal could not be approved because that would give the Austrians power to decide where and how new investments would be made in the Soviet Union, something that central planners had to control; in short, it was a bad precedent.

Abalkin argued for the deal, pointing out the need for flexibility, but Pavlov sternly rebuffed him, insisting on central control.[24]

Nonetheless, Smolensky was undeterred. He was involved in a 1.2-billion-ruble liquid gas deal; he was drafting papers and making contacts with the ministries.

"What do you want for yourself out of all this?" I asked.

"I want to live normally," he said. "I want other people to live normally. For two years, I've tried to buy my apartment. Always there are excuses: 'We have to give it to invalids,' or whatever. So I say, 'Give me another apartment, a bigger one. I'll pay more; let it cost twenty thousand rubles or sixty thousand rubles.' And for my bank, I want equal rights with state banks. Now, we don't have them. They are always giving us trouble."

"Is it worth all the trouble?" I asked.

We were a couple of feet apart, leaning our elbows on a mantlepiece in the anteroom of his office. He looked at me, shaking his head, as if I had simply not understood what really made him tick.

"In spite of the headaches, the past two years have been the best in my life," he said.

"Why?"

"Because I worked for years inside the state system and that work is absolutely boring. I got sick of sitting in meetings with my eyes closed, sleeping.

"But *this*." He smiled triumphantly. "This is life!"[25]

THE "CIVILIZED" CAPITALIST

Mark Masarsky is Gorbachev's model for managing cooperatives. He combines socialist idealism with the business know-how and self-reliance of a capitalist. If Gorbachev's gamble on private enterprise is going to pay off, it will hinge on entrepreneurs like Masarsky.

He is not a speculator, making money off high interest rates or buying up goods in short supply and then marketing them for a fast profit. He runs what Gorbachev's entourage approvingly calls a "production cooperative"—that is, he produces things that are in short supply: roads and houses. He deftly walks a tightrope, doing business with the state, keeping favor with the local authorities, and yet preserving enough autonomy to manage his own business and turn a handsome profit, which he shares with his workers.

Masarsky, who has the close-cropped, clean-cut zeal of an Eagle Scout, calls his cooperative "socialist capitalism." He likes to quote Lenin, who said at the time of his New Economic Policy that socialism is a society of "civilized cooperators." Masarsky considers it "civilized" that his salary is only two and a half times the pay of his average worker. In short, he is a capitalist who sparkles with good citizenship.

For Masarsky, running a cooperative is a family tradition—after a gap of sixty years. In the 1920s, his grandfather ran a small cooperative that made building materials. The cooperative was liquidated in 1928, and Masarsky's grandfather was forced into a collective farm. In the Khrushchev era, Masarsky himself tried to make capitalism live side by side with socialism; he belonged to an experimental group that collectively operated a Siberian gold mine. But that experiment was shut down by Brezhnev. Gorbachev has given him a new opportunity.

Running a cooperative is also a function of Masarsky's disillusionment with the system.

As a boy, he was a Stalinist zealot, so caught up with ideological fervor that he became a local hero for catching a "spy." It was 1951, at the peak of the Cold War, and the Stalinist press, having fomented spy mania, told loyal Soviet citizens to look out for suspicious strangers dressed in trench coats with turned-up collars and taking notes. As a boy of eleven, young Mark spotted such a character outside his school, summoned his classmates, and they all surrounded the intruder until he could be marched off to custody by a militia officer. Masarsky was then drawn into a high political ritual of Stalinist times: The youthful informer was called to a regional meeting to receive a special award as the region's most outstanding Young Pioneer. As he approached the stage, he was stunned to see his "spy" about to give him the award. The man was a senior education official; he had been outside the school making an inspection on the day that Masarsky caught him "spying."

"I remembered him, but apparently he did not remember me because I had been in a crowd of children that day," Masarsky recalled. "I was in a state of shock. I took the award and left. I then understood that the adults had fooled us all. I no longer accepted everything they told me as the absolute truth."[26]

Masarsky's next shock was the shock of his generation: Khrushchev's denunciation of Stalin in 1956. Born in 1940, Masarsky marks Khrushchev's secret speech as his "political birthday," the moment when his eyes really opened. Paradoxically, as a philosophy student at Moscow State University in 1962, he ran afoul of Khrushchev. Masarsky had taken too literally Khrushchev's talk of pluralism of opinions; he did not understand that this did not include criticizing Khrushchev himself. He was expelled from the university for organizing a freewheeling discussion of the famous art exhibition at the Manezh Gallery, at which Khrushchev exploded against abstract paintings. Two years later, after Khrushchev was ousted, Masarsky was reinstated at the university; by then, he had worked in a factory and learned to fend for himself in the tough Soviet economy.

Masarsky is a born leader. He is not physically imposing, but rather short, trim, and compact. Nor is he charismatic; he speaks without flair or humor. He is very serious, a sort of Soviet Jimmy Carter: a manager, an organizer, a technocrat; well intentioned and quick to smile, but a bit pedantic. He can walk into a room of his own employees without attracting special attention, or demanding it. But it is a mistake to underestimate him: He has the ingenuity, drive, and tenacity to get what he wants.

Money is not the key to Masarsky's business, as it was in the case of Smolensky's bank. In addition to Masarsky's knowledge of how to get things done in the Soviet system, the keys are bricks and politics.

For example, Masarsky not only has high-level connections in Moscow, but he nurses close relations with the regional political leaders in Novgorod, the city southeast of Leningrad where Masarsky's cooperative is headquartered. People proposed that Masarsky run for people's deputy from Novgorod—against the regional Communist Party boss; but he chose not to, for fear he would win and alienate the local political hierarchy. In fact, the deputy chief of the Novgorod regional government, Vladimir Kondratev, had given Masarsky his big business break: the chance to buy a brick factory and to receive a 1-million-ruble loan from a state bank to get his business started.

The site of Masarsky's cooperative was a former prison factory at which three hundred inmates used to turn out about twelve million bricks a year. The prison population dwindled and the state turned the place over to Masarsky in December 1987. His deal was to deliver twelve million bricks to the state; any surplus was his to sell. So he brought in new machinery, hired ninety workers at good pay, and within two years, he had doubled the production. His political connections paid off.

So did the bricks, which, I learned, are not a simple commodity in the Soviet economy. Picking up a brick outside his plant, Masarsky instructed me on how cooperatives do business under Gorbachev's *perestroika*.

Bricks are in terribly short supply, so if Masarsky wanted to, he could charge steep prices for them and make a quick profit. But if he took that option, the state would make him pay heavy taxes and disqualify his cooperative from receiving certain state supplies. Masarsky preferred to pay lower taxes, keep on good terms with state suppliers, and charge the state's fixed, low prices.

"But how can you build a business that way?" I asked.

"This is *valuta*, hard currency," replied Masarsky, gesturing with his brick. "Bricks are better than money. I can use them to barter for whatever I need to build up my co-op. I sell four million bricks to the Volsky Automobile Factory for the fixed state price, and I make it part of the deal that they must sell me trucks, earth movers, and other equipment that I cannot get from the state. I pay them, of course, but that is how I get the machinery that I need. I sell a million bricks to the Leningrad Gas Enterprise and they promise to deliver me nine million cubic meters of gas above what I already get, and they grant me a credit of three hundred thousand rubles for five years. So I can add another line of brick ovens and be guaranteed enough gas to operate them."[27]

"We began two years ago with no moving equipment," said Yuri Kaplan, Masarsky's chief engineer. "Now we have one hundred twenty pieces—trucks, bulldozers, cranes, excavators. When I look at all that, I am amazed. Two years ago, the most private property you could own was a motorbike or a car. Now we have all this."[28]

For Masarsky, the brick factory is the foundation of a larger business. Already he has launched a road-building operation, with its own asphalt and cement factories; he gets good contracts from the regional government. He also gets contracts to build houses for a Soviet ministry. In two years, his output jumped from 8 million to 24 million rubles; he now has 750 workers, some building houses, some building roads, others making bricks. They have come from all over Russia, lured by high pay: an average of 1,000 rubles a month, roughly five times the normal factory worker's pay in state enterprises. They have left their families behind, and live in former prison dormitories as temporary quarters. Masarsky has promised to build them homes of their own, telling them what a good investment real estate is. As an appetizer, he turned the prison's former maximum-security section into a health club, with saunas and a small pool.

OWN YOUR OWN HOME

Masarsky's dream is to use his bricks to build private housing in a program that he calls Own Your Own Home. Construction is a particularly fertile field for cooperatives, because the housing shortage is so acute and because the former housing minister, Yuri Batalin, decided in 1989 that 40 percent of all construction should be done by cooperatives. Since then, Masarsky has been studying photographs of model homes in Western architectural magazines.

For all his ingenuity, Masarsky is stymied because he cannot obtain a steady supply of lumber to make his dream houses. All the lumber in Novgorod is controlled by the regional lumber trust; its deputy director is Aleksandr Bokhan, a veteran of the state sector. For several months, Masarsky tried leasing and operating one of Bokhan's lumber mills, but it did not pan out. The state demanded all but a tiny fraction of the output, leaving no lumber for Masarsky. So he gave the lumber mill back to Bokhan. A few months later, in September 1989, when I was in Novgorod, Masarsky was trying to arrange a partnership with Bokhan, and he took me along.

"At the moment we are limited by state orders, so there is no solution for Masarsky's situation," Bokhan explained to me. "They will fire me if I do not fulfill the state plan. I have no other way except doing what I am told. In order to give him lumber, I would have to produce more, but I don't have the resources to do that."[29]

"But this is *perestroika*," I said, prodding Bokhan. "Gorbachev says things are supposed to be worked out at the local level. Can't you work something out?"

Bokhan laughed.

"Yes, of course, everything is possible—*if* Moscow will untie my hands."

"So it's not possible," I said. "You can't solve it without Moscow."

"You are right," he nodded. "So far it is impossible. He [Masarsky] wants lots of wood. In the quantities he needs, it is impossible."

Masarsky took me out to the lumberyard. We found only about fifteen workmen; there had been nearly one hundred when Masarsky was running the place. It was a huge yard with great stacks of timber and a sawmill beside a railroad track. As I looked around, I found it hard to understand how Bokhan could claim that he lacked the resources to increase his output and supply Masarsky.

"The state is a monopolist, not capable of taking advantage of its wealth because nobody wants to work hard for it," Masarsky commented. "We have workers. If we combined his resources and my skills, we could have a treasure here. Leasing is not a solution—we should own this business. This lumber should find its way into the marketplace. Owned by the state, it lies dormant; it belongs to everybody and nobody."

We were standing on a platform overlooking a sea of timber. As he talked about the unused wealth in the lumberyard, Masarsky began doing a pantomime.

"The state and I, we are like two fighters," he said. "His feet are stable. He stands firmly on the ground, he has resources. But his hands are tied."

Masarsky pantomimed the state, feet planted solidly and securely, but his body immobile, arms hugged around his torso.

Then, suddenly, he switched to standing on one leg, wobbling all about, flapping his arms, mimicking himself and his co-op.

"I can do with my hands whatever I want," he said, "but I stand on only one leg. But I need two: One is brick, the other is lumber. With only one, I can't make it."[30]

Without the lumber, Masarsky cannot build houses his own way for his own customers. He has to build them for the state, according to the state's orders, at the state's fixed prices, and using inferior materials supplied by the state. He took me out to see some houses that were under construction in Grigorevo, a village not far from Novgorod. Yuri Kaplan, the chief engineer, pointed out some problems.

"The construction elements are soaking wet and soggy," he said. "We have nothing to cover them with because the roofing material never comes on time. The window frames arrive, made of raw, green wood, so they warp as they dry. It's hard to put in the glass. It takes a lot of effort to make the window right, a lot of manual labor."

Next, we went to see some finished homes paid for by the Ministry of Irrigation, which rents them cheaply to its local workers. They were a row of ten little cracker boxes made of gray bricks. These were brand-new houses, but there was a hitch. Masarsky explained that his builders could do no more than rough-finish them. The shortage of building materials was so severe that even a powerful ministry could not obtain what was needed for its own project. The solution: Give the tenant a token sum of 200 rubles and let him finish the job.

We walked into several homes; they were shells, far from ready for occupants—rough, ugly walls, primitive floors, no fixtures. In one, we found a young blond Russian, tools in hand, at work in his kitchen, the rough walls plastered with newspapers. Everywhere there was work to be done. Clearly, 200 rubles would not finish the job—*even if* he could get the necessary materials.

"The ceilings are a disaster," the tenant, whose name was Volodya, told me. "When you walk around in the attic, you feel them wobble. As for painting, before we could do it properly, my wife and I had to smooth the walls by gluing newspapers on them."

"How about the floors?" I asked.

"The floor doesn't seem very sturdy either," Volodya replied. "Unfortunately, I can't open the basement now to show you. Fungus is growing under the floors in the basement. It's very wet there. How long will this house last? I don't know."

Masarsky, who was listening, was terribly embarrassed. All his frustration with the state-run economy burst out.

"We won't build these homes anymore," he said. "We have refused to continue working on this kind of project, although it seems very easy to do. The house is made of prefab sections. A year ago, we were tempted by the simplicity of this design, but then we realized. . . ."

He interrupted himself and gestured at the hapless tenant. "Look, he's not my customer," Masarsky went on. "I never met him before. My customer is the state. The state ordered this house. The state approved it. And the state is pleased! We could have continued this arrangement with the state, but we don't want to work for the government anymore. It's not even profitable for us. Standing in front of a customer, we are ashamed. The bureaucrat who approved the project doesn't live in this house."

"Do you think you could build better houses—let's say for him directly?" I asked.

"If he pays me, of course," Masarsky replied.

Masarsky was moving out the front door. "Nobody is happy with this," he muttered. "I'm not happy, the renter is not happy. And I am saying the state should not be happy, but—"

"I say the state is happy, all right," interjected Volodya. "They have decided that before the year 2000, each of their workers here gets either an apartment or a house. So here"—he gestured at the row of houses—"ten families got housing. But the state doesn't care whether the families are happy or not. They made a check, filled a square."

We were outside the house now, and Volodya's brother Viktor joined the conversation. "Volodya used to live in one room with a family of three. He didn't have any choice. He was given this house and he took it."

"So we have to change the customer," insisted Masarsky. "It should not be the state, but an individual home owner, a paying customer. Why shouldn't the state give him a mortgage, let's say for fifty years?"

"Let there be capitalism," said Viktor. "Sort of socialist capitalism. But still . . . capitalism."

Masarsky nodded as he left the site, troubled but undaunted. He could not go on building these shoddy houses, and if Bokhan would not supply him with lumber, he had another idea. He was already negotiating with the head of a major electronics factory in Novgorod to build five hundred homes, and he knew the factory had enough clout with the regional government to obtain lumber. He was endlessly inventive, working out a joint venture for foreign sales of construction materials with Yugoslav and Austrian partners; already lobbying local authorities to try to get Novgorod declared a free-trade zone to stimulate foreign trade and investment; working with other leaders in the cooperative movement to strengthen their influence with the national government in Moscow.

I asked him if the risks were not too great in a Communist state to achieve his dreams. He agreed there were hurdles: first, getting workers to see themselves as both employees and shareholders and therefore to have a personal stake in making the cooperative a success; then the obvious risks of trying to develop "a free market inside an economy without a market" and run by people like Bokhan.

The biggest risk, he said, "is the social and political one: Some people do not believe in *perestroika*. But for me, it's the only chance. After this, I won't have another chance. I'm nearly fifty. This is my swan song."[31]

THE BATTLE ROYAL

Mark Masarsky put his finger on the heart of the cooperatives' problem. They have become the focus of a social and political battle royal that will decide the future direction of the Soviet economy. Masarsky and his compatriots are fighting to preserve and expand the opportunity Gorbachev has given them. Their foes see them as the dawning specter of a capitalist revival. In fact, people like Nina Andreyeva, the neo-Stalinist, speak derisively of "the restoration"—meaning the restoration of capitalism and the old conservative order in Russia. So the fate of cooperatives has political as well as economic ramifications.

From a tiny base, cooperatives have grown since 1987 at a stunning rate. And that remarkable success has made them a focus of controversy. The figures tell the story: at the end of 1989, there were 193,000 cooperatives; they employed 4.9 million people, produced 40.4 billion rubles' worth of goods and services, and accounted for roughly 10 percent of the country's retail trade.[32] And they kept expanding through 1990. Despite the fact that most cooperatives were still in the start-up phase in 1989, collectively they paid the state 1.6 billion rubles in taxes that year, and, sensitive to accusations that they were mere profit-mongers with no social conscience, they made charitable contributions worth 226 million rubles.[33]

In cooperatives, the average pay was 528 rubles a month, more than double what average state-factory workers were making.[34] The profile of the average co-op member was striking: young, well educated, and highly skilled—a natural risk taker. According to one survey, roughly three quarters of those in co-ops were under forty-five; two thirds had completed higher education; and three fourths had previously held managerial jobs in state industry, such as shop superintendents, department heads, or restaurant directors, or had worked as engineers and technicians.[35]

In its short history, the shape of the co-op movement has changed, the size and importance of its enterprises has grown. The mom-and-pop restaurants, bakeries, and repair shops that appeared when Gorbachev first eased conditions are now overshadowed by more substantial endeavors. Construction co-ops like Masarsky's have become the most numerous and financially the most important. Textile and consumer-goods manufacturing have joined the consumer-service industry, along with a surge of cooperatives doing scientific research and development and providing technical goods and services.

Entire factories, each with several hundred workers, have broken off from major industrial enterprises to form cooperatives that lease their plants and machinery from the parent firm with the intention of buying out their facilities within five years. By one government estimate, 60 percent of the Soviet cooperatives operate this way, a trend that has been gathering momentum.[36] Typical of more recent developments, I was told by Andrei Smirnov, secretary of the Cinematographers' Union, that sixty new independent film studios have been formed in the past two years, most of them cooperatives. Smirnov, who got Prime Minister Ryzhkov to sign off on regulations to protect them, predicted that by 1993 these independent studios would be making more films than the established state studios.[37]

Tankred Golenpolsky, who in 1988 left the State Publishing Committee to organize an information and book-marketing cooperative, spoke for many when he declared: "Give us five more years of this and you won't recognize this country—it will have gone beyond the point of no return."[38]

Despite their success, or rather because of it, the cooperative movement and the new breed of Soviet entrepreneur are constantly under fire, plagued by official obstructionism and the target of virulent political attacks. Many government officials regard cooperatives with deep suspicion, seeing them as vehicles for thieves and embezzlers of the Brezhnev era who want to launder money from illicit gains. Of course, there have been abuses by new cooperatives, although the fuzzy legal situation makes it hard for anyone to know for sure that he is following the rules.

The national government, split internally over whether cooperatives are good or bad, has zigzagged between promoting and blocking co-ops. In March 1988, just as Gorbachev was about to sanction cooperatives legally, the Ministry of Finance pushed through a 90 percent tax rate. After some Supreme Soviet deputies warned that this would kill Gorbachev's experiment before it got started, the government withdrew the tax law; later, the maximum tax rate was set at 35 percent. In December 1988, the Council of Ministers pushed through another law, barring cooperatives from a slew of activities—running private schools, making or marketing videos, running broadcast networks, manufacturing weapons or ammunition, making alcohol, narcotics, or jewelry from precious metals, and providing medical care for cancer, drug addiction, or any kind of surgery.

Medical co-ops were the prime victims of these new restrictions. They had rapidly become one of the most widely used forms of cooperatives, but the new restrictions were so tight that forty-five hundred medical co-ops went out of business in the wake of the new law.[39] Health Minister Yevgeny Chazov was their outspoken foe. "They produce nothing new, they work in our institutions, use our equipment, use our staff after hours, and they drain away our best specialists," he told me angrily one afternoon. "We don't need them. If they continue, the service to nonpaying patients will deteriorate. . . . Besides, they're unmanageable."[40] Despite Gorbachev's preferences, Chazov's position had great sway with the cabinet and the Supreme Soviet.

In conservative political strongholds, regional governments have carried out campaigns. In Uzbekistan, nearly two thousand cooperatives were shut down by the authorities in that republic; more than twenty-three hundred were closed in Kazakhstan; another thousand in Krasnodar Territory, not far from Gorbachev's home region of Stavropol, where two hundred were closed.[41] Even where officials did not formally decide to shut down co-ops, they applied the squeeze: They refused to register new ones or dragged out the process, denying them space to operate, harassing them with inspections and petty intrusions.

"There is no tradition of law in this country, so some powerful official can strangle a cooperative in five minutes—there are sixty-four thousand ways to do it," said a friend of mine, Oleg Smirnoff, a Soviet representative of Pepsi-Cola. "A cooperative is private enterprise in a state economy. That's like a newspaper inside a prison: It cannot operate freely."[42]

By accounts too numerous to cite, state enterprises and Gossnab, the State Committee for Material and Technical Supply, have not delivered raw materials and supplies to cooperatives that abide by the state pricing system, something they are legally required to do. The press is full of stories about cooperatives paying off local officials—an almost inevitable consequence of the uncertain rights of cooperatives and the petty bureaucrats' life-and-death power over the co-ops' fate. Oleg Smirnoff told me about one cooperative that had built a swimming pool in a district of Moscow under a 1-million-ruble contract, only to have the district government decide to expropriate the pool. The government promised to repay the million rubles, but Smirnoff said the cooperative, including some people whom he knew, simply lost another million rubles that they had paid in bribes to officials, contractors, and suppliers to get the job done. Another friend, a tall slender Russian who worked for an advertising cooperative, said that in Moscow to get office space "takes a bribe of three hundred rubles per square meter."

Cooperatives have also become primary targets of criminal-protection rackets. A rash of incidents were reported in the Soviet press in early 1989—the firebombing of the Come In and Try It restaurant; the torture of the manager of the Sokol Cooperative, coupled with a death threat unless he paid 50,000 rubles in protection money; similar threats to private taxi drivers at Moscow airports. Moscow's police have been hard pressed to keep up with the anti–co-op mafia.[43] Scores of Moscow co-ops united to form an association to combat racketeers, but I was told that plenty still make protection payments to be free of violent harassment.

"THE HONEST MILLIONAIRE"

However menacing, the new organized crime in the Soviet Union is a less serious long-term problem for cooperatives than popular and official hostility. A poll done by *Izvestia* in early 1990 illustrates the cloud under which cooperatives operate: Only 15 percent were strongly in favor of co-ops; twice that many were hostile, with the rest in between or uncertain.[44] From my experience, that in-between group includes many people who are still quite uneasy with private entrepreneurs.

At the Communist Party Central Committee, Leonid Dobrokhotov defined the opposition to cooperatives as ideological, economic, and personal.[45]

The ideological opposition hates cooperatives because it regards them as the start of a dangerous, immoral slide toward capitalism and exploitation, and toward abandonment of a socialist system that has protected the little people. These feelings are especially strong among older Communists, from high Party officials like Yegor Ligachev to members of the rank and file like Nina Andreyeva; they are also strong among the United Front of Russian Workers, a conservative Russian nationalist group, and among trade-union officials, who are trying to stay in office by playing on blue-collar workers' fears that their subsidized socialist welfare is about to disappear in the jungle of the marketplace.

Economic opposition is moved primarily by outrage over what is seen as unbridled greed on the part of some cooperatives. People gave me examples from personal experience or the press: co-ops that corner the market in ordinary T-shirts, print on them little slogans or designs, and then jack up the price five- or tenfold; trading co-ops that buy fruits and vegetables cheap in Uzbekistan and sell them at sky-high prices in Russia; others that wangle a way to import Western computers and reap enormous profits.

State enterprises, angry at the competition from more efficient cooperatives, also feed the economic opposition to co-ops. But more than vested interests and Communist prejudices are at work; dislike of profiteering predates the Bolshevik Revolution. In czarist times, the landed aristocracy and the peasantry showed a disdain for the Russian merchant class as *gryazny*—tainted by the pursuit of profit. Nowadays, pervasive shortages make for enormous profits, and they fuel widespread public anger at the profiteers.

A classic case in point for many Soviets was the self-proclaimed "honest millionaire," an experienced scientific researcher and inventor-turned-entrepreneur named Artyom Tarasov. In early 1989, he confessed on Soviet television that he had paid 90,000 rubles in Communist Party dues, which, since dues are 3 percent of earnings, meant that he had earned 3 million rubles the previous year. The public's shock and horror were enormous, especially when the details came out. His cooperative, Tekhnika, which was comprised of a team of scientists, inventors, and computer programmers, managed to export usable industrial waste and Soviet-built trucks, earning $10 million in the West, and then used that money to import thirty-five hundred computers that it sold for 184 million rubles.[46] When Tarasov revealed himself, the Ministry of Interior launched an investigation to uncover stolen state property. Tarasov contended that everything had been done aboveboard, according to Soviet law, and that his computer prices were 60 percent less than what state import monopolies charged. No wrongdoing was ever proven, but Tekhnika's assets were frozen for more than a year by the Ministry of Finance, and Tarasov had to let more than one hundred employees go. It was as if Tarasov had to be punished for having made all that money.[47]

The personal opposition to cooperatives mentioned by Dobrokhotov—and obviously felt by Tarasov—derives from sheer envy. People cannot stand to see anyone doing much better than they are, so instead of joining up, they blame co-ops for everything: "There's no sugar, because cooperatives bought it all"; "You can't find meat—it's all in the cooperative restaurants"; "Prices are going up because of the cooperatives"; "The co-ops are messing up the whole system." Never mind that cooperatives are still a small fraction (about 3 percent) of the Soviet economy, or that all these problems existed before cooperatives took hold. The envy factor makes cooperatives convenient scapegoats, and some Communist Party officials are only too happy to deflect the rage of the masses away from the apparat and onto the cooperatives.

That suggests a fourth basic opposition to cooperatives—the political hostility of Party and government officials. The issue, perhaps not obvious at first glance, is power. Cooperatives are clearly a threat to state planners and state enterprises; their very essence is a challenge to the old economic system. But cooperatives are also a threat to the political hierarchy, and Gorbachev's aides have suggested that he intended that. As Dobrokhotov put it, cooperatives represent democratization of the economy, and that promotes democratization of the political system.

Gleb Orlikhovsky, business manager for the cooperative film studio Fora Film, talked about this threat, and the political schizophrenia of the apparat, which is caught between Gorbachev's orders and its own survival.

"The authorities are crazy, illogical," Gleb fumed to me one evening. "They want the economy to grow, and the cooperative movement is the only way to get this economy moving, but they resist it."

"Why?" I asked.

"Because they are against the whole style of work in cooperatives," he said. "The cooperative creates a different psychology, a different mentality in people. Working for a cooperative makes people independent, free. They feel they can stand on their own. This changes their lives. They quit the Party. They think, 'What do I need this swamp for?' And that's not what the system wants. The whole system is built on dependence—not independence. It's built on people's dependence on government agencies. That's what the bureaucrats don't want to see change. If it changes, then the bureaucrats and the Party lose power."[48]

Probably the most aggressive public foe of cooperatives has been Ivan Polozkov, former regional Party boss in Krasnodar Territory, and now Party chief for the whole Russian republic.

"Cooperatives are a social evil, a malignant tumor—let us combat this evil in a united front," Polozkov declared at a major regional meeting, a tape of which was later shown on local television. He was prepared to override Gorbachev's Law on Cooperatives: "We can't simply do nothing when people are protesting against this vandalism and shamelessness. We must hold public meetings and rallies a thousand strong to resolve this question. . . . We must base our actions on reality, not on the law."[49]

Polozkov was on a rampage. He publicly scolded the director of a state farm who sold five tons of meat to a cooperative, which then made sausages out of the meat and sold them in other regions. He rapped the knuckles of the director of a state enterprise for buying batteries from a cooperative. He reprimanded judges for sticking to the letter of the law and demanding proof of concrete crimes by cooperatives before closing them down. Hard on the heels of Polozkov's diatribe, the regional soviet shut down, by fiat, 322 cooperatives.

When *Moscow News* sent a reporter to investigate how local authorities could ignore the law, one senior official, Nikolai Kharchenko, shot back: "What has the law to do with it? We are acting in the interests of the people." Polozkov's number two, the head of the regional government's executive committee, Nikolai Kondratenko, defended the old economic system. "At this stage, we won't survive without command methods," he said. "Sometimes I tell myself, all right, I will no longer use pressures, but when I see that things go amiss, I am ready to push aside any cooperative, relying in this on people's support."

The *Moscow News* reporter pointed out the enormous inefficiencies of the local state and collective farms: Seventy-eight thousand head of cattle worth 51 million rubles perished; 40 million rubles lost due to substandard production; annual losses from 320,000 tons to 390,000 tons of fruits and vegetables through spoilage in the fields. He questioned the vague charges of bribery and corruption against the cooperatives who were buying produce from the state and collective farms.

"Enough of this empty talk—we are on the offensive," boomed Kondratenko. "My people have the right to know who is robbing them. As long as I live, I'll show no mercy to speculators and grabbers. I want my children to come to my grave, when I die, without any feeling of shame."[50]

In the fall of 1989, Polozkov and other conservatives in the Supreme Soviet moved to kill the entire cooperative movement. For several days, the national parliament debated the issue, with such government officials as Deputy Premier Leonid Abalkin vigorously defending cooperatives, but conceding the need for better regulation. In the end, the Supreme Soviet banned "trading cooperatives" that did no more than buy items and resell them without adding in any way to their value. The rest of the cooperative movement was left untouched. In March 1990, at the Congress of People's Deputies, Polozkov was back with another assault on the cooperatives, calling them "a mafia . . . [who] compare with Brezhnev's extortioners." He implied there was a cabal, made up of cooperative millionaires and the liberal Soviet media, that was protecting co-ops and helping them plunder the state. And he made a surprisingly bold attack on Gorbachev's *perestroika:* "The dirt appearing now will be as bad as that during the period of [Brezhnev's] stagnation."[51]

The cooperatives have fought back politically and in the courts, an unusual new development of the Gorbachev era. During that same March 1990 session of the Congress of People's Deputies, Vladimir Tikhonov, a deputy and also president of the All-Union Association of Cooperatives, told me that the cooperatives had recently won two important legal cases, including one against Polozkov. The state procurator for the Russian republic had ruled that the regional government under Polozkov had to pay 30–40 million rubles in damages to cooperatives that had been illegally shut down. In the other case, brought by the "honest millionaire" Artyom Tarasov, the prosecutor's office ruled that the state had to return 108 million rubles in frozen assets to his cooperative, Tekhnika, which was still seeking another 200 million rubles in damages from the Ministry of Finance, the state bank, and the Ministry of Justice, for forcing the co-op out of business without legal cause.

"Bit by bit," Tikhonov said, "laws are beginning to work. Thank God.

These Party bosses have accused the cooperatives of being a mafia that is sowing social discord and plundering the people. We say *they* are the ones who are causing discord and robbing the people. Now, finally, we can show that they are committing crimes, and we have official bodies stating that. This is a very important development for us."[52]

Tikhonov, whose association has set up a management school and now publishes a monthly newspaper, *Kommersant,* has great ambitions for the cooperative movement, in tourism, in scientific and technical enterprises, and in the foreign sale of products now cast off as waste by Soviet state industry and agriculture—for example, he said, more than three hundred thousand tons of petrochemicals, eighty-nine million animal hides, half of the nation's cut timber. Tikhonov, an early adviser to Gorbachev on agricultural economics, but now impatient with the cautious pace of Gorbachev's reforms, spearheads a group of Supreme Soviet deputies who push cooperative interests in the parliament and with the cabinet.

At the top, cooperatives have had important backing from Gorbachev, Prime Minister Ryzhkov, Aleksandr Yakovlev, and Vadim Medvedev. The Politburo faction that opposed them, including Yegor Ligachev, Viktor Chebrikov, and Mikhail Solomentsev, were gradually eased out, Ligachev being the last to leave, by retirement, in July 1990. The new Politburo included Ivan Polozkov, an outspoken foe of cooperatives. Nonetheless, the legal and administrative climate improved for private entrepreneurs during 1990.

In early March, the Supreme Soviet granted individual citizens the right to own small-scale factories for the first time since Lenin's New Economic Policy in the 1920s. The law did not use the words "private property," still a taboo in Soviet socialism, but it revoked what had been a constitutional ban on individuals owning "means of production." It specifically authorized "individual labor"—in addition to cooperatives— in farming, handicrafts, and the service sector, and, in an especially important departure from past practices, it allowed small factory owners to hire a small number of workers. The new law also cleared the way for wide use of stock plans so that workers could purchase state enterprises, and for the first time it provided legal protection for private property against confiscation by the state.[53]

Two months later, in late May, Gorbachev issued a presidential decree to promote private construction, ownership, and sale of housing. For the first time in six decades, individuals were permitted "to own, use, dispose of, and inherit land plots with buildings."[54] Previously, individuals could own a single apartment or house, but the land belonged to the state; any resale was under the control of local authorities. Gorbachev's decree was an obvious effort not only to reduce the backlog of at least fourteen million people on waiting lists for better housing, but also to sop up billions of rubles of private savings by selling off state apartments. Gorbachev ordered the Council of Ministers by September 1, 1990, to draft measures to encourage a private housing market. He specifically ordered arrangements for the sale of state apartments, for bank loans, and for the rental of state construction equipment to individuals and small businesses, to promote private construction.[55]

Experience showed that issuing decrees was no guarantee of reform. But the takeover of city governments in Moscow, Leningrad, and more than a dozen other key cities by democratic reformers in the spring of 1990 led to the easing of local restrictions on cooperatives. Gorbachev, moreover, was undeterred by vocal right-wing opposition to them, and seemed determined to help the growing private sector expand.

Back in mid-1988, after the original Law on Cooperatives was passed, economist Leonid Abalkin had predicted privately that by the end of the century there would be thirty million people working in the cooperative sector, producing close to 20 percent of the nation's overall output.[56] It was a highly ambitious goal, but two years later, Gorbachev was still on track—one of the few areas of economic reform where he was following up his bold rhetoric with action. That is true, in good measure, because in this sphere he was backed by Prime Minister Ryzhkov, who had dragged his heels on liberalization in industry and agriculture. Aleksandr Yakovlev, Gorbachev's alter ego in the leadership, was another formidable supporter; "cooperative socialism" was his slogan for moving toward a mixed economy like Sweden's.

During a crescendo of conservative attacks on cooperatives in October 1989, Yakovlev was optimistic about the expanding role of the private sector.

"We're increasing private and cooperative construction," he said, adding prophetically: "That will progress; it's just a question of time. As for food, I think we'll move more quickly on leasing land and individual farming. There are very serious obstacles facing cooperatives. . . . People criticize 'speculative cooperatives'; they have created a bad impression for the entire cooperative movement. But the cooperative movement must develop. We won't move ahead without it."[57]

PART FOUR

THE EMPIRE
TEARING APART

*G*orbachev inherited not only a country that was failing economically but one that was fragmented, a country whose embittered peoples had been secretly seething with national tensions.

For seven decades, one of the major conceits of Communist propaganda was the indissoluble unity of more than one hundred different Soviet nationalities. Lenin had asserted that under the unifying bonds of Communism, nationalism would wither away as a force. But he had allowed a contradiction in Communist policy: He sought cultural assimilation, but he allowed cultural pluralism. Over time, intellectuals in various republics found meaning in their own national cultures and traditions; the Soviet Union was not a melting pot.

It is often true that a system that has been under pressure for a long time, such as the Soviet empire has, bursts at its weakest points when that pressure is abruptly released. That is what happened when Gorbachev suddenly relaxed the system of political repression, introduced the ferment of *glasnost,* invited a new grass-roots activism from the Soviet peoples, and assaulted old ideological canons.

Minority nationalities began exploding: ethnic civil war between Armenians and Azerbaijanis; the "singing revolutions," which became drives for political independence, in the Baltic republics of Lithuania, Estonia, and Latvia; bold nationalist movements in Moldavia, Georgia, and later, in the Ukraine; much slower-moving nationalism coupled with sporadic interethnic violence in Uzbekistan, Kazakhstan, Tadzhikistan.

All of this nationalist hatred and turmoil caught Gorbachev off guard. In fact, his initial outlines for reform had not even included the issue of nationalities or anticipated the ethnic ramifications of political change, though others had years ago spotted interethnic tension as the Achilles' heel of the Soviet empire.

To make matters worse, Gorbachev's political experience left him ill prepared for dealing with nationalist upheavals. His career had been narrower than those of Brezhnev or Khrushchev, who had done political work in minority republics. Except for his years in Moscow, Gorbachev had spent his entire career in Stavropol, a region dominated by Russians and Russo-Ukrainians, with only a smattering of highland tribes. So Gorbachev had risen to the top without being forced to learn ethnic politics.

Out of inexperience, then, he made simple political mistakes that fed hard feelings in Armenia, in Uzbekistan, in the Ukraine. More important, he did not grasp how deeply felt and powerful were nationalist feelings and protests, until it was too late. Sometimes he did not differentiate much between peaceful and popular political change, and ethnic violence, often taking nationalism as a challenge to his power.

"As a matter of self-criticism," he said finally, after five years in power, "one has to admit that we underestimated the forces of nationalism and separatism that were hidden deep within our system . . . creating a socially explosive mixture."[1]

For us, as well as for Gorbachev, it is important not to oversimplify, not to assume that turmoil in one republic signals an urge to secede, or that one secession inevitably will bring fifteen. National awareness and the drive for self-determination differ from one region to another: The Baltics have been far ahead of Central Asia in seeking to leave the Russian sphere; violence in the Caucasus and the Islamic regions has been against other nationalities, not the Russians. And Russia, late to erupt with nationalist demands, has now forced the reshaping of the entire union to the top of Gorbachev's agenda.

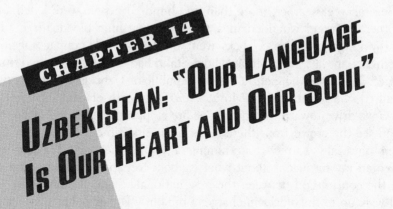

CHAPTER 14
UZBEKISTAN: "OUR LANGUAGE IS OUR HEART AND OUR SOUL"[1]

"You know, in Russian the term
for cotton worker is cotton *rabochy—rab*
for short. Well, there is another Russian
word *rab,* which means slave. So a
cotton worker is a cotton slave."[1]
—Abdur Rahim Pulatov
Uzbek Nationalist Leader
October 1989

"This is our rage, our protest. . . .
We want to arouse our authorities
and our people, . . . to make them rise up
and say, 'We can't live like this anymore!' "[2]
—Shukhrat Makhmudov
Filmmaker
October 1989

Tashkent, Sunday morning, October 1, 1989—I hear that Birlik, the nationalist popular front of Uzbekistan in Soviet Central Asia, is planning an unauthorized rally in Lenin Square, the huge, hallowed parade ground of the Uzbek Communist Party.

As my film crew and I circle the area, we see busload after busload of gray-uniformed Soviet riot police, armed with shields, helmets, and nightsticks. There are easily several hundred police—an overwhelming force.

The Uzbek authorities, plenty of Brezhnev-style Old Guard leaders among them, are tough and nervous. They are clearly in no mood to brook trouble from the popular front, a new grass-roots movement of Uzbek intellectuals and young people.

Several weeks earlier, more than one hundred people were killed and another thousand wounded in a terrible interethnic bloodbath in the nearby Fergana Valley. Uzbeks went on a two-week rampage against Meshkhetians, a Turkic people whom Stalin had exiled decades ago from Soviet Georgia to the Central Asian Republic of Uzbekistan, twenty-five hundred miles southeast of Moscow and just north of Afghanistan.

As we drive toward the square, we are stopped by a cordon of police; I can see the crowd from there. This is the first time that our crew has been physically barred from filming a public meeting. The barriers heighten my suspicions about what is about to happen, and my urge to see the confrontion between the new nationalists and the old order.

I walk up to the officer in charge, a big burly Uzbek police major, and explain that we are from American public television, and that we are filming a documentary on the impact of Gorbachev's reforms on the Soviet people.

"This square is closed," he snaps.

"But you've got people in there—it's your people," I protest. "This is *glasnost.* It's democratization. It's what Gorbachev says is supposed to go on in this country. Why can't we go in?"

"Look—the square's closed," he repeats. "You can go there in an hour. You can't go there now."

"But we're in your country at the invitation of the Communist Party Central Committee in Moscow," I continue. "They told us it's an open country. We're not interested in anything secret. Why can't we go in and cover it?"

"Go over and talk to the big boss," he says, pointing to another approach route to the square, several blocks away.

It's an obvious stall, but we have no choice. We follow his directions and take our van near a large park, where there are even more police buses. In the square, I can see the police massing around the demonstrators. They do not seem to notice us, so we climb over some small barricades and walk toward the crowd.

The mood is turning ugly. The glint I see in the eyes of the police-unit commanders says they are itching to give these young political rebels a thrashing. Lines of khaki-uniformed troops and gray-uniformed riot police are closing, like a vise, around the demonstrators, about to make mass arrests. It is October, but the sun beats down as if it were July in New

York. The 90-degree heat simmers off the pavement, parching throats and
fueling the tension.

As we move toward the crowd, I can barely see the dark hair of student
demonstrators somewhere in the center of the tightening ring of police
helmets. The scene makes my stomach churn: In years of reporting, I have
seen police close in on peaceful demonstrators from Birmingham, Alabama, to Cairo, to Saigon, to Paris. I brace for the sounds of billy clubs
cracking young Uzbek heads.

Our crew splits up: Producers David Royle and Oren Jacoby head off
with Rustam Initiatov, our guide from Uzbek television, to get permission
for our filming; cameraman Jean de Segonzac, sound man Scott Breindel,
and I begin filming, working our way toward the speakers, who are standing on the steps of a gigantic statue of Lenin. Somehow we climb up on
the pedestal of the Lenin statue before anyone can stop us.

Jean gets a few shots of the crowd and of a police officer harassing an
Uzbek cameraman and his wife before the police catch sight of our crew.
They turn on us, ordering us off the platform. As we retreat, Jean keeps
filming; out of nowhere a plainclothes police agent slaps his hand on the
camera lens. I demand to know who he is and why he is interfering. He
shows me credentials: Major Lipshchak, Ministry of Internal Affairs.

"We have a city decree against unsanctioned meetings and this is an
unsanctioned meeting," he says testily. "You have to get out of here. You
are violating state order and discipline."

We do not move, and Lipshchak becomes aggressive, grabbing me by
the arm and demanding our film. I wrestle free, then argue with him,
trying to divert his attention and give the camera crew time to change
film and hide the roll Jean has shot. Royle and Jacoby reappear, but
Rustam is nowhere to be seen. We are surrounded by police. Lipshchak
is still after our film, which is now hidden under Scott Breindel's jacket.
The police threaten us with arrest. They form a tight wedge around us
and start removing us from the square.

As we are being ejected, fresh detachments of troops rush past us. I
glance at a twenty-story state office building overlooking the square, and
notice huge red banners bearing the portraits of Marx and Lenin; from
windows and balconies, a few people peer down on the melee. We are now
a couple of hundred yards from the square, dragging our feet, hoping for
a break.

Suddenly, without explanation, the tension eases; the police ring
around us melts away. Some unseen chief has given a signal; the plainclothes agent who had blocked our camera and the head of the police
detachment walk away, leaving us alone. Turning back toward the square,

we sense that the authorities have decided to let Birlik go through with the rally. Regiments of troops and police still surround the square, but they make no mass arrests; they hold their positions, in formation, but do not interfere. Shields and billy clubs are lowered.

We make our way slowly back into the square, threading a path through a crowd of four or five thousand demonstrators now sitting on the asphalt, listening to speakers who are using a bullhorn from a spot just beneath Lenin's feet. For Uzbekistan, it is a good-sized demonstration, but by comparison with those in other republics, it is pretty small. Most of the demonstrators are university students or young workers in their shirt-sleeves.

Paradoxically, the powers-that-be have given the nationalist speakers from Birlik a second audience: the rank-and-file Uzbek soldiers and police-men who, except for their uniforms, look identical to the young demon-strators. I am fascinated to see hundreds of young police caught up in the speakers' appeals for a new national consciousness among the Uzbeks, long one of the most politically docile Soviet national minorities. The speeches are hardly inflammatory; Birlik's demands are modest. *Birlik* means unity, and its simple act of calling the Uzbeks to speak out and act in their own interests threatens Communist leaders accustomed to giving orders to the masses.

"Comrades, we appeal to you: Unite and consolidate," declares a mid-dle-aged man with a fringe beard, Abdur Rahim Pulatov, the head of Birlik. "We have come together to struggle for democracy, for a better future. The Uzbek people must finally take control of its own land. We must feel that we are the true masters."[3]

Other speakers protest the economic rape of Uzbekistan, Moscow's demands for ever-larger outputs of raw cotton—cotton that activists say has swallowed up Uzbekistan's precious water, distorted its farm economy, ruined its ecology, and left the people and the land impoverished.

"The Communist Party Central Committee has wasted all our trea-sures and keeps taking away all the fruits of our land," protests a vibrant young woman. "A future generation is going to ask us: 'What were you doing at that time? What were you thinking about? How did you get us into this situation? Where's our wealth?' And what will we answer them? How could we look them in the eye?"

Our Uzbek guide, Rustam, who had reappeared after we were seated, whispers to me: "Look at the militia. Look at how intensely they are listening. What she is saying is going right into their hearts. You can see it in their faces."

BLACKLISTING BIRLIK NATIONALISTS

At the core of Birlik's protest that day, its second in a fortnight, and at the heart of its effort to rouse the Uzbek people, is a very simple but significant demand: Restore Uzbek as the official state language.

After seven decades of Soviet rule and previous decades of domination by czarist Russia, the long-obedient, subservient Uzbeks are finally rebelling against Russification—Russian on their television screens, Russian in their schools, Russian in their newspapers, Russian in their government and commerce, Russian on the street signs—even in small villages where many people speak only Uzbek—Russian as the language of science or necessary in making a career, the teaching of great Russian writers of the nineteenth century at the expense of writers from the Uzbeks' own past.

Linguistic discrimination is a tender issue in Uzbekistan, a region larger than both Germanies put together, with a population of twenty million people. (In numbers, Uzbeks rank third, behind Russians and Ukrainians, among the more than one hundred recognized nationalities of the Soviet Union.) So when Birlik appeared out of nowhere in November 1988, encouraged by Gorbachev's new freedoms, it was a language protest by six hundred students from Tashkent University that galvanized it.

Uzbek intellectuals have a long list of language grievances. A writer named Nuraly Kabul told me angrily that Uzbekistan has far fewer children's books in its native language than do other major Soviet nationalities.[4] Shukhrat Makhmudov, the Uzbek cameraman whom we saw filming the Birlik rally, revealed that film scripts for Uzbek movies must be submitted in Russian, in part to accommodate Russian censors.[5] Uzbek medical students complained that their studies are all in Russian, even though many go work in villages where the peasants speak only Uzbek. So much advanced education in Uzbekistan is taught in Russian that its rural students are handicapped in the competition for admission, because training in Russian is weaker in the countryside than in the cities. Mohammed Salikh, an Uzbek poet, told me Uzbek graduate students doing doctoral work on Uzbek language and culture must submit their theses in Russian and defend their theses before a panel of Uzbek scholars—in Russian![6] From many people I heard that it is impossible to buy a typewriter in the Uzbek language; Uzbeks have to buy Russian typewriters and then spend 50 or 60 rubles to have the keys modified for Uzbek.

So it was little wonder that the Birlik demonstrators that day were carrying red-and-white banners declaring: UZBEK LANGUAGE FOR THE REPUBLIC; ATTENTION TO LANGUAGE IS ATTENTION TO OUR STATE; and OUR LANGUAGE IS OUR HEART AND OUR SOUL. On one banner, someone had crossed out a Communist Party boilerplate slogan THE PLANS OF THE PARTY ARE THE PLANS OF THE PEOPLE, and substituted a popular-front slogan: NO, THE DEMANDS OF THE PEOPLE MUST BE THE PLANS OF THE PARTY.

The banners were all written in Arabic script, because Uzbeks are a Turkic people, whose religion over the centuries was Islam and whose written script was Arabic. Fifty years ago, under Stalin, the Uzbek language was Russified, literally transcribed into the Russian Cyrillic alphabet, which was used in so-called Uzbek-language newspapers.

Birlik was now pressuring the government of the Republic of Uzbekistan to take two steps: restore the primacy of Uzbek over Russian, and return Uzbek to its original, pre-Stalin form.

Although such steps had been taken in other minority republics, in some cases years ago, Uzbekistan's political leaders were resisting; they were old-fashioned Party loyalists used to taking orders from Moscow. Their efforts to suppress that morning's demonstration were typical of their resentment toward the new democratic forces released by Gorbachev. In the end, they had acquiesced, perhaps because we foreigners were filming, or, more likely, because some Party official had been smart enough to see that a bloody crackdown would serve Birlik's cause by making its leaders popular martyrs.

That did not mean, however, that the Communist Party rulers of Uzbekistan were bending to Birlik's will or even accepting the existence of a grass-roots popular-front movement. Several hours after the rally, Abdur Rahim Pulatov told me how hard it had been to get Uzbeks, long a politically docile people, to stand up in the face of repressive measures by the authorities.

That morning, he said, police had attacked the first wave of demonstrators arriving at Lenin Square: Several people were arrested; others were clubbed and wounded. Pulatov himself, a slender forty-four-year-old scholar who worked at the Institute of Cybernetics in Tashkent, had left the fracas limping. But in spite of injuries, he had been determined to reach Lenin Square, what he called "the sacred turf" of Communist power in the Uzbek capital of Tashkent, to show the authorities that the movement could not be shut down. In his eyes, simply to have held that demonstration was a psychological victory.

Pulatov described a campaign of official harassment against Birlik. Activists had been denounced in the press by high officials, and economically blacklisted. Rafik Nishanov, installed by Gorbachev as Uzbekistan Party leader from January 1988 to September 1989, had attacked the new Uzbek nationalists for promoting a non-Communist political and cultural renaissance and for pressing economic and ecological protests. In one broadside, he declared: "Deformations revealed under *glasnost* and democratization have seriously disrupted social equilibrium and stability."7 On other occasions, Nishanov accused liberal Uzbek intellectuals specifically of "linguistic chauvinism," of needlessly whipping up hysteria and public passions about the Uzbek economy and ecology, and of flirting with pan-Turkism, an ominous potential rival for Communist ideology.8

With such accusations, Pulatov said, the authorities were trying to intimidate people, to keep them from joining Birlik by painting it as extremist.

"The authorities," he said, "try to create the stereotype that we are fighting the whole [Soviet] system. Our people are very scared of being labeled 'anti-Soviet' or 'anti-Party.' They are even more fearful when somebody calls them 'nationalists.' In the past, any movement for national self-awareness has always been suppressed as 'nationalistic.' At my institute, they had meetings where I was criticized by my colleagues for my actions. We know some others who were fired, lost their jobs, were given a hard time at work. So the pressure is really strong against our members. Popular fear of the political leadership is very strong, you see, because the government has been our only employer. We have had no private sector. If somebody was fired, he remained on the street with no means of survival. So fear is great."9

As a result, Birlik set its first priority, not simply to address the most pressing Uzbek problems, but to rouse Uzbeks from political passivity into new, self-conscious nationalism.

"The main goal of our movement is to educate people, to raise their social consciousness and their political activism," Pulatov explained. "Only the people themselves can stand up for their own rights. . . . Our movement will be virtually powerless if the people keep on hibernating politically. So our main goal is to awaken the people, to turn our people into a politically active society."

DEMOGRAPHIC TIME BOMB

This is precisely what worries Moscow: the danger that the great slumbering giant of fifty million Muslim people in Central Asia is awakening, and stretching against the bonds—and the bondage—of empire.

Three things, above all, trouble the men in the Kremlin and ordinary Russians: the explosive population growth in Central Asia; the influence of Islam; and the difficulty of melding this huge region, still strange,

Oriental, and underdeveloped in its economic and political life, with the relatively more advanced world of European Russia, the Ukraine, and the Baltic republics.

To outsiders, Uzbekistan and its oasis cities—Samarkand, Bukhara, Khiva, and Tashkent—evoke the legendary Silk Route to the Orient, the famous caravan highway of Marco Polo. Uzbekistan is a region rich in history and exotica: traces of man found near Samarkand that date back one hundred thousand years; excavations of an ancient urban settlement at Khiva that is five thousand years old; the site near Tashkent of the Battle of Talas, where, in 751, the Arabs stopped an invasion by the Chinese and marked the outer frontier of Arab civilization; the treasures of Islamic art and architecture dating back six centuries.

Samarkand, located 170 miles southwest of Tashkent, is such a natural crossroads on the Eurasian landmass that it has been a plum choice for conquerors throughout the ages. It was captured in 329 B.C. by Alexander the Great; it was sacked in A.D. 1220 by Genghis Khan and the Mongolian Golden Horde; and then it was resurrected 150 years later by Tamerlane, the great warrior-king, who made Samarkand the prosperous capital of his sprawling Central Asian realm of towering mountains, long rivers, inland seas, and trackless wastes. Tamerlane's grandson, the scholar-astronomer Ulun-Beg, built a famous observatory at Samarkand, and made the oasis city the center of Muslim civilization in all of Central Asia.

Even today, behind the drab, cookie-cutter look of Soviet urban construction, Uzbekistan and the rest of Central Asia are a world apart from the European regions of the U.S.S.R. The peoples are of Turkic origin: Their copper-colored skin, almond-shaped eyes, and dark hair make them look as though they have stepped out of Mongolia, Iran, Afghanistan, or northwest China. Despite the efforts of Stalin and his successors to uproot the Muslim religion, these people still find their roots in Islamic culture. Their open bazaars are afire with dazzling colors and alive with the pungent aroma of fresh spices. Their territory is immense—more than one sixth of the Soviet landmass, an entire subcontinent as large as all of Western Europe, and comprised of five of the fifteen Soviet republics: Uzbekistan, Kazakhstan, Kirghizia, Tadzhikistan, and Turkmenistan.

And their population is multiplying at what Muscovites consider alarming rates. Some call Central Asia a demographic time bomb. The deep anxiety of Russians is that they are close to becoming a minority in their own country (145 million out of a total population of 285 million). When the issue arises in the intimate talk around kitchen tables or in restaurants in Moscow, Leningrad, Yaroslavl, or Sverdlovsk, Russians will say with bitterness that they can only afford, and can only find apartment space for, one child, whereas Uzbeks, Tadzhiks, Kazakhs, and other Central Asians commonly have four, five, eight, even ten children. Russians say too many children put a drag on living standards, and they widely resort to multiple abortions; Uzbeks glory in many children, as a supposed symbol of fertility and wealth, and they largely shun abortions. The absolute population figures still favor the Russians, but the trends are running against them. Between 1979 and 1989, the population of the Russian republic grew 7.2 percent, from 138 million to 147 million; the population of the five Central Asian republics grew more than three times as fast (23 percent), from 40 million to nearly 50 million.[10]

Each year, as the Soviet army takes in its draft recruits, the complement of young Central Asians grows. I have heard Uzbeks complain that they are bearing too much of a burden and that their boys were sent first to die in Afghanistan; I have heard the Russians reply that the Uzbek troops were too friendly with their fellow Muslims the Afghans, and had to be replaced by more reliable Russian boys; I have heard the parents of young draftees from Lithuania and Estonia say that the dark-haired, dark-skinned Uzbeks form gangs inside the army and beat up the blond, fair-skinned, Scandinavian-looking recruits from the Baltic republics.

Although Communist ideology was supposed to render national differences irrelevant and, through the solidarity of the international proletariat, make nationalist feelings wither away, in Central Asia it has not worked out that way. The people may not be rebellious, but they have practiced cultural passive resistance; they have clung to their customs in spite of all the official efforts to uproot traditions and homogenize the Soviet peoples.

Each time I visited Soviet Central Asia during my years as a Moscow correspondent in the early seventies, I was struck by how much more this region resembled countries to the south, from the Arab world to Persia, rather than the Soviet heartland. Arriving in Uzbekistan, I felt that I was stepping out of a European culture into the underdeveloped Third World; Uzbekistan was less like a subdivision of a modern superpower than like a foreign colony.

In Central Asia more than anywhere else in the Soviet Union, I had a sense of Imperial Russia. The regional capitals were the outposts of empire: They were as obviously under the political heel and economic diktat of a powerful, distant culture as Gaul had been under the heel of Rome, or as India and Egypt had been under the sway of the British Raj—until, in the years after World War II, Gandhi and Nasser liberated them, psychologically and politically. Like the British in Delhi, the Russians had put down a strong beachhead in Tashkent: In the seventies, the city's population was 40 percent Russian, and Russians outnumbered Uzbeks. Nonetheless, the pull of traditional culture was strong.

Most striking, perhaps, was the subdued but tenacious hold of Islam. All but a token handful of mosques had been closed, but Islamic customs had hung on, including arranged marriages, extravagant dowries, ritual animal slaughter, periodic fasting, unabashed male supremacy, elaborate family and tribal networks, the tendency of prominent Communist officials to insist on a traditional Islamic burial with a mullah chanting prayers at their funerals. When I visited Uzbekistan in 1972 and 1974, I found young people who observed the monthlong Islamic fast of Ramadan followed by the feast of Bairam. On great feast days, thousands of people would show up at shrines, such as the tomb of Tamerlane in Samarkand. The Soviet campaign to provide education had largely wiped out illiteracy, but a comparable ideological drive had fallen so far short of squelching Islam that former Uzbek Communist Party leader Sharaf Rashidov constantly called for greater efforts to "overcome religious survivals."[11]

In the early eighties, Moscow's worries were compounded by the rise of Islamic fundamentalism in Iran under the Ayatollah Khomeini. Muslims in Central Asia did not share the radical Shiite faith of Iran; they were from the Sunni sect. Even so, Moscow feared the pull of Islam on its people. After the Soviet invasion of Afghanistan, Brezhnev defended the action on grounds of a supposed threat to the Soviet Union's southern regions, and his spokesman railed against the radio propaganda of "reactionary Islamic organizations abroad."[12]

The underlying political danger for the Kremlin is that somehow Islam can become a vehicle for uniting the diverse peoples of Central Asia in some form of pan-Turkism. Under the czars, the whole region was known as Turkestan. In the early twentieth century, there was a pan-Turkic movement, a force for modernization that at one point rivaled Communism. In the late twenties and thirties, Stalin subdued nationalistic rebels and hill tribes by force and controlled the entire region with the classic imperialistic divide-and-conquer strategy. He split Turkestan into separate republics, none of which had ever been an independent nation before, including Uzbekistan. Even Gorbachev's proconsuls have shown alarm at even the slightest flicker of pan-Turkism in Central Asia today. Rafik Nishanov, for nearly two years Uzbekistan's Communist boss, attacked Uzbek intellectuals for glorifying figures whom he derided as "apologists for pan-Turkism and national narrow-mindedness."[13]

COTTON COLONIALISM

When I returned to Uzbekistan fifteen years later, in 1989, not much had visibly changed. It still seemed an exotic, backward province. With its immense cotton fields and their plantation culture, with its relentless sun, its backbreaking labor, its dry, dusty roads, its terrible sickness, its desperate rural poverty, its feudal political system, Uzbekistan reminded me of the Egypt I had known in the mid-sixties. The one new element was a tiny, budding cultural revival. I sensed a people trying to return to their own roots, a colony struggling to lift the burden of alien rule.

To Uzbek activists, the chief villain was King Cotton—what the Russians call "the white gold of Uzbekistan." Under Moscow's relentless pressure, Uzbekistan's cotton output had increased tenfold in the seven decades since 1917; by the mid-1980s, it totaled something like 5.5 million tons, two thirds of the entire Soviet cotton crop.

The Uzbek nationalists, with their social-science lingo, argued that the "cotton monoculture" had ravaged their land, destroyed their normal agriculture, ruined their ecology, left their soil so leached with salt that hundreds of thousands of peasants fell sick from drinking polluted, saline water. Uzbeks blamed what poet Mohammed Salikh called Moscow's "cotton colonialism" for corrupting their whole society.

In truth, under Brezhnev's crony Sharaf Rashidov, who ruled the republic like a feudal lord for a quarter of a century until his death in 1984, wholesale political corruption became the plague of Uzbekistan, infecting every pore of society, every crevice of the economy, every political echelon from the village to the district, to the city, to the region, to the republic, to the ministries in Moscow, to the Politburo (Rashidov and possibly others), and into Brezhnev's family.

"There was a pyramid of corruption, a whole criminal mechanism that developed over the last twenty years."[14] This according to Telman Gdlyan, the jaunty, arrogant, relentless investigator put on the case in 1983 by Yuri Andropov, the former KGB chief who became national Party leader.

Gdlyan's exposé became the most sensational criminal prosecution of the eighties. In early 1989, a tribunal in Moscow sent a slew of high officials to jail, including the number two figure in the national police, Brezhnev's son-in-law Yuri Churbanov, the first deputy minister of internal affairs. Gdlyan accused Churbanov of taking 657,000 rubles in bribes to cover up corruption at lower levels; the court sentenced Churbanov to twelve years in the gulag.[15] Uzbek kingpin Rashidov escaped into the grave, but Gdlyan nailed his successor, Inamshon Usmankhodzhayev, who had supposedly been brought in as Party boss to clean house. Gdlyan got him fired and convicted of bribe taking and coverups.

On a rainy Saturday afternoon, while forty thousand of his supporters staged a mass rally just outside the Kremlin walls, Gdlyan laid out for me the inner workings of the Uzbek cotton scam. He paced around his office, as if fancying himself a Soviet Humphrey Bogart, smoking slowly, deliberately, talking with tight-lipped confidentiality through the smoke, his tone laconic, understated; but he was more dapper than Bogart in his well-tailored, olive-tone suit and vest.

"Moscow provoked this situation, this crime—namely, Brezhnev and his clique in the Politburo," he said. "They simply imposed on Uzbekistan a totally unrealistic cotton quota—a quota of six million tons. They simply took this number out of nowhere, frivolously. One of our records describes the [Party] plenum at which Rashidov was promising to produce five and a half million tons of cotton. Brezhnev whispers his name—he says, 'Sharafchik [Rashidov's most intimate nickname], please, round it up. Add half a million more.' Rashidov, being a political prostitute rather than a leader, immediately answers, 'Yes, yes, Comrade General Secretary. We in Uzbekistan will produce six million tons of cotton.' That was the way it was done—'voluntarily,' as we used to say."[16]

Brezhnev's quota, impossible to fulfill in reality, spawned phantom crops, phony records, false bookkeeping, a pyramid of lies, thievery, bribes.

"If the promises were made at the top level without any material basis, false reports became inevitable. And false reports, you understand"— Gdlyan pantomimed with his palm out—"means a 'fast ruble,' bribery. So this massive mechanism of crime starts working from the very bottom and goes straight to the top. . . . The plan quotas are handed down by the government—totally unrealistic numbers. Equally unrealistic reports of fulfilling the quota come back immediately. There is no cotton, but government money is paid for it anyway. A part of the money goes into this one's pocket, a part of it goes to his boss, and his boss is paying his boss, and that's how it goes—all the way up to Moscow. So these false reports pushed people into making a fast ruble.

"They were even hiding hundreds of thousands of acres of cotton fields—never registered anywhere. Whole cotton fields were hidden and cotton harvested from them was also sold to the government for money. This sort of thing requires a total mechanism of crime, including the state authorities, starting with the local farm chairman, the local government collector, and ending in the office of the first Party secretary of Uzbekistan. Layer by layer, people were dragged into this criminal activity. There were hundreds of thousands involved in this crime—a scale that terrified us."

One state prosecutor who handled Gdlyan's cases estimated that between 1978 and 1983, Brezhnev's final five years, the state paid more than 1 billion rubles for cotton that was never produced.[17]

Gdlyan, who is given to hyperbole, may have exaggerated how many people were guilty of lining their pockets in this massive scam, but the clannish nature of Uzbek society, with its personal networks and informal ways of doing business, was fertile soil for mass corruption. By less self-serving reports than Gdlyan's, so many people were involved that tens of thousands were purged from the Uzbek Communist Party; and at least three thousand Uzbek police officers were fired as a result of Gdlyan's probe.[18]

Gdlyan's sensational disclosures of the "Uzbek mafia" made him unpopular in Uzbekistan, but a folk hero back home in Moscow; he was an easy winner in the elections of spring 1989 and served in the Congress of People's Deputies, the superparliament. By mid-1989, he and his co-investigator, Nikolai Ivanov, had the temerity to point an accusing finger at Yegor Ligachev, second in line in Gorbachev's Politburo, as being implicated in the Uzbek schemes. In his interview with me, Gdlyan mentioned Ligachev, four other former Politburo members, and several of Ligachev's aides, on whom he claimed to have evidence.

For months a hot controversy swirled: Ligachev thundered denials and vowed to have Gdlyan's head; people came forward charging that Gdlyan's investigative team had extracted confessions by brutal means. Gdlyan would not retreat. The Communist Party Central Committee eventually cleared Ligachev, and expelled Gdlyan and Ivanov from the Party. The state prosecutor and a commission of the Supreme Soviet said Gdlyan had not produced sufficient proof against Ligachev, but he stuck by his charges, infuriated that the prosecutor's office had broken up his investigative unit.

"Both East and West have criminal organizations," Gdlyan said to me philosophically. "But the nature of your *mafiosi* differs from ours. Your groups are purely criminal. Here, you cannot become an overnight millionaire without being part of the political power structure. To steal millions here, it's a must to have a state seal, a government position, and a limo, for official status."

SLAVERY AND THE STING OF SALT

Moscow's cotton colonialism not only corrupted Uzbek political life, but contaminated the Uzbek economy and the personal lives of Uzbeks as well. It ravaged the environment, adulterated the region's water supply, poisoned the health of millions, and blighted the lives of Uzbek farm workers, especially the women and children—more so than in any other large region that I visited in the Soviet Union.

"The cotton monoculture was a very convenient instrument for enslaving our people," said Abdur Rahim Pulatov, the Birlik leader. "You know, in Russian the term for cotton worker is cotton *rabochy—rab* for short. Well, there is another Russian word *rab,* which means slave. So a cotton worker is a cotton slave, and in Uzbekistan the cotton monoculture has also been the culture of cotton slavery."[19]

For years, Uzbek leaders and the Soviet press trumpeted cotton as the "gold" of Uzbekistan. But very little of that gold trickled down to Uzbek farm workers; by government statistics, 45 percent of Uzbekistan's workers—and farm workers are at the bottom of the heap—earn less than the Soviet subsistence wage of 75 rubles ($125) a month.[20] By the reckoning of Uzbek nationalists, Uzbek cotton farmers make only 16 kopeks (22 cents) an hour for their work, about one fourth as much as those who work on Soviet grain farms.[21] In addition to that level of poverty among farm workers, Uzbekistan has an estimated one million unemployed, and one of the highest unemployment rates in the country—22.8 percent, according to *Pravda.* [22]

Uzbeks insist that their farmers could do better financially if they could market cotton for themselves, at their own prices, rather than being forced to supply cotton to Moscow, at prices dictated by Moscow; or, they say, let us stop growing so much cotton and return to the farm crops for which Uzbekistan was renowned, a rich and profitable variety of tropical fruits and vegetables.

But the price of the cotton monoculture is reckoned in more than rubles; it is also reckoned in human and environmental terms. In the name of record cotton harvests, the ecology of Uzbekistan has been tragically destroyed. Cotton, constantly in need of irrigation, has literally been sucking the region dry. The water level of the republic's great rivers, the Amu Darya and the Syr Darya, has fallen dramatically. Not far from Urgench, I saw what was left of the Amu Darya River, once more than a quarter of a mile across and now several slender currents fifty and sixty yards wide, winding among the sandbars. Near Bukhara, I saw trucks driving in the riverbed; bridges ridiculously spanning great mud channels;

old riverbanks standing ten feet high, like out-of-place fortifications for peasant villages.

The greatest tragedy of all, however, is the Aral Sea, once a great inland saltwater body, now dying for lack of water from its emaciated tributaries. The Aral Sea is one of only a handful of places that Soviet authorities would not let us film, perhaps out of embarrassment over the ecological disaster. Once 25,676 square miles in size, more than the combined size of the states of Massachusetts, Connecticut, Rhode Island, and New Hampshire, it has lost 60 percent of its former size. Aralsk, the Urals' main fishing port, which used to provide one tenth of the entire Soviet fishing catch, now sits nearly forty miles from shore.[23] The new shores are vast salt beds. From the sky it looks as if a huge powdered doughnut encircles the shrunken sea. Winds lift the salt powder, and for hundreds of miles around, salt-filled air stings the eyes, clogs the lungs, and poisons the earth. Salt rains down, back into the shrunken rivers; river water, used for irrigation, salinates the soil; river water, used by humans for drinking, attacks the liver and corrodes the intestines.

In sum, the pernicious cotton monoculture has destroyed the precious working of the water cycle of Uzbekistan—and the normal healthy cycle of human life as well.

"The cotton monoculture is an evil thing for our people," Timur Pulatov, a popular Uzbek writer, said mournfully. "It has been killing us—first of all, killing our soil, weakening it. You know when you plant the same crop every year, the land, the earth, becomes exhausted. Cotton is a very powerful plant because it drains everything from the soil."[24]

The cotton monoculture has also been killing people, both through the relentless abdominal corrosion from salt in the water, and also through the pesticides and defoliants sprayed on the plants to fight the boll weevil and other borers. So much is infected by this toxic combination that at the hotel in Urgench, tourists are warned not only against drinking the water, but also against eating fresh fruits and vegetables; no matter how well they are washed, they have been contaminated by the irrigation water in which they have been grown.

Infants are the primary victims of this diseased ecology: Uzbekistan's infant mortality rate is one of the highest in the world. In Central Asia, most rural hospitals and clinics lack hot water; medical syringes are either nonexistent or used many times over; sanitation is abysmal and sewage stands stagnant. In the Karakalpak region, adjacent to the Aral Sea, more than one infant in ten dies; for Uzbekistan as a whole, the infant mortality rate is 43.3 percent, which puts it virtually on a par with Guatemala and Cameroon.[25]

Disease, like political corruption, is endemic. At the ancient city of Khiva, Mayor Bakhtiar Normetov told me that the health problem was so overwhelming, the Uzbek health system could not begin to cope with it. He said that as many as 70 percent of the adults and 80 percent of the children in the province were chronically ill.[26] That seemed hard to believe, but someone tipped me off to a massive survey that had just been completed in Khorezm Province, in which Khiva and Urgench are located. Several hundred medical workers had found that infectious diseases were rampant—typhus, dysentery, and hepatitis—not to mention gallstones, anemia, kidney problems of all kinds. The health teams checked 387,919 persons: 72 percent were sick—279,753 in all, including 101,216 children.

Years of exposure to foul air, water polluted with salt, sewage, and chemicals, the medical report said, have "exhausted the ability of the human organism to adapt. That is why we have a most unfavorable prognosis for the health of the people in this province, especially for women and children."[27]

FOR UZBEK WOMEN: SELF-IMMOLATION

"This is our rage, our protest. . . . We want to arouse our authorities and our people, to make them look at themselves as they really are, to make them rise up and say, 'We can't live like this anymore!' "[28]

Shukhrat Makhmudov is a forty-year-old Uzbek cameraman and film producer who has found new ways to promote Uzbek nationalism under Gorbachev's *glasnost*. Along with his wife, Raizeta, who is a film editor, he has worked for the official state documentary studio in Tashkent since his 1972 graduation from the State Film Institute in Moscow. For the first time in their lives, they feel liberated from the confines of official propaganda and able to show the truth to the Uzbek people.

"For many years, you see, they've only been shown how wonderful life was in Soviet Uzbekistan, how happily our women worked, how many doctors and engineers there were among them, how joyfully they picked that magnificent snow-white cotton," Shukhrat said sarcastically.[29]

Although not members of Birlik, Shukhrat and Raizeta are caught up in the burgeoning nationalist feelings of Uzbek intellectuals; they are using documentary films to help Uzbeks rediscover their cultural roots and face the terrible realities of their lives.

"We are not just critics; we feel strong compassion for our people's pain," said Shukhrat, a short, dark-haired, good-looking man with soft

Oriental features. "We do not make films with a cold eye and a cold heart. We feel with our people—it's *our* anguish too. We do not simply try to raise problems to be critical. We want our films to make people's lives better."

In the past two years, they have produced several powerful films on Uzbek life. In *Khudzhum,* they broke one taboo by exposing the exploitation of poor, uneducated women workers in a Samarkand textile factory. The film was named after a women's movement in the 1920s that aroused the Muslim women of Central Asia to cast off their veils, and the film was shot in the same factory where Khudzhum had held protests against exploitation under capitalism. Shukhrat's point was that seventy years of Soviet rule had not ended that exploitation. In a second film, *The Dignity and Mystery of a Smile,* the Makhmudovs shattered another taboo by portraying prostitution in Tashkent, and not just any prostitution, but prostitution of teenage girls.

"Raizeta and I make movie after movie of this kind because there are many people who are indifferent [to these things]," Shukhrat told me. "Somebody has to be involved, has to move. Somebody has to support *perestroika.* If everyone just keeps silent, just grumbles, who will act?"

Shukhrat and Raizeta took very seriously their social duty to forge a new outlook among Uzbeks. "You see, we ourselves create our people—by our social system, by our policy, by our morals," Shukhrat told me. "We created our people the way they are today—so obedient. I don't want to continue making this sort of people anymore. And doing the best we can, we'd like to create a new generation, with a new morality."[30]

I first saw Shukhrat and Raizeta at the Birlik rally in Lenin Square, arguing with the police, who were trying to stop them from filming. They were gathering footage for a new film on Uzbek nationalism, to be called *Point No. 5*—the place in a Soviet internal passport for a citizen's nationality: Russian, Ukrainian, Uzbek, Armenian, Jew, and so on.

Cotton figured prominently in their story, so our crew arranged to go and film with them at the Engels Collective Farm outside Samarkand. It was October—harvest time—but I saw no combines in the fields. Later on I would learn that the machinery was ineffective; its first harvesting run left so much cotton on the plants that the bulk of the work had to be done by hand, sometimes four and five times, as the crop matured. In the fields, I saw women (almost no men) slaving away in the blazing sun: doing ten or twelve hours of backbreaking labor, weeding the parched, dusty earth with a little hand-scythe, or, hunched over, dragging long harvest bags between their legs, plucking cotton from the plants, boll by boll.

At the farm's clinic we saw evidence of chronic sickness among cotton farmers. One woman, with an anemic infant, complained of stomach troubles and needed to be hospitalized, but she could not afford to miss work; so she and the sick child headed for the fields, with little medical relief. The doctors told us that toxic defoliants had been used too heavily, attacking the livers, kidneys, lungs, and other organs of the cotton pickers.

From there, Shukhrat headed for the primary school. In room after room, students said they would head for the cotton fields after school. All hands were needed; age was no barrier. At midday, as we filmed the smallest children having a school lunch of noodle soup under a portrait of a smiling Lenin, Shukhrat bent over one table of tots.

"Do you pick cotton too?" he asked a pretty little girl with bangs and no front teeth.

She nodded.

"How do you pick it? Show me."

She plucked an imaginary boll.

"Are you going after school to pick cotton?"

"Yes," she said.

"These little kids are already picking cotton and helping their parents at home," Raizeta told me.

"How old are they?" I asked.

"They're six years old," she replied, shaking her head. *"Six years old."*

Several hours later, in the fields, Shukhrat found a girl named Delfusa whom we had seen in school, a sturdy fifteen-year-old, toting a nearly full cotton bag. She had obviously been at work since school let out at two-thirty. By now, it was close to six.

"For how much longer are you going to work?" he asked her.

"Another half hour," she said. "Then I'll go home and I'll help my mother."

"And then what?" he asked.

"Then I'll do my homework," she said.

"Will there be time left to do homework?" he asked.

"Well," she said, "not much time."

"You're helping your parents," he observed. "You're not forced to pick, are you?"

Kneading her hands, she showed the tension. Clearly the money she made was crucial for her family, even at 7 cents a pound.

"Look," she said, "it's hard for our parents."[31]

With the others, she dragged her harvest bag over to the weighing machine. Her father, a truck driver, was weighing cotton for a group of children. The sense of exploitation was overwhelming as these children trudged home at dusk.

But if anything epitomizes the despair of the Uzbeks, it is the plight of the women, which was captured in the most powerful of Shukhrat and Raizeta's films, *The Flame.*

"The dirtiest, toughest jobs, the most difficult jobs in the Soviet Union are always given to women," Raizeta declared with obvious anger. "And that's true in Uzbekistan too. But here it's even much more extreme. The situation is much worse here. . . . In our movie *The Flame*, we say that everything starts with the woman, and when women are dying, a nation is finished."[32]

In *The Flame*, Shukhrat and Raizeta tell a terrible story about Uzbek women who commit suicide by setting themselves on fire out of despair over their lives. It is a protest both against the exploitation and misery foisted on the poorest, most defenseless elements of Uzbek society by cotton colonialism, and against the conservative, male-chauvinistic ways of Uzbek and Islamic culture. On the farm that we visited, the nurses in the clinic told us that one twenty-four-year-old woman had burned herself to death just two months earlier. Shukhrat said that in eighteen months, more than 360 women in Uzbekistan chose to die in this horrible fashion—two every three days.

"They just pour kerosene on themselves and burn to death," Raizeta said, "because their lives are unbearable, because of oppression, because they can't live the way they want to. It's an extreme form of protest."[33]

Their movie is terrible to watch, young women still covering most of their faces with veils, desperate eyes peering at the camera, marching to work in the unbearable summer heat, flashing to scenes of ambulances, and then female patients, arms and legs akimbo, rolled into the emergency rooms, their bodies covered with burns.

"It's painful to realize that today, after so many years of the Soviet regime's existence, practically nothing has changed," said Raizeta. "It's very hard to watch, very hard to accept."

"You have two daughters," I said to them. "What is your dream for them?"

"My dream," Shukhrat said simply, "is that neither my children nor my grandchildren will ever have to make movies about the self-immolation of women—ever!"

"EVERYONE SEEMS TO BLAME THE RUSSIANS"

The attacks of Uzbek nationalists on Moscow's cotton colonialism have fed a slow but steadily rising feeling against the Russians. Such frictions could become explosive in Tashkent, the Uzbek capital, which is a very Russified city. Back in the 1950s, Russians were a majority there, comprising 52 percent. By the 1970s, I found that Russians still outnumbered Uzbeks, though they had dropped to 40 percent of the population, as rural Uzbeks and other Central Asians came into the city[34]; and now their share is believed to be lower, but the exact figure is kept secret because the Russian presence is such a touchy issue.

In December 1986, anti-Russian feeling exploded in Kazakhstan after Dinmukhammed Kunyayev, the Kazakh Party boss for many years, was removed. Gorbachev replaced him with a Russian, Gennady Kolbin, violating an unwritten rule of Soviet politics—that the local Party leader in each republic must be of that republic's nationality. Moscow normally put a Russian in as second in command, the man generally regarded as the real boss, who ran things for the Kremlin. But the fiction of local leadership had to be maintained; when Gorbachev ignored that rule, the resulting riots in Alma-Ata, the capital of Kazakhstan, showed how close to the surface anti-Russian feelings were. Nothing so dramatic and violent happened in Uzbekistan, but anti-Russian sentiment has nonetheless been on the rise.

For years Russians prided themselves on having modernized Uzbekistan's educational system and economy, but even in the Brezhnev years, a few daring Uzbeks chided Moscow for exploiting the republic, extracting its wealth without plowing earnings back into local industry. They pointed out that 95 percent of the Uzbek cotton was shipped to textile plants outside Central Asia; only 5 percent was processed at home.[35] Uzbeks and other Central Asians resented the crude regional allocation of economic functions, with heavy industry located mainly in the European parts of the country, Siberia and the north exploited for their rich mineral deposits of gold, diamonds, oil, natural gas, iron, coal, and Central Asia for its cheap manpower. Under Gorbachev, some Uzbeks became more outspoken.

"Emotionally everyone seems to blame the Russians," said Abdur Rahim Pulatov. "I, for one, disagree with that, but I have to say that the anti-Russian mood is growing. And if we don't solve our problems, this mood will grow."[36]

In the seventies, I had come to know one Russian couple in Tashkent very well: a famous composer, Aleksei Kozlovsky, who, with his wife,

Galina, had been exiled there by Stalin in the 1930s. Like many thousands of Russians, the Kozlovskys had made Uzbekistan their home, never returning to Russia proper. Kozlovsky turned his exile into creative joy, training Uzbek musicians, conducting their orchestra, and composing symphonies that mixed Uzbek musical themes with classical European music. The Kozlovskys lived in a small home, surrounded by the kind of wild, unkempt garden that Russians love; their home became a haven for famous Russians, such as the poets Boris Pasternak and Anna Akhmatova, and also for many cultured Uzbeks. Kozlovsky died several years ago; when I went in 1989 to see Galina, white-haired and in her late seventies, she was losing her eyesight but still intellectually vigorous and creative. But she was feeling isolated and lonely.

"How is life, Galina?" I asked. "Has it changed much?"

"Frightfully," she said in her perfect English, learned as a diplomat's daughter.

"Yes, how?"

"Oh, Hedrick, it's difficult even to tell you," she said. "Very, very unhappy—the surroundings are not nice. I'm not used to such feelings, because all of my life that we lived here, my husband loved the people, and I also. They were very kind and very nice and good-natured."

"Do you still have Uzbek friends?" I asked. "People of your generation?"

"No," she said.

"What's happened?"

"They are unfriendly to Russians," she said. "They want us to go away. How can I go away if I have lived here forty-four years? They are dissatisfied, like everybody in this country. All the wrong things that were done by the government are ascribed to the Russians, because it was Moscow that dictated how they should live, what they should do, what they . . . how much cotton they must produce.

"There are whole regions that are absolutely poisoned. The mothers can't feed their newborn babies with their milk because the milk is full of salt. The salt comes from the dying great Aral Sea, one of the wonders of Central Asia. It's a pool now—no more a sea. All the salt is evaporating, and it's blown all about the country, and people are dying."[37]

DIFFIDENT NATIONALISM: NO SECESSION

For all the frustrations of the Uzbeks, their nationalist movement is fairly modest in size and ambition. Birlik's leaders claimed half a million followers out of twenty million people, but from my travels that seemed an exaggeration. The hard-core activists are the intellectuals, students, and a smattering of young workers who show up, five thousand or six thousand strong, at Birlik rallies. Their popular support is probably twenty times that number, but hardly half a million.

Politically, Uzbekistan is very conservative. Central Asia as a whole is reminiscent of the American Deep South on the racial issue in the early sixties: Throughout the eighties the hard-liners dominated the government; they tolerated some liberal protests, but kept pretty tight limits on activists; and so far, the great mass of people have not gotten swept up in the nationalist movement as people have in Armenia, Georgia, the Baltic republics, or Moldavia.

From Moscow's vantage point, Central Asia and its delegates to the People's Congress of Deputies are the hard-core Old Guard who solidly back Gorbachev against the radical reformers. The Uzbek intellectuals and journalists whom I met were very frustrated with their stand-pat deputies, who had won election the old way—unopposed—and who rarely bothered to take part in the political debates of the liberated all-union parliament. They sat silently, passively, taking their cue from the Party leader (Gorbachev) as they always have, voting with him even when he moved against their wishes. That is the tradition of Communist Party discipline.

At the local level, the liberal intelligentsia were even more frustrated by the rigidity of Uzbek leadership, its shying away from debate with the emerging democratic elements.

"The leaders of our republic, and of our province, and of our *raikom*, district Communist Party Committee, all have the Stalinist way of thinking," complained Kurambai Matrizayev, head of Urgench radio and television. "It's very hard for these people to change. It's very hard for Gorbachev to break their habits. They should watch Gorbachev on television and see how he allows deputies to disagree with him, to offer criticism. Our leaders should take a lesson from him. But they do not. They criticize the way I work as the local chairman of television and radio, because my nature is to be democratic, to talk with my people, to listen to those who work with me. But the Party bosses tell me: 'This is wrong. You are a weak leader. You've got to be tougher.' "[38]

Compared with the rest of the Soviet Union, Central Asia is so underdeveloped politically as well as economically that the new nationalists lapsed behind their counterparts in other regions. Their first objective was simply to stir a sense of nationhood among the Uzbeks, who had not been a separate nation before the Bolshevik Revolution; under the czars, they had been lumped with the rest of Central Asia in what was known as Turkestan. In the seventies and eighties, Uzbekistan was still a polyglot nation, an amalgam of Uzbeks, Russians, and other Central Asian peoples, especially Tadzhiks. So Uzbek nationalists tried to encourage a sense of Uzbek nationhood and pride. Their methods were fairly basic, with restoring the primacy of the Uzbek language as the first major step.

In Bukhara, Akhurnjan Safarov, an anthropologist at the local pedagogical institute, was doing his part by heading a drive to remove Communist names from city streets and restore prerevolutionary names or name streets for Central Asian folk heroes. "We had a national hero, Bukhana, who led our people against the Arab invaders in the eighth century, or Mahmoud Tarabin, who headed our people's uprising against the Mongol invaders," Safarov told me. "So why not name our streets after these national heroes—to educate our youth in the spirit of patriotism?"[39]

Even more politically daring was the effort to honor people such as Abdurauf Fitrat, an Uzbek writer, musician, historian, and revolutionary who had written works proclaiming pan-Turkic ideals in the 1920s. He had later collaborated with the Communists, but was arrested in 1938 during Stalin's purges, and shot in 1944. In the late 1950s, Fitrat was formally rehabilitated—declared innocent of any political crime; nonetheless, as a Turkic nationalist, he was still treated negatively in the Soviet press for the next thirty years.[40] Under Gorbachev, Professor Safarov and others have gotten a local high school renamed in Fitrat's honor and have made plans to publish two volumes of his works in 1991. Safarov had other projects too, such as reintroducing traditional Uzbek and Turkic fairy tales and children's games.

"Everyone is asking now, 'Who is the real me?' People are looking for their roots," Safarov said. "That's my personal reason for getting involved in these studies."

Another important revival movement is taking place among Muslims. In Samarkand, the mosque where I had seen two hundred or three hundred worshipers back in the seventies was filled with fifteen hundred worshipers at midday on a Friday in October 1989. There was an energetic new imam leading the prayers, though several worshipers told me it was still impossible for them to get the Koran and Islamic prayer books. And I saw only a sprinkling of young people in the sea of wizened graybeards bending in prayer to Mecca. The absence of the young embarrassed the mullah, Imam Mustafakhan Melikov, when I asked about it; a few moments later, in his sermon, he used the presence of our film crew to harangue the elders.

"You are being photographed by Americans," he told them. "Why don't you bring more children to our prayers? Why don't you bring those who are not working or in school? Bring them to the holy place and attract them to Islam."[41]

At the Islamic seminary in Bukhara, its graying rector, Haj Mukhtar Abdulayev, told me the number of his students had tripled from 40 to 125 in the years since Gorbachev had come to power, and that, within the past year, more than eighty mosques had been reopened in Uzbekistan[42] (Stalin had closed twenty-six thousand mosques[43]). From his description, the curriculum seemed limited to strict fundamentalist training. Both the imam in Samarkand and the rector at Bukhara struck me as men of extremely traditional views.[44]

In Tashkent, there was a push to shake up the Islamic Church establishment, widely regarded as a nest of Soviet puppets. In February 1989, a popular protest in Tashkent forced Moscow to remove the official head of Islamic affairs in Central Asia, Grand Mufti Babakhan. His replacement was slightly more progressive; still, the Islamic leaders whom I met knew little and cared less about the goals and activities of Uzbek nationalists and their secular cultural revival. The more liberal Birlik activists saw the reviving Islamic Church as a conservative rival rather than a partner in rekindling Uzbek nationalism and modernizing its culture.

Poets and writers such as Mohammed Salikh, tall and striking in his all-white tropical shirt and trousers, have stirred people with poetry readings on historic and nationalistic themes. His is a conservative, pro-Islamic kind of nationalism, playing on traditional themes, less secular and modern than that of Pulatov, the Birlik leader, or the Makhmudovs. In a region where the oral tradition is still important, especially in the countryside, it was typical of Salikh to remark that "poetry is still very influential—very useful for awakening people." And so were some new nationalist songs like those written by Dadhon Khassan. In the Uzbek Writers' Union, Salikh and Dadhon sang me a shy duet of several of Khassan's songs: "Turkestan, Koz Khamseh" ("Wake Up"), and "Usbegim" ("My Uzbek"), with the words *If you call yourself a son of your motherland, don't give away your language to others,* " and the refrain

> *Raise your head,*
> *Open your eyes . . .*
> *Join us in our ranks,*
> *Even if you must risk your life.* [45]

Initially, I took it as a sign of the relatively primitive stage of the Uzbek nationalist movement that Salikh and Dadhon had not seen the movies of Shukhrat and Raizeta Makhmudov. In fact, the authorities were keeping the Makhmudovs' films from the public eye. *Khudzhum,* about the exploitation of women factory workers, had been intended for an Uzbek women's conference, but after Party officials previewed the film, they barred it from being shown. Parts of the film about teenage prostitution were broadcast on Moscow television, but not in Uzbekistan. *"The Flame* has been shown only once on Tashkent television—at midnight," Shukhrat said, "and that was only a Russian-language version—not Uzbek. There were thousands of letters sent to the station with demands to rebroadcast *The Flame.* Tashkent television was going to show it again this month [October 1989] but the new first secretary of the Uzbek Communist Party, [Islam] Karimov, called the television officials and told them, 'No more upsetting themes on television. They cause people anxiety. We want people in a good mood.' "46 Shukhrat and Raizeta had to resort to private showings to film clubs and interested groups; the Party's ideologists kept their social criticism out of state-operated movie theaters.

Such restrictions checked the influence of Uzbekistan's new democratic activists, slowing their pace. As the Baltic nationalist movements were winning elections, defying Moscow, and proclaiming independence, the Uzbeks were pushing for reinstatement of their language. Other republics were well ahead of the Uzbeks in demanding "economic sovereignty" in 1988 and 1989; the main Uzbek economic demand was a reduction of the cotton quota and an opportunity to diversify agriculture. It took three years, Mohammed Salikh told me, just to get Brezhnev's fantasy target of 6 million tons of cotton reduced to 5 million, which was what many Uzbeks assumed was the actual peak output. It was a genuine triumph, then, in the fall of 1989, when Moscow agreed that the target for 1990 would be 4.5 million tons.47 Salikh was also encouraged by Karimov's promise to give farm workers a pay raise and let them have slightly larger private plots to farm.

Indeed, in the spring of 1990, the Uzbek leadership, especially the new prime minister, Shukrulla Marsaidov, picked up the theme of "economic independence" from Uzbek nationalists, angrily condemning Moscow's "manipulation" of financial figures to make it look as though the Uzbek economy were subsidized, whereas he claimed it provided three times as much to the central economy as it got back.48

After Gorbachev declared his willingness in mid-June 1990 to tolerate more regional autonomy and to renegotiate the 1922 treaty forming the Soviet Union, the new Uzbek leadership began to try to catch up with other republics. On June 20, Uzbekistan became the eighth Soviet republic, and the first in Central Asia, to declare its "sovereignty"—asserting that its laws would take precedence over Soviet laws, though that seemed hopeful rhetoric, rather than a sign of secessionist intentions. Of more practical consequence was the economic alliance signed in late June by the five Central Asian republics, and aimed at gaining more regional and local control of the economy. At least initially, this was a brand of federalism that Gorbachev had indicated he could tolerate. Nor did it produce any dramatic confrontations. As Mohammed Salikh remarked, "We are doing all this without dramatizing the process, without playing to the crowds."[49]

Toward the radical wing of Birlik, the authorities became more repressive. Police used force to break up a rally of more than five thousand demonstrators in a suburb of Tashkent in March, brought charges against Abdur Rahim Pulatov, the head of Birlik, after the demonstrators burned some local office buildings, and issued emergency decrees banning further demonstrations. Periodically, there were terrible explosions of interethnic violence in Central Asia—in Fergana in Uzbekistan, in Kazakhstan, Tadzhikistan, and Kirghizia. But these seemed to burst suddenly out of economic despair, and then disappear. Aside from such random incidents, Central Asian nationalism was relatively diffident; it posed no great threat to Moscow.

"So long as the Communist Party is in power here, there are going to be only small changes," observed Anvar Shakirov, a well-traveled linguist at Samarkand University. "In Uzbekistan, there is a certain characteristic of people: They are yes-men, especially the leaders. It's a very Oriental trait. They watch for what people want up above them. They never say no to higher-ups. So that means for real changes we need a new type of leader, people elected from below, not appointed from above."[50]

Never, in my conversations with Uzbek activists, did I hear any talk of secession from the Soviet Union. For all their unhappiness with Moscow's "cotton colonialism," Uzbeks still felt dependent upon the Russians. They had not really broken out of the colonial mentality—as their peers had done in Georgia, Moldavia, or the Baltic republics. Central Asia was far more politically conservative than other regions. In the elections of March 1990, Uzbekistan's Communist establishment easily maintained its power, and Birlik split into two factions. More important, perhaps, many people became cynical about the practical impact of *glasnost* and the benefits of reform.

"The excitement over *glasnost* and democracy has dissipated," Raizeta Makhmudova told me during a visit to Washington in May 1990. "When it was new, people were in ecstasy at all the new things that were possible to say and do and see. But now, people notice that it has brought nothing new in their lives. People have become disenchanted and so they are not ready to defend *glasnost* and democracy. Public feeling coincides with the desire of the apparatus to maintain the old controls."[51]

CHAPTER 15

ARMENIA AND AZERBAIJAN: A SOVIET LEBANON

"In this country, we have only a single right—the right of territory. This is the sole right of the republic, of our nation. . . . So a fight over territory became a fight for our worth, our dignity as a people, as a nation."[1]
—Rufat Novrozov
Azerbaijani Economist
March 1990

"Today it is very important to understand . . . whether this city really belongs to us, whether this country really belongs to our people. All these things should become a reality at last. And for us, there is no turning back."[2]
—Ashot Manucharyan
Armenian Teacher
July 1989

In the Armenian capital of Yerevan, my first stop was to be School No. 183, but when we arrived, I was certain the driver had made a mistake. We were in a cul-de-sac of a high-rise ghetto. Before me stood what looked like a condemned building: a dismal, squat, two-story structure that had seen better days. It was in a canyon of dull, gray tenement apartments, faced with a mottled-gray stone that gave the entire district a melancholy appearance.

I had heard that School No. 183 was the most exciting and celebrated school in Armenia today, and I had expected something modern, something emblematic of the dramatic resurgence of nationalist spirit in Armenia. But this place looked bombed out, abandoned, dead.

Soviets make a fetish of official titles and name plates, but no plaque designated this building as a school. Several front windows were broken, and the sidewalk was littered with glass, loose rocks, and other debris. There was no hint of a playground, not a blade of grass.

"This doesn't look like a school," I said to the driver. "Are you sure this is the right place?"

An elderly Armenian and a man of few words, he merely nodded. To make his point, he turned off the engine, leaned back, pulled out a cigarette, and prepared to wait. Seeing my consternation, he flashed me a toothy grin.

I got out and approached the building but I could not open any door. It took considerable bellowing before someone finally came to let me and my companions in, even though the school principal and some teachers were supposedly expecting us. The main foyer had an eerie, lifeless feeling. It was summer, so the students were gone, but more than that, the place had been stripped clean, almost as if it had been vandalized.

Down the hall and around the corner, I finally detected some signs of life. Chairs and desks were stacked up against a wall; an electrician was replacing a ceiling light fixture. From one room came the sound of hammering: someone doing repairs. Apparently the front foyer was so naked because the school was undergoing what the Soviets call *remont*, a major repair job.

Farther on, I heard sounds of music, and upstairs I came across some teachers, Armenian women, dancing in a circle in the hallway, arms on each other's shoulders. They were following the directions of a slender, bearded male instructor, and moving to the rhythms of a simple, old-fashioned folk melody played on an ancient Armenian instrument that sounded like a recorder.

Like many Soviet facades, the exterior of School No. 183 had been misleading, but in a way that was the reverse of what is usually the case. Mostly, the facades of Soviet buildings exaggerate the importance and success of the institutions, but in this case, the dead exterior hid a dynamic interior: The school was a seedbed of ferment. Officials there had an intense commitment to the school that was highly unusual for Soviet

teachers. They had close, proud ties with the neighborhood, and a democratic spirit that stimulated student activism. In a bare office with two
desks and a broken phone, the young principal, Ashot Bleyan, explained
how School No. 183 was revolutionizing the Armenian educational system
by reviving ancient Armenian culture—music, folk art, language, dance;
he and his staff were creating a startling new curriculum. In other republics, people dreamed about revamping their schools; here, people were
doing it.

From past experience, I knew that in minority republics, the Soviet
system provided two sets of schools: "Russian" schools, in which courses
were all taught in the Russian language, and "national" schools, in which
the main language was that of the local nationality, with Russian taught
as well. School No. 183 was a national school; it had twenty-three hundred
Armenian students and two hundred Russians. What bothered Bleyan
was that even this "Armenian" school had been forced into a Russian
mold.

"As you know, all over this country, schools have the same curriculum,
the Soviet curriculum, which is created in Moscow," Bleyan told me. "It's
the same program, same concepts, same textbooks, same courses. Nationality doesn't matter. In music, for example, the program is the same for
Russia, the Ukraine, Moldavia, Armenia. The system allows for a few local
idiosyncrasies—but minimal. The music taught is Russian. Our children
have had to learn the music of composers of the past seventy years [the
Soviet period]. Armenia has a musical tradition of two thousand years,
which we feel our Armenian children should absorb—to understand what
it is to be Armenian."[3]

To many Russians, this would sound brash and offensive. Rarely did a
Russian travel with us, but that day, a Russian from the State Committee
for Television and Radio in Moscow, German Solomatin, was with us. As
Bleyan spoke, I could sense Solomatin's tension: He was irked by Bleyan's
charge that Russians had suppressed Armenian culture. Solomatin was
supposed to be a neutral, silent observer, but he could barely contain
himself. Finally, he picked on Bleyan's manner of speech, trying to put
him down as uncultured.

"You're a principal—why don't you speak better Russian?" Solomatin
demanded.

Bleyan had been speaking in Russian as a courtesy to me, because I did
not understand Armenian. His speech was clear and correct, though his
choppy, singsong Armenian pronunciation was less than linguistically
pure. Solomatin was pouncing on that flaw.

Bleyan bristled, conscious that he was being insulted in front of foreign guests.

"I don't think I speak Russian badly," he replied, barely suppressing his anger. "I *teach* Russian," he added, "as a *second* native language."

Solomatin started to take issue, because Russians think of their own language as first above all others, but he was shouted down by four or five other Armenian teachers in the room. The flash of anger on both sides reminded me how close to the surface nationalist feelings were. As voices rose, I cut in and asked the principal to go on with what he had been saying.

"We have redesigned the concept of the 'national' school," Bleyan resumed, coldly turning away from Solomatin. "We want to know who we are and where we are. This means reworking our school textbooks, and programs for literature, music, history, arithmetic, for everything. So our teachers have prepared two Armenian songbooks and two new musical textbooks. We are doing the same thing in literature. Our written literature starts from the fifth century. We have folklore, poetry, and literature, written in our classical language, Grabar, from which our modern regional dialects come. Now, with our new curriculum, our students can study Grabar starting in the fifth grade."

It sounded innocent enough. But I knew from my travels how radical it was to establish a genuine Armenian curriculum, and then to make the curriculum at School No. 183 a model for all of Armenia. Clearly, more was at stake here than mere academics; School No. 183 was stripping away the dominant Russian culture and endowing a new generation with a vibrant national consciousness. Only two or three other minority peoples—in the Baltics and Soviet Georgia—could rival the Armenians in forcefully asserting their national culture and identity.

Moreover, School No. 183 was more than a center of cultural renaissance—it was a hotbed of political rebellion. Its staff was perhaps the youngest in the whole U.S.S.R.: Bleyan, the principal, was only thirty-three, and the average age of the teachers was thirty. Moreover, they were almost all political activists. The teachers had gone on political strikes, and had rallied hundreds of high school students to join them. They were a vocal force in Yerevan.

Five of the school's staff had been arrested in the Soviet crackdown against Armenian nationalists in December 1988. Two were members of the now famous Karabakh Committee, eleven Armenian intellectuals who had spearheaded a popular movement demanding Armenian control over Nagorno-Karabakh, an enclave of Armenians located deep within the neighboring republic of Azerbaijan. But at School No. 183, they did not call it Nagorno-Karabakh; they gave it the ancient Armenian name—Artsakh.

The school was in fact an apt metaphor for Armenia itself. On the surface Armenia appeared to be destroyed, demoralized after the earthquake of December 1988, which had left 300,000 people homeless, and bloody anti-Armenian pogroms in Azerbaijan that had sent another 160,000 Armenians from their homes, fleeing for their lives. But physical appearances were misleading; Armenia—and the school—were full of democratic energy and expectation.

In the hallway outside the principal's office, I noticed a brightly colored wall mural, done in the style of Armenian folk art, not in the stilted style of Soviet socialist realism. The mural poked fun at an ugly green Soviet dragon, pictured as undulating through the hills of Armenia, its back crawling with Soviet army tanks and troops, symbolizing the military curfew and occupation after the mass protests over Karabakh. But standing over the dragon was a conqueror bigger than life: General Adranik Zorovar, a nineteenth-century Armenian hero, drawn with a dashing Armenian mustache. Still closer to heaven, beneath a rising, hopeful sun, loomed Armenia's sacred high ground, Mount Ararat, long ago annexed by Muslim Turkey. Except that in this mural, the painters had placed on its peak the Christian cross of the Armenian Orthodox Church.

"Extremists is what they call us," Bleyan said with a touch of pride. "That's what the Soviet press has nicknamed School No. 183—*extremists.*"

POLICE RAIDS AND DEATH THREATS

One of the least violent but most influential of the school's "extremists" is Ashot Manucharyan, the deputy principal, who, when I visited in June 1989, had just emerged from five months in a KGB prison in Moscow.

Ashot had been a prime mover in creating School No. 183's new curriculum. He had also been a prime mover on the Karabakh Committee. When he came out of jail, he was forbidden by Soviet authorities to continue his political activities and was ordered not to go outside Yerevan, but he quickly said he intended to violate his parole by going to address a political rally in the hill town of Hrazdan, about an hour's drive from Yerevan. He invited me and my colleagues Oren Jacoby and David Royle to come along.

"You may see me arrested again," he said matter-of-factly. "I have announced publicly that this restriction on me is a political measure, not a legal one, and I will not accept it."[4]

I found Ashot Manucharyan to be an unusually idealistic and public-spirited young man, outspoken but soft-spoken; not a firebrand, but firm and gently persuasive. Others told me that Ashot's quiet integrity and relentless devotion to ordinary people had inspired great popular trust. From his parents, both teachers, he had learned a strong commitment to public service. Years before, he had become an idealistic young member of the Communist Party, and in 1986 he was elected a deputy in the Armenian Supreme Soviet. His inspiration to public activism, he said, had come from his father.

"Until he was forty, my father was a very brave man, and very outspoken," Ashot said, adding with a soft smile: "He has only changed as he has gotten older.

"The KGB frightened him terribly last December, when I was arrested the first time [very briefly]. After my release, I went into hiding for nearly a month. Every night, they would come to our apartment at two or three A.M., to check for me, and it frightened my parents. After the second arrest—when I was in jail for a long time—my wife and my mother became fighters for my release; they became political activists. But my father . . . he never forbids me to go out, but he will ask me, 'Why do you give this speech?' or 'Must you go to that meeting?' He worries about me."

"How about you," I asked. "Do you worry?"

"Am I ever afraid? Yes, of course—I'm only human. Sometimes I feel fear. But less for myself. I really worry about my family."[5]

During his five months in Moscow's Butyrky Prison, Ashot was not mistreated, but he was kept incommunicado. No communication with the outside was permitted, except for one visit from his sister. He was put in a cell with a murderer, an armed robber, and an Uzbek official who had embezzled 300,000 rubles. What he found most unbearable was the ban on family contact. He had left his wife pregnant; his second son was born while he was in jail. At the public's urging, the child was named David, a symbolic Armenian David who would stand up against the Soviet Goliath.

The boy, now three, still stares at strangers with large, frightened brown eyes; Ashot's wife, Bibishan, bitterly remembers the police harassment.

"They would burst into our place after midnight and search the place," she recalled. "And we protested: 'Hey, you are Soviet people, not fascists. What right do you have to burst into our apartment on Sundays?' My father-in-law was very sick. We had to call the ambulance three or four times after these searches. He felt he was dying. I was on the verge of miscarriage. It was hysteria. I wouldn't wish anything like that on my worst enemy. Then [after they took Ashot] we were waiting. We were counting seconds, and then weeks. We wanted to have him back, especially the boy who wanted to hear his bedtime story and didn't want to go to bed without seeing his father. The boy became very nervous. That night [of his arrest], there was one soldier wearing a bulletproof vest and armed with a nightstick. The boy was half asleep when he suddenly saw these strangers, after midnight, and he kept saying: 'I hate them all, they took my daddy.' "

Ashot's face hardened as he listened. "You know, sometimes I felt moments of hatred—a desire to kill them all," he said. "Such a powerful hatred. They were subhumans, really. But I simply don't like to hate."

"He's just too honest, too sincere," his wife observed. "He wanted this freedom and *glasnost* so much, even during his student years. So when this fresh breeze started blowing, he couldn't keep away from politics."[6]

Ashot was constantly on the go, organizing relief for the earthquake victims, talking with students, putting pressure on the Yerevan City Council, negotiating privately with Party leaders, campaigning against them in public.

"I am not a soldier by nature," he told me, "but like all of my people today, I am a soldier in a political revolution. . . . We all want to become a country of free people, where human dignity is not a stranger, where the feeling of freedom is common. . . . My people were the first to raise their heads [under *perestroika*], and it purified them. People don't want to live the way they did, often doing things against their own will. And you know, the slave who is aware of his slave mentality is not a slave anymore."[7]

Ideas tumbled out of Ashot during our seventy-five-mile-an-hour drive up into the hills in a little car called a Zhiguli, a Soviet-model Fiat; the car shook terribly as it bounced over the bumpy roads.

Having been thrown out of the Communist Party for his independence, Ashot was deeply disillusioned with Soviet Communism. Though not an advocate of capitalism, he was a democrat to the core, more a democrat than a Karabakh fanatic. He believed the Soviet political and economic system was rotten, and was in favor of establishing a multiparty system, of giving land back to the peasants, and of fighting the corruption in Armenian politics—corruption not yet as bad as in Uzbekistan, but bad enough, he said, so that people paid bribes of 150,000 to 400,000 rubles to buy jobs as district Party leaders. He pointed out an Armenian teahouse along the highway; he said two political thugs had threatened to kill him there because he had been campaigning against a powerful Communist Party leader in the nearby town of Charensavan. They had told him never to show his face again in the town; Ashot had actually gone ahead and finished his campaigning, but after their threat, he said, "I told them I would be in the main square of Charensavan the next day at three o'clock, if they wanted to find me."

"What happened?" I asked.

"Nothing," he said with a shrug.[8]

For Ashot, it was just one of many little confrontations with the "mafia" of traditional Armenian Communist politics, an inevitable by-product of his challenge to the old political system.

When we reached Hrazdan, an industrial city of roughly fifty thousand, several hundred people had already gathered in an open field, mostly men in dark work clothes. Some militia officers stood in a huddle next to nearby apartment buildings, but they made no move to interfere. Ashot climbed a little ridge overlooking the field and was handed a microphone; at his appearance, the crowd chanted, "Artsakh! Artsakh! Artsakh!" punctuating each cry by hurling their right arms into the air. It was an Armenian ritual and rallying cry.

The crowd energized Ashot, who had been in a reflective mood. In the peaceful, slanting afternoon sun, the chants began to rise. Ashot was the teacher: He tutored and instructed them, patiently, thoughtfully, but powerfully. He spoke quietly, but his tone grew sharp when he talked of the injustice to Armenians in Karabakh, and, further, the political and economic corruption in Armenia itself. He reminded the people that not only had Armenians been arrested, but the Soviet army and national police had killed peaceful demonstrators in nearby Georgia. He attacked the Party and KGB for trying to silence the little people. As he warmed to his themes, the crowd responded. Moving among them, I could hear vows of revenge, muttered death threats to Azerbaijanis over the issue of Karabakh.

But Ashot did not play the demagogue; he did not pander to ethnic hatred. He warned against escalating violence, and tried to channel the passions of Armenian nationalism to the cause of democracy, justice, and reform.

"We must know why innocent people were killed in Georgia. Our authorities must answer. . . . We must decide who should have the power: the people or the Party Central Committee. . . . We must express everything that is in our hearts. We cannot keep it inside anymore. The time has come when we must act—and move forward. We all underwent great changes in this last year and a half. This period was more significant to our lives than the last one hundred years."[9]

"TERRITORY IS OUR SOLE RIGHT"

Karabakh, of course, was the issue that had galvanized Armenian nationalism from 1987 onward. It is what made the Armenians, as Ashot Manucharyan observed, the first of the Soviet peoples to explode, once Gorbachev's *glasnost* gave them freedom to speak. Karabakh became the lightning rod for all the discontent of the Armenians, discontent with economic misery, with the corruption and arrogance of their political leaders, with the pollution of their environment. For Armenia, Karabakh became what cotton was for Uzbekistan.

Except that Karabakh had roots deep in Armenian history; it was a long-suppressed territorial grievance that electrified the masses, and that instantly made it a cause célèbre for the entire nation of Armenians. And Karabakh was much more: It was an aching wound, a symbol of the injustice done to the Armenian nation by Soviet rulers and, before them, by the Turks; it was a holy cause for the Christian Armenians against the Islamic peoples that surrounded them; it was an icon of Armenian suffering through the centuries. In a very real sense, Karabakh is a microcosm of Armenia.

Karabakh is an Armenian island engulfed in a surrounding sea of Azerbaijanis, who are an ethnic blend of Persian and Turkic peoples, Islamic in their culture and religion. Armenia is an island of Christianity virtually surrounded by Islamic peoples: Turkey to the west, Iran to the south, Azerbaijan and all of Soviet Central Asia to the east. Only on the north is it bordered by another Christian nation, Soviet Georgia. In Armenia, there are about 3 million Armenians, and another 1.5 million are scattered around the U.S.S.R.; the Soviet Union has ten times as many Turkic people—42 million—plus another 54 million in Turkey itself.

Historically, this area of the Caucasus, the land bridge connecting Europe and Asia, has seen unending conflict. The Armenians have endured centuries of persecution. They lost about a million people in Turkey during the massacre of 1915, a mass slaughter that drove the Armenians into the arms of czarist Russia and then into alliance with the Bolshevik Revolution; Russia, under any banner, became Armenia's protector against the Turks.

Hanging at Etchmiadzin (the Vatican City of the Armenian Orthodox

Church) is a massive painting, a tapestry, that captures Armenia's view of itself. It depicts the heroic Armenian nation fighting off violent attacks from fierce soldiers on all sides, most of whom wield the characteristic curved swords of Turkish or Islamic warriors.

The Armenian church at Etchmiadzin is the cultural and emotional heart of the Armenian nation. The pageantry of its priests, celebrating mass in black hoods and purple robes, draws Armenians from all over the world, captivated by its rich ceremony and paying homage to the Catholicos, or Patriarch, of the world Armenian Church. Records and relics mark Armenia as the first Christian nation, converted in 303, several decades before the Emperor Constantine declared Christianity the official religion of the Roman Empire.

The Church survived for the past seventy-five years by accommodating to Communist rule and working out a live-and-let-live arrangement. When I visited Armenia in the seventies, I found that many Communist Party officials were clandestine believers whose relatives had church baptisms and weddings in defiance of official atheism. There were thirty thousand baptisms performed a year, I was told. In 1971, Catholicos Vasgen II claimed that nearly half the Armenian people were church-goers, although others said that was an exaggeration.[10] When I saw him again in 1989, Vasgen II estimated that under the more open conditions of *glasnost*, 50–60 percent of the urban population and 80 percent of the rural population were Christian believers.[11]

With the church as the principal vessel of Armenian language, culture, and national cohesion, Armenians maintained a strong sense of national identity, even in the darkest years of Communist rule. Their republic is ethnically the purest of all fifteen major political regions of the U.S.S.R.: Ninety-four percent of Armenia's population are Armenians, according to the 1989 census. Its historical traditions have been well preserved; its national archive, the famous Matenadaran Library, is an unusually rich repository of chronicles and ancient manuscripts, all written in Armenia's distinct script, testimony to the people's pride in their long history.

By contrast, Azerbaijan is a relatively young nation that never enjoyed a clear and coherent history or a distinct national identity to match Armenia's. In what is now Azerbaijan, the ancient Greeks found a mingling of innumerable tribes; the region later became a province of Persia. The Arab conquest in the eighth century brought Islam; then came occupation by the Mongol invaders; later, after the rule of an independent khan, the region became the site of continual battle between Persians and Ottoman Turks. In 1829, czarist Russia annexed northern Azerbaijan, leaving the southern portion around Tabriz to Persia.

Paradoxically, perhaps, this checkerboard history and mixed heritage has left modern Azerbaijanis extraordinarily sensitive to what they see as the territorial integrity of their republic: their primary claim to nationhood. As one highly Russianized Azerbaijani, a young economist named Rufat Novrozov, explained to me, "In this country, we have only a single right—the right of territory. This is the sole right of the republic, of our nation." Stalin, he said, had stripped all the minority nationalities of everything else. "Territory was all we had left," he said. "They could not change our territory without our agreement. So a fight over territory became a fight for our worth, our dignity as a people, as a nation."[12]

Novrozov and other Azerbaijanis acknowledged their weak sense of nationhood. Said Novrozov: "When Azerbaijanis meet each other, they ask, 'Where are you from?' And people answer, 'I'm from Nakhichevan or Karabakh or Kazakh'—from provinces, not from Azerbaijan. They have stronger regional loyalty than national loyalty. In general, we thought of ourselves as Turks."

For many Azerbaijanis, then, the political—and eventually the military—struggle with Armenia over Karabakh has become a test of Azerbaijani national legitimacy; and also a catalyst for a developing Azerbaijani nationalism, a path to a new and stronger national identity. The Armenian challenge for control of Nagorno-Karabakh is both a threat and a stimulus. "The fight for Karabakh," Novrozov said, "is a fight for national [self-] determination, in the form of a fight for territory."

Azerbaijan had been awarded control over Nagorno-Karabakh by Stalin in July 1921, after a confusing period of revolution, civil war, and nationalist uprisings. In 1905 and again in 1918, the Armenians and Azerbaijanis had fought over Karabakh and Nakhichevan, another contested territory. By the early 1920s, the census showed Karabakh was 95 percent Armenian in population; but Azerbaijanis claim that it was originally dominated by their people through the eighteenth century, and that the Armenians arrived only in the nineteenth century.

To Armenians, Stalin's decision was a horror, a double cross; earlier in 1921, the regional Bolshevik leadership had decided to give Karabakh to Armenia. A few Armenians, and even some Russians, suspect Stalin of having acted with satanic purpose, knowing the Karabakh issue would rile the Armenians and keep these two nationalities forever at dagger points.

In a wider sense, the explosion over Karabakh in the 1980s was a natural consequence of the very concept of the Soviet multinational empire. During the Bolshevik Revolution, Lenin was looking for allies against the czarist regime, and he bargained for the support of the minority peoples on the fringes of czarist Russia by promising them autonomy and self-determination once the czar was overthrown. After the Revolution, first Lenin and later Stalin carved up the political map along ethnic lines, clustering Armenians together, Georgians, Ukrainians, Uzbeks, and so on. But inevitably, there were demographic pockets that did not fit a neat map; people who did not match their neighbors. And this was especially true in the Caucasus and Central Asia, where peoples and tribes had moved and mingled for centuries. Karabakh was one of those demographic pockets where the local population did not match its neighbors.

What made Armenians acutely sensitive to the fate of Karabakh in the 1980s was the painful example of Nakhichevan, another province that Stalin had awarded to Azerbaijan. Its population had also once been mainly Armenian, but over several decades of the twentieth century, Azerbaijanis had become the majority through a deliberate program of resettlement: Armenians left, Azerbaijanis moved in. Nowadays, Armenians point with alarm to a similar, though slower trend in Karabakh—the Armenian share of the population has fallen from 95 percent in 1921 to 75 percent in 1981. Armenians with whom I talked were deathly afraid that Karabakh would be forever lost through what they derisively termed "Azerbaijanization." Moreover, Armenians, from taxi drivers to the Communist Party leader Suren Arutunyan, accused the Azerbaijani government in Baku of deliberately letting Armenian towns and villages in Nagorno-Karabakh become run down, of refusing to spend money on schools, hospitals, housing, and other facilities, in hopes of provoking an Armenian exodus from Karabakh.

Periodically, the Armenians' frustration had erupted in the Brezhnev years; they made repeated efforts to get back their "lost territories" of Karabakh and Nakhichevan, through private appeals to Party leaders in Moscow, letter-writing campaigns, and public demonstrations. On April 24, 1965, the fiftieth anniversary of the Turkish massacres, one hundred thousand people demonstrated in Yerevan in what began as an officially sanctioned gathering and then grew into spontaneous demands for the "territories."[13] That same year, forty-five thousand Armenians in Karabakh signed a petition to the Soviet Council of Ministers, seeking reunification of Karabakh with Armenia. Years of Stalinist repression had not snuffed out nationalist passions; when Gorbachev's *glasnost* lifted the political lid, the Armenians were the first people to seize aggressively upon the new openness.

COLD-BLOODED MURDER

It was almost immediately after Gorbachev's accession to power in 1985 that Armenians began bombarding the new leadership with appeals to return Karabakh and Nakhichevan. In 1987, the Karabakh Committee was formed to lobby Moscow and organize public support in Armenia. That fall Armenia became the site of the first large public demonstrations of the Gorbachev era, the central issues being Karabakh and industrial pollution. But the real explosion of public protest came in early 1988, after the Armenians felt they had been deceived by Gorbachev, triggering a campaign that would force the ouster of Communist leaders in both Armenia and Azerbaijan and set Armenia once again on the path to war with its neighbors.

The Armenians had high hopes that Gorbachev, with his democratic approach, would let the Armenian majority in Karabakh determine its own destiny and rejoin Armenia. After lengthy private negotiations with the Communist Party Central Committee in Moscow, there was great excitement in Armenia at a December 1987 report in the French Communist newspaper *L' Humanité.* The paper quoted Armenian economist Abel Aganbegyan, an adviser to Gorbachev, as telling the Armenian community in Paris that Moscow—presumably meaning Gorbachev—had decided to settle the issue of the Nagorno-Karabakh situation, and to return the province to Armenia. Aganbegyan's statements, repeated in the Soviet press, hit like thunder in the Azerbaijani capital of Baku.

The Azerbaijani leadership warned Moscow that any change on Karabakh would not only bring hundreds of thousands of Azerbaijanis into the streets, but would inflame all of Soviet Central Asia. This was an ominous threat to the Kremlin, and many Soviet officials, for fear of opening up a Pandora's box, opposed any change in territorial arrangements in the Caucasus. Across the country, there were at least thirty-five significant territorial disputes; a change in one area was sure to invite pressures on other disputed territories, a nightmare for Moscow. Nonetheless, the Armenians were on the offensive, and on February 20, 1988, the regional soviet, or council, of Nagorno-Karabakh, dominated by Armenians, called for transferring the region to Armenian control. The Soviet Politburo immediately rejected and condemned this move as an "extremist" action. Yerevan reacted with an eruption of demonstrations more massive than the Soviet Union had seen since the Bolshevik Revolution. On February 25, between half a million and a million people assembled in downtown Yerevan, carrying banners that proclaimed KARABAKH IS PART OF ARMENIA! and KARABAKH IS A TEST CASE FOR *PERESTROIKA*![14]

In Azerbaijan, emotions flamed out of control, and on February 27, a mob of young Azerbaijani toughs went on a bloody rampage against Armenians in Sumgait, a city about thirty miles from Baku. After three days of looting and murder, thirty-two people were dead, hundreds were wounded, and tens of thousands had fled for their lives.

When I visited Sumgait, Azerbaijani officials admitted to me that it is a breeding ground for violence—a tough industrial town with high unemployment, inadequate housing, terrible pollution from thirty-two chemical plants and other heavy industry, and what officials called "criminal elements"—meaning ex-convicts legally barred from living in Baku.[15]

On each of the three terrible days, Azerbaijani rallies charged with emotion had been held in Lenin Square, in front of Sumgait City Hall, and city leaders took part. Armenian refugees told me later that the mobs had been sent out by official leaders in Sumgait to hunt Armenians. After the violence, Sumgait's mayor and Party boss were fired for incompetence, but their successors insisted to me that the old officials had not fomented the violence. They acknowledged that those officials had been slow and ineffective in controlling police and city authorities; but they contended that emotions had been fired up, not by local officials, but by the accusations of Azerbaijanis, who had come to Sumgait with stories of having been chased out of Armenia and Karabakh.[16]

The bloodbath in Sumgait changed the dynamics of the Karabakh dispute: It was a nightmare, publicized worldwide, and, in sharpening hostilities on both sides, it propelled both into an escalating cycle of violence.

In Sumgait, I talked with Azerbaijanis who had given shelter to terrified Armenians, and outside Yerevan, I talked with Armenian survivors, who described the carnage. One young woman, Irina Melkunyan, who had hidden for hours in a neighbor's bathtub, told of hearing the mob breaking down doors, hurling furniture out the windows, starting bonfires. She had married into a family in which five people, including her husband, were murdered: mother, father, daughter, and two sons.[17] A middle-aged woman, Asya Arakelyan, told me how she had tried to escape into the apartment of a Russian woman across the hall, but had been chased down by a gang wielding bicycle chains, knives, and hatchets.

"The Azerbaijanis came, all dressed in black," she said, trying to control her terror as she relived the trauma. "They went through every building, looking for Armenians and shouting slogans—'Death to Armenians,' 'We'll annihilate all the Armenians. Get them out of here.'

"They broke down our apartment door and my husband and I escaped. Our Russian neighbor took us to her place. They smashed and burned everything in our place, and then came, with a bullhorn, and told us to come out in the name of the law. I was close to the door and they hit me first with their crowbar. They grabbed me and started pulling me down-stairs, outside, to the courtyard. They threw me down, ripped my dress, and started wildly beating me with anything they could lay their hands on. And those axes and knives—it was terrible. They had a big knife and they threatened to cut my head off. When I looked up, I understood they were about to kill me. So I raised my arm in self-defense, and they slashed open my arm with their huge knife."[18]

She showed me how she had shielded her head, exposing a terrible scar, nearly a foot long, a slice all across the soft flesh of her underarm. We were sitting knee-to-knee in a tiny room, and I could feel her begin to cry. When I reached out to comfort her, she seized my hand, telling me through her tears that the Azerbaijani mob, taking her for dead, had thrown a rug over her.

"Then they dumped some gasoline over my body and burned me," she said. "I didn't know that, right next to me, they had gone at my husband. They hacked him with an ax and burned his body. Practically next to me. Only I did not know it then."

She glanced at a nearby dresser, where she had a framed portrait of her husband, a nice-looking man in his fifties, dressed in a business suit. The sight of him was too much to bear. She broke into sobs, her body throb-bing.

"I was there for hours, losing consciousness," she went on haltingly. "Rain started. It stopped the fire. . . . When I came to, it was dark. I was bleeding. My back was all burned. . . . Finally, my younger son came to me. 'Mama, Mama, what happened to you?' I lifted my head with diffi-culty and told him to run: 'Go away or else they will kill you.' He asked me not to move and went for an ambulance. There were Azerbaijani cars all around. He asked them to take him to the ambulance, but they wouldn't help. . . . Later, much later, the boy came back with a truck."

Considering it a miracle that Asya Arakelyan was alive, the Armenians called her the "Madonna" of Sumgait.

For some, the bloodbath at Sumgait was a modern reenactment of the Turkish massacre of 1915. A journalist named Armen Oganesyan, a trim, steely, violently passionate Armenian nationalist, said:

"If you know Armenian history, you should know that Armenians were always victims—always paying with their lives, with their lands, with their possessions, going through endless genocides, endless manslaughters, end-less bloodshed." As Armen spoke, his brown eyes were burning. "Right now you see a so-called minigenocide, because Azerbaijanis are like Turks, and their pan-Turkic ideology sees Armenia as the big obstacle to their unity, to achieving the goals of pan-Turkism. People want to present all this as Christians against Muslims and vice versa. I have nothing against Islam, but when someone wants to use religious fanaticism as a political weapon, causing the death of children and old people, it becomes a crime."[19]

I saw Armen several times; he took me to other groups of refugees, showed me his articles about Sumgait, explained his desperate attempts to see justice done, seethed with raw fury that only a few minor punishments had been meted out against the Azerbaijani perpetrators. His pain was understandable, but to me he seemed a fanatic who was nursing and spreading hatred. Ashot Manucharyan was trying to turn the pain and passion of Karabakh toward reform, whereas Armen Oganesyan was turning it toward revenge. He said to me that his ethic was Old Testament: an eye for an eye.

Sadly, it was easy to find victims on the other side. By the summer of 1989, when I reached the Caucasus, about 200,000 Armenians had fled from Azerbaijan, and about 160,000 Azerbaijanis had fled from Armenia. Most of these Azerbaijani refugees were concentrated in Baku, where their anger fueled the already heightened tensions. There were still about 200,000 Armenians living in Azerbaijan, but virtually all of the Azerbaijanis cleared out of Armenia as a result of waves of Armenian violence and intimidation, especially in October and November 1988.

In a very plain Baku apartment, I talked with an Azerbaijani family, the Guliyevs, whose twenty-eight-year-old son, Magaran, had been attacked by Armenians in Massis, a city about twenty miles from Yerevan, and not far from their former village of Zangiler, where there had been periodic violence. By the family's account, Magaran Guliyev's murder was as brutal, savage, and cold-blooded as that of Asya Arakelyan's husband.

As tensions had risen in Armenia through the summer of 1988, the Guliyev family, like many Azerbaijanis, had begun preparing to move to Baku. Coming back from Baku, their older son, Magaran, was set upon at the Massis railroad station by Armenians, who attacked him and his uncle with hammers, axes, and screwdrivers.

"They were hiding, a group of them," Mrs. Guliyev said she was told by the uncle, who somehow survived. "My son got off the train and they attacked him and my brother. My brother fell down; they thought he was dead. So they beat my son, hammered him several times, and threw his body in some water [near the station]. It was sort of a swamp. A soldier found him, saw him still breathing, and brought him to the hospital. In three days, they called us from the hospital and said: 'There's a dead man here. Come and take him.' "

The victim's body was buried immediately, but after a couple of weeks his family decided to take his body with them to Azerbaijan, and they had his body exhumed. "There were many Armenians around, including the heads of the local militia, Babahanyan and Iskandaryan, and many soldiers," said Mushtur Guliyev, the surviving son. "They were all saying, 'All the Turks should be killed. . . . All the Azerbaijanis should be caught and killed this way—have their heads cut off.' "

The family was sitting around a rough wooden table in the courtyard of their apartment building—mother, father, brother, two sisters, wife, and small child. Their grief hung in the summer air, thick and heavy. The father, a gray-haired workman, was crying openly, as were the women.

"When I went to get my son's body, there was a militiaman, named Makhachiyan, who asked me: 'Why are you crying? Is this not enough for you? We should have annihilated all of your kind, as we did this one.' "[20]

THE EROSION OF COMMUNIST POWER

Along with the spasms of violence in Armenia and Azerbaijan, the drumbeat of guerrilla war was rising in Nagorno-Karabakh through 1988 and 1989—the planting of land mines, arson, villages blockading each other, strikes, ambushes, shoot-outs like that between the Hatfields and the McCoys. In November 1988, the Soviet army imposed martial law and a curfew in Yerevan and Baku, but several thousand troops could not keep the peace in the mountains of Karabakh. The death toll mounted, building ineluctably toward civil war.

First Gorbachev tried to ban the Karabakh Committee, then he cracked down, arresting its leaders in December 1988 and January 1989, and at the same time arresting the most outspoken Azerbaijani nationalists. But by mid-1989, he let these activists free, and there was an upsurge in nationalist activity in Armenia and Azerbaijan. In both capitals, the cancer of Karabakh was sapping the strength of the Communist Party, undermining the foundations of its rule.

Alarmed by the massive unrest in early 1988, Gorbachev had fired Party leaders in both republics and installed his own choices; but as Moscow temporized, satisfying neither the Armenians nor the Azerbaijanis, populist leaders took politics into their own hands. Party leaders were driven by the need to keep up with the masses in the streets. Under popular pressure, the Armenian Supreme Soviet declared Karabakh part of Armenia; the Azerbaijani parliament angrily rejected that move. In each capital, Party leaders were caught between Moscow's demands to control "extremists" and somehow pacify the new democratic activists, and the pressures of mass demands for justice—and victory—on Karabakh.

"I find myself in a very difficult situation," Suren Arutunyan, first party secretary of Armenia, confessed to me. "I have no right to intervene in the internal affairs of a neighboring republic, Azerbaijan. On the other hand, I have no moral right to remain indifferent. . . . A constructive solution must be found. Postponing a solution will do no good. You cannot keep one hundred seventy-five thousand Armenians living in Nagorno-Karabakh [apart from Armenia] by force. For seventy years, they have felt oppression. They have been humiliated as a nationality, unable to learn the history of their people, to study their language, artifically separated from the rest of their nation."[21]

Hotheads like Armen Oganesyan kept the pot boiling, fueling the passions of conflict. Moderates like Ashot Manucharyan sought to use popular pressures to persuade the government to accept democratic reforms, to clean up political and economic corruption, to protect the environment, to help the poor.

In July 1989, when I was there, Yerevan was in turmoil over daily reports that Azerbaijanis had blocked all the roads into Nagorno-Karabakh, an act of civil war. Each day brought rumors and reports of new casualties. Ashot led a group from the Karabakh Committee and the Armenian Supreme Soviet to a Yerevan City Council meeting; although he was not a council member, his popular following gave him clout in the corridors of government. Ashot directed his team like a congressional floor leader, from a seat on the aisle halfway back in the hall; others checked with him before going up to the podium. One colleague arrived from Karabakh, and Ashot counseled him not to inflame emotions in the hall. Gradually, Ashot and his group took the political initiative away from the mayor and Party leaders, bargaining for a resolution appealing for immediate action from Moscow to lift the road blockade, and chiding the Communist Party for doing too little.

Suren Arutunyan, the Armenian Party leader, admitted to me that the Party faced a "crisis of trust" in Armenia; the damage had been done, he said, over many years. Arutunyan was Gorbachev's man, part of Gorbachev's new generation of reformers; for several years he had worked in Moscow under Aleksandr Yakovlev, a principal architect of Gorbachev's reforms.

"To be candid, in our republic, the Communist Party and Soviet bodies have lost a good part of their authority," Arutunyan conceded during a long conversation in his large, well-furnished office. "Our people have great doubts about our capabilities. . . . In the early stages of *perestroika,* we underestimated the severity of our interethnic problems. . . . I tell you honestly, the overwhelming majority of our political leaders were not prepared to meet the problems which we now face. Our personalities were formed under quite different conditions. Very abruptly, everything has changed."

Arutunyan echoed Gorbachev's impatience with the inability of the Party Old Guard to adapt. "I am especially indignant when Party officials, who are called to lead *perestroika,* drag behind events," he said. "I'm quite critical of my own performance. . . . It is hard to find new people. Each new appointment is real torture for me, because our resources are so limited."[22]

In his late forties, his hair prematurely silver, Arutunyan was a good deal more modern-minded than Party leaders in Central Asia. He was opening contacts with reformers and intellectuals; shortly before our get-together, he had gone for a meeting with Yerevan University students, and wound up enduring an unprecedented five-hour question-and-answer session. His own children were university age: His twenty-three-year-old daughter was studying at Yerevan University, and his nineteen-year-old son was doing his compulsory two years of military service with the KGB border troops. I asked Arutunyan if he had trouble keeping up with the thinking of the younger generation.

"My son's thinking is more modern, more flexible than mine," he replied. "When I talk with him, I can't help feeling like a conservative. And that's not easy for me to admit."

Very unusual for a Soviet Communist leader in his openness, he offered to introduce me to his family, and when I returned to Yerevan a month later, he invited me, my wife, Susan, and our film crew to dinner. He was living in an elaborate government guest house, guarded and behind walls. The family were very gracious; Arutunyan's wife and daughter were dressed for a party, while his son, more informal, wore slacks and a short-sleeved shirt. The boy had his father's self-confidence and directness.

I asked him if the student generation regarded the Karabakh Committee, an obvious challenge to his father, as important.

"Yes, very important," he said. "And the students trust them."

"More than you trust the older generation?" I asked. "More than you trust your parents?"

"You mean my father?" he asked, raising an eyebrow. "I can tell you that the chasm that opened during the [Brezhnev] period of stagnation between the leaders and the people is very hard to overcome. You see, there is *still* mistrust of the leadership."

"During the period of stagnation," Arutunyan interjected, trying to correct his son and deflect the criticism.

But the son stood his ground.

"Before, and now, over all these years," the young man insisted. "We cannot take for granted anything our leadership says. But the Karabakh Committee represents the people."

Arutunyan smiled gamely, and after his son's obvious put-down, he lectured the young man and me.

"Don't idealize the Karabakh Committee," he advised. "I don't fully share some of my children's views here. The committee people aren't always right, due to their political inexperience. . . . But we must engage in the widest possible dialogue with these informal organizations. We must cooperate with them and make compromises."

"You know, there's a member of the committee named Ashot Manucharyan," I said. "Can you work with him or not?"

"What do you mean, 'can or cannot'?" Arutunyan shot back. "We invited him [to meet with us], and he made a lot of remarks and proposals at our session. We have no choice. We have to work with him."[23]

The willingness of a Communist Party leader to work with a grass-roots leader, especially one recently released from a KGB prison, was an indication both of these extraordinary times in the Soviet Union, and also of how compelled Arutunyan felt to combine forces with genuine populists in order to regain the popular following the Communist Party had lost.

"For the first time in my professional life," he said to me, "I have discovered the genuine power of the masses. Sure, theoretically I knew it was there. I read Marx and Lenin and other theorists. But now I see that history is really only created by the masses."[24]

Arutunyan was pursuing an intelligent strategy: seeing Ashot Manucharyan as an ally against the escalation of violence. Even as the Yerevan City Council meeting was droning on that afternoon, emotions over the blockade of Karabakh spilled out into the streets. Thirty or forty thousand people gathered below the hilltop where the Matenadaran Library was situated. Other speakers whipped up popular feelings, but Ashot warned against being "dragged again into this dirty game of bloodshed.

"We are not talking about secession from the Soviet Union, about political separation," he told the crowd. "We are talking about our future as a nation. Today it is very important to understand whether our way is right, whether this city really belongs to us, whether this country really belongs to our people. All these things should become a reality at last. And for us, there is no turning back."[25]

PRIVATE ARMS, PRIVATE ARMIES

Gorbachev, stuck between past policy and his present preachings, equivocated on Nagorno-Karabakh. He satisfied neither Armenia nor Azerbaijan nor Nagorno-Karabakh, thereby ensuring a steady crescendo of violence. Past policy dictated that no Soviet borders could be changed for fear of setting a dangerous precedent; Gorbachev's new politics of *glasnost* and democratization proclaimed the goal of self-government and self-determination, which is what the Armenians in Karabakh desperately wanted: a referendum to decide their own future. But it was also a step sure to inflame the Azerbaijanis.

Gorbachev took a middle course. In January 1989, on the advice of the famous physicist-democrat Andrei Sakharov, he suspended the powers of the two political bodies that had been at loggerheads in Karabakh—the Azerbaijan republic's overall control of Karabakh, and the local, Armenian-dominated provincial council—and he put the province of Nagorno-Karabakh under Moscow's direct rule. In the short run, that cooled Armenian hotheads, but as time dragged on, it placated no one. The Armenians still wanted Karabakh joined to their republic; the Azerbaijanis demanded its return to their control. Moscow was caught in between, fearful of disappointing the Armenians with their influential foreign communities in Paris, Los Angeles, and throughout the Middle East and Europe, but also afraid of angering the Azerbaijanis, and the Muslim peoples of Central Asia and the world at large.

"Applying self-determination would cause a bloody explosion in Azerbaijan—a great, bloody explosion," said Leonid Dobrokhotov, a Central Committee official familiar with the leadership's thinking. "In Armenia, the tension is also rising. There's no radical decision that can be taken. This problem is like Northern Ireland or Lebanon. These problems go on and on. If we satisfy one side, the other will explode."[26]

The price for Gorbachev of neither resolving the problem nor halting the violence was terrible. There was a flow of almost daily casualties and unending criticism of Moscow; and people lost confidence in the central government's ability to protect its citizens. Gorbachev was leaving people to their own devices, implicitly encouraging Soviet citizens to take law and order into their own hands.

There was a wider, more dangerous lesson in the conflict in the Caucasus too: that in a multinational empire organized along the lines of ethnic republics, roughly sixty-three million Soviet citizens were living outside the frontiers of their own national republics; they were ethnic minorities, living in regions dominated by and legally under the control of other nationalities, who might turn on them. Roughly half of these people were Russians; the other half were Uzbeks living in Kirghizia, Meskhetians living in Uzbekistan and Kazakhstan, Armenians and Azerbaijanis living in each other's republics—in each case victims of mass violence during the Gorbachev years. From 1987 to 1990, the death toll from periodic violence by ethnic majorities against local minorities rose into the hundreds.

In recent years, the volume of arms in private hands has grown astonishingly in the Soviet Union. By one Soviet estimate, there were at least fifteen to seventeen million unregistered guns in the nation in 1989,[27] and Paul Goble, an American specialist on Soviet nationality problems, estimated the figure to be more like thirty to forty million.[28] According to another account, there is a black market in guns in almost every major Soviet city, with virtually any item from the Soviet military inventory on sale. In Odessa, "fifty to eighty rubles will buy a grenade, five hundred to eight hundred rubles will buy a pistol. Add two hundred rubles for ammunition." Ports and border areas are reported to offer foreign firearms. In Baku, a visiting American scholar was told that American M-16's were for sale at the city's "midnight market."[29] As the conflict escalated in the Caucasus in late 1989, whole carloads of weapons disappeared from military stocks into the hands of guerrilla armies.

Under the pressures of rising conflict and public tension, the unraveling of Communist authority was even more dramatic in Azerbaijan than in Armenia. When I was in Baku in mid-July 1989, an Azerbaijani Popular Front was just about to organize formally and to marshal mass support. Toward the end of 1988, a group of Baku intellectuals had started to set up a democratic-style popular front, similar to those in other republics, to promote Gorbachev's political and social reforms. A familiar combination of cultural and religious repression, economic discontent, environmental pollution, anger at a corrupt local leadership, and a sense of colonial exploitation [Moscow's buying oil from Baku at a small fraction of the world market price] all provided fertile soil for a grass-roots movement. In late June 1989, some of the most extreme nationalists, arrested six months earlier, were released from prison.[30] Close to 160,000 Azerbaijani refugees from Armenia had concentrated in and around Baku, many without jobs and adequate housing, a festering mass of discontent. Azerbaijani workers were riled by their own grievances, as well as by the Karabakh issue. These forces fused into an explosive combination once the Azerbaijani Popular Front was formally proclaimed on July 17, 1989.

Far more rapidly than any other mass movement in the Soviet Union, the Azerbaijani Popular Front shot from obscurity into having a hammerlock on power. Within two months, it was dictating terms on Karabakh and on Azerbaijani sovereignty to the Communist Party hierarchy. Its leverage came from the emotional fission created by the Karabakh issue, the mass of unemployed refugees in Baku, and its declaration of an economic blockade of Armenia proper as well as of Nagorno-Karabakh. Initially, Communist Party leader Abdur Rahman Vezirov had refused to recognize the front, disparaging its leaders as hooligans and extremists and ignoring its demands—that the military curfew imposed by the Soviet army be lifted; that there be immediate general elections, economic sovereignty for the republic, and restoration of full Azerbaijani administrative control of Nagorno-Karabakh.[31]

"Moscow has to take a hard line against Armenians," a front leader, Abdulfaz Aliyev, declared. "They have not found a solution and are only trying to please the Armenians. Innocent people are suffering in that region [Karabakh] the way the situation is now."[32] Later, Aliyev added: "We simply will not relent on this issue. It is our land, and that is that."[33]

Beginning in late August, the front showed its muscle with a string of mass demonstrations and labor strikes; a two-day general strike in August closed sixty enterprises. But its most menacing display of raw power was the stranglehold it clamped on the entire republic of Armenia.

On September 4, 1989, the front announced that it was imposing a total road and railroad blockade on Armenia to force the national government to return Karabakh to Azerbaijani rule. Armenia was especially vulnerable: Its trunk lines from the rest of the country ran through Azerbaijan, bringing in 85 percent of its freight. My Armenian contacts said that rail traffic had been squeezed since mid-July, but the situation became acute in the fall. The Armenian economy nearly came to a halt: There was no gasoline for private cars, transport, or farming, and the fall harvesting came to a stop. Ambulances and the militia were put on minimum rations.

Because of the lack of grain, the bread shortage became acute; no outside food supplies were getting through. Armenian farmers were killing their livestock because they did not have enough fodder to keep the animals alive. All kinds of goods stacked up on the rail lines, even housing materials and supplies for the victims of the Armenian earthquake. The

Soviet press reported that about four hundred trains with sixty thousand cars were idle.[34]

By mid-September Gorbachev's hand-picked Communist Party leader Vezirov bowed to the front's pressures and agreed, in effect, to share power. On September 13, he signed a "protocol" with Azerbaijani Popular Front leaders, accepting most of their demands, including the demand for a special session of the Azerbaijani Supreme Soviet, to pass a law on sovereignty, in which the republic reserved the right to defy federal authority and reaffirmed its constitutional right to secede. The law was passed ten days later.

"We don't advocate leaving the Soviet Union," said one director of the front, Nadzhaf Nadzhafov. "Our position is that if the conditions are right, we can live in the Soviet Union. But if the conditions are not right, that clause on secession would be our last resort."[35]

In return for concessions, the front was supposed to lift the rail embargo, but it did not. At a critical Communist Party Central Committee meeting in Moscow on September 19, Gorbachev not only thundered his disapproval at Baltic talk of secession, but he gave the Azerbaijanis, without naming them, an ultimatum. "Where a threat has arisen to the safety and lives of the people, we will act decisively, using the full force of Soviet laws," he declared.[36] Effectively, the Kremlin gave the Azerbaijanis forty-eight hours to back down. But they were not intimated and, inexplicably, Gorbachev did not follow through on his threat. The rail blockade continued until October 11, when the Azerbaijanis suspended it on condition that Moscow dissolve its special government committee for Karabakh. Moscow did not act, and the blockade was immediately reimposed—and extended to Soviet Georgia, because the Georgians had refused to collaborate with the Azerbaijanis. The Armenians accused Moscow of intentionally letting the blockade continue so as to bring Armenia to its knees. But the rest of the country was suffering too: The Soviet press reported that more than one million tons of freight, food, and supplies transiting the Caucasus for other places in the country were blocked.

By early October, military combat in and around Karabakh had escalated to undeclared civil war, between what amounted to private armies on both sides, equipped with weaponry provided to them by blood brothers inside the Soviet army. One senior Soviet official called the conflict "a homemade Lebanon," a bitter communal war that was drawing increasingly on combat-tested veterans of the Soviet war in Afghanistan, no longer amateurs armed with hunting weapons but troops trained by Moscow for heavy combat.[37] When a civilian helicopter from Armenia landed at Gadrut in Nagorno-Karabakh, inspectors found that it was carrying grenades, explosives, detonators, rifles, hunting weapons, gunpowder, parts for anti-aircraft weapons, and instructions for operating heavier weapons. The two sides had graduated from rifles and land mines to machine guns, anti-tank weapons, helicopters, armored cars, anti-aircraft guns. In one very graphic report in mid-October, Moscow television showed railroad engines with great gaping holes or mangled by anti-tank weapons. The deputy prime minister of Armenia complained that bridges were being blown up and there was "continuous strafing of trains."

On November 28, 1989, the government in Moscow yielded to the bloody, costly Azerbaijani stranglehold: With Armenian deputies boycotting the session, the all-union Supreme Soviet voted to end Moscow's direct rule over Nagorno-Karabakh and to return the disputed province to Azerbaijani control.

Rather than easing the situation, that decision seemed to exacerbate tensions. Armenia's Supreme Soviet defiantly proclaimed a United Republic of Armenia, embracing Karabakh and even including it in the 1990 Armenian budget. The rail blockade eased, off and on, but killings, sabotage, and kidnappings continued sporadically until the next terrible explosion, on January 13, 1990, in Baku.

In a bloody echo of the carnage at Sumgait, mobs of Azerbaijanis, many of them the unemployed refugees massed in Baku, went on another anti-Armenian rampage. A state of emergency was declared, but Azerbaijanis told me that they saw violence take place in the presence of Soviet troops; apparently the force occupying Baku, eleven thousand army and national-police troops, did not intervene during the three days of the anti-Armenian pogrom.

Only a week later, *after* the violence had subsided because virtually all of the Armenians in the city had fled, did Gorbachev send twelve thousand more troops into Baku to quell the Azerbaijani nationalists. The films I saw of that operation, which took place overnight on January 19–20, showed a brutal, overpowering assault: tanks and armored personnel carriers spraying apartment buildings with gunfire, tracers fired back from Azerbaijani snipers on rooftops, civilian buses riddled with machine gunfire, rows of passengers slumped against the windows, forever motionless. Some top leaders of the Azerbaijani Popular Front were arrested. More than one hundred Azerbaijanis were killed, and a million people turned out two days later to mourn them and denounce Gorbachev.

Gorbachev's crackdown turned the rage of Azerbaijan against the Russians, for it was Russian troops who had invaded. Elmira Kafarova, chairman of the Azerbaijani Supreme Soviet, condemned the Soviet action as "a gross violation of Azerbaijani sovereignty" and vowed that "the Azerbaijani people will never forgive anyone for the tragic way their sons and daughters have been killed."[38] The Azerbaijani Supreme Soviet demanded the withdrawal of Soviet forces within forty-eight hours. In Moscow, demonstrators outside the Defense Ministry carried banners saying: GORBACHEV HANGMAN, STOP THE TERROR IN BAKU; NO—TO OCCUPATION. In Baku, Azerbaijanis held rallies to burn their Communist Party cards. Even in Moscow, at the Supreme Soviet, Gorbachev came under fire for sending in the troops without consulting the national parliament.

Defense Minister Dmitri Yazov belatedly gave a political justification for the operation: The troops, he said, were sent into Baku "to destroy the organizational structure" of the Azerbaijani Popular Front, which, according to Yazov, was running a network of forty thousand armed militants who had been on the verge of overthrowing Soviet authorities in the region.[39] Indeed, front members had seized control of the police station and city offices in Lenkoran, near the Iranian border on the Caspian Sea, on January 11, and two days later, a huge demonstration in Baku had called for the ouster of the republic's Communist Party boss, Vezirov.[40] Gorbachev's delay in ordering troops into Baku was taken as evidence by Azerbaijanis that he had acted not for what the world took as the humanitarian motive of saving the Armenians but for the political motive of saving the Communist regime in Baku.

"In Baku, I have seen two kinds of assassinations," said Azerbaijani economist Rufat Novrozov, who works closely with Russian scholars at a prestigious institute in Moscow, but was in Baku during the events of January. "I saw many things, and it was a horror. First, the assassination of Armenians, then the assassination of Azerbaijanis. It was personal terrorism, then it was state terrorism, government terrorism."[41]

In the aftermath of the invasion, sensational evidence surfaced that Party and police hard-liners in Moscow and Baku may have been plotting a provocation to bring on Gorbachev's crackdown. According to a detailed account pieced together by Bill Keller of *The New York Times,* the police and KGB had advance knowledge that an anti-Armenian pogrom was in the making, but they did nothing to stop it; local Communist Party officials initiated the creation in January of an Azerbaijani paramilitary organization, the so-called National Defense Committee, in order to discredit the Azerbaijani Popular Front by making it appear more violent than it was, and Viktor Polyanichko, the second-ranking Communist Party leader in Azerbaijan—a Ukrainian, and Moscow's most trusted agent in Baku—had for a year or more encouraged Azerbaijanis to form a popular front. Once it was formed, he had tried to turn it toward a militant, chauvinistic direction, hoping to provoke violence and thereby justify Moscow's intervention with force.[42]

Azerbaijanis with whom I talked scoffed at Yazov's charge that the front was bent on toppling Communist rule. They insisted that all they wanted was a change in Party leadership and a democratic chance to compete for power; that they did not want to stage a coup d'état.

"Now we have a coup d'état," commented Novrozov, who is from the moderate wing of Azerbaijani nationalists. "There is no Azerbaijani state, no Azerbaijani government, no Azerbaijani leadership. Now, there is military power. . . . The Soviet invasion showed the real attitude of Moscow toward Azerbaijanis. Gorbachev would never do the same thing in the Baltic republics. Gorbachev wants to look like a democrat in Europe, in the world, and the Baltic republics have very close relations with European countries. . . . Their [Moscow's] relationship with Muslims is not the same. They think the Muslims are not clever people, but foolish, stupid people, and only Russia can be the leader of this nation. . . . I think that Russia, the Soviet Union, has lost Azerbaijan forever. . . . People will never forget the crime in Baku."[43]

Huge Soviet occupying forces have settled into a long, sullen occupation to keep order in Baku and Yerevan, although there is periodic violence, especially in the hills of Nagorno-Karabakh. In late May 1990, Armenian nationalists clashed with a Soviet troop train arriving in Yerevan; the gun battle left twenty-two dead.[44] In late July, Gorbachev ordered all nationalist vigilante groups and armies to disband and surrender their arms within fifteen days; Vadim Bakatin, the Soviet minister for internal affairs, estimated that ten to twenty thousand Armenians were connected with illegally armed bands, and he said others had put the figure as high as one hundred thousand. Gorbachev's order met defiance from the Armenian Supreme Soviet, filled with nationalist supporters; the legislature rejected Gorbachev's proclamation on grounds that it "contradicts the Armenian people's natural right to self-defense," as well as the United Nations Charter.[45]

So the legacy of Gorbachev's policies in the Caucasus is a new hatred of the Russians and a turning away from Communist Party leaders. After the new nationalist coalition occupied public buildings in March, Suren Arutunyan was replaced as Armenian Party chief, evidently because the Kremlin felt he could not cope with the situation.[46] By August 1990, a forty-five-year-old leader of the Karabakh Committee, linguist Levan Ter-Petrosyan, was elected to the top post in the republic—chairman of the Armenian Supreme Soviet. Gorbachev agreed to turn over to Ter-Petrosyan the task of trying to collect arms from bands of armed Armenians—a sign of how far he had been forced to yield real power to grass-roots leaders.[47] For by the fall of 1990, Gorbachev was confronted with an Armenian government that had been elected on a platform of seeking independence. Nearly three years of frustrating protests had left the Armenian people suspicious that Mother Russia could no longer be counted on as Armenia's ultimate protector against the "Turks."

In Azerbaijan, only a few extremists had talked about secession in 1989 but a year later, well-educated, highly assimilated moderates such as Rufat Novrozov discussed it openly. Deep down, however, they seemed to want to stay in the Soviet Union, provided they were allowed to run Azerbaijan themselves, to revive their culture and their economy as they saw fit.

Only grudgingly did Gorbachev accede to demands for genuine home rule in Azerbaijan or Armenia. He refused to bend to the bloodletting of violent extremists on both sides, and it was unclear whether he would move far enough to satisfy more peaceful political radicals. Moreover, he dared not suspend martial law and military occupation in the Caucasus for fear that that would bring on full-fledged civil war.

CHAPTER 16

LITHUANIA: BREAKING THE TABOO OF SECESSION

"If the world accepts one country being oppressed by another country, using aggression to establish some unjust status quo, then violence will rule the world—not the principles of international law and justice."[1]

—Vytautas Landsbergis
Lithuanian Leader
July 1989

"There is no absolute freedom in this. We have embarked on this path, and I am the one who chose to go ahead with it. My own personal fate is linked to that choice. The two states [Lithuania and the U.S.S.R.] must live together."[2]

—Gorbachev, June 1990

The most insistent and menacing challenge to the unity and integrity of the Soviet state came, ironically, not from Central Asia with its fifty million Muslims, and not from the boiling civil war in the Caucasus, nor from the Ukraine, the second-largest of the Soviet republics. It came from tiny Lithuania.

It came not violently, but peacefully, and it came not from the implicit power of hundreds of thousands of people massing in the streets, nor from the terror of rampaging mobs, but from the very means that Gorbachev had chosen for political reform—the ballot box.

The confident, well-organized skill with which the Baltic national movements in Lithuania and neighboring Estonia and Latvia won elections not only demonstrated far greater political sophistication than that exhibited by national movements elsewhere in the Soviet Union, but gave political revolt in the Baltics a legitimacy that was impossible for Gorbachev to deny.

The first democratic victories in the Baltics actually produced what Gorbachev wanted: a dynamic new thrust for reform in the most economically and politically advanced region of the Soviet Union, the region he hoped would become the showcase and model for reform for the rest of the country. But the tempo of political change in the Baltics, sitting on the edge of Eastern Europe, was extremely swift, and soon the Baltic peoples, especially the Lithuanians, were pushing beyond the limits of Gorbachev's plans for reform. For in spite of preaching the gospel of democracy and self-determination, Gorbachev found the consequences unpalatable when Baltic nationalism veered toward independence, secession, and the breakup of the Soviet empire.

The first powerful jolt of the Baltic earthquake came in the election of March 26, 1989—the first free election in the Soviet Union in seven decades, and the first in the Baltic states since Stalin and the Red Army had annexed them in 1940. It was the nationwide election for Gorbachev's new parliament, the all-union Congress of People's Deputies.

With a camera crew, I watched the voting and interviewed people positively spilling over with enthusiasm for the new politics. For the first time in their lives, they were voting in elections that were not a charade. They had a choice, an alternative to the hand-picked Communist Party candidates: a slate of candidates from Sajudis, the Lithuanian nationalist movement.

"It is so different this time," one middle-aged worker told me. "Before, we voted just to get our names checked off. [Voting was compulsory.] I could cast [identical] ballots for my entire family, for my whole building. That's how it was before. But *today*, we're really electing. We're choosing the candidates we prefer."

Neither Lithuania nor any other part of the Soviet Union had electronic voting machines, so the ballot counting was slow. Preelection polling was unknown, and people were not even sure whether the count would be honest. In many parts of the country, the Party apparatus had blocked alternative candidates from running. But in Lithuania, Sajudis had developed a strong enough following to ensure a fair election. And besides, members of the Lithuanian media, many of them reformers, were watching the proceedings like hawks.

It was morning before the tally was complete, and a small crowd had gathered outside the modest old building in downtown Vilnius, the capital of Lithuania, where Sajudis had its second-story, walk-up office. The Baltic peoples, especially the Lithuanians, are cool and unflappable, accustomed to bearing disappointment and hardship stoically; they are rarely given to public exuberance. But this morning, there was excitement in the air.

When a Sajudis staff aide emerged to post the results of the election on a bulletin board, the crowd demanded that he call out the returns. And so, one by one, he read off the names of the Lithuanian government and Party officials who had always been rubber-stamped in past elections:

"Chairman of the Supreme Soviet—defeated."

The crowd let out a whoop.

"Chairman of the Council of Ministers—defeated."

Cries of "Look at that!"

"Secretary of the Communist Party—defeated."

More cheers.

"Another secretary of the Communist Party—defeated."

Shouts of approval.

And so on down the line: deputy prime ministers, the head of the Lithuanian Gosplan, the Communist leader of Vilnius, a particularly unpopular Stalinist leader of one city district, the head of a pro-Russian movement opposing Sajudis—one big name after another, beaten by political newcomers.

In an incredible sweep, Sajudis, which had held its founding congress only five months earlier, in October, had won thirty-one out of forty-two seats; eight were still to be contested in runoffs, and in that second round, Sajudis won all eight. So Sajudis finally emerged with thirty-nine out of Lithuania's forty-two deputies.

Because these elections were for seats in the new all-union parliament in Moscow, not for posts in the Lithuanian government itself, government and Party officials in Lithuania had not been literally thrown out of their jobs; the Communist Party still held official power.

But the Communist Party had been thoroughly rejected and discredited. Political upheaval in Lithuania was running *ahead* of what turned out to be the dramatic unraveling of Communist power in Eastern Europe that took place in the fall of 1989. The unofficial opposition—Sajudis—had overwhelmed the Soviet Communist Party in Lithuania as convincingly as Solidarity, the Polish labor movement, would defeat the Polish Communist Party three months later.

No one, not even the optimists in Sajudis, had expected such a stunning victory. Without actually controlling the Lithuanian government, Sajudis could now drive the political agenda as the recognized voice of the people in Lithuania.

The crowd on the sidewalk was jubilant beyond words, and incredulous.

"It's wonderful . . . it's wonderful," a man with a lush red beard kept repeating, like a small boy who has just opened a Christmas present that exceeds his wildest imagination.

"This means we will live with hope," said a broad-faced grandmother in a mohair hat, tears welling up in her eyes. "We trust Sajudis."

"Down with the Stalinists—that's what it means," said a burly man with a mustache.

"Sajudis stands for the sovereignty of Lithuania," the grandmother insisted, "for economic and political sovereignty—the end of occupation."[3]

THE TRADE SECRET OF A SOVIET EDITOR

In the Lithuanian language, *sajudis* means a spontaneous "coming together," a meeting of the minds as well as a social coalescing. That literally is what happened in the case of the Lithuanian nationalist movement.

Sajudis had emerged, in the summer of 1988, simultaneously with popular-front movements in the neighboring Baltic republics of Estonia and Latvia. All three had developed more swiftly than nationalist movements elsewhere in the Soviet Union. Their strategy had been shrewd: Forming themselves as broad umbrella organizations, they had invited all to join, welcoming Communists as well as anti-Communists, and all nationalities. They were also careful not to call themselves political parties or to define themselves as the official opposition, even though in time that is how they came to function. And the Baltic popular fronts had presented themselves as champions of *perestroika,* as allies of Gorbachev and Gorbachev-style reformers in the battle against the Party's Old Guard.

When I asked why politics were moving so much faster in the Baltics than elsewhere in the Soviet Union, people would say, "Because we're more European than the others."

Lithuanians, Latvians, and Estonians see themselves as part of Europe and of European culture. Not only are they geographically close to Germany, Poland, and Scandinavia, but they are more attuned to the politics of self-determination than are the Slavic peoples of Russia and the Ukraine, or the Turkic peoples of Central Asia. They are more inclined to look Westward than inward.

In the seventies, when my Moscow friends traveled to the Baltics, a favorite region for vacationing and shopping, they would say they were "going West," because the Baltics had a higher standard of living, more interesting art and fashions, and a Western feel to the architecture of their cities and to their manners and attitudes. In the Baltics, Muscovites felt they could escape the drabness of Soviet life; they could find an Old World charm in the cobbled streets of Tallinn in Estonia, Vilnius and Kaunas in Lithuania, and Riga in Latvia. The green, rolling countryside reminded me of the American Midwest: tree-lined fields dotted with solid, well-kept individual farms, or *khuttors,* as they are known in the region, instead of the clustered, log-cabin villages of the Russian heartland.

It is this European spirit, this European atmosphere, and this dream of being once again a part of Europe that has given special thrust to the Baltic movement for independence.

In politics and economics, the Balts look askance at the Russians, with their long centuries of authoritarian rule, their submission to the czar, to "the center," as the heart of Communist power in Moscow is colloquially known.

"The Russians do not understand what is happening here," Arvydas Juozaitis, a Lithuanian political scientist and a young leader in Sajudis, told me on Election Day. "We have information that Gorbachev and others in the Politburo think of Sajudis as a shadow of the Lithuanian Communist Party. They cannot conceive of a grass-roots movement actually starting from below. They see reform as coming from above. They have a primitive political culture."[4]

Intellectuals in the Baltic republics point with pride and nostalgia to their period of political independence, from 1918 to the Stalinist conquest in 1940. Lithuanians treat this period as a golden age of Baltic democracy, overlooking the fact that the final thirteen years of this period were characterized by single-party, hard-line, right-wing rule.

Through most of their history, Estonia and Latvia, often known together as Livonia, had fallen under foreign rule: by Denmark, by the Teutonic Knights from what became known as Prussia, then by Sweden, and finally by Russia's Peter the Great. Lithuania had a more independent tradition; in 1321, under Grand Duke Vytautas Gediminas, Lithuania conquered all of Byelorussia and half of the Ukraine, including Kiev and reaching down to the shores of the Black Sea. Gediminas's son linked

Lithuania to Poland, a union that lasted for three centuries. When Poland was carved up in 1795, Lithuania fell under czarist Russia. So Baltic independence has been episodic, but the last episode, the twenty-two years of independence between the world wars, has been a catalyst to the new nationalist fervor.

In the 1989 elections, Sajudis was the most dramatically successful of the three Baltic movements, partly because it was the most cohesive and best organized, but also because Lithuanians more clearly dominate their republic demographically than Estonians and Latvians do theirs.

After World War II, Stalin deliberately watered down the ethnic purity of the Baltics, sending in waves of ethnic Russian settlers, and two other Slavic peoples, Ukrainians and Byelorussians, to work in newly built Soviet factories there; the Baltic states sit astride a natural invasion route to Russia, and Stalin considered the Slavs more politically dependable than the Balts. By 1989, Latvians comprised only 52 percent of their republic's population of 2.7 million; Estonians 61 percent of Estonia's 1.6 million people; and Lithuanians 80 percent of Lithuania's 3.7 million.[5]

As small nationalities, the Balts felt especially vulnerable to this immigration of Russians and other Slavs, and feared extinction as peoples. And it was this fear that won their nationalist movements near-universal support among their own communities.

The Estonian Popular Front was the first in the Soviet Union to develop a master plan for its republic's economic autonomy. And in November 1988, it was the first to push a declaration of sovereignty through its parliament: Estonian laws were to take precedence over Soviet laws; no law passed in Moscow would have force unless it was confirmed by Estonia. By acceding to this daring measure, the Estonian Communist Party leadership maintained public credibility at a time of nationalist fervor, and that credibility helped it to contain the political challenge posed by the Estonian Popular Front.

In Lithuania, a parallel move was blocked and postponed by the Communist leadership under Algirdas Brazauskas. So there, the Communist Party won a temporary victory, but it cost the Party popularity, and would contribute to its downfall in the 1989 elections. And if Sajudis was temporarily defeated on this issue, it nevertheless won a string of other victories: the declaration of Lithuanian as the official language of the republic, the resurrection of the national flag and anthem from the independence period, and publication of a political program calling for a "neutral, independent, and demilitarized Lithuania," though acknowledging that secession was a theoretical goal.

In 1989, for the first time under Soviet rule, Lithuania openly celebrated the anniversary of its independence, February 16, 1918. Two hundred thousand people gathered in Kaunas to witness the restoration of the Liberty statue in Unity Square. Vincentas Cardinal Sladkevičius, who had been exiled from Kaunas for thirty-three years, made a radical call for Lithuanian independence, and Brazauskas, first secretary of the republic's Communist Party, had come around enough to declare that "Lithuania without sovereignty is Lithuania without a future."[6]

It was a far cry from the Lithuania of the seventies. Even in the Brezhnev era, there had been Lithuanian political protests: In 1972, when I was visiting, two young men had burned themselves to death and seventeen thousand Lithuanians had signed a petition to United Nations Secretary General Kurt Waldheim, charging religious repression by Soviet authorities. As always in Lithuania, religion and nationalism were intertwined, and the Communist press warned of the danger of "religious fanaticism."[7]

On a trip to Vilnius, I had wanted to attend and photograph a Sunday mass, to see who dared take part in religious services. I wondered whether it was only the old, or was it also younger people. The main cathedral was closed, but other churches were functioning, and I had inquired at my hotel about how to get to a service. Saturday evening, I went out to dinner, leaving my camera inside my locked suitcase. The next morning, I found the camera still inside the locked suitcase, but the lens had been smashed, hit with a blunt instrument in several places. Obviously, the authorities did not want more publicity about Catholic activism in Lithuania.

And now, in February 1989, the Communist Party leader was sharing the same platform with the long-exiled Catholic cardinal.

In addition to Sajudis's election sweep, what impressed me more than anything else, on my return to Lithuania in 1989, was the Sajudis newspaper: Its circulation was one hundred thousand. In a country where the Communist Party jealously controlled the press, I found it remarkable that any other political movement could have a weekly newspaper with such a large readership. The openness of the paper, the topics it raised, its defiance of Moscow and of local Communist Party leaders, indeed its continued existence, marked Sajudis apart from the other national movements I had seen.

"If we had enough newsprint, we could sell three hundred thousand," said the editor, Romouldas Ozolas. "But we can't get enough paper."[8]

By profession, Ozolas is a philosophy professor at Vilnius University. He was one of the founders of Sajudis, and is a member of its inner leadership, but he was quick to admit, "We are not politicians—we are amateurs. We still have to grow local politicians. So far we don't have any, because you cannot call [Communist] ideologues politicians."

Slender, angular, and outspoken, Ozolas is a quick-witted scholar who enjoys the game of politics. Experience editing a stuffy academic journal had won him the post of chief editor of what quickly became the most popular newspaper in Lithuania—*Atgimimas,* which means "Renaissance" or "Rebirth." Even its Russian-language edition had a circulation of thirty thousand; and all across the republic, it spawned fifty smaller, local imitations.

"Our movement could not exist without our newspaper," Ozolas told me. "Our one hour of Sajudis on television is a big help. But our people have great faith in the printed word, a strong tradition of reading, especially the older people. It is the press that really unites the people."[9]

When the first issue of *Atgimimas* appeared on September 16, 1988, the authorities did not bother to censor it. In the spirit of *glasnost* and Lithuanian nationalism, they let it have newsprint and access to the Communist Party printing plant. Two months later, after the paper had attacked the Lithuanian parliament as "an autocracy" that violated the new spirit of democracy by refusing to pass a declaration of Lithuanian sovereignty, the Communist leadership imposed censorship. Hard-liners began harassing the newspaper, denying it use of the Party printing plant (despite the fact that Ozolas was a member of the Politburo) and trying to cut off its paper supply. Conservatives in Moscow wanted *Atgimimas* shut down.

"They called all our suppliers, their paper factories in Russia, and now nobody wants to sell us paper, even though we are prepared to pay triple the normal price," Ozolas told me. "I do not know what we will do. Newsprint is their way of backing us into a corner."[10]

By July 1989, simply getting out each issue had become Ozolas's biggest headache. Printing the paper at a book-publishing house had become erratic; issues came out two and three weeks late, often stacked up one behind another. As Ozolas found new sources of newsprint, Moscow tracked them down and choked them off. It was political trench warfare.

Still, I saw people reading fresh issues of *Atgimimas;* and despite censorship, it was still raising the most explosive issues—Soviet military occupation, the secret protocols of the Hitler-Stalin pact under which Stalin occupied the Baltic states, questions of economic and political sovereignty.

Knowing the power of "the center" in this highly centralized economy, I asked Ozolas how he managed to get paper.

"We have so-called socialist entrepreneurship, which means the possibility for organizations to make direct barter deals," he replied. "We're ready to pay for paper with beef, or, let's say, with bricks."

An echo of the cooperatives: Bricks and beef were in short supply, and therefore worth more than money—worth enough to entice some Soviet paper factory into supplying contraband newsprint to political radicals in Lithuania.

"But," I asked, "where does an editor-in-chief lay his hands on beef or bricks to exchange for newsprint?"

A smile crossed Ozolas's face: "This is the trade secret of a Soviet editor-in-chief."[11]

DON'T CROSS THE "RED LINES"

The man who felt the brunt of the Sajudis political offensive, and who was reeling from the movement's election sweep in March 1989, was Algirdas Brazauskas, Lithuania's Communist Party leader, a Gorbachev-style reformer and an experienced Party official with a popular touch.

I found Brazauskas an unusually agile politician, especially for a Party leader. He had been installed by Gorbachev in October 1988 after he had dared to appear at nationalist rallies that his Old Guard predecessor had tried to suppress. Like Gorbachev in Moscow, Brazauskas was trying to readjust Party policy to the rapidly changing popular mood. In November 1988, he had blocked the parliamentary move to make Lithuanian laws supreme over Soviet laws; a few months later, he recognized this as a tactical mistake and shifted his position.

Brazauskas looks as immovable as a Notre Dame fullback. He is a handsome blond heavyweight who had been an Olympic sailor and a track athlete in his youth and is still athletic in his fifties. His personal warmth, easy approachability, willingness to admit the Party's past mistakes, and instinct for moderation made him popular among ordinary Lithuanians, and Russians living in Lithuania saw him as their protector. Moscow saw him as its anchor at a time of rapidly shifting tides. Ardent nationalists had no use for him, because he was a Communist, but the more pragmatic wing of Sajudis saw Brazauskas as a useful buffer, a go-between for them with the Kremlin, until they had built up enough strength to take over power, and negotiate for themselves.

I came to see the political evolution of Algirdas Brazauskas as symbolic of Lithuania's move toward independence.

I met Brazauskas on the morning after the Communist Party's electoral defeat in 1989. The leaders of Sajudis had cannily left Brazauskas and his like-minded deputy, Vladimir Beryozov, without challengers, sensing that if they were beaten, the Kremlin would replace them with hard-liners. So Brazauskas had been spared personal humiliation. Still, he was stung by the Party's defeat, and I was frankly impressed that in such circumstances he had enough grit and poise to do an on-camera interview with an American correspondent.

Months later, Brazauskas admitted to me that the election debacle had been his darkest moment, but on the morning after, he was gamely trying to maintain a facade of confidence, although he allowed that the pace of change baffled him.

"Just a year ago, it was difficult to imagine that such things could happen in our republic," he said. "It all started only eight months ago."

I asked him if the election had not indicated the Party's loss of public trust, its control of events.

"Yes," he replied candidly. "I would say it means *perestroika* should speed up its tempo. People want to see faster results. . . . We should speed the creation of a state governed by law. We should speed up economic reform."

At one point, Brazauskas tried to draw some comfort from the convenient fiction that Sajudis was not calling itself a political party. But later he conceded, "We do have a political opposition, but I don't see any tragedy in that. We have to learn democracy."

On the most crucial issues, however, Brazauskas sounded Moscow's line. I asked him what he had meant by his very nationalist-sounding comment a few weeks earlier that Lithuania without sovereignty was Lithuania without a future.

"I meant that as part of the Union family of republics, each republic should have its own political sovereignty, its own constitution, system of law, system of education, cultural life," he said. "Independence means that a self-sustaining republican [economic] system should be established, that our republic's economy should . . . [set our own] prices, system of payment, our national budget."

In short, he was in favor of Lithuanian autonomy *within* the Soviet Union. And he had limits—what he called "red lines"—that could not be crossed.

"We can join [Sajudis] up to a certain point," he said, "but if someone speaks about leaving the Soviet Union, that would be considered stepping over the line. . . . Sovereignty within the Soviet Union—this is the only realistic sovereignty we can think of, considering how our economy is integrated into the framework of the Soviet Union."

Other steps that he rejected, other red lines, were "an independent currency, or withdrawal of Soviet troops from the territory of Lithuania."[12]

Nonetheless, while Brazauskas held the formal reins of power, he clearly understood that Sajudis was setting the agenda, and pushing the pace of change. He saw that he could govern only by forging a partnership with the moderate wing of Sajudis, and in fact he had met with their leaders just before he saw me. He was being pulled along by events, but he was desperately trying to set limits, to slow the pace, to avoid a fateful collision with Moscow.

At that stage, even the leaders of Sajudis were being coy about their ultimate goals. Like Brazauskas, most of them talked about "sovereignty," implying autonomy within the Soviet Union, rather than about "independence," meaning secession. For some, this was a matter of conviction; for others, it was a tactical movement.

"Are you for staying in the union or are you against that?" I asked Ozolas.

"This question is like asking whether God exists or not," he parried.

"Oh my God," I groaned. "This is life, not metaphysics."

"Well," he answered, "what I am trying to say is that there is no nation in the world that would willingly give up its independence. But to call for that now, when one can be decapitated for that very comment, would be politically unwise."[13]

GUDRI LAPÉ—"THE CLEVER FOX"

When I returned to Vilnius three months later, in June, and again in July, the tempo had quickened; Lithuanian nationalism had gained new momentum. The democratic mood was so much further advanced than it was in other parts of the Soviet Union that coming to Lithuania was like coming to another country. Talk of independence was in the air; Ozolas was no longer worried about being "decapitated" for discussing secession. The Lithuanian parliament had passed a sovereignty law giving it veto power over Soviet laws; it had proclaimed that all property in its territory should be Lithuanian, not Soviet. In Moscow, people were still arguing over the one-party system, but in Lithuania there was already a Democratic party, a Peasant party, a Christian Democratic party, an Independence League.

In one of the most dramatic developments, the Lithuanian Komsomol, or Young Communist League, made up of young people from high school to age thirty-five, severed its ties with Moscow in mid-June and declared itself an independent organization. To Lithuanians, this was an important symbolic break, a harbinger of things to come. My contacts at Lithuanian television, Audrius Braukyla and Algis Jacobinas, said that, as the Communist Party's youth arm, the Komsomol would not have acted without some encouragement from the Party itself. In defiance of Moscow officials who had come to impose the Soviet line, the Lithuanian Komsomol had renounced Marxism-Leninism as its official doctrine, endorsed freedom of conscience, admitted Catholic believers, and passed a program calling for Lithuania's becoming an "independent democratic state outside the Soviet Union."

There were many other straws in the wind. The Catholic Church now had a regular Sunday-morning slot on weekly television and had won official recognition of twelve holidays. Schoolboys were quitting the Communist Young Pioneers to join the Boy Scouts, which had just been reestablished. Lithuanians had formed their own Olympic Committee, and wanted to send a separate team to the 1992 games.

In dozens of ways, large and small, Lithuanians celebrated the rebirth of their national spirit. On June 24, St. John's Eve, Lithuanians outside of Kaunas sang and danced the whole night through, around a bonfire in the traditional pagan Festival of the Dew; for four decades this celebration had been banned by Communist authorities as a dangerous public gathering. In major towns and cities, statues and monuments commemorating pre-Communist heroes were restored. On Bald Hill, overlooking Vilnius, Lithuanians restored the Monument of the Three Crosses, erected in 1916 to martyrs in Lithuania's past and clandestinely dynamited by Stalinists one night in 1950. They also restored the famous statuary ripped down from the pediment of the central cathedral by the Stalinist regime.

In moves full of political significance, Communist names were stripped off the main streets and replaced with the old pre-occupation names. The sixty-mile highway connecting Vilnius and Kaunas, called Red Army Avenue by the Soviets, once again became Volunteer Avenue, honoring the Lithuanian volunteers who had defended the country's independence in 1918. In downtown Vilnius, the main street was no longer Lenin Prospekt but Gediminas Street, for Lithuania's most renowned grand duke.

If one individual personified this nationalist revival, it was Vytautas Landsbergis, chairman of Sajudis. At first glance, Landsbergis seemed an unlikely rival to Brazauskas, and an even more unlikely challenger to Gorbachev, the champion of media-age politics. Gorbachev radiates power, and Brazauskas is a lion of a man, but Landsbergis is a classic intellectual: a slightly stooped and otherworldly fifty-eight-year-old music professor, an unremarkable-looking figure in glasses, rumpled suits, sensible shoes, wispy mustache, and goatee. He teaches musicology at Vilnius Conservatory; next door is the Lithuanian KGB, in an almost identical building, which students impishly nicknamed "Conservatory Number Two."

Landsbergis projects neither power nor charisma, but rather the quiet, serious, reflective manner of an academic who has written nine books and is an accomplished pianist. Even on his cherished topic of Lithuanian independence, his speeches are dry, thoughtful, didactic discourses, rather than passionate orations. Everything about him is understated—except his message.

"He is not Ronald Reagan, he is not handsome, he is not smooth, he is not especially articulate," Romouldas Ozolas conceded. "But he is principled, and firm in his convictions and morality. And right now we do not have the luxury to choose a [chairman] who can both put forth ideas and have a pretty face."[14]

Landsbergis's hallmarks are a deep and abiding patriotism, a lifelong commitment to Lithuanian identity and the renaissance of Lithuanian culture, a tenacious devotion to the cause of the republic's independence. He comes from a long line of Lithuanian patriots; both his grandfathers fought Russian domination during the nineteenth century. In his artistically furnished five-room apartment, ample by Soviet standards, Landsbergis has an oil portrait of his maternal grandfather, Jonas Jablonskis, a linguist who ardently defended the Lithuanian language after it was outlawed by the czars. His paternal grandfather, Gabrielus Landsbergis, a journalist and playwright, opposed czarist rule as a writer for an underground newspaper that was published in Lithuanian; he wound up imprisoned and deported for his nationalist activities. During World War II, his father, Vytautas Landsbergis, Sr., a prominent architect and public figure during the period of Lithuanian independence, fought in the underground against the Nazi invaders.

The Soviet occupation came first, in June 1940, and even now, half a century later, it remains a vivid memory to Landsbergis, though he was only eight years old at the time. He remembers how his older brother, Gabrielus, looked at the first Soviet units, which evidently included a large contingent of soldiers from Central Asia, and whispered: "Look—the Mongols have arrived."[15]

During the Soviet-occupation years, Landsbergis did not become an outspoken dissident, though friends such as Ozolas emphasize that, unlike many Lithuanian intellectuals, Landsbergis "never submitted to the Soviet yoke." In fact, Landsbergis devoted his academic life to the quiet defense of Lithuanian culture. To Landsbergis, as to many Soviet intellectuals, culture and politics have always been inextricably connected; protecting one's national culture became a substitute for political activity. Landsbergis was part of a small, private, inbred world of Lithuanian intellectuals, mostly Catholics (though he is Protestant), whose primary goal was to nourish the flame of Lithuanian culture in the face of relentless Russification and Sovietization. His speciality was the Impressionist symphonies and paintings of the turn-of-the-century Lithuanian composer and painter Mikalojus Čiurlionis.

"You have to understand that, for many years, cultural activity meant political activity," Landsbergis observed. "By protecting our culture, we also protected our national identity. Otherwise, we would have been Russified—first in language and later in thinking."[16]

That same fierce and unyielding spirit brought him to the fore in Sajudis in November 1988, when Moscow was bent on splitting Sajudis and undercutting its growing strength. Landsbergis, with his quiet manner and strong convictions, became a unifying influence. Others looked up to his skill as a conciliator among various factions. Moreover, his calm exterior hid inner forcefulness, a strong sense of purpose and direction, and a surprisingly canny feel for public opinion and political strategy. He soon earned the nickname *Gudri Lapė*, which in Lithuanian means "clever fox."

"Landsbergis is very clever; he is a cool thinker," conceded a political adversary, senior Communist Party official Justas Paleckis. "He plays chess very well. He can see a lot of moves ahead. On the negative side, maybe he is too caught up in Lithuania before the Second World War, that cultural framework, that way of thinking. Maybe his life as a musician and theoretician left him with too little contact with Moscow and politicians abroad. Because he seems not to take into consideration events outside Lithuania."[17]

It is true that Landsbergis has tunnel vision when it comes to his dreams for Lithuania. Yet my first encounter with him, late one evening in July 1989 at the Vilnius airport, was on his return from America, where he had talked with members of Congress and visited Western embassies, and shortly before he was to head off for Sweden to try to further develop foreign support. The next day, over a breakfast of tea and toast in his kitchen, I asked Landsbergis about his goals for Lithuania.

"We are looking for Lithuania as an independent state, as we were up until 1940," he said. "I'd like to see all of Eastern Europe evolving toward a community of free, independent countries, and I'd like to see Lithuania, Latvia, and Estonia finding their places within this community."

"But is it possible to secede?" I asked.

"We do not need to secede. We are not a part of the Soviet Union, under international law. The annexation of 1940 gives no legal grounds for our being in the Soviet Union. We are a part in some practical way; we are ruled from Moscow. But we do not feel ourselves part of the Soviet Union."[18]

In short, Landsbergis and Sajudis argued that the Hitler-Stalin pact of 1939, which carved up Eastern Europe and handed the Baltic republics to the U.S.S.R., was an act of piracy; that the puppet governments which supposedly appealed for Soviet intervention were artificial creations of Moscow; and that the Soviet army illegally annexed Lithuania by force. By that same logic, the United States refused for half a century to recognize the incorporation of the Baltic states into the Soviet Union. Such logic was crucial, moreover, to Lithuania's challenge to Gorbachev. Landsbergis and Sajudis felt they were righting a historical wrong: Since the Baltics were never freely joined to the Soviet Union, they did not need to secede legally, but merely reclaim their independence. To expect more of them, according to Landsbergis, was a travesty of history and international law.

"If the world accepts one country being oppressed by another country, using aggression to establish some unjust status quo," Landsbergis said to me, "then violence will rule the world—not the principles of international law and justice."

"What will you do about the Soviet troops in Lithuania?" I asked. "I have seen Sajudis demonstrations and petitions demanding, 'Occupiers, Go Home.'"

On this touchy issue, Landsbergis had devised a shrewd strategy for asserting Lithuanian sovereignty, without dismissing Moscow's defense concerns. He did not demand immediate withdrawal, pointing out to me that Poland was a sovereign nation, with Soviet forces on its territory—but by Polish consent. The first step, therefore, was to get Moscow to acknowledge that its forces were in Lithuania only by permission of a sovereign Lithuanian government.

"We are now planning a charter project that will define the presence of Soviet troops in Lithuania as temporary," he said, "and that will enable us to set the conditions for their presence here."

Lithuania's economic survival as an independent country was another big question mark. The republic was known for high-quality farm products, electronics, and other light industry, but as of 1989 its "exports" went overwhelmingly to the rest of the Soviet Union. I wondered how far Lithuania would go in cutting these economic ties. And how would little Lithuania survive economically in a world where West European countries were combining into Europe '92?

"As of now, Lithuania is only a colonial adjunct of the Soviet economy; it cannot administer its own economy," Landsbergis answered. "Lithuania can never be isolated from its neighbors. It was never our intention to cut all connections with the Soviet Union. We will use our natural resources, our normal economy, in connection with the Soviet Union, but we will also look for new avenues to widen our contacts with the West."

One major concern raised by the Kremlin was the fate of the Russians, Poles, and other nationalities who comprised 20 percent of Lithuania's population. I knew that Lithuanians resented longtime Russian residents who had never bothered to learn the Lithuanian language, and they wanted to stop further immigration. The Lithuanian parliament was considering a new law to confer citizenship and the right to vote only on ethnic Lithuanians, or residents of five years or more. On immigration, Sajudis advocated that enterprises pay a 20,000-ruble head tax for each new worker brought into the republic. My question was whether Landsbergis and Sajudis wanted the Russians to go home.

"We don't want to drive anybody out," Landsbergis said. "We're not trying to stop people from coming here, but we want to control our immigration. We want to know what is happening to our demography, to foresee the trends."

Finally, how did Landsbergis size up Brazauskas?

"I think he's a good person and his intentions are good," Landsbergis replied. "We see his outlook and his political line changing."

It was true that on some topics Brazauskas was shifting into line with Sajudis; he agreed with the head tax on new workers; he had accepted a de facto multiparty system; and he was discussing the idea of separating Lithuania's Communist Party from Moscow's. Moreover, he was now openly talking about partnership with Sajudis—"we listen to their advice; they're helpful to our government," he told me. But he was not ready to share power formally. There were still major differences.

When I saw Brazauskas at his summer vacation home near the Lithuanian port of Klaipėda in July 1989, he took sharp issue with Sajudis's petitions calling for the removal of Soviet troops. That was utterly "unrealistic," short of general disarmament in Europe, he said. In terms of the economy, he had shifted in favor of a separate Lithuanian currency, as a step toward greater financial autonomy, but he differed with Landsbergis about Lithuania's ability to survive economically as a separate nation. He accepted the Sajudis view that the "notorious" Hitler-Stalin pact of 1939 violated international law, but insisted Sajudis could not simply turn the clock back.

"We have to take the present reality into consideration, the existence of the Soviet Union," he said to me. "It is impossible to start from 1939 again." In short, eight months before Lithuania would declare its independence, Brazauskas was strongly opposed to secession. His strategy was to push for transformation of the Soviet Union into "a union of free republics, a union of free states."[19]

And Brazauskas was growing impatient with Moscow. The pressure of being pulled in opposite directions by Gorbachev and Sajudis was getting to him. He could feel the need to deliver tangible signs of autonomy, especially on the economy, in order to check the growing sentiment for independence. But Moscow was not moving fast enough, and he feared that Gorbachev and his advisers did not really grasp "the political importance" of their rigidity: how Moscow's refusal to relax tight central control was fueling nationalist impatience in Lithuania.

To me, Brazauskas sounded less hopeful of holding the line for Moscow and the Communist Party than he had in March. I took his mood as a measure of how rapidly he felt events were moving, and how little time he felt there was to prevent a fateful collision between Gorbachev and Lithuanian nationalism.

Other Lithuanians, I found, were watching Brazauskas closely. They were asking, "In the showdown, will Brazauskas be Moscow's man or ours?"

RUSSIAN ISLANDS IN A BALTIC SEA

As Landsbergis had indicated, an especially delicate problem for Baltic leaders was posed by the Russians living in their midst: their long-term future in the region and their political reaction to Baltic self-determination. They could disrupt the whole trend of events.

The problem was substantial: 2.6 million of the 8 million people living in the Baltic republics in 1989 were non-Baltic peoples—1.6 million Russians and a million Poles, Ukrainians, Byelorussians, and others.[20] The backbone of the region's work force in heavy industry, especially in Latvia, was Russian; Russian and Ukrainian directors and engineers ran the biggest plants. In general, the loyalties of these groups have run strongly to Moscow; drastic political change, let alone secession, threatened the good life these people enjoyed in the Baltic region, and that made them unhappy.

Baltic political activists were acutely sensitive to the dangerous consequences of violence between their peoples and Russians. Leaders of all three Baltic movements went to great lengths to avert, limit, and defuse physical clashes, fearing that any incident could be seized upon by hardliners in the Kremlin as a pretext to order Soviet troops to crush Baltic nationalism, as Gorbachev had done with the Azerbaijanis in Baku. I heard of several cases where leaders of Sajudis or the Estonian Popular Front moved swiftly to keep small incidents from escalating, even persuading their own people to drop charges in order to keep nasty sparks from spreading.

In fact, while it frequently angered Gorbachev that Baltic nationalists were challenging his pace of reform, threatening, as he saw it, not only the fate of *perestroika* but his own political survival, the Baltic movements spared him the bloody carnage of the Caucasus and Central Asia. For the politics of Baltic nationalism were cool, not hot, and cool politics kept political violence to a minimum.

Yet even without bloodshed, there were interethnic tensions: Some Russians spoke of encountering animosities on a personal level; large numbers were roiled by the sudden requirement that they learn Lithuanian, Estonian, and Latvian as the new languages of government and commerce; many were fearful of being forced to leave the region, to give up good jobs and living conditions; others worried that if they stayed, they would be denied equality. The state-run media in Moscow, in making a case against Baltic sovereignty, portrayed Russians and other Slavic peoples in the Baltics as persecuted minorities. Russian workers, teachers, and industrial managers in the Baltics formed their own political organizations—Interfront in Estonia and Edinstvo ("Unity") in Lithuania and Latvia.

In February 1989, Edinstvo held a rally of eighty thousand people in Vilnius to protest demands by Sajudis to have Lithuanian replace Russian as the republic's official language. A month later in the Estonian capital of Tallinn, Interfront turned out fifty thousand people against "creeping counterrevolution undermining socialism in Estonia and in the Baltic region."[21] By June, Edinstvo was urging Moscow to set up a commission to investigate Lithuanian steps toward establishing sovereignty, and in July, thousands of Russian factory and shipyard workers in Tallinn went on strike to protest Estonian demands for economic autonomy. Some of the protests only hardened Baltic feelings against Russians.

I came across a microcosm of these problems in the Lithuanian town of Snieckus, and at the nearby Ignalina nuclear reactor.

Situated seventy miles northeast of Vilnius, Snieckus is a little island of Russians in the heart of the most beautiful lake region in Lithuania—a huge open region nicknamed "Lithuanian Switzerland." With its massive trucks and huge highway signs in Cyrillic (differing from the normal Latin script on highway signs), Snieckus rises up out of nothing, a town created from scratch thirteen years ago, a product of Soviet industrialization and colonization. It has become a privileged enclave of the prestigious Ministry of Atomic Power—a special economic zone, one of the choicest residential areas in the Soviet Union. Its high-rise apartment blocks are well built, attractively laid out, and comfortably furnished; its stores are better stocked than those in normal cities; it has far more cars per capita than Vilnius, and a nearby lake with a beach; there is a huge fancy high-tech disco, and a $5 million Olympic-sized gym.

The *raison d'être* for Snieckus is the Ignalina nuclear reactor. Since 1977, some thirty-five thousand people have come there to build the reactor, work at the reactor, or support the work force—95 percent of them are Russians or Russian-speaking.[22]

All across the Soviet Union, there are literally hundreds of industrial projects like Ignalina. To Russians and to the "center" in Moscow, these are proud symbols of economic progress bestowed by the Kremlin on local regions. But to Lithuanians, Snieckus is an unwanted Russian colony, an ethnic invasion, and the Ignalina nuclear plant an ecological disaster, sullying one of the most unspoiled regions of all Lithuania. To them Snieckus is a symbol of precisely what they hate about Soviet control: a conquering power seizing the choicest terrain for its own purposes, without the consent of the local nationality.

After the nuclear accident at Chernobyl in April 1986, the plant at Ignalina, built on the Chernobyl model, became a target of the Lithuanian environmental movement, a core element of Sajudis. Initially, Moscow planned for four 1,500-megawatt reactors at Ignalina, to provide electric power for Lithuania, Latvia, and parts of Byelorussia. Two were in operation by the time of the Chernobyl accident, and a third was under construction. But grass-roots politics intervened: A string of protests climaxed on September 17, 1988, when six thousand Lithuanians formed a human ring around the entire facility. They demanded a halt in construction, and inspection of the two operating reactors, because of a recent fire and reported radiation leaks. Under this pressure, Moscow suspended construction of the third unit.[23]

By the time I visited Ignalina in July 1989, Anatoly Khromchenko, the plant director, doubted that the third and fourth reactor units would ever be built. Despite the privileges that Snieckus offered, Khromchenko said he was having trouble luring young atomic specialists from the top institutes in Moscow, Leningrad, and Sverdlovsk to work there, and some of his younger engineers were leaving. Lithuanians had practically stopped working at the plant; they comprised only 3 percent of the plant's two thousand workers.

"What's the problem?" I asked.

"Maybe they're scared," he replied, implying fear of radiation hazards.

"Isn't it also because of the political tensions?" I ventured.

"Well, certainly, the tension is there," Khromchenko conceded. "One can feel it in the press all around: Russians are called occupiers; other terms are also used. They suggest we get out. The tension is definitely there."[24]

Silver-haired and fifty-six, Khromchenko had been in Snieckus since 1977, but he said that he had never bothered to learn Lithuanian. Now, with Lithuanian become the official language, he had set up a course for his two hundred top managers and engineers, and he was studying the language himself—slowly and with great difficulty.

Other Russians told me that Snieckus had lost the once-optimistic morale of a high-prestige project.

"We're worried," said Aleksandr Zharik, a blond activist in Edinstvo who had denounced Lithuanian activism in a letter to the Soviet press. "There is a campaign against Russians here in Lithuania. We are accused of many things. . . .

"When I came here in 1986, local people came and talked to us as friends, as fellow citizens of the Soviet Union. They treated us as equals. But recently, as the national resurgence began, some 'comrades' began to feel superior to other nationalities, and they told us, 'The Russians should go.' . . . Once, there were leaflets here, calling for killing Russians, but we responded calmly. Nobody was worried. It happened on a weekend. Everyone went fishing. Nobody wanted to fight. Our people are very responsible. They have common sense. They can face a difficult situation. . . . So, we are going to stay. It remains to be seen what will happen in the long run, but so far we'll stay. We built this town and we're going to live here."[25]

Not only are Soviets much less accustomed than Americans to career mobility, but Snieckus is a good deal that is hard to match elsewhere.

"To leave this place means starting all over again from scratch," Valery

Antipyevt, another worker, pointed out. "It's not only a question of getting a job, but you have to arrange for an apartment, move all your possessions. It's not that simple.

"I've been working here twelve years. Where should I go? I don't have the slightest idea." He shook his head. "And to achieve such a high standard of living, it's not so simple. People have apartments here, *dachas*, garages. Everyone has his vegetable garden, a little orchard, a good harvest. It would be hard to give up this land. I'm afraid people won't give it up."

Like the reactor boss, Antipyevt was having trouble learning Lithuanian, and he clearly did not like it. "It's pretty hard," he said. "You have to have a lot of free time in the evening to prepare your homework. And still, two times a week are not enough to learn it."

For Russians, who are accustomed to setting the rules, to being at home anywhere in the Soviet Union and to expecting the locals to speak their language and to be grateful to them, it was a shock to be told that they had to adjust to local conditions. The new terms of life were not only abhorrent; they were also hard to comprehend. Suddenly the Russians felt like strangers, aliens in what they saw as their own country.

"Until recently," Antipyevt said, "we could never imagine that we could become some sort of a foreign body among the Lithuanian people."[26]

COLLISION COURSE

That same gulf of widening incomprehension separated Gorbachev and Moscow from the Baltic states, especially Lithuania, as 1989 wore on. The Russian leadership in Moscow—and Gorbachev's team was predominantly Russian—simply could not grasp that they were now viewed as foreigners by the overwhelming majority of people in the Baltic republics. They could not fathom how rapidly the desire for sovereignty had become a determination to achieve independence.

But there were ample signals of "independence fever" in the Baltics in the fall of 1989. The most powerful and dramatic was the massive demonstration on August 23—the fiftieth anniversary of the Hitler-Stalin pact.

For half a century, Moscow had denied the existence of any secret deal between Hitler and Stalin to divide up Eastern Europe and the Baltics. Throughout most of 1989, the three Baltic republics had been gathering documents from the German government, calling for an official Soviet investigation into the Hitler-Stalin pact, and issuing appeals for official renunciation of the secret protocol on the Baltics.

Five days before the demonstration, in an evident effort to placate Baltic nationalists, Politburo member Aleksandr Yakovlev told *Pravda* that "without a doubt," Hitler and Stalin had secretly and illegally divided up Eastern Europe, including the Baltics. But Yakovlev, who headed a parliamentary commission investigating the matter, contended that the secret pact had no significance for the future of the Baltic republics because, he claimed, the Baltic states had freely joined the Soviet Union.[27] He was alluding to the actions of puppet governments set up by the Soviets.

Six weeks later, twenty-two members of Yakovlev's twenty-six-member commission issued a report declaring the Hitler-Stalin pact "null and void" and asserting that the panel's findings had been "distorted" by the Party leadership, obviously meaning Yakovlev.[28]

On August 23, more than one million people formed a human chain 370 miles long: a "freedom chain" linking the three Baltic capitals. People joined hands and passed on the word "Freedom" until it had traveled, from one person to the next, the entire distance from Tallinn (Estonia) in the north, through Riga (Latvia) in the middle, to Vilnius (Lithuania) in the south. The participation of one million people meant virtually one out of every five Latvians, Lithuanians, and Estonians took part—someone from every family.

The Kremlin's reaction was thundering and abusive, an explosion of fury at Baltic "extremists," ignoring the fact that there was such mass participation in a peaceful event. In a long, stinging statement, the Communist Party Central Committee accused Baltic nationalists of exploiting "democracy and openness" in order to incite "the peoples of the Baltics to secede from the Soviet Union." And it added an ominous warning: "Things have gone far. . . . The fate of the Baltics is in serious danger. People should know into what abyss they are being pushed by nationalist leaders. The consequences could be disastrous . . . if the nationalists manage to achieve their goals. The very viability of the Baltic nations could be called into question." The Kremlin also knocked its own minions in the region—the Party and government leaders, who were accused of "losing heart" and "playing up to nationalist sentiments."[29]

The statement was an obvious throwback to the old-style Kremlin ideological denunciations, and since Gorbachev was out of Moscow on summer vacation, the initial temptation in the Baltics was to blame it on Yegor Ligachev, then leader of the hard-line Politburo faction. But within days, spokesmen announced that Gorbachev had personally approved the statement. At the time, Gorbachev was under fire from hard-liners, and he may have gone along to appease them; but he was also obviously angered at the Baltic challenge. In response, Baltic Communist leaders like Lithuania's Algirdas Brazauskas tried to find a middle position; nationalists like Vytautas Landsbergis held their ground.

"This statement was an attempt to frighten us with political terror and to ignite hostilities against us," Landsbergis said. "But we long ago decided that this is something we must do—fight for our independence. We're not extremist, and we are not violent, but we are determined."[30]

Other issues were pressing Brazauskas to align more closely with the nationalists. One was the military service of Baltic youth. Scores of young Lithuanian recruits, drafted into the Soviet army, were deserting: They were coming home with terrible stories of beatings and abuse by other soldiers, especially Central Asians, who took Moscow's anger out on individual Lithuanian recruits. In one sensational case, Arturo Sokolauskas, a young Lithuanian, had been forced by other soldiers to stand guard for seventy-two hours, without sleep; in addition, he had been beaten, abused, and gang-raped. Crazed by their hazing, Sokolauskas had shot all eight dead. In a case given national publicity, he had gone on trial and been committed to a mental institution; his father had declared that he would not let his younger son serve in the army. The incident had occurred in 1988, but the issue was kept alive by a documentary circulated in 1989 by Lithuanian filmmaker Algimantas Zukas.[31]

Sajudis and the Baltic popular fronts were demanding that Baltic recruits be given the right to serve on their home territory. Brazauskas took up the issue with Defense Minister Dmitri Yazov, but Yazov would not agree,[32] further roiling Lithuanian opinion.

On the economy, Brazauskas was moving closer to Sajudis, constantly pressing for economic autonomy, for each republic to control all property within its territory, for the power to make investment decisions and take administrative command of local industry away from the ministries in Moscow. Prices were another bugaboo: The Baltic republics felt that Moscow's pricing system worked to their disadvantage. Moreover, the Baltic peoples knew their standard of living was higher than that elsewhere in the country, they could see the Soviet economy sinking, and they did not want to be dragged down. Kazimiera Prunskiene, a Sajudis leader appointed by Brazauskas as Lithuania's deputy premier for economics, shared Lithuanian anxieties with Pavel Bunich, a reform economist in Moscow in the fall of 1989.

"If we knew that in two or three years the Soviet economy would turn around and we could live like real people, we would stay in the Soviet Union," Prunskiene told Bunich. "But we don't believe that you'll be able to get on your feet in two or three years. We think we will have to go independent, leave the Soviet Union. We understand that the first couple of years will be very hard for us. But after that, we will reorganize our economy and get on our feet. We'll be all right."[33]

All these pressures were working on Brazauskas. He was walking a tightrope between Lithuania's yearnings for independence and Moscow's fulminations against "nationalist hysteria" and "separatism." Through the fall of 1989, as Communist rule in Eastern Europe was crumbling, there was a steady flow of defectors from the Communist Party in Lithuania. Brazauskas kept trying to persuade Moscow to give the Baltics flexibility; Gorbachev was letting Eastern Europe go, but holding on tight to the Baltics. He summoned Brazauskas and the other two Baltic Communist Party leaders to a face-to-face session on September 14 and laid down the law: no split in the Soviet Communist Party.[34] Economic reforms proposed in the Supreme Soviet left the Baltics far from satisfied.

The final straw was the Communist Party Central Committee plenum on September 19–20. "Talk of secession is an irresponsible game," Gorbachev declared. "Those calling for it are no more than adventurists."[35]

Gorbachev used the occasion to spell out what the minority republics could *not* do, not what they could do. By scheduling the plenum, he had raised expectations of new liberal measures, especially for the Baltics; but now he dashed those hopes. He appeased Party hard-liners by making big concessions to the Russian republic, the bastion of Old Guard strength, at the expense of other republics. And he yielded to the arguments of Prime Minister Ryzhkov and his central planners, who opposed giving more autonomy and economic power to the Baltic republics and other minority regions. For Communist leaders in the Baltics, the session was an unmitigated disaster; it proved that Sajudis and the popular fronts had been right: It was impossible to trust Moscow. That plenum further radicalized opinion in the Baltics.

In the immediate aftermath, Brazauskas staved off the radical faction in his own party that wanted a split from Moscow. The Lithuanian Party was constantly under fire—for the repressions and deportations of Lithuanians after World War II, for the heavy hand of Soviet rule, for the Soviet military presence, for economic failures, for suppression of Lithuanian culture, for constantly bowing to Moscow's will. As pressures from below mounted, Politburo members were on the phone from Moscow hammering Brazauskas to stay in line; Gorbachev exhorted him to maintain Party unity.

"I can't give you the exact quote," Brazauskas told me later, "but everything led to the conclusion that the Party must be one, only unity; there can't be organizational changes. It would weaken our Party in Lithuania. We would lose authority."[36]

Brazauskas was on a knife edge, facing the most difficult and politically dangerous step of his career: crossing one of his own "red lines" by leading the Lithuanian Communist Party to declare its separation from the Communist Party of the Soviet Union. On December 20, he could hold out no longer, and led the breakaway from Moscow.

"We had to decide if we were going to depart from the trends among the people or move with them," Brazauskas explained. "And what else does the Party live for? It has to be for the people. We were deeply convinced that . . . only in this way could we become a political force that people could believe in. . . . You can't constantly answer [accusations] and feel guilty. At some point, you have to do something."

The morning after, the wrath of Moscow fell on Brazauskas. Gorbachev poured forth a string of public denunciations. The private phone calls, Brazauskas told me, were even more blistering—not only from Gorbachev but from other enraged members of the Politburo, who cursed Brazauskas as a traitor.

"I had to listen . . . to things that I had never heard before in my entire fifty-seven years," he told me. As he remembered those phone calls, his entire face and neck reddened.

It is easy for Westerners to underestimate the importance of the Lithuanian Communist Party's break with Moscow. But for many Lithuanians, that declaration of independence was a prelude, a springboard toward political independence for Lithuania as a whole.

Gorbachev understood the stakes, and after his fury had subsided, he flew to Lithuania in a bold and daring effort at personal persuasion. As Lithuanians pointed out, this was the first time a Soviet leader had visited the republic in fifty years. Gorbachev made a desperate plea against secession: "We must look for a solution together. If somebody succeeds in splitting us apart that means trouble. . . . You remember that."

In his topcoat, gray fedora, and scarf, and with his gray-faced wife, Raisa, always at his side, Gorbachev barnstormed across Lithuania like a Western politician, engaging in give-and-take with the street crowds. He prodded workers to think twice about their economic future alone in the world; he lectured people across the hood of his car, reminding them that their actions could upset his entire *perestroika*, even topple him from power.

"There is no absolute freedom in this," he cautioned. "We have embarked on this path, and I am the one who chose to go ahead with it. My own personal fate is linked to that choice. The two states must live together."[37]

But his jawboning did not seem to move the Lithuanian people, and by the end of his visit, Sajudis leaders thought Gorbachev and the Politburo were bending their way, preparing to accept independence. Yuri Maslyukov, a centrist in the Soviet Politburo, told factory workers that Lithuanians had the legal right to secede under the Soviet constitution, and that force would not be used to prevent them. In an interview with Swedish television, Yegor Ligachev, the leading Politburo hard-liner, ruled out the use of force. "Tanks cannot solve such problems," he said.[38] Gorbachev himself noted the emergence of multiple political parties in Lithuania, and while that was still not technically permitted, he dismissed it as no "tragedy." But he urged Lithuanians to wait for Moscow to pass a law outlining procedures for secession—a move denounced by Sajudis as "a propagandistic trap" designed to stall the process, and sure to be loaded with conditions that would make actual secession impossible.

"[Gorbachev] understood after being in Lithuania that Lithuania will not be part of the Soviet Union," Romouldas Ozolas told me later. "Before that, he thought it was the opinion of only a few people— 'extremist professors,' he called us. But after he was in Lithuania, and after he talked with the workers, he was convinced that Lithuania would behave only the way that we had said."[39]

In short, Gorbachev's mission seemed too little, too late. For Lithuanians, the question about independence was no longer "if," but "when."

Lithuania, like other republics, was due to elect a new parliament in February and March 1990. Sajudis, campaigning on a platform of swift independence, won seventy-two of the ninety races settled in this first round of balloting; the second-round races were staggered, but enough had been settled by March 10 for Sajudis to control 97 of the 141 seats in the parliament, and for the Brazauskas wing of the Communist Party to have twenty-five seats. What is more, Brazauskas had now crossed the final red line: He was now on record for independence. The die was cast.

On March 10, the day before the new parliament was to convene, Brazauskas and Landsbergis met with their partisans. Ideology seemed to have been stood on its head: The elite of the Vilnius Communist Party, summoned by Brazauskas to the city's modern, Scandinavian-style symphony hall, looked like prosperous, well-fed bourgeois businessmen in their well-cut suits; the Seimas, or council of Sajudis, meeting in a plainer auditorium, looked like a much less well-heeled collection of college professors and political upstarts. The proletariat was nowhere to be seen.

Brazauskas prepared his legions for a new role—giving up power and going into the opposition. "I would like to invite all not to be saddened, not to be depressed, but to feel that we are an honorable opposition, that there is room for honorable opposition," he told them.[40] He declared his own intention to vote, the next day, for independence.

But in a long and thoughtful interview, he told me that the prospect of an economic squeeze by Moscow worried him. "People are very upset, very nervous, high-strung," he said. "It's very dangerous for society, and people don't see their future. What's going to happen next? Where are we going? What are we going to get? What are our relations with our neighbors going to be? Is this going to elicit some countermeasures?"[41]

At a packed meeting of Sajudis, Landsbergis told the nationalists to be ready to govern and to hold together. He was, typically, calm and professorial.

That last day seemed unusually quiet for the eve of a revolution. I talked with Landsbergis; he was too exhausted, too busy with last-minute questions about parliamentary procedure to be elated. Amid other rumblings, there were reports that the Soviets were going to seize the port of Klaipėda on the Baltic Sea. Landsbergis went to the radio station to appeal for calm from all major communities, broadcasting first in Lithuanian, then in Russian and Polish; he was accomplished in all three languages.

Gorbachev had not used the two months since his visit to Vilnius to pass any law on secession, but there was strong likelihood that he would do so at the Congress of People's Deputies on March 12. The Lithuanians wanted to act first.

Lithuania's new Independence Day, March 11, went according to script. Crowds cheered Brazauskas and Landsbergis as they came for the opening session of the parliament. Both were nominated for the chairmanship, the new leader of Lithuania. It was a choice between experience in dealing with Moscow and a clean break with the past. By what amounted to a 91–38 party-line vote, Landsbergis was elected. As Landsbergis proceeded to the dais, Brazauskas looked oversized and out of place at his small desk, seven rows back. He blushed, gritted his teeth, and gamely applauded. It was a hard day for him.

Weeks later, Gorbachev insinuated that the Lithuanian declaration of independence was done in the dark of night, as if it were an act of stealth. That was not the case. The whole procedure was wide open, to the Soviet press as well as to Lithuanian and foreign journalists. The actual vote came at close to 11 P.M., not out of any clandestine motive but because the assembly, heavy with college professors, took forever with technicalities. Under Landsbergis's tutoring, the delegates were careful not simply to declare independence, but also to reassert Lithuania's former independence and to revive the 1938 constitution of the Republic of Lithuania.

At the climactic moment, the delegates broke into applause at their own daring—in defiance of Moscow, of Gorbachev, of Soviet might. As a red, yellow, and green Lithuanian flag was unfurled behind the dais, the entire hall rose and solemnly sang the old Lithuanian national anthem. Landsbergis shyly turned to hug the new vice chairmen of the assembly, and the hall broke into cheers of "Free Lithuania! Free Estonia! Free Latvia!"

Outside in the courtyard, where Lithuanian flags were snapping in a sharp Baltic wind, workmen removed the Soviet hammer-and-sickle seal from the main doorway of the parliament building, and a crowd of several hundred people, who had braved hours of cold for this moment, began stomping on the Soviet emblems. Landsbergis emerged into what seemed his first terrifying moment as the new leader of Lithuania. I saw his smile turn into a look of anxiety as the crowd surged forward to engulf him with applause and flowers. A ring of guards, who had wanted to ferry him through the crowd, gave up and ushered him into the building. Long into the night, people in the courtyard mobbed individual deputies with joy as they came out, and families hugged each other.

Gorbachev's reaction was not immediate; in Moscow, he was preoccupied with establishing the new office of the Soviet presidency and with getting himself elected. Then, on March 15, four days after the Lithuanian declaration, he pushed through the Congress of People's Deputies a secession law requiring a popular referendum, a five-year wait, and final approval by the all-union parliament, a condition that nationalists everywhere regarded as intolerable because it gave Moscow a veto over their right of self-determination.

Gorbachev demanded that Lithuania revoke its declaration of independence, and with that began the denunciations and the pressures that Brazauskas and Landsbergis had anticipated: Soviet tanks rumbling through the streets of Vilnius, leaflets dropped from Soviet army helicopters warning of disaster and telling Lithuanians to turn back, the bloody seizure of Lithuanian youths who had deserted the army and taken refuge in a hospital, the occupation of Communist Party buildings, and the seizure of a Lithuanian printing plant. Soviet guards were posted at industrial installations, which were ordered by Moscow not to obey the new Lithuanian government. On April 18, Moscow turned off Soviet oil supplies to Lithuania's only refinery at Mazeikiai, and on the next day it cut off 85 percent of Lithuania's supply of natural gas. As the economic embargo widened, Lithuanians took to riding bicycles, scrimping on fuel and supplies, and quietly working out barter trade for some supplies with the cities of Moscow, Leningrad, Lvov, and parts of Siberia where democratic groups had won control of local governments in the March 1990 elections.

At times, the siege teetered perilously close to a violent crackdown, which Gorbachev told the United States he was holding in check. Undoubtedly he was restraining some hard-liners, but the campaign of pressure against Lithuania was his policy. It had all the earmarks of his earlier damnation of the August 23 demonstration and the December 20 Communist Party break. Gorbachev has a temper; he has often reacted sharply to what he takes as a challenge to his personal authority and his own political timetable. His response to the Lithuanian crisis followed that pattern: He accused the Lithuanians of trapping him with a unilateral act and savaged them for not taking time to negotiate—although he had been reluctant to consider independence, let alone negotiate the terms for secession. He insisted that his law on secession, passed *ex post facto*, be followed.

Moreover, Gorbachev's public blustering evinced a sense of personal affront at Lithuania's action and Landsbergis, with his quiet defiance and stinging quip that "the spirit of Stalin is walking the Kremlin again"; this obviously enraged Gorbachev, and he was bent on both putting down this upstart and preventing Lithuania's political sedition from starting a chain reaction in other republics. He was determined not to allow a precedent.

The Lithuanian leaders had expected some such reaction from Gorbachev; where Landsbergis had miscalculated was in the reaction of the West. He had counted on diplomatic recognition from some countries, hopefully the United States. He had proven himself a master at marshaling the moral force of public opinion inside Lithuania, first against Brazauskas and then against Gorbachev. He understood that he was in an unequal fight against the might of the Kremlin, and he had counted on outside opinion—both in other Soviet republics and in the West—to offset that might. But he had not prepared the ground well enough. The other Baltic republics did not join or applaud the Lithuanians; instead, they initially criticized them for excessive haste. In the West, President Bush and other leaders offered neither recognition nor clear-cut support. The White House kept public pressure on Gorbachev not to use large-scale military force, although it tolerated lesser moves; and Landsbergis irked Western leaders by comparing their hesitancy to the appeasement of Hitler by the Western powers at Munich in 1938.

It was Kazimiera Prunskiene, newly installed as prime minister, who won some outside support when she was sent in mid-April on a mission abroad to secure foreign oil. Denmark received her as a head of government; Norway and Canada dickered with her about ways to supply oil; important committees in the United States Congress, where conservatives threatened to tie trade concessions for Gorbachev to an end of his Lithuanian embargo, gave her a prestigious reception. Finally, President Bush, trying to avoid angering Gorbachev, but needing some way to show his involvement, received Prunskiene as a private citizen.

She was submitted to the indignity of a personal search of her purse and belongings at the front gate, and Mr. Bush fended off her entreaty to act as a mediator between Moscow and Vilnius. Nonetheless, her long and widely reported hour with the president constituted a kind of de facto White House political recognition.[42] In London, Prime Minister Thatcher saw her too. Prunskiene, the epitome of competence and pragmatic pursuit of her goals, seemed to succeed where Landsbergis had not. She rose in popularity at home, and slowly Lithuania's isolation eased.

In May, the Baltic states revived their solid front, putting more pressure on Gorbachev. Estonia and Latvia made their own declarations of independence, though more cautiously than Lithuania, promising Moscow they would negotiate and take their time. Moldavia's parliament gave a vote of support to Lithuania. Then came endorsements from some Moscow and Leningrad political liberals. What finally turned the tide was the election on May 29 of Gorbachev's political nemesis, the radical populist Boris Yeltsin, as chairman of the parliament of the Russian republic. While Gorbachev was in Washington meeting with President Bush, Yeltsin met with Landsbergis and other Baltic national leaders, promising them support and trade, if necessary. Yeltsin wasted no time in pushing through the Russian republic parliament a declaration of Russian "sovereignty" that made the laws of the republic superior to the all-union laws passed by the federal parliament.

In short, what had begun as an isolated challenge from Lithuania had broadened so much that Gorbachev was forced to the bargaining table. Yeltsin's action threatened Gorbachev's base of power in the largest, most populous, most important republic in the union. Once again, Gorbachev showed his capacity to shift his position in the face of new realities.

On June 12, some ninety-three days after the Lithuanian declaration of independence, he sat down with his erstwhile challengers, Yeltsin and the three leaders of the Baltic republics, as well as with the leaders of the other eleven republics, and began to spell out plans for a much looser Soviet confederation. He softened his demands for Baltic political retractions. No longer did he insist that they revoke their declarations of independence; he would settle for temporary suspension of those declarations and the laws passed to implement them. And in a gesture toward Lithuania, Prime Minister Ryzhkov told Prunskiene that Moscow was allowing an increase of natural-gas supplies to a Lithuanian fertilizer plant.[43]

Gorbachev finally reopened the oil pipeline and ended his other trade sanctions against the rebellious Lithuanians on June 30, the day after their parliament had agreed to suspend their declaration of independence for one hundred days. They had acted after Gorbachev had pledged to start negotiations on independence.[44] Later, he tried to lure them into joining discussions on turning the Soviet Union into a looser federation, but all three Baltic republics refused to take part. They felt they had Gorbachev moving on the track toward their independence and they were not prepared to compromise, especially after Lithuania had faced down his embargo.[45]

Step by step, Gorbachev had been forced to give ground, but in the process he had made Lithuania an object lesson to other republics; they could not merely declare independence and expect to exit the Soviet Union. At least in the short run, his tactic worked; other republics issued declarations of "sovereignty" but not "independence," indicating that they wanted more freedom—but within the union. For the Baltics, Gorbachev seemed to be saying that if all his enticements failed, he was willing to make an exception and to break the taboo on secession.

CHAPTER 17

BACKLASH IN MOTHER RUSSIA

"Russophobia has spread into the
Baltic countries and Georgia, and it is
penetrating into other republics. . . . [W]e
are tired of being the scapegoats,
of enduring the slurs and the treachery.
. . . Live with us or not, just as you
like, but do not behave arrogantly
toward us."[1]

—Valentin Rasputin
Russian Writer
June 1989

"We need a holy, dynamic Russia. . . . It
is bad . . . to have a weak, lame Russia. A
great country cannot have a weak center,
a weak heart. Our culture is sick."[2]

—Stanislav Kunyayev
Russian Editor
September 1989

In Mother Russia, at the heart of the Soviet empire, the rising demands
and aspirations of the minority republics in Central Asia, the Caucasus,
and especially in the Baltics, have stirred a backlash of ethnic Russian
nationalism.

Under some Newtonian law of politics, actions at the fringes of the

Russian empire have created a strong reaction at the core. In Moscow, and across the central Russian heartland, I encountered bitterness, an exaggerated sense of grievance among Russians that the Lilliputians were pushing the Russian Gulliver around, and that this was grossly unfair, because under Soviet rule, Russia proper had sacrificed and suffered more than all the others had.

Long before Gorbachev came to power, some Russians were working quietly at Russia's cultural revival. In the seventies under Brezhnev, I had seen the restoration of a few famous churches and historical monuments. Even Stalin, who destroyed so much of the Russian past, had preserved the Hermitage Museum and the czarist palaces in Leningrad. He was playing on the Russian autocratic tradition, resuscitating Peter the Great and even Ivan the Terrible to justify his own imperial tyranny. Later had come the Russian environmental movement, and the prose of the "village writers"— the *derevenshchiki,* who had celebrated the purity of life in the Russian countryside, writing in a natural prose style free of the cant of Soviet ideology. Under Gorbachev, these trends had accelerated. But by 1989, something new surfaced—a sharp edge of resentment among fervent Russian nationalists, a reaction against what they called "the little peoples." Since the seventies, a small band of writers, painters, filmmakers, and other intellectuals had from time to time insisted that a cultural, economic, and political injustice had been done to Russia. But political controls suppressed these feelings among the larger Russian public. Now these smoldering Russian grievances appeared quite openly among farmers, workers, and pensioners, in the military, and in the upper reaches of the Communist Party, where open Russian nationalism had previously been taboo.

One rainy Saturday morning in October 1989, I was interviewing Yuri Prokofyev, Moscow's Communist Party first secretary. We were discussing the difficulties of *perestroika.* When I mentioned that Russians were complaining that current political trends favored minority nationalities and were unfair to the Russian republic, the largest and most powerful of the fifteen union republics, Prokofyev suddenly became animated.

"It's not fair right now—I agree with that," he shot back. "If we take all of our history, then Russia has gotten less than the others from the country's internal development. If we take the Baltic republics, then all of the industry that they have now was built with the resources and funds of the union as a whole. If you look at the rural areas—agriculture in the Ukraine, the Baltic republics, and Central Asia—people there are on a higher level and better provided for than peasants in Russia.

"If we compare Russia, for example, with England as a colonial power—England squeezed everything out of the colonies and dominions to create a great empire . . . but it turns out Russia is far more backward. It put everything it could into the colonies, if you can call them that, and now they're talking about seceding. And Russia is left, if you'll excuse me, with a bare butt."[3]

The vehemence of Prokofyev's response surprised me, because he is not normally prone to political bluff and bluster; he is polite and business-like—a Party technocrat. Given the accusations that I had heard in Uzbekistan, Azerbaijan, Armenia, and Lithuania about Russian suppression of local cultures and exploitation of local economies, it was odd to hear a high Russian Party official complaining that the ruling majority was persecuted too. But I knew that Prokofyev was not just posturing; his comments reflected a feeling among ethnic Russians that they, too, had been victimized under Stalin, and now other nationalities were unjustly accusing them of imperial sins.

Perhaps no moment in the new Soviet politics captured their anger more vividly than a speech given by the extremely popular Siberian writer Valentin Rasputin at the first session of the Congress of People's Deputies in June 1989.

Rasputin is a gifted storyteller who writes of the Russian countryside and of the lives of simple people in Russian villages. In the seventies, he emerged at the forefront of the village writers, gaining both a popular following and a measure of official favor from Brezhnev, who was sympathetic to Russian nationalist feelings. Although not a Party member, Rasputin was especially admired by the conservative wing of the Party for writing books and stories that affirmed Russian virtues and values and rejected Western influences. By the mid-eighties, he had grown in stature and popularity, even among liberal urban intellectuals, who considered his politics right-wing and chauvinistic but loved his literature; his books sold as many as two million copies each.

Rasputin's voice came from deep in the Russian heartland, and he commanded a large audience, especially when he was given the platform of the nationally televised session of the new Soviet parliament.

He began by delivering a warning about the dangers of excessive democracy, and a powerful indictment of the moral decay brought on by the permissive sensationalism of modern mass culture, a refrain from his famous short novel *The Fire*. Published in 1985, the book portrayed Russia teetering on the edge of a cultural abyss.

Then Rasputin moved on to talk about how Russia was being unjustly attacked by upstart nationalists on the periphery.

"Russophobia has spread into the Baltic countries and Georgia, and it is penetrating into other republics," he declared. "Anti-Soviet slogans are being combined with anti-Russian ones. Emissaries from Lithuania and Estonia are carrying them to Georgia, creating a united front. From there, local agitators are being sent to Armenia and Azerbaijan. . . . The activities of the Baltic deputies, who are attempting to introduce, by parliamentary means, amendments to the constitution which would allow them to part from this country, are readily noticeable here at the Congress."[4]

Rasputin had a Russian riposte, dripping with sarcasm, to throw back at the Baltic secessionists—one that played to resounding applause among the conservative, and mainly ethnic Russian, majority at the Congress:

"Would it be better perhaps for *Russia to leave the union* [sharp applause in the hall], considering that you blame it for all of your misfortunes, and considering that its weak development and awkwardness are what are burdening your progressive aspirations? Perhaps that would be better?

"This, incidentally, would also help us solve many of our own problems, both present and future. [More applause.] We still have a few natural and human resources left—our power has not withered away. We could then utter the word 'Russian' and talk about national self-consciousness without the fear of being labeled 'nationalistic.' . . . [Warm applause.]

"Believe me when I say that we are tired of being the scapegoats, of enduring the slurs and the treachery. We are told that this is our cross to bear. But this cross is becoming increasingly unwieldy. . . . The blame for your misfortunes lies not with Russia but with that common burden of the administrative-industrial machine [created by Stalin], which turned out to be more terrible to all of us than the Mongolian yoke, and which has humiliated and plundered Russia as well, to the point of near suffocation. . . .

"Live with us or not, just as you like," Rasputin told the Baltic secessionists, "but do not behave arrogantly toward us. Do not harbor ill for those who have not earned it."[5]

Rasputin's message resonated profoundly among Russians, far beyond the halls of the Congress of People's Deputies. For many months, his speech was triumphantly echoed by Russian nationalists, especially his trump card: the taunt that Russia should go it alone, secede from the union. Russians saw this as more than a bitter joke; they saw it as a warning to the others. Russian secession, they felt, would knock the other nationalities flat, and the mere threat of it would bring them to their senses, and make them appreciate Russia's importance. For Russia comprises half the population and two thirds the landmass of the Soviet Union; it has been the center, the command point, the bridge, the glue that held the rest together, gave it a framework and a foundation. This was the Russia of Stalinist times—the "elder brother" to the "little peoples."

As Yuri Prokofyev remarked to me, the other republics were "tied hand and foot" to Russia; without Russia, he sniffed, they would be only a union of "dwarf governments."

At first glance, such lamentations seemed inappropriate, coming from the people who had for so long ruled the roost. The Russian people, Russian history, Russian culture, Russian politicians, government officials, engineers, scientists—they have dominated the entire country. This was especially true under Gorbachev. In Brezhnev's time, the Politburo had included several members from non-Slavic nationalities, but except for Foreign Minister Eduard Shevardnadze, who was from Georgia, the non-Slavic minorities had disappeared under Gorbachev. His Politburo was the most Russian since the Bolshevik Revolution, and so was his Council of Ministers.

Yet oddly enough, many Russians spoke with envy of Georgians, Lithuanians, Armenians, Estonians, or Ukrainians, because they all had the trappings of nationhood: their own parliaments, their own languages, their cultural traditions, national histories, their own academies of sciences, even their own Communist Parties. By contrast, the Russians complained that the Russian republic had no academy of sciences, no Russian encyclopedia, no Russian television network, no Communist Party to call its own. These Russians overlooked the fact that Pushkin and Tolstoy were the country's most revered writers; that schoolchildren of all nationalities had to learn the Russian language; that Russian culture and history were taught all over the country; that Moscow television, broadcast in Russian, was the medium of the entire country; that the whole economy and all the major political institutions were commanded by Russians.

Instead, unhappy Russians would point out to me that whenever there was a poster of children from the fifteen Soviet republics, the others all wore their national costumes but the Russian child wore the Soviet Komsomol uniform of blue suit and red scarf. For them, that epitomized how Russia had been forced to surrender its identity on the altar of the Soviet Communist state.

What Russian patriots were doing was drawing an important distinction between Russia and the Soviet Union, between Russian culture, history, and traditions and the culture, history, and values of the Soviet era, the Soviet regime. Under Lenin and especially under Stalin, Russia had been subsumed into the Soviet Union; the Soviet state had treated the two as one and the same for seventy years; for that matter, that is how most Russians had regarded themselves. Moscow television, the Academy of Sciences, and the Communist Party were assumed to serve Soviet and Russian interests simultaneously; the regime saw no distinctions, which is what the other nationalities had so long resented.

But now, under Gorbachev's new freedoms, the Russians, like the other nationalities, were saying that many decisions taken in the Soviet interest had worked against Russia and the Russians. They resented Stalin for having cast himself as a Great Russian nationalist, especially since he was born a Georgian; they hated his exploitation of Russian nationalism in the service of the Soviet state. The most sophisticated and liberal of them knew that Stalin's nationalism was a throwback to the dynastic creed of the conservative czars, a creed in which the nation and nationalism were identified with the state, with the ruler.

The new Russian nationalism of the eighties and nineties was radically different: It was anti-statist, romantic. The nation and nationalism were embodied in the people, in the Russian folk, their culture, and their beloved Russian countryside. Pure Russian nationalists, like nationalists in other regions, wanted to crack the Soviet facade, to break out of the statist mold, and they wanted to reassert Russian culture and Russian identity.

"GRAINS OF TRUTH"

For many Russian nationalists, their cause begins with grieving over what has been lost. And few have done that more movingly than Vladimir Soloukhin, who, like Valentin Rasputin, is a writer. Now in his middle sixties, Soloukhin grew up in a peasant hamlet outside of Vladimir, about 115 miles northeast of Moscow.

Vladimir is famous in the history of Old Russia, a city founded in 1108, as the power of Kiev was waning. The gently rolling meadows around Vladimir, the almost white skies of summertime, are a classic image of central Russia. Soloukhin has poetically evoked that countryside, its peasant life, and his own boyhood in a series of lyrical but candid accounts of the region, starting in 1962 with a work that he called *Vladimir Country Roads*.

In 1989, I found him summering in the village of his birth, at work at a simple wooden table in a corner of a plain, second-floor bedroom in his boyhood home. A two-story log cabin, it had bare floors, simple iron-frame beds, a lamp, no indoor plumbing, and a dirt road out front.

"I write by hand," Soloukhin told me, "and then give my manuscript to a typist."

Soloukhin is a large man of ample frame, broad face, slow speech, and kindly blue eyes; he has about him a comfortable lack of pretense. Long ago, he had moved to Moscow and become a prominent writer, but he still had little use for coat and tie. He wore old pants and a short-sleeved shirt as he slowly walked the paths of his village, gazing at the green fields or stopping by a small cemetery in the woods. He liked to sit, as country people do, on a bench in front of an *izba,* or log cabin, and visit with the neighbor ladies. Or he would stroll to the pond behind his home, watch the ducks paddle or the women kneel down on the opposite bank to do their washing by hand. In summertime, it was a tranquil pastoral scene, a relief from Moscow. But Soloukhin was angry; he found village life hard and dreary, and his hometown almost dead.

"You can't imagine how hard life has become for these people," his wife, Rosa, said. "The one country store only works two hours a day. They have nothing to sell."

"No meat, no fish, no chickens," Soloukhin said.

"Not even a bar of soap for the last six months!" his wife cut in. "No dresses, no clothes."

"They eat what they grow themselves," he said. "And when we come from Moscow, we bring a carload of groceries from the city. We're about out now."[6]

It was a wild idea—bringing food from the city to farm country. I pointed to a cow ambling along the village path, and Soloukhin told me there were only a couple of cows in the village, not enough to provide milk for everyone.

He pointed to a spot where his boyhood school had once stood. There was no replacement for the old school; there were not enough children. Homes were abandoned.

What was it about his writing that made it so popular? I asked. What were his millions of readers looking for?

"Grains of truth," he said.

"Read my books: *Letters from the Russian Museum,* or *Dart Boards on Icons,"* he went on. "My readers want somebody to tell them the truth about what is going on. Today it's easier. Everyone is talking. But when I started writing, in the sixties, seventies, nobody was talking about things. . . . People need the truth, the truth about our countryside. Nobody before had mentioned that our countryside is deserted, that there are eight hundred thousand abandoned homes [in central Russian villages]. Nobody ever mentioned that there were no peasants anymore, that the process of destruction of the peasantry was a success. Only the word 'peasant' exists. There are some agricultural workers who work on the collective farm for a salary, and that's it. . . .

"This is my home, my native village where I was born, and every year I see that less and less remains. It was destroyed by all those years of hunger, by all those Five-Year Plans, by the collectivization. . . . And my experience is typical. In my books, people see . . . themselves, their childhood, their villages, their homeland. They look for that and find it, because our experience is all the same. We are all Russia.

"The Soviets came. The Soviet Union is an international state. And the first governments of this country, in 1917, '18, '19, were decidedly non-Russian. They were multinational governments. The state banner was the world revolution; even our anthem was called 'The Internationale.' Everything Russian had to be suppressed. Why did they destroy ninety-two percent of our churches? Because they had to neutralize the national feelings of Russians. Why were all the towns and villages renamed? In order to weaken the national feelings of Russians. The new government and new state had one goal: to liquidate all these Russias and Georgias and Latvias and so on. And they began with the Russian nation.

"Let me quote Trotsky to you. He said: 'Russia is like a woodpile which we will add to the fire of the world revolution.' "[7]

It was this devastation, this rural poverty in central Russia, that Yuri Prokofyev had had in mind when he said that Russia had suffered more than the other republics, and that the farm regions of the Russian heartland were worse off than other regions.

But the desecration that offended Soloukhin most, even though he was not a religious believer, was the destruction of the village church next door to his home. Its walls were still standing, but it was a shell, in ruins: All the statuary and icons had been pillaged, the murals had been defaced and scraped off the walls, the floors were a dungeon of debris. Weeds towered over Soloukhin's head as he led me through what had once been a churchyard, and into the abandoned hull.

"Our village has existed since the twelfth century, and since the twelfth century we had our Church of the Holy Mother," he said. "This particular building was erected in 1847. It served our village and fourteen neighboring villages. I was baptized here. All my ancestors were baptized in this church, married here, buried here. This church was the fortress of our spiritual life. Around the church was the cemetery, with the graves of our fathers and grandfathers and great-grandfathers. . . ."

Soloukhin's parish church was first assaulted in the thirties, under Stalin.

"It was in 1931—I was small then, six years old, but I remember it," he recalled. "The women went on strike—they tried to blockade the road. But the workers went up to the bell tower and threw the bells down, and took them away. The church continued to be active. It was closed in 1961, under Khrushchev. By then, people didn't even bother to resist."

Soloukhin led us into the dim interior, dust rising through shafts of sunlight from the rubble on the floor. He gazed up at the naked, dingy, crumbling walls, and imagined this church as it had been: a vessel of Russian culture, art, history, and the embodiment of the town's spirit, its heritage, and the story of its people, their births, marriages, funerals.

"There were lots of monuments [here], wonderful marble monuments. There were icons from the sixteenth and seventeenth centuries, pieces of art for our village," he said. "It was like the Louvre . . . the Louvre museum, with ancient books and icons. And look at what has become of all that. This. . . . It's horrendous. It's a devastation. This is the disaster of today's Russia. . . . Film this, film *this*. It's a symbol of Russia today. Russia used to have thousands and thousands of churches, and they're all—ninety-two percent of them—like this."

Soloukhin saw it as his mission to tell this story of the Russia that once was, "to awaken Russian national self-awareness, to write books, to make speeches, to make people feel their own history. For years, we've been told that before 1917 we had nothing but misery and darkness. However, we had a great empire, a great culture, a rich country. So one must tell people the truth, that Russia wasn't poor. It was a rich country and the culture was great—Dostoyevsky, Tolstoy, Borodin, Mendeleyev, dozens of others."

As he talked, Soloukhin reminded me of Aleksandr Solzhenitsyn, whom I had met several times in the seventies, when he was still in Moscow. He, too, had preached the greatness of czarist Russia.

"I know him personally," Soloukhin said. "I esteem him highly as a writer. I like the firmness of his principles. I like his outlook. His position is firm and he is a monarchist."

"Do you agree with him?" I asked, knowing that Soloukhin had been a Communist Party member since 1952.

"Yes," he said. "I am a monarchist, and a vehement one."

"Why?" I asked.

"Because I think this is the best way of ruling this country."

NATIONALISM—AN IDEOLOGY FOR COUNTERREFORM?

Unlike the nationalist movements in most of the minority republics, Russian nationalism has no single unifying movement such as Sajudis in Lithuania, the Karabakh Committee in Armenia, the popular fronts in several republics, or the Ukrainian movement known as Rukh. Nor does it have a single policy focus, such as secession in Lithuania or recovering Nagorno-Karabakh in Armenia. In the minority republics, the unifying force of nationalism is an opposition to "the center"—a common antipathy toward Moscow's domination. But in Russia, nationalist feelings sprawl across the political spectrum, from left to right to extremist right. The nationalist cause is a divisive one.

In the minority republics, the general process of political liberalization and the urge for national self-renewal are mutually reinforcing. But in Russia, Gorbachev's drive for greater democracy has brought upheavals and disorder that grates against the most basic instinct of traditional Russian nationalists—for Russia to be ruled with an iron hand. So, as reform has progressed, divisions among Russian nationalists have sharpened.

There is a strong and ongoing conflict between liberal and moderate Russophiles, who seek a Russian cultural flowering under a new democratic system that is tolerant toward other nationalities, and the right wing of Russian nationalism, which is disdainful, even hostile, toward the minority nationalities and hankers for a dominant, authoritarian Russia. In elections and opinion polls, there is strong evidence that the moderates have far wider support among the populace, but the right wing is more vocal, more aggressive, more organized; despite its small numbers, it is the driving force of Russian nationalism, and in a volatile situation it is the more dangerous element.

Conservative Russian traditionalists like Solzhenitsyn, Rasputin, and Soloukhin are anti-Marxist; as Russian purists, they reject the Communist system. But like hard-line Communists, they have an urge for absolutism, for a strong hand at the top; they advocate a strongly centralized Russian state, with an emphasis on unity, cohesion, and order. Their politics are a throwback to the past; their grand dream is to put a czar back on the throne and reinstitute Russian Orthodoxy as the state religion, and if that is too impractical, at least to reimpose strong rule from the top. They reject Western-style pluralism, which Solzhenitsyn once derisively called "democracy run riot."[8]

The more moderate wing of Russian nationalists are anti-Stalinist; they seek a democratic Russia with a mixed market economy. Their primary interest is cultural, not political, and they advocate Russia's cultural revival, not its political domination of others. They want to revive their cultural heritage, to emphasize those elements of the Russian past (such as individual religious faith and the moral power of Russian art and literature) that strengthen Russian culture and would speed the downfall of Stalinist authoritarianism. And they support Gorbachev's drive for democracy. They are modern in their thinking, and open to the world at large; therefore, they oppose the political absolutism of the Russian Right, as well as its romantic urge to pull back into Holy Russia, away from the modern world.

For the moderates, nationalism raises dilemmas: They are torn between loyalty to the Soviet Union and loyalty to Russia. Other nationalities see aggressive Russian nationalism as a threat; it is offensive to moderates and liberals, who value pluralism and tolerance even as they pursue Russia's cultural revival. In fact, the moderates dislike the term "Russian nationalism"; they prefer to be called "patriots."

Dmitri Likhachev, the aging patron of the moderate wing, explained it this way: "For me, patriotism is the love of one's country, while nationalism is the hatred of other peoples."[9]

This attitude is typical of the moderates: They openly support the idea that other nationalities should assert their rights, whereas conservative Russian nationalists like Rasputin bitterly resent the new, self-assertive nationalism of minority republics and openly criticize "the little peoples."

Finally, the extremist wing of Russian nationalism, on the far right, stands against Gorbachev. It is reactionary, bent on imposing strong authoritarian order, and on finding villains and scapegoats for the present Soviet crisis. Extremist Russian nationalism veers into anti-Semitism and toward fascism.

For Gorbachev, the most serious political threat in Russian nationalism has been that, with the steady loss of popular faith in Communism, Russian nationalism might become a rallying cry for political hard-liners of all stripes. At a time of economic disintegration and political confusion, nationalism is a simple ideology capable of sweeping up millions of ordinary Russians in its undertow. The primary danger has been that right-wing Russian nationalists would form a reactionary alliance with neo-Stalinists in the Party, the army, and the police, each side dismayed by the chaos let loose by Gorbachev and determined to halt the process of reform in order to reimpose discipline. In this role, Russian nationalism could become what Alexander Yanov, an American specialist on the Soviet political Right, called "the ideology of counterreform."[10]

Gorbachev and his advisers are aware of this risk. Even before interethnic tensions rose sharply in 1989 and 1990, Gorbachev made an open bid for support among the natural constituency of Russian nationalism by fashioning alliances with its moderate intellectual leaders and by dramatic moves of cooperation with the Russian Orthodox Church.

With Gorbachev's blessing, Dmitri Likhachev, a revered academician with impeccable credentials as a Russian patriot and environmentalist, became chairman of the Soviet Cultural Foundation, and Gorbachev's wife took a seat on the board. One of the organization's main functions is the restoration of Russian historical monuments and buildings—a primary goal of many moderate nationalists.

Gorbachev also had another older moderate nationalist, the respected writer Sergei Zalygin, installed as chief editor of *Novy Mir*, the most prominent liberal literary magazine in Moscow. Like Likhachev, Zalygin was a strong advocate of protecting and preserving the Russian environment, and his writing celebrated the Russian countryside and the Russian past. Zalygin had been one of the leaders in a sacred Russian cause—the battle against a plan to reverse the northward flow of Siberian rivers so the water could be diverted to the hot, dry Islamic republics of Central Asia. In this battle, Zalygin had teamed not only with conservatives like Rasputin and Soloukhin, but also with liberal, anti-Stalinist writers like Andrei Voznesensky and Yevgeny Yevtushenko, who were opposed to the Russian Right.

Zalygin's democratic instincts made him a rival to the right-wing nationalists. At *Novy Mir*, he promptly moved to steal their thunder, publishing a series of articles on Russian philosophy during the nineteenth century, an important theme for cultural revivalists. He included the work of Nikolai Berdyayev, who favored a synthesis of Slavic and Western values.[11]

Zalygin also moved to publish the political icon of the Russian Right, Solzhenitsyn. Characteristic of a liberal, Zalygin began by publishing large portions of *The Gulag Archipelago*, Solzhenitsyn's biting indictment of Stalinist terror. Neither Zalygin nor Gorbachev could afford to leave Solzhenitsyn to right-wing nationalists to champion. It was a political coup for them both to publish Solzhenitsyn in a liberal journal, and not to leave the cause and the voice of Russian nationalism solely to the Right.

THE CHURCH: THE GOLDEN CUPOLAS

Gorbachev's most important and widely heralded gesture toward Russian nationalist sentiments was to declare an end to the Communist Party's ideological war against the Russian Orthodox Church, and to cast himself as an advocate of a religious revival in Mother Russia.

For the masses of ordinary Russians, especially those in rural areas, nationalism begins with love of country and reverence toward the Church. Throughout the Soviet period, the Orthodox Church survived by accepting a circumscribed existence, occasionally exploited by political leaders; Stalin even used the Church in World War II as a force to rally Russian patriotism. But generally the Church has been under siege from the atheistic propaganda of the Party. Publicly, at least, it was long relegated to tokenism, and left to *babushkas*, old women; to clerics; and to appearances at international peace conclaves, where its prelates proclaimed Soviet goodwill. Gorbachev, whose mother and grandmother were believers, altered the atmosphere, gave the Church new legitimacy, and opened up new opportunities. In doing so, he was going after the heart and soul of Russian nationalism.

In April 1988, Gorbachev held an important symbolic meeting with the late Patriarch Pimen and other leaders of the Church, an encounter that was widely publicized as the first meeting of a Communist Party leader with the Church hierarchy since World War II. Gorbachev gave his political blessing to the reopening of hundreds of Orthodox churches, and to the return of other sanctuaries, such as Moscow's Danilov Monastery and Kiev's Pechersky Monastery, which had been seized by the state under Stalin, Khrushchev, and Brezhnev. The Kremlin museum also turned religious relics over to the Orthodox Church, in ceremonies shown on *Vremya*, the main evening newscast, to 150 million viewers. And finally, in June 1988, Gorbachev allowed a week of celebrations of the millennium of the Orthodox Church. While he himself did not take part, his wife, Raisa, was a conspicuous participant at the main opening ceremonies, which were held on June 10 at Moscow's Bolshoi Theater. Orthodox believers, not only in Russia but also in the Ukraine and Byelorussia, where the Orthodox Church is strong, came to regard Gorbachev as their advocate and protector.

"We understand *perestroika* as the means of our spiritual resurrection as well as our economic development and our cultural reawakening," Metropolitan Filaret, head of the Orthodox Church in Kiev, told me. "The Church has ceased to be considered an obstacle to the development of socialist society. It has become a facilitator of this development."[12]

In 1988 and 1989, the metropolitan said, the Orthodox Church had opened two thousand parish churches all over the Soviet Union; eighteen hundred of them were old churches like the one in Soloukhin's village, and two hundred were brand new. This was the first big addition in many years to the eighty-five hundred functioning Orthodox churches already in existence. The rapid expansion, which cost the Church tens of millions of rubles in repairs and renovations of old sanctuaries, had caused a shortage of priests; and so, Filaret said, the Church was adding new religious seminaries in Minsk and Kiev, to the three that were already operating, as well as religious academies for choral singers, psalm readers, and others.

Beyond that, Filaret said, there was a widening of the Church's sphere of public activity: Church leaders were permitted to be elected to the Congress of People's Deputies, to appear on television, to meet with scholars, to expand Church publications; they could engage in such social activities as running charitable organizations, working in hospitals, joining campaigns against illiteracy and alcohol abuse. Even under more difficult conditions, Filaret said, the Church had baptized thirty million people from 1971 to 1988; and he was confident of an even stronger surge now, especially since the Soviet people were suffering from "a spiritual vacuum."

Moreover, in a not-so-subtle promotion of the Church's role in support of Mother Russia's imperial ambitions, Metropolitan Filaret emphasized that the Church had strength in several republics besides Russia—in the Ukraine, Byelorussia, Moldavia, Estonia, and Latvia, among others. (In fact, I remembered Lithuanian friends complaining that even in Vilnius, there were more Orthodox than Catholic churches.) The bonding promoted by the Church was particularly strong among the three Slavic nationalities, Filaret said. "We have mutual roots in ancient *Rus*—Russians, Byelorussians, and Ukrainians all drink from the same source," he observed. "Our church is truly multinational. The role of the Russian Orthodox Church as a unifying factor is characteristic throughout our one-thousand-year history."

For many nonbelievers, the Russian Orthodox Church is the embodiment of Russian history and culture, a repository of art, music, and architecture as well as religion. For me, too, one of the treasures of driving through Old Russia, near Vladimir, Suzdal, Rostov, and Yaroslavl, was to see the gentle, onion-shaped cupolas of Orthodox churches, blue, green, or gold, rising over the open fields and villages below. I could understand why people happily dedicated their labor to restoring old churches.

On the southwestern edge of Moscow, in what used to be the village of Zolotaryova and what is now a sea of fifteen-story tenement apartments, I found a crew of ten workmen restoring the Church of the Archangel Michael, built in 1740. In the seventies, Zolotaryova had been a mere cluster of peasant homes. Now it looked as overpopulated as Cairo or Calcutta. The red-brick church, with its five cupolas, had long been used to store grain, and later as a metal workshop. In the eighties, as Moscow's housing blocks swallowed up the region, the church was spared, because the metro system ran underneath it; otherwise, it probably would have been demolished to make room for yet another apartment block.

"Look at all those deformities, those ugly boxes," said Vladimir Galitsky, gesturing at the apartments. "I dislike them intensely."

Galitsky was an engineer by training, an architect by avocation, formerly a specialist on architectural theory at the Institute of History. By mid-1989, he was a government administrator, but his passion was restoring churches. He spent his spare time supervising the restoration of the Church of the Archangel Michael, his jewel among the "junky boxes" of modern Moscow.

He studied old books on church architecture, obtained money from the Orthodox Church for gold plating for the cupolas, shouted to the workmen high on the scaffolding, instructing them on how to place the cross once again on the highest cupola.

"It is important to me personally to restore such beauty," he said, "and to know that after our work is done, people can enjoy this beauty." His young daughter was excited just to see the golden cupolas reappear. His mother, a believer, had made him promise, virtually on her deathbed, that he would work to restore the church.

"It is important to me because I love history—the history of the Russian people, of other nations," Galitsky said. "I feel great respect for historic landmarks. So it was very important to me to help restore it. It was created by the people and the people need it back. This history will help people to be educated, to develop their morality, their culture. . . .

"And when you look at this shrine, it's beautiful. It's like the music of Beethoven or Bach."[13]

In the heart of Moscow, others were at work trying to revive the old, prerevolutionary face of the city, which had been largely destroyed by Stalin, Khrushchev, and Viktor Grishin, the Moscow Party boss of the Brezhnev era. One of the most popular grass-roots movements in Russia is the All-Russian Society for the Preservation of Historical and Cultural Monuments; its Moscow branch alone claims eight hundred thousand dues-paying members. It was a far larger body than similar groups I ran across in Uzbekistan, Armenia, Georgia, the Ukraine, Lithuania, and Estonia. And yet, Aleksandr Trefimov, the chairman of the preservation society's Moscow branch and a professor at the Moscow Art Institute, told me that the other republics are far ahead of the Russians in restoration.

"Unfortunately, we only began to follow their example recently," Trefimov said. "Previously, the trend in Moscow, and in Russia as a whole, was to get rid of these landmarks."

We were strolling through an old section of Moscow called Staraya Sloboda, near the home of wealthy prerevolutionary textile magnate Sava

Morozov. Trefimov told me how the preservation society had privately raised funds and gotten city permission to restore the classical residences of Morozov and other prerevolutionary merchants and aristocrats along Old Aleksei Street (still called that by local people, although it had been renamed Communist Street by the Bolsheviks). Farther on, we came to Malaya Vorona, Little Crow Street, where Trefimov and his organization were trying to revive some of the former charm of the city by renovating a run-down warren into a renovated quarter of cafés, ateliers, artistic workshops.

Trefimov was infuriated that Party leaders had ordered the demolition of old sections of Moscow. For more than twenty years, he had been fighting the encroachment of cheap modern buildings, such as the concrete-slab worker dormitories that loomed overhead. He was fighting a rearguard battle.

"Destruction of the old architecture was a terrible thing." A middle-aged academic, Trefimov suddenly turned emotional as he described the cultural crudeness of Communist leaders. "Ancient Moscow cannot be restored. It cannot regain the urban landscape that London or Paris has today. Those cities all have their national faces, while Moscow does not. . . . This disturbs our people, and so masses of people have come to our organization, because there is a certain instinct for self-preservation in people."

Trefimov was a moderate nationalist; like other liberals, he supported the cultural renaissance of other nationalities. "First you must respect other cultures and then you will respect your own," he told me. But his passion for preservation of things Russian was desperate.

"For us, it has really become a matter of life and death," he said. "Let me give you an example: Why did the Mongolians, who were so strong militarily and had a large population, why did they suddenly cease to matter as a nation? The reason is that the Mongolians were much lower in their cultural level than the nations they conquered. So these Mongolians were actually absorbed by the cultures of the nations they conquered in war."

"As a Russian, are you really worried that this could happen to your culture?" I asked.

"Yes, as a Russian, I am afraid of this possibility," he answered. "If our national culture is alive, we can sleep peacefully. But if it is not, our nation will disappear. If the progress of our cultural restoration remains as slow as it has been, we will risk, if not total disappearance, then the loss of our national cultural face. And eventually it will disappear in toto."[14]

"WE NEED A GREAT RUSSIA"

These relatively modest concerns of the moderate nationalists—restoring historic Moscow, protecting the Russian environment, reviving old writings, giving religious believers new freedom—fitted in easily with Gorbachev's attempts to create a more democratic Soviet socialism. But such limited aims did not satisfy the angry Russian Right, the more combative, fundamentalist wing of Russian nationalism. Deep down, the right wing would like to halt reform, turn back the clock, and bring back an iron fist at the top.

The Russian Right sees itself as battling not merely against the devastations of the past, but the moral depredations of the present. As Eastern Europe has thrown off the Communist yoke, it has moved to borrow from the politics and economics of the West; but as Russian nationalists anticipated the collapse of Communism at home, they went the other way—not Westward, but inward. They were at war not only with Bolshevism, but with the whole process of modernization: urbanization, industrialism, twentieth-century technology, the influence of the West. In Siberia, some of their Luddite supporters have gone about smashing computers.

Self-pity is the engine that drives this brand of Russian nationalism, a self-pity that lays the blame for Russia's apocalypse on others: on the Soviet system, on Gorbachev's reforms, on the pernicious influence of Western mass culture, on minority nationalities, on Jews. Russian nationalists reject the charge that Russians, ruling the empire, are responsible for their own fate. Paradoxically, even as the Russophiles berate the Soviet system for their misery, some are defensive about Stalin, as if blaming Stalin were blaming Russia too—because Stalin is so widely regarded as the quintessential Russian despot.

In the eyes of Russian nationalists, seven decades of Communism have left Russia not only materially impoverished but poorer in spirit as well. The heart of Russia became a wasteland—tens of thousands of villages abandoned, Russia's natural riches of oil, gas, timber, and gold plundered by economic ignoramuses running the Kremlin, and sold off to foreigners for a pottage, its churches desecrated, its treasury depleted, its monarch executed, and its once great intelligentsia scattered all across the globe. It has had to endure the trauma of almost mindless industrialization and urbanization, a plummeting birth rate, rampant alcoholism (about forty bottles of vodka a year for every man, woman, and child), a rising crime rate, and one of the highest abortion rates in the world—an average of six abortions for every adult woman.[15]

This catalog of suffering has left the Russian Right not only feeling victimized but searching for a new faith. Its sense of crisis has spawned a slew of new Russian organizations whose very names reflect the hunger for a new belief in Russia: Fatherland, Memory, Patriot, Fidelity, Renewal. In their street rallies, they fly the flag of the patron saint of Old Russia, Saint George slaying the dragon. On November 7, 1989, in the west Siberian oil city of Tyumen, Russian nationalist demonstrators mocked the political turmoil set loose by Gorbachev's *perestroika:* The huge red banner they carried quoted the hard-line czarist minister Pyotr Stolypin: THEY NEED GREAT UPHEAVALS, BUT WE NEED A GREAT RUSSIA![16]

Right-wing nationalists nurse the concept of Holy Russia, a nation with a special historic mission: a Third Rome, after Rome and Constantinople, called in the modern era to propound a Third Way, a Russian way between capitalism and communism. One of the most romantic statements of the Russian credo was Aleksandr Solzhenitsyn's *Letter to the Supreme Leaders,* in which he invoked a mystical celebration of Holy Russia. Written in 1973, before he was exiled to the West (which he termed "spiritual castration"), Solzhenitsyn's open epistle to the leadership urged Russians to cast off the false god of modern technology and "the dark, un-Russian whirlwind" of Marxist ideology, to shed Moscow's East European empire and its non-Russian republics, and to turn inward, away from Europe, to develop the Russian hinterland. Invoking the soul-soothing silences, the human scale, and the moral goodness of the Russian villages, Solzhenitsyn urged the Kremlin leaders to turn away from industrial mass production and to reduce the economy to small-scale; to reduce all dwellings to two stories—"the most pleasant height for human habitation."[17]

The cultural leaders of the Russian Right today yearn for Solzhenitsyn's return from his exile in Cavendish, Vermont. They openly admire him as a prophet of Russian fundamentalism. *Nash Sovremennik,* the literary bible of the right wing, proudly ran his essay "Live but Do Not Lie" in the fall of 1989.

Echoing Solzhenitsyn, Stanislav Kunyayev, the editor of *Nash Sovremennik,* told me: "We need a holy, dynamic Russia. If we achieve that, our other republics will be better off. It is bad for them to have a weak, lame Russia. A great country cannot have a weak center, a weak heart. Our culture is sick. Our young people have been pulled away from their roots. Now they are attracted to a cosmopolitan culture in which America, with its rock and roll, plays a very large part."[18]

Characteristically, the Russian Right is better at lashing out at what it is against, than at spelling out what it is for. Generally, it is against a market economy, against the enrichment of speculators, against joint ventures with Western businesses, against free-trade zones, which nationalists fear will be exploited by multinational corporations. "Our essayists say a free market will not work," Kunyayev said. "It will lead to mass unemployment and turmoil. We must go very slowly, by stages. In the meantime, we must maintain the firm state structure." The one Gorbachev economic reform that wins applause from the Russian Right is returning land to the peasants; nationalists see that as a way of reviving the Russian heartland.

But they view Gorbachev's venture in democratization with fear and disdain. Their spokesmen use the Soviet parliament to broadcast their cause, but they are ill at ease in such a Western institution as a legislature. On an evening in September 1989, in honor of Sergei Vikulov, who retired after twenty-one years as chief editor of *Nash Sovremennik*, the outspoken nationalist writer Vasily Belov drew fervent applause from several hundred well-heeled sympathizers by flailing the new Soviet democrats:

"The prophets of democracy are telling us again and again that the Russian people are fools in everything. Oh, you fly-by-night democrats, Mother Russia is so tired of you all! We are so tired of your screams, of the wailing and whining from foreigners. We do not need any of it. We will make it on our own."[19]

As Kunyayev and Belov indicated, nothing causes more profound dismay among right-wing nationalists than what they see as the loss of moral values in Russia, and the invasion of materialism and mass culture from the West: Western music videos, jeans, television, rock and roll, American cigarettes, and explicit sex in movies.

"Before the advent of television, our people were the vehicles of their own culture," Sergei Vikulov, then still editor of *Nash Sovremennik*, told me in mid-1989. "They had it in the depth of their souls. . . . Now I can see enormous contrasts from ten years ago. Before, when I went to my home village in the Russian north, I could see the people singing folk songs, dancing folk dances in the village club, playing roles in some folk plays. Now everyone sits by the TV and stares at it. They watch what they are shown, and even when they can't sit any longer, they still watch TV. And what are they shown?"

This man in his mid-sixties, in a dark suit and dull tie, gave me a look of disgust, slouched his hips suggestively, then put one hand on his pelvis and reached out the other as if holding an imaginary guitar:

"They are shown those crazy guitars producing that strange sound. . . . *Ah-uh-ah-uh-ahhhhhhh!* And those crazy dancers who are dancing barefoot on tables. Can you understand it? Our poor old women clutch at their heads in frustration and ask: 'What is this? Who are these people and why do they display such behavior?' They can't understand what they are being offered."[20]

Valentin Rasputin was even more hostile toward Western influences, complaining about "the moral permissiveness and lustfulness, the unscrupulousness and sensationalism of the mass media.

"Our young people perished senselessly in Afghanistan, and they are being maimed just as senselessly in the undeclared war against morality," he fumed. "We are observing almost open propaganda of sex, violence, and liberation from all moral norms. . . . Have you noticed? . . . Just as the voice of the announcer fades away, after reporting human misfortunes and sacrifices, the television screen becomes filled with the cacophony of frenzied music. . . . Where does it go from here? A children's sex encyclopedia containing pictures which would make even an adult uncomfortable. . . ."

Russia, Rasputin warned, was in danger of repeating the fall of the Roman Empire.[21]

A NEW BATTLE OF STALINGRAD

In their fury and frustration, the right-wing nationalists launched a campaign against Gorbachev's most liberal economic advisers and reform economists, such as Tatyana Zaslavskaya, Abel Aganbegyan, Leonid Abalkin, and Nikolai Shmelyov. And they went after the most progressive elements of the Soviet media. Since early 1987, cultural warfare has raged between Right and Left—a surrogate battle reflecting internal fights in the upper reaches of the Party hierarchy.

War was declared in March 1987 at a meeting of the Writers' Union of the Russian republic, a stronghold of the Russian Right. The two top officials of the union, the writer Sergei Mikhalkov and the writer and filmmaker Yuri Bondarev, threatened to unleash "a new Battle of Stalingrad" against liberal editors, who were publishing negative works about the Russian past and present.[22] With Stalingrad, Bondarev was evoking not only the old dictator's name (the city is now called Volgograd) but the battle in which the Russians, backed against the wall, repulsed the Nazi invaders.

Carrying out their threat, the Russian Right lashed out at Soviet television, and went after liberal newspapers such as *Moscow News* and *Sovetskaya Kultura*. But their primary targets were Vitaly Korotich, chief editor of *Ogonek* (the liberal flagship of Gorbachev's *glasnost*), and Anatoly

Anayev, who had turned the monthly *Oktyabr* into a hotbed of liberal attacks on the Soviet system. Right-wingers tried endlessly to get those two editors fired, without success—presumably because both were protected by Aleksandr Yakovlev, Gorbachev's chief ally in the Politburo for cultural affairs.[23] Yakovlev has long been a bête noire of the Russian nationalists; in 1972, he lost a high Central Committee post because of an article warning against the dangers of Russian nationalism. More recently, in his rebuttal to the neo-Stalinist Nina Andreyeva, he derided crude peasant patriotism as *"kvas* patriotism" (named for a favorite Russian peasant brew).[24]

But the Russian Right, too, had powerful allies in the hierarchy. Many high-ranking Russian officers in the Soviet military are widely regarded as their silent partners, and even patrons. The ability of right-wing organizations like Pamyat ("Memory") to get permission for demonstrations near the Kremlin is widely taken as evidence of support for the right wing within the police and KGB. But it was Yegor Ligachev, the most durable right-wing antagonist in Gorbachev's Politburo, who gave his blessing to some of the pet concerns of the Russian Writers' Union in mid-1987. He endorsed the group's battle against the liberal press, especially its resistance to attacks on Soviet classics, as well as its concern that the West was attempting to foist bourgeois mass culture on the Soviet Union.[25] Since that time, the Russian Right, especially the right-wing writers, have been widely seen as surrogates for Ligachev and more reactionary members of the Party's Old Guard.

In ideological terms, this is a strange political alliance; Russian nationalists and neo-Stalinists begin as polar opposites. Russian nationalists are angry at the Soviet system for its destruction of their homeland; the Orthodox Church is their ideological anchor and they hang religious icons in their homes. Many of them openly praise the czarist regime overthrown by the Bolsheviks, and they hold special admiration for the czarist prime minister Pyotr Stolypin. For neo-Stalinists, believing Communists, not only czarism, but Stolypin in particular, are anathema, and the Church their ideological enemy.

What has created this marriage of convenience is a shared disgust and alarm at the chaos that has followed in the wake of Gorbachev's democratic reforms; the urge to restore order and bring Russia back under strongman rule; mutual distaste for market economics; common mistrust or rejection of the West; powerful patriotism; and mutual determination to see Russia and the Soviet Union prevail against the threat of disintegration. In this alloy, the two most important elements that forge unity among hard-liners in the army and KGB, neo-Stalinists in the Party, and the new Russian Right are the instinct for order and the Imperial Russian urge to hang on to every scrap of territory within the U.S.S.R.[26]

The Russian Right has poured forth the ideology of counterreform from a handful of publications, including two controlled by the Writers' Union: the newspaper *Literaturnaya Rossiya* and the literary monthly *Nash Sovremennik* (which means "Our Contemporary," its nineteenth-century name). Aligned with them have been two neo-Stalinist publications, *Sovetskaya Rossiya*, the Communist Party newspaper that printed the neo-Stalinist attack on Gorbachev by Nina Andreyeva; and *Molodaya Gvardiya* (*Young Guard*), which runs a steady screed against the liberal press and such liberal leaders as Aleksandr Yakovlev.

Nash Sovremennik has gathered together such village writers as Valentin Rasputin, Vasily Belov, Vladimir Soloukhin, and Viktor Astafyev, most of whom are enormously popular with the Russian reading public. Astafyev's novel *The Sad Detective* had a print run of 2.75 million; it viewed Russia's cultural decline with alarm. Belov's polemical novel *Everything Is Still to Come* had a similar massive printing; it depicted the Western-oriented Soviet intelligentsia as being in the clutches of an insidious Jewish-Masonic conspiracy. By comparison, Gorbachev's book *Perestroika* sold about 300,000 copies in the Soviet Union.

There is a similar mass response to the exhibitions of the Russian nationalist painter Ilya Glazunov, who is a vain, garrulous, chain-smoking painter who effusively advertises prerevolutionary family connections with the St. Petersburg aristocracy and crams his apartment with imperial artifacts. Two million people saw Glazunov's month-long exhibition in Moscow in June 1986; one and a half million more attended when it moved to Leningrad that October. What draws the crowds are Glazunov's realistic portrayal of themes of eternal Russia: churches, Russian princes battling invaders, poor village women, and such works as *Return of the Prodigal Son*, a portrait of a young Russian in Western jeans returning to his home in Russia, where there are icons on the walls. In the summer of 1988, Yegor Ligachev showed up at one of Glazunov's exhibits, in a gesture of endorsement for the artist's nationalistic work.

ANTI-SEMITISM AND PAMYAT

Right-wing Russian nationalists are obsessed, as their writings and conversations testify, with what they see as the excessive influence of Jews in Soviet society. Despite their denials, anti-Semitism lurks barely beneath the surface of the Russian Right. It is another element of their politics that allies them with such Communist Party neo-Stalinists as Nina Andreyeva.

In terms of Soviet history, however, the Russian nationalists have their own special viewpoint. Both Soloukhin and Vikulov suggested to me that the Bolshevik Revolution was not really a Russian revolution at all but rather the work of a multinational cabal led by Jews, mainly Trotsky; and, of course, it was based on a theory by another Jew, Marx. Some Russian nationalists have even offered the fantastic theory that Lenin's grandfather was Jewish; many make the incorrect claim that Jews dominated the Bolshevik Party leadership in its early years. Stanislav Kunyayev suggested to me that Trotsky was really the evil genius behind Stalin's terror of the thirties, even though Trotsky was then in exile.

"Stalin did not invent the concepts of rigid dictatorship, forced collectivization, and enslavery of the peasantry," Kunyayev said emphatically. "He got those ideas from Trotsky."[27]

Others, disregarding the fact that Jews were prime targets of Stalin's purges, have come up with the incredible theory that Stalin was duped by those around him, and that the purges were really the work of Stalin's sinister lieutenant Lazar Kaganovich, a Jew.

"I think today that Jews here should feel responsible for the sin of having carried out the Revolution, and for the shape that it took," Valentin Rasputin asserted. "They should feel responsible for the terror. For the terror that existed during the Revolution and especially after the Revolution. They played a large role, and their guilt is great. . . . In this country, those are Jewish sins because many Jewish leaders took part in the terror, in the repression of the kulaks, of the peasants, and so on."[28]

Nowadays, Russian nationalists hold Jews responsible for many problems. In a polemic so popular with Russian nationalists that it has been reproduced and spread all across Russia, Igor Shafarevich, a prominent mathematician and Russophile, accused the Soviet Jews in mid-1989 of stirring up a current wave of Russophobia.[29] A few months later, in December 1989, the Russian Writers' Union debated whether to withdraw recognition of its Leningrad branch because it had too many Jewish members, and to admit a much smaller rump group of Russian nationalists.[30] In March 1990, a group of Russian nationalists, including Stanislav Kunyayev, published a letter in the right-wing newspaper *Literaturnaya Rossiya* that asserted Jews were deliberately stirring up anti-Semitism in the Soviet Union in order to make it easier for them to emigrate.[31]

It is a short step from these accusations to the activities of Pamyat, the extremist right-wing splinter group that has been most openly associated with anti-Semitic protests and has stirred fears of incipient Soviet fascism.

Pamyat developed in 1979 as an informal group within the moderate All-Russian Society for the Preservation of Historical and Cultural Monuments. But it turned extremist under Dmitri Vasiliyev, a photographer and a minor actor in Soviet movies, who is a powerful, bombastic speaker. Starting in 1986, Vasiliyev made a series of violently angry, reactionary, often anti-Semitic speeches, which were recorded and circulated around the country. He brought Pamyat into public view as an independent entity with a demonstration in May 1987.[32] Soon, the organization invited comparison with German Fascism because its members wore black T-shirts and military greatcoats, and carried a banner with the double eagle of the Romanov dynasty and zigzag bolts of lightning that evoked Nazi swastikas.

I found Vasiliyev a more truculent, vitriolic version of the Russian Right intellectuals. He is a bullish, barrel-chested Russian, who affects collarless peasant blouses; a natural street demagogue, he speaks at a high decibel level and knows how to arouse a crowd to passion. It would have been easy to dismiss Vasiliyev—except for his message; except for the hundreds of people at Pamyat street demonstrations; except for periodic incidents of violence perpetrated in Pamyat's name.

Every charge Vasiliyev made was more shrill than anyone else's. Others spoke of Russian suffering; Vasiliyev told me Russians have suffered "the most cruel political genocide." The Bolshevik Revolution was, to him, a Jewish conspiracy; the czarist regime was "a million times better." He agreed, seriously, with Rasputin that Russia should secede from the Soviet Union. Despite Russian dominance of the leadership, he complained, "We have no Russian ruling Party organ, no Central Committee. We are deprived of our own anthem, our banner, our national seal. Even the word *Russia* is not in use today."[33] He told others that the Communist Party Central Committee, the Soviet legal system, and the media were controlled by Jews, "who are masterminding the systematic destruction of Russian culture."[34]

In late 1989, on Soviet television, Vasiliyev called for the restoration of the monarchy and said that he would not mind being the new czar.[35]

However outlandish, he worried both liberals and the Soviet police—although some Jews feared that he had a tie-in with the police and that was how he escaped arrest. In January 1989, Vitaly Korotich, the liberal editor of *Ogonek*, told me, a group of young toughs shouting the name *Pamyat* and rabid anti-Semitic slogans broke up an election meeting that was preparing to nominate Korotich for people's deputy. In fisticuffs that broke out between Korotich's supporters and the intruders, the invaders called Korotich a "kike" and called out, "Korotich, you Jew, give back your silver coins."[36] (Korotich is not Jewish.)

Periodically, Soviet authorities warned Vasiliyev that he and Pamyat risked prosecution under Article 74 of the Russian republic's criminal code that bars "incitement to national discord." The city government ignored Vasiliyev's efforts to have Pamyat registered as a legal organization, though that did not halt the activities of Pamyat or other groups, liberal or right-wing. And hate incidents continued to occur intermittently; Sasha Kuprin, a young documentary producer who works for *Ogonek*'s television unit, told me he had been beaten up one night by four men who said they were from Pamyat. They left him with a concussion. He thought the attack was prompted by a film he had made about right-wing violence. At a Jewish restaurant, Chez Youssef, Russian nationalists had staged noisy, disruptive fights and insulted the owner; its outdoor buffet stand was burned down and the restaurant was forced to close.[37] Vasiliyev denied any Pamyat connection with the fire; in fact, he denied that Pamyat was in any way anti-Semitic.

There were new spasms of violence in early 1990, and panic spread among Moscow Jews after a Pamyat raid on a group of liberal writers, the so-called April Committee, as they were meeting at the Soviet Writers' Union building on January 18, 1990. About three dozen young thugs, wearing Pamyat badges and chanting anti-Semitic slogans through megaphones, stormed into the meeting and attacked and seriously wounded several older writers. Then, threatening a pogrom on May 5, the Feast of Saint George, they stalked out, shouting: "Next time, we'll come with submachine guns, not megaphones!" Outside, police hustled the gang away, but made no arrests, according to witnesses.[38] However, the incident was widely condemned by high authorities, and warnings against any anti-Semitic violence were issued by the KGB, the prosecutor's office, and many media outlets. No pogrom took place on May 5.

Pamyat's mass support has always been a mystery. Its demonstrations have usually drawn only hundreds or at best a few thousand people, never any massive crowd. In early 1988, Vasiliyev claimed that the organization had twenty thousand members in Moscow, with chapters in thirty other Russian cities.[39] KGB security officers have called that a wild exaggeration; in early 1990, a top KGB officer put Pamyat's membership at "no more than two hundred members in Moscow and only about one thousand in the whole country."[40] It is said to be organized in secretive cells, making its membership hard to calculate. Liberal Russophiles like Dmitri Likhachev have advised against underestimating the danger of a small, clandestine, violent minority. In the spring of 1990, as Gorbachev was striving to get himself elected to the new Soviet presidency, Likhachev warned of the dangerous alternative on the right. He called it "the party of Pamyat" but he meant much more than Vasiliyev and his band of thugs. Likhachev was referring to a wider alliance that embraced the broader Russian Right, and the right wing in the Communist Party, including not only Yegor Ligachev, but rising new figures as well.

"In our country now, the most powerful organization is the Communist Party, and then 'the party of Pamyat,' " he said. "It's an insignificant percentage, but they are very vociferous people. And we know that the [German] Fascist party was also vociferous and represented a minority. . . . Nevertheless, they can seize power because they are organized."[41]

I asked Aleksandr Yakovlev, whom Vasiliyev had marked as enemy number one of Pamyat, whether it was a dangerous group.

"I think to some extent, yes," he replied. "Not Pamyat itself, alone. I think most responsible people there are concerned with monuments, alcoholism, ecology—so, fine. There is also a group of leaders who want to push their activities into the political sphere; they are looking for guilty people. But that's alien to a true Russian. Anti-Semitism, nationalism— that's alien to Russians, especially the intelligentsia."[42]

THE HIGH-STAKES POLITICS OF NATIONALISM

Even so, the political power of the angry Russian Right, and its not-so-hidden allies within the Soviet power structure, became dangerous enough for Gorbachev, during the stormy fall of 1989 through the spring of 1990, to feel the need to outflank and co-opt Russian nationalism. Spurred on by Russian nationalists, provincial Communist Party leaders such as Boris Gidaspov in Leningrad, Leonid Bobykin in Sverdlovsk, and former Moscow Party boss Lev Zaikov were pressing for a separate Communist Party organization for the Russian republic—a demand that Gorbachev understood not only as a reflection of the poisonous political frustration of the Russian masses, but also as a tactical threat to his personal power.[43]

In 1988 and early 1989, the reformist, liberal wing of Soviet politics had been on the upsurge; late 1989 brought the right-wing reaction.

New organizations sprouted up and mushroomed: Edinstvo ("Unity"), with Nina Andreyeva as its figurehead leader; Otechestvo ("Fatherland"), a more respectable version of Pamyat; the United Front of Russian Workers, which sought to organize the Russian blue-collar workers as a mass base of the Russian Right and to mobilize them against Gorbachev's economic reforms. In October 1989, a group of twenty-eight Russian nationalist deputies from the Supreme Soviet met in Tyumen, in west Siberia, to form a parliamentary caucus to fight "reverse discrimination" by other nationalities against Russia. Their main grievances were that Russia's oil, gold, and other natural resources were being exploited by other parts of the country, and that Russians were becoming a minority in the Soviet Union because of rapid birth rates in Central Asia and elsewhere. The Tyumen group issued a declaration that directly attacked Gorbachev's policies—criticizing him for letting the army be discredited; for lowering the level of "state patriotism"; and for dismantling strong executive rule, a bulwark of the Russian state for centuries.[44]

Gorbachev catered to these growing pressures. He might not have understood the power of nationalism in the minority republics, but as a Russian, he understood that nationalism had a powerful pull on his own, discontented people, who were looking for someone to blame and something new to believe in. He could not afford to let the power of Russian nationalism be turned against him personally, as Party rivals seemed determined to do.

Gorbachev made his move in September 1989, at the often-postponed Communist Party Central Committee meeting on nationality issues. He stole the thunder from the right wing by taking a strongly pro-Russian slant. In his opening speech, he promised to set up a "Russian Bureau" in the Communist Party to appease the nationalists; he made a concession to the demands of the Siberian lobby, which wanted more power granted to regional authorities; and he pledged other changes in the "state structure" of the Russian republic. Most of all, in a clear effort to defuse Russian discontent, Gorbachev woefully detailed the sacrifices made by Russia for the sake of the union.

He reminded all the minority republics that economic integration had brought benefits to all.

And then, typical of his style, Gorbachev warned the Communist Party regulars not to carry the lamentations about Russia's misfortunes too far! "If somebody claims that . . . Soviet power has not wrought essential changes, as compared to prerevolutionary Russia, he is engaged in dishonest distortion of reality, intended to whip up nationalist passions and to motivate various extremist demands."[45]

Having made his bow to the right, Gorbachev put himself in charge of the Party's new Russian Bureau, and he got three conservatives purged from the Politburo, including the former KGB chief, Viktor Chebrikov, who sympathized with hard-line Russian nationalists. At the end of 1989 he also indicated willingness to start setting up a Russian Academy of

Sciences, a Russian Ministry of Internal Affairs, Russian trade unions and publishing houses.

The Russian Right was not placated. Its appetite was whetted, its politics made more brazen. Economic recession, and Gorbachev's ending the Communist Party's constitutional monopoly on power in early February 1990, served to further cement the alliance between the nationalists and the Communist Party neo-Stalinists. In late February, just ten days before elections all across Russia, several thousand right-wingers jammed a hockey stadium outside Moscow and jeered Zionists, "foreign exploiters"—and Gorbachev. Members of Pamyat peddled their creed; vendors sold czarist symbols and booklets decrying the exploitation of Russia by other Soviet republics, liberals, Jews, and the current Soviet leadership. And the main speaker, Nina Andreyeva, accused the West of "infecting" the "Russian motherland" with AIDS and pornography. Then she declared that the Communist Party should have demanded Gorbachev's resignation, and the ouster from the Politburo of his allies Aleksandr Yakovlev and Eduard Shevardnadze, at its latest meeting.[46]

Still, Gorbachev continued to court the Russian Right. After he engineered his own election to the presidency in March 1990, he took the astonishing step of bringing two Russian nationalists into his new, powerful, ten-member presidential council. In the company of such official heavyweights as Yakovlev and Shevardnadze, Prime Minister Nikolai Ryzhkov, the heads of the KGB and Defense Ministry, no self-proclaimed nationalist had enough rank to serve on the council. Nonetheless, either as a concession to nationalist strength or as a maneuver to co-opt the Right, Gorbachev put on his council two particularly tart-tongued nationalists: Valentin Rasputin (the only non-Party member on the council); and Veniamin Yarin, a worker from Sverdlovsk, who as a Supreme Soviet deputy had become an aggressive right-wing critic of reform.[47]

Ironically, however, the noisier the Russian Right became and the more Gorbachev appeased it, the worse it did with the voters in Soviet elections. Its mass support, always a question mark, turned out to be very thin—perhaps because many ordinary Russians hear echoes of Stalinism in the rhetoric of hard-line Russian nationalists.

In 1989, candidates from Pamyat and the Russian Right fared badly in the first nationwide parliamentary elections; none of their prominent candidates had been elected. In the March 1990 elections, their weakness among the masses was once again exposed. The fulminating right-wing Writers' Union leader Yuri Bondarev lost a race for people's deputy in the Russian republic on his favorite battleground—Stalingrad (Volgograd). In the Moscow city elections, *Nash Sovremennik* editor Stanislav

Kunyayev and the Russian nationalist painter Ilya Glazunov were also beaten. Right-wing nationalists won only 10 out of 460 seats in the city council; they did no better in Leningrad.

The new democratic Soviet Left outmaneuvered both the Right and Gorbachev's Communist Party. Sensing the powerful populist pull of Russianism, social democratic reformers organized a bloc that they called Democratic Russia, shrewdly playing to the two opposite populist tendencies among Russian voters—the urge for democracy and Russian nationalist feelings. And they swept into power in cities such as Moscow, Leningrad, Sverdlovsk, Gorky, and Volgograd. Thus, by stealing Russophile rhetoric to attack the Communist Party and by promising more local rule, the democratic Left turned the politics of Russian nationalism against its creators.

The final irony was that Boris Yeltsin, not Mikhail Gorbachev, stole the Russian nationalist thunder. After the March 1990 elections, Yeltsin emerged as the populist champion of the "underdog" Russians—the defender of Russian sovereignty against Gorbachev and the hated Soviet Party apparat.

Running for election to the Supreme Soviet of the Russian republic, Yeltsin won 80 percent of the vote against eleven rivals in his home city of Sverdlovsk, in the Ural Mountains—deep in the Russian interior. (Soviet law permits running where you choose and holding elected office at two levels.) Yeltsin had once again demonstrated more popular support than any other figure in Soviet politics. By comparison, Gorbachev has never entered a contested popular election.

After his Sverdlovsk victory, Yeltsin was set on becoming elected the leader of the Russian republic. He ran for the post on a program of more rapid reform, greater autonomy for the Russian republic, a renegotiation of Russia's relations with the central government and other elements of the Soviet Union, the creation of a separate, convertible Russian currency, the establishment of a Russian KGB independent of the Soviet KGB, and the closing of nuclear test sites in the Russian republic. This was heady brew for Russians, who had watched six other republics race ahead of them in demanding sovereignty and autonomy from "the center."

For this most dramatic stage of his political comeback, after a year's work in the new politics, Yeltsin had a host of allies in the Russian parliament, more than two hundred deputies from the Bloc of Democratic Russia, one third of the assembly.

Gorbachev now suddenly saw the power of Russian nationalism coming at him from Yeltsin's democratic, pro-market Left instead of the authoritarian, anti-reform Right. He moved to squelch the challenge, to block

Yeltsin's election as chairman of the Russian parliament. He lashed out at Yeltsin as a "political swindler," who put forth phony claims of being able to solve the country's problems and was guilty of ideological heresy. Among Party members, the overwhelming majority in the parliament, Gorbachev tried to discredit Yeltsin by accusing him of peddling the "corrosive acid" of separatism and "anti-socialist" politics.

"A serious analysis will show that what he [Yeltsin] is offering under the banner of restoring Russia's sovereignty is a call for the breakup of the union," Gorbachev told the deputies. "[This is] an attempt to separate Russia from socialism, which is not mentioned once in Comrade Yeltsin's speech. . . . Socialism hasn't even found a place in the title of the Russian Soviet Federated Socialist Republic. . . . He suggested that from now on it be called the Russian Republic. There's no longer any 'socialism' or 'Soviet' power there."[48]

Against Yeltsin, Gorbachev used a right-winger and Russian nationalist as a stalking horse—Ivan Polozkov, the hard-line Party chief of Krasnodar Territory, who had previously attacked Gorbachev's economic coopera-tives as a "malignant tumor."[49]

But Yeltsin's popular pull was too strong. After two deadlocked votes, pro-Yeltsin telegrams from the people flooded the deputies, tipping the balance narrowly in Yeltsin's favor. On May 29, 1990, Yeltsin became the chairman of the Russian parliament, the top-ranking elected official in a domain that stretches from Leningrad to Vladivostok. That made him, next to Gorbachev, the second most potent political figure in the country. Yeltsin wasted no time in getting the Russian parliament to declare its sovereignty.

For a moment, it seemed as though Yeltsin's election had turned the politics of Russian nationalism on its head by putting the nationalist cause in the hands of moderates and liberals. But the Russian Right was not to be denied.

Right-wing Communists, relentlessly pushing for the revival of a sepa-rate Russian Communist Party, were no longer appeased by Gorbachev's token gestures. They outmaneuvered him while he overextended himself with the new Soviet presidency, with economic problems, with globe-trotting diplomacy. The right-wingers called a founding congress of the Russian Communist Party in Leningrad in June 1990, and Gorbachev was forced to attend or risk surrendering the field to his conservative critics. As it was, Gorbachev had to endure a thunder of criticism—charges that he was introducing capitalism, catering to the West, and had squandered Russia's victory in World War II by giving away Eastern Europe. And then he acquiesced while the right-wing elected its new darling, the feisty, bantam-sized Polozkov, to be the leader of the Russian Communist Party.

Gorbachev was now confronted on both sides by newly elected rivals, each flying the banner of resurgent Russian nationalism, and using it for contrary purposes. He was being pulled in opposite directions.

With a revived Russian Communist Party, the right wing had gained an organizational power base of national dimensions. Its mass support was limited; its political muscle was in the Party apparatus and among senior army generals who were increasingly critical of Gorbachev in public. And in Polozkov, it had an aggressive new leader, an advocate of slowing reform and consolidating strong, centralized rule at the top.

On Gorbachev's left was Boris Yeltsin, a liberal nationalist—indeed, more liberal than nationalist—who was determined to use Russian nationalism for the liberal objective of weakening the Kremlin and centralized economic controls, and also for challenging the grip of the right-wing apparatus.

As soon as he was elected the leader of the Russian republic, Yeltsin reached out to forge links with the leaders of the Baltic republics. This had a powerful impact on Gorbachev, putting new pressure on him to accommodate the centrifugal forces of nationalism tearing at the very fabric of the Soviet Union.

On June 12, 1990, Gorbachev was finally forced, belatedly and reluctantly, to sit down with the leaders of all fifteen republics and begin the serious reallocation of power between the central government and its constituent republics. Seven decades after Lenin had promised the minorities self-determination, Gorbachev was being dragged into putting that promise into practice. His policy of *glasnost* had set free the powerful urges of ethnic nationalism; and now the power of nationalism, in Russia and around the periphery, was compelling Gorbachev to reshape the very structure of the Soviet state in a desperate effort to prevent its total disintegration.

PART FIVE

The Taste of Democracy

*I*n politics, Gorbachev was far bolder than in economics or in dealing with the rising challenge of minority nationalities. To modernize his country, he knew that he had to break up the Stalinist power structure that still ruled with an iron grip. He had to move the Soviet Union from dictatorship toward democracy.

In this arena, Gorbachev was the opposite of Deng Xiaoping in China; Deng believed it was possible to have economic reforms, to modernize his country by giving regions, enterprises, and individual peasant farmers more economic freedom and flexibility, without granting political freedoms.

Gorbachev, urged onward by Aleksandr Yakovlev, concluded that political and economic reforms went hand in hand. If he was to energize his people and to engage them in rejuvenating their country, he had to give them a stake, a voice, and a role in making policy. Gorbachev did not promise full democracy; his slogan was "democratization."

Without understanding initially how far he would have to go, Gorbachev knew he needed a housecleaning in the Communist Party and an end to the Party's diktat over every facet of Soviet life. His purpose was to disperse power.

Yakovlev and other Party reformers understood that this approach would inevitably require stripping the Communist Party of its monopoly on political life and opening the way to a multiparty system. As Gorbachev embarked on his reforms, he did not intend to go that far, and indeed for close to five years he shied away from that. Only when confronted by the swift overthrow of hollow Communist regimes in Eastern Europe and by the democratic pressures within his society, was he finally persuaded.

Democratization came slowly; except for the Party, Soviet society was a political vacuum. It lacked the institutional framework for democracy. It lacked even the basic building blocks for what John Stuart Mill and John Locke called a "civil society"—a multitude of self-generated, self-sustaining voluntary associations representing various popular interests. What Russians called the "Party state" dominated everything.

So Gorbachev had to stimulate popular initiative and engagement—first with informal groups, then with elections, next with a rejuvenated parliament that genuinely debated and ratified or rejected policy, and finally by forcing the Party to give up its legally guaranteed supremacy.

Yet even though Gorbachev was the catalyst of a massive political change, he had only a general notion of where he was going; by the admissions of his closest advisers, he had no stage-by-stage blueprint for political reform. His lurches first this way and then that way were evidence that he was improvising as he went along.

Several times he initiated reforms only to resist their natural consequences. Repeatedly, he was overtaken by the forces that he let loose and the process that he had initiated. More radical reformers outflanked him, impatient with his conservatism and constantly pressing him to go faster than he wanted.

Quite deliberately, he placed himself in the political center—between the radical reformers who were pressing him to go faster, and the hard-line Party *apparatchiki,* who controlled the organs of state security as well as the government ministries and regional Party committees, and who did not want to let go of their power. He tried to reform the Party from within, but ultimately discouraged, he created the new Soviet presidency and forced the Party to relinquish its control at the pinnacle of power.

CHAPTER 18
GRASS-ROOTS ACTIVISM: REINVENTING POLITICS

"*Perestroika* is not manna from heaven. Instead of waiting for it to be brought in from somewhere, it must be brought about by the people themselves."[1]
—Gorbachev, June 1988

"We found out that our opinion counts. You see, Gorbachev gave us some sort of belief in ourselves. A belief that *we* could do it."[2]
—Viktor Zakharov
Carpenter
March 1989

Ivanovo is a rough industrial city in central Russia, a seedbed of revolt among the Russian blue-collar proletariat under the czars, and a provincial bastion of hard-line Communist orthodoxy even in the nineties.

When I arrived in Ivanovo in 1989, Party leaders still ruled like feudal lords. They opposed Gorbachev's push for change, tenaciously clinging to power and, in open defiance of Moscow, they resisted the new politics of pluralism.

Ivanovo's political traditions favored the Communist status quo. Even though the city was only about 150 miles northeast of Moscow, people in the capital thought of it as a provincial center in the silent depths of Russia, largely untouched and uninfluenced by the outside world. It was a hard, self-contained nugget of Stalinism.

Party bosses still preached the catechism of Ivanovo's revolutionary past, the city's long ties to the industrial workers' movement. It is the kind of city Marx had in mind when he summoned the workers of the world to unite and to throw off their chains. A century ago, Ivanovo became the Russian Manchester, an industrial sweatshop, the core of the Russian textile industry. During seven decades of Soviet power, its industrial muscle grew: Its population tripled to more than half a million, and its industry expanded, adding manufacturing and machine building.

With a large industrial work force, Ivanovo was one of the first Russian cities to spawn a Marxist proletariat, and thus was a natural stronghold of the Communist Party. In the 1880s, Ivanovo seethed with industrial discontent and labor activism. More than a decade before the Russian Revolution, workers there formed trade unions; during the 1905 uprising against czarist rule, Ivanovo's workers dared to establish some of Russia's first *soviets*, or workers' councils, which operated much like union strike committees defending Ivanovo's textile workers.

So, both before and during the 1917 Revolution, Ivanovo was in the vanguard of the Bolshevik movement. In the Soviet era, the city was a paradigm of iron-fisted Stalinist rule, tolerating neither deviation nor dissent. Even in the Gorbachev years, the city lays proud claim to the Bolvshevik title "Motherland of the First Soviets," and its schoolchildren, wearing the blue uniforms and red scarves of Communist Young Pioneers and standing rigidly at attention, take turns as the honor guard at an eternal flame and other monuments to the Revolution.

"Because the Party hailed this as 'the city of the first soviets,' they beat us down, beat our independence out of us," observed Leonid Slychkov, a slender intellectual in his forties who specializes in Russian literature and restoration of old Russian buildings. "In the 1930s, Ivanovo was a center of Stalinism."[3]

I went to Ivanovo with a film crew in March 1989, two days before the first nationwide elections under Gorbachev, precisely because Ivanovo was such an Old Guard stronghold. I was curious to see if Gorbachev's political reforms had pushed out into the conservative Russian hinterland. And I stumbled onto something entirely unexpected, something that the Party bosses desperately did not want me and my camera crew to film.

"THERE'S A BIG FREEZE HERE"

As we headed out to observe election campaigning in the rural regions around Ivanovo, a young man tipped us off that there was a hunger strike going on at a local church. When we returned at day's end, the city was pitch black, but we noticed a crowd outside the fence of a large, brick church building. I asked our Soviet driver to stop, but he ignored me. At our hotel, I asked to be taken back, but the driver refused. The Ivanovo television official escorting us pointedly advised that we had only a couple of hours for dinner before our night train left for Moscow; he dismissed the crowd as merely people waiting for trolleys. Our Moscow television escort, Eddie Baranov, said we had a right to go look, but he warned that local authorities would take great offense, since our announced plan was to cover the elections. I insisted nonetheless, but the driver, who may have been working for the police, again refused to take us to the church. It took twenty minutes of haggling before he relented.

From the seventies, I knew that reaction well. Whenever there was a public protest, the reflexive instinct of police and Party, especially in the provinces, was to cover it up, deny its existence, and stonewall.

It was after 9 P.M., late for a sidewalk gathering in a provincial Soviet city in March. But a couple of hundred people were still there—agitated, milling about, talking in low voices, peering through the iron railing of the fence that surrounded the church. Gray-uniformed militiamen moved among the crowd, keeping people from spilling into the streets, but making no arrests. The church gates were all closed, the church itself was closed, but when trolleys paused at the intersection of Friedrich Engels Avenue and Sarmento Street (named for a Mexican revolutionary), almost no one got on. People were drawn to the hunger strike; the mere existence of a spontaneous democratic protest was unprecedented and exciting for Ivanovo.

Young people quickly informed me that four hunger strikers, all women, were lying on the church steps; they were demanding that this Russian Orthodox church, closed for half a century, be reopened. Seventy feet away in the darkness, the women were hard to make out, let alone film. Marty Smith and I decided to spend the night and film in the morning. Our Ivanovo hosts were furious. They made strenuous efforts to get us out of town, insisting that there were no hotel rooms, no transportation to Moscow the next day, and that we were exceeding our original plans. I filibustered past the time of our train departure, and then miraculously the hotel found first one bed, then three, then enough for all six of us. My fear, harking back to the seventies, was that the KGB would arrest the hunger strikers and they would be gone by morning.

Shortly after 7 A.M. we were at the church. It was a tall, imposing shrine made of dark-red brick; its five green cupolas loomed against a turbulent El Greco sky, dominating the downtown landscape. Officially, this was known as the Church of the Presentation, but everyone called it the Red Church. At one time, the Red Church had obviously been the main Russian Orthodox church in Ivanovo; but Stalin had nationalized it in 1938. For the last four decades, it had housed local-government archives. In all, people told me, Ivanovo had once had twenty-eight working churches; now it had only one—on the outskirts, eight miles from downtown.

To avoid the scrutiny of militia patrols, I went around to the far side of the church to climb over the fence, and made my way to the portico, where four women were lying under coats and blankets, half dozing. They looked pale and immobile. One was reciting Psalm 17. Another woman nearby, who was relaying messages to the hunger strikers and circulating a petition on their behalf, told me the hunger strike was in its fourth day.

On the church doors over the four women hung a handwritten banner: ANNOUNCING A HUNGER STRIKE. FROM THE 21ST OF MARCH, WE WILL NEITHER EAT NOR DRINK UNTIL THE OPENING OF THE RED CHURCH. WE ARE PREPARED TO DIE IN THE MOTHERLAND OF THE FIRST SOVIETS.

The women were Larissa Kholina, a fifty-year-old dentist; her twenty-eight-year-old daughter, Rita Pilenkova, a philologist who was working as a hospital aide; Valeriya Savchenko, a forty-six-year-old jurist, who said that she was forced to work as a cleaning woman because, due to her beliefs, authorities would not let her practice law; and Galina Yakhukovskaya, a fifty-year-old sympathizer from the distant Kuban region.

Under Gorbachev's new policies, such churches were to be returned to believers, but Ivanovo Party leaders were resisting, and the hunger strikers were forcing the issue. They told me that five months of appeals to local officials had yielded nothing, although the Council for Religious Affairs in Moscow had agreed that the Red Church should be given to a newly formed congregation.

"Did you personally go to Moscow?" I asked.

"Yes, we were in Moscow—last November twenty-third," said Larissa Kholina, a sturdy woman whose oval face was wrapped in a soft gray scarf.

"And they promised you they would reopen this church?"

"They registered our request and gave us an official certificate."

"And what did the local authorities say?"

"They said we should stop even dreaming about it," she said. "We think this church should be given to the people, and if our death would speed the decision, it will be all right. We thought that only death would bring the authorities to their senses."

"Russia itself will die without its faith, its religion," her daughter, Rita, added.

"The authorities told us that if we choose to die, that's our right," said Valeriya Savchenko, in a weak voice.

"What about Gorbachev?" I asked.

"Well, we are thankful to him," Larissa said, "because he started all of this. He said actually there is a need to reopen churches."

"Did you send him a letter?" I asked.

"Yes, we did," Larissa answered.

"Did you get an answer?"

"Unfortunately, nothing," she said. "Our letters probably never reached him. You know this bureaucratic machinery stands between him and us."[4]

I could understand their frustration but I also saw it as a mark of Gorbachev's new liberalism that this act of religious and political defiance against local authorities was allowed to continue—and that we were not blocked from filming it. Fifteen years earlier, I'd seen small political protests in Moscow, but they were quickly shut down and the demonstrators exiled to Siberia.

Local officials refused to see me that day, and I left Ivanovo shortly thereafter. I was caught up in the national elections and their aftermath, and the Moscow press printed nothing about the outcome in Ivanovo. In May, we tried again to contact the Ivanovo political leadership, but they would not even deal with us.

"These people are afraid of everything and they are embarrassed, so they get aggressive," explained Nikolai Shishlin, a Gorbachev spokesman and speech writer at the Communist Party Central Committee in Moscow. "They don't know how to handle these poor women who want the church, and they don't know how to handle you."[5]

Through the Central Committee staff, Ivanovo's Communist Party leaders sent word for me and my crew to stay out of Ivanovo and warned that we would be arrested if we returned. I went back anyway with the film crew in May.

Larissa Kholina, her daughter, Rita, and Valeriya Savchenko told me that their hunger strike had ended after sixteen days, but only after promises of action from city officials.

"A representative of the city executive committee came and talked to us for four hours," Larissa said. "He was trying to convince us to give up the hunger strike, saying the question would be resolved in the course of the month."

"And so you ended it?" I asked.

"Yes, we believed him. . . . After all, he is a *Communist,*" Larissa said sarcastically, mocking the Communist claim to honesty. "So we stopped the hunger strike and that was announced in the local newspaper, *Leninist.*"

Larissa had lost twenty-eight pounds and Rita twenty-four during the hunger strike; it had taken them a month to recover.

But the impasse over the Red Church remained. The women said that a compromise had been vetoed by the top Party boss of Ivanovo, a crusty hard-liner named Mikhail Knyazyuk, and his circle of Party apparatchiks.

"They gave us nothing, even though they had to, under the law," Larissa snorted. "They were supposed to provide us with at least a temporary building."

"These people were brought up in the atmosphere of Stalinism," Rita interjected, "and of course, they cannot change their mentality. They cannot 'restructure' themselves."

"So *perestroika* isn't working out here?" I suggested.

"Oh, *perestroika* is stuck in the mud here," Larissa said, shaking her head.

Rita grimaced, as if in pain. "All four wheels—stuck," she said.[6]

The local church hierarchy, having survived decades of Communist rule by avoiding confrontation, offered no comfort. The bishop, who had been in Ivanovo for thirty-eight years, was reluctant to pressure the Party leaders over the Red Church. Other priests said at least four new churches were desperately needed to accommodate several thousand believers, but Bishop Amvrosi, a staunch conservative, was cautious.

"To resort to extremism would be unwise," he told me. "We advised our parishioners just to wait. This is not a fast process. One should really be patient."

He had filed a petition for reopening the church but was opposed to public protests and hunger strikes.

"This hunger strike surprised us here in the Church very much," said the bishop, a large man in his sixties in flowing purple robes and with wispy white hair and goatee. "Maybe in secular life it has become trendy in the twentieth century—a hunger strike here, a hunger strike there. But I personally wouldn't bless a hunger strike as the means to achieve their goals. That is not exactly compatible with our Orthodox faith. And I was worried about their health."[7]

A young priest, whose name happened also to be Amvrosi but was no relation to the bishop, had backed the hunger strike. For that, he had been denounced in the press and falsely accused of sexual improprieties; hecklers had repeatedly appeared outside his home. Father Amvrosi suggested that Party leaders found it hard to accept reopening the Red Church because it would be such a prominent symbol of their political failure.

"Inevitably young people will go to church and it will become their gathering place, which will nullify seventy years of the Party's atheistic propaganda," he said. "Their goal has been to close churches, not open them. And, you see, the spirit of Stalinism is still with us. . . . There is a big freeze here. These local leaders want to violate the spirit of *perestroika*. They cannot comprehend the new trend."[8]

Moreover, their defiance was a classic illustration of the difficulties Gorbachev was having in implementing his reforms. Ivanovo's Party chiefs had no fear of retribution for refusing to carry out Gorbachev's policy; they evidently had protectors in Moscow. In fact, that summer Konstantin Kharchev was forced out after five years as head of the Council for Religious Affairs in Moscow, because Party hard-liners considered him too liberal. Kharchev told the Moscow press that some KGB and Communist Party Central Committee officials were sabotaging Gorbachev's policy on religion; he specifically accused Ivanovo's Party bosses of applying a vindictive policy in violation of the law.

"The members of the apparat don't forget their defeats," Kharchev said, evidently alluding to Gorbachev's support for religion. "This is plainly vengeance against believers and all people who have supported their just demands."[9]

Nonetheless, the hunger strike had been a spark; people told me that it had awakened Ivanovo politically. Local newspapers had become more daring, and began writing articles openly critical of the Party leadership, though one reporter was afraid to meet me for fear of official retaliation. A factory newspaper published a poll showing a majority favored reopening the church; three of Ivanovo's eleven deputies to the national congress supported the hunger strikers. A few informal groups were organized to push other issues, such as protecting the environment, restoring old buildings, and making local government more democratic. These became the nucleus for a popular-front movement.

"Suddenly people started to take an interest in the public life of the city," said the philologist and restorer Leonid Slychkov. "It was the hunger strike that awakened people."

Despite this trend, Ivanovo's officials were still in a truculent mood six months after the hunger strike, although Moscow's Council for Religious Affairs had once again agreed to return the Red Church. Mayor Anatoly

Golovkov, finally agreeing to see our team, admitted how much the hunger strike had upset the apparatus.

"Frankly speaking, I would say that it was very unpleasant and very unexpected," said Golovkov, a self-confident man in his early forties with close-cropped hair and cold blue eyes. "They caught us unaware. This is the first time that it happened in our city. We didn't know what to do. We didn't know how to talk to these women. The Party committee decided that their method was simply unacceptable. We tried to persuade them to take other approaches, but they didn't agree."

The central question, of course, was not tactics but policy: Why hadn't Ivanovo authorities simply turned over the church?

"That's not a simple question," Golovkov replied. "I would say there are three reasons. The first is my own personal attitude. I was raised an atheist. It is my deep conviction. And we have to be careful about the current trends going on in the Soviet Union. The second reason is that there is now a state archive located in the church, and it isn't possible to move the books for a year or more. And the third reason is that the church is located on one of the busiest city streets. We think it would not be acceptable to open this church on this very busy street. . . . I don't know what it's like in your country, but here, it's not always the best people who gather around a church. There are all sorts of wretched people who come and hang around by the fence or in the courtyard. It's simply not possible . . . not acceptable in the center of the city to have that kind of service going on."[10]

The word "power" was never used, but as the interview wore on, it became clear that power was the real issue. The Party hierarchy objected to surrendering its monopoly on power. It objected to bowing so obviously to grass-roots pressure, and it regarded the prospect of open ideological competition with the Church as distasteful.

The predicament of the Party apparatchiks in Ivanovo was a microcosm of the country as a whole. In the end, the Party bosses in Ivanovo had to give way to the squeeze from Gorbachev above and the popular pressures from below.

Mayor Golovkov squirmed and stalled in the fall of 1989, a time when the Party was lashing back at its foes; he said it would take a couple of more years before the archives could be moved.

Yet in March 1990, when I returned again to Ivanovo, I found that an important change had taken place: A priest and a group of worshipers, including Larissa Kholina and Rita Pilenkova, had been allowed to convert part of a building on the grounds of the Red Church into a small chapel for services. The archives were still in the church, and the worshipers were impatient to get their hands on the church proper. The priest, himself an artist, was already preparing new icons for the Red Church, and it was clear that the spontaneous public protest that I had witnessed a year earlier had gathered enough public support to force the old system to give way, however slowly.

FREEDOM OR ANARCHY?

Ivanovo's experience was typical of political evolution under Gorbachev. As he began his reforms, the country as a whole was virtually a political vacuum. It lacked political institutions independent of the Communist Party. The Party was the guiding force for everything: In Ivanovo it ran the city government, dictated religious policy, used what were essentially "company trade unions" to manipulate the proletariat, turned the city soviet into an empty showcase, a tool of the Party apparat instead of a people's forum.

The contrast between the Soviet Union and Poland, for example, is stunning. For decades, Poland has had a Catholic Church that was an ideological refuge and a base for political activism as well as a countervailing force to the Communist regime. Poland had a small private economic sector in farming and services. And most important, the independent Solidarity trade-union movement had a decade to develop as an alternative power base to the Communist Party—*before* Solidarity won the elections of 1989.

Soviet society lacked an independent political infrastructure, and so it had to begin virtually from scratch. Except for tiny bands of dissidents, religious believers, or would-be Jewish emigrants, the Soviet people were politically passive—and Russians were particularly so. They accepted politics as the province of the *vlasti,* the powerful; it was practiced in secret and then perpetrated on the masses. People at large never dreamed of participating.

"Politics is like the weather—it comes from on high," one of my Russian friends remarked during the seventies. "There's nothing that we can do about the weather except adjust—bundle up on cold days, wear raincoats when it rains, and wear light clothes when it's warm. The same with politics. *They* make the politics," he said, raising his eyebrows and tossing his jaw upward, to indicate the higher-ups, "and *we* adapt."

That resistance to democracy, even mistrust of democracy, as I commented before, has been embedded in the Russian psyche by a long history of absolutism under both czars and commissars. Russians have known precious little of such essential ingredients of democracy as moderation, constitutionalism, division of powers, rule of law, or restraint either by rulers or by revolutionaries. Political tolerance is not a typical Russian trait. Their politics has been given to extremes: iron rule or bloody revolt. This experience has left them with an abiding fear of chaos, disorder, of things careening wildly out of control, and therefore a strongly felt need for Authority to maintain order and to protect the people from violence and upheaval. As David Shipler, an experienced and talented observer of Russia, commented, there is "no authority without authoritarianism, no order without oppression, no change without upheaval."[11]

Many Russians have inherited from their turbulent and bloody past an inbred fear of freedom. Older Russians shudder, for example, at the twentieth century, which has brought them revolution, civil war, famine, massive purges, and two wars fought on Russian soil. A study of their own history has also taught Russians that pushing protests, taking liberties as it were, can provoke a violent crackdown from on high. Moral: Too much freedom has terrifying consequences.

Fear of freedom also arises from the fact that Russians sense that they are all anarchists in their souls. Democracy requires responsibility, the rule of law, a sense of compromise, a sense of self-restraint coming from within the individual, whether ruler or ruled. But history has not taught Russians the habits of compromise or restraint; theirs has been winner-take-all politics. And so they have a gut anxiety that others will use freedom against them; they find it hard to trust each other to use it responsibly.

So to a greater extent than Westerners, Russians have been relieved when order was imposed on them; and in the great mass of Russians, authoritarianism has bred passivity. It has made them submissive, unaccustomed to exercising individual liberties, and accustomed instead to a system of rules decreed from on high. As anyone who has lived among them knows, they delight in breaking those rules; despite surface appearances, they are not by nature a disciplined, Teutonic people. But their instinct for petty, clandestine defiance of authority is sometimes mistaken by outsiders for a suppressed democratic spirit. In a few people, perhaps; but more frequently it is something else—almost a child's game against powerful parents, a safety valve, a personal struggle to get away with an infraction by covertly bending the rules, rather than an open, democratic assertion that the people are sovereign.

Take seat belts: Traffic rules in Moscow require wearing them in private cars, though not in taxis. Even though a private motorist can be fined 5 rubles on the spot for failing to use his seat belt, practically no one uses them. To avoid fines, people simply pull the belts across their chests and let them dangle. Whenever I attached my belt and suggested that they were useful safety devices, Muscovites laughed me off. Not just a few people—everybody. All of them regarded seat belts as one more bureaucratic gimmick to plague their miserable lives. They never stopped to consider whether the belts made sense.

One day, I was with Sasha Lyubimov, a well-known TV personality from the show *Vzglyad*, and he hitched a ride for both of us from a woman designer. She was awed by his presence. We chatted in a mixture of Russian and English so that by the time he got out, the woman knew I was a foreigner. As I slid into the front seat vacated by Sasha, I threw the seat belt over me without connecting it. She looked over at me with a laugh and remarked, "Ah, I see you are a real Muscovite already. You don't bother to fasten your seat belt. You know our customs."

I laughed too, and then I noticed that her car was missing the bottom connector for the seat belt.

"Most people have the proper equipment," I said. "You don't even have all the equipment."

She laughed again.

"It's not necessary," she said. "Who needs it? We prefer to have our seat belts unattached. We like to pretend we're using them whenever the police are watching us. It's our little game with the authorities. We Russians love to play such tricks on the authorities."

It was a typical Soviet attitude: Rules are made to be broken, if you can get away with it. Life is a game: we and they. They make the rules and we break them. It is a game of absolutist politics, not of democracy—the individual cheating the system, instead of confronting the powers-that-be to demand reform or a better life. That is the traditional way of Soviet politics—breaking rules, not changing them or relaxing them.

In a democracy, people demand and expect greater freedoms, but if the citizenry does not have an inbred sense of responsibility and self-restraint, the system breaks down and freedom leads to anarchy. I recall seeing a sign at the border of Franco's Spain back in the 1950s: THERE CAN BE NO FREEDOM WITHOUT ORDER. Reading this, as I was, in a fascist dictatorship, I considered it a slippery pretext for totalitarian rule: Dictatorships use the demand for law and order to justify repression. To me, Franco's slogan was offensive, and alien, because in fact his regime—like Stalinist Russia—set order in opposition to freedom. Yet actually, in Western society, we take both order and freedom for granted and feel little need to make a fundamental choice between them.

Except for the Civil War more than a century ago, we Americans have not known war on our own soil. We have not experienced mass civic

conflict in which cities have been demolished and millions of people have
perished. In our bones, we do not know the price of such disorder. Our
system is stable, and a structure of social order exists, despite periodic
eruptions of racial violence or mass demonstrations over such issues as the
Vietnam War. We have learned that these events do not threaten the
fundamental stability of our institutions and the essential security of our
society. And after centuries of Anglo-Saxon and Roman legal traditions,
we have an internal sense of restraint.

For the most part, we are a law-abiding people, whose infractions of the
rules come at the margins—traffic speeding, cheating on income taxes,
using the office phones for personal calls. Only the mass drug problem
carries the threat of real social disorder, of the unraveling of our social
structure. It causes panic because it is a dark, menacing force, unpredictable and uncontrollable. We feel vulnerable because we cannot guarantee
our own safety or, worse, that of our children. It is at this point that we
come closest to an instinctive understanding of the Russian panic about
social chaos, and of their wariness toward democracy. Given the choice
between order and a freedom that risks chaos, vast masses of Russians
choose order—and they have done so for centuries.

Prior to Gorbachev, the episodes of democracy in Russian history were
few, limited, and ultimately unsuccessful. In 1825, there was an abortive
uprising of czarist officers, known as the Decembrists, who were pressing
for the abolition of serfdom, and the creation of a constitutional monarchy
and an elected legislature. They wound up hanged or in exile. Another
period of reforms took place under Czar Alexander II, who freed the serfs
in 1861; but he was assassinated on the day he signed a decree approving
a representative assembly. From 1906 to 1917, under the popularly
elected legislative Dumas, there was a period of economic and political
pluralism, of independent farmers and a flourishing press, but this attempt
at constitutional government was so fragile that it crumbled under the
assault of the Bolsheviks.

So Gorbachev's political reforms were not only challenging a power
structure determined to defend itself, they were bucking the accumulated
weight of Russian history. As the hunger strikers in Ivanovo discovered,
reformers had to fight not only a powerful institutional enemy but also
deeply embedded conservative attitudes and popular inertia.

"Democracy is something you learn gradually," Vladimir Pozner said
to me. "It's a process. It cannot be decreed. I mean we, the Soviet people,
are not a democratic people. We have not had a democratic heritage. You
look back in Russian history—what democracy? It's something you have
to learn to use. Some people in our country are more democratic than

others. But if you look at our reaction when we don't like something—say we don't like a movie, people will say, 'You should ban that movie.' When they don't like what someone is saying on television, they will say, 'He shouldn't be allowed to say that.' Such a reaction is spontaneous."[12]

Given my own experience with Soviet political passivity in the seventies, what surprised me in the eighties was how many people quickly grasped at the new freedom that Gorbachev offered—not to overturn the system, but to assert some basic demands.

Before Gorbachev, there had been a spontaneous, unofficial environmental movement to save Siberia's famous Lake Baikal from industrial pollution; there had been a few groups devoted to restoring Russian historical monuments. And there were tiny clusters of dissidents operating at the fringes of society, whose sympathizers in the Soviet mainstream shunned them for fear of police reprisals.

As a result, many Western experts, and Soviets themselves, were astonished by how rapidly political initiative crystallized under Gorbachev. His call for political pluralism clearly tapped into a hunger for independent activity at the grass roots that almost no one had anticipated. In his first year or two, most new political activity was either at the dissident fringe or still modest and devoted to such politically safe goals as historical or environmental preservation.

But from 1987 onward, all kinds of unofficial, informal groups mushroomed almost overnight—the most sensational being the popular-front movements in the Baltic republics and other minority regions. In the mainstream of Soviet life there were suddenly hundreds of new groups: the *afghantsi,* Afghan war veterans lobbying for proper health care, for preferred treatment as consumers, and for understanding from the home folks; in the Ukraine, a group called Zelenni Svet ("Green World"), protesting pollution and nuclear-power stations in populated areas; Memorial, a nationwide network dedicated to rehabilitating and aiding victims of Stalinism and raising money to build them a national memorial; a Leningrad group called Spaseniye, or "Salvation," whose proclaimed goals were to preserve monuments of history and culture and to democratize public life; in Moscow, groups like Civic Dignity, the Club of Social Initiatives, People's Action, Democratic Perestroika. Later came groups like the Union of Lawyers, independent associations of cooperatives or peasant farmers, and some upstart reformers among military officers who formed a group called Shield.

In April 1987, Boris Yeltsin, then Communist Party boss of Moscow, allowed members of 148 different groups to meet in Moscow's famous Hall of Columns, site of some of Stalin's show trials. The nonstop, sophomoric debates of these suddenly liberated Russians were called a "kinder-garten for democracy" by one organizer.[13] A year later, a similar meeting of about 100 different groups led to the formation of the Democratic Union, which openly declared itself an opposition party, even though opposition parties were still illegal.

By early February 1988, *Pravda* estimated that the Soviet Union had about thirty thousand unofficial or informal groups, or *neformalny*, in Soviet shorthand.[14] That statistic was misleading because it included vast numbers of tiny little rock-music fan clubs and clubs of sports fans. Nonetheless, by the end of 1988 there were probably several thousand microgroups concerned with social, political, religious, environmental, and nationalistic issues. The most potent new grass-roots movement to emerge in 1989 was that of striking coal miners in Siberia, the Ukraine, Vorkuta, and Karaganda. The massive walkout by some 150,000 miners in July—the first truly large-scale labor strike since the Bolshevik Revolu-tion—brought the government to its knees, forcing promises of higher pay, better working and living conditions, and more rapid economic reform. Some of the strike leaders used their new muscle in regional politics and talked of forming an independent trade union.

Initially, the national Communist leadership was not only tolerant but approving of grass-roots activism; as a response to Gorbachev's program of democratization, it was evidence of popular engagement in public life. From the Party's perspective, the more the merrier. Proliferation of mi-crogroups meant less of a threat to the Party, because in the early phases, none of the groups was large or extensively organized; moreover, as tiny atoms of political action, all competing with one another, they were vulnerable to domination by the Party or manipulation by the KGB.

Yet the longer-term implications of these embryonic cells of democracy were more threatening to the Party apparat. This was Gorbachev's pur-pose: to use these new "informals" as a populist force to pressure and cow the hard-line apparatchiks. Indeed, as the groups became bolder, and as some, like the popular fronts and striking miners, began to merge into larger coalitions, to reach for wider mass appeal and challenge the Party frontally, hard-liners—not only in Ivanovo, but in Moscow and around the country—began sounding the alarm.

By February 1989, things had moved so far that former KGB chief and Politburo member Viktor Chebrikov could no longer contain his worries. On a visit to Moldavia, where a popular front had begun to rival the Party, Chebrikov lashed out at grass-roots activism.

"Individual, so-called informal associations are doing considerable harm," he declared. "While demagogically declaring their support for *perestroika,* they hinder it by their actions. There are outright anti-social-ist elements who are trying to create political structures opposed to the Communist Party of the Soviet Union. We must, of course, react to such attempts and actions. . . . We must deal a sharp, public rebuff, from a Marxist-Leninist position, to the leaders of informal groups which seek to push the masses on the road to anarchy and lawlessness, on the road to destabilization, on the road to creating legal and illegal structures opposed to the party."[15]

BRATEYEVO: NO GRASS GROWS

Gorbachev was on the opposite tack, encouraging people to demand better government and become politically active, and never more ardently than at the Nineteenth Communist Party Conference in June 1988. In the immediate wake of that conference, one of the most dramatic battle-grounds between the Party and grass-roots activists was an ugly, polluted district known as Brateyevo on the southern outskirts of Moscow.

In Brateyevo, I encountered a citizens' grass-roots movement that re-minded me of neighborhood politics in New York City—but to see it in Russia was astonishing, because it seemed to flare into the open, out of nowhere. The residents, provoked by the arrogant disdain of city authori-ties and the Party apparat, coalesced into an unprecedented "Self-govern-ing Committee." They waged tenacious trench warfare that was ultimately much more dangerous to the Communist Party apparat than were Ivanovo's hunger strikers.

The four women of Ivanovo had the limited objective of trying to reclaim a church. In Brateyevo, the people were after control over devel-opment of their "microdistrict" of sixty thousand residents and they were after long-term political influence. And their movement became a model for scores of other Moscow districts and for people in many other cities.

The issue in Brateyevo was the environment, a pressing concern all across the country, an issue almost as widespread and powerfully felt as the urge for religious revival. As in Western countries, environmental concerns have spawned some of the largest and most successful popular protests in the Soviet Union, blocking industrial development and con-struction of nuclear plants.

Brateyevo is a natural target—and breeding ground—for grass-roots activists. It epitomizes the worst in the Soviet urban landscape. It is a massive, cheerless, twenty-story tenement project choked by the pollution of the heavy industry that surrounds it: a huge petrochemical refinery that supplies half of Moscow's gasoline; an enormous coking plant that converts coal to industrial coke; and half a dozen other large factories that poison the air with acid fumes and billowing gray smoke. The area is a kind of instant slum: barren of greenery, prefab tenements aging and cracking before they are occupied, large metal power stanchions marching right through the residential area, their wires humming and snapping. Industrial silt has piled up on the banks of a nearby river, which is too filthy for swimming and exudes a swampy, malodorous stench.

After dinner in Brateyevo late one evening, I stepped out on my hosts' balcony to look at the exhaust flame from the tower of the petrochemical plant about half a mile away. I began coughing and my eyes watered. My Soviet friends were less afflicted only because they had adjusted to the sting in the air and the foul odor. My host, Haik Zulumyan, a philosophy professor, who is a beautiful classical pianist as well as a fan of American jazz pianist Oscar Peterson, told me that many people in Brateyevo, especially the elderly, are constantly sick and dizzy from the industrial pollution.

"We exist here, but you can't call it life in the normal sense," a group of 192 high school students wrote in an appeal to the local district council. "Grass doesn't grow in this area. Trees are dying. The air smells like a chemical laboratory. Gas exhaust from the oil refinery causes headaches, dizziness, loss of attention. It is hard to exercise here. Many gasp for air even after light exercise. We have no place for leisure. Brateyevo has no public facilities. The neighborhood cinema is ten bus stops away."[16]

Brateyevo was originally planned as an industrial zone; the Moscow city health department ruled in the early 1980s that it was unfit for human habitation because of surrounding industry and a water table just below the land's surface. But Party leaders and city bureaucrats, desperate for new housing space, ignored the health warning and ordered a huge apartment region built; they began moving thousands of people into the area in 1985.

"There was not enough housing space, no place to build," Yuri Prokofyev, who became Moscow Party leader after Brateyevo was built, told me in self-defense. "We used to have only five or six air-monitoring stations for such a large city. The officials simply didn't pay attention to this sort of thing in the past."[17]

To make matters worse, city planners saved money by scrimping on stores, service shops, schools, kindergartens, and clinics in Brateyevo. So the few facilities provided have been hopelessly overcrowded. School No. 27 in Brateyevo has the largest student body in Moscow—but not by plan.

"It was designed for eleven hundred seventy-six students, but we have twenty-three hundred students and by 1991 we will have thirty-two hundred students," said Tatyana Sivilna, the principal. "We have to use three shifts, and still the average number of students per class is forty-five. The school cafeteria cannot service all the students, so our kids cannot eat normally. There is no fresh air in the school. There is no point in talking about the quality of our education in these conditions. . . . Our region has twenty-three thousand children but it doesn't have any sports facilities. No playgrounds."[18]

Muscovites could have easily foreseen this overcrowding. But because of the terrible housing shortage, many people—especially those who had been living elsewhere in cramped communal apartments with several small children—grabbed at the chance to move to Brateyevo.

"We were seven years on the waiting list, and when our turn came they named Brateyevo," explained Nina Shchedrina, a school librarian. "We came to look around and didn't like it very much, but we didn't have any choice."[19]

"WE STARTED FEELING LIKE HUMAN BEINGS"

Public patience in Brateyevo boiled over when the Moscow city government began in May 1988 to implement plans for twenty-one more industrial projects within Brateyevo's already smog-choked district. They were to include the largest printing plant in all of Europe; a huge warehouse for bulk raw materials; a regional depot for subway trains; a large park for trolley buses; a transportation terminal for handling millions of passengers from city subway and bus lines bound for Moscow's most heavily used domestic airport at Domodyedovo; plus a collection of light-industrial plants and major scientific and research institutes.

"Suddenly I began to realize that I was in a very dangerous place," Nina Shchedrina recalled. "I have a son. I'm trying to raise him to be strong and healthy. I was worried about his health and the health of my husband. So I started making phone calls. I called the district executive committee and the district council. They kept saying, 'Oh, there's nothing terrible here. Everything will get better.' But things got worse. I came to the conclusion that the authorities were simply not defending my interests. . . . And I saw an announcement over by the store saying that whoever was interested in improving the ecological situation should come to a meeting. So I decided to go and I took a girlfriend."[20]

That first meeting, on July 12, 1988, led to organized protests. But instead of heeding the citizens' complaints, local authorities pressed ahead with construction and switched to what Nina called "a strategy of silence." As she said, "They figured the less we knew, the better. Everything was done secretly, done very quickly. They worked at night, on three shifts, so that people would not notice what was going on. But we noticed, and we took more steps."

On July 27, the activist group in Brateyevo called for picketing the construction sites. In a country where democracy has never taken root and where citizens normally bow before the might of the state, it was a daring and unprecedented step. Even in cosmopolitan Moscow, citizens are not easily roused to political causes. Decades of repression have conditioned them to be passive and cynical. But in Brateyevo, people were so angry at intolerable living conditions, and their committee so well organized, that they ran picket lines around the clock for five days. In all, several hundred people took part, many using their bodies to block trucks from bringing in materials for construction. The picketers had a guitar and cooked food at night. A young law professor, Sergei Druganov, coached them on how to avoid arrest and helped keep the militia at bay.

The Brateyevo protest quickly attracted attention from local Moscow television, the national TV show *Vzglyad,* and such liberal newspapers as *Moscow News, Komsomolskaya Pravda,* and the weekly *Ogonek.* Nina Shchedrina, who has the classic blond good looks of a Russian worker-heroine cast at Mosfilm Studios, was shown on television blocking the path of huge dump trucks.

"We can't put up with any more," she declared. "We want to recall our formally elected deputies and nominate deputies who live here and breathe this air. We want them to understand all our problems and our pain."[21]

Publicity helped the cause, and construction was temporarily suspended. It was a stunning moral victory. Druganov and other leaders took Brateyevo's case to the Moscow City Council and to local officials in the Red Guard District, where Brateyevo is located. Brateyevo's Self-governing Committee demanded a permanent halt to the construction; it developed an alternative plan for a green belt of parks, playgrounds, and athletic facilities around the apartment complex; and it called for the removal of the petrochemical and coking plants, the worst offenders in terms of pollution.

A series of angry meetings ensued with the Red Guard District leaders. "There were some very tense moments, because truly this was breaking the old stereotypes [of Soviet politics]," Yevgeny Pavlov, chairman of the district council, told me. "We thought they were not raising the issue properly, and they thought the executive committee and the district Party committee . . . should move more quickly."

Sergei Druganov accused the Party of ducking the problem and hiding behind the district council and its executive committee, though under the Soviet system these official bodies traditionally take orders from the district Party boss—in this case an old-fashioned apparatchik, Vyacheslav Zheltov. Months later, Nikolai Pilyayev, a Party secretary, admitted to me that Druganov was right.

"This was the first time we had to deal with these kinds of questions," Pilyayev said. "When the people talked of a bad ecological situation and objected to construction, it was new for us. We had never come up against it before. . . . We were somewhat passive at first. We just ignored those people."[22]

To step up the pressure, the Brateyevo Self-governing Committee called for a public referendum to put Brateyevo's residents on record—choosing between the city's industrial zone and Brateyevo's plan for a green belt. The committee was breaking new ground; Soviet law had no provision for public initiatives or referendums. For maximum participation, the committee wanted to hold the referendum on March 26, 1989—the national Election Day. The local bosses were in an uproar; in a sternly worded private letter to Druganov, they banned the referendum and warned that the militia would be called out to maintain order.

This angered Druganov and the Brateyevo Self-governing Committee, who had been careful to keep their protests peaceful and orderly. When I attended their meeting three days before the election, they were furious at local officials.

"They painted us as a band of extremists," Druganov fumed.

"There are lots of people coming to warn us and make dirty hints," added philosophy professor Haik Zulumyan, who was a co-chair.

"They spat in our face," said a balding, goateed plumber, a bit of a Lenin look-alike. "What kind of *perestroika* is this?"[23]

At this point, Gorbachev's political reforms were just beginning to take root, and I found the willingness at that meeting to confront the powers-that-be quite remarkable. These were ordinary people—a plumber, a carpenter, a driver, a woman pensioner, a teacher, a librarian, some rank-and-file Communist Party members—so emboldened by Gorbachev that they were talking about taking power away from local Party overlords.

"Somehow we started feeling like human beings," said Viktor Zakharov, a carpenter with thoughtful eyes and a great mane of white hair.

"We are not a crowd anymore—we're individuals. We're a group united by mutual interests."

"And we have gotten some self-respect, which is very important," injected Pyotr Kolesnikov, the goateed plumber.

"We found out that our opinion counts," Zakharov said to me. "You see, Gorbachev gave us some sort of belief in ourselves. A belief that *we* could do it."

"He gave us some sort of feeling that we are free to say whatever we think," said Vyacheslav Lomkain, a mechanic. "Before, we said only what they wanted us to say. We were cautious. Now we have a feeling that somebody is really listening to us, taking us into consideration."

The problem was that the "somebody" was Gorbachev, not the local bosses who had just banned the referendum. So the committee drafted a new protest against the ban and demanded that "this discriminatory decision be changed, since it violates the basic human rights of the sixty thousand Brateyevo residents."

Eventually, the local authorities agreed to a referendum—not on Election Day, as residents wanted, but a week later; they were counting on a low turnout once the novelty had worn off. On referendum day, Haik Zulumyan made the rounds of the apartment development with a bull-horn, summoning the voters; people trooped in a light snowfall to School No. 998. The turnout was high and the vote overwhelmingly for the committee.

Unfortunately, the results had no legal power, only the force of a recommendation. As Sergei Druganov complained, "Now we have many laws which are either not enforced or laws ratified stillborn, or simply an absence of laws. All this means that our social relations, our civic life, function very poorly." But to press their cause, the Brateyevo activists demanded a hearing before the district council, a local assembly with 315 members representing the six hundred thousand people in the Red Guard District. Brateyevo comprised 10 percent of that population, but the council—elected before the Gorbachev reforms—included not a single deputy living in Brateyevo.

Moreover, district officials had lined up a barrage of experts from ministries, from the airline Aeroflot, from the city transportation network, from the Moscow architect's office—all of whom pushed for the industrial projects. Nikolai Borisevich, head of the city architectural office that had mapped out the Brateyevo industrial zone, argued that industry would bring jobs (though there was a shortage of labor in the district) and that, as a concession, one industrial site had been moved five hundred yards farther from the apartment area. A health official asserted that the city had no hard scientific evidence that Brateyevo's health problems were worse than in other regions, though he conceded all were in bad shape. Transportation experts insisted that the subway depot, trolley-bus park, and transfer terminal were vital to the city.

Haik Zulumyan protested that the debate was stacked because there were so many powerful state interests trying to drown out the will of the people. "Their budgets consist of billions of rubles and this power gives rise to their self-righteous mentality, which disregards the interests of individuals," he complained. He quoted scientists as saying that there were cancer-causing agents in the Brateyevo air; and finally, he read off the results of Brateyevo's referendum: 21,972 in favor of the green belt, only 38 for industrial development. But Sergei Druganov was denied a chance to speak for several hours and, though normally phlegmatic, he sharply chided the chair. Others from Brateyevo burst out in frustration that only two of their leaders got to speak.

"Comrade deputies," shouted Pyotr Kolesnikov, the outspoken plumber with the goatee, "we are sitting here listening only to those who were registered to speak. Please, listen to us, listen to the public. There were only two people who spoke from our committee."

"Please relax, comrade," the chair replied. "There are fifty people on the list."

"I'm also on the list!" Kolesnikov snapped back, and he turned to his colleagues. "They are not going to let us speak."[24]

What most angered the Brateyevo activists was that district leaders had manipulated the agenda so that the projects were voted on one by one and not as a package, as they wanted. They left the session grumbling.

"Nothing has changed—unbelievable!" blurted out one activist. "The one with the power wins."

"With one-party rule, nothing will change," echoed another. "There used to be repressions and the repressions continue. This blah, blah, blah can go on for another five years."

I talked later with Pavlov, the chairman of the district council. "In the council," I said, "the residents of Brateyevo asked for a simple vote for or against the industrial zone. Why wasn't that possible?"

"You're right that the vast majority of residents expressed their desire not to build these industrial developments," said Pavlov, who had gained experience in deflecting pointed questions. "The council shared that viewpoint. But we had to take into account the opinion of all the deputies. And the deputies thought that this was not only in the interest of the area but in the interest of all of Moscow."[25]

In the end, Brateyevo residents had to settle for less than they wanted.

Some projects, such as the mammoth printing plant and the industrial warehouse, were killed; but the subway depot and the trolley-bus park were given the go-ahead. The local district government pledged to spend 2 million rubles to develop recreational facilities and plant trees; another 1 million rubles was given to Brateyevo's Self-governing Committee to administer. What is more, self-governing committees sprang up quickly in thirty-eight other districts in Moscow, and in many other cities.

Across the country, Soviet environmental protests have scored many local and regional victories over the past three or four years. Russian activists have blocked a scheme to reverse the northern flow of several Siberian rivers for industrial purposes. By Gorbachev's count, environmentalists have shut down roughly one thousand industrial enterprises that manufacture everything from chemicals and metals to pencils, paper, and pharmaceuticals.[26] Environmentalists have been especially effective in fighting the nuclear-power industry, where the government has felt on the defensive.

Since the Chernobyl accident in April 1986, anti-nuclear protests have forced the shutdown of the Metsamor atomic plant in Armenia and halted expansion of reactors at Chernobyl and Khmelnitsky in the Ukraine and Ignalina in Lithuania. They have forced the government to abandon plans to build new reactors at Odessa, Kharkov, Chigirin, and the Crimea in the Ukraine; near the Russian cities of Volgograd and Krasnodar; and near the Byelorussian capital of Minsk. Overall, some 30,000 megawatts of planned nuclear capacity has been abandoned or postponed since Chernobyl; public protests have also interrupted nuclear-weapons testing at Semipalatinsk in Kazakhstan.[27]

Local Green movements have been operating all over the country, and a Green party has been formed in the Ukraine. And while a well-organized national environmental movement has been slow to take shape, Gorbachev's reforms have clearly empowered activists on this issue probably more than any other. In terms of mass support, the Greens rival or surpass the striking coal miners and their demands for economic reforms and independent trade unions, though environmentalists have won fewer sensational headlines than have the miners.

Brateyevo is a good example of how grass-roots environmental protest can affect Soviet political life. Its Self-governing Committee was an excellent political training ground. In fact, the longer-term *political* consequences of the struggle over Brateyevo's industrial pollution were perhaps more significant than the *environmental* gains won for this woefully polluted community.

Old-style Soviet politicians lost out; the district Party boss, Vyacheslav

Zheltov, and Nikolai Pilyayev, the district Party secretary whom I met, were fired. Yuri Prokofyev, who as Moscow Party leader was their overseer, told me bluntly: "There are some people who are used to the administrative method—giving commands or carrying out orders—and they can't give it up. They simply can't work another way. We have to find work for them outside the Party."[28] Yevgeny Pavlov, the district council chairman, ran for reelection in 1990, but lost.

On the other side, the citizen-amateurs succeeded as politicians: Nina Shchedrina, the librarian, won election to the district council in March 1990; Haik Zulumyan, the philosopher, was elected to the Moscow City Council, where he became chairman of the committee on self-government; and Sergei Druganov, the lawyer, won a seat in the Supreme Soviet of the Russian republic.

As Druganov observed, these political results and the psychological changes among people in Brateyevo were probably the most important consequences of the grass-roots revolt against the new industrial zone once planned for Brateyevo.

"What's going on is a radical restructuring of people's way of thinking, a radical *perestroika* of a person's relationship to society," Druganov asserted.

"People are beginning to comprehend that things depend on every individual. If everyone does not participate in *perestroika*, then nothing will happen in the end. . . .

"We understand that we have to fight. We have to stand up for our rights."[29]

CHAPTER 19

ELECTIONS: CROSSING OUT PARTY BOSSES

"Press on, comrades—we from above, you from below. This is the only way *perestroika* can happen. Just like a vise. If there's pressure from only one side, it won't work."[1]

—Gorbachev, February 1989

"Everyone was pessimistic. . . . They thought, Nothing will come of this. It was all unknown territory for us. Our first task was to battle the apparatus. Our second task was to activate the population."[2]

—Yelena Zelinskaya
Leningrad Campaign Organizer
April 1989

The election of March 1989 was a watershed for Soviet society, a historical divide that marked the beginning of a new political era and Gorbachev's move toward a new political order.

That election was the single most powerful catalyst of change in political *perestroika*. By starting the shift of power away from the Communist Party, it launched the transformation of the Soviet political system.

By world standards, the election process was unfair and imperfect. It was intended by Gorbachev as a modest, controlled, incremental step *toward* democracy; it was not truly democratic. Out of 2,250 new deputies, 750 were reserved for the Communist Party, the Komsomol youth organization, trade unions, and other professional groups. The election procedures were manipulated by the Communist Party apparat to protect its power and cripple embryonic democratic forces. In 399 districts, Party officials ran unopposed, and in many regions, such as Armenia and Central Asia, the elections were run the old way. In fact, the great majority of those elected to the new Congress of People's Deputies were Party regulars and loyalists trained by a lifetime of discipline to follow the leader.

Still, the election of March 1989 was like lightning crackling across a long-darkened sky. It struck the foundations of the Soviet power structure like thunder, sending shock waves through the Party establishment.

It was the first election in seven decades with a choice. There were 1,101 election districts that had competition, and 2,895 candidates in all.[3] After years of fabricated unity, of meaningless elections for the Party's designated candidates, the novelty of choice galvanized people from Leningrad to the Pacific Far East. To a far greater degree than anyone, including Gorbachev, anticipated, the chance to reject Party bosses was a powerful magnet; it pulled together democratic movements in the Soviet Union's most important political centers—Moscow, Leningrad, Kiev, Minsk, the Baltic republics. It spawned television debates; it heard calls for a multiparty system; it unearthed army colonels and lieutenants who openly opposed the older generation of generals and called for the end of the Soviet military draft (and in self-defense, some generals advocated student deferments). It forced high officials for the first time to lay out their views, answer questions about how they got cars and apartments, and whether they believed in God.

In the end, the election demonstrated that even when the process was stacked in favor of the Party, it was possible to defeat high Party officials around the country and elect a new wave of radical reformers. The election left the public incredulous, exhilarated, and astonished by its own power.

In the wake of that election began the real shift of power away from the Communist Party and the slow development of a national parliament to challenge the Party's monopoly on control. By lifting a new coterie of reformers and political amateurs to the national stage, the election was the genesis of a political opposition, unsteady and disorganized at first, and certainly no match for the Party machine, but increasingly challenging and purposeful.

In time, the forces set loose by Gorbachev in that election outraced him and his designs for reform. His political offspring harangued him for being too timid and too tied to the Party's Old Guard, and they pressed him toward bolder and more ambitious measures. He was dragged along, repeatedly, reluctantly, by the forces legitimized by the election he had called.

That election, and the first session of the Congress of People's Deputies that followed it, made it all but impossible for Party diehards to halt the momentum of reform or to turn back the path of Soviet history. Short of someone's repeating Stalin's bloody murder of millions, that election and its political consequences made *perestroika* permanent.

That had been Gorbachev's intention, not from the start of his reign but by mid-1988: to use competitive elections to shake up the Party apparatus, open up avenues for new blood to flow into the political system, and at the same time build public support for economic reform by drawing masses of people into public life and giving them a stake in *perestroika*. On the economic side, he did not succeed; but on the political side, he succeeded more than he intended.

As the election approached, Gorbachev traveled the country, preaching his cause, spurring people on to new activism. In a nationally televised encounter on the sidewalks of Kiev, the Ukrainian capital, he invited ordinary people to help him break the yoke of the entrenched bureaucracy.

"Press on, comrades—we from above, you from below," Gorbachev declared. "This is the only way *perestroika* can happen. Just like a vise. If there's pressure from only one side, it won't work."

"The old officials should be replaced!" people shouted.

"Officials should develop from the process of *perestroika,*" Gorbachev shot back. "We should replace the old ones. But where will we get new ones?"

Then he added with a shrug and a grin, "If only we could bake them, like pancakes."[4]

PLAYING THE "GAME OF DEMOCRACY" FOR REAL

Nowhere in all of Russia was Gorbachev's call to action more eagerly or effectively answered than in Leningrad, probably because its politics were so polarized. The city had a long tradition of hard-line Party leaders—from Stalin's henchman Andrei Zhdanov to Gorbachev's onetime Politburo rival Grigory Romanov. Over the decades, crude, iron-fisted rule had bred a festering discontent among a proud but suppressed intelligentsia, many of whom saw themselves as heirs to the European intellectual traditions of czarist St. Petersburg. On the political Right were the neo-Stalinist legions represented by Nina Andreyeva, the teacher whose manifesto had denounced *perestroika;* on the Left were people such as the feisty, independent-minded television producer Bella Kurkova.

In early 1989, feelings were particularly raw because the city government under Mayor Vladimir Khodyrev had decided to raze some old buildings, including the famous Hotel Astoria, once known as the Angleterre. In a city that nurses memories of its imperial past, people considered it a sacrilege to destroy one of the favorite landmarks of old St. Petersburg, still a popular symbol with Leningraders. Khodyrev's decision, backed by the regional Party boss Yuri Solovyov, had provoked the first spontaneous demonstrations in Leningrad in early 1988 and, when he ignored popular feelings, new outbursts in 1989.

"We knew that feelings against the apparatus were extremely powerful; we knew the whole city hated Solovyov," said Yelena Zelinskaya, a soft-spoken writer in her mid-thirties and one of the main organizers of the anti-Party campaign in the spring of 1989. "I hate Khodyrev—he's my personal enemy for what he did to the Hotel Angleterre. We knew the city hated him. Never have we lived so badly in Leningrad. Our living standards under Solovyov are lower than under Romanov and the others before him. Sugar is rationed. Can you imagine—my baby cannot get enough sugar? Our air is worse than ever. Our water is dirtier. Our job [in the election] was to channel the rage of the people against the apparatus.

"So we decided to take part in the election—without hope," Zelinskaya admitted to me. "Everyone was pessimistic. People were frightened. They thought, Nothing will come of this. It was all unknown territory for us. Our first task was to battle the apparatus. Our second task was to activate the population. We had to talk people into taking part in the election. People did not normally participate. I myself had never voted before. But the election campaign was a way to mobilize people, a way to advertise our democratic movement, a way to develop our political muscles."[5]

By that spring, Leningrad was burgeoning with informal groups, from environmental coalitions like Epicenter, Delta, and the Council for Ecological Culture, to historical groups like Salvation and Peterburg, and political organizations like the Leningrad branch of the International League of Human Rights and Club Perestroika. In January 1989, several hundred activists from these various groups met at the House of Writers and formed a democratic coalition that called itself Election '89. They began to draw up a list of candidates, and they formed several committees

to manage the campaign: a legal advisory group to help candidates overcome the obstacles of getting nominated, a "psychological" group to
coach candidates on how to conduct a campaign, a third group to draft
a common program, a fourth group on mobilizing voters and instructing
them how to vote for the first time in a multiple-choice election.

In Leningrad, as elsewhere, the provincial Party leadership resorted to
tricks and maneuvers to block the nominations of rival candidates. Gorbachev's procedures required a two-stage process—first, nomination by factories, institutes, hospitals, farms, and then approval at district meetings
run by the Party or governmental apparatus. Several top officials, including Leningrad Province Party boss Yuri Solovyov, a junior member of the
Politburo, managed to stymie all would-be rivals, and to run unopposed.
Nonetheless, there was still a chance to defeat them: The election law
required the winner to get at least 50 percent of the vote, and it gave
voters the right not only to vote *for*—but also *against*—a candidate. If
enough people crossed out a candidate's name so that he sank below 50
percent, he lost.

Leningrad's Election '89 coalition targeted the Party's unopposed leaders just as vigorously as it pushed its own nominees in contested races.
Yelena Zelinskaya, with her relentless determination and fervent distaste
of the Party apparat, had built an extensive network of friends and contacts from her university years, and from living at the fringe of dissident
politics in the Brezhnev era. Out of her high-ceilinged apartment near one
of Leningrad's canals, Zelinskaya ran a precinct-by-precinct get-out-the-
vote operation that would have done her credit at the Iowa caucuses in
an American presidential campaign. For a nation that had not known a
democratic election for seventy-two years, hers was a very sophisticated
nuts-and-bolts political operation.

On Election Day, March 26, 1989, Zelinskaya had controllers at every
precinct and district, checking the flow of voters; at night, after the polls
closed, these controllers monitored the vote count, and kept her informed
by phone—a sheer miracle given the vagaries of the Soviet phone system.
The regional and city Party leadership, never having faced a challenge of
any kind before, were confident of victory. Soundings by Party organizations at the district and precinct level assured Yuri Solovyov of at least
60 percent of the vote.[6] But by 1 A.M., well before the Party had a full
count, Yelena Zelinskaya knew that even though Solovyov had no opponent, he had fallen!

Two days later, the Party's own newspaper, *Leningradskaya Pravda*, ran
the results: Solovyov had gotten just 45 percent of the vote. There had
been 109,000 people for him, but 133,000 others had gone to the trouble

of crossing out his name—a real testimony to public anger at the Party apparat.[7]

What is more, the voters rejected the entire slate of high Party and city officials, seven in all: Solovyov and his deputy; city Party leader Anatoly Gerasimov and Mayor Vladimir Khodyrev; the leader of the provincial government and his deputy; and the Leningrad regional military commander. After the May 14 runoffs, the anti-Party coalition had elected a slate of reformers, including Anatoly Sobchak, a Leningrad University law professor; Yuri Boldyrev, an outspoken twenty-eight-year-old engineer; Boris Nikolsky, editor of the literary magazine *Neva*, which in January 1989 had printed a scathing attack on the Communist Party, even faulting Gorbachev; and Nikolai Ivanov, a federal investigator who had accused Politburo member Yegor Ligachev of corruption.

Leningrad Party leaders were stunned. As the Soviet press reported, "Literally to the last hour they believed they would win."[8] Some Party officials blamed the press and Leningrad television for biased coverage. Gerasimov admitted the Party had been complacent and had ignored the public's desires when making policy decisions. Solovyov said that the Party "didn't take into account the psychological conditions of the population," especially the need to improve living conditions. Khodyrev blamed everyone but himself.

It was the most stunning blow to the Party's prestige since the Bolshevik Revolution. "I believe it will have a very long-term impact," Boris Nikolsky told me. "Before the election, people thought that this was a 'game of democracy' put on by the leaders. They thought it would come out as elections used to come out, all arranged by the bosses. Now people realize that they have the power to express their opinions and to have an impact."[9]

It was, in Zelinskaya's words, "a real revolution"—the first in Leningrad since the Bolshevik assault on the czar's Winter Palace in 1917.

MOSCOW: COMEBACK FOR BORIS YELTSIN

The elections were also devastating for the Party in Moscow; not only did the hand-picked mayor and some high officials lose, but the Party failed to stop the irrepressible voice of populism—Boris Yeltsin, the hard-driving provincial Party boss who had first been brought to Moscow and promoted into the Politburo by Gorbachev in 1985, and then had been broken by Gorbachev in 1987 for being too brash, too outspoken, too radical a reformer.

To Westerners, Yeltsin might seem a raw, bullish demagogue, but to the Russian man in the street, Yeltsin is a natural for the new politics of *glasnost.* He is a rough-talking, hard-drinking, no-nonsense construction engineer–turned–Party boss, a strapping man with a beefy Russian face, a sharp tongue, and a talent for self-promotion. He has a way of voicing, and igniting, the civic rage of the Russian masses.

Born in a village near the Ural Mountain city of Sverdlovsk in 1931—the same year Gorbachev was born—Yeltsin has had a rebellious streak since childhood. Now silver-haired, he can be charming as well as boorish. He is bright, tireless, and undaunted, a demanding boss and a dangerous foe. At important government and Party meetings, he seems to thrive on confrontation; he will slash at an opponent, and then flash a tight grin and arch an eyebrow at his victim.

By his own account, Yeltsin is prickly, sharp-tongued, and difficult; he appropriately titled his autobiography *Against the Grain.* At Politburo meetings, he felt like an alien, an outsider, and he would provoke the two top men, Ligachev and Gorbachev, with his combative ways. At one session, on September 12, 1987, Yeltsin reported, he made twenty separate criticisms of Gorbachev's proposed speech for Revolution Day—"which caused [Gorbachev] to explode. . . . I was amazed that anyone could react so hysterically to criticism."[10] Gorbachev's aides tried to cast Yeltsin as primarily a foe of Ligachev, with Gorbachev in the center. But Yeltsin's primary challenge was directed at Gorbachev, both publicly and privately.

Yeltsin pushed Gorbachev beyond the breaking point at a Central Committee meeting in October 1987; this was a moment of Party self-congratulation, and Yeltsin was the skunk at the tea party. He rose to tell the Party bosses that "in the eyes of the people the Party's authority has drastically fallen," to chastise the Party for going slow on *perestroika,* and to warn against leaving Gorbachev "totally immune from criticism," because such adulation could bring a new "cult of personality"—a chilling echo of the euphemism once used to describe Stalin's dictatorship. Yeltsin anticipated the onslaught against him—stinging accusations and political excommunication.

Overnight, Yeltsin had become a folk hero. Fired from his high posts but spared a Stalinist execution or exile, he had been given a sinecure post in the Ministry of Construction, and now in the election of March 1989, he was attempting his political comeback. He was running as the voice of the people for the post of at-large deputy from the entire city of Moscow, the single largest election district in the country.

Better than any other politician of the Gorbachev era, Yeltsin had found how to turn earthy barrages against the privileged arrogance and bureaucratic incompetence of the Party elite into vote-getting appeal. Yeltsin's platform called for the Party to be subordinate to the new, popularly elected Congress of People's Deputies, for an end to privileges for Party members, for direct elections at all levels, including head of government, for the rule of law, for popular referendums, for abolition of many ministries, for cancellation of big industrial projects, and for postponement of the space program. Yeltsin cast himself as the people's David against the Party's Goliath.

The Party apparat did everything it could to destroy Yeltsin, and each step backfired, only making him more popular. When the Party threw red tape at his candidacy, he outfoxed them. When the Central Committee accused him of violating Party rules and appointed a commission to investigate, he turned his candidacy into a referendum on the Party establishment. During a televised debate, all the hostile questions were targeted at Yeltsin; one of his backers found out that the questions had been stacked and written not by ordinary listeners but by Party apparatchiks, and he went on another television show to expose the fraudulent debate. When the police, under Party orders, tried to block a Yeltsin rally in Gorky Park, the crowd swelled and marched on city hall, carrying signs that demanded, HANDS OFF YELTSIN!

Each obstacle thrown in Yeltsin's path only served to inflame public opinion; the Party dug its own grave, building up Yeltsin as the people's champion. Valentin Chikin, the anti-Yeltsin editor of the hard-line *Sovetskaya Rossiya,* told me an amusing anecdote about his eighty-four-year-old mother, who was confused by having to make a choice for the first time in her life. Chikin coached her to vote against Yeltsin; but to keep it simple, he instructed her simply to leave the first line—for Yevgeny Brakov, the general director of the Zil automobile factory—and to cross out the second line, Yeltsin; this would count as a vote for Brakov.

A couple of days after the election, Chikin saw his mother.

"Did you vote, Mama?" he asked.

"Yes, certainly," she said, grinning proudly.

"Did you do what I told you?"

"I crossed out the first line and left the second name," she said, grinning again.

"Oh, Mama," Chikin groaned, "that's the opposite of what I told you. Why did you do that?"

"I talked with the people in my building," she chirped. "They were all for Yeltsin. He's for the people. So I decided to vote for Yeltsin too."[11]

Under his political umbrella, Yeltsin brought together forces that intellectual reformers have always had trouble combining: blue-collar workers and the intelligentsia, pensioners and students.

"I'm voting for Yeltsin," said Eddie Baranov, a veteran of Moscow television, "because he's the first one in sixty years to raise his voice and shout out what he thinks. I need *him,* against *them.*"[12]

Yeltsin touched off an avalanche of public rage that buried the Party. He got five million votes—89.44 percent of the total—a stinging rebuff to the Party leadership, Gorbachev included.

"The Party Central Committee did not expect these results," commented Roy Medvedev, the dissident historian who had written about Stalin's terror, and had emerged from the twilight zone to win election himself. "There are people elected whom they did not want—Yeltsin, for example. He's a problem for Gorbachev. He's had a great triumph."[13]

For all its imperfections, the election of March 1989 was the most democratic ever held in the Soviet era up to that point. As Roy Medvedev said, there were stunning upsets all across the country. Some 399 candidates, mostly Party and government officials, had run unopposed, and 195 of them were rejected. In the debris of that election lay the political ruins of three dozen regional Party bosses in Russia, the Ukraine, and Byelorussia, plus the mayors of Moscow and Leningrad, and city leaders in Kiev, Minsk, Kishinev, and Alma-Ata. Sajudis, the national front in Lithuania, swept to victory over the Party; popular fronts scored powerfully in Latvia, Estonia, and Moldavia, as did anti-Party coalitions in Russian cities such as Yaroslavl, Sverdlovsk, and Kuibyshev.[14]

The Party's image of invincibility had been shattered, despite the roadblocks it threw at its new opponents. Many people called the election a referendum against the Party, but Gorbachev's circle construed it more narrowly—as a vote against the Old Guard apparat.

"It's very good they weren't elected," asserted Aleksandr Yakovlev, referring to the Party bosses who had been beaten. With Gorbachev, Yakovlev had co-authored the strategy of using elections to purge the Party from below.

"I know [the losers] and it's great, a terrific example of people voting correctly," he exulted. "Out of the thirty-six, to be honest, I only felt a bit bad for two of them."[15]

Gorbachev seems to have been as surprised as others by the force of the populist vote, but he seized on it as evidence that his revolution from above had now been met by a popular upsurge. "The elections demonstrated that *perestroika* has ceased to be a cause mostly for enthusiasts and trailblazers," he asserted. "We can say that today it has become a truly nationwide movement."[16]

Gorbachev was right: Literally tens of millions of people had taken part in a Soviet election for the first time in decades with some sense that their vote counted for something. And the election had vaulted many new reformers from around the country onto the national stage. Leningrad had a strong slate, as did Moscow: people such as economist Oleg Bogomolov, criminal investigator Telman Gdlyan, political scientist Sergei Stankevich, historian Yuri Afanasyev, and scientific technician Arkady Murashev, an advocate of a multiparty system. The Academy of Sciences elected the world-famous dissident physicist Andrei Sakharov, sociologist Tatyana Zaslavskaya, space scientist Roald Sagdeyev, radical economists Nikolai Shmelyov, Nikolai Petrakov, and Pavel Bunich. From other regions and organizations came radical editors such as Yegor Yakovlev of *Moscow News* and Vitaly Korotich of *Ogonek*, poet Yevgeny Yevtushenko, and economist Gavril Popov, the future mayor of Moscow.

No one could be sure in advance, because no one outside the Communist Party was organized enough to take a nose count, but some reformers guessed they had more than 300, perhaps as many as 400, like-minded deputies in the new Congress—a minority among 2,250, but a large enough group of activists to affect the course of debate and to have a strong impact on the national television audience.

"The big surprise for Gorbachev is that there was such a grass-roots upheaval," commented Boris Kurashvili, a scholar at the Institute of State and Law and a daring exponent of reform under Brezhnev. "There will be independent, unmanageable deputies in the new People's Congress—I figure twenty percent.

"Ten percent is enough to have an opposition that can be heard," Kurashvili emphasized. "There will be enough to form an opposition, an independent bloc."[17]

CHAPTER 20

CONGRESS: GENESIS OF AN OPPOSITION

"Gorbachev is justifiably regarded as the man who launched *perestroika,* . . . [but] he finds it difficult to understand that he is no longer the only leader of *perestroika.* They are cropping up all around the country."[1]

—Yuri Afanasyev
Congress Deputy
July 1989

"This is not *real* democracy. The atmosphere was very different from previous Supreme Soviet sessions. . . . The delegates . . . put tough questions to Gorbachev and he had to reply. They had their own proposals. . . . So that is . . . *significant* democracy, but not *real* democracy."[2]

—Roy Medvedev
Supreme Soviet Deputy
May 1989

Virtually on the eve of the new superparliament, the Congress of People's Deputies, one hundred thousand people held a rally near Moscow's Lenin Stadium to support the new liberal deputies and to listen to their ringing denunciations of the Party apparatus. The speakers included many of the most influential reformers elected to the Congress: members of the Moscow group, the Leningrad slate, popular-front deputies from the Baltic republics, radicals from the Ukraine, the Ural Mountains, and Siberia.

Heady with victory, they were gearing up for the Congress, demanding more radical change, more power to the people. For seventy years, the Supreme Soviet had been among the world's most supine legislative bodies—no one casting a negative vote, except for a rare smattering in mid-1988. The reformers were now intent on putting life and spine into this moribund institution.

"*Perestroika* in the old sense is ended—the reform from above is ended," said Boris Kagarlitsky, a leader of Moscow's popular front, which had organized the rally. "We are coming to the beginning of the popular revolution. But it will be a dangerous process, and that can also end tragically."

"Why is it dangerous?" my colleague Louis Menashe asked.

"Because we are now seeing . . . the people beginning to show their teeth to the bureaucracy. Still, the bureaucracy has more teeth. It's still much stronger."[3]

The thirteen-day Congress—unprecedented in Soviet history—was an open clash of two contending forces, two casts of mind: a loose, disorganized collection of newly elected radicals bent on challenging the old system and forcing reform, and the loyalist Old Guard, derisively nicknamed by the reformers "the aggressively obedient majority," determined to protect its power and to contain what it saw as an upstart rabble. Between them, playing one force off against the other, using the Left to prod the Right to change, activating the Right to hold the Left in check, and always steering a conservative majority to follow his lead, was the ringmaster—Mikhail Gorbachev.

The Congress opened on May 25, 1989. At a minimum, liberals and radicals wanted democratic procedures, especially open debate and an open agenda. The old power establishment had other designs. It wanted the Congress merely to perform the perfunctory chores of electing Gorbachev as the legislative chairman, in effect Soviet president, and of selecting 542 of its own members to serve in the Supreme Soviet, as the permanent legislature to enact laws and approve policy. (The Congress was a special body, sitting only twice a year.) Over the objections of reformers, who wanted a testing examination of Gorbachev's policies before any vote, Gorbachev rammed through his agenda; debate was put off until the end.

No sooner was the vote taken than the reformers were protesting; their moral leader, physicist Andrei Sakharov, was on his feet, demanding to be heard. Sakharov was even more stooped than I had remembered from the seventies, when I used to watch him at his kitchen table sipping tea from a saucer and nibbling little sour green apples, or when I listened to his vibrant defense of human rights against some new repression by Brezhnev and Andropov. In those days, Sakharov's podium had been his small apartment on Chkalova Street, KGB cars down on the road, agents watching who came and went, his wife, Yelena Bonner, interrogated day after day, his stepchildren harassed. He was then ostracized by other academicians, and shunned by his own children and his former wife. Sakharov had braved it all—the cheap slanders and the vicious hypocrisy—remarkably without bitterness. I had marveled at him; he was a saint—fearless, untiring, always prepared to sacrifice himself for others. His manner was gentle, but he was morally uncompromising. In time, I came to admire Andrei Sakharov more than any other human being I had ever met.

Now, his appearance as spokesman for a budding, still inchoate democratic opposition at the Congress signaled the political transformation taking place. It was incredible to see him in this setting, a massive ceremonial hall with thousands of red seats, and a presidium of two dozen members sitting in polished wooden benches stretching across an opera-sized stage, which was dominated by a huge white plaster statue of Lenin.

There stood Sakharov, once defiled and exiled, now a revered public figure, clearly respected—by Gorbachev, among others—as a voice of reason and conscience. Sakharov's shoulders were hunched, his head rimmed by a wispy fringe of hair, his hearing weak, and his step unsteady. He was a heroic but frail figure; now sixty-eight, he had aged badly during nearly seven years of brutal exile in Gorky, where he and his wife were cut off from almost all human contact and had to stage a hunger strike to get decent medical treatment. His wife later told me how suffocating it had been to have guards accompany them to the bread store and keep people away, or to have doctors force-feed them in the hospital. Through it all, Sakharov's independent spirit remained unbroken, and even if his voice now quavered, his message was clear. On this day of days, he supported Gorbachev, but for Sakharov, free, democratic debate was not a matter of majority approval of an agenda—it was a point of principle.

"I think we *must* have a discussion," Sakharov said with direct simplicity. "We would *disgrace ourselves* before our entire people if we did otherwise. *We cannot do otherwise.* This is my profound conviction. . . . We cannot allow elections to be held in a formal manner. In these conditions, I do not consider it possible to participate in this election."[4]

WHAT ABOUT YOUR WIFE?

As Sakharov finished and before the chairman could curtail discussion, a dozen other reform deputies had crowded to the front of the chamber, shouting to be recognized. Gorbachev, sitting beside the temporary chairman, seemed to acquiesce momentarily. Seizing the instant, they began to barrage him with questions.

Marju Lauristan, outspoken leader of the Estonian popular front, said she saw no alternative to Gorbachev but had several tough questions "which I would like answered before I can vote with peace of mind":

What political and legal guarantees for self-determination by minority republics would Gorbachev put into the Soviet constitution? When had he personally found out that army troops with trenching shovels and gas were being used against peaceful demonstrators in Tbilisi on the night of April 8?

And finally: "Do you personally consider the use of the army for punitive operations against civilians to be compatible with democracy and the rule of law in our country?"[5]

Other questions were more personal.

"There has been a great deal of talk about your building a country *dacha* in the Crimea," asserted Aleksandr Shchelkanov, a fifty-year-old deputy from Leningrad. "Millions now watching on TV should be given a straight answer, and only you can give it."[6]

Leonid Sukhov, a motor-pool driver from Kharkov, stunned the entire hall by asking what was on many lips—a question about the influence of Gorbachev's wife, Raisa.

"I compare you not to Lenin or Stalin but to the great Napoleon, who . . . led his people to victory, but owing to sycophants and his wife, transformed the republic into an empire," Sukhov said. "Apparently you are unable to avoid the adulation and influence of your wife. I am willing to vote for you—but just heed these critical comments."[7]

A whole string of delegates, especially younger ones from Moscow, Sverdlovsk, Leningrad, and Ivanovo, pressed Gorbachev to give up his post as general secretary of the Communist Party, if he wished to serve as head of government.

"I cannot understand how it is possible to combine the two functions," complained Sergei Zvonov, a twenty-six-year-old Komsomol leader from Ivanovo. "That concentrates too much power in the hands of one man, which is contrary to democracy."[8]

As I watched from the press gallery, I knew that no other Soviet leader since Lenin would have brooked such a public challenge. But Gorbachev had obviously decided to allow his critics and questioners their day, to let his openness to challenge serve as an example to other government and Party officials, to let it serve as a school in democracy for the nation at large.

At one point, Gorbachev—who had simply assumed the chairmanship of the session without election—was abruptly reminded that in a society of laws, power and privilege have their limits. As he was addressing the presidium, Aleksei Levashov, a young political scientist from Leningrad, strode to the podium and interrupted Gorbachev, refusing to recognize his authority to head the proceedings.

Gorbachev (to the presidium): "Don't worry, we agreed that all presidium members will preside in turn . . ."

Levashov: "Comrade deputies, according to the constitution . . ."

Gorbachev (to Levashov): "Just a minute—I haven't given you the floor."

Levashov: "It's the [election] commission chairman who should give me the floor."

Gorbachev: "Just a minute. I'll give you the floor, but just the same you should ask for it first. You should show respect to the Congress and the presidium. Please go on, introduce yourself."

Levashov: "Comrade deputies, according to the constitution . . ."

Finally, after a couple of hours, Gorbachev left the chairman's seat, came down to the lectern, and gave an impromptu twenty-three-minute speech, answering some questions, ignoring others.

"I am in favor of dialogue," he said. "All of us today are just learning democracy. We are just now shaping our political culture."

He launched into a general defense of *perestroika,* but acknowledged that it was "moving with difficulty." He said the Communist Party should get out of trying to run the economy, spoke in favor of giving republics more sovereignty, but also urged interethnic harmony. Then he turned to the personal items.

"I accept your businesslike criticism as comradely remarks—I am open to that," Gorbachev said. "The *dacha* question, since it has been raised directly that way, I have said already that in my life, in my whole life, neither I nor members of my family have ever had, or now have, any personal country homes. As far as state *dachas* are concerned, they are made available to the government leadership . . . and the Party has built retreats for high officials. Perks exist everywhere, comrades. . . . Let's set up a Supreme Soviet commission; let's make an inventory. . . ."

On the "painful" question of bloodshed in Georgia, Gorbachev equivocated. "The army should do the army's job," he declared, but he added that that job was to maintain stability, not to "pacify the people." He disavowed personal responsibility, claiming that he had learned about the army's violent use of force only the morning after it had occurred, a reply that met with some audible skepticism.

Gorbachev sidestepped the question about Raisa, made no concession to demands that he relinquish his Party post, and did not address fears that he would have too much power. His only gesture was the assurance that "I will not exploit my present [Party] position or my future [government] position. . . . I will fight . . . to prevent what has happened in our country from ever happening again."[9]

This scenario was far short of the general policy debate demanded by radical reformers. Still, Gorbachev's willingness to allow for Q-and-A was a gesture to them and a symbolic bow to the concept that the nation's leadership had to answer to the elected parliament—an important precedent used later by the liberals.

When it came to selecting a chairman for the new Supreme Soviet, Boris Yeltsin was nominated along with Gorbachev, but Yeltsin tactfully withdrew. Then, to great surprise, Aleksandr Obolensky, an unknown construction engineer from Apatita, a town north of Leningrad, nominated himself as an alternative to Gorbachev. Amid murmuring in the hall, Obolensky laid out a progressive program calling for an independent judiciary, a constitutional court, cutting the power of ministries, firing the finance minister because of his hostility to cooperatives, and making the soviets, or regional assemblies, superior to the Communist Party and executive authority all across the country. Obolensky, feeling all elections should be contested, offered his nomination as a matter of principle.

"I am well aware I have no chance of winning," Obolensky said, "but I want us to have a precedent for holding elections. The voters who elected me demand this."[10]

Obolensky caught everyone off guard. His speech brought spontaneous applause from liberals, and uncomfortable chatter from the claque of conservatives Gorbachev had installed near the front of the hall.

The ensuing debate and the vote on whether to allow Obolensky's candidacy led to the first real test of sentiment in the Congress. When it was over, 689 deputies voted for the principle of competition; 1,415 deputies voted against even allowing a rival to run against Gorbachev.

So Gorbachev ran unopposed and got 96 percent of the vote (2,133 in favor, 87 opposed). Liberals grumbled about looking like rubber-stamp assemblies of the past.

In fact, once Gorbachev was installed, he railroaded through his agenda, ensuring the election of hand-picked lieutenants to all the key leadership posts in the Congress and the Supreme Soviet. He used the obedient majority to block any challengers; all races were uncontested.

So the die was cast by Gorbachev's alliance with the impregnable conservative majority. Even if they sometimes disagreed with Gorbachev, the loyalists understood that their only hope for holding power was to maintain unity and discipline behind Gorbachev. Radicals could debate, could score points against Gorbachev, against government policy, against the system—and their use of that opportunity was important for shaping public opinion and for firmly establishing the practice of open disagreement. But Gorbachev held the high cards; anytime that he wanted to swing the tide, he could signal his wish and manipulate the obedient majority. The solid regiments of Party loyalists and careerists were ready to do his bidding, as they always had been, from Lenin to Stalin to Brezhnev and Chernenko.

"This is not *real* democracy," the historian-now-deputy Roy Medvedev commented to me that afternoon. "The atmosphere was very different from previous Supreme Soviet sessions, where all people did was listen. The delegates today put tough questions to Gorbachev and he had to reply. They had their own proposals and positions, and the country could see that. So that is a significant change for us—it's *significant* democracy, but not *real* democracy."[11]

THE SOVIET NEW BREED

Sergei Stankevich, one of the sharp, new activist Moscow radicals, agreed with Medvedev. "We have no chance to change the general course of events during this Congress . . . because we are in a minority," he told me during an afternoon recess. "We would like to have more profound changes, deeper changes. But we are in the minority now. And our main task now is not to become a majority. That's unrealistic. [Better] to show our people a real alternative."[12]

Stankevich is typical of the Soviet new-breed politicians. Whatever his frustrations, for him the politics of summer 1989 were a dream come true. Slender, clean-cut, and serious, Stankevich looks twenty-three, but he is in his upper thirties. As a political scientist, he had been studying parliamentary government, mainly the U.S. Congress, for fifteen years in dusty archives, most recently at the Institute of History. But in all that time, he had never been to America, never seen a live, functioning Western parliament. Suddenly, Gorbachev's new politics gave Stankevich the wholly unexpected opportunity of becoming a real politician, of testing his skills as a power player.

As a student at Moscow State University, Stankevich had steered clear of the Communist Party. He was skeptical of Communist orthodoxy, turned off by the corruption of the Brezhnev era, and disillusioned by the Soviet invasion of Afghanistan. As a teenager, he admired many things in the West and considered himself part of the Beatles generation. "I learned English so I could understand the Beatles' songs," he told me with a shy grin. In 1987, Stankevich had been drawn into the Communist Party as part of the "Gorbachev wave," his idealism excited by the prospect of reform. He soon joined other radical Communists in a group called Inter-Club, which wanted to reform the Party from within.

Only in January 1989 did Stankevich decide belatedly to run for the Congress of People's Deputies; he was one of many academics and political amateurs who came out of the woodwork. Angered by attacks on Boris Yeltsin by the Party apparatus, Stankevich organized—and publicized—a telegram of support to Yeltsin from several young reform candidates. Back then, climbing on Yeltsin's bandwagon was an act of some courage for such a junior Party member; in fact, his district Party organization considered expelling Stankevich for his generally liberal, Westernized politics. Stankevich was running against the Party hierarchy, as a strong advocate of making the popularly elected legislatures, the soviets, more powerful than the Party.[13]

As Stankevich had expected, his defense of Yeltsin and his own positions were very popular moves. They marked him apart from rivals in a multicandidate race in Cheremushkinsky District, a sprawl of urban housing on the south side of Moscow. To his own surprise, he made it through the first round into a runoff, and then he won the second round to gain a precious seat in the Congress. Suddenly he had become a celebrity, appearing on television, addressing large crowds. Now, with his knowledge of parliamentary procedure and a certain poise bred from facing down competition, Stankevich was a rising young comer among the Moscow radicals.

He felt that if the reformers were too small a minority to compete for high posts, they should make the session a public test of Gorbachev's commitment to democratization. Like other reformers, he wanted Gorbachev to repeal anti-democratic laws, such as a decree that put restrictions on public meetings and rallies; it had been approved in July 1988 by the old Supreme Soviet. In the provinces, and sometimes in Moscow and Leningrad, hard-line bosses and police chiefs had used the decree to ban democratic rallies and to arrest organizers; liberals wanted the decree suspended. On the first day, they demanded a vote but Gorbachev, who had a way of ignoring unwelcome proposals, refused.

During a recess, I caught up with Yeltsin to ask his reactions to the session so far. He was unhappy. I asked him whether he thought ordinary people in Moscow would be satisfied.

"No, they will be deeply dissatisfied," Yeltsin retorted, eyes flashing, head bobbing over a whirl of reporters who were crushing in on both of us. "I think you will have a chance to see on the Moscow streets. There is a good reason why the authorities decided to refrain from making any decisions during the Congress on the issue of street demonstrations. They are pretty well aware that there are lots of Muscovites ready to go out and demonstrate."[14]

Late that evening, as the session was ending, Stankevich tipped me off that two thousand of his supporters were holding a rally near Pushkin Square in the heart of Moscow, and he was going to meet with them. Together, we walked fifteen blocks from the Kremlin up Gorky Street. "My voters came to me and said we must go there immediately," Stankevich told me. "There is a real possibility for bloody conflict. We should try to help these people."

When we got there, we could hear the crowd, but in the darkness, all we could see at first were clouds of rising dust and several rings of police, some in riot gear, with helmets and billy clubs. One group of demonstrators had planned to march on the Kremlin, but the police had surrounded them. Now, they were penned inside the police rings.

As we approached, I could hear shouts.

"Long live freedom of assembly!" someone cried.

"Respected citizens, please roll up your flags and leave the square," commanded a police officer over a bullhorn. "Your meeting is over. Stop violating public order."

"Never, comrades!" came back the retort. "We'll hold to the last man. We won't stand for it."

Once Stankevich showed his deputy's badge, the police cordon opened to let us through. A few yards farther on, the crowd engulfed us, pressing in like a vise, chanting rhythmically, "Stan-kay-vich! Stan-kay-vich!" Then a babel of shouts, angry accusations, and a melee over a megaphone that was being passed to Stankevich. Fearful that the first sign of a scuffle would be used by the police as a pretext to make arrests, he used it to try to calm the crowd.

"I ask you . . . be calm, if possible," he shouted through the megaphone. "Don't get hurt or do anything rash."

Above the din, Stankevich gave a shouting report to his voters. He told of reform proposals, of the voting, of the demands made, of the reformers' frustration at the rigidity of the hard-line majority.

"They spat in our faces," he declared.

A plump woman, obviously a rally leader, took back the megaphone and tongue-lashed Stankevich for the reformers' failure to wring concessions from Gorbachev. It was obvious from her comments, and those of others, that these people had followed the live telecast of the Congress in detail, with the fresh enthusiasm of people long denied that privilege and hungry to use it well. It was also obvious that these people saw the Congress as the voice of the people and they were angry that it was being manipulated by Gorbachev and the hard-liners.[15]

The demonstration lasted until 3 A.M. The police were not violent, but they made a few arrests. The menacing atmosphere was enough to prompt Stankevich and other liberals to take the issue of free assembly and the anti-rally decree back to the Congress floor the next day. But when Stankevich went to the rostrum to make his report, conservative deputies drowned him out with rhythmic applause, a typical Soviet harassment tactic.

Like all the new Soviet breed, Stankevich speaks with a refreshing and almost naïve candor that lacks the polished platitudes of many American politicians. He is unvarnished, direct, thoughtful, rather resembling Jimmy Carter, though instead of singsong, he is given to a matter-of-fact monotone that would worry an American media adviser. Yet beneath Stankevich's academic exterior, there is a hard self-confidence that rises to a challenge. On that morning, he bristled when he sensed that his political manhood was being rudely tested.

"They were trying to dump me," he recalled later. "I was very angry at that moment. I understood that besides these two thousand delegates in this hall, millions of people were in front of their TV sets and they [would] judge me by my every word and gesture. It was an unforgettable feeling. I knew I had to defend my position, that I could not lose face in this situation, this real conflict. I understood: If I lose face, I cannot be a real politician. People will not trust me."[16]

Facing down his challengers, Stankevich turned to Gorbachev, demanding that he bring order to the hall.

"I am asking that respect be shown to deputies," Stankevich said.

Gorbachev backed him. "We're going to go very slowly if you keep interrupting," he warned the other deputies.

"This anti-democratic tendency of drowning out speakers at the Congress is impermissible," declared Stankevich, his voice rising toward a shout.

One of the old-line deputies, sitting in the front row, shot back: "He's too young—too young to teach us."

Stankevich heard the taunt; it was a spur, a stimulus to counterattack.

"Excuse me—are you talking to me?" he retorted. "I ask the chairman to stop the anti-democratic actions that unfortunately are becoming fashionable here. It's a disgrace. I have been sent here by three hundred and eighty thousand voters, and you have no right to shut me up."

Stankevich was not only protecting himself; he was also trying to force Gorbachev to stop the conservative majority from doing what it had done the first day: clap and talk in order to rattle liberal speakers and drown them out.

"I will try to conduct this Congress in an organized fashion so it doesn't degenerate into a farce," Gorbachev declared.

"I didn't see the police dispersing the rally," said Stankevich. "Still, some actions must be taken. Some space in Moscow must be set aside for the people to gather, to learn the news and meet with deputies. It's absolutely essential for the normal functioning of the Congress."

On the heels of his report, reform delegates made another push to put the rally decree to a vote. Gorbachev relented, knowing full well that the conservative majority would not overturn a decree that gave large discretion to local authorities—that is, to themselves and their allies in the apparat. And he signaled his own desire to see the decree sustained, and it was.

After the vote, Gorbachev tried to put a good face on it, to be conciliatory to the radicals by giving a soft interpretation of the decree. "The question is decided, but what does that mean?" he said. "We don't suspend the decree, but the decree does not prevent rallies."[17]

The reformers had hoped for much more from Gorbachev; they had hoped that in promoting the new politics of mass participation, Gorbachev would come out against the decree himself and see it stricken. Many reformers had assumed that since Gorbachev had called the elections in March and had convened the Congress, he would be in their camp most of the time. But the first two days of the Congress had shown just the opposite.

"Gorbachev's mind is unclear to us," Stankevich said, not wanting to write him off completely so early in the session. "He is not fully predictable in his actions. We anticipated that his behavior during this Congress would be more in support of the democratic line, the democratic group."[18]

As the Congress wore on, Stankevich found himself repeatedly on the opposite side from his mentor and hero. His seat was in the sixth row, not far from Gorbachev, and he found that the Soviet president often spotted him voting against his position; he could overhear Gorbachev commenting to aides on the dais, "Well, look, Sergei is against us once again."

After the Congress was over, one national magazine ran a photograph of the two of them, Stankevich and Gorbachev, standing toe-to-toe on the empty dais, talking intently during one of the breaks. Gorbachev had beckoned to Stankevich to come up to the dais for a personal chat; Stankevich had clearly been flattered by such personal attention, especially when Gorbachev showed that he knew something about Stankevich personally, that he had studied the American Congress.

From his reading, Stankevich knew about the charm treatment. He understood that Gorbachev was lobbying him the way that Lyndon Johnson, as president, had shrewdly massaged the egos of younger members of Congress by taking them aside to talk, man to man. Gorbachev was "working" Stankevich, trying to soften his radicalism, trying to win him over to a more centrist position.

"What did he say to you?" I asked Stankevich.

"He said, 'Well, I understand your aims. I understand that you are sincere in your activity. But please don't accelerate the process. Don't push . . . don't push, because maybe we should go steadily. . . . So you should be more moderate, in order to avoid sharp conflict during this Congress.' "

"What was your reply?" I asked.

"Well, my words [were], 'If we stop our activity, the whole Congress will go in the old way and we can lose the trust of our voters. So that if we would like to have really new decisions, we should insist on some radical proposals. They should be heard, at least. They should be heard. They should be taken into account . . . in order to demonstrate the whole spectrum of positions, in order to have more freedom of choice.' "[19]

BRINGING THE GENERAL TO HEEL

All across the nation the reformers were heard, day after day. The Congress was such a hot running political soap opera, providing six or eight hours of live television programming daily, that part of the country simply stopped working. There, before their eyes, people could see the brash young deputies daring to challenge the most powerful figures in the land, Party leaders, ministers, army generals, those accustomed to giving orders and never having to answer for their actions. People were glued to their television sets, and government officials estimated that production nation-wide fell off 20–40 percent during the two weeks of the Congress. For a nation that had never seen real political debate, this was a festival of free expression. And it was the radical reformers who provided the fireworks.

By the second week, they had begun to work together informally as a loose grouping based around the Moscow and Leningrad delegations. They took their cues from people such as Andrei Sakharov, Boris Yeltsin, the radical economist Gavril Popov, and Yuri Afanasyev, a former Party activist and Komsomol apparatchik who now headed a historical institute and was the most tart-tongued radical speaker. It was Afanasyev, hand-some, with close-cropped hair, and powerfully built, who taunted the conservatives for being an "aggressively obedient majority" still mired in a "Stalinist-Brezhnevite mentality" that was "out of step with the times and the needs of the country."

In all, something close to four hundred deputies were part of the loose cluster of reformers, but they were far from an opposition bloc. It was too soon for formal organization; these new deputies were too ill acquainted with each other and with the changing political system to be ready to organize that way. And they had many diverse interests. There was one cluster of nationalist democrats from the three Baltic republics, and some like-minded nationalists from Moldavia, Georgia, the Ukraine, and else-where. There was an even larger group of Russian democrats interested in economic reform, environmental protection, seeing more power given to the soviets or legislatures at all levels of Soviet society, and determined to reduce the power of the Party apparatus and the centralized state.

Some radicals, like Yuri Afanasyev, wanted to pressure Gorbachev, to break with him if need be, to force big changes that would seize power from the Party. Others, such as Stankevich, were more pragmatic, liberal rather than radical; even when Gorbachev blocked them, they saw them-selves as Gorbachev's shock troops against the diehard Right, eager to push him further, faster, but hesitant to treat him as an adversary. They were all moving to open up the Soviet political system and wrest power from the Party-state apparat. Day by day, from the Congress podium, they set about shattering old taboos while the conservative Old Guard cringed in their seats.

In one stinging speech, former Olympic weight-lifting champion Yuri Vlasov savaged the KGB as "a threat to democracy," condemning it for a history of torture, murder, and misuse of psychiatric hospitals to intimi-date free-thinkers. Today, Vlasov said, the KGB was "not a service but a real underground empire which has not yet surrendered its secrets."

Vlasov's father, a committed Communist and diplomat in China, had disappeared in 1953 at the hands of state security. "We must honor the memories of our fellow citizens who were victims of excesses and executions," Vlasov said solemnly.

The strapping former athlete, who was now in his fifties, got a standing ovation from hundreds of deputies when he called for the removal of KGB headquarters from Dzerzhinsky Square in downtown Moscow because of the "unforgettable bloody history of the building." Gorbachev joined the applause briefly when Vlasov said the KGB chairman should be approved by the Congress; but Vladimir Kryuchkov, the head of the KGB, and other members of the Politburo sat with blank stares through his shocking address. It was the sharpest public attack on the KGB in memory.[20]

In a similar vein, Boris Yeltsin called for a new Soviet constitution that would bring the Communist Party under the rule of law, transfer primary power from the Party to the Supreme Soviet and Congress, eliminate the Party's control of the mass media, and provide for direct election of the chief of state. Yeltsin had already been the focus of controversy in the Congress; the Gorbachev-controlled presidium had maneuvered the conservative majority to exclude Yeltsin and Stankevich from membership in the Supreme Soviet, an obviously outrageous move given the fact that Yeltsin represented the largest constituency in the country. The liberals created an uproar, and after another deputy offered to give up his seat in favor of Yeltsin, Gorbachev belatedly sanctioned the move.

Yeltsin's speech was a manifesto for reformers, but the poet Yevgeny Yevtushenko—ever theatrical, in a bright white suit to match the white plaster statue of Lenin—upstaged Yeltsin. Yevtushenko explicitly demanded what was unthinkable to Gorbachev and the Old Guard. He reminded the hall (87.6 percent of the deputies were Communists[21]) that he was *not* a Party member and then called for repeal of Article VI of the Soviet constitution, which enshrined the Party's "vanguard role" in Soviet society and guaranteed its monopoly on power. And he advocated a new amendment to ensure that all citizens—"Party member or non-Party member—have . . . complete equality when being nominated to fill any Soviet state positions, including the highest ones." This struck at the heart of the Party's control of the entire country through its system of *nomenklatura*—the secret appointment of all government officials, heads of industrial enterprises, farms, and top leaders in the army and security services.[22]

One sacred cow after another was skewered. The radicals' irreverence was epitomized by publicist Yuri Chernichenko and historian Yuri Karyakin. Chernichenko had the cheek to publicly mock Politburo member

Yegor Ligachev, whose responsibilities had recently been shifted from ideology to agriculture. "I merely want to ask, as I was asked a hundred and sixty-eight times," Chernichenko demanded to snickering in the hall, "why in a politically essential sector have they placed a man who understands nothing of [agriculture], and who has failed in ideology?"[23] Karyakin called for restoring Soviet citizenship to the exiled writer Aleksandr Solzhenitsyn and then assaulted the holy of holies: He appealed for the removal of Lenin's body from the mausoleum on Red Square, the shrine built by Stalin to glorify the Party dictatorship.

"Lenin himself wanted to be buried beside the grave of his mother at the Volkon Cemetery in St. Petersburg," Karyakin reminded the deputies, but his wishes were ignored, as Karyakin sarcastically recalled—"of course, in the name of Lenin."[24]

But the reformers wanted more than rhetorical victories; their own power rested on mass public support, and their greatest fear was that the power of the army, KGB, and special security troops under the Ministry of Internal Affairs would be used to crush democratic protests and to suffocate the entire reform movement. Fresh in their minds was the brutal crackdown in Tbilisi, Georgia, during the wee hours of April 9, less than seven weeks before the opening of the Congress. They demanded guarantees that troops would never again be used against peaceful rallies and that high officials would be held accountable for such acts of repression.

Protesting the violence in Georgia became the reformers' most successful cause. From the very first moments of the Congress, on May 25, when a Latvian delegate called for a minute of silence to honor the victims of the "Tbilisi massacre," that tragedy became a primary issue. Gorbachev had been asked about his role, and when he disclaimed any advance knowledge of the crackdown, one deputy asked what the point was of having a national leader who could be ignorant of such actions. Eldar Shengelaya, secretary of the Georgian Filmmakers' Union, circulated an amateur videotape that showed tanks and armored cars running down people in the streets; the corpses of women and children, their heads and bodies bloodied, reportedly by troops wielding trenching shovels; and other victims asphyxiated by poison gas.

A Georgian deputy, T. V. Gankrelidze, described the events to the Congress: how at 4 A.M. on "bloody Sunday," after demonstrators had gone to sleep in the central square, troops had sealed off the exits and then staged a brutal assault. "The Tbilisi tragedy revealed the utter bankruptcy of the U.S.S.R. legal mechanism," the deputy declared. He called for the expulsion from the Congress of Colonel General Igor Rodionov, who had commanded the troops in that operation. (As military commander for

Georgia, Rodionov had been elected a deputy from the Georgian district of Borzhomi two weeks before the massacre.)

"Only complete *glasnost* and punishment of those responsible can prevent the catastrophic effect of this tragedy on the moral state of our fellow citizens," Gankrelidze asserted. "Colonel General Rodionov has neither the moral nor legal right to remain a people's deputy for the U.S.S.R. from Georgia."[25]

The charges brought one of the most dramatic showdowns of the Congress: Rodionov, in uniform and with a chestful of medals, made his way to the rostrum, demanding the right to reply. He is an imposing man, with a strong, deep voice and a commanding presence. It was obvious that it rankled him to be called to account before this assembly.

"It is necessary to give a political evaluation of what happened in Tbilisi," he declared. "The deputy who spoke before me said the rally was peaceful . . . [but] there were vile appeals for physical violence against Communists, and anti-Russian and nationalist attitudes were being fanned. . . . All measures of persuasion and appeal to reason [had] been exhausted and there remained the extreme measure—to apply force. . . ."

A voice from the audience shouted: "We have witnesses among the deputies, so you'd better . . ."

The chair cut in: "Just a minute—we have given over the floor. Let him say what he has to say. . . ."

Rodionov: "The situation was very complex. I am sure that the person who spoke here was not present there on the street. I was there from three A.M. . . . and stayed as long as necessary. I saw it all with my own eyes.

"There were mistakes on our side. We were in a hurry. . . . Incidentally, comrades, according to official information, sixteen people died at the site of the tragedy. . . . Not a single one of those who were picked up, and the square was clear by six A.M., not a single one had a cut or a stab wound. Not one of the sixteen."

There was a commotion in the hall and some protests.

Rodionov: "Do not interrupt me! The investigative agencies have gone into this. . . . I am especially disturbed, comrades, by discussion of the use of chemical agents. . . . People talk here about how bad it was in 1937 [at the peak of Stalin's purges], but I think it is worse now than in 1937. Now, people can talk about you on television, write about you in newspapers, and the mass media can defame you, however they wish and without justification."[26]

When Rodionov finished, there was prolonged applause from the obedient majority. But the reaction was far different across the country, and

Gorbachev sensed it. Suspicions had been raised about the Kremlin's role, and Gorbachev sent out a deputy, Politburo member Anatoly Lukianov, to read to the Congress the texts of cables between Party headquarters in Moscow and Tbilisi; these exculpated Gorbachev and put the blame on Georgian Communist Party leaders. The wrangle broadened, in full public view, when the Georgian Party leader, Dzhumber Patiashvili, accused General Rodionov of giving him exaggerated reports of the danger from demonstrators, which tricked him into approving the use of force.

Roald Sagdeyev, a deputy who was Gorbachev's leading space scientist, called the Georgian mess "our Irangate, and General Rodionov is our Colonel Ollie North."[27]

The radicals were on the hunt for a smoking gun, and Gorbachev felt compelled to bow to their demand for a parliamentary investigation. He named Sagdeyev and other reformers to a commission headed by Anatoly Sobchak, a law professor and one of Leningrad's leading radicals. Rodionov was quickly relieved of his command and named head of the General Staff military academy, but his career had clearly been damaged. It was a powerful lesson to the army.

As the parliamentary investigation proceeded, it contradicted the Kremlin's previous denials of Politburo involvement in the events of "bloody Sunday." The radicals had a powerful ally inside Gorbachev's inner circle—Foreign Minister Eduard Shevardnadze, who was also the former Georgian Party chief. Shevardnadze had flown to Georgia to investigate, arriving just as the plans to crack down were unfolding, but evidently he was not informed of the intention to use force until after the fact. *Moscow News* carried an article on September 10, 1989, revealing that Defense Minister Dmitri Yazov had given Rodionov orders for the Soviet troops to use force and that authority had come from Victor Chebrikov, former head of the KGB, who was described as the Politburo "duty man" on the fateful night. Yegor Yakovlev, the editor of *Moscow News*, told me that Shevardnadze had provided information for that article and given it political protection. Ten days later, Chebrikov was thrown out of the Politburo.

The parliamentary inquiry also pointed to Yegor Ligachev, who, while Gorbachev was visiting Britain and Cuba, had chaired a Politburo session on April 7, authorizing the use of troops. Ligachev charged that Gorbachev and Shevardnadze had been at the April 7 meeting—and Anatoly Sobchak publicly accused Ligachev of lying. Nonetheless, Ligachev and Yazov had somehow both survived; Chebrikov and Rodionov became the fall guys.

The radicals could count the Tbilisi affair as their biggest single victory at the Congress. It would take months for the political drama to play out, but the plot line was clear before the Congress closed: High officials were being brought to account by the new political system, and in the end, heads rolled. The reformers had taken Gorbachev literally when he preached the gospel of a new "law-governed state." And on the issue of "bloody Sunday" they had clearly established the vital principle of parliamentary oversight of the government. For a fledgling democratic parliament, that was no mean feat.

THE SOLEMN TREAD OF THE LOSERS

The hard-liners, largely a silent majority during the first week, took out their vengeance later in the Congress session. Their pent-up frustration at the radicals boiled over on June 2 at the most distinguished dissident in the assembly, Andrei Sakharov, for his accusations against Soviet forces in Afghanistan. The humbling of Sakharov was an emotional but calculated display of the power and passion of the right wing. The Old Guard was intent on humbling the reformers on national television and undercutting their power by casting them in the public's eyes as anti-patriotic.

Sergei Chervonopisky, a thirty-two-year-old former major in the Soviet airborne troops who had lost both legs in the war, and one of 120 Afghan war veterans in the Congress, was the first to savage Sakharov. A hand-picked Komsomol delegate from the Ukraine, Chervonopisky lashed out at Sakharov for his charge, in an interview with the Canadian newspaper *Ottawa Citizen,* that Soviet pilots had sometimes fired on Soviet soldiers to prevent them from being taken alive by Afghan rebels.

"To the depths of our souls we are indignant over this irresponsible, provocative trick by a well-known scientist," Chervonopisky declared. He accused Sakharov of trying to discredit the Soviet armed forces and attempting "to breach the sacred unity of the army, the Party, and the people."

Gorbachev and the entire Politburo joined in a standing ovation for Chervonopisky's censure of Sakharov, and again when he concluded with a paean to Communism, a word that he said had not been used enough at the Congress. "The three words for which I feel we must all fight," declared the thundering Afghan veteran, "are *state, motherland,* and *Communism.*"[28]

Gorbachev gave the hard-liners free rein, and speaker after speaker heaped opprobrium on Sakharov. "Who gave him the right to insult our children?" demanded a fifty-year-old farm worker.

"Not a single order or anything like it was issued at the General Staff and the Ministry of Defense, nor did we receive any such savage instructions from the political leadership of our nation," declared Marshal Sergei Akhromeyev, former chief of the General Staff. "All of this is a pure lie, a deliberate untruth, and Academician Sakharov will not find any documents to substantiate it."[29]

A twenty-five-year-old teacher from outside Tashkent told Sakharov: "You have insulted the entire army, the entire people. . . . I have nothing but contempt."

When Sakharov rose to make his own defense, he had to shout to be heard above the boos and catcalls. Just as he had done in the seventies, he faced the angry chorus alone, and he did not flinch or retreat.

"The Afghan war was a criminal adventure . . . a terrible sin," he asserted. "I came out against sending troops to Afghanistan and for this I was exiled to Gorky. I am proud of this exile to Gorky, as a decoration which I received. . . . I have not apologized to the Soviet army, for I have not insulted it. I have insulted those who gave criminal orders to send troops to Afghanistan."

He insisted that no one could accuse him of false accusations until there was a full investigation of his charges.[30]

Gorbachev and Sakharov clashed more directly on June 9. These were the final moments of the Congress, and Gorbachev was putting a favorable gloss on its work, indulging in his characteristic fence-straddling between radicals and regulars. He began by welcoming the "critical spirit, fresh thinking," and "constructive opposition" of the reformers; but he concluded by categorically rejecting their broadside attacks on the Communist Party and warning them against "a struggle against the apparatus."

The conservatives did not even want to let Sakharov speak, but Gorbachev gave him five minutes. And his final assessment was gloomier; he worried that the Congress had failed to achieve a real transfer of power from the self-perpetuating Party-state apparat to the elected parliament, and he warned that concentrating great power in one man, Gorbachev, was "extremely dangerous." As Sakharov laid out a program to halt the KGB's domestic operations, strip the Party of its legal supremacy, and make all high state officials subject to recall by the Congress, Gorbachev told him his time had run out.

Sakharov tried to go on.

"Finish up," Gorbachev scolded.

"I am finishing," Sakharov pleaded. "I have left out a great deal."

"That's all!" Gorbachev chided. "Your time, two time allotments, has run out."

Sakharov mumbled something more.

"All!" commanded Gorbachev. And he cut off Sakharov's microphone.[31]

These two confrontations with Sakharov captured the anger of the Right and Gorbachev's impatience with the reformers. What is more, they displayed the sharp ideological cleavage at the Congress, and in the country as a whole.

But these episodes could not obscure the larger meaning of the Congress. For in spite of Sakharov's anxieties and the obvious limitations of a parliament controlled by a stacked majority of regulars with a vested interest in the status quo, in two short weeks the Congress had altered the political landscape of the Soviet Union.

By letting liberal and radical reformers debate freely, Gorbachev had given the entire nation a schooling in the new politics, via television. He had also begun reshaping the institutional structure of the political system. Admittedly he had held the reins tightly; still, he had begun to shift power away from the closed sanctuaries of the Communist Party hierarchy to the open arena of the new superparliament.

Regardless of what Gorbachev said or of his manipulative tactics, he had conveyed a change in the flow of power by his very presence. There, before the nation, he sat every day for thirteen days, from gavel to gavel, watching, listening every moment, commenting, responding, guiding the whole process. It was a personal tour de force. The picture of Gorbachev with his headphones, his arm gestures, his quick flashes of temper, or his gestures of conciliation all carried a message to ordinary people, and to the Party apparat, that this process, this body, was significant enough for the nation's leader—indeed, almost the entire national leadership—to devote full time to it.

Russians are careful readers of visual symbols. The physical picture of Gorbachev's commitment to the Congress was indelible; it took attention—and power—away from the Party. The Party regulars felt the loss, and eventually came to make this theft of power a major point of contention with Gorbachev.

At a minimum, he had sanctioned the idea of legislative oversight and had shifted the arena of debate, and hence that of policy-making, out of the Party's hands. His move was not direct and complete enough to satisfy Sakharov and the radicals, but it was palpable enough for the Old Guard to feel it.

An episode at the end of the second week of the Congress sticks in my mind. I came out of the Kremlin's Hall of Congresses quickly after the session and found myself among the members of the Politburo and senior

Party officials as they were walking across the Kremlin grounds. Black limousines rumbled over the Kremlin cobblestones, like so many power boats idling up to a dock, ready to ferry the Party VIPs to a Communist Party Central Committee plenum gathering that night. But the leaders kept walking, their security men fending off my efforts to talk to them.

Gorbachev was far ahead, so I could not see his face, but the mood of the others was somber, funereal; there was no animated conversation, no exchange of pleasantries, just a low mutter. Their silent, sober mood spoke volumes. It suggested that the power barons of the Communist Party had been chastened, and irked, by the challenging tone of the reformers; it had been a wholly new experience for them, and now they were walking across the Kremlin grounds with their tails figuratively between their legs. Their whole way of life had come under fire, and they understood from Gorbachev's sanction of the political free-for-all that things could never be the same again.

THE OPPOSITION TAKES SHAPE

Their political nightmares only increased. No sooner did the Congress end its session, than the new Supreme Soviet went to work—the very next day, June 10, 1989—and despite reformers' fears that it would be an old-fashioned captive assembly, it immediately shocked the government. The Supreme Soviet was a 542-member miniature version of the Congress, operating as the permanent legislature, whereas the Congress met briefly twice a year as a constitutional assembly.

As the Supreme Soviet convened, the legislative battle over the Tbilisi affair was fresh in everyone's mind; it set the tone for advice and consent in the Supreme Soviet. The deputies heeded Sakharov's advice that confirmation of government ministers was the legislature's responsibility. Gorbachev had maneuvered approval of Prime Minister Nikolai Ryzhkov from the Congress, but his cabinet faced the Supreme Soviet. Its grilling of Ryzhkov's ministers was so aggressive that eventually three ministers— including one deputy prime minister—were rejected, the nominations of six more were withdrawn by Ryzhkov because of opposition by legislative committees, and two others quit in the face of likely defeat.

No one was more sharply interrogated than Defense Minister Dmitri Yazov. During a five-hour debate broadcast on national television, Soviet viewers saw the extraordinary spectacle of one of the nation's most intimidating figures being subjected to a bold and unrelenting parliamentary inquisition.

Deputies grilled the graying, heavy-set, and slow-moving Yazov about military corruption, discipline problems, violent hazing of new recruits, and poor living conditions for career officers and sergeants. They pressed him to apply student draft exemptions, and to consider ending the draft in favor of a professional army, and they inquired about combat readiness and the size of military forces.

Genrikh Borovik, head of the Soviet Peace Committee, tried to get Yazov on record as opposing further nuclear-weapons testing and acknowledging the dangers of radioactivity. Yazov tried to duck, more than once, and Gorbachev had to prod him to answer directly; eventually Yazov said: "We have to develop weapons; otherwise we will lag behind the U.S."

Among four hundred written questions were several about the size of the armed forces—a figure never publicly revealed. Yazov, hesitating, eyed Gorbachev for guidance.

"Well, I don't think it will be a secret, Mikhail Sergeyevich . . ."

"Go on," Gorbachev nudged.

Yazov said the figure would be 3.7 million after Gorbachev's promised reductions of 500,000 were completed.

Adapting to the new rules of Soviet politics, Yazov said the size of the military budget was for the Supreme Soviet to decide, but he went on record in favor of cutbacks. "I think that is appropriate," he said. "You see, in the end you have so many weapons, mountains of weapons, and you can become a prisoner of those weapons. . . . Naturally, this [reduction] will to a certain extent reduce the combat readiness of the armed forces, but we must perceive combat readiness not in an abstract way but in comparison with other states and blocs."[32]

Nonetheless, Yazov staunchly opposed the demands of Baltic deputies that non-Russian recruits be allowed to serve in their home republics— and they announced that they would vote against him. He also rejected proposals for a professional army. He claimed widespread reports of hazing in the military were exaggerated, but he admitted that the army lacked housing for sixty thousand career officers and sergeants soon due to be mustered out. And he refused to go along with a call from university educators for the release of 176,000 university-level draftees; six days later the Supreme Soviet overruled him and discharged the students.

Several deputies in uniform were among Yazov's sharpest critics. Lieutenant Colonel Viktor Podziruk, a military reformer from the Ivanovo region, accused Yazov of granting the top brass too many perks and cushy retirement, and permitting a system of political patronage. He called for cutting deadwood and chastised Yazov for reducing technical training while protecting political indoctrination units and sports regiments. Lieutenant Nikolai Tutov, a twenty-eight-year-old pilot from Orenburg in western Siberia, was even more outspoken. He said the army was in a quagmire because "Dmitri Timofeyevich Yazov has no real conception of *perestroika* in the armed forces," and he called for Yazov's replacement. Other deputies argued that Yazov was too old, too inflexible, too stuck in the past, and the country needed a younger, more modern-minded chief.

Gorbachev, sensing danger, stepped into the argument; the defeat of his own hand-picked defense minister would be devastating. Trying to save Yazov, Gorbachev admitted shortcomings in the military and endorsed some of the deputies' demands for change. But in an effort to take Yazov off the hook, he asserted that Yazov had inherited a bad state of affairs when he took over in May 1987, and had made improvements; he also pointed out that defense policy was formulated not by Yazov alone, but by the National Defense Council headed by Gorbachev himself.

Only this personal intervention rescued Yazov—and even then Gorbachev had to bend the rules. Confirmation requires a majority of at least 272 votes; Yazov got only 256 yes votes, with 77 against and 66 abstentions. Because there were so many absentees, Gorbachev persuaded the Supreme Soviet to amend its rules and accept a plurality instead of the required majority. But the Supreme Soviet, put on guard, set up a new committee to oversee the Ministry of Defense and KGB.

Victorious, Gorbachev flew off to France, and on the very next day, with Prime Minister Ryzhkov in the chair, the Supreme Soviet rejected Deputy Premier Vladimir Kamentsev, chairman of the Foreign Economic Commission and a key figure in Ryzhkov's plans for reinvigorating the economy through foreign economic projects. Deputies accused Kamentsev of nepotism and squandering the country's raw materials.

The Supreme Soviet sessions attracted so much public interest that the government decided to delay the televised broadcasts until evening, to get people back to work. Wherever I traveled, I found everyone, from scholars and Party officials to hotel maids, with their chairs pulled up in front of television sets until 2 A.M., still incredulously watching the new politics. And then they dragged to work the next morning.

Over the summer months and then in the fall session of the Supreme Soviet, the radicals began to use committees to advance their causes and to critique government policy. The great bulk of policy initiative and legislation still came from the government, but the Supreme Soviet shaped a new pension law and passed its own bill for reducing taxes on cooperatives from 90 percent to 35 percent. In the spring of 1990, it

rejected the unpopular bread and food price increases proposed by Ryzhkov and forced more liberal provisions into his economic reform bill. More
significant, it passed two crucially important initiatives of the radicals: a
law banning censorship and permitting any individual or group to operate
a newspaper or television station; and a law granting wide powers to local
governments, including control of property within their jurisdiction.

By the fall of 1990, the Supreme Soviet was not yet a Western-style
legislature, but it was gradually accumulating power at the expense of the
Party apparatus and the executive branch.

Equally important, the 1989 summer Supreme Soviet session brought
the formation of an organized opposition. In mid-July, Boris Yeltsin called
for formation of a "leftist-radical" group to push for more rapid reform;
he said more than 300 deputies from the larger Congress had expressed
interest. Frustration was forcing the radicals to organize; their demands
for constitutional reforms had been ignored, and they felt at a disadvantage on other issues. So on the weekend of July 29–30, 1989, what became
known as the Inter-Regional Group took shape; some 316 Congress deputies attended its founding session in Moscow, including 90 from the
Supreme Soviet. Another 119 deputies, unable to attend, signified that
they would join.[33] At that stage, they avoided declaring themselves a party
or picking an ideological label; a certain vagueness helped preserve unity
among this diverse group.

The Inter-Regional Group had two main bases of support. One nucleus
was from the Baltic republics, where the national drive for self-determination was the primary interest and rallying cry. It was reinforced by other
nationalist deputies from Moldavia, Georgia, and the Ukraine, who favored republican sovereignty, but were less assertive and less cohesive than
the Baltic delegations. Its second main base was the Russian reformers,
mainly from Moscow, Leningrad, and provincial centers such as Sverdlovsk, Yaroslavl, Novosibirsk, and Volgograd. This element included
economists and budding entrepreneurs whose primary goal was to reduce
the power of ministries and to push market economics; political reformers
whose priority was to build the effective power of the Congress, Supreme
Soviet, and local soviets; journalists who were after legislation that would
end censorship; environmentalists who wanted most of all to fight industrial pollution and the hazards of nuclear power. The Russian reformers
were tolerant of minority nationalists, but they did not support total
independence; and the Balts supported the dispersal of power in Moscow,
but their real interest was regional. So there was common ground among
the constituent groups, but the coalition had its limits.

Equally important, the reformers were divided among radicals and pragmatists. The more fiery radicals like Yuri Afanasyev accused Gorbachev of being paralyzed by fear and of failing to take bold action; they urged the Inter-Regional Group to declare itself an opposition to Gorbachev.

"Gorbachev is justifiably regarded as the man who launched *perestroika* but is no longer capable of being the leader of both the reform and the *nomenklatura* [the Party-state apparat]," declared Afanasyev. "He has to make a choice. He finds it difficult to understand that he is no longer the only leader of *perestroika*. They are cropping up all around the country."[34]

In the same vein, Yeltsin proposed that the Inter-Regional Group demand local, regional, and republican elections in the fall of 1989, to give a new impulse to the democratic movement. (The Party apparat was trying to cancel local elections; Gorbachev leaned toward putting them off until 1990.) Yeltsin asserted that the coal miners' strikes in the Ukraine and Siberia signaled that the public was fed up with talk and wanted faster action for reform. "The people have been disappointed by the Congress and the Supreme Soviet," Yeltsin declared; the miners' strike committees were "embryos of real people's power."[35]

Pragmatic liberals, such as Sergei Stankevich, argued that it was unrealistic for the Inter-Regional Group to force a confrontation with Gorbachev at this stage. Other deputies disagreed with Yeltsin on the issues. The pragmatists saw the role of the Inter-Regional Group not as Gorbachev's opposition, but as a liberal force backing *perestroika* but pressing Gorbachev to move more boldly and to ignore right-wing foot-dragging.

Typical of its diversity, the Inter-Regional Group could not settle on a single leader. It chose five co-chairmen: Yeltsin, Sakharov, Afanasyev, the economist Gavril Popov, a shrewd, low-key strategist, and Viktor Palm, an Estonian scholar who represented the Baltic delegations.

What united these diverse elements most was common hostility to the Party apparatus; their determination to break up the centralized, dictatorial structure of Soviet power and to curb the arbitrary power of the army, KGB, and national police; and their insistence on free assembly, rule of law, and the authority of elected legislatures as guarantees for the pluralistic, democratic politics that Gorbachev had promised.

The more assertive they became, the more warily Gorbachev reacted. As the Supreme Soviet closed its session on August 4, Gorbachev warned the new Inter-Regional Group not to divide the Supreme Soviet nor to create artificial confrontations. The conflict grew sharper in late September. After two days of heated debate on September 23–24, the Inter-Regional Group adopted a platform calling for movement toward a multiparty system, a mixed economy, a free press, and a popularly elected head of government. The platform specifically demanded the abolition of the Communist Party's monopoly on power, and Sergei Stankevich drafted a law to legalize alternative political parties. Having now organized formally, the reform coalition demanded that Gorbachev recognize them as a parliamentary opposition and grant them their own staff, offices, bank account, and newspaper.

Gorbachev had swung to the right that fall, under heavy pressure from Politburo conservatives, and now he lashed back at the radicals. Through aides, he flatly refused their demands for formal recognition and the organizational trappings of an opposition. Stung by their criticism, Gorbachev denounced the radicals on the first day of the fall session of the Supreme Soviet, September 25. Without naming the Inter-Regional Group, he condemned any interference with the efficiency of the Supreme Soviet and warned them against making trouble. And he chastised the reformers for speeches with "too little content and too much harshness, and even simply a disrespectful attitude toward the Supreme Soviet."[36] At a stormy meeting with editors and cultural leaders on October 13, Gorbachev was more vitriolic; he lashed out at the reform deputies, calling them "a gangster group."[37]

Even moderates like Stankevich were dismayed to have their patron turn on them so sharply. Stankevich suggested to me that Gorbachev was exhausted from nearly five years of reform, and that he was so much a prisoner of his own past that he was incapable of moving much further, especially to surrender the Party's guaranteed political supremacy.[38]

So Gorbachev had been overtaken by the forces he had let loose and was now trying to check them, and they were fighting him more openly. They were still a legislative minority, but public pressures were mounting in their favor—the nationalist movements all over the country, and other populist movements, such as environmental protesters and the coal miners' strike committees. Through the fall of 1989, Gorbachev acquiesced in the crumbling of Communist regimes across Eastern Europe, but he grew harsher at home, resisting the nationalists, spurning the Inter-Regional Group. But come the spring of 1990, he responded to the pressure for yet another momentous shift of power away from the Party to the new institutions of government.

ANARCHY OR THE "IRON FIST"?

It was the radical reformers Yeltsin and Sakharov, in speeches to the first Congress, and then collectively in the September 1989 platform of the

Inter-Regional Group, who first proposed a popularly elected president. The reformers saw the presidency as a vehicle for taking power away from the Party, as a counterweight to the Politburo, a means for weaning Gorbachev from the influence of the Old Guard apparat. Amid periodic rumors about the dangers of a military coup or a right-wing plot to oust Gorbachev, moderate reformers saw the presidency as a way of protecting Gorbachev's survival by giving him a legally impregnable base of power.

For months Gorbachev rejected the idea, probably because he knew that the Politburo and other strongholds of Party power would never accept such a surrender of their authority. In a speech to the Supreme Soviet on October 23, 1989, Gorbachev argued against "starting off along the path of switching to presidential power" on grounds that the country's democratic processes were still too feeble to invest such a concentration of power in the hands of one man. That would undermine the effort to build up the authority of the legislature, he said, and divert energies from engaging the people in grass-roots politics.[39]

A little over three months later, in February 1990, Gorbachev had flip-flopped: He seized the idea of a strong presidency and was ramming it through the Supreme Soviet; he called for a special session of the Congress of People's Deputies to pass the necessary constitutional amendments.

The motives for Gorbachev's turnaround were complex. Central Committee officials told me that he was increasingly frustrated by seeing his economic and political reforms blocked by Yegor Ligachev and Party conservatives; a presidency would free him of that albatross. Undoubtedly, too, Gorbachev had in mind the precedent of Nikita Khrushchev; in the early 1960s, Khrushchev had alienated the Party hierarchy by attacking its lines of power, and the Politburo barons had thrown him out on October 14, 1964. Gorbachev had been far bolder than Khrushchev in bringing the Party under assault, and he had faced dangerous rumblings through the fall and winter of 1989–90; Moscow was full of coup talk. So a popularly elected presidency offered him a safer power base.

Most important, however, was the sense of chaos and disintegration in Soviet society: rising crime, the breakdown of the economy, and the widespread disenchantment with *perestroika.* There was a sense that things were falling apart. Nationalist movements were growing more powerful and more willing to challenge Moscow. Generals complained about thousands of Soviet youth ducking the draft, and of thousands more deserting in the republics. The killing of Armenians by mobs of Azerbaijanis in January 1990 had been followed by new outbursts of interethnic violence across Central Asia. Gorbachev himself had complained of "a kind of chain reaction accompanied by an orgy of violence."[40]

That fall and winter, Moscow intellectuals whom I knew talked darkly of the dangers of "civil war" or a violent repression by the army, KGB, and Party right-wingers, a crackdown that they feared would snatch away the precious new freedoms of *glasnost* and democratization. I heard less of this as I traveled out across the country, except in places where there was actual ethnic strife. Nonetheless, the overall sense of social and economic collapse had awakened the desperate Russian fear of disorder—of anarchy—and the reflexive response of the right wing, using what Russians call the "iron fist" to impose order from above.

At the center, in the Central Committee and the Kremlin, officials spoke of a paralysis of power, and the need to fill the power vacuum. "Central power is now much too weak," complained Gorbachev's alter ego, Aleksandr Yakovlev. "We need to strengthen it."[41] No one rival then threatened Gorbachev, but with the economy in such terrible shape, his prestige had fallen. He had lost power in practical terms; his orders were not being carried out—no one's were. The old system of top-down commands had been deliberately shattered, so that the nation's economic structure and the Party hierarchy were no longer functioning effectively, though they still stifled individual initiative; and the new system of democratic self-interest and legislative power had not yet taken hold, to spark spontaneous economic growth and enterprise.

The final straw for Gorbachev was the anti-Armenian violence in Baku. Before he sent in eleven thousand Soviet troops, Gorbachev claimed to have been hamstrung by legal requirements that he first gain the consent of Azerbaijani authorities and of the presidium of the Supreme Soviet, a process that took three or four days. With a strong presidency, Gorbachev's team argued, he could have taken firm action more swiftly. The Baku episode seems to have tipped the balance in Gorbachev's mind and also enabled him to win endorsement of a strong new Soviet presidency from the Communist Party Central Committee and the Party regulars who still dominated the Supreme Soviet.

But Gorbachev, eager to shore up his power and free himself from the constraints of both the Politburo and the legislature, had a serious problem. Legally establishing a presidency required amending the Soviet constitution, and only the Congress of People's Deputies could do that. It was convened on March 12, 1990. Gorbachev wanted swift action, but he could not be sure that he had enough votes. He was handicapped by the changing arithmetic and politics of the Congress. Amending the constitution required a two-thirds vote; in a body with 2,250 members, the magic number was 1,497. But with deaths and absentees, only 2,021 deputies registered for the session. Every single missing deputy made Gorbachev's task harder, because it subtracted from his potential total. Moreover, the deputies from Lithuania—which had just declared its independence on March 11—were attending as observers and were boycotting the vote.

What is more, Gorbachev could not count on support from the Inter-Regional Group, because he had turned their democratic presidency into an office with dictatorial powers, and they were by now very wary of Gorbachev's intentions. One of Sakharov's final warnings had been not to give one leader too much power. With that in mind, the liberals accused Gorbachev of trying to rush through the new presidency without time for proper consideration and careful drafting of the necessary constitutional amendments.

"We can still feel the great totalitarian tradition in this country," protested Sergei Stankevich, after Gorbachev railroaded his presidential bill through a preliminary vote in the Supreme Soviet. "If the law is adopted [by the constitutional Congress] in its present form, the president can do almost everything."[42]

At the Congress, the Inter-Regional Group was split between the "aggressive opposition" and the "constructive opposition"—Stankevich's terms. The aggressive faction, led by Yuri Afanasyev, advocated uncompromising opposition to Gorbachev's proposal; the pragmatic faction, represented by Stankevich, wanted to modify the proposal to make it more reasonable. Stankevich warned the radical caucus that Afanasyev's strategy was impractical and doomed, given the mood of the country. "It is not possible for us to stop it," he told me. "We must try to make it more acceptable. We must save Gorbachev from himself, oppose him and force compromise."[43]

Gorbachev's strategy was to sweeten his package for the radicals by combining it with two measures of great interest to the Inter-Regional Group: new constitutional language on permissible forms of economic property; and the elimination of Article VI, the constitutional guarantee of the Communist Party's political monopoly. He was coupling the presidency with constitutional sanction of a multiparty system. He had already won approval of that package from the Party's Central Committee.

To get his way on the presidency, Gorbachev engaged in more blatant manipulation of the Congress than ever before. When reformers were pressing him too hard, he ignored their requests to speak; if they already had the podium, he would cut off the mikes; more than once, he closed the microphones in the entire hall to lecture the deputies; and he simply refused to allow votes on proposals that did not suit him.

His parliamentary sleight-of-hand—more slippery, as one reporter said, than the tricks of the legendary American House Speaker Sam Rayburn or Senate Majority Leader Lyndon Johnson—reached a climax when Gorbachev duped the Inter-Regional Group on the critical vote to establish the presidency, *before* they had a chance to offer amendments to his proposal from the floor. Gorbachev stood normal parliamentary procedure on its head, and even ignored the rules of the Congress. Under normal procedure, amendments to a proposal are considered first, and then it is voted on as amended. When Gorbachev first put his presidential proposal to a vote on March 13, the reformers thought it was a vote in principle and that there would be a second reading later, after amendments were attached. But Gorbachev whisked the proposal through—it carried easily by a vote of 1,771 in favor, 164 opposed, and 74 abstentions—and then pronounced it adopted as part of the Soviet constitution.[44]

The radicals were outraged when they learned that Gorbachev had hoodwinked them, and that their amendments would now require a two-thirds vote, instead of a simple majority, as the rules required. A stream of radicals vehemently protested Gorbachev's chicanery and demanded another vote.

"This is a parliamentary abomination," Stankevich exploded. "We have violated all the classic parliamentary rules and several of our own rules of procedure."

"It's a circus," fumed Arkady Murashev, a Moscow radical who had voted for Gorbachev's package. "We were manipulated. We didn't know what we were voting for."

Gorbachev, unmoved, coldly cut them off. "This is normal procedure in parliaments all over the world," he said. "The discussion is closed."[45]

The radical reformers were crestfallen. Their only comfort was that Stankevich, with his skill in the intricacies of bill drafting, had been meeting privately with Gorbachev's aides to work out changes in the proposal. And on the night before the vote, he had won acceptance of limitations on the most egregious excesses of Gorbachev's proposal. So those provisions were included in the version approved by the Congress and were now part of the constitution.

Stankevich had a list of amendments aimed at making the Soviet president legally accountable and at curbing his dictatorial powers. Of his list, about half of the key amendments had been accepted. Most important were the inclusion of the legislature's power of impeachment, by a two-thirds vote of the Congress, for presidential violation of laws or the constitution; and also significant limits on the president's powers to issue decrees and to declare a state of emergency.

Gorbachev's draft had granted the president virtually unlimited power to issue decrees and to declare a state of emergency, and then impose direct presidential rule in any region of the country. These provisions legally made the president a czar or dictator, and alarmed the reformers. Stankevich had insisted on language that allowed presidential decrees only "on the basis, and in fulfillment, of the constitution . . . and the laws of the U.S.S.R." On declaration of a state of emergency, Stankevich inserted the requirement that the president must receive a request or gain approval from the local government, or else obtain immediate confirmation of his action by a two-thirds vote of the Supreme Soviet. One exception was made for declaring martial law in the event of a foreign military attack on the Soviet Union.

Other inroads on Gorbachev's draft were accomplished by the liberals. One made it less cumbersome for the legislature to override a presidential veto; another took the authority to appoint a Constitutional Control Commission away from the president and gave it to the chairman of the Supreme Soviet. The Baltic delegates from Estonia and Latvia, whose votes Gorbachev needed badly, bargained for language pledging that the new presidency "does not change the legal position or entail any restriction on the competence of union and autonomous republics," obviously including their constitutional right to secede.

In short, there had been the real politics of compromise. Stankevich was especially pleased with the changes on presidential decrees and the state of emergency. "Those are real limitations on the president," he told me. "They make [Gorbachev's proposal] almost acceptable to me." But progress was fitful; rights won on paper did not always work out in practice. Stankevich was smarting at Gorbachev's high-handed floor tactics, and with other reformers, he was determined to fight for still further restrictions.

The reformers got one important floor amendment through—a provision protecting the chairman of the Supreme Court from removal by the president; but they failed on others because they were boxed in by Gorbachev's procedural trick. A proposal to strike any mention of the Communist Party in the constitution got a vote of 1,067 to 906—positive but not a two-thirds majority.

The most important effort, and the most painful defeat, was a proposal that would have forced Gorbachev to give up his post as general secretary of the Communist Party; the amendment prohibited the president from serving as an official of any party, but again, while the vote was 1,303 to 607, a solid margin of victory, it was short of two thirds (1,497). That so angered the radicals that they demanded a new vote on the original proposal for the presidency. Gorbachev, sensing conservative impatience, shrewdly called for a vote on whether to vote again. That idea went down to resounding defeat.

Stankevich's final effort was a bid to limit Gorbachev to an initial term of two to three years. The new constitutional change provided for a five-year term and popular elections. But with the polls showing a severe drop in his public support, Gorbachev evidently feared a popular vote and wanted his first election made by the 2,250-member Congress. Stankevich and other reformers were willing to vote for him—but only on condition that Gorbachev agree to a short, transitional first term.

"I sent Gorbachev a note saying, 'If the idea of a transitional presidency of two or three years is adopted, then everything will be okay, and a lot of radicals will vote for you,' " Stankevich recalled later. "I stood near the microphone at the front, trying to get recognized. But Gorbachev ignored me. It was a real risk for Gorbachev not to let our proposal come to a vote. He made a big choice: five years or nothing!"[46]

Gorbachev was gambling that he had drawn a stark choice for the Congress: either back him all the way or face anarchy and chaos. It was a typical Gorbachev tactic to force his critics into a predicament where they felt they had no alternative but to side with him, despite strong differences with him.

As reinforcement, just before the vote on whether the Congress should elect the president, Gorbachev sent to the podium two of the most influential voices with the liberals: his Politburo ally Aleksandr Yakovlev and Dmitri Likhachev, the elderly academician with impeccable anti-Stalinist credentials, who is known as a voice of reason. Both made the argument that the country was in too deep a crisis to afford the delay and the divisive turmoil of a popular presidential election.

"The idea of a popular vote is attractive, correct, and legal," Yakovlev conceded, "but any delay can throw us back. . . . I am afraid of a miscalculation that will cost our country and our people dearly."[47]

Likhachev drew a parallel between the situation in 1990 and the situation after February 1917, when Russia's prerevolutionary experiment in constitutional government was undermined by civil turmoil. Sitting in the gallery, I could feel a chill silence descending on the hall as the tall, distinguished, aging scholar spoke.

"I remember perfectly well the February Revolution," said Likhachev, who was a boy of eleven at that time. "I know what people's emotions

are like, and I have to tell you that at the present time our country is swept
with emotions. In these conditions the direct election of a president would
lead to a civil war. Believe me. Trust my experience. I am opposed to a
direct election. The election should be held here and without delay."[48]

The stage was set for Gorbachev, and he came perilously close to losing.
Everyone watched the electronic voting teller attentively: 1,542 for, 360
against, 76 abstentions. Gorbachev's margin of victory was only 45 votes.

Now he had to go through the actual balloting for president. Two other
candidates were nominated by conservatives: Prime Minister Ryzhkov
and Interior Minister Vadim Bakatin; both withdrew in favor of Gorbachev, but not before there were several blistering speeches attacking him,
from both left and right, the liberals worried about Gorbachev's enshrin-
ing one-man rule, and the conservatives condemning him for a country
in ruins.

"We live in a nightmarish situation, in a nightmarish country, under
a nightmarish system of doing things," protested a bemedaled military
officer.

"Every minute he is losing votes of deputies," Vladimir Tikhonov, a
leading reformer, commented to me during a smoke break. "More and
more people are unhappy with the machinery of changing the constitution. Have you ever seen a legislature amend and pass a constitution
orally—with oral amendments? And in just three days? No civilized country operates this way."[49]

I asked Dmitri Likhachev how he thought the people would vote, if
given a chance.

"I doubt Gorbachev would win," he replied. "People are upset about
food. They would vote for someone else—a negative vote in protest
against the government."[50]

That sentiment was palpable in the hall too, and the secret ballot for
the president gave Gorbachev's critics and enemies, including those in the
Party apparatus and the military, a hidden chance to vote against him.

By law, Gorbachev needed votes from at least 50 percent of the total
membership of the Congress. A year before, in the first Congress, Gorbachev had received 96 percent; but as Tikhonov said, support seemed to
be ebbing by the hour.

When the final tally came in, Gorbachev had just 59 percent, an
embarrassingly small majority from this establishment assembly. Out of
2,250 deputies, only 2,000 took ballots—and not taking a ballot was one
way of opposing Gorbachev; 54 ballots were invalid, and 122 did not use
their ballots (again, votes against Gorbachev). Of the ballots cast, 1,329

votes were for Gorbachev, 495 against. But counting the unused ballots, the negative vote was really somewhere between 600 and 800. Obviously, both right-wingers and radicals had opposed him in significant numbers.

The next day, Gorbachev administered the oath of office to himself, promising to uphold the Soviet constitution and pledging a new surge of radical reforms. But the final action of the Congress, a Gorbachev-engineered denunciation of Lithuania's declaration of independence, was hardly a promising beginning: It was a stream of invective, a charade of parliamentary procedure, a throwback to the old obsequious Supreme Soviets of the Stalin and Brezhnev eras; it embarrassed and infuriated my Moscow intellectual friends.

In the immediate aftermath, the reformers were disappointed with the whole process, and fearful that the legislature was still the pliable tool of Gorbachev, on whom almost everything depended. Stankevich, Tikhonov, and others, such as Roy Medvedev and the writer Aleksandr Gelman, openly decried the shortcomings of both the Congress and the Supreme Soviet; Gorbachev and the government had the political initiative, controlled the budget, could manipulate the conservative majority, and the new democrats had only a skeleton staff, an infant newspaper, and the bare framework of organization.

It was, as Medvedev repeated to me, "not real democracy." But as he also observed, the changes were significant.

In a year, from the elections of March 1989 to the Congress of March 1990, Gorbachev had overseen the establishment of a new parliamentary system and a new presidency. In a country where kings and dictators had ruled for life or until some cabal dethroned them, there was now an elected president, with a fixed term of office, a line of succession (the chairman of the Supreme Soviet and the prime minister), and a two-term limit. There were provisions for impeaching the ruler, for passing legislation against his will, and for overriding his veto.

However imperfectly it worked, the Supreme Soviet had shown that it dared to reject government policy and throw out government ministers, and it now had the constitutional power to topple a government—through a vote of no-confidence.

Of course, the system looks better on paper than in reality; Soviet leaders are experts at nice-sounding proposals, but bad at putting them into practice, especially when they cut across the interests of the rulers. Gorbachev was no exception, as he had shown in the Congress. As Stankevich observed to me, "Gorbachev is not a democrat—he is a democratic autocrat."

Still, for a society that has never heeded the rule of law, the changes in the structure and functioning of the government have been momentous.

This was hardly a Western-style democracy, but Gorbachev could no longer exercise power in isolation, like Stalin; he had to operate more like a Western leader, dealing and bargaining with a variety of forces. In May 1990, for example, the Supreme Soviet rejected the price increases and the economic-reform program put together by Gorbachev and Ryzhkov. The Communist Party had no say in the matter—it was losing its grip on power.

The Politburo and the Central Committee were being superseded by the new mechanisms of elected government, a presidency and the Supreme Soviet. Gorbachev had shifted the primary power for ruling the country out of the hands of the Party, and he had tolerated, however reluctantly, the rise of a political opposition.

CHAPTER 21

COMMUNISM: "KNEE-DEEP IN GASOLINE"

"When people see the elated tone . . . in
our press about how bourgeois leaders
praise *perestroika*, it raises questions
in their minds. They remember Lenin's
advice: 'Think twice anytime your class
enemy praises you.' "[1]

—Ratmir Bobovikov
Provincial Party Boss
April 1989

"How is it possible to have a
situation where life is humming all
around, and where vital problems are
being discussed by the people out in city
squares, but certain Party organizations
are still chewing stale gum?"[2]

—Gorbachev, July 1989

No institution in Soviet society had more to lose from Gorbachev's reforms than the Communist Party apparat, what the Russians call the
nomenklatura: the self-selecting, self-perpetuating hierarchy of the Party,
and the inner core of government officials and economic executives who
are named to their posts by the Party. In a famous book, the maverick
Yugoslav Communist Milovan Djilas called this *The New Class.*

These are not rank-and-file Communists, the nineteen million members of the Soviet Communist Party. These are the Party's inner hierarchy, its power elite: the Politburo, the Central Committee, and their staffs, as powerful as the Office of the Presidency in Washington combined with the apparatus of the congressional leadership; the power barons who rule all the republics, provinces, cities, districts, and villages; their legions of apparatchiks; the Party secretaries and Party committees in every farm, factory, coal mine, university, TV station, army unit, KGB detachment; the staffs of hundreds of Party newspapers at every level of society, from *Pravda* to industrial shop-floor leaflets; as well as thousands of Party lecturers, propagandists, speech writers, and instructors constantly agitating on the Party's behalf.

It is a formidable political machine—217,700 full-time employees with an annual budget of more than 2.7 billion rubles (officially $4.5 billion).[3] Add the interlocking echelons of key leaders in the government and in all facets of the economy, all of whom are dependent on the Party's patronage, and you have the *nomenklatura*. Add, too, another million part-time Party workers and lecturers. This is more than any normal political party; it is what the New Left of American politics calls "the power structure," an entire web of power. It is the Party integrated into the governmental and economic structure of the Soviet state, at every level of society. That is what makes the Party-state apparat so difficult to dislodge.

To break the Party's grip on power in the Soviet Union was different from overthrowing Communist rule in Eastern Europe. For one thing, the Communist parties in Poland, Hungary, East Germany, and Czechoslovakia were imposed by the Soviet army, whereas in Russia, the Party came to power out of a homegrown revolution. In Eastern Europe, the Communist Party was an agent of alien rule, a tool of an occupying army, so that when the power force of local nationalism was released, the mass of the nation turned against the Party. That also happened in the minority regions of the Soviet Union; Lithuanians, Armenians, Ukrainians, and others turned against the Party. But Russia was different; for all the grievances of Russian nationalists, a strong Communist Party had meant a powerful Russia, dominating a huge empire. Stalin had played that theme, especially during World War II. Party and nation had been linked; so nationalism was not a force that reformers could use to turn the masses of Russians against the Party.

With the natural instinct for survival of politicians and bureaucrats everywhere, the *nomenklatura* intuitively understood just how much of a threat was posed by Gorbachev's drive to shake up the Soviet system and to bring in new blood. Most of them mistrusted his ulterior motives, despite what he said, and they fought him every time he chipped away at their edifice, or shook the foundations of their power.

But as Gorbachev geared up *perestroika,* the Party was no longer a Stalinist monolith. Since Khrushchev's time, it had included three factions: a small minority of anti-Stalinist reformers, another minority of neo-Stalinist counterreformers, and a majority of conservatives committed to protecting the status quo.[4] Under Gorbachev, the different tendencies multiplied. Party liberals backed reform, convinced it was vital to save the Party; a small radical minority wanted more sweeping reforms. Some conservatives endorsed economic reform only and opposed political changes. The bulk of the *nomenklatura,* politically to the right of Gorbachev, paid lip service to *perestroika* because it was the Party line, but they dug in their heels against assaults on the Party's supremacy and control. They were strongest among the Party machine in the provinces, in the military and the KGB, in the right-wing Party press, in some ministries, and in the Politburo faction led by Yegor Ligachev.

Gorbachev's well-nigh impossible task was to persuade the *nomenklatura* that what was clearly against their individual and collective self-interest in the short run was in the higher interest of the Party over the long run. He tapped into their lifelong habits of unity, discipline, following orders from the top, to try to get them to do what troubled them in the marrow of their bones: to change their ways and gradually surrender some of their power.

Initially, Gorbachev's strategy was to reform the Party from within by drumming out the Brezhnevite Old Guard, by gradually replacing other officials bit by bit, and by carrying out minor periodic purges and cutbacks. But there were so many layers that he could not scrape away the Old Guard fast enough; a new layer replaced the old one. By 1987, pursuing "socialist pluralism," he allowed formation of rival groups, of informal grass-roots organizations, but he wanted to restrict them to the role of junior partners, protecting the Party as the dominant force in Soviet society. Nevertheless, over time, his aides told me, the intransigence of the apparat gradually "radicalized" Gorbachev, and his assaults on its entrenched power became more frontal.

The first real jolt to the apparat's power was the election of 1989.

Before that, Gorbachev had been whittling away at the old structure through press articles that jabbed constantly at Stalinist terror and Stalinist thinking, and through the Nineteenth Party Conference in mid-1988, where he made the *nomenklatura* endure the open challenge of free-thinking reformers. Then, in October 1988, he really cut into their power, with a swift, surgical behind-the-scenes coup at a Party Central Committee meeting. He forced President Andrei Gromyko and three other senior Brezhnev holdovers into retirement; he stripped hard-liner Yegor Ligachev of the ideology portfolio—responsibility over the press and media; he disbanded the Party Secretariat (until then, Ligachev's stronghold); and he began to lop off Central Committee staff departments that dealt with economic management.[5]

Still, these were modest blows compared to the March 1989 elections, which shattered the Party's image of invincibility. With the defeat of several dozen high Party and government officials across the country, the Party had lost face, and the apparat stood in jeopardy of losing their jobs.

"I am convinced that for us the moment of truth has come," conceded Ivan Saly, a burly district Party leader in Kiev, who had fallen victim in the elections and was scrambling to adjust to the new democratic mood. "We can no longer entertain illusions. We have suffered a major political defeat."[6]

At the top, Gorbachev had insulated all but one full member of the Politburo (Vitaly Vorotnikov) from having to face public elections. One hundred VIPs, led by the Politburo, were awarded the Party's "golden seats" in the Congress, though they had to go through the formality of election by the Party Central Committee. Yet even that sanctuary of Party orthodoxy was infected by dissent: Out of a few hundred votes, Gorbachev got twelve negative votes, Aleksandr Yakovlev fifty-nine, and Yegor Ligachev seventy-eight.

But that was nothing compared to the stinging personal humiliation of less exalted, but still important, Party officials who were rejected by the voters. These provincial czars, the *obkom* bosses, as Russians call them— leaders of the *oblast* or provincial Party committees—were publicly humbled. These big shots, used to riding around in limousines, to sitting behind huge desks and giving orders, were suddenly shorn of moral authority, of their pretense of ruling in the name of the people.

"The Party is losing its role as vanguard of the people," Leonid Dobrokhotov candidly admitted to me. Dobrokhotov works as a liberal, reformist supporter of Gorbachev in the Central Committee staff. "The constitution says the Party is the vanguard, but that means nothing. The Party is only the vanguard in the minds of people. Either it has authority, or it doesn't. Either people believe in it, or they don't. That's the Party's problem. We've lost that, and now we have to get it back. . . .[7]

"There's a real division within the Party between the old mentality and the new mentality, between Right and Left," Dobrokhotov remarked to me on a different occasion. "The election result has sharpened this division. The Old Guard, the Right, sees the election as bad, the outcome as grave. The Left sees the election as good, favoring progressive forces that support *perestroika*. Gorbachev is now using a purge from below, rather than forcing people out by a purge from the top."[8]

AN APPARATCHIK TASTES DEFEAT

In Moscow, the highest-ranking Party official to feel the sting of defeat was Yuri Prokofyev, then number two in Moscow, second secretary of the city Party committee. Prokofyev ran in the Kuibyshev District, where he had formerly been the Party leader; he came in third in a three-man race, with just 13.5 percent of the vote. I tried to interview him after the elections, but he kept ducking me; his Party colleagues said he was in a state of shock and depression. When I finally saw him in the fall, he was still bitter about being rejected by his old Party district.

"I worked, I tried, I thought I worked decently, and then when people started to wipe out what was done by the Party in years past, it made me very bitter," Prokofyev told me.

"I was hurt because I had worked in this district for eight years, put all of my efforts into it, to develop it. Some things worked out, not everything, but right now we're finishing the subway station. We've built Houses of Culture for Young Pioneers. We've fixed up many streets, built a new housing development. . . . And of course, the people did not think so highly of it. That was insulting to me. But it taught me how to get used to real political struggle."

When I asked Prokofyev why the public rejected him if he had done so much, he cited their rage over economic shortages, their anger at his taking the Party line against Yeltsin, and the Party's terrible loss of authority, something that hit him the instant he entered the campaign.

"I had low expectations because I had an early sense of the attitude toward Party officials," he said. "To be honest, I didn't expect such strong criticism and such a strong battle against me. After the second or third meeting [with the voters], I sensed that I wasn't going to win. . . . All of the problems in the district—housing, transportation, food—all of that was directed at me. . . . As a Party secretary, I had to justify the situation, rather than criticize it. People wanted me to criticize the Council of Ministers or Gorbachev or the Central Committee. Had I done that, I would have been elected easily."

"What about the privileges of the Party elite that Yeltsin mentioned in his campaign?" I asked.

"What kind of Party privileges do I have?" Prokofyev retorted. "I have a two-room apartment of thirty-five square meters with my wife. Our son lives in a two-room apartment with twenty-nine square meters with his wife and child. What other privileges? I rent a government *dacha* for about five hundred rubles [$833] a year. And I have a car."9

The apartments were hardly Park Avenue–style; yet in a city of tight housing, they were very ample. Many families of five live in less space than Prokofyev shares with his wife. And the idea of a car and a country *dacha* smacks of luxury to Russian workers.

Even though Yeltsin was not a direct rival, he figured prominently in Prokofyev's campaign because the Party had tried so hard to crush Yeltsin.

"People often asked me questions about Yeltsin," Prokofyev said. "I have a negative attitude toward him, because I worked with him shoulder to shoulder for three months in the Moscow Party committee and city council, and I don't think he's democratic. If he comes to power, to the leadership, it would be a repeat of Stalinism, because by nature he's a boss. He likes people to be subordinate to him. He is democratic only in words. When I explained that to people, they didn't accept it. People like what he says. They don't know his essence."

Prokofyev, a man in his early fifties, was a Party career man, a traditional apparatchik. But he was also a new-style leader in the Gorbachev mold; he had gotten the Soviet equivalent of a Ph.D. in economics, and his manner was hardly that of a hard-line Party boss: He was businesslike and thoughtful; short and unimposing—not a desk-pounding ideologue or a right-wing martinet.

In fact, Prokofyev was something of a weather vane among the apparat. He was accustomed to a certain political compass, and he was disconcerted that it no longer guided him. Not only had the election left him scarred, but Gorbachev's *perestroika* had confused him and left him disoriented, as it had many apparatchiks.

"The Party began *perestroika* and decided on several priorities, but in my view, a well-worked-out political and economic platform doesn't exist," Prokofyev complained. "Democracy, *glasnost,* a market economic system—these are only theses right now. So it's hard. Everyone understands *perestroika* in his own way. . . . I think the most important thing is for the Party leaders to decide what they want, what kind of society they want, so that everyone understands. Then we can know who's who: who are the enemies, and who are our supporters."

Prokofyev's personal destiny was uncertain and precarious after the election, though defeat did not require him to surrender his Party post just because he had lost a race for the Congress of People's Deputies. The only body that could dismiss him was the Moscow city Party committee (or a signal from the Politburo bosses, who had kicked Yeltsin out in late 1987). Prokofyev was not fighting Gorbachev or blaming reform for his defeat, and probably for those reasons, he survived his election debacle. By the time I saw him in the fall, he still had his job; but he was defensive when I asked him whom he—and the Party—now claimed to represent.

"In the system that exists, I can say that I represent one-point-two million Communists in this city," he replied.

The bigger issue, it seemed to me, was the legitimacy of the Party itself. As Dobrokhotov had said, the Party had to find ways to win back its claim as the political vanguard.

"Will you run again in local elections?" I asked.

"I don't think so." Prokofyev shook his head. "The chances of winning are pretty slim for Party officials. That will change only if the economic situation changes. If people's lives get better, and they feel some results, then their attitudes will change. Right now, things aren't getting better— unfortunately. It's a very difficult situation for the Party right now."

GETTING RID OF "DEAD SOULS"

The 1989 elections made clear for the first time that Gorbachev's goal was to move power—not all power, but some—from the Communist Party to the government, to the Congress of People's Deputies and the all-union Supreme Soviet. It was a delicate operation, requiring tactical zigzags. The Party was still his own power base, and it was still too formidable a force simply to ignore and leave to its own devices. He could not allow it to slip out of his control and become a solid phalanx opposed to him and to perestroika. If he could not bend the apparat to his will, at least he had to immobilize it, neutralize it. So periodically, like any political leader in the West, he had to tend to his power base, hear out his angry constituents, defend their interests until he had decided whether to try to strip them of still more power.

As part of his general strategy, he decided to open up the workings of the Party apparat to public scrutiny as one way of keeping on the pressure for internal Party reform. Sometimes that tactic worked, and sometimes it backfired, which then allowed the apparat to put pressure on Gorbachev and force him to retreat.

Traditionally, the Communist Party has kept its internal feuds private, thus maintaining the facade of unity. From 1985 well into 1989, for example, Gorbachev and Ligachev went to great lengths to claim that they were in harmony, even though a simple reading of their speeches revealed their conflicts. But after the March 1989 elections, there was such a fractious explosion inside the Party that it could no longer be hidden. Gorbachev suddenly released, in the pages of *Pravda,* what had hitherto been the secret speeches of closed Party Central Committee meetings—in this case the plenum of April 25, 1989—so that the public could see how the provincial bosses had screamed in protest over the elections.

One defeated Party candidate after another took to the podium to heap blame on "political extremists" for leveling scurrilous charges against the Party and for pandering to the public; on the central press for sensational-izing the issue of Party privileges; on the way the Party leadership was allowing the infiltration of Western values and political methods; and on Gorbachev's economic reforms for failing to produce. Several speakers warned Gorbachev that he was pushing democracy too far, opening the door to "anarchy and total license"; they demanded a crackdown against the informal democratic groups that had toppled the Party barons.

"In our province and in Moscow, it has become fashionable to distrib-ute leaflets, posters, and all kind of appeals," said the Moscow Province Party chief, Valentin Mesyats, who lost his election bid. "Let me tell you: These are no childish pranks. These are political slogans which call for the overthrow of Soviet power and the overthrow of the Party. . . . The main thing now is not to retreat."[10]

"Events in the last few years and especially in recent months in the Baltic republics, the Caucasus, Moscow, Leningrad, Moldavia, and other regions, and the slogans now openly printed in our press [by] informal associations, give us no grounds for passivity or peace of mind," warned Ivan Polozkov, the Party chief in Krasnodar Territory, who would be elected a year later as Party leader for the entire Russian republic. "When people . . . call for the entire party to be blamed for Stalin's crimes and hold rallies for the breakup of the U.S.S.R. and the elimination of the Communist Party, when there are calls to hang Communists, not to fulfill government decisions, and to sabotage Soviet laws, and there is no official reaction, then let's honestly admit that we have already gone a bit too far!"[11]

"We must stop trying to pin the mistakes and crimes of individual Communists, leaders included, on the entire Party and its policy . . . stop the discrediting of the elected Party *aktiv* and the groundless censuring of the management apparatus," declared Ratmir Bobovikov, the regional boss in Vladimir Province. "When people see the elated tone of articles in our press about how bourgeois leaders praise *perestroika,* it raises ques-

tions in their minds. They remember Lenin's advice: 'Think twice anytime your class enemy praises you.' "12

In their anger, the defeated Party leaders made the Soviet press their
whipping boy. Azerbaijani Party chief Abdur Rahman Vezirov stooped to
accuse "independent periodicals" of fostering "a kind of ideological AIDS
in our people."13 Others picked up his chant.

Vladimir Melnikov, the Party boss in the Komi republic, candidly
admitted that sugar rationing, the shortage of soap, the erratic supply of
meat, and the lack of modern appliances, children's clothing, and shoes
had contributed to Party losses in his area. There were now mass work
stoppages, hunger strikes, unsanctioned rallies and demonstrations, he
said, some pushed by "extremist-minded elements . . . who come to us
from the center [Moscow]". Then, with an alarm typical of the Party
apparat, Melnikov pointed an accusing finger at the media.

"Was the outcome of the elections not influenced by the well-targeted
salvos that the press and television fired at the first secretaries of provincial
Party committees?" he demanded. "Comrades, look at the movies, look
at our magazines. What has become of patriotism and civic-mindedness?
How are we going to educate our young people? We are raising them in
a totally different spirit. Can this really not worry the ideological staff of
the Central Committee and the Politburo?"14

Yuri Solovyov, the Leningrad Province chief and junior member of the
Politburo, who had led the entire Party slate in Leningrad to ignominious
defeat, admitted to his colleagues: "For understandable reasons, it is not
easy for me to speak today."

Right after his defeat, Solovyov had taken personal responsibility, a
theme he now touched on only lightly. The undercurrent of his remarks
blamed Gorbachev's policies. While Solovyov never mentioned Gorbachev, he said the Soviet president's policy on cooperatives had legalized
speculation and unearned income, "which has gotten out of control." He
said Gorbachev's plan to have workers elect their managers had produced
plant directors "who willy-nilly pander to . . . the syndrome of consumer-
ism, greed, and freeloading." He charged that an "ideological spineless-
ness has infiltrated the Party ranks" and that reformers were trying "to
turn a party of action into a party of debating clubs." And he warned that
the young now saw the Communist Party as "a party of mistakes and
crimes."

Finally, Solovyov invited the right-wing apparat to do battle. As an
alternative to Gorbachev's Congress of People's Deputies, Solovyov proposed "an all-union congress of workers' delegates" with regional rallies
to arouse the masses. It was an invitation to a new political class struggle,

a rallying cry for hard-liners to mobilize a blue-collar counterforce to combat the grass-roots groups of urban intellectuals.[15]

Gorbachev was undeterred—he gave the bleating Party barons a scolding. He took some responsibility for the economic mess, but he also pinned blame on them for the public's anger over disastrous housing, transport, and other consumer services, and he admonished them that it was time to "change their style of work to be closer to the people."

Perestroika, he advised them, would take iron nerves and a steady stomach. Just as his reforms were generating "a powerful movement from underneath," he said, some Party leaders "are beginning to panic and very nearly perceive a threat to socialism." Instead, Gorbachev told them to learn how to work in democratic conditions and to get into "the thick of life"; and he slapped back at Solovyov's dig about the Party becoming a weak-kneed "debating club."

"The party's dialogue with the working people is not weakness or making the Party a discussion club," Gorbachev retorted. "If it is weakness to conduct a dialogue with all segments of the society, then I do not know what courage is."

Gorbachev dismissed the apparat's complaints as "nostalgic yearning for authoritarian methods."[16]

In case they did not get the message, Gorbachev carried out a purge of Old Guard holdovers on the Central Committee—"lame ducks," or, in Russian lingo, "dead souls." These were former Party officials whom Gorbachev had previously fired or demoted from important posts; under Party rules, they kept their seats on the Central Committee until the next Party Congress replaced them—and Party Congresses occurred only every five years.

Gorbachev wanted them off the committee because they were a nuisance, and also a threat; technically, the Central Committee had to approve his policies and it could remove him from his post. In 1985, he had inherited what was essentially Brezhnev's Central Committee; in February 1986, at the Twenty-seventh Party Congress, Gorbachev replaced roughly 40 percent of the Brezhnev holdovers, but close to 60 percent were still around.[17] They were a drag on Gorbachev's reforms and he wanted them out; at that April 1989 Party plenum, he got rid of 110 "dead souls" by "persuading" them to retire.

Since Gorbachev was cutting deadwood, it seemed strange that he did not also purge the Party hard-liners who had lost elections. Aides said that Gorbachev wanted the purge to come from the Party's rank and file; and in a few places that happened. By and large, however, Gorbachev let the defeated barons stay on, including those who had attacked his policies.

Some, such as Yuri Prokofyev, figured out how to work the new, democratic style of politics to their advantage; Prokofyev got promoted to Moscow Party chief when Gorbachev moved out Lev Zaikov, a Politburo conservative, in late 1989.

But Leningrad remained a thorn in Gorbachev's side, and eventually he had to deal with it; Leningrad was far too important a power base, and the defeat of its entire Party slate had been far too visible for Gorbachev to ignore. Moreover, Leningrad Party boss Yuri Solovyov had hardly been contrite at the Party meeting, and he had been even more truculent since then. When I visited Leningrad in June 1989, I heard repeated speculation that Solovyov was on his way out. Instead, he became more defiant; he was reviving Leningrad as a hotbed of hard-line opposition to *perestroika*. Finally, Gorbachev could brook no more. On July 12, he showed up in Leningrad for a Party meeting that fired Solovyov and appointed a successor, Boris Gidaspov, a fifty-six-year-old science administrator, who had won a seat in the March 1989 elections, and whom everyone presumed to be less hard-line than Solovyov.

Gorbachev made Solovyov endure the indignity of sitting beside him during a joint television appearance with Gidaspov, while Gorbachev ran down the failings of the Leningrad Party apparatus and sarcastically derided Solovyov's outdated style of leadership.

His voice heavy with sarcasm, Gorbachev asked how it was possible, in a city such as Leningrad, to have a situation where life was brimming with action and public debate on city squares, "but certain Party organizations are still chewing stale gum?"[18]

THE DANGERS OF "DUAL POWER"

Within the Party, Gorbachev was riding high after the March elections. His political reform was on track, his personal power at a peak. The right wing of the Party apparat was on the defensive, nursing its wounds; it was angry, but cowed.

Power is rarely static, however, and reform never moves in a straight line; it has fits and starts. The power that flows, also ebbs. The tide within the Party turned against Gorbachev in the summer of 1989—and it had been reversed in good measure by events. The entire nation was in upheaval. The *nomenklatura*, which had been shaken in the spring, was now alarmed that the Party was losing control.

The most stunning blow was the wave of mass strikes by coal miners in western Siberia, the Ukraine, around Vorkuta in the north, and near

Karaganda in Central Asia. In mid-July 1989, several hundred thousand miners walked off the job, the first massive strike since the 1920s—with the ominous potential of touching off a popular revolution because of widespread economic despair. The walkout struck fear into the government, which was already anxious to keep the germ of worker unrest from spreading.

Until the strike, the apparat could blame political ferment on the press and the intellectuals, but now the proletariat was lashing out at the Party. The miners were in fury that after seventy years, the Party had failed to deliver on the promises of the Bolshevik Revolution, and that in four years, Gorbachev's *perestroika* had delivered them nothing. With their walkout paralyzing much of Soviet heavy industry, Gorbachev quickly sided with their demands. Prime Minister Ryzhkov promised almost anything—higher pay, fringe benefits, better working conditions, housing, meat, soap—to get the miners back to work.

At the same time, nationalist violence was on the rise between Armenia and Azerbaijan; there were outbreaks in the Ferghana Valley of Uzbekistan; and Baltic nationalists were stepping up their drive toward secession. From the center, it looked as though the Soviet Union were beginning to tear apart.

Closer to home, the *nomenklatura* saw another threat: the danger of what Yuri Prokofyev and others called "dual power"—a rival power base, paralleling the Party, with members free of Party control. The Congress of People's Deputies and the Supreme Soviet were asserting real power, invading the Party's domain, usurping its prerogatives. The legislature was appointing and rejecting government ministers, it was seriously debating policy—and it was doing all this without any guidance from the Party. Only three Politburo members and very few other top apparatchiks were in the Supreme Soviet; obviously Gorbachev was keeping them out.[19] Control was the heart of the *nomenklatura* system—unity under a single central command—and the Party's control of all major political decisions, appointments, policies, was slipping away.

By actually starting to apply Lenin's slogan "All Power to the Soviets," Gorbachev was undermining the essence of the dictatorship of the *nomenklatura*. The nerve endings of Party regulars told them this erosion could be as fatal as the strike of a cobra.

"We say that we're passing over power to the soviets, and that is happening," Yuri Prokofyev snorted. "But then we have to think of what the role and place of the Party is, because two kinds of power can't exist, right? We have to deal with the question of the Party itself so that it does not lose its authority."[20]

Technically, all Supreme Soviet deputies who were Party members (85 percent) were expected to follow the Party's orders. But there was a breakdown in Party discipline: The deputies were defying the Party; they were going their own way—even to the point of demanding removal of the constitutional guarantee of the Party's supremacy in all walks of Soviet life. The apparat found this breach of discipline especially intolerable.

These concerns were gnawing at the apparat when Gorbachev met on July 18, 1989, with the Politburo and 150 regional Party first secretaries. The atmosphere was charged. The anger that had percolated among the regional bosses at the Central Committee meeting in April was now boiling at a higher and more dangerous level—among Politburo members, including Gorbachev's supposed partner in reform, Prime Minister Nikolai Ryzhkov.

Up in arms, Gorbachev's colleagues ganged up on him, citing the nation's political chaos and the erosion of Party power. The chorus of discontent on all major issues had the ominous ring of an incipient cabal:

Lev Zaikov, Moscow Party chief: "[M]any Party committees are losing control of the situation. . . . Wherever you look, there is relentless propaganda of Western values. The news from 'over there' is about luxury cars and villas, shop windows and so on. And our news? Perpetual shortages, law breaking, drug addiction. It is as if *perestroika* had changed nothing, as if we could find no other color except black to paint our own picture."[21]

Vitaly Vorotnikov, leader of the Russian republic: "The point is that *perestroika* is not going the way we want it to and there is mounting criticism among the people. . . . The time has come to change the whole range of [our] precepts."[22]

Yegor Ligachev, ranking Politburo conservative: "Recently there have been calls for a multiparty system. In a federated state, such as the Soviet Union, this is simply fatal. A multiparty system would mean the disintegration of the Soviet federation. . . . [The] Communist Party is the only real political force that rallies and unites all the country's peoples into a union of republics."[23]

Leonid Bobykin, the Sverdlovsk regional secretary, cut close to Gorbachev himself, without naming him. There was "no firm line on ideological questions," he said. "The role of the Central Committee Secretariat has been weakened recently. Obviously we need a Central Committee second secretary."[24]

Bobykin's was the voice of the apparat, alarmed at how Gorbachev had emasculated the very core of its power by disbanding the Secretariat and cutting the Central Committee staff. Bobykin was a hard-line Party veteran who was very close to Prime Minister Ryzhkov. By proposing a new

Party number two, he was raising a direct threat to Gorbachev; it meant Gorbachev's letting go of some power and allowing a pretender to his throne. Gorbachev had moved Ligachev out of that post in October 1988 and had allowed no one to step into his shoes.

Ryzhkov picked up Bobykin's theme, accusing Gorbachev of neglecting the Party; he did not hesitate to lecture Gorbachev under the guise of addressing the Party elite.

"We must do everything to help ensure that [Gorbachev] devotes more attention to his Party duties," Ryzhkov told the gathering. "We must free him from trivial questions, which are bogging him down."[25]

As if Gorbachev had been indulging in trivia; no matter, Ryzhkov was warning Gorbachev—if the Party was going to be saved, and if Gorbachev was going to save himself, he had better defend the citadel, and stop playing around with democratic institutions. Even more pointedly, Ryzhkov, as prime minister, seemed to be telling Gorbachev, as president, to get off his back and stick to Party business.

Ryzhkov's salvo was all the more stunning because he was usually an ally, not a critic, of Gorbachev, although during that summer they had exchanged barbs in public. Gorbachev had invited the Supreme Soviet to rake Ryzhkov over the coals, and the prime minister was paying him back. He had emerged at the moment as Gorbachev's chief antagonist.

The picture Ryzhkov painted was stark: a Party "reduced to self-flagellation and often to open castigation" of its own apparat; a Party blindly stumbling along without a clear strategy; a Party gone soft and losing power; a Party whose leaders were foolishly acting as if nothing had gone wrong.

"So many accusations have been brought against the Party both in our country and abroad—more than ever before in its entire history—that it is in fact losing authority," Ryzhkov declared. "[Yet] despite the loss of authority and of influence over all that is happening in society, willingly or not, we have continued to maintain the illusion that nothing out of the ordinary has happened, that as before the main levers remain in our hands and that using them, we can, as before, with the very same methods, govern . . . the country."

Ryzhkov was alluding not only to the coal mines and minority republics careening out of control, but to power slipping away right under the Party's nose in the Supreme Soviet. It was ironic that the Politburo member in charge of the government was the one to rise to the Party's defense. But Ryzhkov was especially sensitive on this issue because he personally had been humiliated by the Supreme Soviet. His policy had been ripped apart, and his ministers; and he was obviously furious.

"Things are reaching the point where the Party is being relegated to a backseat in public life—this was shown by the elections," Ryzhkov argued.

"In my view, we must acknowledge that the assessment made after the elections is not quite accurate. We overestimated statistics, citing the fact that 85 percent of the elected deputies are Communists. But this quantitative majority means little," he pointed out. "They [have] literally forced their way to the rostrum with their own platforms, programs, proposals, and accusations, often including insinuations against the Party. And the Politburo found itself on the sidelines, in an isolated position, as if it had fallen under seige. . . .

"We need now to find new approaches, new methods, new principles to govern relations among the triangle of power that has emerged today in our system of government—the [Party] Central Committee, the Supreme Soviet, and the U.S.S.R. Council of Ministers. . . . A real and mighty power has appeared in the form of the Congress of People's Deputies and the U.S.S.R. Supreme Soviet. If the Party does not find a way out of this, then it may lose influence over state government.

"Things have not yet reached the point where the slogan 'Party in Danger' is justified. But if we face the truth, we must clearly see that this possibility exists. . . ."[26]

It was a powerful indictment of Gorbachev's policy, coming from the man who was second in power in fact, if not by formal designation. Not only was Ryzhkov prime minister, but opinion polls showed him second to Gorbachev in mass popularity, and his stock was soaring among the *nomenklatura*.

In spite of all this, my Party contacts denied that Ryzhkov was setting himself up as the point man of a political coup against Gorbachev; they said that Ryzhkov, as an economic manager, did not see himself becoming political number one.

Perhaps. I found it hard to gauge from a distance. Most politicians who get close to the top have the ambition to become number one, but the chemistry of Ryzhkov's relations with Gorbachev, who had appointed him and brought him along, might have forced Ryzhkov to suppress that ambition.

If Gorbachev was bothered by this onslaught from his Politburo colleagues, he did not show it. With the supreme self-confidence that has been his most effective armor when he is challenged, Gorbachev took the offensive.

"There will be no return to 'the good old days,' " he bluntly told the hard-liners who wanted to roll back *perestroika*. "It is impossible to decree the Party's authority. . . . Today, authority can only be 'won' " by progressive action.

Gorbachev conceded that it was irresponsible not to worry about the destiny of the Party, but he insisted it was equally irresponsible to become mired in pessimism. He admitted that the turmoil caused by *perestroika* was painful, but he justified that as a necessary by-product of reform aimed at real change.

"This creates extra tension," he said, "but this is what makes these revolutionary years." And he admonished the conservatives that others were able to seize the initiative whenever the Party fell behind the pace of change in society; he exhorted them to bring in new blood. "A renewal of cadres is needed, an influx of fresh forces," he said.

Gorbachev was blunt and unflinching, not even bothering to respond to Bobykin's proposal for a deputy and bypassing most of Ryzhkov's unhappy litany. With sheer force of conviction and personality, he overrode his critics and laid the blame for the Party's predicament squarely at the feet of the apparat.

"How can it happen that a party organization with many thousands of Communists, which possesses its own newspapers, its own professional workers, which possesses everything—suddenly begins to lose the initiative?" Gorbachev asked.

"There is only one reason for this: It means that we are lagging behind. It means that among us somewhere, there's a gap between words and deeds, between the masses and the Party, which—as a vanguard—ought to be out front."[27]

Gorbachev and the apparat had reached a standoff. The *nomenklatura* could not make him halt or reverse his democratic and press reforms; he could not force them to make real political changes. They could not keep him from shifting power to the Congress, but he could not get them to stop blocking his economic program. He was frustrated by their rigidity, but he lacked the power or the will to conduct a wholesale Party purge. They disliked his strategy, but they could not remove him because of his mass support, his power base in the legislature, and because they had no real alternative to his program except a return to Stalinism, which would lead to mass bloodshed.

With neither side content, the battle was bound to resume.

A PLOT AGAINST GORBACHEV?

Something happened between the summer and fall of 1989 to turn Gorbachev around. His rhetoric and his actions swung to the right; retrenchment replaced reform. He became the Party's defender instead of its attacker. It was not wholly surprising for Gorbachev; his path was a series of zigzags, a living testament to Lenin's dictum that revolution is "two steps forward, one step back."

Through that fall, Gorbachev showed personal strain more transparently than ever before. At times, he acted as if he felt he was losing control of events, that the country's social, political, and economic disintegration was overwhelming him. When challenged, he snarled and snapped. He seemed under intolerable pressure from the Party's right wing. At times, he acted like a dictator: He flew off the handle at the leaders of Baltic nationalism; he thundered his outrageous charge that the Inter-Regional Group deputies were "a gangster group"; he called for the resignation of Vladislav Starkov, editor of *Argumenty i Fakty*, for printing a public-opinion poll that made Gorbachev look bad.

At an angry session with senior newspaper editors, Gorbachev spluttered: "Reading the press, you get the feeling that you are standing knee-deep in gasoline. The only thing lacking is a spark."[28]

Anxiety about an impending explosion hung over Moscow in the fall and winter of 1989–90. The city was periodically swept by rumors of an imminent coup against Gorbachev by the Party right wing and the military. In a televised speech at the Congress of People's Deputies the previous June, Gorbachev himself had brought up such rumors, and he had laughed them off, joking that according to rumors, over the past four years "I have died seven times and my family has already been slain three times."[29]

The coup speculation was more insistent in the fall; it broke into print, in mid-August, when *Moscow News* ran an article headlined IS OCTOBER 1964 POSSIBLE TODAY? (alluding to the Party coup that threw out Khrushchev). And its answer was yes. On September 8, the television show *Vzglyad (View)* ran a piece on the political power struggle in the Kremlin. Other articles about the dangers of a coup or a violent explosion between "the upper echelons" of power, meaning the army, and the "grass roots," meaning the masses, appeared in the popular weekly *Ogonek* and the Moscow daily, *Moskovskaya Pravda.* Speaking in Vienna, Georgy Smirnov, a Central Committee official, confirmed "rumors according to which some people in the U.S.S.R. are thinking aloud about overthrowing state and Party chief M. S. Gorbachev."[30]

Because of my experiences in the seventies, when so many Moscow rumors had proven false, I had long been skeptical of such speculation. Now, in the late eighties, there was so much turmoil in the country that people were inclined to believe and say anything. Still, *Moscow News* and *Ogonek* had excellent connections with the liberal faction of the Party leadership—Yakovlev, Shevardnadze, and Party officials who worked under them. The fact that these publications printed such stories was an indication that Gorbachev's liberal allies seriously feared a coup. Printing coup stories was supposed to be prophylactic.

A ranking Baltic Communist Party official, whose chief was very close to Gorbachev and who met with Gorbachev several times in September 1989, told me that there had actually been an attempt by the right-wing faction of the Politburo to oust Gorbachev. He had gone off on a five-week vacation in the Crimea during August; while he was away, Politburo conservatives and the neo-Stalinist Right were particularly outspoken. Leningrad's citizen activist Nina Andreyeva went further than ever before—attacking Gorbachev by name for the first time and calling him a "bourgeois," who was out to destroy socialism. On September 1, Viktor Chebrikov, the Politburo hard-liner who had formerly headed the KGB, delivered a very tough law-and-order speech demanding crackdowns on many fronts. Yegor Ligachev, too, called for repression against "those people who are forever attacking the Party, the Soviet Union, our glorious army, and the security organs."

According to this Baltic Communist contact, who said his information came indirectly from Gorbachev himself, Gorbachev had planned to return from vacation on Sunday, September 10, but he was tipped off by allies in Moscow that a right-wing cabal was afoot, and he came home two days early, on Friday. Everything was prepared for his ouster, my source said, and on either that Friday or Saturday, at a rump meeting of the Politburo, the hard-liners confronted Gorbachev. According to my source, "They said to him bluntly, 'It's time to change,' "—meaning change leadership.

In this version of events, Ligachev was the real power behind the cabal, but Chebrikov took the lead in attacking Gorbachev to his face and demanding a change. The two had been emboldened by Ryzhkov's switch in July, supposedly feeling for the first time that the balance in the Politburo had tipped in their favor. Somehow, Gorbachev managed to face them down—the account is sketchy at best—but personal chemistry is often crucial in those situations. For waverers, Gorbachev was the establishment leader. Nonetheless, during the next fortnight, he was under intense pressure, as each side maneuvered behind the scenes to marshal its forces for a showdown at the scheduled Central Committee plenum on nationalities issues, September 19–20. In the middle of the month, Ligachev supposedly told visiting French Communists that he was confident of an imminent change at the helm.

I never got confirmation of the story that Gorbachev had been pressed to resign by Politburo hard-liners on September 8 or 9, but on September 19, one of Gorbachev's speech writers, Nikolai Shishlin, told me cryptically: "This is a very dangerous time for my boss." Shishlin was tense—awaiting the outcome of the Central Committee session. Gorbachev himself had been quoted on September 16 by Vaino Väljas, the Estonian Communist Party leader, as having said: "*Perestroika* is experiencing one of its most serious and difficult periods, with extremist forces consolidating, and with the conservative wing consolidating."[31] My Baltic contact told me that Gorbachev had indicated to Väljas, an old Party friend, that not just *perestroika,* but he himself was in trouble.

My source reminded me that Gorbachev had made a speech to the nation on September 9, which he called "an open cry to the public for support."

I remembered that speech well. I was in Sverdlovsk and had been so struck by how bad Gorbachev looked—strange for a man coming back from a five-week vacation—that I had pointed it out to my wife, Susan, who agreed. His tone was so alarmist that we were both riveted to the television set. He had an air about him of catastrophe.

"Everything is bound up in a tight knot," he said, ticking off nationality conflicts, economic shortages, public despair—and he saw malicious hands at work.

"We are seeing how attempts to discredit *perestroika* are being made from both the conservative and ultraleftist positions," he told the Soviet people. "From the midst of this discordant choir, scare stories of imminent chaos and arguments about the danger of a coup, or even civil war, may be heard. . . .

"Some would like to create an atmosphere of alarm, of uncertainty. It is difficult to rid oneself of the impression that this is all to someone's advantage. . . .

"In effect, an attempt is being made from conservative positions to impose assessments of the situation that would prompt counteraction against *perestroika.* . . . They call for return to the old command methods; otherwise, they say, there will be chaos."[32]

Gorbachev also disapproved, as before, of what he saw as the excessive zeal of ultraprogressives, whom he accused of demanding a breakthrough "at one gallop, at one stroke."

But the main threat in his mind clearly came from the Right; and to meet it, Gorbachev himself moved to the right. He stole the right wing's thunder by making a very tough law-and-order speech, using almost the identical language that Chebrikov and Ligachev had been using during his vacation.

"We cannot tolerate violations of state, labor, and technological discipline. . . . We cannot tolerate the fact that the national economy is in a feverish state because of interruptions in transportation. . . . I cannot disregard the question of crime. . . . The Supreme Soviet has considered it necessary . . . to increase the number of internal security troops."

What was most striking was his about-face on the Party. After hounding the Party apparat in mid-July to change its ways and bluntly telling it that the Party had to earn authority, here he was, eight weeks later, trumpeting the Party's importance and defending its power.

"The role of the Party, as the uniting, vanguard force of society, is indispensable," Gorbachev declared. "Those who are . . . attempting to undermine the Party's influence, must know that this will not work. We are confident that despite all the criticism directed at the activity of various Party committees and various Communists, the working people have a good understanding of the importance of Lenin's Party for the destiny of socialism."[33]

This was the line Gorbachev took all fall; he sounded like Ligachev. After meeting with the Communist leaders of the Baltic states, where local parties were on the verge of splitting from Moscow, Gorbachev declared: "It would be a grave historical mistake to weaken such a powerful political organism as the Communist Party of the Soviet Union."[34] At the Central Committee session on September 19–20, he preached the gospel of patriotism, scolded aggressive nationalists, and catered to Party conservatives by making concessions to Russian nationalism.

Nonetheless, having survived, he quickly settled scores with the right-wing faction in the Politburo. He purged his enemies—three of five Politburo conservatives: the dangerous Chebrikov; Vladimir Shcherbitsky, the iron-fisted boss of the Ukraine; and Viktor Nikonov, an economic right-winger. Many read Chebrikov's ouster as punishment for ordering the army crackdown in Tbilisi, Georgia; but others insisted it had to be something more, since the whole Politburo, even Gorbachev, was tainted with the Tbilisi episode. My Baltic contact suggested Chebrikov was axed for daring to challenge Gorbachev directly. Ligachev survived, but shorn of his clique.

Even with that tactical victory, Gorbachev showed the strain on a visit to Kiev in late September. During one of his sidewalk conversations with people, someone asked if he wasn't afraid to leave Moscow for fear of a coup. "No, this is . . ." Gorbachev began, but quickly changed the subject. Yet when a woman asked how he managed "to bear a country of so many millions on your shoulders," her worrying reminded him of his mother.

"During the Congress of People's Deputies my mother was listening, and she said, 'Why is he doing all this? . . . He ought to come home to me and drop it all.' "

People all laughed. Gorbachev then turned to the woman, and in an echo of Robert Frost's famous couplet "And miles to go before I sleep,/ And miles to go before I sleep," Gorbachev said with tired reverie and resignation:

"So your words sound to me like my mother's. But you can't [stop], you know. The country believes; people now believe. . . . So it's all the way . . . all the way."[35]

The intense pressure from the right wing pushed Gorbachev to retrench. Many a Party leader has purged rivals, only to adopt their policies. Alarmed by events, Gorbachev aligned himself with the loyalist apparat. His response to challenge was a tough fist, epitomized by his decision to send twelve thousand Soviet troops into Baku in January 1990, not so much to save the Armenian victims of a pogrom, but, as Defense Minister Dmitri Yazov said, to save the Communist Party from being thrown out by the Azerbaijani Popular Front.

That fall and early winter were a gloomy season for radical reformers in the Supreme Soviet. They were appalled by Gorbachev's swing to the right; they despaired of his ever breaking the Party's lock on power. Several told me that they feared Gorbachev was too much a prisoner of his own past, too wedded in his bones to the Party apparat, ever to try for a full democratic reform that would strip the Party of its power monopoly.

CHAPTER 22

THE PARTY: LOSING POWER, LOSING PEOPLE

"The organs of power are so
irresolute. . . . The state, as it were,
belongs to no one. . . . We need a conductor."[1]
—Ivan Polozkov
Provincial Party Chief
March 1990

"If you want to bury the Party,
split the Party, then continue on
this way. Think hard. Think hard."[2]
—Gorbachev, July 1990

"They don't believe the Party is
still the party of the working class.
. . . A certain part is leaving because of
disappointment with the Party
over *perestroika*. The working class has
gotten nothing but empty shelves and inflation."[3]
—Yuri Prokofyev
Moscow Party Chief
June 1990

Gorbachev is restless. He rarely sticks with one approach for long. For he
is powerfully influenced by events.

In the fall of 1989, he clearly felt besieged; his political horizon was
dominated by domestic turmoil, and his reflexive response was to retrench
and get tough. But by early 1990, another reality filled the horizon—the

nightmarish collapse of Communism in Eastern Europe. Gorbachev had let one Communist regime after another crumble, and this had confirmed his view that survival required staying close to the people. His response was to return to the path of reform.

He had seen that where the Communist Party had been rigid, arrogant, aloof, where it could not flow with the tides of history, it was swept away. And he could hardly have failed to ponder the personal fate of such Party leaders as Erich Honecker in East Germany and Nicolae Ceauşescu in Romania, one arrested, the other executed, without realizing that the Soviet Party apparat could drag him down too.

At home in the Soviet Union, the clamor against the Party was rising again as 1989 was ending. In early December, the parliaments of Lithuania and Estonia formally sanctioned multiparty political systems. Simultaneously, forty thousand people held a rally in Leningrad and voted in a mass show of hands to revoke Article VI of the constitution, the one protecting the Party's political supremacy over all Soviet institutions, including the government. In Moscow, Andrei Sakharov called for a two-hour workers' strike on December 10 to demand a vote on Article VI at the upcoming Congress of People's Deputies.

"I think [the Party's] constitutionally fixed exclusiveness is inadmissible, undemocratic, and, judging by everything, undermining the Party's prestige," Sakharov declared.[4]

When the Congress convened on December 12, Sakharov made his move, but Gorbachev blocked him.

Sakharov went to the podium with a sack of mail to demonstrate public support for stripping the Party of its constitutionally guaranteed monopoly of power. At the climax of Sakharov's speech, Gorbachev interrupted, ringing the bell to end Sakharov's time.

Sakharov: "Then I . . . then I . . . I will get telegrams which I have received."

Gorbachev: "Come to me and I'll give you three files containing thousands of telegrams."

Sakharov: *"There are sixty thousand here!"*

Gorbachev (ordering): "That's all."

Sakharov (continuing): ". . . sixty thousand signatures."

Derisive clapping drowns out Sakharov.

Gorbachev: "So let's not press each other, resting on and manipulating the view of the people. Let's not."[5]

Gorbachev, testy and temperamental, wheeled out the obedient conservative majority and put down Sakharov's appeal for a vote on Article VI.

"We don't need to rush things," Gorbachev had said earlier to a Party meeting.

But, tragically, time ran out on Sakharov, two days after their confrontation. On the morning of December 14, he worked with the Inter-Regional Group on issues of reform; that evening, he died of heart failure. Democratic reform had lost its most authentic voice, the reformers their most unifying leader. Gorbachev joined in honoring Sakharov at the Congress.

Most of the time, however, Gorbachev was still sounding and acting like right-winger Yegor Ligachev. Only later did it become clear that he was not so much rejecting fundamental political change as he was jealously asserting his prerogative to control the process, to decide personally when and how he would let certain steps be taken. Eventually, he developed a scheme: If the Party was going to lose power, he would take advantage of that moment to buttress his personal power. He would couple the change in the Party's status with a proposal to establish a new, more powerful presidency.

So, even as he was stifling Sakharov's final attempt to sweep away the Party's legal crutch, Gorbachev was laying the political groundwork to make such a move himself, if he chose. Once again, he was warning the Party that it could afford to ignore the popular will only at its own peril. In a speech on December 10, Gorbachev pointed to the fall of the East European Communists as a fate that awaited the Soviet Party unless it mended its ways.

"Fraternal parties are no longer ruling in Poland and Hungary," he said, and the Communist regimes in East Germany and Czechoslovakia "have largely lost their positions. . . . The Soviet people do not want to put up with the fact that at a time when the normal rhythm of life has been broken, their local and national leaders are often doing nothing."[6]

Under the pull of these new realities, Gorbachev kept shifting. A month later, on January 12, 1990, he flew to Lithuania to try to head off secession, and he was confronted with a multiparty system already in existence, though the Soviet constitution still barred it. He personally met with two Communist parties, the pro-Moscow loyalists and the much larger pro-independence Lithuanian Communist Party. Lithuania also had the powerful nationalist movement, Sajudis, and smaller parties. Although Gorbachev had again rejected a multiparty system as recently as a month before, and had once called it "rubbish," he closed out his two-day Lithuania visit by remarking that he did "not see anything tragic about a multiparty system." A day later, he added, "We should not be afraid of a multiparty system the way the devil is afraid of incense."[7]

Gorbachev tried to make it sound offhand, but it was his first public sanction of a momentous change. Before long, he was pushing this policy as his own.

In early February, Gorbachev summoned the Party Central Committee into session, and once again the conservatives were fuming. On the eve of the session, Moscow saw its largest demonstration since the Revolution—two hundred thousand people just off Red Square, calling for the Party to surrender its constitutional monopoly. Radicals had organized the rally, but held it so near the Kremlin that it had to have Gorbachev's blessing; there was no police interference. What is more, the Party press blossomed with articles favoring a transition to a multiparty system—which suggested political choreography by Mikhail S. Gorbachev.

What Gorbachev was asking the Party itself to revoke was Article VI of the Soviet constitution. It states:

> The Communist Party of the Soviet Union (CPSU) is the leading and guiding force of Soviet society and the nucleus of its political system, of all state and public organizations. The CPSU exists for the people and serves the people.
>
> Armed with the Marxist-Leninist teaching, the Communist Party shall determine the general prospects of society's development and the line of domestic and foreign policy of the USSR, give guidance to the great creative activity of the Soviet people, and place its struggle for the victory of Communism on a planned, scientific basis.
>
> All Party organizations shall function within the framework of the Constitution of the USSR.[8]

When the Central Committee convened on February 5, 1990, Gorbachev proposed that the Party agree to strike Article VI, and to approve a new, strong presidency as a way to ensure centralized order.

The battle was joined along familiar lines; the hard-liners immediately counterattacked.

Ligachev had drawn a different lesson from the nightmare in Eastern Europe. He stressed the loss of empire and the imminent danger of a resurgent Germany, the threat of a "new Munich," which would redraft the postwar frontiers and see East Germany swallowed up by the West. Boris Gidaspov, personally installed by Gorbachev as the Leningrad Party leader and now quickly establishing himself as a new champion of conservatives, defended the apparat. The Party was the only force, Gidaspov said, that "can act as a constructive, consolidating base of our state and as guarantor of a socialist path of development."[9] Valentin Mesyats, the

Moscow Province chief, accused Gorbachev of leading the country down the road to anarchy and voiced outrage that the Soviet leader was assaulting the apparat. "Why is the Central Committee to assume a defensive position?" Mesyats demanded. "The Party began *perestroika*, has led it, and should proceed as its vanguard."[10]

But this was a rearguard effort. Having stripped Ligachev of support in the Politburo, Gorbachev had the big guns on his side this time.

Vadim Medvedev, the ideology secretary, said that unless the Party opened up democratic channels to let the public voice its discontent, the Soviet Party would follow those in Eastern Europe. Foreign Minister Eduard Shevardnadze declared that "a viable party doesn't need a monopoly on power. . . . The power monopoly has played a bad joke on us."[11] Nikolai Ryzhkov, who had swung over to Gorbachev, advised the apparatchiks that "no party has a perpetual monopoly on power." The Soviet Party, he warned, "has lost the combative qualities which are organically inherent in any leading force." To succeed, he said, the Party should get rid of Article VI and fight for popular support.[12] Aleksandr Yakovlev, who more than anyone in the leadership had been the advocate of this change, said simply: "Society itself will decide whether it wishes to adopt our politics."[13]

That was Gorbachev's point. "The Party," he declared, "can exist and play its role as the vanguard—only as a democratically recognized force. This means that its status should not be imposed through constitutional endorsement."[14]

To Party hard-liners, this was the suicidal step they had instinctively refused to take. But at that moment, the Party apparat was reeling, on the defensive from a string of scandals exposing the corruption of the Party bosses that had led from Leningrad to Volgograd, Kiev, Tyumen in western Siberia, and Chernigov in the Ukraine. In Leningrad, the final indignity had been heaped on the former Party boss Yuri Solovyov; he had been expelled from the Party after an investigation disclosed his use of Party influence to buy a Mercedes at a cut-rate price.[15]

So the apparat was on the defensive. Not only was it being goaded by Gorbachev, but it was demoralized by evidence of its waning support among the Party rank and file. Moreover, it was trapped by its own rules and traditions. It operated under Lenin's principle of "democratic centralism," which had the ring of rule from below but the reality of rule from above, and the requirement that the Party faithful follow discipline. In this case, Gorbachev had come to the Central Committee not just with his own policy, but with the collectively approved policy of the Politburo. The Central Committee was discipline-bound to follow the Politburo line and vote for its own funeral. Grudgingly, unhappily, it voted as it was told. Only one vote in the 249-member Central Committee was cast against stripping the Party of its monopoly power—and that was cast by Boris Yeltsin. His complaint was that Gorbachev had not gone far enough.

"We have taken a step of exceptional magnitude," Aleksandr Yakovlev said after the vote. "Power is being transferred from the Party to the soviets."[16]

The Party's surrender of its dominion over every facet of Soviet life was a watershed, but it had not vanished into thin air; it was merely accepting the principle of competition. It was not surrendering actual power, except where rivals were popular and organized enough to win it, and clever enough to dislodge the Party bureaucracy from all the places where it had implanted itself over the decades. A new principle had been established, but an old reality still existed. Theoretically, the state machinery was now liberated from the Party's grip, but the apparatus of the Party was still so tightly intermingled with the apparatus of the state, especially in the army and KGB, that it would take years to disentangle them.

Nonetheless, Gorbachev had achieved a quite remarkable personal victory. As leader of both Party and government, he had been a captive of each. Both the Party and the new Congress and Supreme Soviet hemmed him in politically, from opposite sides, limiting his ability to maneuver. By lifting the Party's dictate from all Soviet institutions and by simultaneously winning the Party's approval for a new presidency (later voted into law by the Congress of People's Deputies), Gorbachev was getting the better of both rivals. As president, he was no longer constitutionally subservient to the Party, and he had greater power to act independently of the Supreme Soviet. So the Party's loss was his gain; he had strengthened his power base apart from the Party, and had put more distance between himself and the increasingly unpopular apparat.

WILL THE PARTY SPLIT?

As the decisive Central Committee session came to a close in early February, Gorbachev's new worry was the polarizing trend of Party politics: Ligachev's right wing versus the left-wing radicals led by Boris Yeltsin. As a catalyst of change, Gorbachev welcomed ferment and debate; it helped him keep pressure on the apparat. But as a centrist and a Leninist, Gorbachev wanted to prevent a split. He might want to reduce the Party's power, but he still saw it as an important institution of stability and cohesion, a check on the radical reformers, ballast against ethnic strife. So Gorbachev warned the Party faithful: "We must all stand together [and] not start dividing into clans and groupings. That way we will ruin the Party and the country."[17]

Gorbachev's words came too late. There were already identifiable factions taking organizational form. In January, the radical reformers in the Party had formed Democratic Platform, a group dedicated to forcing the Communist Party to become more democratic internally and to give up its legally guaranteed dominance in Soviet politics.

In the apparat, radical reformers had limited support—though among the leadership, they regarded Aleksandr Yakovlev as their philosophical patron. But from the Party rank and file, they claimed a mass following, especially among the urban intelligentsia, and that claim seemed legitimate. A senior Central Committee official, Aleksandr Lebedev, told me that the Party's own polling data indicated that 30–40 percent of the rank and file shared the views of Democratic Platform and might side with it if the Party were to split.[18] In June 1990, the weekly newspaper *Argumenty i Fakty* published a poll of 5,326 Party members (probably parts of the same poll) taken by the Central Committee's sociology section, which showed that more ordinary Communists shared the views of Democratic Platform than of the Party's right-wingers. Roughly half indicated their liberal leanings by saying the Party should reject conservatism; only one third took the conservative view that the Party should reject liberal reformers.[19]

At Democratic Platform's organizational session in Moscow on January 20–21, the leadership included the most prominent deputies in the Congress and Supreme Soviet—Boris Yeltsin, Gavril Popov, Yuri Afanasyev, Sergei Stankevich, and Ilya Zaslavsky. In all, the meeting attracted about 450 delegates from reformist political clubs in more than seventy-eight Soviet cities.[20]

The program adopted by Democratic Platform called for drastic changes. First, it demanded internal democracy within the Party: scrapping the Leninist rule of "democratic centralism," revoking Lenin's 1921 ban against organized factions within the Party, requiring multicandidate elections for all Party posts, and barring privileges for Party higher-ups. More broadly, Democratic Platform went beyond advocating a multiparty political system to pressing for the abolition of the *nomenklatura* system and for dissolving all Party organizations in factories, farms, and other institutions, including the armed forces, the KGB, and the police. Its overall goal was to convert a totalitarian party into a parliamentary party, allowing internal competition and then competing with other parties for elected office.[21]

One irony is that this radical reform movement took root in the Higher Party School, organized by Stalin, and for decades the purveyor of Stalinist orthodoxy for Party "cadres"—officials of the apparat. Since Stalin's time, it had been the special educational training ground for promising midcareer Party officials in their thirties and forties, especially those marked by early success for higher leadership posts. In 1990, it had thirty-seven hundred students and four hundred teachers. Ligachev had attended the Moscow Higher Party School; Gorbachev had gone through one of the fifteen branches scattered across the country.

The school's rector, Vyacheslav Shostakovsky, was an ardent advocate of reforming the Communist Party; he cashiered some of the old-line Stalinist faculty and encouraged debate and experimentation. When I made a visit there, the evidence of Shostakovsky's free spirit was everywhere: not only "students" arguing over the destiny of the Party and the tactics of reform, but computer experts doing "after hours" research for foreign joint ventures, and a sociologist working as a consultant for several new Soviet cooperative enterprises. Shostakovsky himself was out making speeches and organizing meetings on behalf of radical change.

Initially, Sergei Stankevich told me, the idealists in Democratic Platform had hopes of getting the Soviet Communist Party to follow the model of the Hungarian Party: to cast off the Old Guard apparat, take a new name, and adopt the policies of European social democrats. Yuri Afanasyev was bluntly skeptical: "My conviction is the Party cannot be reformed." His plan was to lead the organization out of the Communist Party and set up a new party.[22] Vladimir Lysenko, another leader of Democratic Platform, rather cheerfully embraced the idea of a splinter movement. The Party's Central Committee, he declared, is "an empire full of mummies. . . . The dead are overtaking the living. A schism is necessary and inevitable."[23]

Communist Party hard-liners were quite happy to accommodate people of Afanasyev's ilk. In April, the Central Committee issued an open letter to the Party's nineteen million members denouncing Democratic Platform and urging its members to resign, unless they pledged to conform to Party policies. Some Party organizations began throwing out reformers. Although Gorbachev denied there was a purge, he came down hard on Party members who disagreed with the Party's position; he said they should quit, but of their own accord. It was an important moment, because he was siding with the right wing against the liberals, who wanted to do what he had proclaimed as his own goal: reform the Party from within. Afanasyev took Gorbachev's hint and turned in his Party card in mid-April.

Democratic Platform's most prominent deputies, Yeltsin, Popov, Stankevich, Zaslavsky, and others, were elected to city government or to the Supreme Soviet of the Russian republic in March 1990, and they drifted away from the organization. So in the crucial election of delegates to the Twenty-eighth Communist Party Congress, Democratic Platform could not use its best voices to rally support. With the Party apparat controlling the elections, Democratic Platform wound up with only 125 of the 5,000 Congress delegates, a proportion far short of what its mass support would have promised.

THE REVENGE OF THE RIGHT

More menacing to Gorbachev was the resurgence of the right wing; he seriously misjudged its power and purpose after having beaten or seduced it into submission so many times. Each beating and each seduction seemed only to sharpen the apparat's lust for vengeance and for a power base to advance its cause. The chosen vehicle of the regional power barons was a new Russian Communist Party. They had been demanding it ever since their public humiliation in the 1989 elections; after suffering more setbacks in the 1990 elections at the hands of the new democratic radicals, they became more insistent. As their popularity fell, their anxiety and anger grew.

In late 1989, Gorbachev had tried to appease them with token gestures, such as setting up a Russian Party Bureau, but typically, he kept that bureau under his own thumb. He had promised new authority and new institutions to the Russian republic, but the apparat saw that citadel slip through its fingers into the hands of its nemesis, the renegade Boris Yeltsin. Though its own new champion, the provincial Party leader Ivan Polozkov, had run neck and neck with Yeltsin on two ballots for the top position in the republic, Gorbachev had withdrawn him on the third ballot, only to see Yeltsin beat someone more moderate. In the process, however, the Right had shown its strength.

And while Gorbachev was preoccupied with his new presidency, with the economy, and with world diplomacy, the right wing set out to capture the machinery of the Party and challenge Gorbachev's control. Stealing a page from his book, the hard-liners intended to undermine him from below. Their first step was to stack and control elections for the five thousand delegates to the all-union Party Congress; they wanted a majority in order to dictate terms to Gorbachev. Then, before the *all-union*

Party Congress, they planned to found their cherished new *Russian* Communist Party and show their power.

The Leningrad Party organization took the lead in this campaign—Leningrad, shamed by the 1989 elections and publicly humiliated by Gorbachev's quip about a Party organization whose functionaries were still "chewing stale gum." Gorbachev thought he had an ally in Boris Gidaspov, the new Leningrad leader, but he had miscalculated, or else he had been hoodwinked by Ligachev, who still had well-placed agents making appointments under Gorbachev's nose. Gidaspov, an ambitious opportunist, quickly catered to the right wing. Under his protection, and in tandem with the reactionary United Front of Russian Workers, the Leningrad Party apparat organized an "action conference" for the new Russian Communist Party in April; in June, it called the founding Congress.

These machinations got a sudden, unwitting boost from a classic political gaffe by Gorbachev and Ryzhkov. The massive public panic in response to the food-price increases and other economic measures announced by Ryzhkov in late May played directly into the hands of the right wing. Ryzhkov's announcement that bread prices would triple in July and other prices would shoot up in early 1991 gave the apparatchiks the opening they had longed for. Heretofore, not much of the public had been moved by their attacks on Gorbachev's reforms. Now, overnight, people all over the country were aflame with fear over talk of free-market economics; the right-wing apparat, so long a target of the popular mistrust, could pose as the defenders of little people by opposing the Gorbachev-Ryzkhov plan for a "regulated market economy."

Belatedly, Gorbachev woke up, and, sensing the danger of a new Party organization controlled by his opponents, he tried to stop the Right from forming the Russian Party. But he was too late. The process had too much momentum. In order not to let the right-wingers have things all their way, Gorbachev was forced into attending the founding Congress. Hoping to outwit the right-wing apparat, Gorbachev got himself named presiding officer and insisted that the delegates be those elected to the all-union Party Congress. But the apparatchiks had done their spadework while he was neglecting the Party, and they were ready for him. The delegates were in their pocket; out of roughly twenty-seven hundred delegates, more than forty percent were from the apparat.[24] It was, as the disconsolate liberals later lamented, "the apparat Congress."

Even before the Russian Party Congress opened on June 19, 1990, it was clear Gorbachev was in for a siege. Yegor Ligachev had dropped all pretense of unity, and was shrilly attacking Gorbachev on every policy—Eastern Europe, nationalities, market economics, and the role of the Party. At a conference of farm officials, he accused Gorbachev of making "concession after concession" that could lead to the breakup of the Soviet Union and the Party; Gorbachev was in danger of becoming a "president without territory."[25] To halt Gorbachev's move toward market economics, Ligachev demanded a national referendum—socialism or capitalism. He had sounded the keynote.

Like sharks, the right wing relentlessly savaged Gorbachev throughout the five-day Congress. Their invective had never been sharper or more personal. No sooner had Gorbachev made his routine opening statement than the first speaker, Ivan Osadchy, a Congress organizer, accused Gorbachev of pushing the Party toward "suicide." Under his leadership, Osadchy declared, the once-mighty Party had been "reduced to crouching unarmed in the trenches, under massive shelling by anti-socialist forces."[26]

Viktor Tyulkin, Party secretary at Leningrad's Kirov Factory, said Gorbachev's *perestroika* had done so little for the proletariat that there was "a mass exodus of workers" from the Party—seven hundred from his own plant had already quit, and four hundred more had signaled their intention to do so. Tyulkin charged that the Gorbachev-Ryzhkov package would lower the people's standard of living still further. And in what was widely taken as an anti-Semitic slur (Russian nationalists claim Jews have trouble rolling their Russian *R*), Tyulkin mocked reformers such as Democratic Platform leader Vladimir Lysenko as "comrades who have trouble pronouncing the word 'Russian' and frankly have no wish to pronounce the word 'Communist.'"[27]

To an unprecedented degree, military officers, angry over the loss of Eastern Europe, joined the harangue against Gorbachev. Colonel General D. A. Volkogonov bemoaned the lack of a clear strategy to Gorbachev's reforms and the nation's uncertain leadership. Far more harshly, General Albert Makashov gave vent to the anxieties of troop commanders that the Soviet Union was sinking as a world power.

"Germany is reuniting and will probably become a member of NATO, Japan is becoming the decisive force in the Pacific. Only our wise peacocks are crowing that no one is going to attack us," the general declared. He decried the policy of withdrawing Soviet troops from Eastern Europe—"countries that our fathers liberated from Fascism"—and then, to waves of applause from this conclave of hard-liners and self-proclaimed Russian patriots, General Makashov added: "Comrades, the army and navy will be needed yet by the Soviet Union."[28]

When Ligachev's turn came, he sided with the military in denouncing "the collapse of the socialist commonwealth." Then he leveled the grievous charge that Gorbachev had made policy on economic reform, the German question, and Eastern Europe without consulting the Politburo, thus letting policy control slip out of the Party's hands. And he hinted that Gorbachev ought to give up his top Party position. Tongue-lashing the reformers of Democratic Platform, Ligachev warned that "the main danger to the Party today is the destruction of the Party from within."[29]

On several previous occasions when stung by critics, Gorbachev had peremptorily threatened to resign. It was an extreme ploy, designed to get his way and warn his accusers not to go too far lest they lose a leader whom most people considered indispensable. Ligachev had pushed this button. Gorbachev rose to advise his taunters: "I think, comrades, that people are not taking the general secretary of the Party, the president of this country, very seriously. It is not a question of me personally; tomorrow, or in ten or twelve days [at the all-union Party Congress], someone else might be general secretary or Party chairman. To condemn and make accusations, you ought to understand a great deal more."[30]

Gorbachev won a strong round of applause, but little else. In the end, the apparat elected one of its own, Ivan Polozkov, the fifty-five-year-old Party leader in Krasnodar Territory, as leader of the new Russian Communist Party. He was certainly not Gorbachev's choice, but Gorbachev seemed either powerless or too demoralized to stop Polozkov.

Back in mid-March, in a speech laced with stiletto innuendos, Polozkov had made a biting attack on Gorbachev's weak leadership: "The organs of power are so irresolute. . . . The state, as it were, belongs to no one. . . . We need a conductor."[31] Later, Polozkov, a pint-sized true believer with charcoal hair and blunt candor, had needled Gorbachev for lack of ideological conviction. "Gorbachev is too tolerant, too slow. He thinks too much," Polozkov told reporters. "He's too careful."[32]

Now, in June, he reminded the Congress that in the late seventies, when Gorbachev had been the Party leader in Stavropol, he himself had been Gorbachev's overseer from the Central Committee's organizational department, the section that supervised the work of provincial Party organizations. With patronizing approval, he recalled Gorbachev's introduction of reform measures, as if he, Polozkov, had been the tutor. Then he turned on the Gorbachev of today, chiding him for "inconsistency and concessions." And lest anyone misunderstand, Polozkov traced the nation's current problems to a "crisis of leadership."[33]

The apparat's obvious triumph sent Gorbachev's Party supporters into a tailspin and set the radical Democratic Platform group to talking about a mass walkout from the Twenty-eighth Party Congress. Some radicals did not wait. The Leningrad television producer Bella Kurkova and six of her Communist colleagues at *Fifth Wheel* turned in their Party cards right after Polozkov's election. "I could not stand to be in a party that picked Polozkov," Bella told me.[34]

The very thing that Gorbachev had wanted to prevent—the polarization of the Party into left-wing and right-wing factions—had now taken concrete form, and Gorbachev's partisans in the apparat blamed him directly. I found Party centrists such as Moscow Party leader Yuri Prokofyev and liberal Central Committee officials such as Aleksandr Lebedev furious at Gorbachev for having let himself be so outmaneuvered.

"Gorbachev paid little attention to preparations for the Russian Party Congress," Prokofyev spluttered. "No one is paying attention to the Party. Gorbachev went to the United States, Gorbachev met with Thatcher, he was preoccupied with other business, and meanwhile...."[35]

"He was too busy being a global statesman," Lebedev echoed bitterly. "He is not good at organizational politics. He left it to others, and they did a terrible job. It's as if 'his people' were working for someone else. He neglected the very thing he should have done first of all. And now look at the problems we have."[36]

Gorbachev himself was so worried by the resurgence of the right wing and the threat to his own leadership that, according to Lebedev, he tried to get Party leaders to postpone the forthcoming all-union Communist Party Congress. Boris Yeltsin backed postponement, but Gorbachev ran into resistance from other leaders. The right wing was riding high and was not going to let Gorbachev off the hook.

THE POLITBURO'S LAST HURRAH

Gorbachev was right to brace for a blow at the Twenty-eighth Communist Party Congress, but the Party's problems were more serious than the ups and downs of factional infighting. In the country, the Party's prestige had fallen disastrously; it was losing members by the tens of thousands. As the elections of 1989 and 1990 showed, millions of ordinary people—including millions of rank-and-file Communists—were turning their backs on Party leaders; they no longer looked to the Party for national leadership.

In terms of public trust, the Communist Party ranked seventh behind the army, the Russian Orthodox Church, the Supreme Soviet, and even behind the KGB, government ministries, and trade unions, according to an opinion poll taken for the weekly newsmagazine *Ogonek* in May 1990.

Only the police and the Party's unpopular youth arm, the Komsomol, ranked lower. Nearly 60 percent blamed the Party for slowing the country's growth; half held the Party responsible for the current situation being out of control; one third said the Party no longer played a significant role in Soviet life.[37] Another poll, taken by sociologist Yuri Levada's team to measure political tendencies, found that if the country actually had a multiparty system, less than 19 percent would vote for the Communist Party, 11 percent for the Democratic Platform, nearly 10 percent for a workers' party, and 7 percent each for the Greens and for social democrats—all this without any organized parties in opposition. But half of the people could not state any preference, a sign of mass ambivalence about the Party: neither total rejection nor loyal support.[38]

Even more worrisome to Party officials were the rising defections. Since the 1988 euphoric high point over Gorbachev's reforms, the Party had been losing members—at least 259,605 by its own admission in 1989. The exodus was worst in Moscow, Leningrad, the Baltic republics, and the Siberian mining and industrial areas of Kemerovo, Chelyabinsk, and Krasnoyarsk.[39]

Pravda carried letters from defectors. There were old-timers fed up with reform, or the lack of it; liberal intellectuals angry at the Old Guard or Gorbachev; workers feeling cheated. Coal miners held a nationwide congress in the Ukrainian mining city of Donetsk in mid-June 1990 to begin setting up an independent union. And one of their resolutions, passed by a vote of 308–116, showed their disillusionment with the Party, which many workers felt was abandoning its proclaimed blue-collar constituency in favor of apparatchiks, intellectuals, and white-collar workers.

"We do not consider the Communist Party our party," the miners declared. "We call for a mass exit from the Party."[40]

Worker defections alarmed Party officials such as Yuri Prokofyev. In the first half of 1990, he told me, the Moscow Party had lost twenty thousand members—half of them workers. "They don't believe the Party is still the party of the working class," Prokofyev explained. "They don't believe in the Party's social and economic policies. A certain part is leaving because of disappointment with the Party over *perestroika.* The working class has gotten nothing but empty shelves and inflation."[41]

Prokofyev had been in a watch factory that morning; I asked him how the workers reacted to Gorbachev's battle with the right-wing apparat.

"The workers jumped all over me about that," Prokofyev reported. "They said that if the Party is only going to be concerned with its internal problems, and is not worried about society, then why do we need such a party?"

That was an echo of things I had heard and read; in a Siberian newspaper, *Sibirskaya Gazeta,* readers were asked whose interest the Party promoted; 85 percent said the interests of Party functionaries.[42] And in fact, at the Twenty-eighth Communist Party Congress in Moscow, the apparat had stacked the deck—it comprised 48 percent of the delegates; 20 percent were government officials and factory or farm directors and the like; only 7 percent workers and peasants.[43] Party officials tried to make the best of this, calling it a "party of all classes"—precisely what made the blue-collar workers angry.

Gorbachev's aides knew that it would be a miracle if the Party Congress did not produce a new stream of defections, if not an open split. The radicals of Democratic Platform were threatening to quit unless they won drastic changes in the Party rules. Gorbachev was striving to prevent a split, to win a general mandate for his policies, to limit the damage from the right wing, and to bring new blood into the upper echelons. The right wing simply wanted blood; it was after the scalps of the Gorbachev team.

As the Congress convened on July 2, 1990, the tone was set in the opening minutes when Vladimir Bludov, a delegate from the Soviet Far East, called for the immediate removal of the entire Politburo. His proposal was rejected, but the delegates won the right to examine the performances of individual Politburo members, one by one; their grilling was merciless. Prime Minister Ryzhkov and ideology chief Vadim Medvedev were jeered; boos and hisses rained on Leonid Abalkin, the economist; Yuri Prokofyev was so inundated with angry clapping as he tried to defend Gorbachev that he had to start his speech over four times. Several of Gorbachev's allies, Medvedev, Aleksandr Yakovlev, and Eduard Shevardnadze, announced they were resigning from the Politburo, but that did not calm the fury.

Yakovlev sailed more boldly into the right-wing storm than did Gorbachev. "Shaking from our feet the mud of enmity and suspicion that has built up over decades, it is time [for us] to end the [ideological] civil war," he told the hard-liners. "A misfortune happened, for a Party based on a revolutionary idea has turned into a Party of power, . . . a Party of unquestioning obedience, Communist arrogance, and Communist lordliness. . . . It is precisely the backbone of the authoritarian organism that *perestroika* is striving to break, and for precisely that reason it provokes seething hatred among certain strata. . . .

"One can defend dogma for a certain period of time, but no one has yet succeeded in stopping life. . . . Let us remember that not only empty shelves but also empty souls brought about *perestroika* and the demand for revolutionary changes."[44]

Yakovlev's daring speech won strong applause from liberals and moderates but did not halt the right-wingers. On the fifth day, the right-wing scapegoating became so heated that Gorbachev stepped in. "If you want to bury the Party, split the Party, then continue on this way," he remonstrated. "Think hard. Think hard."[45] His firm hand prevented a political lynching on the spot.

As a Westerner, wary of military influence on civilian politics, I found it eerie to see the military so much in evidence—ranks of army generals and colonels in the balcony in their khaki uniforms; the ivory-yellow shirts of naval officers in solid rows; KGB officers with their telltale blue shoulder boards; Major General Ivan Nikulin raking the leadership over the coals for losing Eastern Europe. Aleksandr Yakovlev defiantly faced down the hard-liners, telling them it was popular will that had toppled the Eastern European regimes. "We cannot repeal the fact that the volume of labor production in South Korea is ten times higher than in the North, and that people in West Germany live better than in the East," he declared.[46] Foreign Minister Shevardnadze, accused of being an architect of retreat, told the hall that the armed forces had squandered 700 billion rubles ($1.2 trillion) on excessive military spending, and that arms agreements with the West would net a peace dividend of 250 billion rubles ($400 billion) over the next five years.[47]

Gorbachev could not restrain himself. "Do you want tanks again?" he demanded of the military. "Shall we teach them how to live?" And then, insisting that the military high command had agreed with his policies, he issued a warning to the dissident generals and colonels: "All officials must be loyal to the government. And if they are decent people and they disagree, they must resign."[48]

The politics of the military and the KGB produced one of the most sensitive conflicts of the Party Congress, a debate that cut to the bone of Party power. With 1.1 million Communists in the military and security services, the Party has long used a network of Party committees to ensure political reliability of the armed forces. Radicals from Democratic Platform demanded those ties be cut; they argued that in a law-governed, multiparty state, the military and KGB should be "depoliticized" and Party committees shut down. Their demands had become more insistent after a recently retired KGB officer, Major General Oleg Kalugin, who had once been acting chief of KGB operations in the United States, caused a sensation by asserting in several press interviews that despite efforts to assume a more democratic image, the KGB had been virtually untouched by five years of *perestroika* and was continuing its efforts to penetrate new Soviet political organizations.[49] Kalugin had called for "depoliticization" of the KGB—that is, elimination of the Party network throughout the secret police—and Democratic Platform had taken up its cry, forcing the issue at the Congress.

In full uniform and wearing their medals, Defense Minister Dmitri Yazov and KGB Chief Vladimir Kryuchkov trooped to the rostrum to squelch the idea of eliminating the Party's political network in the armed forces and KGB as a menace to national security. On this litmus issue, Gorbachev opposed reform. Before the Congress, he had signed an order stripping General Kalugin of all his KGB medals and honors. At the Congress, he signaled in his opening speech that he sided with the right wing against the reformers; he would keep the Party and the army bonded.

This underscored a crucial element of Gorbachev's political strategy. Reformers wanted him to quit as Party leader and to concentrate on the presidency, but he refused, and presumably one reason was to have under his thumb the mechanisms that kept check on the army and KGB. For amid national turmoil, a military freed of political restraint was arguably the greatest threat to Gorbachev's survival. Moreover, the military itself was torn by interethnic tensions, and Gorbachev may have seen the Party as the one element of cohesive glue.

But on the flash point of market economics, Gorbachev clashed with the right wing. On the first day, the conservatives had demanded—and won—a vote to have the word "market" stricken from the name of the economic commission of the Congress. Yegor Ligachev lashed out at Gorbachev's economic policies, savaging him for five years of "mindless radicalism."[50] Even Kryuchkov, the KGB chief, warned: "It would be a fatal mistake to thrust the country into the embrace of the elemental forces of the market."[51] Gorbachev chided them all for churlish alarm, and then offered the sop to a swirl of reporters that the leadership should resign in two years if the economy did not improve.

It was Boris Yeltsin, not surprisingly, who had the temerity to walk into the lion's den and tell the right wing that they were "bankrupt," to urge Gorbachev and the Party's moderates to join in "a center-left alliance of all socialist forces to prevent a schism that will otherwise lead to the Party's total defeat." He laid out Democratic Platform's manifesto— liberalize the Party rules, get its cells out of the military and KGB, transform itself from an "apparatus" party to a "parliamentary" party, and change its name to the Party of Democratic Socialism. If the leadership rejected this "one last chance," Yeltsin warned, the Soviet Communist Party would, like those in Eastern Europe, be "left by the roadside." Sheer force of personality won Yeltsin an attentive audience and light applause.[52]

But everyone knew that this was not a serious challenge. Significantly, Gorbachev had already slammed the door shut on all the internal reforms advocated by the radicals. Over their objections, he had reinstituted Lenin's "democratic centralism," and the right wing had backed him solidly. From the outset he had sided with the right wing on all the crucial issues of the Party's internal operation, and privately he had won a fair amount of right-wing support in return.

By the second week, Gorbachev had weathered the worst of the right-wing storm. There was a solid, silent middle at the Congress that had not taken sides in the noisy clashes of the first week; after the first few days, Gorbachev and Yakovlev had lobbied them effectively to keep them solidly behind Gorbachev. Moreover, even the right-wingers understood that they could not afford a power showdown with Gorbachev. He had given them a lot of what they wanted, by protecting the Party's top-down controls and the Party's network in the army, and by rejecting reforms. A pitched battle against Gorbachev would not only unite the Party's Center and Left against the Right, but a nasty internal fight would probably hasten the flow of defections among the rank and file. Gorbachev might be unpopular with the apparat, but he was also irreplaceable for them. His ouster—or, worse yet, an open and unsuccessful attempt to oust him—would only hasten the Party's demise.

So the right wing did not offer a candidate for Party chairman; they might applaud Ligachev's sallies, but they understood that rhetoric was one thing and supreme power was another. So Gorbachev was reelected general secretary without serious opposition.

The real test came on the choice of deputy general secretary: Yegor Ligachev saw one last chance to grab for the Party machinery, and made a lunge; Gorbachev's candidate was his hand-picked Ukrainian leader, Vladimir Ivashko, a Party loyalist with some appeal to the right wing. Gorbachev's team lobbied hard for Ivashko. Said Georgy Shakhnazarov, Gorbachev's aide: "If Ligachev is elected, there will be a collapse."[53] But with Gorbachev once again secure, the Party readily bowed to his will; Ligachev, nearly seventy, was a nostalgic figure, a voice of the past. When the tally was counted, he had been swamped—only 776 were for him, 3,642 against.

In defeat, Ligachev left the field, announcing his retirement to Siberia. And that helped clear the way for an expanded but much less powerful Politburo, with new faces such as right-winger Ivan Polozkov and the centrist Yuri Prokofyev. This was what Gorbachev had wanted—a major change at the upper echelons of the Party. Both the Politburo and the policy-approving Central Committee were virtually all new; out of more than four hundred old Central Committee members and candidate members, fewer than fifty remained. Gorbachev had finally gotten the fresh blood that he wanted, though it would take time to tell how much policy leeway this new body would give him. He had shuffled faces in the past, only to be surprised how little change that had brought.

In any case, Gorbachev had faced down the angry apparat, and had prevailed. As the Congress began, the apparatchiks were full of confidence from their victory in the Russian Party Congress. But this time they were big losers. Gorbachev had conquered them once again, but he had not tamed them once and for all. On the issue of reforming the inner workings of the Party, he had bowed to the Right, not even trying to reform the Party rules to make the Party more democratic. He had brought new blood into the central Party machinery, but the recalcitrant apparat remained entrenched in many bastions of provincial power, in the Russian republic, and also in the Ukraine, Byelorussia, and Central Asia. And their chosen leader, Ivan Polozkov, was not only in charge of the Russian Party apparatus but sitting in the new Politburo.

At the Twenty-eighth Party Congress, Gorbachev also lost the most dynamic and popular wing of the Party. As the Congress ended, he shouted out the Leninist slogan "The Party Lives and the Party Will Live!" But it was a hollow cheer; the Party was already losing its lifeblood. Gorbachev had been unable to preserve unity, to reconcile the irreconcilables within the Party. He had given so much to the Right that he lost the Left, an outcome to which he seemed resigned in advance. He knew the liberals would be disillusioned by how much ground he gave to the right wing, and their reaction was not long in coming.

On July 12, the second-to-last day, Boris Yeltsin strode into the Congress in a dark suit, a written statement in hand. He had given fair warning that he would quit if the Party did not change; still, it was a thunderbolt when he announced his resignation.

To cries of "Shame! Shame!" Yeltsin said that as head of the Russian republic and "in connection with the move toward a multiparty system, I cannot fulfill only the instructions of the Communist Party. As the highest elected figure in the republic, I have to bow to the will of the people."[54] The next day Leningrad Mayor Anatoly Sobchak and Moscow Mayor Gavril Popov followed suit; and then, quickly, prominent radicals such as Moscow Deputy Mayor Sergei Stankevich; Yeltsin's economic adviser, Mikhail Bocharev; and the leaders of Democratic Platform, Vyacheslav Shostakovsky and Vladimir Lysenko, who announced plans to form a new "democratic coalition."

The numbers were not immediately dramatic; but the Party was losing the most effective vote-getters in its ranks, the most energetic reformers, and in some cases the very people whom Gorbachev himself had attracted two or three years before. There were hundreds of others, I knew, from excited conversations I had had before and during the Congress with liberal activists in Leningrad and Moscow and with people from other parts of the country. The comments of Andrei Kortunov, a thirty-three-year-old foreign-policy analyst at Moscow's Institute of the U.S.A. and Canada, were typical and telling.

"Many of us had previously refused to join the Party because we felt our nation's politics were dirty, but we decided in 1987 or 1988 that Gorbachev was making a serious effort to reform our society, and that we should help him," Kortunov told me. "We saw he was threatened from the right. We had a feeling that deep in his soul, Gorbachev was a real liberal, that he was one of us, but he had to hide his real face, he had to play by the rules, or the system would crush him.

"But in the last year, it became clear to us that Gorbachev was not a liberal. Many of us expected him to resign as general secretary of the Party and to separate himself from the Party bureaucracy. But he has not wanted to do that. He is always a consensus seeker; he wanted approval from all sectors of society.

"So, many of us were disillusioned. I have felt a sense of personal betrayal. Yakovlev is more like what I thought Gorbachev would be like. But Gorbachev is trying for a consensus where there is none. It turned out that the Party apparatus today is just like the apparatus five years ago, just like fifty years ago. It puts its interests ahead of the people's interests. Our apparatchiks are like the Bourbons: They forgot nothing because they learned nothing. There's no use dealing with these people. The only way is to fight them from another party—to confront them in political battle."[55]

This disillusionment among the reformers whom Gorbachev had drawn into the Party earlier in his tenure was the price he paid for preventing his own schism with the apparat.

His great achievement at the Party Congress, and one with significance for the future course of reform and the ultimate fate of the Communist Party itself, was stripping the once-almighty Politburo of real power over the government. This had obviously been carefully planned and engineered in private before the Congress opened; Gorbachev's closest Politburo allies were to quit, setting an example for others. The only threat was an effective right-wing revolt and victory by Ligachev. But Ligachev's defeat ensured the success of Gorbachev's plan. For with his retirement, the way was cleared for the entire old leadership, except for Gorbachev, to leave the Politburo.

This meant that at the top of the power pyramid, the Siamese connection between Party and state—the heart of the Party's power—had finally been severed.

When Gorbachev had set up his new presidency in March 1990, he had taken the first major step in moving supreme power out of the Party's hands. But then he had appointed a presidential council as his inner cabinet, and it included half a dozen key figures from the Party Politburo—Prime Minister Ryzhkov, Foreign Minister Shevardnadze, Defense Minister Yazov, KGB Chief Kryuchkov, and his personal adviser, Aleksandr Yakovlev. So even with the presidency in place, there had still been an intimate overlap between Party and state at the highest policy-making level. With that link retained, Ligachev and the rest of the Politburo could demand their say before government decisions were taken.

At the Twenty-eighth Party Congress, with the five key members of Gorbachev's government leaving the Politburo, except for Gorbachev himself, there was no longer any overlap. And there was no reason to consult the Politburo beforehand on government policy; it was left to deal with Party affairs. Moreover, Gorbachev was much less vulnerable to being overthrown by an unhappy Politburo once its power had been reduced.

In sum, the Party Congress was the culmination of an effort Gorbachev had begun with the elections of March 1989, the Congress of People's Deputies that summer, and the presidency set up in March 1990—to shift policy-making power out of the Party into the new institutions of government. The final step was the separation of Party and state at the highest level.

For the Party, already losing mass support among the rank and file, that was an irreparable and potentially fatal loss of power.

CHAPTER 23

CITY HALL: THE NEW POLITICAL ENTREPRENEURS

"The big leaders are too preoccupied with the
fight for power within the Party, so they
don't pay attention to the city level,
they do not consider it a real danger
so far. But I think they make a real mistake."[1]
—Sergei Stankevich
Deputy Mayor of Moscow
June 1990

"This is Leningrad city property. The
running water, sewage, electricity for
Smolny [Party headquarters] are all provided
by the city. If we are not respected,
we can cut off all of the above. Then let
them see how they can get along in that building."[2]
—Anatoly Sobchak
Mayor of Leningrad
June 1990

Many of the leading radicals who quit the Communist Party in the
summer of 1990 had found a promising new arena for actually wielding
power—city hall.

Even before establishing a national political party that could challenge
the fading but still entrenched Communist Party, the reformers could win

majority control of city councils and take charge of an important segment of the political system. As power at the center fragmented, this was an important opening to seize.

At the city level, they could build the infrastructure of democracy and develop new national parties, even a democratic coalition, from the bottom up. City hall was an excellent place to learn the nuts and bolts of making policy, exercising power, and battling the Party apparat for day-to-day authority. It was an ideal stepping-stone for the wave of political newcomers who had flowed into the system after the 1989 election, who had learned to confront Gorbachev, Ryzhkov, and government ministers in the Supreme Soviet, but who were still woefully short of experience in running government themselves.

These reformers were desperate to accomplish something at the local level, instead of merely debating points in the Supreme Soviet and the Congress of People's Deputies, or being outvoted by Gorbachev's obedient majority. Given the feuding and posturing between Gorbachev and the Party's right wing, and the policy stalemate at the top, the radicals wanted to show that a more flexible approach could produce authentic change and improve people's daily lives.

They could chip away at the Party's control of the press and television by bringing out newspapers of their own, or by organizing independent television outlets. While Gorbachev and Ryzhkov wallowed in ideological uncertainty or tried half measures on economic reform, the radicals could use city governments to push free-market economics. They could take practical steps: authorize the sale of unprofitable state enterprises; improve operating conditions for cooperatives; sign deals for foreign joint ventures; encourage private Soviet entrepreneurs by throwing lucrative city contracts their way.

The most canny reform politicians took advantage of Soviet electoral law, which allowed anyone to hold office at two levels of government simultaneously. So they sat in the Supreme Soviet, where they drafted laws that passed power to local governments, and then they got themselves elected to local governments, to carry out the laws that they themselves had written.

Their dream of actually exercising power turned into reality with the elections of the spring of 1990. It was these elections, at the republic, province, city, and district levels, that the apparat had wanted to prevent, and that Gorbachev had agreed to postpone for six months, because the Party bosses knew that they would take another beating.

Some Party officials, such as Yuri Prokofyev, the centrist Party leader in Moscow, and Mikhail Knyazyuk, the hard-line Party boss in Ivanovo, caught on to ways of beating the new democratic election process. They ran as candidates from rural villages, where the Party's machine-style politics still worked among the peasantry. Prokofyev, needing a seat in the Moscow City Council, picked a country town called Butovo, which had only recently been brought within the city limits, and showered it with minor "pork barrel" improvements during the election campaign. So despite his fears about running as a Party boss, Prokofyev managed to win a council seat.

In Ivanovo, Knyazyuk also picked a rural district, from which to get elected to the Russian-republic parliament; on the other hand, Anatoly Golovkov, the Ivanovo mayor who had callously dismissed the hunger strikers trying to reopen the Red Church, was thrown out of office by urban voters. On the morning after the election, he complained to me, choking down his bitterness, that Gorbachev was pushing democracy too fast.[3]

This was a typical result: Party bosses maneuvering to hold power in the countryside, but decimated once again in the heart of the bigger cities. This time, however, the defeat hit home.

In 1989, the race had been for the optional prestige of a seat in the distant national legislature. This time, the stakes were control of local government.

In Moscow, radical reformers from the Inter-Regional Group pulled together a political coalition that united the Moscow Popular Front, the anti-Stalinist association called Memorial, the Moscow Association of Voters, and various ecological groups and democratic political clubs. They shrewdly named their coalition the Bloc of Democratic Russia. As Sergei Stankevich explained, opinion polls had shown that the most powerful trends in Russian politics were pushing people to the left and to the right: toward democratic populism opposed to the power "mafia"; and toward Russian nationalism, which the right wing was trying to appropriate. And so the reformers in Moscow cannily crafted the name "Democratic Russia" to appeal to those two contrary trends.

To build a coalition in the Moscow city government, Stankevich and two other well-known deputies, economist Gavril Popov and Nikolai Travkin, a mathematical physicist, worked Western-style political techniques. All three had become celebrities from their frequent televised appearances at the national Congress and Supreme Soviet; during the 1990 election campaign they made the rounds of Moscow political rallies as media heavyweights. They publicized the Bloc of Democratic Russia; they made speeches for younger allies; they circulated campaign leaflets endorsing less prominent candidates.

What was especially fascinating was the fast learning curve of these new Soviet politicians. On one of my trips to Moscow, Stankevich had asked me how to get American political books about coalition building; he despaired of the Russian penchant for windy philosophizing, and the absence of a knack for the give-and-take of compromise and political organizing. Then he had visited Washington; he had gone around Capitol Hill getting pointers from American politicians such as New Jersey Senator Bill Bradley. Now, only a little more than a year after having emerged from his institute's archives, he was using the coalition-building techniques of the American power game; and he was consulting opinion polls, by then commercially available from Soviet sociologists such as Boris Grushin, one of Yuri Levada's colleagues.

In Leningrad, the precinct-by-precinct operation run so successfully by Yelena Zelinskaya in the 1989 campaign was revived under the banner of Democratic Election '90, which played openly on the growth of anti-Party feeling during the year since the 1989 election. Several candidates from the democratic coalition told me that they survived only by playing down their Party membership. One coalition candidate, a bright forty-year-old ecologist named Konstantin Yarukhin, described the problems he encountered at political rallies.

"People reacted to my being a member of the Party," Yarukhin told me. "They said it was no use talking to me, because I was a Communist. But when I explained to them my ideas of reform, they were pleased and surprised. Other times, people talked with me first, liked my views, and then were astonished when they discovered I was a Party member. It made me think twice about why I am staying in the Party."[4]

As in Moscow, many of the lesser-known candidates in Leningrad rode the coattails of nationally known Supreme Soviet deputies like electrical engineer Yuri Boldyrev and fifty-three-year-old law professor Anatoly Sobchak, who was rated in one opinion poll as the third-most-popular figure in the country, behind Gorbachev and Yeltsin.

In the big industrial city of Sverdlovsk, the slate from Democratic Russia got a shot in the arm from Yeltsin, who had gone home to his birthplace and the region where he had once been the Party leader to run for the parliament of the Russian republic. Sverdlovsk had an active popular front, a very liberal film studio, a thriving youth movement, and a strong team of democratic-minded deputies in the national legislature, led by Gennady Burbulis, a management specialist, and Vladimir Volkov, a Party secretary in a huge machine-tool plant, who had thumbed his nose at the apparat and sided with Yeltsin.

In coal-mining cities such as Kemerovo in western Siberia and Donetsk in the Ukraine, the network of miners' strike committees gave the democratic, anti-Party activists a powerful political base for the election. In other major Russian cities such as Gorky, Volgograd, Tyumen, and Kuibyshev, popular protests against the corrupt practices of local Party bosses in the winter-spring of 1990 fueled the drive of democratic outsiders for control of city hall. In Volgograd, even the new Party leaders who came to power were radicals who aligned with non-Party reformers.

In the Ukrainian capital of Kiev and the ardently nationalistic city of Lvov in the western Ukraine, the rising Ukrainian national movement Rukh, after lagging for a long time behind similar movements in other republics, became a force in the local elections. In the Moldavian capital of Kishinev and the Byelorussian capital of Minsk, popular-front movements organized slates of opposition candidates. And of course in the Baltic republics, the powerful national movements were waiting to pounce on the 1990 elections, to gain control of local and republic governments.

The 1990 election campaign changed the political map of the country. Insurgents scored well in the republican elections throughout the Baltics, in Russia, the Ukraine, Byelorussia, and Moldavia, although only in Lithuania did they win an absolute majority in the national legislature.

But their upset victories at the city level, from Siberia to Leningrad, were stunning.

In Moscow, city government in the capital of world Communism passed into alien hands on April 20, 1990. The Bloc of Democratic Russia, led by Popov and Stankevich, captured 281 of the 442 seats in the city soviet, or city council. The Communist Party was reduced to holding 90 seats, so few that Party boss Yuri Prokofyev admitted to me later that he found it embarrassing to sit in the minority section. The radicals, with more than 60 percent of the seats, elected the pudgy, tousle-haired economist Popov, as the new mayor of Moscow. And they chose Stankevich, the serious-minded young political scientist, as deputy mayor.

In Leningrad, the cradle of the Bolshevik Revolution, Democratic Election '90 won 68 percent of the four hundred seats in the city soviet, and then elected Anatoly Sobchak as mayor. "We were overcome with a feeling of euphoria when we occupied Marinsky Palace [city-council chambers]," Yelena Zelinskaya told me. At first, it was practically like a holiday. "For three days, our deputies all wore their jeans and sweaters," Zelinskaya said. "Then, after three days, they changed into suits and ties and became more businesslike."[5]

In Kiev, the third-largest Soviet city, the insurgents claimed the largest group of deputies, but the balance was so even, between the new forces of democratic nationalism and the more traditional Party regulars, that

it took forty days for the city council to pick a compromise mayor—
Arnold Nazarchuk, the fifty-seven-year-old chief of a local electronics
complex, and his progressive deputy, Aleksandr Mosiyuk, a thirty-five-
year-old professor of physics and mathematics. But the experience of
having to bargain for power and office softened the old battle lines; as one
Kiev editor put it, the independents were radicalizing the Communists.[6]

The central press in Moscow never bothered to publish election returns
from around the country. No political organization save the Communist
Party had a good enough information network to ferret out the results
across the country; and the Party had no desire to publicize its defeats.
Even three months after the 1990 election, the democratic radicals in
Moscow and Leningrad still had only sketchy information, but by their
count, democratic insurgents now dominated city councils in fifteen to
twenty cities—not only Moscow, Leningrad, and Kiev, but also such
major Russian cities as Sverdlovsk, Gorky, Volgograd, Kemerovo, Tyumen, and Kuibyshev. Though still in the minority, independents had also
elected solid blocks of delegates in other places, such as Omsk, Novgorod,
Arkhangelsk, and Krasnoyarsk.[7]

In the Ukraine, the Lvov City Hall fell to an anti-Party coalition, which
elected Vyacheslav Chernovil, a former dissident jailed in the seventies,
as mayor; in Donetsk, the miners won at least 40 percent of the seats;
democrats supposedly prevailed in the major industrial city of Kharkov.
In the Baltics, popular fronts had strong influence in the main cities, as
they did in other republic capitals such as Minsk and Kishinev, where local
Party leaders were rejected by the voters.

There was a fairly consistent pattern. Except in Central Asia, where
little changed, the Party apparat clung to elected power in the outlying
provinces, but in urban areas Party officials either were turned out of city
councils or were confronted with strong new activist minorities of democratic delegates and had to bend to these new political pressures. It was
a sea change; Gorbachev and the Party apparat very quickly began to feel
its effects.

DEFYING GORBACHEV, RIGHT UNDER HIS NOSE

Almost as soon as the first of these new insurgent city councils took office
in April 1990, they showed their independence and their muscle—by
defying the trade embargo that Gorbachev invoked on April 19 in his
attempt to crush Lithuania's bid for independence.

Ironically, Gorbachev's blockade forced the Lithuanians, and the new independent city governments in central Russia, Siberia, the Ukraine, and elsewhere, to make deals behind the Kremlin's back. The embargo had the unintended effect of helping to break down the Kremlin's highly centralized control of the Soviet economy.

The Lithuanians were desperate for Russian oil, gas, and raw materials, as well as for spare parts and industrial goods from the Ukraine, Byelorussia, and Moldavia. So they sent trade delegations to the city governments in Moscow, Leningrad, Lvov in the Ukraine, Kishinev in Moldavia, Minsk in Byelorussia, and as far away as Sverdlovsk in the Ural Mountains and Omsk and Tyumen in western Siberia. And they found that the new democratic-led governments in these places were eager to barter for Lithuanian textiles, clothing, fabrics, bricks, and a variety of services.

Initially, the trade began with private black-market deals on a small scale, but it mushroomed quickly. Before long, as one Lithuanian legislator disclosed, the Lithuanians were sending truck convoys with food to an automobile plant in the Urals and a tractor plant in Minsk, in return for spare parts; and to sawmills in Siberia in return for lumber needed by Lithuanian furniture factories. Another barter arrangement saw newsprint brought to Lithuania from the Komi region of northern Russia, in exchange for Lithuanian publication of Komi's uncensored newspapers.[8] The Lithuanian government cut off its normal food shipments to Soviet military bases and to Soviet contractors, if they abided by Gorbachev's embargo; and they took those supplies and diverted them to friendly business partners. Before long, Lithuanian officials said, they had deals to ship eight thousand tons of meat a month to the new Moscow City Council, and four thousand tons a month to Leningrad, plus deals for substantial supplies of dairy products for both cities.[9]

The new Moscow and Leningrad city councils had been quick to pass resolutions condemning Gorbachev's trade embargo. The Leningrad council had denounced the blockade as an act of aggression that violated international law, and called upon Gorbachev to lift the blockade. In Moscow, democratic-minded deputies had seen the embargo not only as an effort to crush a democratically elected government in Lithuania, but also as an ominous sign of autocratic rule from the Kremlin and an implicit threat to the budding democratic city governments in Russia as well.

Leningrad, as the major Russian city closest to Lithuania (it is within four hundred miles of Vilnius), had been the most anxious to protect the normal flow of commerce with Lithuania. The city council set up the Committee for the Defense of Lithuania and in early April sent one of its members, Aleksandr Seryakov, a tall, wiry physicist who specialized in molecular spectroscopy, to Vilnius to establish trade and political relations with the self-proclaimed independent Republic of Lithuania.

Soon after Gorbachev's embargo had been imposed, Seryakov and Professor Julius Juzelionas, a Lithuanian academic-turned-politician, had swapped lists of goods for barter, because initially Gorbachev's embargo against Lithuania had caused a backlash in Leningrad. For example, Lithuania had stopped supplying fabric to Leningrad textile factories, and production had suddenly dropped. To avoid having its factories shut down, Leningrad had to help the Lithuanians obtain their primary need—fuel—denied them when Gorbachev cut off supplies of oil and natural gas.

In open defiance of Gorbachev's embargo, the Leningrad City Council declared its moral support of Lithuania, and openly authorized Lithuanians with private cars and trucks to buy gasoline in Leningrad. And a larger volume of industrial trade developed privately. City-council deputy Seryakov frequently acted as the middleman to get new barter deals started. Two or three times a week, he told me, he was approached by Lithuanian contacts eager to open up channels of supply in Leningrad.

"Lithuanians came to me because I was part of the delegation that went to Lithuania and addressed their national council, and my speech was televised. So they knew me," Seryakov explained. "Usually, the Lithuanians coming to me were factory managers and collective-farm directors who were asking for gasoline and diesel fuel. Even though we have shortages in Leningrad, I would always try to find them some enterprises which could help them. Normally some kind of deal was struck between an enterprise in Leningrad and the Lithuanian farms. What they trade is their business. I just help them to find each other."[10]

Illicit trade during the Lithuanian embargo had a more important, long-term consequence: It prompted the Leningrad City Council to set up regular trade missions in all three Baltic republics, anticipating the day when they would secede from the U.S.S.R. and become independent states. Leningraders had no question that enduring trade relationships with the independent Baltic states were in their self-interest, and they were not about to let Gorbachev's objections interfere.

"Now, the Leningrad City Council has the right to go into business directly, according to a recently adopted law on local self-government," Seryakov informed me. "On the business side, enterprises buy their products and trade directly with Lithuania on a barter basis. Hopefully that will be more efficient and we can trade on a larger scale, beneficial to the whole city and not just to a handful of factories."

To Seryakov, and to Mayor Sobchak, with whom I talked later, the main point was that Leningrad was asserting its right to establish its own trade relations, as well as protecting the rights of its local enterprises, without getting permission from the Kremlin.

"The Leningrad City Council assumes the power and responsibility," Seryakov said. "Unlike previously, when Moscow governed everything, we are going to run the city ourselves, and establish ties with other regions of the country, directly, without going through the central authorities in Moscow."

His comments sounded as if the democratic reformers were bent on establishing something like the old Hanseatic League, the mercantile association of German and Scandinavian towns and cities that had operated around the shores of the Baltic Sea from the thirteenth century onward.

Those comments were echoed by the radical reformers who took over the Moscow City Council. They had long chafed under what they saw as Gorbachev's excessively centralized control of both the economy and relations with minority republics. And so, like the Leningraders, the Muscovites plunged into trade with Lithuania, in violation of Gorbachev's embargo.

At one point, they had the audacity to run a whole trainload of fuel from Moscow to Lithuania—right under the Kremlin's nose. Sergei Stankevich told me about it late one evening in his city-council office; at the time, the embargo was still in force, so he was reporting about contraband deals.

"We received meat from [the Lithuanians] and we gave them some fuel and some machinery goods," Stankevich said. "We made up a special train with fuel barrels and we sent it to Leningrad. And they redirected the train to Lithuania."

"Where does the fuel come from?" I asked.

"From a Moscow oil-processing plant," he said.

"Which one?"

"Oh, I'm afraid you can't receive such information," he said, a knowing smile creasing the corners of his eyes.[11]

At that point, the radicals were keeping the scope and details of their trade secret, to avoid Kremlin reprisals. But as soon as the embargo was lifted, on June 29, the Lithuanians proudly disclosed their trade with a host of cities: Moscow, Leningrad, Omsk, Smolensk, Saratov, Arkhangelsk, Pskov, Tyumen, Minsk, and even faraway Uzbekistan, not to mention individual factories or enterprises elsewhere. The Lithuanian government claimed that through barter deals with parts of the Soviet Union, and not counting old Soviet contracts, it had imported 892 million rubles' (nearly $1.5 billion) worth of goods during the embargo, and had shipped back an equal volume.[12] If correct, those figures signified a staggering breakdown of centralized economic control, and defiance of Gorbachev—mainly by the new city governments.

"ALL POWER TO THE SOVIETS"

This bold new brand of urban politics had its roots in Leninism; it had been legitimized seven decades earlier by Vladimir Ilyich Lenin himself. In the summer of 1917, during the crescendo that produced the Bolshevik Revolution, Lenin had seen the popularly elected city soviets in Petrograd and across Russia as a crucial springboard to the Bolsheviks' ultimate seizure of power; and he canonized the slogan "All Power to the Soviets." When the provisional government of Prime Minister Aleksandr Kerensky objected, Lenin protested: "Such opposition means nothing but renouncing democracy!"[13] Of course, once Communist control was firmly established, Lenin emasculated the soviets as independent power bases, and ever since, the Party had used them as the window dressing of the "workers' state."

As part of his political strategy, Gorbachev had decided to invest real power once again in popularly elected soviets—first of all, in the Congress of People's Deputies and the Supreme Soviet; and then in soviets all across the country. Gorbachev was repeating Lenin's tactic, using the soviets as vehicles for an assault on the centralized power structure of his day. Lenin used them to fight Kerensky and the remnants of the czarist state; Gorbachev was using them to humble the Party apparat and to fashion a countervailing power to oppose it.

The democratic-minded radicals were quite happy to adapt the tactics of both Lenin and Gorbachev and to use the hallowed scripture of Soviet Communism's patron saint against his own party. Months before the spring elections of 1990, I began seeing radicals and young people wearing T-shirts and sweatshirts emblazoned with ALL POWER TO THE SOVIETS. It had now become a rallying cry for foes of the Party apparatus.

Before the 1990 elections, city soviets had been tools of the Party bosses—in effect, mere puppets. Theoretically, the city Party committee and the city soviet shared power; they often shared office buildings, newspapers, special rest homes, and cafeterias, as well as responsibility and authority. But, in fact, the Party pulled the strings.

The prospect of genuine independence in city hall alarmed the Party apparat, and in several cities it moved to preempt the new reformers. Even

Gorbachev acted alarmed—he immediately stripped the new Moscow City Council of control over street demonstrations and rallies, asserting his personal control on the grounds that "supreme state and government institutions are situated in the Kremlin and other places in the center of the city."[14] Once in office, the new city council protested, immediately appealing to the newly established Soviet Constitutional Oversight Commission to revoke the order, asserting that direct presidential rule was permissible only in the wake of palpable danger to public order.

Gorbachev's move, and other actions by local Party officials, immediately sharpened a sense of confrontation. Moreover, the radicals came into office with the natural instincts of political winners everywhere: They reached for the spoils of victory and fought for control of very practical instruments of power—real estate, the machinery of local government, control of the Party press and television.

In Moscow, the first battle was over the loyalties of the newly elected city deputies themselves. Since the great bulk of them were Communist Party members, the immediate question was whether they would stick with the Bloc of Democratic Russia, which had helped them get elected, or submit to Party discipline.

"It was a real confrontation from the very beginning," Stankevich told me. "Our local Party chief [Yuri Prokofyev] tried to press the Communists [in the city council] but they rejected this attempt. And so we succeeded in consolidating our democratic coalition."

The election of Gavril Popov as mayor of Moscow on April 20 had sealed the psychological break from the Party for the independent-minded deputies, 90 percent of whom were political novices.

Popov immediately became embroiled in the next battle, over the most important buildings in the city of Moscow—buildings that were symbols of political power.

"The Party tried to capture the administrative buildings in Moscow," Stankevich told me. "We have thirty-three districts in the city, and each district has an administrative building. Normally, you can find there the offices of the district council, the district Party organization, and the district Komsomol. The Party made the former city council adopt a decision to transfer these buildings from the soviets to the Party. So we had to counterattack at once. We reversed the old decision. The Party tried to appeal to the courts, but the court didn't accept their suit. So now we are the proprietors."[15]

Prokofyev, the Party boss, had a different version: He claimed that the Party had put up one third of the funds for those buildings, 23 million rubles in all, and that its investment entitled the Party to keep its offices in those buildings. He accused the radical reformers of picking fights with the Party.

"Mossoviet [the Moscow City Council] clearly has an anti-Party stance," Prokofyev said. "They are trying to show the supremacy of the city council and the district councils over the Party in this city."[16]

Stankevich said that it was up to the thirty-three individual district councils to collect rent from their district Party committees, but he voiced confidence that the Party would pay up in 1991, as the Moscow city government began to exercise its new taxing power, under a law passed earlier in 1990 by the Supreme Soviet.

"They will pay rent to the district councils," Stankevich insisted. "Previously, they didn't pay anything—not a single ruble. They will start paying in 1991. For them, it's a very serious situation—because we have new tax authority at the beginning of 1991. We can tax any enterprise, up to a forty-percent rate, and that includes Party enterprises, Party newspapers and printing plants. The Party wants tax credits, favorable treatment, so I think they will agree to pay rent."[17]

The next confrontation came over control of the newspapers. For years, the Moscow Party Committee had jointly controlled two newspapers, the more official morning *Moscow Pravda (Moskovskaya Pravda)*, with a circulation of 725,000, and the more informal and readable afternoon daily, *Evening Moscow (Vechernaya Moskva)*, with a circulation of 625,000. Just before the reformers took over city hall, the Party seized exclusive control of *Moscow Pravda* by simply erasing the city council's name from the newspaper's masthead. Even though the Party offered to continue sharing *Evening Moscow*, the democrats in the city council were furious at the Party's power grab. But initially the Party was unmoved.

"*Moskovskaya Pravda* was always a Party paper," asserted its editor, Valery Lysenko, a staunch Party man. "All the main decisions, on personnel, finances, were made by the Party, even when technically they were joint decisions with Mossoviet. The role of Mossoviet was a formality. Mossoviet itself was a formality."[18]

Mayor Popov decided to insist on either having joint control of the morning paper restored or having the Party pay some compensation. Popov, a short, portly, rumpled professor, likes behind-the-scenes negotiations. He makes tough demands, but he is a bargainer. In this case, he had his eye on setting up an entirely new newspaper, independent of Party influence, to break the Party's dominance of the media. Similar efforts were mounted by democratic city councils in Volgograd, Tyumen, and Sverdlovsk. In Leningrad, the city council had won outright control of one of two daily newspapers formerly controlled jointly with the Party. Volgograd was also ahead of Moscow; both the local province and the local city government started publishing their own independent newspapers in June and July 1990.[19]

In Moscow, as elsewhere, one major problem was that the Party controlled not only the newspapers but the printing plant and the supply of newsprint as well. Prokofyev, a relatively moderate Party leader, decided to make concessions to the new city council, rather than harden the lines of confrontation.

"We will reduce the circulation of our paper by two hundred thousand, to make it possible for Mossoviet to put out its own newspaper," he told me in late June 1990. "We will take this paper from *Evening Moscow*—not from *Moscow Pravda*, which remains the organ of the Party. And we have offered Mossoviet services—our printing plant, office space, and so on—so they can create their own newspaper."

Popov and his people made plans to bring out not one, but two new publications—first, by the fall of 1990, a newspaper called *Stolitsa (Capital)*, starting as a weekly and eventually becoming a daily; and second, in early 1991, a weekly magazine called *Kurant*, an old Russian word meaning "bell chimes," or "time," and evoking the name of one of the oldest newspapers in Russian history, published in the early eighteenth century under Peter the Great.

The breakthrough had taken place. Given the chance to launch its own paper, the city council quickly negotiated and signed preliminary agreements with Western publishing interests (Robert Maxwell of England and Robert Hersant of France) to set up two new printing plants. They began dickering for major Western investments in a new Moscow broadcast center as well. So within four months of organizing itself, the new city government of Moscow had moved swiftly to establish its independence from the Party and the national government in the field of communications. And it put the Party on notice that it was no longer the master, but merely a tenant, in the halls of Moscow city government.

LENINGRAD: WHO OBEYS WHOM?

In Leningrad, the confrontation between the new city council and the Party was sharper and more hostile. Both of the main protagonists, provincial Party leader Boris Gidaspov and Mayor Anatoly Sobchak, were fighters; neither was inclined to yield an inch on the central definition of power in the confusing situation that Gorbachev had created: Who obeys whom?

Gidaspov, unexpectedly put into the top Party job in the summer of 1989, quickly established himself as a proud and ambitious opportunist who was quite ready to side with the Party's right wing against Gorbachev in order to gain influence. He was a promoter of the Russian Communist Party Congress, which Leningrad hosted; and while he was no ironclad conservative, he was a strong Party loyalist. Even though his career had been as a scientist and administrator, not as an apparatchik, when he assumed command of the hard-line Leningrad regional Party hierarchy, he became its spokesman; and in the spring of 1990, he put down a liberal challenge from a Democratic Platform faction within the Leningrad Party.

Before being elected mayor that same May, Sobchak had won a reputation in the Supreme Soviet as a legislator capable of cold logic, fierce independence, and a polemical manner. Debating on national television came naturally to the Leningrad law professor. Powerful people did not intimidate him; he had publicly taken on Gorbachev, Ryzhkov, and Ligachev, individually and collectively, to argue for individual rights, to insist on the rule of law and fair procedures, to oppose the repressive use of force, to attack official corruption. Rather quickly, Sobchak became known as the most effective parliamentarian among the Inter-Regional Group. He led the attack that caused the first minister in Ryzhkov's government to be rejected; he came within two votes of pushing the Supreme Soviet to revoke the Party's monopoly on power—several months before Gorbachev was ready for that step; he ferried a tough report on the army's crackdown in Tbilisi, Georgia, through a committee and then accused Ligachev of lying to the committee; and several times, his crisp debating points caused Gorbachev to send government proposals back to be redrafted, or to drop devious parliamentary tactics.

"I have been a mountain climber and I know there are no absolutely smooth or impenetrable walls in nature," Sobchak once observed. "It's impossible to sit tight when it comes to the life or death of just one person, or the life or death of an entire society."[20]

It was his striking presence—fearless candor, legislative agility, and telegenic good looks—that gave Sobchak national recognition and a popularity that ranked behind only Gorbachev and Yeltsin, within a few months of his arrival on the national political stage in early 1989.

In person, or on television, Sobchak seems too cerebral, too educated, too fast-talking, and too high-pitched in voice to have natural appeal for the Russian masses. Instead of Boris Yeltsin's earthy charisma, Sobchak projects the cooler, blue-eyed, blond appeal of suburban gentry. With his new prominence, he now travels frequently to the West (he was in

Portland, Oregon, getting an honorary degree a couple of days after his election as mayor). Sitting in the baroque and gilded grandeur of his spacious chambers in a former czarist palace, Sobchak looks more Western than Russian in his tweed sport coat, rep tie, and gray flannel slacks. And with the poise and self-confidence of a Speaker of the House at home with Robert's rules of order, he corrals the freewheeling Leningrad City Council, which looks—and is—about as large and as self-absorbed as the U.S. House of Representatives.

Sobchak never had been a deeply committed Communist; he had joined the Party only in 1989, after the government promised to withdraw Soviet troops from Afghanistan. In July 1990, he was one of the first prominent reformers to quit the Party at the close of the Twenty-eighth Party Congress. Well before that he had made it clear that in Leningrad he was ready for a head-to-head fight to bring the Party to heel and to assert the supremacy of the popularly elected city council.

"We will not share power with anyone," he declared shortly after his election. "After we start working we shall see which affairs Party bodies will meddle in. . . . I hope our cooperation with the [Leningrad] Party committee will be fruitful. The main thing is that all power belongs to the soviet. Anyone who would fancy opposing this power should remember the fate of all those who have ever opposed soviet power."[21]

It was characteristic of Sobchak to strike quickly—only a month after assuming office—at the most sensitive nerve: to protest that the KGB was delivering daily reports on Leningrad's internal-security matters to Gidaspov, the Party chief, but not to him as mayor. Sobchak condemned this as a Stalinist legacy and warned the Leningrad KGB to heed the power of the city soviet.

"For decades the army, the MVD [Ministry of Internal Affairs], and KGB were led not by the state, but by the Party," Sobchak complained. "This is one of the most 'fruitful' Stalinist ideas, which enabled Stalin to create 'his' state. Now the point is to restore the state to its original form. . . . For a month already I have occupied the post of chairman of the Leningrad city soviet [mayor], but the daily reports on what is happening in the city are put on the table of Boris Gidaspov. The heads of the administrative bodies do not consider it necessary to supply me with the corresponding information. I informed these comrades that the city soviet will confirm them in their posts and, therefore, they need to make a choice about who governs them—the state or the CPSU [Party]."[22]

Mirroring what had happened in Moscow, Sobchak and the Leningrad City Council immediately got into a fight with the regional Party leadership over control of real estate and other property claimed by the Party through some eleventh-hour finagling by the outgoing city council, which had transferred about fifty major pieces of real estate to other organizations. The reform city council immediately froze those transfers; Sobchak said these were city properties. He demanded control—and in most cases occupancy—of thirty-nine district administrative centers; several czarist palaces and other historic buildings; Lenizdat, the Party's publishing house and the largest printing plant in the city; the Party's hotel and meeting center; its dairy farm, with four hundred head of cattle, which supplied meat and milk to Party cafeterias and to high officials; a sanitarium and several country *dachas* for the Party elite; a fleet of cars and trucks that had long been at the Party's beck and call.

The sharpest confrontation came over the headquarters of the Leningrad Province Party Committee at Smolny, once a nineteenth-century private school, which had been taken over by Lenin during the Bolshevik Revolution as his headquarters. Ever since, the Leningrad Party had occupied Smolny; in fact, to Leningraders, the word Smolny had become synonymous with Party power.

I was told that Gidaspov had had the effrontery to show up at the first city-council sessions, acting like a powerful uncle patronizing his nephews; he had told Sobchak that there was no way the Party could be evicted from Smolny, because the Party had earned the building with the blood of the Revolution. Sobchak retorted: "Those workers and sailors seized Smolny to establish soviet power, not to give it to the Communist Party."[23]

Sobchak was perhaps better able than anyone else to make the city's claim to Smolny and the rest of those properties; he had been one of the architects in the Supreme Soviet of a law that transferred all but certain designated categories of property to local governments, effective June 30, 1990. This law was central to the property claims of city councils in Moscow, Leningrad, and elsewhere.

Cornered and outmaneuvered, Gidaspov escalated the issue to the Kremlin, trying to get Gorbachev to save Leningrad Party headquarters. Finally, just before the June 30 deadline for the transfer of properties, Prime Minister Ryzhkov issued a decree nationalizing all property in the Soviet Union historically linked to Lenin—specifically Smolny and several other Leningrad buildings.

Sobchak threatened reprisal. "This decree is illegal," he argued. "I reject this action. This is Leningrad city property. The running water, sewage, electricity for Smolny are all provided by the city. If we are not respected, we can cut off all of the above. Then let them see how they can get along in that building."[24]

Later, Sobchak tried to pass off his threat as "a joke," but he reasserted his determination to use every measure to establish the contested buildings as city property. "These buildings cannot be considered state property," he told me. "According to the Law on Property, only industries and organizations necessary for the functioning of the nation can be regarded as state property—communications, mass media, central television, defense industries. We are going to fight this decree. We'll hold a referendum, and on the basis of its result, we will appeal to the Russian government [Yeltsin]."

The feisty Leningrad City Council had already shown readiness to take matters directly into its own hands. During a fight with Moscow Central Television over a controversial broadcast, about two dozen deputies had gone to the Leningrad branch of state television and physically asserted the city's authority. Like other institutions, Leningrad television was caught between two masters: the State Committee for Television and Radio, headquartered in Moscow, and traditionally subordinate to the Party, and the city council, which technically had to consent to any appointments of senior Leningrad television officials. Until the reformers took office, that had been a formality. In practice, the ideology department of the Leningrad Party apparat set the policy line for Leningrad television.

What had provoked the showdown was a broadcast scheduled for April 5, 1990: a scripted interview with Nikolai Ivanov, a federal investigator and people's deputy, who had prepared a series of sensational charges of high-level economic corruption that included Gorbachev and his wife.

According to Bella Kurkova, executive producer of *Fifth Wheel*, the Kremlin's television bosses had wanted none of this information on the air, and had given orders to Boris Petrov, chairman of the Leningrad branch of the State Committee for Television and Radio, to block the show. The Leningrad City Council, for whom Ivanov was a hero, had then passed a resolution ordering that the show go on the air, but Petrov had followed Moscow's orders. Despite advance publicity, Ivanov was not allowed in the studio.

The next day, the Leningrad City Council had suspended Petrov from his post and appointed his deputy, Viktor Senin, to replace him; Senin was a member of the city soviet. That evening, about twenty deputies went to the television station with the order to ensure that Ivanov was allowed to broadcast. Petrov fled the station after the deputies confronted him, Senin signed off on the show, and Ivanov went on the air and made his charges.

The episode was not one of the city council's proudest victories; Petrov claimed that the deputies had messed up papers and bodily ejected him. Moscow authorities accused the city council of an illegal seizure of the television station. Nearly three months later, Petrov was still coming to work, because the Kremlin and the city council could not agree on a replacement for him. But the council had made its point; it had broken the Party's and Moscow's control of Leningrad television.

As Bella Kurkova put it, "The Party is losing its tribune and, therefore, the possibility of influencing people. Nowadays, it is the democrats who can influence the people of Leningrad on television."[25]

"SHOW PEOPLE A DIFFERENCE"

The ambitions of the urban democrats went well beyond trench warfare with the Party apparat. In most cities where the insurgents took control, the reformers were bent on moving more rapidly than the national government into a market economy. Worried by the deteriorating economic situation, Sobchak, Popov, Stankevich, and others came into office aware that they had precious little time to demonstrate results before popular disillusionment would engulf them, along with Gorbachev. The more sophisticated understood that their role as critics had spared them responsibility for a year, but that taking control of a part of government made them accountable too.

The Party had lost power because of its dismal record; the reformers had to do better. Like a Western politician, Stankevich remarked shortly after his election to city hall: "My main motto is: Show our people the difference."[26] And he meant basic things such as stopping industrial construction, using funds for better housing, building more schools and health clinics, cleaning up the city, paving streets.

Mayor Popov, a fifty-three-year-old economist whose career had been teaching at Moscow State University and editing an academic journal, also had an unusual streak of pragmatism for a scholar-theoretician. Some Russian colleagues joked that perhaps he was more of a realist than most Russians, because he is of Greek descent. In an early interview as mayor, Popov ticked off five practical priorities: ecology, medicine, housing, city economy, and philanthropy. All of this assumed market economics and encouragement of private enterprise.[27]

In its first three months, the Popov administration moved quickly: It halted the construction of a huge new power station that was unpopular with environmental groups; it hired outside contractors to repave the worst of the city's streets; and, in a grand gesture of municipal largesse, it issued a decree transferring ownership of all state-owned apartments to the renters who occupied them—Muscovites could now legally buy and sell apartments without resorting to black-market subterfuges to evade state regulations.[28]

The most immediately visible project was the repair of the city's ubiquitous and treacherous potholes. Because state construction trusts were notorious for crawling inefficiency, the new city council decided on an innovation: It turned to private cooperatives—not only to get quicker results but to show skeptics the benefits of private enterprise. It set the cooperatives in competition with each other and with state construction gangs on various small projects, and it held out as the prize for best performance a 30-million-ruble contract to repair Moscow's seventy-mile circumferential highway, known as the Ring Road.

The winner of the competition was Stroitel ("Builder"), a private firm run by a tough, cunning, hard-driving, sixty-one-year-old contractor named Vadim Tumanov, a veteran of Stalin's Siberian labor camps. As a teenager in the 1940s, he had gotten into trouble for political dissent, and he had compounded his difficulties by fighting with other prisoners and rifling the camp safe. But after Stalin's death, he was pardoned and released. In the camp, Tumanov had developed a gang of laborers willing to work hard for extra pay, and when he got out, he went into what amounted to private construction for thirty-five years, dodging the state by operating in rural, far-off regions, where, because he got things done, local officials turned a blind eye to his capitalistic ways of doing business. Under Gorbachev, Tumanov came out into the open and become known for good, fast construction work in the Karelia region, north of Leningrad along the Finnish border.

The Moscow City Council lured Tumanov into doing a four-mile stretch of the Ring Road, as a tryout. State construction firms normally completely ignore deadlines, but Tumanov drove his crew of 130 men around the clock for two months, an unheard-of pace for Soviet construction, in order to finish on time. The men worked twelve-hour days and pulled down pay up to 1,200 rubles a month, four times the Soviet average. Tumanov even brought in floodlights for night work; and the city fathers allocated thirty-five trucks and the output of one Moscow asphalt plant to keep the operation going at full speed.

"I am accused of knowing how to make a profit," Tumanov told Francis Clines of *The New York Times*. "There is no secret [to it]. You get organized and you keep initiative alive. . . . Only productivity can save this country—all other talk is garbage."[29]

Tumanov's performance, which drew astonished stares from truckers on the Ring Road, was a classic lesson in free-market productivity. His results were far better, faster, and cheaper than those of state firms—and the work was done on time. It was a showcase for the new city council.

The council's housing giveaway, decreed in late June 1990, did not enjoy such immediate success. Gorbachev's government had previously announced plans to sell people their apartments, in order to sop up billions of rubles of private cash and help close the federal deficit. They were chagrined at being upstaged by Moscow's decision to give away those apartments. Yet simple as that sounded, the mechanics were difficult.

In the interests of fairness, Stankevich told me, the original blanket offer of free apartments was qualified: Up to 120 square feet per person would be free, but surplus footage would have to be paid for. Weeks later, the city had not figured out the correct price, or how to compensate more than one million people who were living in communal apartments with much less than 120 square feet per person. Clearly, the giveaway was a bonanza for most of Moscow's 9.5 million residents; but there was the potential for political backlash if too many others wound up dissatisfied. Many people were complaining that suddenly they were responsible for maintenance.

The most dramatic—and controversial—early action by the Moscow City Council came in the wake of Prime Minister Ryzhkov's announcement in late May 1990 that bread and other food prices were going to rise fast. To control the ensuing panic-buying and the mass influx of frantic out-of-town shoppers, the city council quickly passed a regulation barring outsiders from shopping in Moscow stores. Store clerks were to require shoppers to show Moscow passports. City dwellers were relieved, but the regulation provoked a horrendous outcry from the surrounding countryside. People had long been accustomed to traveling to Moscow to shop, even for staples, because the capital was so much better supplied than their home regions. Traditionally, as many as two million people streamed through the city daily, and panic had multiplied that number. Moscow's action triggered threats to retaliate from nearby farm regions, and other agricultural regions all the way to Uzbekistan—regions from which Moscow got its food. The reformers had unwittingly aroused traditional provincial animosities against Moscow as an elite city, and had put Moscow's winter food supplies in jeopardy.

But disaster turned into opportunity. Forced by the uproar into sitting down face-to-face with angry provincial leaders, the new city council saw a chance to move into business in a big way, bypassing the central planners. For hectic days and nights, Popov, Stankevich, and others negotiated furiously with regional officials from twenty-seven central Russian provinces, including Yaroslavl, Tula, Vladimir, Ryazan, and Kalinin (renamed Tver). They swapped shopping lists that laid out an exchange: machinery, cars, appliances, and manufactured goods from Moscow, in exchange for meat, milk, and farm produce from the surrounding regions.

Then the city council leaders persuaded Prime Minister Ryzhkov to let the council have control over 12.5 percent of the total output of the factories and enterprises located in the city.[30] In the past, those goods had been earmarked by Gosplan and Gossnab for nationwide allocation; Moscow now needed them for its barter deals.

Starting in 1991, the city council had plans to take some of its corporate taxes in the form of goods—trucks, refrigerators, television sets, and the like—and use them to barter with its regional trading partners for food supplies. As Stankevich explained, the city had to resort to barter in goods, because "our money is no good."

So just as Gorbachev's trade embargo of Lithuania had stimulated new trading relations, the crisis over Ryzhkov's proposed increase in bread prices spurred Moscow and its neighbors to develop direct new avenues of commerce. Their trade deal was only an intermediary step toward a market economy, but it helped loosen the grip of the central state apparatus.

This was just the beginning of the Moscow City Council's business ventures. By the fall of 1990, Moscow sent 2,000 city-owned trucks to the Orenburg region in western Siberia to help transport the grain from the harvest, and another 750 trucks to Astrakhan. The old city government had done similar things, but the new city council had a commercial twist: It made Orenburg promise to pay with Siberian grain for the use of trucks. It also got a pledge from Astrakhan to supply vegetables, tomatoes, and melons. Similar deals were made with farming areas just outside Moscow: The city council promised to arrange for factory workers to help gather the harvest, in exchange for a payoff in meat and produce.

On another front, city reformers began to challenge the commercial monopolies of government ministries. They had two goals: to get their hands on hard-currency earnings for the city's treasury, and to provide new openings for private cooperatives or state enterprises capable of adapting to market economics. One target was Moscow's four major airports, which the council wanted to take over with the idea of setting up a municipal agency like the New York Port Authority, and then encouraging the start of smaller, private airlines. When the Ministry of Aviation snubbed the upstart reformers, the Popov-Stankevich team reminded the ministry that the airports were sitting on city land and getting vital city services such as water, electricity, and sewage, and that these services could be withheld unless the ministry turned over the airports, or agreed to heavy user fees in hard currency. That started negotiations in earnest.

"We would like to exploit the airports in a commercial way," Stankevich explained. "It's good business for the city. Why not?"[31]

Another prime target was Intourist, the national tourist monopoly and the bête noire of foreign travelers in the Soviet Union. Its practice was to charge foreign tourists steep hard-currency rates and then pay its Moscow subcontractors in cheap rubles for their work, such as transport, repairs, hotel services. The city council wanted a share of those hard-currency earnings, for itself and for Moscow businesses. As leverage, the council passed a regulation requiring that Intourist pay in hard currency for all services, and that all basic deals be sanctioned by the council. It also made plans to help put other private and state firms into competition with Intourist.

The Moscow reformers came into office with the overall objective of stimulating entrepreneurship. One of the first actions of the city council—echoed in Leningrad, Volgograd, Sverdlovsk, and other big cities—was to make it much easier for Soviet private cooperatives to get started and to operate. Mark Masarsky, the Novgorod house builder, told me in midsummer 1990 that new city governments, even the one in Novgorod, had drastically eased restrictions on cooperatives. What is more, these cities were ready to give business to private firms, unlike their old, hard-line predecessors. Masarsky had come to Moscow looking for a big city contract for renovating old housing.[32]

With the national government bogged down in endless debate about economic reform in mid-1990, the Moscow City Council took on the role of midwife for market economics. The reformers conceived of having the city, with its control of land and property, stimulate the creation of businesses by going into partnership with foreign investors, or with Soviet private firms, acting not only as co-owner and sponsor but also as a political protector for the fragile new market sector. Typical was the role Deputy Mayor Stankevich played in bringing Soviet firms together with Ikea, the Swedish furniture maker, to promote a joint enterprise under the aegis of the city council, which was eager to ease the severe furniture shortage in Moscow.

"Of course, it is not absolutely normal for us to operate in such a way, but since we have almost no economic activity independent of the state, our democratic city councils have to start this activity," Stankevich explained to me. "So in Moscow, we are establishing what we call the House of Trade. It is an incubator for joint ventures, for stock companies, for new independent enterprises. We help create them and give them a legal basis and full opportunity for independent activity. And they give us part of their profits, or part of their product—things the city badly needs—for example, meals for our schoolchildren."

More broadly, Mayor Popov moved to develop an infrastructure for business. The city council set up an employment agency and authorized the opening of a very simple wholesale barter market, to let Soviet enterprises make money from the stocks of spare parts and raw materials they had been hoarding for years. Stankevich traveled to Washington and several European capitals to try to negotiate Western investments for a Moscow Bank for Reconstruction and Development, to help finance the city's ambitious projects and to underwrite mixed Soviet public-and-private companies.

"You see the same kinds of things going on in other cities where democrats are in power—in Sverdlovsk, Kuibyshev, Leningrad, Gorky, Donetsk," Stankevich said. "They try to control the administrative buildings. They try to control local newspapers and establish radio stations. And also they are trying to become real entrepreneurs in their cities, because it is a real life-and-death situation for them."[33]

In Leningrad, the new city council was behind Moscow but moving in the same direction.

Mayor Sobchak told me of Leningrad's efforts to privatize the economy by selling off unprofitable state enterprises, by promoting cooperatives, by making conditions attractive for foreign joint ventures. Sobchak was particularly eager to exploit Leningrad as a tourist center. He was angered that so much of the city's profits from tourism were skimmed off by Intourist and sent to the national government, rather than being kept by the Leningraders who earned them and reinvested in the city. His goal was to develop local competition for Intourist.

Sobchak's big dream was to turn the entire Leningrad region into an economic free zone—to free Leningrad's economy from national regulations, taxes, customs controls, and, above all, the dead hand of Soviet ministries and central planning. The base had been laid: A modest industrial free zone had been established in Vyborg, a city in Leningrad Province on the border with Finland; a dozen foreign firms were already building plants. Sobchak wanted a massive expansion, and on August 1 he got the go-ahead from Boris Yeltsin's Russian republic for setting up banks, stock companies, joint enterprises, and other deals. Nonetheless, he still needed Gorbachev's blanket approval for Leningrad enterprises to market products abroad without deal-by-deal permission from Moscow ministries; and for the city to sell land to foreigners, and set up its own customs zone.[34]

Sobchak told me that in spite of his feuding with the Party apparatus and the ministries, his free-zone concept could succeed. He insisted that it had the ardent backing of Gorbachev's main new economic advisers, Nikolai Petrakov and Stanislav Shatalin.

Nonetheless, reformers like Sobchak, Popov, and Stankevich acknowledge that for all their energy, new ideas, and noble objectives, city radicals have an uphill road. As Popov has warned repeatedly, they must deliver widespread benefits quickly before rank-and-file workers turn against their market reforms as simply a means to line the pockets of a new Soviet bourgeoisie. They confront the ingrained conservatism of the Russians; Sobchak's initial offers to sell off unprofitable state stores and enterprises had very few takers. In the tough world of Soviet bureaucratic infighting and international finance, the radicals are still innocents. They need quick, large infusions of Western capital to show some movement. It is hard to see how they can carve out economic enclaves in the cities independent of the rest of the Soviet economy, without provoking an economic war with the countryside.

What the radicals had going for them in 1990—their first year in power—was the political initiative and popular support. They were the most dynamic element in Soviet society and in the political system; with the disintegration of authority and control at the center, they had wide openings to exploit. Moreover, with the nation's economy in crisis and little prospect of a turnaround, it was in Gorbachev's interest to promote some brights spots to help persuade a skeptical population that market economics has a payoff.

"Gorbachev needs us to succeed," Sobchak asserted. "The country is more interested in this than we are, because it needs a showcase for the benefits of a market economy."[35]

PART SIX

CONCLUSION

CHAPTER 24

THE OUTLOOK: WILL IT COLLAPSE OR WILL IT ENDURE?

"[E]xperience teaches that the most critical moment for bad governments is the one which witnesses their first steps toward reform."[1]
—Alexis de Tocqueville, 1856

QUESTION: What's the difference between the Soviet Union and the United States?
ANSWER: Gorbachev could probably get elected president in the United States.
—Soviet political joke, March 1990

From afar the Soviet Union seems so stricken by tumult, chaos, and uncertainty, that it is easy to discount the profound transformation that has taken place, or to worry that it will all end in disaster and be wiped away. That view misses the magnitude of what has already occurred.

What we have been watching is no less than the most extraordinary peaceful revolution of the twentieth century.

In human history, there have been years of surpassing consequence for the future course of events: the popular revolts of 1848 against the old

order of Europe; the Russian Revolution of 1917; the defeat of Hitler and
the onset of the Cold War in 1945.

The years 1989–90 are of similar historical significance. In 1989, in
what seemed like barely an instant, Eastern Europe threw off Soviet rule
and the alien system of Communist power imposed by the Soviet army.
In that same bright year and in 1990, the old order was shattered inside
the Soviet Union, and Gorbachev set in place political changes of enduring importance, not only for Soviets but for the destiny of mankind.

An era has ended—not simply the era of the Cold War, but the era
of Soviet totalitarianism. It has been felled like a rotting oak. The Communist Party has been stripped of its domination over the entire life of
the nation. The *nomenklatura,* the inner priesthood of the Party-state, has
lost its immunity; it still clings to certain strongholds, but it is in decline.
After popular rejection in two elections, it now sees the Party rank and
file draining away. The Politburo, once the pinnacle of power under
Stalin, Khrushchev, and Brezhnev, has lost its preeminent authority to
new governmental institutions: the presidency, the Congress of People's
Deputies, and the Supreme Soviet, where suddenly, for the first time,
debates and votes count for something.

With the choke hold of fear broken and dissent now tolerated, Russians
are no longer politically passive. They have plunged into election campaigns, mass demonstrations, environmental protests, miners' strikes—all
evidence of a hunger for participation that could not have been predicted
even as late as 1987, two years *after* Gorbachev took power. The breathtaking pace of popular self-emancipation and the growth of grass-roots
activism has outstripped what Gorbachev had intended. Change, initially
decreed from above, now rises more insistently from below. One after
another, eleven republics have declared their sovereignty over the center—though their actions constitute pressure on Gorbachev rather than
their assumption of governing power. The people have chosen fresh,
iconoclastic voices to represent them: Boris Yeltsin, Lithuania's Vytautas
Landsbergis, the new reform mayors, scores of people's deputies, and
hundreds more at the local level. These new populist advocates have dared
to challenge every facet of Soviet power, and in the fall of 1990, they
initiated the first serious stirrings of a multiparty system.

What the world had come to know as the Communist credo lies
discredited. The Soviet leadership has abandoned the messianic dream of
remaking the world according to the gospel of Marxism-Leninism; and at
home, it has admitted the failure of Communism's gossamer promise of
Utopia. Gorbachev has talked of resuscitating Communism in a new

form—as a humane Leninism that to Western ears sounds like democratic socialism. But since the crash of the old credo, no new ideology has taken hold. Nationalism has moved powerfully into the vacuum—a centrifugal and explosive force, not a source of unity or cohesion. That portion of Soviet society, mainly the intelligentsia, for whom the democratic ideal is a sufficient ideology, is still precariously small.

Nonetheless, the free market of ideas is now at work in the Soviet press and on television, and it has spilled into the streets; the police state still functions but it no longer chills ordinary people into silence, nor muffles poets, pundits, or playwrights. Free expression is alive and vibrant; and it has belatedly gained legal anchor and protection from a new law that permits anyone or any group to start a newspaper or to operate a television station, though as a practical matter the Party still controls paper supplies and the only national television channels.

The notion of a "law-governed state," now a refrain of Gorbachev's political catechism, has slowly begun to take practical form. The institutional instruments of democracy—independent courts, an unfettered legal profession, a free press, elections, a two-term limit on the presidency, the process of legislating—all these are in their infancy, and therefore inevitably fragile. But the chances for their survival and growth have been improved by the practical dispersal of authority among contending power centers—the presidency, the legislature, the Party apparat, the new leadership in republic and city governments, the military and the KGB, even masses of striking workers.

In short, these two years have given birth to a rough system of political checks and balances that impose real limits on the exercise of power, by Gorbachev or any would-be successor. As the feudal barons in the Soviet provinces have come to understand, it is no longer possible to move the Soviet people by fiat and fear alone; as Gorbachev has also painfully learned, the new Soviet politics require compromise and collaboration. The old order has been dismantled, even if the new order has not yet taken shape.

THE ECONOMY: THE PRICE OF AMBIVALENCE

Where *perestroika* has conspicuously failed to achieve the most rudimentary and essential transformation is the place where it began—the economy. The rhetoric of reform has filled the air for more than three years, but the old economic mechanism has been little altered. The old channels of central control, the old industrial ministries and their state monopolies, the old inefficiencies of featherbedding, fixed prices, and false accounting, the old habits of Soviet workers, have resisted change.

The Stalinist command system has been damaged but not dislodged. With each passing year, it has functioned less effectively; but nothing has been fashioned to replace it. Cooperatives are in operation, but they are unpopular, especially those that provide services rather than produce goods. Individual property has been written into law, but most people are not yet accustomed to its commercial potential. The language of the market—competition, profits, free prices, and productivity—has come into vogue among urban intellectuals and government circles, but so far these concepts inspire fear, not confidence, among the masses; they cut against the grain of deep-set attitudes.

"The conservativism that has eaten into everyone and into society, like rust, has turned out to be more durable than we expected," Aleksandr Yakovlev confessed to me one afternoon. "Resistance to change has turned out to be very strong. A person gets his two hundred rubles [pay] without really working, and today he's told to work, and he'll get one hundred rubles more. He knows he'll have to *earn* not only those one hundred rubles but the first two hundred, which he used to get without working. To get people to work, economically, democratically, is very hard."[2]

What is more, the tenacity and guile of the bureaucracy have been greater than Gorbachev anticipated, as has the difficulty of purging people of their Stalinist mind-set, their Stalinist habits.

Without question, the task of economic reform is monumental. But Gorbachev himself is considerably to blame for not attacking it more directly at the outset. He missed his best opportunity—during his first two or three years, a time of popular faith in and tolerance toward the new leadership, and the period of his greatest popularity, before public passions had been let loose by *glasnost.* He squandered that precious time trying to find his way. For in his quest for a "more humane socialism," Gorbachev has been crippled by his own ambivalence. In the economy, the realm of policy most critical to his ultimate success, Gorbachev was operating without a blueprint. He knew what he was against, without being certain enough about what he was for, or how to get it.

Gorbachev has changed direction several times. He began in 1985–86 with a conservative drive to strengthen discipline, to fight alcoholism, to set up huge new central agencies, to look to science and technology to produce modernization. He fanned popular expectations of a dramatic turnaround, with sloganeering about economic "acceleration" *(us-*

koreniye) and hopeful talk of competing on the world market within a few years. Unlike Deng Xiaoping in China, Gorbachev did not move quickly to build a mass constituency for economic reform by generating pocket-book results—by giving peasants freedom to earn more and by putting more food on the table for people in the cities.

By 1987, he had shifted from organizational shuffling and demands for discipline to a wholly different tack, the more liberal prescription that he had once advocated as Party leader in Stavropol: decentralization of economic control, more autonomy for industrial enterprises and for regional authorities. Only gradually, in 1988 and 1989, did he edge further toward market economics. But he was moving without the clarity and conviction that he needed to persuade his Politburo colleagues or his people.

He was constantly at pains to reassure both the masses and the Party elite that he would not demand heavy sacrifices or radically alter the status quo. Somehow, magically, life would improve—without pain. In 1987, in his book *Perestroika*, Gorbachev proclaimed with typical buoyant self-confidence that he was "looking within socialism . . . for the answers," and the West should not expect him to adopt capitalism.[3] Later, as he tried more daring experiments, Yegor Ligachev's conservative faction in the Politburo and the Party apparat held him back. But even with the Soviet economy in deep decline, Gorbachev made it clear through 1989 and 1990, in speech after speech, that he himself was shying away from the unpredictable world of supply and demand. He raged at the inefficiencies of central planning; he wanted it to work better, he wanted more flexibility, but he was not ready to scrap it for something radically different.

The parallel drawn by his close friend and colleague Eduard Shevardnadze was to Franklin Roosevelt's drive to lift America out of the Depression with the New Deal, a program to save capitalism by grafting on elements of socialism.[4] Gorbachev's notion of "grafting" on something new was to take half steps, to make piecemeal changes. As late as April 1990, after five years in office, he refused to follow Eastern Europe's plunge into market economics—"shock therapy," his economic advisers called it; he publicly promised the workers that he would not agree to measures that would cost them jobs or shut down plants. He seemed paralyzed by fear of a popular backlash. Gorbachev was discovering that the institutions of democracy could make economic reform harder; the Supreme Soviet, responding to public outcry, swiftly killed badly overdue consumer price increases in late May. So Gorbachev retreated. Only in the fall, worried about being upstaged by Boris Yeltsin, did he begin to redefine his notion of socialism to allow for a transition to genuine markets, free prices, stock companies, and the kind of competitive environment that would lead sometime in the early nineties to a mixed socialist-capitalist economy.

In politics, Gorbachev could bypass the recalcitrant apparat by creating new institutions and by inviting mass involvement in *glasnost* and in the new politics of elections. In economics, he could not bypass the economic apparatus, because he was reluctant to risk setting people free with the new institutions of market economics. In politics, the public was eager for change and he played to its eagerness; in economics, the people were wary of changes and he bowed to their caution.

At each turn, Gorbachev was hampered by the fundamental paradox that *perestroika* is an assault on the state, and its leader is the head of state. He was held back not only by his own ideological ambivalence but also by his dual roles—by trying to play both Luther and the pope, both Master Architect of reform and Father Protector of the system.

TURNING A WEAK HAND INTO GRAND STRATEGY

In spite of all the obvious problems, Gorbachev has already established himself as one of a handful of twentieth-century leaders who have galvanized and transformed their nations, and thereby affected the larger course of history. In terms of his impact on the world, he has put himself in the class of such paramount figures as Roosevelt, Lenin, Churchill, Gandhi, Stalin, Mao, and Adenauer.

Forces of change were gathering within Soviet society before he came to power, but Gorbachev was the indispensable catalyst. He set them loose and thereby transformed the Soviet Union, Eastern Europe, and the world beyond.

Gorbachev was following the Russian tradition of the reformer-czars who created what Russians call "revolutions from above": Peter the Great, who westernized Imperial Russia at the turn of the eighteenth century, or Aleksandr II, the "Czar Liberator," who freed the serfs and initiated the period of "great reforms" late in the nineteenth century.

Yet contrary to Gorbachev's claims that he took over the Kremlin with a clear vision and a well-developed concept for *perestroika*, he was constantly experimenting, defining his path along the way, much as Franklin Roosevelt had proceeded with the New Deal. Both men seized grand opportunities and then nimbly responded to the quixotic course of events. Gorbachev began *perestroika* with a general sense of direction, and then zigzagged his way through history; he had no master plan.

One day, talking with Aleksandr Yakovlev, who was closer to Gorbachev's thinking than any other colleague, I had a chance to put to him the question of whether Gorbachev and his inner circle had begun *perestroika* with an overall plan.

"No," Yakovlev replied. "Yes, and no. There was a clear-cut understanding that what had existed had to be overturned—the authoritarianism, the command-bureaucratic economic system. It was clear that democracy had to be developed, but in what amounts or how? That plan didn't exist. It was clear that we had to return to Lenin's theory that people should rule their affairs. But how could that be done, in what stages? That, of course, wasn't there at the beginning. There was one thing, and the most important: that society would have to radically change its nature—what we call 'renewal.' But we had to find the instruments along the way, in the process of transformation: in politics, the economy, culture, the law, *glasnost*, and democracy. And it turns out that those instruments are very important—no less important than the overall concept."[5]

Gorbachev is propelled by a brimming self-confidence that he can ride over realities that would daunt lesser men, but in his intrepid resolve there is a not-so-obvious and perhaps essential element of naïveté. I have heard his aides describe him as so optimistic and so convinced of his own reasoning that he is naïve about the darker motives of others, a poor judge of how the Russian man in the street will react. At times, they say, he simply shuts out words of caution, not wanting to hear of the obstacles. Yakovlev described to me how innocent he and Gorbachev were, starting out on the road to *perestroika*.

"In 1984, 1985, I had moments of romanticism. I thought that the ideas of *glasnost*, renewal, democracy, would grab the masses," Yakovlev confessed. "But when you think more about those ideas, you see that it couldn't have happened that way. You have to stand on the soil of reality. Over more than sixty years so much conformity appeared in our economy, public life, politics, that you can't break it in one year, or two years, or five."

So Gorbachev's genius is not strategy, but improvisation. He is a brilliant improviser, an instinctive tactician, far quicker on his feet than his rivals, foreign or domestic. His skill is not so much in imposing his will on history as in discerning its flow, guiding it when he can, more often riding the tide.

To say this is not to denigrate Gorbachev. According to historians, some of the modern world's "great visionaries" have operated in the same way. The British historian A.J.P. Taylor, in his biography of Otto von

Bismarck, Germany's nineteenth-century "Iron Chancellor," has suggested that while Bismarck was a genius at political maneuvering, he was often driven by events rather than being their guiding force.[6] My colleague Simon Serfaty of the Johns Hopkins Foreign Policy Institute draws a parallel between Gorbachev and the late President De Gaulle of France, whom Serfaty has described as a masterful opportunist who took advantage of situations inherited from others. "It is precisely such ability to seize the opportunities opened by any new conjuncture which made him a true revolutionary," Serfaty wrote.[7]

Gorbachev, like all great leaders, has gotten credit in hindsight for being a visionary when he was clever enough to abandon those policies that did not work and to play up those that did. In fact, the longer *perestroika* has gone on, the more frequently Gorbachev has had to react to the flow of events rather than dictating their course, the more he has been propelled by the forces he himself released and been forced to catch up, merely to survive. Certainly one of Gorbachev's greatest assets is his personal capacity for change, for learning. He is forever trying something new, ever evolving. In every arena of policy, he has miscalculated, blundered badly, and had to reverse course. What is remarkable is his willingness to cast off failed policies without apology, to cut his political losses, and then to treat the inevitable as if it had been his design.

He is a master of retreat as well as of attack; examples of this ability are legion.

He failed entirely to anticipate that his own policies would release powerful forces of nationalism in the minority republics that would threaten the entire fate of reform. He treated local nationalists with benign neglect, patronizing approval, token appeasement, stinging denunciation, and finally, in Lithuania and Azerbaijan, he tried to crush them with either military force or economic embargo. But when those failed to stem the tide of nationalism, Gorbachev finally made a virtue out of offering other nationalities more of the autonomy they were demanding, and out of negotiating independence for the Baltic republics.

Boris Yeltsin has provided another litmus of Gorbachev. Gorbachev tried to banish and excommunicate Yeltsin, to beat him down; but ultimately, when Yeltsin bounced back with mass support and when Gorbachev needed that popularity to help sell economic reform to a reluctant populace, he allied himself with Yeltsin.

For a long time, Gorbachev treated a multiparty system as political anathema. The persistent pressures of the Inter-Regional Group to strip the Communist Party of its political monopoly provoked him into temperamental outbursts. But in the end, the logic of events forced him to make a 180-degree turn: He adopted the view of the opposition and then became the master persuader who induced the Party to bless this heresy.

Or again, on Eastern Europe, Gorbachev was more realistic and daring than his predecessors in the Kremlin; he saw the region less as a proud empire than as an economic albatross, and so to cut the Kremlin's financial losses and political liabilities, he let it go. But the swiftness of the Communist collapse caught him by surprise, and he vehemently opposed a reunified Germany, and even more adamantly vetoed its membership in NATO. Yet eventually, with West German Chancellor Helmut Kohl by his side, Gorbachev acquiesced both in German unification and NATO membership, and he made it sound as though that were the outcome he had secretly favored all along, if only he had been given the right assurances and some financial aid.

Gorbachev even managed to convert Soviet defeat and withdrawal from Afghanistan into a public-relations triumph at home. Again and again, he has demonstrated that he is an expert at turning a weak hand into grand strategy.

Perestroika could never have advanced so far without Gorbachev's single-minded determination, his will to succeed, his daring, his relentless energy. But it also would have failed without his political agility, his flexibility, his uncanny capacity for survival.

Gorbachev has seemed perpetually in trouble, but he is a master escape artist—a political Houdini, as Bill Keller of *The New York Times* put it—who has not only foiled political rivals but has also confounded the Western Kremlinologists who were too quick to count him down and out. The headlines on their punditry tell the story: GORBACHEV'S LAST SUMMIT (May 1990), GORBACHEV: GOVERNING ON THE RAZOR'S EDGE (December 1989), LIFE AFTER GORBACHEV: THE SOVIETS' GRIM FUTURE (November 1989). But Gorbachev has more political lives than a cat. He defies the political laws of gravity, or to quote *Time* magazine's portrait: "he hang-glides across the abyss."[8]

But not without cost. For all his victories, Gorbachev is no longer the colossus among his own people that he was in the heyday of *perestroika*, mid-1988. Now, like an American president or a West European prime minister who has led his nation through nearly six years of rough times, he has paid a price: The luster is gone, his popularity has plummeted. The right wing blames him for the breakdown of the old order at home and the loss of Eastern Europe. The radical and progressive reformers have been disillusioned by his moderation. And the great mass of ordinary people, seeing no more food in the stores than when he began, have grown cynical toward Gorbachev's promises of a better life. It is a source of wry humor in Moscow, as well as in New York and London and Paris, that Gorbachev is more popular in the West than he is at home.

His fall in popularity should come as no surprise; for more than five years, Gorbachev alone has borne the burden of accountability for the upheaval in people's lives. Both Left and Right were free to finger-point and criticize; only when Yeltsin took over as the leader of the Russian republic, and Popov and Sobchak were elected the mayors of Moscow and Leningrad, did anyone independent of Gorbachev share responsibility for making government work.

By the fall of 1989, I heard people in Moscow suggesting that the Gorbachev era of reform was over; they spoke of Gorbachev as a transitional figure. No longer did they put him on a par with Lenin, whom they saw as an authentic revolutionary, the creator of a new political and economic order. They had begun to call Gorbachev a "Kerensky"—comparing him to Aleksandr Kerensky, the prime minister of the provisional government of 1917, the precursor to Lenin, the leader whose modest tremors of reform prepared the way for the real political earthquake. After five years, these people suggested, Gorbachev was a spent force: He had done much, but he had exhausted his own potential and he was incapable of going further, because he was a prisoner of attitudes drawn from a lifetime under Stalin, Khrushchev, and Brezhnev. It would take someone with a new cast of mind to finish the job, the reformers said, and they had successors in mind—Yeltsin, Sobchak, or Popov. The Right, too, had its new champion, the Russian Party first secretary, Ivan Polozkov.

DARK SCENARIOS

With so much still in flux and so many contradictions in Soviet society, it is impossible to predict how *perestroika* will play out. The disintegration of the old system has gone so far, social turmoil is so widespread, and the economic situation is so precarious that in Moscow, a city of Cassandras, the most articulate people are pessimistic. They are full of dark scenarios—ethnic civil war, an economic crash, a total breakdown of law and order, the emergence of a new right-wing dictator, furious anti-Semitic pogroms, Russian nationalist revanchism lashing out at the world.

At every step of the way, there has been the potential of catastrophic violence—civil war or a bloody revolution. In nearly six years, there have been numerous instances of communal bloodshed and hundreds have been killed. But given the enormity of the changes under way and the passion of the forces unleashed, what is remarkable is not how much but how little mass violence there has been.

It is impossible to dismiss the possibility of mass ethnic bloodshed. Only occupation by twenty-five thousand Soviet army troops has kept Armenia and Azerbaijan from renewing civil war. As president, Gorbachev has commanded the private armies and guerrilla forces in these republics to disband and surrender their arms, but they have defied him, as have guerrilla forces in other republics. Vadim Bakatin, the minister of internal affairs, reported in mid-1990 that there were armed bands operating in Georgia, Moldavia, Latvia, Lithuania, and Estonia, and in Central Asia among Uzbeks, Kirghiz, and Kazakhs.[9] Significantly, Bakatin did not mention Russia, or the Ukraine, the second-largest republic and the only one capable of posing a serious armed challenge to Russia proper.

In terms of governmental stability, what is important is that the violence so far has taken place far from Moscow, outside the Russian republic; and street revolutions rarely topple governments unless they rise within the nation's capital and engage a nation's dominant people.

In Moscow, Gorbachev has allowed large political demonstrations but, with a sizable military garrison in reserve nearby, he has kept order. Even the largest Moscow rallies have been much smaller than the mass marches in East European capitals, and they have never approached the passion of the frenzied mobs that toppled Nicolae Ceauşescu. Nor has Gorbachev tempted fate, as Ceauşescu did when he summoned the masses to the central square of Bucharest to address them, and thereby set the stage for the rampage that led to his own overthrow.

Out across the Soviet Union, violence has been sporadic. The combustion of ethnic tensions has suddenly exploded in some distant region and then died down; in Central Asia, it has sometimes burst into flames and skipped, once, twice, three times, to other places, flaring briefly in each place, but not setting off a general conflagration. Significantly, that kind of violence has broken out almost exclusively in Central Asia and the Caucasus. By comparison, even the viciously anti-Semitic hate-mongering of the right-wing Pamyat group has led to very little actual bloodshed. In most of the country—the Baltics, the Ukraine, Byelorussia, Moldavia, the vast Russian republic—nationalist leaders have explicitly eschewed violence, preaching instead peaceful change. So that while spasms of violence and local conflict will probably continue, it seems unlikely that ethnic tensions will trigger a general civil war.

War or not, the Soviet Union is in the process of disintegration, though that scenario will probably be less drastic than many Westerners imagine. The Baltic republics, with a total population of 8 million, are determined to secede, and Gorbachev is committed in principle to allowing their independence. Other republics where there is widespread sentiment for secession include Georgia (5.4 million) and Moldavia (4.3 million), plus the western Ukraine around the once-Polish city of Lvov, and the Azerbaijani province of Nakhichevan, bordering Iran. It is hard to imagine that Gorbachev would allow all these regions to secede, but even if he did, that would involve no more than 25 million people out of a nation of 290 million.

Many a Western scholar has voiced the view of Timothy Garton Ash that "if history is any guide the decline of empires does not stop half-way,"[10] but it is conceivable that Gorbachev could get away with a partial, peaceful dissolution and still keep the bulk of what is now known as the Soviet Union intact, though with power decentralized.

At present, the prevailing demand of local people in most parts of the country is for their own sovereignty, primarily in economic affairs; almost every republic has been pressing Gorbachev to surrender central power to a looser confederation. Once again, Gorbachev seems to be bowing to the inevitable by negotiating ways to revise the Soviet federal structure. If he not only is willing to make sufficient concessions to reach agreement but succeeds in actually making it function, he could wind up with a new confederation of 265 million people (the Russian republic, the Ukraine, Byelorussia, Central Asia, Armenia, and perhaps others). Smaller than the current Soviet Union, it would still be a continental giant of superpower size.

More menacing to Gorbachev and the fate of his reform movement would be mass civil unrest growing out of an economic breakdown: social outrage turning to anarchy—a general strike crippling the nation's factories and transport system, massive refusal by farmers to deliver crops to the cities, food riots in Moscow and other urban areas, economic uprisings in the Russian heartland that the army could not, or would not, quell.

As the crucial 1990 fall harvest began, the government braced for rising social tensions. Prime Minister Nikolai Ryzhkov sounded the alarm that despite one of the most bountiful growing seasons in recent years, grain deliveries to the government from state and collective farms had fallen behind those in 1989. Such a trend, he warned, could lead to serious food shortages through the winter of 1990–91, possibly sparking civil unrest. Ryzhkov also disclosed a drastic worsening in the supply of consumer goods in the western regions because East European visitors were buying cheaper Soviet goods on the Soviet black market. Industrial plants, Ryzhkov complained, were refusing to abide by state economic plans.[11] And he warned that the country was running out of hard currency and could not import even as much food as in 1989, to make up for any shortfall in the 1990 harvest. In short, the economic crisis was worsening.

For Ryzhkov, schooled in central planning and responsible for making it work, those were disastrous indicators. But in terms of the long-range prospects for reform, aspects of his gloomy report may have pointed to precisely the trends that reform has needed—a further erosion of the old economic order to make way for market economics. As the Lithuanians and the new city governments discovered in the spring of 1990, they could do business with each other, bypassing the central government; now, it seemed, farms, industrial plants, other regions, and republics were pursuing that path too. Ryzhkov's open puzzlement over the odd disappearance of the bountiful grain harvest suggested that many food suppliers were making their own deals and not telling the government.

Unquestionably, food shortages are the tinder of revolution. Lenin's fiery slogan in 1917 was "Peace, Bread, and Land." It was a potentially dangerous moment in September 1990 when Moscow began reporting bread shortages for the first time. But as the past two years have shown, acute shortages of many consumer goods in the Soviet Union do not necessarily trigger revolt. Soviet economic production is down, but not as disastrously as the barren shelves in Soviet stores indicate. The explanation of many Russians is that more and more goods are disappearing from state shops and reappearing in the underground economy. In the seventies, the black market was illegal, but even then it was so vast that I called it a countereconomy. In the nineties, it borders on the legal and is even more massive, perhaps 10–20 percent of the national output. People at all levels are ingenious at finding goods that are "nonexistent." Massive hoarding and under-the-table sales are a fact of life; some people have surprising private stocks. Whenever hard-to-get items appear unpredictably in stores, the lucky shoppers on hand buy out the supply, regardless of their own needs. That has been standard operating procedure for years, accentuated by the latest economic hardships.

A Moscow intellectual told Jim Hoagland of *The Washington Post* in mid-1990 that he had five refrigerators in his apartment, so that whenever perishable goods appeared on the market, he could hoard them. A senior Kremlin official told a Western businessman that one of his civil servants had stockpiled a five-year supply of soap. Some Western economic specialists believe that a twenty-million-ton shortfall of harvested grain that never made it into official channels in 1989 was sold in private trade by Soviet farmers.[12]

That does not relieve the desperate circumstances of the millions of people at the bottom, the pensioners, the rural poor, and unskilled workers. But by world standards, Russians are extraordinarily patient, willing to endure conditions that Westerners, or even Poles, would find intolerable. Moreover, Americans, convinced that the current Soviet economic agony cannot go on for much longer without a social explosion, sometimes forget how long America lay in the grip of the Great Depression: twelve years from the stock-market crash of 1929 until the beginning of World War II in 1941, with the numbers of unemployed ranging as high as sixteen million. Soviet society may be in the midst of such a long and severe stretch of hardship, and the level of political instability that goes with it.

Inevitably, the question arises whether Gorbachev can survive, or whether chaos will produce a new dictator who will turn the clock back to Stalinism.

For the outside world, the worst prospect would probably be the rise of a hard-line Russian nationalist fascism bred of economic chaos, military and political humiliation, and anger at the world's exploiting Soviet weakness—a parallel to Hitler's rise in Germany.

Yet paradoxically, as Gorbachev's mass popularity has fallen, he has become more secure in his position as chief of state. A cabal of Old Guard conservatives in the Politburo seems less threatening; his old Party rivals have been dispersed. Ivan Polozkov, the new Russian Communist Party chief, is a potential point man for a political coup by the right wing, but he does not yet have the stature to challenge Gorbachev, especially after the political rout of the Party's right wing at the Twenty-eighth Communist Party Congress. Moreover, Gorbachev's election to a five-year term as president has put him beyond the Party's power of removal.

Another black scenario that has worried Moscow intellectuals is that senior army generals, alarmed by mass civil unrest, would move against Gorbachev to install one of their own or a hard-line Party figure. Gorbachev has been careful to court the army, by including Defense Minister Dmitri Yazov on his presidential council; and he has kept the Party's political network in the army, as a check on its reliability. Gorbachev is reported to have even more carefully cultivated the KGB, long an institutional rival to the army, so that neither agency could be certain where the other would stand in a power struggle.

But most important, as several knowledgeable civilian politicians told me, the armed forces are no more a monolith than the Communist Party or Soviet society as a whole. The senior generals, the generation among whom the hard-line sentiments seem the strongest, are indoctrinated in the tradition of loyalty to the Party leader—Gorbachev. Among junior and field-grade officers, Party loyalty has less pull, but at these ranks there is a strong and active movement of political democrats and progressives, many of whom think the army should stay out of politics entirely. Another complication stems from the ethnic divisions that tear at the unity of the army as well as at Soviet society in general.

Anatoly Sobchak, who as the reform mayor of Leningrad would presumably be among the first officials arrested in a military takeover, scoffed at the idea of a military coup. His argument to me was that even desperate hard-liners dared not move because of internal political divisions in the armed forces—because they could not count on others to support a move against Gorbachev. I asked about repeated rumors that Colonel General Boris Gromov, former Soviet army commander in Afghanistan and more recently commander of the Kiev military district, was a potential focal point of army plotting. More senior generals, Sobchak told me, dismiss Gromov, who is in his forties, as "a mere boy."

"We have no one in the army strong enough and popular enough to try it," Sobchak said. "To take over the government, you have to have some idea of what to do. You have to be popular with the masses. I know the mood of our people. They would never accept it. The army leaders know that if they tried such a thing, the people would be out in the streets protesting. No, I do not think it will happen."[13]

If the military were tempted, they know that Gorbachev would be a formidable and cunning foe, especially hard to dislodge because of his election as president. Nor is it likely that he would allow civil unrest to reach a point where the army felt compelled to take over in order to preserve law and order. In Azerbaijan, Gorbachev showed willingness to use troops to put down civil strife, and presumably he would not hesitate to do so again, especially if he sensed that riots in the streets were putting his own survival—and the fate of his reforms—in jeopardy.

But assuming for a moment that Sobchak is wrong and a hard-liner did seize power, I cannot imagine a new Stalinist dictatorship. The Soviet system has already changed too much; too many people around the country in the institutions of government and the press now control elements of power for one man to gather all the strings of control. The new populists, Boris Yeltsin in the lead, have demanded that the military stay out of politics and that the Party break its ties with the military, and there is wide popular sympathy for those views. The breakdown of the economy, the erosion of discipline, the power of striking workers—all these are impediments to dictatorial rule. In one republic after another, a would-be dictator would meet mass discontent and resistance. Restoring right-wing totalitarian rule would take years of relentless purges—and I am skeptical that even what remains of the Communist Party, let alone the rest of Soviet society, would stomach that.

REFORM CAN OUTLIVE GORBACHEV

"The politics of the right has no future. Our future is left radicalism. The politics of our country has nowhere to go except to the left."[14]

That was the assessment given me by Interior Minister Vadim Bakatin on July 4, 1990, at the very moment when the right wing was riding high at the Communist Party Congress. I found this judgment especially significant, coming from Bakatin. He is the Soviet Union's top cop, a veteran Party boss from the provinces but more sophisticated than most, a moderate Communist leader who has won favor with both the Party's right wing and Gorbachev centrists.

In Soviet shorthand, Bakatin's term "left radicalism" was the direction staked out by Boris Yeltsin. It was also the direction in which Gorbachev felt pulled by events and by necessity toward the conclusion of his sixth year. Although he had helped bring the left-wing reformers into being and had sometimes blessed their politics, he had long resisted an open alliance.

Nonetheless, by the second half of 1990, Gorbachev was drawn to Yeltsin's politics. Instinct taught him to neutralize his most serious rivals by joining forces; and after Yeltsin's election as the political leader of the Russian republic, people all over the country talked of Yeltsin as a rival and potential successor to Gorbachev. That was something Gorbachev had to take seriously.

After all the Party's efforts to crush Yeltsin, his reemergence at the national leadership level made Gorbachev look, for the first time, less indispensable to the future of reform. And yet Gorbachev and Yeltsin were natural allies; they needed each other, and needed to overcome the bad personal chemistry of their past. As president, Yeltsin would lack something vital that Gorbachev had—the acceptance of the apparat and the military, the Party conservatives who so mistrusted and loathed Yeltsin. Facing such hostility as president, Yeltsin would dangerously polarize Soviet politics.

But Yeltsin had what Gorbachev most desperately lacked—a popular mandate. Yeltsin had risked what Gorbachev had not dared: testing his popularity with the voters. Yeltsin had run twice and come home with millions of votes; he had a mass following and legitimacy that Gorbachev needed. So a Yeltsin-Gorbachev alliance combined populism with establishment power; it was potentially the central symbol of the next phase of *perestroika*.

What is more, Yeltsin had a fresh dynamism that sometimes ebbed in Gorbachev. He had become the primary advocate for nationalist leaders around the country who were pressing for a looser confederation. Yeltsin had accepted Lithuania's bid for independence; he had provided the final straw that broke the blockade against that republic in early June 1990, announcing that Russia would not honor Gorbachev's embargo. Yeltsin had given his blessing to an economic free zone in Leningrad, and to a new independent television network. He had unveiled a plan for a five-hundred-day transition to a market economy: first, legalizing private property, then abolishing government subsidies and selling off state enterprises and stalled construction projects. Only toward the end, when other essential elements were in place, did Yeltsin intend to take the most controversial step—lifting government controls on prices.[15] Yeltsin employed other unconventional maneuvers: To give incentive to Russian farmers to bring in the fall harvest, he offered special coupons that guaranteed purchase of scarce consumer goods.[16]

On virtually every point, Gorbachev had been pushed to accommodate the positions taken by Yeltsin.

In fact, barring a massive upheaval brought on by economic depression, most of the prevailing trends of Soviet politics, as Gorbachev neared the end of his sixth year, pointed not toward retreat, as anxious Moscow intellectuals feared, but toward still further, bolder reforms.

The rudiments of a multiparty system were becoming visible; political pluralism was on the rise all around the country, while the Communist Party was losing mass support. The pressures for political decentralization were more insistent than ever, and Gorbachev was bending to them. The radical reformers in charge of city governments had seized the political initiative, and Gorbachev himself had moved to the left to make common cause with the radical reformers on many issues. One major danger was that they, like Gorbachev, might not be able to deliver economic results fast enough to satisfy the masses; another was that their market economics would produce such inequalities that a backlash would be provoked among ordinary workers who were still stuck in the mentality of "equal poverty for all."[17]

What was most significant was that the entire process of reform had gained a momentum of its own, a momentum that would outlive Gorbachev, whatever his personal fate might be. For the first time, there were political leaders who were committed to democratic reforms and who could be considered potential successors to Gorbachev—either in the near future (Yeltsin) or later on (Popov, Sobchak)—if he managed to finish out his presidential term to 1995. And the odds of Gorbachev's surviving that long politically seemed strong, certainly better than 50-50.

In 1988, I had gone to Moscow wondering whether Gorbachev could make *perestroika* work in the coming two or three years. I left thinking it would take five or ten years. After another two trips, I saw such an enormous social transformation under way that I understood it was bound to take two or three decades at least—a time frame far beyond the reach of any one leader.

Over that long a period, reform was bound to ebb and flow. I could conceive of a conservative retreat, especially in the face of economic disaster and social upheavals; Gorbachev himself might backtrack once again. But if there was a reversal, my sense was that it would be a temporary interruption in the long process of reform. Retreat could last for several years. But if so, my expectation would be that a new, younger generation of reformers—the Stankevich generation, perhaps—would be ready to resume reform's forward thrust. In sum, though the path was certain to be rocky, I came to feel that *perestroika* had a dynamism that assured its own permanence.

Gorbachev has changed our world more definitively than he has changed his own. The transformation that has taken place beyond Soviet borders is irreversible. Eastern Europe's economic future is uncertain, but its political future outside the Soviet empire is not in doubt. Gorbachev's acquiescence in the reunification of Germany and its membership in NATO cannot be revoked by a successor in the Kremlin. A political and historic divide has been crossed.

Given the turmoil inside the Soviet Union, the Soviet army cannot pose a credible military threat to the West or the United States in the years directly ahead. In both Moscow and Washington, the powerful economic demands to reduce military spending will only hasten the process of arms control and cutbacks in nuclear arsenals, and that is a self-reinforcing process. The popular hunger to seal the end of the Cold War cannot be resisted by leaders anywhere.

As if to prove that his intent was global, Gorbachev has not only relinquished the Kremlin's East European empire, but he has also changed its politics in the Third World. Most dramatically, he has withdrawn Soviet troops from Afghanistan. And in the wake of Iraq's invasion of Kuwait, he cut off Soviet arms sales to Iraqi dictator Saddam Hussein.

In all of his foreign-policy moves, and above all, in changing the nature of the Soviet system, what Gorbachev has done for us is change our national agenda. Thanks to Gorbachev's "new thinking," we have been allowed to move from a world dominated by the stark calculus of the arms race and the nuclear first strike, to one concerned primarily with the economics of world trade and competition, and to the issues of human poverty, global warming, the quality of life, and the care of the environment.

The process of change within the Soviet Union is primarily a matter for Soviets themselves; outside influence can only be marginal. But given the delicate balance in the Soviet economy today, the West has a stake—in its own self-interest—in seeing the process of *perestroika* carried forward. Under the new Soviet conditions, that does not mean that the West must ensure Gorbachev's survival or provide aid only to the national government. The rise to power of democratic reformers in the cities, in the Russian republic, in the Baltic republics, and in other regions provides new channels for Western aid and engagement for years to come. These may be more effective avenues in the early nineties for promoting democratic pluralism and market economics than the national government; and the success of regional leaders may determine the national leadership of the next generation. In the interim, Gorbachev still provides a vital protective umbrella for these emerging figures and their reforms.

Gorbachev's dominance of world affairs over the past six years is astonishing, given the weak hand he has had to play. For it is worth remembering that Gorbachev is the leader of a country whose supposed allies were quick to desert the moment they were given a chance; whose diverse nationalities challenge the national government and the fabric of national unity; whose single powerful Party elite constantly menaces the national leader; and whose economy is a disaster.

In spite of all these handicaps, to a remarkable degree Gorbachev has managed to command the political initiative not only in his own country but in the world at large. He has kept our attention riveted on the unfolding drama in the Soviet Union. And he has done it, I believe, by being willing to confront the most fundamental problems that trouble his people and that hold back his nation.

Facing the truth and publicly debating the nation's most acute and vexing difficulties is supposed to be the strength of democracies. Isn't it extraordinary that today this is being done not in the West but in the land of Stalin and Ivan the Terrible?

That is a point worth pondering in democratic societies, where political leaders have not been nearly so candid with their people, nor so daring in their politics.

What Gorbachev is attempting—on a grand scale and in the incredibly short span of one decade—is something genuinely new on this planet, and that explains both the uncertainty of the process and its compelling fascination.

History is full of men on horseback trampling fragile democracies underfoot. But there is no precedent for a single leader attempting the peaceful transition from a dictatorship to democracy.

BOOKS

Aslund, Anders. *Gorbachev's Struggle for Economic Reform.* Ithaca, N.Y.: Cornell University Press, 1989.

Bialer, Seweryn. *The Soviet Paradox: External Expansion & Internal Decline.* New York: Alfred A. Knopf, 1986.

———, ed. *Inside Gorbachev's Russia.* Boulder, Col.: Westview Press, 1989.

Brown, Archie, ed. *Political Leadership in the Soviet Union.* Bloomington, Ind.: Indiana University Press, 1989.

Brzezinski, Zbigniew. *The Grand Failure.* New York: Charles Scribner's Sons, 1989.

Cohen, Stephen F., and Katrina vanden Heuvel. *Voices of Glasnost.* New York: W. W. Norton, 1989.

Directory of Soviet "Informal" Political Organizations and Samizdat Publications. Chicago: Soviet-American Review, 1988.

Doder, Dusko. *Shadows and Whispers.* New York: Random House, 1986.

——— and Louise Branson. *Gorbachev: Heretic in the Kremlin.* New York: Viking, 1990.

Goldman, Marshall I. *Gorbachev's Challenge.* New York: W. W. Norton, 1987.

———. *U.S.S.R. in Crisis.* New York: W. W. Norton, 1983.

Gorbachev, Mikhail S. *Perestroika.* New York: Harper & Row, 1987.

Grossman, Vasily. *Forever Flowing.* New York: Harper & Row, 1972.

Guroff, Greg. *Entrepreneurship and Economic Innovation in Imperial and Soviet Russia.* Princeton, N.J.: Princeton University Press, 1983.

Hewett, Ed A. *Reforming the Soviet Economy: Equality Versus Efficiency.* Washington, D.C.: Brookings, 1988.

Hosking, Geoffrey. *The Awakening of the Soviet Union.* Cambridge, Mass.: Harvard University Press, 1990.

Lenin, Vladimir I. *Collected Works,* Vol. XXX. Moscow: Progress Publishers, 1965.

————. *Collected Works*, Vol. XXV. Moscow: Progress Publishers, 1964.

Lewin, Moshe. *The Gorbachev Phenomenon.* Berkeley, Cal.: University of California Press, 1988.

Mandelstam, Nadezhda. *Hope Against Hope.* New York: Atheneum, 1970.

Marx, Karl, and Friedrich Engels. *Collected Works*, Vol. I. New York: International Publishers, 1975.

Medvedev, Roy. *Let History Judge: The Origins and Consequences of Stalinism* (revised and expanded edition). New York: Columbia University Press, 1989.

————. *On Stalin and Stalinism.* Oxford: Oxford University Press, 1973.

Medvedev, Zhores. *Soviet Agriculture.* New York: W. W. Norton, 1987.

————. *Gorbachev.* New York: W. W. Norton, 1986.

————. *Nuclear Disaster in the Urals.* New York: W. W. Norton, 1979.

Mickiewicz, Ellen. *Split Signals: Television and Politics in the Soviet Union.* New York: Oxford University Press, 1988.

Mirsky, D. S. *A History of Russian Literature.* New York: Vintage Russian Library, 1958.

Morrison, Donald, ed. *Mikhail S. Gorbachev: An Intimate Biography.* New York: Time, Inc., 1988.

Nagel. *Nagel's Encyclopedic Guide: U.S.S.R.* Geneva: Nagel, 1970.

Nahaylo, Bogdan, and Victor Swoboda. *Soviet Disunion: A History of the Nationalities Problem in the USSR.* New York: The Free Press, 1990.

Nove,Alec.*Glasnost in Action: Cultural Renaissance in Russia.* Boston: Unwin Hyman, 1989.

————. *An Economic History of the U.S.S.R.* (2nd revised edition). Middlesex, England: Penguin, 1982.

Popov, Gavril. *Upravleniye Ekonomikoi—Ekonomicheskiye Metody.* Moscow: Ekonomika, 1985.

Pozner, Vladimir. *Parting with Illusions.* New York: Atlantic Monthly Press, 1990.

Remington, Thomas F. *The Truth of Authority: Ideology and Communication in the Soviet Union.* Pittsburgh: University of Pittsburgh Press, 1988.

Robinson, Geroid Tanquary. *Rural Russia Under the Old Regime.* Berkeley, Cal.: University of California Press, 1969.

Sel'skokhozaistvennoye Provisvodstvo v Lichnikh Podsovnikh Khozaistvakh Naseleniya. Moscow: Goskomstat, 1989.

Serfaty, Simon. *France, DeGaulle, & Europe.* Baltimore: Johns Hopkins University Press, 1968.

Shelton, Judy. *The Coming of the Soviet Crash.* New York: The Free Press, 1989.

Shmelyov, Nikolai, and Vladimir Popov. *The Turning Point: Revitalizing the Soviet Economy.* New York: Doubleday, 1989.

Simis, Konstantin. *USSR: The Corrupt Society.* New York: Simon and Schuster, 1982.

Smith, Hedrick. *The Russians* (revised edition). New York: Ballantine, 1984.

Solzhenitsyn, Aleksandr I. *Letter to the Supreme Leaders.* New York: Harper & Row, 1974.

Sumner, B. H. *A Short History of Russia.* New York: Harcourt, Brace, 1949.

Tocqueville, Alexis de. *The Old Regime and the Revolution.* New York: Harper & Brothers, 1856.

Utechin, S. V. *A Concise Encyclopedia of Russia.* New York: E. P. Dutton, 1964.

Vernadsky, George. *A History of Russia.* New Haven, Conn.: Yale University Press, 1954.

Walker, Martin. *The Harper Independent Traveler: The Soviet Union.* New York: Harper & Row, 1989.
———. *The Waking Giant.* New York: Pantheon Books, 1986.
Yanov, Alexander. *The Russian Challenge.* Oxford: Basil Blackwell, 1987.
Yeltsin, Boris. *Against the Grain.* New York: Summit Books, 1990.

ARTICLES

Abalkin, Leonid. "Not Sharing, but Earning." *Ogonek,* Oct. 7–14, 1989.
Andreyev, Sergei. "The Power Structure and Problems of Society." *Neva,* No. 1, Jan. 1989.
Andreyeva, Nina. "I Cannot Forsake Principles." *Sovetskaya Rossiya,* Mar. 13, 1988.
Aslund, Anders. "Gorbachev: Governing on the Razor's Edge." *The Washington Post,* Jan. 28, 1990, pp. C1–C2.
Berdyayev, Nikolai. "Man's Fate in the Modern World." *Novy Mir,* No. 1, 1989.
Bialer, Seweryn, and Joan Afferica. "The Genesis of Gorbachev's World." *Foreign Affairs,* Vol. 64, No. 3, America and the World, 1985.
Borovik, Artyom. "Diary of a Reporter." *Ogonek,* Nos. 28, 29, and 30, Jul. 1987.
Breslauer, George W. "Evaluating Gorbachev as a Leader." *Soviet Economy,* Vol. 5, No. 4, Oct.–Dec. 1989.
Brown, Archie. "Political Change in the Soviet Union: Movement Toward Democracy." *The World Policy Journal,* Vol. 6, No. 3, Summer 1989.
———. "Gorbachev: New Man in the Kremlin." *Problems of Communism,* May–June 1985.
Brumberg, Abraham. "Moscow: The Struggle for Reform." *New York Review of Books,* Mar. 30, 1989.
Brzezinski, Zbigniew. "Post-Communist Nationalism." *Foreign Affairs,* Vol. 68, No. 5, Winter 1989–90.
Condee, Nancy, and Vladimir Padunov. "The Frontiers of Soviet Culture: Reaching the Limits?" *The Harriman Institute Forum,* Vol. 1, No. 5, May 1988.
Dobbs, Michael. "*Perestroika* at a Crossroads in the Soviet Heartland." *The Washington Post,* Jul. 1, 1990, pp. A1, A30.
———. "Gorbachev's Other Face: Lenin Heir and Savior of Soviet Communism." *The International Herald Tribune,* Sept. 22, 1989, pp. 1, 8.
———. "Separatism in Azerbaijan Growing Since Crackdown." *The Washington Post,* Feb. 16, 1989, pp. A1, A36–37.
Dunlop, John B. "The Contemporary Russian Nationalist Spectrum." *Radio Liberty Research Bulletin: Russian Nationalism Today,* Dec. 19, 1988.
———. "Soviet Cultural Politics." *Problems of Communism,* Nov.–Dec. 1987.
Fairbanks, Charles H., Jr. "Gorbachev's Cultural Revolution." *Commentary,* Aug. 1989.
———. "The Soviet Elections in Gorbachev's Political Strategy." Unpublished paper, Summer 1989.
Feshbach, Murray. "Demographic Trends in the Soviet Union: Serious Implications for the Soviet Military." *NATO Review,* Oct. 1989.
———. *Soviet Military Health Issues.* Washington, D.C.: Joint Economic Committee of the U.S. Congress, Fall 1987.

———. "The Age Structure of Soviet Population." *Soviet Economy*, Vol. 1, No. 2, Apr.–June 1985.

———. *Population Trends and Dilemmas.* Washington, D.C.: The Population Reference Bureau, Inc., Aug. 1982.

Fierman, William. "*Glasnost* in Practice: The Uzbek Experience." *Central Asian Survey*, Vol. 8, No. 2, 1989.

Fukuyama, Francis. "The End of History." *The National Interest*, No. 16, Summer 1989.

Goble, Paul. "Gorbachev: Facing the Nationality Nightmare." *The Washington Post*, Mar. 25, 1990, pp. C1, C2.

———. "Soviet Ethnic Politics." *Problems of Communism*, Jul.–Aug. 1989.

———. "The End of the 'National Question': Ideological Decay and Ethnic Relations in the U.S.S.R." Unpublished paper, 1989.

———. "Three Realities in Search of a Theory: Nationalities and the Soviet Future." Unpublished paper, 1989.

Gorbachev, Mikhail S. "Merakh Pseldovataln'novo Osyushesvleniya Agrarnoi Politiki KPSS na Sovremennom Etape." *Izbranniye, rechy i stat'i*, Moscow, 1987.

Hammer, Darrell P. " 'Glasnost' and 'The Russian Idea.' " *Radio Liberty Research Bulletin: Russian Nationalism Today*, Dec. 19, 1988.

Hewett, Ed A. "Is Soviet Socialism Reformable?" *SAIS Review*, Vol. 10, No. 2, Summer/Fall 1990.

———. "American and Western European Approaches to the Soviet Union: Economic Issues." Lecture for the Aspen Institute Conference on U.S.-Soviet Relations, Dubrovnik, Yugoslavia, Aug. 27–31, 1989.

———. "The Dynamics of Economic Reform." Remarks at the conference "Soviet Domestic Change and Geopolitical Strategy Under Gorbachev," Johns Hopkins School of Advanced International Studies, Washington, D.C., Feb. 16–17, 1989.

———. "*Perestroyka* and the Congress of People's Deputies." *Soviet Economy*, Vol. 5, No. 1, Jan.–Mar. 1989.

———. "Gorbachev's Economic Strategy: A Preliminary Assessment." *Soviet Economy*, Vol. 1, No. 4, Oct.–Dec. 1985.

Hough, Jerry F. "Why Gorby is Defying the Pundits' Predictions." *The Washington Post*, Feb. 11, 1990, pp. C1, C4.

———. "Gorbachev's Politics." *Foreign Affairs*, Winter 1989–90.

———. "The Politics of Successful Economic Reform." *Soviet Economy*, Vol. 5, No. 1, Jan.–Mar. 1989.

———. "The Politics of the 19th Party Conference." *Soviet Economy*, Vol. 4, No. 2, Apr.–June 1988.

Jones, Anthony, and William Moskoff. "New Cooperatives in the USSR." *Problems of Communism*, Nov.–Dec., 1989.

Kaiser, Robert G. "Red Intrigue: How Gorbachev Outfoxed His Kremlin Rivals." *The Washington Post*, June 12, 1988, pp. C1, C2.

Keller, Bill. "How Gorbachev Rejected Plan to 'Shock Treat' the Economy." *The New York Times*, May 14, 1990, pp. A1, A10.

———. "Soviet Economy: A Shattered Dream." *The New York Times*, May 13, 1990, pp. A1, A12.

———. "Did Moscow Incite Azerbaijanis? Some See a Plot." *The New York Times*, Feb. 19, 1990, p. A8.

———. "Russian Nationalists: Yearning for an Iron Hand." *The New York Times Magazine*, Jan. 28, 1990.

Klyamkin, Igor. "Why It Is Difficult to Speak the Truth." *Novy Mir*, No. 2, Feb. 1989.

Lapidus, Gail W. "Gorbachev and the National Question." *Soviet Economy*, Vol. 5, No. 3, Jul.–Sept. 1989.

———. "Gorbachev and Reform of the Soviet System." *Daedalus*, Spring 1987.

Legvold, Robert. "The Revolution in Soviet Foreign Policy." *Foreign Affairs*, Vol. 68, No. 1, America and the World, 1988–89.

Menashe, Louis. "Tinker on the Roof." *Tikkun*, Vol. 3, No. 5, Sept.–Oct. 1988.

———. "Repentance." *Cineaste*, Vol. XVI, No. 3, 1988.

———. "*Glasnost* in Soviet Cinema." *Cineaste*, Vol. XVI, No. 2, 1987–88.

Morrow, Lance. "The Unlikely Patron of Change." *Time*, Jan. 1, 1990.

Nitze, Paul H. "Gorbachev's Plan for a Communist Comeback." *The Washington Post*, Jan. 10, 1990.

Parrott, Bruce. "Gorbachev's Gamble: Political, Economic, and Ethnic Challenges to Soviet Reform." *SAIS Review*, Vol. 10, No. 2, Summer/Fall 1990.

———. "Soviet National Security Under Gorbachev." *Problems of Communism*, Nov.–Dec. 1988.

Reddaway, Peter. "Life After Gorbachev: The Soviets' Grim Future." *The Washington Post*, Nov. 26, 1989, pp. C1–C2.

———. "The Threat to Gorbachev." *New York Review of Books*, Aug. 17, 1989.

Remington, Thomas F. "Intellectuals, the 'Middle Class,' and the Drive for Reform." Paper presented to the conference "Soviet Domestic Change and Geopolitical Strategy Under Gorbachev," Johns Hopkins School of Advanced International Studies, Washington, D.C., Feb. 16–17, 1989.

Remnick, David. "Gorbachev: The Glow Is Gone." *The Washington Post*, May 27, 1990, pp. B1, B4.

———. "Comrade Personality." *Esquire*, Feb. 1990.

———. "The Cultivation of Young Gorbachev." *The Washington Post*, Dec. 1, 1989, p. B8.

Ruble, Blair. "The Social Dimensions of *Perestroika.*" *Soviet Economy*, Vol. 3, No. 2, Apr.–June 1987.

Schmemann, Serge. "The Emergence of Gorbachev." *The New York Times Magazine*, Mar. 3, 1985.

Schroeder, Gertrude E. "The Role of Property in Communist Countries: Past, Present, and Future." Unpublished paper, University of Virginia, Aug. 1988.

———. "Anatomy of Gorbachev's Economic Reform." *Soviet Economy*, Vol. 3, No. 3, Jul.–Sept. 1987.

———. "Gorbachev: 'Radically' Implementing Brezhnev's Reforms." *Soviet Economy*, Vol. 2, No. 4, Oct.–Dec. 1986.

Selyunin, Vasily. "Sources." *Novy Mir*, No. 5, May 1988.

Semyonov, V. "Ukrepleniye Ekonomiki Kolkhozov i Sovkhozov." *Finansy SSSR*, No. 9, 1985.

Sheehy, Gail. "Gorbachev, Red Star: The Shaping of the Man Who Managed the World." *Vanity Fair*, Feb. 1990.

Sherlock, Thomas. "Politics and History Under Gorbachev." *Problems of Communism*, May–Aug. 1988.

Shipler, David. "Between Dictatorship and Anarchy." *The New Yorker*, June 25, 1990.

Shmelyov, Nikolai. "New Anxieties." *Novy Mir*, No. 4, Apr. 1988.

———. "Advances and Debts." *Novy Mir*, No. 6, June 1987.

Sinyavsky, Andrei. "Russian Nationalism." *Radio Liberty Research Bulletin: Russian Nationalism Today*, Dec. 19, 1988.

Starr, S. Frederick. "Party Animals." *The New Republic*, June 26, 1989.

———. "A Usable Past." *The New Republic*, May 15, 1989.

———. "Soviet Union: A Civil Society." *Foreign Policy*, No. 70, Spring 1988.

Teague, Elizabeth, and Dawn Mann. "Gorbachev's Dual Role." *Problems of Communism*, Jan.–Feb. 1990.

Tolz, Vera. "Informal Groups and Soviet Politics in 1989." *Radio Liberty Report on the USSR*, Nov. 24, 1989.

———. "Informal Groups in the USSR." *Washington Quarterly*, Winter 1988.

Treml, Vladimir G. "The Most Recent Input-Output Table: A Milestone in Soviet Statistics." *Soviet Economy*, Vol. 5, No. 4, Oct.–Dec. 1989.

Tsipko, Aleksandr. "We Should Not Fear the Truth." *Nauka i Zhizn*, No. 2, Feb. 1989.

———. "Egotism of Dreamers." *Nauka i Zhizn*, No. 1, Jan. 1989.

———. "Perversities of Socialism." *Nauka i Zhizn*, No. 12, Dec. 1988.

———. "The Roots of Stalinism." *Nauka i Zhizn*, No. 11, Nov. 1988.

Van Atta, Don. " 'Full-Scale, Like Collectivization, but Without Collectivization's Excesses': The Campaign to Introduce the Family and Lease Contract in Soviet Agriculture." Revised version of paper prepared for annual meeting of American Association for the Advancement of Slavic Studies, Chicago, Nov. 2–5, 1989.

———. "Theorists of Agrarian *Perestroika*." *Soviet Economy*, Vol. 5, No. 1, Jan.–Mar. 1989.

Woll, Josephine. " *'Glasnost'* and Soviet Culture." *Problems of Communism*, Nov.–Dec. 1989.

Yakovlev, Yegor. "To Halt the Pendulum Is to Stop the Clock." *Moscow News*, Oct. 29–Nov. 5, 1989.

Yanov, Alexander. "Russian Nationalism as the Ideology of Counterreform." *Radio Liberty Research Bulletin: Russian Nationalism Today*, Dec. 19, 1988.

Z. "To the Stalin Mausoleum." *Daedalus*, Winter 1990.

Zavslavskaya, Tatyana. "The Novosibirsk Report." *Survey*, Vol. 28, No. 1, Spring 1984.

NOTES

Author's Note: While many of the translations are my own, I have relied extensively on the *Foreign Broadcast Information Service* and the *Current Digest of the Soviet Press,* referred to in the notes as *FBIS* and *CDSP.* To clarify the distinction between *interviews* and *conversations* in citations: In my *interviews,* I used video or audio recording devices and worked from transcripts; in *conversations,* I took handwritten notes. If the citation refers to *interview* or *conversation,* it is with the author, unless otherwise specified.

INTRODUCTION: AFTER THE WALL CAME DOWN

1. Zinovy Yuryev, conversation with the author, May 27, 1988.

1. THE HIDDEN WELLSPRINGS OF REFORM

1. Mikhail Gorbachev, *Perestroika* (New York: Harper & Row, 1987), pp. 23–24.
2. Tatyana Zaslavskaya, interview with the author, Sept. 26, 1989.
3. Abel Aganbegyan and Timur Timofeyev, director of the Institute of International Labor Studies, interviews with the author, Mar. 7–9, 1988.
4. Zaslavskaya, *op. cit.*
5. "The Novosibirsk Report," in *Survey,* Vol. 28, No. 1 (Spring 1984), pp. 83–108. The formal title of the paper, according to Zaslavskaya, was "The Improvement of Productive Relations and the Social Mechanism of Economic Development."
6. Dusko Doder, *Shadows and Whispers* (New York: Random House, 1986), pp. 169–70, 186–90.
7. "The Novosibirsk Report," *op. cit.*
8. Zaslavskaya, *op. cit.*

2. THE BREZHNEV GENERATION: SLIDE INTO CYNICISM

1. See Marshall I. Goldman, *U.S.S.R. in Crisis* (New York: W. W. Norton, 1983), pp. 109–11. Also, interviews with the author, Jan. 1984.
2. Moshe Lewin, *The Gorbachev Phenomenon* (Berkeley: University of California Press, 1988), p. 49.

3. *Ibid.*, pp. 86, 89, 91, 93, 95.

4. Martin Walker, *The Waking Giant* (New York: Pantheon Books, 1986), pp. xx–xxi.

5. Leonid Dobrokhotov, interview with the author, Sept. 28, 1989.

6. *Ibid.*, Jan. 8, 1990.

7. Hedrick Smith, *The Russians*, rev. ed. (New York: Ballantine, 1984), pp. 684–98.

8. Roy Medvedev, interview with the author, Oct. 9, 1989.

9. Sergei Stankevich, interview with the author, Jan. 8, 1990.

10. Aleksandr Yakovlev, interview with the author, Oct. 9, 1989.

11. Dobrokhotov, interview, Sept. 28, 1989.

12. Vadim Medvedev, *The Administration of Socialist Production: Problems of Theory and Practice* (Moscow: Publishing House of Political Literature, 1983).

13. Anders Aslund, *Gorbachev's Struggle for Economic Reform* (Ithaca, New York: Cornell University Press, 1989), pp. 35–36.

14. Dobrokhotov, interview, Sept. 28, 1989.

15. Yakovlev, *op. cit.*

3. GORBACHEV AND THE KHRUSHCHEV GENERATION

1. Vadimir Tikhonov, interview with the author, Sept. 26, 1989.

2. This account of the Gorbachev family comes from the author's interviews with Gorbachev's uncle Sergei Gopkolo and several elderly residents of Privolnoye, Nikolai Lubenko, Pavel Ignatenko, and Aleksandr Yakovenko, on Dec. 6, 1988; and with a close family friend, Grigory Gorlov, on Dec. 7, 1988.

3. Gorlov, interview with the author, Sept. 8, 1989.

4. Gopkolo, *op. cit.*

5. Zhores A. Medvedev, *Gorbachev* (New York: W. W. Norton, 1986), pp. 22–28.

6. *Ibid.*, p. 26.

7. Antonina Shcherbakova, interview with the author, May 30, 1989.

8. Gorlov, interview with the author, Dec. 8, 1988.

9. Yakovenko, interview with the author, May 30, 1989.

10. *Ibid.*, Dec. 6, 1988.

11. Lyubov Grudchenko, interview with the author, May 30, 1989.

12. Mariya Grevtsova, interview with the author, Dec. 6, 1988.

13. David Remnick, "Comrade Personality," *Esquire*, Feb. 1990, p. 78.

14. *Ibid.*, "The Cultivation of Young Gorbachev," *The Washington Post*, Dec. 1, 1989, p. B8.

15. Ivan Manuilov, conversation with Louis Menashe, Dec. 6, 1988.

16. Mikhail Gorbachev, interview with *Unita*, May 20, 1987, *FBIS*, May 20, 1987, p. R5.

17. Gopkolo, interview, Dec. 6, 1988.

18. Gorlov, interview, Dec. 7, 1988.

19. This description of university life comes from the author's group interview with several of Gorbachev's classmates, Nadezhda Mikhailova, Vladimir Lieberman, Rudolf Kulchanov, Vladimir Kuzmin, and Natalya Rimachevskaya, May 23, 1989; and from a separate interview with Zdenek Mlynar, Mar. 29, 1989.

20. Kulchanov, *op. cit.*

21. Mlynar, *op. cit.*

22. Lieberman and Kulchanov, interview, May 24, 1989.

23. Lieberman, interview, May 24, 1989.

24. Mlynar, *op. cit.*

25. Fridrikh Neznansky, participant in discussion in *Possev*, Nov. 4, 1985, p. 22.

26. Lev Yudovich, in "Gorbachev, New Chief of Russia, May Make a Tougher Adversary," *The Wall Street Journal*, Mar. 12, 1985, p. 1.

27. Mikhailova, Kulchanov, Kuzmin, interview, May 24, 1989.

28. Mlynar, *op. cit.*
29. Neznansky, *op. cit.*
30. Mlynar, *op. cit.*
31. Nikolai Shishlin, conversation with the author, Apr. 30, 1990.
32. Dusko Doder and Louise Branson, *Gorbachev: Heretic in the Kremlin* (New York: Viking, 1990), pp. 2–4.
33. Gorbachev, *FBIS*, Nov. 3, 1987, p. 44.
34. Aleksandr Yakovlev, interview with the author, Oct. 9, 1989.
35. Roy Medvedev, interview with the author, Oct. 9, 1989.
36. Kulchanov, interview, May 24, 1989.

4. HOW DID GORBACHEV MAKE IT TO THE TOP?

1. Zinovy Yuryev, conversation with the author, June 6, 1988.
2. Vladimir and Lydiya Kolodichuk, interview with the author, Dec. 5, 1988.
3. Grigory Gorlov, conversation with the author, Dec. 7, 1988.
4. Viktor Nikitin and Valentina Brelova, interview with the author, Dec. 7, 1988.
5. Gorlov, conversation with the author, Mar. 14, 1990.
6. Brelova, *op. cit.*
7. Zdenek Mlynar, interview with the author, Mar. 29, 1989.
8. Mikhail Novikov, interview with Joyce Barnathan, spring 1988, as research for the author's documentary films on Gorbachev and *perestroika.*
9. Valentin Mezin, interviews with the author, Dec. 6–8, 1988.
10. Konstantin Nikitin, interview with the author, Dec. 6, 1988; and Vsvelod Mukakhovsky and Aleksandr Nikonov, interviews with the author, Apr. 13, 1989.
11. Viktor Postnikov, interview with the author, Dec. 5, 1988.
12. *Ibid.,* Sept. 26, 1989.
13. Gorbachev, "Merakh Psledovateln'novo Osyushesvleniya Agrarnoi Politiki KPSS na Sovremennom Etape," *Izbranniye, rechy i stat'i* (Moscow, 1987), pp. 180–200.
14. *Ibid.,* p. 200.
15. *Ibid.,* p. 199.
16. Postnikov, interview, Sept. 26, 1989.
17. Donald Morrison, ed., *Mikhail S. Gorbachev: An Intimate Biography* (New York: Time, Inc., 1988), p. 103.
18. Yulian Semyonov, interview with the author, Oct. 18, 1989.
19. Sasha Gelman, interview with the author, Sept. 18, 1989.
20. Nikolai Shishlin, interview with the author, Nov. 30, 1988.
21. Vladimir Tikhonov, interview with the author, Sept. 29, 1989.
22. Tatyana Zaslavskaya, interview with the author, Sept. 26, 1989. She said the six were Nikolai Federenko, Aleksandr Nikonov, Vladimir Mozhen, Ivan Lukianov, Tikhonov, and herself.
23. Zaslavskaya, interview, Sept. 26, 1989.
24. Postnikov, interview, Sept. 26, 1989.
25. Roald Sagdeyev, interview with the author, Dec. 15, 1988.
26. Yevgeny Velikhov, conversation with the author, June 6, 1988.
27. Valentin Lazutkin, conversation with the author, Dec. 14, 1988.
28. Aleksandr Yakovlev, interview with the author, Oct. 9, 1989.
29. Gorbachev, speech to scientific and cultural leaders, Jan. 6, 1989, *FBIS*, Jan. 9, 1989, p. 53.
30. Dusko Doder, *Shadows and Whispers* (New York: Random House, 1986), p. 267.
31. Mikhail Gorbachev, *Perestroika* (New York: Harper & Row, 1987), p. 13.
32. Gorbachev, speech, Jan. 6, 1989, *FBIS*, Jan. 9, 1989, p. 52.

5. "WHAT DO YOU THINK?"

1. Yuri Levada, conversation with the author, Mar. 15, 1990.

2. Leonid Sedov, interview with the author, Sept. 25, 1989.

3. Vladimir Shlyapentokh, conversation with the author, Mar. 23, 1990.

4. Levada, op. cit.

5. Levada, Alex Levinson, Lev Gudkov, Aleksandr Golov, Sedov, Boris Dubin, and Nadya Zorlaya, interview with the author, Sept. 25, 1989.

6. Levada, conversation, Mar. 15, 1990.

7. Nadezhda Mandelstam, Hope Against Hope (New York: Atheneum, 1970), p. 13.

8. These polling figures were provided to me by Gudkov, Levinson, and Levada, of the Center for the Study of Public Opinion on Social and Economic Issues, on Apr. 11, 1989, and were later updated.

9. Actually, the Institute of Sociological Research had conducted a poll of 940 Muscovites in May 1988 for The New York Times and CBS News, and found that three of four wanted multicandidate elections and doubted that the Soviet one-party system would permit Gorbachev's promised democratization. See The New York Times, May 26, 1988, p. A1.

6. *GLASNOST:* A MARRIAGE OF POLITICAL CONVENIENCE

1. Gorbachev, speech to Nineteenth All-Union Conference of the Communist Party of the Soviet Union, June 28, 1988, Pravda, June 29, 1988, p. 4.

2. Vladimir Pozner, conversation with the author, June 6, 1988.

3. Karl Marx, "Debates on Freedom of the Press and Publication of Proceedings of the Assembly of the States," Karl Marx: 1835–43, pp. 167–68, Vol. I of Karl Marx and Frederick Engels, Collected Works (New York: International Publishers, 1975).

4. The New York Times, May 22, 1990, p. A10.

5. Gorbachev, speech, Dec. 10, 1984, FBIS, Dec. 11, 1984, p. R6.

7. TROUBADOURS OF TRUTH

1. Tankred Golenpolsky, conversation with the author, June 5, 1988.

2. See Louis Menashe, "Tinker on the Roof," Tikkun, Vol. 3, No. 5, Sept.–Oct. 1988; "Repentance," Cineaste, Vol. XVI, No. 3, 1988; and "Glasnost in Soviet Cinema," Cineaste, Vol. XVI, No. 2, 1987–88, pp. 28–33.

3. The Washington Post, May 25, 1990, p. D2.

4. Vasily Grossman, Forever Flowing (New York: Harper & Row, 1972), p. 203.

5. Artyom Borovik, "Diary of a Reporter," Ogonek, Nos. 28, 29, 30, Jul. 1987.

6. Ibid.

7. Vitaly Korotich, conversation with the author, June 7, 1988.

8. Izvestia Ts.K. KPSS, No. 1, 1989, pp. 138–39.

9. Vasily Selyunin, "Sources," Novy Mir, No. 5, May 1988, p. 169.

10. Aleksandr Tsipko, "The Roots of Stalinism," Nauka i Zhizn, No. 11, Nov. 1988, in Current Digest of the Soviet Press, Vol. XLI, No. 10, Apr. 5, 1989, p. 3.

11. Eduard Shevardnadze, conversation with the author, Dec. 7, 1987.

12. Vasily Pichul, interview with the author, Apr. 29, 1989.

13. Arkady Ruderman, remarks at Yaroslavl Film Club, Sept. 10, 1989.

14. Ibid.

15. Ibid., interview with Sherry Jones, Sept. 13, 1989.

16. The New York Times, June 30, 1988, p. A1.

17. Gorbachev, June 28, 1988, Pravda, June 29, 1988, p. 2.

18. The New York Times, June 30, 1988, p. A13.

8. STALINISM: THE OPEN WOUND

1. Andrei Smirnov, conversation with the author, Mar. 15, 1990.
2. Nina Soboleva, conversation with the author, Apr. 24, 1989.
3. Zenon Poznyak, interview with the author, Apr. 23, 1989.
4. *Ibid.*, Sept. 16, 1989.
5. *Ibid.*, Apr. 23, 1989.
6. Maya Klishtornaya, interview with the author, Sept. 17, 1989.
7. Poznyak, interview, Sept. 16, 1989.
8. *Ibid.*
9. *Ibid.*, Apr. 23, 1989.
10. *Ibid.*
11. *Ibid.*, Sept. 16, 1989.
12. *Ibid.*, Apr. 23, 1989.
13. Yuri Solomonov, conversation with the author, Apr. 27, 1989.
14. Andrei Borovik-Romanov, conversation with the author, June 2, 1988.
15. Soboleva, *op. cit.*
16. Alla Nikitina, conversation with the author, Apr. 21, 1989.
17. Genrikh Borovik, conversation with the author, June 6, 1988.
18. This polling was done through "Project Understanding," a Soviet-American effort jointly run by the Institute of Sociology, Moscow, and Marttila & Kiley, Inc., of Boston. John Marttila shared the results with the author, Apr. 14, 1989.
19. Vadim Andreyenkov, conversation with the author, Apr. 23, 1989.
20. Nina Andreyeva, "I Cannot Forsake Principles," *Sovetskaya Rossiya,* Mar. 13, 1988, in *CDSP,* Apr. 27, 1988, pp. 1, 3.
21. *Ibid.*, p. 4.
22. Valentin Chikin, interview with the author, Apr. 29, 1989.
23. For an excellent early account of this maneuvering, see Robert Kaiser, "Red Intrigue: How Gorbachev Outfoxed His Kremlin Rivals," *The Washington Post,* June 12, 1988, p. C1.
24. Solomonov, conversation with the author, Apr. 29, 1989.
25. Vitaly Korotich, conversation with the author, June 7, 1988.
26. Roy Medvedev, conversation with the author, Dec. 14, 1988.
27. "The Principles of Restructuring: The Revolutionary Nature of Thinking and Acting," *Pravda,* Apr. 5, 1988, p. 2, *CDSP,* Vol. XL, No. 14, May 4, 1988, pp. 1–5.
28. Vladimir Krushin, interview with the author, Sept. 23, 1989.
29. David Remnick, "Gorbachev's Furious Critic," *The Washington Post,* Jul. 28, 1989, p. C1.
30. Andreyeva and Krushin, interview with the author, Sept. 23, 1989.
31. Galina Klokova, interview with the author, Sept. 15, 1989.
32. Oleg Voloboyev, interview with the author, Sept. 15, 1989.
33. Roy Medvedev, author of the most authoritative Soviet study of Stalinism, *Let History Judge* (New York: Knopf, 1972), updated his work in 1989 and recently estimated the Stalinist death toll at forty million. See *Argumenty i Fakty,* No. 5, 1989.
34. Viktoriya Kulikova, interview with the author, May 3, 1989.
35. *Ibid.*, interview with Sherry Jones, Sept. 9, 1989.
36. Leonid Milgram, interview with the author, Sept. 26, 1989.
37. *Ibid.*, interview with Sherry Jones, Sept. 14, 1989.
38. Milgram and students, filmed by Foster Wiley, Sept. 28, 1989.

9. THE MEDIA VERSUS THE APPARAT

1. Bella Kurkova, interview with the author, Sept. 22, 1989.
2. *Ibid.*, conversation with the author, Apr. 4, 1989.

3. *Leningradskaya Pravda*, Apr. 6, 1989.

4. Kurkova, interview, Sept. 22, 1989.

5. Officially at that time, 800 rubles was $1,333, unofficially $133, more than three times a good worker's salary.

6. Kurkova, conversation with the author, Apr. 5, 1989.

7. Zoya Belyayeva, Sasha Krivonos, Natasha Sereva, Tatyana Smorodinskaya, interview with Sherry Jones and Louis Menashe, Sept. 20, 1989.

8. Aleksandr Nevzorov, conversation with the author, Sept. 22, 1989.

9. Tamara Maksimova and Vladimir Maksimov, conversation with the author, Apr. 4, 1989.

10. *Fifth Wheel* footage shown the author, Apr. 4–5, 1989.

11. Kurkova, interview, Sept. 22, 1989.

12. *Ibid.*

13. *Ibid.*

14. Viktor Senin and Kurkova, interview with the author, Sept. 22, 1989.

15. Aleksandr Melnikov, interview with the author, Sept. 5, 1989.

16. Gennady Metyakhin, conversations with the author, Sept. 3–5, 1989.

17. Aleksandr Tsvetkov, Valentina Kurikalova, Dmitri Pushkar, and Yevgeny Kovalev, conversations with the author, May 5 and 11, 1989.

18. Valentin Lazuktin, conversation with the author, Dec. 5, 1988.

19. See Ellen Mickiewicz, *Split Signals: Television and Politics in the Soviet Union* (New York: Oxford University Press, 1988), pp. 89–98.

20. "Dissident Yelena Bonner and the Road to Change," *The Washington Post*, Nov. 16, 1989, p. C16.

21. Anatoly Lysenko, conversation with the author, Nov. 30, 1988.

22. Dmitri Zakharov, conversation with the author, Mar. 15, 1990.

23. DDT, "Revolution," translation by Michele Berdy and Anne Lawrence.

24. *Vzglyad*, June 15, 1989, *FBIS*, June 22, 1989, pp. 73–74.

25. *Vzglyad* footage shown the author, Dec. 12, 1988.

26. *The New York Times*, May 17, 1989, p. A9.

27. Sasha Lyubimov, conversation with the author, Oct. 10, 1989.

28. Zakharov, conversation, Mar. 15, 1990.

29. Yegor Yakovlev, interview with the author, Sept. 27, 1989.

PART THREE: LOOKING FOR *PERESTROIKA*

1. Gorbachev, *Izbrannye rechy i stati* (Moscow: Politizdat, 1987), Vol. 2, p. 86.

2. *Ibid.*, speech to the Twenty-seventh Communist Party Congress, Feb. 26, 1986, *CDSP*, Mar. 26, 1986, p. 12.

10. THE CULTURE OF ENVY

1. Vladimir Pozner, conversation with the author, June 6, 1988.

2. Tatyana Tolstaya, interview with David Royle, Jul. 30, 1989.

3. Andrei Voznesensky, interview with the author, Mar. 13, 1990.

4. Pavel Bunich, conversation with the author, Nov. 2, 1989.

5. Vladimir Kabaidze, speech to Nineteenth All-Union Conference of the Communist Party of the Soviet Union, June 29, 1988, *CDSP*, Aug. 24, 1988, p. 22.

6. Tatyana Zaslavskaya, "The Novosibirsk Report," *Survey*, Vol. 28, No. 1 (Spring 1984), pp. 90ff.

7. Nikolai Shmelyov, "Advances and Debts," *Novy Mir*, June 1987, p. 145.

8. Pozner, *op. cit.*

9. Vladimir Yadov, conversation with the author, Apr. 11, 1989.

10. Igor Beshev, conversation with the author, Sept. 14, 1989.

11. *PlanEcon Report*, Vol. 6, Nos. 7, 8, Feb. 21, 1990, p. 13.

12. Nikolai Y. Petrakov, *Rabochaya Tribuna*, Apr. 24, 1990.

13. Otto Latsis, *Rabochaya Tribuna*, Mar. 27, 1990.

14. "Person Without a Job," *Pravda*, Oct. 31, 1989.

15. Andrei Smirnov, conversation with the author, Mar. 15, 1990.

16. *Ibid.*, Oct. 10, 1989.

17. Rair Simonyan, conversation with the author, Jul. 5, 1989.

18. Leonid Abalkin, "Not Sharing, but Earning," *Ogonek*, Oct. 7–14, 1989, pp. 1–2, 25–27, translated in *Joint Publications Research Service*, Nov. 17, 1989, p. 7.

19. Aleksandr Yakovlev, interview with the author, Oct. 9, 1989.

20. Vladimir Mayakovsky, *Vladimir Ilyich Lenin* (Moscow: Sovetskaya Rossiya, 1981), pp. 42–43.

21. Aleksandr Kuzmin, conversation with the author, Apr. 26, 1989.

22. Galya Zhirnova, conversation with the author, Sept. 11, 1989.

23. Volodya Konoplanikov, conversation with the author, Sept. 12, 1989.

24. Roy Medvedev, *On Stalin and Stalinism* (Oxford: Oxford University Press, 1973), p. 190.

25. See Geroid Tanquary Robinson, *Rural Russia Under the Old Regime* (Berkeley: University of California Press, 1969), pp. 10–11, 64–75, 117–28.

26. Felicity Barringer, Chautauqua at Pitt: The Fifth General Chautauqua Conference on U.S. and Soviet Relations, 1989, Oct. 30, 1989.

27. Dmitri Zakharov, conversation with the author, Mar. 15, 1990.

28. Anatoly Sobchak, conversation with the author, Sept. 23, 1989.

29. Pozner, conversation with the author, Sept. 30, 1989.

30. Nikolai Shmelyov, speech to Third Congress of People's Deputies, Mar. 12, 1990, *FBIS*, Mar. 14, 1990, p. 74.

31. *Ibid.*, "New Anxieties," *Novy Mir*, Apr. 1988, p. 175.

32. Mikhail Gorbachev, speech in Sverdlovsk, Apr. 26, 1990, *Radio Liberty Daily Report*, Apr. 27, 1990, p. 2.

11. WHY THE RELUCTANT FARMERS?

1. Gorbachev, speech to Fourth All-Union Congress of Collective Farmers, Mar. 23, 1988, *CDSP*, Apr. 20, 1988, p. 1.

2. Dmitri Starodubtsev, interview with the author, Sept. 14, 1989.

3. Doak Barnett, conversation with the author, May 2, 1990.

4. Alec Nove, *An Economic History of the U.S.S.R.*, rev. ed. (Middlesex, England: Penguin, 1976), p. 106.

5. Gavril Popov, *Upravleniye Ekonomikoi—Ekonomicheskiye Metody* (Moscow: Ekonomika, 1985), p. 280.

6. See pp. 11, 14, 32, and 33, *Sel'skokhozaistvennoye Provisvodtsvo v Lichnikh Podsobnikh Khozaistvakh Naseleniya* (Moscow, Goskomstat, 1989).

7. *The New York Times*, Mar. 16, 1989, pp. A1, A6.

8. Zhores Medvedev, *Soviet Agriculture* (New York: W. W. Norton, 1987), p. 403.

9. Gorbachev, speech to Twenty-seventh Communist Party Congress, Feb. 25, 1986, *CDSP*, Mar. 26, 1988, p. 15.

10. V. Semyonov, "Ukrepleniye Ekonomiki Kolkhozov i Sovkhozov," *Finansy SSSR*, No. 9, 1985, pp. 3–11.

11. *Ibid.*, *Prodovolstvennaia Programmai Finansy* (Moscow, 1985), p. 113.

12. Georgy Shakhnazarov, conversation with the author, Dec. 15, 1988.

13. Gorbachev, speech to Fourth All-Union Congress of Collective Farmers, *op. cit.*

14. Vladimir Tikhonov, interview with the author, Sept. 29, 1989.

15. *Ibid.*
16. Abel Aganbegyan, conversation with the author, Feb. 27, 1988.
17. M. Vagin, *Sovetskaya Rossiya,* Sept. 29, 1987.
18. Valery N. Romanov, conversation with the author, Jul. 29, 1989.
19. Yevgeny Sokolov, "A Vexatious Fact—Lack of Realism," *Izvestia,* Jan. 28, 1990, p. 2.
20. Zhores Medvedev, *op. cit.,* pp. 16, 42–55, 73–81.
21. V. I. Lenin, *Collected Works* (Moscow: Progress Publishers, 1965), Vol. XXX, p. 113.
22. Roy Medvedev, *Let History Judge,* rev. ed. (New York: Columbia University Press, 1989), p. 230.
23. Nikolai Shmelyov, "New Anxieties," *Novy Mir,* Apr. 1988, p. 165.
24. Nikolai Sivkov, "This Is My Job," *Moscow News,* Jan. 21–28, 1990, p. 6.
25. "To Sivkov's Farmstead," *Izvestia,* Jan. 14, 1990.
26. Semyon Sharetsky, *Sovetskaya Rossiya,* Dec. 30, 1989, p. 6.
27. Shmelyov, "Advances and Debts," *Novy Mir,* June 1987, p. 147.
28. Gorbachev, *Pravda,* June 29, 1989, p. 2.
29. *Ibid.,* Oct. 14, 1988, p. 2.
30. *Ibid., Krasnaya Zvezda,* Feb. 24, 1989, pp. 1–3, *FBIS,* Feb. 24, 1989, p. 59.
31. Yegor Ligachev, *Pravda,* Mar. 3, 1989, p. 2.
32. *The Washington Post,* Mar. 13, 1989, p. A26.
33. *Ibid.,* Mar. 17, 1989, p. A1.
34. Vladimir Dorofeyev, interview with the author, Sept. 13, 1989.
35. Starodubtsev, conversation with the author, May 4, 1989.
36. Lydiya Popova and Starodubtsev, interview with the author, Sept. 13, 1989.
37. Aleksandr F. Orlov, interview with the author, Sept. 13, 1989.
38. Orlov family, group interview with the author, Sept. 13, 1989.
39. Starodubtsev, interview, Sept. 14, 1989.
40. Gorbachev, speech to Fourth All-Union Congress of Collective Farmers, *op. cit.,* p. 6.
41. See V. Bashmachnikov, in group discussion, "The Land Awaits a Proprietor: How We See the Law on Leasing," *Izvestia,* Feb. 14, 1990, p. 1.
42. "The Owner and the Land: The Population's Attitude Toward the Draft Law on Land," *Izvestia,* Feb. 28, 1990, p. 2.
43. Aleksandr P. Vladislavlev, *Moscow Domestic Service,* Apr. 5, 1990, *FBIS,* Apr. 19, 1990, p. 60.

12. THE CAPTIVE CAPTAINS OF SOVIET INDUSTRY

1. Worker, Uralmash Machine Works, interview with Marian Marzynski, Sept. 7, 1989.
2. Mikhail Gorbachev, "On the Party's Tasks in the Fundamental Restructuring of Economic Management," speech to Central Committee plenum, June 25, 1987 (Moscow: Novosti Press Agency Publishing House, 1987), p. 42.
3. President Tito, in Seweryn Bialer, *Inside Gorbachev's Russia* (Boulder, Colo.: Westview Press, 1989), p. 218.
4. Nikolai Shmelyov and Vladimir Popov, *The Turning Point: Revitalizing the Soviet Economy* (New York: Doubleday, 1989), p. 114.
5. "The Uralmash Incident," *Izvestia,* Mar. 23, 1988, p. 3.
6. "A Matter of Chance: What Uralmash Achieved," *Izvestia,* Dec. 15, 1988, p. 2.
7. Igor Stroganov, conversation with the author, Jul. 26, 1989.
8. Gorbachev, *Perestroika* (New York: Harper & Row, 1987), p. 33.
9. *Ibid.,* p. 23.
10. Gorbachev, "On the Party's Tasks," *op. cit.,* p. 47.
11. *Ibid.,* p. 50.
12. Nikolai I. Ryzhkov, *Pravda,* June 30, 1987.

13. Gorbachev, speech in Murmansk, Oct. 1, 1987, *FBIS*, Oct. 2, 1987, p. 29.

14. Stefan Pachikov, conversation with the author, Apr. 18, 1989.

15. Shmelyov, "Advances and Debts," *Novy Mir*, June 1987, p. 144.

16. See Alec Nove, "The Problems of *Perestroika*," *Dissent*, Vol. 36, No. 4, Fall 1989, p. 463.

17. Shmelyov, "Advances and Debts," *op. cit.*

18. Gorbachev, "On the Party's Tasks," *op. cit.*, p. 46.

19. *Ibid.*, p. 45.

20. *Ibid.*, p. 49.

21. Ryzhkov, quoted in Gertrude E. Schroeder, "Anatomy of Gorbachev's Economic Reform," *Soviet Economy*, Vol. 3, No. 3, Jul.–Sept. 1987, p. 226.

22. Gorbachev, "On the Party's Tasks," *op. cit.*, p. 51.

23. For an excellent analysis of the role and views of Prime Minister Nikolai Ryzhkov, see Anders Aslund, *Gorbachev's Struggle for Economic Reform* (Ithaca, N.Y.: Cornell University Press, 1989), pp. 39–43, 62.

24. Zhores Medvedev, *Nuclear Disaster in the Urals* (New York: W. W. Norton, 1979), pp. 4, 16, 22, 164–69.

25. Stroganov, interview with the author, Sept. 8, 1989.

26. Uralmash exit interview, filmed by Jean de Segonzac, Sept. 7, 1989.

27. Georgy Pospelov, conversation with the author, Sept. 7, 1989.

28. Stroganov and working woman, interview with the author, Sept. 9, 1989.

29. Stroganov, interview, Sept. 8, 1989.

30. *Ibid.*, conversation with the author, Jul. 27, 1989.

31. *Ibid.*, interview with the author, Sept. 7, 1989.

32. *Ibid.*, conversation, Jul. 26, 1989.

33. *Ibid.*, conversation with the author, Sept. 8, 1989.

34. *Ibid.*, interview, Sept. 7, 1989.

35. Vladislav Grammatin, Uralmash staff meeting, filmed by Jean de Segonzac, Sept. 8, 1989.

36. Anatoly Osintsev, conversations with the author, Jul. 27 and Sept. 8, 1989.

37. Stroganov, conversation with the author, Sept. 9, 1989.

38. *Ibid.*, conversation with the author, Sept. 7, 1989.

39. Leonid Abalkin, interview with the author, Sept. 21, 1989.

40. *Ibid.*, conversation with the author, Jul. 7, 1989.

41. Grigory Yarlinsky, Gennady Melikyan, Yuri Ivanovich, discussion with Abalkin, Sept. 25, 1989.

42. Abalkin, interview, Sept. 21, 1989.

43. Anders Aslund, "Gorbachev: Governing on the Razor's Edge," *The Washington Post*, Jan. 28, 1990, p. C1.

44. Bill Keller, "How Gorbachev Rejected Plan to 'Shock Treat' the Economy," *The New York Times*, May 14, 1990, p. A1.

45. Gorbachev, speech at Nizhny Tagil, Apr. 27, 1990, *FBIS*, Apr. 30, 1990, p. 114.

46. *Ibid.*, speech in Sverdlovsk, Apr. 26, 1990, *FBIS*, Apr. 30, 1990, p. 117.

47. *Ibid.*, quoted by Tass, May 23, 1990, *FBIS*, May 24, 1990, p. 101.

48. Ryzhkov, speech to the Supreme Soviet, May 24, 1990, *FBIS*, May 25, 1990, pp. 37–57.

49. Stanislav Shatalin and Vladen Martynov, press conference, Washington, D.C., June 1, 1990.

50. Yuri Prokofyev, interview with the author, June 27, 1990.

51. Pavel Bunich, in *Izvestia*, May 29, 1990, *FBIS*, May 31, 1990, p. 57.

13. THE NEW ENTREPRENEURS: TRYING OUT CAPITALISM

1. Oleg Smirnoff, conversation with the author, Apr. 16, 1989.

2. Gleb Orlikhovsky, conversation with the author, Mar. 3, 1990.

3. Aleksandr Yakovlev, interview with the author, Oct. 9, 1989.

4. The Law on Individual Labor Activity, enacted Nov. 19, 1986, was the first general legislation,

later followed by individual decrees on certain areas. See Anders Aslund, *Gorbachev's Struggle for Economic Reform* (Ithaca, N.Y.: Cornell University Press, 1989), pp. 153–54.

5. Gorbachev, speech at Fourth All-Union Congress of Collective Farmers, Mar. 23, 1988, *Pravda*, Mar. 24, 1988, pp. 1–3.

6. *Ibid.*, *CDSP*, Apr. 20, 1988, p. 4.

7. See Aslund, *op. cit.*, pp. 163–67, and Anthony Jones and William Moskoff, "New Cooperatives in the U.S.S.R.," *Problems of Communism*, Nov.–Dec. 1989, p. 29.

8. Gorbachev, speech, March 23, 1988, *CDSP*, Apr. 20, 1988, p. 2.

9. See Alec Nove, *An Economic History of the U.S.S.R.*, rev. ed. (Middlesex, England: Penguin, 1982), pp. 83–92, 102–13.

10. Professor Grossman kindly shared with me findings from Gregory Grossman and Vladimir Treml, Berkeley-Duke Project on the Second Economy of the U.S.S.R., May 20, 1990.

11. Nikolai Shmelyov and Vladimir Popov, *The Turning Point: Revitalizing the Soviet Economy* (New York: Doubleday, 1989), p. 199.

12. *Ibid.* Also see articles in *Izvestia*, Aug. 18, 1985, and *Pravda*, Sept. 5, 1987.

13. Aleksandr Borin, "Podmena," *Literaturnaya Gazeta*, Jul. 15, 1987, p. 11.

14. Hedrick Smith, *The Russians*, rev. (New York: Ballantine Books, 1984), pp. 124–25.

15. *Ibid.*, pp. 125–30.

16. Konstantin Simis, *U.S.S.R.: The Corrupt Society* (New York: Simon and Schuster, 1982), pp. 86–87.

17. Abel Aganbegyan, conversation with the author, Apr. 12, 1989.

18. Sergei Vladov, conversation with the author, Dec. 18, 1989.

19. Igor Stroganov, conversation with the author, Jul. 26, 1989.

20. Stanislav Dailitko, conversations with the author, Jul. 26 and Sept. 6, 1989.

21. Aleksandr Smolensky, conversation with the author, Sept. 19, 1989.

22. Aleksandr Friedman, conversation with the author, Sept. 18, 1989.

23. Smolensky, conversation with the author, Sept. 18, 1989.

24. Valentin Pavlov and Leonid Abalkin, conversation with the author, Sept. 21, 1989.

25. Smolensky, conversation, Sept. 19, 1989.

26. Mark Masarsky, conversation with the author, Sept. 1, 1989.

27. *Ibid.*, Sept. 3, 1989.

28. Yuri Kaplan, conversation with the author, Sept. 3, 1989.

29. Aleksandr Bokhan and Masarsky, interview with the author, Sept. 19, 1989.

30. Masarsky, interview with the author, Sept. 19, 1989.

31. *Ibid.*, Sept. 20, 1989.

32. U.S.S.R. State Committee for Statistics, cited in "Cooperation-89," *Moscow News*, Apr. 1, 1990, p. 10.

33. "Hurdle Race," *Moscow News*, Apr. 1, 1990, p. 10.

34. *Ekonomika i Zhizn*, Jan. 1990, p. 11, *CDSP*, Vol. XLII, No. 3, 1990, p. 23.

35. "Cooperator's Profile," *Moscow News*, Dec. 26, 1989, No. 52, p. 12.

36. Vadim Kirichenko, chairman, State Committee for Statistics, *Moscow News*, Apr. 1, 1990.

37. Andrei Smirnov, conversation with the author, Mar. 15, 1990.

38. Tankred Golenpolsky, conversation with the author, Sept. 19, 1988.

39. *The New York Times*, Mar. 5, 1989, p. 3.

40. Yevgeny Chazov, interview with the author, Aug. 3, 1989.

41. "Hurdle Race," *Moscow News*, Apr. 1, 1990, p. 10.

42. Smirnoff, conversation, Apr. 16, 1989.

43. L. Kislinskaya, "Barrier Against Racketeering," *Sovetskaya Rossiya*, Jan. 26, 1989, p. 4.

44. "Cooperatives: Let Us Explain the System Again," *Izvestia*, Mar. 3, 1990, p. 2.

45. Leonid Dobrokhotov, conversation with the author, Dec. 2, 1988.

46. Vladimir Tikhonov, conversation with the author, Aug. 3, 1989.

47. "A Case Involving Millions," *Moscow News*, Mar. 5–12, 1989, p. 12; and *Trud*, June 13, 1989, p. 2.

48. Orlikhovsky, conversation, Mar. 3, 1990.

49. *Moscow News,* Oct. 1, 1989, p. 5.

50. *Ibid.*

51. Moscow television, Mar. 13, 1990, *FBIS,* Mar. 14, 1990, pp. 51–52.

52. Tikhonov, conversation with the author, Mar. 14, 1990.

53. *The New York Times,* Mar. 7, 1990, p. A1.

54. "Decree of the President of the U.S.S.R.: On New Approaches to the Solution of the Housing Problem in the Country and Measures for Their Practical Implementation," *Pravda,* May 20, 1990, p. 1.

55. *The New York Times,* May 21, 1990, p. A1.

56. Masarsky, conversation, Sept. 1, 1989.

57. Yakovlev, *op. cit.*

PART FOUR: THE EMPIRE TEARING APART

1. Gorbachev, speech to Russian Communist Party Congress, June 19, 1990, *FBIS,* June 20, 1990, p. 90.

14. UZBEKISTAN: "OUR LANGUAGE IS OUR HEART AND OUR SOUL"

1. Abdur Rahim Pulatov, interview with the author, Oct. 1, 1989.

2. Shukhrat Makhmudov, interview with the author, Oct. 5, 1989.

3. Pulatov, Birlik rally, Oct. 1, 1989.

4. Nuraly Kabul, conversation with the author, June 8, 1989.

5. Makhmudov, conversation with the author, Oct. 4, 1989.

6. Mohammed Salikh, conversation with the author, June 12, 1989.

7. Rafik Nishanov, *Pravda Vostoka,* June 17, 1989, p. 2.

8. William Fierman, *"Glasnost* in Practice: The Uzbek Experience," *Central Asian Survey,* Vol. 8, No. 2, 1989, p. 33.

9. Pulatov, interview, Oct. 1, 1989.

10. *Narodnoye khozaistvo SSSR* (Moscow: Financy i statistiki, 1989), pp. 19, 26.

11. Hedrick Smith, "Islam Retaining a Strong Grip on Uzbeks," *The New York Times,* Nov. 22, 1972, p. 8.

12. Bogdan Nahaylo and Victor Swoboda, *Soviet Disunion: A History of the Nationalities Problem in the U.S.S.R.* (New York: Free Press, 1990), p. 217.

13. Fierman, *op.cit.*

14. Telman Gdlyan, interview with the author, Oct. 7, 1989.

15. "Verdict Announced, Problems Remain," *Moscow News,* Jan. 15–22, 1989, p. 5.

16. Gdlyan, *op. cit.*

17. James Critchlow, "Further Repercussions of 'The Uzbek Affair,'" *Radio Liberty Report on the USSR,* May 4, 1990, p. 1.

18. *Ibid.,* p. 20.

19. Pulatov, interview, Oct. 1, 1989.

20. Islam Karimov, *Pravda,* Sept. 22, 1989.

21. Salikh, conversation, June 12, 1989.

22. "Person Without a Job," *Pravda,* Oct. 31, 1989, p. 2.

23. Martin Walker, *The Harper Independent Traveler: The Soviet Union* (New York: Harper & Row, 1989), p. 270.

24. Timur Pulatov, conversation with the author, June 8, 1989.

25. Esther Fein, "In Soviet Asia Backwater, Infancy's a Rite of Survival," *The New York Times,* Aug. 14, 1989, pp. A1, A6.

26. Bakhtiar Normetov, conversation with the author, June 10, 1989.

27. "Sick People—72%; That's What a Medical Study Showed," *Khorezmskaya Pravda*, May 23, 1989, p. 3; see also "Let's Talk About Health," *Khorezmskaya Pravda*, May 18, 1989, p. 3.

28. Makhmudov, interview, Oct. 5, 1989.

29. *Ibid.*, Oct. 2, 1989.

30. *Ibid.*, Oct, 5, 1989.

31. *Ibid.*, field dialogue filmed by Jean de Segonzac, Oct. 15, 1989.

32. Raizeta Makhmudova, interview with the author, Oct. 2, 1989.

33. Shukhrat Makhmudov and Raizeta Makhmudova, interview with the author, Oct. 3, 1989.

34. Smith, *op. cit.*

35. Nahaylo and Swoboda, *op. cit.*, pp. 215–16.

36. Pulatov, interview, Oct. 1, 1989.

37. Galina Kozlovskaya, interview with the author, Oct. 1, 1989.

38. Kurambai Matrizayev, conversation with the author, June 11, 1989.

39. Akhurnjan Safarov, conversation with the author, Oct. 3, 1989.

40. Fierman, *op. cit.*, p. 13.

41. Imam Mustafakhan Melikov, sermon, Samarkand mosque, Oct. 5, 1989.

42. Haj Mukhtar Abdulayev, interview with the author, Oct. 3, 1989.

43. "Islam Regains Its Voice," *Time*, Apr. 10, 1989, p. 99.

44. Melikov, interview with the author, Oct. 5, 1989; Abdulayev, *op. cit.*

45. Salikh and Dadhon Khassan, conversation with the author, Oct. 2, 1989.

46. Shukhrat Makhmudov, conversation with the author, Oct. 4, 1989.

47. Salikh, conversation, Oct. 2, 1989.

48. *Pravda Vostoka*, Mar. 29, 1990, pp. 2–3.

49. Francis X. Clines, "Defiance of Kremlin's Control Is Accelerating in Soviet Asia," *The New York Times*, June 29, 1990, pp. A1, A6.

50. Anvar Shakirov, conversation with the author, Oct. 4, 1989.

51. Raizeta Makhmudova, conversation with the author, May 14, 1990.

15. ARMENIA AND AZERBAIJAN: A SOVIET LEBANON

1. Rufat Novrozov, interview with the author, Mar. 7, 1990.

2. Ashot Manucharyan, speech in Yerevan, Jul. 12, 1989.

3. Ashot Bleyan, conversation with the author, June 17, 1989.

4. Manucharyan, conversation with the author, June 18, 1989.

5. *Ibid.*, interview with the author, Jul. 12, 1989.

6. Ashot and Bibishan Manucharyan, interview with Oren Jacoby, Jul. 11, 1989.

7. Ashot Manucharyan, interview, Jul. 12, 1989.

8. *Ibid.*, conversation, June 18, 1989.

9. Manucharyan, filmed by Oren Jacoby, June 18, 1989.

10. Hedrick Smith, "Soviet Armenian Church Is Confident and Strong," *The New York Times*, Dec. 18, 1971, p. 6.

11. Vasgen II, interview with the author, Jul. 9, 1989.

12. Novrozov, *op. cit.*

13. Mary Matossian, "The Armenians," *Problems of Communism*, Vol. XVI, No. 5, Sept.–Oct. 1967, p. 68.

14. *The Sunday Times* (London), Feb. 28, 1988, p. 1.

15. Afrend Dezhdamerov, Azerbaijan Communist Party Central Committee, interview with the author, Jul. 13, 1989.

16. Sumgait Deputy Mayor Ali Sasanov and Eldar Ismailov, third city Party secretary, interview with the author, Jul. 13, 1989.

17. Irina Melkunyan, conversation with the author, June 20, 1989.

18. Asya Arakelyan, interview with the author, Jul. 9, 1989.

19. Armen Oganesyan, interview with the author, Jul. 9, 1989.

20. Guliyev family, interview with the author, Jul. 15, 1989.

21. Suren Arutunyan, interview with the author, Jul. 10, 1989.

22. *Ibid.*, June 18, 1989.

23. Arutunyan and son, interview with the author, Jul. 10, 1989.

24. Arutunyan, interview, June 18, 1989.

25. Ashot Manucharyan, speech in Yerevan, *op. cit.*

26. Leonid Dobrokhotov, conversation with the author, Sept. 25, 1989.

27. "Vokrug ruzhya . . . ," *Kazakhstanskaya Pravda*, Sept. 18, 1987.

28. Paul Goble, conversations with the author, Oct. 18, 1989, and Nov. 17, 1989.

29. Stephen Sestanovich, "Soviet Chaos: Gunplay," *The Washington Post*, Jul. 23, 1989, p. C1.

30. Aydin Ambertov, Azerbaijani Popular Front spokesman, conversation with the author, Jul. 14, 1989.

31. Mirza Michaeli and William Reese, "The Popular Front in Azerbaijan and Its Program," *Radio Liberty Report on the USSR*, Aug. 25, 1989, p. 30.

32. *The Washington Post*, Sept. 3, 1989, p. A22.

33. *Argumenty i Fakty*, Oct. 1, 1989.

34. "Azerbaijanis End Strike, Let Supplies into Armenia," *The Washington Post*, Oct. 11, 1989, p. A34.

35. Bill Keller, "Nationalists in Azerbaijan Win Big Concessions from Party Chief," *The New York Times*, Oct. 12, 1989, p. A1.

36. Mikhail Gorbachev, speech to Communist Party Central Committee, Sept. 19, 1989, *FBIS*, Sept. 20, 1989, p. 38.

37. *The Washington Post*, Oct. 2, 1989, p. A23.

38. *Ibid.*, Jan. 21, 1990, p. A30.

39. *Izvestia*, Jan. 27, 1990, pp. 1–2.

40. See Elizabeth Fuller, "Gorbachev's Dilemma in Azerbaijan," *RL Report on the USSR*, Feb. 2, 1990, p. 14.

41. Novrozov, *op. cit.*

42. Keller, "Did Moscow Incite Azerbaijanis? Some See a Plot," *The New York Times*, Feb. 19, 1990, p. A8.

43. Novrozov, *op. cit.*

44. *The Washington Post*, May 29, 1990, p. A17.

45. *Ibid.*, Jul. 31, 1990, p. A17.

46. Arutunyan, conversation with the author, Jul. 5, 1990.

47. *The New York Times*, Aug. 10, 1990, p. A3.

16. LITHUANIA: BREAKING THE TABOO OF SECESSION

1. Vytautas Landsbergis, interview with the author, Jul. 24, 1989.

2. Esther Fein, "Gorbachev Urges Lithuania to Stay with Soviet Union," *The New York Times*, Jan. 13, 1990, p. A1; and David Remnick, "Gorbachev Urges Lithuanians Not to Press for Independence," *The Washington Post*, Jan. 12, 1990, p. A1.

3. Lithuanian voters, interviews with the author filmed by Maryse Alberti, Mar. 26–27, 1989.

4. Arvydas Juozaitis, conversation with the author, Mar. 26, 1989.

5. Map, "Ethnicity and Political Boundaries in the Soviet Union," Office of the Geographer, U.S. Department of State, based on preliminary data from 1989 U.S.S.R. census.

6. Algirdas Brazauskas, speech in Kaunas, Feb. 16, 1989, *FBIS*, Feb. 17, 1989, p. 63.

7. Hedrick Smith, "Lithuania Warns of Religious Backlash," *The New York Times*, Aug. 15, 1972, p. 5.

8. Romouldas Ozolas, interview with the author, Mar. 27, 1989.

9. *Ibid.*, conversation with the author, June 21, 1989.

10. *Ibid.*, interview with the author, Jul. 21, 1989.

11. *Ibid.*

12. Brazauskas, interview with the author, Mar. 27, 1989.

13. Ozolas, interview, Mar. 27, 1989.

14. Fein, "Lithuanian to the Core," *The New York Times,* Mar. 26, 1990, p. A8.

15. Landsbergis, conversation with the author, Jul. 23, 1989.

16. Michael Dobbs, "Unlikely Revolutionary Leads Lithuanian Drive," *The Washington Post,* May 7, 1990, p. A13.

17. Justas Paleckis, conversation with the author, Mar. 10, 1990.

18. Landsbergis, interview, Jul. 24, 1989.

19. Brazauskas, interview with the author, Jul. 22, 1989.

20. The Russian populations are drawn from the 1989 census; see *Nationalny sostav naceleniye,* State Committee for Statistics (Moscow: Information Publications Center, 1989).

21. *The New York Times,* Mar. 15, 1989, p. A10.

22. Mayor Rimantas Kumbis, conversation with the author, June 22, 1989.

23. Bill Keller, "Public Mistrust Curbs Soviet Nuclear Power Efforts," *The New York Times,* Oct. 12, 1988, p. A1.

24. Anatoly Khromchenko, interview with the author, Jul. 24, 1989.

25. Aleksandr Zharik and Valery Antipyevt, interview with Oren Jacoby, Jul. 24, 1989.

26. *Ibid.*

27. *Pravda,* Aug. 18, 1989, pp. 1–2.

28. *The Washington Post,* Sept. 30, 1989, p. A16.

29. *Pravda,* Aug. 27, 1989, p. 1.

30. *The New York Times,* Aug. 28, 1989, p. A1.

31. Algimantas Zukas, conversation with the author, June 24, 1989.

32. Brazauskas, conversation with the author, Jul. 24, 1989.

33. Pavel Bunich, conversation with the author, Nov. 1, 1989.

34. *FBIS,* Sept. 15, 1989, p. 26.

35. Gorbachev, *FBIS,* Sept. 19, 1989, p. 38.

36. Brazauskas, interview with the author, Mar. 10, 1990.

37. Fein, "Gorbachev Urges Lithuania to Stay with Soviet Union," *The New York Times,* Jan. 13, 1990, p. A1; and Remnick, "Gorbachev Urges Lithuanians Not to Press for Independence," *The Washington Post,* Jan. 12, 1990, p. A1.

38. Keller, "Buying Time in Lithuania," *The New York Times,* Jan. 13, 1990, p. A1.

39. Ozolas, interview with the author, Mar. 9, 1990.

40. Brazauskas, speech to Vilnius Communist Party, Mar. 10, 1990.

41. Brazauskas, interview, Mar. 10, 1990.

42. Kazimiera Prunskiene, meeting with Washington reporters, May 3, 1990.

43. *The New York Times,* June 13, 1990, p. A18; and *The Washington Post,* June 13, 1990, p. A1.

44. *The New York Times,* June 30, 1990, p. A1.

45. *The Washington Post,* Jul. 29, 1990, p. A19.

17. BACKLASH IN MOTHER RUSSIA

1. Valentin Rasputin, speech to Congress of People's Deputies, June 6, 1989, *FBIS,* Aug. 9, 1989, p. 27.

2. Stanislav Kunyayev, conversation with the author, Sept. 15, 1989.

3. Yuri Prokofyev, interview with the author, Oct. 7, 1989.

4. Rasputin, *op. cit.*

5. *Ibid.*, pp. 27–28.

6. Vladimir Soloukhin and Rosa Soloukhina, conversation with the author, Jul. 18, 1989.

7. Soloukhin, interview with the author, Jul. 18, 1989.

8. See Aleksandr Solzhenitsyn, "Letter to the Supreme Leaders," in Hedrick Smith, *The Russians* (New York: Ballantine Books, 1984), pp. 568–69.

9. Dmitri Likhachev, *Le Nouvel Observateur*, May 8–14, 1987, quoted in John B. Dunlop, "The Contemporary Russian Nationalist Spectrum," *Radio Liberty Research Bulletin, Russian Nationalism Today*, Dec. 19, 1988, p. 4.

10. See Alexander Yanov, "Russian Nationalism as the Ideology of Counterreform," in *RL Research Bulletin, Russian Nationalism Today*, Dec. 19, 1988, pp. 43ff.

11. Nikolai Berdyayev, "Man's Fate in the Modern World," *Novy Mir*, No. 1, 1989.

12. Metropolitan Filaret, interview with the author, Jul. 19, 1989.

13. Vladimir Galitsky, interview with the author, Jul. 17, 1989.

14. Aleksandr Trefimov, interview with the author, Jan. 17, 1989.

15. Alex Alexiev, "Life-Death Struggle for the Soul and Center of Soviet Union," *Los Angeles Times*, Mar. 25, 1990, p. M2.

16. See Bill Keller, "Russian Nationalists: Yearning for an Iron Hand," *The New York Times Magazine*, Jan. 28, 1990, p. 50.

17. Aleksandr I. Solzhenitsyn, *Letter to the Supreme Leaders* (New York: Harper & Row, 1974).

18. Kunyayev, *op. cit.*

19. Vasily Belov, speech in Moscow, Sept. 28, 1989, filmed by Foster Wiley.

20. Sergei Vikulov, interview with the author, Apr. 26, 1989.

21. Rasputin, *op. cit.*, p. 26.

22. Julia Wishnevsky, "*Nash Sovremennik* Provides Focus for 'Opposition Party,'" *Radio Liberty Report on the USSR*, Jan. 20, 1989, pp. 1–3.

23. Even after October 1988, when Vadim Medvedev became the Politburo's nominal chief for press affairs, Korotich told me that he maintained close and regular contact with Yakovlev; other liberals made it clear that Yakovlev was their main protector in the Politburo.

24. Aleksandr Yakovlev, *Literaturnaya Gazeta*, Nov. 15, 1972; and the main rebuttal to Andreyeva in *Pravda*, Apr. 5, 1988, p. 2. Yakovlev subsequently identified himself as the author of the *Pravda* editorial.

25. Yegor Ligachev, quoted in John Dunlop, "Soviet Cultural Politics," *Problems of Communism*, Nov.–Dec. 1987, pp. 51–52.

26. Roman Szporluk, in "Dilemmas of Russian Nationalism," *Problems of Communism*, Jul.–Aug. 1989, pp. 15–35, divides Russian nationalists into two groups: "nation-builders," eager to restore Russia and willing to tolerate separatism among other nationalities, and "empire-savers," determined to hold on to "all of Russia," which they define as the territory of the U.S.S.R.

27. Kunyayev, conversation with the author, Sept. 12, 1989.

28. Rasputin, quoted in Keller, "Russian Nationalists," *op cit.*, p. 48.

29. Igor Shafarevich, "Russophobia," *Nash Sovremennik*, June 1989, pp. 167–92, *CDSP*, Vol. XLI, No. 46, pp. 16–19.

30. *Literaturnaya Rossiya*, Dec. 1, 1989, pp. 2–13.

31. Kunyayev, quoted in *The New York Times*, Apr. 18, 1990, p. A10.

32. Darrell P. Hammer, "*Glasnost* and 'The Russian Idea,'" *RL Research Bulletin, Russian Nationalism Today*, Dec. 19, 1988, pp. 14–15.

33. Dmitri Vasiliyev, interview with the author, Jul. 20, 1990.

34. "Gorbachev's Dead Rival," *The Washington Post*, May 17, 1988, p. A18.

35. Vasiliyev, Moscow television, Nov. 18, 1989, *Radio Free Europe/Radio Liberty Daily Report*, Nov. 27, 1989, p. 7.

36. Vitaly Korotich, conversation with the author, Jan. 15, 1989.

37. Sasha Kuprin, conversations with the author, Jul. 7 and 19, 1989.

38. *Komsomolskaya Pravda*, Jan. 21, 1990; *RFE/RL Daily Report*, Jan. 26, 1990, p. 6.

39. Vasiliyev, interview, *Moscow News,* Nov. 7, 1988, p. 4.

40. KGB Major General Aleksandr Karbainov, quoted in *RFE/RL Daily Report,* Feb. 20, 1990, p. 5.

41. Likhachev, interview with the author, Mar. 4, 1990.

42. Yakovlev, interview with the author, Oct. 9, 1989.

43. Conversations at Central Committee with Nikolai Shishlin and Leonid Dobrokhotov, Sept. 1989, and Anatoly Afanasyev, Moscow Party Committee, Sept. 1989.

44. *The Washington Post,* Nov. 23, 1989, p. A23.

45. Gorbachev, speech to Communist Party plenum, Sept. 19, 1989, *FBIS,* Sept. 20, 1989, p. 32.

46. *The New York Times,* Feb. 24, 1990, p. A6; *The Washington Post,* Feb. 24, 1990, p. A24.

47. *The New York Times,* Mar. 25, 1990, p. 16.

48. Gorbachev, speech, May 23, 1990, *FBIS,* May 24, 1990, p. 105.

49. *The Washington Post,* June 24, 1990, p. A1.

18. GRASS-ROOTS ACTIVISM: REINVENTING POLITICS

1. Gorbachev, speech to Nineteenth Communist Party Conference, June 28, 1988, *Pravda,* June 29, 1988, p. 2.

2. Viktor Zakharov, interview with the author, Mar. 23, 1989.

3. Leonid Slychkov, conversation with the author, May 27, 1989.

4. Larissa Kholina, Rita Pilenkova, and Valeriya Savchenko, interview with the author, Mar. 25, 1989.

5. Nikolai Shishlin, conversation with the author, May 26, 1989.

6. Kholina, Pilenkova, and Savchenko, interview with the author, May 27, 1989.

7. Bishop Amvrosi, interview with the author, May 27, 1989.

8. Father Amvrosi, interview with the author, May 28, 1989.

9. Konstantin Kharchev, interview, *Ogonek,* No. 44, 1989, pp. 17–21.

10. Anatoly Golovkov, interview with Martin Smith, Sept. 26, 1989.

11. See David K. Shipler, "Between Dictatorship and Anarchy," *The New Yorker,* June 25, 1990, p. 43.

12. Vladimir Pozner, interview with the author, June 6, 1988.

13. S. Frederick Starr, "Party Animals," *The New Republic,* June 26, 1989, p. 19.

14. *Pravda,* Feb. 5, 1988, *FBIS,* Feb. 12, 1988, p. 59.

15. Viktor Chebrikov, speech in Kishinev, Moldavia, Feb. 10, 1989, *Pravda,* Feb. 11, 1989, p. 2.

16. Andrei Martinov, delivering petition to Red Guard District Council, Apr. 26, 1989.

17. Yuri Prokofyev, interview with the author, Oct. 7, 1989.

18. Tatyana Sivilna, report to Red Guard District Soviet, Apr. 26, 1989.

19. Nina Shchedrina, interview with the author, Apr. 2, 1989.

20. *Ibid.,* interview with Martin Smith, Sept. 26, 1989.

21. Shchedrina, on *Good Evening, Moscow,* Jul. 29, 1989.

22. Yevgeny Pavlov and Nikolai Pilyayev, interview with the author, Sept. 28, 1989.

23. Sergei Druganov, Haik Zulumyan, Shchedrina, and others, Brateyovo Self-governing Committee, Mar. 23, 1989.

24. Red Guard District Council session, Apr. 26, 1989.

25. Pavlov, interview, Sept. 28, 1989.

26. See D. J. Peterson, "A Wave of Environmentalism Shakes the Soviet Union," *Radio Liberty Report on the USSR,* June 22, 1990, p. 8.

27. *Ibid.;* David Marples, "Growing Influence of Antinuclear Movement in Ukraine," *RL Report on the USSR,* June 22, 1990, p. 18; and Bill Keller, "Public Mistrust Curbs Soviet Nuclear Power Efforts," *The New York Times,* Oct. 13, 1988, p. A1.

28. Prokofyev, *op. cit.*

29. Druganov, interview with Martin Smith, Sept. 27, 1989.

19. ELECTIONS: CROSSING OUT PARTY BOSSES

1. Gorbachev, campaigning in Kiev, Feb. 20, 1989, *FBIS*, Feb. 20, 1989.
2. Yelena Zelinskaya, conversation with the author, Apr. 5, 1989.
3. *Izvestia*, Apr. 26, 1989.
4. Gorbachev, *op. cit.*
5. Zelinskaya, *op. cit.*
6. *Pravda*, Apr. 20, 1989, *FBIS*, Apr. 21, 1989, p. 60.
7. *Leningradskaya Pravda*, Mar. 28, 1989, p. 1.
8. *Sovetsyaka Rossiya*, Apr. 6, 1989.
9. Boris Nikolsky, conversation with the author, Apr. 5, 1989.
10. Boris Yeltsin, *Against the Grain* (New York: Summit Books, 1990), pp. 177–204, especially p. 182.
11. Valentin Chikin, conversation with the author, Apr. 29, 1989.
12. Eddie Baranov, conversation with the author, Mar. 25, 1989.
13. Roy Medvedev, conversation with the author, Apr. 10, 1989.
14. *Izvestia*, Apr. 24, 1989, reported thirty-one *oblast* secretaries defeated, but Aleksandr Yakovlev, in an interview with the author, Oct. 9, 1989, put the figure at thirty-six.
15. Aleksandr Yakovlev, interview with the author, Oct. 7, 1989. Jerry F. Hough, "The Politics of Successful Economic Reform," *Soviet Economy*, Vol. 5, No. 1, Jan.–Mar. 1989, p. 14, reports that thirty-eight *obkom* first secretaries were defeated.
16. Gorbachev, Apr. 25, 1989, *Pravda*, Apr. 27, 1989, p. 1.
17. Boris Kurashvili, conversation with the author, Apr. 13, 1989.

20. CONGRESS: GENESIS OF AN OPPOSITION

1. *FBIS*, Jul. 31, 1989, p. 51.
2. Roy Medvedev, conversation with the author, May 25, 1989.
3. Boris Kagarlitsky, interview with Louis Menashe, May 21, 1989.
4. Andrei Sakharov, Congress, May 25, 1989, *FBIS*, June 13, 1989, pp. 4, 24.
5. Marju Lauristan, Congress, May 25, 1989, *FBIS*, June 13, 1989, p. 23.
6. Aleksandr Shchelkanov, Congress, May 25, 1989, *FBIS*, June 13, 1989, p. 24.
7. Leonid Sukhov, Moscow television, May 25, 1989.
8. Sergei Zvonov, Moscow television, May 25, 1989.
9. Gorbachev, Congress, Moscow television, May 25, 1989, *FBIS*, May 26, 1989, pp. 10, 18–20.
10. Aleksandr Obolensky, Congress, May 25, 1989, *FBIS*, June 13, 1989, p. 13.
11. Medvedev, *op. cit.*
12. Sergei Stankevich, interview with the author, May 25, 1989.
13. *Ibid.*, Sept. 28, 1989.
14. Boris Yeltsin, interview with the author, May 25, 1989.
15. Demonstration, filmed by Jean de Segonzac, sound man Scott Breindel, May 25, 1989.
16. Stankevich, interview, Sept. 28, 1989.
17. Stankevich and Gorbachev, Congress, Moscow television, May 26, 1989.
18. Stankevich, interview with the author, May 26, 1989.
19. *Ibid.*, Sept. 28, 1989.
20. Yuri Vlasov, Congress, May 31, 1989, *FBIS*, Jul. 5, 1989, pp. 33–34.
21. Tass, Apr. 4, 1989.
22. Yevgeny Yevtushenko, Congress, Moscow television, June 1, 1989, *FBIS*, Jul. 14, 1989, pp. 40–42.
23. Yuri Chernichenko, Congress, June 1, 1989, *FBIS*, Jul. 14, 1989, pp. 18–21.
24. Yuri Karyakin, Congress, June 2, 1989, *FBIS*, Jul. 26, 1989, p. 10.
25. T. V. Gankrelidze, Congress, Moscow television, May 30, 1989, *FBIS*, June 3, 1989, pp. 2–5.

26. Col. Gen. Igor Rodionov, Congress, Moscow television, May 30, 1989, *FBIS*, June 30, 1989, pp. 5–9.

27. Roald Sagdeyev, conversation with the author, June 2, 1989.

28. Sergei Chervonopisky, Congress, June 2, 1989, *FBIS*, Jul. 26, 1989, pp. 1–3.

29. Sergei Akhromeyev, Congress, June 2, 1989, *FBIS*, Jul. 26, 1989, p. 4.

30. Sakharov, Congress, June 2, 1989, *FBIS*, Jul. 26, 1989, pp. 3–4.

31. Sakharov and Gorbachev Congress, June 9, 1989, *FBIS*, Aug. 29, 1989, pp. 40–41.

32. Dmitri Yazov, Supreme Soviet, Jul. 5, 1989, *FBIS*, Jul. 6, 1989, p. 43.

33. Tass, Jul. 31, 1989.

34. *FBIS*, Jul. 31, 1989, p. 51.

35. *Ibid.*, pp. 51, 53.

36. Gorbachev, Supreme Soviet, Sept. 25, 1989, *FBIS*, Sept. 25, 1989, p. 49.

37. *Ibid.*, in *The Washington Post*, Oct. 19, 1989, pp. A1, A42.

38. Stankevich, conversation with the author, Sept. 30, 1989.

39. Gorbachev, Supreme Soviet, Oct. 23, 1989, *FBIS*, Oct. 24, 1989, pp. 40–41.

40. *Ibid.*, Supreme Soviet, Feb. 14, 1990, *The New York Times*, Feb. 15, 1990, p. A20.

41. *The Washington Post*, Feb. 28, 1990, p. A19.

42. *The New York Times*, Feb. 28, 1990, p. A1.

43. Stankevich, conversation with the author, Mar. 13, 1990.

44. For an excellent, detailed account, see David K. Shipler, "Between Dictatorship and Anarchy," *The New Yorker*, June 25, 1990, pp. 42–70.

45. Michael Dobbs, "Gorbachev's Tactics Confound Critics of His Proposals," *The Washington Post*, Mar. 14, 1990, p. A22.

46. Stankevich, conversation with the author, June 25, 1990.

47. Aleksandr Yakovlev, Congress, Moscow television, Mar. 14, 1990.

48. Dmitri Likhachev, Congress, Moscow television, Mar. 14, 1990.

49. Vladimir Tikhonov, conversation with the author, Mar. 14, 1990.

50. Likhachev, conversation with the author, Mar. 14, 1989.

21. COMMUNISM: "KNEE-DEEP IN GASOLINE"

1. Ratmir Bobovikov, *Pravda*, Apr. 27, 1989, p. 7.

2. Gorbachev, Moscow television, Jul. 12, 1989.

3. Communist Party Central Auditing Commission Report, Congress, Jul. 5, 1990, *FBIS*, Jul. 5, 1990, pp. 26, 31.

4. See Stephen F. Cohen and Katrina vanden Heuvel, *Voices of Glasnost* (New York: W. W. Norton, 1989), p. 31.

5. See Peter Reddaway, "The Threat to Gorbachev," *New York Review of Books*, Aug. 17, 1989, pp. 19ff.

6. Ivan Saly, *Vechirny Kyiv*, Apr. 10, 1989, *Radio Liberty Report on the USSR*, Aug. 4, 1989, p. 29.

7. Leonid Dobrokhotov, interview with the author, Sept. 28, 1989.

8. *Ibid.*, conversation with the author, Mar. 31, 1989.

9. Yuri Prokofyev, interview with the author, Oct. 7, 1989.

10. Valentin Mesyats, *Pravda*, Apr. 27, 1989, p. 7.

11. Ivan Polozkov, *Pravda*, Apr. 27, 1989, pp. 3–4.

12. Bobovikov, *op. cit.*

13. Abdur Rahman Vezirov, *Pravda*, Apr. 27, 1989, p. 6.

14. Vladimir Melnikov, *Pravda*, Apr. 27, 1989, p. 7.

15. Yuri Solovyov, *Pravda*, Apr. 27, 1989, p. 4.

16. Gorbachev, *Pravda*, Apr. 27, 1989, pp. 1–2, *FBIS*, Apr. 27, 1989, pp. 34–48.

17. See Jerry F. Hough, "The Politics of Successful Economic Reform," *Soviet Economy*, Vol. 5, No. 1, Jan.–Mar. 1989, p. 6.

18. Gorbachev, Moscow television, *op. cit.*

19. See Elizabeth Teague and Dawn Mann, "Gorbachev's Dual Role," *Problems of Communism*, Jan.–Feb. 1990, p. 5.

20. Prokofyev, interview, Oct. 7, 1989.

21. Lev Zaikov, Jul. 18, 1989, *Pravda*, Jul. 21, 1989, pp. 1–4.

22. Vitaly Vorotnikov, Jul. 18, 1989, *Pravda*, Jul. 21, 1989, p. 4.

23. Yegor Ligachev, Jul. 18, 1989, *FBIS*, Jul. 21, 1989, p. 63.

24. Leonid Bobykin, Jul. 18, 1989, *FBIS*, Jul. 21, 1989, pp. 58–59.

25. Nikolai Ryzhkov, Jul. 18, 1989, *FBIS*, Jul. 21, 1989, p. 67.

26. *Ibid.*, pp. 65–68.

27. Gorbachev, *Pravda*, Jul. 18, 1989, p. 1.

28. Gorbachev, in *Moscow News*, Oct. 29, 1989, p. 3.

29. Gorbachev, Congress of People's Deputies, June 9, 1989, *FBIS*, June 12, 1989, p. 53.

30. *FBIS*, Sept. 18, 1989, p. 72.

31. Vaino Väljas, *FBIS*, Sept. 15, 1989, p. 26.

32. Gorbachev, Moscow television, Sept. 9, 1989, *FBIS*, Sept. 11, 1989, pp. 27–29; *CDSP*, Oct. 4, 1989, p. 1.

33. *Ibid.*, p. 27.

34. Gorbachev, *Pravda*, Sept. 16, 1989, *FBIS*, Sept. 18, 1989, p. 39.

35. *Ibid.*, in Kiev, Sept. 28, 1989, *FBIS*, Sept. 29, 1989, pp. 52–53.

22. THE PARTY: LOSING POWER, LOSING PEOPLE

1. Ivan Polozkov, *FBIS*, Mar. 14, 1990, pp. 52, 65.

2. Gorbachev, Twenty-eighth Congress of the Communist Party of the Soviet Union, *The Washington Post*, Jul. 8, 1990, p. A24.

3. Yuri Prokofyev, interview with the author, June 27, 1990.

4. Andrei Sakharov, *FBIS*, Nov. 27, 1989, p. 80.

5. Gorbachev and Sakharov, Congress, Dec. 12, 1989, *FBIS*, Dec. 13, 1989, p. 55.

6. Gorbachev, *Pravda*, Dec. 1, 1989, pp. 1–5; *FBIS*, Dec. 11, 1989, p. 52.

7. *The Washington Post*, Jan. 14, 1990, p. A9; Jan 15, 1989, p. A1.

8. *Keesing's Contemporary Archives*, Dec. 9, 1977, p. 28,702.

9. Boris Gidaspov, Feb. 6, 1990, *FBIS*, Feb. 8, 1990, p. 87.

10. Valentin Mesyats, Feb. 6, 1990, *FBIS*, Feb. 6, 1990, p. 65.

11. Eduard Shevardnadze, Feb. 6, 1990, *FBIS*, Feb. 8, 1990, pp. 55–56.

12. Nikolai Ryzhkov, Feb. 5, 1990, *FBIS*, Feb. 8, 1990, p. 79.

13. *The New York Times*, Feb. 8, 1990, p. 1.

14. Gorbachev, *FBIS*, Feb. 6, 1990, p. 45.

15. *The New York Times*, Feb. 4, 1990, p. A21.

16. *The Washington Post*, Feb. 8, 1990, p. A1.

17. Gorbachev, Feb. 9, 1990, *FBIS*, Feb. 9, 1990, p. 45.

18. Aleksandr Lebedev, conversation with the author, June 27, 1990.

19. *Argumenty i Fakty*, June 23, 1990, p. 2.

20. Francis X. Clines, "In Moscow, Heated Cry for an Opposition," *The New York Times*, Jan. 21, 1990, p. A14.

21. Dawn Mann, "Cracks in the CPSU Monolith," *Radio Free Europe/Radio Liberty Report on the USSR*, June 15, 1990, p. 2.

22. Yuri Afanasyev, *FBIS*, Jan. 30, 1990, p. 62.

23. Vladimir Lysenko, *FBIS*, Apr. 3, 1990, p. 47.

24. Julia Wishnevsky, "Two RSFSR Congresses: A Diarchy?" *RFE/RL Report on the USSR*, July.
6, 1990, p. 2.

25. Yegor Ligachev, *FBIS*, June 18, 1990, p. 55.

26. Ivan Osadchy, *FBIS*, June 19, 1990, p. 88.

27. Viktor Tyulkin, *FBIS*, Jul. 2, 1990, p. 93.

28. Gen. Albert Makashov, *The Washington Post*, June 20, 1990, pp. A31, A36.

29. Ligachev, *The Washington Post*, June 21, 1990, p. A1.

30. Gorbachev, *FBIS*, June 20, 1990, p. 79.

31. Polozkov, *op. cit.*

32. *The Washington Post*, June 24, 1990, p. A30.

33. *Ibid.*, June 23, 1990, p. A24.

34. Bella Kurkova, conversation with the author, June 28, 1990.

35. Prokofyev, *op. cit.*

36. Lebedev, *op. cit.*

37. *Ogonek*, June 16–23, 1990, No. 25, p. 1.

38. *Moscow News*, Jul. 8, 1990, p. 5.

39. *Izvestia Tsk KPSS*, No. 3, 1990, pp. 124–25, cited in *Radio Free Europe/Radio Liberty Report on the USSR*, May 18, 1990, pp. 1–3.

40. *The Washington Post*, June 16, 1990, p. A16.

41. Prokofyev, *op. cit.*

42. *Moscow News*, June 24, 1990, p. 8.

43. *Ibid.*, p. 9.

44. Aleksandr Yakovlev, Jul. 2, 1990, Moscow television, *FBIS*, Jul. 3, 1990, pp. 28–30.

45. Gorbachev, Congress, *op. cit.*

46. Yakovlev, Congress, Jul. 7, 1990, *FBIS*, Jul. 9, 1990, p. 41.

47. Shevardnadze, Congress, Jul. 3, 1990, *FBIS*, Jul. 5, 1990, pp. 7, 9.

48. Gorbachev, Congress, Jul. 10, 1990, *FBIS*, Jul. 11, 1990, p. 8.

49. See *Moscow News*, Jul. 1, 1990, p. 13.

50. Ligachev, Moscow television, Jul. 5, 1990.

51. Vladimir Kryuchkov, Congress, Jul. 3, 1990, *FBIS*, Jul. 5, 1990, p. 16.

52. Boris Yeltsin, Congress, Jul. 6, 1990, *FBIS*, Jul. 10, 1990, p. 1.

53. *The New York Times*, Jul. 12, 1990, p. A12.

54. *The New York Times*, Jul. 13, 1990, pp. A1, A6.

55. Andrei Kortunov, conversation with the author, Jul. 4, 1990.

23. CITY HALL: THE NEW POLITICAL ENTREPRENEURS

1. Sergei Stankevich, interview with the author, June 26, 1990.

2. Anatoly Sobchak, Leningrad radio, June 27, 1990, interview with the author, June 29, 1990.

3. Anatoly Golovkov, interview with the author, Mar. 5, 1990.

4. Konstantin Yarukhin, conversation with the author, June 28, 1990.

5. Yelena Zelinskaya, conversation with the author, June 28, 1990.

6. David Broder, "Home Rule for Kiev," *The Washington Post*, Jul. 15, 1990, p. A23.

7. Conversations with Stankevich, June 26, 1990, Sobchak, June 29, 1990.

8. *The Washington Post*, Apr. 26, 1990, p. A34.

9. *The New York Times*, Apr. 26, 1990, p. A12.

10. Aleksandr Seryakov, interview with the author, June 28, 1990.

11. Stankevich, interview, June 26, 1990.

12. Lithuanian Department of Statistics, "Lithuanian Barter of Lithuanian Products and Goods with the U.S.S.R. during the Blockade," Jul. 12, 1990.

13. V. I. Lenin, *Collected Works* (Moscow: Progress Publishers, 1964), Vol. XXV, p. 154.

14. *The New York Times*, Apr. 21, 1990, p. A1.

15. Stankevich, interview, June 26, 1990.

16. Yuri Prokofyev, interview with the author, June 27, 1990.

17. Stankevich, conversation with the author, Aug. 2, 1990.

18. Celestine Bohlen, "Amid Soviets' Changes, Who Owns the Papers?" *The New York Times*, June 6, 1990, p. A12.

19. Moscow radio, June 23, 1990, *FBIS*, Jul. 6, 1990, p. 64.

20. Sobchak, interview, *Moscow News*, June 10, 1990, p. 5.

21. *Ibid.*, interview, *New Times*, May 29–June 4, 1990, p. 7.

22. *Ibid.*, "Who Obeys Whom?" *Moscow News*, Jul. 8, 1990, p. 5.

23. Bill Keller, "Party, Facing Eviction, Clings to Its Properties," *The New York Times*, June 29, 1990, p. A4.

24. Sobchak, Leningrad radio, June 27, 1990, interview with the author, June 29, 1990.

25. Bella Kurkova, interview with the author, June 28, 1990.

26. Stankevich, conversation with the author, Mar. 12, 1990.

27. Gavril Popov, interview, *Rabochaya Tribuna*, Apr. 22, 1990, p. 5; *FBIS*, Apr. 27, 1990, p. 95.

28. *The New York Times*, Jul. 8, 1990, p. 1.

29. Francis X. Clines, "Private Lesson on Moscow Potholes," *The New York Times*, Jul. 28, 1990, p. A6.

30. Stankevich, conversation, Aug. 2, 1990.

31. *Ibid.*, interview, June 26, 1990.

32. Mark Masarsky, conversation with the author, Jul. 3, 1990.

33. Stankevich, interview, June 26, 1990.

34. Sobchak, conversation with the author, Aug. 8, 1990.

35. *Ibid.*, June 29, 1990.

24. THE OUTLOOK: WILL IT COLLAPSE OR WILL IT ENDURE?

1. Alexis de Tocqueville, *The Old Regime and the Revolution* (New York: Harper and Brothers, 1856), p. 214.

2. Aleksandr Yakovlev, interview with the author, Oct. 9, 1989.

3. Gorbachev, *Perestroika* (New York: Harper & Row, 1987), p. 36.

4. Eduard Shevardnadze, speech to Foreign Policy Association of New York, Oct. 2, 1989.

5. Yakovlev, *op. cit.*

6. A.J.P. Taylor, *Bismarck: The Man and The Statesman* (London: H. Hamilton, 1955), pp. 255–58.

7. Simon Serfaty, *France, DeGaulle, & Europe* (Baltimore: Johns Hopkins University Press, 1968), p. 163–64.

8. Lance Morrow, "The Unlikely Patron of Change," *Time*, Jan. 1, 1990, p. 44.

9. *The Washington Post*, Jul. 31, 1990, p. A17.

10. Timothy Garton Ash, "Ten Thoughts on the New Europe," *The New York Review of Books*, June 14, 1990, p. 22.

11. *The New York Times*, June 23, 1990, p. A6.

12. Jim Hoagland, "The Real Soviet Economy—Underground," *The Washington Post*, June 15, 1990, p. A25.

13. Anatoly Sobchak, conversation with the author, Aug. 7, 1990.

14. Vadim Bakatin, conversation with the author, Jul. 4, 1990.

15. *The Washington Post*, Jul. 21, 1990, p. A1.

16. *The New York Times*, Jul. 27, 1990, p. A6.

17. See Gavril Popov, "Dangers of Democracy," *The New York Review of Books*, Aug. 16, 1990, pp. 27–28.

About the Author

Hedrick Smith's twenty-six-year career with *The New York Times* took him to Vietnam, Cairo, Paris, and Washington, as well as Moscow, where his reporting from 1971 to 1974 won him a Pulitzer Prize. His books include the best-sellers *The Russians* and *The Power Game*. He is a fellow of the Foreign Policy Institute at the Johns Hopkins School of Advanced International Studies. He was chief correspondent of the four-part PBS miniseries *Inside Gorbachev's USSR,* and is a regular panelist on PBS's *Washington Week in Review.* He lives in Maryland with his wife, Susan.

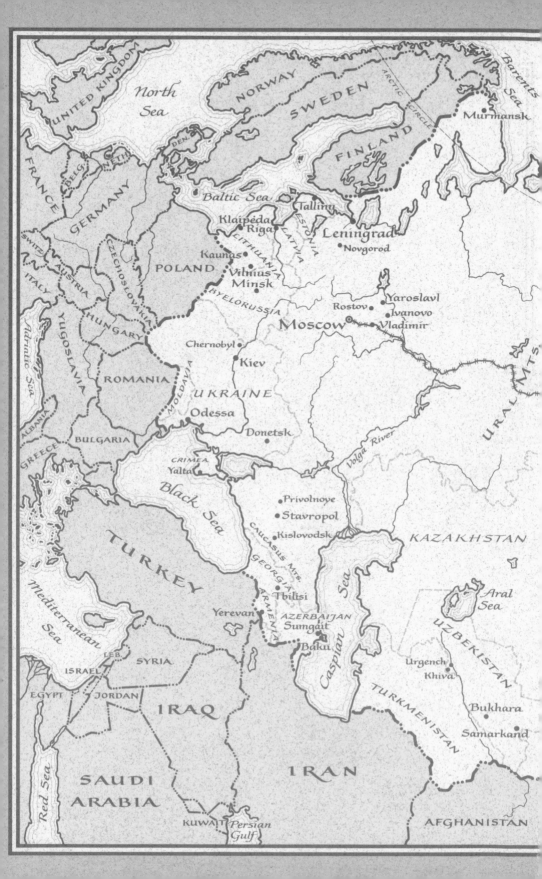